Comprehensive Economics

Comprehensive Economics

Second Edition

Part One: Institutional and Applied

B. V. Marshall M.COM.

Principal Lecturer in Economics
North Staffordshire Polytechnic

Longman   *London & New York*

Longman Group Limited
LONDON
*Associated companies, branches and
representatives throughout the world*

First published 1967
Second edition 1975

ISBN *Complete Cased Edition 0 582 35130 8*
ISBN *Part One, Paper 0 582 35131 6*
ISBN *Part Two, Paper 0 582 35124 3*

*Printed in Great Britain by
Lowe & Brydone (Printers) Ltd,
Thetford, Norfolk*

To my family and former teachers

Preface to the Second Edition

In recent years economics has been subjected to hostile criticism from outside its ranks and to agonising self-criticism from within. Its practitioners have been first elevated to the status of omnipotent witch doctors, then scorned as charlatans. A very real danger is that economics may appear on many student curricula not for any practical, interpretative, predictive function it may have, but as a mental gymnastics discipline – like the compulsory Latin of former days. Another danger is that economists may develop a 'stampede' or 'bandwaggon' syndrome, causing them to flee intellectually from one crisis to another, or to seek comfort on the coat tails of academic trendiness.

Too much blind faith has been put in the ability of the practitioners to identify the relevant problems, ask the right questions and provide the theories and techniques to come up with the right answers. As Sir Eric Roll has put it, in the third edition of his book, 'A History of Economic Thought', economics has experienced an 'erosion of its authority in the world of action' and 'doubt has been expressed whether Economics as a whole is concerned with the right problem'.

Internal criticisms and doubts have revolved, *inter alia*, around the need for economics to be more mathematical, precise and 'scientific', or the need to be more integrated with political and social 'normative' value judgements and less pure, 'positive' or objective. External criticisms have revolved around the need for economics to be more inter-disciplinary and integrated with other social sciences, such as sociology and psychology.

The author believes that some sort of compromise must be found between these competing claims. Economics is a social *study*: much of the behaviour of social groups and institutions is not amenable to prediction in the same way as controlled experiments in the physical science laboratory. As a social study, it cannot be considered solely as a branch of mathematics, substituting complex algebra and calculus in place of simple geometry. It must incorporate a detailed knowledge and understanding of the institutional framework, within which and through which economic forces function, as has long been recognised in the fields of monetary, public finance and international economics. Disillusionment with the theory of the *firm*, for example – usually treated as an excursion into a static fairyland – must give way to an appreciation of the value of more and more realistic models of the firm, reacting to the behaviour of competitors in a changing environment, as a step towards a wider theory of *industrial* structure, conduct and performance. For this broader objective, of course, a detailed familiarity with the institutional environment and problems of industry is essential.

Similarly, the understanding of behaviour by consumers, investors and suppliers; by small, large and publicly-owned firms; by industrialised and less developed countries; by high and low income earners and wealth owners; by different sectors of the labour market, must be enhanced by a parallel understanding and awareness of historical, political, behavioural and sociological disciplines.

Whereas it may not be possible nor desirable to quantify every relationship and interaction in economics, there is nevertheless much scope for the use of mathematical techniques, which often simplify and express the essence of relationships, changes and trends. Furthermore, for the handling of vast amounts of data, for the assessment of probabilities and uncertainties in complex models, for calculating the best methods for achieving a desired result on the basis of precise data and known variables and for calculating the likely effects of changes in numerous recognised variables in a limited model of the economy, there is obviously a need for advanced mathematical and statistical techniques and for highly trained specialists to operate them.

This does not imply, however, that no student may pursue a fruitful, satisfying and creative study of economics unless he or she is able and willing to develop such a high degree of expertise. It is at least as important for the many to achieve an insight into and appreciation of economic forces and relationships and to see their relevance to current problems, large and small, as it is for the few to seek a high degree of specialist operational expertise in mathematical and statistical techniques. The many wish to establish meaningful communication and integration between economics and other social studies (or 'science') disciplines. The few all too often fail to seek or achieve such communication and integration, often fail to see the limitations of their complex models and often, faced with the need to be decisive, appear to suffer from 'analysis paralysis'.

The main aim of this second edition is to provide a thorough, integrated grounding in the major principles of economic theory and their application to institutional and other economic problems of current relevance. To this end it pursues a similar philosophy and structure to those in the first edition – outlined in the preface to it.

The second edition is based on the outline of the first, but is updated and completely rewritten and combines a much more comprehensive approach with a more extensive and more intensive treatment of institutional, analytical and applied topics. Some of the main extensions and additions are as follows:

PART ONE: INSTITUTIONAL AND APPLIED

The sections on population, industrial economics, monopoly and merger policy and State intervention now include topics such as activity rates; the world urban population explosion; regional problems and policy; major changes in the structure of the economy and the input–output matrix; efficiency and size; size and growth; the relationship between type of control and economic performance; problems of the small firm; multinational firms and conglomerates; the problems of technological change; the pricing and investment policies of public enterprise; economic planning and prices and incomes policy.

The sections on international trade, money and banking and public finance now include such topics as opportunity cost and relative factor endowment theories; problems of international liquidity; the Friedman–Keynesian monetary controversy and the transmission mechanism; development of the parallel money markets; problems of defining the money supply; recent policy changes on financial competition and credit control; empirical findings on the economic effects of taxation; recent changes in the taxation system; developments in public spending; the economics of the negative (or reverse) income tax; the 'poverty trap' and 'fiscal drag'.

PART TWO: ANALYTICAL AND APPLIED

The production and price (Supply and Demand or Consumption) theory sections now introduce the student to the mathematical treatment of marginal analysis and include an expanded treatment of capital, the labour market and industrial relations; production functions; revealed preference; more extensive applications of supply and demand analysis.

The theory of the firm section has been expanded, includes further treatment of non-economic theories and contains a new chapter on applications of the analytical tools of theory of the firm – as, for example, in the problem of the marginal cost pricing policies of nationalised industries.

The sections on distribution theory and economic growth have been expanded to include topics such as the use of linear programming in the optimal allocation of resources; growth rates and inflation; the national and international redistribution of income; the pros and cons of economic growth.

The section on the neo-Keynesian model of income determination and the level of activity has been completely rewritten, to include the current controversy on Keynes; the consumption and investment functions and their applications; time lags and the multiplier and accelerator; general equilibrium analysis in the goods, money and labour markets; the analysis of unemployment and wage inflation.

I am deeply grateful for the assistance offered to me by the North Staffordshire Polytechnic library and printing staff and by so many of my colleagues on the teaching staff. In particular, I should like to thank the following colleagues for their interest, encouragement and practical help in researching on problems and sources, in patient explanation and in commenting on parts of the manuscript: Wyn Protheroe, on international trade theory; Dick Ledward, on monetary theory and institutions; Peter Nurse, on the 'poverty trap' and reverse income tax; Mac Speirs and Terry Doughty, on the labour market and industrial relations; Peter Reynolds, my mathematics 'guru'; Rob Macey, on economic growth; Chris Brownless, on the neo-Keynesian model. No blame, of course, attaches to any of these persons for errors and omissions, large or small.

My thanks are also due to many students, present and past, whom I have been privileged to teach. Their anonymous function as sounding-board and seed-bed and their patience have been the source of feedback on pedagogical methods and ideas used throughout this book. If it continues to be of use to a wider circle of students, the foremost debt is to them.

For assistance in the typing of a daunting manuscript I wish to thank Sheila Evans and especially Pat Corfield, for her patience and efficiency.

Finally, my thanks must be noted for generous help, in the grinding chore of proof-reading, by Wendy Spreyer, Jane Glennie, Pam Ryder, Helmi Büscher and my wife, Ann. She and my children, Jonathan and Louise, have had the additional burden of living with me during the lengthy birth-pangs of the second edition.

1974   *B. V. Marshall*

Preface to the First Edition

This book came into being to fill a gap.

Firstly, it is specifically designed as a self-sufficient volume, providing for all the basic requirements of students at both elementary and more advanced levels without the need for specialist books.

Secondly, it consists of two courses in one volume. Stage One is an elementary course for the beginner, suitable for students beginning Economics in the sixth form or a technical college. Stage Two builds upon this and provides a course for G.C.E. A level and first-year degree requirements. The two courses are not consecutive: they are dovetailed together in such a way that each topic is treated first at an elementary and then at a more advanced level. This pattern is maintained throughout the book, the running heads indicating those chapters on each topic which are elementary (Stage I) and those which are more advanced (Stage II). The student can pick out the Stage I material first – passing over the advanced chapters – if he or she is reading for an elementary examination. Later, when reading for a more advanced examination, the student may work through all the Stage II chapters, which follow on from the previous material, and may at any time refer back to the earlier material on a topic. Alternatively, if the student wishes to read right through for an advanced examination he or she can simply work through the whole book, one topic at a time – elementary material first, followed by advanced material.

Thirdly, the book has been planned to be comprehensive in scope and in detail. I believe that all three basic ingredients of economics – Descriptive, Theoretical and Applied – should be given equal emphasis to provide a course which is an integrated whole.

I have taken as a nucleus the three traditional divisions of economic theory – production (or supply), exchange (or value and price), and income distribution (or factor earnings and the size and distribution of wealth created within the economy). It was possible to integrate into these sections of economic theory a great deal of descriptive material and applied, real-life problems, topics and case histories. These provide the student with some of the essential factual background to economic theory, without which it is arid and unreal, and with examples of the context within which theory may be applied in practice.

However, there were certain topics of a mainly descriptive nature which did not fit neatly into any single division of theory. They either overlapped more than one division or lay right outside, or else were so extensive as to merit separate treatment as fields of study in their own right. These topics have been assembled together in Part One of the book, since they constitute much of the essential background against which traditional economic theory may be viewed.

In each case there is a mixture of specialist theory appropriate to the particular topic and of applied problems.

Thus Part One is concerned with the following background fields of study:

Population
Industrial Location, Structure and Organisation
International Trade
Money, Banking and Institutions of the Capital Market
Public Finance
Stages in the Flow of Goods and Services to the Final Consumer

Part Two covers the traditional divisions of economic theory, with suitable descriptive stiffening and the lifeblood of applied problems.

In consequence, the student is taken through a logical, integrated programme of work, involving all the main elements of economics. The distinction between Part One and Part Two arises naturally out of the material and the student should soon become familiar with the layout of chapters in each part.

Fourthly, it has been deliberate policy to show detailed sources of information throughout the text – at both elementary and advanced levels. Extensive lists of further reading and bibliographical details of sources used in the text are provided at the end of each chapter. In addition, each chapter is followed by questions from past examinations, in a sequence which follows closely the layout of material in that chapter. Thus the student, while following the course at either stage, is made aware of extensive sources of material – some of it current and easily obtainable – is shown how to use it and is provided with the basic training necessary to keep up to date.

I would like to record my sincere gratitude to the numerous authors and publishers of current and specialist material made use of in this book and fully acknowledged on each occasion, and to the University of London for their kind permission to reproduce questions from past papers.

Finally, I would like to express my gratitude to my former colleagues and students of Enfield Grammar School – whose cooperation and encouragement made this project possible – and to my students and colleagues at the Portsmouth College of Technology, for their cooperation and criticism at a later stage.

1967   *B. V. Marshall*

Contents

Chapter 3 Some Major Industries

THE COAL INDUSTRY

Stage I

Stage II: Structure and Organisation

THE IRON AND STEEL INDUSTRY

Stage I

Stage II: Structure and Organisation

AGRICULTURE

THE MOTOR INDUSTRY

THE TEXTILE INDUSTRY

Chapter 6 Money, Banking and the Capital Market

Chapter 7 Public Finance

Chapter 8 Stages in the Flow of Goods and Services to the Final Consumer

Acknowledgements

We are grateful to the following for permission to reproduce copyright material and statistical data:

The Athlone Press of the University of London for material from *British Shipping and World Competition* by S. G. Sturmey; The British Iron and Steel Federation (Statistical Services); Cambridge University Press for material from *Concentration in British Industry* by R. Evely and I. M. D. Little, *British Economic Growth, 1688–1959* by P. Deane and W. A. Cole, and *The Structure of British Industry* edited by D. Burn; Central Office of Information (*Britain: an Official Handbook – Broadsheets on Britain*, miscellaneous Reference Pamphlets and Fact Sheets, and *D.E.A. Progress Report*); The Cotton Board (Statistics Department); *The Daily Telegraph and Morning Post*; Department of the Treasury (*Bulletin for Industry*); *The Economist*; Sir Robert Hall; Lloyds Bank Ltd (*Lloyds Bank Review*); Midland Bank Ltd (*Midland Bank Review*); National Savings Committee (*Monthly Bulletin of Statistics and Economic Information*); *The Observer*; Princetown University Press for material from *The Growth of Public Expenditure in the United Kingdom* by Alan T. Peacock and Jack Wiseman; Routledge and Kegan Paul Ltd for material from *The Logic of British and American Industry* by Professor Sargant Florence; Royal Statistical Society; The Shipbuilding Employers' Federation; The Society of Motor Manufacturers and Traders Ltd; the *Statist*; Sweet and Maxwell Ltd for material from *Ownership, Control and Success of Large Companies* by Professor Sargant Florence; the United Nations Department of Economic and Social Affairs (*Population Studies No. 28*); and the University of London, for past examination questions.

The author is grateful to the following for particular help and information:

J. McDonnell, Statistics Department, National Coal Board; E. P. Pearce, Iron and Steel Statistics Bureau; J. Malcolm, Survey and Economics Department, The National Farmers' Union; D. C. Shaw, Economics and Statistics Department, The Textile Council; A. Fitch, Economics Information Section, International Wool Secretariat; J. R. Barton, Shipbuilders and Repairers National Association; J. P. Cashman, Statistics Department, Lloyd's Register of Shipping.

Copyright material in tables, figures and footnotes is acknowledged throughout in the text.

Abbreviations used in Footnotes

A.E.A.	American Economic Association
A.E.R.	*American Economic Review*
Ann. Abs. Stat.	*Annual Abstract of Statistics*
B.B.C.B.	*Broadsheets on Britain: Changing Britain* (Central Office of Information)
B.B.L.A.	*Broadsheets on Britain: Looking Ahead* (Central Office of Information)
B.B.R.	*Barclays Bank Review*
B.E.Q.B.	*Bank of England Quarterly Bulletin*
Brit. O.H.	*Britain: an Official Handbook*. Annual
Bull. Ind.	*Bulletin for Industry* (Information Division of the Treasury)
C.O.I.	Central Office of Information
C.O.I. Ref.	*C.O.I. Reference Pamphlets*
C.U.P.	Cambridge University Press
D.B.R.	*District Bank Review*
D.E.A. Pr. Rep. Econ.	*Department of Economic Affairs Progress Report: Economic*
D.E.A. Pr. Rep. Ind. and Reg.	*Department of Economic Affairs Progress Report: Industrial and Regional*
D.T.	*Daily Telegraph*
Econ.	*The Economist*
E.J.	*Economic Journal*
E.P.R.	*Economic Progress Reports* (The Treasury)
F.S.B.	*Fact Sheets on Britain* (C.O.I.)
F.B.E.	*Fact Sheets on Britain and Europe* (C.O.I.)
F.T.	*The Financial Times*
J.L.E.	*Journal of Law and Economics*
J.P.E.	*Journal of Political Economy*
J. Roy. Stat. Soc.	*Journal of the Royal Statistical Society*
L.B.R.	*Lloyds Bank Review*
M.B.R.	*Midland Bank Review*
M.B. Stat. Econ. Inf.	*Monthly Bulletin of Statistics and Economic Information* (National Savings Committee)
Min. Lab. Gaz.	*Ministry of Labour Gazette*
M. and W.S.R.	*Moorgate and Wall Street Review*
N.W.B.Q.R.	*National Westminster Bank Quarterly Review*
O.U.P.	Oxford University Press
Obs.	*The Observer*
P.E.P.	Political and Economic Planning
Q.J.E.	*Quarterly Journal of Economics*
R.E.S.	Royal Economic Society
S.M.M.T.	Society of Motor Manufacturers and Traders
S.T.	*The Sunday Times*
Stat.	*Statist*
T.B.B.E.	*Treasury Broadsheets: Britain's Economy*

PART ONE

1. Population
Stage I

1. General

It seems appropriate that a study of economics, covering as it does the theoretical and descriptive analysis of how human communities 'earn their living' and evolve methods and institutions to enter into the resultant production-exchange relationships, should start with an examination of the communities themselves: the population. Population is the essential backcloth against which economics may be viewed, the human environment in which an economy functions. It is an important factor of production; it exercises choice and makes production and exchange decisions; it generates the forces which make a dynamic economic world out of a mere geophysical environment.

Population problems have always been experienced in human communities. In attempts to strike a balance between the size and constitution of the population and the available natural resources various methods have evolved over the millennia, ranging from infanticide and contraception to polygamy.

In Great Britain in 1086 it would appear, from the information in the Domesday Survey, that the population numbered about 2 million. By 1690, according to the estimates of Gregory King, it had reached about 7 million. The intervening centuries, marked by a high birth-rate, a high death-rate, plagues and political and religious tensions, contained periods of slow growth and periods of stagnation and decline. This state of affairs seems to have prevailed all over the world until the eighteenth century.

During the two-and-a-half centuries since 1700 the population of Great Britain increased seven-and-a-half times, and in 1961 revised population 'projections' or forecasts envisaged a population of about 62 million by the year 2000 – a ninefold increase in three centuries. During the nineteenth century a similar change took place in other European countries and colonisers of European descent in overseas territories also increased rapidly. Most of this increase appears to be due to improvements in health, hygiene, nutrition and medical science and the consequent reduction in the death-rate amongst European peoples. Not until the twentieth century did the same improvements manifest a marked effect on the non-European populations of the world. Thus from 1700 to about 1900 the balance of a fast-increasing world population shifted in favour of European peoples. During the twentieth century, however, the rate of population growth amongst the peoples of western Europe has fallen rapidly, due to several economic and social factors, although the death-rate has continued to fall. In southern and eastern Europe, South America, Africa and Asia, on the other hand, the improvements which had earlier affected western Europe began to exert a tremendous influence. The result has been what is sometimes referred

3

to as a population 'explosion', this time with the balance overwhelmingly in favour of the non-Europeans.

According to the Report of the Royal Commission on Population, 1949, world population in 1750 was 728 million, of whom about 78% inhabited Africa and Asia. By 1900 world population had reached 1,608 million, of whom the same two continents contained about 65%.[1] Since then, however, world population has been approaching the 3,000 million mark, and some forecasts envisage a figure of 6,000 million by the year 2000, of which North America, Europe and Russia will contain a gradually diminishing proportion.

The first official census of population for Great Britain was taken in 1801. It confirmed what earlier investigators had suspected, that the population in England, Wales and Scotland had risen during the eighteenth century by about 50%, or over 3½ million, to reach 10½ million. Population was by then a matter for public concern, and censuses were taken every ten years thereafter, except in wartime 1941.

Three years before the first census, T. R. Malthus (1766–1834) published the first systematic theory on population, entitled *An Essay on the Principle of Population as it affects the Future improvement of Society*. Malthus had noticed the unprecedented rise in Great Britain's population and the consequent cultivation of less fertile marginal land to feed it. His theory in its crudest form held that food supply increased in arithmetic progression (1, 2, 3, 4, etc.) whilst population increased in geometric progression (1, 2, 4, 8, 16, etc.). He later diluted the precise mathematical connection between the two rates of growth, but his thesis continued to claim that food supplies lag behind the number of mouths and that the great mass of people would live at subsistence level. It would follow that any increase in the means of subsistence would lead to an increase in surviving births and a subsequent fall in the standard of living. He forecast that an excessive population would be eliminated by 'misery': starvation, wars and plagues. The only solution he could see was 'moral restraint': later marriage and smaller families.[2]

In fact these results did not occur in nineteenth-century Britain, despite an even faster rate of population growth than that noticed by Malthus. This was partly because Malthus had not foreseen the increasing productivity in the manufacture of goods which enabled Britain to purchase food from abroad. Nor had he foreseen the great improvements in technique of the Agricultural Revolution and the vast lands of the New World and Australia. Furthermore, it appears that after a certain rise in the standard of living and education, a trend to smaller families set in.

With regard to this period, the Royal Commission Report states that the growth of numbers in Europe stimulated the development of modern industry and trade and the development of overseas territories by emigration and investment. Great Britain took a leading part in this process and 'the growth of her population in the nineteenth century was an essential condition of her becoming and remaining a strong and rich nation, the centre of a great Commonwealth,

---

[1] *Royal Commission on Population Report*, 1949, p. 7.

[2] In 1882 Francis Place, stimulated by the debate about human perfectibility between Malthus and Godwin, published his *Illustrations and Proofs of the Principle of Population*. This work was of prime significance in being the first systematic English exposition of the doctrine of contraception as a means of birth control. See 'The original Neo-Malthusian', *Econ.*, 14 Oct. 1967, p. 186.

a large Colonial Empire, and a commercial system whose ramifications covered the whole world'.[1]

Because the rate of growth in the British population was slowing down in the interwar period, the Royal Commission made a thorough investigation into the whole question of the trends of population and family size and their relationship with the national interest. It would seem that the higher postwar rate of growth, once considered to be a temporary phenomenon, shows no sign of abating. A similar phenomenon is apparent in North America and western Europe.

As for the rest of the world, the population explosion which Malthus forecast was delayed until the twentieth century. Now, however, this problem is exercising the brains of economists, scientists, governments and United Nations agencies.

In Britain, in 1971, steps were taken to formalise the coordination of Government policies with population projections. A Select Committee of the House of Commons had earlier advocated a special office to advise on population. The Government responded by announcing in July 1971 the appointment of a panel of independent and Government experts, backed by the staff of the Cabinet Office.[2]

2. The Rate of Population Growth

(a) **Birth-rates, death-rates, natural increase, migration and actual or net increase**
The keys to an understanding of the processes by which a population increases or diminishes, with all the social, economic and political consequences that such changes entail, are the relationships between the birth-rate and death-rate of that population, the rate of migration, the pattern of marriage, the rate of reproduction and the size of family.

For the greater part of the nineteenth century the annual birth-rate of the British population was about 35 per thousand persons (3·5%) and the annual death-rate was just over 20 per thousand (2·0%). During the last thirty years of the century both death-rates and birth-rates were falling, but there was little change in the difference between them, known as the rate of natural increase. This rose from 12 per thousand in 1851 to 15 per thousand in 1881 (due to a greater fall in death-rate than in birth-rate). Then it fell to 11 per thousand in 1901, because birth-rate fell faster than death-rate.

After 1911 the birth-rate started to fall very rapidly. Despite a brief rise after World War I it reached by World War II a level less than half the nineteenth-century rate. Life expectancy rose for all age groups during this period, because of improving economic, social and medical circumstances. This fact, allied with the falling birth-rate, tended to accentuate the average age of the population, which had started to rise after 1881. Consequently, the general death-rate of the 'ageing' population remained nearly stationary at about 12 per thousand. Thus in the interwar period the rate of natural increase fell to less than 5 per thousand.

After World War II the birth-rate rose to 20·7 per thousand in 1947 then fell to 15·4 per thousand in 1955, slightly higher than the prewar level. After 1955 it rose gradually, reaching a peak of 18·7 per thousand in 1964. This, allied with the fairly constant death-rate and rising life expectancy rate, resulted in an expansion in the rate of natural increase and a growth in both the lower and upper age groups. From 1964 there was a gradual decline in the birth-rate,

[1] *Report*, p. 218.
[2] *Econ.*, 31 July 1971, p. 22.

1. POPULATION [1]

which fell to 16·6 per thousand in 1969.[1] These fluctuations in the birth-rate have played havoc with official projections of the future population, which have had to be revised with every change in the trend.

Numerous reasons have been suggested for the vagaries of the birth-rate, ranging from a combination of hot summers and income tax rate reductions as causal factors in the 1956–64 upward trend,[2] to improved methods of contraception, the Abortion Act of 1967 and an apparent decline of female fertility in the later years of marriage as causal factors in the post-1964 downward trend.[3] Figures 1.1 and 1.2 below illustrate the birth-rate, death-rate and life expectancy trends since 1871.

Apart from the effects of birth-rates and death-rates on natural increase, the actual change in the size of a population is affected by migration, inwards or outwards. The balance of migration will result in a net gain or a net loss.

Since the beginning of the nineteenth century Britain has experienced a marked net loss by migration. It has been estimated that 25 million people born in the British Isles have migrated to the United States and Commonwealth countries. However, large numbers of Europeans have come to Britain since the 1880s. The net loss by migration since 1871 from the present area of the United Kingdom (i.e. ignoring Eire) has been about 3 million. From 1871 to 1931 there was a net loss in every census period, amounting in all to 3½ million. From 1931 to 1951 there was, for the first time, a net gain, amounting to about ½ million. In fact there were about ¾ million incomers in all, consisting mainly of British subjects returning home and ¼ million aliens (refugees from the Nazis, and French, Polish, Belgian, Dutch, Czechoslovakian and Norwegian servicemen, after the German conquests early in World War II). During the intercensal period 1951 to 1961 there was again a net loss, but of only 97,000, despite the fact that the

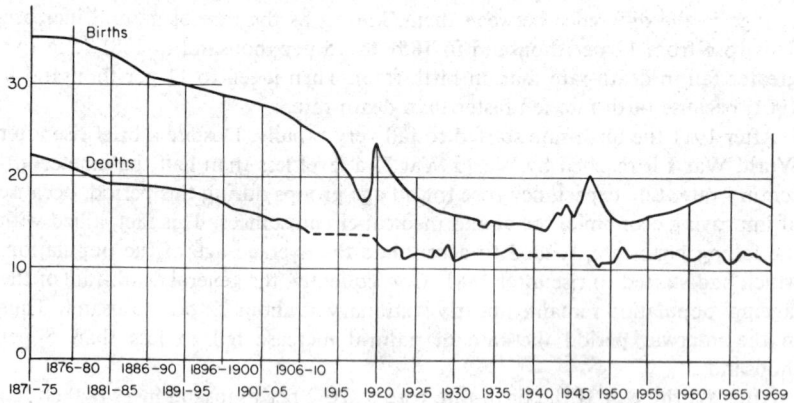

Fig. 1.1. *Birth-rates and death-rates in Great Britain (per 1,000 population) (1871–1969)*

(Source: *Britain: an Official Handbook*, 1971; *Ann. Abs. Stat.* No. 107, 1970)

[1] *Ann. Abs. Stat.* No. 107, 1970.
[2] *Econ.*, 24 June 1967, p. 1336.
[3] *D.T.*, 13 Jan. 1970 and *Econ.*, 17 Aug. 1968, p. 41.

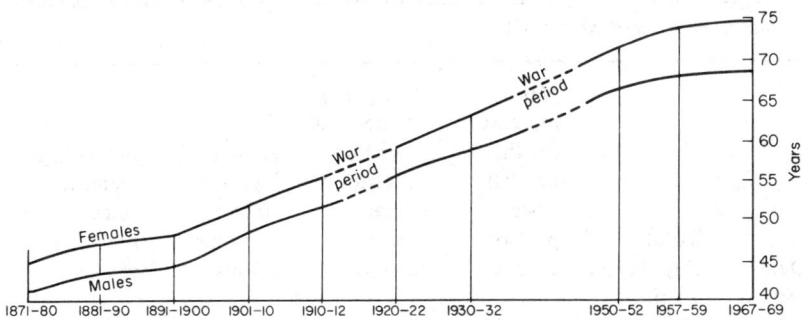

Fig. 1.2. *Expectation of life at birth in England and Wales (1871–1969)*
(Source: *Britain: an Official Handbook*, 1971; *Ann. Abs. Stat.* No. 107, 1970)

migration flows were greater than ever. Net annual outflow to Commonwealth countries reached a peak of 87,000 in 1952, but this was followed by an intensified inflow from the Commonwealth, mainly the West Indies. In fact about 450,000 Commonwealth immigrants entered Britain from 1955 to mid-1962, from the West Indies, Asia, Africa and the Mediterranean.[1] For the United Kingdom as a whole, the net gain by migration between 1951 and 1961 was only 12,000: England and Wales gained 387,000 but Scotland lost 282,000 and Northern Ireland 93,000.[2] Much of the movement was within the United Kingdom. Nevertheless, the Government introduced the Commonwealth Immigrants Acts of 1962 and 1968 in order to restrict entry of Commonwealth citizens and U.K. citizens who have no close links with Britain. In 1965 there was a net U.K. loss of 77,600[3] and in 1969 a loss of 87,000 but these figures exclude the movement between the U.K. and the Irish Republic: in the year to mid-1969 this resulted in a net inflow of 25,000.[4]

The combined effect of birth-rates, death-rates and migration may be seen from Table 1.1.

Bearing in mind the fact that the population of Northern Ireland has remained almost stationary at about 1½ million, due to migration to mainland Britain and the Commonwealth, we see that in almost every censal period up to 1901 the rate of population increase was falling slightly but that the actual increase was rising in absolute terms. From 1901 to 1941 there was a rapid fall in the percentage increase and in the actual increase. This coincides with the drastic fall in the birth-rate after 1911. From 1941 to 1961 the percentage increase rose from 4 to 5 and there has been a big rise in the actual population increase. This coincides with the generally rising postwar birth-rate.

The influence of migration on these rapid changes in the population trends has been of minor significance. The decisive part in the slowing down of British population growth in the interwar period was played by birth-rates and death-rates. In each decade from 1871 to 1911 the natural increase was about 4 million, but in the interwar period it fell to less than 2 million.

[1] *D.T.*, 29 June 1962.
[2] *Ann. Abs. Stat.*, No. 107, 1970.
[3] *Ibid.*
[4] *D.T.*, 4 Sept. 1970.

1. POPULATION [I]

Table 1.1 *Population of Great Britain* (*thousands*) *1801–1971* (*Great Britain=* *England, Wales and Scotland*)

Date	Total Population	Natural increase (births– deaths) since previous census	Net gain (+) or net loss (−) by migration since previous census	Actual increase since previous census	Percentage increase since previous census
1801	10,501				
1811	12,206			1,505	14·3
1821	14,092			2,086	17·1
1831	16,261			2,169	15·4
1841	18,534			2,273	14·0
1851	20,817			2,283	12·3
1861	23,128			2,311	11·1
1871	26,072			2,944	12·7
1881	29,710	3,895	−257	3,638	13·9
1891	33,029	4,138	−819	3,319	11·2
1901	37,000	4,094	−122	3,971	12·0
1911	40,831	4,586	−755	3,831	10·3
1921	42,769	2,797	−859	1,938	4·7
1931	44,795	2,588	·−562	2,026	4·7
1941	46,605 (est)	1,160 (est)	+650 (est)	1,810 (est)	4·0
1951	48,854	2,361	+112	2,249	4·8
1961	51,284	2,325	+105	2,430	5·0
1971*	53,937	2,653	NIL	2,653	5·2

(Based on *Royal Commission on Population Report*, 1949; *Ann. Abs. Stat.*, No. 107, 1970; *Econ.* 21 Aug. 1971, p. 20)

* =Provisional figures.

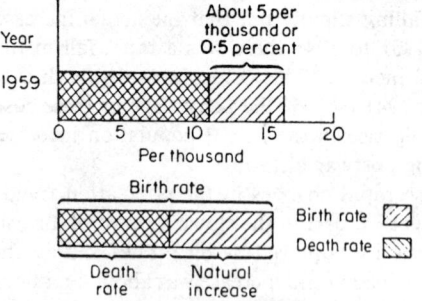

Fig. 1.3. *Rate of natural increase per 1,000, Great Britain*

A simple graphic way of comparing birth-rates, death-rates and natural increase rates for any given year is to superimpose, in a bar diagram, one rate upon the other. The balance will be a rate either of natural increase or decrease. If, as in the case of Great Britain, this annual rate of increase is about 5 per thousand, it is useful to bear in mind that this implies a percentage increase of 0·5 per year. This will produce, roughly, a 5% rate of growth in ten years.

For the same year, 1959, the U.S.A., Japan and Singapore, for example, showed much higher rates of natural increase per thousand, or percentage growth rates (see Fig. 1.4).

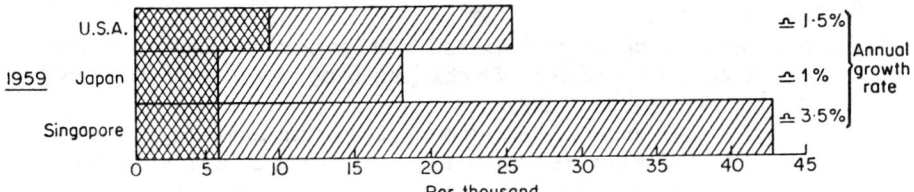

Fig. 1.4. *Rates of natural increase per thousand and growth rates per cent* (*1959*) (Based on 'The menace of over-population' by A. S. Parkes, *New Scientist*, 8 June 1961)

(b) Marriage, family size, fertility and reproduction rates

We have considered, so far, the major factors of birth-rates, death-rates and migration and their effects upon natural and actual (or net) increase. The next step is to examine briefly those factors which influence the birth-rate itself, subjecting this positive, dynamic element in the population analysis to some-times violent changes.

Basically the birth-rate will be determined by the number and pattern of marriages (itself influenced by social custom, legislation and economic circum-stances) and by the pattern of family size (which in turn is influenced by custom, social and economic conditions and natural fertility).

(i) MARRIAGE

Between 1871 and 1947 the proportion of people of both sexes in Great Britain aged 45–54 who were or had been married remained very stable. It varied between 85·2 and 88·5 per cent. Although the proportion eventually marrying remained so stable, the ages at which they married varied a great deal. This is ascertainable from the marriage rates for individual years. Between 1871 and 1911 the proportion of married persons in the age group 20–24 fell from 28% to 19%. In the same period the proportion of married persons in the 50–54 age group dropped from 88% to 86%. Thus the proportion ultimately marrying during the normal childbearing period varied only slightly, whilst the general tendency was to marry at a later age. From 1911 onwards there has been an increase in the married section of the 20–24 age group, reflecting a tendency to marry at a younger age. This has been reinforced in the post-1945 years by the greater economic opportunities for the young and by the provisions of the Welfare State.

As most births occur to married women, it follows that the changing trends in age at marriage will affect the proportion of the childbearing period during which married women will be able to bear children. The variations in marrying age during this period were not, however, sufficient to exert a dominant influence on the rapidly falling birth-rate, after 1911, and on the rising birth-rate since World War II.

9

The percentage of married women in the 20–24 age group rose from 25·4 in 1938 to 57·2 in 1969. Whilst this has resulted in recent years in an increase in the number of children born to women under 30 years of age and in the total number of annual births, the point should be noted that the divorce rate is highest for girls marrying in their teens, being twice as high as for women aged 20–24 at marriage.[1]

(ii) FAMILY SIZE

The dominant cause of change in the birth-rate has been the change in family size. In fact, any lasting influence of a changing marrying age would ultimately be felt in the average size of family.

A decline in the number of children born per married couple began among the married couples who were born at about 1850. Couples born before then, starting families in the mid-Victorian era, each produced about six surviving children. Couples starting families after 1860 gradually reduced the average size of their families, until with couples married between 1925 and 1929 the average size was 2·2 (see Table 1.2). This reduction in family size proceeded fastest amongst the higher occupational categories. The families of manual workers married between 1900 and 1930 have consistently been about 40% larger than those of non-manual workers (see Table 1.3(a) and (b), pp. 11 and 12). There have also been differences due to religion and regional custom. Couples married since the early 1930s appear to have halted the reduction in family size. Recent data suggests some slight increase in family size in Britain, but this is obscured by the birth-rate fluctuations since the late 1950s.[2] At the European Population Conference in Strasbourg, August 1971, it was suggested that there was an apparent trend towards a standard family size in Europe, regardless of parents' religion, nationality or economic circumstances. This had fallen to just over two children, and the central factor behind the shrinkage was the increase in the married female labour force.[3]

Table 1.2 *Changes in size distribution of families (1860–1946)*

Number of children born	Marriages taking place about 1860 (based on 1911 Fertility Census of England and Wales.) (%)	Marriages taking place in 1925 (based on 1946 Family Census of Great Britain.) (%)
0	9	17
1	5	25
2	6	25
3	8	14
4	9	8
5	10	5
6	10	3
7	10	2
8	9	1
9	6	0·6
10	8	0·4
Over 10	10	0·3

(Source: *Royal Commission on Population Report* 1949)

[1] *Brit. O.H.*, 1971, p. 10.
[2] *Ibid.*, p. 10.
[3] 'The shrinking Euro family', *S.T.*, 29 Aug. 1971.

(iii) FERTILITY

The Royal Commission found that there is no positive evidence of a decline in the biological reproductive capacity of the population, which might explain the post-1911 fall in the birth-rate. The main and probably only cause of this fall was the spread of deliberate family limitation.

During the nineteenth century there were powerful economic, social and cultural forces working against the continuance of an uncontrolled birth-rate. Urbanisation, the Factory and Education Acts and the spread of the factory system all helped to undermine the importance of the family as a productive unit and/or to increase the economic burden of children upon their parents. The growth and spread of scientific knowledge and of female cultural, economic and political emancipation paved the way to the desirability for and acceptance of family limitation.

In the period since World War II a definite trend towards earlier marriage has been noted. This, allied with a tendency to start families earlier in the marriage has resulted in a raising of the birth-rate during the past few years. As there is a lower limit to the age at which females can marry, the possible effect on the birth-rate of mere earliness of marriage is limited. Furthermore, if there is no real change in average family size, this high birth-rate, boosted by earlier births, will not be maintained in the future.

Nevertheless, earlier marriage does increase the risk of larger families on account of the length of the potential childbearing period and also of the greater physical reproductive capacity of younger couples. There are also several other factors which support the view that postwar marriages might be tending towards bigger families. For example, there are signs that opinion is turning against the very small family. For various reasons the small family is less fashionable than it used to be. This phenomenon has been observed throughout the western politico-economic world. Also, Government action, exercised through a more secure employment policy, welfare services, redistributive taxation (family allowances, etc.), food subsidies and free education, has lessened the economic disadvantages of parenthood.

Table 1.3 *Size of completed families*

(a) *Average size of completed families of women in various social classes who married 1851–61, as percentage of the average for all classes. (Based on 1911 Fertility Census of England and Wales.)*

Social class		% of average for all classes
I	Professional and higher administrative in finance and commerce	86
II	Employers in industry and retail trade	98
III	Skilled workers	101
IV	Intermediate between III and V	100
V	Unskilled labourers	105
VI	Textile workers	99
VII	Miners	110
VIII	Agricultural labourers	106

1. POPULATION [1]

(b) *Estimated average size of completed family, manual and non-manual workers, according to period of marriage.* (*Based on 1946 Family Census of Great Britain – Provisional Figures.*)

Date of marriage	Non-manual workers	Manual workers	Ratio of 3 to 2 (%)
1	2	3	4
1900–09	2·79	3·94	141
1910–14	2·34	3·35	143
1915–19	2·05	2·91	142
1920–24	1·89	2·73	144
1925–29	1·73	2·49	144

(Source: *Royal Commission on Population Report*, 1949)

(iv) REPRODUCTION RATES

During the interwar period of discussion about the population problem a special index was evolved to measure the extent to which the number of children born to any generation of adults is sufficient to replace that generation. This replacement measurement is known as the Net Reproduction Rate (NRR). It had been realised that the rate of natural increase is misleading, because although a population may increase in size, this may be due to an increase in the upper (non-reproductive) age groups, whilst at the same time the younger, potentially reproductive age groups might be diminishing. Therefore the basis for future replacement or expansion might be declining. The net reproduction rate eliminates the distorting effect of any current age distribution, which might alter in time, upon the estimable future population. NRR may be based on the 'productive' female population, and takes into account the current fertility and mortality rates of various age groups. The result is an index of the proportion of live female children born to any given generation of females. It is really a Maternal Net Reproduction Rate. During the period 1935–38 the Maternal NRR was 0·81 (i.e. the female population of Great Britain in the childbearing age was replacing itself in that period only to the extent of 81 %). The generation of girls born about 1840 had a Maternal NRR of 1·4 (i.e. they had 40 % more daughters than were necessary to replace themselves).

It is possible to produce a Paternal NRR – and for the period 1935–38 this was 0·90.

As the current mortality rates, which are used in estimating NRR may alter in the future, the Registrar-General for England and Wales has evolved an index based on the probability of falling mortality rates. This, of course, forecasts a higher survival rate and this index, known as the Effective Reproduction Rate, is usually one-tenth or two-tenths of one per cent higher than the NRR.

The Maternal NRR and the Paternal NRR may be combined into a Joint Net Reproduction Rate (see Table 1.4).

Table 1.4 *Joint net reproduction rates, Great Britain (1935–48)*

1935–38	0·85
1939	0·85
1940	0·81
1941	0·80
1942	0·89
1943	0·94
1944	1·03
1945	0·93
1946	1·12
1947	1·23
1948	1·07
1939–48	0·97

(Source: *Royal Commission on Population Report*, 1949)

From Table 1.4 it may be seen that at current fertility rates the population from 1935 to 1938 was only replacing itself to the extent of 85%. The Joint NRR rose from 1944 to reach 1·23 in 1947, the peak birth-rate year. It has since declined somewhat, but is still greater than 1. For the period 1944 to 1948 Joint NRR averaged 1·08, and for the ten-year period 1939–48 it was 0·97. Thus the prewar population was not replacing itself, to the extent of 15%. The postwar population up to 1948 had been producing a surplus – but the overall population for a ten-year period was just falling short in replacement. The generation born during World War II (1939–45) and marrying during the 1960s appears to be exceeding full replacement, due mainly to the increased proportions of women getting married and of children surviving to adult life.[1]

3. Age and Sex Distribution

(a) Age distribution

Population is a dynamic, changing thing and may be visualised as a flow, passing through various five-year stages, which we shall refer to as age groups, ranging from '0–4' to '85 and over'. This flow, the dynamic population, is determined by birth-rates and death-rates and is influenced by migration. When natural increase or decrease rise or fall, the flow is altered. However, it is not sufficient to know how the total volume has changed. The composition of the flow (the proportions in various age groups, male and female) has profound economic implications. For example, if we roughly divide the population into '0–14' (below working age), '15–64' (working age) and '65 and over' (above working age), a change in the birth- and death-rates would affect not only the size of the population but also the proportion of working to non-working population, of old to young. It would, furthermore, affect the average age of the population and also the numbers of males and females who will eventually pass through the reproductive cycle.

[1] *Brit. O.H.*, 1971, p. 10.

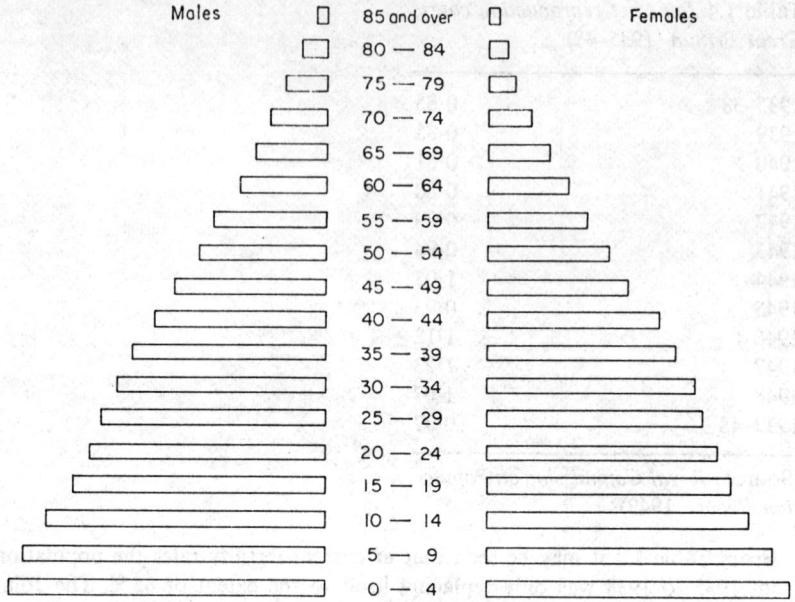

Fig. 1.5. *Stable population age pyramid (high birth- and death-rates)*

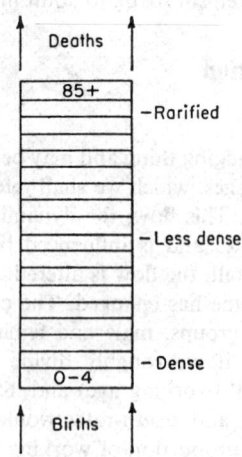

Fig. 1.6.

To grasp thoroughly the basic mechanics of age distribution, in the context of dynamic population changes, it would be useful to bear in mind the following terms:

Ageing population   rising average age.
Younger population   falling average age.
Increasing population   refers to size.
Declining population   refers to size.

The term 'constant' refers either to size or to average age.

In the case of a population which remains relatively constant in size and age distribution because of a high birth-rate and an equally high death-rate, the population graph will show a pyramid structure. Each higher age group has less members than the previous one, due to natural loss. Furthermore, because of the greater risk of death as age increases, each age group loses proportionately more members than the preceding one. The pinnacle will be the '85 and over' group, including the last survivors. Such was the typical age distribution for most countries of the world prior to 1700, viz. fairly constant populations, flowing from one age group to the next, losing members at each stage (see Fig. 1.5). The higher the mortality rate for any group, the flatter the curve at that level.

If we now visualise the population flow as passing through a tube, on which the age groups are marked, we would get a certain density of members at each different level on the tube, e.g. dense at bottom level, where new arrivals enter; rarefied at top level, where last survivors leave (see Fig. 1.6). With a population of constant size and age composition the flow lines, indicating births and deaths, would be parallel.

Using this simple diagram, we may now venture into a brief analysis of the main ways in which the variables ageing, younger, increasing and declining may be related. The results may be superimposed upon the 'constant' population pyramid, to show the main likely effect on the age pattern. We shall use the following symbols:

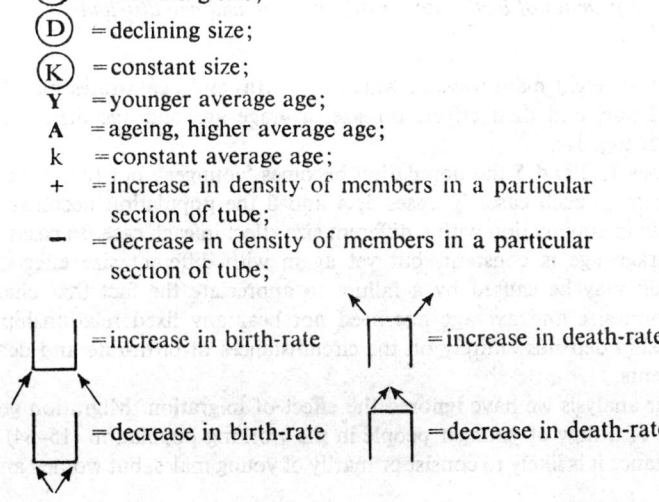

  (I)   = increasing size;
  (D)   = declining size;
  (K)   = constant size;
  Y   = younger average age;
  A   = ageing, higher average age;
  k   = constant average age;
  +   = increase in density of members in a particular section of tube;
  —   = decrease in density of members in a particular section of tube;

  = increase in birth-rate   = increase in death-rate

  = decrease in birth-rate   = decrease in death-rate

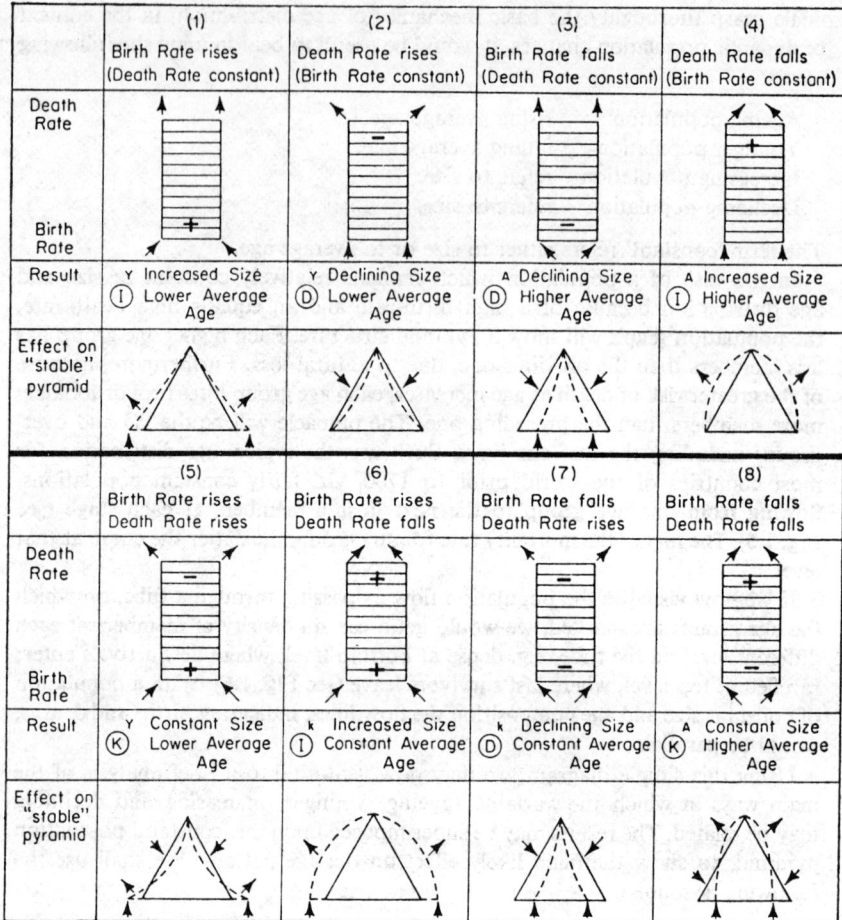

Fig. 1.7. *Dynamics of birth-rate, death-rate, size and age distribution*

There are eight main ways in which the birth- and death-rates may be combined. These, and their effects on size, average age and age distribution are shown in Fig. 1.7.

In cases 1, 2 and 5 the population becomes 'younger', but the effect on size is different in each case. In cases 3, 4 and 8 the population becomes 'older', but again in conjunction with a different size effect in each case. In cases 6 and 7 the average age is constant, but yet again with different size effects. Much confusion may be caused by a failure to appreciate the fact that changes in population size and average age need not bear any fixed relationship. Their relationship depends entirely on the circumstances of birth-rate and death-rate movements.

In our analysis we have ignored the effect of migration. Migration generally consists of a flow of younger people in the working population (15–64). In the first instance it is likely to consist primarily of young males, but women and some older dependants may follow. Thus a net gain from migration would tend to increase the proportion of younger working males – lowering the average age; a net loss would have the opposite effect.

The age distribution of Great Britain in 1891 formed a pyramid in which every group was smaller than the younger one, not only because of the mortality loss but also because there had been a period of expansion in size, during which every new generation was larger than the preceding one. Thus every age group was descended from a smaller generation than was the group below it. As this population had increased mainly due to a fall in the death-rate (birth-rate started to fall in the 1870s), there was already a noticeable 'beehive' effect in the age groups 0–30 (born since 1860) – indicating a smaller proportionate mortality loss in each of those five-year groups (see Fig. 1.8).

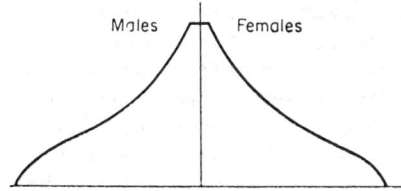

Fig. 1.8. *1891 Great Britain age pyramid*
(Source: *Royal Commission on Population Report*, 1949)

By 1947 the results of the post-1911 falling birth-rate and falling natural increase had caused the base of the population pyramid to narrow down. At the same time, mortality rates for persons up to 45 years of age had fallen very much since 1891, and had risen for age groups over 65. The combined result was a narrowing of the base and flattening of the peak, leaving a bulge higher up, with a maximum width in the 35–39 age group. This group, mostly born prior to 1911, was descended from a larger intake than those which followed. There was, however, a larger number in the 0–4 group, due to the postwar expansion in the birth-rate (see Fig. 1.9).

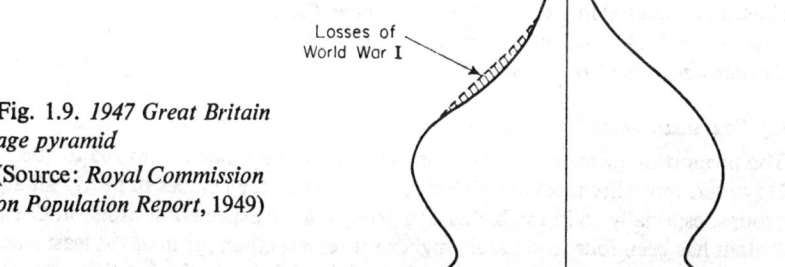

Fig. 1.9. *1947 Great Britain age pyramid*
(Source: *Royal Commission on Population Report*, 1949)

There was, moreover, a noticeably lower proportion of males as compared with females in the age groups 45–69 – reflecting the heavy male losses during the 1914–18 war, some thirty years previously.

The general effects, therefore, felt by 1891 and 1947 had been a flattening of the pyramid and a narrowing of its base, respectively. Both influences tended to raise the average age of the population, which was under 27 years in 1891 and

17

over 35 years in 1947. Thus in 1891 33% of the population was below 15 years of age and 4·5% was above 65 years of age. By 1947 the proportions were 21·3% and 12·5% respectively.[1]

Although a bigger proportion of the population was of working age (15–64) in 1947 than in 1891 (66·2% and 62·5% respectively), this group was tending to move upwards into the non-working section, leaving a relatively smaller group to take its place. By mid-1969 the proportions for the United Kingdom as a whole were:[2] 0–14 — 23·8%; 15–64 — 63·5%; 65 and over — 12·7%.

Thus although the higher postwar birth-rate has raised the proportion of under-15 dependants who will eventually form part of the working population – the proportion by 1969 of working age had fallen. These figures are summarised in Table 1.5.

Of course, the rise in the birth-rate following World War II, raising the 0–14 group to 23·8% in 1969, has not only paved the way to a proportionately bigger working population in the near future. It has also laid the foundations for a further rise in the birth-rate and expansion of population, at such time as these young people move up into and enlarge the reproductive age groups. (This assumes that there is no fall in average family size.) Also, the presence of these numerous young people – who, unless birth-rates fall for some reason, will be followed by even more numerous young entrants – is gradually reducing the average age of the population as a whole. Therefore the general death-rate, which started to dip in the late 1950s, should continue to fall slightly, at least until this recent bulge reaches the over-65 age group at the turn of the century. Both these tendencies have the effect of raising the rate of natural increase.

Table 1.5 *Proportions of working and non-working population (Great Britain)*

	1891	1947	1960	1969
0–14	33	21·3	23·3	23·8
15–65	62·5	66·2	65·1	63·5
65 and over	4·5	12·5	11·6	12·7

(Based on material in the *Royal Commission on Population Report*, 1947; *Abstract of Statistics; The Economist;* and *Britain: an Official Handbook*, 1971)

(b) **Sex distribution**

The proportion of male to female births does not vary much from 105 to 106%. However, mortality rates are higher for males than for females in nearly all age groups, especially so in the higher age groups. (The expectation of life in Great Britain has been four to six years higher for females than for males at least since 1871.) Thus in a normal population, free of the influences of migration and war (which affect males rather more than females) there would continue to be an excess of males over females up to about the age of 50, after which the male rate of loss would result in a gradually declining proportion of elderly males to females. The net result would be an excess of total females over total males. Yet from the mid-nineteenth century to the mid-twentieth century there was an

[1] Based on *Royal Commission on Population Report*, 1949, p. 14.
[2] *Ann. Abs. Stat.*, No. 107, 1970.

excess of females in the 15–49 age group, the important one from the reproductive point of view. This was mainly due, before 1914, to the net loss from migration and overseas service in the colonies. Then the 1914–18 war took a heavy toll of young and middle-aged men. The proportion of females to males in this age group was 107% in 1851. It rose to 108% in 1911 but quickly increased to 113% in 1921, gradually falling to 106% by 1939, by which time many of the earlier members of the group had moved higher up. In 1947 the relationship was 102%, closer to the 'normal' ratio.[1]

Preliminary findings of the 1971 census show that the overall preponderance of females to males had fallen slightly from 108 to 100 in 1951 and 107 to 100 in 1961 to 105·8 to 100 in 1971 – the closest relationship since 1881.[2] The fall in stillbirths and infant mortality in recent years has tended to reduce the former preponderance of females in all age groups. The age at which females outnumber males has now advanced to about 45. However, the mortality rates for males tend to be higher in most age groups: linked to the more marked lengthening of life expectancy for females as compared with males, this results in an increasing preponderance of the former in the 70+ age groups (166% in 1961 and 186·6% in 1970).[3]

4. Economic Results of a Changing Population

This field of study and its bearing on the national interest constituted one of the main preoccupations of the Royal Commission on Population, which reported in 1949. It does, of course, have the utmost bearing on all countries at all times. Any thinking person must at times wonder whether his community is growing too large or too small; whether it is growing too young or too old.

Any change in population size will involve changes in the age distribution. As we saw in Fig. 1.7, the change in size bears no fixed relationship to the change in age composition. This relationship depends upon the factors causing the change in size, viz. birth- and death-rates and migration. Size may rise whilst average age increases. It may also rise while average age decreases, or even while overall average age remains stable (because of an increase in both upper and lower age groups).

Size may also fall while average age decreases, increases or remains stable overall. Furthermore, size may remain constant while average age either increases or decreases.

Therefore we shall not attempt to present a rigid list of 'consequences' for each of these eight situations, but rather to examine some of the consequences of changing size and of changing age distribution as such. Any individual situation may then be considered on its merits.

(a) Changing size

It seems appropriate here to illustrate some comparative changes in the size of various populations over the years. They may serve as a background, against which some of the general economic consequences may be viewed (see Table 1.6).

1 *Royal Commission on Population Report*, 1949, p. 97.
2 *Econ.*, 21 Aug. 1971, p. 20.
3 *Brit. O.H.*, 1971, p. 10; 'Male mortality' chart in *Econ.*, 28 Oct. 1967, p. 373; 'Why men die sooner', *S.T.*, 15 Nov. 1970.

1. POPULATION [1]

Table 1.6 *Comparative size changes in various populations (1650–1950)*
(in millions)

	1650	1800	1850	1900	1950	1966
Great Britain	6	10	21	37	49	52¼
U.S.A.	–	5	23	75	152	197
Germany	14	20	35	54	68	76
Japan	?	?	30	45	83	99
France	16	27	35	41	42	49
Italy	13	17	24	32	47	52
Ireland	1	5	6½	4½	4⅓	4½

(Source: G. N. Clark, *The Seventeenth Century*, ch. *1*; Colin Clark, *Population Growth and Land Use*, ch. 3)

(i) DECLINING POPULATION

1. The amount of land per head (available for cultivation, building space, etc.) would rise.

2. Available natural resources, raw materials, etc., per head would rise. The smaller population would have a reduced demand for domestic food production, building space and raw materials. It would consequently be possible to reduce imports of food and materials and to relieve or improve the balance of payments position of the particular country. Apart from the reduced total demand for building space, food and materials, it would be possible to concentrate production on the more accessible sites, more fertile land and more accessible sources of raw materials and to reduce the exploitation of submarginal, high-cost sites and fields.

3. The contracted markets for industrial and agricultural products would reduce the scope for division of labour (specialised labour, equipment and techniques) and for large-scale production and the economies which flow from it.

The significance of this point would depend upon the per head accumulation of capital in the particular population. In a society where capital accumulation was low, the contracting population would generate a smaller demand for 'social capital' (investment in schools, hospitals, subsidised housing, etc.) and would release these scarce resources for much-needed investment in productive equipment and techniques.

If the society had a high per head capital accumulation, some of these resources might be idle because of the reduced stimulus to invest. Such a crisis of confidence would reduce the level of economic activity and increase unemployment.

However, provided that agencies and channels for funnelling these surplus resources were brought into operation, there would be opportunities to release them to countries which were capital-deficient, such as the emerging nations of Africa, Asia and South America.

(ii) INCREASING POPULATION

1. Land per head of population would fall.
2. Available raw materials per head would fall.

The combined effect of these two trends would be to necessitate imports of food and raw materials (thus worsening the balance of payments position) and to push the margin of building, extraction and agricultural production to high-cost sites and fields.

3. The increased population, however, would create larger markets for agricultural and industrial commodities, making possible an extension of the division of labour and large-scale production. This, allied with the stimulus to investment in new capital equipment and new techniques could result in increased productivity, a high level of activity and a reduction in unemployment.

Again, the significance of this point would depend to a great extent on the capital accumulation per head of population.[1]

The results mentioned above would be expected to follow in a society with a high capital accumulation per head. Where it was low, however, the increase in population might swallow up the available resources in the form of technically non-productive social capital investment (houses, hospitals, etc.). It might not be possible to take advantage of large-scale economies by investing in more productive, capital-intensive methods.[2]

But, the capital-deficient country might still exploit the advantages of productive investment if it were possible to tap the surplus funds of high-capital countries, to provide an already built-up reserve of funds, equipment and food.

(b) Changing age distribution

(i) YOUNGER AVERAGE AGE

1. Whether the population is increasing, declining, or constant, if it is tending towards a lower average age there will be a smaller proportion of the total in the groups above working age. This will involve a relative reduction in the burden on the working population of welfare services (pensions, old-age homes, hospitals, etc.) for the old. There may be, temporarily, an increase in the burden of welfare services for the young, such as antenatal services, welfare foods, education and so on, but eventually the increased proportion of preworking age will themselves join the labour force.

2. A younger population would be more flexible and capable of adapting itself to the needs of technological change, both from the point of view of its educability and because the young tend to have a smaller stake in capital ownership and would therefore tend to be less cautious with regard to technology.

3. Mobility of labour would tend to increase both from one trade to another and from one geographical area to another. The largest element in migration consists of younger people. This mobility need not be due entirely to people being willing to give up one job for another, but would be increased by the very fact that a greater proportion of the population would be new entrants to the labour force. These could be attracted from declining to expanding industries or into new skills at the training stage.

4. Apart from the change in welfare services and products there would be a change in the pattern of consumption away from products and services catering for the adult and old to those catering for the young (e.g. proportionately less

---

[1] See 'People, not population', *Econ.*, 5 Sept. 1964, pp. 892–3.

[2] For an interesting assessment of the economic effects of immigration see K. Jones and A. D. Smith, *The economic impact of Commonwealth immigration*, N.I.E.S.R./C.U.P., 1970; W. Keegan, 'Immigration: Measuring the impact on the economy', *F.T.*, 2 July 1970; 'The immigrant balance sheet', *S.T.*, 5 July 1970; 'Immigrant sums', *Econ.*, 4 July 1970, p. 49; 'Immigration: some economic effects', E. J. Mishan and L. Needleman, *L.B.R.*, July 1966; 'Immigration: long-run economic effects', E. J. Mishan and L. Needleman, *L.B.R.*, Jan. 1968.

motor cars, bath-chairs and luxuries such as carpets, fashionable clothes, foreign travel, etc., and proportionately more perambulators, children's and teenagers' clothes, pop records, etc.). This would involve not only a readaptation of the industrial framework of the particular country, but also a more stable demand pattern, as the requirements of the young are not so liable to fluctuations of taste and fashion as are those of the adult.[1]

5. Less competition for promotion among a proportionately smaller middle-aged section of the population.

(ii) AGEING POPULATION

The consequences of a rising average age, whatever the parallel development in total size of the population, would be the reverse of those mentioned above, viz.

1. A greater proportionate burden on the labour force of welfare services for the old and a diminishing burden of welfare services for the very young.

2. Less flexibility and ability to adjust to technological innovation and change.

3. Reduced mobility of labour and an increase in the need for governmental aid in retraining workers, in facilitating their physical movement to areas of expanding industry and in attracting newer industries to areas of declining industrial activity.

4. A change in consumption patterns from goods and services for the young to goods and services for the adult and aged.[2]

5. Greater competition for promotion and greater frustration, possibly leading to demands for a reduction in the retirement age, which would further reduce the proportion of the population of working age.

(c) Optimum population

As has been seen in (a) (i) and (ii), the effects of increasing or decreasing markets depend upon the available capital resources per head of the population. This relationship is closely bound up with the concepts of economic 'under-population', 'overpopulation' and 'optimum population'. These concepts refer not to mere numbers but to the relationship between the labour force and other factors of production (viz. the stock of natural resources and equipment). When there is such a relationship that the existing amount of labour, combined with other factors available, yields a greater per head production (is more productive) than would either a higher or a lower population, then the population is said to be of optimum size and age distribution.

It follows that a country with a higher population than this would be economically overpopulated, regardless of the actual numbers involved. Similarly, a country with a lower population than would achieve maximum average productivity with available resources would be economically underpopulated. These concepts, therefore, are not applicable for all time to any given population. If the supply of other factors of production alters in relation to the labour force; if the age composition and labour force alter; if techniques change; then, the concept of the degree to which a country is economically populated might alter over the course of time.

[1] See J. P. Lewis, 'Young people and the pattern of the economy', *L.B.R.*, Oct. 1961, pp. 33–42; 'The "new" industries of Britain', *Conjoncture* (Société Générale Economic Digest), no. 110, Dec. 1968; 'Young big spenders', *F.T.*, 26 Nov. 1970.
[2] 'Lessons of the falling birth rate', *D.T.*, 12 Dec. 1966; 'Why fewer babies mean slower growth', *Obs.*, 23 May 1971.

5. British Population Forecasts

The Royal Commission on Population noted in 1949 that, on the basis of the size and constitution of the population then, and of the birth-rate, mortality rates and pattern of family size then current, the population could be expected to grow by a few million during the next two decades and to reach a maximum by about 1977, followed by a slow decline and ageing.

It viewed such a prospect with alarm, concluding that 'a replacement size of family is desirable in Great Britain at the present time. It is impossible for policy, in its effects as distinct from its intentions, to be "neutral" on this matter since over a wide range of affairs policy and administration have a continuous influence on the trend of family size.'[1] The Commission went on to advocate measures to promote family welfare and reduce the economic disadvantages of parenthood. These measures included financial assistance (free grants, reductions in income tax, children's allowances in salary scales, etc.); family services (home helps, sitters-in, day nurseries, etc.); improved maternity service facilities (investigation and treatment of infecundity, anaesthetics for mothers, increased attendance by midwives, etc.); housing (better town and country planning, better design, improved local authority assistance to couples with children, etc.); education (preparation for family life and educational effort to inform public opinion of the facts of population trends and its consequences).

Population forecasts for the United Kingdom, made in 1955, when the postwar birth-rate appeared to be settling down to the prewar pattern, envisaged a figure of 52·2 million by 1965, a peak of about 53·5 million by the early 1980s and a gradual decline thereafter to 52·8 million by 1995.

From 1955, however, as we have noted previously, the birth-rate per thousand persons in the population had been rising, reaching 18·7 in 1964. As a result, the actual number of births each year rose by about 25,000, reaching 1,015,000 in 1964 (see Fig. 1.10). The causes of this increased birth-rate were earlier marriage and earlier reproduction in married life. It is not yet certain whether or not there is a lasting trend towards larger family size, but certainly natural fertility is higher in younger couples and the likelihood of large families becomes greater in a longer married life.

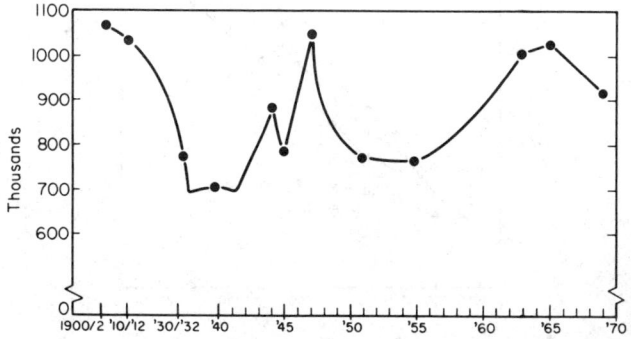

Fig. 1.10. *Live births per year* (*United Kingdom*)
(Source: *Ann. Abs. Stat.*, 101, 1964, and 107, 1970)

[1] *Report*, p. 226.

1. POPULATION [1]

Consequently the 1955 forecast for 1965 was already surpassed by mid-1960 and the 1955 'maximum' estimate for the early 1980s was reached by the end of 1964. Whereas the 1955 forecast predicted a population of 52·8 million by the end of the century, forecasts made in 1965 envisaged 74·66 million by that date (see Fig. 1.11). With the subsequent fall in the birth-rate and actual number of live births after 1964, however, the population projections or forecasts have had to be revised annually. The mid-1969 projection for the year 2001 was about 8 million lower than that of 1965, having fallen to 66·5 million. This figure remained unaltered in the forecast made at end-1971.[1]

It is estimated that by the end of the century, even if the birth-rate declines somewhat (as a result of the changed age distribution of the population by then) the annual number of births will be about 1·1 million, which would be more than were born annually at the beginning of this century, when population was less than 40 million and birth-rate was about 27 per thousand. Thus the present rate of natural increase, approximately 5 per thousand (or 0·5% of a population greater than 50 million) will yield an increase each year of about ¼ million–⅓ million – resulting in over 65 million by the close of the century, six people for every five living at the end of the 1950s. Whereas it appeared, before and just after World War II, that the future increase in the British population during the second half of the twentieth century would be about a quarter of the actual increase during the first half, it now seems that this increase will be at least as great as that in the first fifty years.

Apart from the increase in size, the forecasts now suggest some interesting

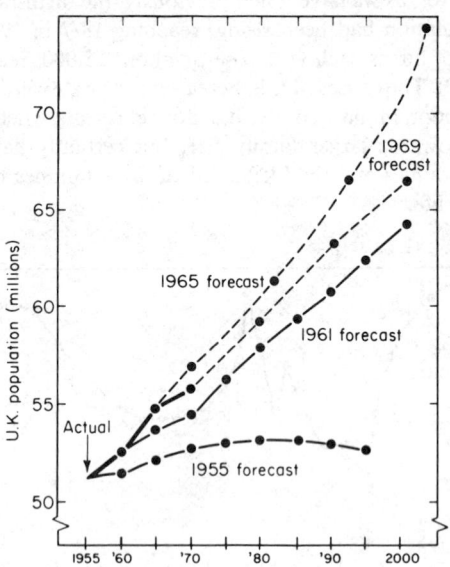

Fig. 1.11. *United Kingdom population forecasts*
(Source: *Econ.*, 29 September 1961; *Ann. Abs.
Stat., 107, 1970*)

[1] *Ann. Abs. Stat.*, 107, 1970 and *F.T.*, 11 Nov. 1971.

changes in the age distribution of the population (see Table 1.7). Thus from 1970 to 1980 the population of working age (15–64) should increase by 1·5 million, from 35·3 to 36·7 million. Those below working age (0–14) should rise by 0·5 million from 13·4 to 14·0 million, and those above working age (over 65) should increase by 1·0 million from 7·1 to 8·1 million. Those of working age will, therefore, form a smaller proportion of the total population, which will be of higher average age as the middle-aged bulge of the late 1950s moves up and is succeeded by the less numerous survivors of the interwar generations. From 1980 to 2000 the middle-aged bulge of the late 1950s will have disappeared and the high-birth

Table 1.7 *Population changes by age group in U.K.* (*mid-1969 projections*)

	0·6 2·4	☐ = 1970
0–14 years	13·4	
	1·4 5·2	▨ = 1980
15–64 years	35·3	
	1·0	▨ = 2000
65 + years	7·1 ▨ −0·05	
Total	55·87 3·0 7·6	
	(millions)	

(Based on *Ann. Abs. Stat.*, 107, 1970)

bulge which followed World War II will have moved up. Thus the 15–64 group should increase by 5·2 million to 42 million, the over-65 group should fall to 8·0 million and the 0–14 group should increase by 2·4 million to 16·5 million. The working population will, therefore, become relatively bigger and the average age will fall somewhat, due to the relatively smaller old-age groups and the continuous large inflow at the base of the age pyramid.[1]

6. Geographical Distribution

When examining the distribution of the British population over the area of the United Kingdom, several lines of approach may be utilised:
1. The distribution by country.
2. The distribution between urban and rural in each country.
3. The distribution by major administrative 'Standard Region'.
4. The distribution in areas of highly concentrated population or conurbations around the biggest cities.

The surface area of the United Kingdom is about 93⅓ thousand square miles. With a population of 52⅔ million in 1961 this gives a population density, on average, of 571 persons per square mile – one of the highest in the world. This population is not, however, evenly distributed. Nor is the uneven distribution pattern static. There have been many changes during this century in the rates of growth of various areas, largely due to internal migration.

Table 1.8 illustrates the geographical distribution pattern for the United Kingdom at various censal periods from 1921 to 1969.

From 1921 to 1931, although the total United Kingdom population increased,

[1] 'The future population', *E.P.R.*, 12 Feb. 1971; 'The British population', *D.E.A. Pr. Rep. and Reg.*, 43, Aug. 1968; 'The year 2000', *Econ.*, 17 May 1969, p. 26; chart in *Econ.*, 22 June 1968, p. 49.

that of Wales and Scotland actually declined, because the net loss from migration to other parts of the United Kingdom and abroad was greater than the natural increase. From 1931 to 1961 the populations of all member countries increased, but the greatest increases were still in England, particularly in the South-East, West Midlands, South-West and East Midlands administrative standard regions. The smallest increase was in Wales (see Table 1.8).

In the South-East Home Counties, from 1951 to 1961, Greater London experienced a net loss in population, while the rest of the region, roughly equivalent in numbers to Greater London, gained about five times as much, in absolute terms. From 1961 to 1966 this shift from the inner urban area of Greater London and into the Home Counties continued (see Fig. 1.12). The fastest-growing counties were West Sussex and Essex, followed by East Sussex, Kent, Berkshire and the Isle of Wight.

Between the 1961 and 1971 censuses all the conurbations except West York-

Table 1.8 *Geographical distribution of the U.K. population (thousands)*

	Area in square miles	1921	1931	1951	1961	1969	1981 (pro-jected)
Urban and Rural Districts							
England and Wales							
Urban districts	8,302·2	30,035	31,952	35,336	36,872	38,386	
Rural districts	50,046·3	7,851	8,000	8.422	9,223	10,441	
TOTAL	58,348·5	37,886	39,952	43,758	46,095	48,827	51,833
Scotland							
Cities and burghs	470·3	3,311	3,362	3,563	3,646	3,707	
Landward areas	29,941·8	1,572	1,481	1,534	1,533	1,488	
TOTAL	30,412·1	4,883	4,843	5,097	5,179	5,195	5,347
Northern Ireland							
Urban districts	92·8	638	678	720	771	840	
Rural districts	5,359·0	619	602	643	656	673	
TOTAL	5,451·8	1,257	1,280	1,363	1,427	1,513	1,646
Standard Regions of							
England and Wales							
North	7,470·7	3,019	3,037	3,138	3,250	3,346	3,433
Yorks and Humberside	5,481·1	4,095	4,307	4,527	4,635	4,811	4,959
North-West	3,085·7	6,022	6,196	6,447	6,567	6,770	7,040
East Midlands	4,702·2	2,337	2,511	2,887	3,100	3,349	3,742
West Midlands	5,024·4	3,504	3,743	4,423	4,758	5,145	5,516
East Anglia	4,851·6	1,211	1,233	1,382	1,470	1,657	1,941
South-East	10,584·4	12,317	13,537	15,127	16,271	17,295	18,281
South-West	9,135·0	2,725	2,794	3,229	3,411	3,730	4,099
Wales	8,016·4	2,656	2,593	2,599	2,644	2,725	2,822
Conurbations							
Greater London	616·4	7,488	8,216	8,348	8,183	7,703	
West Midlands	268·8	1,773	1,933	2,237	2,347	2,441	
West Yorkshire	484·6	1,614	1,655	1,693	1,704	1,727	
South-East Lancashire	379·6	2,361	2,427	2,423	2,428	2,433	
Merseyside	150·3	1,263	1,347	1,382	1,384	1,342	
Tyneside	90·2	816	827	836	855	840	
Central Clydeside	300·2	1,638	1,690	1,758	1,802	1,746	

(Sources: *Ann. Abs. Stat.*, no. 107, 1970; *Brit. O.H.*, 1971)

shire followed the same trend as Greater London, and lost population at a faster rate than during the 1951–61 decade. From 1961 to 1971 the main area of population growth was the belt of country from the Midlands to the Solent and the South-East. West Suffolk had the fastest rate of growth, but in absolute terms Essex headed the list, with a gain of 250,000 people.[1]

These changes in the geographical distribution of the United Kingdom population are closely associated with gradual changes in the structure of the economy and in the resultant occupational redistribution of the labour force between different industries in different parts of Britain.

The United Kingdom population is predominantly urban and suburban. In England and Wales only about one-fifth live in 'rural districts'; in Scotland only about two-sevenths live in 'landward areas'; in Northern Ireland about nine-twentieths live in rural districts. Most of the increases in each of these countries since 1911 have been in urban districts (England, Wales and Northern Ireland) and in cities and burghs (Scotland). This implies that a migration trend in each country, from country to town, has been superimposed on the migration trend from Wales, Scotland and Northern Ireland to England. This trend away from rural areas proceeded most rapidly during the nineteenth century, due to the

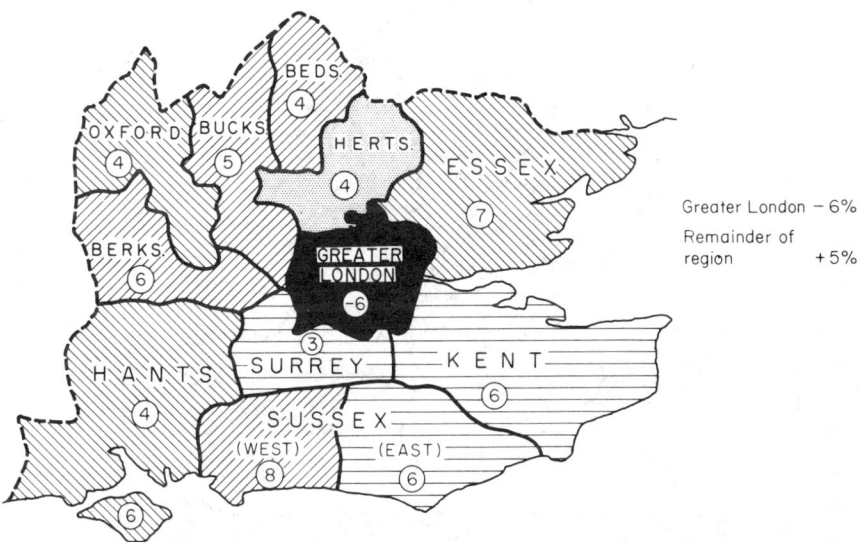

Greater London − 6%
Remainder of region + 5%

Fig. 1.12. *Population shifts in the south-east of England, 1961–66 (percentage changes)*
(Source: *Econ.* 4 Jan. 1969).

labour requirements of the newly developing industries. By the turn of the century three-quarters of the United Kingdom population lived within urban administrative areas, over half of them in the seven great conurbations. Since 1921 nearly 40% of the United Kingdom population has lived in these conurbations (see Fig. 1.13), whose centres are London (Greater London), Manchester (South-east Lancashire), Birmingham and Wolverhampton (west Midlands),

[1] *Econ.*, 21 Aug. 1971, p. 20.

Glasgow (central Clydeside), Leeds and Bradford (west Yorkshire), Liverpool (Merseyside) and Newcastle upon Tyne (Tyneside). These conurbations are not precise administrative areas but are continuously built up and economically interdependent areas.

Greater London contains the largest single concentration of population. In turn it is the social and economic magnet and dynamo for a still wider area.

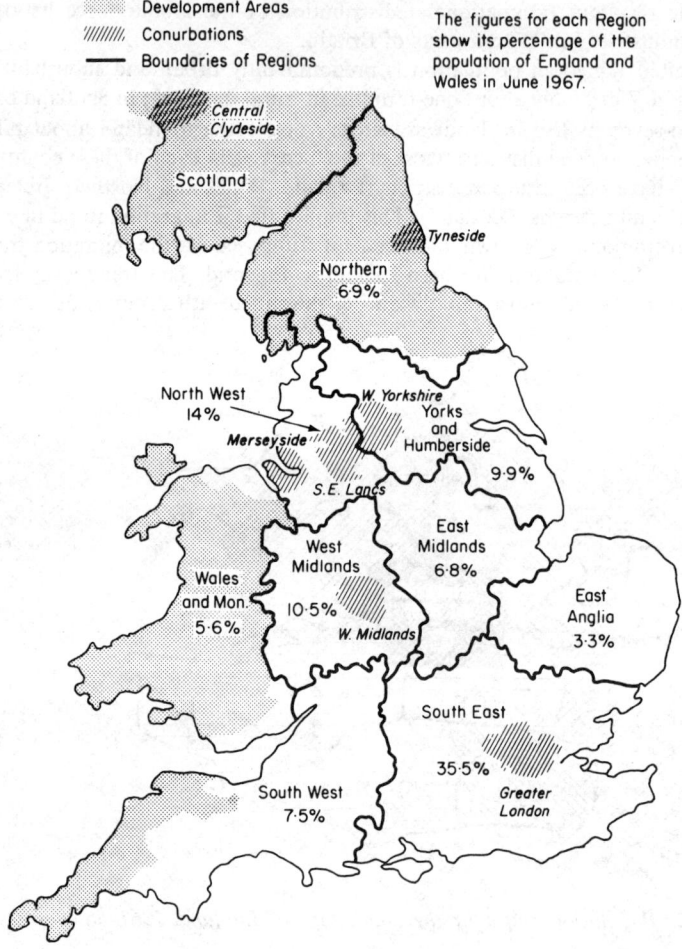

Fig. 1.13. *Regions, Conurbations and population distribution* (Source: *B.B.C.B.*, No. 17, Feb. 1968)

From 1939 to 1951 the former County of London lost about 2–3 millions, consisting mainly of people who gave up homes in the centre of the conurbation. The outer suburban fringes of the conurbation and the Government-sponsored new towns in the Home Counties received these migrants from the centre of the conurbation. During the 1950s this process continued and from 1951 to 1961 the County of London decreased in population by 5%, whilst the population of

Hertfordshire, for example, increased by 37%. Many of the people who moved to the fringes of the conurbation and beyond still work in London and commute daily. This process has been facilitated by progress in rail transport and by the increase in private car ownership.

The extent of population mobility may be gauged from the finding that in 1966 10·7% of residents in Great Britain – for purposes of work, housing or study—had changed their address during the preceding year: 33% had moved in the previous five years and 4·2% had moved between England and Scotland or Wales, or from one region to another during the period 1961–66.[1]

Apart from the spread of car ownership, the development of commuter public transport and the spread of private property developments to meet the demand for housing, an important factor in the process of dispersal and mobility has been the planned transfer of population to the new towns (see Fig. 1.14 and Table 1.9).

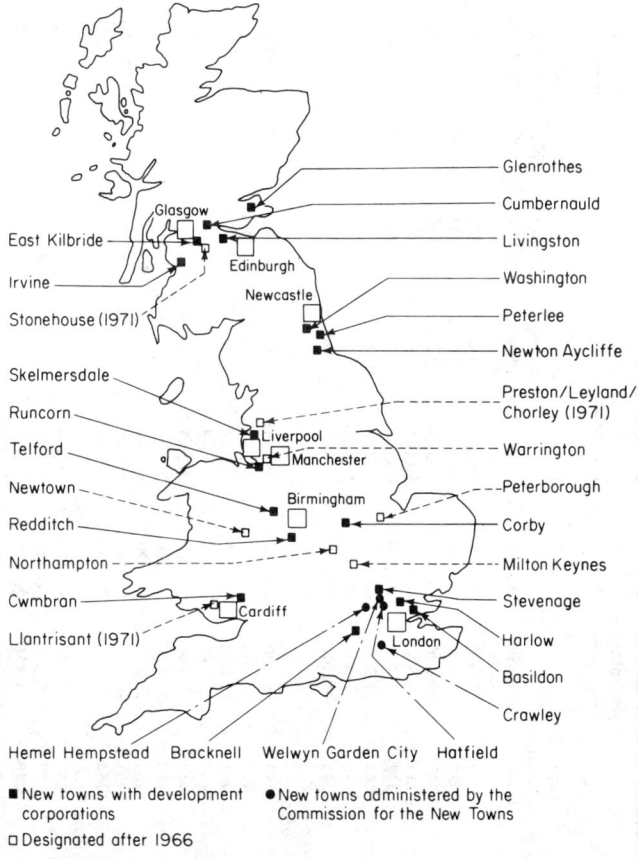

Fig. 1.14. *New towns in Great Britain, 1971.*
(Based on material in *D.E.A. Pr. Rep. Ind. and Reg.*, 24, Jan. 1967; *Brit. O.H.*, 1971; *Conjuncture*, 122, Dec. 1969)

[1] *Brit. O.H.*, 1971, p. 16.

30

Table 1.9 *Progress in the New Towns (to 30 September 1966)*

Town	Year of Designation	Population Original	Population Present	Population Ultimate	New Dwellings Completed	New Dwellings Under construction	New Industries No. of firms	New Industries No. employed by new firms	New Schools	New Shops	New Office Space (sq. ft.)	Estimated Capital Expenditure £
London's New Towns												
Basildon	1949	25,000	70,797	106,000	14,998	1,422	121	19,784	35	318	112,715	58,767,000
Bracknell	1949	5,000	25,965	60,000	6,041	431	29	7,803	13	101	269,192	23,420,000
Crawley	1947	10,000	63,062	75,000	13,534	150	86	17,335	24	293	355,950	32,787,000
Harlow	1947	4,500	70,905	80,000	17,817	1,673	94	16,124	29	290	204,968	54,144,000
Hatfield	1948	8,500	24,149	29,000	4,092	293	15	1,023	14	96	93,582	10,972,000
Hemel Hempstead	1947	21,000	67,177	80,000	12,868	96	65	11,392	30	308	374,936	40,219,000
Stevenage	1946	7,000	58,766	80,000	14,475	875	60	16,521	29	300	249,746	46,600,000
Welwyn Garden City	1948	18,500	43,165	50,000	6,034	395	54	5,120	20	123	166,804	17,319,000
Other New Towns in England and Wales:												
Corby	1950	15,700	45,574	75,000	6,059	643	24	3,918	20	190	56,924	18,400,000
Cwmbran	1949	12,000	38,330	55,000	6,506	896	15	528	15	150	37,950	21,242,000
Telford	1963	21,000	21,000	90,000	—	9	7	21	—	—	—	3,211,000
Newton Aycliffe	1947	60	17,138	45,000	4,929	279	—	2,192	10	74	16,120	10,956,000
Peterlee	1948	200	19,817	30,000	5,541	4	21	—	16	74	33,304	14,263,000
Redditch	1964	29,000	29,000	90,000	—	—	—	—	—	—	—	2,995,000
Runcorn	1964	28,500	28,500	90,000	—	—	—	—	—	—	—	1,932,000
Skelmersdale	1961	10,000	13,249	80,000	478	1,210	25	2,416	1	4	30,865	10,107,000
Washington	1964	20,000	20,000	80,000	—	•	—	—	—	—	—	781,000
Scottish New Towns												
Cumbernauld	1955	3,500	21,812	70,000	5,167	1,055	41	5,303	7	32	15,592	24,537,000
East Kilbride	1947	2,500	50,937	100,000	13,156	1,672	117	12,453	13	138	62,175	39,511,000
Glenrothes	1948	1,150	20,871	75,000	5,578	977	20	3,600	9	71	53,384	18,335,000
Irvine	1966	30,000	30,000	85,000	—	—	—	—	—	—	—	—
Livingston	1962	2,063	3,300	100,000	441	1,043	8	531	1	—	36,000	8,893,000
Total		275,173	783,514	1,625,000	137,714	13,123	802	126,064	286	2,562	2,170,207	459,391,000

(*Source: D.E.A. Pr. Rep. Ind. and Reg.*, 24, Jan. 1967)

During the 1960s a great deal of attention began to be paid to the need for coordinating public strategy on population, industrial location and development and employment policy on a regional basis. The two most pressing needs were the problems of planning for the future industrial, commercial and population pattern of the South-East region and of relieving the unemployment problems of the fringe regions by way of planning for better balanced growth.

Between 1964 and 1966 Economic Planning Councils and Boards were established in Great Britain – eight in England and one each for Scotland and Wales.[1] All have completed and published major reports on their regions and have outlined medium and longer-term strategies on population, industry and employment.[2] An important development in the context of regional planning has been the concept of the 'growth centre'. This has been defined as an urban core and its surrounding commuter area, capable of growth. It is a trigger-point or centre of economic dynamism, at which investment, development of services and diversification of economic activity should be concentrated, so as to generate self-sustaining growth for the whole region.[3]

7. Occupational Distribution

The proportion of a population which is gainfully employed will be influenced by factors such as the age distribution (proportion of infants and aged people); legislation (minimum working age, pensionable age, etc.); family pattern (large families – wives cannot work; small families – wives may be able to work, etc.) level of affluence (indigent – all potential breadwinners may be required to work; affluent – heads of households may be sufficient to provide for their dependents); social custom.

The distribution of a labour force between various types of occupation and between various individual jobs will be influenced by such factors as the state of technical knowledge, the accumulation of capital per head of population, the relative advantages possessed by various occupations, the general level of affluence and the processes of economic and technological change.

The working population may be split up into the following main categories:

PRODUCTION OF GOODS (Primary and secondary activities)
(a) Primary Extraction: (1) agriculture; (2) mining and quarrying; (3) fishing
(b) Manufacturing: (1) process; (2) assembly.
(c) Public utilities (gas, electricity and water).
(d) Construction.

PROVISION OF SERVICES (Tertiary activities)
(a) Commercial.
(b) Direct: (1) private; (2) public: (i) civilian; (ii) military.

---

[1] Fig. 1.13.
[2] See *Brit. O.H.*, 1971, pp. 236–7; *B.B.C.B.*, 17, Feb. 1968. The most important of these – the Strategic Plan for the South-East – produced in 1970, was approved in principle by the Government in October 1971. It was an attempt to bring together the various economic, social and other factors involved in the long-term planning of the region, by way of a flexible strategy designed to concentrate future development in selected growth areas at varying distances from London (see *F.T.*, 13 Oct. 1971; *Econ.*, 30 May 1970, pp. 52–3).
[3] *D.E.A. Pr. Rep. Ind. and Reg.*, 47, Dec. 1968.

The proportion of a working population engaged in the provision of services provides an index of economic, social, political and military interest. For example, a poor economy could not support many people engaged in private direct services, such as entertainers, psychiatrists, doctors and teachers. A police state might have a relatively large proportion of people engaged in public direct services, such as the police force, the armed forces and an inflated civil service.

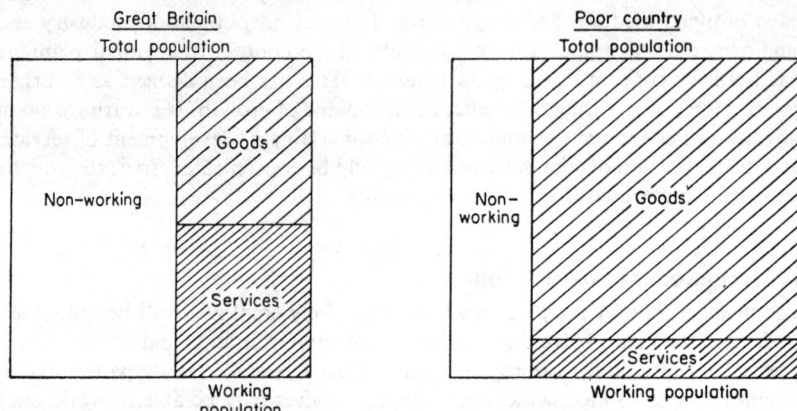

Fig. 1.15. *Working population and occupational distribution*

Thus we have two simple indexes of economic significance, when examining the occupational distribution of any country: the proportion of the total population in gainful employment and the proportion of the occupied population providing commercial and direct services. Fig. 1.15 illustrates simply the case of Great Britain, a prosperous, industrialised country, where about 48% of the total population are gainfully employed and about 48% of those people are providing services. Also illustrated is the case of an imaginary country, poor and with a backward economy, where most of the population are obliged to work in production (primarily extraction and manufacturing) and which can support only a small proportion of persons in service occupations.[1]

The working population of the United Kingdom consists of people who are in or seeking gainful employment and who are either self-employed or work for a wage or salary. It includes all persons of normal working age (15–59 for women; 15–64 for men) who are able and willing to work and nearly 1¼ million older people who are still at work. It includes, therefore, part-time workers, members of the armed forces and persons registered as unemployed. It excludes children under 15 years of age, disabled and retired persons, students of working age who are receiving full-time education, housewives not wishing to work and persons of private means not wishing to work.

[1] Some cases of excessive expansion in the tertiary or services sector have been noticed in some developing countries – reflecting either superficial employment (or 'disguised unemployment') or precocious, distorted development, due to the growth of economic relationships with more developed regions (see P. Bairoch and J.-M. Limbor, 'Changes in the industrial distribution of the world labour force, by region, 1880–1960', paper in *International Labour Review*, 98, Oct. 1968, p. 325; 'The poor world's cities', *Econ.*, 6 Dec. 1969, p. 57).

Apart from the size of the working population and its relationship to the total population, economists are keenly interested in the 'activity rate' or 'labour force participation rate'. This generally relates to the proportions of the male or female population eligible for employment (over the age of 15) who are registered as being in, or seeking, gainful employment.[1] This activity rate is calculated as:

$$\frac{\text{No. of persons in the working population}}{\text{No. of persons aged 15 and over in the population}} \times 100$$

Activity rates may also be established for particular sections or age groups in the population above 15 years of age. The patterns of activity rates for males and females in various age groups during the period 1951 to 1966 may be seen in Fig. 1.16. It will be seen that whereas most of the male rates have been fairly steady, that of the 15–24 females has followed a downward trend and those of the 25–44 and 45–59 females have followed upward trends.

There was a fall in the over-65 male rate, as against a rise in the over-65 female rate. The general overall rate in 1951 was 54·6% and this rose to 57·4% in 1966, largely due to the increase in the female activity rate, which rose from 35·4% to 40·5%. Table 1.10 shows the average male and female activity rates over the period 1951–1966 in the pre-1966 administrative standard regions: there were variations of 19·1% for males and 15·1% for females.

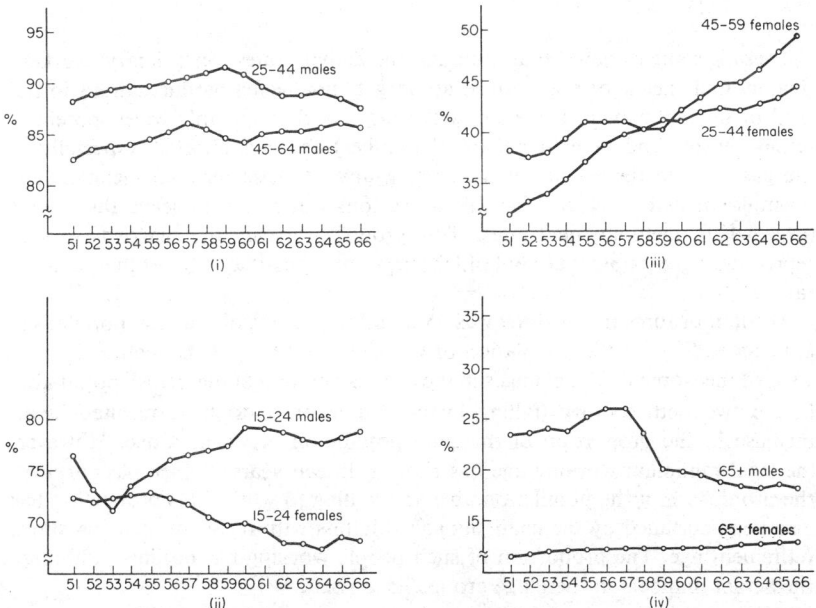

Fig. 1.16. *Great Britain activity rates, 1951–66*
(Source: B. A. Corry and J. A. Roberts, 'Activity rates and unemployment; the experience of the United Kingdom 1951–66', *Applied Economics*, No. 3, 1970, p. 182)

[1] See L. C. Hunter and D. J. Robertson, *Economics of Wages and Labour*, 1969, pp. 145–50; B. A. Corry and J. A. Roberts, 'Activity rates and unemployment: the experience of the United Kingdom 1951–66', paper in *Applied Economics*, No. 3, 1970, pp. 179–201.

Table 1.10 *Regional activity rates, 1951–66*

Region	Males %	Females %
South-East	75·627	37·501
South-West	64·249	27·540
Midlands	81·825	41·096
North Midlands	76·518	34·088
East and West Ridings	80·825	36·857
North-West	80·532	41·758
North	78·227	28·443
Scotland	78·391	36·660
Wales	71·290	25·502
Northern Ireland	61·813	33.559

(Source: B. A. Corry and J. A. Roberts, 'Activity rates and unemployment: the experience of the United Kingdom 1951–66', *Applied Economics*, No. 3, 1970, p. 185)

There is some evidence that although the activity rates for 'primary' workers (mainly male heads of households) are largely unaffected by fluctuations in the level of unemployment, those for 'secondary' workers (mainly wives, potential school leavers and older members of families) are thus affected, especially in the case of female secondary workers. Many of these may be ineligible for unemployment benefit and for this or various other reasons leave the labour force when unemployment rises. This group, primarily the married women, represents a great potential pool of labour, were it possible to boost their activity rate.

The labour force in mid-1969 was 25·2 million, 47·5% of the total population. It included 73% of the population of working age (91% of the men and about 53% of the women). The changes in the age distribution of the British population in the twentieth century (falling birth- and death-rates) have resulted in an increase in the proportion of the total population of working age. However, the legal minimum working age has risen to fifteen years[1], which has curtailed the proportion of the population able and willing to work. This proportion has also been curtailed by the changing social habits with regard to persons above retirement age. The proportion of such people working has declined, although the actual numbers in these age groups have risen.

An O.E.C.D. study in 1967 made some interesting international comparisons with regard to rates of increase in populations of working age, in actual working populations and in the 'dependency ratios' or proportions of inactive to active populations (see Fig. 1.17), for the period to 1980. Britain's general activity rate was likely to go up, but so was the dependency ratio.

[1] The raising of the minimum school-leaving age in 1973 was expected to cause a sharp reduction in the 15–24 activity rate and in the size of the working population in the following year.

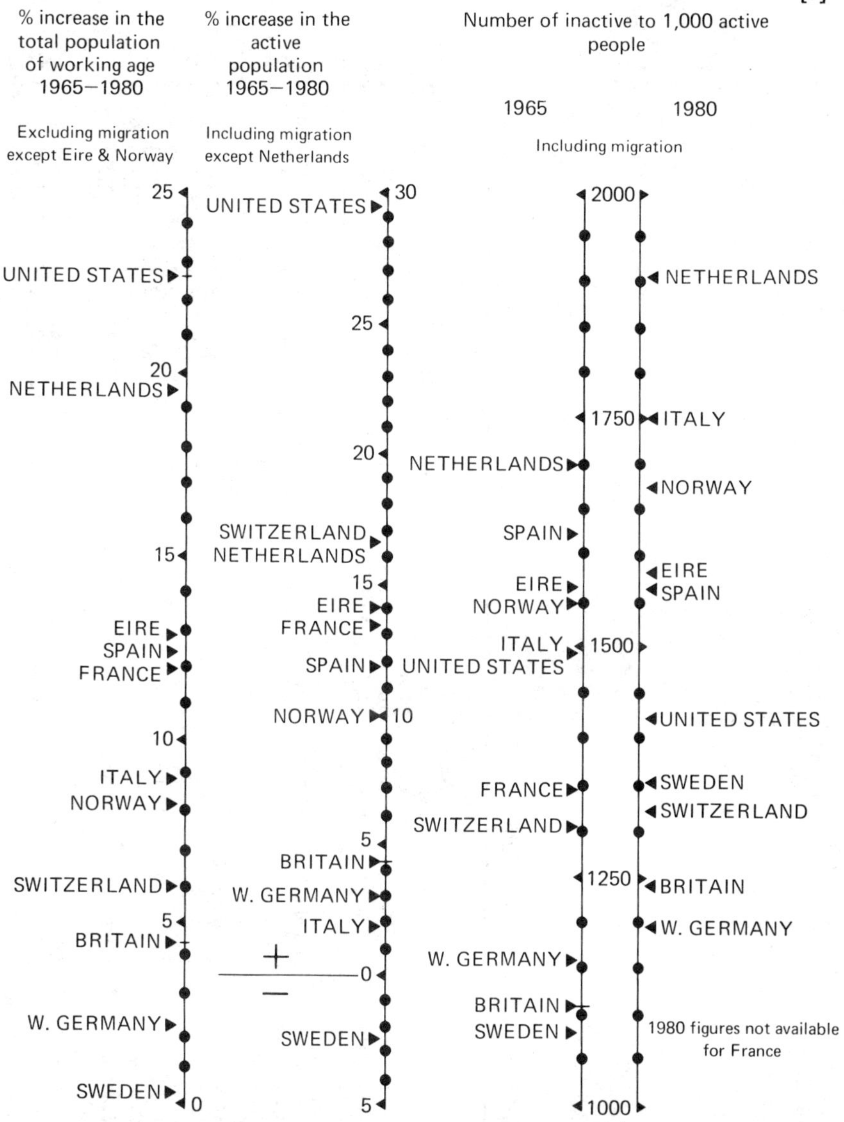

% increase in the total population of working age 1965–1980

Excluding migration except Eire & Norway

% increase in the active population 1965–1980

Including migration except Netherlands

Number of inactive to 1,000 active people

1965   1980

Including migration

25
UNITED STATES ► 30

UNITED STATES ►

◄ 2000 ►

◄ NETHERLANDS

25

20
NETHERLANDS ►

◄ 1750 ◄ ITALY

20
NETHERLANDS ►

◄ NORWAY

SWITZERLAND
15 ◄ NETHERLANDS

SPAIN ►

◄ EIRE
◄ SPAIN

15
EIRE ►
FRANCE ►

EIRE ►
NORWAY ►

EIRE ►
SPAIN ►
FRANCE ►

SPAIN ►

ITALY ◄ 1500 ►
UNITED STATES

NORWAY ► 10

10

◄ UNITED STATES

ITALY ►
NORWAY ►

FRANCE ►

◄ SWEDEN
◄ SWITZERLAND

5
BRITAIN ►

SWITZERLAND ►

SWITZERLAND ►
5
BRITAIN ►

W. GERMANY ►
ITALY ►

◄ 1250 ◄ BRITAIN

+
— 0

W. GERMANY ►

◄ W. GERMANY

W. GERMANY ►

SWEDEN ►

BRITAIN ►
SWEDEN ►

1980 figures not available for France

SWEDEN ► 0

5

◄ 1000 ►

Fig. 1.17. *Populations of working age, working populations and dependency ratios, 1965–80*
(Source: *Econ.*, 4 Feb. 1967, p. 427)

There has not been much change in the proportions of working men in age groups 20–64 during the present century. Among women, however, there has been a steady increase in the proportions employed in the age group 15–59, the most significant element being an increase in the employment of married women,

35

Table 1.11 Industrial distribution of the occupied population.

Occupational Classification	England & Wales 1841 % of working pop.	1901 % of working pop.	Great Britain 1939 No. ('000s)	1939 % of working pop.	Mid-1961* No. ('000s)	Mid-1961* % of working pop.	Mid-1969 No. ('000s)	Mid-1969 % of working pop.
[a] Extraction:								
Agriculture, forestry and fishing	22·8	9·0	950	4·81	947	3·85	600(est.)	2·4
Mining and quarrying	3·0	5·8	873	4·42	729	2·96	442	1·75
[b] Manufacturing:								
Chemicals and allied trades			294	1·49	542	2·2	528	2·1
Metals, engineering and vehicles			2,812	14·2	4,476	18·2	4,469	17·75
Textiles	35·4	32·6	1,002	5·07	839	3·41	696	2·77
Clothing			752	3·81	589	2·39	501	2·0
Food, drink and tobacco			654	3·31	832	3·38	850	3·37
Other manufactures			1,301	6·59	1,638	6·66	2,199	8·75
Total in manufacturing			6,815	34·5	8,917	36·3	8,953	35·7
[c] Public utilities:								
Gas, electricity, water			242	1·23	376	1·53	397	1·58
[d] Construction	6·1	8·1	1,310	6·63	1,592	6·47	1,446	5·77
Total in production	67·3	55·5	10,190	51·6	12,561	51·1	11,838	47·2

(A) Production of Goods

[a] Commercial and Private Direct:									
Distributive trades	28·4 ⎱		2,887	14·6	3,309	13·5	2,702	10·75	
Professional, financial and miscellaneous services	⎰	32·7	2,225	11·3	5,048	20·5	5,552	22·2	
Transport and communications†	2·9	9·3	1,233	6·24	1,686	6·86	1,552	6·16	
[b] Public direct:									
(i) Civilian:									
National Government Service	0·6 ⎱	1·4	1,465‡ ⎱	7·42	512	2·08	558	2·22	
Local Government Service	⎰		⎰		749	3·05	820	3·27	
Total in civil employment	99·2	98·9	18,000	91·4	23,865	97·1	23,022	92·0	
(ii) Military:									
H.M. Forces	0·8	1·1	480	2·43	474	1·93	380	1·52	
Total in Services	32·7	44·5	8,290	42	11,778	48	11,564	46·2	
(C) Registered Unemployed	—	—	1,270	6·43	251	1·02	483	1·92	
Total Working Population	100	100	19,750	100	24,590	100	25,207	100	
Total Population ('000s)	15,914	37,000	46,467		51,250		53,500		
Working Pop. as % of Total Population	?	?	42·5		48		47·5		

(B) Services

* 1961 figures are based on the Standard Industrial Classification, introduced in 1958.

† Transport and Communications classified as commercial and private direct, as the direct element was mostly private until nationalisation of the railways and road haulage.

‡ Includes 80,000 in Civil Defence, National Fire Service and Police.

N.B. 1969 figures are based on the new Standard Industrial Classification, introduced in 1968. For all groups *except* Agriculture, Forestry and Fishing figures are for *employees* only. Of the total employers and self-employed (1,744,000) 200,000 have been estimated as part of the Agriculture, Forestry and Fishing labour force. 1,544,000 should be added to the remaining figures to arrive at the Total Working Population.

(Sources: Colin Clark, *Conditions of Economic Progress*; *Ann. Abs. Stat.*, 84 and 107; *Brit. O.H.*, 1962 and 1971)

especially since the beginning of World War II. Fig. 1.18 illustrates the comparative crude activity rates of female populations in several countries in 1961 and 1962 – the ratios representing working females as percentages of total females.

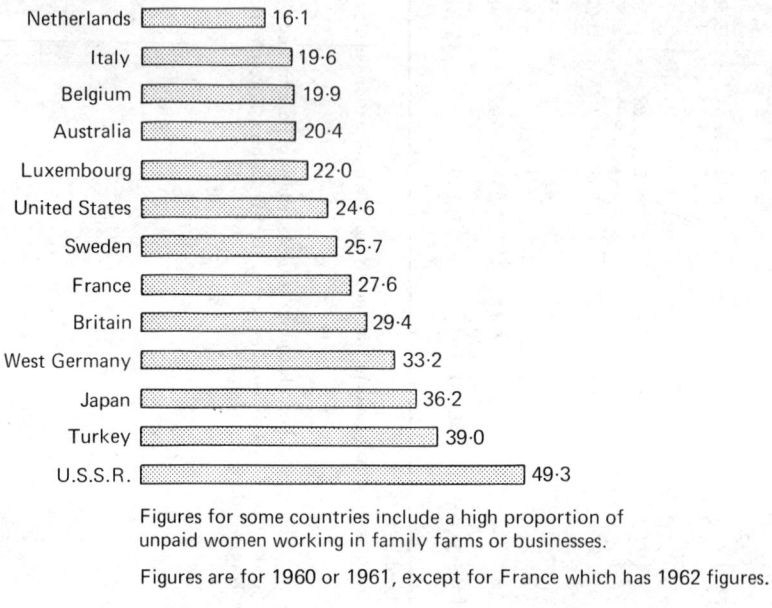

Netherlands	16·1
Italy	19·6
Belgium	19·9
Australia	20·4
Luxembourg	22·0
United States	24·6
Sweden	25·7
France	27·6
Britain	29·4
West Germany	33·2
Japan	36·2
Turkey	39·0
U.S.S.R.	49·3

Figures for some countries include a high proportion of unpaid women working in family farms or businesses.

Figures are for 1960 or 1961, except for France which has 1962 figures.

Figures for Britain do not include Northern Ireland.

Fig. 1.18. *Percentages of the total female population at work in Britain and twelve other countries*
(Source: *D.E.A. Pr. Rep. Ind. and Reg.*, 25, Feb. 1967)

The proportion in Production of Goods as a whole in mid-1969 was just under half (47·2%) – not much change since before World War II but much less than in 1841 (67·3%). The proportion in Services as a whole was 46·2% – not much greater than in 1901 (the 1939 figure was 42%, but was distorted by the high unemployment figure and the preparations for war), but much higher than in 1841 (32·7%).

Within these broad categories, however, there were several highly significant changes in the distribution of the labour force. Table 1.11 shows this distribution at the sixty-year periods 1841–1900, 1901–61 and for the immediate prewar year, 1939. This permits long-term comparisons to be made for the period since the middle of the nineteenth century, and also permits a short-term comparison to be made with the period just before World War II.

The salient points which emerge are as follows:

1. A decline in the proportion engaged in agriculture, forestry and fishing. This process has been less rapid since 1901 than between 1841 and 1901.

2. An increase in the proportions engaged in construction and in mining and quarrying, from 1841–1901, followed by a decrease to about the original level by 1961.

3. A considerable increase in the numbers employed in the distributive trades, and a general increase in the proportions employed in providing other commercial and direct services, both private and public.

Within this general trend there was a considerable decline in indoor private domestic service, in which the number of women employed fell by about 1 million between 1901 and 1951. There was a general increase in administrative, technical and clerical employment, including public administration (local and national), especially in the employment of women in clerical work. Fig. 1.19 gives some indication as to the deployment of female labour in 1961. Transport and communications increased, proportionately, from 1841 to 1901 but then declined somewhat. This expansion of 'white collar' employment is, in fact, superimposed upon the whole field of production. From 1948 to 1961 the proportion of 'white collar' workers in industry rose from 15% to 23% and the proportion of manual workers declined accordingly.[1]

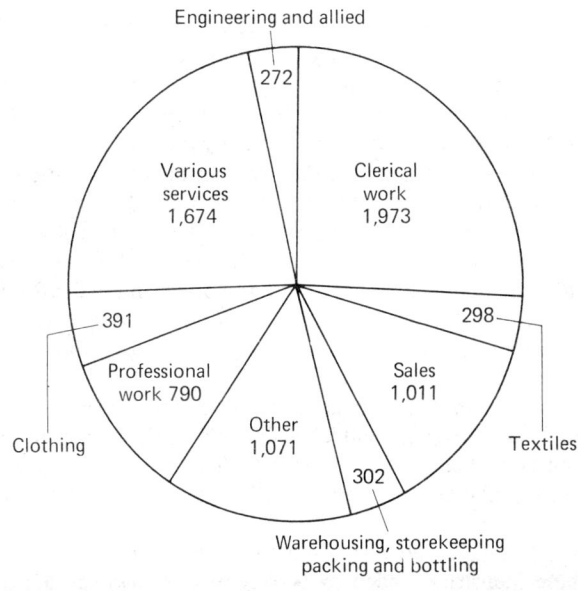

Fig. 1.19. *Where Britain's eight million women workers were employed in 1961* (Source: *D.E.A. Pr. Rep. Ind. and Reg.*, 25, Feb. 1967)

4. An overall increase in the proportion employed in manufacturing. Within this general trend there was a decline in the proportions employed in some old-established manufacturing industries of the North, such as cotton textiles, clothing and shipbuilding (part of engineering). There was a large increase in the proportions employed in the metals, engineering and vehicles group, and the chemicals group. Employment in these industries just about doubled between 1931 and 1951, and since then has increased by another 10%. Expansion in the

[1] *Obs.*, 24 June 1962.

manufacturing group has been most rapid in sections using more productive techniques, making relatively new types of products, such as cars, plastics, aircraft, electrical and electronic apparatus. The two world wars gave a stimulus to some of these industries, which were not tied to the old sources of power in the North but could use electricity and other power sources closer to their markets farther south.

The reasons for these changes are varied, but they are interconnected, being part of the changing economic environment in which the population lived and worked.[1]

The decrease in agricultural employment is closely bound up with the development of industry, in which technical productivity rose fast enough to raise average income per head of the population, more of whom were attracted into urban industries. Some consequences of this were that the country was enabled to concentrate more on manufacturing industrial products and could import foodstuffs; a smaller proportion of rising average income was spent on essential foodstuffs; the drift of labour to the towns and the high, competitive industrial wages obliged farmers to invest in mechanical techniques, which replaced men and also raised production.

In the case of the other extractive industries, coal expanded in the nineteenth century because of the immense requirements for industry and for export markets. During the twentieth century, however, export markets were either lost to new competitive producers or to new sources of power (which also competed for the attention of the more southerly located new home industries). Also, rising labour costs stimulated the progress of mechanisation. Quarrying is closely linked with the requirements of the building industry. During the nineteenth century the building industry had to keep pace with an expanding population, and the quarrying industry supplied much of the materials. During the twentieth century population growth slowed down and so did the demand for building materials. Furthermore, new materials came into use, which competed with the quarried products. Again, too, rising labour costs stimulated mechanisation, which tended to replace labour.

The construction industries expanded, as mentioned above, in the nineteenth century, then encountered a general fall in demand. Perhaps even more important was the stimulus of higher wage costs, which induced firms to adopt newer techniques, using relatively less labour and more productive methods and/or machines.

As Britain specialised more and more in the manufacturing of industrial products, these industries tended to benefit from economies of scale and of localisation. Productivity per man increased, generally, and therefore production rose even faster than employment in manufacturing industries. Markets throughout the world provided the stimulus to industrial expansion. This in turn led to higher average income per head of the home population, which devoted a relatively smaller part of its spending power to the necessities of life and a greater part to items with what is called a high income-elasticity of demand, viz. manufactured goods and services. During the inter-war period some of the old staple industries 'declined' in the sense that employment

---

[1] For further analysis and exposition of the changes since 1900 see G. G. C. Routh, 'The changing pattern of employment since 1900', paper in B. C. Roberts and J. H. Smith, eds., *Manpower Policy and Employment Trends*, 1966, esp. pp. 44–5.

in them fell relatively and absolutely as they faced dwindling markets and increased competition from foreign producers and from new products, materials and fuels. This process has been accentuated by the quest for new techniques and machines to replace progressively more costly labour and to increase productivity per man. Capital, management skill and labour have been attracted during the twentieth century into the 'expanding' industries, which often supplied products for which income-elasticity of demand was high or which reaped the benefits of great technological advances.

The service group as a whole has expanded but various elements in it have had a chequered career. With the increases in goods available and personal incomes, the distributive services have expanded to cope with the sheer volume of commodities and to cater for the more exacting requirements of the consumer. Financial services such as banking and insurance expanded to cater for the rest of the world and to provide efficient institutions to channel surplus capital from savers to investors. A more affluent society has experienced a high income-

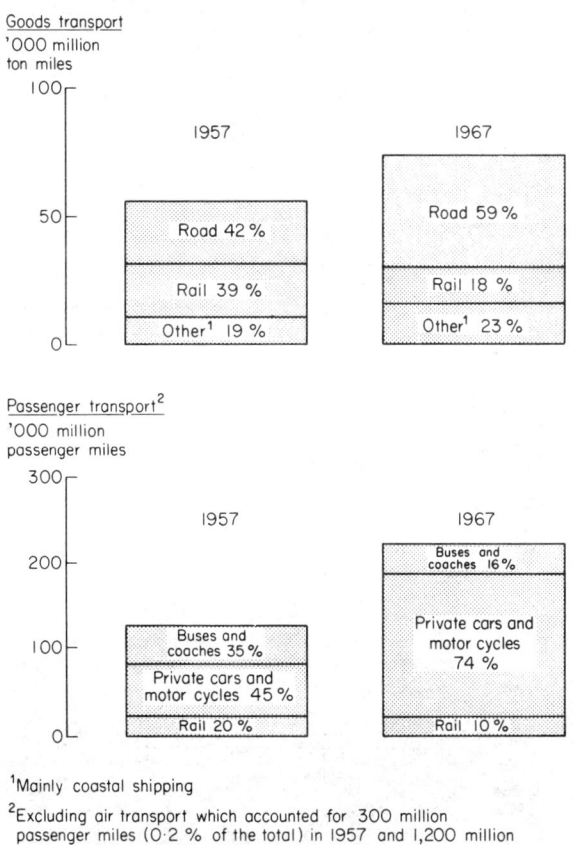

[1]Mainly coastal shipping

[2]Excluding air transport which accounted for 300 million passenger miles (0·2 % of the total) in 1957 and 1,200 million passenger miles (0·5 % of the total) in 1967

Fig. 1.20. *The changing pattern of inland transport in Great Britain*
(Source: *D.E.A. Pr. Rep. Ind. and Reg.*, 53, June 1969)

elasticity of demand for the direct private services of entertainers, the catering trade, doctors, lawyers, accountants, psychiatrists and other professional people. Nevertheless, rising wages, greater scope for female industrial and clerical work and the gradual reduction of inequalities of wealth and income by the State (through progressive death duties and income tax) have reduced the supply of and demand for female domestic service. Transport and communications improved and expanded considerably during the nineteenth century, with the development of railways and steamships. The partial decline during the twentieth century has been in regard to employment rather than volume of service. This

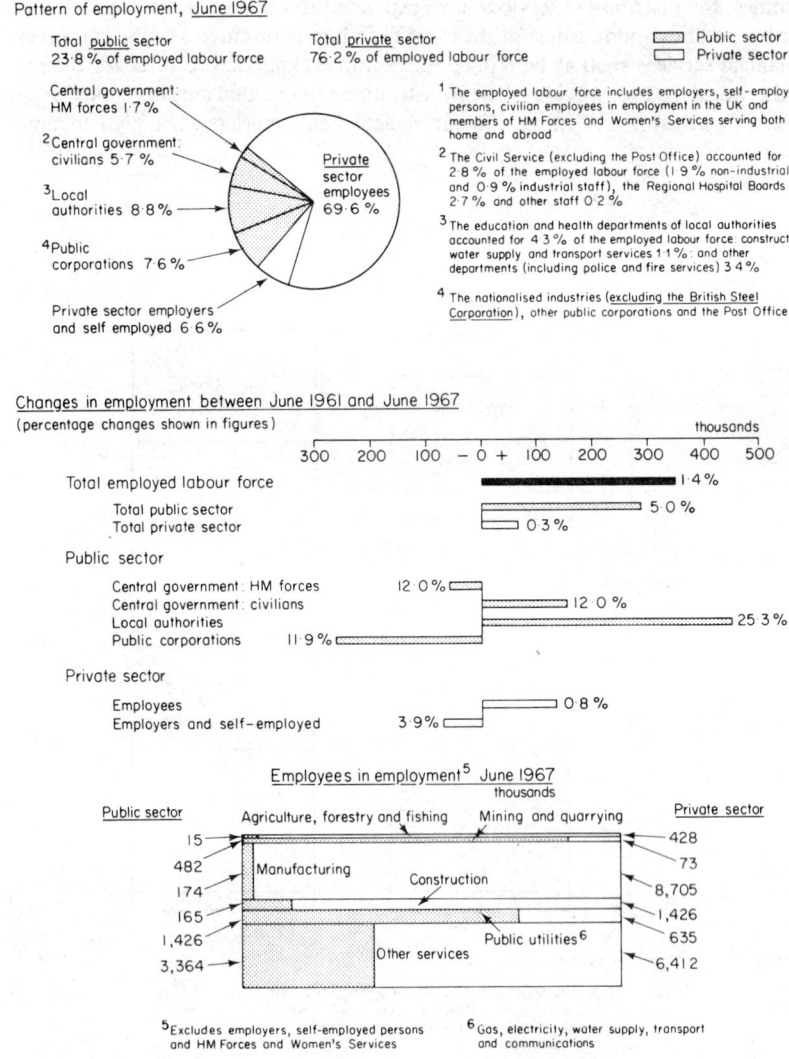

Fig. 1.21. *Employment in the public and private sectors (U.K.), 1967* (Source: *D.E.A. Pr. Rep. Ind. and Reg.*, 48, Jan. 1969)

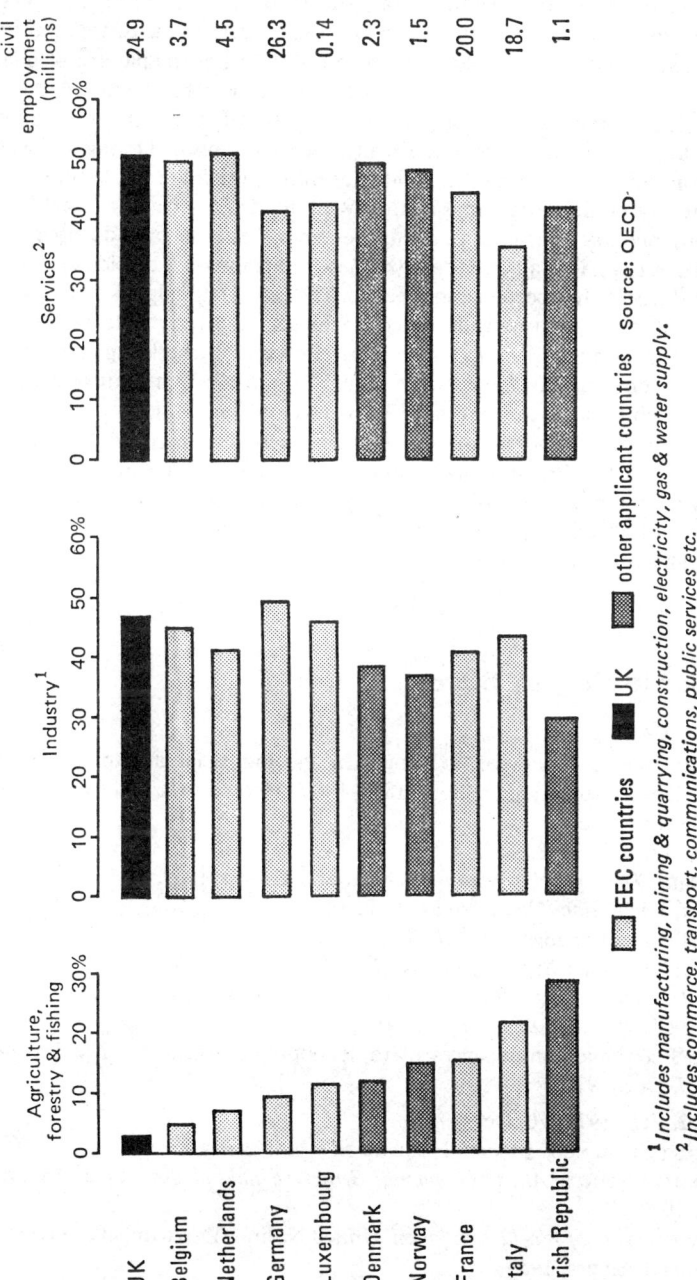

Fig. 1.22. *Total civil employment in three main sectors, 1969*
(Source: *E.P.R.*, 20, Oct. 1971)

43

has been largely due to the great labour-saving improvements in techniques (telephone, telegraph, etc.). Railways have surrendered a share of their market to motorised road transport but they have lost a great deal to the private motorist (a case of self-service). Fig. 1.20 gives some indication of the pattern of inland transport in 1967 and the changes which occurred during the previous decade.

The encroachment of the State, in regard to taxation and its effect on the demand for domestic services, has already been mentioned. During the whole period, and especially during the twentieth century, the State has become more and more involved in economic affairs. Welfare services (such as health and education) military expenditure, roads, research, location of industry policy, tariff regulation, nationalised industry – these are some of the fields of activity in which the State has become more active. The result (stimulated by two world wars) has been a great expansion in the machinery of government, the National and Local Government services and H.M. Forces. A detailed picture of the extent and constitution of the public sector in mid-1967, indicating the main changes which took place from mid-1961 is given in Fig. 1.21.[1]

In conclusion, it may be of interest to note the comparison between the distribution of the British working population amongst the major industrial sectors with those of other Western European countries, all of which, with the exception of Italy and the Irish Republic, had higher per capita national incomes in 1969. This is made in Fig. 1.22.

8. Further Reading and Sources

Applied Economics, No. 3, 1970.

P. BAIROCH and J.-M. LIMBOR, 'Changes in the industrial distribution of the world labour force, by region, 1880–1960'. *International Labour Review*, Vol. 98, Oct. 1968.

B.B.C.B., 17, Feb. 1968.

B. BENJAMIN, *Demographic Analysis*. Allen and Unwin. 1969.

L. BOWEN, *Population*. Nisbet and C.U.P. 1954.

'The challenge of change'. *N.W.B.Q.R.*, Nov. 1971.

C. CLARK, *Population Growth and Land Use*. Macmillan. 1969.

D.E.A. Pr. Rep. 8. Aug. 1965; 9. Sept. 1965; 24. Jan. 1967; 25. Feb. 1967; 47. Dec. 1968; 48. Jan. 1969; 53. June 1969.

S. ENKE, 'Economic consequences of rapid population growth'. *The Economic Journal*, Dec. 1971.

E.P.R. 12. Feb. 1971; 20. Oct. 1971.

P. SARGANT FLORENCE, *Labour*. Hutchinson's University Library.

P. SARGANT FLORENCE, *Atlas of Economic Structure and Policies*, vol. 2. Pergamon Press. 1970.

The Future Growth of World Population. United Nations Department of Economic and Social Affairs, 1958.

L. C. HUNTER and D. J. ROBERTSON, *Economics of Wages and Labour*. Macmillan. 1969.

[1]Further details of the growth and constitution of Central Government employment may be found in *Econ.*, 11 Sept. 1971, p. 74 and 2 Jan. 1971, p. 51.

K. JONES and A. D. SMITH, *The Economic Impact of Commonwealth Immigration*. N.I.E.S.R./C.U.P. 1970.

R. K. KELSALL, *Population*. Longman. 1970.

L.B.R., Oct. 1961; July 1966; Jan. 1968.

'Manpower and employment trends in the future'. *M.B. Stat. Econ. Inf.* (National Savings Committee) Sept. 1964.

F. PLACE, *Illustrations and Proofs of the Principle of Population*. Allen and Unwin. 1967.

R. PRESSAT, *Population*. Watts & Co. 1970.

B. C. ROBERTS and J. H. SMITH, eds., *Manpower Policy and Employment Trends*. L.S.E. 1966.

T. K. ROBINSON, *The Population of Britain: Key Discussion Book 5*. Longmans/ I.E.A. 1968.

Royal Commission on Population Report, Cmd 7695. H.M.S.O. 1949.

'Women in Employment', *B.B.L.A.*, July 1964.

9. Past Examination Questions

1. What are the main causes and effects of immigration? (Autumn 1957)
2. During the past century the general trend in the United Kingdom has been for both the birth-rate and the death-rate to decline. What are the causes and effects of this trend? (January 1965)
3. Discuss the ways in which the exceptionally high birth-rate of 1947 in Britain will affect the demand and supply of goods and services. (Summer 1962)
4. Discuss the main trends in the age distribution of the United Kingdom at the present time. (January 1959)
5. It has been stated that the population of this country is gradually ageing. What does this statement mean? Explain the causes of this trend and suggest the economic consequences which it is likely to have. (Summer 1952)
6. In 1931 about 29% of our population was over the age of 45. It is estimated that in 1960 38% will be over the age of 45. What effects may this have on our industrial life? (Autumn 1953)
7. Account for the growing importance of the 'teenage market'. In what ways does it affect the pattern of production? (January 1963)
8. Write short notes on the following:
   (a) Age-distribution of the population. (Summer 1963)
9. The average age of the population of the United Kingdom is increasing. In what ways is this likely to affect the available labour supply? (Summer 1964)
10. Write short notes on . . . the following:
    (a) Sex-distribution of the population. (Summer 1961)
11. The following figures relate to the density of population per square mile: Westmorland 84; Sussex 699; Lancashire 2,716. Comment on these figures, and give reasons which help to explain the differences in the densities of population. (Summer 1961)
12. Describe the geographical distribution of population in England and Wales, and then indicate briefly why the density of population varies in the way you have described. (Summer 1953)

1. POPULATION [I]

13. Describe the geographical distribution of population in England and Wales, and explain its main characteristics. (Summer, 1956)

14. Describe the geographical distribution of the population of Scotland *or* Wales *or* south-east England. Give reasons which help to explain how this distribution came about. (Summer 1959)

15. Describe broadly how the occupational distribution of the working population of this country differs from that of fifty years ago. Give the main reasons for the changes. (Augumn 1952)

16. Describe the main features of the present-day economic structure and activities of the metropolitan area. (Autumn 1957)

17. How may changes occur in the size of the working population? (Summer 1958)

18. Giving examples, explain why it is that in some occupations in the United Kingdom the majority of workers are men, and that in others the majority are women. (Summer 1960)

19. Large numbers of farm workers are leaving the agricultural industry of the United Kingdom each year. Explain this movement, and outline its effects on agriculture. (Summer 1961)

20. Describe in outline the occupational distribution of the British population. (Summer 1963)

21. Name and account for some of the most important ways in which the occupational distribution of the population of the United Kingdom has changed since 1939. (January 1964)

1. Population
Stage II

1. World Population Prospects

'The value of population projections is no longer disputed. It is now common-place that, if a plan for social and economic development is to have any chance of realistic implementation, it requires a parallel assessment of the dynamics of population growth.' This statement prefaces a United Nations study, *The Future Growth of World Population*, published in 1958. Its significance is more readily appreciated if we bear in mind that world population had reached an estimated 300 million by A.D. 1000, had slowly risen to about 728 million by 1750 and 1,550 million by 1900, has since leaped up to about 3,632 million by 1970, and is estimated to be heading for about 7,000 million by the year 2000. By 1970 world population was expanding by about 70 million annually, and, at an average rate of approximately 2 per cent compound would, on current trends, double in about 35 years. The highest rates of growth were in Kuwait (8·3% – including 4·2% from net immigration) and Costa Rica (3·8%): the slowest growth rates were in East Germany (0·3%) and Hungary (0·4%).[1]

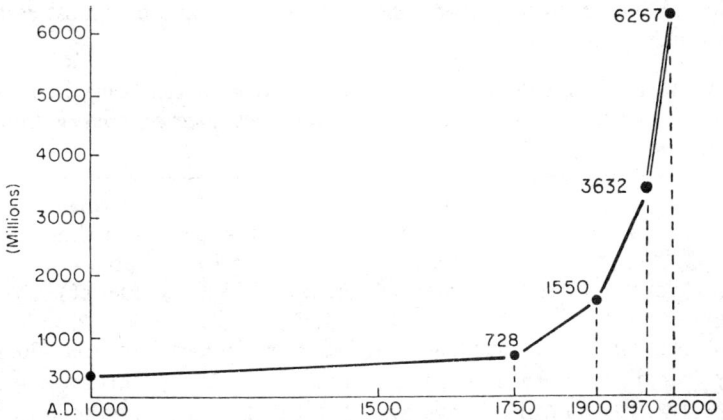

Fig. 1.23. *Past and future growth of world population* (*medium assumption*) (Based on *The Future Growth of World Population*, U.N., 1958, and A. S. Parkes, 'The Menace of over-population', *New Scientist*, 8 June 1961)

[1] *F.T.*, 9 April 1970 and 15 Oct. 1971; *United Nations Monthly Bulletin of Statistics*, Sept. 1971; *U.N. Statistical Yearbook for 1970*, p. 28.

47

1. POPULATION [II]

Most of the likely increase to 4,457 million by 1980 was likely to occur in the less economically developed regions – with birth-rates of between 2·4 and 2·5 per cent, as against rates of between 1·1 and 1·2 per cent in the economically advanced countries.

One of the most urgent problems emerging in the 1970s was the rapid pace of urbanisation and urban immigration, which was even more pronounced in the less developed countries – despite the lack of industrial infrastructure and job opportunities to support the massive influx. It has been estimated that the urban population of the world will double from 990 million in 1960 to 1,780 million in 1980.[1]

This forecast figure for the end of the twentieth century would represent a twenty-fold increase in the last 1,000 years of human history after nearly 200,000 years of almost static population (see Fig. 1.23). Three-quarters of this increase would have occurred during the twentieth century. The United Nations study found that by projecting the present rate of population increase 600 years into the future, the concentration of human beings on the earth's land surface would be one to each square metre – standing room only. 'It goes without saying', continues the survey, 'that this can never take place. Something will happen to prevent it.' The survey stresses the need for a conscious application of human thought to the slowing down and controlling of this massive growth, which has, in its turn, been made possible by recent developments in human knowledge.

For the major areas of the world, population estimates were made for each quarter century from 1900 and were projected forward to A.D. 2000 (see Table 1.12). Then the percentage rates of growth for each quarter century were worked out on a 'medium assumption'. It was found that the percentage increase for the world as a whole has been rising and will continue to do so at an accelerating speed (23% from 1900–1925; 64% from 1975–2000.) The rates of increase differ, however, for the various regions.

Fig. 1.24 illustrates the regional dispersion of birth-rates over most parts of the world.

Table 1.12 *Past populations and projected populations of continents, A.D. 1900–2000 (in millions), with percentage changes each quarter century (medium assumption)*

Year	World No.	% incr.	Asia No.	% incr.	South America (incl. Mexico) No.	% incr.	Africa No.	% incr.	Europe (incl. U.S.S.R.) No.	% incr.	Northern America (excl. Mexico) No.	% incr.	Oceania No.	% incr.
1900	1,550	–	857	–	63	–	120	–	423	–	81	–	6	–
1925	1,907	23	1,020	19	99	57	147	22	505	19	126	56	10	57
1950	2,497	31	1,380	35	163	65	199	35	574	14	168	33	13	36
1975	3,828	53	2,210	60	303	86	303	52	751	31	240	43	21	59
2000	6,267	64	3,870	75	592	95	517	71	947	26	312	30	29	40

(Based on figures in *The Future Growth of World Population*, U.N., 1958)

[1] *F.T.*, 19 Feb. 1970; 'The poor world's cities', *Econ.*, 6 Dec. 1969, pp. 56–70.

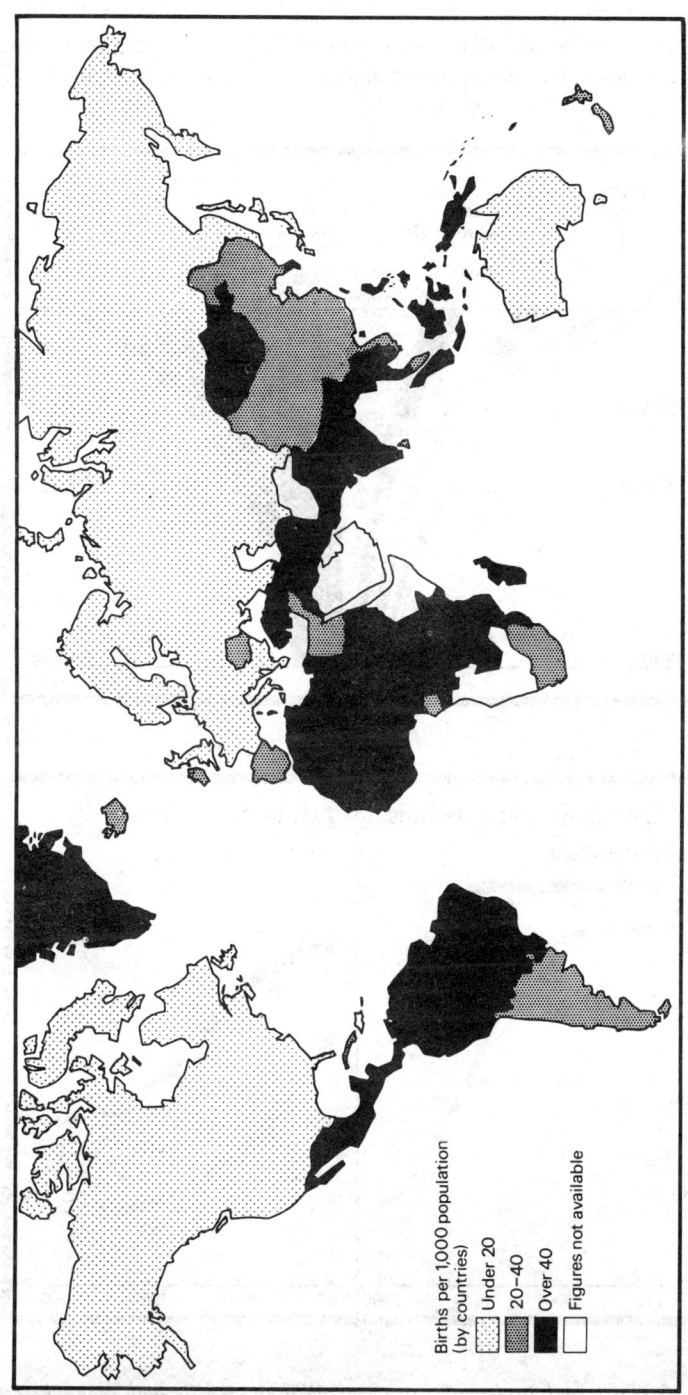

Fig. 1.24. *Regional distribution of birth-rates*
(Source: *Econ.*, 5 April 1969, p. 54)

Births per 1,000 population
(by countries)

Under 20
20–40
Over 40
Figures not available

1. POPULATION [II]

The composite effect of the trends in birth-rates and death-rates on the changing regional balance in world population may be seen from Fig. 1.25(a) and (b).

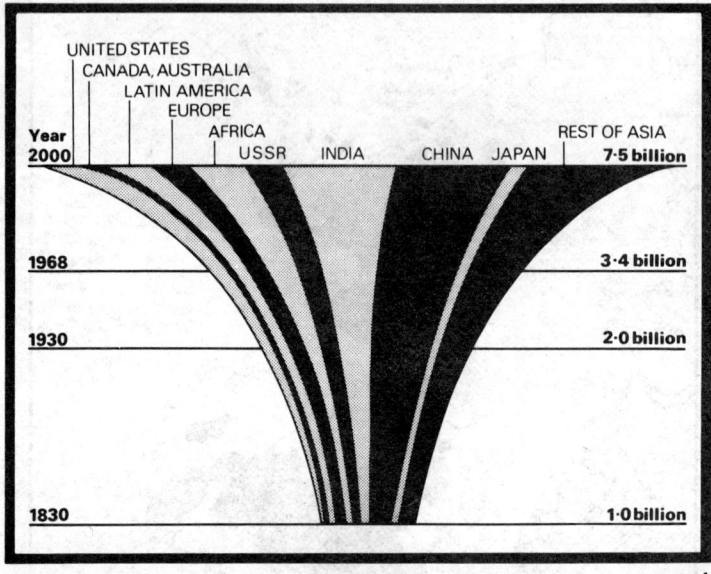

A

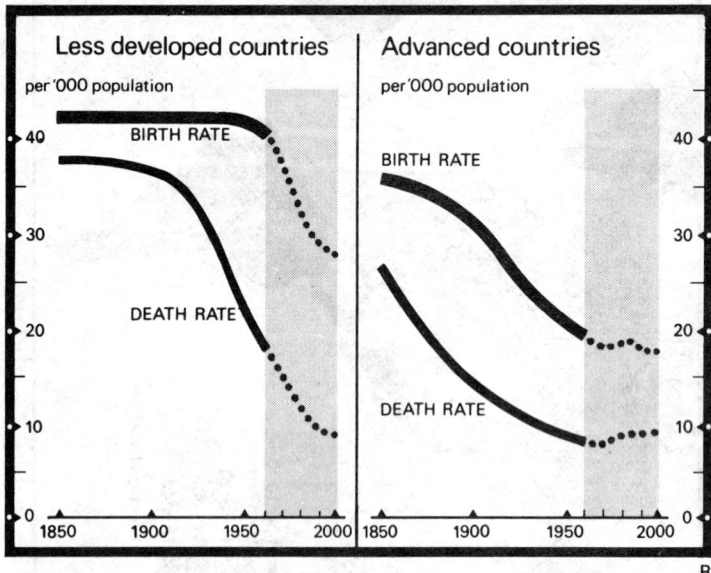

B

Fig. 1.25. *Past and projected world population growth and dynamic causes: regional analysis*
(Source: *Econ.*, 20 Dec. 1969, p. 53)

In considering the carrying capacity of the world, its ability to support this future population, it is important to bear in mind the present distribution of land and population in the major areas. Europe (including U.S.S.R.), North America (excluding Mexico) and Oceania cover about 45% of the land area of the world and contain about 30% of its population. Asia (excluding U.S.S.R.), South America (including Mexico) and Africa cover about 55% of the Earth and contain about 70% of its population. The populations of the last three areas, however, are increasing at a much more rapid pace than the first three. Thus by the year 2000 the 45% of the world covered by Europe, North America and Oceania will contain about 20% of world population. The 55% of the world covered by Asia, South America and Africa will contain about 80% of the total population (see Fig. 1.26). The proportion of world population in Asia alone (about 20% of world land area) will increase from just over half now to just under two-thirds in A.D. 2000.

Year	World	Asia %	S. America %	Africa %	Europe (incl. U.S.S.R.) %	N. America %	Oceania %
1900	100·0	55·3	4·1	7·7	27·3	5·2	0·4
1925	100·0	53·5	5·2	7·7	26·5	6·6	0·5
1950	100·0	55·2	6·5	8·0	23·0	6·7	0·5
1975	100·0	57·7	7·9	7·9	19·6	6·3	0·5
2000	100·0	61·8	9·4	8·2	15·1	5·0	0·5

Fig. 1.26(a). *Continental distribution of population (1900–2000)*
(Source: *The Future Growth of World Population*, U.N., 1958)

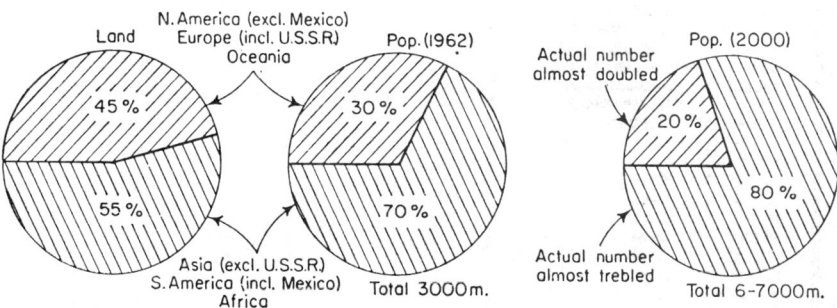

Fig. 1.26(b). *Land and population distribution by continents*

Not only does this raise general problems as to the possibility of techniques in agricultural and industrial production being able to keep pace with the increases in world population. It also highlights the dichotomy existing between the technologically advanced continents and the technologically underdeveloped ones. Because of the relative overpopulation of Asia, the technologically under-developed continents as a group already contain more population in proportion

51

to land area than the technologically advanced continents. By the end of the century they will, unless birth-rates fall considerably, contain proportionately even more.[1] In view of their weaker economic ability to expand resources, skills and production, the increase in population densities, both absolute and relative, will pose immense problems of economic development and social change.[2] It has been estimated that the percentage of Gross National Product which needs to be invested, just to maintain per capita income, is about double the rate of net population increase (see Fig. 1.27). This highlights the problem facing the capital-deficient developing regions, which tend to have birth-rates far higher than those in the more prosperous countries of the world.

Fig. 1.27. *Population growth, real income and investment*
(Source: *Econ.*, 20 Dec. 1969, p. 53)

[1] See also 'Galloping population', *Econ.*, 8 May 1965, pp. 650–1.
[2] For an extremely relevant and informative analysis of how the occupational and industrial structure of the world's labour force has been changing since the late nineteenth century, see P. Bairoch and J.-M. Limbor, 'Changes in the industrial distribution of the world labour force, by region, 1880–1960', *International Labour Review*, Oct. 1968.

A more precise appreciation of the problems of population density may be achieved by cutting across continental groupings and dividing the world into areas which correspond to present population density and projected rates of growth. The results of the United Nations survey were as follows:

1. *Low density, moderate growth:* Northern America; Temperate South America; Australia and New Zealand; U.S.S.R.

2. *Low density, rapid growth:* Africa; Central America; Tropical South America; South-west Asia; The Pacific Islands.

3. *High density, moderate growth:* Europe (excluding U.S.S.R.); Japan.

4. *High density, rapid growth:* The Caribbean; Central South Asia; South-east Asia; East Asia (excluding Japan).

The differences in rates of growth are linked very closely to differences in birth- and death-rates. The result is that age distribution will be affected differently in various parts of the world. The projected continental age distributions (quoting U.S.S.R. separately) for 1975 compared with those of 1950 are shown in Table 1.13.

Table 1.13 *Projected world and continental changes in age-distribution (1950–75)*

	1950(%)			1975(%)			
	Under		Over	Under		Over	Trend in
Continent	15	15–59	60	15	15–59	60	average age
World	37	56	7	38	54	8	K (constant)
Africa	42	54	4	41	54	5	A (ageing)
North America (excluding Mexico)	27	61	12	28	56	16	A (ageing)
South America (including Mexico)	40	54	6	42	52	6	Y (younger)
Asia (excluding U.S.S.R.)	40	55	5	41	54	5	Y (younger)
Oceania	30	59	11	31	55	14	A (ageing)
Europe (excluding U.S.S.R.)	26	62	12	24	59	17	A (ageing)
U.S.S.R.	33	59	8	30	59	11	A (ageing)

(Based on *The Future Growth of World Population*, U.N., 1958)

The analysis is based on age groups 'under 15', '15–59' and '60 and over'. The middle group, representing the population of working age (according to western European conventions) should fall by 2% for the world as a whole, whilst each other group will rise by 1%. The average age, however, will remain more or less constant. South America and Asia will attain a slightly lower average age. The population of Africa, the third technologically underdeveloped continent, will age slightly. The populations of the other areas will age to a much greater extent.

The general economic implications of these changes in population size and average age, in both technologically advanced and underdeveloped countries, have been surveyed in 1.1.4.[1]

[1] See also 'Resources for the Future', *Econ.*, 28 Dec. 1963, p. 1335.

1. POPULATION [II]

The magnitude of the problem on a worldwide scale is, however, enormous. Far-reaching advances in technology may be made and applied to food and industrial production (e.g. extracting protein from grass; 'farming' the seas, etc.). [1] As may be seen from Fig. 1.28, the proportion of land area under cultivation is still relatively small and the yields in most of the less developed areas are well below those in the advanced countries. Colin Clark has estimated that far from posing an intolerable burden on the world's natural resources, population growth could, as in the past, provide an effective stimulus to agricultural and economic development. The potential, he believes, is enormous and even with efficient present-day methods the world could support 47,000 million people on American-style diets or 157,000 million at Japanese dietary standards. Indeed, he makes a case for a reduction in the expansion of agricultural production in the West, which tends to reduce the market for producers in less prosperous countries – doing more harm even than industrial protectionism. [2]

Great progress must be made in the creation and development of international institutions for funnelling surplus products, capital and skills from the advanced to the underdeveloped nations. An international conference on the rôle of science in aiding underdeveloped nations was held in Israel in 1960. It concluded that capital was not the only major requirement. A realistic policy, it was decided, must rest on the triple planks of progress in the spheres of health, education and technique, in that order. Poor health made for weakness, apathy and ignorance; ignorance made for a high birth-rate and distrust of new techniques – stony ground for the efficient use of capital, however obtained. Progress in these fields would eventually lead to increased capability for capital accumulation in the underdeveloped nations, who were advised how to pull themselves up 'by their own boot strings' by investing available capital in what would be, in the long run, the most fruitful fields.

Of course, continued improvements in the field of health would tend to decrease death-rates even more. Unless birth-rates are correspondingly reduced, the world population 'explosion' would accelerate. The crux of the problem is, of course, a concerted effort to reduce birth-rates, especially in the technologically underdeveloped regions of high density and rapid growth. Otherwise, even 'the rich' may face the prospect of ceasing 'to become richer', and 'the poor' will most certainly 'become poorer'. At the United Nations Conference on Trade and Development, held in Geneva in 1964, it was agreed that the 'less developed' countries should seek the removal of trade barriers, and preferential treatment for their exports. 'Trade, as well as aid' was the slogan. [3]

An indication of the extent of international concern at the ecological and social dangers in the growth of population may be seen in the establishment, in 1971, of a U.N. Fund for Population Activities (U.N.F.P.A.), with the object of pursuing a World Plan of Action for the U.N. Second Development Decade. [4] Attention has been drawn, however, in the debate on population problems, to

---

[1] See Lord Fleck, 'Feeding the 6,000 million', *D.T.*, 12 Jan. 1963.
[2] C. Clark, *Population Growth and Land Use*, Macmillan, 1969; *Econ.*, 15 July 1967, p. 221; C. Clark, 'Too much food?' *L.B.R.*, Jan. 1970.
[3] World conference on development, *B.B.L.A.*, April 1964; G. Patterson, 'Would tariff preferences help economic development?', *L.B.R.*, April 1965, pp. 18–20; for further details on post-U.N.C.T.A.D. developments and implications, see H. G. Johnson, *Economic Policies Towards Less Developed Countries*, 1967, esp. chs. 5 and 6.
[4] *F.T.*, 9 March 1971.

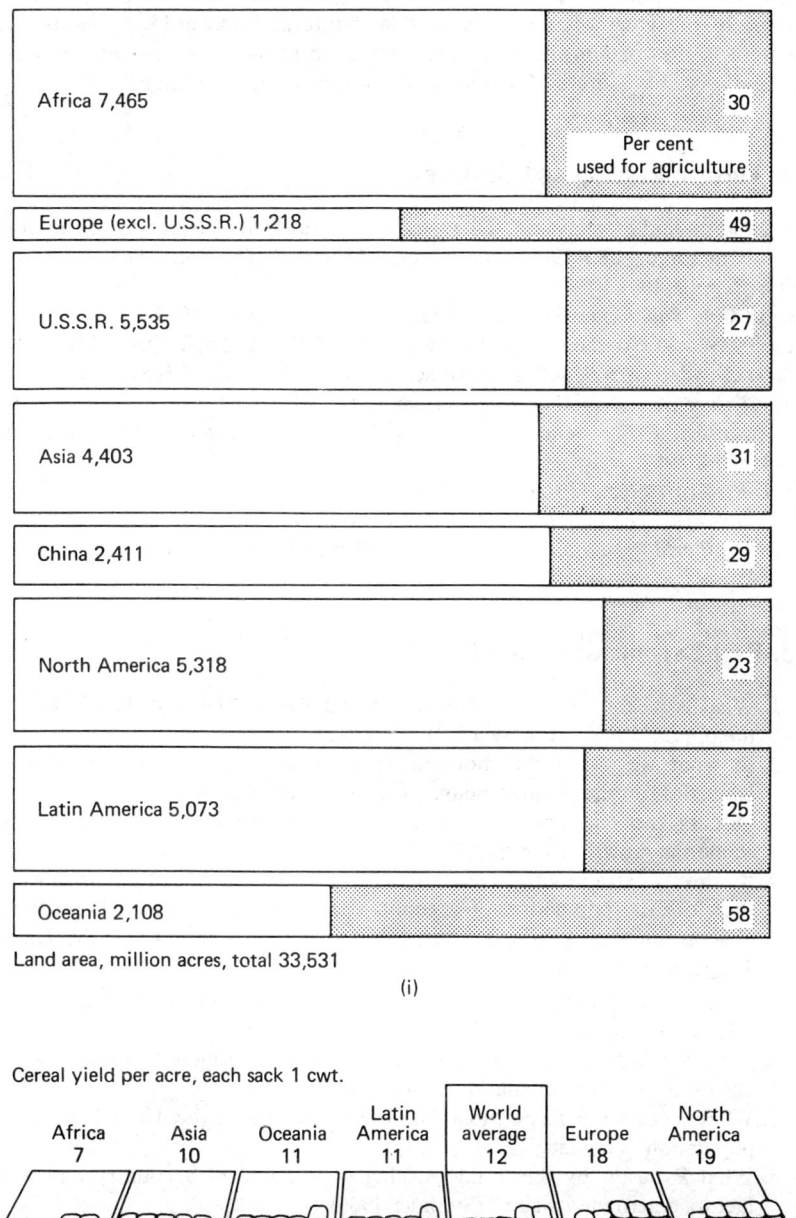

Land area, million acres, total 33,531

(i)

Cereal yield per acre, each sack 1 cwt.

			Latin	World		North
Africa	Asia	Oceania	America	average	Europe	America
7	10	11	11	12	18	19

(ii)

Fig. 1.28. *World land area, agricultural use and crop yields; regional analysis* (*1962*)
(Source: *B.B.R.*, Aug. 1967)

55

the need for pursuing urgent social reforms and land redistribution policies in some of the areas of unemployment, agricultural backwardness, disease and illiteracy; the curtailment in the rate of growth in numbers was seen as one of several possible sources of action, and not as a panacea solution.[1]

2. Further Reading and Sources

P. BAIROCH and J.-M. LIMBOR, 'Changes in the industrial distribution of the world labour force, 1880–1960'. *International Labour Review*. Oct. 1968.

B.B.R. Aug. 1967.

C. CLARK, *Population Growth and Land Use*. Macmillan. 1969.

C.O.I., 'World Conference on Development', *B.B.L.A.* April 1964, H.M.S.O.

'The crowded world', series of articles in *Punch*. 1, 8 and 15 Nov., 1961.

The Future Growth of World Population, U.N., 1958.

H. G. JOHNSON, *Economic Policies Towards Less Developed Countries*. Allen and Unwin. 1967.

L.B.R., April 1965; Jan. 1970.

A. S. PARKES, 'The menace of over-population', *New Scientist*, 8 June 1961.

P.E.P., *World Population and Resources*. Allen and Unwin. 1964.

3. Past Examination Questions

1. What is meant by 'the danger of overpopulation'? Discuss its relevance in the present time. (January 1964)
2. In what ways can the more advanced economies help underdeveloped countries to raise their standard of living? (Summer 1959)
3. Discuss the relationship between population growth in a country and economic growth. (Summer 1962)
4. 'For every extra mouth to feed there is soon an extra pair of hands to work: therefore the population of a country can never be too big.' Discuss this proposition with particular reference to your own country or the United Kingdom. (Summer 1961)
5. What would be the economic effects of an increasing rate of growth of population? (Summer 1963)
6. What would be the probable economic effects of an increase in the average age of a country's population? (January 1960)
7. What factors are responsible for recent changes in the United Kingdom population? (January 1965)
8. What is meant by the 'total working population' of a country and what factors determine its size? (Summer 1956)
9. What factors determine the supply of labour to the economy as a whole? (Summer 1962)
10. Describe briefly the 'industrial' distribution of population in the U.K. (or your own country) and discuss the economic forces which have determined that distribution. (January 1963)

[1] *Ibid.*, 8 Oct. 1971.

11. Discuss the advantages of the division of labour and illustrate your points by reference to the present day occupational distribution of population in the United Kingdom. (Summer 1959)

12. 'A falling proportion of the labour force employed in agriculture is usually associated with a rising standard of living.' Discuss. (Summer 1959)

13. What future trends do you expect in the occupational distribution of the population of your country (or the United Kingdom)? (Summer 1960)

14. Explain how changes in the occupational distribution have affected the geographical distribution of population in the United Kingdom during the last fifty years. (January 1960)

15. Discuss the effect of the expansion of light industries in the United Kingdom on the geographical distribution of its population. (Summer 1958)

16. What have been the main changes in the geographical distribution of population in the United Kingdom since the war? Explain the chief causes of these changes. (Summer 1961)

17. Why was there a southward movement of the industrial population in this country in the interwar years? (Autumn 1952)

2. Location, Structure and Organisation of Industry Stage I

1. Expanding and Declining Industries During the Interwar Period

During the nineteenth century great concentrations of population grew around the major coalfields of Britain, specialising on a narrow range of what became staple industries. Examples of these were:

Lancashire	cotton spinning and weaving;
South Wales	coal-mining and iron and steel production;
North-east Coast	coal, iron and steel, heavy engineering, shipbuilding;
West Cumberland	coal, iron and steel, and shipbuilding;
Clydeside	coal, shipbuilding and heavy engineering;
Stoke-on-Trent	coal-mining and pottery
Belfast	shipbuilding and linen

Those areas thrived upon this specialisation, so long as their respective industries were growing. At the same time they were severing links with industries formerly located in their vicinities, and became heavily dependent on a few sources of employment, quite unlike areas of diversified industry, such as the London and Birmingham regions.

Between the two world wars several of the old-established staple industries contracted in size and relative importance. They included coal-mining, iron ore mining, pig-iron production, steel smelting and rolling, shipbuilding and repairing, cotton spinning and weaving, lace and wool and worsted. At the same time the Midlands (Birmingham region) and the south-east (including Greater London) experienced a rapid development, particularly in new industries such as motor vehicles, electrical apparatus, scientific instruments, heating and ventilating apparatus, electrical engineering, aircraft, rubber, silk and rayon.

The declining industries were mostly heavy trades, localised near the coalfields and/or near the coast. They relied to a great extent upon the export trade which had been built up before World War I. They contracted largely because of a reduction in foreign demand and because of increased competition from new and old manufacturing countries and from new sources of power and materials.

An important example is the cotton industry. Before World War I Britain was the predominant cotton yarn and textile exporter, although other countries, such as America, India and Japan, had started their own textile industries. During the war those countries were sheltered from British competition and received a stimulus to expansion. After the war, Britain was faced with more powerful rivals, equipped with modern machinery and techniques, who had 'moved in' on her former export markets. Other customers were, by then, treading the path to self-sufficiency in textile production.

58

2. LOCATION, STRUCTURE AND ORGANISATION OF INDUSTRY [I]

The financial crises of the interwar period obliged the staple industries to seek to force down wages. This resulted in strikes and discontinuity of production, which aggravated their besetting problem of chronic excess capacity, further reduced their capacity to compete and gave a boost to foreign competitors.

The industries which expanded were enjoying the benefits of newer, more dispersed sources of power (e.g. oil and the electricity grid system), newer raw materials and newer techniques. Several became dependent upon scientific research and a continuous process of scientific development. They tended to cater for the internal home market and were concerned mainly with light finished goods or components. Consequently the transport costs pull of the coalfields and ports was weakened, whilst the pull of the south-east and Midlands (in terms of diversified components industries, large internal markets, relatively high *per capita* spending power, semi-skilled labour and freedom from 'slump neurosis') grew stronger. Despite the resultant migration from the old-established areas of declining industry to the 'new frontier' areas of expanding industries, the relative slowness of this migration produced a dichotomy between the chronically depressed areas of the North and Wales and the relatively prosperous south-east and Midlands. This problem was tackled by Government attempts to attract diversified industries to the 'Special Areas', as they were called.

From this brief survey some interesting points emerge.[1] First, various locational factors, prior to World War I, had contributed to the localised nature of a few staple industries in certain narrowly specialised regions. Secondly, a different set of locational factors was, during the interwar period, attracting newer industries away from the old areas to regions farther south. Thirdly, the resultant changes in occupational distribution of the population were accompanied, *via* internal migration, by changes in the geographical distribution of the British people. Fourthly – superimposed upon these gradual trends, and working against them – there was the locational pull, back to the depressed areas, of Government policy and measures. This locational attraction had a socio-political basis, but was exercised through economic incentives, such as financial assistance and Government-subsidised factory rents.

Despite the unfortunate consequences – upon certain industries and groups of people – of this period of structural unemployment and industrial change, the economy as a whole emerged, before World War II, in a healthier condition. Nevertheless, investigations by Dr Rostas[2] show that by 1936–37 productivity in the American economy was at least twice as high as in Britain, largely due to the greater stimulus of the American industrial depression (the consequences of which were much more severe than the British depression) towards technical innovation. The Board of Trade figures for employment and production in Britain between 1929 and 1937 were as follows:

	Employment	Production
1929	100	100
1932	90	80
1937	115	125

[1] For a further analysis of the important changes which took place in the British economy during the 1930s, see H. W. Richardson, *Economic Recovery in Britain, 1932-39*, 1967 (reviewed in *Econ.*, 1 April 1967, p. 51) and D. H. Aldcroft, *The Inter-War Economy: Britain, 1919–1939*, 1970 (reviewed in *Econ.*, 12 Dec. 1970, pp. 62–3).

[2] L. Rostas, *Comparative Productivity in British and American Industry*, 1948. For further data on comparative productivities in the pre-World War I and interwar periods, see Sir Alec Cairncross, ed., *Britain's Economic Prospects Reconsidered*, 1971, p. 105.

Thus by 1937 employment had risen from 90 (depression) to 115 and production had risen even more, from 80 to 125. Both total production and productivity per person employed had increased. (Between 1911 and 1938 productivity rose by about 50%.)

The censuses of production figures illustrate this improvement in productivity in another way. Net output per person employed (i.e. value of gross output, less cost of materials and fuel) in all census industries was £212 in 1924; it fell to £211 in 1930; it rose to £225 in 1935.[1]

A fuller appreciation of the implications of the process of structural and locational change, which continues all the time, may be enhanced by a review of locational factors, patterns and policy.

2. Factors Influencing Location

Historically, the major technical and economic locational attractions for industry were raw materials and sources of power. Thus the swift-flowing Pennine streams provided water power for local industries, many years ago. With the development of steam power, coal assumed great importance as an industrial fuel. Because of its heavy, bulky nature and the fact that its entire weight was used up in the power process, there was a strong locational attraction, for the developing industries, towards the coalfields.

Another important locational factor is the proximity of markets. There has always been a tug-of-war between the pull of the market and that of materials and power. In the case of the iron and steel industry, raw materials and fuel were both available near the coast. The possibility of importing raw materials and exporting finished products from near-by ports added to the locational pull of the northern coastal areas and also attracted ancillary industries.

Gradually, as industries gravitated towards certain regions, labour migrated to them and local skills were developed. These pools of skilled labour in turn exercised a locational attraction for similar industries. Although some regions came to specialise on a narrow range of industries, it did not automatically follow that all localised industries determined the industrial character of their surroundings. The Midlands, for example, is the major centre for vehicle production, but it nevertheless has a variegated industrial life.

In connection with the locational pulls of markets, fuels, materials and pools of skilled labour, Weber expounded a theory based on transport costs. He claimed that industries will be located in such a way as to result in the minimum total ton-miles of transport to and from the industry. This thesis rests on 'weight-losing' and 'weight-gaining' principles. Thus if materials and/or fuel are heavy, but lose weight in the process of production, then rather than transport them to distant plants, they will be used at source and the lighter product will be transported to the market. Conversely, if the product gains weight in the process of production and is heavier than its main materials and fuel, then transport costs will be lower if the product is made in dispersed centres near the markets. One such case is beer, which gains weight from water, the final product being far heavier than the malt and hops contained in it. Beer, then, is not localised in Kent but is produced near the main markets. It must be stressed, however, that the transport cost factor is relative to the value of the product. In the case of beer, transport costs would be relatively, as well as absolutely, high. Whisky,

[1] *Ann. Abs. Stat.*

on the other hand, has a much higher value–weight ratio. Consequently, whisky production is much more highly localised than beer, the resultant transport costs being relatively low.

This raises an important point. Weber's transport cost principles would apply strongly to heavy, bulky products with a low value–weight ratio, and they help to explain the dispersed nature of such industries. However, many cases of localised industry exist and prosper not because of Weber's weight and transport cost principles but rather because of economies of local concentration.[1] These external economies of localised concentration (arising not within particular firms and plants but between them) include skilled labour pools, specialist services, efficient distribution (because purchasers can 'shop around'), and, above all, a division of labour between linked products, processes and services in close proximity with one another (known as 'partial integration').

To sum up, the main technical and economic factors influencing the location of industry are:

1. Proximity and distribution of climatic conditions, raw materials, fuel, labour and markets.
2. Absolute and relative transport costs to and from the industry, resulting in 'material-orientated' or 'market-orientated' location.
3. Advantages of 'partial' integration in localised areas, even when the original locational attractions have become exhausted.

It is important to note that constant improvements in technique, making for more productive use of fuels and materials (which therefore lose less weight, relative to the product) tend to weaken their locational pull. This process is reinforced by the improvements being made in transport efficiency and the flexibility of the transport system, which tend to reduce the relative importance of transport costs. The locational pull of coal, the traditional, localised source of power, is being further weakened by the gradual development of alternative dispersed sources of power, such as oil and National Grid electricity.

Considering also the fact that original location decisions are sometimes made for non-technical and/or non-economic factors (such as personal attachment to a home locality; physical availability of suitable accommodation; personal acquaintance with suppliers or customers, etc.), it seems likely that there will be more and more scope for such general factors to influence locational decisions in future.

Nevertheless, despite the progressive weakening of technical and economic factors, and the increasing scope for more general, short-term factors, there has not been much general dispersion of industries as a whole. The vast conurbations and agglomerations of industry still tend to attract and hold plants and firms, although in a more diversified mixture than before. This seems to point to the overriding factor of the pull of 'partial integration' of specialised processes and products in localised areas, regardless of the historical reasons for that localisation – what Professor Sargant Florence calls 'the dead hand of past technical conditions'.

[1] For an interesting exposition of the role of 'resource endowment' and the principle of 'circular and cumulative causation' in the location of manufacturing industry, see N. Kaldor, 'The case for regional policies', *Scottish Journal of Political Economy*, Nov. 1970.

3. Location of Industry in Britain

The location of British industry falls into ten broad geographical areas. These are as follows:[1]

GREATER LONDON AND THE SOUTH-EASTERN REGION

London, one of the world's three largest cities (with New York and Tokyo) and one of the world's three largest ports (with New York and Rotterdam) is situated at the head of navigation on the Thames estuary. It is Britain's capital and probably the most important financial centre in the world. The working population of Greater London and the urbanised fringe areas up to forty or fifty miles from Charing Cross numbers over 5 million, nearly half of whom are in manufacturing industries. London is the main British centre for the production of clothing, food and drink, printing, films, furniture, art materials, precision instruments and many other specialised products. In many of these industries small firms predominate and the average size of manufacturing firms is well below the national average, particularly in the County of London. London's outer ring, especially, is an important area for light engineering, chemicals and consumer goods and it also has some heavy engineering plants. In the periphery of the London conurbation and in the new urban development outside it industry has been expanding rapidly, particularly electronics and many consumer goods industries. Some of the largest aircraft plants are in this area and two of the major motor vehicle manufacturers have factories at Dagenham, Luton and Dunstable. Oil refineries, shipyards and a variety of engineering works are situated along the lower Thames and Medway estuaries.

SOUTH-WEST AND WEST ENGLAND

Bristol, the largest city in the area is a leading port and an industrial centre with aircraft, food processing, tobacco, paper, paint and other industries. Aircraft and engineering plants are situated in Gloucester; railway and engineering works are situated in Swindon, Wiltshire; ship repair yards, oil refineries and other industries are situated near Southampton; Plymouth has an important dockyard and other light industries; the Cotswold valleys produce West of England woollen and worsted cloths.

EAST ANGLIA AND LINCOLNSHIRE

This is the most important agricultural region, with regard to employment, and one of the most productive. Ipswich and Grantham are noted for agricultural machinery and implements; Norwich is noted for footwear and food manufacture; there has been a rapid development of food canning and freezing, mainly based on locally grown produce; Scunthorpe, in Lincolnshire, is an important and growing centre for steel-making; Grimsby and Yarmouth are important fishing centres and have extensive fish processing plants.

THE MIDLANDS

The major Midlands industrial area consists of the conurbation centred on Birmingham and Wolverhampton (including parts of Staffordshire, Worcestershire and Warwickshire), where there is a wide variety of industries, especially the manufacture of metals and metal goods, motor vehicles (at Coventry, Birmingham and Oxford), electrical and engineering products, jewellery and

[1] *Brit. O. H.*

rubber products. Other industrial towns outside the main conurbations include Leicester, with hosiery, clothing, footwear and footwear machinery; Derby, with general engineering, locomotives and aero-engines; Nottingham, with light engineering, lace, drugs and tobacco; Rugby, with electrical engineering; Northampton, with footwear and engineering; Kidderminster, with carpets; Corby, in Northamptonshire, with an expanding steel industry, originally based on local deposits of iron ore; Peterborough, with large engineering works. The north-west of this region contains the richest coalfield in Britain, with the highest output per man. It continues into Yorkshire.

YORKSHIRE

The West Riding contains most of the industry of this area. About 90% of the country's worsted industry and the greatest proportion of its woollen industry are found here. Bradford is the main city for worsteds and is the commercial centre for the whole wool trade. Morley and Leeds specialise in cheaper cloths; Batley, Dewsbury and Cleckheaton specialise in heavy cloth; Huddersfield produces fine woollens and Halifax produces carpets; Leeds is the commercial capital of the area and has a large clothing industry and a range of engineering products. Sheffield is a centre for heavy engineering and high quality steels, cutlery and tools. About one-fifth of Britain's coal comes from this area's coalfields. York produces chocolate and confectionery and has important railway shops; Hull is one of the world's largest fishing ports and has many manufacturing industries, including engineering, vegetable oil processing, paints and sawmilling.

LANCASHIRE

Manchester, as well as being the commercial centre of the cotton textile industry, is one of the chief centres of electrical and heavy engineering, machine tools and dyestuffs in Britain. Most of the cotton yarn is spun at Bolton, Oldham, Rochdale and Stockport (in Cheshire). Weaving is carried out at Burnley, Nelson, Blackburn, Colne, Accrington and Darwen. Both spinning and weaving are carried out at Preston and Bury. A wide variety of industries has developed in this area and they are now far more important than cotton. They include food, drink, tobacco, chemicals, metals and metal goods, engineering and electrical goods (including printing, textile and electrical machinery), and motor vehicles. The Lancashire coalfield lies in the Manchester–Wigan part of the region. The Manchester Ship Canal facilitates a big volume of overseas trade and links Manchester with Merseyside, passing through the industrial towns of Warrington, with metal industries such as wire-drawing; Widnes, with chemicals; Ellesmere Port, with oil refinery installations. Glass is manufactured at St Helens, north of the Canal; Liverpool, the second port in Britain, is a great commercial and insurance centre and comes next to London as a centre for processing imported foodstuffs and raw materials, especially flour milling, soap manufacture, sugar refining and rubber products. One of its older industries is ship repairing, whilst at Birkenhead shipbuilding is a major industry. Many of the new industries in the region have become established in the Liverpool area, particularly on the Government-fostered industrial estates. They include electrical engineering and the manufacture of other heavy industrial equipment. Shipbuilding is important in Barrow, in the north-west of the county and linoleum is an important product of Lancaster.

NORTH-EAST ENGLAND

The coal industry is important in Northumberland and Durham. Tyneside and Wearside come next to Clydeside as shipbuilding and ship-repairing centres. Ships are also built at Hartlepools and on Tees-side. Iron and steel plants are situated at Consett, in County Durham, and in the Middlesbrough area, which is also Britain's most important chemicals centre. Tyneside is especially noted for heavy electrical equipment. Industries in the area have become greatly diversified since 1937, as a result of Government-sponsored industrial estates. They include mining and other machinery, rolling mill plant, machine tools, ropes, glass, clothing and scientific instruments.

SCOTLAND

The densely populated area of Clydeside, which includes Glasgow, is Britain's largest shipbuilding and marine engineering centre. Mainly in the north Lanark-shire area steel plants are situated, specialising in steel plate and heavier products. On Clydeside a wide variety of engineering products is made, including earth-moving equipment, locomotives, air-conditioning plant, industrial valves, food-processing machinery and commercial vehicles. The coalfields of the Lothians, Fife, Ayr and Lanark produce about one-tenth of Britain's coal, but in general they are high-cost fields and their future hangs in the balance. Edinburgh, Scotland's capital and second largest city, has printing, brewing, rubber and engineering industries. The British jute industry is concentrated almost entirely at Dundee, which also produces office machinery, clocks and watches, refrig-erators and manufactured food. Several light industries are situated in Aberdeen, a fishing port and Scotland's third city. Kirkcaldy, in Fife, is an important centre for linoleum manufacture. High quality tweeds and knitwear are produced in the border towns in the south; the north of Scotland is Britain's only significant source of hydro-electric power; north-east Scotland has Britain's largest con-centration of whisky distilleries.

WALES

Coal-mining, particularly the extraction of special coals, such as anthracite and steam coal, remains the chief source of employment in Wales. However, the area produces many types of capital and consumer goods such as engineering products and electrical goods, metal goods and chemicals. The steel industry in Wales supplies most of Britain's tinplate and a large proportion of its sheet steel. Since 1937 many new industries have been established on the Government-sponsored industrial estates, including plastics, synthetic fibres, clothing, electronics and light engineering. In North Wales a number of light industries are situated in the coastal and other towns, particularly Wrexham.

NORTHERN IRELAND

The largest shipyard in the United Kingdom is situated in Belfast, the capital city. Besides the traditional industries of the area, such as linen, shirt-making, ropes, tobacco and general engineering, there are marine engineering and aircraft construction. In recent years new industries have been introduced, such as man-made fibres, electrical equipment and food canning.

These geographical areas do not coincide exactly with the administrative 'standard regions' and economic planning regions. However, the map in Fig. 2.1

superimposes the regional boundaries over the distribution of industrial employment. From this it may be seen that the Greater London region, the North-West and West and East Midlands regions predominate in industrial employment.

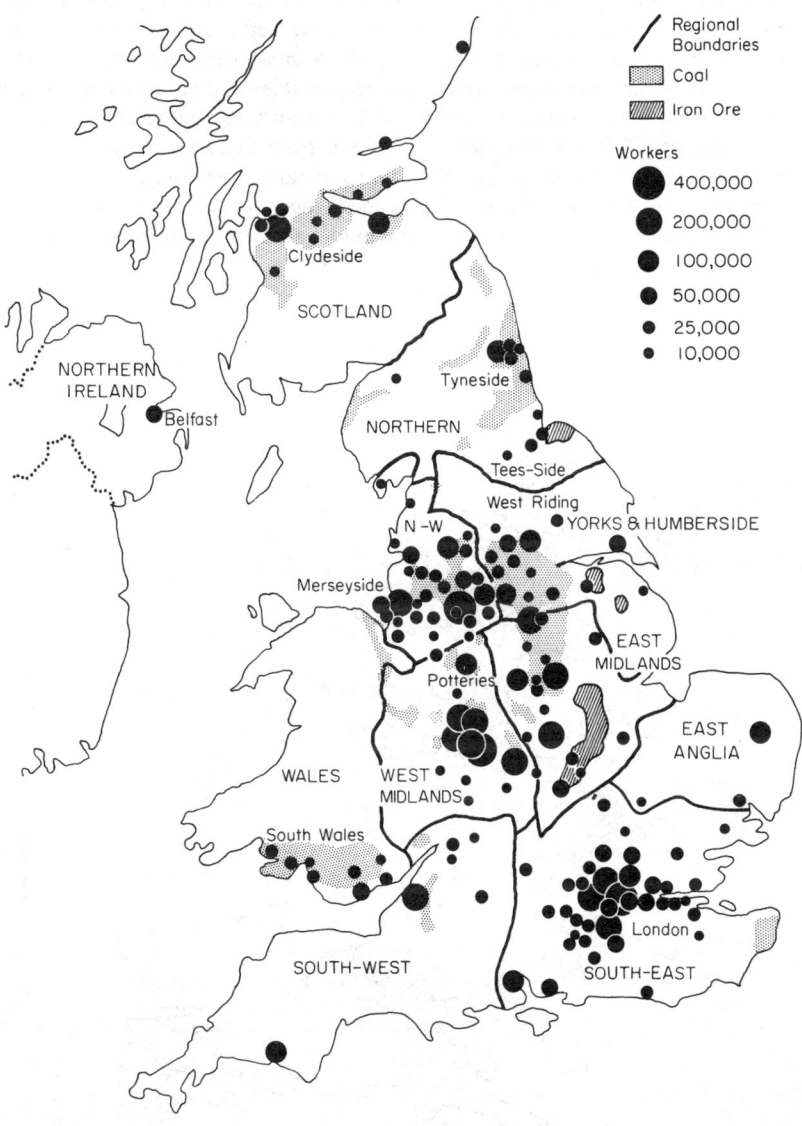

Fig. 2.1. *Location of industrial employment*
(Source: *Brit. O.H.*, 1962)

4. Location of Industry Policy

(a) Before World War II

As a result of the acute economic depression in the early 1930s in west Cumberland, the north-east coast, South Wales and the Clyde valley, the Government embarked upon a policy of positive measures for the alleviation of local unemployment. Under the Special Areas (Development and Improvement) Act of 1934 and an amending Act of 1937, these areas were designated Special Areas. Special Commissioners were made responsible for their development and improvement, and industry was attracted to the areas by inducements such as loan facilities, Government grants, and the lease of factories by Government-financed, non-profit-making Trading Estate companies (see Fig. 2.2). One of the major problems in these areas was their dependence upon a narrow range of coal and capital investment industries, which employed men rather than women. In

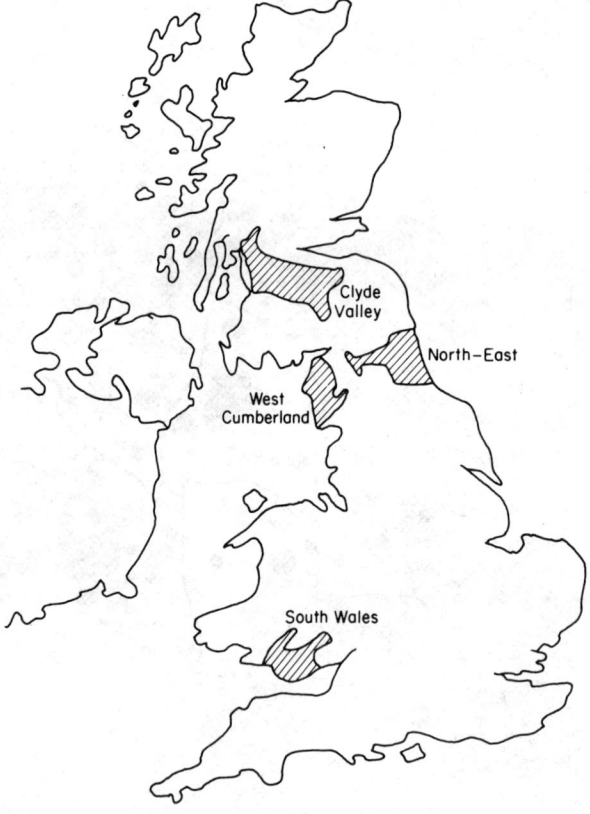

Fig. 2.2. *Pre-World War II Special Areas*
(Source: G. McCrone, *Regional Policy in Britain*, 1969, p. 94)

times of cyclical economic depression a great proportion of the men were unemployed, whilst the women continued to be unoccupied. A major task, therefore, was that of mixing light and heavy industry so as to achieve a more varied balance. This, in turn, however, was liable to the danger that too varied a mixture might discard potential economies of local specialisation. What needed to be done, therefore, was to permit the continuance of a variety of localised industries, which employed a cross-section of the population and were not economically unstable; to introduce variety into 'unstable' areas of localised industry; to avoid the double fault of excessive development in areas of both highly localised and varied industry – which (as in the London area) resulted in high and steady levels of employment at the cost of congestion, slums, long journeys to work and other social nuisances.

(b) After World War II

1945-1960 . After World War II the Government gave the Board of Trade statutory power, under the 1947 Town and Country Planning Acts, to ensure that new industrial development was consistent with 'the proper distribution of industry'. Any new industrial building or extension exceeding 5,000 square feet in area must be authorised by a Board of Trade development certificate. This power has been used to discourage the expansion of industry in the Greater London and Birmingham areas.

In addition, after World War II the Distribution of Industry Acts of 1945 and 1950 renamed the special areas 'development areas'. They were enlarged and added to, and the Government's powers of assistance were increased (see Fig. 2.3). The Board of Trade took over the Special Commissioners' powers to build and let factories in these areas; the Treasury had powers to make loans or grants to firms unable to obtain them through normal channels; the Board of Trade factories were built and managed by Industrial Estate companies, which had unpaid directors, appointed by the Board of Trade.

The Distribution of Industry Acts did not apply to Northern Ireland, because the Northern Ireland Parliament passed its own legislation to build factories for rent or sale and to provide grants and loans. The Board of Trade treats Northern Ireland as a development area, guiding and encouraging new industrial projects there. As a result, from 1945 to 1962, 162 firms started production in Northern Ireland for the first time and 106 expansion schemes were put into effect, together providing employment for over 40,000 people.[1] Preference is also given to Northern Ireland in the placing of Government contracts.

As a result of the successful operation of the development areas, the general employment position in them had improved by 1958. By the end of 1958, of the total of over 400 million square feet of new industrial buildings and extensions (in the over 5,000 square feet category) built in Great Britain since 1945, 27% had been in the development areas, which employed only 18% of manufacturing industry workers.

Since 1947, in order to coordinate the work of the Board of Trade with that of the Ministry of Town and Country Planning (which, through the local planning authorities, is responsible for the siting of industrial premises), the local planning authorities were authorised to prepare development plans for their own districts. Also, the New Towns Act of 1946 made provision for the

---

[1] *Brit. O. H.*, 1962, p. 264.

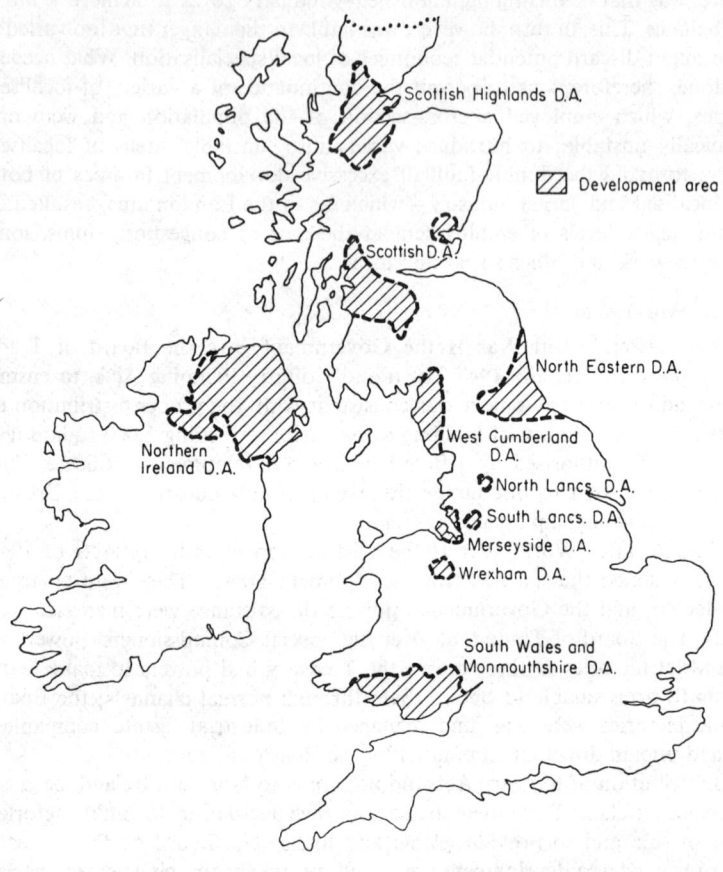

Fig. 2.3. *Development Areas of the United Kingdom, 1945–60*
(Source: A. Ferriday, *A Regional Geography of the British Isles*, 1956, p. 346)

housing of populations, not only of the development areas (Cwmbran in Wales; Glenrothes in Scotland; Aycliffe and Peterlee in England), but also of Greater London (Stevenage, Crawley, Basildon, Hatfield, Hemel Hempstead, Bracknell, Harlow and Welwyn Garden City).

Government assistance was not limited, after 1945, to the development areas. Other areas of persistent unemployment received attention from the Board of Trade, which has tried to steer suitable 'footloose' industries to them. In such areas and in new or expanded towns, factories have been built by local authorities; in rural and fishing areas in need of manufacturing industry, the

Development Commission has financed the building of factories for industrial firms prepared to go there.

Because by 1958 the general employment position in the development areas had improved, the Government was able to tackle more vigorously the problem of relatively high, persistent unemployment in certain places both in and outside the development areas, particularly in Scotland, West and North Wales and some coastal districts in England. In July 1958 the Government acquired powers under the Distribution of Industry (Industrial Finance) Act to enable financial assistance to be given, on the recommendation of the Development Areas Treasury Advisory Committee, to firms which would give employment in places of high and persistent unemployment, whether in or outside the development areas.

1960-1966. By 1960 the general position in the development areas had improved to such an extent that the 1958 legislation was simplified and strengthened by the Local Employment Act, which came into effect on 1 April 1960. According to this Act, the Government's powers of assistance were vested in the Board of Trade. The industrial estate companies in the development areas were replaced by three industrial estate management corporations, one for England, one for Wales and one for Scotland. They were controlled and financed by the Board of Trade. The Board of Trade drew up a list of unemployment 'black spots' or 'development districts' – places where high and persistent unemployment existed or was expected. This list was more realistic than the previous D.A.T.A.C. list, compiled since 1958, being shorter and covering less of the country. The D.A.T.A.C. list and the original development areas had covered about 20% of the British insured working population, but the new list covered areas where about 12% of the insured working population live. The Board of Trade was empowered and instructed to offer a number of inducements to industrialists to settle, or expand their activities in, the development districts. These inducements included the building of factories for sale or lease on favourable terms; loans and capital grants towards working capital and initial equipment; or grants (through the appropriate Government departments) to local authorities for clearing derelict or neglected sites and for improving basic services. The new scheme was to be flexible. The Board of Trade could add to the list new localities which became or were likely to become eligible; it could also de-schedule localities where the employment position improved. Furthermore, it was to pay regard to 'the proper diversification of industry' in a district and also to the circumstances not only of the district in general, but also of any particular class of persons in it. The Board of Trade was to produce an annual report on its use of the powers under the Act.

The Act did not apply to Northern Ireland, where the original scheme there was still in effect.

In response to a rise in unemployment during the winter of 1962–63 in Merseyside, the north-east and Scotland, the 1963 Local Employment Act was passed, to provide the Government with greater powers of inducement for industrial siting. The Board of Trade was empowered to offer grants amounting to 25% of building costs and 10% of plant and machinery costs to firms establishing or expanding activities in the development districts. The Development Districts as

2. LOCATION, STRUCTURE AND ORGANISATION OF INDUSTRY [1]

at 1965 may be seen in Fig. 2·4, with the regional planning boundaries superimposed.[1]

Between 1964 and 1966 the Government established the machinery of regional planning, which was to set in motion a swing in policy away from the 'district'

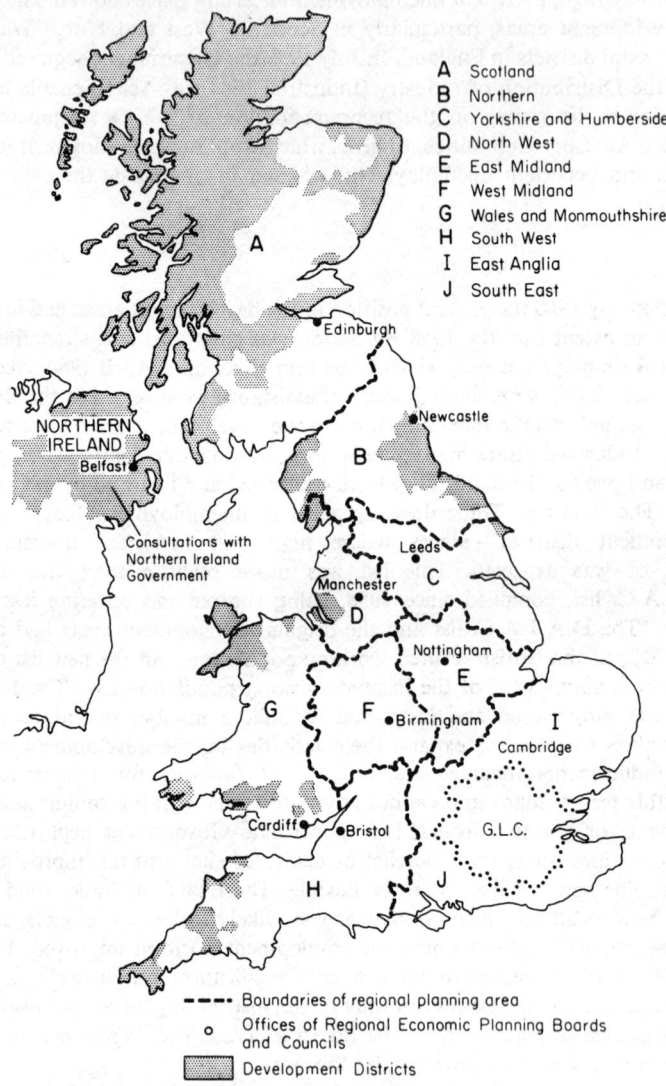

A Scotland
B Northern
C Yorkshire and Humberside
D North West
E East Midland
F West Midland
G Wales and Monmouthshire
H South West
I East Anglia
J South East

- - - - Boundaries of regional planning area
  o   Offices of Regional Economic Planning Boards and Councils
  ▨   Development Districts

Fig. 2.4. *Development districts and Economic Planning Regions, 1965*
(Source: *Brit. O.H.*, 1968, p. 18)

[1] In 1968 a B. of T. research study indicated the major trends in locational movement of manufacturing firms from 1945 to 1965. About 438,000 jobs were created in moves to 'peripheral areas', corresponding to the Development Areas. For further details see *DE.A. Pr. Rep. Ind. and Reg.*, 44, Sept. 1968 and *The Movement of Manufacturing Industry in the United Kingdom, 1945–65*, H.M.S.O., 1968.

approach to a regional scale of operation, aimed at strengthening the national economy by planned, efficient use of productive resources and an improvement in the economic and social conditions within each region.[1]

Post-1966: (i) *Development Areas:* The 1966 Industrial Development Act abolished the post-1960 Development Districts and established new Development Areas – the most extensive yet specified. These covered about one-fifth of Britain's working population (Northern Ireland has its own, very similar industrial incentives legislation) and about 40% of the land area. This compares with about one-sixth of the working population covered by the Development Districts as at 1966. The powers available under the 1960 and 1963 Local Employment Acts were extended: tax incentives on depreciation allowances were discontinued, but cash grants for industrial building were raised, in certain cases, to 35% and for plant and machinery to 40%. Other extensions of 1960-63 assistance included financial assistance *via* loans on the recommendation of the Board of Trade Advisory Committee; removal grants; the provision of factories on advantageous terms for sale or rent (in some cases rent-free for two years). Local authorities could obtain Government capital grants covering 85% of the cost of clearing derelict sites and the improvement of basic services. The Department of Employment and Productivity (formerly the Ministry of Labour) could provide help with the cost of training and transferring workers in the Development Areas. The control exercised by Industrial Development Certificates was tightened: the limit on exemption was reduced from 10,000 sq. feet generally to 5,000 sq. feet (3,000 sq. feet in the Midlands and the South-East), with some exemptions in Development Areas.

In 1967, because of the additional unemployment problem caused by closures in some coal-mining areas, the Government designated them as Special Development Areas – corresponding roughly to the prewar Special Areas – which were to receive priority treatment. This included up to five years rent-free in Board of Trade factories; loans at moderate interest rates on the balance between building grants and costs; operational grants for three years. Also, in 1967, a Regional Employment Premium was offered to employers of manufacturing workers in the Development Areas, which was in addition to the Selective Employment Tax rebate on all manufacturing employees. A major reason for this was that the S.E.T. tended to penalise the labour-intensive services industries and the capital grants to favour the capital-intensive industries: as a major problem in the Development Areas was unemployed labour, it was felt that some inducement or subsidy should be provided for employment-creating, labour-intensive manufacturing industry.[2]

In October 1970 the Government made an important change in the type of Development Areas assistance, by announcing a switch from investment grants to a system of tax allowances on investment in industrial plant and machinery and in buildings. Certain types of the former in Development Areas were to benefit from totally tax-free depreciation; the latter were to benefit indefinitely

[1] *Economic Planning in the Regions*, D.E.A., H.M.S.O., 1968; 'Old and new industrial areas in Britain', *M.B.R.*, May 1964, pp. 3–10; G. McCrone, *op. cit.*, pp. 142–66.

For further comment and analysis see *Brit. O. H.*, 1971, pp. 251–2; McCrone, *op. cit.*, pp. 126–42; Colin Clark, 'Industrial location and economic potential', *L.B.R.*, Oct. 1966; B. J. Loasby, 'Making location policy work', *L.B.R.*, Jan. 1967; 'Progress in the Development Areas', *Board of Trade Journal*, 28 Oct. 1966.

from a 44% initial tax-free depreciation allowance.[1] The Regional Employment Premium was to be discontinued as of September 1974.

The reasons given were the high and increasing cost of these forms of regional differential, the scale of which may be seen from Table 2.1. In July 1971 it was announced that the discrimination against service industries was to be relaxed in the Development Areas: free depreciation tax reliefs were to be extended to immobile plant and machinery used in service industries in these areas.

Table 2.1 *Aid to Development Areas* (Total cost of special regional assistance to industry over and above that available nationally)

	£ million					
	1963/64	'64/65	'65/66	'66/67	'67/68	'68/69[1]
Investment grants[1]	–	–	–	–	72	85
Regional Employment Premium	–	–	–	–	34·1	100
Selective Employment Premium	–	–	–	[8·4][3]	[25][3]	25
Local Employment Acts[4]	16·9	28·2	29·8	44·0	45·0	50
Industrial training[5]	–	–	neg	0·8	0·9	3
Miscellaneous[6]	–	–	0·1	0·1	1·5	2·9
Free depreciation[2]	–	3	45	25	4	neg
Total aid to industry	**17**	**31**	**75**	**70**	**156**[7]	**265**[7]
Land clearance etc.[8]	0·3	0·8	0·8	0·7	1·3	2·1

(Source: *D.E.A. Pr. Rep. Ind. and Reg.*, 55, Aug. 1969)

In March 1971 the Special Development Areas were extended (see Fig. 2.5) and the operational grants were increased to as much as 30% of eligible wage and salary costs during the first three years.

On the occasion of the March 1972 Budget the Government, in its White Paper *Industrial and Regional Development* (Cmnd. 4942), modified its Development Area policy considerably. Free (i.e. 100%) initial tax-free depreciation allowances on (new and secondhand) plant and machinery were to be extended to all parts of the country and the 30% initial tax-free allowances on new industrial buildings were to be raised to 40% in all parts of the country, whereas this rate had hitherto applied only to the Development Areas. In order to preserve a differential between the D.A.s and the rest of the country, the I.D.C.s were abolished within the Areas and plant and machinery investment grants were to be restored in those areas. Development grants for new industrial building were also restored, at 20% in the D.A.s and 22% in the Special D.A.s – the same rates as for new plant and machinery. The annual cost of the new incentives extending to the rest of the country was estimated at £115 million in 1973–74, rising to £450 million in 1975–76, whilst those applying to the D.A.s, Special D.A.s and Intermediate Areas (see below) were estimated to cost between £250 million and £300 million. A subsidiary incentive lay in the innovation that the tax-free depreciation allowances were to be given on the full amount of capital expenditure, even

[1] *E.P.R.*, 10 Dec. 1970; *D.T.*, 28 Oct. 1970.

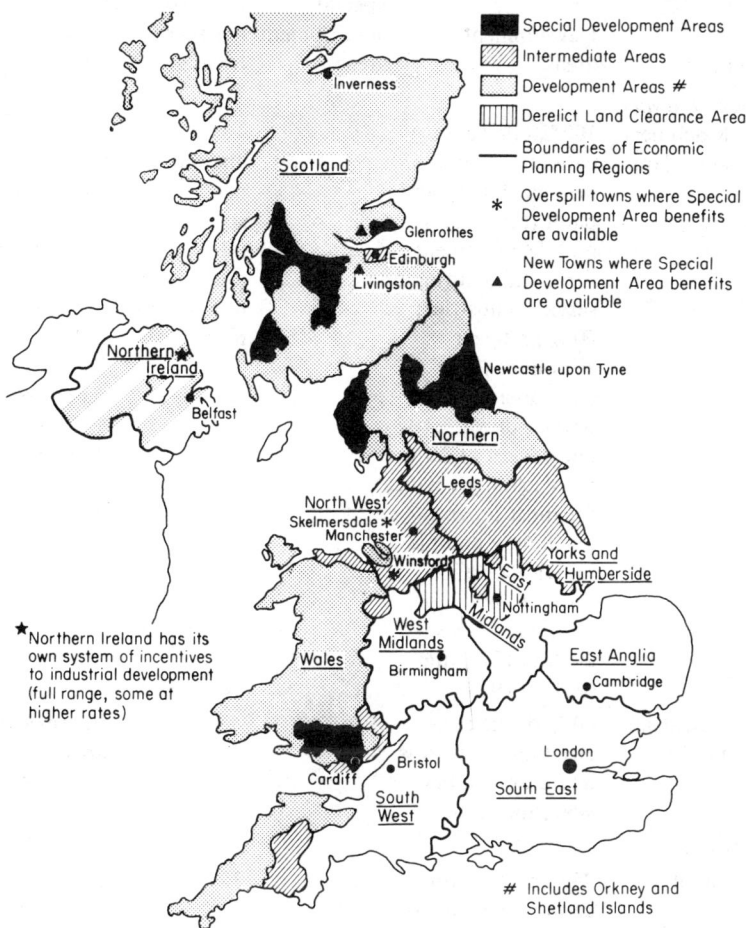

Special Development Areas
Intermediate Areas
Development Areas #
Derelict Land Clearance Areas
Boundaries of Economic Planning Regions
* Overspill towns where Special Development Area benefits are available
▲ New Towns where Special Development Area benefits are available

*Northern Ireland has its own system of incentives to industrial development (full range, some at higher rates)

Includes Orkney and Shetland Islands

Fig. 2.5. *Assisted Areas, 1972*
(Source: *D.E.A. Pr. Rep. Ind. and Reg.*, 55, Aug. 1969; *D.T.*, 17 March 1971 and 26 Oct. 1971; *Econ.*, 17 July 1971, p. 81 and 15 Jan. 1972, p. 57; *F.T.*, 23 March 1972)

when part of this may be financed by regional development grants for buildings, plant or machinery.

The Industry Bill, published in May 1972, also provided for the buildings, plant and machinery grants to apply to already established firms, as well as newcomers. In addition, 'selective financial assistance' was to be available for safeguarding employment and as an aid to efficiency, expansion and growth. This selective aid was to be available in the D.A.s, Special D.A.s and Intermediate Areas (estimated annual cost about £75 million by the mid-1970s) and also to firms in the rest of the country, when in the 'national interest' (up to a total of £550 million). Both service and manufacturing firms were eligible and the aid

73

Table 2.2 *Incentives to all areas as at January 1972*

Incentive	Development areas	Special development areas	Northern Ireland	Other
1. Tax allowances:				
(a) Machinery and plant	100% allowance on capital spending on new machinery and plant (other than mobile equipment) for manufacturing and service industries; 60% first-year allowance (and subsequent annual writing-down allowances of 25% on the declining balance) for most other machinery and plant; initial allowance raised to 80% for spending between 20 July 1971, and 31 July 1973		Tax allowances on net spending (after any grants) as in development areas	60% first-year allowance on most items, then 25% a year on declining balance. Temporarily raised to 80% (see development areas for dates)
(b) Industrial buildings	44% of the construction costs (less any grant) in first year; thereafter, 4%			Intermediate areas: 44%; other: 30%
2. Grants:				
(a) Building	35% or 45% for certain new undertakings		35–55%	25–35%; intermediate areas only
(b) Operational (for new incoming industry only)	nil	30% of eligible wage and salary cost during first three years	Negotiable contribution	nil
(c) Machinery and equipment	nil	nil	20–40%	nil
3. Regional employment premium:	£1·50 a week for every male adult employee; lower rate for other workers			nil

(Source: *Econ.*, 15 Jan. 1972, p. 57)

would be in the form of bonus, grants or guarantees on 'any terms or conditions'.
(ii) *Intermediate Areas:* In 1969 the Hunt Committee, set up in 1967 to investigate the special economic problems of the 'intermediate' or 'grey' areas, which lay outside the Development Areas, reported. The 1970 Local Employment Act, which followed, extended to the designated Intermediate Areas special assistance similar to, but more limited than, that extended to the Development Areas by the 1960 and 1963 Local Employment Acts. This included factory building grants, additional provisions for industrial training and help in a programme for the clearing of derelict land. Also, the I.D.C.s were to be made available to these areas on the same basis as in the Development Areas. In March 1971 additional areas were designated Intermediate Areas (see Fig. 2.5).[1] The full range of incentives to all areas as at January 1972 may be seen in summary form in Table 2.2. The March 1972 White Paper, referred to above, also initiated important changes in the Intermediate Areas. They were extended, geographically, to include all of the North-West, Wales and Yorkshire and Humberside not already designated for special assistance. The 20% investment grant rate, for new industrial buildings only, was to be operative: Derelict Land Clearance areas not absorbed into the Intermediate Areas were to benefit, temporarily (i.e. for two years) from the same 20% building grants.

(iii) *Regional Policy:* The ten Regional Economic Planning Councils, supported by their Economic Planning Boards, set up between 1964 and 1966 have all published reports. The most far-reaching regional study has been the third major report on the South-East (see Fig. 2.6) – *A Strategic Plan for the South-East* – published in 1970[2] and accepted in principle by the Government in October 1971, along with a reconsideration of locational incentives and of the 'growth centre' concept.

In fact, all the elements of the New Towns and the Development, Special Development and Intermediate Areas constitute strands in the fabric of regional policy. There has, nevertheless, been a great deal of criticism of the scope and nature of regional policy and planning[3], which call into question matters such as the advisability of tampering piecemeal, with sometimes conflicting policy measures, in an intricate economy; the possible conflict between incentives to capital mobility as opposed to labour mobility; the possible further congestion of old industrial areas, whose social capital or infrastructure may often be obsolete; the pressure to locate new industry in areas determined by the historical decline of obsolete industry; the lack of certainty and knowledge as to how and why and for how long policy is being operated; the cost-effectiveness of dispersing population and industry, in order to reduce congestion in the prosperous regions, by dogmatically creating job-opportunities in problem areas by means of expensive incentives and possibly at the cost of completely inhibiting investment which may only be worthwhile in the more affluent areas.

[1] *D.E.A. Pr. Rep. Ind. and Reg.*, 52, May 1969 and 55, Aug. 1969; 'Aid for regions: blank cheque', *Econ.*, 13 May 1972, pp. 104–7.
[2] 'The South-East—20 years on', *Econ.*, 30 May 1970, pp. 52–3.
[3] R. C. Tress, 'The next stage in regional policy', *The Three Banks Review*, March 1969; E. G. West, 'Regional policy: fact and fallacy', *L.B.R.*, April 1966; H. W. Richardson, *Regional Economics*, 1969; W. F. Deedes, 'Second thoughts on regional planning', *D.T.*, 21 June 1966 and 23 June 1966; F. Broadway, *State Intervention in British Industry: 1964–68*, Ch. 11; N. Kaldor, 'The case for regional policies', *Scottish Journal of Political Economy*, Nov. 1970; 'Cities for 3,000 million people', survey in *Econ.*, 8 July 1967, pp. 114–21.

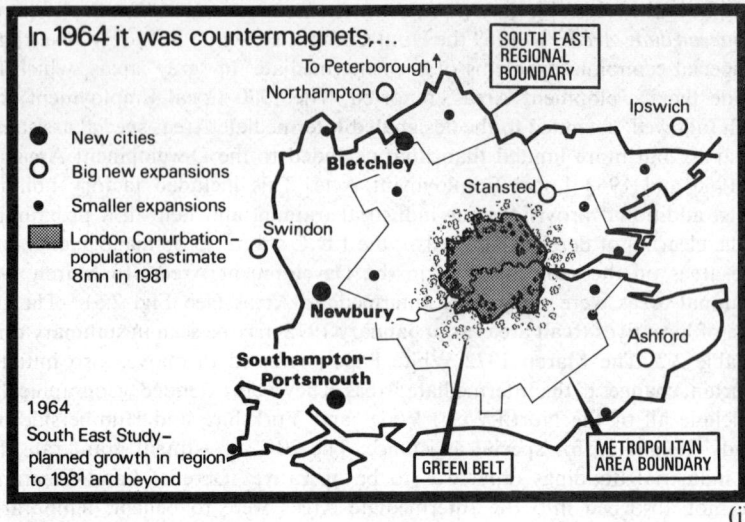

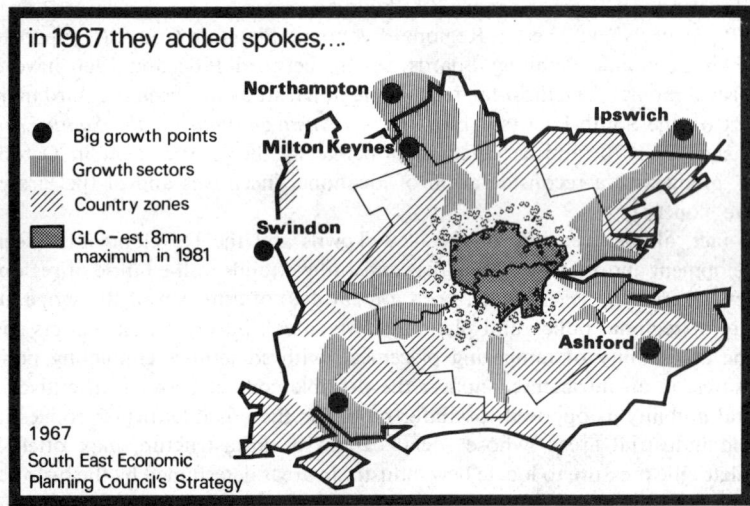

Fig. 2.6. *Evolution of plans for the South-East*
(Source: *Econ.*, 30 May 1970, p. 53)

In October 1971 an important step was taken by the Government, whereby it announced a phased decentralisation of planning work from London to the regional offices, which were to become 'mini Whitehalls'. The aim was to achieve a comprehensive approach, within each region, to problems of planning and environment, with more regional decisions taken locally.[1] In the March 1972 White Paper, referred to above, it was announced that a new, coordinating Industrial Development Executive, headed by a Minister for Industrial Development, was to be established. It would incorporate all the divisions in the Department for Trade and Industry which were concerned with regional

[1] *D.T.*, 26 Oct. 1971.

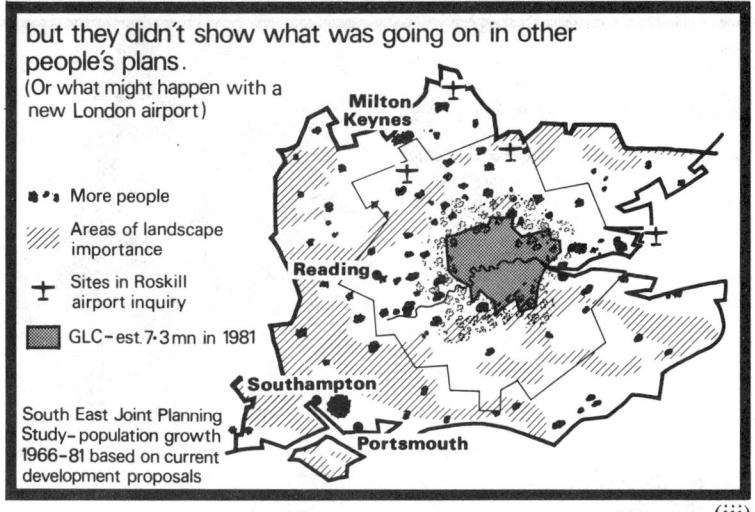

but they didn't show what was going on in other people's plans.
(Or what might happen with a new London airport)

■ ● ● More people

Areas of landscape importance

✛ Sites in Roskill airport inquiry

GLC – est. 7·3 mn in 1981

South East Joint Planning Study – population growth 1966–81 based on current development proposals

(iii)

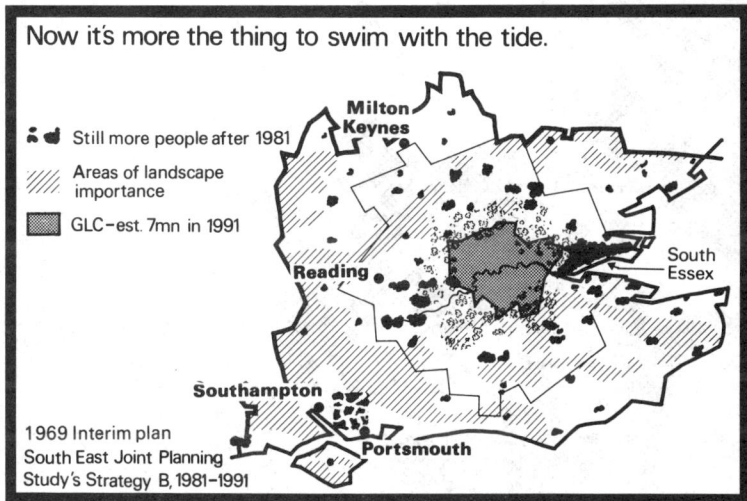

Now it's more the thing to swim with the tide.

▲ ◢ Still more people after 1981

Areas of landscape importance

GLC – est. 7 mn in 1991

1969 Interim plan
South East Joint Planning Study's Strategy B, 1981–1991

(iv)

Fig. 2.6. (contd.)

development, as well as with small firms and key sectors such as chemicals, textiles, machine tools and shipbuilding.

During the 1970s the problems of industrial location and regional policy in Britain are coming more and more to be seen in the wider context of Western European regional problems.[1] As may be seen in Fig. 2.7, most of these problem areas are either regions of declining industry, outer periphery regions or internal frontier areas. With regard to British membership of the E.E.C. and its impact on British regional problems, there are dangers that the central areas of the enlarged Common Market – the South-East of England, the Ruhr, Belgium, Rotterdam

[1] 'Regional problems compared', *Econ.*, 29 Aug. 1970, pp. 45–53; 'Regional policy', *Econ.*, 24 July 1971, p. 71; 'The poor always with us', *Econ.*, 16 Oct. 1971, pp. 72–3.

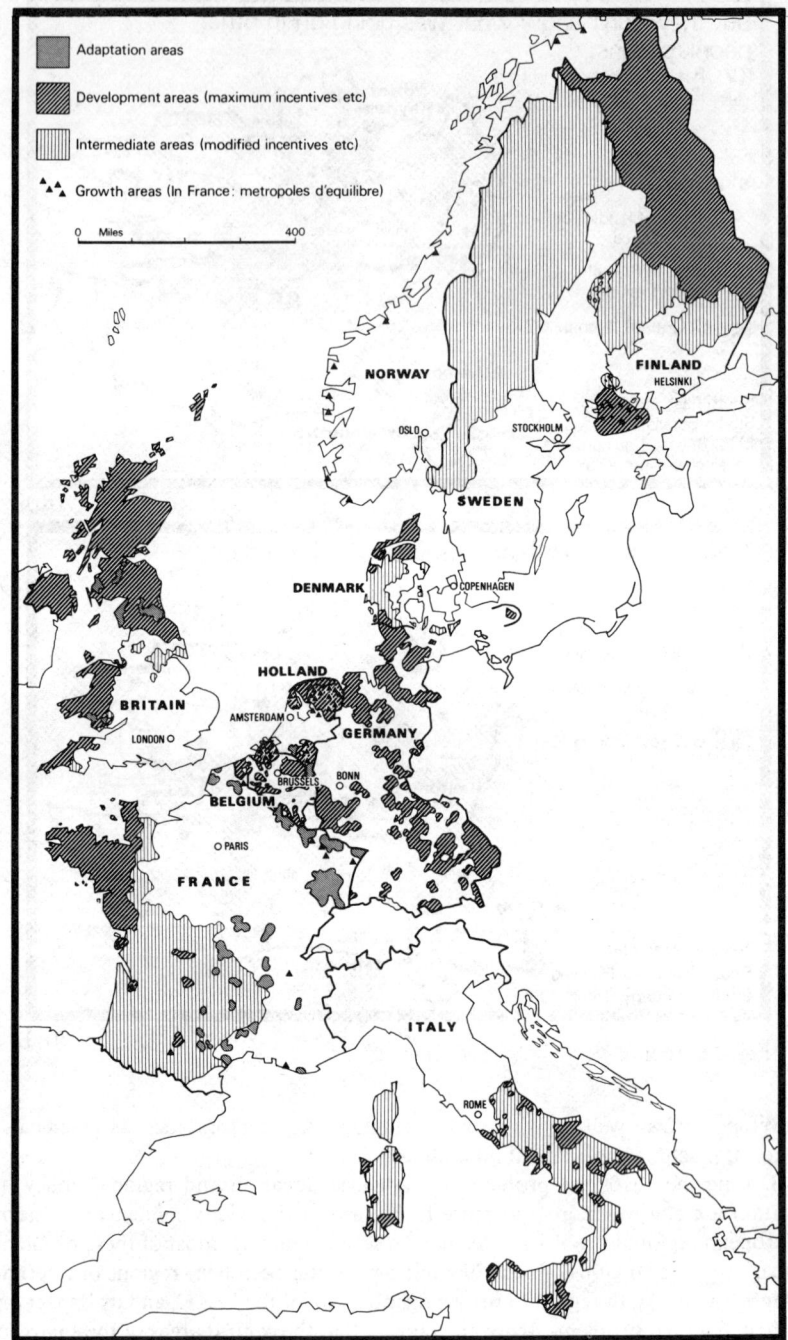

Fig. 2.7. *Problem areas in Western Europe*
(Source: *Econ.*, 29 Aug. 1970, p. 45)

and the Paris region – might develop at the expense of the peripheral regions: also, that the element of control, within the U.K., exercised by Industrial Development Certificates might be neutralised by firms' opening branches on the Continent instead of in the U.K. Development Areas.[1] The E.E.C. member countries have been operating regional controls and incentives similar to those in Britain, but in 1971 discussions took place amongst Ministers for Regional Planning to establish a common policy, which would also embrace Britain. It was hoped that British entry would break the deadlock exerted by France, which had preferred to pursue sovereign policies. In October 1971 agreement in principle was reached that unbalanced development of the European 'heartlands' and dereliction of the fringe regions should be avoided and that common rules should persuade investors to give priority to these outlying regions and deter them from playing off one country against another.[2]

5. Further Reading and Sources

D. H. ALDCROFT, *The Inter-War Economy: Britain, 1919–39.* Batsford. 1970.

G. C. ALLEN, *The Structure of Industry in Britain.* Longman. 1961 (2nd edn. 1966).

R. J. BALL, Investment Incentives, *N.W.B.Q.R.*, Aug. 1973 (sep. Appendix).

F. BROADWAY, *State Intervention in British Industry: 1964–68.* Kaye and Ward. 1969.

A. J. BROWN, 'Surveys of applied economics: regional economics, with special reference to the United Kingdom'. *The Economic Journal.* Dec. 1969.

T. W. BUCK, 'U.K. regional policy: a plea for more information'. *Moorgate and Wall Street Review.* Autumn 1970.

SIR ALEC CAIRNCROSS, ed., *Britain's Economic Prospects Reconsidered.* Allen & Unwin. 1971.

G. CHETWYND, 'The North-East: a case study in regional development'. *L.B.R.* Oct. 1963.

C. CLARK, 'Industrial location and economic potential'. *L.B.R.* Oct. 1966.

C.O.I. Regional Measures. B.B.L.A. H.M.S.O. Feb. 1964.

D.E.A. Pr. Rep. Ind. and Reg., 1. Jan. 1965; 3. Mar. 1965; 44. Sept. 1968; 52. March 1969; 55. Aug. 1969.

D.E.A. Pr. Rep. 7. The Location of Offices Bureau. July 1965.

E.P.R. 10, Dec. 1970.

D. EZRA, 'Regional Policy in the European Community'. *N.W.B.Q.R.* Aug. 1973.

F.B.E. 11, July 1971; 12, Sept. 1971.

P. SARGANT FLORENCE, *Investment, Location and Size of Plant.* Cambridge University Press. 1948.

P. SARGANT FLORENCE, *The Logic of British and American Industry.* Routledge & Kegan Paul. 1953.

E. M. HOOVER, *The Location of Economic Activity.* McGraw-Hill. 1948.

Industrial and Regional Development, White Paper. Cmnd 4942. H.M.S.O. March 1972.

'Industrial dispersal'. *P.E.P.* XXXI. 485. Feb. 1965.

N. KALDOR, *The case for regional policies. Scottish Journal of Political Economy.* Nov. 1970.

[1] *F.B.E.,* 11, July 1971 ('Free movement of labour') and 12, Sept. 1971 ('Regional policy and your job').
[2] 'Save-the-regions plan by Six', *D.T.,* 26 Oct. 1971; also *F.T.,* 5 Nov. 1971.

2. LOCATION, STRUCTURE AND ORGANISATION OF INDUSTRY [1]

B. J. LOASBY, 'Making location policy work'. *L.B.R.* Jan. 1967.

G. MCCRONE, *Regional Policy in Britain.* Allen and Unwin. 1969.

C. MANSELL, 'The regional development dilemma'. *Management Today.* Jan. 1972.

'Must we always take work to the workers?' *L.B.R.* Jan. 1964.

'Northern Ireland: underlying progress in development'. *M.B.R.* Aug. 1963.

H. W. RICHARDSON, *Economic Recovery in Britain, 1932–39.* Weidenfeld and Nicolson. 1967.

H. W. RICHARDSON, *Regional Economics.* Weidenfeld and Nicolson. 1969.

H. H. SCHOLEFIELD and J. R. FRANKS, 'Investment incentives and regional policy'. *N.W.B.Q.R.* Feb. 1972.

D. STEELE, *More Power to the Regions.* Young Fabian Pamphlet. March 1964.

BOARD OF TRADE, *The Movement of Manufacturing Industry in the United Kingdom, 1945–65.* H.M.S.O. 1968.

R. C. TRESS, 'The next stage in regional policy'. *The Three Banks Review.* March 1969.

E. G. WEST, 'Regional policy: fact and fallacy'. *L.B.R.* April 1966.

T. WILSON, ed., 'Papers on regional development'. (Supplement to the *Journal of Industrial Economics.* 1965).

6. Past Examination Questions

1. What are the main factors which determine the location of a factory? Give examples of these by referring to specific factories. (Autumn 1952)
2. What factors determine the localisation of an industry? With reference to any *one* industry, how have these factors changed since 1900? (Summer 1964)
3. What do you think would be the economic effects if, owing to technical advancement, the cost of air transport became less than the cost of sea and rail transport? (Summer 1959)
4. Why do industries such as the cotton textile industry of Lancashire, the pottery industry of Staffordshire, or the Yorkshire woollen industry, continue to be located where they originally started, although the advantages which they then possessed can now be obtained elsewhere? (Autumn 1953)
5. What are the advantages likely to be enjoyed by a new pottery factory if it is located in or near Stoke-on-Trent rather than elsewhere? (Summer 1956)
6. Describe the main features of the present-day economic structure and activities of the metropolitan area. (Autumn 1957)
7. Why are steel-producing firms concentrated in comparatively few centres in the United Kingdom, whereas breweries are dispersed throughout the country? (Summer 1960)
8. What problems would face a manufacturer if he transferred his factory from the centre of a large industrial city to a New Town? What advantages might he derive from this change? (January 1963)
9. Discuss the economic effects of the provision of an extensive network of motorways in the United Kingdom. (Summer 1963)
10. Write short notes on . . . the following:
    (a) Localised industries. (Summer 1963)
11. Write a short survey of the main industries in the region in which you live, and account for their presence there. (January 1965)

2. LOCATION, STRUCTURE AND ORGANISATION OF INDUSTRY [I]

12. Consider, giving examples, the dangers of an industry being concentrated in one particular part of the country. (Summer 1952)

13. 'It is better to bring jobs to the workers rather than to move workers to the jobs'. Discuss. (Summer 1955)

14. Write short notes on . . . the following:
    (a) Development Area. (Autumn 1952)

15. What do you understand by a 'development area'? Give examples and state what measures have been taken by the Government to help these areas. (Summer 1953)

2. Location, Structure and Organisation of Industry Stage II

1. Measurement of Location and Localisation

A detailed analysis of regional occupational distribution and regional specialisation is made in Table 2.3 below. This relates to employees only, but they form over 94% of persons engaged in civil employment. Comparisons have been made of the structure of employment in the major Orders, or officially classified groups of industries (according to the pre-1968 Standard Industrial Classification) in the Standard Regions (as they were in 1961) and in Great Britain as a whole. Construction, public utilities and services, serving dispersed markets, have been grouped together. Where the percentage employed in a particular group of industries in any region is higher than the national average, the region is said to 'specialise' in that group. The eastern and southern regions have been combined, in the table, because the Ministry of Labour compiled the relevant statistics in that way. The degrees to which regional percentages are higher than the national average have been worked out, and are shown as 'L.Q.s' or Location Quotients.

The London and south-eastern region, for example, has 1·2 times the national average in construction, public utilities and services, largely because of the location there of the Civil Service, the financial institutions of the City and the multitudinous head offices of business firms. The highest degrees of specialisation are for metal goods in the Midland region (3·8); shipbuilding and marine engineering in the northern region (3·9); mining and quarrying in the northern region (3·5); mining and quarrying in Wales (3·4); and metal manufacture in Wales (3·4).

It must be borne in mind that much higher degrees of specialisation are obscured by the fact that Table 2.3 refers to large regions and entire groups of industry. The more detailed the analysis, the smaller the area and the finer the delineation of a particular industry, the higher will be the degree of specialisation reached in certain localities. For example, whilst textiles have a specialisation degree of 2·5 in the north-western region, the spinning and doubling of cotton, flax and man-made fibres have a Location Quotient of 6·0 in that region. In the East and West Ridings region textiles as a whole have an L.Q. of 2·9, whereas the woollen and worsted industry has a specialisation degree of 8·9.

Whereas Table 2.1 analyses the occupational distribution in the various Standard Regions, compares it with that of Great Britain as a whole and arrives at comparative Location Quotients, Table 2.4 analyses the percentage concentrations of each group of industries in the various regions, comparing them with the percentage of total employment in each region. Where the proportion of a particular group of industries in a particular region is higher than the percentage

Table 2.3 Occupational distribution and degrees of specialisation: Regional analysis (end-May 1961): 1958 Revised Standard Industrial Classification. (Numbers to nearest thousand: based on employees only; employers and self-employed not included)

Group of Industries	Order	London and SE No.	%	LQ.	E and S No.	%	LQ.	S–W No.	%	LQ.	Mid No.	%	LQ.	N Mid No.	%	LQ.
Agriculture, Forestry and Fishing	I	68	1·2		144	5·9	2·2	68	5·4	2·0	44	2·0		65	4·2	1·6
Mining and Quarrying	II	13	0·3		5	0·2		18	1·4		56	2·5		119	7·6	2·3
Food, Drink and Tobacco	III	182	3·2		88	3·6	1·0	60	4·7	1·3	72	3·2		56	3·6	1·0
Chemicals and Allied Industries	IV	131	2·4	1·0	50	2·0		11	0·9		29	1·3		24	1·5	
Metal Manufacture	V	35	0·6		21	0·9		5	0·4		147	6·6	2·3	67	4·3	1·5
Engineering and Electrical Goods	VI	599	10·3	1·1	248	10·2	1·1	81	6·4		297	13·2	1·4	145	9·2	
Shipbuilding and Marine Engineering	VII	21	0·4		36	1·5	1·4	22	1·7	1·5	0·5	0·0		3	0·2	
Vehicles	VIII	142	2·5		149	6·1	1·6	84	6·6	1·7	222	10·0	2·5	69	4·4	1·1
Metal Goods not elsewhere specified	IX	101	1·6	1·0	30	1·2		7	0·6		215	9·6	3·8	18	1·1	
Textiles	X	29	0·5		16	0·7		14	1·1		39	1·7		121	7·7	2·1
Leather, Leather Goods and Fur	XI	19	0·3	1·0	3	0·1		4	0·3	1·0	6	0·3	1·0	5	0·3	1·0
Clothing and Footwear	XII	143	2·5		49	2·0		26	2·1		23	1·0		89	5·7	2·3
Bricks, Pottery, Glass, Cement, etc.	XIII	59	1·1	1·3	31	1·3		11	0·9	1·0	89	4·0	2·6	27	1·7	1·1
Timber, Furniture, etc.	XIV	94	1·7		43	1·8	1·4	17	1·3		22	0·1		17	1·1	
Paper, Printing and Publishing	XV	242	4·3	1·6	74	3·0	1·1	35	2·8	1·0	32	1·4		26	1·7	
Other Manufacturing Industries	XVI	91	1·6	1·1	30	1·2		15	1·2		41	1·8	1·3	15	1·0	
Construction, Public Utilities and Services	XVII–XXIV	3,702	65·5	1·2	1,420	58·3	1·1	787	62·1	1·1	906	40·5		699	44·6	
Total		5,670	100	—	2,436	100	—	1,266	100	—	2,238	100	—	1,565	100	—

(Table 2.3 contd.)

Group of Industries	Order	E and W Ridings No.	%	LQ	N-W No.	%	LQ	Northern No.	%	LQ	Scotland No.	%	LQ	Wales No.	%	LQ	GB No.	%
Agriculture, Forestry and Fishing	I	30	1·6		26	0·9		32	2·5		98	4·5	1·7	23	2·4		599	2·7
Mining and Quarrying	II	130	6·9	2·1	50	1·7		150	11·6	3·5	89	4·1	1·2	108	11·1	3·4	738	3·3
Food, Drink and Tobacco	III	71	3·8	1·0	130	4·4	1·2	35	2·7		99	4·6	1·3	21	2·2		813	3·6
Chemicals and Allied Industries	IV	41	2·2		127	4·2	1·7	59	4·5	1·9	38	1·8		25	2·6	1·1	534	2·4
Metal Manufacture	V	105	5·6	2·0	43	1·4		64	4·9	1·7	58	2·7		92	9·5	3·4	637	2·8
Engineering and Electrical Goods	VI	147	7·7		295	9·8	1·0	105	8·1		168	7·8		49	5·0		2,133	9·5
Shipbuilding and Marine Engineering	VII	7	0·4		37	1·2	1·1	56	4·3	3·9	66	3·1	2·8	5	0·5		253	1·1
Vehicles	VIII	47	2·5		111	3·7		15	1·1		37	1·7		18	1·9		894	3·9
Metal Goods not elsewhere specified	IX	72	3·8	1·5	57	1·9		12	0·9		28	1·3		23	2·4		563	2·5
Textiles	X	204	10·8	2·9	277	9·2	2·5	20	1·5		107	5·0	1·3	17	1·8		843	3·7
Leather, Leather Goods and Fur	XI	7	0·4	1·3	10	0·3	1·0	3	0·2		4	0·2		2	0·2		63	0·3
Clothing and Footwear	XII	64	3·4	1·4	103	3·4	1·4	31	2·4		31	1·4		14	1·4		573	2·5
Bricks, Pottery, Glass, Cement, etc.	XIII	32	1·7	1·1	47	1·6	1·0	18	1·4		23	1·1		11	1·1		347	1·5
Timber, Furniture, etc.	XIV	23	1·2		32	1·1		12	0·9		25	1·2		6	0·6		290	1·3
Paper, Printing and Publishing	XV	36	1·9		88	2·9	1·1	15	1·1		58	2·7	1·0	10	1·0		616	2·7
Other Manufacturing Industries	XVI	11	0·6		63	2·1	1·5	12	0·9		19	0·9		12	1·2		308	1·4
Construction, Public Utilities and Services	XVII–XXIV	859	45·7		1,508	50·3		664	51·0		1,207	56·2	1·0	533	55·0	1·0	12,286	54·7
Total		1,885	100	–	3,003	100	–	1,302	100	–	2,155	100	–	970	100	–	22,490	100

(Based on material in *Ministry of Labour Gazette*, March 1962)

84

Table 2.4 *Degrees of Regional Concentration and Overall local Concentration of Various Industries (end-May 1961): 1958 Revised Standard Industrial Classification (N.B. Based on employees only. Employers and self-employed not included)*

Group of Industries	Order	London &SE 25·2 Reg. Conc %	LQ	E&S 10·8 Reg. Conc %	LQ	S-W 5·6 Reg. Conc %	LQ	Mid 10·0 Reg. Conc %	LQ	N Mid 6·9 Reg. Conc %	LQ	E&W Ridings 8·4 Reg. Conc %	LQ	N-W 13·4 Reg. Conc %	LQ	Northern 5·8 Reg. Conc %	LQ	Scotland 9·6 Reg. Conc %	LQ	Wales 4·3 Reg. Conc %	LQ	Sum of + Deviations	Coefficient of Localisation
Agriculture, Forestry and Fishing		11·5		24·0	2·2	11·5	2·0	7·4		10·8	1·6	5·0		4·3		5·3		16·4	1·7	3·9		29·8	0·3
Mining and Quarrying	I	1·8		0·7		2·4		7·5		16·1		17·8	2·1	6·7		20·3	3·5	12·1	1·2	14·6	3·4	45·9	0·46
Food, Drink and Tobacco	II	22·5		10·5		7·4		8·8		6·9		8·7	1·0	15·9	1·2	4·2		12·2	1·3	2·6		7·2	0·07
Chemicals and Allied Industries	III	24·5		9·4		2·0		5·4		4·4		7·7		23·7	1·8	11·0	1·9	7·0		4·7	1·1	15·8	0·16
Metal Manufacture	IV	5·5		3·3		0·8		23·0	2·3	10·5		16·8	2·0	6·8		10·1	1·7	9·2		14·4	3·4	39·4	0·39
Engineering and Electrical Goods	V	28·0	1·1	11·6	1·1	3·8		13·9	1·4	6·8		6·9		13·8	1·0	4·9		7·8		2·3		7·9	0·08
Shipbuilding and Marine Engineering	VI					8·7	1·6	0·2		1·2		2·6		14·6	1·1	22·0	3·8	26·0	2·6	2·1		40·5	0·4
Vehicles	VII	8·2		14·4	1·3	9·4	1·7	24·7	2·5	7·7		5·3		12·4		1·7		4·2		2·0		25·2	0·25
Metal goods not elsewhere specified	VIII	15·9		16·7	1·5	1·3		38·1	3·8	3·3		12·8	1·5	10·0		2·2		5·0		4·1		32·5	0·32
Textiles	IX	17·9		5·2		1·7		4·6		14·4		24·1	2·9	32·8	2·5	2·3		12·6	1·3	2·0		45·6	0·46
Leather, Leather goods and Fur	X	3·4		1·8		6·2	1·1	10·0	1·0	8·0		10·4	1·2	15·8	1·2	4·0						11·3	0·11
Clothing and Footwear	XI	30·2	1·2	5·2		4·5		4·0		15·6		11·2	1·3	18·0	1·3	5·5		6·7		3·3		16·1	0·16
Bricks, Pottery, Glass, Cement, etc.	XII	24·9		8·5		3·1		25·5	2·6	7·7		9·2	1·1	13·4	1·0	5·2		5·4		2·5		17·1	0·17
Timber, Furniture, etc.	XIII	17·0		8·9		5·7	1·0	7·4		5·9		7·9		10·9		4·3		6·7		3·0		11·2	0·11
Paper, Printing and Publishing	XIV	32·3	1·3	14·8	1·4	5·7	1·0	5·1		4·2		5·9		14·2	1·1	2·5		8·6		2·2		16·2	0·16
Other Manufacturing	XV	39·3	1·6	12·0	1·1	4·9		13·2	1·3	4·8		3·5		20·6	1·5	3·8		9·5		1·7		14·6	0·15
Construction, Public Utilities Industries	XVI	29·4	1·2	9·8														6·0		3·9		6·6	0·07
Utilities and Services	XVII–XXIV	30·0	1·2	11·6	1·1	6·4	1·1	7·4		5·7		6·8		12·2		5·1		9·8	1·0	4·3	1·0		

(Based on material in *Ministry of Labour Gazette*, March, 1962)

of total employment in that region, then there is said to be a regional concentration of that industry in that region. The degree to which the regional concentration of an industry is higher than the regional proportion of total employment is also known as the Location Quotient. Where the L.Q.s are greater than 1, they are shown in the table. It will be noted that the Table 2.3 'degree of specialisation' L.Q.s and the Table 2.4 'degree of regional concentration' L.Q.s are strikingly similar. In fact, where they occasionally differ slightly, it is only because numbers are given to the nearest thousand in Table 2.3 and percentages of regional distribution and concentration in both tables are to one decimal place. With more detail they would be identical, and so we shall treat them as such.

Thus, in Table 2.3 we find that the textiles group of industries has 'specialisation' L.Q.s of 2·1, 2·9 and 2·5 in the north Midland, East and West Ridings and north-western regions respectively. In Table 2.4 the same group of industries has exactly the same 'concentration' L.Q.s in the same regions. Again, with a more detailed breakdown of the geographical and/or industrial classification, we would find instances of higher concentration L.Q.s in various localities.

Definitions of the two L.Q.s and of the Coefficient of Localisation (arrived at in Table 2.4) are as follows: with regard to the regional Location Quotients, encountered above, it was noted that the 'specialisation' L.Q. would be identical with the 'concentration' L.Q., although each is calculated in a different manner.

In fact, the specialisation L.Q. (Table 2.3) is a measurement of the extent to which a particular region specialises in a particular industry, as compared with its average specialisation in the country as a whole. This is regardless of the relative size of the occupied population in the region. The comparison is one of relative proportions employed in a particular industry. The specialisation L.Q. may be expressed as:

$$\frac{\text{Proportion of A region's labour force in AN industry}}{\text{Proportion of Nation's labour force in AN industry}}$$

Thus 10% of the Midland region's labour force is employed in the vehicles industry, but only 3·9% of the whole nation's labour force. The specialisation L.Q. is therefore $\frac{10}{3\cdot9} = 2\cdot5$.

The concentration L.Q. (Table 2.4) measures the extent to which a particular industry is concentrated in a particular region, compared with the proportion of all industry there. It therefore measures whether the region contains more or less than its 'fair share' of that industry, and may be expressed as:

$$\frac{\text{Proportion of AN industry in A region}}{\text{Proportion of ALL industry in A region}}$$

Thus 24·7% of the vehicles industry is situated in the Midlands region, but only 10·8% of the total labour force is there. The concentration L.Q. is therefore $\frac{24\cdot7}{10\cdot8} = 2\cdot5$.

The reason why both L.Q.s are identical is that if a region both specialises in a certain industry and also has a certain proportion of the nation's total labour force, then it will contain a specific proportion of that particular industry. In other words, the Midlands region specialisation L.Q. of 2·5 for vehicles, combined with its 10·0% of the national labour force, give it 24·7% of the vehicles industry. This percentage regional concentration in turn gives a concentration L.Q. of 2·5. Table 2.5 illustrates employment and specialisation L.Q.s for the West Midlands region in 1970. This bar diagram indicates an alternative method of showing the occupational structure of a region.

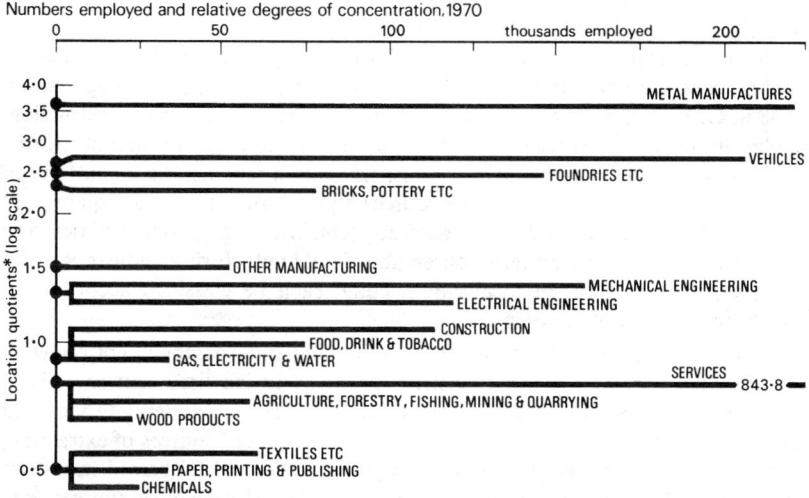

Table 2.5 *Specialisation L.Q.s in the West Midlands Region, 1970*
(Source: *Econ.*, 12 June 1970, p. 78)

Apart from this dual purpose measure of industrial location or specialisation in a specific region, Professor Sargant Florence and A. J. Wensley of the University of Birmingham developed a measurement of **overall** local concentration of an industry, called the Coefficient of Localisation. This measures the cumulative extent to which an industry is regionally overconcentrated. Whenever the regional concentration is higher than the proportion of the national labour force in that region, the excess or 'plus deviation' is noted. The plus deviations are added together throughout the regions, giving a cumulative percentage of excessive concentration. For simplicity, this figure is rendered as a unit. Thus, four regions (east and south, south-west, Midland and north Midlands) have excessive concentrations of the vehicles group. The sum of their plus deviations (from the regional averages of total employment) is 25·2% or 0·25. If the industry were spread throughout the regions exactly according to their relative labour forces, there would be no plus deviations and the Coefficient of Localisation would be 0. If the industry were 100% concentrated in an area which had only 1% of the nation's labour force, the plus deviation (and the only one) would be 99% or 0·99. The maximum possible Coefficient of Localisation would be 100% or 1.

Just as with Location Quotients, the Coefficient of Localisation will be higher, the more refined the definition of a specific industry or the smaller the region considered. For example, the bricks, pottery, glass and cement group has a low coefficient of 0·17. However, the pottery industry alone has a coefficient of 0·72. 82% of the industry is situated in the Midlands (which has 10% of the national labour force). It is much more localised than bricks, glass and cement.

2. Location Patterns and 'Movement' of Industry

Table 2.4 supports, in its modest but limited way, with more recent material, the results of a comparative study of British and American industry before World War II, made by Professor Sargant Florence.[1]

This noted that both countries showed a fairly high degree of localisation in mining (coal, 0·50 in G.B.; 0·65 in U.S.A.); moderate localisation in agriculture (0·38 in G.B.; 0·33 in U.S.A.); dispersed localisation in quarrying, construction, public utilities and services; widely varying localisation in manufacturing industry. All but manufacturing industries had a characteristic pattern of location, being 'rooted' to extractive sources (agriculture, mining and quarrying) or 'tied' to dispersed consumer markets (construction, public utilities and services). The location patterns observable in manufacturing industries, with their respective degrees of localisation, could each be classified according to the predominant motive force.

Thus highly localised industries, such as spinning and weaving of cotton, wool and worsted, were 'swarming' industries, attracted to localised centres without reference to sources of extraction or consumer markets, Moderately localised industries, such as iron and steel, were 'rooted' to localised sources of extraction, being material-orientated, on the basis of transport costs. Dispersed industries with low localisation were either 'rooted' to scattered extractive sources (e.g. bricks) or 'tied' to scattered consumer markets (e.g. bread). Industries, the demand for whose services and products was derived from other industries (e.g. textile packing and textile machinery) could be described as 'linked'. The degree of localisation of linked industries would follow that of the parent industry. There remained many 'footloose' industries whose location patterns could not be pinned down to any specific factor. These were industries (such as electrical machinery, television tubes and other light assembly industries using unskilled and semi-skilled labour and dispersed sources of power, such as National Grid electricity), which could be situated almost anywhere, provided that there was a potential labour force. They were not dependent upon local markets (tied) or local materials and/or sources of power (rooted). They were not particularly attracted to any localised centre of industry (swarming), and their products usually had a high value-weight ratio, which minimised the effect of transport costs. The 'footloose' type of industry is, in fact, the most amenable to economic planning.[2]

In connection with the classification of these dynamic factors making for location patterns, it is important to mention the 'movement' of industry, which is said to have taken place in nineteenth-century Britain (when it 'moved' North) and is taking place in twentieth-century Britain (when it is 'moving' South). This 'movement' is not due to a physical uprooting of plants and firms, but rather

---

[1] Included in his later book, *The Logic of British and American Industry*, 1953.

[2] For further development of the theme of location policy, in the context of the locational attractions of the 'growth' areas of the country, see C. Clark, 'Industrial location and economic potential', *L.B.R.*, Oct. 1966; A. C. Hobson, 'The great industrial belt', *E.J.*, vol. 61, Sept. 1951.

to the fact that in some areas certain industries have prospered and expanded, whilst in other areas certain industries have contracted and withered. The result has been a change in the locational balance, which produced the nineteenth-century industrial concentrations and highly localised areas in the North, and is producing a shift in balance to the highly localised conurbations of the Midlands and the London area during the twentieth century.

Table 2.6 *Comparative localisation of fifteen out of the twenty-one largest manufacturing industries in G.B. (1935) and U.S.A. (1939)*

Great Britain		Coefficient of localisation		United States of America	
Relative size	Census of production industry			Census of manufacture industry	Relative size
1	Wool and worsted	0·66	0·54	Woollen and worsted	8
2	Motor and cycle manufacturing	0·45	0·62	Motor vehicles	1
3	Cotton spinning	0·69	0·73	Cotton yarn	20
4	Printing and bookbinding	0·25	0·27	General commercial printing (job)	16
5	Cotton weaving	0·72	0·70	Cotton broad woven goods	3
6	Wholesale tailoring	0·30	0·37	Men's and boys' suits, coats, etc.	9
7	Iron and steel (roll and smelt)	0·42	0·51	Steelworks and rolling mills	2
8	Hosiery	0·48	0·52	Hosiery – full fashioned	15
9	Bread and cakes, etc.	0·22	0·14	Bread and other bakery products	7
11	Boot and shoe manufacturing	0·58	0·44	Footwear (except rubber)	6
12	Furniture	0·25	0·34	Furniture (household, except upholstered)	18
15	Silk and artificial silk	0·41	0·59	Rayon	21
17	Newspaper	0·30	0·20	Newspapers, publishing and printing	17
20	Timber (sawmilling), etc.	0·25	0·65	Sawmills, veneer mills, etc.	4
21	Paper	0·25	0·40	Paper and paperboard mills	11

(Based on material in P. Sargant Florence, *The Logic of British and American Industry*, 1953)

3. Localisation of Industry

Apart from similarities in the location patterns of similar Orders or groups of industry in Britain and America, the above-mentioned study also noted that similar individual industries also tended to have the same location pattern in both countries, despite the great differences in geography and climate. Of the twenty-one largest manufacturing industries (as measured by employment) in Great Britain (in 1935) and in the United States (in 1939), comparative figures were obtained for fifteen which were very similar in both countries, with regard to their range of products, or scope. Of these fifteen, all but one, the timber and sawmilling industry, showed a remarkable similarity in localisation coefficient (see Table 2). The discrepancy in this industry was largely due to the fact that it is a 'material-orientated' industry, subject to a strong transport cost factor and rooted to the extractive sources (viz. dispersed ports of entry in Britain and less dispersed local extraction in the U.S.A.).

Of the twenty most highly localised industries in Great Britain and America, most were in localisations of long standing, but very few were either material-orientated or market-orientated. In Britain, out of the twenty most localised industries, only tinplate (near the South Wales iron and steel works), the iron and steel industry itself, and fish-curing could be considered as material-orientated; more were market-orientated; jute, the most highly localised of all (in Dundee), receives its raw materials from distant places and sends its products all over Britain and the world. In America, also, only three industries (out of the twenty most highly localised) were material-orientated. They were turpentine (near the cotton-seed source in the south), oil-cake and fish canning. Of the remainder, only textile machinery and agricultural implements could be considered as linked to special, localised markets.[1]

The facts seem to point to the overriding supremacy of the pull of a localised area – with its concentrated demand for, and division of labour between, linked processes, products and services in separate plants. This conflux of specialised plants in close proximity produces external economies which are very similar to the internal economies of a single, large plant. In addition, the burden of decision-taking and administration is spread over several firms, and the profit incentive applies at more points than it would in a single firm. Thus transport costs between separate plants in the complex will be outweighed by these advantages of localised concentration or 'partial integration' between firms and plants in close proximity.

4. Sub-localisation within an Area

Apart from the theoretical assumptions made in the previous section, with regard to the advantages of localisation, facts are available, which point to the structure of localised concentrations of industry. To be efficient, a localised area must have a balanced complex of specialist processes and products, each of which will be localised to a certain extent within the general area of allied or linked industries.

A study – based on the 1931 Census of Population – of the Birmingham and Black Country conurbation, the Lancashire cotton industry and the London area electrical industries,[2] revealed a marked degree of 'spot' localisation of certain processes within general, localised areas of allied industries.

[1] *The Logic of British and American Industry*, 1953, pp. 83–4.
[2] P. Sargant Florence, *Investment, Location and Size of Plant*, pp. 63–78.

In the case of the Birmingham and Black Country conurbation, twenty-eight local authorities were involved, of which six were county boroughs. Seventeen main Census of Production industries had high location quotients in this area plus Coventry, and twelve of them were related metal industries (closely linked with one another). Whilst the main metal industries were found to be ubiquitous throughout the area, and especially so for earlier, common processes and components (such as founding, forging, galvanising, tubes, nuts, bolts, etc.), industries making specific final metal goods (such as motor cars, pins, stoves, jewellery, etc.) were very closely localised in certain parts of the conurbation. Dudley, for example, had an L.Q. of 83·8 for chains and anchors; Wolverhampton an L.Q. of 50·0 for locks. Industries and sub-industries were technically linked or integrated. It was also found that the cocoa, chocolate and sugar confectionery industry was localised in the area. As this industry employed twice as many women as men, it had presumably drifted to the area as a footloose 'balancing' industry, taking advantage of the available supply of female labour.

With spot localisation, transport costs between plants in early processes are kept down to a minimum, not exceeding very much those within a single large plant.

5. Structural Definitions

The three most important structural and organisational concepts with which we are concerned are 'the industry', 'the firm' and 'the plant'.

There are various ways of considering the term 'industry'. Does it include agriculture, services and other non-manufacturing activities? Is it defined as a group producing identical products, or using the same raw materials, the same type of skilled labour or the same type of technological process? Is it based upon the weight of materials used, upon the weight of the product produced, or upon the power of machinery used? In fact, all these things will influence the location, interconnections and forms of organisation of various industries. For purposes of securing uniformity and comparability in the statistics published by Government departments in the United Kingdom, a Standard Industrial Classification has been adopted by the Government, and is used as the basis for the Censuses of Production, Distribution and Population, for Department of Employment and Productivity, Department of Trade and Industry and other official statistics. The S.I.C. was first adopted in 1948, was modified in 1958 and achieved its present form, after further modifications, in 1968. The process of reclassification allows for the increasing importance of certain industries. For example, whereas in the 1958 S.I.C. there were 24 Orders or groups of industry, with 152 Minimum List Headings or individual industries, the 1968 S.I.C. contains 27 Orders and 181 Minimum List Headings.[1] Whereas the 1958 S.I.C. grouped Engineering and electrical goods into one Order, the 1968 S.I.C. creates three Orders, viz. 'Mechanical Engineering', 'Instrument Engineering' and 'Electrical Engineering'. Also, the 1968 S.I.C. creates a separate Order for 'Coal and Petroleum Products', which were primarily included in the 1958

[1] For further details see Appendix 1 of *Ann. Abs. Stat.*, No. 107, 1970 and *D.E.A. Pr. Rep. Econ.*, 56 Sept. 1969.

Order for 'Chemicals and Allied Industries'. Furthermore, there has been some reclassification of Minimum List Headings and optional sub-divisions as between one Order and another. For example, the 1968 S.I.C. Order for 'Food, Drink and Tobacco' now includes 'Milk bottling and processing' and 'Tea blending' (formerly in the 'Distributive Trades' Order) and 'Vegetable and animal oils and fats' (formerly in the 'Chemicals and Allied Industries' Order).

The S.I.C. classifies all forms of civilian employment by industry, approximating very closely to the definition put forward by Professor Sargant Florence in 1929: 'An industry is any kind of transactions (e.g. production) usually specialised in by a number of plants who do not usually perform much of any other kind of transaction.'

The method of presentation consists of listing twenty-four Orders of industry or major industrial groups, commencing with 'Agriculture, forestry, fishing' and ending with 'Public administration'. Each Order is split up into Minimum List headings, or separate trades within the group, e.g. Fishing. Some of the Minimum List headings are divided into optional subdivisions, where more detail is required, e.g. Sea fishing.

The full list of industrial Orders is as follows:

I. Agriculture, Forestry, Fishing	*(Extraction – Primary group)*
II. Mining and Quarrying	
III. Food, Drink and Tobacco	
IV. Coal and Petroleum Products	
V. Chemicals and Allied Industries	
VI. Metal Manufacture	
VII. Mechanical Engineering	
VIII. Instrument Engineering	
IX. Electrical Engineering	
X. Shipbuilding and Marine Engineering	*Manufacturing – Secondary group)*
XI. Vehicles	
XII. Metal Goods not elsewhere specified	
XIII. Textiles	
XIV. Leather, Leather Goods and Fur	
XV. Clothing and Footwear	
XVI. Bricks, Pottery, Glass, Cement, etc.	
XVII. Timber, Furniture, etc.	
XVIII. Paper, Printing and Publishing	
XIX. Other Manufacturing Industries	
XX. Construction	*(Construction and Public Utilities)*
XXI. Gas, Electricity and Water	
XXII. Transport and Communication	– Handling of goods
XXIII. Distributive Trades	– Distribution of goods
XXIV. Insurance, Banking, Finance and Business Services	– *(Services – Tertiary group)* – Finance
XXV. Professional and Scientific Services	– Private direct
XXVI. Miscellaneous Services	
XXVII. Public Administration and Defence	– Public direct

There is a certain amount of economic logic in the sequence of Orders on the list, which ranges from the 'primary' (or extractive) industries, through the 'secondary' (or manufacturing) industries, then those which bridge the gap (construction and the public utilities) and finally the 'tertiary' (or service) industries. Furthermore, within the manufacturing (secondary) group, the first Orders to be listed are those containing predominantly 'processing' industries (III–VI), followed by Orders which contain predominantly 'assembly' industries (VII–XII). Of the seven remaining manufacturing Orders (XIII–XIX), four are 'mixed' – containing *both* processing and assembly industries (XIII, XIV, XVII and XVIII), while three are predominantly 'assembly' groups (XV, XVI and XIX), which might more logically be placed in sequence with Orders VII–XII.

The 'firm' is the basic governing unit in an organisational analysis of industry. As a firm may own or control[1] many productive units or 'plants', it is not a suitable basic unit for a structural analysis. The S.I.C. avoids this pitfall by ignoring ownership (or firms) and by taking the plant or establishment as its unit of classification. Although many plants produce more than one product, they are classified according to their principal product. If at a particular address under the control of one firm there are several clearly defined Departments, engaged in different industries (e.g. a manufacturing department, a sales department and a transport department), each department is treated as a separate plant in a separate industry. Flexibility is maintained by virtue of the 'principal product' classification. In real life there is a continuous change in industry. Plants gravitate from one group of products to another, either because of fairly quick breakthroughs in technology or invention or by gradually developing a lesser part of their activities and withdrawing from others. Official statistics based on the S.I.C. record this process of mutation at such time as the principal activity of a plant has moved from one Order or Minimum List heading to another.

6. Location, Investment Intensity and Size of Plant

Apart from noting the total size of an industry, a structural analysis will show the typical size of plant in that industry, since the plant is the productive unit from which the industry's output comes and in which the labour force is employed. There are, however, various ways of considering size as an index which will give an insight into the structure, organisation, technical background and importance of an industry.

Size of plant may be measured by the volume or value of output, by the volume of raw materials used, by the value of assets employed, by the value of mechanical equipment used, by the power of mechanical equipment per worker, or by the number of workers employed. None of these measures will correspond exactly with another; none is a perfect yardstick for all possible circumstances in which a particular study might be made. The most easily obtained statistics

---

[1] Control is loosely defined as more than 50% of voting power in subsidiary firms and/or plants. In fact, various forms of association exist, through which influence or even control may be exercised, but the most clear case of nominal or formal control is as here defined.

are those for employment, and, although there are cases where a small number of workers with much expensive equipment (e.g. in an oil refinery, atomic energy station or automated plant) may produce a high value of output, employment is a good general indication of probable size of output. Usually if short-term changes occur in employment they will be reflected in output. Employment, therefore, is the criterion by which we shall measure the physical size of plant.

Another useful index, not of physical size but of technological processes is intensity of investment, or mechanisation. Here we must distinguish between the intricacy and value of machinery and its power. Power, measured as horse-power per worker, results from the type of process (heavy or light, processing or assembly) as well as the extent of mechanisation (so much 'machinery' per worker). In fact, an assembly industry might very well have a high intensity of investment in intricate, expensive machinery which may not be very powerful. A processing industry might have less expensive equipment (i.e. a lower intensity of investment) but with more horsepower. Professor Sargant Florence found that, despite the fact that the general level of horsepower per worker was twice as high in America as it was in Britain, in both Britain and America processing industries tended to have twice the horsepower of assembly industries. It is neces-sary, therefore, to consider 2 h.p. in a processing industry as being equivalent to 1 h.p. in an assembly industry, when making comparisons of investment intensity.[1]

With these two indexes – size (as measured by employment) and horsepower per worker (investment intensity) – we have some very useful tools for examining the physical structure and technological background of industries.

The above-mentioned study investigated the relationship between location, investment intensity and size of plants in America and Britain. Of the twenty-one largest industries in Britain and America before World War II, seventeen were similar industries, for which typical size grades were worked out.[2] (N.B. For two of these seventeen industries, electrical machinery and iron and steel castings, the localisation coefficient was not available for America. They are not, therefore, included in Table 2.6 which lists the other fifteen similar industries.) Of these seventeen largest similar industries, eight had the same typical size grade and two had a neighbouring grade. In the case of the remaining seven, each one registered 'no typical size' in either one country or the other. These similarities existed in spite of the fact that there were great differences in economic and geographical circumstances in the two countries.

The size grades used were as follows:

Small (1)   60% of employees in plants with less than 100 workers.
Smallish (2) 50% of employees in plants with 50 to 200 workers.
Medium (3)   50% of employees in plants with 100 to 500 workers.
Largish (4)   50% of employees in plants with 500 plus workers.
Large (5)   50% of employees in plants with 1,000 plus workers.

[1] P. Sargant Florence, *The Logic of British and American Industry*, p. 68.   [2] *Ibid.*, p. 24–5.

The eight industries with equivalent size grades were:

Motor vehicles (5);
Iron and steel rolling and smelting (5);
Silk and Rayon (4);
Cotton spinning (3);
Paper and paperboard (3);
Bread (1);
Men's and boys' tailoring $\Big\}$ no typical size grade.
Hosiery

The two industries with neighbouring grades were:

Cotton weaving (G.B. 4; U.S. 5);
Electrical machinery (G.B. 5; U.S. 4);

The seven differing industries were:

Timber (sawmilling) (G.B. 2; U.S. none);
Footwear (G.B. none; U.S. 3);
Wool and worsted (G.B. 3; U.S. none);
Iron and steel castings (G.B. none; U.S. 3);
Printing (G.B. none; U.S. 1);
Newspapers (G.B. 4; U.S. none);
Furniture (G.B. none; U.S. 3)

Bearing in mind the close similarity in localisation of most of these American and British industries, it is interesting to see the remarkably close size relationship of plant in the two countries, despite the great differences in their physical and economic circumstances.

In order to throw more light on the relationship between location and size, a study was made of ninety-one British and eighty-four American manufacturing industries.[1] The conclusions reached were that in both countries, the smaller the typical plant prevailing in an industry, the lower did its localisation coefficient tend to be. In Britain, medium and largish sized plants tended to have the highest coefficient of localisation (0·50 plus), whilst large plants tended to be less localised (0·40–0·49). In America, medium, largish and large plant industries tended to have the highest localisation coefficients.

When a similar study was made of the relationship between investment intensity (or mechanisation) and size in 86 British and 155 American manufacturing industries,[2] it found a definite correlation between the degree of mechanisation (measured by h.p. per worker, where 1 h.p. in an assembly industry is equivalent to 2 h.p. in a processing industry) and size. The larger the typical plant size, the greater did the degree of mechanisation tend to be. This seems to support the view that a high investment intensity is generally only worth while if the plant is large enough to use each machine to capacity.

The two studies mentioned above would appear to indicate that small, dispersed markets lead to small, dispersed plants with low mechanisation; larger markets lead to larger, more localised and more highly mechanised plants.

[1] *Ibid.*, p. 71. [2] *Ibid.*, p. 69.

However, British experience (supported to some extent by American experience) tends to indicate that given the large market a very intensive localisation pattern leads to the medium size of plant, supported by small plants producing specialist allied products and processes. In other words, the highly localised pattern of medium and small plants provides external economies similar to the internal economies of a very large plant, which has integrated, auxiliary processes. High localisation becomes more and more feasible as the transport system becomes more flexible and relatively less costly. The industry with very large plants of medium localisation will have smaller transport costs, in total, but will bear a heavier burden of management responsibility, as decision-taking is concentrated into fewer and bigger units.

With regard to the relative importance of plant size in manufacturing employment, some interesting conclusions may be drawn from the available 1935 and 1959 figures (see Table 2.7).

Table 2.7 *The size distribution of British manufacturing establishments* (*1935 and 1959*)

Size (No. of Employees)	1935 (Census of Production)				1959 (April/May)			
	Plants No.	%	Employees No. ('000s)	%	Plants No.	%	Employees No. ('000s)	%
1– 10	132,338	73·0	536	9·3	150,000	73·5	1,134	12·8
11– 99	37,614	20·7	1,318	23·2	40,020	19·7	1,584	17·9
100–499	9,750	5·4	2,015	35·3	12,052	5·9	2,492	28·0
500–999	1,047	0·6	719	12·6	1,524	0·73	1,048	11·9
1,000-plus	533	0·3	1,106	19·6	1,144	0·55	2,611	29·4
All Sizes	181,282	100	5,694	100	204,740	100	8,869	100

(Sources: *Census of Production*, 1935; *Min. Lab. Gaz.*, Sept. 1959; A. Armstrong and A. Silberston, 'Size of plant, size of enterprise and concentration in British manufacturing industry 1935–58', *Journal of the Royal Statistical Society*, Series A (General), vol. 128, part 3, 1965. Figures for plants with 1–10 employees are estimates.)

In both periods nearly three-quarters of plants were very small, employing 1–10 workers. They only employed a small proportion of manufacturing workers, but this proportion was higher (12·8%) in 1959 than in 1935 (9·3%). All other plant sizes from 11–999 employed a smaller proportion of manufacturing workers (57·8%) in 1959 than in 1935 (71·1%), despite the fact that they, too, constituted almost the same proportions of all plants in 1959 as in 1935. Plants employing over 1,000 workers constituted twice the proportion of all manufacturing enterprises in 1959 as compared with 1935, but even so they were only 0·6% of the total. Nevertheless, they employed 29·4% of the workers in 1959 as compared with 19·6% in 1935.

These figures would seem to show a gradual trend towards plants of larger size, in terms of employment, whilst at the same time very small plants continue to constitute almost three-quarters of the total, employing a slightly growing proportion of the workers (one-eighth). Employment in both very large and very small plants has grown relatively, at the expense of other plants, particularly in the ranges 11–500.

A high proportion of the bigger establishments in 1959 were in the heavier process and assembly industries. (Of all employees in plants with more than 10 workers, 60% of vehicles employees, 51% of metal manufacture employees, 47% of engineering, shipbuilding and electrical goods employees were in plants of 1,000 plus.) The average size of plant in industries making consumer goods was smaller than the average for manufacturing industries as a whole. In the textiles group of industries, only 13% of employees were in plants of 1,000-plus; in clothing industries the figure was 7%. In textiles 53% of employees were in plants of 100–500; in clothing the figure was 44%. The clothing industry, in fact, had the highest proportion of employees in plants of 11–99: 37% as compared with 20% in all manufacturing industry. (Again, these figures refer to the 7,735,000 employees in plants with over 10 workers, for which the Ministry of Labour collected data.)[1]

Over the period 1935–58 the number of plants with 10+ employees increased much less than did output, and in the later years was actually falling. In most industries the trend was towards fewer, but larger plants. If the average size of plant is taken as a very rough index, the only industrial group in which this did not increase was textiles. Furthermore, the number of plants in the largest size category present in each industry (e.g. 400+ in timber, but 5,000+ in aircraft) has risen in all groups apart from textiles, clothing and footwear; the average size of these largest plants has been increasing, and they have been employing a higher proportion of the total labour force than formerly.[2]

Apart from the size differences between different Orders of industry, there were striking variations in the regional distribution of plant sizes, reflecting the locational pattern of various industries. Of the employees in plants of 10-plus, the average proportion in plants of 1,000-plus for Britain as a whole was 34%. Regional proportions in plants of 1,000-plus ranged from 25% in the East and West Ridings to 40% in the northern region. In the North-eastern and Merseyside Development Areas (as they were at that time) nearly 50% of '10-plus' employees were in plants of 1,000-plus.[3]

Difficulties in making interperiod comparisons of firm size are caused by the fact that 1935 data relate to 'firms', which constitute one or more plants operating under the same trading name, whereas later data refer to 'business units' or 'enterprises', which constitute units of common ownership and control (i.e. firms as defined in this chapter). Nevertheless, detailed comparisons are possible for the period 1954–58. The results[4] indicate that out of 115 manufacturing industries, in 101 – employing 91% of the labour force – the number of 'enterprises' fell: the total numbers of both plants of 10+ and 'enterprises' decreased, but the latter showed the most marked reduction. In 101 out of 115 industries – employing 88% of manufacturing labour – the number of plants per 'enterprise' rose: for all manufacturing industry the ratio rose from 1.38 to 1.43.

Although a comparison of firm size distribution is not possible between 1935 and 1958 for individual industries or groups, it is possible for manufacturing industry as a whole: see Table 2.8.

---

[1] For a much more detailed breakdown of the output and distribution in different plant sizes, analysed by industry for 1958, see Armstrong and Silberston, *op. cit.*
[2] *Ibid.*
[3] *Min. Lab. Gaz.*, Sept. 1959.
[4] Armstrong and Silberston, *op. cit.*

Table 2.8 *The size distribution of enterprises in British manufacturing industry, 1935 and 1958*

Size (No. of Employees)	Number of Enterprises		% of Employment		% of Net Output	
	1935	1958	1935	1958	1935	1958
1–499	n.a.	n.a.	50·5	35·9	47·4	31·5
500– 999	1,021	993	8·9	9·2	8·6	8·6
1,000– 1,999	528	488	9·1	9·1	9·3	9·4
2,000– 9,999	358	395	17·8	21·0	19·9	22·4
10,000–19,999	34	42	6·0	7·5	6·1	8·2
20,000–49,999	16	24	5·9	10·0	7·3	11·6
50,000+	2	8	1·8	7·3	1·4	8·3

(Source: A. Armstrong and A. Silberston, 'Size of plant, size of enterprise and concentration in British manufacturing industry, 1935–58, *Journal of the Royal Statistical Society*, Series A (General), vol. 128, part 3, 1965.)

These figures indicate that not only is there a heavy and growing concentration of manufacturing employees in plants of 500-plus, but that there is also an even greater concentration of employees in big multi-plant firms. These big firms control all the big plants and many of the lesser ones. (Section II.11 will deal with the extent of concentration of control by firms.) Plants, then, are tending to be controlled by fewer firms, and the extent to which many industries are becoming dominated by a small number of 'giant' firms – stimulated by the merger boom of the 1960s – appears to be increasing.

7. Efficiency, Size and Growth of Plants and Firms

The size of plants and firms may be extended by increasing the scale of production of a product, process or service (specialisation) or by integrating various products, processes or services. (These avenues will be examined in Section II.9.)

There are various advantages to be derived from sheer size, as the trend towards larger plants and firms might suggest.[1] Generalisations are, however, strewn with pitfalls. It does not follow, for example, that great size would be beneficial to every plant. Neither does it necessarily follow that the small-plant firm will itself be small.

There are, however, certain general principles of efficiency which may be applied to the concept of 'structural size' of both plant and firm. Structural size itself is a by-product of the scale of activity – that is, of the scale of production in the plant and the scale of operation within the firm, the organisational unit.

It is necessary to point out here that many economists examine efficiency (of size, or scale of activity) on a functional basis.[2] They identify maximum efficiency with the optimum financial, marketing and risk-taking functions. For purposes of a general economic theory of the firm this is very useful, but in the context of

[1] See C. Pratten and R. M. Dean, *The Economies of Large-scale Production in British Industry* 1965.
[2] E.g. E. A. G. Robinson, *The Structure of Competitive Industry*, 1945.

a structural analysis of industry it is less useful. It results in vagueness as to whether each function is being considered within the framework of a plant, firm or combination of firms.

The most important structural principles of efficiency – first elucidated by Professor Sargant Florence – flowing from the scale of plant 'production' and firm 'operation' activities are:

1. The Principle of Bulk Transactions.
2. The Principle of Massed (or Pooled) Reserves.
3. The Principle of Multiples.

The principle of bulk transactions applies to both productional and operational scale and refers to the economy of dealing in big quantities, if the cost factor does not increase proportionately. This principle applies to such activities as the purchase of materials, power and products in bulk, the negotiating of long-term contracts (e.g. for transport facilities) on advantageous terms, the reduction in overhead costs per unit of production by using specialised equipment to the full, and a host of others. It also applies to physical things. For example, if the size of a container (such as a cargo ship, goods waggon, blast furnace, etc.) is increased, the volume increases proportionately more than the surface area. Thus cost of materials, at least, does not increase proportionately with the increase in capacity.

The principle of massed or pooled reserves refers to the advantages of productional (plant) and operational (firm) scale. It is manifested in the fact that the total reserves of labour, capital, materials and other stocks which need to be held for uncertain future commitments are smaller when there is large-scale, coordinated activity, than would need to be held for several smaller, unco-ordinated scales of activity. For example, a large plant or firm with coordinated planning and control need keep fewer stocks of a particular spare part or product than would several smaller plants or firms in total. Whereas each smaller plant or firm must hold enough in reserve to act independently in an emergency, the larger plant or firm can switch over the requisite item, from a centrally controlled stockpile, to whichever section of the plant (or whichever plant in the firm) is in need. This principle applies to multiple stores, multi-plant manufacturing firms, department stores (plants) and big, coordinated manufacturing plants.

The principle of multiples refers to the indivisibility of various items of machinery and equipment, various processes and techniques, and various skilled individuals. If any of these cannot be broken down, then they will be less costly if utilised to capacity. The high cost of a particular machine; the high cost of an electronic computer at head office, or of a research laboratory; the high salary of a brilliant executive or research worker – all these specialised factors of production will only be worth while if used to the full. Then their overhead cost will be spread over a large range of production (plant) or operational (firm) activity. It follows, therefore, that the large firm or plant will be able to employ such indivisible factors to the full, whereas the small firm or plant will not. Furthermore, such indivisible factors can only be efficiently employed in multiples of a certain size, and this can only be done by the large productional or organisational unit.

Apart from these general principles of the efficiency of structural size in plant and firm, there are various ways of measuring such efficiency in terms of returns and costs. These measures refer, basically, to the concept of 'returns' minus 'costs'. This concept of efficiency may be applied in the monetary sense, where the value of production, compared with the cost of factors, indicates monetary productivity (or the cost per unit of production) and overall profits. In the physical sense the concept measures the volume and quality of production in relation to the volume of factors, viz. physical productivity and returns to scale. In human, psychological or 'welfare' terms it compares the social utility or satisfaction derived from any given productive activity in relation to the sacrifice of alternatives and the social effort or inconvenience involved. The monetary 'profits' measurement is, in practice, only applicable to the firm, the organisational and accounting unit. The monetary ('cost per unit') measurement of productivity is applicable to both plant and firm. The physical ('returns to scale') measurement of productivity is also applicable to both plant and firm, but because of the difficulty in imputing the physical return to each individual factor, it is not very amenable to precise use. The welfare measurement of efficiency is applicable, in the field of public policy decisions, to the firm and the entire industry (e.g. with regard to monopoly control, service to the public, location of industry policy, etc.)

If we wish to go further, in testing the efficiency of structural size and in checking and comparing the results in different plants and firms, we may adopt the following criteria: (a) the test of survival; (b) the test of growth.

Various studies have been made in Britain, America and India,[1] which support the general conclusions to be inferred from Table 2.7 and the other figures quoted with it: that employment is becoming concentrated into bigger plants and even bigger firms; that large plants and firms tend to survive and grow; that the profits of large firms tend to be higher, and fluctuate less, than those of smaller firms in the same industry; and that large firms must be generally more efficient than small firms in the same industry.[2] In 1962 the Board of Trade published its findings on an investigation into the growth of companies. This covered nearly all the companies quoted on the Stock Exchange, over the period 1958–60. Apart from noting a general growth in concentration of control – (quoted companies fell in number by about 10% from nearly 2,900 to just over 2,600 and net assets rose by 39% to £13,500 million) – the report concluded that the fastest-growing firms tended to have *three* common characteristics: they were already large; they earned a high rate of return on their assets; and they had tended to go to the capital market for a large proportion of their finance, rather than depending upon undistributed profits, retained in reserves.[3]

If size is so advantageous to the plant and firm, the question may be asked: 'why does not the biggest plant in each industry grow until it encompasses the whole industry, and why does not the biggest firm in the economy grow until it controls all those "one-plant" industries?' In other words, why do we not have something approximating to the 'pure monopoly' of economic theory, the single

[1] E.g. M. M. Mehta, *Structure of Cotton-mill Industry of India*, 1949; W. L. Crum, *Corporate Size and Earning Power*, 1939; P. Sargant Florence, *Ownership, Control and Success of Large Companies*, 1961; *The Working Party Report on the British Jewellery and Silverware Trade*, 1946.

[2] R. Lancier, 'Size in European business organisation', *Stat.*, 18 Dec. 1964, pp. 781–2, summarises findings of the *Patronat Francas* on size and success in U.S. and European industry.

[3] 'Company assets, income and finance in 1960', Board of Trade, H.M.S.O., 1962 – summarised in the *Board of Trade Journal*, 3, vol. 183, No. 3428.

firm which produces everything (and in fact, produces everything in 'one-plant' industries)?

The answer to this is basically twofold. First, 'one-plant' industries are not the general rule because a 100% localisation in one plant would not result in economies sufficient to outweigh the diseconomies of the resultant transport costs and management strain. Furthermore, the historical fact that many plants came into being in each industry, controlled by many firms which do not wish to relinquish their identity and control, results in the continuance of the multi-plant industry, even though it may be 'partially integrated' in a localised area. Secondly, despite the process whereby plants which cater for a sufficiently large market tend to reap internal economies of scale, and grow, many different firms control these plants. Though the big firms grow bigger, expanding (by large-scale specialisation or by integration of processes and/or products) *via* capital accumulation or by absorbing smaller plants and firms or by merging with other firms, the process is usually limited to the general confines of a particular industry or group of industries. The hypothetical result of such growth would be 'one-firm' industries, because other giants will be blotting out the horizons in other fields. The result might eventually be a balance of power between a few firms, each controlling (or sharing control of) one or more multi-plant industries; in other words, a few multi-plant/one-industry (and possibly multi-industry) firms. Again, however, there is present the limiting factor of management strain.

A great deal of learned debate has revolved around the relationship between *size* and *growth*, since there has been much evidence which conflicts with that of the studies noted above. For example, in March 1971 the National Economic Development Office (N.E.D.O.) submitted a paper to the National Economic Development Council which cast serious doubt as to the correlation of increasing profits with increasing size.[1] Yet, in the past, N.E.D.O. had been an enthusiastic supporter of the principle of large size in business organisation. The Confederation of British Industry disputed this stand and supported the virtues of large size, but nevertheless admitted the currently low general profitability of big firms – explaining this as being due to long-term planning and expenditure on research and development. It appears that the technical economies of scale in production are somewhat limited, that economies of scale in marketing and finance are much more relevant, and that management diseconomies (as in the giant civil aviation firms) tend to cancel out the technical scale economies. It is worthy of note that much of the merger activity in the late 1960s was in the formation of conglomerates, aimed at ensuring financial and marketing economies, rather than economies of large scale production. Furthermore, for 1970, only one of the 100 largest companies in Britain (assessed by turnover) was present in the top 10 (assessed by profitability).

If we examine the relationship between *growth* and *profitability*, and between *growth* and *productivity*, the evidence is somewhat easier to evaluate. Firstly, *growth and profitability* seem to be fairly clearly correlated. On the one hand, the more successful and profitable firms will find it easier to raise external capital on the issues market; on the other hand, they would be better able to 'plough back' or self-finance, if they wished; yet again, under competitive pressures, they may find that only by breaking into new fields and diversifying (and thus

[1] *Econ.*, 6 March 1971, p. 80.

growing) are they able to retain their profitability: these factors tend to support the conclusions of the Board of Trade study, noted above.[1] Secondly, *growth and productivity* (or rather output growth and the rate of growth in labour productivity) appear also to be fairly clearly correlated. This relationship, referred to as 'Verdoorn's Law', has been subject to differing interpretations and differing policy arguments. These centred on whether it was market expansion and growth in total output which led, *via* scale economies, etc. to higher productivity, or whether it was technological progress, stimulated by market forces and/or competitive pressures, which resulted in higher productivity, which in turn led to lower costs, greater sales and higher output. The Nicholson and Gupta study of 138 U.K. industries over the period 1948–54 suggests that the predominant causal relationship, for that period, ran from productivity improvements to output growth[2].

It is when we seek evidence of a correlation between *growth* and the *size of firm* that the picture becomes hazy. In fact, the various empirical studies and the evidence of numerous recurrent cases indicate that there is no general systematic relationship between size and the rate of growth of firms or their profitability performance ratios. This lack of association between size and growth has led to the suggestion that it is a random phenomenon, influenced by the particular circumstances, market forces, historical factors, management experience, product mix, etc. of the individual firm. There is much evidence in favour of 'Gibrat's Law of Proportionate Effect', which implies that there is a tendency for the *dispersion* or spread of profit rates in each size grade of firm to vary inversely with the size grade. In other words, the range of profitabilities tends to be wider amongst small firms (some of which may be amongst the most highly profitable and some amongst the least profitable), whereas among the largest firms there tends to be a greater stability and narrower range of profit rates.[3] Numerous reasons may be advanced to explain this phenomenon. For example, the small firm may be in a sheltered, specialised market, with minimal fixed cost overheads; the large firm may be much more diversified than small firms tend to be, and may suffer or alternatively benefit from a 'swings and roundabouts' effect, whereby the average profit rate disguises some extremes; the large firm may be much more cautious than the small, and may thus tend to avoid extreme losses and extreme gains; the large, diversified firm may be able to counteract adverse market trends by pruning losses and expanding profitable areas, viz., by improving its internal efficiency.

Economic, physical and technological reasons, then, uphold the continual existence of the small plant. Added to these is the historical fact that many of what are small plants at the moment may be in the process of growing into larger ones. Nevertheless, small plants do not necessarily coincide with small firms. A large firm may control several small plants. What is it, then, which explains the continued existence of the small firm, when so much evidence points to the advantages of size? This question will be dealt with in the next section.

[1] For further data, see R. E. Caves, ed., *Britain's Economic Prospects*, 1968, pp. 295–6 and K. D. George, *Industrial Organization*, 1971, pp. 63–5.
[2] Caves, *op. cit.*, pp. 297–8.
[3] For further data see F. V. Meyer, D. C. Corner and J. E. S. Parker, *Problems of a Mature Economy*, 1970, pp. 17–23 and K. D. George, *op. cit.*, pp. 65–6.

8. Reasons for the Continued Existence of the Small Firm

Despite the fact that the 'mortality rate' for small firms is higher than for large firms, the small firm continues to survive as a high proportion of the total. Most small firms are one-plant firms, predominating particularly in retailing, agriculture, building, servicing (e.g. garages), short distance road haulage and other trades requiring little machinery, serving small, local markets or specialising in allied processes and products in centres of local concentration.

There is always present the personal profit incentive, which ensures that there is an elastic, seemingly inexhaustible supply of entrepreneurs, willing to take risks and make management decisions.

Some of the overriding reasons for the existence of the small firm, either retarding its growth or underwriting its continued survival are:

(a) The great need for capital militates against the small firm, especially as machinery and new techniques become necessary under competitive conditions. The small firm is a more risky investment than the large firm, and whereas the big concern can seek capital in the cheaper, long-term capital market, the small firm must either slowly plough back profits or must rely upon the more expensive short-term capital market.

(b) It takes time for big firms to accumulate capital and grow. Meanwhile, the small firm is given a respite in the struggle for survival.

(c) Sometimes the burden of capital expenditure on equipment is removed (e.g. the renting of specialist machinery from other firms).

(d) Sometimes the small firm is relieved of the expense of conducting individual research, the results of which may be provided by Government establishments or trade associations.

(e) The social prestige attached to 'being one's own boss', fortified by the personal profit incentive and the skilled man's fear of being unemployed, ensure an elastic supply of entrepreneurs, willing to take big risks and to work for small returns (in the short period, at least), providing good quality 'cheap management'.

(f) In localised areas the small firm may be able to subcontract to a larger firm, concentrating on a specialist process or product.

(g) Sometimes the small firm is purposely tolerated by the big firm (or firms) in an industry, to serve as a cloak of respectability for monopolistic practices, under which oligopoly price-leadership may be practised.

(h) Wholesalers and other specialist middlemen may save the small firm the marketing expense of developing a sales organisation. These middlemen also provide the link between the small firm and the big supplier, who might not sell small quantities direct to the small firm.

(i) The advantages of bulk transactions may be achieved directly by the small firm, when it collaborates with others to negotiate joint bulk purchase agreements.

(j) The small firm builds up a fund of goodwill with other firms, which is fortified by the desire of 'bosses' to be in contact with other 'bosses' rather than hired personnel. 'Bosses' usually feel that things will be more efficiently accomplished through the 'principal to principal' channels.

(k) Imperfections in the labour market, whereby certain types of labour might be immobile – less able to move into higher-paid jobs elsewhere and willing to accept lower pay, longer hours or less congenial conditions – favour the small firm.

It is important to note that though the 1935 and 1959 figures for small plants (reflecting fairly closely the distribution of small firms) showed that they constituted 73% of the total in both periods, the actual number of plants was higher in 1959. This underlines the fact that the 'population' of small firms is by no means static. Many of them are spurious and in the process of dying; others are one-time large firms, which are growing smaller; others are embryonic large firms in the process of growing.

As was noted above, however, the study by Armstrong and Silberston showed that in 101 out of 115 British manufacturing industries there was an actual decline in the number of plants with 10+ employees over the period 1954–58. This finding is more in keeping with that of the Bolton Committee of Inquiry on Small Firms[1] – the first rigorous investigation of the role and problems of small firms in this country – which reported in November 1971. The report defined small businesses differently for different industries (e.g. less than 200 employees in manufacturing; less than 25 employees in construction, mining or quarrying; less than 5 vehicles in road haulage; less than £50,000 p.a. turnover in retailing) and found that their numbers had been declining in recent years, largely as a result of inevitable technological changes and changes in the size of the market.

As defined by the Committee, there were 820,000 small firms, accounting for 14% of the Gross National Product and 18% of the net output (value added) of the private sector. If agriculture and the professions were included, numbers reach 1¼ million with 19% of G.N.P. and 29% of the working population, which is larger than the entire public sector of the economy. The report emphasised the role of the small firms as innovators from which new, larger companies grew, and described this as the 'seed-bed' function. Their fundamental problem was that of raising money to start up. Nevertheless, deserving cases could obtain capital, with the help of organisations such as the Industrial and Commercial Finance Corporation, but all face the problem of having to retain a larger proportion of earnings to finance expansion than do larger firms.[2]

An interesting study of the small firm's struggle to survive, in an ever thickening atmosphere of concentration of control, was made in France in 1962.[3] It found that 60% of manufacturing and 90% of distribution enterprises were small or medium in size. Under the added pressures of the Common Market these small enterprises (particularly the 100,000 industrial and 1 million commercial enterprises in the P.M.E. – General Confederation of Small and Medium Enterprises) were adopting vigorous measures of self-defence and self-improvement. These included cooperative agreements embracing production, buying, export, research and financing, on professional, local and regional levels. The study concluded by expressing confidence that the small firm would survive by reason of its liking for risk, its ingenuity and sense of personal responsibility, the elasticity granted by its limited size, and its quality of private enterprise.

---

[1] *Report of the Committee of Inquiry on Small Firms* (Bolton Report), Cmnd 4811, H.M.S.O., 1971.
[2] *Econ.*, 6 Nov. 1971, p. 88, and B. Hollowood, 'The small business and the economic climate', *N.W.B.Q.R.*, Feb. 1970.
[3] This appeared in the journal of the *Patronat Français* (French Employers' Federation) in June 1962, and was reviewed in *The Times* of 19 June 1962 under the title 'Small business surviving in France'.

9. Integration and Standardisation

Large structural size in a plant or firm reflects the scale of productional activity in the plant or operational activity in the firm. These extensions in the scale of activity are made through the processes of integration and/or standardisation.

Integration is a diversification of products and processes. It is an extension of the 'scope' of productive activity vertically (over consecutive linked processes), horizontally or laterally (over various materials and products), or diagonally (over various auxiliary services). This diversification of scope may occur within the plant and/or within the firm as a whole.

Standardisation represents a specialisation of management and resources on a product, process or service, *via* batch- or mass-production methods or by flow-production techniques. It is an extension of the division of labour – of the 'scale' upon which a particular operation is performed: a specialisation which brings in its train internal economies. This form of activity seems very suited to certain industries in which repetitive mechanical operations can be performed, reducing the burden of overhead costs of equipment each time that equipment is used. The degree to which production in a plant or firm need be standardised depends upon such things as the size of the market, the location of the market, the location of the plant and the resources available in the plant and the firm. For example, if there is only a small market for mink fur bathing trunks, a small firm with one small plant may very well be highly specialised on the production of that luxury article, using machinery and techniques of the *requisite* capacity. However, if the product were taken up by a large firm with several large plants, production might only be economically feasible in a small part of one of those plants. This does not mean that less efficient methods will be adopted, as compared with the previous example. Specialised machinery and techniques of the requisite capacity may be used, but the whole plant, and indeed the whole firm will not be specialising on that one product. Standardisation will have been carried out to the optimum *feasible* extent, but it will only represent a fraction of the productive activities of the plant and firm with large resources.

Very few cases occur, in fact, where a whole firm (or even whole plant) specialises on one single process, product or service. Carried to a theoretical but absurd conclusion, 100% specialisation would result in entire firms, with all their constituent plants, performing one solitary movement out of the thousands necessary to complete a single product, process or service. Clearly, then, some form of integration takes place in most plants and firms, even if only the integration of several motions which result in the completion of one single product or process. Yet each stage in that activity might be standardised, using specialised techniques or equipment of the requisite capacity. Standardisation, then, is a question of degree, based upon the extent of the market, the extent of the scale at which a particular product, process or service is performed, and the relationship of these factors to the total resources of the plant and the firm.

Some of the major technological or cost of production economies of standardisation within plants are the 'learning effect' (or 'practice makes perfect'); the once-for-all set-up costs for production lines; the regulated matching of supply with demand by avoidance of unpredictability. The area-volume relationship, known by the shorthand engineering term' the 0·6 rule', refers to the slower rate of increase in surface area of capital equipment as its capacity or volume rises. This same bulk transactions principle may be adopted much more widely, however, as it was during World War II, when Operations Research studies showed that more effective destroyer protection could be given to a few large convoys than to several small ones. It is important to recognise that there are various dimensions or ways of considering standardisation. Firstly, it may refer to the scale of production of an individual product. Secondly, it may be extended by lengthening the production run or period over which the product is produced. In practice, many of the empirical studies on economies of large-scale plant production indicate that in most industries the cost reductions tail off fairly quickly, to reach a critical size called the minimum optimum (or efficient) scale, against which costs at any suboptimal scale may be compared.[1]

Some of the major organisational or operational benefits of standardisation within firms lie in managerial economies, research and development economies, marketing (selling and distribution) economies, financial economies, rationalisation economies and the stabilisation or ironing out of fluctuations in market forces.[2]

The balance of evidence seems to point to *operational* economies of scale or standardisation rather than to *technological* or plant production economies of scale as the more important factor behind the size of firms and the degree of seller concentration or market concentration. Nevertheless, large organisations face the problem of coordinating the efforts of hierarchies of managers: managers may attempt too much, or establish excessively wide spans of control; communications may become slow and inaccurate, the workforce alienated and its morale low. Such problems have been experienced by some of the giant 'multinational companies', which at one time attempted to meet them by decentralising into national companies, each operated by a sort of local baron. With the increasing complexity and interdependence of international operations, however, this practice has tended to be replaced by a reversal to sharper centralisation: this in turn has been facilitated by the increasing availability of computer facilities for coordination and information processing.

Integration (or diversification) is sometimes thought to be the opposite of standardisation, as if it were a hostile phenomenon. In fact this is so only if integration occurs to the detriment of the fullest extent of standardisation which is feasible in any given circumstance. If, for example, integration of one sort or another occurred in a plant or firm of limited resources, with the result that one or all of the activities of that firm or plant were not performed to the maximum extent which was economically feasible, then it could be said that 'scope' was militating against 'scale'. On the other hand, a large firm with vast resources might integrate several activities within each or between each of its plants,[3] and if each of those activities is performed to the maximum scale which is economically justified, then 'scope' and 'scale' will be complementing each

[1] For further data see A. Silberston, 'Economies of scale in theory and practice', *E.J.*, March 1972 (supplement); C. F. Pratten, *Economies of Scale in Manufacturing Industry;* J. S. Bain, *Barriers to New Competition*, 1956, ch. 5; C. F. Pratten and R. M. Dean, *The Economies of Large-scale Production in British Industry*, 1965; D. Swann and D. L. McLachlan, *Concentration or Competition: A European Dilemma?*, 1967, pp. 13–15.

[2] C. F. Pratten, 'The merger boom in manufacturing industry', *L.B.R.*, Oct. 1968.

[3] For details of diversification by tobacco firms – into fields such as ice-cream and crisps (like tobacco, perishable consumer goods requiring vast distribution networks) and also teaching machines – see 'Creeping diversification', *Econ.*, 25 July 1964, p. 418.

other. Where 'scope' is practised in such a way that the 'scale' of any activity is not economically reached, there is justification for 'dis-integration' – a reduction in scope, and an increase in the scale of the remaining activities.

Some of the advantages of, and motives for integration of various types, within plant or firm, are as follows:

(a) Common costs in producing products, processes or services. Examples of this are common research units, sales organisation, and management organisation, which may not be used to capacity unless extended over diversified activities; common costs in producing to capacity an early process, product, service or material which at a later stage (by vertical integration) is used in a wide range of products, etc. (in lateral integration); common costs in producing to capacity, at a later stage, a product or process (after vertical integration with several earlier processes, products, materials, etc., which are each produced in lateral integration). These common costs may be visualised in a diagram such as Fig. 2.8.

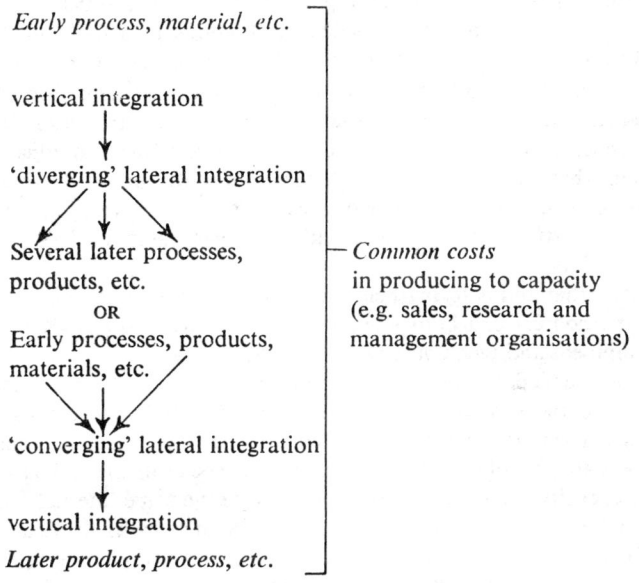

Fig. 2.8. *Common costs in vertical, 'diverging' lateral and 'converging' lateral integration.*

When considering examples of lateral or vertical integration it may sometimes appear to lack any logical relationship between similar products or processes, or successive stages in the productive and distributive process. Nevertheless, there may very well be a 'functional congruity' or similarity in the business processes or operational characteristics involved. One of the major problems to be noted in cases of vertical integration of successive processes is that of *balance* between the processes. Due to the differing technical capacities of different units of equipment, the firm may have to choose between continuing to 'buy in' some of that stage from competing outside producers, or having to sell off some of its surplus at that stage to competing outside customers.

(b) Technique and quality may make vertical integration desirable, as where there are economies to be gained from continuous processes within the plant (such as in an integrated steel plant, where heat is conserved and utilised, and where the metal is worked whilst still hot), and where there are advantages in being able to control quality at various stages, even down to the distribution of the final product to the consumer.

(c) Desire to supply a comprehensive range, to secure consumer loyalty, is a very strong incentive to lateral integration. Retailers and other early consumers appear to prefer to deal with suppliers who keep a wide range of products. This also minimises the risk of fluctuations in supply and demand.

(d) Security is another important motive and advantage of integration: the ensuring of stability of sources and outlets, by vertical integration,[1] and the reduction of competition and promotion of monopolistic power over markets by lateral integration.

(e) Stability of profits is also an important motive for diversification: firms in industries which are prone to cyclical fluctuations in activity might wish to expand into more stable industries, so as to 'smooth out the profit cycle.'[2]

Apart from the disadvantages of over-integration, where diversification of scope is achieved at the cost of insufficient scale or standardisation (viz. internal diseconomies within the plant and/or firm), there is the additional social disadvantage that integrated firms, whether innocently or by 'buying up' competition, may assume such proportions as to restrict entry by competitors and/or exert strong monopolistic influence over factors of production and markets.

Granted that ultimate markets of varying extents exist, the big firm with sufficient resources can both integrate and specialise most efficiently, with the best equipment and techniques which may be required.

Two problems flow from this observation. Firstly, granted the same markets, what should the firm with smaller resources do? If it integrates to the same extent, each activity will be conducted on a smaller scale. Although smaller equipment and techniques of lower capacity may be available and may be worked to their capacity, they are not likely to provide the same internal economies of scale that the bigger firm will secure. Therefore the smaller firm has the choice, either of earning smaller profits by integrating and using lesser equipment and techniques to capacity, or of not integrating and performing fewer activities, each one on a bigger scale. If, on the other hand, lesser techniques and equipment are not available (indivisible factors – principle of multiples), then it would be doubly unwise to integrate to the same extent as the bigger firm. Equipment and techniques would be too costly and/or not used to capacity.

Secondly, to what extent will an individual plant in a firm perform integrated activities? Apart from the factors outlined above, relating to the resources available in the firm and the consequent total of integrated activities feasible

[1] For an analysis of an interesting example along these lines see D. F. Dixon, 'The development of the solus system of petrol distribution in the United Kingdom, 1950–1960', *Economica*, Feb. 1962.
[2] C. George, 'Why diversify?', *Stat.*, 14 Aug. 1964, pp. 432–4; E. T. Penrose, *The Theory of the Growth of the Firm*, 1966, p. 105.

amongst its plants, the number of those integrated activities which it is economically feasible to integrate in any one plant will be affected by the location of that plant. As was pointed out in Section II.6, the more highly localised plant in an industry tended to be of smaller size than the plant of medium localisation. This stems from the fact that an area of localised small and medium plants, where linked processes, products and services exist in close juxtaposition, manifests 'external economies of scale' much the same as the internal economies of scale in a single, highly integrated, large plant. There is, in the area of localised industrial concentration, a process of the 'partial' integration (or 'localised dis-integration') of small and medium plants, each under independent management. The strain on the management factor is eased; small plants can benefit from the principle of multiples by specialising on auxiliary products and processes with equipment which is used to capacity on orders from several outside firms; the outside firms are each saved the expense of financing the purchase of such indivisible specialist equipment, which none of them might have been able to use to capacity; each plant is enabled to perform fewer activities, each one on a larger scale than would be possible outside the localised area. Thus, the localised area of 'linked' and 'swarming' small and medium plants is a substitute for the larger, integrated plant. Each plant can specialise on fewer, standardised products, processes and services with a more efficient use of management and, possibly, of other resources.

10. Advantages of Different Plants and Firms

Apart from the three major structural principles of efficiency, which encourage large size in both plant and firm (through integration and/or standardisation), various functions were mentioned in Section II.7, whose efficiency varies with the extent to which they are performed. A clearer appreciation of the practical application of these efficiency principles and functions of size may be achieved by examining some actual structural cases.[1] For this purpose we shall use the following symbols:

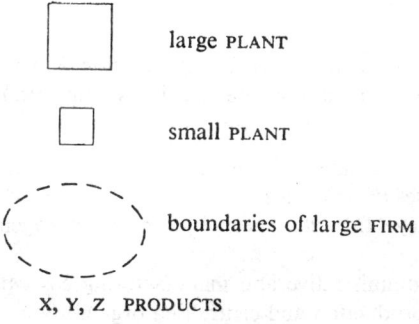

large PLANT

small PLANT

boundaries of large FIRM

X, Y, Z   PRODUCTS

THE LARGE FIRM

[1] Along the lines developed by J. W. Jenks (and Clark) in *The Trust Problem*, 1919, and P. Sargant Florence, *The Logic of British and American Industry*.

The principles of operational efficiency (bulk transactions, massed reserves and multiples) are at work, as in the following instances:

(*a*) Cheaper financing costs (reputation, Stock Exchange and long-term capital).
(*b*) Common use and full and flexible utilisation of specialised management, patents, brands, advertising, etc.
(*c*) Efficient use of research and other media for accumulation and dissemination of knowledge and skills over the whole organisation.

THE LARGE PLANT

The three efficiency principles of plant production and other factors are at work, promoting internal economies:

(*a*) The execution of decisions is more efficiently controlled and coordinated in one large plant than in several small ones.
(*b*) Transport economies are felt in the elimination of cross-freights between processes and products when these are in juxtaposition.
(*c*) The large establishment may have enough waste materials to make full use of available skills, equipment, management and residual power in the manufacture of by-products.
(*d*) Auxiliary repair, maintenance and tool-making services may be employed to capacity on the premises, and therefore more quickly (and possibly more cheaply) than if called in from outside.

THE LARGE FIRM, WITH ONE LARGE PLANT, MAKING ONE PRODUCT OR PROCESS

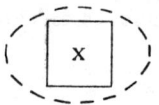

Internal economies made in the plant's production activities and the firm's operational activities (through the three efficiency principles) would include all those in cases 1 and 2, plus the following:

(*a*) The fulfilling of customers' orders more promptly, through coordinated control of all activities in one place.
(*b*) Greater efficiency, through specialisation in management, labour and equipment.
(*c*) The cutting of administrative and manufacturing costs per unit of output, through large-scale production and centralised organisation.

THE SMALL PLANT

The advantages of the small plant, as such (not to be confused with the small firm), rest primarily on the dispersed location of materials, markets and labour,

110

difficulties and expense in the transportability of materials and/or the product, or discontinuity in the supply of factors of production or in demand for the product.

THE LARGE FIRM, WITH SEVERAL SMALL PLANTS, EACH PRODUCING THE SAME PRODUCT OR PROCESS

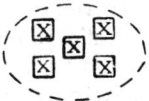

Apart from the advantages listed in cases 1 and 4, there are advantages of specialisation (perhaps in dispersed locations).

(*a*) The filling of customers' orders promptly from the nearest plant.
(*b*) The exchange of comparative cost-accountancy information between the plants.
(*c*) Availability of a pool of skilled management and labour for flexible use between plants.

THE LARGE FIRM, WITH SEVERAL SMALL PLANTS, EACH PRODUCING A DIFFERENT PRODUCT OR PROCESS

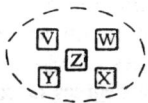

This structure does not have the advantages of large-scale, specialised production. The advantages are primarily those of the large firm (case 1) and of integration (lateral and/or vertical), viz. common costs, technique and quality control, comprehensive range, security and stable profits.

11. Evidence of Monopolistic Concentrated Control

Whilst the previous sections of this chapter have referred to the structural size of plants and firms, the advantages of such size and the avenues leading to increases in size, it must be borne in mind that control of industry is not only vested in 'the firm'. Furthermore, 'the firm' is not always a clear-cut unit of industrial government or organisation.

The nominal firm, operating under a certain name, may itself be controlled in a number of ways by a firm of a different name. It may also be controlled in a number of ways by more than one individual or firm, each of whom may exert an influence elsewhere in the industrial structure. Furthermore, with or without these manifestations of 'vote control' and/or 'wirepulling' by outside interests, the nominal firm may act in concert with other firms, willingly or unwillingly, as leader, partner or satellite.

The net result is that the 'external government of industry' – control of industry which is exercised beyond the confines of the nominal firm – has complex ramifications. We have already noted that the basic structural unit in the productive activity of an industry is 'the plant' and that 'the firm' is the basic organisational unit of control, which may cut across more than one industry.

It would be as well to add a third dimension, that of 'the monopolistic group'. This is the unit of 'concentrated control', or of external government (control extending beyond the nominal limits of 'the firm'). Here we shall note some of the evidence of the extent of concentrated control in the organisation of individual industries, exercised by monopolistic groupings of the few largest firms. From studies made on the basis of 1935 census statistics in Britain and America[1] it appears that a similar pattern of concentration of industrial control was present in both countries, because of similarities in physical, technological, supply and demand circumstances, which seem to have outweighed national differences in resources, markets and customs. A study was made of 234 British and 275 American manufacturing industries of all sizes to see what proportion of their workers was employed in the three largest firms in Britain and the four largest in America. The main points which emerged were:

	American industries (%)	British industries (%)
(i) Degree of concentration (%)		
0–19	27	25
20–34	23	27
35–49	23	19
50–69	15	15
70 +	12	14

The average degree of concentration in both countries was 35%.
(ii) In both countries, the largest industries tended to have lower degrees of concentration than the smaller ones.
(iii) In both countries the highest degrees of concentrated control tended to be in similar industries, and the lowest degrees of concentration also tended to be in similar industries.

Some of the most highly concentrated industries in Britain were: condensed milk (94%); sewing and shoe-making machines (93%); wallpaper (90%); matches (89%); cigarettes (88%); zinc smelting (86%); cast iron and steel pipes (84%); non-beet sugar (83%); petroleum (82%); explosives (81%); gramophones (81%); rayon (80%); vegetable oil (seed-crushing) (79%); batteries (78%); candles (77%); rubber tyres (76%); spirit distilling (74%); beet sugar (72%); margarine (72%); wrought iron and steel tubes (71%); photographic apparatus (70%); bicycles (70%); motor cycles (63%); and linoleum (64%).

A more recent study by Evely and Little of the 1951 census figures in Britain[2] indicated that in most of the trades which were highly concentrated in 1935, concentration had increased. Also, the degree of concentration had risen in many other industries. Nevertheless it was not certain that concentrated control had increased for industry as a whole since 1935. One useful innovation in this study was the classification of industries not only by degrees of concentration, but also by the number of firms and the relative size of the largest firms. This brought out the fact that not only was 10·7% of total employment in industries with 67%+ degrees of concentration, but that these were industries in which the three largest firms were big in comparison with the others, and/or there were

[1] H. Leak and A. Maizels, 'The structure of British industry', J. Roy. Stat. Soc., 1945, pp. 144–99; Report of the U.S. National Resources Committee, The Structure of the American Economy 1939, Part I, App. 7.
[2] R. Evely and I. M. D. Little, Concentration in British industry, National Institute of Economic and Social Research, Economic and Social Studies, No. 16, 1960.

very few firms. The significance of this fact lies in the resultant possibility of price-leadership or collusion. Fairly 'competitive' industries – where concentration was medium or low, where the top three firms were not relatively big and where there were many firms, accounted for 27·2% of employment. Such conditions were least conducive to monopolistic practices. The remaining 62·1% of employment was in industries where the degree of competitiveness (on the basis of concentration, relative size of the top three and number of firms) varied between these two extremes.

Despite the similarities between the 1935 and 1951 patterns of concentration of control in industry, it must be noted that there have been changes in the membership of the 'Big Threes' in various industries. S. J. Prais, for example, pointed out[1] that between 1948 and 1952 there was a 12% turnover in the membership of the 100 largest British firms. There is probably a strong link between this finding and the fact that the above-mentioned study by Evely and Little could find no definitive proof of a general increase in concentrated control in British manufacturing since 1935.

The fact that ambitious and growing firms are continually entering upon the scene, tumbling other firms off their 'status pedestals', is one of the chief factors retarding the development of concentrated control. On the one hand we find – especially in industries suffering from decline or surplus capacity – a process of amalgamation for security into larger firms, or less formal types of combination and concentration. On the other hand we find other firms growing and surging to the top, having mastered new techniques or found new solutions to chronic problems. These newcomers to the 'status scene' either change places with earlier members or syphon off some of the labour force into their own growing activities. W. Fellner, in his book *Competition Among the Few*, ascribes one of the chief limits to concentration of control to 'changes in relative strengths', stemming from progress in innovation and inventiveness.

We have, so far, dealt with concentration of control within the structure of individual industries. Due, however, to the overlapping of some firms into several industries, and the various forms of cooperation and collusion which exist outside 'the firm', it is useful to bear in mind the fact that there are wider ramifications of concentrated control, extending beyond the yardstick which we have applied to individual industries. These ramifications and the problems they pose will be dealt with in Chapter 4, after certain industries have been examined in detail.

12. Summary

We have traced in the preceding sections a methodological framework for the location, structure and organisation of industry.

It was found that there were connections between location, investment intensity (or mechanisation) and size of plants; between integration, standardisation and size of plants and firms; and between the degrees of concentrated control in similar industries in Britain and America. These findings seem to point to the overriding influence of similarities in technological factors (type of process), the pull of localised production centres and the vagaries of supply and

---

[1] S. J. Prais, 'The financial experience of giant companies', *E.J.*, June 1957. For details of the 300 largest U.K. firms in 1965, see 'Britain's Largest Business Groups: The Times 300', *The Times*, 21 June 1965.

demand conditions in both countries, as compared with the differences in customs and in the location of resources and markets.

We may summarise our findings briefly as between factors influencing plant location and plant structure of an industry on the one hand, and the organisational framework of an industry on the other.

(a) Plant location and plant structure

The factors influencing location, or SITE are primarily physical and economic: the dispersion of markets, materials and fuel; the weight and bulk of materials, fuels and products; the flexibility of the transport system; the relationship of transport costs to total costs; the type of industry – 'rooted', 'footloose', 'swarming' or 'linked'; the existence of a localised area of industrial concentration, etc.

The main factors influencing investment intensity or H.P. per worker are technological: type of process – extraction, process or assembly; degree of integration (SCOPE) and degree of standardisation or specialisation (SCALE), which are in turn influenced by the size of markets, available resources and techniques used.

(a) *Physical, economic and technological factors*

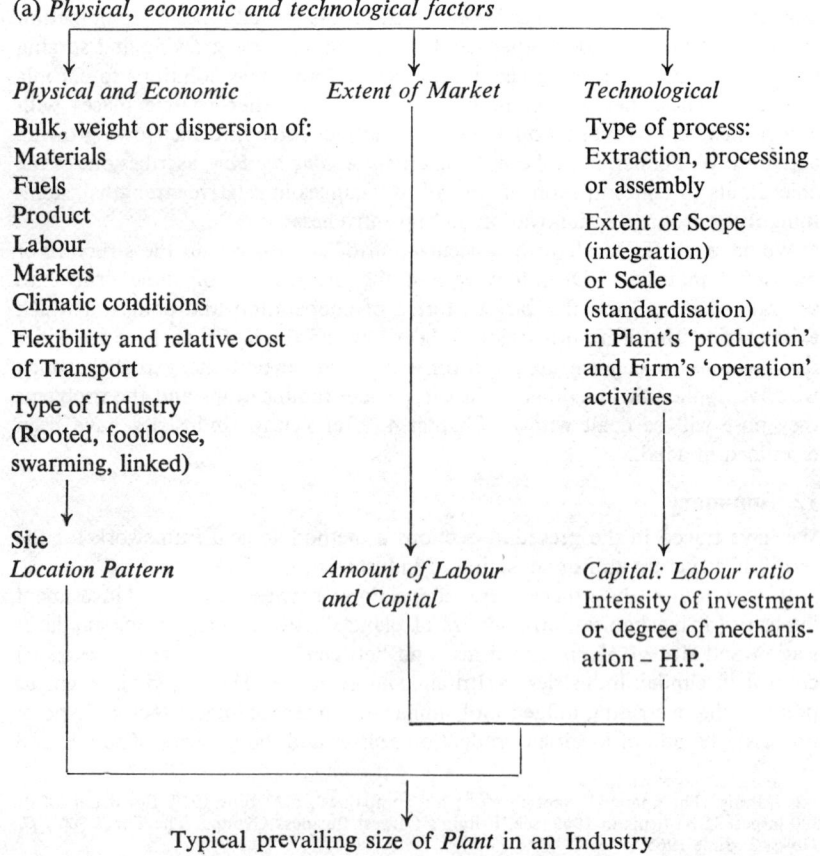

Physical and Economic   *Extent of Market*   *Technological*

Bulk, weight or dispersion of:
Materials
Fuels
Product
Labour
Markets
Climatic conditions

Flexibility and relative cost
of Transport

Type of Industry
(Rooted, footloose,
swarming, linked)

Type of process:
Extraction, processing
or assembly

Extent of Scope
(integration)
or Scale
(standardisation)
in Plant's 'production'
and Firm's 'operation'
activities

Site
Location Pattern

*Amount of Labour
and Capital*

Capital: Labour ratio
Intensity of investment
or degree of mechanisation – H.P.

Typical prevailing size of *Plant* in an Industry

(b) *Non-physical/economic/technological factors*

Past and present management ⎤
Age of controlling firm ⎥   *Differences* in *sizes* of *Plant* within an
Length of time in the industry ⎥ — *industry*
Degree of inventiveness ⎥
Experience ⎦

Fig. 2.9. *Factors influencing plant location and plant structure in an industry*

Investment intensity, influenced by scope and scale factors, has a close bearing on SIZE of plant, but this influence is diluted by the parallel influence of location or site. High localisation is a substitute for the large plant. The confluence of h.p. and site considerations make for the differences in typical plant size between different industries. The reasons for wide variations in plant size within a particular industry must be sought in non-physical/economic/technological factors. These are such things as age of controlling firm, time of entry into the industry, the quality of past and present management, the effects of experience of trade fluctuations, etc. (see Fig. 2.9).

Table 2.9 *Scheme for appraisal and comparison of the structure and organisation of industries*

ASPECT	DATA
General description	1. Employment
	2. Output
	3. No. of Plants
	4. No. of Firms
Geographical (site)	1. Location Pattern of the Industry,
	2. Coefficient of Localisation,
	3. Factors influencing Location Pattern.
	4. Type of Industry ('footloose' 'rooted', etc.)
Technological structure	1. Major Divisions of the Industry
	2. Type of Process (extraction, processing, assembly, etc.)
	3. Scale, Scope, and Investment Intensity (h.p.)
	4. Typical Size of Plant (*Unit of Production*)
Organisation: (*a*) *Internal*	1. Typical Size of Firm (*Unit of Internal Organisation*)
(*b*) *External*	2. Concentration of Control (% of production and/or employment in largest firms, associations or combinations)
	3. Tiers of Authority (representative organisations of labour, employers and/or State).

(*b*) **Organisational framework**

Whilst in general there are definite economies to be derived from larger size (increases in the extent of a plant's PRODUCTION activities and/or a firm's OPERATION activities – these increases being in scope or scale), and indeed a trend towards larger plants and firms, there is still room for small firms (which will, of course, have small plants), especially in 'management-intensive' fields, where management initiative is being provided cheaply, where small, distinctive and specialised markets occur, and where relatively cheap, immobile labour pools may be tapped.

The 1935 studies in Britain and America showed a close similarity in the degrees of control concentrated in a few big firms in similar industries in both countries. This indicates that apart from the general advantages of large size which may be reaped by a big firm (regardless of how many industries it is operating in), there are similar factors of a physical, technological, supply or demand nature at work in similar industries in different countries, which tend to result in a particular pattern of concentrated control amongst the firms in a particular industry.

Whilst the basic structural unit of production in an industry is the plant, and the basic unit of internal organisation is the firm, the unit of external government or concentrated control, outside the confines of the nominal firm, is the monopolistic grouping of firms in associations or combinations of various types, or in dominant positions by virtue of their size.

13. Scheme for Appraisal and Comparison of the Location, Structure and Organisation of Industries

Whilst some of the various ramifications of the external government of industry – control beyond the limits of the simple firm – will be dealt with later on, in Chapter 4, it seems appropriate here to present a brief scheme (see Table 2.9), by which different industries may be compared in respect of their location, technological structure and organisation.

14. Further Reading and Sources

A. ARMSTRONG·and A. SILBERSTON, 'Size of plant, size of enterprise and concentration in British manufacturing industry 1935–58'. *Journal of the Royal Statistical Society.* Series A (General) vol. 128, part 3. 1965.

J. S. BAIN, *Barriers to New Competition.* Harvard U.P. 1956.

A. BEACHAM and L. J. WILLIAMS, *Economics of Industrial Organization.* Pitman. 1961.

BOARD OF TRADE, *Company Assets, Income and Finance in 1960.* H.M.S.O. 1962. *Board of Trade Journal.* 3. vol. 183, no. 3428.

R. E. CAVES, ed., *Britain's Economic Prospects.* Brookings/Allen and Unwin. 1968.

W. L. CRUM, *Corporate Size and Earning Power.* Harvard U.P., 1939.

G. CYRIAX, *Monopoly and Competition.* Institute of Economic Affairs. Key Discussion Book No. 1. 1965.

D. F. DIXON, 'The development of the solus system of Petrol Distribution in the United Kingdom, 1950–1960'. *Economica.* Feb. 1962.

R. EVELY and I. M. D. LITTLE, *Concentration in British Industry.* C.U.P. 1960.

W. FELLNER, *Competition Among the Few.* Cass. 1966.

P. SARGANT FLORENCE, *The Logic of British and American Industry.* Routledge & Kegan Paul. 1953.

P. SARGANT FLORENCE, *Investment, Location and Size of Plant.* C.U.P. 1948.

P. SARGANT FLORENCE, *Ownership, Control and Success of Large Companies.* Sweet & Maxwell. 1961.

P. SARGANT FLORENCE, *Post-War Investment, Location and Size of Plant.* C.U.P. 1962.

K. D. GEORGE, *Industrial Organization: competition, growth and structural change in Britain.* Allen and Unwin. 1971.

A. C. HOBSON, 'The great industrial belt'. *The Economic Journal.* Vol. LXI. Sept. 1951.

B. HOLLOWOOD, 'The small business and the economic climate'. *N.W.B.Q.R.* Feb. 1970.

J. W. JENKS (and CLARK), *The Trust Problem.* Putnam. 4th Ed. 1919.

P. S. JOHNSON, *Industrial Structure.* Longman. 1970.

M. M. MEHTA, *Structure of Cotton-mill Industry of India.* 1949.

F. V. MEYER, D. C. CORNER and J. E. S. PARKER, *Problems of a Mature Economy.* Macmillan. 1970.

NATIONAL BUREAU OF ECONOMIC RESEARCH, *Business Concentration and Price Policy.* Princeton U.P. 1955.

D. NEEDHAM, *Economic Analysis and Industrial Structure.* Holt, Rinehart and Winston. 1969.

E. T. PENROSE, *The Theory of the Growth of the Firm.* Blackwell. 1966.

S. J. PRAIS, 'The financial experience of giant companies'. *E.J.* June 1957.

C. F. PRATTEN, *Economies of Scale in Manufacturing Industry.* C.U.P. 1971.

C. F. PRATTEN, 'The merger boom in manufacturing industry'. *L.B.R.* Oct. 1968.

C. F. PRATTEN and R. M. DEAN, *The Economies of Large-scale Production in British Industry.* C.U.P. 1965.

Report of the Committee of Inquiry on Small Firms (Bolton Report). Cmnd 4811. H.M.S.O. 1971.

E. A. G. ROBINSON, *The Structure of Competitive Industry.* Nisbet & C.U.P. 1945.

A. SILBERSTON, 'Economies of scale in theory and practice'. *E.J.* March 1972 (Supplement).

D. SWANN and D. L. MCLACHLAN, *Concentration or Competition: A European Dilemma?* Chatham House/P.E.P. 1967.

H. TOWNSEND, *Scale, Innovation, Merger and Monopoly.* Pergamon. 1968.

U.S. NATIONAL RESOURCES COMMITTEE, *Structure of the American Economy.* 1939. Part I, App. 7.

M. A. UTTON, *Industrial Concentration.* Penguin. 1970.

L. W. WEISS, *Case Studies in American Industry.* Wiley. 1967.

15. Past Examination Questions

1. Explain with examples why some industries are highly localised while others are carried on in small units scattered throughout the country. (Summer 1953)

2. What are the main economic activities carried on near where you live? Why do they take place there? (Summer 1952)

3. What factors would influence a prospective producer of washing machines in deciding the location of his factory? (January 1963)

4. What determines the extent to which closeness of a market for the product affects the location of a plant? (Summer 1964)

5. Describe and explain the factors which determine the location of the main

firms in the motor car industry in the United Kingdom. (Summer 1960)

6. 'The troubles of Britain's declining industries are not due to their own inefficiency, but to the development of new industries in Britain.' Discuss. (Summer 1961)

7. Why were there depressed areas in South Wales and northern England between the world wars? (Summer 1957)

8. Why is the level of unemployment greater in some areas than in others? Refer in your answer to conditions in the United Kingdom. (Summer 1959)

9. Why were some areas in the United Kingdom suffering the effects of higher than average levels of unemployment in 1959? Illustrate your answer by examples. (Summer 1960)

10. In the light of the influences governing the location of industry, do you consider it has been wise to encourage firms to go to Development Areas rather than to encourage people to move out of them? (Summer 1954)

11. Explain the advantages and disadvantages of inducing firms to locate new plants in areas of 'high and persistent levels of unemployment'. (Summer 1960)

12. 'The Government should so plan the location of industry that new industries are set up where the old ones are dying.' Discuss. (Summer 1962)

13. Say what is meant by localised unemployment. What policies might be used to remove it? (Summer 1963)

14. Why may large scale production lower unit costs? (January 1964)

15. If you were a businessman about to build a new factory, what considerations would affect you in deciding how large to build it? (Summer 1953)

16. What are internal and external economies of scale? Why do they occur? (Summer 1962)

17. If there are economies to be gained by large-scale production, why does one not find a single firm producing the entire output of each industry? (January 1963)

18. In what areas of the economy does the small business still survive and why? (Summer 1951)

19. 'Though larger firms may be more efficient than smaller firms it is difficult to see why smaller firms should ever be more efficient than larger firms.' Discuss. (Summer 1963)

20. Discuss the advantages and disadvantages of integration of firms. (Summer 1958)

21. Why are petroleum companies in the United Kingdom acquiring petrol filling stations? (Summer 1958)

22. Why do some radio manufacturers not produce their own valves? (January 1963)

23. What is the effect of scientific advance on the structure of industry? (Summer 1961)

24. Why are some industries more competitive than others? Illustrate your answer with examples drawn from United Kingdom industry. (Summer 1961)

25. 'Monopoly is in the public interest because large-scale production is efficient.' Comment. (Summer 1961)

26. Is the number of firms in an industry a good indicator of the strength of the producers' monopoly? (January 1963)

27. 'Monopolies must be desirable, for they arise from the economies of large-scale production.' Comment. (Summer 1964)

3. Some Major Industries

THE COAL INDUSTRY: Stage I

1. Technical Background

The first point to note about the coal industry is that the product is not homogeneous. There are great differences between the properties of coal mined in different coalfields, and even in different mines in the same coalfield. Each type of coal has different uses according to the calorific value (based mainly on carbon content), caking properties (tendency to become plastic on heating, producing a hard coke residue for metallurgical purposes) and the proportion of volatile matter (e.g. sulphur and ash, for the creation of gas). The coals range from anthracite (high calorific carbon value, low caking properties, and low content of volatile matter) down to the high volatile, low caking and low calorific coals. They are graded downwards according to decreasing calorific value, decreasing caking properties and increasing volatile content. For example the third main grade is Coking Steam Coal (high calorific value, high caking properties and low volatile content). The ninth main grade is High Volatile Weakly Caking coal. Despite the fact that each particular grade of coal is best suited for a particular use, there is a great deal of interchange by end-users, according to the changing relative prices of different grades.

Where the value of a particular type of coal to the user is based upon the properties mentioned above, these properties have no direct bearing on the actual costs of production. Costs of production vary from one coalfield to another and from one mine to another. Thus a high-cost mine may produce coal of low commercial value, whilst a low-cost mine may produce highly valued coal. This consideration has a bearing on the future of the industry, with regard to the planning of production and pricing policy.

Apart from a small and reducing amount of coal produced by opencast mining (planned to fall to 2 million tons annually), most British coal is deep-mined. This involves the sinking of expensive shafts, for access and ventilation.

British coal is generally at a depth of more than 1,000 feet (305 metres). At such depths conditions are hot, ventilation costs are high, gas is generated, and the risk of disaster from explosions is high. This makes for high insurance costs.

Absenteeism is relatively high in coal-mining, due to the rigorous conditions of work, which adversely affect health and efficiency.

The differences in costs already mentioned stem from the fact that coal seams vary in thickness and accessibility from one field or mine to another. As they are worked they become increasingly inaccessible. Layers of rock have to be removed to reach the coal seams, and this unproductive work increases as the most accessible seams are worked out. This factor is an important inducement

119

to mechanisation in the cutting, loading and conveying of coal, in an effort to keep down rising labour costs.

Apart from the high cost of ventilation, there is the cost of lighting and the provision of underground transport. The traditional pattern of British mining, with a multiplicity of owners and individual underground transport systems, each working on a 'room and pillar' system (parallel borings interconnected by horizontal cuttings, now being changed to 'longwall advancing', or working of the coalface on a broad, advancing front) tended to make transport in British mines much more costly than on the Continent, where straight roads were run through bigger, concentrated holdings. The 1945 Reid Committee on the coal industry reported that whereas the average haulage worker in Holland handled 25 tons per day, 25% of haulage workers in Britain could only handle 5 tons.

The age of the mine, the amount of accessible coal left in it, and plans for its place in the future activity of the industry as a whole, all affect decisions on how much capital to sink into tunnels, ventilation equipment, transport underground and housing for the coalminers.

A long-standing problem, inherited by the National Coal Board from the prewar industry, is the insularity and immobility of coalminers in most districts. These factors bedevil both labour relations within the industry and plans for the reorganisation of production.

2. History and Development

During the twentieth century it has been becoming more difficult and expensive to extract coal, whilst at the same time competition from alternative sources of power has been growing. Nevertheless, coal still supplies nearly three-quarters of Britain's primary energy, the other one-quarter being provided by oil, and to a lesser extent by water power and nuclear energy.

Great changes have taken place in the production of coal and the pattern of its use since 1913. Total production rose from approximately 10 million tons in the period 1800–10 to 80 million in the period 1850–60, 147 million in 1880, 225 million in 1900, and reached a peak of 287·4 million tons in 1913, of which one-third (98·3 million) was exported or used in ships' bunkers and 189·1 million were used at home. Employment in the coal industry in that year was 1,107,000.

Early development, as compared with other countries, contributed to the relative difficulty in working the seams, and the consequent necessity to maintain productivity per man by means of a high level of investment.

Furthermore, after World War I, foreign and shipping demands for British coal fell. This was a result of the emergence of alternative fuels, such as oil; competition from Holland, Poland and Japan, who had stepped in to fill the breach whilst Britain was engaged in the war effort; and more efficient fuel techniques, which resulted in a reduced consumption of coal per unit of production.

By 1925 production had fallen to 243·2 million tons, but 172·7 were still used at home. The total used abroad (exported and used in ships' bunkers) had fallen to 70·5 million tons. In 1929, the peak pre-slump year for Continental coal production, British production had only risen to 257·9 million tons, of which 177·3 million were used at home and 80·6 million abroad. Employment, which had reached a peak of 1,260,000 in 1924, had fallen to 1,087,000 in 1925 and reached 932,000 in 1929.

During the trade slump which followed, production and employment suffered greatly. By 1933 production reached 207·1 million tons (150·4 used at home, 56·7 used abroad), a fall of approximately one-fifth. Employment in mid-1932 had fallen by 41% to 550,000, but rose by the end of 1933 to 772,000.

The best year of the 1930s was 1937, when production was 240·4 million tons, of which 56·3 million went abroad and 184·1 were used at home. Employment had remained fairly stable at 778,000. This production was secured more efficiently than that of 1929 and 1933. Whereas output per man-year was 277 tons in 1929 and 268 in 1933, it had risen to 309 tons in 1937. In 1929 output per man-shift was 1·08 tons; in 1937 it was 1·17 tons.

The improvements in productivity from the time of the depression to the beginning of World War II were achieved by reducing the labour force, increasing the process of mechanisation in cutting and conveying, and by a gradual process of amalgamation of smaller into larger units, carried out under the shadow of various Government-sponsored rationalisation schemes, in an attempt to solve the problem of excess capacity. Were it not for the fact that industrial production had been expanding, the amount of coal used at home would not have remained as stable as it did, and the industry's problems would have been even more formidable.

The nationalisation of the coal industry in 1947 was intended to solve the industry's problems of excess capacity, irrational pattern of production, bad labour relationships and lack of capital for mechanisation.

The National Coal Board have embarked upon a course of concentrating production on the most efficient fields and pits and extending the process of mechanisation into loading as well as cutting and conveying.

The average thickness of coal seams fell from 51 in. (1,300 mm.) to 49 in. (1,250 mm.) between 1946 and 1960, but as production becomes concentrated on the more workable seams this has since risen back to 51 in. (1,300 mm.) in 1971. The thickest seam in 1971 was in Northumberland – 12 ft. 6 in. (3·8 m.): the thinnest was in Durham – 1 ft. 6 in. (0·46 m.).

Production was at a postwar peak of 222 million tons in 1956 and fell gradually by about one-third to 142·4 million tons in 1970–71. The number of mines operated by the N.C.B. fell from 850 to 292 during this period; exports fluctuated between the 1953 peak of 16·6 million tons to a 1967–68 low point of 2·0 million tons; the labour force fell from the postwar peak of 724,000 in 1948 to 287,200 in 1970–71; output per man-year rose from 298 tons in 1956 to 463 tons in 1970–71, whilst output per man-shift increased from 1·23 tons to 2·21 tons. This has been achieved by rationalisation, reorganisation, research and development and mechanisation. By March 1970 92% of deep-mined coal was obtained by mechanical cutting and power-loading techniques. Remote control techniques have also been developed and research is being done on new techniques, such as 'retreat mining'.[1] Nevertheless, the 1967 Fuel Policy White Paper forecast a coal production target of about 120 million tons by 1975, and the N.C.B. in March 1969 informed the Select Committee on the Nationalised Industries that to achieve its long-term objective it needed to raise output per man-shift to 2·55 tons (51 cwt) by 1970–71. Future viability depends greatly, therefore, on continued productivity increases and further concentration on the most economic pits and coal faces and on low-cost opencast mining.

During the late 1960s the N.C.B. involved itself in a variety of diversified

[1] 'The coal-face revolution', *D.T.*, 20 Oct. 1971 and 'Is coal making its comeback?', *The Sunday Times*, 12 Sept. 1971.

activities, some of them in coal-based chemical industries. These were seen as logical developments into profitable areas, with which coal was technologically connected.[1] In October 1971 Lord Robens, former N.C.B. Chairman, suggested the development of N.C.B. growth along the lines of the 'coalplex' concept, being researched in the U.K. and U.S.A., viz., an integrated power and chemical complex, based on coal.[2]

The salient points brought out above are summarised in Table 3.1.

Table 3.1 *Production, exports, productivity and manpower in the British Coal Industry*

Year	Output (million tons)	Used at Home (million tons)	Used Abroad (million tons)	No. of mines	Labour force (thousand)	Output per man-year (tons)	Output per man-shift (tons)
1913	287·4	189·1	98·3	3,024	1,107	260	0·98
1925	243·2	172·7	70·5	2,479	1,087	224	0·90
1929	257·9	177·3	80·6	2,146	932	277	1·08
1933	207·1	150·4	56·7	1,782	772	268	1·12
1937	240·4	184·1	56·3	1,807	778	309	1·17
1945	182·8	176·4	6·4	1,570	709	246	1·00
1956	222·0	217·6	9·7	850*	703	298	1·23
1959	206·0	201·9	4·1	789*	665	294	1·33
1961	190·5	191·8	5·8	698*	575	315	1·45
1962	197·4	191·2	4·8	669*	551	342	1·55
1963	195·8	194·0	7·5	611*	524	346	1·64
1964	193·6	187·1	6·0	576*	498	361	1·72
1965/6	182·8	181·1	3·6	483*	455·7	380·7	1·81
1966/7	173·0	169·9	2·5	438*	419·4	390·4	1·83
1967/8	170·9	165·5	2·0	376*	391·9	413·8	1·95
1968/9	160·6	165·0	3·1	317*	336·3	453·9	2·13
1969/70	147·4	159·1	3·5	299*	305·1	456·7	2·17
1970/71	142·4	148·3	3·0	292*	287·2	463·0	2·21

* Only includes mines worked by the N.C.B. Excludes small mines, licensed out, with less than thirty men underground.

(Sources: *Econ.*, 4 Aug. 1962; N.C.B., *50 Questions and Answers on British Coal*, 1962; D. Burn, *The Structure of British Industry*, 1958, vol. 1, p. 117; *D.T.*, 4 and 16 Jan. and 30 Apr. 1962; N.C.B. *Annual Reports;* N.C.B. *Memorandum*, Nov. 1971)

3. Location

There are eighteen coalfields in the United Kingdom, three of which account for about three-quarters of total production and one of which accounts for nearly half of the total output: see Table 3.2.

[1] *D.T.*, 29 May 1969.
[2] 'A long-term use for coal', *F.T.*, 14 Oct. 1971.

Table 3.2 *Coalfields in the U.K., in order of importance, with the 17 controlling N.C.B. Areas and output percentages for 1969/70*

Coalfields	N.C.B. Areas	% of 1969/70 output
Yorkshire, Derbyshire and Nottinghamshire	— North Yorkshire Barnsley Doncaster South Yorkshire North Derbyshire North Nottingham South Nottingham	49·5
Northumberland and Durham	Northumberland North Durham South Durham	14·7
South Wales (including Somerset and Forest of Dean)	West Wales East Wales	9·1
South Derbyshire and Leicestershire Warwickshire	South Midlands	6·7
North Staffordshire Cannock and South Staffordshire Shropshire	Staffordshire	6·2
Lancashire Cumberland North Wales	North Western	5·0
Lanarkshire Ayr and Dumfries The Lothians	Scottish South	4·6
Fife	Scottish North	3·4
Kent	—	0·8

The geographical location of the coalfields and their allocation amongst the 17 N.C.B. administrative Areas are illustrated in Fig. 3.1. Also shown are the number of pits and employees in each Area, percentage of total 1969/70 output from each Area and 1969/70 Area profits or losses. Also shown is the new Oxfordshire coalfield, verified in August 1971, which added 5 billion tons to British reserves – 50% of those hitherto known. Unfortunately, the new reserves may not have arrived at a suitable time to ensure their commercial exploitation.[1]

The geographical location of these fields and their allocation amongst the nine administrative Divisions of the National Coal Board (following the nationalisation of the industry in 1947) may be seen in Fig. 3.1.

[1] *Econ.*, 14 Aug. 1971, p. 68.

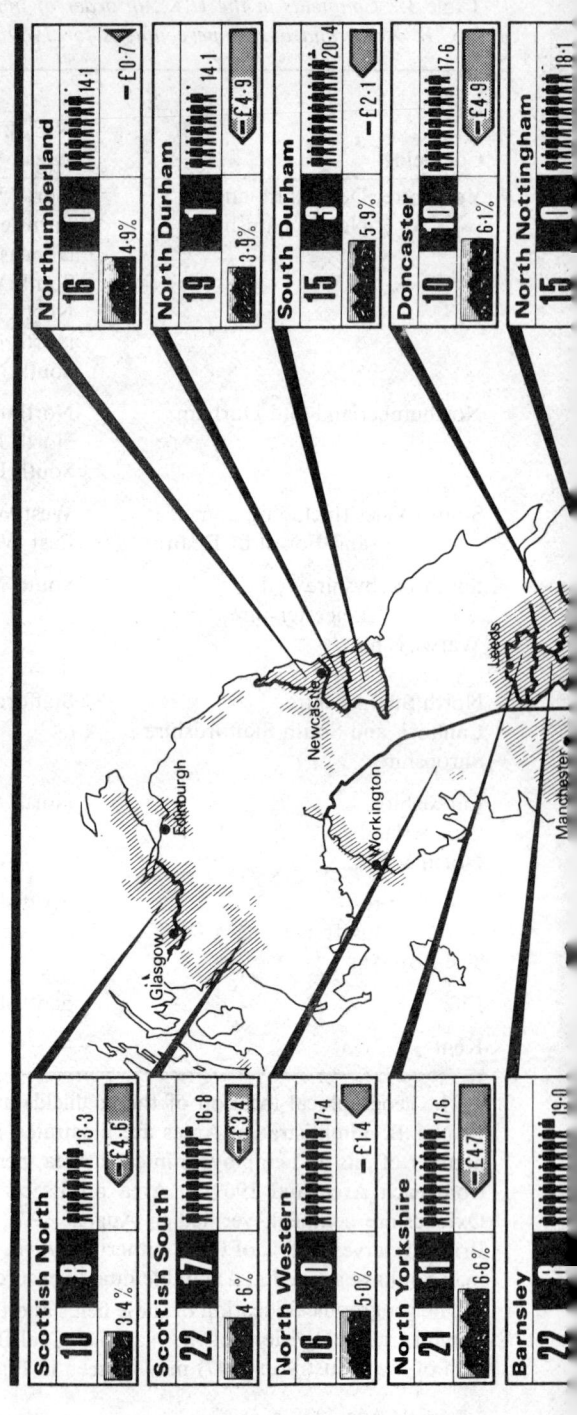

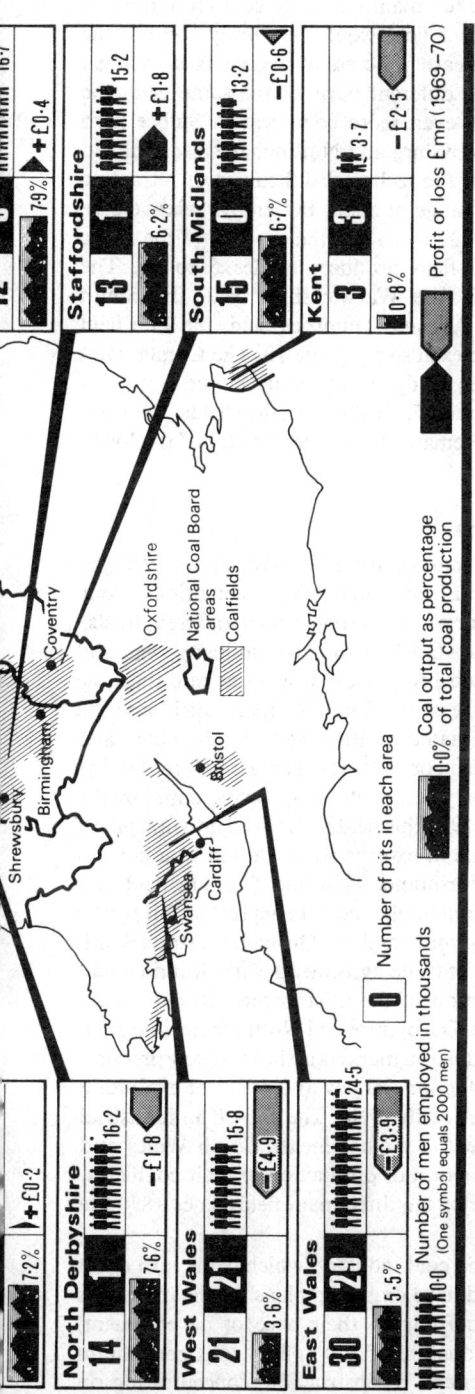

Fig. 3.1. *Coalfields, N.C.B. Areas and their relative importance*
(Source: *Econ.*, 14 Nov. 1970, p. 68, and 14 Aug. 1971, p. 68)

In most of the coalfields several of the ten main grades of coal are mined. A full list of all the grades found in each coalfield would needlessly confuse the student. In view of the vast differences in ease of access to the seams as between one field and another, and even between different parts of the same field, the results in terms of costs and returns are even more complicated. Suffice it to note at this point that the Yorkshire, Derbyshire and Nottinghamshire coalfield is the main field which suffers least from the technical difficulties of retracting seams. It produces the lower half of the range of coals, but enjoys relative ease of access. The South Wales coalfield produces coals in the top half of the range and the Northumberland and Durham field produces grades 5 to 10. The Cannock and South Staffordshire field, the Warwickshire field, the South Derbyshire and Leicestershire field, the Ayr and Dumfries field, the Fife field and the Lothians field all produce almost exclusively grade 10. The Cumberland field produces grade 7; the North Wales field, mostly grade 8; the Forest of Dean field, grade 9; the Somerset field, grade 6. Of the five other fields, the Kent coalfield produces grades 2 to 5 and the remainder produce several of the lower grades.

4. Changes in Location of Production

It is inevitable that changes in the various markets for different coals and changes in the relative ease of extraction in different fields will result in fluctuations, from one period to another, in the relative importance of production in different fields.

During the period before World War I, when the coal industry was still expanding, the three main fields expanded production at a faster rate than the others. This was particularly so in the case of the South Wales coalfield and the Northumberland and Durham field, situated as they were on the coast and catering for about three-quarters of British coal exports. The Yorkshire, Derby-shire and Nottinghamshire field, with easily accessible coal, was favoured by the proximity of the industrial Midlands. By 1914 this field had moved into first place.

In the interwar period the steep decline in exports was reflected in a curtail-ment of production, especially in the Northumberland and Durham field and the South Wales field – the latter, supplying bunker coal, being further hit by the changeover in ships from coal to oil. Northumberland and Durham overtook South Wales in the production league by reason of trade agreements with Scandinavian countries, and because of the sterner action of the mine owners in depressing conditions of employment. The Yorkshire, Derbyshire and Nottinghamshire coal-field, catering mainly for domestic and industrial markets in the relatively prosper-ous Midlands, continued to increase production, largely as a result of exploiting the deep coal of the south-eastern section of the field. The fall-off in industrial demand in the areas of high unemployment in the north-east, South Wales and Scotland further contributed to the contraction of production in their coalfields.

The changes in the relative importance of the three main fields since 1870 are shown in Table 3.3.

Since the postwar nationalisation of the coal industry, which came into effect in January 1947, the National Coal Board have drawn up plans for the industry's future and have classified the mines according to their pace of development. The 1950 Plan for Coal envisaged a production of 240 million tons per annum by 1961–65, as a result of reorganisation and reconstruction, concentrating on larger, more productive units, with new sinkings and increased mechanisation.

This estimate was reduced, in 1956, to 230 million tons by 1965. At the end of 1960 the estimated future coal target was reduced by the Chairman of the N.C.B. to 200 million tons by 1965.[1] This reduction in planned estimates was influenced largely by the increasing share taken by oil as a primary source of British fuel requirements since the war. From 1956 to 1960 the share of oil increased from 15% to 25%.[2] Following the 1967 Fuel Policy White Paper, the target for 1975 was again cut back to 120 million tons. By 1970 the increasing inroads made by oil in the total energy mix (47% of about 330 million tons coal-equivalent, as compared with 42% for coal) and the increasing relative price-competitiveness of oil for electricity generation had resulted in suggestions that a 1980 target of about 80 million tons – erased from earlier drafts of the 1967 White Paper because of its likely effects on the industry's morale – might very well become realistic.[3] Such is the confusion of the changing situation, however, with the exploration of North Sea gas and oil, that by end-1971 the 1980 N.C.B. target share for coal, out of an enlarged total energy mix of about 430 million tons coal–equivalent, had risen to between 32% (or 140 million tons) and 26% (or 110 million tons). The repercussions of the lengthy 1972 coal strike may, however, result in a downward revision of the target share for coal[4]: one post-strike estimate envisaged a target as low as $12\frac{1}{2}$% or 55 million tons for 1981 (see Fig. 3.2). It was conceded, however, that contraction, or the threat of it, might encourage management and workers to improve machinery maintenance and intensity of utilisation, thus making more pits commercially viable, reducing costs and maintaining a larger share for coal. Many of the privately-owned U.S. pits have per head productivity five times higher than the N.C.B. average, largely due to more efficient maintenance practices for mine machinery.[5]

The cumulative surpluses and deficiencies in the major deep-mining regions and for the opencast mining, coal products and brickworks sectors are shown in Fig. 3.3. For purposes of comparability with data for earlier years, the Areas have been grouped as closely as possible within the boundaries of the nine pre-1967 N.C.B. Divisions.[6]

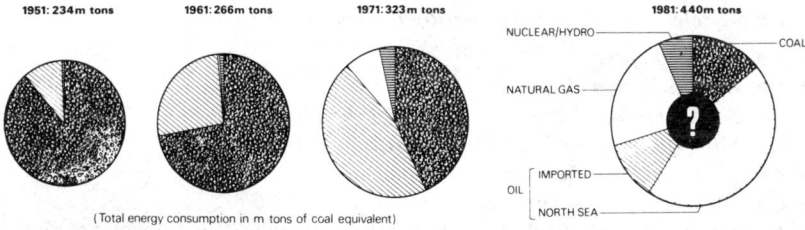

Fig. 3.2. *Britain's changing fuel mix*
(Source: *Econ.*, 1 April 1972, p. 58)

[1] *The Times*, 6 Dec. 1960.
[2] *Brit. O.H.*, 1962, p. 275.
[3] *F.T.*, 12 Jan. 1970.
[4] *Econ.*, 4 Dec. 1971, p. 77; 'The true cost of propping up coal', *Obs.*, 20 Feb. 1972.
[5] 'Energy: where is Britain heading?', *Econ.*, 1 April 1972, pp. 58–9.
[6] For further data on 1963–71 changes in productivity, absenteeism and tonnage lost through disputes, for numbers of pits and employees at end-1971 and for regional profits and losses for 1970–71, see charts in *Econ.*, 8 Jan. 1972, pp. 53–4.

Table 3.3 *Changes in the relative importance of the three main coalfields since 1875*

	1875	1913	1937	1971
Yorkshire, Derbyshire and Nottinghamshire C.F.	2	1	1	1
Northumberland and Durham C.F.	1	3	2	2
South Wales C.F.	3	2	3	3

Fig. 3.3. *N.C.B. losses and gains since nationalisation. January 1947 to 1970/71 (£ million)*
(Source: *N.C.B. Annual Report, 1970/71*, vol. 2, pp. 6, 7)

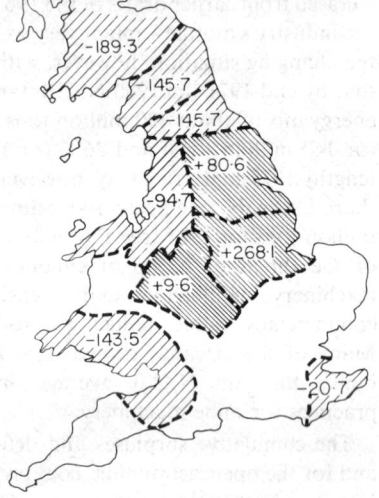

Cannock
Opencast   + 112·5 (1952–1970/71)
Coal Products + 16·3 (1963/64–1970/71)
Brickworks   − 1·1 (1962–1970/71)
TOTAL   − 107·9

▨ Cumulative surplus (£M)
▨ Cumulative deficit (£M)

5. Further Reading and Sources

Footnote references to daily and weekly journals are not repeated.

N.C.B. *Annual Reports.*
N.C.B. *Coal in Britain Today*, 1971.
N.C.B. *The Coalfields of Britain: Location of the Main Types of Coal.*
N.C.B. *Fifty Questions and Answers on British Coal*, 1961, 1962.
N.C.B. *Memorandum*, May 1965.
N.C.B. *20-Year Review of the Coal Industry: 1947–1966/67.*
E. S. SIMPSON, *Coal and the Power Industries in Postwar Britain.* Longmans. 1966.

THE COAL INDUSTRY: Stage II: Structure and Organisation

1. Interwar Problems, Combination and State Intervention

The major problems facing the coal industry after World War I may be listed as follows:

(*a*) embittered industrial relations and deficient channels of communication between labour and management;

(b) excess capacity, inelastic supply conditions and price instability in an industry in which a great deal of capital was inextricably sunk and in which more was needed as seams became exhausted and less accessible;

(c) lack of rational organisation in the ownership and working of a multiplicity of mines;

(d) long-term competition from export competitors, from increasing efficiency in fuel-using techniques and from newer, more flexible and sometimes cheaper sources of power.

During the years immediately following World War I domestic prices for coal were kept down by Government control, whilst export demand on the Continent was high and resulted in inflated prices for the coal quotas permitted for export. The trade depression which followed in 1920 brought down export prices for a while, but they rose again during the sixteen-weeks' U.S.A. coal strike in 1922 and during the French occupation of the Ruhr in 1923. As a result, wages were relatively higher than in many other industries and the labour force became artificially expanded. Towards the end of 1924 a greater degree of normality in the world coal supply had been established and this depressant to the British coal industry was fortified by the return to the Gold Standard at an inflated rate of exchange for sterling, which tended to make British export prices high in terms of foreign currency. The Government granted a subsidy of £23 million to the mine owners for nine months from August 1925, but when it ended the owners became involved in a bitter and grossly mishandled dispute over wages and hours of work. This led to the General Strike and a seven-month stoppage in the coal industry, which weakened its competitive position still further. By this time the German and Polish coal industries had been reorganised on more rational lines and productivity had been raised in those and other European coal producing areas.

During the late 1920s the industry in Britain suffered from great price instability, which was influenced by the heavy burden of overheads, fluctuations in demand for a multiplicity of different coals, fierce price competition and difficulties in storing large stocks or in curtailing production. This factor led to attempts at price control by loose associations of mine owners, based on the cartel system developed by the Rhenish-Westphalian Coal Syndicate of the Ruhr. The most notable attempt was the 'Five Counties Scheme', operated in the Midlands in 1928 on a voluntary basis. Each member was given a basic tonnage and a monthly quota for production; a levy of threepence per ton was raised on coal mined, and from this a subsidy of two shillings per ton was granted on coal exported from the area. Apart from this scheme of direct control over output, other schemes for output and price control were tried in Scotland and South Wales. These schemes tended to fail because of the individualism and lack of cohesion amongst the members.

The first major step of Government intervention in the industry came with the Coal Mines Act of 1930, which attempted to compel the industry to strengthen control over prices and output, established a Coal Mines Reorganisation Commission for the reorganisation and amalgamation of the mines, repealed the statutory eight-hour day and created a National Industrial Board to discuss wages. A Central Council of colliery owners was set up to fix quarterly production quotas for the various districts and to coordinate the work of the District Executive Boards, which determined the standard tonnage for each mine, the proportion of that to be produced each month, and the minimum prices for various types of coal. Quotas were transferable between districts; the subsidising of exports by levies was abolished; and in 1934 restrictions on quotas for export were raised and were kept separate from home market quotas. In 1936 the Government pressed the industry into establishing coordinated central selling organisations in each district. The long-term effects of these measures were to preserve the inefficient firms, to lower general efficiency and to delay a national reorganisation of the industry into bigger, more productive units.

The second major step in Government intervention came in 1938, with the nationalisation of royalties. In an attempt to facilitate the compulsory amalgamations which the 1930 Act had failed to do, and also to relieve the industry of the burden of paying royalties, the surface landowners' rights to extract royalties were bought up by the State for £66½ million. At the same time a new Coal Commission was established with powers to compel reorganisation. Its activities, however, were disrupted by the advent of World War II.

During World War II the industry again came under Government control. In 1944 a Technical Advisory Committee was set up and issued the Reid Report in 1945. This called for a complete reorganisation of the industry to eliminate uneconomic units and to make possible the thorough mechanisation of the rest. It recommended the establishment of a body to carry out the necessary administrative changes.

Largely on the basis of the Reid Report, the third major step in Government intervention was taken in 1946 with the passing of the Coal Mines (Nationalisation) Act, which came into effect in January 1947. Under the Act, a public corporation, the National Coal Board, was set up to administer the industry. The N.C.B. members are appointed by the Government. Under the Act the Board were entrusted with securing the efficient development of the nation's coal production, with making coal available in such quantities and at such prices as may seem to them best calculated to further the public interest, and with seeing that over an average of good and bad years the industry pays its way. Compensation amounting to £164·6 million for the mines and their immediate equipment was paid to the former owners. In addition about £224 million has been paid for houses, railways, brickworks, by-product plants, coke ovens and other coal industry ancillaries. The Board are responsible for redeeming the capital value of this compensation and for paying the interest on it. During the first fourteen years of operation, the N.C.B. paid £300 million in interest and £74 million of the principal. These payments have to be provided before the Board can declare their annual surplus or deficit. The N.C.B. is empowered to raise capital, including working capital, by borrowing from the Secretary of State for Trade and Industry, the statutory limit being (in 1971) £900 million. Internal resources account for the major proportion of investment, however. Capital reconstruction of the industry's finances was provided by the 1965 Coal Industry Act, as a result of which £415 million of the industry's accumulated deficit was written off. By end-March 1970 the total liabilities outstanding – for which interest is payable to the Secretary of State – totalled £689·7 million. The N.C.B. have the exclusive monopoly to mine coal in Great Britain, but they may license the working by private firms of 'small mines', employing not more than thirty underground workers. Apart from the main statutory duties listed above, the Board have the additional duty of ensuring the safety, health and welfare of the industry's employees.

2. Structure of the Industry
(a) Number and size of plant

When the N.C.B. took over the administration of the coal industry there were about 1,500 mines, employing 697,000 workers, producing 190 million tons (including 9 millions of opencast coal), with an output per man-shift of 1·03 tons. By 1961 there were 1,150 mines, employing 562,000 workers, producing 190·5 million tons, with an output per man-shift of 1·45 tons. Of these, 698 were operated by the N.C.B., the remainder being worked under licences. By 1970/71 mines operated by the N.C.B. had been reduced to 292, with a labour force of 287,200, producing 142·4 million tons. The peak year for closures was 1968/69 when 55 pits employing 27,000 men ceased working. These 292 mines in 1970/71 were all controlled by the seventeen Area Directors, except for three in Kent, which were controlled by a general manager. A typical Area is, in fact, a large industrial concern. They produce, on average, nearly 10 million tons of coal per year, employ up to 20,000 men and have an average turnover of about £50 million.

This reduction in the number of mines and workers was allied with an increase in mechanisation (particularly in the loading process, which was almost entirely manual in 1946), to result in increased productivity per man.

The Reid Committee had advocated the merging of individual mines into compact units of manageable size, and the Samuel Commission of 1925 showed that larger mines were generally more productive. Nevertheless, a breakdown of the statistics provided by their report showed that such large mines were more common in the newer, developing coalfields, where conditions of extraction were easier. Furthermore, the 1952 figures of the Ministry of Fuel and Power's *Statistical Digest*, 1953, showed that some of the highest outputs per man-shift (40 cwt and over) came from some mines employing less than fifty workers and from only eight of the 528 mines employing more than 500 workers.[1]

Despite these anomalies, arising out of the variegated natural conditions prevailing in the industry, the fact remains that the expensive mechanical techniques necessary to raise productivity can only be utilised efficiently in large units, working to capacity, so as to minimise unit costs.

By 1972 the N.C.B. was leasing about 200 small mines, under licence to private enterprise owners and groups. These may employ no more than thirty underground workers, and so the largest employ about sixty persons in all. About eighty of these licensed mines were in South Wales, about thirty in Scotland and the rest scattered about the coalfields. In 1971 the private mines produced about 1¼ million tons, compared with 2½ million tons in 1969. Half is sold to power stations.[2]

(b) Concentration of production

As we saw earlier, 49·5% of production in 1969/70 came from the Yorkshire, Derbyshire and Nottinghamshire fields. The Northumberland and Durham field provides about 15% and the South Wales field about 9%.

[1] Reviewed in *The Structure of British Industry*, ed. D. Burn, vol. 1, pp. 140–1, 1958.
[2] *D.T.*, 4 Feb. 1972.

Of the 1,334 mines operated by the N.C.B. and under lease in 1952, the North-Eastern Division (Yorkshire coalfield) controlled 146. It had the second highest output per man-shift, the second lowest costs per ton and the fourth largest estimated reserves. By mid-1962 it had an accumulated profit of £89·4 million. The East Midlands Division (Nottinghamshire and North Derbyshire field and South Derbyshire and Leicestershire field) controlled 104 mines. It had the highest output per man-shift (o.m.s.), the lowest costs per ton and the third largest estimated reserves. Its accumulated profits by mid-1962 were £178 million. The Northern (Northumberland and Cumberland) Division controlled 97 mines, had the fourth highest o.m.s., the fourth lowest costs per ton and the seventh highest reserves. By mid-1962 it had an accumulated deficit of £37·1 million. The Durham Division controlled 159 mines, had the eighth highest o.m.s., the seventh lowest costs per ton and the lowest reserves. It had a cumulative deficit of £72·5 million by mid-1962. The South Western Division (South Wales coalfield) controlled the greatest number of mines: 322. It had the lowest o.m.s., the highest costs per ton and the largest estimated reserves. Its cumulative deficit was £87·8 million by mid-1962, despite the fact that it enjoyed the highest proceeds per ton (355p).[1]

3. Administrative Organisation

In May 1971, towards the completion of successful British negotiations to join the European Economic Community, Britain was formally assured that her eventual membership of the European Coal and Steel Community (E.C.S.C.) need not require any major alteration in the form of ownership or organisation of the N.C.B.[2] Nevertheless, the E.C.S.C. would eventually assume a supranational authority over the industry.

Within the existing framework established by nationalisation, Parliament has ultimate authority. The Secretary of State for Trade and Industry, who appoints the members of the N.C.B., is responsible to Parliament. The Minister may give directions of a general character to the Board on matters affecting the public interest; he has to give his approval to programmes of reorganisation and development and to the exercise and performance of the N.C.B.'s functions of training, education and research. The Board must provide the Secretary of State with information and the facilities to verify such information.

Apart from the ultimate external control exercised by Parliament, the 1946 Act aimed at providing a channel through which consumers could exert an influence on the N.C.B. Accordingly, two consumers' councils were set up, the Industrial Coal Consumers' Council and the Domestic Coal Consumers' Council. The membership of the former represents the N.C.B. and industrial consumers, merchants and bulk suppliers of coal, coke and manufactured fuel. The latter council represents similar bodies, concerned with the domestic markets. Both councils have the duty of considering any matter affecting the sale or supply of these fuels. They may report on these matters to the Secretary of State, when necessary.

The internal organisation of the industry is based on the 'line-and-staff' or hierarchical and advisory principle. There is a direct line of command from the

[1] Based on Burn, *op. cit.*, p. 115 and *Obs.*, 3 June 1962.
[2] *F.T.*, 6 May 1971.

N.C.B. to the individual mine *via* the seventeen Area Directors (and one general manager, for Kent), the Deputy Directors and Production Managers (in control of mining operations), and the individual colliery managers. From April 1967 Divisions and Groups ceased as managerial units. The new pattern adopted was a streamlined three-tier pattern, with N.C.B., Areas and Collieries, in place of the old five-tier pattern with N.C.B., 9 Divisions, 41 Areas, 160 Groups and individual Collieries. At each level, from the N.C.B. downwards, there were, at first, staffs of functional advisory experts dealing with production, labour problems, marketing, finance, manpower and welfare and science, responsible primarily to the management at that level. The Fleck Committee, appointed in 1953 by the N.C.B. to report on its organisation, found in 1955 that the basic principles of organisation were correct, but that members of the N.C.B. and the Divisional Boards should assume responsibility right down the line for a particular function. This recommendation was later adopted. There are now twelve functional departments (see Fig. 3.4) in the three-tier pattern adopted in April 1967.

Provision was made in the 1946 Act for joint consultation. The National Union of Mineworkers is the biggest trade union in the industry. It participates with the smaller unions in the consultative committees at each colliery, in some areas, in each division, and in the National Consultative Council in London. The colliery manager is chairman of the pit committee; at all higher committees the Board themselves are represented.

The N.C.B. do not have a monopoly of sales or distribution. About half the industrial market is supplied direct from the seven Regional Sales Offices. In some regions the Board sell direct to householders from their seventy-nine Sales District retail depots. Most of the wholesale and retail distribution is, however, in the hands of private firms.

4. Price Policy

The N.C.B. have interpreted their duties under the 1946 Act as being to price coal on the basis of overall average cost. Furthermore, relative prices are intended to reflect the qualities of the various grades and their worth to consumers. House or domestic coals are sold in the twenty-three zones into which the country is divided. Within each zone the prices are uniform, calculated on the national average cost, plus the average of transport costs to selling points in the zone. Industrial coals are given a points value, based on calorific and caking properties. This is combined with a national average cost for the particular grade at the pit-head, and there is a 'coalfield adjustment' to the price, to average out transport costs of that coal to its various markets.

There has been much controversy over the policy of 'average costing'. As long-term costs are tending to rise, marginal cost is higher than average cost. Whereas in a free market price would equate demand with marginal cost for each grade and each pit, causing supply to respond to demand fluctuations, under the present system this process is hindered. The least efficient or submarginal pits are not immediately seen to be making a loss; the more efficient are not immediately seen to be making a profit. Closures and/or expansion are not forced upon the N.C.B. on the basis of profitability in individual pits from year to year. During the first ten years of nationalisation demand (at prices based on average cost) tended to exceed supply (see Fig. 3.5 on p. 135). Consequently,

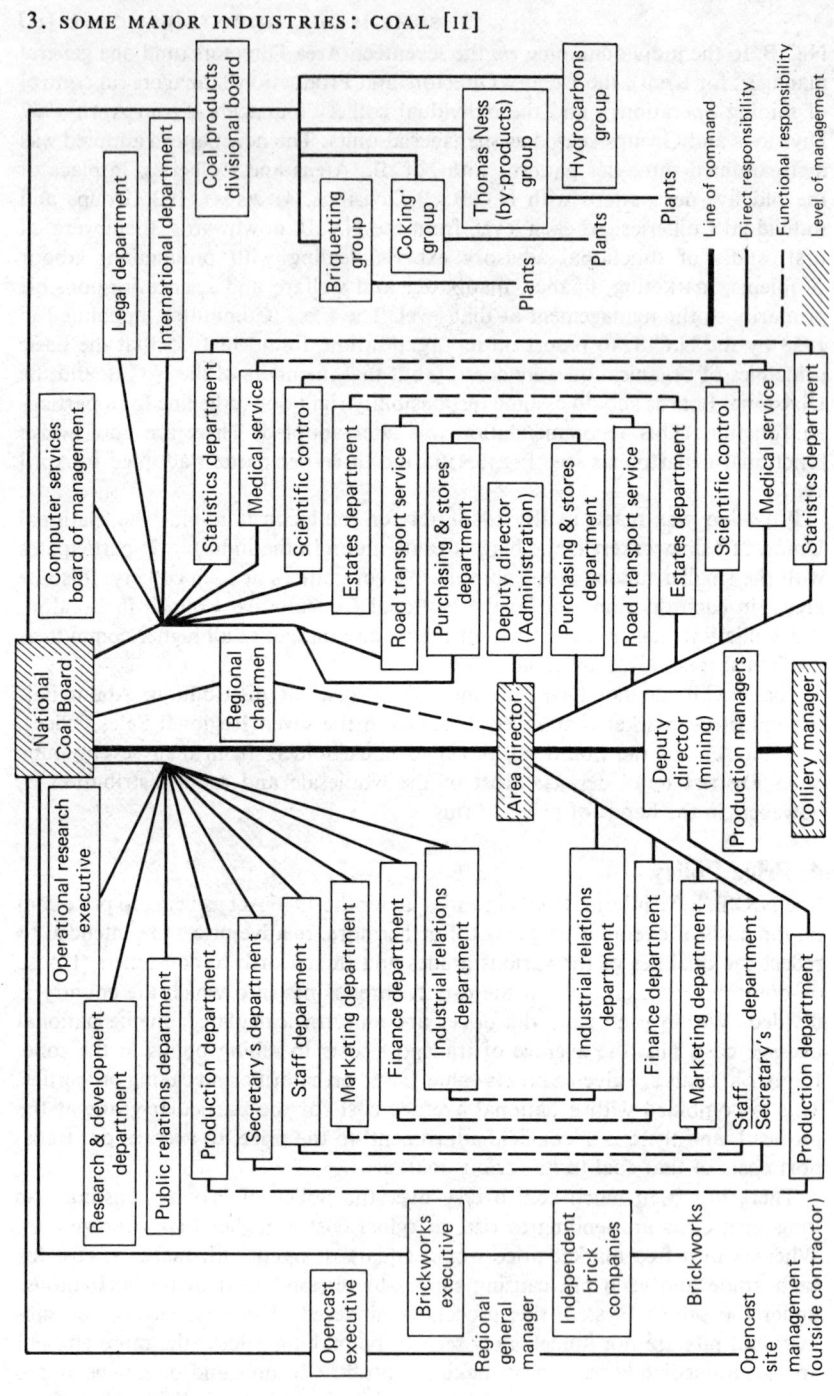

Fig. 3.4 *N.C.B. organisation from April 1967*
(Source: *Public Relations Department, N.C.B.*

the industry did not receive the 'surplus profit' which would have accrued if prices had been based on marginal costs. The N.C.B. were, in fact, subsidising other industries, such as iron and steel. They could have accumulated profits to finance reorganisation and mechanisation. Since 1956 demand has tended to fall short of supply, at average cost prices (see Fig. 3.5). The N.C.B. have been obliged to curtail capacity and concentrate production on fewer, more mechanised and more productive pits, as stockpiles of unsold coal mounted up.[1] Coal consumption declined by 12% from 1951–61, whilst oil consumption trebled.[2]

In favour of average cost pricing is the argument that a nationalised industry must be expected to bear costs which would not be born by private industry. These might be justified as being in the national interest, as, for example, by subsidising industries which use coal; by preserving a valuable national asset at a higher level of production than would be possible at marginal cost pricing; by keeping to a minimum the social dislocation of drastic pit closures. On the other hand, it may be argued that had higher prices been charged, based on marginal cost, then not only would reduced demand and output have caused the industry to contract by rationalising output much sooner on to the most efficient pits, but also the N.C.B. would have been able to accumulate financial surpluses, which could have eased the social problems of contraction and might have financed profitable diversification into other ventures.

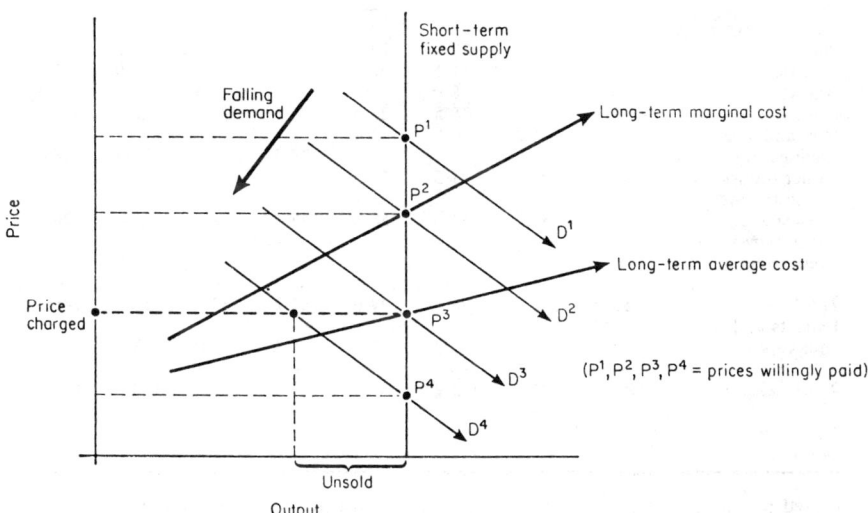

Fig. 3.5. *Implications of average cost pricing.*

5. The Main Users of Coal

Between 1947 and 1956 inland coal consumption in Britain rose by an average annual rate of 3 million tons. From 1956 to 1959 inland sales fell sharply, and large stocks were created. This was largely due to more efficient utilisation of

[1] See C. Jones, 'Coal caught in transition', *Stat.*, 4 June 1965, pp. 1545–6 (with charts).
[2] *Econ.*, 8 Sept. 1962, p. 947.

coal and increased competition from oil. Output has been curtailed and demand since 1960 has exceeded supply, and stockpiles have been reduced. Table 3.4 shows the pattern of production, inland consumption and exports between 1947 and 1970/71. There has been a big reduction in the use of coal by the gas industry, the railways, iron and steel, engineering and domestic and miscellaneous categories, but a large increase in its use by the electricity industry. This is now the industry's biggest market, accounting for about 50% of sales.

Opencast mining was reduced during the years of stockbuilding, but, since the rundown in stocks has occurred, it was planned to bring opencast production up to about 10 million tons in 1971/72. As it is completely mechanised, opencast is highly productive and profitable. Between 1960 and 1970 average opencast cost was £4·55 per ton, as compared with £5·20 for deep-mined coal: the operating profit was £1·17½ per ton.

Table 3.4 *Production, inland sales and exports (1947–1970/71 (million tons)*

	1947	1958	1960	1963	1964/65	1967/68	1969/70	1970/71
Production								
Deep-mined	186·6	201·5	186·0	189·7	185·5	163·8	140·8	134·1
Opencast	10·0	14·3	7·6	6·1	7·0	7·1	6·6	8·3
Total Production	196·6	215·8	193·6	195·8	192·5	170·9	147·4	142·4
Inland Consumption†								
Gas	22·7	24·8	22·3	22·1	19·7	13·6	6·0	3·5
Electricity	27·1	46·1	51·1	66·8	68·5	69·2	75·9	73·5
Railways	14·6	10·3	8·9	4·9	3·5	0·6	*	*
Coke ovens	19·8	27·8	28·5	23·5	25·6	23·2	25·5	24·7
Iron and steel	8·7	4·2	3·8	2·4 ⎫				
Engineering and				⎬ 24·7	20·0	20·8	18·5	
other industries	31·0	29·5	27·5	23·5 ⎭				
Domestic and miscellaneous	61·1	59·7	54·6	50·8	45·0	38·9	27·0	24·0
Other conversion industries	–	–	–	–	–	–	3·9	4·2
Total	185·0	202·4	196·7	194·0	187·2	165·5	159·1	148·3
Exports and ships' bunkers	5·5	4·9	5·5	7·6	5·4	2·0	3·5	3·0
Total Consumption	190·5	207·3	202·2	201·6	192·6	167·5	162·7	151·3
Change in Stocks	+6·1	+8·5	−8·6	−5·8	−0·1	+3·4	−15·3	−8·9

(Based on material in *Brit. O. H.*; *Ann. Abs. Stat.*; N.C.B., *50 Questions and Answers on British Coal*, 1961; N.C.B. *Annual Reports*)
* Included in Domestic and miscellaneous.
† From Dec. 1970 includes imported coal.

6. Further Reading and Sources

Footnote references to daily and weekly journals are not repeated.

Coal Mining: Report of the Technical Advisory Committee (Reid Committee), Cmd 6610. H.M.S.O. 1945.

P. SARGENT FLORENCE, *Industry and the State*. Hutchinson's University Library. 1957.

N.C.B. *Annual Reports and Accounts.*

N.C.B. *Coal in Britain Today.* 1971.

N.C.B. *50 Questions and Answers on British Coal.* 1961.

N.C.B. *Report of the Advisory Committee on Organization* (Fleck Committee). 1955.

N.C.B. *20-Year Review of the Coal Industry: 1947-1966/67.*

E. S. SIMPSON, *Coal and the Power Industries in Postwar Britain.* Longmans. 1966.

N.C.B. *Report of the Advisory Committee on Organization* (Fleck Committee). 1955.

ROYAL COMMISSION ON THE COAL INDUSTRY. *Report.* 1925.

THE IRON AND STEEL INDUSTRY: Stage I

1. Technical Background

Commercial iron and steel are different forms of the same metal, in which the impurities have, by various processes, been controlled and adjusted. Carbon is the key element. Metal with more than 2% carbon is usually known as iron; with under 2% of carbon it is usually termed steel.

The smelting of iron ore, before the eighteenth century, was performed with charcoal. The resultant product was a bloom, having a steel shell and iron core. The latter was cast into moulds or hammered until it was malleable. This process was slow and costly in terms of timber.

During the eighteenth century the Darbys of Shropshire successfully applied pit coal as a fuel, in the form of coke. The resultant pig iron was suitable for cast-iron hollow-ware. In 1783-84 Henry Cort developed a technique for producing malleable iron, which hitherto had to be hammered. This was by means of the puddling furnace, which was coal-fired, and in which the impurities were removed from pig iron. In 1790 Homfray developed the refinery, in which surplus silicon was removed from the pig iron before the puddling stage. This vastly reduced the amount of pig needed to produce a given amount of wrought iron. By 1800 the steam engine using coal was supplanting water power in the various processes, such as rolling. These developments away from timber (charcoal) and water power to coal had repercussions on the location of the industry.

Demands for quality, fuel economy and speed fostered further technological developments during the nineteenth century, which led from the production of wrought iron to that of steel. The major innovations in this respect were as follows:

(*a*) In 1856 Sir Henry Bessemer developed the steel converter process, in which molten pig could be turned into steel without additional fuel. Carbon and silicon were removed from the molten iron by forcing air through it. This was much quicker than the puddling process, and the finished product was far more durable and versatile.

(*b*) By 1869 Siemens and Martin had developed the open hearth steel furnace, in which an intensely hot flame was directed from burners on to the materials in the hearth. This process could be used for steel scrap, as well as pig.

137

(c) In 1878 Gilchrist and Thomas developed the 'basic process', in which both the Bessemer and Siemens-Martin techniques could utilise ores with a high phosphorous content, which were plentiful and cheap in Britain. The furnaces were lined with a basic material, refractory bricks, to produce this basic steel. Acid steels are still produced for certain purposes, but mild basic steel is cheaper and more workable.

Since those early developments, there have been modifications and improvements. For example, electric arc furnaces are increasingly being used, in which the open hearth heat process is generated by an electric arc, producing intense heat and being useful for smelting scrap and producing special steels; in the Bessemer converter process, the Kaldo and L.D. techniques, in which oxygen replaces or boosts the air flow, are being increasingly used.

The main processes and resultant products are summarised in Fig. 3.6.

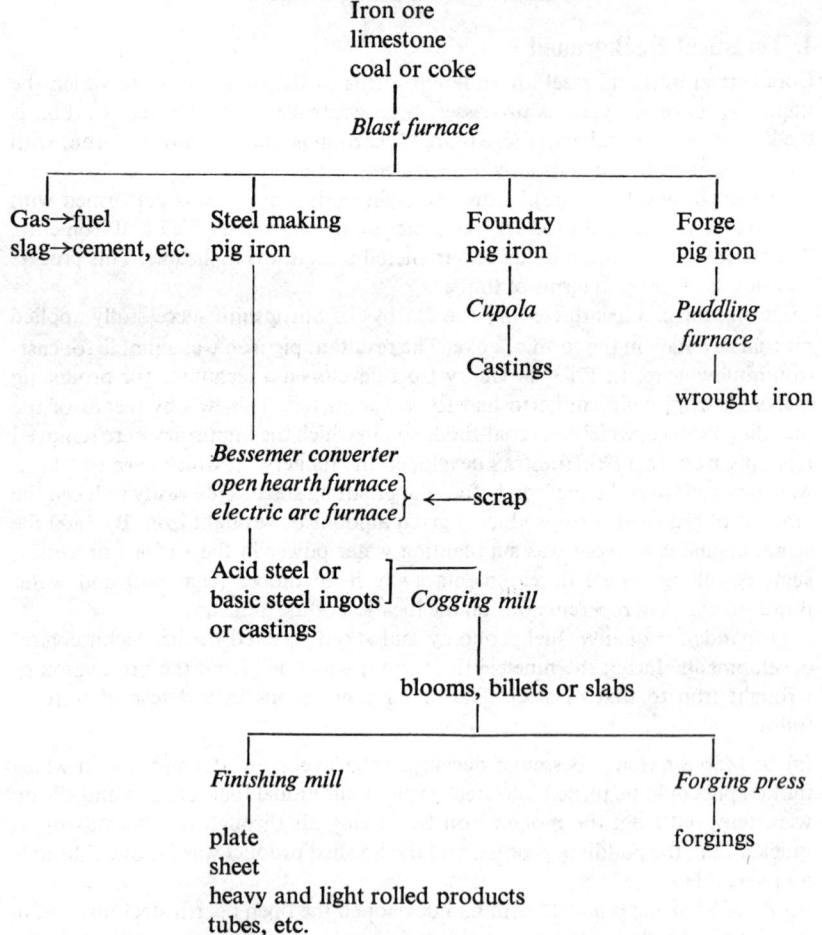

Fig. 3.6. *Iron and steel processes*

Steel is really a family name, covering a multitude of compositions and alloys. The finished steel is turned out in a wide variety of shapes, but for general purposes the finishing stages of the industry may be classified into four main sections:

1. Flat steel plates, sheets and tinplate.
2. Heavy rolled steel products (sections, bars, rails, beams, girders, etc.).
3. Light rolled steel products (sections, medium and narrow strip, bars, rods for wire).
4. Steel tubes.

There are many other miscellaneous shapes, produced by castings and forgings.

In all stages of iron and steel making, the capital investment required for plant is very high, due to the factors of heat, weight and pressure. Great economies may be reaped from vertical integration of processes, such as in heat conservation and reduction of transport costs (from 4 to 6 tons of raw materials are used to produce 1 ton of finished steel). Great economies may also be reaped by enlarging the scale of production at each process. According to the finished product and the site, an integrated steel plant will cost from £80 to £130 per ton of capacity, or up to £15,000 per worker employed. However, as the degree of integration and the size of steel plants increases it has been found that the capital cost per ton of capacity falls.[1] This is an additional factor making for the increasing size and integration of new plant. Any works which is to make full economic use of equipment must nowadays operate on a scale of at least 1 million tons annually.[2]

In view of the great amount of capital involved in the industry, location decisions are very important. An error made in siting a new plant uneconomically is not easy to put right. A great deal of capital will be sunk in the project.

2. History and Development

In 1865 United Kingdom crude steel production was 0·10 million tons. In 1870 it was 0·22 million tons, compared with a world production of 0·51 million. By 1900 it was 4·90 million (world production 27·69).

World War I stimulated steel production in the belligerent states and in others which wanted to be self-sufficient. In 1920 the ratio of U.K. to world production had fallen to 9·07 million out of 71·42 million tons. After the postwar recovery in world steel production in 1924–25, the British industry suffered from excess capacity and was producing only 7·33 million tons in 1930 (world production 93·59 million). In 1938 U.K. production rose to 10·40 million tons.

---

[1] *Development in the Iron and Steel Industry; Special Report, 1961, Iron and Steel Board, 1961*, pp. 22 and 113. For further data and results of technological studies on the iron and steel industry, see C. F. Pratten and R. M. Dean, *The Economies of Large-scale Production in British Industry*, 1965, ch. 4, and C. F. Pratten, *Economies of Scale in Manufacturing Industry*, 1971, ch. 12.

[2] *Development in the Iron and Steel Industry; Special Report, 1961, Iron and Steel Board, 1961*, p. 99; 'Rationalising steel', *Stat.*, 30 July 1965, p. 291. The previously mentioned study by Pratten and Dean considered that the minimum optimum plant sizes and their relative shares of U.K. total capacity in 1964 for bulk steel production and sheet steel production were 2 million tons capacity (7%) and 3 million tons capacity (50%), respectively. Due to the pace of technological change, these optimal capacities were revised considerably upwards in the later study by C. F. Pratten, *Economies of Scale in Manufacturing Industry*, 1971, ch. 12.

From 1945 to 1970 crude steel production increased by about 136% (11·82 million tons to 27·9 million tons). During the same period world production rose from 112·83 million tons to 583 million tons. By 1970 world capacity was chronically in excess of actual production: the consequent export competition was leading to suggestions for price stabilisation agreements and 'orderly markets'. The U.K. steel industry lay in fifth place after the U.S. (115 million tons), U.S.S.R. (113 million tons), Japan (90 million tons) and West Germany (43 million tons). The relative importance of the major steel producing countries and of the major European steel firms may be seen in Fig. 3.7.

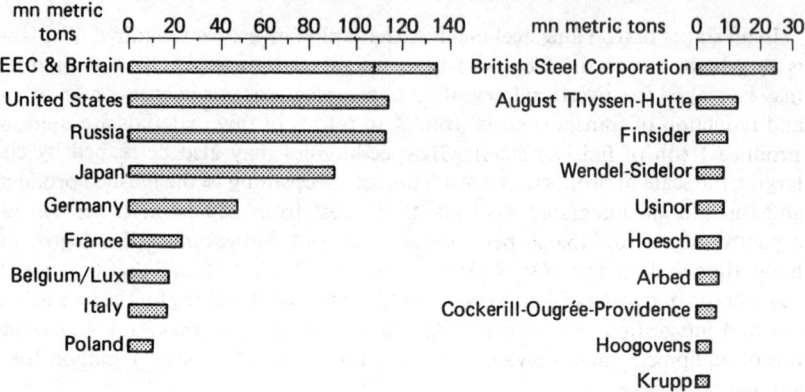

Fig. 3.7 *Relative importance of the major steel producers.*
(Source: *Econ.* 9 Oct. 1971, p. 74)

In the production of pig iron, which rose from 6·76 million tons in 1938 to 17·4 million in 1970, a relative change towards imported ores was noticeable. During the same period consumption of imported ore rose from 4·63 million tons to 19·6 million tons. Consumption of home ores, which have a much lower iron content, rose from 11·72 to 17·06 million tons in 1960 and fell to 11·7 million tons in 1970.

In steel making, the consumption of pig iron rose from 4·84 million tons in 1938 to 16·0 million in 1970; consumption of scrap rose from 6·13 million to 15·1 million tons.

Since World War II the labour force in bulk steel production (i.e. excluding iron foundries) has been expanded (from 218,000 in 1946 to 326,000 in 1960 to 337,000 in 1970) but there has been a relative decline in the proportion of process workers and a relative increase in the proportion of maintenance and administrative workers (which were, by 1960, 49% of the total). This decline in process workers has been mainly in the sheet and tinplate processes, where mechanisation progressed most.

In both iron and steel output has risen faster than manpower, since World War II. The rise in productivity per man in iron foundries from 1954 to 1960 was 22%. The annual pig iron output per blast furnace rose from 68,600 tons in 1938 to 299,400 tons in 1970. The rise in productivity per man-year in steel from 1954–70 was 33%; annual output per open hearth furnace rose from

36,500 tons in 1938 to 102,800 tons in 1970. In both iron and steel combined, the output per man-hour worked rose by 37% from 1954–64 and has continued to increase.

This increase in productivity has been made possible by heavy capital investment and new techniques. From 1946 to end-1960 £1,113 million was spent on development. In 1961 £199 million was spent – out of schemes totalling £500 million, approved by the Iron and Steel Board and due for completion by the end of 1965. Between 1955 and 1967 over £1,750 million was spent on capital development, raising capacity to 31 million tons.

The British Steel Corporation, which took over thirteen major steel firms, with more than 90% of crude steel capacity (but much less in special steels) and about 70% of the industry's labour force on re-nationalisation in mid-1967, embarked on a £1,000 million investment programme from 1968–75, aimed at raising capacity to between 30 and 34 million tons by 1975 – of which about 20 million would represent new capacity, thus permitting a closing down of about 14 million tons of old plant capacity. Much of this investment has been heavily criticised in having been geared to the further development of existing sites (termed 'heritage' development), particularly the 'Anchor' scheme at Scunthorpe (based on the existence of large blast furnaces) and at Llanwern and Port Talbot in South Wales and on Teesside. These were found to be cheaper to develop than new, integrated, deepwater coastal sites, but with the exception of Port Talbot and Teesside they do not have deepwater docking facilities and are not ideally sited for the use of cheap, high grade imported ores. Furthermore, some of the 'heritage' capacity which they absorb will become obsolete and have to be replaced: by then the new extensions will present further 'heritage' investment attractions, and so the vicious circle of suboptimally efficient investment might continue.[1] By end-1975 the B.S.C. was expected to have expanded Scunthorpe, Port Talbot and Teesside into three complexes, operating at about the 7 million tons per year level. However, this contrasts with projects in Japan for deepwater coastal plant capacities in the 15–20 million ton range, with capital costs per ton capacity of about £30 (compared with £100 in the U.K.) and with labour productivity in terms of crude steel per man-year of about 600–700 tons (compared with under 150 tons in the U.K.).[2]

In 1971 the B.S.C. and the Government were considering £1,700 million development plans for the period 1975–80. A maximum capacity of 43 million tons was envisaged, after discarding the remaining 8 million tons of open hearth capacity. The extra 20 million tons of new capacity was to be centred on Teesside, where further £700 million, 7 million ton extensions would create a 12 million ton complex, and a £1,000 million, 12 million ton new, deepwater coastal complex somewhere along the south-east coast – probably Foulness, Sheerness or the Portsmouth–Southampton area, with easy access to the Home Counties and north-west Europe. In March 1972, these development plans were in danger of being shelved.[3] In May 1972 the Minister for Industry announced the Government's decision on the planned capacity for 1980. This was to be

---

[1] K. Warren, 'Coastal steelworks – a case for argument?', *The Three Banks Review*, June 1969; 'How British steel lost its appeal', *Obs.*, 26 Sept. 1971; 'Steel men say goodbye to the seaside', *S.T.*, 13 July 1969.
[2] *Obs.*, 26 Sept. 1971, *op. cit.*
[3] *S.T.*, 19 March 1972; 'Steel supply: the arithmetic of the '70s', *F.T.*, 11 May 1972; 'Now it's a steel contraction plan', *Econ.*, 13 May 1972, pp. 89–90.

between 28m. tons and 36m. tons – the first figure representing the Government's more pessimistic view of the B.S.C.'s ability to increase exports and retain its home market share and the latter figure representing the B.S.C.'s more optimistic view. Decisions on major new projects and locations were expected by late 1972.

Blast furnace sizes have been increased; large-scale 'tonnage' oxygen plant has been developed to supply the gas more cheaply and to cater for the L.D. and Kaldo Bessemer techniques and for speedier processes in open hearth production; larger electric arc furnaces have been developed to produce special alloy and stainless steels; developments have been made in continuous castings, which allows slabs and billets to be formed directly from molten steel, omitting the expensive cogging mill process; developments have also occurred in the computer control of processes, in vacuum treatment processes, in continuous ironmaking processes and continuous spray steel-forming and in the direct reduction of iron ore without the use of coking coal (in which there was a world shortage) and with the use of gas, oil or solid fuel. A hoped-for break-through in this respect was in the development of low-cost electricity.[1]

The salient points in this section are brought out in Table 3.5.

3. Location

Transport costs are of the utmost significance to the iron and steel industry. From 4 to 6 tons of raw materials are required for each ton of steel produced; nearly 10% of the price of steel delivered to users in Britain is accounted for by transport costs and about 50% of production costs consist of raw materials. The location of plant is therefore of fundamental importance to the economical operation of the industry.

The ideal location would be within easy reach of raw materials, fuel, water, labour and markets for the finished products, reinforced by their function as a source of scrap. Because of the 'weight-losing' factor, the greatest pull has been, and continues to be, from raw materials.

The competing pulls are influenced by changes in technique. The change from charcoal to coking coal, for example, altered the direction of the locational pull of fuel. The relative strength of this pull, however, is lessened as more efficient usage of coal takes place (in 200 years coal requirements per ton of pig iron have fallen from 10 tons to 1·4 tons in 1920 and 0·85 tons in 1960). Iron ore require-ments have not changed much for any given type of ore, but the exhaustion of non-phosphoric home ores in the old centres has led to greater dependence on imported ores and scrap. Furthermore, 2 to 3 tons of ore are required per ton of pig iron, making the relative pull of ore much stronger than that of coal. The trend towards bigger, integrated plants has reinforced the pull of raw materials, and has made correct siting of new works more important. Water is an important raw material, used in several processes. As much as 126 tons per ton of steel may be required, but with expensive recirculation plant this may be cut down to about 4 tons, thus reducing the relative pull of water supplies.

Where old sites have lost some of their original advantages, they may still exert a stronger pull than new sites, such as Northamptonshire and Lincolnshire,

[1] *Econ.*, 11 Jan. 1969, p. 57; *Obs.*, 16 Oct. 1968; *D.T.*, 1 Feb. 1968; *F.T.*, 20 March 1969, 24 Nov. 1971, 11 Oct. 1971, 13 April 1970.

Table 3.5 *Production, labour, productivity, investment and processes in the Iron and Steel Industry*

	Units	1870	1900	1920	1938	1945
Production						
World crude steel production	mill. tons	0·51	27·69	71·42	–	112·83
U.K. crude steel production	,,	0·22	4·9	9·07	10·40	11·82
Pig iron production	,,	–	–	–	6·76	–
Imported iron ore consumed	,,	–	–	–	4·63	–
Imported manganese ore consumed	,,	–	–	–	–	–
Home ore consumed‡	,,	–	–	–	11·72	–
Pig iron consumed in steel making†	,,	–	–	–	4·84	–
Scrap consumed in steel making§	,,	–	–	–	6·13	–
Labour						
Number on pay roll‡‡ (excluding iron foundries)	thous.	–	–	–	222	–
Number at work**‡‡	,,	–	–	–	–	–
Productivity						
Iron foundry production	mill. tons	–	–	–	–	–
Iron foundry pay roll	thous.	–	–	–	–	–
Pig iron output per furnace††	'000 tons	–	–	–	68·6	–
Steel output per man-year	'54 = 100	–	–	–	–	–
Steel output per open hearth furnace	'000 tons	–	–	–	36·5	–
I. & S. output per man-hour§§	'54 = 100	–	–	–	–	–
Investment						
Capital expenditure (current prices)	£m	–	–	–	–	–
Capital expenditure (1964 prices)	,,	–	–	–	–	–
Crude steel capacity	mill. tons	–	–	–	–	–
Crude steel capacity scrapped	,,	–	–	–	–	–
New steel capacity installed	,,	–	–	–	–	–
Blast furnace capacity	,,	–	–	–	–	–
Blast furnace capacity scrapped	,,	–	–	–	–	–
Blast furnace capacity installed	,,	–	–	–	–	–
Pattern of steelmaking processes						
Open hearth production	%	–	–	–	–	–
Bessemer (including VLN) production	,,	–	–	–	–	–
Electric production	,,	–	–	–	–	–
Pneumatic (L.D., Rotor, Kaldo) production	,,	–	–	–	–	–
Others (Tropenas and Stock Converters) production	,,	–	–	–	–	–
Oxygen consumption in I. & S. industry	m. ft.³	–	–	–	–	–

* 53 week statistical year, except world crude steel production, which is based on the calendar year.   § Steel scrap and cast iron scrap.   † Molten and cold.

‡ Raw ore and raw equivalent of calcined ore.   ** Excludes members on holiday and away sick, etc.

†† 1960 onwards includes the weighted output of iron made at integrated steelworks.   *P* Provisional.

‡‡ Labour from 1957 to 1964 excludes labour employed in the production of welded tubes over 16 in. outside dia.

§§ Crude calculation on basis of labour force and crude steel and pig iron production.

After 1967 (renationalisation) the I. & S. Statistics Bureau figures are for the public sector only: D.E.P. national figures are not strictly comparable to B.I.S.F. pre-nationalisation data.

Table 3.5 Production, labour, productivity, investment and processes in the Iron and Steel Industry (cont.)

	Units	1946	1954	1955	1956	1957	1958*	1959	1960
Production									
World crude steel production	mill. tons	—	220·4	265·7	279·3	288·0	267·0	300·7	339·2
U.K. crude steel production	„	—	18·5	19·8	20·7	21·7	19·6	20·2	24·3
Pig iron production	„	7·76	11·9	12·5	13·2	14·3	13·0	12·6	15·8
Imported iron ore consumed	„	5·90	12·7	12·3	13·7	15·4	13·6	12·4	16·1
Imported manganese ore consumed	„	—	0·4	0·4	0·4	0·3	0·3	0·3	0·5
Home ore consumed†	„	12·76	15·9	16·4	16·4	17·0	14·9	14·8	17·1
Pig iron consumed in steel making†	„	6·09	9·8	10·5	11·2	12·0	10·8	11·1	13·9
Scrap consumed in steel making§	„	7·65	10·3	11·1	11·2	11·5	10·4	10·9	12·6
Labour									
Number on pay roll‡‡ (excluding iron foundries)	thous.	281	300·5	309·3	318·6	321·4	298·9	308·7	326·1
Number at work**‡‡	„	—	290·2	299·2	308·4	311·0	289·2	298·6	315·8
Productivity									
Iron foundry production	mill. tons	—	3·7	3·9	3·9	3·7	3·5	3·5	4·0
Iron foundry pay roll	thous.	—	142·4	145·6	139·8	136·9	125·5	127·1	130·9
Pig iron output per furnace††	'000 tons	—	118·6	126·4	131·9	145·5	146·8	160·6	185·4
Steel output per man-year	'54 = 100	—	100·0	106·3	108·6	110·0	102·9	106·5	115·5
Steel output per open hearth furnace	'000 tons	—	58·0	60·1	61·1	64·7	71·1	74·4	77·5
I. & S. output per man-hour§§	'54 = 100	—	100	...	...	...	...	...	123
Investment									
Capital expenditure (current prices)	£m	15·33	52	58	75	95	105	99	146
Capital expenditure (1964 prices)	„	—	77	81	96	114	124	115	165
Crude steel capacity	mill. tons	—	18·9	20·2	21·3	22·5	23·7	24·1	25·8
Crude steel capacity scrapped	„	(Cumulative 5·87) →							
New steel capacity installed	„	10·35	(Cumulative 17·32) →						18·88
Blast furnace capacity	„								
Blast furnace capacity scrapped	„	(Cumulative 6·37) →							
Blast furnace capacity installed	„	(Cumulative 14·9) →							
Pattern of steelmaking processes									
Open hearth production	%	—	87·7	87·3	87·2	87·7	87·6	85·8	84·5
Bessemer (including VLN) production	„	—	6·3	6·5	6·3	6·0	6·0	7·0	8·0
Electric production	„	—	5·0	5·5	5·9	5·6	5·8	6·7	6·9
Pneumatic (L.D., Rotor, Kaldo) production	„	—	—	—	—	—	—	—	0·1
Others (Tropenas and Stock Converters) production	„	—	1·0	0·7	0·7	0·7	0·6	0·5	0·5
Oxygen consumption in I. & S. industry	m. ft.³	—	...	...	—	—	4,672	6,864	9,667

Table 3.5 *Production, labour, productivity, investment and processes in the Iron and Steel Industry (cont.)*

	Units	1961	1962	1963	1964*	1970*
Production						
World crude steel production	mill. tons	348·0	351·9	376·9	395·0	P 583·0
U.K. crude steel production	,,	22·1	20·5	22·5	26·2	27·9
Pig iron production	,,	14·7	13·7	14·6	17·3	17·4
Imported iron ore consumed	,,	14·7	13·0	14·3	17·6	19·6
Imported manganese ore consumed	,,	0·4	0·4	0·3	0·4	0·4
Home ore consumed	,,	16·5	15·3	15·0	16·3	11·7
Pig iron consumed in steel making†	,,	12·6	12·1	13·3	15·7	16·0
Scrap consumed in steel making§	,,	11·5	10·5	11·7	13·4	15·1
Labour						
Number on pay roll‡‡ (excluding iron foundries)	thous.	317·5	304·8	304·9	316·9	337·0
Number at work**‡‡	,,	306·9	294·3	294·9	304·9	n.a.
Productivity						
Iron foundry production	mill. tons	3·8	3·5	3·7	4·1	3·8
Iron foundry pay roll	thous.	127·2	121·3	119·8	122·7	116·0
Pig iron output per furnace††	'000 tons	179·8	186·8	228·6	257·0	299·4
Steel output per man-year	'54 = 100	106·0	104·8	111·4	120·9	133·0
Steel output per open hearth furnace	'000 tons	78·9	89·6	95·2	100·4	102·8
I. & S. output per man-hour§§	'54 = 100	...	...	...	137	
Investment						
Capital expenditure (current prices)	£m	199	170	77	55	excludes
Capital expenditure (1964 prices)	,,	214	178	79	55	schemes costing less
Crude steel capacity	mill. tons	26·5	27·7	28·6	29·7	than £100,000
Crude steel capacity scrapped	,,	...	...	...	...	
New steel capacity installed	,,	...	...	...	...	
Blast furnace capacity	,,	...	...	...	...	
Blast furnace capacity scrapped	,,	...	...	...	...	
Blast furnace capacity installed	,,	...	...	...	...	
Pattern of steelmaking processes						
Open hearth production	%	83·2	81·6	76·0	70·5	47·2
Bessemer (including VLN) production	,,	8·5	8·7	7·8	6·6	1·0
Electric production	,,	7·5	7·2	9·2	11·2	19·5
Pneumatic (L.D., Rotor, Kaldo) production	,,	0·3	2·1	6·7	11·4	32·2
Others (Tropenas and Stock Converters) production	,,	0·5	0·4	0·3	0·3	0·1
Oxygen consumption in I. & S. industry	m. ft.³	10,915	16,968	23,468	29,983	40,550

(Sources: *Development in the Iron and Steel Industry: Special Report, 1961*, I, and S. Board; *Development in the Iron and Steel Industry: Special Report, 1964*, I. and S. Board; *The British Steel Industry*, B.I.S.F., 1962 and 1964; *Steel in the 1960s*, B.I.S.F.; Memorandum from B.I.S.F. Statistical Services Dept., May 1965; *Iron and Steel Industry Annual Statistics for the United Kingdom, 1970*, Iron and Steel Statistics Bureau; *Ann. Abs. Stat.*)

which have raw materials. This is because immense investment of capital has been sunk in them, which cannot easily be transferred elsewhere. Also they tend to develop external economies or special advantages, such as the provision of services, the growth of skilled labour pools, etc.[1]

Following the pre-B.S.C. industry report of the Benson Committee it became clear that the Clyde Valley and Shotton (Flintshire) would not be expected to grow appreciably as iron and steel producing areas. The main band of plants

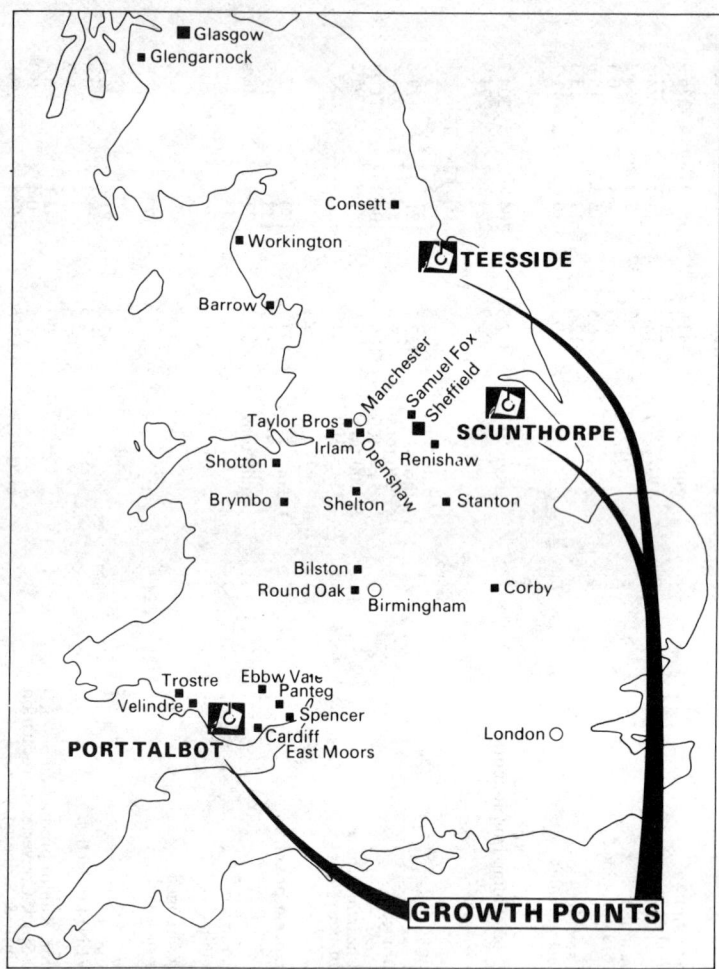

Fig. 3.8. *Location of the iron and steel industry.*
(Source: *Econ.* 25 Jan. 1969, p. 58)

---

[1] 'British steel', *Econ.*, 30 July 1966, pp. 454–5; *Econ.*, 5 Aug. 1967, pp. 512–3; *Econ.*, 25 Jan. 1969, pp. 57–8.

from the North-West, through the Midlands to the South-East was visualised as continuing steel production, largely based on scrap from nearby industrial markets: many plants in the finishing processes were obsolete and tied to declining industries; many blast furnaces were based on declining reserves of low-grade ores and/or were too far from coastal access to cheap, high-grade imported ores. This left the three areas of South Wales, Teesside and Humberside as the major growth points for pig iron, crude steel and finished steel (see Fig. 3.8). The B.S.C.'s £3,000 million development plan, announced in December 1972,[1] visualised this second major stage in the industry's rationalisation as leading to a capacity of 33–35 million tonnes by the end of the decade and 36–38 million tonnes by 1985. The five major existing steel plants at Port Talbot, Llanwern, Scunthorpe, Lackenby and Ravenscraig were to reach optimum capacity: a new steel complex was to be located on the south bank of the Tees.

Lancashire and Flintshire have no local ore, but the Manchester Ship Canal provides access to imported ores. The heavy centres of population and industry in the Midlands and Lancashire constitute a source of scrap and outlets for the sheet and light rolled products.

Yorkshire and the Sheffield area rely now mainly on Scunthorpe pig iron and scrap. Original location here was due to local ores, forests for charcoal, coal and fast-flowing streams for power and water. The Sheffield district produces high value alloy steels and complex forgings, as well as cutlery and machinery. Local skills exert a strong, retentive locational pull.

Table 3.6 *Regional production of pig iron and crude steel, 1970, with sources of supply (thousand tons)*

Region	Pig Iron Production	Crude Steel Production	Pig Iron used		Scrap used
			Molten	Cold	
North	3,681·5	4,750·7	3,082·1	147·5	2,021·8
Yorks. and Humberside	3,337·9	7,228·0	3,093·4	249·1	4,589·0
E. Midlands	1,449·3	1,088·3	835·3	37·8	354·3
South-East	304·0	38·0	–	0·1	39·3
Wales	5,796·5	8,448·1	5,312·4	373·6	3,905·1
West Midlands	649·3	2,063·2	482·4	161·6	1,651·0
North-West	355·8	922·6	338·2	42·0	683·5
Scotland	1,818·2	3,330·3	1,290·8	559·2	1,877·3
TOTAL	17,392·6	27,869·2	14,434·6	1,570·9	15,121·3

(Source: *Iron and Steel Industry Annual Statistics for the United Kingdom, 1970,* Iron and Steel Statistics Bureau.

The North-East Coast, which was the biggest steel producer before World War II, is now third, after South Wales and the Yorkshire and Humberside region. The industry was originally attracted by Durham coking coal and local Cleveland ore. It is still the biggest pig iron producer, using mainly imported ore. Access by sea, a heavy concentration of population, shipbuilding and heavy engineering industry (as markets and source of scrap) and local skills tend to exert strong secondary locational attractions.

[1] *Steel: British Steel Corporation: Ten Year Development Strategy,* Cmnd 5226, Feb. 1973. espec. paras. 6–10, 17–19, 31–2, 35.

Scotland relies primarily on imported ores and scrap. The original attractions were black band ironstone and local coking coal. In view of limited supplies of coking coal now, and exhausted ore deposits, retention of the industry here is due mainly to accessibility by sea to foreign ores, local skills and concentrations of shipbuilding and heavy engineering industry and population as markets and scrap suppliers.

The Black Country originally offered the attractions of Staffordshire ore, charcoal supplies and limestone. Once the biggest steel smelting district in Britain, it now has no local ore. Some comes from Oxfordshire, but most raw material comes from local scrap. Present locational attractions are the concentration of metal-using industries as markets and sources of scrap and local skills. Because of the distances from the coast, transport costs are kept to a minimum by concentrating on specialist finishing processes. A great deal of crude steel is brought in from other districts to be processed by the specialist plants here, the emphasis being on high value-to-weight products.

South Wales and Monmouthshire once had the advantages of local ore in the Brecon Beacons and suitable coal in the valleys. The older plants in the valleys have, as local ores became exhausted, gone over to imported scrap and pig iron and scrap from other districts. These cold metal plants produce mainly semi-finished steel. The area continues to hold steel plants and has attracted many new ones since the end of the 1930s. The new plants, attracted by access to imported ores, local coal, water, skilled labour and the near-by motor industry in the Midlands, are sited mainly near the ports, are primarily concerned in producing strip, sheet and tinplate, and are generally fully integrated, large-scale plants.

4. Changes in Location of Production

(a) Ore production

The pattern of home ore production has altered considerably in the last 100 years. In 1857, out of a total production of 9,573,000 tons, almost all (9,515,000) came from the old fields. These were the basis for the original industry. By 1907 the old fields were producing 10,080,000 tons out of a total of 15,732,000. There had been a big decrease in almost all these fields, but a threefold increase in the Yorkshire, Northumberland and Durham area (6·3 million) and a 50% increase in the Cumberland and Lancashire area (1·69 million). Meanwhile, over a third of total production came from new fields. Northamptonshire produced 2,689,000 tons; Lincolnshire produced 2,152,000 tons and Oxfordshire, Rutland and Leicestershire produced 811,000 tons.[1]

By 1960 the remaining old fields were only producing 900,000 tons out of a total of 17 million. Half of this was in the Cleveland field and the rest was mainly from the North-West coast and partly from the Glamorgan field. More than 95% came from the newer fields. Of these, Northamptonshire remained the largest producer, at 8·46 million tons; Lincolnshire was second, with 5·6 million;

[1] *Steel*, July 1958, B.I.S.F.

Oxfordshire produced 1·33 million tons and Rutland and Leicestershire 0·79 million.[1]

(b) Pig iron production

The change in the pattern of home ore production, even though accompanied by an increase in imports of higher content ore from abroad to the old pig iron centres, has resulted in a change in the pattern of pig iron production. The low content of British ores in the newer fields increased the locational pull of ore in relation to that of coal.

From the 1870s to World War I the North-East Coast increased its share of pig iron production from 29% to 38%. Scotland was still second by World War I; output in South Wales and Staffordshire had declined, through exhaustion of local ores; production in the new iron ore areas had reached 41% of the total.

Since World War I there has been a shift in emphasis from old inland centres to the coast, for access to imported ores, especially in South Wales and Scotland. The locational pull of the low-content new fields increased their share of total pig iron production by World War II. However, the increasing emphasis since then on imported ores has reduced the relative share of these areas as compared with the coastal centres. It was about 31% in 1960 and fell to about 8% in 1970.

(c) Steel production

Prior to World War I the most important steel centres were the North-East Coast (22%), South Wales (20%), Scotland (15%) and Sheffield (14%). The 'new' areas produced 13% of total steel output.[2] Since World War II South Wales has moved into first place, Yorkshire and Humberside is second, the North-East Coast is third and Scotland is fourth. All rely heavily on locally processed imported ore. Sheffield relies mainly on cold scrap and pig iron from other districts. Table 3.6 gives details of pig iron and crude steel production, with pig iron and scrap usages, analysed by region.

5. Sources of Imported Ore

In 1913 the largest sources of British ore imports were Spain and Spanish North Africa. Next came French North Africa, followed by Sweden.

By 1937 French North Africa had moved into first place, followed by Sweden and Spanish North Africa. The most important changes since World War II have been the relative increase in supplies from Canada (4% in 1937, 19% in 1960) and the relative decrease in imports from French and Spanish North Africa (34% in 1937, 20% in 1960). Sweden's share fell from 33% in 1937 to 28% in 1960, but it had moved into first place. The additional imports expected by the Iron and Steel Board by 1965 were likely to come mainly from Sweden, Canada and West Africa.[3]

[1] *Development in the Iron and Steel Industry*, pp. 71–2.
[2] *The Structure of British Industry*, 1, p. 276.
[3] *Development in the Iron and Steel Industry*, pp. 5, 81.

6. Further Reading and Sources

Footnote references to daily and weekly journals are not repeated.

BRITISH IRON AND STEEL FEDERATION, *The British Steel Industry*, B.I.S.F. 1962 and 1965.

B.I.S.F., *Steel in the 1960s: Developments by the Companies.*

B.I.S.F., *Steel Review* No. 11, July 1958.

B.I.S.F., Statistical Services Department. *Memorandum*, May 1965.

CENTRAL OFFICE OF INFORMATION, *the United Kingdom Iron and Steel Industry*, *F.S.B.* R.4735/D/8. C.O.I. 9161.

C.O.I. *The United Kingdom Steel Industry*, R.4930. C.O.I. 1961.

DEPARTMENT OF TRADE AND INDUSTRY, *Steel: British Steel Corporation: Ten Year Development Strategy*. Cmnd. 5226. H.M.S.O. Feb. 1973.

IRON AND STEEL BOARD, *Development in the Iron and Steel Industry: Special Reports*. 1961 and 1964. H.M.S.O.

Iron and Steel Industry Annual Statistics for the United Kingdom, 1970: Iron and Steel Statistics Bureau.

B. S. KEELING and A. E. G. WRIGHT, *The Development of the Modern British Steel Industry*. Longmans. 1965.

C. F. PRATTEN, *Economies of Scale in Manufacturing Industry*. C.U.P. 1971.

C. F. PRATTEN and R. M. DEAN, *The Economies of Large-scale Production in British Industry*. C.U.P. 1965.

Stat., 30 July 1965, p. 291.

Steel: Background to the News, No. 14, pub. by the *News Chronicle*. 1958.

K. WARREN, 'Coastal Steelworks – A Case for Argument?'. *The Three Banks Review*. June 1969.

THE IRON AND STEEL INDUSTRY: Stage II: Structure and Organisation

1. Protection and Public Policy[1]

During the early years of the twentieth century the British iron and steel industry, supplying capital goods to other industries, was particularly vulnerable to fluctuations in demand. The heavy capital investment involved created a great burden of overhead costs; these, and the cost of restarting costly heat processes, once dampened down, tended to compel the industry to continue production as long as prime or working costs could be covered. These inelastic supply conditions – excess capacity in times of falling demand – resulted in violent price fluctuations. Furthermore, the British industry relied heavily on exports. It was dispersed, had lost some of its early locational advantages, was not very integrated, and was falling behind the newer German, French and American industries in comparative efficiency. The expanding American industry was stimulated by the growing home market. The continental producers had well protected home markets, once supplied by Britain; they could maintain prices by

---

[1] For a brief but competent survey, see *An Account of the Principal Trade Association in the Steel Industry*, B.I.S.F., Sept. 1963. Appendix I: 'Evolution of the Federation'.

cartel arrangements; and they could cut prices to gain access to export markets, including the unprotected British market.

After World War I increasing competition from abroad and from new entrants at home stimulated the process of amalgamation and vertical integration within the industry. The motives were varied: the 'buying up' of competition, the quest for security and control over supplies and of markets, and economies of integrated processes. The industry made repeated requests for tariff protection, but the Government took the view that rationalisation along efficient lines was the most vital need, and that a protective tariff might inhibit such a process if it were granted first.

The great trade depression of the early 1930s forced the pace of events. It was decided in 1932 to grant tariff protection, but the Import Duties Advisory Committee was formed to ensure that the public interest was served, to make recommendations on import duties and to exert pressure on the industry to reorganise itself. A temporary duty of $33\frac{1}{3}\%$ *ad valorem* was imposed on imports of iron and steel, to be renewed if satisfactory reorganisation schemes were produced. The first important result was the formation of the British Iron and Steel Federation in 1934, primarily to foster reorganisation schemes and to represent the industry in dealings with the I.D.A.C. In 1935 the B.I.S.F. was reconstituted with greater powers and with an independent chairman from outside the industry. Also in 1935 the Government, by using the tariff as a lever, induced the European Steel Cartel to come to terms with the B.I.S.F. with regard to a quantitative limitation on imports into Britain.

This additional measure of protection committed the industry to supplying most of the country's needs. Investment projects were put in hand, but the industry was not compelled to abandon or run down plant in the old, high cost locations and to invest in the newer home ore fields. This emphasis of investment plans on avoiding dislocation of established sites was partly due to the pull of capital already sunk there, and partly to political considerations relating to unemployment problems in the depressed areas.

During World War II the industry came under Government control. After the war the industry was officially supervised by the Iron and Steel Board. In 1949 the Iron and Steel Act nationalised the main part of the industry, which came under public ownership in February 1951, when the securities of about ninety companies and their subsidiaries were transferred to the Iron and Steel Corporation of Great Britain.

The process of nationalisation was halted later that year, when the Conservatives came to office, pledged to denationalise the industry. This was done by the Iron and Steel Act of 1953. An Iron and Steel Holding and Realisation Agency was appointed by the Treasury to assume ownership of the nationalised companies from the I.S.C., and to resell them to private ownership. The 1953 Act also set up the Iron and Steel Board, which is appointed by and responsible to the Minister of Power. Its main functions are to exercise a general supervision over the industry 'with a view to promoting the efficient, economic, and adequate supply under competitive conditions of iron and steel products'.

The Iron and Steel Act 1967 brought into public ownership in July 1967 fourteen major iron and steel companies under the British Steel Corporation. Excluding Richard, Thomas and Baldwins, which was already publicly owned. the takeover compensation to shareholders was £650 million. The B.S.C. encompassed about 90% of British crude steel output and 70% of the labour force. [1] However, the private sector, consisting of about 200 companies, produced most of the special steels and accounted for 30% of the total value of steel production. Since vesting day the B.S.C. has transferred a half share in one of its holdings (Round Oak Steel Works, Ltd.) to Tube Investments, Ltd. By mid-1968 the B.S.C. had thirty-nine crude steel producing works, of which twenty-one were fully integrated.

Renationalisation also left the B.S.C. with plants in constructional engineering (twenty with 9,000 employees in March 1970) and in chemicals (four with 1,400 employees in March 1970).

In 1971 consideration was given to the 'hiving off' of some of B.S.C.'s special steels, constructional engineering, chemicals and other miscellaneous activities to private buyers, but it was decided not to split up the main iron and steel-making activities into two or more multiproduct companies, largely because of the need to develop large, integrated plants, which would be beyond the financial reach of smaller successor bodies to the B.S.C. The borrowing ceiling for 1971–72 was raised to £300 million and the overall borrowing limits were increased from £500 million to £650 million.[2]

2. Structure of the Industry: Number and Size of Plant

In almost all iron and steel processes there are very definite advantages of large-scale production. Improvements in blast furnace technique result in an increase in the typical size. In 1945 a blast furnace hearth diameter of 20 feet (6·1 metres) was considered to be very large; by 1965 it was regarded as small, whilst 30 feet (9·1 metres) and over is large. Developments in steel furnace techniques have also led to speedier production on a larger scale. It is generally considered that economies of scale and integration can be increased until a plant reaches a capacity of 3 to 4 million tons annually.[3]

There is scope for smaller works, producing special steels, sections, forgings and castings. Also, some recent developments, such as continuous casting (which eliminates the need for ingot moulds and cogging mills), oxygen blasts with Bessemer converters and open hearth furnaces and electric furnace adaptation to cheaper grades of steel, using cheap scrap and electricity, tend to reduce the need for greater size.

The trend is, however, towards more fully integrated, generally larger plants. The 1951 Census recorded 398 establishments in the Iron and Steel (Melting and Rolling) categories, which comprise most of the industry. These included 51 blast furnace plants, and 231 tube, sheet and tinplate plants, many of which were classified as separate establishments but were, in fact, parts of integrated plant. From 1946 to 1964 the number of iron-making (blast furnace) plants fell from 53 to 36; the number of steel making plants fell from 105 to 96. However, whereas in 1946 no plants existed with a capacity of 1 million tons or more, there were

[1] D.T., 1 May 1965; 'The steel industry', D.E.A. Pr. Rep. Ind. & Reg., 42, July 1968.
[2] For further details see F.T., 28 April 1971; Econ., 29 May 1971; D.T., 29 June 1971.
[3] For further details see C. F. Pratten, Economies of Scale in Manufacturing Industry, esp. pp. 103–22, and Pratten and Dean, op. cit.

eight in 1963, accounting for 40% of total crude steel production. In the finishing stages, concentration of production was most spectacular in sheet and tinplate. Whereas in 1937 total sheet steel (1·3 million tons) came from fifty plants, the 3·5 million current output in 1963 was provided by five plants. Whereas in 1937 the total output of tinplate (0·9 million tons) came from thirty-four plants, in 1963 the current output of 1·2 million tons was provided by two plants. [1]

By 1964 there were 310 physically distinct plants, of which 250 covered only one of the three major operations (iron making, steel making and steel shaping). Thirty-seven works performed two major operations, whilst twenty-three were fully integrated plants, performing all three major functions. [2]

Some idea of the progress made in modernising productive capacity in the industry since World War II may be gained from Table 3.7.

Of the 398 main establishments in 1951, a quarter produced only 1·8% of net output and employed 10–49 workers each (the average being 28). One-seventh produced nearly 70% of net output and employed 70% of the labour force in establishments of 1,000 workers or more. Production was further concentrated into seven plants (one fifty-seventh) employing over 4,000 workers each, which employed 19% of the labour force and produced 19% of net output. [3]

There is considerable range in the size of plant in various processes and also in the productivity per person in plants of differing size. Highest net outputs per employee were recorded not in the largest works (with the relatively greatest amount of capital per head), but in plants with 11–24 employees, followed by plants with 300–399 employees.

Table 3.7 *Degree of plant modernity in the iron and steel industry, 1965–66*

Product	Category A %	B %	C %	Unclassified %	Total '000 tons
Pig iron	56	37	6	1	22,800
Crude steel	59	35	4	2	33,500
Billets	60	31	5	4	10,700
Plates	83	14	2	1	4,220
Sheets	96	0	1	3	4,470
Tinplate	97	0	3	0	1,500
Wire rods, etc.	83	16	0	1	2,320

Category A: *first class modern plant in a good location*
Category B: *efficient though older plant and smaller-scale modern plant*
Category C: *old plant capable of some years of useful life in conditions of high demand but otherwise of doubtful viability*
(Source: *Steel Review*, 35, July 1964, B.I.S.F.)

[1] *Steel: Leave Well Alone*, B.I.S.F., June 1964, pp. 7–8. [2] *Ibid.*, p. 7.
[3] *The Structure of British Industry*, vol. 1, p. 280.

The wide discrepancies between average capital investment per worker and productivity in different size grades are linked with such factors as suitability of location, degree of integration, the techniques used and the proportion of old equipment used (which detracts from possible economies of scale and integration).

In 1970 the industry contained 71 blast furnaces, of which 69 were operational

Table 3.8 *Regional organisation of the B.S.C. up to March 1970*

Company	Location of works
MIDLAND GROUP	
English Steel Corporation Ltd	Sheffield and Manchester
G.K.N. Steel Co. Ltd	Scunthorpe
The Park Gate Iron and Steel Co. Ltd	Rotherham and Sheffield
Richard Thomas & Baldwins Ltd	Scunthorpe
The United Steel Companies Ltd	Scunthorpe, Barrow, Sheffield, Rotherham and Workington
Crude steel output in 1966: 5·8m. tons	
Numbers employed in 1966: 68,500	
NORTHERN AND TUBES GROUP	
Consett Iron Co. Ltd	Consett and Jarrow
Dorman, Long & Co. Ltd	Middlesbrough and Redcar
Skinningrove Iron Co. Ltd	Saltburn
South Durham Steel and Iron Co. Ltd	Middlesbrough and West Hartlepool
Stewarts and Lloyds, Ltd	Bilston, Lanarkshire, Corby, Nottingham, Wolverhampton and Oldbury
Crude steel output in 1966: 5·6m. tons	
Numbers employed in 1966: 95,500	
SCOTTISH AND NORTH-WEST GROUP	
Colvilles Ltd	Glasgow, Motherwell and Ayrshire
John Summers & Sons Ltd	Stalybridge, Stoke-on-Trent and Shotton
The Lancashire Steel Corporation Ltd	Irlam and Warrington
Richard Thomas & Baldwins Ltd	Warrington
Crude steel output in 1966: 4·6m. tons	
Numbers employed in 1966: 47,400	
SOUTH WALES GROUP	
G.K.N. Steel Co. Ltd	Cardiff
Richard Thomas & Baldwins Ltd	Brierley Hill, Ebbw Vale, Pontypool and Newport
The Steel Company of Wales Ltd	Port Talbot, Newport, Llanelli and Swansea
Crude steel output in 1966: 6·1m. tons	
Numbers employed in 1966: 57,100	

(Source: *D.E.A. Pr. Rep. Ind. & Reg.*, 42, July 1968)

at any one time; 39 were under 24 feet (7·3m.) in diameter: 12 were over 28 feet (8·5m.) in diameter. The number of steel furnaces in existence in 1970 was 622 (compared with 657 in 1969): 414 of these were electric furnaces, 167 open hearth and 41 were convertors.[1]

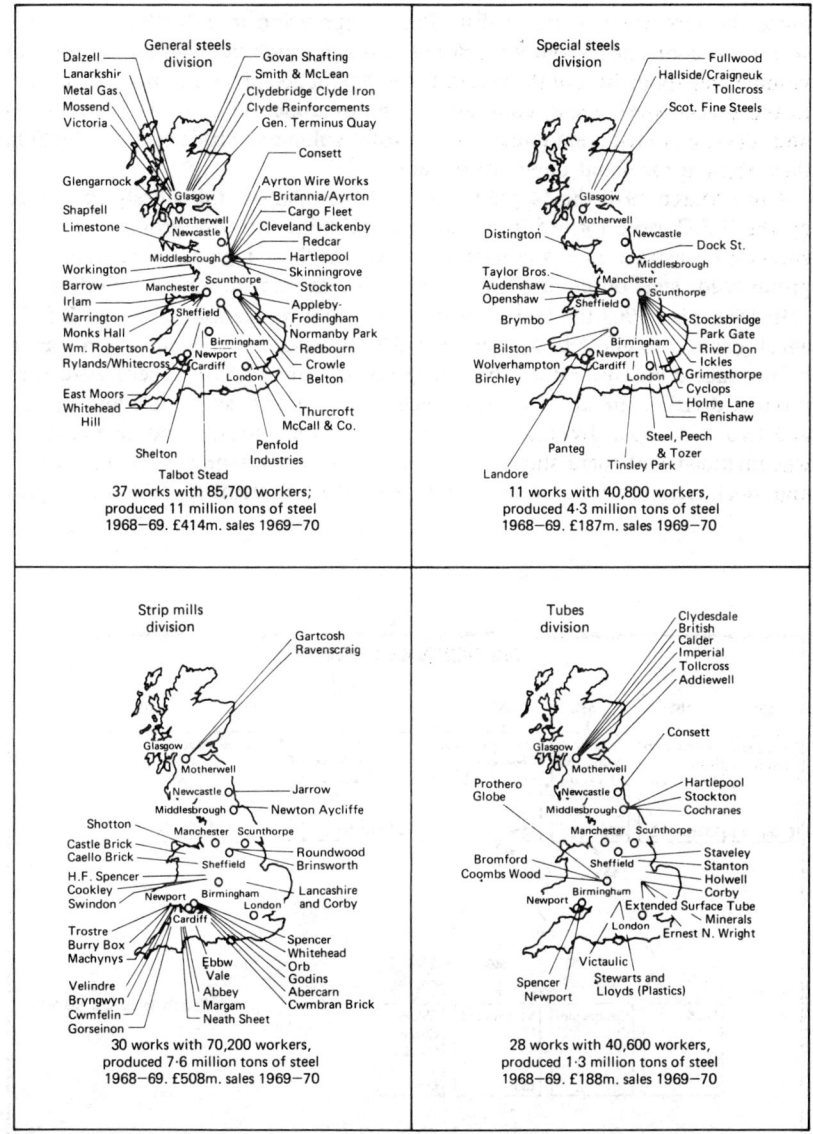

Fig. 3.9 *B.S.C. organisation and plant location*, March 1970
(Source: *The Sunday Times*, 22 March 1970)

[1] *Iron and Steel Industry Annual Statistics for the United Kingdom, 1970, op. cit.* Tables 22 and 29.

3. Administrative Organisation

(a) Concentration of control

Since the formation of the British Steel Corporation in July 1967 the public sector has controlled about 90% of pig iron and crude steel output, in terms of volume and about 70% of the labour force. About 200 private companies, mostly in the special steels areas, continue to employ about 30% of the labour force and, despite contributing under 10% of total volume in crude steel production, they account for about one-third in value.

Until March 1970 the 14 pre-vesting date companies still entirely controlled by the B.S.C. were formed into four regional administrative groups. Table 3.8 shows the separate company names involved in these regional groups, and the group crude steel output and employment figures prior to renationalisation.

In December 1969 the Government agreed to a reorganisation of the B.S.C., which came into effect in March 1970. The basis of the reorganisation was to be product divisions, rather than geographical distribution. There were four product divisions in steel – general steels, special steels, strip mills and tubes – and two additional divisions for constructional engineering and chemicals. It was intended that there should be a minimum of overlapping. Estimated iron and steel turnover for the year September 1969–September 1970 was £1,344

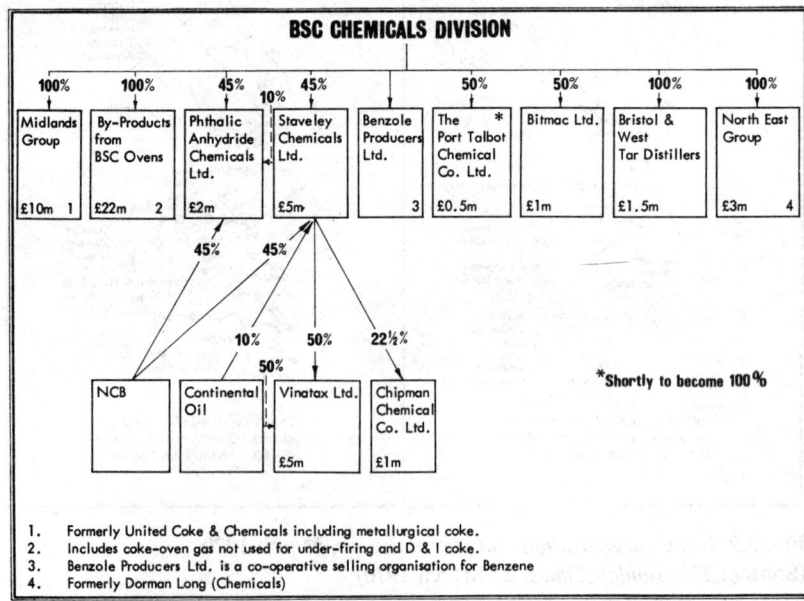

1. Formerly United Coke & Chemicals including metallurgical coke.
2. Includes coke-oven gas not used for under-firing and D & I coke.
3. Benzole Producers Ltd. is a co-operative selling organisation for Benzene
4. Formerly Dorman Long (Chemicals)

Fig. 3.10 *B.S.C. Chemicals Division at end-1970*
(Source: *F.T.*, 23 Nov. 1970)

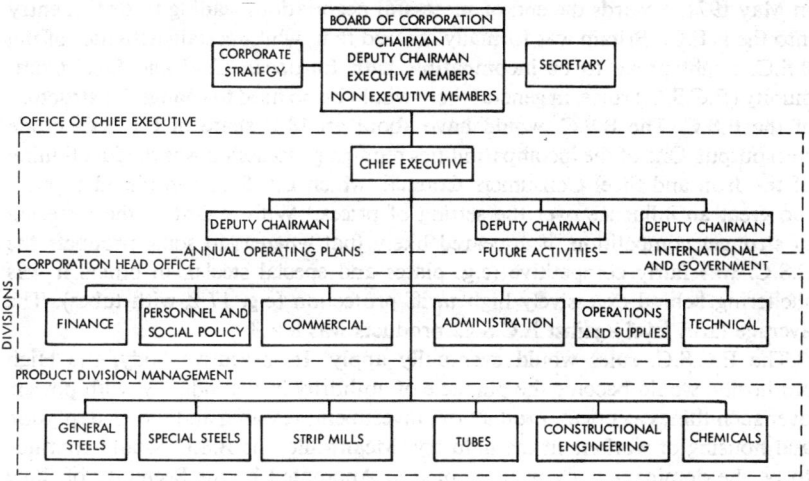

Fig. 3.11 *B.S.C. organisation chart as at end-1971*
(Source: *F.T.*, 7 Oct. 1971 and 13 April 1970)

million, compared with £1,071 million in 1967/68. Of this, the largest proportion
was from the strip mills division (£508m. or 39·2%), followed by general steels
(31·9%), tubes (14·5%) and special steels (14·4%). At end-June 1969 the number
of employees in all four steel divisions was 237,300.

The locations of the constituent plants in the four steel divisions are shown
in Fig. 3.9. The ramifications of the B.S.C. chemicals division, as at end-1970,
are illustrated in Fig. 3.10.

In October 1971 the B.S.C. announced further rearrangements at and just
below Board level, aimed at clarifying the distinction between policy-making
and control over day-to-day operational activities. The functions of financial
planning and of operations and supplies were to be more logically separated:
the old administration division was to be dismantled and Board members, whilst
retaining areas of special interest, were to be relieved of executive responsibilities.[1]
The Chief Executive Officer was to exercise control over day-to-day performance
of the product divisions and the head office functional departments.[2] Fig. 3.11
shows the B.S.C. organisation structure at end-1971.

The private companies in the industry are in some respects complementary
to the activities of the B.S.C. In 1970, whereas they accounted for only 7% of
crude steel output, their share of high-value alloy steels was 36%: their shares
of some non-alloy finished products ranged from 27% for tubes to 90% for
bright bars: for some alloy finished products it was as high as 93% (high-speed
and tool steels). This high value-to-weight production accounts for their one-
third share in total turnover.[3]

[1] *F.T.*, 18 Dec. 1969 and *S.T.*, 22 March 1970.
[2] *F.T.*, 7 Oct. 1971.
[3] *Ibid.*

157

In May 1971, towards the end of successful negotiations leading to British entry into the E.E.C., Britain was formally assured that, whilst certain activities of the B.S.C. might prove to be incompatible with European Coal and Steel Community (E.C.S.C.) rules, in general there would be no need to change the structure of the B.S.C. The B.S.C. would have about an 18% share of E.C.S.C. crude steel output. One of the incompatibilities requiring discussion was the functioning of the Iron and Steel Consumers Council, which E.C.S.C. considered to have too great an influence over the setting of prices.[1] With regard to the fostering of stronger competition, it appeared likely that whereas in some products the B.S.C. was fairly competitive (e.g. plates and special steels), in others it was sheltering behind excessively high tariff protection (e.g. 17% with tubes). The average tariff level against E.C.S.C. products was 8%.[2]

The E.C.S.C. rules would eventually apply. Its executive body, the High Authority, would become the pinnacle of authority in the industry, with powers over such things as prices, production, investment, research and the readaptation and housing of workers in the industry. Meanwhile, the B.S.C. would continue to be the dominant body in the industry. Appointed by the Secretary of State for Trade and Industry, its specific duties include promoting the efficient and economic supply of iron and steel products; exports; research and development; the financial affairs of the public sector.

The chief representative body for the 200 or so firms in the private sector is the British Independent Steel Producers' Association. These firms consider that they are capable of providing a competitive and efficient role within the E.C.S.C., but recognise the need to adapt to the Treaty of Paris rules for one set of products (crude and semi-finished steel, hot-rolled products and cold-rolled sheet) and to the Treaty of Rome rules for the rest.[3]

Table 3.9 *Trade unions in the iron and steel industry, 1969*

	Total members	Foremen and 'White-collar' members
Unions recognised nationally by the B.S.C.		
Iron and Steel Trades Confederation	105,400	11,750
Natl. Union of Blastfurnacemen	19,600	300
Transport and General Workers	17,500	3,200
Natl. Union General & Municipal Workers	12,800	400
Natl. Craftsmen's Co-ordinating Cmtte.	22,300	2,300
Amalgd. Union of Building Trade Workers	3,000	Not known
Unions offered local recognition by the B.S.C.		
Clerical and Admin. Workers' Union	3,500	3,500
Assocn. of Scientific, Technical & Managerial Staffs	4,100	4,100

(Source: *F.T.*, 15 Jan. 1969)

[1] *F.T.*, 6 May 1971.
[2] *F.T.*, 11 Oct. 1971.
[3] *Ibid.*

Industry-wide scientific and technological research is conducted by the B.S.C.'s Inter-Group Laboratories, with an annual expenditure of about £10 million.[1]

The major trade union in the industry is the Iron and Steel Trades Confederation, with 105,400 members in 1969. A variety of other unions is represented, as shown in Table 3.9. The most significant development in recent years has been the inroads made in the recruitment of the white-collar steel workers (7,600 out of 18,000) by two white-collar unions which have gradually achieved local recognition by the B.S.C. As the industry becomes more automated and labour functions more supervisory, the influence of the traditional steel unions may be expected to wane.[2]

4. Price Policy

Price policy proved to be a complex subject after the vesting of the B.S.C. An attempt to introduce a new feature into the pre-nationalisation structure – a loyalty rebate – was quashed after protests from E.F.T.A. and most major customers. The Iron and Steel Consumers Council must approve of price changes. The operation of price policy by the B.S.C. is strongly influenced by its capital structure and interest charges. If these could be written off or reduced, the standing charges on each unit of production would be lower. Another major problem is that not only is the B.S.C. in competition with the private producers, but also they constitute one of the major B.S.C. markets for intermediate products, which they process further.

In February 1969 the largest of the private firms, Thomas Firth and John Brown, strongly criticised the B.S.C.'s pricing policy: B.S.C. had proposed price increases in the carbon and sheet steel sectors, in which it had a more than 50% market share, but for the alloy steels sector, in which it held a less than 50% market share, it proposed price reductions of up to $12\frac{1}{2}\%$. The B.S.C. frankly explained that it was aiming to win over some of the private sector's customers, by undercutting in alloy prices. It appeared anxious not only to conduct a price war against the private sector, but also to follow this up with a possible buying up of some further parts of the industry still in private hands.[3] The private firms generally pursue a policy of following the market-leader, B.S.C., although they officially have pricing freedom.

In January 1970 the B.S.C. requested approval for price increases of up to 15%, averaging 11–12%. It claimed that this would reduce the B.S.C.'s losses and burden on the taxpayer, and would lead to a period of stable prices. The Treasury was expected to set a financial target of 10% net rate of return (after depreciation) on the £700 million of 'public dividend capital', which it held in B.S.C. and the projected price increases were expected to yield about £120 million in extra revenue in a full year. The Iron and Steel Consumers Council

---

[1] *Brit. O.H.*, 1971, p. 276.
[2] 'The steel industry's cleft stick', *F.T.*, 15 Jan. 1969.
[3] *F.T.*, 12 Feb. 1969.

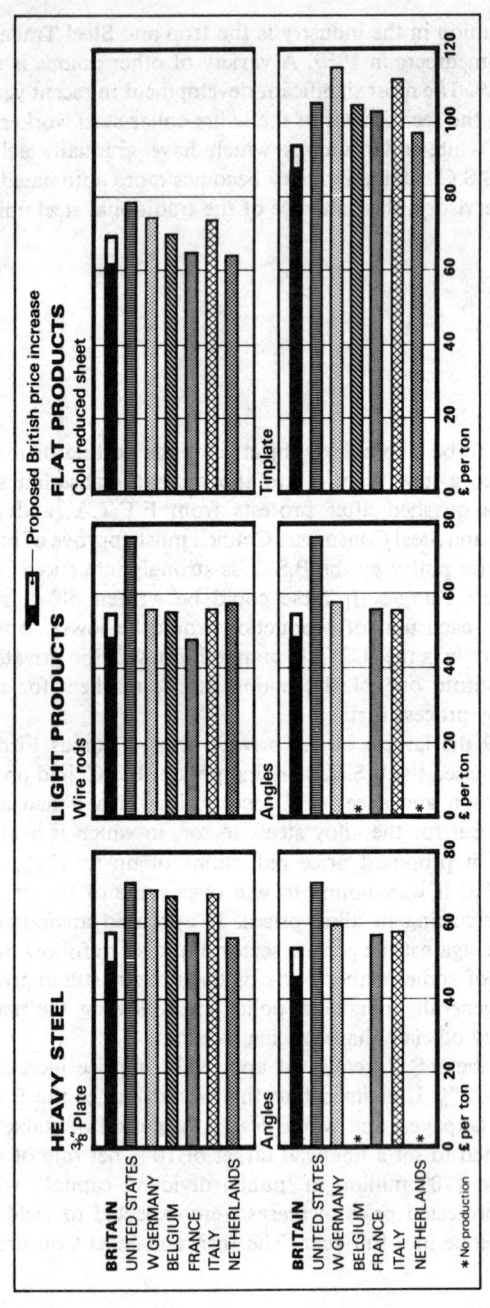

Fig. 3.12 *Comparative steel prices, January 1970*
(Source: *Econ.*, 24 Jan. 1970, p. 55)

approved of the price increase application,[1] which would have resulted in comparative steel prices as shown in Fig. 3.12.

As mentioned above, E.C.S.C. applies Treaty of Paris pricing rules to one set of products and Treaty of Rome rules to the rest. The Paris rules, applying to crude and semi-finished steel, hot-rolled products and cold-rolled sheet, require the publication of basing-point prices, with freight rates published separately and dependent on the location of each consumer. The U.K. practice has been to quote all-in final prices. In so far as the Paris rules infringe upon the private sector in the U.K., it is thought unlikely to cause much distortion, since most of their operations are geographically close-knit – in Sheffield, the Midlands and South Wales – and their market centre of gravity is in the Midlands.[2]

5. The Main Users of Steel

Whereas crude steel output in 1970 totalled 27·9 million ingot tons, net deliveries of finished steel to home consumers amounted to only 17·78 million tons, to which were added 990,000 tons of imports. Exports were 3·24 million tons.

The main users were stockholding merchants, industrial plant and steelwork constructors, the motor industry, further processing users in the steel industry itself, wire manufacturers and the shipbuilding industry. Details of the deliveries of finished steel from 1965 to 1970 are given in Table 3.10.

Until 1957 home market shortages of steel led to restrictions on direct exports, but since 1958 these restrictions have been removed. In 1961 direct exports of steel were 4·16 million tons in ingot equivalent (2·986 million tons of finished steel). The main markets for finished steel were the Commonwealth countries, which took more than two-fifths of direct steel exports (New Zealand, 172,900 tons; India 162,000 tons, Australia, 101,000 tons; Canada, 101,000 tons). This proportion has declined from the figure of 55% in 1957, whilst exports to Europe have been rising. In E.F.T.A. the largest customers were Sweden (156,700 tons) and Norway (124,700 tons); in E.E.C. the Netherlands were the biggest customer (106,900 tons). In the Western Hemisphere group, the largest customer was the U.S.A. (127,500 tons). In 1970 the direct exports of finished steel (3·24 million tons) were valued at £347·8 million: the area distribution was North America (£64·7 million), Sterling area (£85·9 million), Western Europe (£142·3 million) and rest of world (£54·9 million).[3] During recent years world output and competition in export markets have been increased by the growing output of the newer producing countries and the establishment of steel production in many developing countries. Demand for steel in traditional markets has not grown as fast as major producers had expected and Japan has increased its share of world steel exports (7% in 1958, 25% in 1966). Apart from stimulating changes in the pattern of trade distribution, this process has led some major exporters to seek

---

[1] *D.T.*, 10 Jan. 1970; *F.T.*, 21 Jan. 1970; *Econ.*, 24 Jan. 1970, p. 55.
[2] *F.T.*, 11 Oct. 1971.
[3] *Ann. Abs. Stat.*, No. 108, 1971.

outlets within their competitors' domestic markets and to open up production subsidiaries abroad, within their export markets. [1]

Table 3.10 *Finished steel (all qualities). Deliveries to consuming industries, merchants and exports: 1965-1970*

Thousand tons

Industry Group	1965	1966	1967	1968	1969	1970
Net Home Deliveries:						
Coal Mining	463·7	439·0	475·5	380·4	398·2	409·3
Food, Drink and Tobacco	77·6	87·7	90·6	92·3	90·0	88·9
Chemicals and Allied Industries	103·9	112·4	101·8	92·2	83·3	84·0
Iron and Steel:						
Repair and Maintenance	147·8	115·6	104·3	114·6	111·0	129·9
Further Manufacture	637·0	715·0	713·4	875·7	1,101·4	1,093·3
Ironfoundries	48·1	57·9	46·4	56·0	48·0	54·8
Agricultural Machinery	131·5	116·5	106·8	114·2	127·9	124·3
Metal-working Machine Tools and Engineers' Small Tools and Gauges	85·2	85·0	74·8	82·1	102·9	129·8
Contractors' Plant and Quarrying Machinery and Mechanical Handling Equipment	293·6	247·4	225·3	250·7	252·2	239·8
Other Machinery (including office machinery, refrigerators and textile machinery and accessories)	490·2	454·7	399·6	402·3	415·4	391·3
Other Non-Electrical Engineering	385·5	374·6	326·6	352·8	377·4	344·8
Industrial Plant and Steelwork	1,666·1	1,466·6	1,329·6	1,320·1	1,331·7	1,371·2
Tools, Implements, Instruments, Cutlery, Watches and Clocks	82·6	82·7	73·1	83·1	96·5	96·3
Electrical Machinery	318·6	275·5	231·2	236·6	228·6	235·3
Domestic Electric Appliances (excluding refrigerators)	77·8	82·1	65·2	82·6	83·8	98·1
Other Electrical Goods and Apparatus	156·3	156·6	142·7	163·7	165·7	134·4
Shipbuilding and Marine Engineering	585·1	531·1	417·8	507·0	574·5	534·7
Motor Vehicle Manufacturing (including parts and accessories)	1,870·2	1,692·0	1,567·8	1,797·1	1,801·7	1,799·0
Motor Cycle, Three-wheeled Vehicle, Pedal Cycle, Perambulator Manufacture and Repair	57·1	50·4	44·9	51·0	49·7	43·5
Aircraft Manufacture and Repair	28·9	32·6	26·8	24·0	21·6	20·5
Manufacture and Repair of Railway Rolling Stock by British Railways	130·8	101·1	88·5	85·5	91·7	101·1
Manufacture and Repair of Railway Rolling Stock by all other makers	89·7	88·5	67·5	50·7	42·5	61·2
Bolts, Nuts, Rivets, Screws, etc.	230·6	209·1	220·4	233·6	217·5	213·5
Wire and Wire Manufactures	1,242·6	1,102·8	1,045·0	1,127·5	1,183·4	1,267·5
Cans and Metal Boxes	596·8	654·3	658·3	726·6	691·5	666·3
Metal Furniture	102·1	95·1	88·7	84·8	82·5	75·6
Metal Windows and Door Frames	99·8	85·3	82·4	82·3	74·0	70·2
Drop Forgings, etc.	761·6	686·6	629·2	709·3	813·1	799·2
Industrial and Domestic Hollowware	184·2	170·4	146·2	160·0	185·1	182·2
Metal Industries, n.e.s.	690·9	646·3	588·1	673·0	750·7	679·2
Construction (building and civil engineering)	794·0	587·3	589·4	590·3	630·3	653·7
Gas, Electricity and Water	83·9	108·6	128·7	74·7	89·1	104·8
Transport and Communication	217·2	167·1	155·5	166·0	168·4	168·1
Other U.K. Consumers	319·3	283·2	219·4	222·5	255·9	293·4
Stockholding Merchants	3,003·5	2,749·9	2,756·0	3,260·1	4,382·0	4,939·8
Unallocated:						
(a) Home Produced	26·5	24·2	21·9	20·0	18·5	20·1
(b) Imports (incl. welded tubes over 16 in. o.d.)	502·0	739·9	1,160·8	1,346·1	1,083·6	990·1
(c) Second-hand Material	58·8	58·8	58·8	58·8	58·8	60·0
Total	16,841·1	15,733·9	15,269·1	16,750·3	18,280·1	18,769·2
Exports by Producers	3,349·6	3,286·3	3,711·6	3,946·7	3,373·8	3,239·8
Total Net Deliveries	20,190·7	19,020·2	18,980·7	20,697·0	21.653·9	22.009·0

(Source: *Iron and Steel Industry Annual Statistics for the United Kingdom, 1970,* Iron and Steel Statistics Bureau)

[1] *F.T.,* 19 Dec. 1970, 'Foreign approach to set up steel plant in U.K.'; 'Trans-national steel', *Econ.,* 19 Oct. 1968, p. 71.

6. Further Reading and Sources

B.I.S.F. *Steel in the 1960s: Developments by the Companies.*

B.I.S.F. *The Britisn Steel Industry*, 1962 and 1965.

B.I.S.F. *Current trends in development policy.* Oct. 1962.

B.I.S.F. *The British Iron and Steel Federation: An account of the principal trade association in the Steel Industry.* Sept. 1963.

B.I.S.F. 'Steel pricing', supplement in *Steel Review.* July 1964.

B.I.S.F. *Steel: Leave Well Alone.* June 1964.

B.I.S.F. *Steel Review.* 35. July 1964.

C.O.I. *The United Kingdom Steel Industry.* R.4930. 1961.

C.O.I. *The United Kingdom Iron and Steel Industry.* F.S.B. R.4735/D/8. 1961.

D.E.A. *Pr. Rep. Ind. & Reg.* 'The Steel Industry,' 42. July 1968.

W. K. V. GALE, *The British Iron and Steel Industry.* David and Charles. 1967.

IRON AND STEEL BOARD, *Development in the Iron and Steel Industry: Special Reports.* H.M.S.O. 1961 and 1964.

B. S. KEELING and A. E. G. WRIGHT, *The Development of the Modern British Steel Industry.* Longmans. 1964.

C. F. PRATTEN, *Economies of Scale in Manufacturing Industry.* C.U.P. 1971.

C. F. PRATTEN and R. M. DEAN, *The Economies of Large-scale Production in British Industry.* C.U.P. 1965 (espec. ch. 4).

'Regulation in steel manufacture', *M.B.R.* February 1963.

C. K. ROWLEY, *Steel and Public Policy.* McGraw-Hill. 1971.

Steel: Background to the News. No. 14, pub. by the *News Chronicle.*

AGRICULTURE: Stage I

1. Background

Despite the drift from country to town during the past century, agriculture, when considered as a single industry, remains one of Britain's largest and most important industries, with a labour force of nearly 1 million on about half a million holdings.

In 1970 out of the 60 million acres (24·28 million hectares) of land in the United Kingdom, 46·6 million (18·85) were farmed (17·8 [7·28] million for arable farming, 12·2 [5·26] million for permanent grass and about 16·6 [6·72] million for rough grazing). The rough grazing land has a low potential output (about one-sixth that of arable land), but is useful for sheep. The proportion of rough grazing is about one-sixth of the agricultural land in England and Wales, about one-quarter of that in Northern Ireland and about three-quarters of that in Scotland. Arable and permanent grassland are sometimes referred to as improved land, suitable for cultivation. The distribution of this and of rough grazing is based on the extreme variety of soils in the United Kingdom. The lowlands and river valleys are generally fertile and vary in soil texture from clay to loam, silt and peat; many areas in the west and north have poor, thin soil overlying hard rock.

Social changes in the past half-century have changed the pattern of rural life in England and Scotland. Where hitherto the majority of farming land consisted of

163

estates of a few hundred acres and upwards, let to tenants in farms of varying size, these being interspersed with some owner-occupied farms, nearly half Britain's farms today are owner-occupied. An important factor in this change has been the imposition of heavy estate duties.

In general, British farms produce a variety of products, but in many districts a particular pattern or specialisation predominates.

Whereas in Scotland the tenant is free to plough out any grassland on his farm, the tradition in England and Wales has been that 'old grass' belongs to the landlord and cannot be ploughed. This is called permanent grass, as opposed to rotational or temporary grass, grown and ploughed out by the tenant.

Part of the technical background to the industry is its dependence on the fluctuations of weather, markets, pests and disease.

2. Recent Developments

During the interwar period, 1930 marked the trough of a long depression in British agriculture. By 1939 there had been a general decline in agricultural activity, and much formerly cultivated land had reverted to grassland.

During this period attempts were made within the industry to strengthen its bargaining power and solve some of its perennial problems. The mass of unorganised small farmers had, by 1930, formed separate National Farmers' Unions in England, Wales, Scotland and Northern Ireland; breed societies were formed to protect the interests of stock breeders; numerous young farmers' clubs were formed; a chain of research stations was set up, and educational courses were established in universities, colleges and farm institutes.

Since World War II a great deal has been done to mitigate the risks to which agriculture is prone, especially with regard to pests and diseases and the vagaries of the market. Much of this progress has been due to the efforts of science and the self-help of farmers' organisations, but the greatest factor has been the strengthening of the Government's rôle as a wartime controller, financial supporter and guarantor (under the Agriculture Acts of 1947 and 1957), and provider of technical and advisory services.

The results of these developments have been many and varied. During World War II much permanent grass was ploughed up, and by 1944 arable land area had risen from 12·9 million acres (4·22 million hectares) in 1939 to 19·3 (7·81) million. By 1960 this had declined to 18·0 (7·28) million acres, due to a partial return to permanent grass. Nevertheless, the total area under tillage (11·2 million acres [4·53 million hectares]) and the area under temporary grass (6·8 million acres [2·75 million hectares]) were 2·4 million acres (0·97 million hectares) and 2·7 million acres (1·09 million hectares) respectively higher than in 1939. The use of this increased arable land has also changed. In England and Wales the old system of crop rotations has been abandoned in favour of a cropping system which allows a high proportion of cereals, sugar beet and potatoes, with short or medium term 'leys' (temporary sowing under grass). With improved grass management over the country as a whole, there has been a tendency towards longer leys.

The freer importation of feeding stuffs since World War II has, in conjunction with improved grass management, permitted a general trend towards the building up of cattle and sheep stocks. Production of livestock products and all the main crop products has increased since the war (the agricultural net output of all holdings was 79% higher in 1960–61 than the average for the prewar years. By 1964 net agricultural output was estimated as 108% higher than the prewar average: by 1970, on the basis of a new, updated index, it was estimated as 6% higher than the 1964–67 average.[1] These increases have been greater than the 10% population increase since 1939. In consequence, the United Kingdom now produces over half its food, in terms of value, as compared with one-third before World War II. Of products which can be produced in temperate climates such as Britain's, two-thirds are produced at home. Table 3.11 illustrates the change in the degree of self-sufficiency in principal foods, by weight, in relation to total supplies made available to the public.[2] It must be noted that the pattern of consumption has altered somewhat since prewar days. Furthermore, in 1945 food rationing was still in force and total supplies were low in relation to the prewar and post-rationing years.

Table 3.11 *Degree of self-sufficiency in food production: percentages of principal food supplies in U.K. provided by home agriculture*

Food product	Prewar average	1945	1963	1970
Wheat and flour for human consumption	23	32	41	45
Oils and fats	16	7	13	13
Sugar	17	32	23	30
Carcase meat and offal	51	50	69	73
Bacon and ham (not canned)	32	38	38	40
Butter	9	8	10	14
Cheese	24	10	43	45
Condensed milk	70	59	95	94
Dried milk (whole and skimmed)	59	49	56	70
Shell eggs	71	87	98	99
Milk for human consumption (liquid)	100	100	100	100
Potatoes for human consumption	96	100	93	96

(Source: *Britain: an Official Handbook*, 1962 and 1965; N.F.U. *Memorandum*, Nov. 1971)

The Price Review White Paper for 1971 forecast that the value of agricultural output (1970–71) would be £2,496 million, to which would be added £140 million in production grants and other credits. Total expenses were estimated at £2,047 million, leaving a net income of £589 million for the one-third million holdings – an average of about £1,750 per holding. Labour costs were the largest item of expense until 1953–54, but since then feedingstuffs have moved into first place. Nevertheless, whilst the number of farm labourers had fallen by over one-third since 1960, the increased responsibilities of those remaining forced up wages by nearly 70%.[3] Livestock and livestock products account for two-thirds of

[1] *Brit. O.H.*, 1971, p. 301..
[2] For a useful analysis of consumption, production and imports, see *D. E. A. Pr. Rep. Econ.*, 48, Jan. 1969 and 55, Aug. 1969.
[3] *Brit. O.H.*, 1971, p. 307.

farmers' income, and horticultural products, although using only 4% of arable land (0·7 million acres [0·28 million hectares]), provide one-third of income from crops of all kinds (see Table 3.12).

Despite the fact that aggregate net farm income was estimated at £359 million in 1960–61 and £589 million in 1970–71, as compared with £56 million in 1937–38 and £192 million in 1946–7, this increase has to be viewed against changes in the purchasing power of the £ and vagaries in the weather from year to year. Taking these factors into account, it has been estimated that real net income was only 5% higher in 1960–61, than in the immediate postwar years whilst the real income of the community as a whole went up by about 40%:[1] it was only 4% higher in 1969–70, as compared with 38% for the community as a whole. Profitability varies between different sizes and types of farm and even amongst similar farms. It appears to vary according to the quality of management, the quality of land and size. There is a marked tendency for small farms to show a higher profit per acre than large ones, this being due to the more intensive and efficient personal management of the small farmer. The average net income for different types of farm was, in the late 1960s, between £5 and £16 per acre (£2·02 and £6·47 per hectare). Exceptions were pig and poultry farms and horticultural holdings, with higher net incomes, largely due to more intensive methods and dairy and arable farms, where net incomes are almost always higher than on stock-rearing farms, which are generally larger than other types and situated on poorer land.

Increased productivity has been achieved partly as a result of increased mechanisation. Whereas 430,000 workers were employed in 1970 as compared with 804,000 in 1939, the number of tractors quadrupled and the number of combine harvesters increased about seventy-fold between 1942 and 1970 (116,830 to 513,000 and 1,000 to 69,000 respectively).[2]

Table 3.12 *Farm income and outlay, 1960–61 and 1970–71*

Outlay	£ million		Income	£ million	
	1960/61	1970/71 (est.)		1960/61	1970/71 (est.)
Labour	312½	361	Milk and milk products	349½	498
Rent and Interest	105	203	Fatstock	435	744
Machinery	215½	318	Eggs and poultry	251	332
Feedingstuffs	343	649			
Fertilisers	115	163	Farm crops	258	458
Other	178	353	Horticultural products	133	286
			Other	54½	46
Total	1,269	2,047	Total	1,481	2,364
Net income	359	589	Production grants, sundry receipts and other credits	121	132
			Increase in value of farm stocks and work in hand	26	140
Total	1,628	2,636	Total	1,628	2,636

(Source: *Annual Price Review, 1961*, Cmnd 1311; *ibid.*, 1971, Cmnd 4623)

[1] *The British Farmer*, 18 Nov. 1961; N.F.U., *Memorandum* 1797/70, 1970, p. 3.
[2] *Ibid.*, and *Brit. O.H.*, 1971, p. 308.

Fig. 3.13. *Highlands, uplands and lowlands of the United Kingdom*

Increased mechanisation and more efficient techniques involve heavy capital investment, much of which is provided by the 'ploughing back' of profits. Investigations have shown that in England and Wales in 1968–69 capital investment per acre ranges from £10 to £60 (£4·04 to £24·24 per hectare); in Scotland it ranges from £3 (£1·21) on hill sheep farms to £50 to £60 (£20·23 to £24·24) on lower ground farms. Dairy farms are more capital-intensive than

167

other types of stock farms; machinery accounts for a large part of the capital investment per acre (about £20 on dairy and arable farms and £7 on stock rearing farms [£4·24, £8·09, and £2·83 per hectare]).[1]

Production and productivity increases since prewar days are summarised in Table 3.13.

3. Location of Agricultural Production

Britain may very roughly be divided into a pastoral west (hills, valleys and fairly heavy rainfall), and an arable east (lowlands and lighter rainfall). However, too rigid a classification would be misleading, because beef and dairy cattle and sheep are reared in some eastern districts, and oats and potatoes are grown in some

Main wheat areas

Fig. 3.14. *Main areas of wheat production in the United Kingdom*

western districts. Furthermore, some areas grow crops primarily for sale, while others grow crops primarily for feeding their livestock. There is much overlapping of the arable crop areas and the livestock areas, but not so much overlapping of the saleable arable crop areas and livestock areas.

Location of production may best be understood if reference is first made to the topography of the United Kingdom (Fig. 3.13). As the prevailing winds are warm, wet south-westerlies, the hillier western areas of Britain tend to receive more rainfall than the lower eastern areas.

[1] *Brit. O.H.*, 1971, pp. 307–8.

Most crop production (especially crops for sale), is carried on in the east and south-east of England, but potatoes are also grown in the peaty lands of south Lancashire, in Northern Ireland, and as far north as south-eastern Scotland and Northumberland. Oats are grown in eastern and south-western Scotland, Cumberland, Northern Ireland, Lancashire, south-west Wales and Devon (see Figs. 3.14–3.18). Horticultural crops are grown in a wide variety of areas (see Fig. 3.19). Though occupying only about $2\frac{1}{2}\%$ of crop and grassland, they have a high value per acre. Market gardening has grown up around most large centres of population, due to market and time factors (perishable goods). It is also conducted in many rural areas of south-west and south-east England, where favourable soil and climatic conditions are present. Glasshouse production (mainly tomatoes) is concentrated in the Lea valley (near the London market) and the Worthing district of Sussex. Hops for the brewing industry are concentrated in the Kent–

Main barley areas

Fig. 3.15. *Main areas of barley production in the United Kingdom*

Sussex and Herefordshire–Worcestershire areas. Hard fruits are grown in south, south-west and east England and County Armagh, where the risk of late frost is minimised. Soft fruits have varied locations, with plums concentrated in Kent and Worcestershire, blackcurrants in Norfolk, cherries in Kent, strawberries in Norfolk, Kent and Hampshire. On the other hand, 80% of raspberries are cultivated in east-central Scotland (primarily in the Blairgowrie district).

Dairy cattle are reared mainly on the wet coastal fringes, lowlands and undulating uplands of Northern Ireland, south-western Scotland, the north-west, Midlands, south and south-east England and South Wales. Beef cattle are reared and fattened mainly in the Midlands and also in areas too hilly or too dry for dairy cattle (e.g. north-eastern Scotland, parts of Northern Ireland, Devon

Table 3.13 Livestock, use of land, production and productivity in U.K. agriculture

	1939	Pre-war average	1960	1960–61	% Increase	1964	1970
Acreage (million acres)							
1. Cereals	5·3	—	7·7	—	45	8·5	9·4
2. Total tillage	8·8	—	11·2	—	27	11·5	12·1
3. Temporary grass	4·1	—	6·8	—	66	6·9	5·7
4. Permanent grass	18·8	—	12·8	—	−32	12·3	12·2
5. Total arable land (2 + 3)	12·9	—	18·0	—	39	18·4	17·8
6. Total crops and grass (2 + 3 + 4)	31·7	—	30·9	—	−2½	30·7	30·0
7. Rough grazings	16·5	—	18·3	—	11	—	16·6
Employed Labour Force ('000)	—	825	693	—	−16	584	430
Machinery							
Tractors	—	50,000 (1942)	417,000	—	833	435,000	513,000
Combine harvesters	—	1,000 (1942)	48,000	—	4,800	55,000 (1963)	69,000 (1969)
Crop production ('000 tons)						(1964–65 est.)	
Wheat	—	1,651	—	3,064	81	3,639	4,169
Rye	—	10	—	18	90	25	13
Barley	—	765	—	4,241	454	7,404	7,410
Oats	—	1,940	—	2,058	6	1,325	1,198
Mixed corn	—	76	—	219	191	101	253
Potatoes	—	4,873	—	7,158	47	6,952	7,363
Sugar beet	—	2,741	—	7,215	163	6,218	6,311

[Table 3.13 contd.]

			(1958–60 average)			(1962/3–1964/5 average)	(1968/9–1970/1)
Crop yield per acre							
Wheat (cwt)	–	17·8	27·2	–	53	33·3	31·2
Barley (cwt)	–	16·5	24·9	–	51	28·8	27·6
Oats (cwt)	–	16·1	20·5	–	27	22·9	26·2
Mixed corn (cwt)	–	15·7	20·9	–	33	24·7	25·5
Potatoes (tons)	–	6·7	8·0	–	12	8·8	10·3
Sugar beet (tons)	–	8·2	14·1	–	73	13·0	13·9
Livestock (millions)	(1939)		(1960)			(1964)	(1970)
Dairy and Beef cattle (cows and heifers)	3·9		4·8	–	23	4·9	5·4
Other cattle	5·0	–	6·9	–	38	6·7	7·2
Sheep	26·9	–	27·9	–	$3\frac{3}{4}$	29·6	26·1
Pigs	4·4	–	5·7	–	$29\frac{1}{2}$	7·4	8·1
Poultry	74·4	–	103·0	–	$38\frac{1}{2}$	118·4	143·4
Horses	1·1	–	0·2(G.B.)	–	–82	n.a.	n.a.
							(F = Forecast)
Livestock products						(1964–65)	(1970–71F)
Eggs (million doz.)	–	545	–	1,043	92	1,219	1,233
Beef and veal ('000 tons)	–	578	–	772	$33\frac{1}{2}$	803	963
Mutton and lamb ('000 tons)	–	191	–	241	$26\frac{1}{3}$	249	221
Pigmeat ('000 tons)	–	368	–	634	$72\frac{3}{4}$	857	869
Wool ('000 tons)	–	34	–	36	6	–	–
Milk (million galls.)	–	1,556	–	2,445	$57\frac{2}{5}$	2,480	2,702
Livestock product yields						(1963–64)	(1970–71)
Eggs (per hen)	–	148	–	188	$26\frac{2}{3}$	196	$216\frac{1}{2}$
Milk (galls. per Dairy cow, England and Wales)	–	560	–	765	$36\frac{3}{5}$	770	850
						(1963–64 est.)	
Index of net agricultural output on all holdings	–	100	–	179	79	208	–

(Based on material in *Monthly Digest of Statistics; The British Farmer*, 18 November 1961; *Annual Review and Determination of Guarantees*, Cmnd 2621, 1965; N.F.U., *Memoranda*, May 1965 and Nov. 1971.)

and Cornwall). Some of these dairy and beef areas are helped by the presence of oat production (e.g. Northern Ireland, Devon, Cornwall, Lancashire, Cumberland, south-western and north-eastern Scotland). Lancashire and eastern Scotland have the additional advantage of local potato production.

Sheep-breeding is located almost exclusively in the rough, hilly areas of southern Scotland, northern England, Wales, the Cotswolds and Northampton Uplands, north Devon and Cornwall, and the North and South Downs. Overlapping of dairy and beef cattle takes place in coastal south-western Scotland, Cumberland and the east Midlands; it occurs with beef cattle in north Devon and Cornwall and with dairy cattle in the North and South Downs (see Fig. 3.20).

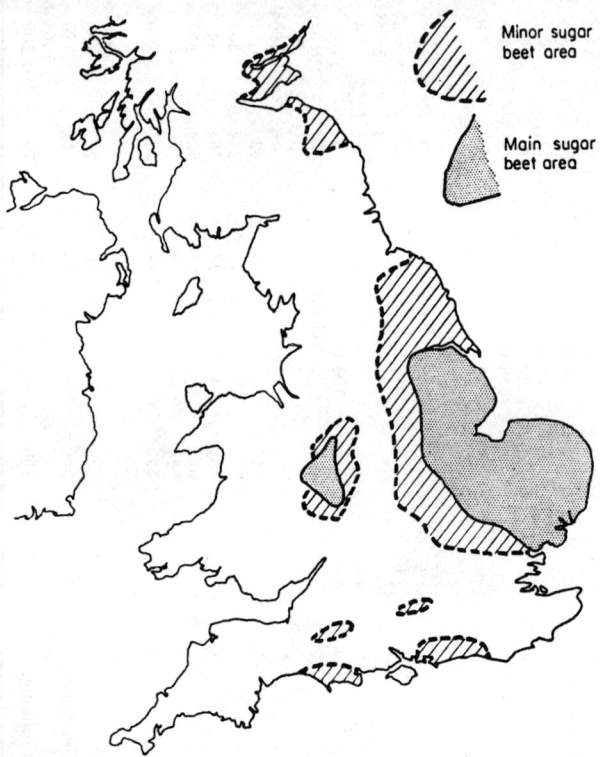

Minor sugar beet area

Main sugar beet area

Fig. 3.16. *Main areas of sugar beet production in the United Kingdom*

4. Further Reading and Sources

Footnote references to daily and weekly journals are not repeated.

Annual Review and Determination of Guarantees. H.M.S.O.
'Britain's Agriculture Today', *M.B.R.* Aug. 1968.
Britain's Agriculture Today, booklet. Midland Bank. 1968.
'British agriculture in the world setting'. *Bulletin for Industry* (Information Division of the Treasury). 166. Sept. 1963.
M. CAPSTICK, *The Economics of Agriculture.* Allen & Unwin. 1970.

A Century of Agricultural Statistics, Great Britain 1866–1966. H.M.S.O. 1968.

C.O.I. *Agriculture in Britain. B.B.L.A.* H.M.S.O. June 1964.

C.O.I. *Britain in Brief.* C.O.I. 1961.

D.E.A. Pr. Rep. Econ. 48, 'Agricultural expansion', Jan. 1969.

D.E.A. Pr. Rep. Econ. 55, 'The food we eat', Aug. 1969.

A. FERRIDAY, *A Regional Geography of the British Isles.* Macmillan. 1956.

G. HALLETT, *The Economics of Agricultural Policy.* Blackwell. 1968.

D. METCALF, *The Economics of Agriculture.* Penguin. 1969.

A. MURRAY, *The British Isles: Where, How and Why.* Collins. 1960.

NATIONAL FARMERS' UNION, *The British Farmer.* 18 Nov. 1961, pub. by N.F.U. of England and Wales.

NATIONAL FARMERS' UNION. 1970. *Memorandum 1797/70, Econ. G. 106.*

Fig. 3.17. *Main areas of potato production in the United Kingdom*

AGRICULTURE: Stage II: Structure and Organisation

1. The Increasing Rôle of the State

Government policy has influenced the fortunes of agriculture since the protection-ist era of the Corn Laws. With the advent of a free trade policy in the mid-nineteenth century this protection was removed. The increased food supplies from the New World and the Antipodes resulted in an excess of supply over demand. The Government did not raise a protective barrier for this industry (whose relative importance in the economy was declining) against such imports because of the effect this would have on the cost of food to the industrial popu-

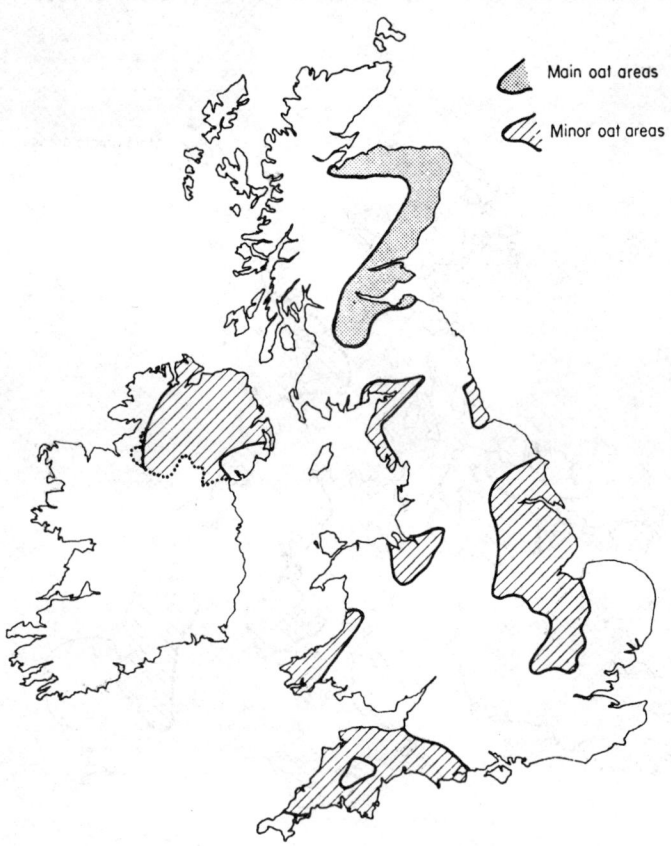

Main oat areas

Minor oat areas

Fig. 3.18. *Main areas of oat production in the United Kingdom*

lation and on the purchasing power of the primary producers who were markets for exports of manufactured goods.

During the depression of the 1930s, however, agriculture at home and abroad suffered badly, because of its comparatively inelastic supply conditions. Home agriculture faced intensified competition from the falling prices of imports. The

174

pressure for State assistance grew, and Government agricultural policy was directed to supporting home agriculture.

Various forms of protection and direct financial assistance were developed. For wheat and livestock, commodity commissions were established to administer Government subsidies and other types of direct financial assistance; sugar beet factories were taken over by the British Sugar Corporation; for milk, pigs, hops and potatoes, marketing boards were established, controlled by the producers, with powers to regulate marketing; for beef cattle, subsidy payments were introduced in 1934 to encourage production; for barley and oats, assistance to producers was granted in 1937, when the Government assumed powers to pay acreage subsidies.

Agriculture was closely controlled by the State during World War II and the

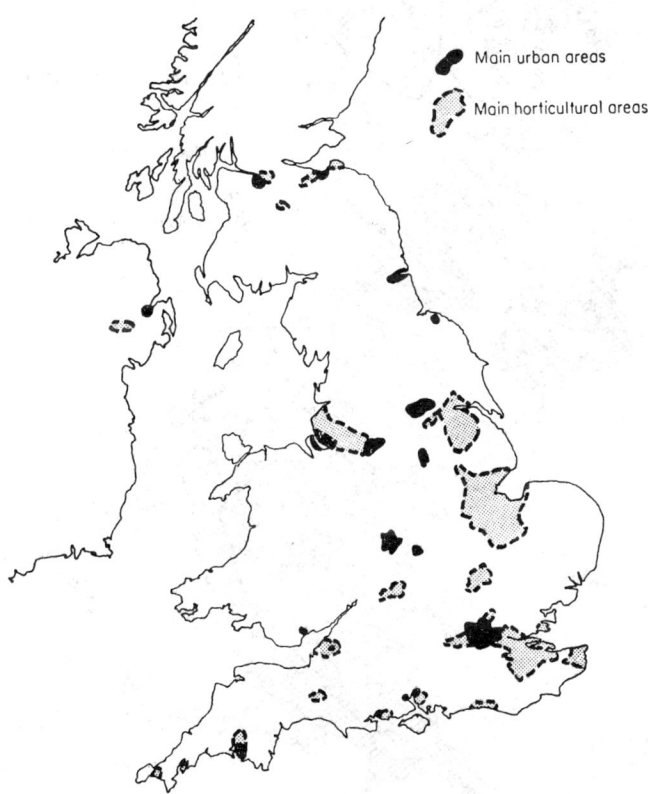

Fig. 3.19. *Main areas of horticultural production (market gardening, hard fruit, soft fruit, and hops) in the United Kingdom*

immediate postwar years. The functions of the marketing boards and commodity commissions were superseded by the system of Government fixed price purchases and controlled price sales, and rationing.

After the war Government policy, conditioned by strategic considerations and wartime experience, was revised and formally enunciated in the 1947 Agriculture Act. Section I set the objective as being 'a stable and efficient agricultural industry capable of producing such part of the nation's food and other agricultural produce as in the national interest it is desirable to produce in the United Kingdom, and of producing it at minimum prices, consistent with proper remuneration and living conditions for farmers and workers in agriculture and an adequate return on capital invested in the industry'. The main instrument for securing this objective was the Government's power to provide guaranteed prices for the main agricultural products, calculated by means of annual price

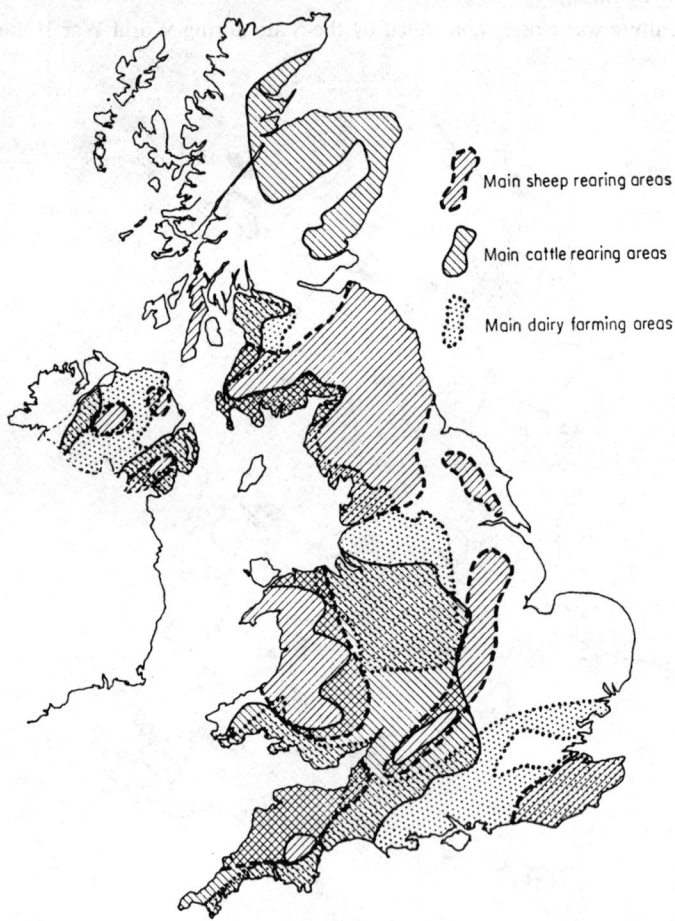

Main sheep rearing areas

Main cattle rearing areas

Main dairy farming areas

Fig. 3.20. *Main dairy-farming, cattle-rearing and sheep-breeding areas in the United Kingdom*

reviews. The general method of price support was that of deficiency payments, whereby the Government paid producers the difference between the average market price and the guaranteed price. The Government also provides research and advisory services and various grants and subsidies for fertilisers, land drainage, hill farming, farm improvements, etc. Farmers are expected to maintain efficiency in husbandry and estate management. Until they were repealed by the 1957 Agriculture Act, the Government had powers of supervision, direction and dispossession to secure this objective.

Until 1954, when rationing was abolished, State policy was aimed at encouraging an expansion of production and a return to the traditional pattern of farming, using the incentive of 'production objectives' and fixed price increases at the annual reviews (which do not cover horticultural products), which injected £40 million additional working capital each year. After 1954 policy changed to an emphasis on a more discriminate pattern of expansion, with more economic production of types and qualities demanded by the market – in particular beef, mutton, lamb and home-grown feedingstuffs. By 1957 the objective of a 60% production increase had been achieved. Attention turned to long-term measures, and the 1957 Agriculture Act provided long-term assurances to farmers by limiting the extent of any reductions which may be made in guaranteed prices and production grants in any one year. It provided grants for modernising fixed equipment, and in 1960 grants were made available for horticultural buildings and equipment.[1]

In 1964 the Agriculture and Horticulture Act gave the Government discretionary powers to impose minimum import prices for agricultural and horticultural products and these powers have been used in connection with cereals and eggs and egg products. The new policy was embodied in the 1964 *Annual Price Review* White Paper, which gave a further impetus to the use of 'standard quantity' targets, extending their application, backed up by controls on imports and import prices, to cereals and meat. The major objective was to control the open-ended Exchequer deficiency-payment price support. The 'standard quantity' arrangements for wheat and barley were abolished in 1968 and 1969 respectively. The Agriculture Act of 1967 carried further the policy of restructuring the industry into larger and more efficient units. Its provisions included amalgamation grants (60%) and annuities and lump sum retirement grants to small farmers of uncommercial holdings, who withdrew from the industry. This Act complemented an official report, published in 1966, which classified farming units into four categories, based on standard labour requirements and using the standard man-day as the unit of measurement. Commercially viable units were the medium and large categories, with more than 600 standard man-days. The standard man-year is 275 standard man-days.[2]

In 1968, following the Economic Development Committee for Agriculture report on agriculture's import-saving role, the selective expansion plan for the industry, announced in 1965, was extended to 1973, mainly in regard to cereals, potatoes, meat, milk, poultry, eggs and horticultural products.[3] The Agriculture

---

[1] For further details of Government policy, its effects on agriculture and the proposals of the 1965 National Plan, see 'Retirement offer to small farmers', *D.T.*, 5 Aug. 1965; 'Capital revolution on the land', *ibid.*, 29 Nov. 1965; 'Agriculture's place in the plan', *ibid.*, 20 Sept. 1965.

[2] For further data, see *Brit. O. H.*, 1971, pp. 308–12; 'Political algebra and U.K. agricultural policy', *N.W.B.Q.R.*, Feb. 1969, p. 65; D. Metcalf, *The Economics of Agriculture*, ch. 7; *Britain's Agriculture Today*, loc. cit., p. 3.

[3] 'Agricultural expansion', *D.E.A. Pr. Rep. Econ.*, 48, Jan. 1969; 'Agricultural expansion and the U.K. balance of payments', *N.W.B.Q.R.*, Feb. 1970; *Agriculture and Import Saving*, Hill Samuel Occasional Paper No. 5, Feb. 1970.

Act of 1970 was introduced to rationalise the production grants system by creating a unified capital grant scheme.

The 1971 Annual Farm Price Review was introduced against a background of possible E.E.C. entry and of existing policy to fortify farmers' incomes over the next three years by progressively raising the proportion of their incomes from market prices, as opposed to deficiency-payment price support. It raised the guaranteed prices for all review commodities except rye and eggs, reducing that for the latter: the only production grants to be increased were the hill and upland sheep subsidies and the incentives to eliminate the brucellosis disease. The annual cost to the Exchequer of price support and direct grants has varied from £206 million in 1955–56, when deficiency payments were first introduced, to £343 million in 1961–62 and £229 million in 1966–67: in 1970–71 it is estimated at £343 million. The proportion of direct *grant* support to deficiency payment *price* support has gradually risen to almost equality.[1]

The 1972 *Annual Farm Price Review* increased farm price guarantees by £70½ million and capital grants by £1½ million, although it was estimated that the industry's costs had risen by only £48 million on guaranteed commodities. This really represented an increased Exchequer commitment of £49 million and was undertaken as a policy measure to encourage the industry to increase production on the eve of E.E.C. entry, especially in livestock, by providing cash for expansion. It was also felt that higher guaranteed prices would tend to bring actual market prices up to a level nearer to those in the E.E.C.[2]

2. The Structure of Production: Number and Size of Farms

The number of agricultural holdings in the U.K. was 510,000 in 1955, 450,000 in 1965 and about 340,000 in 1970. Of these, almost half are 'very small' units (less than one standard man-year requirement), farmed mainly as a part-time occupation: they account for less than 10% of total output and 10% of total acreage and average 16 acres [6·47 hectares] (crops and grass) in size. Of the 190,000 full-time farming units in 1970, about 90,000 are 'small' (one to two man-years), accounting for about 15% of total output and 20% of total acreage and average 62 acres (25·08 hectares) in size. About 56,000 are 'medium' (2–4 man-years), accounting for about 25% of total output and 30% of total acreage and average 130 acres (52·60 hectares) in size. About 40,000 are 'large' (more than 4 man-year requirement), accounting for about 50% of total output and 40% of total acreage and average 300 acres (121·38 hectares) in size. Of these, the 5,000 largest farms contribute about 18% of total output.

There has been a reduction, in recent years, of about 4,000 per annum in the number of 'very small' holdings. In England and Wales the average size of full-time holdings is 160 acres (64·73 hectares): they number about 150,000. In Scotland the average size of the 22,300 full-time holdings is 170 acres (68·78 hectares) and that of the 18,000 full-time holdings in Northern Ireland is about 70 acres (42·46 hectares).

Alongside the reduction in the number of holdings there has been a trend towards larger farms: from 1954–64 the number of farms of more than 500 acres

---

[1] See *Econ.*, 20 March 1971, pp. 17–18. For detailed analysis of Exchequer support, see *Britain's Agriculture Today*, pp. 5–6.
[2] See *F.T.*, 2 and 16 March 1972.

[202·30 hectares] (crops and grass) rose from 3,650 to 4,950.[1] In 1969 a farm conference speaker claimed that the ideal farm of the future would be a family holding of up to 500 acres [202·30 hectares] of arable land (crops and grass), run without hired labour.[2] The 1967 Agriculture Act had been expected to result in about 6,000 amalgamations per year. By the end of 1971 only 2,600 had been approved, and the current annual rate was only 800–900. As a result, amalgamation incentives were improved in the Agriculture (Miscellaneous Provisions) Bill, published in November 1971. It proposed amalgamation grants on an acreage basis, instead of on the basis of remodelling expenditure, and the fifteen-year restriction on the breaking up of amalgamated farms was reduced to four years The Government was also expected to increase the cash grants to farmers who were prepared to leave the industry.[3]

Most farm labour consists of the occupier and his family. A survey made in 1941–43 showed that 44% of the holdings in England and Wales larger than 5 acres had no regular workers, apart from the farmers and their wives. Thirty-six per cent of such holdings had one or two workers and 3% had ten or more. Fifty-three per cent of the crops and grass area consisted of holdings with under three regular workers (other than farmers and their wives); only 13% of the acreage was in holdings with ten or more workers.[4] By 1968 the average number of male employees on full-time holdings was 1·8 (compared with 2·1 in 1963). A 1970 report[5] found that between 1963 and 1968 90,000 sought employment outside the industry: 25,000 retired and were not replaced, and about 30,000 became self-employed farmers. It was thought possible that soon there could be more farmers than farm employees. The most rapid recent losses were from large farms, which, however, find it easier to adapt their systems. In effect, because of changing relative prices of labour and other factors, capital and land had been substituted for labour.

The pattern of predominantly small farms limits the scope for specialised labour and techniques, but results in a great deal of personal control and initiative. These conditions favour the higher profitability per acre in the small farm than in the large, where the possibilities of specialisation are outweighed by the problems of administration and the resultant strain on the management factor.

3. Administrative Organisation

(a) Concentration of control in production

The pattern of farm ownership and tenure is significant. Returns made in 1950 for the World Census of the United Nations Food and Agriculture Organisation[6] indicated that in England and Wales about 36% of holdings were wholly owner-occupied, 49% wholly rented and 15% part-owned and part-rented; the proportion of owner-occupiers was higher in holdings of less than 5 acres, but was

---

[1] For further data see *Britain's Agriculture Today*, loc. cit., pp. 9–10; *The Changing Structure of Agriculture*, H.M.S.O.; 'Facing the future: the agricultural estate', *N.W.B.Q.R.*, May 1971; *Brit. O.H.* 1971, pp. 299–300; *D.T.*, 22 June 1970; *F.T.*, 26 June 1970.
[2] *D.T.*, 13 Feb. 1969.
[3] *F.T.*, 5 Nov. 1971.
[4] *The Structure of British Industry*, vol. 1., p. 3.
[5] *F.T.*, 8 May 1970 and *The Changing Agricultural Labour Force: Implications for Training*, Newcastle University, 1970.
[6] *Brit., O.H.*, 1960.

fairly constant amongst larger holdings. In Scotland, about 36% of all holdings were wholly owner-occupied, 60% wholly rented and 4% part-owned and part-rented. In Northern Ireland all farmers either owned their holdings or were in the process of assuming ownership. The general pattern, therefore, is for about one-third of farmers to own their own land, but for most of the remainder to be tenants, operating the farm and owning the stock, crops and movable equipment, whilst the landlord owns the land, buildings and fixed equipment and is responsible for maintenance and improvement.

The ownership of estates which are let to tenant farmers is mostly in the hands of private individuals or family trusts, but the Crown, the Church Commissioners, the local authorities, the National Coal Board and other private and public companies hold considerable areas. Despite the concentration of land ownership in these individuals and bodies, the actual number of private and public companies involved in agricultural production was assessed at only 3,600 in 1952–53.[1] In 1959 it was estimated that about 2% of the 220,000 holdings in England and Wales (about 4,500) were run by joint stock companies: the proportion in the South-East and near the Wash exceeded 5%[2]. The number of partnerships was probably higher. The 1941–43 surveys, mentioned in Section 2, showed that in England and Wales 266,600 holdings over 5 acres (2·02 hectares) were one-farm firms, and only 24,000 farms were operated in groups, by 10,000 firms. In Scotland, in 1947, a higher proportion of 'multi-plant' firms existed, controlling 3,300 of the 30,400 full-time farms.[3] The commonest type of firm in agricultural production, therefore, is the individual farmer, who is generally also the manager, whether owner or tenant of the land. By 1970 about half the farms in the U.K. were owner-occupied.[4]

There are many reasons for the persistent structural and organisational pattern of predominantly small, single-farm firms. Larger farms do tend to achieve higher returns on medium-term and short-term 'tenant's capital' than do smaller farms, largely because of economies of specialisation, bulk buying of factors and the relative ease of obtaining capital. On the other hand, net returns on management and risk-bearing (after allowing for interest charges and remuneration for personal and family labour) do not appear to be significantly higher on larger farms than on smaller ones. This appears to be due mainly to the steeply rising relative importance, difficulties and cost of management on larger units, and also to the greater risks of uncertainty in prices, weather, etc., as size of farm rises.[5] The small farm, therefore, tends to be more intensively worked and to have a higher net profitability per acre than the large farm (see Table 3.14). Capital requirements are large, in relation to output, and as credit for expansion tends to be difficult to raise, farmers tend to restrict investment decisions to projects which lie within the scope of their personal ability to manage. Under the Agriculture (Miscellaneous Provisions) Act, 1963, 33⅓% capital grants may be made by the State towards buildings and capital equipment for use by farmers' cooperative machinery syndicates.

Under the provisions of the 1967 Agriculture Act the Agricultural and

[1] *The Structure of British Industry*, vol. 1., p. 5.
[2] *Britain's Agriculture Today*, p. 10.
[3] *The Structure of British Industry*, vol. 1, p. 4.
[4] *Brit. O.H.*, 1971, p. 299.
[5] *The Structure of British Industry*, vol. 1., pp. 22–4. Also see 'Changes in Britain's agriculture', *loc. cit.*, pp. 19–20

Horticultural Cooperation Scheme was launched: this incorporated and extended grants for co-operative production and marketing projects. In recent years syndicates of farmers have been formed in some areas to purchase and share the use of equipment and machinery. By 1968 over 900 machinery syndicates were in existence: N.F.U. credit companies had been formed in over forty counties, to assist in financing the purchase of equipment by them. Official grants to syndicates, towards the cost of buildings to house grain or machinery, were available.

The salient features of this section are brought out in Table 3.14.

Table 3.14 *Distribution of U.K. farms by size, employees and net income, 1966–1970*

Size category	Standard employee man-day requirement	No. of units	% of total acreage	% contribution to total output	Av. acreage per farm	Av. male employees per farm	Av. net income per farm	Av. male employees per acre	Av. net income per acre
	less than					*less than*	(£)		(£)
Very small	275	150,000	10	10	16	1	687	1/16	43
Small	275–599	90,000	20	15	62	1–2	1,066	1/62–1/31	17
Medium	600–1,199	56,000	30	25	130	2–4	1,773	1/65–1/32	13
Large	1,200+	40,000	40	50	300	4+	3,000	1/75	10

(Source: *Britain's Agriculture Today*, pp. 9–10, 12–13; 'Facing the future: the agricultural estate,' *N.W.B.Q.R.*, May 1971; *Brit. O.H.*, 1971, pp. 299–300; *D.T.*, 22 June 1970; *F.T.*, 26 June 1970.)

(b) Concentration of control in marketing

To fortify the weak bargaining position of the mass of small producers, who would otherwise be fiercely competing with similar products under fairly inelastic supply conditions (in the short run), the Government set up marketing boards for many commodities. These operate under the 1958 Agricultural Marketing Act, which consolidated earlier legislation.

The boards are producers' organisations, with statutory powers to regulate the marketing of their products. By 1972 there were four marketing boards – for hops and potatoes (both of which established production quotas), milk (which operated a revenue-pooling system for producers) and wool (which implemented the Government's guaranteed-price subsidy scheme). All, except for potatoes, are sole buyers of the regulated product (or regulate all contracts between sellers and first buyers). In potatoes, it exercises broad control over general marketing conditions, leaving producers free to deal individually with buyers. Until 1964 there were boards for tomatoes and cucumbers, similar to that for potatoes, exercising broad control: in April 1971 the Egg Marketing Board (sole buyer type, implementing a guaranteed-price subsidy scheme) was replaced by a more general Eggs Authority, restricted to 'support buying', to upholding the market price and to general market matters. Separate marketing boards operate in Northern Ireland for milk, pigs and seed potatoes.[1]

For horticultural products, since the demise of the Horticultural Marketing Council (1960–62), grants of up to one-third are available for the modernisation of major wholesale markets, national statutory grades are being introduced for

[1] *Brit. O.H.*, 1971, p. 315; 'Case for marketing boards revived', *F.T.*, 29 Jan. 1971; 'Taxpayers down on the farm', *D.T.*, 29 Nov. 1968.

many products and the Apple and Pear Development Council publicises home-grown fruit.[1]

For sugar, the British Sugar Corporation contracts to buy the whole sugar beet crop from a specified area at fixed prices, according to the annual price review. The corporation arranges market-sharing agreements with the refiners, for the sale of its refined sugar on the basis of world prices. Commonwealth sugar imports are purchased and sold commercially by the Sugar Board, under the Commonwealth Sugar Agreement. A levy on home-produced and imported sugar entering the home market is used to finance deficits resulting from the joint transactions of the board and corporation. A distribution payment is given when surpluses are made.

Suggestions have been voiced for statutory marketing boards for cereals and livestock, as a means of controlling supply and price and thus reducing the need for 'fallback guarantees' or price-deficiency subsidy payments. In regard to cereals, mainly the product of the bigger farms and in which Britain is not self-sufficient, sale at fixed prices through a single channel might well appeal to farmers. In regard to livestock, the control of marketing would be much more difficult: animal output is much more unpredictable than is the case with cereals and so a marketing board would require considerable financial backing. As at 1972, the Home-Grown Cereals Authority, established under the 1965 Cereals Marketing Act, operates in this area: it provides marketing intelligence, operates a bonus scheme, has reserve trading powers and aims to improve marketing efficiency in home-grown cereals. The 1967 Agriculture Marketing Act established the Meat and Livestock Commission, charged with promoting greater efficiency in the production, marketing and distribution of livestock and livestock products (excepting dairying and fleece wool). One of its most important executive functions is to evolve a general scheme of carcase classification: it has no trading functions in livestock or meat.

The Government has, in recent years, aimed at encouraging more efficient marketing in agriculture, and the 1961 annual review proposed that funds should be provided for research into and development of marketing techniques.[2] These proposals were incorporated into the 1962 annual price review in March 1962 (Cmnd 1658). The Agriculture (Miscellaneous Provisions) Act of 1963 confirmed these proposals, and allowed for expenditure of £1½ million during an experimental period of three years. The grant ceiling was later raised to £2 million and the scheme extended to March 1971. This Act indicated a trend away from direct price support subsidies to direct grants, intended to encourage a more efficient production pattern and marketing system for agriculture.[3]

The scope and necessity for cooperation in marketing is becoming recognised by the industry as a counterweight to its weakness on the production side and to the increasing bargaining power of its large customers. A report published in October 1971 found that agricultural cooperatives were suffering from a chronic shortage of capital in the industry, as compared with commercial competitors, with regard to investment and trading projects.[4] Nevertheless, the Central

[1] For further data on the horticulture section of the industry, see *Britain's Agriculture Today*, Part 3.
[2] *Annual Price Review*, 1961, Cmnd 1311.
[3] For further discussion of support policies and the policy of reducing reliance on price-deficiency payments, see 'A question of timing', *Econ.*, 12 Dec. 1970, p. 24; Metcalf, *op. cit.*, ch. 7; 'Dearer food policy', *F.T.*, 18 Dec. 1970.   [4] *F.T.*, 19 Oct. 1971.

Council for Agricultural and Horticultural Co-operation has been gradually extending and widening its grant aid to marketing cooperatives, especially for the benefit of small farmers and for the improvement of efficiency.[1] The fourth annual report of the C.C.A.H.C., in May 1971, revealed that during 1970–71 £1·1 million was granted to 592 cooperative projects: the most popular type was silage groups, of which over 300 were grant-aided during 1970–71.[2] In March 1969 the Deputy Chairman of C.C.A.H.C. announced that since 1945 the agricultural cooperative movement's annual turnover had risen by 725% (compared with a 238% rise in aggregate farm income) to over £300 million.[3]

(c) Tiers of authority

Britain's entry into the European Economic Community (Common Market) would result in its Council of Ministers' making ultimate decisions on policy for British agriculture. The Council of Ministers would become the pinnacle of the pyramid of supervisory authority.

Meanwhile Government policy is exercised through the agricultural ministers (the Minister of Agriculture, Fisheries and Food for England and Wales; the Secretary of State for Scotland; the Home Secretary for Northern Ireland, who is responsible for United Kingdom aspects of Northern Ireland agriculture). These agricultural ministers have under them a number of advisory committees. In England and Wales the ministry is divided functionally, each division dealing with a particular subject or service and operating through local offices, grouped into eight regions. There are County Agricultural Executive Committees, whose duties include the promotion of technical development and advising the minister on local aspects of policy. In Scotland, the Secretary of State's agricultural functions are executed through the Department of Agriculture and Fisheries, with the assistance of eleven Agricultural Executive Committees. Northern Ireland has its own Minister of Agriculture, responsible for local aspects of agriculture, under whom is an agricultural executive officer in each county.

The agricultural ministers review State policy and support for the industry in the annual review, each February. Special interim reviews are possible, if considered necessary by the ministers. For the reviews, the ministers must consult with the three farmers' unions and must consider such factors as production trends, market requirements, world market prospects, the cost of subsidies, the trend in profits, increasing efficiency, changes in production costs, trading relations and the national economic situation. The guaranteed prices decided upon are for cattle, fat sheep, fat pigs, eggs, wool and milk during the following year, and for cereals, potatoes and sugar beet, harvested in the current year. 'Production grants' are made for various kinds of production or practice, such as for ploughing up grass, fertilisers and lime, calves (subsidy), hill cows (subsidy), small farmers, farm improvement, hill farming, farm drainage and water supply schemes. Capital grants are also made for farm improvement, buildings and equipment and for amalgamations, cooperative projects and marketing research.

The agricultural ministers assist the Ministry of Housing and Local Government (in England and Wales) and the Department of Health (in Scotland) in pursuing Government policy with regard to land use.

[1] F.T., 30 April 1969 and 30 April 1970.
[2] F.T., 19 May 1971.
[3] F.T., 13 March 1969.

Various agricultural credit facilities for specific purposes are encouraged and supported by the Government.[1] In England and Wales, the Agricultural Mortgage Corporation, Ltd, which provides long-term finance for the purchase or improvement of agricultural property, receives some Government support. In October 1971 the Corporation announced a scheme for short-term loans of eight to ten years' duration for immediate spending for expansion, in addition to its existing long-term loans of up to forty years' duration.[2] In Scotland, the Scottish Agricultural Securities Corporation, Ltd, which receives government support, makes loans for agricultural purposes. In Northern Ireland, no loans are advanced for land purchase, but for a wide range of agricultural purposes they may be obtained from the Agricultural Loans Fund, administered by the Ministry of Agriculture, financed out of public funds.

The State also provides advisory services and research and education services, through such bodies as the Ministry of Agriculture's Agricultural Development and Advisory Service[3] and the Agricultural Research Council, which conducts its own research and also makes grants to universities and other institutions.

Within the industry itself, the main bodies are the three National Farmers' Unions, the marketing boards, the cooperatives and the individual firms, most of which are single-farm units.

In the field of hired labour, which is a relatively small element, when compared with the employer-employee ratio in other industries, the weak bargaining position of what is often casual or seasonal labour is fortified by the presence of the Agricultural Wages Boards, which fix minimum wage rates and conditions of work.

In the other factor markets conditions vary from the State monopoly over rail transport, through oligopoly in the production and supply of fertilisers (I.C.I. and Fisons), and oligopoly in tractor and heavy machinery supply, to imperfect competition in the supply of feedingstuffs (influenced by advertising), and full competition in the supply of livestock and insurance. The State, however, influences the fertiliser, feedingstuffs and seed markets by means of the subsidies and production grants.

4. The Impact of the Common Market

Between 1962 and 1966 the basic foundations of the E.E.C.'s Common Agricultural Policy (C.A.P.) were elaborated: C.A.P. eventually emerged as a highly protective commercial policy. By 1972 it was covering cereals (wheat, rye, barley, maize and rice); pigmeat, beef and veal; poultry and eggs; milk and milk products; sugar; fruit and vegetables; wine. The dual purpose of the policy is firstly, to maintain a high level of farm incomes and secondly, to modernise and restructure E.E.C. agriculture.

Income protection is sought by way of 'target' or support prices fixed above the world level of market prices – by variable protective levies on imports and by export subsidies. If the market price drops below the 'target price', local intervention agencies can buy up surpluses at the 'target' or 'intervention' price. The intervention subsidies are financed by F.E.O.G.A. (the European Agricultural Guidance and Guarantee Fund): about 90% of this central fund is spent

[1] 'Finance for farming', *M.B.R.*, Feb. 1965, pp. 3–10.
[2] *F.T.*, 14 Oct. 1971.
[3] *F.T.*, 26 Feb. 1971.

on agriculture and it is financed from all the member States' levies on food imports, all their customs duties on goods and a proportion of their V.A.T. (Value Added Tax) revenue.

The restructuring and modernising of E.E.C. agriculture is to be sought by way of the Mansholt Plan, as it was modified and adopted in March 1971. This originally aimed at a 12% reduction in agricultural acreage by 1980, a decrease of 3·6 million in the agricultural occupied population, pensions for farmers, consolidation of the least efficient units into larger units and increased mechanisation. The much watered-down Plan adopted was to be implemented regionally, but faces many political problems in execution.[1] The need for such changes is highlighted by comparison with British agriculture. E.E.C. farmers and farm employees (11 million) constitute 14% of the E.E.C. occupied population but contribute only 8% to E.E.C. Gross National Product. In 1968 the average size of the 5·7 million E.E.C. farms was only 27 acres [11·34 hectares] (compared with about 160 acres [64·74 hectares] for full-time holdings in England and Wales): almost 87% were 50 acres (20·23 hectares) or less and 66% were 25 acres [10·12 hectares] or less; 80% of the 4 million dairy herds in the E.E.C. contained 10 cows or less: the 'ideal' farm, suggested by High Commission officials, was approximately the current England and Wales average – 150–175 acres [60–70 hectares] with about 50 cows.[2] One of the major reasons for the problem of agricultural surpluses in the E.E.C. has been the inefficient farm size: target prices high enough to protect the small farmer have encouraged the more efficient, larger farmers to produce more and more.

Britain's entry into the E.E.C. should have significant implications. Firstly, farmers would have to rely on higher market prices and 'intervention buying', instead of on price-deficiency Exchequer support. Secondly, British agriculture would be subject to C.A.P. and the E.E.C. High Commission. Thirdly, either Britain would become a vast importer of E.E.C. commodities, switching its imports from traditional external suppliers, or British farmers would have a strong incentive to produce more, at higher market prices, thus increasing British self-sufficiency and reducing imports and the subsequent repaying of import levies to F.E.O.G.A. In the former event, British entry would reduce the burden of financing C.A.P., as regards the other members of the E.E.C. This, in turn, would relax the pressures on E.E.C. agriculture, making for reconstruction.[3]

For British agriculture itself, there are three main problems:

(i) the diminution of United Kingdom sovereignty in granting protection;
(ii) the method or protection and price determination;
(iii) the extent of protection.

(i) Ultimate decisions on agricultural policy would be taken by a qualified majority vote in the Council of Ministers of all member countries, some of which might have problems and interests quite different from those of Britain.

---

[1] A. L. Lougheed, 'The common agricultural policy and international trade', *N.W.B.Q.R.*. Nov. 1971; *D.T.*, 8 Feb. 1972. *Econ.*, 10 Oct. 1970, p. 60.
[2] *Ibid*; 'How the Common Market works', *Obs.*, 11 July 1971; *Econ.*, 10 Oct. 1970, p. 60; 'E.E.C. agricultural reform', *F.T.*, 5 Feb. 1971. (*N.B.* Compare this 'ideal' with that envisaged for Britain, viz., about 500 acres of crops and grass.)
[3] Lougheed, *op. cit.*; *Econ.*, 10 Oct. 1970, p. 60 and 15 May 1971, pp. 52–3; 'The logic of E.E.C.'s farm policy', *D.T.*, 29 June 1971; 'Moving closer to the Common Market system', *F.T.*, 22 July 1970; 'Agriculture and fisheries', *F.B.E.* No. 7, June 1971.

(ii) The Continental system of protection is for agreed and protected prices, the efficiency of which would depend on the resultant amount of production and the disposal of any surpluses. The British system, which the farmers' unions wish to retain, is for annual reviews, agreed prices and subsidy payments for deficiencies in actual market prices. The farmers also wish to retain adequate protection for non-review commodities, especially horticulture, and to retain the various producer marketing organisations.[1]

(iii) The British farming organisations fear that price support would be lower in E.E.C. than out of it. The N.F.U. President maintains that E.E.C. is about 90% self-sufficient, and that price policy might be directed against excess production. On the other hand, G. McCrone[2] contends that price support in Britain is not high, and results in the farm prices of all products except milk and eggs (and in some years, sugar beet) being below those of Germany, and not much higher

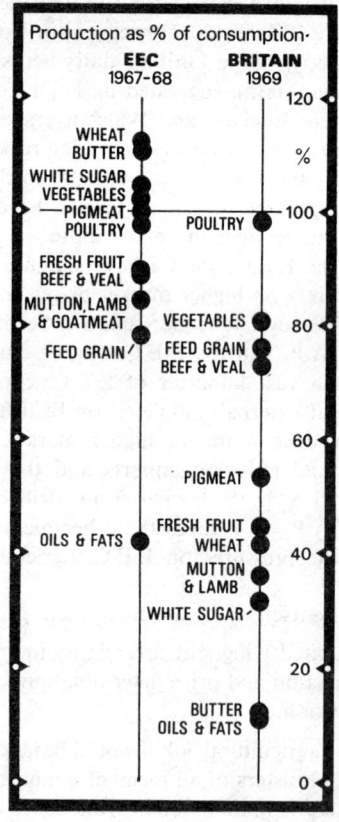

Fig. 3.21. *Agricultural self-sufficiency in Britain and the E.E.C.: production as percentage of consumption*
(Source: *Econ.* 10 Oct. 1970, p. 60)

---

[1] N.F.U. President, 'British agriculture and the Common Market', *British Farmer*, 7 July 1962.
[2] *The Economics of Subsidising Agriculture*, G. McCrone, 1962.

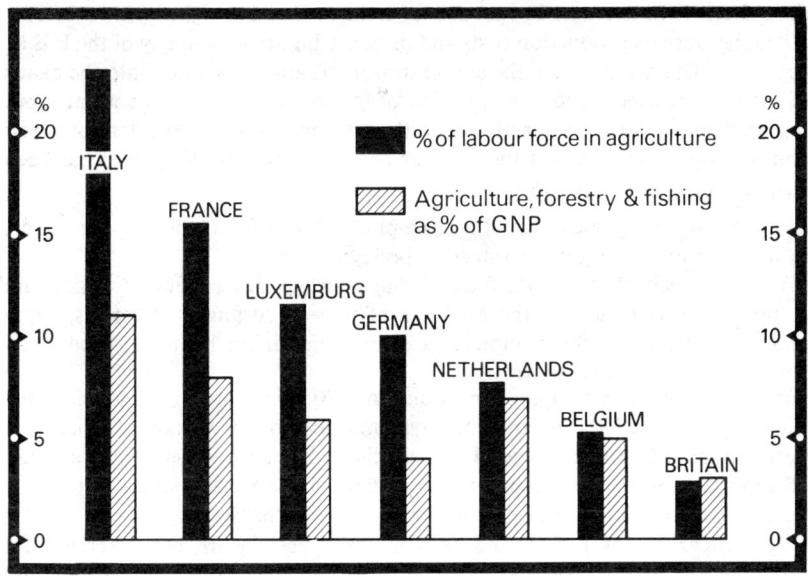

Fig. 3.22. *Agricultural efficiency in Britain and the E.E.C., 1968*
(Source: *Econ.* 10 Oct. 1970, p. 61)

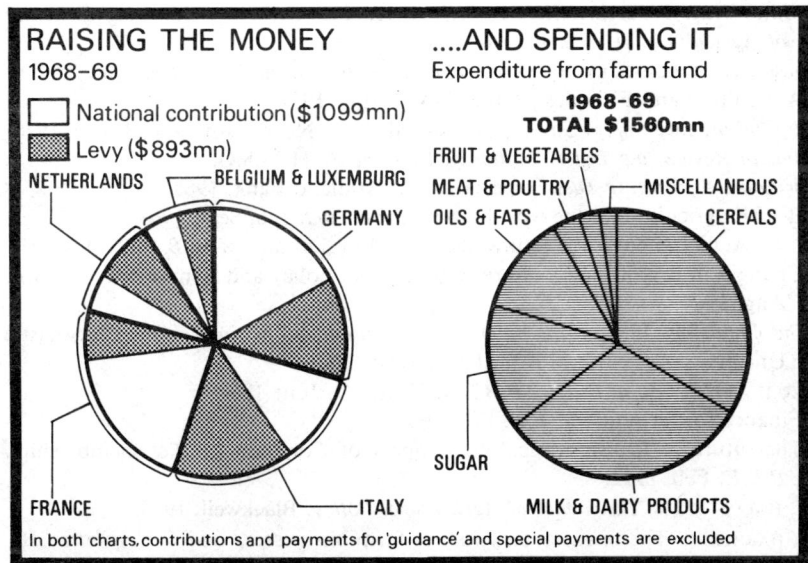

Fig. 3.23. *E.E.C. central agricultural fund revenue and expenditure*
(Source: *Econ.* 10 Oct. 1970, p. 61)

than the E.E.C. average. Production of milk in Britain might have to be curtailed, because its production costs and price are higher than in any of the E.E.C. countries. This would entail the concentration of milk production into the hands of the most efficient producers and also of farmers who have no alternative but to supplement their other activities with milk production.[1] Furthermore, Self and Storing[2] point out that the case for protecting the British farmer has been exaggerated on three grounds:

(i) the strategic argument would best be pursued by a food storage programme, rather than an agricultural production policy;
(ii) the argument that a world food shortage necessitates a sheltered agriculture at home is invalidated by the existence of present surpluses of cereals, sugar and dairy products: the economic case for maintaining high-cost production with subsidies is therefore weak;
(iii) the argument that support, resulting in a 70% increase in output since the war, has improved the balance of payments position, is weakened when it is borne in mind that this increased self-sufficiency has been largely at the expense of imports from the Commonwealth members of the Sterling area: Britain has tended to have a balance of payments surplus with the Sterling area.

A comparison of E.E.C. and British self-sufficiency in major agricultural products and relative agricultural efficiency, and an analysis of central fund revenue and expenditure may be seen in Figs. 3.21 to 3.23.

5. Further Reading and Sources

Footnote references to daily and weekly journals are not repeated.

AGRICULTURAL DEPARTMENTS IN THE UNITED KINGDOM, *The Changing Structure of Agriculture*. H.M.S.O. 1970.

MINISTRY OF AGRICULTURE AND FISHERIES, *At the Farmer's Service*. 1962.

'Agriculture and Fisheries', *F.B.E.* No. 7. June 1971.

Agriculture and Import Saving, Occasional Paper No. 5. Hill Samuel. Feb. 1970.

Annual Review and Determination of Guarantees. H.M.S.O.

Britain's Agriculture Today, special study. Midland Bank. 1968.

'British agriculture in the world setting'. *Bull. Ind.* 166. Sept. 1963.

A. A. CALDER, 'Facing the future: the agricultural estate'. *N.W.B.Q.R.* May 1971

'Changes in Britain's agriculture: Government policy and farm output'. *M.B.R.* Aug. 1964.

The Changing Agricultural Labour Force: Implications for Training. Newcastle University Agricultural Adjustment Unit. 1970.

C.O.I. *Agriculture in Britain*. *B.B.L.A.* H.M.S.O. June 1964.

'Finance for farming'. *M.B.R.* Feb. 1965.

'The future of British Agriculture: impact of Common Market membership'. *B.B.R.* Feb. 1972.

G. HALLETT, *The Economics of Agricultural Policy*. Blackwell. 1968.

A. HARRISON, 'The financial structure of farm businesses,' *SSRC Newsletter*. 20. Oct. 1973.

[1] 'Farmer's diary', *D.T.*, 13 Nov. 1961.
[2] P. Self and H. J. Storing, *The State and the Farmer*, 1962.

A. L. LOUGHEED, 'The common agricultural policy and international trade'. *N.W.B.Q.R.* Nov. 1971.

G. MCCRONE, *The Economics of Subsidising Agriculture.* Allen & Unwin. 1962.

D. METCALF, *The Economics of Agriculture.* Penguin. 1969.

NATIONAL FARMERS' UNION, *Information Service.* Vol. 20. 1. 1965. (Special edition on 1965/6 Annual Review.)

N.F.U. PRESIDENT, 'British agriculture and the Common Market'. *British Farmer.* 7 July 1962.

T. PHILLIPS and C. RITSON, 'Agricultural expansion and the U.K. balance of payments'. *N.W.B.Q.R.* Feb. 1970.

S. J. ROGERS, 'Political algebra and U.K. agricultural policy'. *N.W.B.Q.R.* Feb. 1969.

P. SELF and H. J. STORING, *The State and the Farmer.* Allen & Unwin. 1962.

THE MOTOR INDUSTRY: Stage I

1. Technical Background

The boundaries between the motor vehicle industry and other branches of engineering are not easy to define. The industry could be said to cover the manufacture not only of motor cars and commercial vehicles, but also tractors, works trucks, trailers, caravans, marine and industrial engines, transport service equipment and the components and accessories incorporated in them. Generally however, the industry is considered to cover the assembly of motor cars (including taxis) and commercial vehicles, and the manufacture of their components.

From modest beginnings the motor vehicle industry has grown, since World War II, to become one of the most important industries in the economy, a large employer of labour, an important customer of other industries, and one of the major sources of export earnings.

The motor industry is an assembly industry, but none of the manufacturers of finished vehicles is self-sufficient. Of the 20,000 (at least) parts in the average vehicle, about 60% of the final value of motor assembly production is still represented by materials, components and services bought out from over 1,000 component manufacturers and firms in the iron and steel and general engineering industries.[1] Great economies of scope or integration exist for manufacturers to supply their own components, but this depends upon the scale of their output being sufficiently large to warrant integration. Among the products most frequently bought out are bodies, electrical equipment, tyres, wheels, brakes, bearings, castings, pressings and drop forgings. Much vertical integration has taken place within the few largest firms in recent years, but none has reached the degree of integration achieved by the largest American producers. On the other hand, the parallel development of the main component manufacturers, catering for several firms, has enabled them to specialise, enjoying economies of large scale standardisation.

The assembly nature of the industry, the element of standardisation in components, and the flow-production techniques which gradually evolved, have influenced the location of the industry and changes in the location pattern.

Benz and Daimler began the manufacture of motor cars in Germany in 1885

---

[1] C. F. Pratten, *Economies of Scale in Manufacturing Industry*, ch. 14, p. 134.

and 1886. In America the motor industry received a great stimulus in its early days from the favourable home market conditions of high income per head, and from the fact that, on the supply side, American engineering trades had developed production techniques to manufacture 'interchangeable' or standardised parts. The latter factor enabled American manufacturers to adopt mass-production methods right from the start, and the availability of competing outside suppliers of standardised parts reduced the risk of monopoly control over components supplies. It also relieved the assemblers of the need to invest in component production.

In Britain, the larger engineering firms were not very keen on the 'interchangeable' principle, and concentrated mainly on heavy equipment. Coventry, Birmingham and Wolverhampton, however, had by the last quarter of the nineteenth century become centres of a wide range of engineering products. These, in turn, had led to the localisation there of the cycle industry. Due to the seasonal character of the demand for cycles, some firms engaged in that industry began to turn to motor vehicle production (lateral integration) to supplement their output.

The beginnings of the motor industry in Britain are marked by the entry of the English Daimler and Lanchester companies in 1896. Between 1900 and 1914 many firms entered the industry, such as Rolls-Royce, Napier, Albion, Rover, Humber, A.E.C., Dennis, Hillman, Crossley, Austin, Morris, Standard, Armstrong Siddeley, Ford and Vauxhall. Most of these had previously been general engineering companies, but some, such as Rover, Humber, Dennis and Morris had been cycle manufacturers. The new industry needed skilled labour, alloy steels, electrical fittings, pneumatic tyres, and the products of the brass, screw, nut, bolt, tube, leather, spring and paint trades. The west Midlands was particularly well suited to provide these products, and the numerous independent manufacturers there adapted themselves to the needs of the motor vehicle assemblers.

The first goods-carrying motor vehicle produced in Britain was the three-ton Napier, in 1902.

The pattern of the industry until 1911 was marked by the lack of standardisation, the large number of small producers, producing a considerable number of their own parts, the large number of models and the small number of highly priced vehicles. The Ford Motor Company of Great Britain was the first firm to produce vehicles on a large scale, with the introduction of the model 'T' Ford. Other manufacturers soon began to introduce flow-production techniques, using standardised parts. After World War I, the decade 1920–30 was marked by the efforts of British motor vehicle firms to reorganise their production methods for the large-scale production of cheaper, standardised vehicles.

During the period since World War II a significant development has been the great advance in production methods and factory layout. This has been most pronounced amongst the larger vehicle and component manufacturers. Plants have become increasingly automated, and a high degree of mechanisation has been achieved even in medium-sized and smaller plants.

The industry is one of the chief customers for machine tools, required for the numerous processing and assembly stages. Early processes involved in shaping the metal parts include pressings (e.g. bodies), forgings (e.g. crankshafts) and castings (e.g. cylinder blocks). Later processes involve machining parts into their final shape.

The assembly stages are complex, but may be split into three phases. First comes the construction of components (e.g. dynamos and carburettors) from their constituent parts. Secondly, these components are assembled into more complex units (e.g. engines and bodies) in the vehicle plant's sub-assembly department. Thirdly, the complete vehicle is assembled. The number of assembly stages performed by the vehicle manufacturer depends on the degree of integration he has achieved. This will be influenced by his scale of output.

Increasing use is being made, by the larger producers, of automatic transfer machines, to speed up the flow-production processes. These were first installed by Morris Motors of Oxford in 1923,[1] but they were successfully applied for the first time by American motor plants after World War II. They consist of a number of multihead 'tool stations', which form an automatic flow-production line in which precise operations are automatically performed, the processed part being automatically moved on to the next 'station'. These automatic transfer machines are arranged in sequence on either side of conveyor belts. The conveyor belts themselves are arranged in sequence, so that the 'flow tributaries' automatically deliver the main components to the main assembly line at the exact moment required. In consequence, precise coordination and timing may be achieved, permitting the incorporation of accessories and trims to suit individual customers' requirements. Furthermore, operational speeds can be controlled; economies in handling time can be achieved; productivity can be increased; reliance on skilled labour is reduced. During the 1960s one of the major developments in assembly operations has been the introduction of more automated methods and tools. For one U.K. manufacturer it was estimated that for rates of output up to 80 vehicles per hour per assembly line labour costs per unit were 12% less, and capital costs per unit 18% less than at rates of 30 vehicles per hour. Above eighty per hour efficiency was adversely affected by the speed of the line. At the other extremes, one leading European assembler estimated the maximum rate of production at only sixteen per hour per assembly line, whereas in the U.S. lines with a capacity of more than 120 vehicles per hour have been built. Another U.K. assembler estimated the effect of assembling a mix of models on an existing line as a reduction in capacity of about 8%[2]. On the other hand, at least one Japanese assembler has succeeded, by sophisticated computer-controlled automated coordination, to assemble more than twenty different models on a single assembly line, as if they constituted a normal mass-production flow, as quickly as a conventional line could handle a single standard model.[3]

The smaller firms do not usually produce on a sufficiently large scale to use such capital-intensive techniques and special purpose equipment. They tend to use more general purpose machinery and a correspondingly larger proportion of more highly skilled labour.

2. History and Development

After the introduction of the model 'T' Ford in 1911, produced on a relatively large scale, several other inexpensive models came into production, including Singer and Morris. Production of cars and commercial vehicles rose from 19,000 in 1911 to 34,000 in 1913 (of which, Ford 6,000; Wolseley 2,500; Morris, Austin,

[1] *British Motor Vehicle Industry*, p. 11.
[2] C. F. Pratten, *loc. cit.*, p. 139; also 'Vegas held up', *Econ.*, 12 Feb. 1972, p. 48.
[3] *Stat.*, 30 Dec. 1966, p. 10; *Econ.*, 20 Jan. 1968, p. 47.

Singer and Rover 1,000 each). Compared with 1913 production in the U.S.A. (485,000) and even France (45,000), this was still comparatively small. During World War I the industry was geared to war needs, and the home market was protected by the imposition in 1915 of an *ad valorem* duty on imported cars.

During the decade 1920–30 American-style flow-production methods were increasingly adopted by many firms. Morris and Austin became serious challengers of Ford. Despite new entrants to the industry, mergers and bankruptcies resulted in the number of firms falling from eighty-eight in 1922 to thirty-one in 1929. Output of cars rose from 71,000 in 1923 to 182,000 in 1929; output of commercial vehicles in that period expanded from 23,604 to 56,458. Absolutely and relatively, exports rose, from 5,278 cars and taxis and 1,483 commercial vehicles in 1923 to 33,792 and 8,451, respectively, in 1929. By 1929, when total output was 238,805 vehicles, the U.S.A. produced 5·3 million, Canada 263,000, France 253,000 and Germany 156,000. Morris, Austin and Singer accounted for 75% of car output; Morris and Ford were the largest producers of commercial vehicles.

The British motor vehicle industry suffered much less than that of other countries during the world trade depression which started in late 1929. In fact, by 1933 total output was 286,000, about 50,000 more than in 1929. The relative prosperity of the industry in Britain was due to several factors. First, British motor vehicles were, until 1947, taxed according to their horsepower, which was rated according to the piston area of the engine; the petrol tax here encouraged fuel efficiency and small engines; insurance premiums were heavier on cars with large engines. Consequently, British manufacturers tended to concentrate on small-engined cars, which were not competitive in the U.S.A. and other markets, where large-engined cars were demanded. However, these factors tended to protect the home market from imports of large-engined foreign cars. During the depression the low running costs of British cars gave them added protection in the home market and also increased their competitiveness in foreign markets, in many of which fuel taxes were increased. Secondly, the U.S.A. market was relatively saturated, and demand was largely for replacement vehicles. During the depression U.S.A. demand for replacements tended to be postponed. In Britain, on the other hand, the market had hardly been scratched. In fact, despite the high level of unemployment generally, real income per head rose during the depression, largely due to falling import prices (improving terms of trade) and falling domestic prices. This factor was reinforced by the high income-elasticity of demand experienced for vehicles, whereby, as real incomes rose, the demand for vehicles rose proportionately more, albeit at the expense of other commodities. Thirdly, falling U.S.A. output entailed rising costs per unit. This made American vehicles less competitive with British cars in export markets. Added to this were the effect of the depreciation of many currencies in relation to the dollar (following the abandonment of the gold standard in 1931), and the further effect of the widespread imposition of *ad valorem* protective tariffs throughout the world.

After the depression the industry continued to expand, reaching a prewar peak of 493,000 vehicles (379,000 cars and 114,000 commercial vehicles) in 1937. By then Britain was the second largest producer in the world, while America (3·9 million cars, 891,000 commercial vehicles in 1937) and France did not regain their pre-1929 levels of output until after World War II. In 1931 exports of cars and taxis had fallen to 18,992, but commercial vehicle exports were hardly affected, reaching 5,429. By 1937 exports were still higher than in 1929, both absolutely and relatively, reaching 78,113 cars and taxis and 21,072 commercial vehicles.[1] The 1930s saw a continuance of the process of concentration of production and control in the industry, into bigger plants and fewer firms. There was a large proportionate growth in the output of medium-priced and medium-powered cars, to cater partly for export markets and partly for changing tastes in the domestic market. By 1938 the number of independent firms had shrunk to twenty, six of which were responsible for 90% of car and 80% of commercial vehicle production. The Big Six were, in order of size as car producers: Nuffield (Morris), Austin, Ford, Vauxhall, Rootes and Standard. As light commercial vehicle producers Vauxhall (acquired by General Motors of U.S.A. in 1926) was the most important, followed by Rootes.

During World War II the industry was again turned over to military production. A great boost to total capacity was given by the extension of plants to produce specialised vehicles, tanks, aero engines, etc. By 1944, out of a total vehicle production of 132,955, goods vehicles (mainly for the Services) accounted for 99⅛%.

After World War II there were significant increases in concentration of control, production, productivity, proportion of output exported, capacity, reduction in the number of models, and the use of common components.

In 1952 Austin and Nuffield merged to form B.M.C. (the British Motor Corporation); A.C.V. (Associated Commercial Vehicles) have absorbed Crossley, Park Royal, Maudsley and Thornycroft and the A.E.C. Leyland acquired Albion in 1951, Scammell in 1955, and Standard-Triumph at the end of 1960. In mid-1962 Leyland-Standard-Triumph, producing a wide range of vehicles, from saloon cars to the heaviest commercial vehicles, announced a merger with A.C.V., the second largest producer of lorries and buses. This produced the biggest heavy vehicle group in the world, with sales of £150 million annually and assets of £120 million.[2] In 1956 Rootes acquired Singer; Jaguar acquired Daimler in 1960 and Guy Motors in 1961. During the late 1960s the main features of the British motor industry began to crystallise. In 1965 B.M.C. merged vertically with the body panel-making firms Pressed Steel and Fisher-Ludlow, which, due to capacity exceeding B.M.C.'s requirements, continued to supply competitors both in Britain and abroad. The following year it took over the Jaguar group, to expand its range of products and become B.M.H. – British Motors (Holdings) – amalgamating the three main sectors of activity.[3] At the end of 1966 the Leyland group took over the last main independent car producer, Rover, to extend its range of lighter products and pool overseas marketing and servicing facilities.[4] In 1967 the American firm, Chrysler, gained formal control of the Rootes group, thus bringing about half the British motor industry under American control.[5] During 1967 it was becoming apparent that the Leyland group had to expand in order to survive: this could be achieved either by creating new capacity for mass-produced cars and a lighter range of vans and other commercial vehicles or by merging with an existing group whose range and output would complement its own. Also, B.M.H. was experiencing problems of insufficiently rationalised

[1] *British Motor Vehicle Industry*, p. 4.   [2] *D.T.*, 6 June 1962.
[3] *D.T.*, 12 July 1966.   [4] *D.T.*, 13 Dec. 1966.
[5] *D.T.*, 11 Jan. 1967.

management, capacity and output: there were fears that it, too, would come under American control. For reasons such as these, in 1968 the two groups merged to form the British Leyland Motor Corporation.[1]

The process of vertical integration, stimulated by increases in output, has included several vertical mergers between motor firms and component firms. In 1969 B.L.M.C. further rationalised its vertically integrated control over Pressed Steel and Fisher-Ludlow, achieved in 1965, by linking and coordinating their output with that of the Austin-Morris division of British Leyland, in particular at the Cowley (Oxford) complex.[2]

Production reached and surpassed the prewar (1937) peak by 1948, with 508,117 vehicles (334,815 cars and taxis; 173,302 commercial vehicles). The largest proportionate increase by then had been made by commercial vehicles. In 1950 cars and taxis reached the half-million mark for the first time, and commercial vehicles passed the quarter-million mark. By 1955 production of cars and taxis reached 897,560 and commercial vehicles reached the figure of 339,508. In that year, total vehicle output was 146% higher than in 1948, but labour had only increased by 16·5% (from 284,000 to 331,000), indicating a much higher productivity per man employed in the industry.[3]

Some of the factors making for the growth in production and exports during the period since World War II were as follows: first, capacity had been expanded during the war years, and this was available for peacetime production; secondly, there was a pent-up demand at home and abroad for motor vehicles, both private and commercial; thirdly, there was a dollar shortage in most countries, which, together with the high domestic demand for U.S.A. and Canadian vehicles, resulted in low supply and demand conditions for those vehicles; fourthly, production in European vehicle industries had been dislocated by the war; fifthly, high and rising real income at home and abroad extended the demand for vehicles; sixthly, expansion in the steel industry (especially in sheet steel) made supplies more readily available for the industry. For some years restrictions were imposed, during the export drive, on the number sold in Britain, and the motor vehicle industry participated in the high degree of concentration of British manufacturing resources on export markets.

By 1960 total vehicle production reached 1,810,700, of which cars and taxis were 1,352,728 and commercial vehicles were 457,972. Both groups had expanded almost fourfold since 1938. In 1961 contraction in home and overseas demand caused total output to fall, to 1,464,134. However, the loss was suffered by car and taxi output, which fell to 1,003,967, whereas commercial vehicle production rose slightly to 460,167. Employment in mid-1961 among the motor vehicle manufacturers and their main suppliers was 415,000.[4] Several thousand others were employed by firms which supplied components to the motor vehicle and other industries, and were not classified as being in the motor vehicle industry itself. This represented a decrease in productivity per man since 1955 (labour increased by about a quarter, whereas production was less than one-fifth higher). but motor firms were tending to hold on to their labour during the cyclical fall in demand. In fact, plans were already in force for additional capacity.

By 1960 the industry had invested about £150 million in expansion and re-

---

[1] For further details see *S.T.*, 21 Jan. 1968; *D.T.*, 25 Jan. 1968; *Econ.*, 28 Sept. 1968, pp. 56–7.
[2] 'Streamlining for the future at Cowley', *D.T.*, 24 April 1969.
[3] *British Motor Industry*, 1958, p. 7.
[4] *British Motor Vehicle Industry*, pp. 7–12, 22.

equipment. In 1960 plans were announced by the larger firms in the industry for expansion projects costing a further £200 million, guided by the Board of Trade to areas of high unemployment, to bring capacity to more than 2·3 million cars and taxis and 600,000 commercial vehicles (and tractors). Corresponding expansion plans by many producers of components, specialised cars and heavy commercial vehicles were also put in hand. The industry was confident that long-term prospects for demand at home and abroad were good, despite the progress being made by foreign manufacturers.

In the event, production during the 1960s did not fulfil manufacturers' expectations. The highest level of production was reached in 1964, with 2,332,376 units (cars, 1,867,640; commercial vehicles, 464,736). Only in the case of commercial vehicles was the 1964 level ever reached again during the decade, with 465,720 in 1969. Throughout the period annual production fluctuated, but the lowest level was achieved in 1967, with 1,937,119 units (cars, 1,552,013; commercial vehicles, 385,106). For 1970 production was 2,098,498 units (cars, 1,640,966; commercial vehicles, 457,532). Employment was 484,000 in 1964, 477,000 in 1967 and 520,000 in 1970.[1] Thus it may be seen that whereas the number of production units fell by 17% from 1964 to 1967, employment fell by only 1½%: productivity per man was much lower in the latter period. Similarly, whereas the number of production units fell by 10% from 1964 to 1970, the labour force actually rose by 7½%: productivity per man was even lower than in 1967. These data illustrate the importance of rationalisation, high levels of capacity utilisation and profitability in the industry: it was largely to bring these about that many of the mergers of the 1960s were effected.

There have been significant changes since World War II in the number of vehicles exported and the proportion of total output exported. Whereas in 1937 (the peak prewar export year) less than one-fifth of car, taxi and commercial vehicle output was exported, in 1948 68% of car and taxi output and 43% of commercial vehicle output were exported. By 1950 these proportions had risen to 76% and 55%, the highest ever. During the next decade, although the numbers exported rose, the proportions of total output exported fell. In 1960, 569,916 cars and taxis (42%) and 145,525 commercial vehicles (32%) were exported. By 1961 these proportions had changed to 37% (370,758) for cars and taxis, but to 36% (167,905) for commercial vehicles.[2] In 1961 Britain was the world's largest exporter of commercial vehicles.

In 1964 38% of cars and commercial vehicles were exported; in 1967 36·3% of cars and 35% of commercial vehicles were exported and in 1970 44·1% and 38%, respectively. For 1970, 43·3% of total output was exported, valued at £729·6 million: one-third of this value was accounted for by commercial vehicles, in the export of which Britain had fallen to second place, with 190,125, after Japan (316,000), closely followed by West Germany (179,170).[3]

The reductions, since the early postwar years, in the proportions of vehicles exported, have been accompanied by a strong tendency for home demand to rise. New registrations for cars reached a peak of 1,215,929 in 1964; for commercial vehicles the peak of 244,735 was reached in 1969; for hackney carriages

---

[1] *The Motor Industry of Great Britain, 1971*, pp. 26–8; *Ann. Abs. Stat.*, Nos. 104, 1967; 107, 1970; and 108, 1971.

[2] *British Motor Vehicle Industry*, p. 12.

[3] Based on material in *The Motor Industry of Great Britain, 1971*, pp. 26–8.

the peak year was 1949 (postwar replacements).[1]

Another factor accompanying this reduction in the proportions of output exported has been the change in the British share of world output. Britain maintained her position as the second largest producer until 1956, in which year she was overtaken by West Germany, and was closely followed by France. Since 1956 the relative positions of the world's leading producers have altered dramatically. Where as in 1956 Canada was fifth (467,864 units), Italy sixth (315,793 units) and Japan seventh (111,066 units), for 1970 the relative positions were as follows:[2]

> 1st – U.S.A.   (8¼ million)
> 2nd – Japan   (5,289,157 – of which ⅖ were commercial vehicles)
> 3rd – W.Germany (3,842,247 units)
> 4th – France   (2,750,086 units)
> 5th – U.K.   (2,098,498 units)
> 6th – Italy   (1,854, 252 units)
> 7th – Canada   (1,193,572 units)

The salient points in this section are reproduced in Table 3.15.

Table 3.15 *Output, exports and labour in the motor vehicle industry*

Year	Cars and taxis Prod. ('000)	Expts. ('000)	% Expd.	Commercial vehicles Prod. ('000)	Expts. ('000)	% Expd.	Total Prod. ('000)	Expts. ('000)	% Expd.	Labour ('000)
1911	–	–	–	–	–	–	19	–	–	–
1913	–	–	–	–	–	–	34	–	–	–
1923	71·4	5·28	7·4	23·6	1·48	6·3	95·0	6·76	7·1	–
1929	182·3	33·8	18·6	56·46	8·45	15·0	238·8	42·24	17·8	228 ⎫
1931	159·0	19·0	12·0	67·3	5·43	8·1	226·3	24·42	10·7	194 ⎪
1933	220·78	41·02	18·6	65·5	10·87	16·6	286·29	51·89	18·0	218 ⎬ †
1937	379·31	78·11	21·2	113·95	21·07	18·5	493·26	99·18	20·2	335 ⎪
1938	341·02	68·26	20·0	103·85	15·47	15·0	444·88	83·72	18·8	358 ⎭
1944	2·1	–	–	130·85	–	–	132·95	–	–	–
1948	334·81	226·02	68	173·3	74·25	43	508·12	300·27	59·2	284 ⎫
1950	522·51	398·12	76	261·16	143·89	55	783·67	542·01	69·0	300 ⎬ ‡
1955	897·56	388·39	43	339·5	139·81	41	1,237·07	528·21	42·7	331 ⎭
1960	1,352·73	575·32	42·5	457·97	167·95	36·7	1,810·7	743·27	41	436
1961	1,003·97	401·8	40·4	460·17	162·78	35·4	1,464·13	564·58	38·5	415
1962	1,249·43	551·0	44·1	425·1	155·34	36·5	1,674·53	706·34	42	429 (Oct.)
1963	1,607·94	649·17	40	403·78	164·9	39	2,011·72	814·07	38·5	454
1964	1,867·64	705·75	37·8	464·74	179·4	36	2,332·38	885·15	38	484
1967	1,552·01	563·74	36·3	385·1	139·4	35	1,937·12	703·14	36·2	477
1970	1,640·97	722·86	44·1	457·53	190·1	38	2,098·5	912·96	43·3	520

† Employment in construction and repair of motor vehicles, cycles and aircraft.
‡ Includes employment in manufacture of cycles.
(Based on material in *British Motor Vehicle Industry*, 1962; *British Motor Industry*, 1958; Memorandum from S.M.M.T., May 1965; *The Motor Industry of Great Britain*, 1971, pp. 14–17, 28; *Ann. Abs. Stat.*)

3. Location of the Motor Vehicle Industry

There have been important changes in the locational balance of the industry since its early days in the west Midlands. The first main surge was southwards, mainly towards London and the Home Counties, and was associated with the large-scale flow-production techniques which were increasingly applied from the

[1] *Ibid.*, p. 53.
[2] Based on material in *ibid.*, pp. 44–7.

1920s onwards. A secondary movement during this period was the gradual emergence of Lancashire as an important centre for components manufacture, associated with the decline in the cotton industry, which made available factory buildings and labour. This process was given added stimulus during World War II, as wartime requirements grew. The second main surge has been taking place since 1960, primarily towards Merseyside, South Wales and Scotland. These locational changes are discussed below.

There was still a high degree of regional concentration of employment in the industry in mid-1961. The Midlands region, primarily Birmingham and Coventry, continued to employ 36% of the labour force. London and the south-east, including Dagenham, accounted for almost 20%. The eastern and southern regions, including Luton in the east and Oxford and Cowley in the south, employed a further 21%. Lancashire accounted for 8·4%, mostly in components, but this labour force should gradually increase as the new Merseyside expansion projects for assembly and components take shape.[1]

(a) Early days

As outlined in Section 1.1, the west Midlands possessed many locational advantages for the motor vehicle industry. These included access to all parts of Britain, a wide variety of industrial products, many light engineering firms, and a pool of labour skilled in the upholstery, plating, key, chain, watchmaking and cycle industries. The early start of assembly and specialist component firms in this region resulted in a locational pattern which has continued to generate its own locational pull, especially for the production of quality vehicles, and components. The relative importance of the region declined, however, with the movement southward of assembly plants and firms and the movement to Lancashire of component plants and firms.

(b) Interwar years

The adoption of mass-production assembly methods by many firms, following the 1911 example of the model 'T' Ford, weakened the locational attraction of the west Midlands skilled labour pool, especially for assembly. The new methods required large numbers of unskilled and semi-skilled labour, and areas nearer to the markets of London, the south-east and the Continent, provided such labour, which was cheaper than that of the skilled workers of the west Midlands. Vauxhall, for example, when it first came from London to Luton, had access to a labour force amongst which effective trade union organisation was weak. There was little industry in the area, apart from the straw hat trade, which was dying out and employed a large proportion of female labour.[2] For Vauxhall of Luton, Morris of Oxford and Ford of Dagenham, suitable labour for their production methods was available; large markets were near at hand; cheap land was available for extensive plant layouts, needed for flow-production; components were available from the near-by Midlands and the London area. In addition, Ford wished to produce its own steel for stamped bodies and Dagenham was suitably situated on the Thames for the importation of coal and iron ore and for the shipment of finished vehicles. Gradually many components firms followed the industry southwards. These included extensions of existing Midlands

---

[1] *Min. Lab. Gaz.*, Mar. 1962.
[2] 'Labour problems in the motor industry', *F.T.*, 11 Mar. 1960.

firms, subsidiaries of the assembly firms and new, independent firms, such as Pressed Steel (bodybuilders) at Cowley and Swindon. By the mid-1930s these three of the six largest assembly firms were producing most of their output outside the west Midlands.

In Lancashire there had for some time been a variety of engineering trades, stimulated by textile machinery manufacture. Ford, in fact, began production of the model 'T' in Old Trafford, Manchester, in 1911 and Jaguar began in Blackpool. As the cotton industry declined, a wide variety of trades supplied components to the motor vehicle industry, and were centred primarily in Burnley, Chapel-en-le-Frith, St Helens, Speke, and the environs of Manchester. These products included tyres, brake linings, windscreens, springs, lamps, batteries, upholstery, fabrics, wiring, cables, sheet steel and tyre cord.[1]

During the interwar period and after World War II vehicle assembly plants were established by major and minor firms in areas as scattered as Langley and Doncaster (Ford), Abingdon and Cowley (B.M.C.), and Preston, Watford and Glasgow (Leyland, Scammell and Albion). Components plants were also set up in South Wales (B.M.C., Lucas, Pressed Steel and Smiths), Southampton (Ford), Leeds (A.E.C.), Bath (Simms) and Maidstone (Rootes).

(c) Locational Changes during the 1960s

Since 1960 many assembly and components firms have completed projects for the construction of plants in areas away from the Midlands and the south. The locational factors in this process were:

(a) the presence of existing and planned steel strip mills (Newport in South Wales and Ravenscraig in Scotland);
(b) the developing domestic markets in the north and Scotland;
(c) the provision of Government subsidies, under the Local Employment Act, in conjunction with the permissive powers of the Board of Trade with regard to Industrial Development Certificates, used to guide the industry to areas of relatively high unemployment.

The three areas selected for future development were:

1. MERSEYSIDE. An integrated Ford plant at Halewood, near Liverpool, with an initial capacity of 200,000 cars per annum; a B.L.M.C. factory at Kirby; a B.L.M.C. components plant at Speke; a Vauxhall component, truck and van plant at Ellesmere Port; a Lucas component plant is also planned for the area. Liverpool is a near-by outlet for exports; the Shotton strip mill is near-by for body materials; the near-by Lancashire and Yorkshire market provides an outlet for the finished products. Other components are available from Lancashire and the Midlands.

2. SOUTH WALES. A B.L.M.C. car body pressings and radiator plant near Llanelly; a B.L.M.C. 'Land-Rover' assembly plant at Cardiff. Components are available from local and Midland factories; local sheet steel is available; labour and export facilities are additional locational factors.

3. SCOTLAND. A Chrysler plant at Linwood, for the assembly of small cars; a B.L.M.C. plant at Bathgate for tractors and heavy commercial vehicles; a

---

[1] 'Report on the changing North-West', *The Times*, 6 Dec. 1960; 'North West: To remake a region', special survey in *Econ.*, 15 May 1965.

Fig. 3.24. *Location of existing and projected plants in the motor vehicle industry*
(Source: S.M.M.T. Memorandum)

3. SOME MAJOR INDUSTRIES: MOTOR [1]

B.L.M.C. plant at Dumbarton, for commercial vehicles; a Pressed Steel plant at Linwood, for the production of vehicle bodies. Locational factors present here are a labour pool, the steel strip mill at Ravenscraig and the local market. The motor industry 'Little Neddy' (Economic Development Council) reported in 1969 that despite problems of lower productivity and labour troubles – particu-

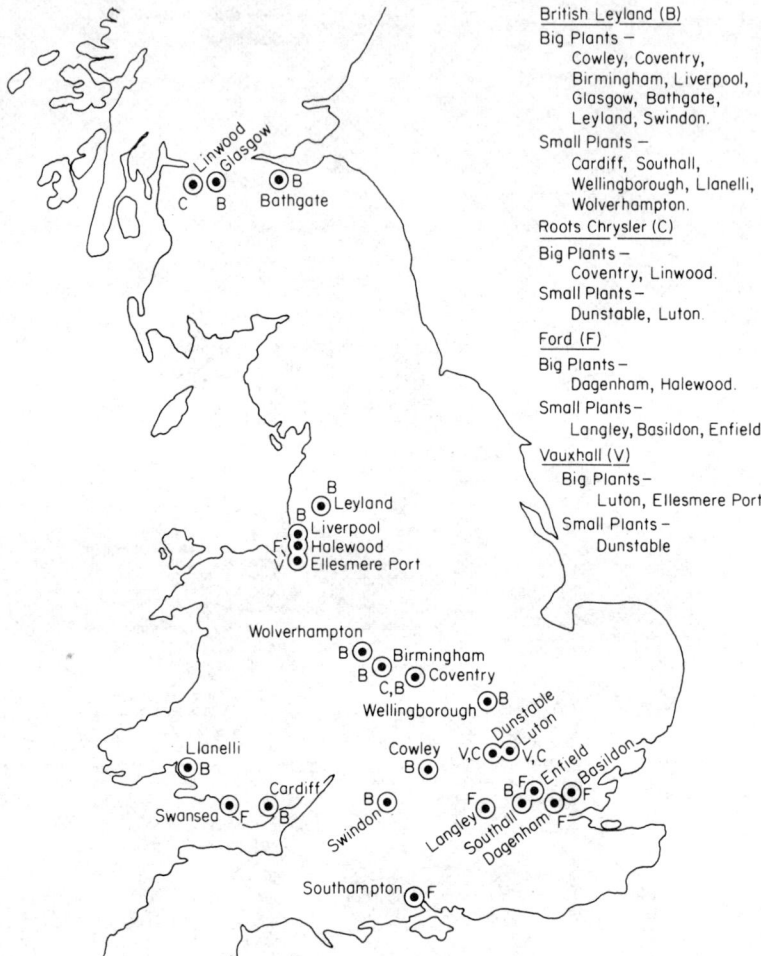

Fig. 3.25. *Location of main plants of the 'Big 4' assembly firms, 1970*
(Source: *S.T.*, 21 Dec. 1969; *F.T.*, 16 Feb. 1970)

larly on Merseyside – the Government policy of steering investment projects to the development areas had created about 41,000 new jobs between 1960 and 1965. It made no secret of the fact that some manufacturers moved reluctantly: the major locational factor in their case was the use of the I.D.C. powers by the Government.[1]

[1] *D.T.*, 10 April 1969.

The location of the main assembly and components plants in the industry may be seen in Fig. 3.24. The location of the main plants of the four largest motor vehicle assembly firms may be more clearly seen in Fig. 3.25. A much more detailed presentation of the plant location of B.L.M.C., which accounts for about half the British motor industry's output, is shown in Fig. 3.26.

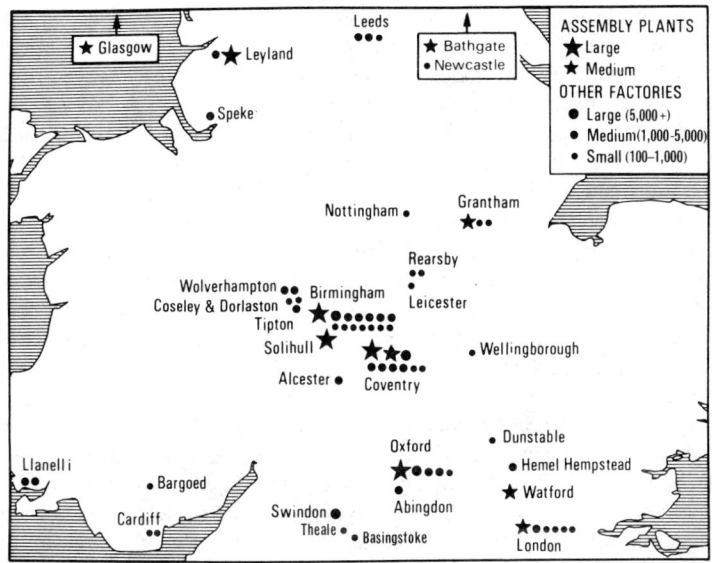

Fig. 3.26. *Location of major and minor plants of the British Leyland Motor Corporation, 1970*
(Sources: *Econ.*, 21 Sept. 1968, p. 92; *S.T.*, 22 Nov. 1970)

4. Further Reading and Sources

Footnote references to daily and weekly journals are not repeated.

A. G. ARMSTRONG, 'The Motor Industry and the British Economy', *D.B.R.* Sept. 1967.

'The British motor industry'. *Economic Digest.* 1964. Société Générale.

Bull. Ind. No. 172. March 1964. Information Division of the Treasury.

C.O.I. *British Motor Vehicle Industry.* 1962.

The Financial Times, Annual Review. 1960.

MINISTRY OF LABOUR. *Min. Lab. Gaz.* H.M.S.O.

'North-West: to remake a Region'. *Econ.* 15 May 1965.

C. F. PRATTEN, *Economies of Scale in Manufacturing Industry.* C.U.P. 1971.

A. SILBERSTON, 'The motor industry 1955–1964'. *Bulletin of the Oxford Institute of Statistics.* Nov. 1965.

SOCIETY OF MOTOR MANUFACTURERS AND TRADERS, *The Motor Industry of Great Britain, 1971.* S.M.M.T. 1971.

THE MOTOR INDUSTRY: Stage II: Structure and Organisation

1. Standardisation and Integration[1]

The processes involved in motor vehicle manufacture are complex and varied, as was seen in Stage I, Section 1. They range from engineering processes (the working of metal with machine tools) to assembly of components and vehicles. In most of these processes economies of scale or standardisation are significant, but they are greater in some processes than others. These differing potential economies of large scale are extremely important, in so far as they influence decisions with regard to plant location, integration (lateral and vertical), standardisation, variety of models, frequency of model styling changes, and the frequency of innovation in mechanical features.

In engineering processes the potential economies of large-scale, standardised production are greatest, mainly because they permit the use of specialised machine tools (such as automatic transfer machines), and the use of specialised flow-production techniques. These latter are an improvement on batch-production techniques, but they require a really large scale of production to be economically utilised. Specialised tools and techniques can also be applied to other processes, such as component assembly, body pressing, foundry and casting work, and final vehicle assembly. However, such processes as spraying and upholstery manufacture, requiring skilled labour and craftsmanship, do not offer such great economies of scale. The optimum output, or length of production run necessary to achieve minimum costs, is lower for such processes than for the others. For body pressing dies, the useful life is about 250,000 bodies; engineering machine tools have a life of about ten years. Thus for a long production run of about 500,000 or more, body styling changes could be made, without adding significantly to costs, but mechanical innovation would be more costly because of the larger optimum output of the engineering tools.[2] The 1971 study by C. F. Pratten, mentioned previously, has drawn attention to the effects of changing technology on the optimal scales of various processes and types of equipment. For body shell production, it appears that presses are capable of outputs of up to a million units, if spread over five years (at 200,000 per annum): the main increase in costs would be tooling repair. The maximum economies of scale for body production are estimated at 1 million – whether at long runs of 0.2 million for five years or shorter runs of 0·5 million over two years: of course, the same total output, in the former case, might involve additional marketing problems. Castings and forgings were considered to be optimal at a rate of 100,000 per annum; engineering processes for engines and transmission equipment were thought to be optimal at about 0·25 million per annum; assembly lines were optimal at about 300,000 units per annum, the reduction in unit costs, as compared with outputs of 100,000 p.a., being 12% for labour costs and 28% for capital costs; for bought-out materials and components the main advantage of large scale volume was found to lie in the use of more than one supplier and the consequent increase in competition between them, with the result that for volumes over 100,000 p.a. there could be a price advantage of about 10%; in regard to paint spraying, referred to earlier, one company found that an annual

---

[1] For an excellent review of the problems of standardisation and integration, see the series of articles in the supplement of *Econ.*, 23 Oct. 1965, especially pp. vii, viii, x, xiii, xiv and xxvii.
[2] 'Cars: Does innovation pay?' *Econ.*, 15 Dec. 1962.

scale of production of at least 0·25 million was required to justify a satisfactory paint plant which could meet their standards.[1]

These factors help to explain various developments in the industry. For example, the larger independent component firms have standardised their products to a very high degree, as with dynamos, starters, batteries, locks, pistons, lighting equipment, wheel drums, tyres, etc. Before World War II, for example, Lucas made forty-eight different dynamos, thirty-eight starter motors and sixty-eight distributors: they now make only three or four of each.[2] Another development has been the reduction of models by the vehicle assembly firms. This has permitted them to plan for longer production runs, using specialised machines and flow techniques in body pressing and vehicle assembly. Though the larger British manufacturers of vehicles still tend to produce more models than the American 'Big Three', and more than the larger Continental producers, they do attempt to minimise this diseconomy by using standardised component parts in different models, by keeping basic body changes to a minimum, by retaining engine and chassis types for as long as possible, and by offering instead superficial variety in the form of minor grill and exterior 'trim' modifications and a choice of body colours and upholstery (where long production runs are not so vital). Complete retooling for new models, which costs several million pounds, is thus minimised. In 1964, for example, B.M.C. produced about seventy different models, the Rootes Group produced about twenty models, Ford about thirty models and Vauxhall about ten. However, one basic body was often used for four or five different models, which differed only in interior fittings and exterior trims.[3]

Faced with so many differing economies of long production runs in different processes, it appears to be difficult to determine the optimum output for a motor vehicle. Some costs seem to fall indefinitely, as is apparent with American Ford and Chevrolet cars, which are each produced in excess of 1 million and are much cheaper than similar cars produced on a smaller scale. Other optima are met at much smaller outputs. The above-mentioned study by Pratten estimated the overall economies of scale for two situations. The first was the four-year production run of one basic model and its variants at one site, using existing as well as new equipment. It was found that the greatest economies (11%) would be achieved over the annual output range 100,000 to 250,000 units: over the range 0·25 to 0·5 million, costs would fall by a further 5% and from 0·5 million to 1 million by only a further 3%. Thus, up to 100,000 units falling costs would be experienced in forgings and castings, bought-out materials and components, painting, assembly line operations, engine and transmission production and body pressings. Between 100,000 and 0·25 million, costs would continue to fall in painting, assembly, engines, transmissions and body pressings. From 0·25 to 0·5 million, most of these economies would have been exhausted, apart from body pressing and through coordinating duplicated equipment in parallel. From 0·5 to 1 million all equipment would be duplicated, thus leaving scope only for economies of coordination (see Fig. 3.27). The second case (see Fig. 3.28) was

[1] Pratten, *op. cit.*, pp. 134–40.
[2] *Report on Proceedings*, National Advisory Council for the Motor Manufacturing Industry, 1947, p. 11; 'Car components', *Financial Times*, Motor Supplement, 15 Oct. 1962; 'How to build a Jaguar', *Obs.*, 29 Oct. 1961; 'And now price competition', *Stat.*, 3 Apr. 1964, p. 35.
[3] *British Motor Vehicle Industry*, p. 5; 'The British motor industry, *Conjoncture: Economic Digest*, No. 62, Dec. 1964, by Société Générale.

the four-year production run of three basic models and their variants and five basic engines: 60% of total output was assumed to be in one of the three basic models. The major features noticed were the higher initial overhead costs, for any given total annual output, as compared with the single model case, and the continuing fall in units costs up to about 2 million: at this level of annual total production, ex-works cost would be similar to that of the single model produced

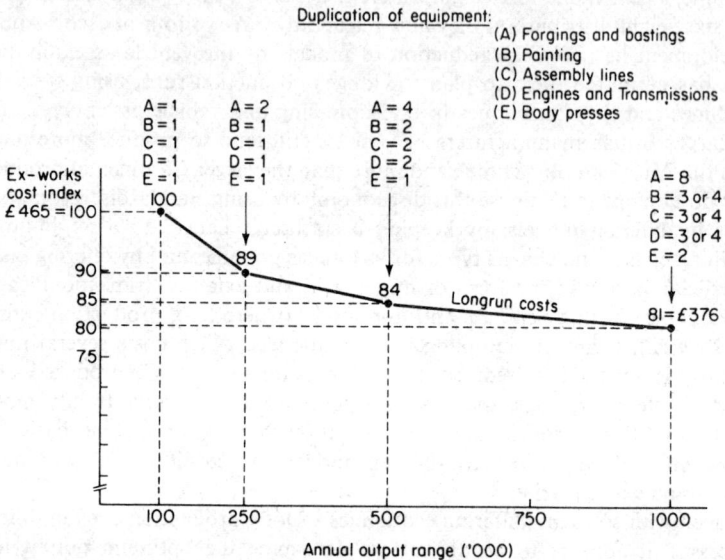

Fig. 3.27 *Scale economies and duplication of equipment: one basic vehicle model (with variants) on four-year production run. (N.B. model in range 1000–1200 cc.)*

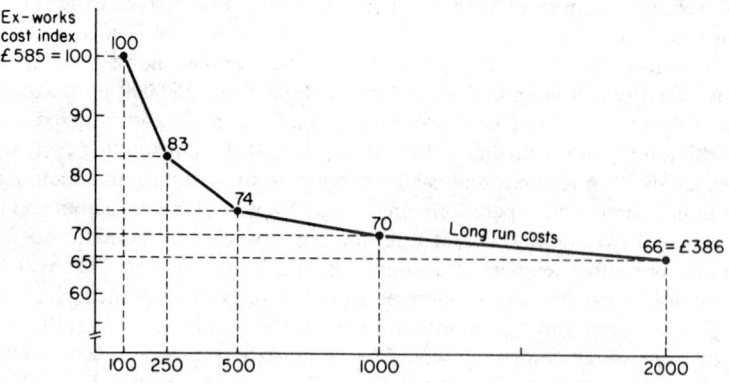

Fig. 3.28. *Scale economies with three basic models (with varients) and five basic engines on four-year production run. (N.B. Three-fifths of output in model range 1300 cc, one-fifth at 1000 cc, one-fifth at 1800 cc.)*

(Based on material in C. F. Pratten, *Economies of Scale in Manufacturing Industry*, pp. 140–3.)

at an annual rate of 1 million.[1] Other factors, such as flexibility in the use of equipment and scope for the spreading of technological improvements and costs could further increase these scale economies and reduce costs.

With the introduction of a completely new model style, with novel technical innovations (as in the case of the Morris 1100 in 1962), the tooling costs are likely to be double those of introducing a new body style only (using existing components). However, it has been estimated that a production run of 500,000 would be sufficient to bring down the additional overhead to £5 per car (experience of B.M.C. Minis and Ford Anglias).[2] Pratten found that where several variations of a model are introduced, the body tooling costs for a model designed for a substantial share of the market could be in excess of £5 million.[3] When British Leyland introduced the Maxi, a completely new model with a new engine, more than £20 million was invested in its production.[4] When it introduced the Marina range in 1971 it invested £45 million, but about £30 million of this was due to the complete stripping and re-equipping of the Cowley plant: £7 million went into a new gearbox plant, but this was to serve more than one model.[5] This latter case illustrates the difficulty in distinguishing between capital costs attributable solely to the introduction of a new model and those due to expansion and replacement of capacity, which would have been incurred, regardless.

West European experience of long production runs on some models is of great interest. By February 1965 nine models had been produced in excess of 1 million, and two more were closely following. They ranged from the Volkswagen 1200 cc – 6·5 million, mainly since 1945 – to the B.M.C. Mini – 1 million since 1959. They were followed by the Ford Anglia (950,000 since 1959) and the Ford Cortina (700,000 since 1962).[6] By February, 1964 Ford were able to reduce the price of the Anglia. By then it had been produced in excess of three-quarters of a million: initial tooling costs had been largely written off, and production had been switched to the new, highly automated, £30 million plant at Halewood, Merseyside.[7] By February 1964 B.M.C. had become Europe's largest producer of vans and lorries, having exported nearly three-quarters of a million to 190 markets since 1945. Production of lorries from the Bathgate works, Scotland, at which lorry production had been concentrated since August 1961, was nearing the planned target of 50,000 per year.[8] In 1964 annual production of the B.M.C. 1100 reached 250,000 and that of the Ford Cortina reached 230,000.[9]

Apart from standardisation, the factors of lateral and vertical integration are very important. Lateral integration dates back to the early days, when cycle, engineering and other firms entered the industry. Despite the tendency of many firms, especially the smaller ones, to dis-integrate and specialise on a narrow range, for the larger firms with sufficient resources the desire to be competitive and to provide a wide range of vehicles is still strong. Many of the mergers in the industry have been aimed at an extension of the range of vehicles (lateral integration) combined with a reduction in the number of vehicles in each range (standardisation). The Leyland-Standard-Triumph and Leyland-B.M.H. mergers were recent examples of such motives.

As the larger assembly firms have expanded their output, they have been increasingly able to take advantage of economies of vertical integration, by

---

[1] Pratten, *op. cit.*, pp. 140–3. [2] 'Cars: Does innovation pay?', *Econ.*, 15 Dec. 1962.
[3] Pratten, *op. cit.*, p. 135. [4] *D.T.*, 24 April 1969. [5] *F.T.*, 27 April 1971.
[6] *Stat.*, 5 Feb. 1965, p. 385. [7] *D.T.*, 4 Feb. 1964. [8] *D.T.*, 7 Feb. 1964.
[9] *Stat.*, supplement on the Motor Industry, 2 Apr. 1965, p. 3.

which large-scale production economies in each process may be combined with additional security in the supply of key components, such as body pressings. Such were the motives behind the 1953 merger of Briggs Motor Bodies into Fords, the 1965 merger of Pressed Steel-Fisher-Ludlow with B.M.C., the 1958 acquisition of Mulliners of Birmingham by Standard-Triumph and the establishment of British Light Steel Pressings as a subsidiary of Rootes.[1] Similar extensions of vertical integration with a wide range of components manufacture have taken place to varying extents within all the main vehicle assembly firms. Apart from full financial integration, however, there has been a great deal of *de facto* integration. For most individual components the motor firms tend to deal with only one or two outside firms, and many of them use the same standardised parts.

Mergers, concentration and rationalisation among the assembly firms have been accompanied by similar developments among the component suppliers. There are still several thousand of these and a major assembly firm may well obtain parts and services from 4,000 different suppliers. One such development occurred in 1968 when Lucas bid to take over Simms Motor Units – diesel fuel pump producers – to add to its C.A.V. subsidiary. This type of development is motivated by reasons such as the desire to match the output growth and buying power of firms such as British Leyland; the mounting cost of duplicating research and development; the increasing scale optima of much component-producing equipment – only economical if used to supply on a large scale; the desire to keep pace with the assembly firms' worldwide assembly and distribution networks.[2] Due to major problems of breakdown in supplies and dependence on near-monopoly major and minor component firms, some of the assembly firms have been induced to seek alternative sources, either by producing their own components (as in the case of British Leyland, which in 1967 started to produce its own starter motors, regulators and alternators, instead of buying them from Simms and C.A.V. (Lucas)),[3] or by establishing contractual relationships with small firms, to produce to the assembler's specifications, or by establishing dual supply sources from foreign producers – especially in Japan.[4] It is quite likely that an important reason for British Leyland's decision in 1969 to produce and market 'Unipart' accessories and replacement parts for every major British motor car was its desire to utilise its components capacity more intensively than if it were to satisfy its own requirements only.[5]

2. Structure of the Industry: Number and Size of Plant

For various reasons it is not possible to state precisely how many plants are engaged in the motor vehicle industry. Apart from the plants of the main vehicle assembly firms and the major components manufacturers, there are thousands of plants which cater only partly to the motor vehicle industry, as in the case of textile plants and thousands of others producing minor components and trims. The official classification only includes as being in the motor vehicle industry

---

[1] *British Motor Vehicle Industry*, p. 7.
[2] *F.T.*, 24 March 1969; *Econ.*, 10 Feb. 1968, p. 64; 'Components for some motor mergers', *S.T.*, 4 Feb. 1968.
[3] *Econ.*, 4 Nov. 1967, p. 543, and 10 Feb. 1968, p. 64.
[4] 'Car makers' revolt', *Econ.*, 11 July 1970, pp. 53–4 and 13 July 1968, pp. 66–8; *S.T.*, 2 May 1971 and 26 April 1970; *F.T.*, 2 Oct. 1969, 17 Sept. 1970, 29 March 1971; *D.T.*, 3 Oct. 1968.
[5] *D.T.*, 21 Oct. 1969.

those plants devoted mainly to the industry. Even in the case of plants devoted primarily to the industry, the wide range of technical processes and degrees of standardisation and integration results in a correspondingly wide range of plant sizes. These range from the vertically integrated Ford plant at Dagenham (employing over 25,000 workers) and the large components plants of Lucas, to the small assembly plants (such as Lotus) producing specialised cars, and the small components plants, in the jewellery district of Birmingham.

More is known of the number of plants in the main assembly and components firms. On the assembly side these firms are Ford, Vauxhall, Chrysler and British Leyland. Some of their plants are integrated for components and assembly; others are primarily assembly plants and some are components plants. On the components side the main firms are Lucas, Smiths, Simms, Ferodo, G.K.N. (for castings and forgings), Pilkingtons (for glass), Automotive Products (gearboxes), Birmid Qualcast (for castings), Dunlop, Avon, Firestone, Goodyear, India and John Bull. These major firms contained, in 1961, 22 motor vehicle assembly plants (some of them vertically integrated to some extent, as with Ford's Dagenham plant and Vauxhall's Luton plant) and 51 components plants. When expansion plans were complete, these numbers increased to 34 and 57.[1] These plants account for more than 95% of the total British output of finished vehicles and probably at least as high a percentage of components (by value) produced in Britain.

Typical size of plant is another point which cannot really be ascertained. Certainly, the plants referred to above will constitute the largest in the industry. Some light has been thrown on this matter, however, by a Ministry of Labour investigation of plant size in manufacturing industry in April 1959. It found that in the Vehicles group or Order of manufacturing industries, 60% of the total number of employees were in the 3·1% of plants with 1,000 employees: 48·5% of employees were engaged in the 1·7% of plants employing over 2,000 workers.[2] These findings must be qualified by the fact that the Vehicles Order of industry also includes aircraft, motor cycles, locomotives and perambulators. However, they do indicate the tendency of the major plants to large size. In 1963, of the 1,255 plants with more than 25 employees in the major sectors of the motor industry, 26 with more than 4,000 employees accounted for 48% of the labour force; 70 with 1,000 to 4,000 accounted for 29%; 254 with 100 to 1,000 accounted for 18% of the labour force and the 905 plants in the 25 to 100 range employed only 5% of the labour force.[3] Amongst the Big 4 assembly firms British Leyland, with about 180,000 employees (of whom about 135,000 were manual workers) had in 1970 about 70 plants, 11 of them assembly plants. Because of the close proximity of many of these (e.g. 30 in the Birmingham–Coventry complex – an example of 'partial integration' – with almost 90,000 employees), and their specialisation on different processes, it is not very meaningful to quote plant sizes. Ford, however, had 25,000 at Dagenham and 12,000 at Halewood out of a total of 7 plants employing 47,000 manual workers. Chrysler had 18,700 manual workers in its 4 main plants and Vauxhall had 30,000 in its 3 main plants.[4]

[1] Based on material in S.M.M.T. chart, 'Location of motor plants'.
[2] Min. Lab. Gaz., Sept. 1959.
[3] Pratten, op. cit., p. 133.
[4] S.T., 21 Dec. 1969, and 22 Nov. 1970; Econ., 21 Sept. 1968; F.T., 16 Feb. 1970, 7 Jan. 1971 and 25 Feb. 1971.

More light is thrown on this trend towards large plant size in the major sections of the industry when we consider the immense tooling costs incurred in a major assembly or component plant. For example the new Rootes die-casting and assembly plant at Linwood, Scotland, for the construction of a new small car was estimated to involve a total expenditure of £23½ million. [1]It has been estimated that the cost of equipping a factory to make a new component (such as automatic transmission or disc brakes) are in the region of at least £4 million.[2] Such high capital-intensity is only economical in the large plant producing for a wide market.

3. Administrative Organisation

(a) Concentration of control

There is a high degree of concentrated control in the motor vehicle industry, which is particularly noticeable in the final assembly stage. Of the assembly firms whose plants were mentioned in the previous section, four – sometimes referred to as the 'Big Four' – employ about 85% of assembly workers and produce over 99% of the vehicles of all types. These firms are British Leyland Motor Corporation (B.L.M.C.), employing about 180,000 people and producing in 1970 46% of total vehicles; the Ford Motor Company, with 28% of total production; Vauxhall Motors, 14%; Chrysler (U.K.), 12%. One may even refer to the 'Big Two' (B.L.M.C. and Ford), because they now produce about 75% of the cars and about 70% of the commercial vehicles made in Britain.

In the production of cars (and taxis) B.L.M.C. is responsible for about 48%, Ford about 27%, Vauxhall about 11%, Chrysler about 13%. These firms cater primarily for the mass-produced popular car market, but they also make mass-produced sports cars. Of the 10 or so firms outside the Big Four, producing less than 1% of car output, the largest are Lotus and Reliant.[3]

In the production of commercial vehicles, it is important to note in this context that the value of these vehicles rises steeply with their size and complexity. Many of the heavier vehicles are made to special order. Over 80% of commercial vehicles (by number, but not by value) are vans and trucks below 6 tons carrying capacity. Nearly all of these are mass-produced by B.L.M.C. (38% of total), Vauxhall (22% of total), Ford (31% of total) and Chrysler (7% of total). A few specialist producers are responsible for the remaining output of heavy commercial vehicles, such as Foden and E.R.F. of Sandbach, Cheshire.

Of the thousands of firms involved in the industry, 966 were officially classified as constituting the industry in 1968. Of these the sixteen main assembly and component firms controlled almost three-quarters of the labour force (73%)[4]: employment amongst the Big Four assembly firms has been noted in Section 2, above.

As has been pointed out earlier, many of these major assembly firms are quite highly integrated, and produce many of their own bodies and components. This becomes increasingly feasible as their scales of production rise. Nevertheless,

1 *British Motor Vehicle Industry*, p. 9.
2 'Cars: Does innovation pay?', *loc. cit.*, p. 1136; 'Lucas subsidiary starts £13m. expansion programme', *F.T.*, 10 April 1970.
3 The Motor industry of Great Britain, 1971, *loc. cit.*, pp. 30–1. For a discussion of British Leyland's fluctuating market shares since the merger, see *S.T.*, 16 Jan. 1972. *N.B.* In 1970. imports accounted for 14% of total U.K. home market sales (*Econ.*, 1 May 1971, p. 66).
4 Pratten, *op. cit.*, p. 133.

even the most highly integrated firms obtain a significant proportion of their components (by value) from outside producers. This has enabled many of the thousands of components producers to standardise their range, catering simultaneously for several assembly firms. In turn, this has led to a high degree of concentrated control in the production of many important components by some large firms.[1] The importance of some of these key firms is immeasurably greater than their size would suggest, because a restriction of their supplies can halt production in the assembly firms. Even where the component firm has no outright monopoly control, the assembly firm cannot quickly switch over to different equipment from alternative suppliers. This vulnerability is intensified by the tendency of assembly firms to keep the minimum of capital tied up in stocks. Examples of key component firms are Lucas (55,000 employees and, before the B.L.M.C. merger, the largest employer in the industry) for electrical equipment and Girling brakes; Vandervell and Glacier Metal for engine shell bearings; Automative Products, for Borg and Beck clutches and Lockheed brakes; S. Smith and Sons, who supply instruments for over 90% of British vehicles, and control K.L.G. Sparking Plugs. As a result of the oligopolistic and sometimes monopoly conditions of supply in the components field, the Monopolies Commission started an investigation in 1957 on 'the supply of electrical equipment for mechanically propelled land vehicles'.[2] Despite the short-term power of the key components firms, it must be noted that as the major assembly firms expand, they can exert increasing long-term influence upon their components suppliers. In fact, apart from their ability to switch over to other suppliers, after a time-lag, they wield the ultimate power of being able to produce components themselves[3] (see Section 1, above).

(b) Tiers of authority

Though the State is not represented by any supervising body, it wields important influence through several factors. First, the Department of Trade and Industry has the power to restrict the granting of Industrial Development Certificates for expansion projects involving more than 5,000 square feet of factory floor space. This power has been used to influence the siting of new plants in Merseyside, South Wales and Scotland. Secondly, the Government can influence finance for car purchases, through action on interest rates and hire purchase controls. Thirdly, the Government exerts important influence through the medium of the motor vehicle duty. This was, from 1910 to 1947, based on the horsepower of cars, and had an effect on the type of car produced; for commercial vehicles it is based on weight and upon the type of licence issued. The licences are designed to restrict vehicle operations to approved needs, and to eliminate wasteful competition. Under the 1968 Transport Act goods vehicles not exceeding 3·5 tons gross loaded weight were exempted from licensing: over 3·5 tons they required operators' licences, and eventually a quantitative control was to be applied to vehicles over 16 tons gross weight, used for specific purposes.[4] Fourthly, the Government wields tremendous influence over demand by virtue of the

[1] 'Car components', *Financial Times*, Motor Supplement, 15 Oct. 1962; *Econ.*, 11 July 1970, p. 53.
[2] *Obs.*, 29 Oct. 1961.
[3] For details of modernisation and expansion programmes in the industry, as at July 1964, see *The British Motor Industry: News Bulletin*, 0220, July 1974, S.M.M.T.
[4] *Brit. O.H.*, 1971, pp. 340–1.

purchase tax, imposed on passenger cars. This was introduced at $33\frac{1}{3}\%$ in 1941; since then it has fluctuated to as high as $66\frac{2}{3}\%$. Fifthly, the Government may influence home market demand for British vehicles by its tariff policy towards other countries. As the market share of imported cars in the U.K. has risen from about 4% in 1962 to 14% in 1970 (more than the home market sales of either Vauxhall or Chrysler),[1] this factor might be expected to become increasingly important.

The main trade association in the industry is the Society of Motor Manufacturers and Traders (S.M.M.T.), founded in 1902. It represents all the assembly firms, the larger component manufacturers and larger dealers. The S.M.M.T. provides statistical, legal, technical, press and public relations services to the industry, and represents it in discussions with Government departments. It has an overseas department and travelling representatives; it also organises an annual International Motor Exhibition and a biennial International Commercial Motor Exhibition.

Other organisations in the industry, some of which overlap with the wholesalers and retail distributors are: the British Transport Vehicle Manufacturers Association; the Institute of British Carriage and Automobile Manufacturers; the Tyre Manufacturers Conference Ltd.

On the distribution side, the major organisation is the British Motor Trade Association, founded in 1910 to maintain wholesale and retail prices laid down by the producers. During the highly competitive years of the early 1930s the manufacturers made it compulsory for their agents to join the B.M.T.A., and instituted a fixed allowance system for part-exchanges. Collective enforcement of such a scheme is now forbidden by the 1956 Restrictive Trade Practices Act. Other distributive organisations for the 10,000 retail dealers and main distributors are the Motor Agents Association, Ltd, the Motor Factors Association, the National Federation of Vehicle Trades, and the Scottish Motor Trade Association.

In the employment field, the majority of manufacturers are members of the Engineering and Allied Employers National Federation. They are parties to agreements negotiated between the Federation and the unions, although there is no national wage agreement for the motor vehicle industry as such. Ford and Vauxhall, however, do not belong to any such national negotiating body. Trade unions represent nearly all the workers in the industry. Most of these unions are affiliated to the Confederation of Shipbuilding and Engineering Unions, but they are not exclusively motor industry unions. The four main unions are the Transport and General Workers' Union, the National Union of General and Municipal Workers, the Amalgamated Engineering and Foundry Workers' Union and the National Union of Vehicle Builders. There are also many craft unions, such as the Electrical Trades Union, which cater mainly for skilled workers.

4. The Emerging Pattern of the World Motor Industry

When considering the emerging pattern of British and overseas motor vehicle production, several factors must be borne in mind. First, past performance; secondly, present degree of saturation; thirdly, future plans for expanded capacity.

In 1950 Britain was the world's second largest motor vehicle producer, after the U.S., with 783,672 units, followed by France (357,552), West Germany

[1] *The Motor Industry of Great Britain, 1971*, pp. 99–102.

(306,064) and Italy (127,847). In 1970 the ·U.K. was fifth: Japan (31,597 in 1950) had surged into second place with 5·25 million, after the U.S. (8·25 million).[1]

The degree of saturation (or density of car ownership) on the passenger car market differs from one country to another, but the great potential markets of the early 1960s have to a large extent been tapped by 1970: whereas the number of persons per car in 1960 were U.S. 3, Canada 5, Sweden 8, U.K. 11, France 11, West Germany 16 and Italy 38 – in 1969 the figures were U.S. 2·2, Canada 3·1,

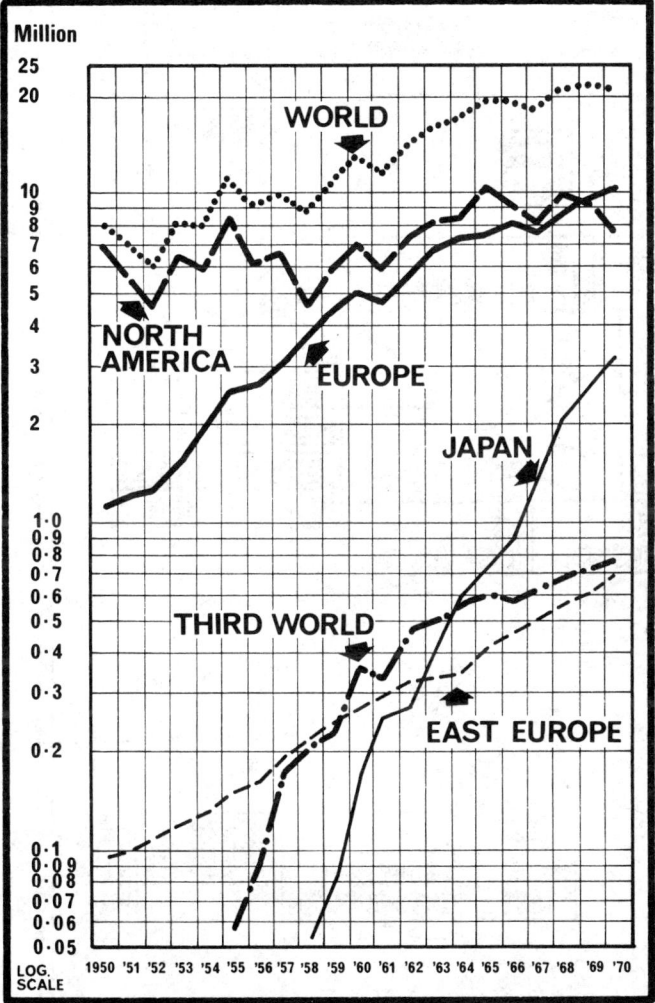

Fig. 3.29. *World motor car production 1950–70.*
(Source: *F.T.*, 29 Oct. 1971)

---

[1] *The Motor Industry of Great Britain, 1971, loc. cit.*, pp. 44–7. Also see N.E.D.O. report, *Japan: its Motor Industry and Market*, H.M.S.O., 1971, and 'Business brief', *Econ.*, 12 June 1971, pp. 64–5.

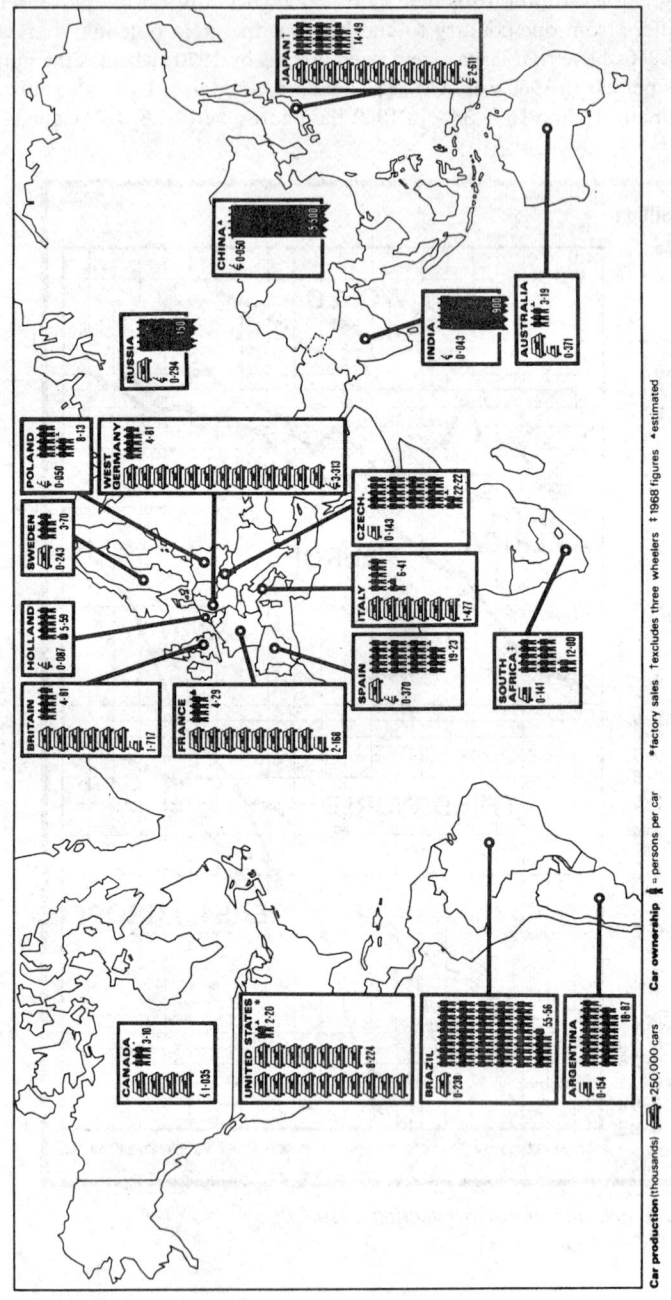

Fig. 3.30. *Distribution of world motor car production and car ownership, 1969*
(Source: *Econ.*, 17 Oct. 1970, pp. vi–vii)

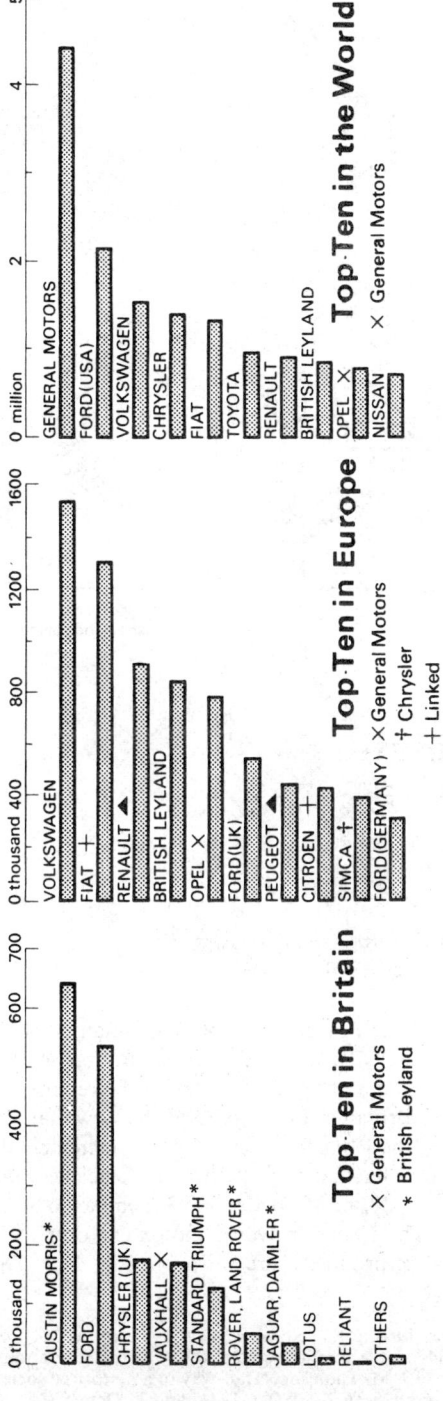

Fig. 3.31. *The major motor car producers, 1969*
(Source: *Econ.*, 17 Oct. 1970, p. xiii)

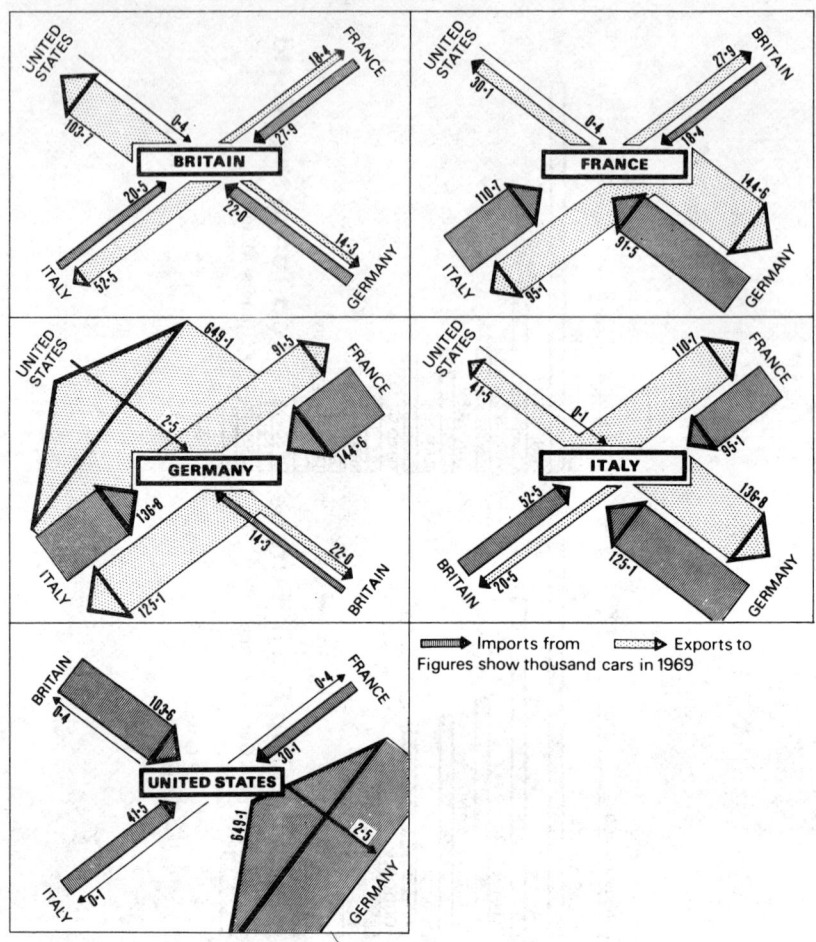

Fig. 3.32. *Multilateral trade in motor cars, 1969*
(Source: *Econ.*, 17 Oct. 1970, p. xv)

Sweden 3·7, U.K. 4·81, France 4·29, West Germany 4·81 and Italy 6·41.[1] By the beginning of the 1970s the degree of saturation in Western Europe had reached the level of that in the U.S. in 1929, just before the Great Depression. In October 1971 the chairman of Fiat expressed the view that the European market had changed during the 1960s from one of steady incremental growth (about 7% per annum) to one of fluctuating growth and replacement demand. He foresaw future growth of only 2% or 3% per annum[2] – similar to that in the U.S. market during the 1950s. The trends in world motor car output from 1950 to 1970, when 22 million were produced, are shown in Fig. 3.29. The pattern of world

---

[1] *F.T.*, *Annual Review*, 1960, p. 77; *Econ.*, 17 Oct. 1970, pp. vi–vii. For data on population and car densities and on the implications of the growing saturation levels, see *Econ.*, 27 March 1971, p. xiii, and J. M. Thomson, 'Half-way to a motorized society', *L.B.R.*, Oct. 1971.
[2] 'An anxious eye on growth', *F.T.*, 29 Oct. 1971; and 27 Oct. 1971.

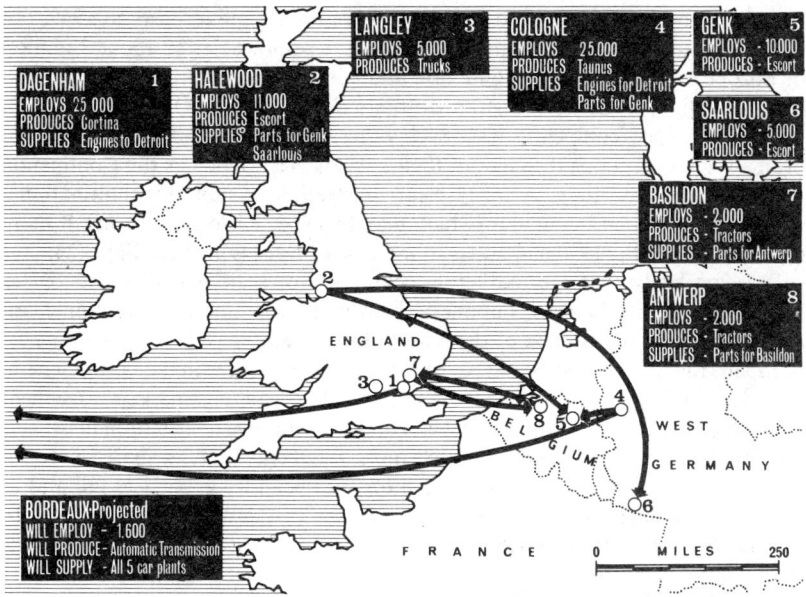

Fig. 3.33. *Coordination of multinational plant operations: Ford*
(Source: *F.T.*, 25 Feb. 1971)

motor car production and of car ownership for 1969 are as shown in Fig. 3.30. The major car producers in Britain, Europe and the world as a whole are shown in Fig. 3.31.

The growth of the industry during the 1960s has been accompanied by a great deal of competition, an increasing degree of consumer selectivity and sophistication, and a great deal of multilateral trade in motor vehicles between the major producers themselves. Fig. 3.32 shows the pattern of motor car imports and exports between the U.S., Britain, West Germany, France and Italy, in 1969. This increasing total size and the competitive pressures to which it gives rise have stimulated, during the 1960s, a series of national and international mergers and inter-company agreements amongst assembly firms and components firms. Examples of these have been the Chrysler merger with Rootes in Britain and Simca in France; the tyre merger between Dunlop of Britain and Pirelli of Italy; the Volkswagen merger with N.S.U. and its Auto-Union subsidiary in West Germany; the joint production and purchasing agreements between Renault and Peugeot in France; the financial stake in Citroen of France by Fiat of Italy; the joint component production agreements between Ford and Borg-Warner of America and Nissan and Toyo Kogyo in Japan; the financial and production links between Ford of America and Isuzu of Japan; the merger between British Leyland and Innocenti of Italy.[1]

As may be seen from Figs. 3.29 and 3.31, the Big Three U.S. firms and their

---

[1] *F.T.*, 16 Dec. 1969, 1 June 1970, and 29 Oct. 1970; *Econ.*, 4 July 1970, p. 71, 24 July 1971, p. 79, and 15 March 1969, p. 76; *S.T.*, 29 Sept. 1968, 23 March 1969, and 25 July 1971; *D.T.*, 25 Oct. 1968.

overseas subsidiaries produced between them about 9 million cars in 1969, out of a world total of about 22 million. They were responsible for about 2 million of Europe's 9·5 million car production and 0·87 million of Britain's 1·7 million car production.[1] Whereas General Motors tends to keep its Opel and Vauxhall operations apart, competing with each other, Chrysler and Ford tend to co-ordinate the operations throughout their subsidiaries – much as the Continental merger firms have done. A fairly clear illustration of how this multinational coórdination of plant activities (which may be expected to become much more common during the 1970s) operates in the case of Ford is given in Fig. 3.33.

It seems likely that the marketing economies of scale will prove to be far higher than the technical economies which make for minimal optimum plant and firm size, in the context of the world motor industry. Whereas the Big Two in Japan (the Toyota and Nissan Groups) and the Big Three in the U.S. (General Motors, Ford and Chrysler) have sufficient shares of big markets to benefit from such marketing economies and can operate extensive distribution networks, the European motor industry is much more fragmented, being shared between about twenty major firms in 1970. As intra-European trade barriers fall and as worldwide competition and, possibly, excess capacity grow, it may be expected that much more rationalisation by mergers will ensue during the 1970s. Some of the more successful and profitable companies, producing specialist and luxury vehicles (e.g. Alfa Romeo, Volvo, B.M.W. and Daimler-Benz) may retain their independence, but some, such as Rover and Peugeot, have already been affected.[2]

5. Further Reading and Sources

Footnote references to daily and weekly journals are not repeated.

A. G. ARMSTRONG, 'The motor industry and the British economy'. *D.B.R.* Sept. 1967.

'The British motor industry'. *Conjoncture: Economic Digest* 62. Société Générale. Dec. 1964.

C.O.I. *The British Motor Vehicle Industry.* 1962.

The Financial Times Annual Review, 1960.

'Motor vehicles'. *Bull. Ind.* 172. March 1964.

NATIONAL ECONOMIC DEVELOPMENT OFFICE, *Japan: its Motor Industry and Market.* H.M.S.O. 1971.

C. F. PRATTEN, *Economies of Scale in Manufacturing Industry.* C.U.P. 1971.

Society of Motor Manufacturers and Traders, *The British Motor Industry News Bulletin.* 0217, June 1964; 0220, July 1964.

S.M.M.T. *The Motor Industry of Great Britain, 1971.* 1971.

J. M. THOMSON, 'Half-way to a motorized society'. *L.B.R.* Oct. 1971.

---

1 For details of the location and world distribution of the Big Three and their subsidiaries, for the European locations of these and of plants in the other large firms, and for the changing shares of the Big Three in U.S. total production, see *F.T.*, 8 April 1969; 'Far flung production lines', *Econ.*, 9 July 1966, p. xvi; *Econ.*, 10 April 1971, p. 48.

2 'Questions of scale will be paramount', *F.T.*, 16 Dec. 1969; 'An anxious eye on growth', *F.T.*, 29 Oct. 1971; 'Room for four car makers?', *D.T.*, 25 Aug. 1970.

THE TEXTILE INDUSTRY: Stage I

1. Technical Background

According to the Standard Industrial Classification, the textiles Order of industry covers much more than the traditional cotton, woollen and worsted trades. Such trades as jute; production of man-made fibres; rope, twine and net; hosiery and other knitted goods; lace; carpets; narrow fabrics; made-up textiles; and textile finishing are included in the Order. Furthermore, because of the strides made in recent years in the development and production of man-made fibres, the spinning and weaving (but not the production) of these and flax are now officially classified as being linked with cotton. During the 1960s the traditional lines of demarcation between the cotton, the woollen and worsted, and other textile industries have become increasingly blurred. There has been a great deal of technological integration of various subdivisions of the textile industry, largely consequent on the increasing use of man-made fibres[1] and of new machinery – mainly in the knitting section – which can handle man-made fibres, cotton or wool. These links may be seen in Fig. 3.34. In 1968 the share of man-made fibres in total world textile fibre consumption was 72%. In the U.K. it was 29% in 1958, 54·5% in 1968, 57·5% in 1970: the forecast for 1975 was 65%.[2]

This chapter, however, will be restricted to the traditional sub-divisions of the cotton industry and the woollen and worsted industry, covering spinning, weaving and finishing processes and including man-made fibres spun and woven. These industries, in fact, accounted for about 52% of employment in the textiles Order of industry in 1970.[3]

The main processes in cotton, woollen and worsted are:

(a) spinning the fibre into a yarn (accompanied by 'doubling' – twisting together two or more strands of yarn);

(b) weaving the yarn into cloth;

(c) converting or finishing the woven cloth into piece goods.

There are several subsidiary processes at each of these main stages, and some of them, like the 'combing' of worsted tops (removal of short fibres and arrangement of the longer fibres into a continuous band of parallel fibres), are often performed by specialist plants and firms, which may not continue the rest of a major process.

The scope for economies of scale at each process and of integration of processes differs according to the type and quality of cotton yarn or cloth and also differs as between woollen and worsted production. The implications of the technical background have, indeed, exerted a significant effect on the patterns of location, structure and organisation of these textile trades.

Most of the major technical innovations in textiles were introduced during the eighteenth century in Britain. In response to the bottleneck in the woollen weaving process Kay's 'flying shuttle' was introduced in 1733, and gradually spread to the cotton industry. Spinning was speeded up after 1765 by Hargreaves'

---

[1] For further discussion of the technological homogeneity induced by man-made fibre developments, see 'A time for reappraisal' and 'Man-mades in the melting pot', *F.T.*, 13 Jan. 1970; 'Get together', *Econ.*, 7 Nov. 1970, pp. 80–1.

[2] *Cotton and Allied Textiles: a report on present performance and future prospects.* Vol. 1, Textile Council, pp. 6, 11; *Econ.*, 22 Nov. 1969, p. 69.

[3] *Min. Lab. Gaz.* Mar. 1962. N.B. Statistics put out by the industries give much lower figures because part-time workers are included as halves.

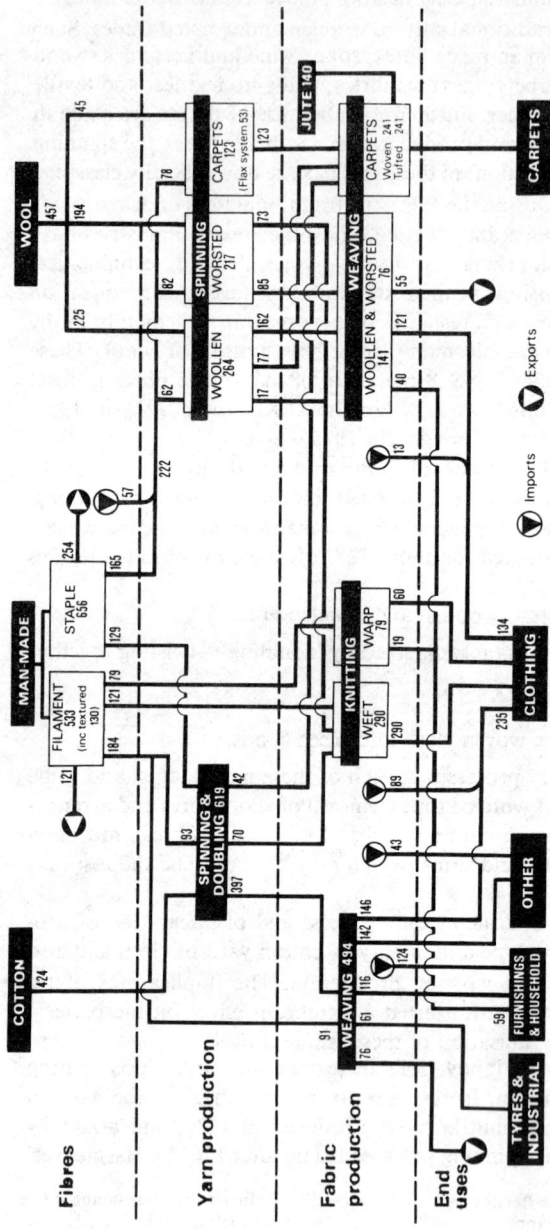

Deliveries of raw materials, yarns and fabric in 1968 in millions of pounds weight

The chart shows how the traditional subdivisions of the textile industry are breaking down. The two main divisions, historically have been cotton (Lancashire) and wool (Yorkshire). The reasons why the distinction is breaking down are (a) the growing importance of man-made fibres as a new raw material and (b) the introduction of machinery (principally knitting machinery) that can handle equally well yarn made from man-made fibres, from cotton and from wool. For simplicity flax and jute have been excluded from the chart. So have wool combing and top making (two of the earlier intermediate processes in wool manufact-ure before the spinning stage). So has lace (made from cotton) and some other end-uses. Some carpet-making operations have been eliminated. The figures (compiled by the textiles little neddies together) give only a rough guide. They come from several sources, and take no account of stock changes and time lags. For these and other reasons the figures often do not add up to the totals shown. Man-made fibre is extruded in filament form. It can either be used in that way, or after texturising (which gives bulk and stretch) or be chopped up into staple and then spun.

Fig. 3.34. *Technical unification of major sectors of the textile industry: the impact of man-made fibres and multi-fibre machinery.* (Source: *Econ.,* 14 March 1970, p. 63)

218

'spinning jenny', and during the latter half of the eighteenth century further improvements were made in cotton spinning machinery and the application of water and steam power to them (e.g. Arkwright's water-frame, 1769, and Crompton's 'mule', 1774–79). Innovations were made in the subsidiary processes of spinning and finishing. The cotton gin, introduced in America in 1793, speeded and cheapened the process of procuring raw cotton. The weaving process was rather slow in catching up with the increases in capacity made on the spinning side. Cartwright's power loom, patented in 1784, became commercially competitive with hand weaving by 1822.[1] Apart from minor improvements, no fundamental innovation was to follow. The pattern of factory machine production spread quickly in the cotton industry and was adopted more slowly by the wool and worsted industry. Difficulties were experienced in adapting machinery to wool and worsted production, but worsted spinning was more amenable to mechanical application than were worsted weaving and woollen spinning and weaving. Furthermore, until the advent of Australian wool supplies in the 1830s, raw materials were not sufficiently plentiful to stimulate large-scale factory production. Also, the wide variety of cloths made (particularly in woollens, where the range of fibre mixtures was very extensive), and the conservatism of an old-established industry tended to hold back the widespread use of machinery.

In cotton, the factory system and resultant production developed quickly, as did home and export markets. The requirements of widely varied, specialised markets gave a stimulus to specialised production in the weaving section. This led to a requirement for specialisation in yarn production, which in turn, was made possible by technical considerations. These lay in the relative uniformity of raw cotton fibres, whereby large-scale, standardised production of yarn could be carried on. The result of economic (market) stimuli and technical possibilities was a pattern of horizontal specialisation by merchants of raw cotton or cloth, spinners, weavers and finishers, who concentrated on particular narrow ranges, in particular processes, for highly specialised markets.

The horizontal pattern of specialisation was not merely confined to plants and firms, but also to districts. Certain areas concentrated on spinning, others on weaving; certain towns specialised in coarse cloths or yarns, others on fine cloths or yarns.

In woollen and worsted, technical and economic factors operated differently. First, the raw material is not standardised, as are the various types of cotton fibre.[2] Difficulties in grading make for difficulties in the organisation of raw material purchases. Samples must be inspected before purchase, then auctioned. In the processing stages, the subsidiary processes of washing and carding are common to both the woollen and worsted trades; thereafter the processes diverge. The worsted trade uses the combed 'tops' of parallel, long fibres from merino and fine, cross-bred wool. These are fairly standardised, and so are the yarns and cloths produced from them. Worsted yarn is used for knitwear and is woven into suit, dress, and waterproof cloths. Thus the worsted trade tends to split up into a pattern of horizontal specialisations, like the cotton industry, with plants and firms concentrating on a particular range of a particular process. This is especially so in worsted spinning, with specialist combers and spinners,

---

[1] W. T. Shackleton, 'A new look at the structure of the industry', paper at the Cotton Board Conference, 1956.
[2] 'Wool seeks an identity', *Econ.*, 8 Aug. 1964, pp. 567–8; *Stat.*, 20 Sept. 1963, pp. 850–1.

who also cater for a large export market in 'tops' and yarns. The woollen trade uses a wide variety of lower grades of wool: the 'noils' or short fibres discarded from worsted 'top' combing: mungo and shoddy (ground worsted and woollen waste rags); broken 'tops'; hair, cotton, silk, jute and man-made fibres. These fibres are usually shorter than those used in worsted production; they are not combed out; and there is a great diversity of qualities, mixtures and types of yarn and cloth which may be made up from them. Woollen yarn is used for the manufacture of tweeds, flannels, overcoatings, blankets and many industrial cloths. Consequently the scope for large-scale specialisation of process is restricted, as compared with the worsted or cotton trades, and plants tend to perform most of the main and subsidiary processes of spinning and weaving, to suit their requirements.

The finishing trades for woollen and worsted goods, as for cotton goods, provide scope for large-scale specialisation, due to continuity of processes and standardised techniques.

The types of capital investment required for the various processes of textile manufacture have important implications. As mentioned above, the finishing processes, involving chemicals, dyestuffs, etc., offer scope for large-scale operation. Increases in scale can often be achieved more efficiently with larger, more complex equipment. In finishing, therefore, the most efficient plants will tend to be those requiring quite heavy capital investment. Such plants will not be easily available to countries embarking upon textile production. In spinning and weaving, however, the scale of activity may be increased efficiently merely by adding to existing spindles and looms, which do not have to be replaced by larger, faster equipment. This factor makes it possible for countries with scarce capital resources but plentiful labour to start textile production and to add gradually to their capacity. True, more expensive, faster units of equipment can be utilised (such as the high-draft ring spindle and the automatic loom), but even these are limited in unit size and complexity. Furthermore, they are useful for the large-scale production of standardised, cheap yarns and cloths, but less useful for variegated, high quality products, for which the more adaptable, slower, smaller units of equipment still have a place. Some recent developments in textile machinery and techniques, which speed up the rate of production and reduce the labour requirement per unit of production, are 'break spinning' or 'open end' spinning in cotton, the high-speed circular loom (which weaves a 'tube' of cloth), the high-speed 'shuttleless' loom and the high-speed 'reverse twist' wool spinning machine.[1] By extending the scale of production at their particular process stage, this type of development makes it increasingly feasible for a few big firms with large, vertically integrated plants to handle several processes in textile production.

One interesting development in man-made fibres was announced in 1968 as heralding the obsolescence of much of the textile industry during the 1970s. This was 'heterofilaments', in which 'fibres within fibres' had cores and sheaths of different composition and could be bonded together, eliminating the knitting or weaving process.[2]

---

[1] *Cotton and Allied Textiles*, pp. 14–15, 198–200; *F.T.*, 12 May 1970 and 17 June 1970; *S.T.*, 7 Dec. 1969.
[2] *D.T.*, 13 March 1968.

2. History and Development: Cotton

East Indian cotton goods (calico derives from the term 'Calcutta cloth') were introduced to Britain during the seventeenth century, and quickly found favour. It was not until the eighteenth-century innovations, mentioned above, that the industry became firmly established in Britain, but once it did, it began to supply the world with cotton goods. From the outset the industry tended to concentrate in Lancashire, but it also overlapped into Cheshire, Derbyshire, the West Riding and Scotland.

Power-driven textile machinery, first developed and applied to mills in Britain, permitted her to capture world markets for cotton goods during the nineteenth century. By the middle of the century cotton exports, by value, constituted about half Britain's total exports.[1] By 1912–14, U.K. cotton exports of 7,000 million square yards (seven-eighths of total output) of cloth accounted for about two-thirds of world trade in cotton piece goods. At the peak year of 1914 about 60 million spindles were in use (of which 10 million, or 25% in 'mule equivalent', were ring spindles) and about 800,000 looms (mostly adaptable Lancashire looms).[2] The labour force totalled 620,000 operatives in spinning and weaving and over 80% of the output of this labour force and machine capacity was devoted to the export trade. Nevertheless, cotton employed directly only about one-fifth of Lancashire's labour force, although a great many subsidiary and ancillary trades were dependent upon cotton.

Moreover, the cotton industry had become firmly established on the Continent and in the U.S.A. World War I cut off many of Lancashire's underdeveloped and industrialised customers and hastened the process of self-sufficiency, which spread to countries like Japan, China and India. After World War I Lancashire was stimulated for two years by a worldwide shortage and demand, but after 1920 she met powerful competition from some of her old customers. The depression of the 1930s hastened the decline in international trade and in the Lancashire cotton industry's relative share in it. The emerging foreign cotton industries were protected by tariff barriers against British exports. A significant feature of this period was the fact that looms were reduced at a faster rate than spindles, which suffered more from excess capacity. Competition between spinners became very fierce during the 1920s and early 1930s.[3] Nevertheless, exports of yarn (as opposed to total production) did not suffer as much as cloth exports, because they were generally special qualities, destined largely for the more sophisticated Continental and American markets.

To deal with the problems of excess capacity in spinning, the Lancashire Cotton Corporation was formed in 1929, as an amalgamation, set with the task of buying up about one-fifth of spindle capacity (10 million spindles) and about 30,000 looms. It succeeded in buying up 9 million spindles, and had scrapped half of them by World War II. Another move was made by the Government's institution of a Spindles Board in 1936, to control the removal of redundant spindles in an orderly fashion.[4] The culmination of the process of horizontal mergers in spinning, weaving and finishing, and of numerous planned measures taken during the interwar period was the passing of the Cotton Industry (Re-

---

[1] *F.S.B.*, R.4735/D/5, C.O.I., 1961.
[2] Shackleton, *op. cit.*, p. 4. (*N.B.* 1 ring spindle is taken as 1½ 'mule' spindle equivalents.)
[3] *Ibid.*, p. 4.   [4] *Ibid.*, p. 4.

organisation) Act in 1939. It established machinery to fix compulsory minimum prices, to reduce competition, but World War II prevented the scheme from coming into operation.

By 1937 production of yarn and cloth had fallen drastically. Yarn production (2,000 million lb in 1912/14) was down to 1,358 million (cotton) and 21 million (man-made fibre and mixture); exports (210 million lb in 1912) fell to 159. Cloth production had fallen to 4,122 million linear yards (3,640 million cotton and 482 million man-made fibre and mixture); exports had fallen to 25% of world trade in cotton piece goods and stood at 2,001 million square yards (1,921 million cotton and 80 million man-made fibres and mixture).[1] Spindles had been reduced to 44 million, looms to 505,000 and operatives in spinning and weaving to 390,600. Contraction continued in 1938, to 300,300 operatives.[2] 495,000 looms and 42 million spindles were in place, but only 70% were working.[3]

Home demand increased slightly during this period, but, in view of the fact that both population and *per capita* income were rising, it would appear that the income-elasticity of demand for textiles was low. The fall in production to almost half the pre-1914 figure was entirely due to the contraction of export markets, more so for cheap cottons than for high quality goods.

After World War II there was an increase in output in almost all sections of the industry, to meet the worldwide postwar demand. The peak year was 1951. In that year employment in spinning and weaving was 318,000; the number of spindles installed was 33·6 million (mule equivalent); the number of looms was 389,000.[4]

In 1952 there was a slump in world demand for textiles, but recovery began in 1953, and by mid-1954 employment and production had almost recovered to the 1951 level (286,460 employees in spinning and weaving; 32 million (M.E.) spindles and 361,000 looms; yarn production 997 million lb, of which 44 million lb was exported; cloth production 2,775 million linear yards, of which 812 million square yards were exported).[5] Since 1955 employment, production, looms, spindles and exports have been falling.

In July 1959 the Government introduced the Cotton Industry (Reorganisation) Act, a plan for reorganising the spinning, doubling and weaving sections of the industry. The first stage was to grant two-thirds compensation to manufacturers who scrapped surplus machinery by April 1960. The remaining one-third was to come from a levy on the industry, administered by the Cotton Board. The second part was to encourage re-equipment with approved new machinery by a 25% grant, provided that expenditure was incurred by July 1962. By mid-1962 the number of spindles had been reduced to 10·1 million (ring equivalent). Of the 6·89 million raw cotton spinning spindles actually in use, 5·65 million were modern ring spindles. The number of looms had been reduced to 156,000 (mostly in Lancashire, of which 42,700 were fully automatic). This represented a reduction of more than one-third on weaving capacity and nearly half of spinning and doubling capacity, since 1959.[6] Progress in re-equipment, however, has not been so marked. In his address to the annual Conference of the Cotton Board in October 1962 the retiring Chairman, Lord Rochdale, stated that approval had

[1] *F.S.B.*, R.4735/D/5.   [2] *Ann. Abs. Stat.* No. 84.
[3] *The Structure of British Industry*, vol. 2, p. 188.
[4] *The Structure of British Industry*, vol. 2, p. 203, and Shackleton, *op. cit.*, p. 5.
[5] *Ibid.*, p. 5; *F.S.B.*, R.4735/D/5; *The Structure of British Industry*, vol. 2, p. 203.
[6] Source: *The Cotton Board Quarterly Statistical Review*, No. 66.

been given for re-equipment schemes amounting to £116 million, but only £18·3 million of re-equipment had actually taken place.[1]

In June 1960 the Government announced an additional scheme, whereby up to two-thirds compensation was offered for the complete scrapping of production units in the finishing trades by December 1961. By mid-1962 employment in the finishing section had reduced from 37,400 in 1960 to 30,600.

In 1960 yarn and cloth exports were valued at £62·9 million (1·8% of U.K. exports), compared with £181 million in 1951. The Commonwealth took two-thirds of these. In 1959 imports (mainly grey cloth imports from Asian countries) were valued at £36 million.

In 1961 measures were taken to protect the home market from low-cost oriental cotton goods. Imports from Japan and China were subjected to quota, and under a G.A.T.T. agreement imports from India, Hong Kong and Pakistan were voluntarily limited to an annual upper limit, which was extended in 1962 until the end of 1965.[2] Also in 1961, U.K. cotton yarn and cloth production accounted for about 20% of west European production (E.E.C., 70%; rest of E.F.T.A., 10%).[3]

During the 1960s employment, equipment and production in the industry continued to contract. Quotas on cotton textile imports from Commonwealth producers were extended until 1972 and tariffs were levied on non-Commonwealth Asian cotton textile imports and on woven and knitted man-made fibre textile imports from most countries,[4] in an attempt to give some security to the industry and to counteract some of the cost differentials between the home industry and lower-cost foreign competitors. In 1969 the Textile Council (for cotton and allied textiles) produced a report on the industry, giving projections of its future structure. This criticised the 1959 Act as having penalised firms which had already scrapped obsolete equipment and as having done little to improve long-term profitability and efficiency: many firms which had re-equipped had failed to realise hoped-for improvements in profitability, because markets were changing and were being eroded by imports, knitwear and other forms of fabric production.[5] Labour costs were noted as the main reason for higher costs in the British industry, which in yarn were a quarter to one-third higher, and in grey cloth a quarter to three-sevenths higher than costs in Portugal and the Far East. Spinning was the weakest section, mainly because the major technical developments had occurred in that section and had been adopted much more readily by overseas competitors.[6] The Report also called on the Government to replace the quotas on Commonwealth cotton textiles with a tariff. This was coupled with a forecast of a major reduction in the number of firms in the industry by 1975, of the need for drastic improvements in productivity and of the need for an extension of Development Area grants to the traditional cotton textile regions. The Government decided to introduce tariffs and to phase out the quotas by early 1972. By late 1971, however, the industry considered that the tariff would

---

[1] Cotton Board, C.B.347/62.
[2] *Ibid.* For details of proposals by the Board of Trade in September 1965, for a final five-year period of protection during which the industry is to become viable, see C. Jones, 'Cotton gets another five years', *Stat.*, 17 Sept. 1965, p. 771.
[3] A. M. Alfred, address to 1962 Cotton Board Conference, Cotton Board, C.B.346/62.
[4] 'Aiming for a new structure in textile tariffs', *F.T.*, 24 March 1969.
[5] See *Cotton and Allied Textiles: a report on present performance and future prospects*, vol. 1, Textile Council, para. 576.
[6] *Ibid.*, paras. 577–8.

be inadequate, and requested an extension of the quota. In December 1971 the Government acceded to this request, extending the specific quotas on India and Hong Kong and the 'Global quota' on other developing countries.[1] In June 1970 the Government approved of loans of £10 million to aid re-equipment and mergers in small and medium-sized companies, but this was threatened with premature termination at the end of 1970 when the Industrial Reorganisation Corporation, administering the scheme, was wound up.[2]

In its final annual *Review* (No. 38, June/July 1971) the Textile Council detailed the developments in the industry since its 1969 Report and compared them with that report's projections. Firstly, productivity had fallen below the forecast level: output per head in spinning in 1970 was about 5% greater than in 1968, but in weaving there was almost no improvement, whereas the Report forecast about 10% per annum productivity increase in both areas. In finishing, output per head was static, compared with a 3% per annum forecast improvement. Secondly, the Report had forecast an expansion in the U.K. fabric market of about 4% between 1967 and 1970. This seems to have been maintained, but the market share of knitted fabrics had increased by 10%, as compared with the 5% forecast. Thirdly, the proportion of man-made fibres used in the major processes did not expand as much as had been forecast. The proportion used in spinning (25·5% in 1968) was 28·5% in 1970, as compared with the 35–40% 1975 forecast, but the proportion used in weaving only rose from 15% in 1968 to 16% in 1970 (1975 forecast, 30%). Fourthly, whereas employment in spinning, weaving and doubling was forecast to contract by about 8·5% per annum from 1968 to 1975, the contraction was only 6% per annum up to mid-1971. This slower than forecast reduction in employment, with output below the forecast level (and a slower than forecast reduction in machinery) combined to cause productivity to lag. In finishing the annual decline in employment (5·5%) exceeded the 3% forecast. The proportion of male workers in spinning, doubling and weaving rose from about 46% in 1968 to 52% in mid-1971, in line with the 1975 forecast of about 60%. Fifthly, the reduction in machinery between 1968 and mid-1971 was well behind the forecast rate. For example, ring-equivalent spindles only fell from 3·9 million in 1968 to 3·4 million in mid-1971 (1975 forecast, 1·7 million). However, only 88% of the mid-1971 spindles were actually in use, and progress in shift-working, for maximum utilisation, had not been as rapid as envisaged. Nevertheless, the rate of decrease in looms was about in line with the forecast: they fell from 90,000 in 1968 to 67,500 in mid-1971 (of which only 85% were in use), whereas the forecast for 1975 was 45,000. Sixthly, the restructuring of the industry did not seem to have proceeded as quickly as forecast: the number of production units fell from 686 in all sectors in 1968 to 590 in mid-1971 (1975 forecast, 290–310) and the number of firms fell from 375 in 1968 to 329 in 1970 (1975 forecast, 120–150), despite the reductions in looms and finishing employment. Progress was made in vertical integration, particularly between spinning and weaving and between finishing and converting, but there was noticeably little between weaving and converting.[3]

The salient facts and trends noted in this section are brought together in Table 3.16.

---

[1] *Econ.*, 23 Oct. 1971, p. 86; *F.T.*, 9 Dec. 1971.
[2] *F.T.*, 16 June 1970; *D.T.*, 4 June 1970 and 5 Nov. 1970.
[3] *Textile Council Review*, no. 38, June/July 1971, pp. 3–12; *Cotton and Allied Textiles*.

Table 3.16 Production, capacity, employment, imports and exports in the Cotton Industry

	Units	1912	1937	1951	1954	1957	1960	1964	1967	1970
Employment*										
Spinning[a]	'000's	622 ⎫	176	148	135	116	88	66	49	45
Weaving	'000's	⎬	187	143	132	108	85	67	51	43
Finishing	'000's	88	–	48	45	41	37	29	24	22
Total	'000's	710	n.a.	339	312	265	210	162	124	110
Capacity[a]										
Spinning – spindles	m. ring-equivalent[b]	40·9	29·4	22·4	21·1	18·1	8·8	5·8	3·8	3·5
Looms	'000's	786	505	389	366	293	167	130	98	75
Output										
Single Yarn – cotton	m. lb.	1,983	1,358	968	842	727	596	508†	308†	277†
– spun man-made fibre and mixture	,,	–	19	109	155	149	155	146†	117†	163†
Cloth – cotton	m. lin. yd.	8,050	3,640	2,201	1,994	1,628	1,294	1,035†	745†	686†
– man-made fibre and mixtures	,,	–	482	759	781	660	617	610†	530†	530†
Exports										
Yarn – cotton	m. lb.	243·9	159·0	65·5	40·4	37·6	21·1	15·3	11·7	14·1
– spun man-made fibre	,,	–	0·1	4·8	4·4	5·4	3·9	6·3	6·5	17·8
Cloth – cotton	m. sq. yd.	6,913[c]	1,921	864	637	456	327	210	143	129
– man-made fibre	,,	–	78	218	175	111	54	91	75	118
Imports										
Yarn – cotton	m. lb.	8·4	3·0	31·7	10·7	14·7	38·7	40·9	39·3	36·8
– spun man-made fibre	,,	–	–	0·9	0·7	0·8	0·5	2·3	6·6	11·9
Cloth – cotton	m. sq. yd.	108[c]	50	376	267	416	728	767	660	480
– man-made fibre	,,	–	25	99	67	74	58	93	125	164

[a] Including waste spinning and doubling.
[c] Million linear yards.
* Part-time workers counted as halves from 1951 onwards.

[b] Counting one-ring spindle as equivalent to 1¼ mule spindles.
[a] Postwar figures relate to machinery in place in running mills at year end.
† 53-week year.

N.B. Owing to the differing sources, the prewar figures for employment, capacity and output cannot be regarded as being completely comparable with the post-war figures. Equally, changes in definition mean that the export and import figures are not completely comparable throughout. In particular, from 1960 onwards textiles are classified in the trade statistics according to the fibre which predominates by weight. 1967 and 1970 figures for exports include small quantities for re-export.

(Sources: *Quarterly Statistical Review*, Cotton Board and Textile Council; *Fact Sheets on Britain*, R.4735/D/5, W. T. Shackleton; *A New Look at the Structure of the Industry*, The Cotton Board; *The Structure of British Industry*, vol. 2, C.U.P., 1958; *Annual Abstract of Statistics*, H.M.S.O.; Memorandum from The Cotton Board Statistics Department, May 1965)

3. History and Development: Woollen and Worsted

The woollen and worsted trades are the oldest of Britain's manufacturing industries, being based in earlier days on local wool supplies. Until the rise of cotton in the early nineteenth century, woollen and worsted goods constituted the largest item of U.K. manufactured goods exports. The industry as a whole has maintained a leading position in world trade (particularly the worsted section) and is still one of the largest of the world's wool textile industries.

With the gradual change from domestic to factory production, which followed upon the evolution and introduction of machinery, the centre of the industry moved from East Anglia and south-west England to the East and (particularly) West Ridings of Yorkshire, attracted by suitable soft water, water and coal, power and labour.

At about the same time, the practice of breeding sheep for mutton was growing, and gradually the fine wool produced in Britain declined in importance. Imports came in from Saxony, Australia and other regions, and the British clip of coarser mutton-sheep wool gravitated to such trades as carpet manufacture.

Unlike the cotton industry, which in its peak years exported mainly to underdeveloped countries, the woollen and worsted industry exported mainly to countries or colonies of European descent, and these were the first to develop industries of their own. Thus woollen and worsted suffered from foreign competition and self-sufficiency in export markets from the 1870s – earlier than cotton.

This competition was felt more keenly by worsted (particularly cloth) than by woollens, because foreign manufacturers were more easily able to produce standardised worsted cloths than worsted tops and yarns and variegated woollen products.

Before World War I Britain was exporting about 40% of her woollen and worsted cloth (225·9 million square yards out of 572·5 million square yards), about 15% of her woollen and worsted yarns (87 million lb out of 565·1 million lb) and about 14% of her worsted tops (41·9 million lb) out of 304·5 million lb).

After World War I, up to 1924, Britain maintained her relative position as a manufacturer of worsted and woollen goods, and increased her share of world trade in these products. Yet home production was below the prewar level in fabrics, due largely to changes in home demand (substitute fabrics, shorter dresses, etc.). Yarn production was higher and tops production only slightly lower, because of a maintenance of exports in tops and an increase in home demand for yarn for the growing knitwear and hosiery trades. After 1924 Britain's share of world trade fell relatively and absolutely, due to greater foreign competition and self-sufficiency. The losses were less pronounced in tops than in other products, as Britain supplied to foreign manufacturers. Production of yarn continued to be higher than prewar levels; tops production continued to be slightly below the prewar level; fabrics continued below the prewar level, this time because of a loss of foreign markets.

Since World War II the industry has faced increasing competition from foreign producers and from the growing knitwear industry. The increasing importance of man-made fibres has not only resulted in a decline in the usage of wool, but has also blurred the boundaries of the industry, as multi-fibre textile machinery and the use of wool and man-made fibre mixtures have led to some overlapping of processes and products with the cotton textiles and knitwear sectors.

By 1970 the production of worsted tops, which reached a peak in 1960, had dropped to below the pre-World War II level. Yarn production has fluctuated slightly and by 1970 was below the prewar level: fabric production had almost continuously declined during the period to about three-fifths of the pre-war level.

In 1969 the most comprehensive study of the industry to date was issued as a report of the Wool Textile E.D.C.[1] The report indicated the relatively low profitability of the U.K. industry, compared with competitors such as Japan, Portugal, South Korea and South Africa in both the home market and foreign markets. Between 1960 and 1968 the U.K. share in world exports of tops fell from 40% to 22%; for woollen and worsted yarn it fell from 18% to 14%; for woven wool fabric it fell from 26% to 18%. In the home market, imports of woven wool fabrics doubled in quantity and increased their share of total home consumption from 5% to 13%. These trends were reflected in the reduced consumption of virgin wool, which fell from about 480 million lb in the mid-1950s to about 380 million lb in the late 1960s.

Three major factors lie behind these trends: they interact on each other and feature strongly in the report's forecast of future developments in the industry. Firstly, the impact of the growth in knitted fabric production, processed outside the industry, has caused woollen and worsted woven fabric production to fall by 2·5% per annum from 1960 to 1968. Whereas in 1955 knitted fabrics constituted 28% of wool textile fabric production, by 1965 their share rose to 42%: the forecast for 1975 was for a 66% knitted fabric share.[2] As the industry supplies worsted yarns of wool and man-made fibre mixture for knitting and as modern wool textile machinery can handle such yarns, it is expected that the industry will increasingly integrate with knitted goods production, as some cotton textile firms have done. Secondly, the significant incursions of man-made fibres into the industry's products have resulted in changes in the industry's production processes and in the markets for its traditional products. The E.D.C. report forecast a rise in the man-made fibre share in yarn production from 188 million lb in 1967 (37%) to 304 million lb in 1975 (53%).[3] This development has resulted in a movement into the industry of outside firms, such as Coats Patons (from the cotton industry) and Courtaulds and I.C.I. (from the man-made fibre sector). Also, some firms in the industry have integrated horizontally into other sectors of the textile industry, as in the case of Bulmer and Lumb (Holdings) Ltd., a Bradford firm which in 1963 took over Bolten Eagle (Holdings) Ltd., a firm with both wool and cotton interests in Yorkshire, Lancashire and the Leicestershire knitting region.[4] Thirdly, the chief structural flaw in the industry, noted in the 1969 Report, was excess capacity and undersized, suboptimal units. Numerous small firms with obsolete, written-off equipment and minimal fixed overhead charges were undercutting prices set by more efficient firms and making it difficult for them to recoup overhead charges on modern equipment. For example, in yarn production a firm with only operating costs (for materials, labour, etc.) to cover could survive on a production of 100 lb per hour, whereas a firm using new machinery would require 1500 lb per hour to cover its overheads.

[1] *The Strategic Future of the Wool Textile Industry*, Wool Textile Economic Development Committee.
[2] *F.T.*, 28 April 1971, survey on double jersey knitting; E.D.C. *Report*, para. 12.4.
[3] E.D.C. *Report*, para. 6.9; *F.T.*, 2 June 1969, 'Synthetics force Yorkshire to rethink old attitudes'; 'The fortunes of wool', statistical charts, *B.B.R.*, Nov. 1967.
[4] R. A. Bowman, 'The structure of the United Kingdom wool textile industry', *Quarterly Review of Agricultural Economics*, Jan. 1970, p. 43.

Thus during a recession the former type of firm, despite its inferior technical ability, could nevertheless cut prices below the level at which the latter could compete. These marginal firms which could enter or leave the production scene were largely responsible for price instability. The Report advocated a policy of acquisition and the liquidation of excess capacity, and also policies of narrow specialisation (particularly in tops and yarns) and highly efficient multi-shift operation, as methods of strengthening marketing activities. An interesting conclusion was that, 'there is no future in this industry for the firm that will make anything for anybody, at any price'.[1]

The Report's principal recommendations[2] included an increase in the output of converted tops, worsted and semi-worsted yarns and non-woven fabrics, a decrease in the output of combed tops and woollen woven fabrics and a diversification into knitted fabrics;

an investment of about £40 million by 1975 in re-equipment and modernisation in high-profit projects;

an increase in shift-working and other practices to improve productivity and wage levels;

a 17% reduction in manpower by 1975, largely made possible by higher productivity and natural wastage, with an increase in the proportion of male employees from 51% to 56%;

a target of 80% in the home market share of woollen woven fabrics and of 95% in the share of other products;

a reduction of 40% in the number of independent firms, to increase plants to a viable size, mainly by way of horizontal integration amongst small firms: scope for some further vertical integration amongst the larger firms existed, but the Report was not in favour of much change in this direction, particularly on the part of the major man-made fibre suppliers. The major objective was not so much the achievement of large scale technological economies – since this would detract from the variety, design and quality which were positive attributes of the industry – but rather the creation of financially strong companies;

an increase in direct selling, particularly overseas, with the formation of joint marketing companies, where necessary.

Some of the salient points in this section are brought out in Table 3.17.

4. Location of the Cotton Industry

(a) General

Though the cotton industry, in its early days, took root in the Clyde valley, the West Riding of Yorkshire and the Nottingham district, it was always concentrated in the Lancashire area and adjacent counties of Cheshire and Derbyshire. The other districts possessed existing textile skills; the Glasgow and West Riding areas also had a humid climate, suitable for the thin cotton yarns; the West Riding also had water power and soft water (useful for bleaching, dyeing and other processes) from the millstone grit of the Pennines. Lancashire, however, possessed all these advantages. In addition, its soil was poor, and farmers took to domestic cotton spinning and weaving to supplement their income.

As the new mechanical techniques developed in the cotton industry, it became

[1] E.D.C. *Report*, paras. 15.1–15.3; 'Knitting Yorkshire together', *Econ.*, 14 June 1969, p. 72.
[2] E.D.C. *Report*, p. xi; also see 'Wool textiles – an industry examined', *D.E.A. Pr. Rep. Ind. and Reg.*, 53, June 1969.

Table 3.17 *Production, capacity, employment and exports in the Woollen and Worsted industry*

	1912	1924	1937	1950	1957	1960	1963	1964	1965	1966	1967	1968	1969	1970
Production														
Tops (million lb)	304·5	285·5	278·5	344·9	349·0	356·7	346·2	322·0	304·7	292·7	264·0	293·2	295·9	274·1
Yarn (million lb)	561·1	554·5	565·8	556·0	538·2	546·5	552·0	562·1	548·7	536·0	497·5	538·5	534·4	499·2
*Fabric (million sq. yd)	572·5	440·0	445·5	450·3	394·1	367·1	325·4	325·4	323·0	302·3	294·5	294·7	286·2	257·4
Exports														
Tops (million lb)	41·9	41·1	40·2	73·0	85·4	95·9	100·1	81·9	71·7	72·5	62·2	70·3	77·1	72·3
Yarn (million lb)	87·0	65·9	41·4	35·2	29·9	32·8	33·9	32·1	30·1	29·5	27·7	31·6	35·5	34·9
*Fabric (million sq. yd)	225·9	221·5	122·8	117·3	109·0	98·2	89·0	89·2	88·5	76·9	71·1	78·2	78·4	64·5
Employment ('000)														
Combing	⎱ 250 (est.)	⎱ 120 (est.)	⎱ 216·6	⎱ 221	13·2	13·0	10·8	9·9	9·4	8·8	7·9	7·9	7·7	6·4
Worsted Spinning					51·6	52·4	47·2	44·1	42·5	39·2	35·1	35·3	34·9	30·1
Worsted Weaving	⎰	⎰			28·4	27·3	24·3	23·4	22·4	21·6	19·6	18·9	17·9	15·8
Woollen Spinning	⎱ 130 (est.)	⎱ 130 (est.)			22·3	22·4	21·8	21·0	21·1	20·5	22·8	23·5	22·5	20·1
Woollen Weaving	⎰	⎰	⎰	⎰	40·4	37·6	33·3	32·4	31·0	29·0	25·2	23·8	22·2	19·9
Minor Production processes and finishing					8·4	7·3	7·7	7·2	6·8	6·2	5·4	5·3	4·6	3·9
Total	—	—	—	—	164·3	160·0	145·1	138·0	133·2	125·3	116·0	114·7	109·8	96·2
Capacity														
Combs ('000)	—	—	—	—	2·3	2·3	2·1	1·9	1·7	1·7	1·5	1·4	1·4	1·2
Worsted Spindles (mill.)	—	—	—	—	2·8	2·7	2·4	2·3	2·2	2·1	1·9	1·8	1·7	1·5
Woollen Spindles (mill.)	—	—	—	—	2·0	1·9	1·6	1·6	1·5	1·5	1·3	1·3	1·2	1·2
Looms ('000)	—	—	—	—	55·9	47·4	39·7	37·9	36·1	33·6	31·9	29·6	28·3	25·6

* Excludes blankets.

(Based on material in *Fact Sheets on Britain*, R.4735/D/6, 1961; *Brit. O.H.*, 1962; *The Structure of British Industry*, vol. 2, 1958; *G. C. Allen, British Industries and their Organisation*, 1959; *Ann. Abs. Stat.*: Memoranda from International Wool Secretariat, May 1965 and Oct. 1971)

more and more concentrated in the Lancashire area, which soon generated its own locational pull in the form of economies of local concentration. With the advent of steam power, the local coal reserves exerted an attraction to the industry; the growth of exports and the introduction of raw cotton supplies from America generated an extremely strong pull to the Lancashire area, with its western position, in close proximity to Liverpool. This factor was fortified by the construction of the Manchester Ship Canal, completed in 1894. A pool of skilled labour was built up; many ancillary industries (finishing, packing, textile machinery, etc.) grew up in the area; Manchester developed into a specialist merchanting centre.

The Glasgow area enjoyed many of Lancashire's original advantages, but developed greater comparative advantages in the production of ships, iron and steel products, etc. The West Riding area gradually developed greater comparative advantages in the production of woollen and worsted products. The Nottingham area gradually concentrated on lace and hosiery, the thicker threads of which did not tend to snap in the drier climate of the area.

In mid-1961, the north-west contained just over 75% of cotton spinning, doubling and weaving employees; Scotland contained about 7% (mostly in spinning and doubling: Paisley is an important sewing thread centre); Yorkshire contained about 7% (mostly in weaving); the north Midland region contained almost 3% and the Midland region about 2%.[1]

(b) Specialisation within the Lancashire area

Largely as a result of the high degree of horizontal specialisation which developed in the industry, a process of regional and district sub-specialisation has grown up in Lancashire. Manchester is the commercial centre for the finished products; Liverpool deals with the raw cotton imports, and contains the Cotton Exchange; the north-east part of the region concentrates on weaving; the south-east concentrates on spinning. Within each of these regions there is a district and town specialisation. Within the spinning region, Haslingdon and Rochdale specialise on waste spinning; Rochdale and Oldham on medium and coarse yarns; Bolton and the Manchester environs on fine yarns; Stockport on doubling. In the weaving region, Preston, Blackburn and Nelson produce most of the rayon and mixture cloths; Preston also concentrates on fancy cloths, sheetings and fine shirtings; Blackburn and Burnley specialise on plain cloths; Nelson and Colne specialise on dress fabrics. The finishing trades tend to concentrate in the central part of the area, but many finishing plants are scattered throughout east Lancashire, drawing their chemicals from the near-by Warrington, Widnes and Runcorn area (see Fig. 3.35).

(c) Sources of raw cotton imports

More than four-fifths of the raw cotton used in Britain's cotton industry is of medium staple ($\frac{7}{8}$ to $1\frac{1}{4}$ inches in length). In 1959 the main sources of its supply were the U.S.A., Nigeria, Peru, Iran, Mexico, the U.S.S.R., Turkey and Brazil. Long staple cotton, used for fine yarns, comes principally from the Sudan, Egypt, Aden and Peru. Short staple cotton (less than $\frac{7}{8}$ inch in length) comes mainly from Pakistan, Burma and India. In 1959 the total value of raw cotton imports (300,000 tons) and cotton waste imports was £68·1 million, of which 24% came from the U.S.A.[2]

[1] Min. Lab. Gaz., Mar. 1962.   [2] F.S.B., R.4735/D/5

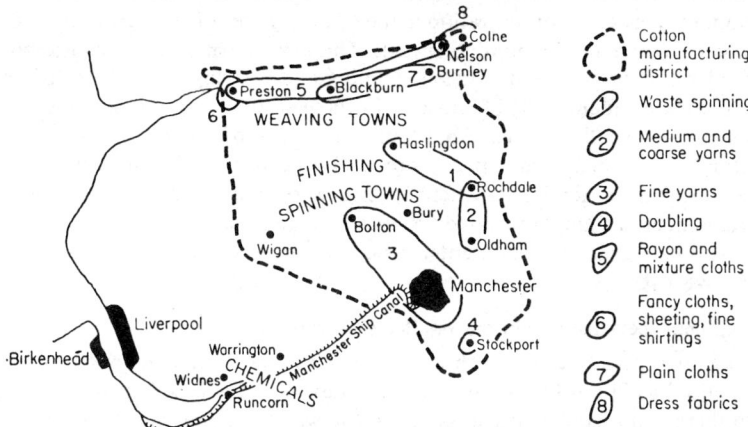

Fig. 3.35. *Location of the Cotton Industry and regional specialisation in the Lancashire area*
(Based on: *The British Isles: Where, How and Why*)

5. Location of the Woollen and Worsted Industry

(a) General

In its early days, woollen and worsted was a domestic industry, using local raw materials. It was scattered throughout Britain according to available supplies of soft water and wool, but was centred mainly in East Anglia, Scotland and the south-west of England.

Following the gradual change to factory production after the late eighteenth century, the centre of the industry moved north, particularly to the West Riding of Yorkshire.

Some of the locational factors which attracted the industry predominantly to the West Riding were: plentiful supplies of wool from the Pennine sheep; soft water from the Calder and Colne rivers, flowing through millstone grit; supplies of cheap labour; a willingness to adopt new, mechanical methods, as opposed to the conservatism of the old areas; fast-flowing Pennine streams to provide water power; access to ports for the export trade and, gradually, for the increasingly important raw material imports. With the advent of steam power, local coal reserves were an added locational attraction.

Scotland and the west of England retained a certain amount of woollen production, and came to specialise in high quality goods, such as West of England tweeds and Witney blankets, and Scottish tweeds, knitwear and scarves.

In 1969, of the 1,289 establishments or plants in the industry (over half of which were in one-plant firms) 78% were in Yorkshire and the North (with 82% of the labour force), 12% were in Scotland (with 11% of the labour force), 2·5% in the West of England (with 2% of manpower) and 7·5% in Wales and the rest of England (with 5% of manpower).[1] More fully integrated plants can exist more easily in isolation, whereas more fragmented plants need the proximity of allied processes in a localised area. Woollen plants tend to be more fully

[1] E.D.C. *Report*, pp. 23, 50–1 and 56.

integrated, and worsted plants tend to be horizontally specialised. These factors account for the heavy concentration in the Bradford area of worsted plants – 80% of which were entirely non-integrated. There is a particular localisation of worsted wool combing and worsted spinning and weaving in the West Riding, which contains about 90% of capacity in these sections, as well as about two-thirds of the woollen trade. About three-quarters of combing capacity and one-third of worsted yarn capacity are in Bradford itself. Woollen plants tend to be scattered in Scotland – where a third were fully integrated and many of the remainder partially integrated – Lancashire and the West of England (which both also had some worsted plants), Leicestershire and the 'heavy woollen' area of the West Riding.

(b) Regional specialisation in the woollen and worsted industry

The regional specialisation which has grown up in the Yorkshire area is not so pronounced as in the Lancashire cotton industry, and is based on the fact that while there is horizontal specialisation in the worsted trade, mostly in the west and north, there is a high degree of integration of processes in the woollen section, in the east and south. In the worsted region, Bradford is the commercial

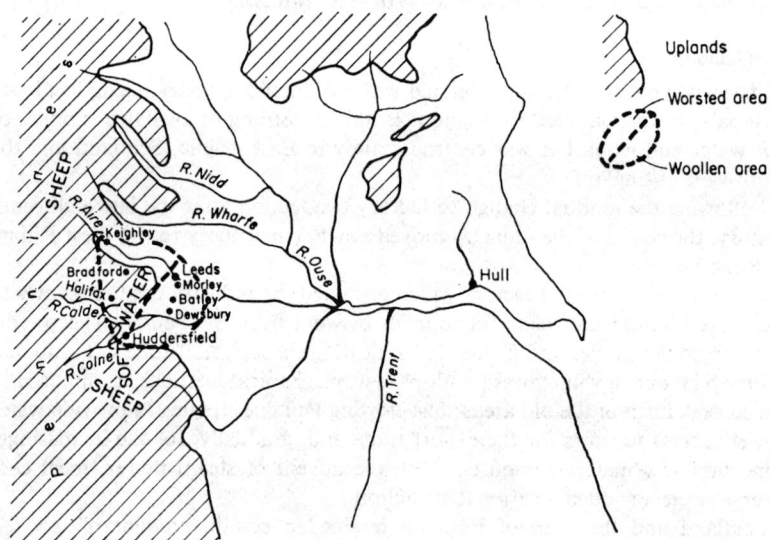

Fig. 3.36. *Location of the Woollen and Worsted Industry and regional specialisation in the West Riding area*
(Source: *The British Isles: Where, How and Why*)

centre, also doing most of the wool combing. Along with Halifax and Keighley it produces a wide variety of worsted yarns and worsted dress fabrics. Huddersfield produces high quality men's worsteds and also high quality woollen fabrics. In the woollen area (which overlaps on to Huddersfield) Batley and Dewsbury, the main centres, concentrate on most of the processes involved in cheaper, simpler woollen fabrics. Leeds and Morley are less important producers of woollens. There is thus less district specialisation in the vertically integrated woollen trade than in the horizontally specialised worsted section (see Fig. 3.36).

In the west of England the industry (predominantly woollen) is situated in a group of towns in the region of, and including, Stroud, Trowbridge and Witney.

In Scotland the industry is located in clearly defined areas, according to local specialisation. The border area of the south of Scotland is the main centre (tweeds, scarves, knitwear, etc.). Other areas are the district between Aberdeen and Inverness, the Hebrides (Harris tweeds), and the district north of the Forth.

(c) Sources of raw wool imports

Most U.K. wool production consists of the coarser fibre, mainly useful for carpets. Merino and cross-bred wool for apparel yarns and fabrics is mainly imported. Of the 1960 imports (647 million lb), valued at £150 million, Australia supplied 266 million lb, valued at £56·5 million; New Zealand supplied 162 million lb, valued at £35·6 million; Argentina supplied 54·8 million lb, with a value of £9·8 million; and South Africa supplied 48·4 million lb, valued at £9·7 million. Re-exports of raw wool amounted to 48·1 million lb with a value of £10·6 million, and went mainly through the London Wool Exchange to European wool and worsted manufacturers.[1]

6. Further Reading and Sources

Footnote references to daily and weekly journals are not repeated.

R. A. BOWMAN, 'The structure of the United Kingdom wool textile industry'. *Quarterly Review of Agricultural Economics*. Jan. 1970.

C.O.I., *The United Kingdom Cotton Industry. F.S.B.* R.4735/D/5. 1961.

C.O.I., *The British Wool Textile Industry. F.S.B.* R.4735/D/6. 1961.

THE COTTON BOARD, *Introducing Cotton*, pamphlet.

The Cotton Board Harrogate Conference, 1962; addresses by A. M. Alfred, C.B.346/62 and by the Chairman, C.B.347/62.

The Cotton Board Quarterly Statistical Review.

D.E.A. Pr. Rep. Ind. and Reg., 53, June 1969.

M. M. EDWARDS, *The Growth of the British Cotton Trade, 1780–1815*. Manchester U.P. 1967.

INTERNATIONAL WOOL SECRETARIAT MEMORANDUM, May 1965.

J. and S. JEWKES, 'A hundred years of change in the structure of the cotton industry'. *The Journal of Law and Economics*. Oct. 1966.

C. MILES, *Lancashire Textiles: a case Study of Industrial Change*. C.U.P. 1968.

A. MURRAY, *The British Isles: Where, How and Why*. Collins. 1958.

W. T. SHACKLETON, 'A new look at the structure of the industry: Cotton's new look'. Cotton Board Conference, 1956.

THE TEXTILE COUNCIL, *Cotton and Allied Textiles: a report on present performance and future prospects*, vol. 1. 1969.

The Textile Council Quarterly Statistical Review.

WOOL TEXTILE ECONOMIC DEVELOPMENT COUNCIL, *The Strategic Future of the Wool Textile Industry*. H.M.S.O. 1969.

[1] *F.S.B.*, R.4735/D/6.

THE TEXTILE INDUSTRY: Stage II: Structure and Organisation

1. THE COTTON INDUSTRY

(a) Structure of the Industry: Number and Size of Plant·

In general, cotton spinning, weaving and finishing have tended to be carried on in specialised plants, along the lines of horizontal technical specialisation. An analysis, by the Ministry of Labour, of plant size in manufacturing industry in 1959 showed that in textile trades generally, 53% of employees worked in plants of 100–500 employees, as compared with 20% in all manufacturing industry.[1]

At end-1968 there were 130 plants engaged in spinning, 390 in weaving and 166 in finishing.[2] In spinning, the average plant had 29,000 spindles at an average rate of 68 hours per week. The 1975 forecast was for 60 to 70 plants with an average of 26,150 spindles operating for an average of 112 hours per week. By 1971 there were still 119 plants, averaging 26,550 working spindles at 83 hours per week. In weaving, the average plant used 220 looms, averaging 69 hours per week. The 1975 forecast was for 140 to 150 plants using an average of 310 looms for 94 hours per week. The economically feasible scale would be 500 looms, but the 1975 forecast envisaged that 25% of looms would be 'shuttleless', and that 80% of total output would be in units larger than the 310 loom average, working for up to 144 hours per week – the balance being accounted for by smaller scale, specialised units, working shorter hours. By 1971 there were 322 units with an average of 186 working looms at 71·4 hours per week: only about 5·3% of these looms were 'shuttleless'. In finishing, there were 166 plants in 1968: these were forecast to reduce to 90 by 1975, and by 1971 had only fallen to 149.[3]

Two major problems involved in the structure and restructuring of the industry are firstly, the existence of excess capacity in the form of small, specialist spinners, weavers and finishers, with small plants operated on a commission basis for many of the 850 'convertor' firms in 1968 (in 1971 there were about 730, of whom 550 each converted less than 0·06% of the industry's total cloth throughput).[4] Many of these small plants were operating fully depreciated and obsolete machinery at a low degree of intensity, and thus posed a problem of price instability in the industry. Secondly, there is the problem of whether rationalisation should proceed on vertical or horizontal lines. Much of the vertical integration by 1968 was commercial – the financial ownership of capacity in various processes – rather than full, technical coordination. In addition, there is the problem of balance between the processes. Due to the narrower range of standardised raw materials and yarns in the spinning sector, the much greater diversity of cloths in the weaving sector and the significant technical scale economies in finishing, much vertical integration will of necessity be out of balance: the spinning section of a vertically integrated plant will probably supply outside customers and the finishing sections will probably both take in work from outside, for customers, and send out work to specialist finishers. Much of the debate about vertical *versus* horizontal integration hinges on their respective merits of greater coordination and control as compared with greater flexibility and diversity of product. The 1969 Report concluded that there would

---

·[1] *Min. Lab. Gaz.*, Sept. 1959.
[2] *Textile Council Review*, 38, June/July 1971, p. 11.
[3] *Ibid.*, pp. 10–11 and *Cotton and Allied Textiles*, paras. 536–51.
[4] *Cotton and Allied Textiles*, para. 549; *F.T.*, 30 Sept. 1971.

still be room for small-volume plants, horizontally specialised, but that the balance for the major part of the industry was strongly tilted in favour of vertical organisation, especially for bulk production – due to factors such as increasing capital intensity in production, increasing optimal scales in finishing, increasing emphasis on product and technical innovation and the increase in risk associated with these developments.[1] An important point made in the Report was that despite the increase in capacity represented by modern spindles and looms, worked very intensively, they are still relatively small indivisible units, so that many are used even in small plants. Thus the major scale economies tend to be operational – in staffing, management and marketing. Depending upon the degree of variety or standardisation, the optimal size of spinning plant would therefore be about 30,000 to 40,000 spindles working three shifts (112·5 hours) and for weaving plants would be about 500 modern looms.[2]

With regard to the implications of standardisation, the Report examined relative costs in the industry in Britain and overseas. Its labour productivity as compared with the U.S.A. was 1 : 2·8, although for all types of industry the ratio was 1 : 3. This appeared to be due largely to the fact that most U.S. spinning and weaving plants specialise on a single product, whereas in Britain and Western Europe spinning plants, for example, often produce up to thirty varieties. In general, the performance of the better plants in Britain, as compared with other main competitors, was relatively weakest in spinning (labour productivity about two-thirds of that in E.E.C. countries and half that in the U.S.A.), less weak in weaving (labour productivity about four-fifths the E.E.C. level and less than half the U.S.A. level): in finishing, however, Britain had lower costs than any other country except the U.S.A.[3]

(b) Administrative Organisation

(i) Concentration of control

Significant changes have taken place in the pattern of administrative control in the industry, since the 1959 restructuring policy, and further developments are likely to continue in the future.

Between 1961 and 1968 the total number of firms engaged in the industry declined by about 40% from 1,887 to 1,138. This magnitude of contraction was similar both for horizontally specialised firms with one principal activity and for vertically integrated firms with more than one principal activity. By 1968 the number of specialist firms (1,572 in 1961) had fallen to 941: the number of integrated firms (315 in 1961) had reached 197. Of these 197 firms, 139 had two principal activities and 58 had three or more principal activities. The net result of such multiple-process integration was to cause the aggregate of firms involved in the various processes (1,408) to exceed the actual number of firms in the industry.

Thus in 1968 there were 49 specialist spinning firms (including waste spinners) with 35% of spinning spindles and 27% of waste spindles: there were 54 integrated firms in these activities, controlling 64% of spinning spindles and 72% of waste spindles. The 95 specialist weavers controlled 22% of the looms, whilst 184 integrated weaving firms controlled 78% of the looms. The 670 specialist

---

[1] *Cotton and Allied Textiles*, paras. 518–38.
[2] *Ibid.*, paras. 335, 556.
[3] *Ibid.*, ch. 5.

converting firms (who buy 'grey' cloth and order it to be processed to their specifications, usually on a commission basis) accounted for only 29% of converting throughput, whilst 177 integrated convertors accounted for 71% of total throughput. There were 49 specialist fabric finishing firms with 29% of the labour force in that sector, and 52 integrated finishers with 71% of the labour force. In doubling, 34 specialist firms controlled only 23% of doubling spindles: the specialist spinners and weavers had 15% and the more vertically integrated firms controlled 62%. In yarn finishing, 44 specialist yarn finishing firms employed 51% of the labour force while specialist weavers and fabric finishers employed 6% and the more fully integrated firms employed 43%.[1] The details of this 1968 control pattern, showing the changes since 1961, are given in Table 3.18.

Of the 103 firms involved in spinning in 1968, about 40 were primarily waste spinners: the remaining 63 spinners proper were forecast to contract to between 25 and 30 by 1975. By late 1970 they still numbered 56. The 279 firms involved in weaving were forecast to contract to 100 in 1975: by late 1970 they still totalled 240. The 101 fabric finishers (1968) had only fallen to 94 by late 1970, as compared with the forecast of 30 by 1975.[2]

As may be seen from Table 3.18, the only specialist sector firms to increase their share of total capacity from 1961 to 1968 were the spinners (3% increase). The specialist weavers, convertors and fabric finishers lost 6%, 15% and 33% of total capacity, respectively. The groups of firms which made most progress in concentrating their control of industry capacity were the integrated spinner/weaver/convertor/finishers and, to a lesser extent, the weaver/convertor/finishers.

Since 1957 there has been more horizontal integration into larger firms in each section, aimed at the creation of larger groups which can specialise on a narrower range of qualities and finishes.

With regard to vertical integration of plants within firms, in 1956 there was quite a lot of integration between the weaving and converting sections, but not much between these and spinning. About a quarter of cloth production was converted by the firms which produced it. However, in the U.S.A. (and other countries) spinner/weaver/converter integration accounted for about two-thirds of cloth production.[3]

Since then there has been an increasing trend towards the vertical integration of firms, both formal (by merger) and by contractual agreement (as in the case of some multiple store organisations). This latter trend was encouraged at the 1963 Cotton Board Annual Conference by the head of Combined English Mills, who called upon firms to 'think vertically' and coordinate their activities, as well as merging formally.[4]

A major argument for vertical integration of control in the industry is that fluctuations of activity in the producing sections farthest from the consumer might be less violent if these producers had more scope for framing policy on sales promotion, pricing, and stocking of the finished cloth.[5]

1 *Cotton and Allied Textiles*, p. 153.
2 *Ibid.*, pp. 113–16; *Textile Council Review*, No. 38, June/July 1971, p. 11.
3 Shackleton, *op. cit.*, p. 10.
4 *Stat.*, 25 Oct. 1963.
5 'Chairman's address to the 1962 Cotton Board Conference, p. 7; Sir Cuthbert Clegg, 'A new shape for Britain's cotton industry', *D.T.*, 29 Nov. 1961.

Table 3.18 *Vertical integration in the U.K. cotton and allied textile industry: the changes between March 1961 and October 1968*

	Number of firms		Principal activities										Other activities	
			Spinning spindles (mn. ring-equiv)		Waste spindles (000)		Looms (000)		Converting (mn. sq. yd)		Fabric finishing (employment)(000)		Doubling spindles (000)	Yarn finishing (employment)(000)
	1961	1968	1961	1968	1961	1968	1961	1968	1961	1968	1961(a)	1968	1968	1968
Firms with one principal activity														
Spinners (inc. waste spinners)	76	49	2·78 *32%*	1·33 *35%*	164 *23%*	115 *27%*					(c)		67 *8%*	
Weavers	171	95					47 *28%*	19·1 *22%*		(b)			55 *7%*	0·1 *2%*
Convertors	1,123	670							900 *44%*	446 *29%*				
Fabric finishers	84	49									18·4 *62%*	6·0 *29%*		0·2 *4%*
Firms with two principal activities														
Spinner/Weavers	23	20	0·25 *3%*	0·19 *5%*	66 *9%*	40 *9%*	4 *2%*	2·8 *3%*					58 *7%*	
Weaver/Convertors	185	106					47 *28%*	22·1 *25%*	240 *12%*	133 *9%*			40 *5%*	
Convertor/Finishers	17	13							55 *3%*	24 *2%*	1·8 *6%*	0·7 *4%*		
Firms with three or more principal activities														
Spinner/Weaver/Convertors	37	19	2·88 *33%*	0·45 *12%*	228 *32%*	67 *16%*	27 *16%*	7·6 *9%*	147 *7%*	43 *3%*			250 *30%*	— *1%*
Spinner/Weaver/Convertor/Finishers	26	15	2·84 *32%*	1·78 *47%*	247 *35%*	200 *47%*	31 *18%*	26·5 *30%*	467 *23%*	623 *41%*	⎱ 9·6 *32%*	12·5 *60%*	175 *21%*	1·4 *35%*
Weaver/Convertor/Finishers	27	24					12 *7%*	10·0 *11%*	244 *12%*	255 *17%*	⎰	1·6 *8%*		0·3 *7%*
Other firms														
Doublers	59	34											190 *23%*	
Yarn finishers	59	44												2·0 *51%*
TOTAL:	1,887	1,138	8·75	3·75	705	423	168	88·3	2,053	1,522	29·8	20·9	834	4·0

(a) Partly estimated.
(b) One firm, yardage included against 'convertors'.
(c) One firm, employment included against 'finishers'.

(Source: *Cotton and Allied Textiles*, p. 153)

237

At the 1962 Cotton Board Conference a call was made for more vertical integration into groups capable of rationalising production, and of financing and controlling their own marketing. It was suggested that there should be nine large groups of this type, each controlling about a quarter of a million spindles and 5,000 looms, producing about 100 million square yards of cloth and converting about 140 million square yards.[1]

An attempt to weld the horizontal layers in the industry into fewer, more efficient, vertically integrated firms was made by I.C.I. and Courtaulds in 1963. They sponsored the 'Northern Scheme', designed to combine English Sewing Cotton, Tootals, Combined English Mills, Lancashire Cotton and Fine Spinners and Doublers. The scheme did not materialise. The two firms then jointly financed the two largest weavers of filament yarns – English Sewing Cotton and Carrington and Dewhurst – to bring about further vertical moves. Following the unsuccessful 1961 bid by I.C.I. to take over Courtaulds, the two companies proceeded in different ways. I.C.I. has developed 'bridgeheads of efficiency' in the industry, by financing takeover mergers by Viyella International. Courtaulds have been following a policy of more direct involvement, by integrating formally with spinning companies, thus procuring stable outlets for man-made fibres and stronger control over the types and qualities of yarn spun.

In July 1964 Viyella bid for Combined English Mills, the third largest spinning group in Lancashire. The following week Courtaulds bid for the two largest spinning groups – Lancashire Cotton and Fine Spinners and Doublers. The three groups accounted for almost 40% of total spinning capacity. In August 1964 English Sewing Cotton bid for the integrated group of Barlow and Jones. By mid-1964 about a quarter of Lancashire yarn and about one-third of its cloth were based on man-made fibres, and the Courtaulds bid gave it control of about 25% of total yarn production.

During June 1964 Viyella bid for Bradford Dyers, the world's largest textile finishing company. Integration in the highly capital-intensive finishing sector – running, on average, at only 40% of capacity – provided the advantages of being able to iron out some of the effects of the textile stock cycle, and of being able to recruit some efficient managerial talent.

From mid-1963 to mid-1964 about twenty-five mergers were announced, involving textile companies. Courtaulds alone had made more than a dozen acquisitions. With the 1964 bids Courtaulds would have become the largest integrated textile group in the world, with assets totalling £370 million in interests ranging from the fibre to the end product. With its bids for Bradford Dyers and Combined English Mills, Viyella was on the way to becoming the most efficient of the integrated textile combines. Whereas Viyella's acquisitions represented vertical integration *backward* from the marketing end, those of Courtaulds represented vertical integration *forward* from the source of raw material. Together with the English Sewing Cotton group, they controlled, by late 1964, 40% of the industry's finishing capacity, about half its spinning capacity and about 15% of its weaving capacity. Also, they had strong interests in the fast-growing knitting field and in merchanting.

From 1967 to 1970 the process of rationalisation and concentration of control gathered momentum. In 1967 I.C.I. started to disengage from its financial links

---

[1] A. M. Alfred, address to the 1962 Cotton Board Conference, p. 11.

with Viyella, which was complaining at the sluggishness of I.C.I., its lack of a dynamic philosophy about the integration of fibres and textiles and its lack of success in marketing.[1] In 1968 Viyella made an unsuccessful bid for English Sewing Cotton. One of the reasons for the failure of this bid was that Viyella's policy was to integrate backward, from market to intermediate product, whilst that of E.S.C. was to integrate forward to the market, as far as retailing. Partly as a response to this bid, E.S.C. merged in 1968 with Calico Printers Association (C.P.A.), to form English Calico.[2] After this development and at the time of the above-mentioned Report, the degree of vertical integration and concentration in the industry had resulted in the four largest firms' controlling about 40% of the industry's major activities. The next twenty largest firms controlled about another 17% of major activities, but eight of these firms were almost exclusively engaged in only one major activity (see Tables 3.19 and 3.20). In 1969 Courtaulds made an abortive bid to take over English Calico. I.C.I. strongly resisted this threat to its own fibre market and the Government imposed a merger standstill between any of the four largest Lancashire firms – Courtaulds, Viyella, English Calico, Carrington and Dewhurst – and the largest non-Lancashire firm, Coats Patons (sewing thread and yarn producers). I.C.I. was prompted to a more dynamic intervention policy in the industry, and sponsored an anti-Courtaulds proposal for a consortium of English Calico, Carrington and Dewhurst, Viyella, Nottingham Manufacturing, Klinger and Lister. In this it had the approval of Marks and Spencer, anxious to avoid too great a dependency upon Courtaulds.[3] Meanwhile, in March 1969 Courtaulds took steps to strengthen its marketing position by forming the first voluntary trading groups for independent textile and clothing retailers, called 'Gain', *via* four of its textile wholesalers, acquired in its 1967 incursion into textile distribution.[4]

In 1970 the Government announced its policy on the industry's structure – the Lever plan – in which it approved of part of I.C.I.'s 1969 consortium plan, *viz.* that I.C.I. should be permitted to sponsor the merger of Viyella with Carrington and Dewhurst, subject to limits on I.C.I.'s shareholding and representation on the board. This vertical merger proceeded in 1970, linking the second and fourth largest firms in the industry with I.C.I., the second largest fibre producer. On this occasion the new Carrington Viyella group departed from former Viyella policy to the extent of moving its headquarters to London, to strengthen its marketing activities by being closer to home and overseas customers.[5] Early in 1970 the possibility was discussed between I.C.I. and Courtaulds that they should merge their fibre interests into a 'British Fibre Corporation', to meet the overseas challenge of giants such as Du Pont (U.S.), A.K.Z.O. (Holland) and other potential groupings. This would have linked, *via* fibres, Courtaulds' textile interests with I.C.I.'s chemical interests. Following the Lever policy I.C.I. announced that it was no longer interested in the project, which had similarities with the abortive 1961 merger bid.[6]

[1] I.C.I. – Viyella', *Econ.*, 29 July 1967.
[2] *S.T.*, 11 Feb. 1968; *D.T.*, 5 March 1968; *F.T.*, 25 June 1969.
[3] 'The textiles blockade', *Econ.*, 19 July 1969, pp. 61–4; *D.T.*, 17 Jan. 1969; *F.T.*, 31 Jan. 1969 and 1 July 1969.
[4] *D.T.*, 19 March 1969.
[5] *S.T.*, 1 Feb. 1970 and 29 March 1970; *F.T.*, 30 Sept. 1971.
[6] For further discussion see *F.T.*, 7 Jan. 1970 and 11 March 1970.

3. SOME MAJOR INDUSTRIES: TEXTILE [II]

Table 3.19 *Degree of concentration in the woollen and worsted industry, 1968*

	Top 4 companies *	Next 20 companies *	Top 24 companies *
	percentage of activity		
Spinning	47	23	70
Weaving	33	15	48
Fabric finishing (employment)	53	14	67
Converting (excluding surgicals)	28	14	43
Total employment †	36	19	55

* As measured by employment in spinning, waste spinning, doubling, weaving, yarn finishing and fabric finishing.
† Excluding employment in converting.

(Source: *Cotton and Allied Textiles*, p. 16)

Table 3.20 *Estimated shares of top four firms in total U.K. output of cotton and allied textiles and knitted fabrics mid-1968 (percentages)*

	Court-aulds	Viyella	English Calico	Carring-ton & Dewhurst	Total
Spinning					
(ex. Waste spinning)	30	7	8	2	47
Weaving					
Total	12	5	6	10	33
(Filament)	(22)	(5)	(4)	(29)	(60)
Fabric finishing					
Bleaching (ex. surg. dressings)	4	8	6	2	20
Dyeing	12	36	5	9	62
Printing	9	12	38	2	61
Converting					
(ex. surgicals)	7	6	8	6	28
Knitting					
Warp	35	17	4	8	64
Weft	15	5	2	small	22

(Source: *Cotton and Allied Textiles*, p. 16)

It would seem that by 1970 the major phase of integration between large firms in the industry was over. The four largest groupings, Courtaulds, Carrington Viyella, English Calico and Coats Patons, accounted for about one-third to one-half of total industry sales: their major task would be to rationalise their activities and achieve efficient technical integration and marketing. Other mergers had meanwhile been proceeding between medium and small firms – such as in the Spirella, Vantona and Klinger groups – and these are likely to continue in the future.

An interesting overseas example with which to compare the British industry's giants is Burlington Industries – the largest textile firm in the U.S. and the world. It concentrates primarily on yarns and cloth and in 1968 alone invested more in modernisation and expansion than did the U.K. government in its reconstruction policy for the entire industry in Britain over the period 1959–64.[1] A 1968 international comparison of concentration and control is provided by Table 3.21, from which it may be seen that spinning was more concentrated in the U.K. than in most overseas countries and that looms were less concentrated in integrated firms than in most overseas countries. Furthermore, there was less integration between weaving and converting in the U.K. than in any other Western country and commission finishing was more important in the U.K. than in most other countries.[2]

(ii) Tiers of authority

In the context of Common Market membership it seems likely that the European Commission would assume a supranational role in the industry in Britain. In July 1971 the Commission committed itself to a policy on the future of the E.E.C. textile industry which was anti-protectionist and aimed at restructuring the industry on more competitive lines, using a wide range of instruments available within the Community framework.[3]

From 1948 to 1972 the major administrative bodies in the industry were the Cotton Board and, later, its successor the Textile Council. These were statutory coordinating bodies, representing trade unions and employers' organisations and financed by levies. The Textile Council, wound up in 1972, was a Development Council and did not, therefore, have functions relating to terms and conditions of employment. Its functions included provision of statistics, provision of training in work study techniques, consultancy on design and fabrics and information on exports. It cooperated on policy issues between employers' and trade union representatives.

In late 1970 the Government reconsidered the feasibility of the Textile Council, in view of the increasingly blurred boundaries of the industry.[4] It was decided to establish in 1972 a pan-textile voluntary body, to replace the Textile Council, to be called the British Textile Confederation.[5] When first established in January 1972 it encompassed the cotton and allied, wool, man-made fibre and textile converting sectors of the textile industry. It was hoped that hosiery, carpet, clothing, jute and flax sectors would eventually join. It was to represent member organisations in dealings with the E.E.C., was to have no role in relation to conditions of employment, and was to concern itself with foreign trade policy and with a common commercial policy for the enlarged E.E.C. Of its forty members, twenty were to be trade union representatives and twenty were to represent employers' associations.[6]

As far back as the 1962 Cotton Board Conference the Chairman had proposed a single employers' federation and a single trade union for the industry. The advent of the pan-textile B.T.C. might be expected to stimulate developments in

---

[1] *Econ.*, 31 May 1969, pp. 50–1; *S.T.*, 1 June 1969.
[2] *Cotton and Allied Textiles*, pp. 159, 12.
[3] See 'EEC: pattern for textiles', *Econ.*, 31 July 1971, p. 64.
[4] *D.T.*, 1 Dec. 1970; *F.T.*, 1 Dec. 1970.
[5] *F.T.*, 7 Oct. 1970, 4 May 1971; *D.T.*, 29 Dec. 1970.
[6] *F.T.*, 20 Jan. 1972.

Table 3.21 *Comparative structure of the cotton and allied textile industries, 1968*

	Per cent of spindles in firms with more than 100,000 spindles	Per cent of looms in, firms with more than 1,000 looms	Per cent of employees in firms with more than 1,000 employees*	Per cent of industry owned by three largest firms		Per cent of industry owned by spinner/weavers		Per cent of looms owned by weaver/finishers
				Spindles	Looms	Spindles	Looms	
U.K.	51	41	46	35	15	59	36	42
France	n.a.	n.a.	n.a.	20	23	(57)	(50)	Small
West Germany	(24)	27	n.a.	(13)	(10)	54	65	47
Italy	31	29	41	13	(3)	65	55	25
Netherlands	n.a.	65	67	79	51	(90)	70	(75)
Belgium	n.a.	Small	(30)	48	(18)	62	(30)	n.a.
Sweden	–	38	29	67	75	88	69	Very large
Austria	–	15	33	28	31	62	69	58
Switzerland	23	8	27	30	21	48	49	(30)
Portugal	–	3	n.a.	13	8	78	n.a.	n.a.
U.S.A.	Large†	(85)	n.a.	22	(25)	(75)	(85)	Large
Canada	81	90	74	88	93	93	100	(100)
India	21	(25)‡	(87)§	5	(2)‡	71	(45)‡	n.a.
Pakistan	(11)	(33)‡	n.a.	(13)	(21)‡	76	(98)‡	(98)‡
Hong Kong	–	6	n.a.	(26)	(12)	74	36	Small
Japan	63	(15)	(25)	20	6	(63)	15	n.a.

Figures in brackets are tentative estimates.

* Excluding finishing employees.

† Nearly half the spindles are owned by firms with more than 300,000 spindles each.

‡ Power-looms only.

§ Excluding the non-integrated weaving sector.

(Source: *Cotton and Allied Textiles*, p. 159)

this direction. The unions were discussing, in 1969, the feasibility of a single trade union for the textile industry, and this was echoed in the 1969 Report.[1]

Scientific and technical research is carried out by the Cotton, Silk and Man-Made Fibres Research Association, formed in April 1961 by a merger of the British Cotton Industry Research Association (Shirley Institute) with the British Rayon Research Association.

2. THE WOOLLEN AND WORSTED INDUSTRY

(a) Structure of the Industry: Number and Size of Plant

In 1968 1,289 plants in the industry replied to the Wool E.D.C.'s questionnaire. They accounted for 91 % of total employment in the industry. Plants accounting for the other 9 % of employees were mostly small, commercial or dormant.

Of the 1,289 plants, 358 or 28% were commercial plants. Most of these commercial plants had less than 10 employees: very few had more than 30 employees. Of the 931 production and processing plants, 83% had between 32 and 320 employees: very few had more than 1,000 employees. Integrated plants tended to be larger than single-sector plants, but there was a wide variation in size in most sectors (see Table 3.22). The concentration of total employment, of course, was weighted in the direction of larger-sized plants. For example, the largest number (19) of the 43 integrated worsted mills was in the size band 101–320, but the greatest overall number of employees was in the 1,001–3,200 size band: the average plant size was about 550 employees.[2]

It was found in 1968 that the degree of horizontal integration was very similar in both the woollen and worsted sectors (or 'systems') in the industry. On the other hand, the degrees of horizontal specialisation and vertical integration differed strongly. Generally, integrated woollen processes are feasible because the output levels of economic process units are much more in balance than is the case with worsted. Skill, variety, quality control and specialist blending of materials tends to result in batch production, right through several processes. Finishing plant is less complex and more adaptable than in the worsted system, and so many woollen plants are integrated from material preparation to finishing. 57% were integrated to some extent: very few were horizontally specialised in activities such as tweed weaving or spinning for the hosiery, hand-knitting and carpet sectors.

In the worsted system there are strong economic and technical factors which have influenced horizontal specialisation, such that only one-fifth of plants were vertically integrated. Firstly, economies of scale were such that the balance between different processes was not possible for a self-sufficient internal sequence of operations. In tops production, the optimal batch size was about 10,000 lb to 12,000 lb. This influenced the optimal plant sizes, which varied from 800 lb per hour capacity for fine tops to 1,600 lb per hour capacity for converted tops. In worsted yarn spinning, optimal batch size varied for different yarns from about 4,000 lb to 10,000 lb and optimal plant sizes for different yarns varied from a capacity of 330 lb per hour for fine yarns to a capacity of about 750 lb per hour for hard knitting yarns. In worsted weaving, the optimal plant size was shown to be between 160 lb per hour capacity for fine cloth and 800 lb per hour capacity

---

[1] *F.T.*, 29 May 1969; *Cotton and Allied Textiles*, pp. 191 and 195.
[2] E.D.C. *Report*, pp. 49–51.

for bulk cloth. In finishing processes the optimal capacities ranged from 0·4 million lb per year for fine worsted tops to 1·8 million lb per year for bulk worsted yarns.[1]

Thus a combing plant of economic size would produce enough tops for several spinning plants. Secondly, worsted spinners supply about 60% of their yarn to sectors such as hosiery, carpets, etc., outside the weaving stage. By preserving their separate identity they retain freedom of action and pass on to the combing plants some of the risks of wool price fluctuations. Thirdly, weavers generally require a wider range of yarns than could be produced economically by a single spinning plant, and therefore their freedom of action is enhanced by non-integration. Finally, worsted cloth requires a variety of specialist finishing operations which, except for the fine Huddersfield trade, are more economically performed by outside specialists. The E.D.C. report found that in the current trading situation there was little incentive for vertical integration in the worsted system.[2] It recommended a continuing process of rationalisation and plant closures, especially in the worsted and finishing sectors, so as to reduce the current total (1968) of 1,470 plants to about 950 by the mid-1970s.

Table 3.22 *Size distribution of plants in the wool textile industry, 1968*

Division	Number of establishments answering the questionnaire								
	1–3 em-ployees	4–10	11–32	33–100	101–320	321–1,000	1,001–3,200	3,201–10,000	Totals
Combers and recombers	–	2	3	12	23	2	1	–	43
Worsted spinners	–	1	8	36	65	16	–	–	126
Woollen yarn producers	1	6	9	32	13	–	–	–	61
Worsted weavers	–	6	16	50	34	4	–	–	110
Woollen weavers	4	3	17	26	9	3	–	–	62
Integrated worsted mills	–	–	–	6	19	13	5	–	43
Integrated woollen mills	2	3	11	41	85	21	1	–	164
Woollen and worsted mills	–	1	10	21	24	7	–	–	63
Dyers and finishers	–	–	21	47	20	1	–	–	89
Rag and waste processors	5	17	17	13	–	–	–	–	52
Scourers and carbonisers	2	7	7	6	1	–	–	–	23
Burlers and menders	2	20	28	11	1	–	–	–	62
Topmakers	4	6	16	5	2	–	–	–	33
Merchants, brokers and stockists	108	119	70	25	2	–	–	–	324
Fellmongers	–	7	12	14	1	–	–	–	34
TOTALS	128	198	245	345	299	67	7	–	1,289

(Source: *E.D.C. Report*, p. 50)

---

[1] *Ibid.*, pp. 53, 156–8, 165–7, 175–7, 188–90, 197–8, 252–3.
[2] *Ibid.*, p. 53.

(b) Administrative Organisation

(i) Concentration of control

In 1968 the number of firms in the industry which completed the E.D.C. questionnaire was 877: they accounted for 91% of employees and very few medium or large firms were included.

Of these 877 firms, three-quarters (668) were single-plant firms: the other 209 shared 621 plants, with an average of 3 plants each. 80% of the single-plant firms had less than 100 employees, and only 4% had more than 320: about half of the multi-plant firms had more than 100 employees, and more than a quarter had more than 320. Between December 1964 and December 1967 the number of employees in the industry had fallen by 15%, but the number of firms had been reduced by 18%, this indicating a perceptible trend to larger firm size. Of the 262 firms which disappeared, about 200 were employing less than 100 workers and 28 were in the 100 to 150 size range, this indicating a relatively high death rate for small firms.[1]

The patterns of vertical integration in woollens and of horizontal specialisation in worsted, noted in the production structure, are reflected in the activities of the controlling firms. In the worsted system only 18% of firms had multiple activities, whereas in woollens 66% were vertically integrated. With regard to the 18% of integrated worsted firms, the Report noted that in recent years this had been an increasing trend, but had often resulted in financial rather than technical integration: many weaving plants in such firms were still buying some or all of their yarn from outside suppliers. In the U.S., on the other hand, most worsted firms were integrated, including the 6 most important firms: these 6 had also integrated horizontally into the cotton and man-made fibre industries, and the second largest was also the largest woollen manufacturer. Nevertheless, even in the U.S. there were still a few important specialist combers, and the integrated firms tended to consist of large numbers of relatively small, specialised plants, rather than big, technically integrated, multi-process plants.[2]

In 1967 92% of firms in the industry were private companies, their number having fallen by 21% since 1964. These private companies employed only 46% of the labour force, their payroll having fallen by 28% since 1964. Public companies had increased since 1964 by 20% and their labour force had suffered less than a 2% reduction. In consequence, over half the labour force (54%) was in the 5% of firms in the 500+ size groups: of these 5%, 4% were public companies (with 47% of employees) and 1% were private (with 7% of employees).[3]

The period 1956-68 saw a reduction in the number of firms in all sectors, but the increase in concentration of control amongst fewer firms proceeded more rapidly in the worsted system, largely *via* horizontal mergers, to achieve scale economies in production and marketing.

Motives for concentration related mainly to finance and excess capacity. Financial pressures in a declining market have led to many marginal firms' withdrawing or selling out. Furthermore, small firms lacked the capital to finance technical modernisation at the scale needed to operate economically. Excess capacity, especially in the weaving sectors, has reduced the viability

---

[1] E.D.C. *Report*, pp. 49–52.
[2] *Ibid.*, pp. 53–4.
[3] *Ibid.*, pp. 54–5. Data on links with, and control by, firms in other industries are also given.

of borderline or marginal firms, leading them to fall out or sell out to firms capable of modernising and operating on a more efficient scale.

The initiative for mergers has come from firms within and outside the industry. Examples of initiative from within are the horizontal integration of Woolcombers Ltd – the largest combing firm – with several top makers, in 1965 and 1966, and its backward integration with a central buying organisation in Australia; and the forward integration of the top maker, Illingworth Morris, with Huddersfield Fine Worsteds, in 1963. Examples of initiative from outside the industry have been the loans, share purchases and complete takeovers by I.C.I. Fibres, Viyella, Coats Patons and Courtaulds, and the 1965 acquisition of a Huddersfield

Table 3.23 *Major wool textile firms, 1968 (figures relate to 1967 financial year)*

Firms	Net assets £000	Gross return on net assets %	P/E ratio	Dividend yield
Worsted topmakers and combers				
Woolcombers	6,616	—	—	3·8
Aire Wool	2,604	5·0	14·3	5·6
G. R. Herron	743	—	—	—*
Worsted spinners				
Bulmer & Lumb	4,175	9·1	14·9	6·4
J. Haggas	548	35·2	11·4	4·6
Worsted spinners and weavers				
West Riding	10,333	14·4	26·1	5·9
Parkland	4,604	13·1	14·7	6·5
Tulketh	2,754	0·2	—	4·4
Hield Bros	2,312	12·9	11·9	6·7
Kelsall & Kemp	2,297	13·3	10·1	6·0
Woollen spinners and weavers				
Troydale	2,687	12·4	8·4	7·7
John Crowther	2,565	8·0	8·7	7·9
Mohair spinners and weavers				
Jeremiah Ambler	2,744	10·3	—	—*
J. Foster	2,508	10·5	14·7	9·7
R. Clough	2,236	12·3	8·2	9·4
General groups				
Illingworth Morris	12,384	5·8	22·5	11·1
Lister	11,652	7·6	17·0	4·7
Outsiders with an interest				
Coats Patons	141,120	13·7†	16·7	4·8
Courtaulds	320,176	10·1†	15·1	5·1
Viyella	52,484	8·7†	15·9	6·3

(Source: *Econ.*, 17 Feb. 1968, p. 59)

worsted firm by English Sewing Cotton – the first step in its creation of a wool processing division.[1]

The major firms in the industry in 1968, specialists, integrated firms and outsiders with an interest, were as shown in Table 3.23.

The E.D.C. *Report* recommended that apart from plant closures and modernisation, the main future developments in integration should be horizontal, between those small and medium firms which would be committed to long run production of bulk products, and should be accompanied or preceded by strong marketing policies: specialist production, in all its diversity, should remain in small firms.[2] The *Report* also considered it inadvisable for the few large companies, in particular the man-made fibre producers, to indulge in a vertical takeover race in order to secure their outlets, as the character of the industry would be adversely affected.[3]

The *Report* forecast that, along with the contraction in the number of plants, there would be a 40% reduction in the number of firms, between 1968 (1,000) and the mid-1970s (600). This contraction and increasing concentration should occur mainly in the worsted sectors, the finishing sectors and the commercial group (see Table 3.24).

An interesting comment on the large groupings in the industry, against the advice of the 1969 E.D.C. *Report*, was made in January 1972 by Joe Hyman, Chairman of John Crowther (woollen spinners and weavers) and ex-chairman of Viyella. He stated, in a speech to the Bradford Textile Society, that the solutions required for the Yorkshire industry would not be found in large groupings,

Table 3.24 *Forecast changes in the structure of the wool textile industry (as at 1969)*

Division	Number at present		Number in mid-1970s	
	Organisations	Establishments	Organisations	Establishments
Combing and recombing	20	50	15	30
Worsted spinning	65	140	35	90
Woollen yarn production	35	70	20	40
Semi-worsted yarn production		10		10
Worsted weaving	60	120	25	60
Woollen weaving	35	70	20	40
Knitting	—	—	—	20
Integrated worsted	30	50	25	40
Integrated woollen	130	170	80	120
Woollen and worsted	60	70	40	50
Dyeing and finishing	100	120	60	70
Others	465	600	280	380
TOTAL	1,000	1,470	600	950

(Source: E.D.C. *Report*, p. 263)

[1] R. A. Bowman, 'The structure of the United Kingdom Wool Textile Industry', *Quarterly Review of Agricultural Economics*, Jan. 1970, pp. 43–4. Also see 'Next, wool textiles', *Econ.*, 17 Feb. 1968, pp. 58–9.
[2] E.D.C. *Report*, pp. 254–5.
[3] *Ibid.*, p. 261; Bowman, *op. cit.*, p. 44; 'Master plan for wool: Coats Patons' wool interests' *S.T.*, 14 Jan. 1968.

claiming that scale and size – particularly in horizontal mergers – have failed to bring about any improvement in profitability, and certainly not in return on capital.[1]

(ii) Tiers of authority

The implications for the entire textile industry of E.E.C. membership and the developments towards a pan-textile body – the British Textile Confederation – were outlined in the section on the cotton industry.

Before 1972 there was a broad spectrum of process-orientated and employers' associations, which supported the Wool Industries Research Association. They provided various export services and other central services through the Wool Textile Delegation. The employers' federations also linked up in the Wool and Allied Textile Employers' Council to negotiate with the numerous trade unions in the industry, who were represented by the National Association of Unions in the Textile Trade. The Wool Textile Delegation and the Wool and Allied Textile Employers' Council also provided central services, such as statistics, management services and public relations.[2] The E.D.C. *Report* did refer to the existence of too many federations and trade unions in the context of the increasingly blurred boundaries of the industry. It forecast that amalgamations would occur during the 1970s. Attention was drawn to the possibility of a complete amalgamation of the central organisation with those of other textile sectors, but the *Report* considered that the industry should concentrate its resources on its own affairs during the coming years of internal reorganisation and change. It suggested a new Combined Central Federation, representing all the process and employers' federations, to replace the existing Council and Delegation. The unions were also reviewing their structure and functions.[3]

3. Further Reading and Sources

Footnote references to daily and weekly journals are not repeated.

BOARD OF TRADE, *The Wool Working Party Report.* H.M.S.O. 1947.

R. A. BOWMAN, 'The structure of the United Kingdom Wool Textile Industry'. *Quarterly Review of Agricultural Economics.* January 1970.

C.O.I., *The United Kingdom Cotton Industry.* F.S.B. R.4735/D/5. 1961.

C.O.I., *The British Wool Textile Industry.* F.S.B. R.4735/D/6. 1961.

The Cotton Board Harrogate Conference, 1962: addresses by A. M. Alfred, C.B.346/62 and by the Chairman, C.B.347/62.

J. and S. JEWKES, ' A hundred years of change in the structure of the Cotton Industry'. *The Journal of Law and Economics.* Oct. 1966.

C. MILES, *Lancashire Textiles: a Case Study of Industrial Change.* C.U.P. 1968.

C. F. PRATTEN, *Economies of Scale in Manufacturing Industry.* C.U.P. 1971.

W. T. SHACKLETON, 'A new look at the structure of the industry: Cotton's new look'. The Cotton Board. 1956.

THE TEXTILE COUNCIL, *Cotton and Allied Textiles: a report on present performance and future prospects,* vol. 1. 1969.

The Textile Council Quarterly Statistical Review.

Textile Council Review.

TEXTILE ECONOMIC DEVELOPMENT COUNCIL, *The Strategic Future of the Wool Textile Industry,* H.M.S.O. 1969.

---

[1] *F.T.,* 12 Jan. 1972.   [2] E.D.C. *Report,* pp. 56–61.   [3] *Ibid.,* pp. 263–4.

THE SHIPBUILDING INDUSTRY: Stage I

1. Technical Background

Shipbuilding is basically an assembly industry, incorporating in the final product a wide range of components produced by other industries. The component requirements of the shipbuilding industry are complex, and the United Kingdom economy is well adapted to meet them. It has been estimated that as many as 300 specialist sub-contracting firms may be called upon to meet the requirements of one particular ship construction order. In the case of the £29 million Cunard liner Q.E. II, launched in 1967, it was estimated that over 1,000 firms – from small sub-contractors to Colvilles, suppliers of £1 million worth of sheet steel – would eventually have been involved in its construction and fitting out.[1] Consequently, thousands of workers, often remote from the main shipbuilding area, contribute to the final product. The work of outside contractors has been estimated to account for from two-thirds to three-quarters of the total cost of some ships.[2]

In addition to the steel industry, a wide range of industries is involved in supplying the numerous components required by the shipbuilders. Many specialist companies, supplying equipment such as marine engines, valves, pumps, fittings, etc., are largely dependent upon and linked with the industry and are usually situated in the main shipyard areas.

Closely linked with shipbuilding are ship-repairing and the construction of marine engines. Many firms have integrated two or all three of these main activities; in particular, half of the large firms in the ship-repairing section also build ships; many shipbuilders, including most of the largest, produce marine engines. In 1965, of the 27 major shipyards, 13 had the facilities to build large marine engines.[3]

One of the most notable features of the U.K. industry is the wide variety of its output, covering large passenger liners, oil tankers, ore carriers, specialised cargo ships, colliers, coasters, dredgers, trawlers, tugs, river vessels, barges and naval vessels ranging from large aircraft carriers to dockyard tugs.

A consequence of this great variety of products is that in most cases it has been the custom to build to special order, to the shipowner's requirements. Allied with this is the fact that the site of the average shipbuilding yard is limited, and can only hold a limited number of orders at one time. The net result has been to reduce the chances of reaping great economies of large-scale batch production. In recent years, however, methods have been evolved, especially abroad, of producing standardised designs for sale 'off the peg', and of speeding up production and increasing its volume by constructing prefabricated sub-assemblies indoors, for speedy final outdoor assembly in the yard. In this context two dimensions of technical scale economies have been significant. One relates to the degree of standardisation or production-line manufacture of a limited range of standardised and semi-standardised ships. Such 'series production' is particularly suitable for the yard whose capacity does not extend beyond the range of medium-sized ships. The other relates to the actual unit size or scale

---

[1] *S.T.*, 17 Sept. 1967.
[2] *British Shipbuilding*, Information Office of the Shipbuilding Employers' Federation, 1962, p. 3; *Econ.*, 24 March 1962, p. 1150; also see *Shipbuilding Inquiry Committee (Geddes Committee) 1965–1966 Report*, 1966, para. 4.
[3] *Stat.*, 5 Feb. 1965, p. 382.

of ships built. With regard to standardisation, the technique was originally developed during World War II, with the American Liberty ships. These American production engineering methods were further developed by the Gotaverken yard in Sweden, which established a straightthrough, flowline process. Both traditions were enthusiastically and successfully adapted by the Japanese industry, which was able in the 1960s to offer fixed price contracts, even under conditions of materials costs and wage increases. Automated pre-fabrication techniques have evolved for more efficient production of 'off-the-peg' ships and for the production of standardised sections, to be used in a variety of semi-standardised ships.[1] With regard to unit size, there has been an immense growth in the size of tankers and bulk ore carriers, designed since World War II. The largest tanker designed in 1956 was 31,000 deadweight tons (DWT) costing about $125 per ton: in 1969 the largest was 300,000 DWT, estimated to cost about $67 per ton. The largest design submitted to Lloyd's in 1970 was a Japanese design project for a 500,000 ton tanker. The scale economies of large ships are not limited to building costs, but also extend to transport costs per ton of cargo. If the cost index for 25,000 DWT tankers is taken as 100, it falls to 43 for 100,000 tons, 24 for 300,000 tons and 23 for 400,000 tons[2] (see Fig. 3.37). On the basis of pre-tax profitability on capital employed, over the period 1958–69 ore carriers averaged a 10·5% return, while other bulk carriers, tankers and cargo liners averaged between 4% and 5%: general purpose tramps and composite liners reached 2% and passenger liners had a zero rate of return. Yet between 1958 and 1967 only 28·3% of new ships were in the former group (only 4·5% being ore carriers).[3] A trend in recent years has been towards the commissioning of multi-purpose ships, known as OBO ships (ore, other bulk and oil), which can take on a variety of cargoes. This achieves a compromise between the scale utilisation economies of single-cargo ships and the degree of flexibility which shipowners require.[4] In 1966 Associated Shipbuilders of Tyneside were seeking patent rights on a technique claimed to be capable of building ships to take 1 million tons of cargo.[5] However, by 1968, serious structural stress problems were being encountered in the launching and performance of ships over 200,000 DWT, which were proving very expensive to rectify.[6] Such structural problems and that of single-cargo inflexibility may constitute eventual diseconomies of scale.

A further consequence of the diversified output and traditional custom of building to special order has been that marine engines have had to be tailored individually to each ship. There has been little scope for standardised batch production by specialist marine engineering firms, and many shipbuilders have maintained their own integrated marine engine works, only going to specialist firms for products which they could not supply themselves. On the other hand, the existence of a marine engine works in a shipbuilding firm often leads it to cater to

[1] *Econ.*, 16 Dec. 1967, p. 1161, 24 Feb. 1968, p. 67, 14 Oct. 1967, p. 195, 2 March 1968, pp. xxii–xxiii, 4 April 1970, p. 76, 24 Jan. 1970, p. 60, 5 June 1971, p. 83; *Stat.*, 10 Feb. 1967, p. 224; *F.T.*, 9 Oct. 1969, 9 Jan. 1970.
[2] *Econ.*, 1 June 1968, p. 75, 2 March 1968, p. xiv, 8 June 1968, p. 79 and 5 Feb. 1972, p. 67; *Lloyd's Register of Shipping Annual Report*, 1970, p. 17; also *Report of the Committee of Inquiry into Shipping (Rochdale Report)*, 1970, Cmnd 4337, p. 156.
[3] *Econ.*, 9 May 1970, p. 64.
[4] *Ibid.*, 7 Feb. 1972, pp. 72–4.
[5] *D.T.*, 17 Sept. 1966.
[6] *Ibid.*, 18 April 1968 and 27 Jan. 1970.

(a) Growth in tanker size

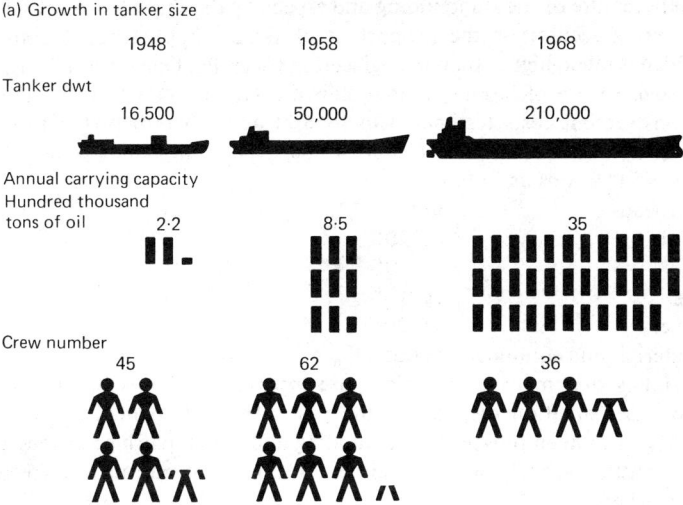

Note: Carrying capacity on voyages from East Mediterranean to NW Europe only

(b) Effect of size of tanker in transport cost

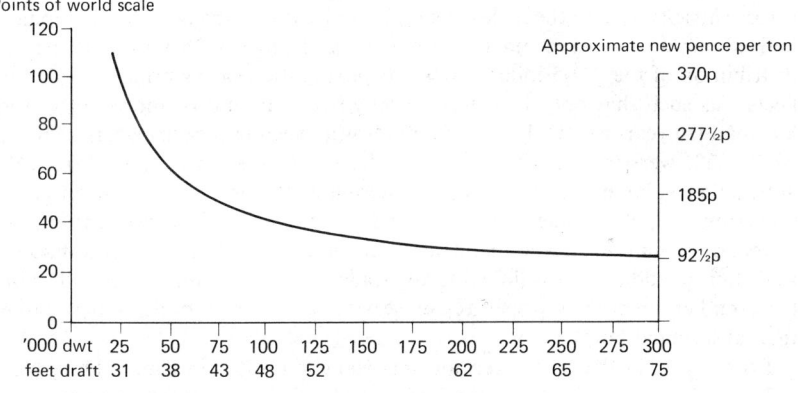

Fig. 3.37. *Tanker size and economies of scale*
(Source: *Shipbuilding and Shiprepairing*, C.I.R. Report No. 22, Cmnd 4756, 1971)

other shipbuilders when the works are not fully occupied. With regard to vertical integration generally, the dependence of shipyards on outside suppliers and contractors, referred to above, has generally been assumed to be a factor outside their control. Yet it should be noted that the Japanese producers, doubling their capacity in the 1970s while European yards stagnate, have been able to predict costs and give fixed-price contracts. This is largely due to their high degree of control and coordination of supplies, by contractual arrangements (or contractual vertical integration).[1]

[1] 'Beyond control?', *Econ.*, 21 Aug. 1971, p. 65.

3. SOME MAJOR INDUSTRIES: SHIPBUILDING [1]

An important feature of the shipbuilding and especially the ship-repairing and marine engineering sections is the proportion of skilled, apprenticed labour employed, which is much higher than in engineering generally. One result of this, and of the extensive use of labour, is that shipyard labour costs form a high element of construction costs (estimated in 1966 at about a fifth of the total finished cost of a cargo vessel). The Geddes Report listed the major costs for most ships over 5,000 tons as follows:[1]

Shipyard overheads	about 10%
Shipyard labour	15–20%
Steel	15–20%
Main engines	10–15%
Other machinery	15–20%
Other hull materials and equipment	about 20%

A further result is that many craft unions are involved, and this has led to some notorious demarcation disputes in the past.[2] In 1971 manual workers constituted 83% of total employees in shipbuilding and ship-repairing: of these, craft workers constituted 68% of shipbuilding, 60% of ship-repairing and 65% of combined workers.[3]

Another important feature of the industry is that it produces durable capital equipment, the demand for which is subject to violent fluctuations. The normal life of the product is about ten to fifteen years; thus the annual replacement rate is for only about 7% to 10% of existing ships. There is a constant danger of excess capacity, due to the inelastic supply conditions in the industry (equipment and labour do not have much alternative employment). In mid-1970 the age distribution of the 227·5 million tons comprising the world's principal shipping fleets was such that only 11% were twenty-five years old or more: 58% were less than ten years old. Only 4% of tankers were aged twenty-five years or more, whilst 62% were less than ten years old. Demand for ships is derived from the anticipated volume and character of international trade and is influenced by Government policies – such as on tariffs, subsidies and investment grants. Demand for ship-repair and maintenance facilities is similarly subject to fluctuations but, in addition, it is linked to the trade of ports at which ships call. Also, large tankers increasingly seek repair services along their trade routes, rather than at terminal ports.[4]

Britain has, in the past, been an important innovator in shipbuilding technology. She had a firmly established industry in the sixteenth century, and this was expanded by the stimulus of foreign trade in the seventeenth and eighteenth centuries, and the growth of the Royal Navy. Ships at that time were constructed of timber, and the industry was attracted to the estuaries of southern England, where local and imported timber, tallow and other materials were available.

The modern shipbuilding industry dates back to the mid-nineteenth century, when iron-clad, steam-driven vessels were introduced. Iron ore and coal deposits

[1] Geddes Report, para. 129.
[2] For example, see 'Shipyard men threaten demarcation row', *F.T.*, 10 Feb. 1970; also see Geddes Report, para. 2.
[3] *Shipbuilding and Shiprepairing*, C.I.R. Report No. 22, p. 23.
[4] *Lloyd's Register of Shipping Annual Report*, 1970, pp. 104,107; also see *Shipbuilding and Shiprepairing*, p. 9.

exerted a local attraction northwards. Britain led the way in the development of steam-power and the substitution of steel for iron in shipbuilding. These revolutionary technical developments permitted Britain to forge ahead, as they led to ships of greater size and speed. Backed by the most advanced metallurgical and engineering industries in the world, by skilled labour in the north, and by coastal iron-ore and coalfields, Britain produced most of the world's merchant shipping during the 1890s. At the beginning of the twentieth century high-speed traffic was revolutionised by the adoption of the steam turbine, developed in 1894 by Sir Charles Parsons.[1]

2. History and Development

By 1892–94 the U.K. was producing about 1 million gross tons of shipping annually – over 80% of the world total. Early in the twentieth century modern shipbuilding industry was established in other countries, much of it assisted by State subsidies. U.K. output continued to rise, but was forming a smaller proportion of the world total. By 1910–14 output averaged 1·6 million gross tons annually, but was only 60% of the world total.[2]

During World War I Britain concentrated on naval ships and built additional berths, greatly enlarging capacity. Foreign countries, particularly the U.S.A. and neutral countries, made even larger additions to capacity, with the result that by 1918 world capacity was double the 1914 figure. Furthermore, many of those countries were forging ahead of Britain in the adoption of oil-burning diesel engines, to replace coal-burners for propulsion.

From 1918 to 1933, the turn of the interwar trade depression, the industry was subjected to unparalleled cyclical fluctuations of demand. Up to 1920 the industry was stimulated by the backlog of suppressed demand, and in 1920 U.K. launchings reached a record level of 2·1 million gross tons, 40% of which was for export. Output in 1920 included the Fullager, the first all-welded ocean-going vessel. After 1920 demand declined below the 1914 level, and in 1923 U.K. launchings only totalled 650,000 gross tons, about 40% of world production. After 1923 demand for British ships again rose, and average annual launchings from 1923 to 1927 were 1 million gross tons, representing 50% of the world total. Demand was sustained until the depression (end of 1929), but the general fall in world demand for shipping, which followed, resulted in a 1933 world output of only 500,000 tons, of which only 26½% (133,000 gross tons) were launched in the U.K. After 1933 demand for British shipping expanded and by 1938 U.K. launchings again reached 1 million gross tons, 34% of the world total.[3]

During the interwar period shipyards were operating well below capacity (which had expanded during the 1914–18 war), and even during the relatively prosperous years after 1923 there was about 30% unemployment in the industry's labour force. The shipbuilders took steps to concentrate output in fewer yards and to buy up and scrap obsolete and excess capacity. There was a stimulus to horizontal integration (by mergers and trade association) and to vertical integration (between shipbuilders and steel manufacturers and between shipbuilders and marine engine builders).

After World War II there was again a pent-up world demand for merchant shipping and for ship-repairing. Allied losses during the war were about 20

---

1 C.O.I., *The United Kingdom Shipbuilding Industry*, R.4801, 1960, p. 2. 2 *Ibid.*
3 *Ibid.*, p. 3.

million gross tons, of which 11·5 million were suffered by the U.K. By 1952 orders on U.K. shipbuilder's books (stimulated by the Korean war) were at the record level of 7 million gross tons. 1955 and 1956 saw another heavy inflow of new orders, and by mid-1957 (stimulated by the Suez crisis) outstanding orders had again reached about 7 million gross tons, equivalent to about five years' output. For the whole period 1946–56 orders on hand averaged 3 million gross tons, or two years' work. Until 1955 Britain remained the world's largest producer of ships, but since then it has been outstripped by Japan, particularly, and by Sweden and West Germany, and is closely followed by France and Spain. From the mid-1950s to 1970 U.K. launchings have been between 0.9 and 1·3 million tons: the general relaxation in orders after the Suez crisis was followed by a surge in new orders after devaluation of sterling in 1967. By the end of 1970 total orders were for 4·9 million tons – about four years' output – one of the highest levels for a decade. This compared with 32·2 million tons on order in Japan. During the ten years to end-1970 U.K. shipyards completed 1,975 merchant ships, totalling 11 million tons, with a basic value of £1,446 million, plus £370 million worth of naval vessels, plus £550 million worth of merchant and naval repair work.[1] Nevertheless, these results, accompanied by further rationalisation and shipyard groupings, were giving cause for concern. Many yards had lost heavily on fixed-price contracts in competition with Japan, and had taken orders barely covering prime costs, in order to keep resources in use, and productivity was low in relation to major competitors, as reflected in the turnover, or ratio of launchings to total orders: for Japan this was about 180%, for West Germany and Sweden about 100%, but for the U.K. about 66%.[2]

During the postwar period the British shipbuilding industry has spent about £200 million on the modernisation, reconstruction and extension of its yards.[3] The capital cost involved in reorganising yards to produce all-welded ships, with undercover construction, prefabrication and mechanical conveyance of sections, is heavy. One shipyard alone has estimated that the modernisation cost would be about £17 million; other yards have undertaken schemes involving projects costing over £5 million.[4] In 1965 discussions were begun between eleven U.K. shipyards on the pooling of resources to design a production-line ship which might compete with the Japanese in price and efficiency. In 1966 the Government was inviting tenders for a 'split ship', designed like an articulated lorry, with detachable engine room and bridge, to put Britain in the forefront of shipbuilding technology. In 1968 the first British standard design, series production or production-line cargo ship, the SD14, was launched. In June 1970 the managing director of Upper Clyde Shipbuilders forecast at an international symposium at The Hague that world shipping demand would rise. However, it would be vital for firms to undertake detailed market research and to plan ahead to meet exact requirements. A range of ships, from passenger liners to cargo ships to naval vessels in one yard was no longer feasible: even the formation of individual yards into groups was not enough; the need was for each yard to specialise on

[1] *British Shipbuilding*, memorandum of Shipbuilders and Repairers National Association, 1971, pp. 9, 3–4; also *Shipbuilding and Shiprepairing*, pp. 10–11.
[2] *Shipbuilding and Shiprepairing*, p. 12; *F.T.*, 10 Dec. 1969 and 9 Nov. 1971; *Econ.*, 18 April 1970, p. 16; *S.T.*, 26 April 1970; 'Inquiry into shipbuilding', *Econ.*, 20 March 1965, p. 1294.
[3] *British Shipbuilding*, 1971, p. 2.
[4] 'Agreement on Clyde "super yard" expected soon', *F.T.*, 14 Oct. 1969; 'Shipbuilding in Britain', *M.B.R.*, May 1969, p. 6.

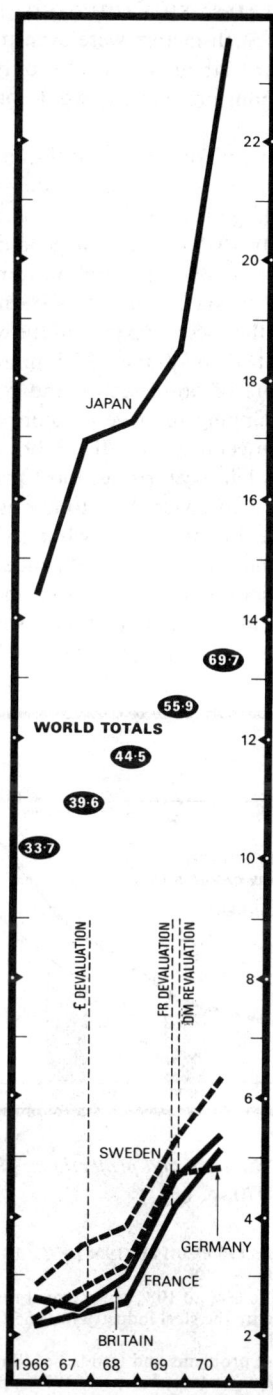

Fig. 3.38. *Ships on order or under construction: mn gross tons (at end Sept. 1970).*
(Source: *Econ.*, 14 Nov. 1970, p. 65)

vessel type and size limit. Such factors were even more important than labour productivity. Since shipyard labour costs were only about one-fifth the total, even a 10% increase in labour productivity would only result in about 2% total cost reduction.[1]

Since World War II many foreign countries, particularly Japan, Sweden, Holland, West Germany, Norway, France and Italy have expanded and modernised their shipbuilding industry. World capacity in 1962 was estimated to exceed demand by 30%.[2] In 1970 world tonnage launched passed the 20 million ton mark for the first time: of the 21·7 million tons, 48% was built in Japan. World orders outstanding totalled more than 7·8 million tons (see Fig. 3.38), about 3½ years' work, and the excess capacity of the early 1960s had disappeared. Annual output was about 10% of the 227·5 million tons of existing world merchant shipping: the rate of obsolescence and replacement was expected to rise[3] and a total world shipping tonnage of more than 500 million tons was forecast for the end of the century (see Fig. 3.39). A major problem was that labour and materials costs had been rising: most producers, with the exception of Japan, have been failing to cover their total costs. Consequently, very few yards, even in Japan, were finding it worthwhile to expand capacity further. It seems that the economic and technological influences at work are likely to result in a worldwide rationalisation of the industry into fewer but larger yards, concentrating on series-production, standardised ships, of which an increasing proportion would be OBO multi-purpose types.[4] With regard to the U.K.'s

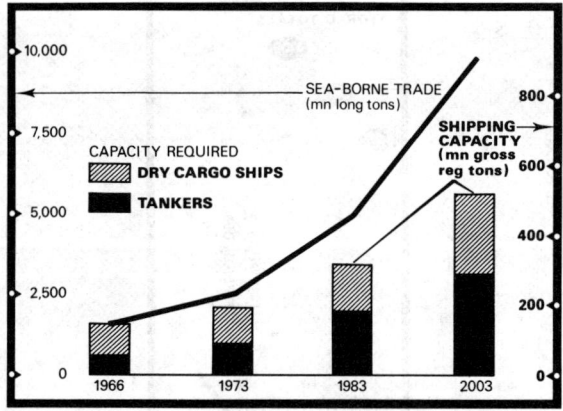

Fig. 3.39. *World shipping capacity and projections, 1966–2003*
(Source: *Econ.*, 14 Nov. 1970, p. 65)

1 *D.T.*, 22 March 1965, 29 Sept. 1966, 20 Feb. 1968; *F.T.*, 18 June 1970.
2 See *Stat.*, 26 Feb. 1965, p. 590.
3 Compare the 10- to 15-year life (7% to 10% replacement rate) in 1970 with the 25-year life (4% replacement rate) estimate by the steel industry in 1965 (see 'Inquiry into Shipbuilding', *Econ.*, 20 March 1965, p. 1293).
4 For further discussion of these problems and trends, see 'Shipbuilding', *The Times*, 12 Feb. 1969; *Lloyd's Register of Shipping, Annual Report*, 1970, pp. 97, 104; *F.T.*, 13 Nov. 1969, 1 June 1970, 27 Jan. 1971, 29 April 1971; 'Shipbuilding: the world's sickest industry', *Econ.*, 14 Nov. 1970, pp. 64–5; 'Should Europe build ships?', *Econ.*, 27 March 1971, pp. 71–2; 'German shipyards', *Econ.*, 19 Feb. 1972, pp. 72–5.

prospects in this stringently competitive world industry, a useful criterion of competitiveness is the percentage of production exported. In 1970, when she was in fourth place in the production league, the U.K. exported only 15%: the percentages exported by her main competitors were Japan 61%, Sweden 85%, West Germany 56%, France 38% and Spain 48%.[1]

Foreign yards have been improving their productivity, relative to Britain's; they have been offering shorter completion dates and lower prices. On the other hand, some, like Italy, Germany and France, have enjoyed Government subsidies, tariff protection, or tax concessions.[2] Some, like Sweden and Holland, avoid the 'demarcation' disputes which trouble British shipbuilding, by having single industrial unions, representing all the workers in the industry. Many adopt three-shift, 'round-the-clock' working, to cut down overheads, speed up production times and raise productivity.[3]

In 1960 the British industry set up a committee to consider ways and means of improving productivity and developing research. The committee reported in March 1962 that British technical facilities were generally quite as good as those of her foreign competitors. They found, however, that management and labour efficiency were of a higher standard abroad than in Britain. Some of the reasons suggested were the foreign achievements of greater sales-consciousness; more thorough preparation for construction; greater accuracy in prefabrication; cheaper steel, other materials and subcontracting work; greater flexibility and interchangeability of labour; better labour relations; better training of apprentices and better supervision and management.[4]

With regard to the demand exerted by British shipowners, who vitally influence shipbuilding, a 1962 study by Dr Sturmey,[5] has concluded that although the Government had not helped the shipping industry by providing specialist advice, 'the industry itself had done little in this direction – there was no collection of data on costs and results; no studies are made of the economics of shipping operations'. He suggested that the industry had suffered from a failure of competitive imagination. He listed specific faults, which flowed from the change from the tough, ruthless management of the Victorian era to the large, over-capitalised, inflexible 'family' managements of the twentieth century, subject to nepotism and lacking the competitive spirit.

In March 1966 the *Report of the Shipbuilding Inquiry Committee, 1965–1966* (Geddes Report) was published. This had been stimulated by the fall-off in orders in 1964 and aimed at assessing future demand and changes in the industry's structure. The Report was limited to yards building vessels of 5,000 gross tons minimum and to the production of engines usually installed in such ships. The Report concluded that the world market for ships had expanded and would continue to do so, and that the U.K. industry should be able to increase its share, producing about 2·25 million gross tons by 1972–75. Some of the main recommendations concerned structural reorganisation, public financial assistance and

1 *Lloyd's Register of Shipping, Annual Summary,* 1970.
2 For details of the various types of grants, subsidies, loans, indirect assistance and tariff protection afforded by the main shipbuilding nations, see 'Who gives subsidies, and how', *Econ.,* 2 March 1968, p. xxxi; 'Pampering on the high seas', *Econ.,* 11 Oct. 1969, pp. 62–3; 'On the burning deck', *Econ.,* 5 Feb. 1972, pp. 66–7.
3 *D.T.,* 15, 16, 17 Jan. 1962.
4 *Econ.,* 24 March 1962, p. 1150; *Shipbuilding in Britain,* p. 8.
5 S. G. Sturmey, *British Shipping and World Competition,* 1962.

improvements in trade union structure and practices and in labour relations. With regard to structure, it was recommended that the major yards should form groups of about five yards, each yard specialising in a particular type of vessel. Each group would have about 8–10,000 operatives, producing about 400,000 to 500,000 gross tons annually: there would be two groups in the North-East and one or two on the Clyde. While Belfast constituted a special problem, it was possible that some individual yards isolated from the major areas could be included in other groups. Such groups would provide a viable framework of large, centralised organisations, within which resources could be used more efficiently in activities such as marketing, design, purchasing and more flexible labour utilisation. State participation in ownership, except as a temporary expedient, was decried.[1]

Marine engine works were found to be fragmented, uneconomic, usually in or closely associated with shipyards and often doing general engineering work on a commission basis. The Report suggested a separation of main engine works from shipyards, concentrated in about four large plants, each with sufficient throughput to benefit from large scale, rationalised production methods.[2] The Report recommended the formation of a Shipbuilding Industry Board to guide this reorganisation and administer about £67·5 million of temporary financial assistance, recommended for shipbuilding credits and for regrouping and transitional losses. It rejected the idea of permanent credit assistance for shipbuilding, such as that provided by the Shipbuilding Credit Scheme in 1963 (which granted £75 million of ten-year credits to British owners buying new U.K. ships).[3]

The Report was accepted by the Government, but two major policy changes were made. First, the Shipbuilding Industry Act of 1967, which established a Shipbuilding Industry Board, gave the Board power to recommend cheap credit loans to British shipowners ordering from U.K. yards. The limit on these credits was set at £200 million by the 1967 Act: this was raised to £400 million by the 1969 Shipbuilding Industry Act and to £700 million by the 1971 Shipbuilding Industry Act, which set the termination date for the Shipbuilding Industry Board as end-1971. The Board, during its five-year life dispensed to the shipbuilders and main engine builders £19·2 million of its £20 million limit in grants, but only £21·5 million of its £32·5 million limit for loans and State shareholdings.[4] Secondly, the Board was authorised by the 1967 Act to acquire shares in any of the new shipyard groups as an alternative to, or in addition to providing grants or loans.

In regard to the industry's reorganisation after the Geddes Report, there has been a significant trend towards consolidation into larger groups. One shipbuilding group was formed in 1968 on the Upper Clyde, taking in the Fairfield yard (which in 1966 had been temporarily taken over by a consortium of private interests, the State and the trade unions). One group was formed on the Lower Clyde, one in the Leith-Dundee region, one on the Tyne and Tees region, two on the Wear, and one on the south coast (Vosper Thorneycroft – formed shortly

---

[1] *Report of the Shipbuilding Inquiry Committee, 1965–1966* (Geddes Report), Cmnd 2937 1966, ch. 18.
[2] *Ibid.*, ch. 11.
[3] *Ibid.*, ch. 26.
[4] For further details see *Obs.*, 19 Feb. 1967; *Econ.*, 7 Dec. 1968, p. 71; *D.T.*, 16 Feb. 1967 and 23 April, 1971; *F.T.*, 15 Dec. 1971; *Shipbuilding and Shiprepairing, loc. cit.*, paras. 50–51.

before publication of the Report). Further concentration has been suggested, including a single group for the Clyde, an Irish Sea group linking Belfast, Barrow and Birkenhead, and a single Tyne-Tees-Wear group. Reorganisation has also taken place in main engine production. Medium- and high-speed diesels were concentrated into four large groups, but slow-speed diesels were fragmented into nine firms in four areas. The Board had suggested their concentration into four specialist firms, but strong arguments have been made in favour of regional groupings, each producing engines of several designs.[1]

Nevertheless, groupings and rationalisation did not solve the industry's problems, and the State has been involved in what has been termed a 'lame duck' exercise to bolster up several firms financially. The most protracted problems were suffered by Upper Clyde Shipbuilders – the largest group, with the largest losses. In 1969 the State, a 48% shareholder in U.C.S., had to provide £13 million to avoid the group's liquidation, despite orders worth £100 million. A major problem appeared to be massive overmanning. In 1971 the Yarrow naval yard was given a £4·5 million loan and sold back to private control. In 1971 protracted discussions, with workers 'sitting in' to prevent yard closures, were initiated as to the future size and constitution of the truncated group, renamed in 1972 Govan Shipbuilders. A further £35 million of State finance had to be provided. In 1970 the Vickers ship-repair yard at Hebburn, on the Tyne (in the Tyne-Tees Swan Hunter group), one of the most modern in the country, was closed down because of financial difficulties. In 1970 the future of Harland and Wolff of Belfast was in jeopardy. Eventually, in 1971, the State took over its finances, whilst leaving it theoretically in private hands. In 1970 and 1971 the Birkenhead yard of Cammell Laird received £9 million in State loans and a 50% State shareholding.[2] In 1970 the ship-repairing sector of the industry made a plea for fiscal and financial assistance and preferential treatment.[3]

During the late 1960s and early 1970s the relative success of Japanese competitors – despite worldwide rising costs – to keep to fixed-price contracts had led them to increase capacity, while U.K. and Continental yards were slipping behind in productivity, profitability, new capacity investment and modernisation. Depressed world freight rates in 1971, due to increasing competition by shipowners, was leading to a fall-off in new orders – a situation similar to that ten years earlier. In 1971 a prominent shipbuilder expressed the view that a clear, farsighted Government policy for shipbuilding should be decided upon, which would determine whether there should be a shipbuilding industry in Britain and, if so, how big it should be and where it should be sited. In 1972 a leading shipbuilder proposed a wider-ranging common European joint shipbuilding and shipping policy, with strong elements of protection – particularly from Japanese competition. He made the point that both sectors were indivisible and that this

---

[1] Memorandum of Shipbuilders and Repairers National Association, 1971, pp. 6–7; 'Shipbuilding in Britain, *loc. cit.*, pp. 9-10.
[2] *Shipbuilding and Shiprepairing*; *loc. cit.*, paras. 52-55; *D.T.*, 3 Sept. 1970 and 4 Nov. 1971; *F.T.*, 2 Dec. 1970 and 12 Feb. 1971; *Econ.*, 7 June 1969, p. 67; 6 March 1971, p. 87, 4 Dec. 1971, p. 87 and 12 Feb. 1972, p. 70;
[3] *F.T.*, 1 Oct. 1970. In fact, the March 1972 Budget made provision for the industry to receive the first £50 million of selective assistance, in the form of a 10% subsidy on new ships over 100 gross tons, built in 1972: the subsidy was to taper off to 4% in 1973 and 3% in 1974 (*S.T.*, 26 March 1972).

was appreciated and backed up by policy and links between owner and builder in Japan [1].

The salient facts in this section are brought out in Table 3.25 and Figs. 3.40 and 3.41.

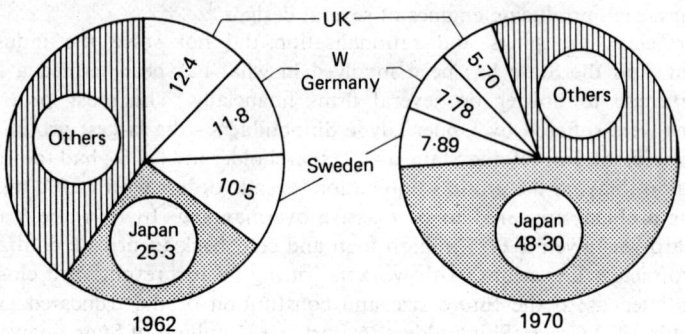

Fig. 3.40. *Percentage shares of world shipbuilding output*
(Source: *Lloyd's Register of Shipping*)

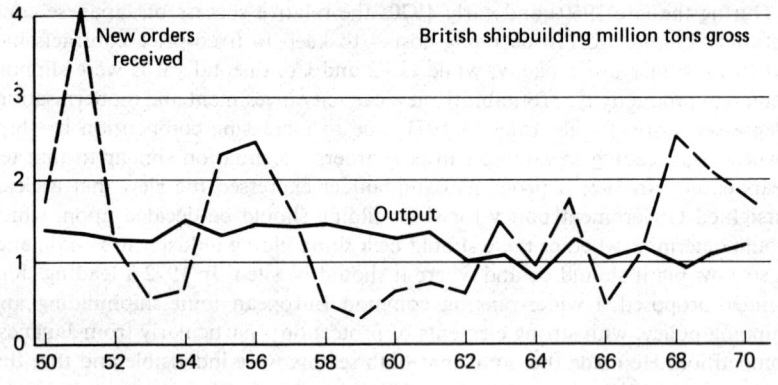

Fig. 3.41. *U.K. output and new orders*
(Sources: Output – *Lloyd's Register of Shipping*. New orders – *Shipbuilders and Repairers National Association*)

[1] *Econ.*, 1 Dec. 1962, p. 949 and 4 Dec. 1971, p. 87; *F.T.*, 1 Oct. 1970, 4 and 11 Nov. 1971 and 8 Jan. 1972.

Table 3.25 *Output of merchant shipping; exports and employment in the U.K. Shipbuilding Industry*

Year	U.K. launchings (million gross tons)	U.K. launchings as % of world total	U.K. exports as % of launchings	Labour (thousands) Shipbuilding and ship-repairing	Marine engineering
1892–94 (av.)	1·0	80·7	–	–	–
1898–1902 (av.)	1·44	62·8	–	–	–
1910–14 (av.)	1·66	60·6	–	–	–
1920	2·06	35·1	41·2	–	–
1923	0·65	39·3	2·9	151·0	51·5
1923–27 (av.)	1·01	50·1	15·4	–	–
1933	0·133	27·2	9·1	–	–
1938	1·03	34·0	19·8	140·0	52·8
1946	1·12	53·3	10·3	229·1	72·0
1951	1·34	36·8	44·9	223·2	79·5
1956	1·38	20·7	31·4	235·3	88·3
1959	1·37	15·7	8·4	221·0	84·3
1960	1·33	15·9	11·0	210·6	81·2
1961	1·19	15·0	23·6	200·0	75·5
1962	1·07	12·8	15·4	191·1	72·7
1963	0·93	10·9	30·6	177·1	65·0
1964	1·04	10·1	14·3	166·7	61·0
1965	1·07	8·8	12·7	167·3	56·9
1966	1·08	7·6	28·3	166·5	52·4
1967	1·30	8·2	55·2	168·1	49·8
1968	0·90	5·3	52·9	164·4	43·0
1969	1·04	5·4	37·0	166·6	40·2
1970	1·24	5·7	15·0	170·8	36·7

(Sources: *Lloyd's Register of Shipping – Annual Summaries of Launches; Ministry of Labour Gazette; Shipbuilding and Shiprepairing*, C.I.R. Report No. 22, p. 10)

3. Location of the Shipbuilding Industry

(a) Early days

At the beginning of the nineteenth century New England, with its ample supplies of timber, was the world's chief shipbuilding centre. In Britain, the industry, based on wooden sailing ships, was concentrated from its early days in the river estuaries of southern England, particularly the Thames, utilising local raw materials and materials imported from the Continent. An additional locational attraction to the south in the early days was the fact that the main trading routes were to the Continent. The coastal trade, however, resulted in some shipbuilding being carried on in northern districts. This factor was strengthened by the requirements of the local fishing industry and, later on, by the favourable location of these districts for imports of shipbuilding materials from the Baltic.

(b) Iron and steam

With the introduction, during the nineteenth century, of iron and steel ships using coal for steam power, the main centres of production moved to suitable deep-water sites at the coastal coalfields and steel centres of the north of England and Scotland.

There are now four major shipbuilding centres:

(i) The north-east coast of England, along the lower reaches of the rivers Tyne, Wear and Tees, and at Blyth. This area has been producing about 45% of U.K.

261

output since World War II. The Tyne and Wear areas produce about 80% of the whole area's output;

(ii) The River Clyde, in Scotland. This area has produced over one-quarter of U.K. output since World War II;

(iii) Belfast, which is responsible for about 10% to 15% of U.K. output;

(iv) The north-east coast of England, at Barrow-in-Furness and Birkenhead. This area produces about 6% to 10% of British output, most of which comes from Birkenhead, on Merseyside.[1]

Each of these areas has facilities for building warships and all types of merchant ships, from passenger liners and tankers to small coasters and cross-Channel steamers.

Less important shipyards are located in the Southampton area, Bristol, East Anglia, the Humber and along the estuaries of the rivers Forth and Tay in

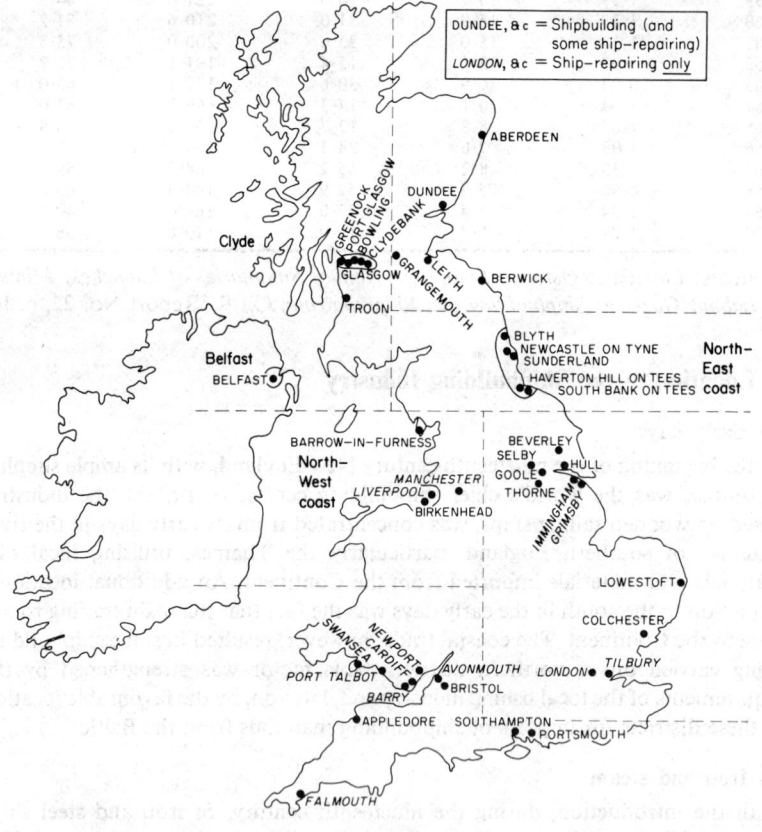

Fig. 3.42. *Location of shipbuilding and ship-repairing in the U.K.*
(Source: *Shipbuilders and Repairers National Association Memorandum, 1971*)

---

[1] *The United Kingdom Shipbuilding Industry*, p. 6.

Scotland. Smaller craft, such as fishing vessels, yachts, barges and harbour craft are built in numerous places along the coastal fringe and on inland waterways.

Repair yards and dry docks are attracted to both the main shipbuilding areas and the main shipping traffic terminals, and therefore ship-repairing is much more dispersed than shipbuilding. Furthermore, being susceptible to the shifting pattern of trade through the various ports, the location of ship-repair activity is much less stable than that in the construction sector, which is still dominated by the developments of the industrial revolution. In 1971 the most important areas were the North-East (mainly on the Tyne) and the Mersey, each with almost 20% of total ship-repair employees. Next came the Thames (about 15%), Scotland (about 10% – mainly on the Clyde), the Humber (about 10% – mainly at Hull and Grimsby), Southampton (about 10%) and the South-West (about 10% – mainly at Falmouth).[1]

In mid-1961, of the 184,440 employees in shipbuilding and ship-repairing in Great Britain, 24·7% were in Scotland; 22·4% in the north-east; 13·3% in the north-west; 13·9% in the eastern and southern regions. Marine engineering was closely linked to shipbuilding in its locational pattern. Of the 68,270 employees, 29·7% were in Scotland; 21·2% in the northern region; 18% in the north-west; 15·4% in the eastern and southern regions.[2]

Table 3.26 shows the relative output of the main shipbuilding centres from 1959 to 1970. The locations of the main shipbuilding and ship-repairing centres in the U.K. are shown in Figure 3.42. Details of the yards on the Lower and Upper Clyde (where important problems of reorganisation and structure have arisen)

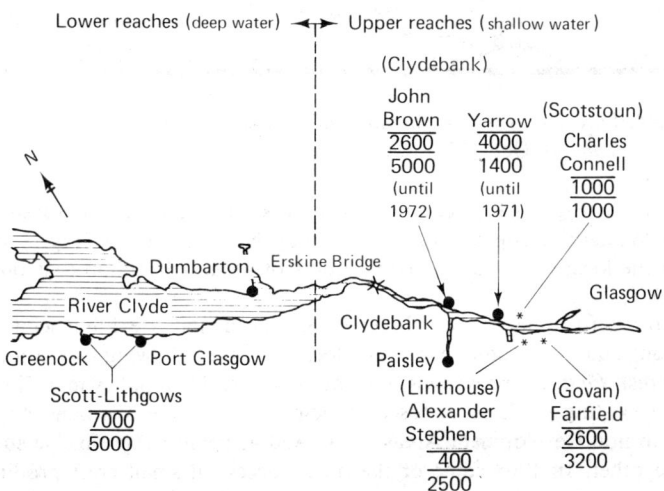

Fig. 3.43. *Shipbuilding on the Clyde, 1971*
(Source: *Econ.*, 19 June 1971, p. 70)

[1] *Shipbuilding and Shiprepairing*, para. 42.
[2] *Min. Lab. Gaz.*, March 1962.

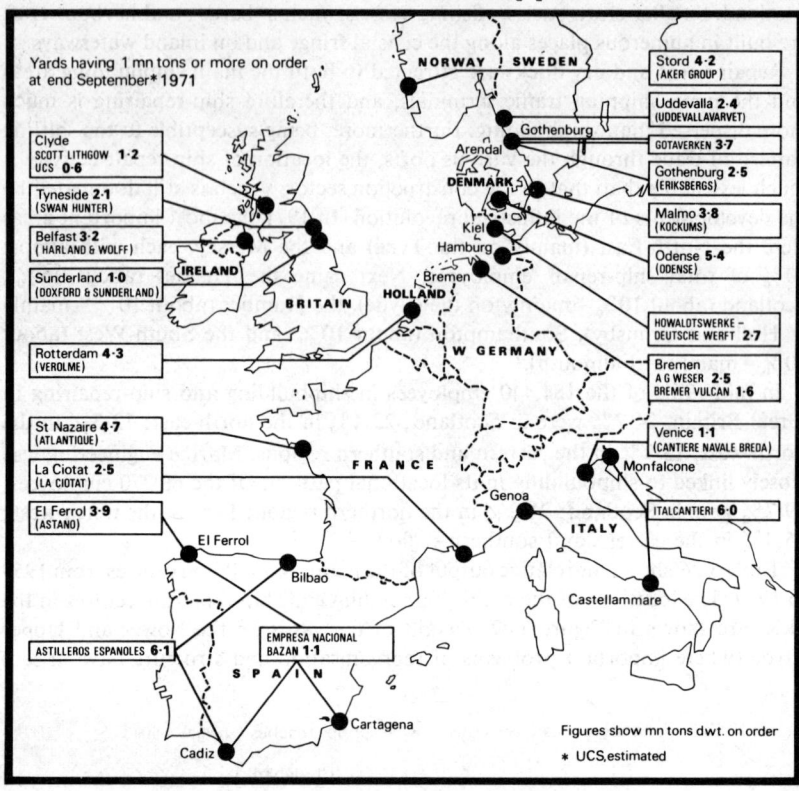

Fig. 3.44.·*Location of major shipyards in Western Europe, 1971*
(Source: *Econ.*, 16 Oct. 1971, p. 68)

are given in Fig. 3.43. A comparison between the industry in Britain and her major Western European competitors may be facilitated by Fig. 3.44, which shows the location of yards having orders of at least 1 million tons on hand in late-1971.

With regard to factors which have influenced and are influencing location decisions and the viability of existing locations, the following two points may be of interest. *First*, the provisions of location and regional policy may discriminate against existing yards as opposed to new yards, on the one hand and against yards in non-Development Areas (or D.A.s) as against those inside such areas, on the other. In 1968 some of the most successful small craft producers and exporters in Yorkshire, East Anglia and on the South Coast claimed that Development Area aid to the ten out of forty yards in D.A.s, which competed with them, resulted in a labour cost differential of 12·5% to 15%. Firms outside the D.A.s had built-in disadvantages of up to £118,000 per year, which could result in a £12,000 differential in tendering for a stern trawler. Yet several of the non-D.A. yards were in areas of high unemployment.[1] In late-1971 in- dustrialists on Clydeside claimed that some of the new Special Development

[1] 'No-subsidy shipyards plea for equality', *D.T.*, 10 Jan. 1968.

264

Area provisions for Clydeside (which included an extra 10% building grant and 30% payroll subsidy) were applicable only to newcomers and not to existing firms. Not only were wage structures being distorted, but also there was no incentive to established industry to diversify or expand on Clydeside.[1] Much was done to remove these anomalies in the Industry Bill, published in May, 1972. The credit ceiling for the industry was raised to £1,000 million, with power to increase it to £1,400 million and it was to be applied to offshore platforms and rigs as well as to ships proper. Also, the post-1972 Budget regional development grants for capital expenditure on plant, machinery and buildings, were to apply to existing firms as well as to newcomers. Furthermore, additional 'selective financial assistance' in the form of loans, grants or guarantees was to be available for firms outside the assisted areas (in the 'national interest') as well as for firms within them.

Secondly, there is room for debate as to the merits of developing existing sites and those of locating yards at new 'green field' sites. The Geddes Report noted that some U.K. yards suffered from lack of space and narrowness of their river, but considered that by methods such as building in sections these disadvantages in large ship construction could be overcome. It found no grounds, on balance, for thinking that 'green field' sites would be an economic investment.[2] The issue was revived in 1972 by the managing director of Appledore Shipbuilders, giving the Blackadder lecture on the economics of shipbuilding at Newcastle-upon-Tyne University. He considered that a basic miscalculation of the Geddes Report was the decision that no new yards were needed. He called for the creation of four or five completely new, medium-sized shipyards, possibly on existing ship-building rivers, using dry docks already there, as an alternative to propping up existing yards which were in financial difficulties. The new yards – with the Government as equity holder or as lessor or as lender of capital without repayment until the yards were in use – would build sophisticated, medium-sized specialist ships, rather than compete in the cheap labour market with giant tankers. His own firm was profitable, and whereas 60% of the U.K. industry in 1970 had only £825 worth of fixed assets per worker, his firm made more

Table 3.26 *Location of shipbuilding production in the U.K.*

Area	Proportion of total gross merchant tonnage			
	1959 (launched) %	1961 (completed) %	March 1965 (under construction) %	1970 (completed) %
River Clyde	28·0	24·6	29·5	26·5
River Tyne	18·8	23·0	⎫	27·5
River Wear	18·1	18·4	⎬45·2	12·6
River Tees	8·4	10·0	⎭	7·9
River Mersey	6·5	3·5	6·0	6·4
Barrow	3·0	1·7	4·1	–
Belfast	8·7	13·4	10·6	15·1
Other districts	8·5	4·4	4·7	4·2

(Based on material in *The United Kingdom Shipbuilding Industry*, C.O.I.; *British Shipbuilding*, the Shipbuilding Employers' Federation; *Stat.*, 30 May 1965, p. 1201; *Memorandum* of Shipbuilders and Repairers Association, 1971).

[1] *F.T.*, 13 Oct. 1971; *D.T.*, 12 May 1972; *Econ.*, 13 May 1972, p. 104.
[2] Geddes Report paras. 245, 13.

efficient use of labour with £3,000 worth of fixed assets per worker: Appledore had premises for 25,000 ton vessels and was designing a yard for vessels of up to 70,000 tons, at a capital cost of £10–12 million.[1]

4. Further Reading and Sources

C.O.I., *The United Kingdom Shipbuilding Industry*, F.S.B. R.4735/D/12. 1961.

C.O.I., *The United Kingdom Shipbuilding Industry*, R.4801. 1960.

COMMISSION ON INDUSTRIAL RELATIONS, *Shipbuilding and Shiprepairing*, Report No. 22. Cmnd 4756. H.M.S.O. 1971.

Committee of Inquiry into Shipping: Report (Rochdale Report), Cmnd 4337. H.M.S.O. 1970.

D.E.A. Pr. Rep. Ind. and Reg. 16. 'The future of shipbuilding', May 1966.

Lloyd's Register of Shipping: Annual Report, 1970.

Lloyd's Register of Shipping: Annual Summary, 1970.

J. R. PARKINSON, 'The financial prospects of shipbuilding after Geddes', *Journal of Industrial Economics*. Nov. 1968.

SHIPBUILDING EMPLOYERS' FEDERATION, *British Shipbuilding, Memoranda*, 1962 and 1965.

SHIPBUILDERS AND REPAIRERS NATIONAL ASSOCIATION, 1971. Information Office Memorandum of *British Shipbuilding*.

'Shipbuilding in Britain', *M.B.R.*, May 1969.

'The shipbuilding industry', *Conjoncture*. April 1966. Société Générale.

Shipbuilding Inquiry Committee, 1965–1966: Report (Geddes Report), Cmnd 2937. H.M.S.O. 1966.

S. G. STURMEY, *British Shipping and World Competition*. Athlone Press. 1962.

THE SHIPBUILDING INDUSTRY: Stage II: Structure and Organisation

1. Structure of the Industry: Number and Size of Plant

According to the 1963 Census of Production, the shipbuilding, marine engineering and ship-repairing industry accounted for less than 2% of total sales and net output in manufacturing industry and employed about 2·5% of the labour force. Some yards undertook repairs, built marine engines and undertook non-marine work, and so a detailed analysis of shipbuilding industry activity was not possible. The Geddes Report found that there were sixty-two shipyards in the U.K. in 1966. It concerned itself with the twenty-seven of these which regularly built vessels of 5,000 gross tons or more: they accounted for about one-third of net output and one-third of employment in the industry. Their combined sales of £159 million in 1963 were only a fraction of those of some individual firms such as I.C.I. (£720·2 million), B.M.C. (£444·1 million) and Courtaulds (£227·7 million). The other thirty-five yards were of two classes: those building mainly vessels for coastal or river transport, fishing, ferries, dredgers, tugs, etc. of less than 5,000 tons and those which specialised in ship-repair and maintenance.[2] The twenty-seven large yards were more significant in terms of new ship construction: about 75% of the 65,000 workers employed

1 *D.T.* and *F.T.*, 22 Feb. 1972.
2 Geddes Report, paras. 7–11.

in new shipbuilding were in the twenty-seven yards covered by Geddes, and they accounted for about 90% of U.K. total tonnage completed (over 80% by value) during the six years 1960–65.[1]

According to the Ministry of Labour survey of plant size in manufacturing industry in April 1959,[2] 47% of employees in the engineering, shipbuilding and electrical goods industries were employed in plants of more than 1,000 workers. This compares with 33·7% in manufacturing industries as a whole. On the other hand only 4⅓% of plants in this group of industries were in the size range of 1,000 employees and over. Although the pattern for shipbuilding is somewhat disguised by the other two industries included, the general point emerges that only a small proportion of all shipbuilding plants are large, but they employ about half the labour force.

Of the 49,000 new shipbuilding employees in the twenty-seven largest yards in 1966 18,000 were in the nine largest yards in the North-East (Tyne, Wear and Tees); 16,000 were in the nine largest yards on the Clyde and 6,000 were in the Belfast yard of Harland and Wolff.[3] The twenty-seven largest yards had seventy-five berths.[4] Thirteen of the yards also engaged in both repair work .and marine engine building: nine others were engaged in repair work and one other was engaged in engine building. The annual capacities of the twenty-seven largest yards ranged from 10,000 tons (Yarrow & Co. on the Upper Clyde) to 250,000 tons (Swan, Hunter & Wigham Richardson, Ltd on the Tyne): their total claimed annual capacity was 2·3 million tons, more than double the average tonnage launched by the entire industry during the early 1960s and indicating a high degree of excess capacity.[5]

When the Minister of State, Board of Trade, returned in 1965 from a tour of inspection of the Japanese shipbuilding industry, one of the reasons he gave for the relative success of firms in that country was that marine engine production and installation were rationalised. Other factors making for success were that custom-built ships were available to meet customers' requirements, whilst very efficient production control and planning throughout the industry were apparent.[6]

By 1971 there were about sixty yards in the U.K. building vessels of 100 gross tons or more: of these, fifteen could build ships in excess of 50,000 DWT; eight were capable of building 100,000 ton ships, six could build up to 150,000 tons and three in excess of 250,000 tons. The rest were concerned with smaller, more specialised vessels.[7] In May 1969 Swan Hunter, on the Tyne launched the first 250,000 ton vessel in Britain, the Esso Northumbria. This increase in the scale of production was significant in that it was launched from a traditional slipway, in a period when there were indications that giant tankers were creating diseconomies of large scale by outgrowing the facilities specially built to produce them.[8] In fact, the Geddes Report had looked at this problem, and concluded that by launching at an angle or by changing the layout of berths and craneage, narrowness of river and shortness of berth might not represent insurmountable limits to the size of ships: in fact, three yards (Harland and Wolff, Swan Hunter

[1] Ibid., paras. 11, 12.
[2] Min. Lab. Gaz., Sept. 1959.
[3] Geddes Report, para. 319.
[4] Stat., 27 April 1964, p. 556 and 5 Feb. 1965, p. 382; Econ., 20 March, 1965, p. 1294.
[5] Geddes Report, Appendix D.
[6] D.T. 14 Jan. 1965.
[7] British Shipbuilding, 1971, p. 2.
[8] 'Icebergs ahead for oilbergs', S.T., 4 May 1969.

and Vickers at Barrow) were pinpointed as being capable of 200,000 DWT launches with little further capital expenditure.[1] Since then Harland and Wolff, assisted by an £8 million loan from the Shipbuilding Industry Board, has constructed a new building dock and associated facilities, capable of building ships up to 1 million DWT, and the Swan Hunter group has devised a method of building 1 million ton tankers in sections.[2]

In 1971 there were about 100 ship-repairing plants and about sixteen marine engine building works.[3]

2. Administrative Organisation

(a) Concentration of control

Prior to the post-Geddes reorganisation of the industry there were over fifty separate member firms in the Shipbuilding Conference (the pre-1967 central trade association), controlling over sixty yards. The five largest firms controlled sixteen of the major yards, with seventy-five births, and each of these firms had an annual capacity of more than 200,000 tons of merchant or naval shipping. Apart from these resources, there are twice as many shipyards and berths in other companies in Scotland, Belfast and the north, as well as the numerous yards around the Bristol Channel, the south coast, the Thames and the Humber, with facilities for small ships.[4] In 1964 the six largest firms were responsible for about half the total output of ships and had each produced over 100,000 gross tons in at least one post-war year.[5] Not all the twenty-seven largest yards studied by Geddes were independently owned: some belonged to groups which had a range of interests in other fields such as engineering, steel, investment finance and shipping.[6]

In the ship-repairing section of the industry, fourteen large firms controlled about 73% of U.K. activity. Of these fourteen firms, half were also engaged in shipbuilding.[7] Some of the work they performed consists of 'ship-surgery', such as joining together the bow of one ship and the stern of another, or the insertion, between bow and stern, of a large, prefabricated mid-section. Such complex work requires extensive construction capacity, and provides a stimulus to vertical integration with shipbuilding itself. The Geddes Report found that repair work had been more profitable than new building and, if conducted in a building yard, could afford more flexible use of resources. However, it could also lead to under-utilisation of resources, and so the Report recommended that groups should have an interest in repair work, provided that it did not distract attention from the main shipbuilding activities and was separately managed.[8]

In marine engine building there were sixteen firms engaged in main engines at the time of the Geddes Report and there were still sixteen in 1971. In 1966 twelve of these main engine builders, including three of the six largest, were

[1] Geddes Report, para. 13.
[2] *British Shipbuilding*, 1971, p. 2; 'Shipbuilding in Britain', *M.B.R.*, May 1969, p. 10; *D.T.*, 19 Sept. 1966.
[3] *British Shipbuilding*, 1971, p. 2.
[4] *Stat.*, 10 Jan. 1964, p. 116.
[5] *F.S.B.*, 4735/D/12.
[6] Geddes Report, para. 15.
[7] *F.S.B.*, R.4735/D/12.
[8] Geddes Report, paras. 117, 321.

integrated or closely associated with shipbuilding and were involved in the fourteen engine building/shipbuilding plants mentioned above, thirteen of which also engaged in ship-repairing. A thirteenth engine building firm – John G. Kincaid & Co on the Lower Clyde (one of the six largest) – was not completely independent of shipbuilders: several shipbuilding firms held shares in it.[1] Geddes found that the savings in transport costs and the control over delivery, resulting from integration of engine building with ship construction, did not justify integration. It concluded that there was too much fragmentation of engine building and not enough specialisation: many firms built only three or four engines annually and the two largest producers – Harland and Wolff and the Richardsons Westgarth Group – each averaged eight or twelve engines from 1961 to 1965, as compared with an average annual output by the three largest overseas competitors, during the same period, of between twenty-two and thirty-six. It recommended four specialist plants, independent of the shipbuilding firms, each with an annual production capacity of about 300,000 horsepower.[2]

Horizontal integration, in the form of amalgamations, has resulted in the growth of most of the larger firms in the industry. Many of these mergers were preceded by periods of close trading association and tacit understandings, which still exist in many sections of the industry.[3]

Diversification into activities unconnected with shipbuilding was noted in some firms by the Geddes Report, undertaken to maintain employment and to utilise existing facilities. It suggested that such activities should only be continued if they did not overextend the firms' finances or distract management from shipbuilding operations: the grouping of yards was held to facilitate this specialisation of effort by creating greater efficiency and stability of orders.[4]

With regard to vertical integration backwards, with suppliers (such as steel) and forwards, with shipowners, the Report noted that some of the strongest competitors in Japan and West Germany had such links. In the U.K., in 1966, five of the main shipbuilding firms were owned by groups with other interests and two were owned by shipowners, yet they were not generally more profitable than the other firms in the industry. Similarly, the integration of some shipbuilding with engine building had not conferred a higher degree of success, and it was recommended that these particular activities should in future be separated. Some advantages were found in vertical integration, such as flexible internal pricing, technical efficiency from the unified planning of a series of processes and strength and stability from greater size and the spreading of investment over a wider range of processes. On the other hand, disadvantages existed, such as the masking of inefficiency in one process with strength in another. The Report concluded that the major concern of the industry should be its shipbuilding operations, unencumbered by forward or backward commitments, and also that most of the advantages of vertical integration could be achieved through contractual commercial relationships – or informal vertical integration. Vertical integration was neither the only nor the best way to proceed, and the Report did not recommend it.[5]

1 *Ibid.*, Appendices G and D; *British Shipbuilding*, 1971, p. 2.
2 Geddes Report, paras. 201–23.
3 *The Structure of British Industry*, vol. 2, p. 105.
4 Geddes Report, para. 323.
5 *Ibid.*, paras. 336–9.

As was mentioned earlier, the Report recommended the amalgamation of firms and yards into about five groups – two in the North-East, two on the Clyde and the other at Belfast. Each group would have about five or six specialised yards – each employing 1,500 to 2,000 men on shipbuilding. Groups would therefore have 8,000 to 10,000 shipbuilding operatives and aim at annual outputs of 400,000 to 500,000 gross tons. These should be able to compete with Japanese and Swedish firms: in Japan the six groups with annual launchings of at least 250,000 gross tons accounted for 71·3% of total output, whilst in Sweden the two such groups accounted for 75%. Whereas the thirty-four firms in Japan with less than 100,000 gross tons annual launchings represented only 8·8% of the total and the twenty-one such firms in Sweden represented only 6·2%, there were forty-nine U.K. firms in this category, accounting for 57·2% of total launchings.[1]

Since the Geddes Report the administrative organisation of the industry has been radically rationalised. Between 1960 and 1970, for example, the number of firms building ships of 400 feet or more in length fell from about thirty-six to twenty-six as a result of mergers and closures. In Scotland alone the number of individual shipbuilding firms or groups declined from 23 in 1964 to eight at the end of 1969.[2] The Commission on Industrial Relations (C.I.R.) Report No. 22 on Shipbuilding and Shiprepairing in 1971 limited its scope of reference to firms concerned with ships of at least 100 gross tons, usually eligible for membership of the Shipbuilders and Repairers National Association (S.R.N.A.). The 110,000 employees in 1971 according to this definition (75,000 in shipbuilding and 35,000 in ship-repairing) were employed in 255 firms (mostly single-plant firms) – seventy-five in shipbuilding and 180 in ship-repairing: of these, the thirteen largest groups and individual companies controlled about fifty-five yards and employed 85,000 or over 75% of the total.

Only eleven of the thirteen largest firms in the industry (as defined by the C.I.R.) were involved in shipbuilding and they employed 67,000 or about 90% of the building employees: of these, the four largest accounted for 55% and the seven largest for over 75%. Apart from these eleven firms, there were only two others which employed more than 1,000 each (not being, of course, amongst the top thirteen in the combined industry): in addition, ten other firms in ship-building, with 250 to 500 employees each, accounted for about 3,000 shipbuilding employees, and the remaining 3,000 such employees were scattered amongst about fifty smaller firms.

In ship-repairing there was a much lower concentration of control. Only eight companies and groups had more than 1,000 employees in ship-repairing: the seven largest accounted for just about 50% of the total, and at least twenty-six firms were required to reach the 75% control of employment attained by the top seven shipbuilders. Of these seven largest repairers, only six were members of the top thirteen firms in the combined industry and only three were also members of the top seven builders. After the eight firms with more than 1,000 employees, about twelve, mostly single-plant firms, each had about 500 to 750 employees. Each was independent of other ship-repairers, but most had links with ship-building, shipping or engineering firms. These twenty firms controlled about 70% of ship-repairing employees, the remaining 30% being scattered amongst

1 *Ibid.*, paras. 312–20.
2 *F.T.*, 3 Nov. 1969, and 13 Oct. 1970.

about 160 small, specialist firms, mostly dispersed in and around ports where they undertook minor repair work on vessels between voyages.[1] At the time of the C.I.R. Report, Upper Clyde Shipbuilders employed about 10,000 in shipbuilding. At the time it went into liquidation in 1971 it employed about 8,500 in its four yards – *viz.* Clydebank (John Brown), Linthouse (Alexander Stephen), Scotstoun (Charles Connell) and Govan (Fairfield). In February 1972 the Government

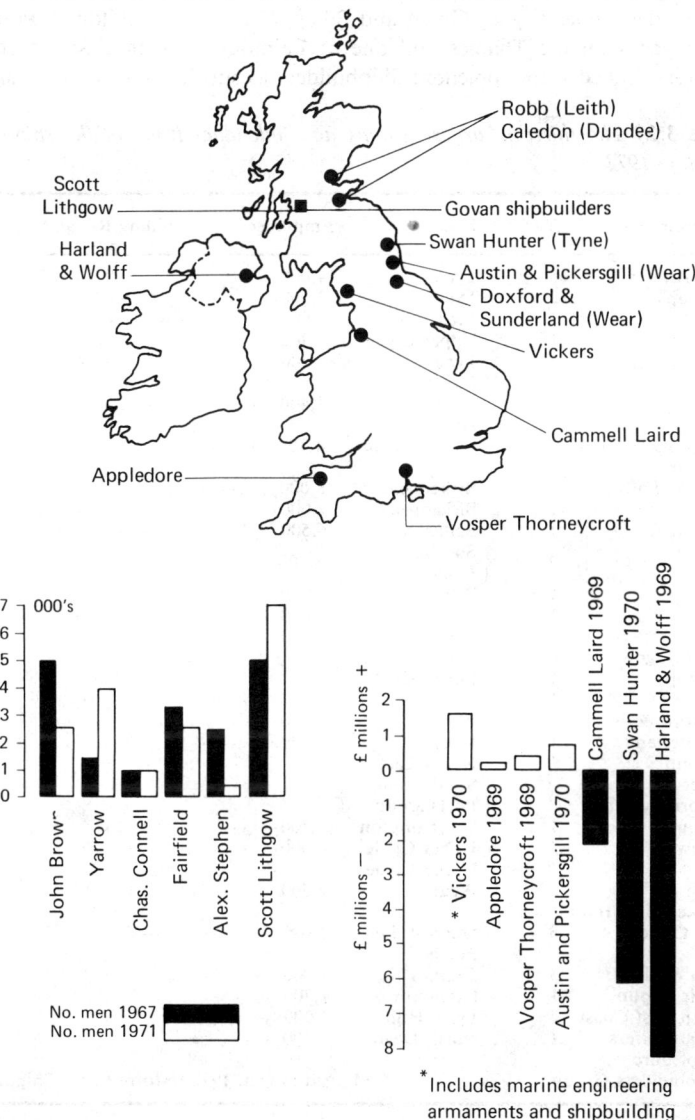

Fig. 3.45. *Major groupings and firms in the shipbuilding industry, 1971* (Source: *Obs.*, 20 June, 1971)

[1] *Shipbuilding and Shiprepairing*, C.I.R. Report No. 22, paras. 35–40.

finally decided to supply another £35 million for working capital and modernisation to the reconstituted company, Govan Shipbuilders, which was not to include the Clydebank yard: this was to be closed down or sold off. The other three yards would have a combined labour force of about 4,300.[1] The location of most of the thirteen largest firms in the combined shipbuilding and ship-repairing industry in 1972 is shown in Fig. 3.45. The omissions are Yarrow & Co. on the Upper Clyde; Green and Silley Weir (no shipbuilding) with three repair yards on the Thames and one at Falmouth; North East Coast Ship-repairers (linked with Appledore Shipbuilders as subsidiaries of the Court Line

Table 3.27 *The thirteen largest groups and individual firms in the shipbuilding industry, 1971*

Group or firm	Yards	Location	Employees	Building	Repair	Engines
Swan Hunter	5	Tyne	14,000 · · · · · · · · *			
Group	2	Tyne	2,500 · · · · · · · ·		*	
	1	Tees	2,000 · · · · · · · · *————*————*			
	1	Upper Clyde	900 · · · · · · · ·		*————*	
	1	Tyne	200 · · · · · · · ·		*————*	
	3	{ Forth, Tyne, Humber }	1,400 · · · · · · · *————*			
Govan Shipbuilders Group	3	Upper Clyde	4,300 · · · · · · · · *			
Cammell Laird	1	Birkenhead	8,000 · · · · · · · · *			
	1	Birkenhead	2,000 · · · · · · · ·		* ·	
Harland & Wolff	1	Belfast	6,500 · · · · · · · *————*			
	2	{ Southampton, Liverpool }	3,200 · · · · · · · · · · · · · · *			
	1	Belfast	3,000 · · · · · · · ·			*
Vickers	1	Barrow	7,000 · · · · · · · · *			
	1	Barrow	5,000 · · · · · · · ·			*
Scott Lithgow	6	} Lower Clyde {	5,500 · · · · · · · · *			
Group	1				*	
	1		1,500 · · · · · · · ·			*
†Doxford &	3	Wear	5,000 · · · · · · · · *			
Sunderland	1	Wear	2,500 · · · · · · · ·		*	
Group	?	North-East	? · · · · · · · ·			*
Vosper	3	{ Southampton, Portsmouth }	3,000 · · · · · · · · *			
Thorneycroft						
Group	1	Southampton	1,500 · · · · · · · ·		*	
Yarrow	1	Upper Clyde	3,000 · · · · · · · · *			
	?	Upper Clyde	? · · · · · · · ·			*
Austin &	2	Wear	2,500 · · · · · · · · *			
Pickersgill Group						
Robb Caledon	3	{ Dundee, Leith, Forth	2,000 · · · · · · · · *————*			
Green & Silley	3	Thames	1,000 · · · · · · · ·		*	
Weir Group	1	Falmouth	1,700 · · · · · · · ·		*	
†North East Coast	4	Tyne, Hull	2,000 · · · · · · · ·		*	
Shiprepairers/	1	North Devon	500 · · · · · · · · *			
Appledore						
Shipbuilders Group			† Merged in Oct. 1972 to form Court Shipbuilders.			

(Source: Based on material in *Shipbuilding and Shiprepairing*, C.I.R. Report No. 22, 1971, pp. 147–50)

[1] *F.T.* 29 Feb. 1972; *D.T.*, 29 Feb. 1972; *Shipbuilding and Shiprepairing*, loc. cit., p. 147; also 'U.C.S.: £6,000 a job', *Econ.*, 12 Feb. 1972, p. 70; *Econ.*, 4 Sept. 1971, p. 67; *Econ.*, 29 Jan. 1972, pp. 66–7.

shipping firm) with three repair yards on the Tyne and one at Hull. Details of the thirteen largest firms in the combined building and repair sectors in 1971 (adjusted for the 1972 Govan arrangement on the Upper Clyde), showing the major elements of vertical integration within the firms and constituent plants, are provided in Table 3.27. In October 1972 the Court Line's Appledore Shipbuilders Group and N.E. Coast Shiprepairers merged with the Doxford and Sunderland group, to form Court Shipbuilders.[1]

With regard to marine engine building, as was mentioned earlier, medium-speed and high-speed engine production had been concentrated into four large groups by the late 1960s, but slow-speed diesel production was still fragmented amongst nine firms in four areas – the Clyde, Sunderland, Belfast and Barrow. These groups and individual firms together comprised the sixteen marine engine building firms in existence in 1971.

(b) Tiers of authority

Until 1967 there were two major organisations in the industry, *viz.* the Shipbuilding Conference, founded in 1928 as the industry's national commercial trade association and the Shipbuilding Employers' Federation, established in 1899, which dealt with labour relations, consultation and negotiation in conjunction with the shipbuilding trade unions. In addition there were the Dry Dock Owners and Repairers Central Council, representing ship-repairers at national level and the National Association of Marine Engine Builders, the central commercial organisation of the principal U.K. marine engine builders.

In May 1967 the S.C., S.E.F. and D.D.O.R.C.C. were merged into the Shipbuilders and Repairers National Association, to which the N.A.M.E.B. was affiliated. The S.R.N.A. is concerned with both commercial and labour relations aspects of the U.K. shipbuilding and ship-repairing industry. It is considered to be better able to handle the increasingly complex economic developments concerning the industry than were the former separate organisations.

On general matters such as wages and hours negotiations, affecting all employees in the industry, the S.R.N.A. deals at national level with the Confederation of Shipbuilding and Engineering Unions. This is the major trade union body in the industry, to which about twenty-four unions are affiliated: of these, about fourteen are directly connected with shipbuilding and associated activities. On problems at national level, affecting all employees of a particular class, the S.R.N.A. consults with the specific union or unions concerned.

Negotiations on day-to-day matters are conducted in the yard, between representatives of the employers and workers, but in the event of a failure to reach a settlement, the next stage is a conference between the local employers' association and representatives of the union or unions directly concerned: only if this fails to bring agreement is the matter referred at national level.

Apart from negotiations on pay and conditions of work, there is provision for joint consultation: in late 1966 a Joint Industry Consultative Committee was established, comprising representatives of the S.R.N.A. and of the C.S.E.U. It also has its counterparts at yard and district levels.[7]

[1] See *D.T.*, 12 Oct. 1972, for further details.
[1] *British Shipbuilding*, 1971, pp. 10–11 and *Shipbuilding and Shiprepairing*, paras. 3, 5, 81–93, 94–143, and pp. 144–6.

Lloyd's Register of Shipping supervises the survey and classification of merchant ships of all nationalities, by means of a world-wide organisation of surveyors. The Register classifies over half the world's merchant tonnage. It is now an independent organisation, voluntarily maintained by the shipping community. Its committee of management consists of shipowners, shipbuilders, marine engineers, marine underwriters and other specialists.

Large-scale research is carried out for the whole industry by the British Shipbuilding Research Association (B.S.R.A.), formed in 1944 by the Shipbuilding Conference and the Department of Scientific and Industrial Research. It deals with research on naval architecture, marine propulsion engineering, ship-repairing and production and computer applications. With regard to the latter, it is worthy of mention that defining and designing the types of ships required to serve shipowners' future requirements, in the light of changing world trade patterns, is a vital aspect of B.S.R.A.'s work. This is becoming increasingly a joint effort between designer and computer. On-line design techniques, which enable designers to explore wide ranges of ship types and to identify the optimum for a particular use, are well advanced. B.S.R.A. is financed by the shipbuilding industry, together with a Government grant and assistance from the shipping industry.[1]

The State is, of course, an important element in the tiers of authority. As sponsor of the Shipbuilding Industry Board, until 1972 and as the policy maker on grants, loans, subsidies, regional assistance, naval orders, tariff protection, etc.,[2] it has wielded great influence over the survival and prospects of the industry. It is also a major shareholder in firms such as Govan Shipbuilders and Harland and Wolff.

3. Further Reading and Sources

Footnote references to daily and weekly journals are not repeated.

COMMISSION ON INDUSTRIAL RELATIONS, *Shipbuilding and Shiprepairing*, Report No. 22, Cmnd 4756. H.M.S.O. 1971.

Committee of Inquiry into Shipping: Report (Rochdale Report), Cmnd 4337. H.M.S.O. 1970.

Lloyd's Register of Shipping: Annual Report, 1970.

J. R. PARKINSON, 'The financial prospects of shipbuilding after Geddes'. *Journal of Industrial Economics*. Nov. 1968.

SHIPBUILDERS AND REPAIRERS NATIONAL ASSOCIATION, *British Shipbuilding*, memorandum of 1971.

'Shipbuilding in Britain', *M.B.R.* May 1969.

Shipbuilding Inquiry Committee 1965–1966: Report (Geddes Report), Cmnd 2937. H.M.S.O. 1966.

---

[1] *British Shipbuilding* p. 5.
[2] For an outline of some of the main areas of State influence, see 'Cooling the subsidy war in shipbuilding', *Econ.*, 28 Feb. 1970, p. 79. Also see *Shipbuilding and Shiprepairing*, paras. 28–34.

PAST EXAMINATION QUESTIONS ON VARIOUS INDUSTRIES: Stage I

1. Why do industries such as the cotton textile industry of Lancashire, the pottery industry of Staffordshire, or the Yorkshire woollen industry, continue to be located where they originally started, although the advantages which they then possessed can now be obtained elsewhere? (Autumn 1953)
2. Discuss the present-day problems of *one* of the following: coal-mining; shipbuilding; rail transport. (Summer 1964)
3. Explain the importance of the British coal-mining industry and describe how it is organised. (January 1965)
4. Describe the location of the major centres of the steel industry in Great Britain. What do you consider would be the main factors determining the location of a new steelworks? (Summer 1958)
5. Why are steel-producing firms concentrated in comparatively few centres in the United Kingdom, whereas breweries are dispersed throughout the country? (Summer 1960)
6. The electrical equipment industry and the heavy iron and steel industry are two of the major industries of this country. Why is the former industry well distributed throughout the country, while the latter is highly localised? (January 1964)
7. Before 1939 Britain imported the bulk of her food and raw materials for industry. (a) How did she pay for them? (b) To what extent has the position changed in the postwar years? (January 1963)
8. 'The development of a new industry often causes short-run unemployment, but in the long run it usually increases employment.' Discuss this statement, using the development of the motor vehicle industry in the twentieth century as the basis of argument. (January 1963)
9. Describe the location, and account for the factors determining it, in respect of *either* dairy farming *or* the woollen and worsted industry in England. (Autumn 1957)
10. Describe carefully the location of the shipbuilding industry in the United Kingdom. Give reasons which help to account for the location of *one* important shipbuilding centre. (Summer 1962)
11. Write a short survey of the main industries in the region in which you live, and account for their presence there. (January 1965)

Stage II: Structure and Organisation

1. Write a note on the problem of coal. (Summer 1952)
2. Is coal in Britain too cheap and hence wastefully used? What considerations are relevant to forming an opinion on this subject? (Summer 1954)
3. Compare the main features of the general organisation of (a) coal mining and (b) the steel industry in the United Kingdom. (Summer 1959)
4. How and why is public control exerted over the U.K. iron and steel industry? (January 1964)
5. Contrast the economic organisation of the United Kingdom's agricultural industry with that of the United Kingdom's steel industry. (Summer 1960)

6. What have been the causes of the rapid increase in the British output of agricultural products during the last twenty years? (Summer 1959)

7. In what ways does the government influence the U.K. agricultural industry at the present time? Give your own assessment of these policies. (Summer 1963)

8. Outline the main economic problems facing either the British coal-mining industry or the British cotton industry. (Summer 1960)

9. Examine the main economic problems of the textile industries in Britain. (Autumn 1956)

10. Discuss the organisation and problems of any *one* of the following industries: rail transport, cotton, motor-vehicle manufacture, or agriculture. (Summer 1953)

11. *Either* (*a*) discuss the nature of and reasons for the present problems of British Railways, *or* (*b*) briefly outline the present transport system of your country and assess the main changes likely in the future. (Summer 1961)

12. Explain why the chemical industry of the United Kingdom has expanded more quickly in recent years than the textile industry. (Summer 1961)

13. Examine the main economic problems of the fuel and power industries in Britain. (Summer 1956)

14. Give an account of the relative size, location, and organisation of any one British industry. (Summer 1952)

15. Describe the structure and organisation of any one of Britain's newer industries. (Summer 1956)

16. Discuss the structure of any one industry. (Autumn 1956)

THE CHANGING STRUCTURE OF THE ECONOMY
Stage II[1]

1. Changes in the Relative Importance of the Main Industrial Groups

As was pointed out in Stage I.7 of Chapter 1, in regard to occupational distribution, the industrial structure of Britain has, over a long period, been undergoing significant changes, both within the main divisions of production and service occupations and between those two divisions. Major individual industries were then examined, to throw more light on the causes and effects of this process of industrial change.

In general, it may be said that in an expanding economy, such as Britain's, where both the total national income and income per head have risen over the years, industrial change comes about in four main stages. These stages have been observable in Britain.

(*a*) Agricultural production must be increased by more productive methods, so as to free labour and resources from the land into other occupations. This stage was achieved in Britain by the Agricultural Revolution and access to the agricultural surpluses of Australia, New Zealand and the New World.

(*b*) Factors of production can flow into manufacturing industry, in which technological improvements and economies of scale are able to give high yields. As one market becomes saturated, so factors flow into other industries.

[1] No Stage I to this section.

(c) A distribution system and a transport and communications network develop, to facilitate the growth of agricultural and industrial production and to convey the resultant output to its markets.

(d) As surpluses are achieved in the production of food and industrial goods and as their markets become saturated, there is a release of labour and resources into service industries.

A recent study by Deane and Cole[1] throws much light on this subject. They show that the average real income per head of population increased about seven-fold between 1688 and 1959.[2] At the same time agriculture fell from being Britain's largest industry until it employed only about 4% of the working population; raw materials extraction, manufacturing, utilities, and construction rose in importance to employ almost half the working population, but in recent years they have been marking time, whilst services have come to assume about equal importance.

Within the manufacturing group itself great changes have taken place. Textiles, one of the early 'growth' industries, has declined drastically since World War I. Its lead in exports and employment (28·2% of the manufacturing labour force in 1891; 11·5% in 1951) has passed to metals, machinery and vehicles – the production of durable consumer goods and producer goods (4·3% to 45·5%). Other less striking changes have been the growth of the chemicals group (1·7% to 5·1%) and of the food, drink and tobacco group (4·1% to 8·7%).[3]

The service sector has also witnessed internal changes, with the fall in domestic and personal service (from 15·8% of the working population in 1891 to 2·2% in 1951) and the rise in professional, financial, distribution, local and national government services (7·1% in 1891; 21·9% in 1951).

The United Nations publication, *World Economic Survey, 1961* indicates that most industrialised nations appear to have a similar pattern of manufacturing and service groups, with the latter rising in relative importance and agriculture diminishing, relatively. Furthermore, its findings indicate that, despite the wide disparities in industrial output growth rates in different countries, similar industries tend to be expanding fastest all over the world. The two main factors generating expansion in the 'growth' industries appear to be the expansion of exports and the ability to achieve technical progress through capital investment. These two factors stimulate higher productivity, but they require the smooth transfer of factors of production out of industries which are contracting (due to saturation of demand, change of tastes or technical obsolescence), into the growth industries.

With regard to the relative decline in agriculture and the relative rise in the services sector, some caution must be exercised against uncritically accepting such trends as an index of economic progress and sophistication. An excessively truncated agricultural sector may result in a distorted economic structure, with too little self-sufficiency, and may intensify balance of payments problems, as E. A. G. Robinson has pointed out.[4] A high proportion of employment in services may represent a form of 'concealed unemployment' and/or may be a premature phenomenon, not backed up with a well-balanced secondary sector

[1] P. Deane and W. A. Cole, *British Economic Growth, 1688–1959*, 1962.
[2] *Ibid.*, p. 3.
[3] *Ibid.*, p. 146.
[4] E. A. G. Robinson, 'The changing structure of the British economy', *E.J.*, Sept. 1954.

and representing a distortion of economic activities, as has been pointed out by Bauer and Yamey.[1] Bairoch and Limbor found such a hypertrophy or excessive, premature development of the tertiary sector in developing countries: this constituted an element of distortion in the economies of these countries, due to their maintaining economic relations with more developed economies for more than a century.[2] This controversy over the significance of the tertiary or services sector has had important policy implications in Britain. The Selective Employment Tax (S.E.T.) was introduced in 1966 and had as one of its major objectives the redeployment of labour from services into manufacturing. The philosophy behind it is generally attributed to Professor Kaldor,[3] who considered that Britain's economy was suffering from 'premature maturity', had exhausted the potential of past growth before achieving high productivity, and required a displacement from supposedly low-productivity service industries to high-productivity manufacturing industries, allied with technological innovation and economies of scale by way of international specialisation. Others have considered that some service industries have a high level of productivity and contribute extensively towards a healthy balance of payments and that many manufacturing industries have been overmanned and would increase productivity per employee by reducing their labour force.[4]

As has been pointed out by K. D. George,[5] the changes in overall sector shares in manpower and output as between *all goods* (primary, secondary, construction and public utilities) and *all services* indicate a relative fall in the service sector share in the volume of output, from 57% in 1924 to 48% in 1964. With regard to manpower, during the interwar period there was a relative rise in the service sector share, which did not result in a corresponding increase in its relative output share: this was largely due to the underemployment of surplus labour in the low-wage services groups. During World War II and the early postwar period there was a reversal to the 1924 manpower position, with 52% in goods and 48% in services in 1951. By 1964 services were rising again, relatively, and had reached 50%. This compares with the sustained rise in the services manpower share in the U.S., where it was 47% in 1929 and 58% in 1965. A comparison of major sectoral manpower shares in 1969 as between the U.K. and E.E.C. and other applicant countries is given in Fig. 3.46. From this it may be seen that although several countries had a similar services share to that of the U.K., the U.K.'s Agriculture, forestry and fishing section of the goods sector was unusually small. In the U.K. during the period 1951 to 1964 the goods sector increased its share in the real volume of output (or the value of output, as measured at constant prices) from 50% to 52%, with a manpower share reduction from 52% to 50%. However, because of the faster rise in services prices during this period, the share of services in the value of output (at current prices) rose from 50% to 52%.

---

[1] P. T. Bauer and B. S. Yamey, 'Further notes on economic progress and occupational distribution', *E.J.*, March 1954.
[2] P. Bairoch and J.-M. Limbor, 'Changes in the industrial distribution of the world labour force, by region, 1880–1960', *International Labour Review*, Oct. 1968, esp. p. 325.
[3] N. Kaldor, *Causes of the Slow Rate of Economic Growth of the United Kingdom*, 1966; see also C. F. Pratten, *Economies of Scale in Manufacturing Industry*, 1971, p. 321 and 'Premature maturity', *Stat.*, 11 Nov. 1966, p. 1139.
[4] 'Tory "swing to service sector",' *F.T.*, 19 Sept. 1969.
[5] K. D. George, *Industrial Organization*, 1971, ch. 1.

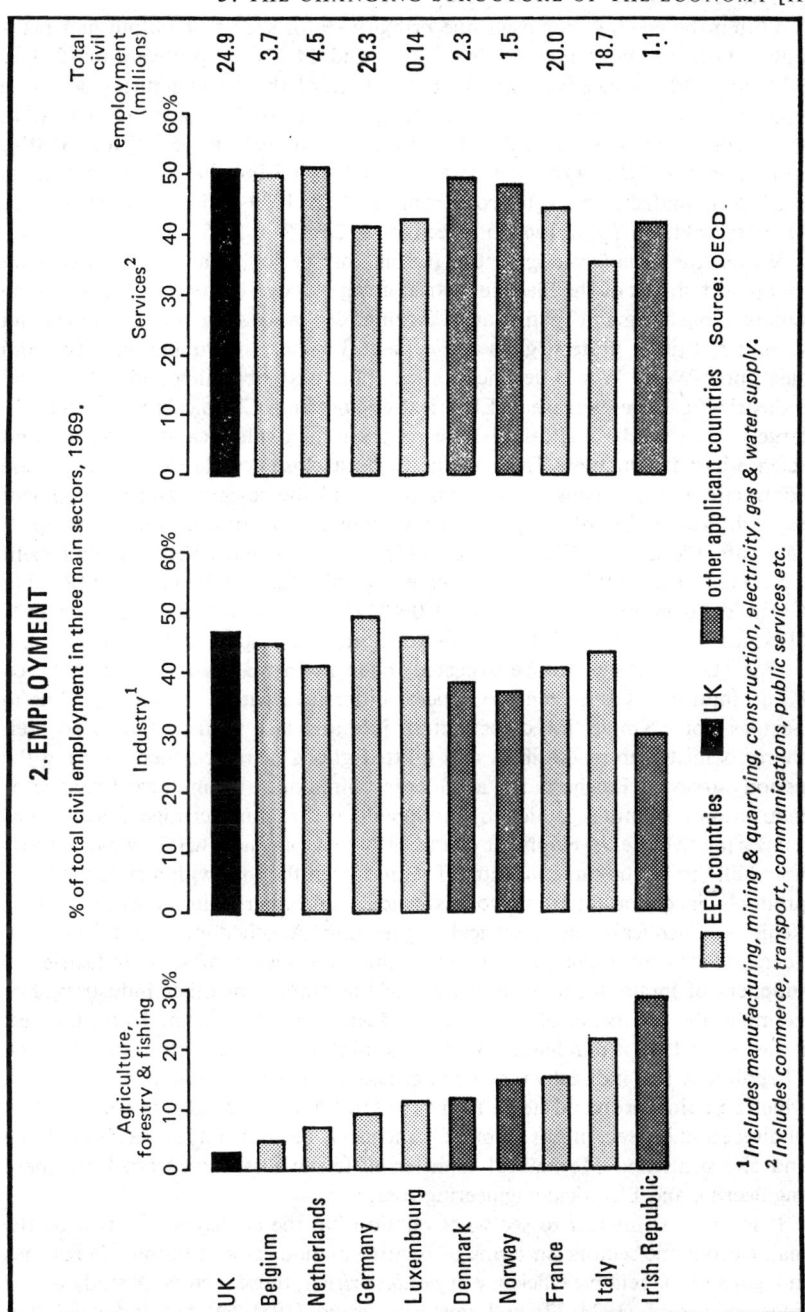

Fig. 3.46. *Percentage of total civil employment in three main sectors, 1969*
(Source: *E.P.R.*, 20, Oct. 1971)

Within the *goods* sector itself, the primary sector shares of output and manpower both fell continuously, from 12% and 14·3%, respectively in 1924 to 7% and 6·3%, respectively in 1964: the share of the manufacturing sector in output rose continuously, as it did in manpower, apart from a temporary fall in the 1930s (from 24·5% and 31·2%, respectively in 1924 to 35·7% and 35·0%, respectively in 1964). Over the period 1929 to 1965 the share of manpower in the U.S. manufacturing sector rose from 22·8% in 1929 (influenced by the Great Depression) to 26·7% in 1947, but declined to 25·9% in 1965.[1]

Within the *manufacturing* sector, during this period, changes in the relative manpower shares of the main industrial groups draw attention to the following points: a big decline in Textiles and Clothing; decline or stagnation in Timber and furniture, Bricks, pottery, glass and cement, Leather and rubber and Iron and steel; post-World War II decline or stagnation in Shipbuilding and Other metal industries; a large increase in Electrical engineering, Chemicals and Vehicles – largely due to technological advances in these high-value, capital-intensive and science-based industries. There seems to be a close correlation between these contractions and expansions in manpower and the research and development expenditures in British and American industrial groups in 1962: Group A (Aircraft, Electronics, Chemicals, Machinery, Instruments, Vehicles, etc.) spent 3·5% (U.K.) and 6·0% (U.S.) as a percentage of sales in 1962; Group B (Rubber Ceramics, Iron and steel, etc:) spent 0·4% (U.K.) and 0·7% (U.S.); Group C (Textiles and clothing, Timber and furniture, etc.) spent 0·24% (U.K.) and 0·17% (U.S.).[2] As might be expected, changes in manpower shares between broad industrial groups tend to conceal differences within the groups: thus in Textiles, for example, the older cotton, jute and lace industries reduced their shares, whilst man-made fibres and knitted goods increased theirs, during the period surveyed. Furthermore, as George points out,[3] technological change or innovation constitutes a 'hidden component' in structural change, inasmuch as it may involve the development of radically new products within what appears nominally to be the same industry. This has been the case with a stream of new products, incomparably more sophisticated than hitherto, in industries such as Vehicles, Chemicals and Electrical engineering. Another important factor influencing structural change is the close interdependence of some industries as suppliers of inputs to, and purchasers of the outputs of other industries. For example, the expansion of the Motor industry has affected the Iron and steel industry: in 1968 it purchased 13·6% of total iron and steel output directly, and 17% directly and indirectly (i.e. *via* intermediate products from other industries, which contained iron and steel). From 1963 to 1968 Motor industry consumption of direct and indirect inputs from Iron and steel, Textiles and leather, Oil refining and chemicals and Mechanical engineering fell, whilst those from Instrument engineering and Electrical engineering rose.[4]

It is of great interest to see what relationship the changing *structure* of the major economic sectors (in terms of relative manpower and output shares) has in regard to the relative efficiency or *productivity* in those sectors. A study of the interwar period (1924–37) and postwar period (1951–64) has indicated that

1 *Ibid.*, pp. 15–18.
2 R. E. Caves, ed., *Britain's Economic Prospects*, 1968, p. 482.
3 *Industrial Organization*, p. 19.
4 *Economic Trends*, No. 207, Jan. 1971, pp. xl–xli.

whereas the annual increase in productivity per unit of all inputs in the economy rose from 0·9% to 1·5% – an increase of 0·6% in the rate of growth – the increase in productivity growth in manufacturing was only 0·2% for labour (whilst for all inputs it actually fell from 2·4% to 1·8% per annum), whereas in services and distribution the increase in the growth of labour productivity was 1·9% and for all inputs was 1·1% (rising from – 0·4% to 0·7% per annum).[1]

Thus most of the overall postwar improvements in productivity were accounted for by the services sector. The less marked gains in overall factor productivity in all sectors were largely due to the greatly increased capital intensity in most sectors. Some of the major implications of the relationships between structural change and productivity growth are firstly, that the generally high postwar level of demand has had a favourable effect on productivity growth; secondly, that labour has tended to move from low-wage, low-productivity, low-value sectors to high-wage, high-productivity sectors, particularly within manufacturing; thirdly, that there have been pressures on all industries to introduce labour-saving techniques. The major part (over 80%) of the 1·3 million workers released from declining industries (0·42 million) and added to the labour force (0·9 million) between 1960 and 1965 went into services: despite the significant gains in services productivity, S.E.T., introduced in 1966, was aimed at stimulating even further the efficient utilisation of labour in this sector.

A study by W. E. G. Salter, added to by W. B. Reddaway,[2] of the prewar and postwar periods drew attention to some interesting relationships between productivity and structural change in respect of *individual* manufacturing industries. First, both prewar and postwar, those industries which expanded their output fastest also showed the highest gains in output per head. However, some industries which declined also showed above-average increases in labour productivity, as in the case of blast furnaces and jute in the earlier period and of footwear and cotton spinning in the postwar period. It would appear that adversity exercises a stimulus to efficiency in declining industries, such that the most successful survivors aim, through mergers, vertical integration and scale economies (as in Textiles during the 1960s), to secure a larger share of the shrinking market. Secondly, for most industries there was a tendency for those with above-average or below-average output growth rates, prewar, to follow a similar pattern in the postwar period. Such was the case with electricity, chemicals and glass, which expanded, and with leather, jute, cotton and coal, which contracted. Finally, for most industries there was no such persistency in good or bad productivity performance, but rather a discrepancy between prewar and postwar productivity. Such was the case with rubber – persistently above average, prewar and below average, postwar – and with footwear (prewar below, postwar above).

A study of changes in the industrial structure of Great Britain between 1954 and 1962, made by Sir Robert Hall[3] confirms the major trends and their implications, referred to above. A detailed breakdown of manpower, output, productivity and exports changes during the 1950s, analysed by industry, and

1 George, *op. cit.*, pp. 21–3.
2 W. E. G. Salter, *Productivity and Technical Change*, 2nd edn., 1966, Appendix A and addendum 'The Post-War Scene', by W. B. Reddaway. Also appraised in George, *op. cit.*, pp. 25–31.
3 Sir Robert Hall, 'Changes in the industrial structure of Britain', *L.B.R.*, Jan. 1963.

the major sectoral contributions to the Gross Domestic Product (G.D.P.) from 1907 to 1970 is provided in Table 3.28. Sir Robert Hall's findings and those of the U.N. *World Economic Survey, 1961*, referred to above, in regard to the similar pattern of growth rates in different countries, were given further support by R. E. Caves. By comparing manpower changes in seven similar U.S. and U.K. industrial groups between 1954 and 1962, he found striking similarities in all except Vehicles, Food, drink and tobacco, and Clothing and footwear. In general, the 'shaking out' of manpower and its reallocation to the faster-growing industries had proceeded more speedily in the U.K. than in the U.S. For example, Clothing and footwear, Textiles, and Mining and quarrying declined by 4%, 18% and 18%, respectively in the U.K. and by -7% (i.e. net increase), 13% and 18%, respectively in the U.S.: on the other hand, Engineering and electrical goods increased by 23% in the U.K. and only 18% in the U.S.[1]

Percentage changes in the labour force of industries accounting for nearly 60% of civil employment in Great Britain during the period mid-1953 to mid-1963 are shown in diagrammatic form in Fig. 3·47.

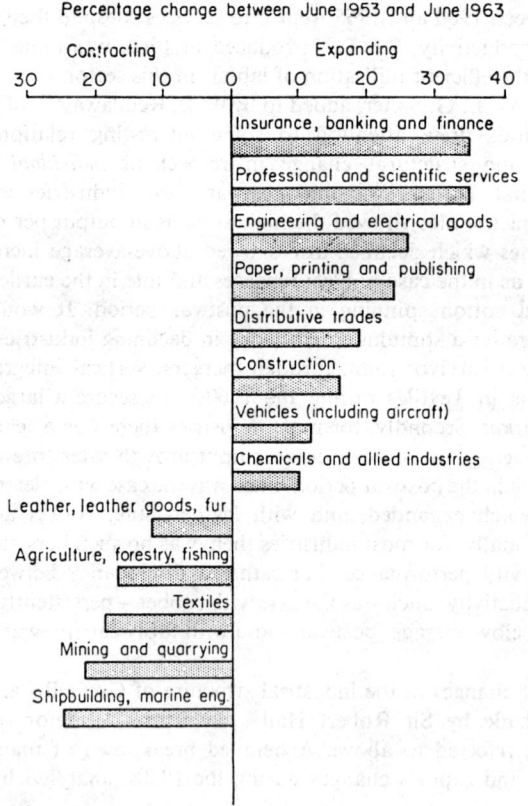

Fig. 3·47. *Relative changes in employment, June 1953–June 1963*
(Source: *Bulletin for Industry* 174, May 1964)

[1] Caves, ed., *op. cit.*, p. 294.

Table 3.28 Relative changes in the Industrial Structure of Britain

Sector	Order	Percentage change in labour force (G.B.) (1954–1962) +	Exports mid-'62 (1954=100) Volume	Exports mid-'62 Value	Productivity mid-'62 (1954=100)	% Annual growth in output (1950–1960)	% Contribution to U.K. Gross Domestic Product (1950–1960)	1907*	1957*	1970*
Extraction	Agriculture, Forestry and Fishing	− 12·8	—	—	—	—	5·1	6·5	4·5	3·2
	Mining and Quarrying	− 17·9	—	—	109	3·3	3·3	6·5	3·8	1·7
Manufacture	Metal Manufacture	} + 9·1	} 126	142	} 100	} 4·3	} 36·8	} 8·9	} 2·9	} 34·2
	Metal Goods			—	114					
	Engineering and Electrical Goods	+ 22·9	151	202	117				} 8·4	
	Shipbuilding and Marine Engineering	− 17·3	—	109	119					
	Vehicles	+ 11·8	139	159	111	2·7		4·6	4·4	
	Food, Drink and Tobacco	+ 9·9	129	131	134	6·0		1·1	3·7	
	Chemicals	+ 10·0	213	171	117	4·3		1·8	2·7	
	Paper, Printing and Publishing	+ 19·3	125	134	120	1·8		} 8·6	2·4	
	Clothing and Footwear	− 3·6	84	89	111	−0·9			1·5	
	Textiles	− 18·2	74	79	—	−2·1			3·0	
	Miscellaneous (including Leather Products)	} + 3·1	—	—	—	−2·1		} 2·7	} 3·8	
	Timber and Furniture		—	—	—	−2·4				
	Non-metal Mineral Products		—	—	—					
Public Utilities	Gas, Water and Electricity	+ 3·8	—	—	142		2·4	1·7	2·5	3·1
Construction	Construction	+ 10·9	—	—	115		5·7	4·0	5·9	6·3
Services	Financial, Scientific, Professional and Miscellaneous	+ 12·1	—	—	—		} 46·7	} 42·5	12·8	9·1
	Distributive Trades	+ 12·4	—	—	—				12·4	10·7
	Transport and Communications	− 1·8	—	—	—			10·2	8·7	8·4
	Local Government	+ 12·2	—	—	—			} 3·2	} 9·6	} 11·9
	National Government	+ 11·2	—	—	—					
Total		+ 12·3 / − 10·5	—	—	—	3·5	100	—	—	—
Overall Balance		6·2	—	—	—	—	—	—	—	—

* = Before providing for depreciation and stock appreciation.

(Based on material in *Lloyds Bank Review*, January 1963; *Ann. Abs. Stat.*; P. Dean and W. A. Cole, *British Economic Growth: 1688–1959*, C.U.P., 1962)

Percentage changes in the output of some major industries during the period 1954 to 1962, and the relative size of their output in 1958 are shown in diagrammatic form in Fig. 3.48.

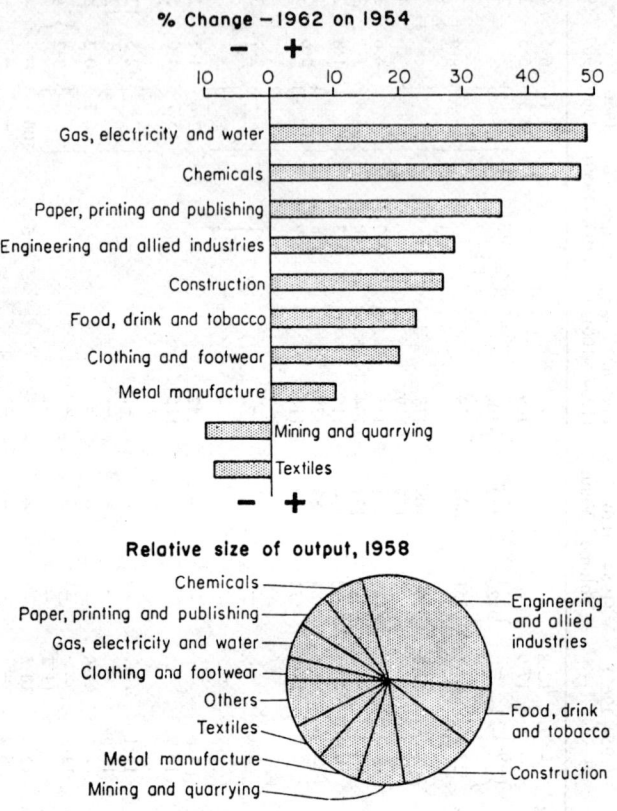

Fig. 3.48. *Changes in output of major industries*
(Source: *Growth and Change, B.B.L.A.*, September 1963)

The structural changes outlined above have, of course, been reflected in the changing contributions of the various industries and major Orders to the G.D.P. The main dimensions of these changes were included in Table 3.28. The new Index of Industrial Production, introduced in 1969 and using the post-1968 Standard Industrial Classification, attempts to show such changes in industrial output (*viz.*, Mining, Manufacturing, Construction and Gas, electricity and water). This sector accounts for about 45% of the total G.D.P.: both Industrial Production and G.D.P. are measured at constant factor cost (or prices), so as to indicate 'real' output. The weights given to each industry by the Index are in proportion to its net output (or value added) contribution to the G.D.P. Table 3.29 lists the weights used in the post-1969 Index of Industrial Production. Those for manufacturing industries are based on the 1963 Census of Production: those outside manufacturing are derived from a variety of sources. These weights are

284

Table 3.29 *Relative sector contributions to the G.D.P.*

	Index of G.D.P. at constant factor cost 1963 Weights %	Index of Industrial Production	
		1958 Weights %	1963 Weights %
Mining and quarrying	*2·4*	7·17	5·58
Manufacturing industries	*32·9*	74·83	74·94
Food, drink and tobacco	—	8·60	8·44
Coal and petroleum products	—	0·90	0·74
Chemicals and allied industries	—	5·88	6·36
Metal manufacture	—	6·85	6·01
Mechanical engineering	—	⎫	9·04
Instrument engineering	—	⎬16·69	0·97
Electrical engineering	—	⎭	6·81
Shipbuilding and marine engineering	—	2·18	1·54
Vehicles	—	7·91	8·05
Other metal goods	—	4·21	4·85
Textiles	—	5·82	5·64
Leather, leather goods and fur	—	0·41	0·43
Clothing and footwear	—	2·95	2·71
Bricks, pottery, glass, cement, etc.	—	2·81	2·90
Timber, furniture etc.	—	1·99	2·10
Paper, printing and publishing	—	5·47	5·88
Other manufacturing industries	—	2·16	2·47
Construction	*5·6*	12·59	12·71
Gas, electricity and water	*3·0*	5·41	6·77
Total industrial production	**43·9**	**100·00**	**100·00**
Agriculture, forestry and fishing	3·4		
Transport and communication	9·1		
Distributive trades	10·9		
Insurance, banking, finance and business services	7·1		
Professional and scientific services	8·1		
Miscellaneous services	7·8		
Public administration and defence	5·6		
Ownership of dwellings	4·1		
Total Output (G.D.P.)	**100·0**		

(Source: Based on material in *D.E.A. Pr. Rep. Econ.*, 56, Sept. 1969 and *E.P.R.*, 14, April 1971)

3. THE CHANGING STRUCTURE OF THE ECONOMY [II]

(I)

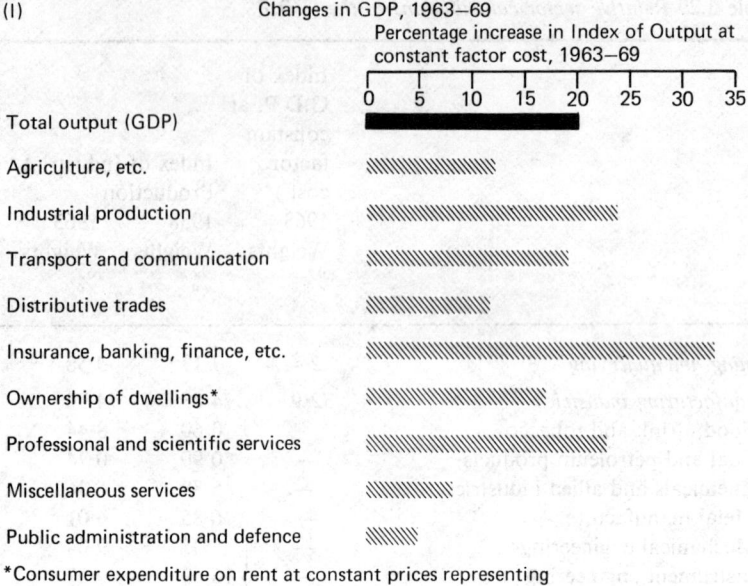

Changes in GDP, 1963—69

Percentage increase in Index of Output at constant factor cost, 1963—69

Total output (GDP)

Agriculture, etc.

Industrial production

Transport and communication

Distributive trades

Insurance, banking, finance, etc.

Ownership of dwellings*

Professional and scientific services

Miscellaneous services

Public administration and defence

*Consumer expenditure on rent at constant prices representing house ownership and occupation

(II)   Changes in industrial production, 1948—71

	1963 Weights per cent	Change in output 1948—71 per cent
Mining and quarrying	**5·6**	**− 21**
Manufacturing industries	**74·9**	**+ 110**
Food	5·5	+ 74
Drink and tobacco	2·9	+ 87
Coal and petroleum products	0·7	+ 374
Chemical and allied industries	6·4	+ 306
Metal manufacture	6·0	+ 46
Engineering industries	16·8	+ 182
Shipbuilding	1·5	− 34
Vehicles (inc. aircraft)	8·1	+ 164
Other metal goods	4·9	+ 39
Textiles, leather and clothing	8·7	+ 34
Bricks, pottery, glass, cement, etc.	2·9	+ 98
Timber, furniture, etc.	2·1	+ 113
Paper, printing and publishing	5·9	+ 111
Other manufacturing industries	2·5	+ 222
Construction	**12·7**	**+ 74**
Gas, electricity and water	**6·8**	**+ 250**
All industries	**100·0**	**+ 100**

Fig. 3.49. *Percentage changes in sector contributions to total output, 1963–69 and in industrial production, 1948–1971*
(Source: *E.P.R.*, 14, April 1971 and 30, Aug. 1972)

compared with those of the superseded Index, based on the 1958 Census. Table 3.29 also shows the 1963 weights of all sectors, used in the Index of G.D.P. (or Total Output), measuring 'real' output at constant factor cost. Fig. 3.49 indicates the major changes in sector contributions to the G.D.P., at constant factor cost, between 1963 and 1969 and the more detailed changes in industrial production, between 1948 and 1971. The changing annual output growth rates for the various sub-periods from 1948 to 1971 are shown for most industries or groups, in Fig. 3.50. For the manufacturing sector, manpower changes from 1963 to 1968 are shown in diagrammatic form in Fig. 3.51. From this it may be seen that Vehicles, Chemicals, and Metal manufacture joined the group of declining industries, in terms of manpower. In all these Orders the value of net output increased at less than the average for all manufacturing industry: allied to a more efficient utilisation of labour and proportionately greater increase in labour productivity (measured in net output per head), this resulted in a reduced demand for labour in these industries.

An interesting observation on structural and technological change and their implications for manpower was made by the chairman of the Conservative party's trade union advisory committee, in late-1971. He found that between

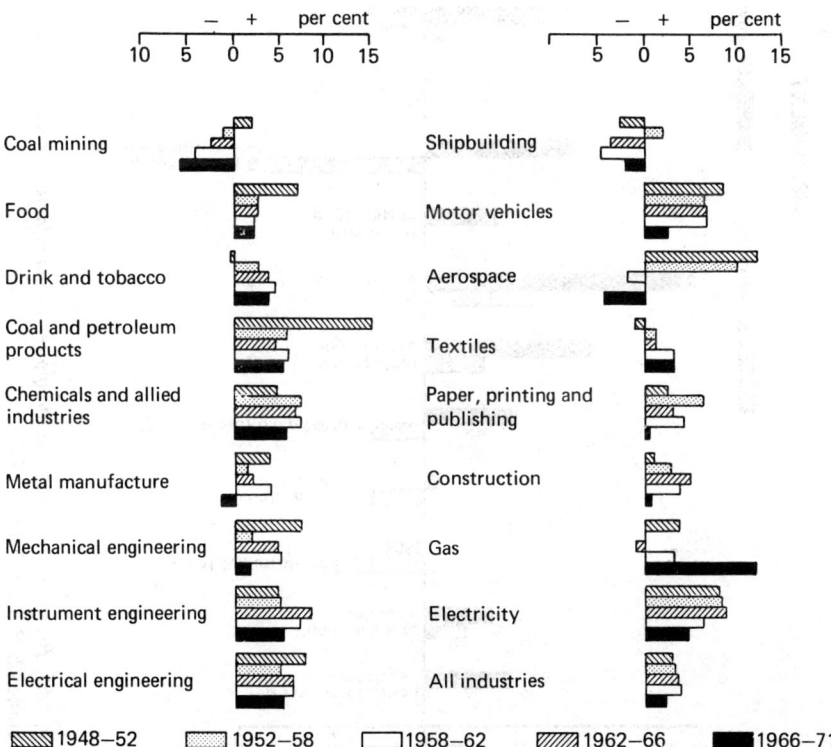

Fig. 3.50. *Annual output growth rates in selected industries, by sub-period, 1948–1971*
(Source: *E.P.R.*, 30, Aug. 1972)

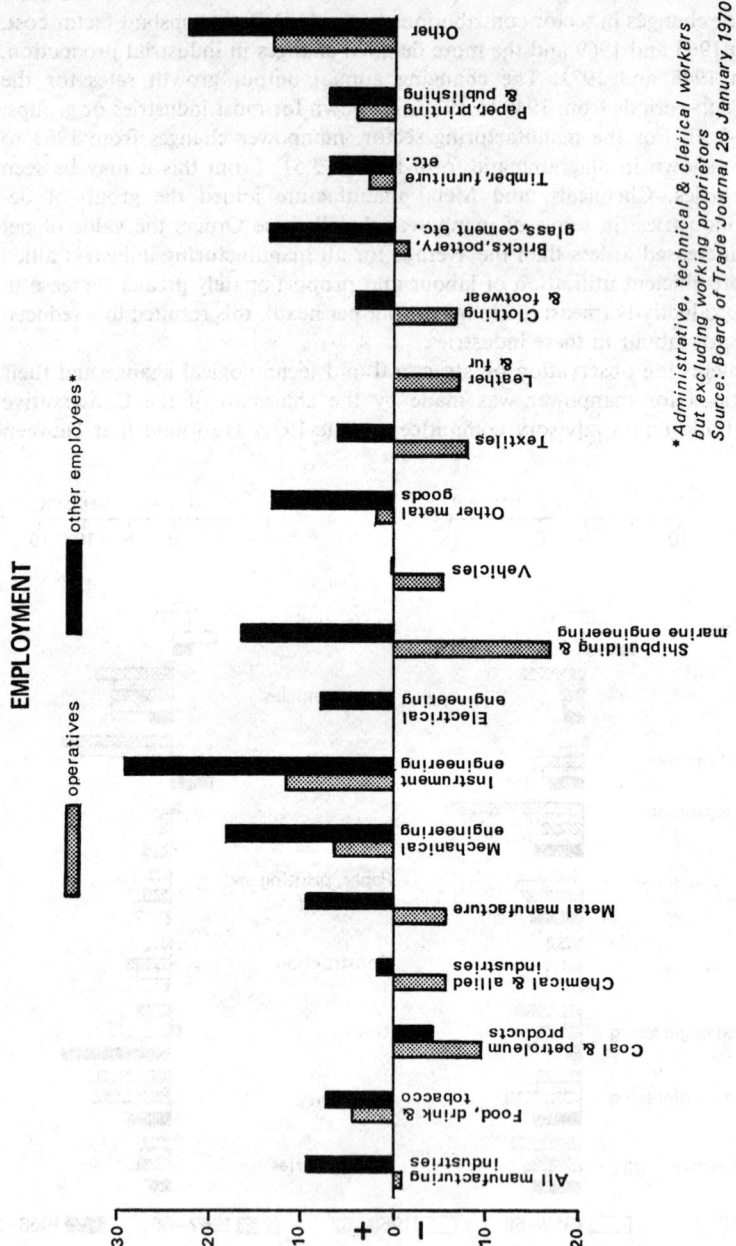

EMPLOYMENT

operatives   other employees*

Other	
Paper, printing & publishing	
Timber, furniture etc.	
Bricks, pottery, glass, cement etc.	
Clothing & footwear	
Leather & fur	
Textiles	
Other metal goods	
Vehicles	
Shipbuilding & marine engineering	
Electrical engineering	
Instrument engineering	
Mechanical engineering	
Metal manufacture	
Chemical & allied industries	
Coal & petroleum products	
Food, drink & tobacco	
All manufacturing industries	

*Administrative, technical & clerical workers
but excluding working proprietors
Source: Board of Trade Journal 28 January 1970

Fig. 3.51. *Percentage changes in manpower in manufacturing industry, 1963–68*
(Source: *E.P.R.*, 3, March 1970)

1963 and 1970 total real output in the goods sector (i.e. according to the Index of Industrial Production) had risen by 24% but labour productivity (output per head) had risen by 31%. The result had been a fall in the sector's labour force of 5%. In key sections of the goods sector the results were as follows:

	Total output	Output per worker	Manpower
Gas, electricity and water	+49%	+60%	− 7%
Textiles	+25%	+52%	−18%
Mining	−18%	+37%	−40%

It appeared that the contracting industries had been equally affected by the trend towards greater mechanisation and science-based efficiency: he forecast a continuance of 'technological unemployment', which would require new types of solution.[1] These findings, of course, reinforce those of Salter's study, referred to above, on the interwar and postwar periods.

One of the major features of the processes of technological and structural change outlined in this section has been the 'deepening' of capital invested in industry – the increased capital intensity in goods and services industries. This has affected the capital–labour ratio, labour productivity and general input (or factor) efficiency and employment. As has been noted, even declining industries with shrinking markets have participated in this process, which has, in turn, accelerated their rate of manpower shedding. However, the immense cost of technological change and science-based increases in capital intensity tend to raise overheads or fixed costs. Thus industry tends to become more sensitive to fluctuations in market demand, which may result in reduced capital utilisation or 'capital idleness'. Industries experiencing severe and/or prolonged excess capacity or capital under-utilisation might become more prone to contraction to a more viable size: the pressures towards 'rationalisation' and elimination of excess capacity might be expected to intensify. This will increasingly hasten the process of structural change and the balance of relative importance of different sectors of the economy.

An interesting study of capital utilisation in the manufacturing sector of the U.K. economy between 1958 and 1969 has shown[2] that most of the industries in which manpower declined during the period had experienced very high degrees of capital under-utilisation. For example, where the lowest rate of utilisation for all manufacturing was 92·1% (in 1963), it was 74·8% for Motor vehicles (1958), 76·1% for Metal manufacture (1963), 79·7% for Shipbuilding and marine engineering (1964), 80·5% for Leather, fur, clothing and footwear and 85·7% for Textiles. Furthermore, whilst the 'peak' range of capital utilisation for all manufacturing during the period was 97·5% to 100·0%, all these groups were in the range of 90·0% to 95·5%, with the exception of Textiles (97·5% to 100·0%), which had been radically restructured during the latter part of the period.

---

[1] *D.T.*, 18 Oct. 1971.
[2] M. Panić, 'Capital utilisation in the manufacturing industry', *N.W.B.Q.R.*, Feb. 1972. For discussion of a related problem, see M. Panić and R. E. Close, 'Profitability of British Manufacturing Industry' *L.B.R.*, July 1973.

With regard to the problems of efficient utilisation of industrial capital and the rationalising and restructuring of industry, mention should be made of the Industrial Reorganisation Corporation (I.R.C.). This was set up in 1966, with resources of up to £150 million, to promote industrial efficiency and reorganisation. It was decided to disband it in 1970, but during its lifetime it was instrumental in furthering large mergers in industries such as motors, electrical engineering and electronics, wool textiles, mechanical engineering, paper and board, ball bearings and special steels. Its powers were backed up by the 1968 Industrial Expansion Act, which extended existing Government powers (to support research and development) to the production and marketing activities of firms, by the injection of funds through the purchase of shares. There has been much controversy over the pros and cons of the I.R.C.'s activities, much of it centred around the extension of horizontal mergers among already dominant firms and the consequent increase in monopoly power.[1]

2. Relative Importance of Some Major Industries

This section attempts to draw together the relevant points brought out in preceding sections, so as to show the relative significance of the industries which have been covered in detail. These industries are coal; iron and steel; agriculture; motor vehicles; cotton; woollen and worsted; shipbuilding. The main points to be summarised concern their significance as employers of labour; the value of their output; their importance in the balance of payments, as importers and exporters; their interrelationships with other industries as customers or suppliers.

In 1954 a detailed analysis was made of the import and export significance of the major industrial groups.[2] It was found that all except public administration were involved in the import and export of goods and services: their output was closely concerned with the balance of payments. Their relative significance in this respect is summarised in Table 3.30.

During the period 1960 to 1970 many of the key basic industries in the U.K. had much lower rates of output expansion (or, as in the case of coal, contraction) than was the case of their E.E.C. counterparts. As may be seen in Fig. 3.52, U.K. growth varied between one-fifth and one-third that of the E.E.C. industries, and only in the case of electricity generation did U.K. growth approach that of the E.E.C.

Changes in the industrial structure, insofar as they are affected by international market forces, technological change and international economic groupings, might be expected to intensify during the next decade or so. In general, two important trends are apparent, both of which have implications for British membership of the E.E.C. First, there appear to be economic pressures to shift the balance of productive capacity in the conventional manufacturing industries (including motor cars) to the less developed and lower-wage countries. This might be increasingly resisted by the developed countries, by protective devices such as motor car safety regulations, subsidies (as in shipbuilding) and other non-tariff measures. Secondly, there is a tendency for the developed countries to

---

[1] Caves, ed., *op. cit.*, pp. 319–21; *Brit. O.H.*, 1971, p. 239; F. Broadway, *State Intervention in British Industry, 1964–68*, 1969, *loc. cit.*; *D.E.A. Pr. Rep. Ind. and Reg.*, 40, May 1968, *Reorgcorp*, London; *D.E.A. Pr. Rep. Econ.*, 54, July 1969, *IRC – second year*.
[2] *Input–Output tables for the United Kingdom in 1954*, 1961, H.M.S.O.

Table 3.30 *Relative significance of the major industrial groups on the balance of payments* (*1954*)

	0–10%	11–25%	Over 25%
Imports as a percentage of output (1954)	Public administration (nil) Mining (5%) Gas, Electricity, Water (5%) Services (6%) Construction (9%)	Engineering (11%) Agriculture, Forestry, Fishing (19%) Other manufactures (19%) Food, Drink, Tobacco (21%) Metal manufactures (23%)	Textiles, Leather, Clothing (28%) Chemicals (29%)
People employed in Gt Britain, Nov. 1962	14·2 million	7·8 million	2·0 million

	0–10%	11–25%	Over 25%
Percentage of output exported (1954)	Public administration (nil) Construction (3%) Agriculture, Forestry, Fishing (4%) Food, Drink, Tobacco (5%) Gas, Electricity, Water (10%)	Services (18%) Other manufactures (20%) Mining (21%)	Textiles, Leather, Clothing (29%) Chemicals (31%) Engineering (34%) Metal manufactures (35%)
People employed in Gt Britain Nov. 1962	5·1 million	12·5 million	6·4 million

(Source: *Trade expansion: Why?*, *B.B.L.A.*, March 1963)

concentrate more on knowledge-processing and other science-based industries of a more sophisticated and capital-intensive nature: this, however, requires large initial home markets on a continental scale. British membership of E.E.C. might reduce the barriers to its exports of conventional manufactures, in the first case, and might grant it access to production and markets for more sophisticated products, in the second case. A recent survey on the prospects for various U.K. industries, consequent upon E.E.C. membership found, *inter alia*, that Motors and components and Textiles were likely to gain from membership, whilst Shipbuilding and Steel were likely to be largely unaffected, unlike Domestic appliances and Machine tools, which were likely to lose some of their market share.[1]

[1] 'The economics of entry', *Econ.*, 6 May 1967, p. 542; *Econ.*, 30 Oct. 1971, p. 12; 'The winners and losers in Europe', *Econ.*, 6 Nov. 1971, pp. 80–81.

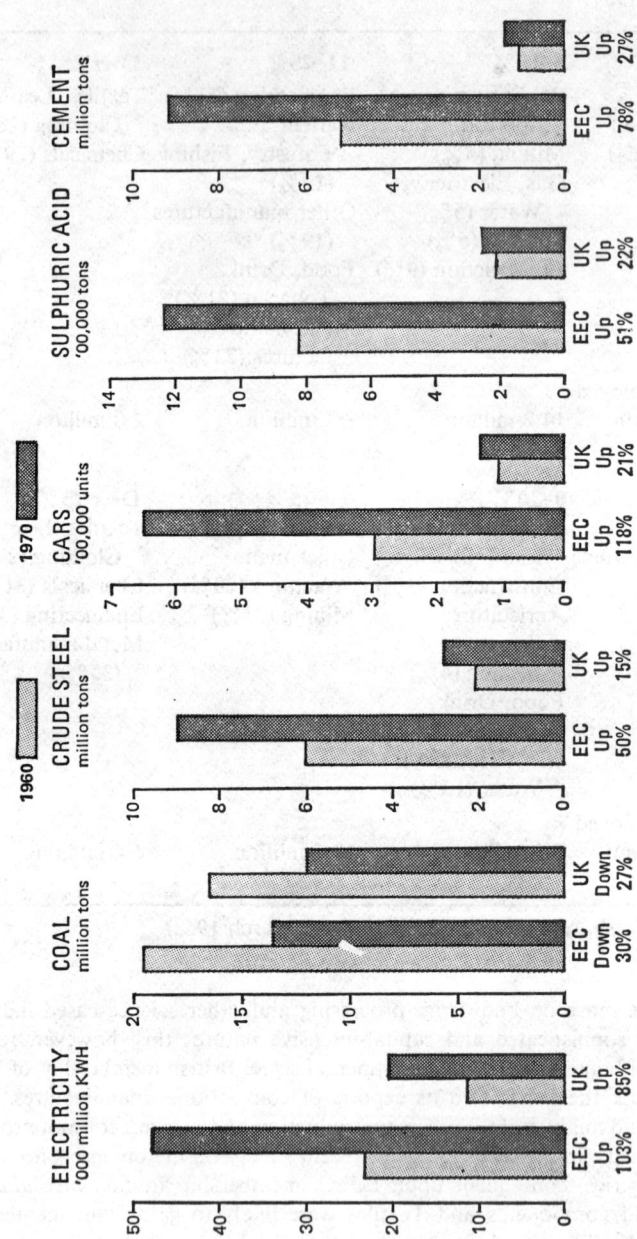

Fig. 3.52. *U.K. and E.E.C. output changes in some basic industries, 1960–70* (Source: *E.P.R.*, 20, Oct. 1971)

Labour costs, imports and exports

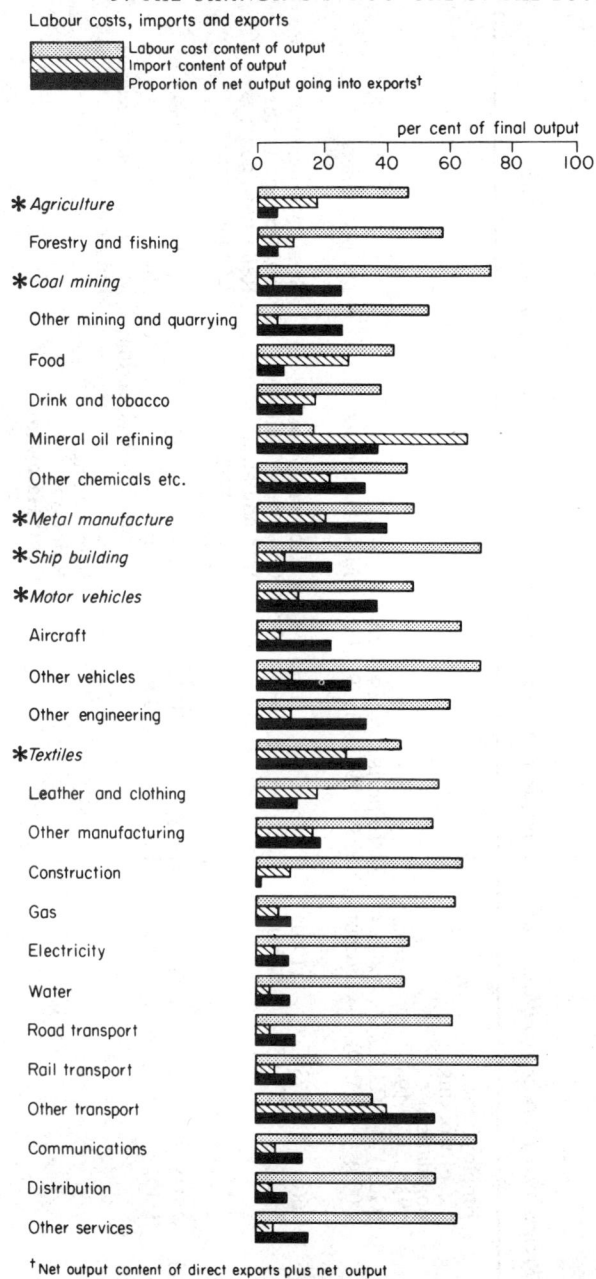

Fig. 3.53. *Direct and indirect labour cost content, import content and exports of major sectors in the U.K. economy, 1963*
(Source: *D.E.A. Pr. Rep. Econ.*, 48, Jan. 1969)

293

Table 3.31 *Prewar and postwar significance of some major U.K. industries in employment, output, imports and exports*

Industry	Employment (% of working population) 1939 (G.B.) ('000)	1961 (U.K.) ('000)	Gross value of output	Imports 1939	1961	Exports 1939	1961	Main customers	Main suppliers
Coal	766 3·9%	575 2·25%	(1961) £855m			(1935–38) 8·0	0·5	Electricity; Coke ovens; Gas ovens; Railways; Iron and steel; Engineering; Domestic.	Steel; Mechanical engineering; Timber; Railway wagons; Locomotives.
Iron and Steel	251·5 1·3%	307 1·2%	(1961) £1,000 m	(1938) 1·3	2·3	(1938) 8·9	5·5	Constructional engineering; Mechanical engineering; Motors; Shipbuilding; Railways; Coal; Hardware.	Coal; Shipbuilding; Mechanical engineering; Industrial plant.

								Markets	Inputs
Agriculture	Approx 1 m 4·8%	Approx 1 m 4·05%	(1961) £1,507 m (net value £772·8 m)			(1938) 0·85	1·1	Domestic; Breweries; Manufactured food.	Fertilisers; Machinery; Feedingstuffs.
Motors	Approx ¼ m 1·3%	415 1·6%	(1961) £1,000 m			4·0	11·7	Domestic services; Extractive; Manufacturing.	Sheet steel; Rubber; Paint; Glass; Mechanical engineering.
Cotton	348·8 1·8%	270 1·1%		4·1	1·4	11·1	1·5	Clothing; Tyres; Soft furnishing.	Mechanical engineering; Man-made fibres.
Wool and Worsted	214·5 1·1%	203 0·8%		4·8	2·8	6·0	4·0	Clothing.	Mechanical engineering; Man-made fibres.
Shipbuilding	183 0·9%	200 0·8%	(1946–61) Merchant £2,342 m Repairs £1,000 m Naval £325 m			(1938) 1·8	2·4	Shipping (Tankers, Passenger, Cargo); Iron and Steel industry; Coal industry.	Steel; Marine engineering.

3. THE CHANGING STRUCTURE OF THE ECONOMY [II]

With regard to the major industries covered in detail in previous chapters, the outlines of some of the basic changes in their manpower, output and direct shares of total imports and exports are provided in Table 3.31 for the prewar and postwar years 1939 and 1961. With regard to these industries in 1963, as the provisional input – output statistical analysis showed, Coal mining had the largest labour cost element (as direct and indirect factor input involved in the activities of the industry and in the intermediate products and services which it purchased from other industries). Textiles had the lowest labour cost element. On the other hand, Textiles had the highest import cost content as a direct and indirect input, whilst Coal mining had the lowest. As might be expected, Metal manufacture (previously Iron and steel) had the highest proportion of net output exported, directly as iron and steel or indirectly, as iron and steel in the exported products of other industries. Agriculture had the lowest proportion of net output exported. A summary of some of the data from the provisional input – output tables for the economy in 1963 is shown in Fig. 3.53.

A more recent appraisal of the relative significance of the six industries referred to above is possible on the basis of the provisional input – output tables for 1968.[1] From these has been derived Table 3.32. which compares the direct and indirect labour cost contents, import contents and proportions of net output exported, as between 1963 and 1968. The most significant changes were an increase of 4·9% in the labour cost content of Coal mining; a decrease of 3·3% in the import cost content of Agriculture and an increase of 3·1% in that of Motor vehicles; a reduction of 3·3% in the proportion of net output exported of the Coal mining industry and an increase of 2·2% in that of Shipbuilding.

The input–output analysis is a method of tracing the flows of final goods and intermediate goods and services between different industries and sectors of the economy. The sources of each industry's inputs and the destinations of its outputs are determined, to give a bird's-eye-view of the complex inter-relationships within the economy. Apart from the direct inputs and outputs, there are also indirect ones, as, for example, the labour content in the coal input

Table 3.32 *Direct and indirect labour cost content, import content and exports of some major U.K. industries, 1963 and 1968*

INDUSTRY	Labour cost content (%)				Import content (%)				Net output exported			
	Direct		Indirect		Direct		Indirect		Direct		Indirect	
	1963	1968	1963	1968	1963	1968	1963	1968	1963	1968	1963	1968
Agriculture	20·1	16·7	25·2	24·9	8·3	5·5	9·3	9·7	3·0	3·6	3·8	4·4
Coal mining	59·6	63·5	13·7	14·7	0·8	0·8	2·8	3·3	3·7	1·5	13·8	12·6
Iron and steel	30·0	31·9	24·0	22·9	7·0	7·8	4·3	6·2	14·8	15·5	25·1	24·9
Shipbuilding, etc.	44·4	45·1	25·9	25·9	2·2	3·1	5·0	6·7	17·3	22·4	7·2	4·3
Motor vehicles	28·8	31·2	29·3	28·3	2·0	3·6	6·6	8·2	39·9	40·3	2·4	2·8
Textiles	38·0	35·2	8·6	15·1	21·0	19·4	2·5	3·4	26·1	24·5	5·3	6·5

(Source: Based on material in *Economic Trends*, Nos. 178, Aug. 1968, 207, Jan. 1971 and 212, June 1971)

[1] 'Provisional input–output tables for 1968', *Economic Trends*, No. 207, Jan. 1971 and No. 212, June 1971.

INPUTS (Purchases from) ↓ / OUTPUTS (Sales to) →	Agriculture 1	Forestry and fishing 2	Coal mining 3	Other mining and quarrying 4	Food 5	Drink and tobacco 6	Mineral oil refining 7	Coke ovens 8	Chemicals, etc. 9	Iron and steel 10	Non-ferrous metals 11	Mechanical engineering 12	Instrument engineering 13	Electrical engineering 14	Shipbuilding, etc. 15	Motor vehicles 16	Aerospace equipment 17	Other vehicles 18	Other metal goods 19	Textiles 20	Leather, etc. 21	Clothing and footwear 22	Bricks, etc. 23	Timber and furniture 24	Paper and printing 25	Other manufacturing 26	Construction 27	Gas 28	Electricity 29	Water 30	Transport 31	Communication 32	Distributive trades 33	Miscellaneous services 34	Public administration 35	TOTAL INTERMEDIATE OUTPUT 36	FINAL BUYERS: CURRENT EXPENDITURE: Consumers 37	FINAL BUYERS: CURRENT EXPENDITURE: Public authorities 38	FINAL BUYERS: GROSS DOMESTIC CAPITAL FORMATION: Fixed 39	FINAL BUYERS: GROSS DOMESTIC CAPITAL FORMATION: Stocks 40	EXPORTS 41	TOTAL FINAL OUTPUT (37–41) 42	TOTAL OUTPUT (36–42) 43	
1 Agriculture					897	42															15															979	839	43			70	965	1944	1
3 Coal mining								138															17					57	314							595	177	35			12	219	813	3
5 Food	438																																											5
7 Mineral oil refining										30										12																								7
8 Coke ovens										103																																		8
9 Chemicals, etc.	121									40						23				129																								9
10 Iron and steel			34									357		77	39	222			303								168									1345					254	291	1635	10
11 Non-ferrous metals										64						69																												11
12 Mechanical engineering			41							74					19	52				22																								12
14 Electrical engineering															13	115																												14
15 Shipbuilding, etc.																															36					60		158	158		108	421	481	15
16 Motor vehicles, etc.												24																			33			65		223	353	63	600		831	1838	2061	16
19 Other metal goods															65	167																												19
20 Textiles									28				13			25						261		30	25	62	14						94	18		634	668	21			432	1128	1762	20
23 Bricks, etc.	25									32																																		23
24 Timber and furniture																51																												24
25 Paper and printing																				24																								25
26 Other manufacturing																114				21																								26
27 Construction	47		21																																									27
28 Gas										39																																		28
29 Electricity	24		32							64						22				34																								29
31 Transport	22		18							75						32				57																								31
33 Distributive trades	172									54					14	60				53																								33
34 Miscellaneous services	55														24	65				86																								34
36 Imports of goods and services	108		7							143					21	119				367																								36
37 Sales by final buyers (scrap, etc.)										48																																		37
38 TOTAL GOODS AND SERVICES	1123		239							921					250	1212				878																								38
39 Taxes LESS subsidies	–199		–0·5							26					–4	31				22																								39
40 Income from employment	326		510							510					217	640				620																								40
41 Gross profits and other trading income	694		65							179					18	177				242																								41
42 TOTAL INPUTS	1944		813							1635					481	2061				1762																								42

Table 3.33 *Input–output flow matrix for selected U.K. industries, 1968* (£ million)
(Source: Based on material in *Economic Trends*, no. 207, Jan. 1971)

to the Iron and steel industry and the iron and steel content in the various components which are inputs of the Motor vehicles industry, purchased from other sectors.

A summary of some of the data in the 1968 provisional input – output tables, insofar as the six major industries which have been covered previously are concerned, is given in Table 3.33. It shows the major relationships between the six industries and between them and the rest of the economy, as customers of and suppliers to each other. For example, Motor vehicles was a customer of the Iron and steel and of the Textile industries; it was both a customer of and supplier to the Transport industry and the Miscellaneous services sector. In Table 3.33 the vertical *columns* 1 to 35, down to *row* 38, indicate the purchases by each main industry of its intermediate products or services (i.e. inputs) from other industries. The extensions of the columns into *rows* 39 to 41 indicate the other input or factor costs (employment income and profits) and the addition for taxes on expenditure (a sort of Government factor cost) and the deduction for subsidies (which have effectively reduced the input or factor costs). The horizontal *rows* from columns 1 to 35 indicate the destinations of each industry's output, or its sales to other industries of its intermediate goods and services; *column* 36 shows the value of this intermediate output; *columns* 37 to 41 show the values of each industry's final outputs, purchased by final buyers (including exports), which are totalled in column 42; *column* 43 indicates the total value of each industry's total sales and output, both intermediate and final.

3. Further Reading and Sources

P. BAIROCH and J.-M. LIMBOR, 'Changes in the industrial distribution of the world labour force, by region, 1880–1960'. *International Labour Review*, vol. 98, no. 4. Oct. 1968.

P. T. BAUER and B. S. YAMEY, 'Further notes on economic progress and occupational distribution'. *E.J.* March 1954.

F. BROADWAY, *State Intervention in British Industry, 1964–68*. Kaye and Ward. 1969.

R. E. CAVES, ed., *Britain's Economic Prospects*. Allen and Unwin. 1968.

C.S.I., *National Income and Expenditure* (Blue Book). H.M.S.O.

D.E.A. Pr. Rep. Ind. and Reg., 40, May 1968.

D.E.A. Pr. Rep. Econ., 48, Jan. 1969 and 54, July 1969.

Economic Trends, 178, Aug. 1968; 207, Jan. 1971; 212, June 1971. C.S.O. H.M.S.O.

E.P.R., 4, April 1970, 14, April 1971 and 30 Aug. 1972.

K. D. GEORGE, *Industrial Organization*. Allen and Unwin. 1971.

Input–Output Tables for the United Kingdom. H.M.S.O.

N. KALDOR, *Causes of the Slow Rate of Economic Growth of the United Kingdom*. C.U.P. 1966.

M. PANIĆ, 'Capital utilisation in the manufacturing industry'. *N.W.B.Q.R.* Feb. 1972.

M. PANIĆ and R. E. CLOSE, 'Profitability of British Manufacturing Industry.' *L.B.R.* July 1973.

C. F. PRATTEN, *Economies of Scale in Manufacturing Industry.* C.U.P. 1971 (ch. 35).

E. A. G. ROBINSON, 'The changing structure of the British economy'. *E.J.* Sept. 1954.

W. E. G. SALTER, *Productivity and Technical Change,* 2nd edn. C.U.P. 1966.

TREASURY, 'Changing patterns of employment'. *E.P.R.* 41, July 1973; 42, Aug. 1973.

World Economic Survey, 1961, U.N. Publication: 62.II. C.I. U.N. Dept. of Economic and Social Affairs.

4. Past Examination Questions

1. Outline and explain the main changes in the relative importance of the major British industries in this century. (Summer 1962)
2. 'The troubles of Britain's declining industries are not due to their own inefficiency, but to the development of new industries in Britain.' Discuss. (Summer 1961)
3. 'A falling proportion of the labour force employed in agriculture is usually associated with a rising standard of living.' Discuss. (Summer 1959)
4. What is the effect of scientific advance on the structure of industry? (Summer 1961)
5. Can the relatively high rate of unemployment in the north of the United Kingdom be cured by a general increase in effective demand? Give reasons for your opinion. (Summer 1964)
6. Outline the broad changes in the composition of United Kingdom exports over the last fifty years. What is the relationship between these changes and those in the industrial structure of the United Kingdom over the same period? (January 1965)
7 Explain why the chemical industry of the United Kingdom has expanded more quickly in recent years than the textile industry. (Summer 1961)

4. Concentration of Control and Public Policy Stage II*

1. Introduction

In Chapter 2, Stage II.11 evidence of the extent of monopolistic concentration of control in industry was examined. The unit of concentrated control was taken as the small group of independent single firms or combines (where single firms had controlling interests in subsidiaries). It was pointed out, however, that the unit of concentrated control, the monopolistic grouping, could be much wider in scope. It may consist of firms voluntarily combined in varying forms of association, or of firms with varying degrees of influence and formal control in other firms.

This chapter touches on the various types of formal combination and voluntary association, which constitute the wider units of concentrated control, and examines some of the problems of such monopolistic power and public policy towards them.

Voluntary associations may be established merely to propound the opinions of a particular trade; they may also aim, however, at the control of price, quality or innovations, and may lead up to quite extensive collusion, such as exists in various types of formal combination.

The degree to which monopolistic power may be established is influenced by the following factors:

(a) the importance of the product to the consumer and/or the firms involved;
(b) the fewness of firms in the particular trade; which depends upon such factors as capital requirements and conditions of entry;
(c) the control of raw materials, patents, tariff protection and the desire for security.

The advantages of monopolistic power are mainly in the direction of potential economies of scale and/or of vertical integration: the dangers lie principally in the direction of potential exploitation of consumers and labour, the smothering of innovations and the social and political consequences of powerful vested interests, and are more likely to flow from lateral integration, where this occurs in the quest for power or control.[1]

* There is no Stage I to this chapter.
[1] One recent study has suggested that the growth in concentration may result in about three-quarters of private sector industry being controlled by about 21 giant national companies by the end of the 1970s: each would dominate a major sector of the economy. The trend, it has been suggested, is quite marked and is underlined by recent merger experience and by certain characteristics of managerial behaviour and motivation, viz. to escape the competitive discipline of free market forces and to pursue a 'growth ethos'. Important implications would follow with regard to pricing policies, market power and investment policy. (See G. Newbould and A. S. Jackson, *The Receding Ideal*, 1972.)

An important manifestation of the concentration of control in recent years, which has generated a great deal of controversial debate, is the growth of *multinational companies*. These may be defined as enterprises which, through direct private investment, own or control production (of services or goods) facilities in more than one country. The basic economic justification for their establishment is the profitable manipulation of particular resources, markets and products: they arise as a response to specific economic advantages of economic integration on an international scale, shifting factors of production across national frontiers, in order to overcome some of the elements of imperfect competition existing in world trade – *viz.* differences in the prices of goods and factors; hindrances to the free movement of capital, goods and services; and product differentiation. Some of the potential disadvantages or dangers of such companies are the inefficient control of resources by those which have outgrown their optimum size; the tendency of some to become inflexible and bureaucratised or institutionalised; the possibility of excessive control over the economies of primarily recipient countries (especially developing countries); the possibility that these companies may not react in accordance with the wishes of the host country to its economic policies, and may avoid constraints on their conduct by intra-group transfers, pricing strategies, and other manipulations. Multinational company activities are of three basic types:

(*a*) 'backward vertical', cost-orientated activities, to obtain cheaper, more reliable sources of materials or intermediate products;

(*b*) 'forward vertical', market-orientated activities, as an extension of the company's sales function;

(*c*) 'horizontal' activities, either non-integrated, duplicated production in the various countries or integrated production, whereby each subsidiary undertakes a particular process or range of components or where each produces a different range of finished products: in both cases the subsidiaries trade with each other.[1]

On the basis of U.S. experience, it appears that of the 187 major American multinationals (i.e. all amongst the 500 largest U.S. firms and each with subsidiaries in six or more countries) the ones with activities of types (*a*) and (*b*) above – primarily seeking markets or raw materials – had the lowest profitability and growth achievements by 1966: they also tended to be less reliant on heavy advertising and skilled manpower (as with textiles and iron and steel) than the more successful ones, such as motors, drugs, petroleum refining, chemicals and electrical equipment.[2] By the 1970s three-quarters of the growth in sales and production of multinationals over the preceding twenty years had been accounted for by American- and British-owned and controlled firms, but Continental European and Japanese multinationals were experiencing faster growth rates. Of about 300 multinationals in 1972, 187 were American (controlling 2,000 of the 2,500 foreign subsidiaries of the 500 largest U.S. firms), about 30 were British and Dutch, about 30 belonged to other European countries and about 50 were multinational banks and insurance groups. The largest, General Motors, had

---

[1] For further data see N. Macrae 'The future of international business', special survey in *Econ.*, 22 Jan. 1972; J. H. Dunning, 'The multinational enterprise', *L.B.R.*, July 1970; 'Multi-national companies', *B.B.R.*, Aug. 1971; M. Zinkin, 'Multi-national companies', *M. and W.S.R.*, Autumn 1968; T. E. Chester, 'Large organizations – their role in the U.K. economy' *N.W.B.Q.R.*, Aug. 1971; R. Bailey, 'International corporations and developing countries' *N.W.B.Q.R.* Aug. 1970; 'Corporate families and their problem children' *D.T.* 18 Jan. 1972.

[2] Macrae *loc. cit.* p. xxiv.

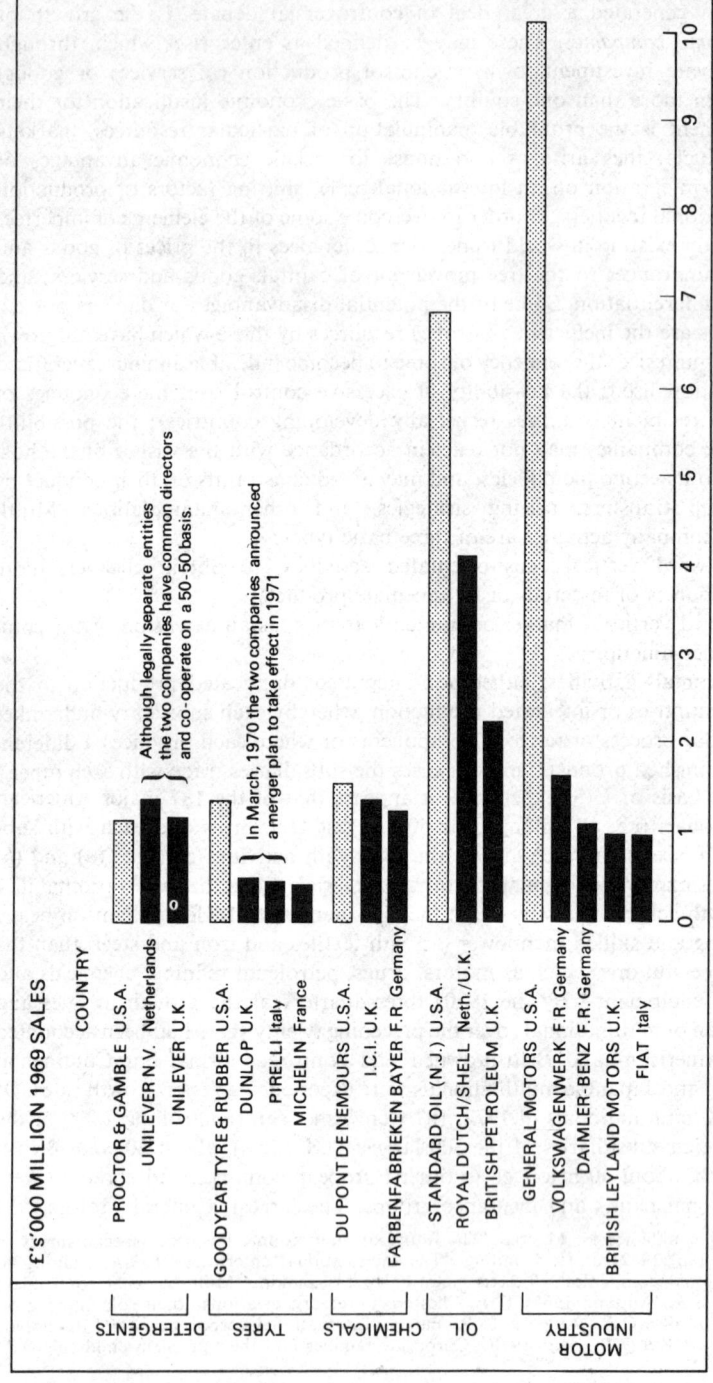

Fig. 4.1. *Multinational companies in selected industries; some major U.S. and other competitors*
(Source: *B.B.R.*, Aug. 1971, p. 51)

annual sales of more than $25 billion, exceeding the net national incomes of all except about twelve countries. The annual sales and output of the foreign subsidiaries of the 300 multinationals, estimated at about $300 billion, exceeded the gross national product (G.N.P.) of all countries except the U.S. and the U.S.S.R.: nearly two-thirds of this was accounted for by American firms, who controlled about 55% of the total assets of the 300 multinationals (the U.K. controlled about 20%), and the value of sales of these U.S.-controlled foreign subsidiaries had risen to about five times that of total U.S. visible exports. The growth in foreign output of the multinationals since the 1950s had been about 10% per annum – twice the growth rate in world GNP and 40% faster than the growth in world exports.[1] Fig. 4.1 gives some examples.

It seems to be a fairly general assumption that the recent growth rates of the multinationals, especially in the technologically advanced, knowledge-creating and knowledge-processing, faster-growing industries must lead, by the turn of the century, to the control of over half the world's total output by the 200 or 300 largest multinationals: this process is visualised as beginning with national mergers, then regional groupings and finally supranational enterprises.[2] Nevertheless, one interesting study has concluded that the trends in technology and communications are such that many of the largest multinationals which do not split up into component parts may face financial failure, like obsolescent economic dinosaurs: the prototype of the future would be fairly small, wholly 'transnational' companies of a new type, which specialise on the international coordination of specialist services, product development and design, marketing, etc., by way of local organising subcontractors. Some support for this view may be derived from a study of the 500 largest U.K. firms in 1970/71 – which found no strong evidence that large organisations were intrinsically more or less efficient than small ones – and from a study of the 500 largest industrial firms in the capitalist world between 1957 and 1967 – which found that the American, like the British firms, grew more slowly than Continental firms in seven out of eight industries, and that whereas the U.S. multinationals had an average sales revenue of about $1 billion, it was the smaller U.S. firms, with turnover between $150 million and $500 million, which grew fastest.[3]

The main types of combination and association may best be classified by the length of the period of association: some are temporary, some transitional and some permanent.

2. Forms of Combination and Association
(a) **Local and national trade associations**
1. Non-price-fixing type
    (i) Pressure groups
    (ii) Product associations
2. Price-fixing type
    (i) Manufacturing associations
    (ii) Resale Price Maintenance agreements

TEMPORARY

---

[1] *Ibid.*, p. xxi and Dunning, *loc. cit.*, p. 21.
[2] 'Multi-national companies', *B.B.R.*, Aug. 1971; Dunning, *loc. cit.*, Macrae, *loc. cit.*, and Chester, *loc. cit.*, p. 24. For a discussion of the problems of the 'host' country in benefiting from multi-national technology, see also J. H. Dunning and M. Steuer, 'The effects of United States direct investment in Britain on British technology', *M. and W.S.R.*, Autumn 1969·
[3] See Macrae, *loc. cit.*, pp. viii, xxi and xiii; Chester, *loc. cit.*, pp. 32–35; R. Rowthorn and S. Hymer, *International Big Business 1957–1967*, 1971, pp. 84–5.

3. More fully coordinated trade associations – national cartels ⎤

(b) **International cartels** ⎬ TRANSITIONAL
1. Primary products
2. Manufacturing ⎦

(c) **Combines, trusts or mergers** ⎤
1. Interlocking minority shareholdings and/or interlocking
   directorates ⎬ PERMANENT
2. Holding companies
3. Outright mergers ⎦

(a) **Local and national trade associations**

Some of the general activities and devices noticeable in various types of trade association are as follows:

COMMERCIAL: the regulation of trading practices and the provision of common services.
1. Price control, *via* 'minimum price schedules', 'information agreements', 'open price registers', 'bid filing', 'price-leadership', etc.
2. 'Fair trading' agreements
3. Market-sharing
4. Joint selling
5. Output control, *via* quotas and compensation for non-production, financed by joint levies
6. Profit-pooling
7. Joint purchases of raw materials, etc.
8. Exclusive agencies
9. Loyalty rebates
10. 'Basing-point' systems, for standardising freight charges
11. 'Credit-rating' bureaux
12. Unified terms of sale
13. Debt-collecting
14. Litigation and arbitration
TECHNICAL: provision of common services
15. Schemes for elimination of redundant capacity
16. Research and statistics
17. Standardisation
18. Patents pools
19. Planning of investment projects
EXTERNAL: representations to the outside world
20. Cooperation with, and representations to Government departments
21. Joint public relations and advertising activity
22. Joint negotiations with trade unions on wages and conditions of work

The framework within which any of these activities is performed ranges from unwritten gentlemen's agreements to overall collusive planning.

Associations for the provision of common services, representations to the outside world, and negotiations with trade unions cover most of British industry.

Associations which deal with the regulation of trading practices do not cover the whole of British industry, but they have expanded greatly in number and scope during this century. They generally tend to cover particular products or processes. Many firms which deal with a wide range of products or processes belong to several trade associations. However, membership of trade associations does not necessarily cover all the products and processes of the member firms.

The number of trade associations providing common services and regulating trading practices is not known precisely, but Hilton noted about 500 in Great Britain in 1919. An investigation by Political and Economic Planning (P.E.P.) in 1944 referred to trade associations as the most significant recent development in the modern economic structure. Another P.E.P. survey on industrial trade associations between 1953 and 1956 noted 1,300, which varied greatly in importance, structure and activities. About 240 of them were concerned with the suppression of price competition.[1] By the end of 1960 about 2,340 restrictive trade agreements had been registered under the 1956 Restrictive Trade Practices Act.[2]

Before World War I there were few trade associations in Britain. The main reason for this was probably the prevalence of small firms, operating under highly competitive conditions. Furthermore, the home market was not protected against imports, and the major industries were vitally involved in the competitive export field. Even in retail distribution competition was still strong. Despite the gradual establishment of resale price maintenance by manufacturers, there was little direct selling from producer to retailer, and improvements in communications tended to intensify competition by disseminating knowledge of the market.

After World War I trade association activity increased, largely due to the decline in the relative importance of export markets and the increasing importance of the home market. Many manufacturers developed their own sales organisations, thus weakening the functions of the wholesaler. Moreover, the difficult conditions of the depression years stimulated combined action and a favourable public opinion towards protectionism. This process was furthered by the abandonment of a free trade policy after 1931. Further, there was a general trend to increasing size in plants and firms, due to technological and other economies, which increased the degree of concentration of control and resulted in an increase of market imperfection. Lastly, the experience of the war itself had shown the Government that it was sometimes convenient to deal with industries which 'spoke with one voice' through representative organisations.

Parallel to the growth in the number of trade associations there was an extension of their coverage of firms in particular trades. Also, there was an increase in the range of activities and functions performed by trade associations. There were also many vertical amalgamations of trade associations (such as between distributors and manufacturers),[3] and lateral amalgamations of particular product associations.

Despite the fact that technological and market conditions have gradually favoured oligopolistic trade association collusion, and despite the evolution of

---

[1] *Industrial Trade Associations: activities and organisation*, P.E.P., 1957.
[2] *Brit. O. H.*, 1962, p. 274.
[3] e.g. **Society of Motor Manufacturers and Traders.**

stronger forms of such collusion, it must not be assumed that all trade associations are collusive and against the public interest. Many are primarily pressure groups, and/or provide common services, and/or deal with labour matters.

1. NON-PRICE-FIXING TYPE

(i) Pressure groups

There are about 1,500 regional and local employers' organisations and about seventy-five national federations in the United Kingdom, dealing with labour negotiations on wages and conditions of work. Most of the national federations, until 1964, were affiliated to the British Employers' Confederation (B.E.C.), which represented employers on labour questions which affected industry generally. About 8,500 individual firms and 280 national trade associations (covering 40–45,000 firms) were members of the Federation of British Industries (F.B.I.). This was the national body which represented British industry on economic, commercial and industrial questions, but not on labour matters. It had several regional branches in the main industrial cities. Some organisations affiliated to the F.B.I. which dealt with labour questions were also affiliated to the B.E.C. Both the B.E.C. and the F.B.I. cooperated on questions of common interest.

About sixty-six trade associations, and over 5,000 manufacturing firms (mainly small and medium in size) constituted the National Association of British Manufacturers (N.A.B.M.). It also had regional branches.

In 1964 the B.E.C., F.B.I. and N.A.B.M. decided to merge into a unified national body, the Confederation of British Industry.[1] The C.B.I. was formed on 14 September 1965. By 1971 the C.B.I. membership consisted of about 11,500 firms and about 200 manufacturers' trade associations and employers' federations, with twelve nationalised public corporations, which are industrial associates. It is the central body representing British industry nationally and internationally (as, for example, on the Council of European Industrial Federations). Its representatives also sit on a number of Government advisory committees, on other statutory bodies and on voluntary bodies concerned with issues affecting industry. Two major developments in recent years have forced the C.B.I. to re-examine its role. One has been the abolition of Resale Price Maintenance (RPM) in 1964 and the 1956 Restrictive Trade Practices Act, which generally outlawed the coordinating of price-fixing arrangements: these developments have tended to eliminate one of the basic objectives of many trade associations. The other has been the development of productivity bargaining at plant level, which has been undermining the role of employers' organisations in national wage agreements. The C.B.I. was urged by the Report of the Royal Commission on Trade Unions and Employers' Associations (Donovan Report) in 1968 to foster an orderly and efficient system of industrial relations. Accordingly, in 1969 the C.B.I. decided to aim at a more rational coordination of the numerous employers' organisations and manufacturers' trade associations: many of these were seen to have outlived their original objectives and were not geared to the provision of sophisticated services, and increasing Government intervention in industry was deemed to require more effective representation by

[1] *D.T.*, 16 July 1964; 'A single voice for industry', *Stat.*, 12 Feb. 1965, p. 453; 'Trade associations,' *ibid.*, 19 March 1965, p. 793.

industry. In 1970 the C.B.I. Director-General announced the intention of making the C.B.I. a policy-making body – an initiator rather than a passive reactor to events. Later that year it was decided that the formal talks which had been conducted between the C.B.I. and the T.U.C. should be translated into a regular 'dialogue', with closer informal contact at official level. Recent manifestations of this more active role have been the C.B.I. injunction in 1971 to 500 leading firms to adopt a 5% ceiling on price rises and the C.B.I.'s early support for British entry into the E.E.C. On occasion, some manifestations of its active role have aroused accusations that it has been becoming 'elitist' in tone.[1]

Ninety-three local chambers of commerce and seventeen overseas British chambers of commerce are affiliated to the Association of British Chambers of Commerce.[2] In Scotland there is a parallel central organisation, the Council of Scottish Chambers of Commerce. They are open to producers and traders, and function to promote local trade and industrial interests. The C.B.I. and the Chambers of Commerce often cooperate on matters of joint concern.

The basic aims of these 'pressure group' type trade associations are:

(a) the general promotion of local and national trade interests;
(b) the collection and dissemination of statistics and the provision of general informative services;
(c) the promotion and support of favourable local and national legislation.

(ii) *Product associations*

These are trade associations of producers only, which are neither pressure groups nor price-fixing. Their basic functions are:

(a) The collection and distribution of statistics;
(b) 'Price-filing' – the establishment of open price registers, whereby members may see what prices competitors charge;
(c) Uniform methods of accounting, whereby common formulae may be established for such matters as overheads: this helps small firms to avoid mistakes in judgment;
(d) Standardisation programmes, whereby the members may agree on common policy with regard to qualities, varieties, etc.: this helps to eliminate wasteful variations of the product and permits a greater scale of production and lower costs for each member firm.

This type of trade association is quite common in the U.S.A., where anti-monopoly legislation is much stricter than in Britain, and often serves as a substitute or cover for more formal types of collusion. In Britain, where actual collusion is easier, this type of association usually consists of small firms, in conditions where the possibilities of collusion are limited and where the main aim is to benefit from the association's services.

2. PRICE-FIXING TYPE

(i) *Manufacturing associations*

These are trade associations of producers in which there is informal collusion in the short period with regard to a particular product. They are temporary

[1] See *Brit. O.H.*, 1971, p. 242; *D.T.*, 14 June 1968, 4 Jan. 1969 and 27 May 1970; *Econ.*, 19 July 1969, p. 59; *F.T.*, 16 Oct. 1969, 6 Feb. 1970 and 5 Nov. 1971.
[2] For details of the largest, the London Chamber of Commerce, with its 70 specialist sections, see 'The London Chamber of Commerce', special survey, *F.T.*, 11 May 1970.

oligopolies, usually dominated by a large producer, who acts as price leader. Sometimes the price leader has other and more important commitments in other product fields. The *ad hoc* association may be more important to the smaller members, but may simply be convenient for the price leader. He may resist full collusion in order to maintain freedom of action, for example, in case the interests of the product in question clash with his other activities. An example of this type of trade association is the Electrical Light Fittings Association. This organisation replaced the more fully collusive Electric Lamp Manufacturers Association (E.L.F.A.), which was disbanded in 1958, after being reported on in 1951 by the Monopolies Commission and because of the provisions of the Restrictive Trade Practices Act of 1956. The members evaded the Restrictive Practices Court by means of an 'information agreement', whereby they informed each other of price changes envisaged. This was the case in February 1963, when the price leader (A.E.I. Lamp and Lighting) started a price increase of 5% to 10%, which was instantly followed by the other members. Officially, price changes were stated to be the result of 'independent and spontaneous' decisions by each firm.

By 1968 Thorn Electrical, once an aggressive outsider, had merged with A.E.I. to form British Lighting Industries, which had over one-third of the market: with the other members of E.L.F.A. it controlled 97% of the lamp market, and in consequence was subjected to a second Monopolies Commission investigation. The Report, in 1968, found that although the group's activities were only a shadow of those of the pre-1951 cartel, price competition was still weakened. B.L.I. and G.E.C. were able to obtain components at lower prices than their competitors; all manufacturers sold basically the same range; consultation and the exchange of technical information still took place; recommended prices still applied; different firms gave almost identical discounts, as a result of price and discount consultations. Consequently, despite the absence of formal discussion, the general effect was 'to eliminate any uncertainty a manufacturer might have about what his competitors are doing'. E.L.F.A. denied the Commission's claim that recommended prices were against the public interest and that prices would fall if the practice were forbidden, and rejected the suggestion that they should sell long-life bulbs to the public (such as those sold to the N.C.B. since 1962). In fact, it was one of the smaller lamp producers, Crompton Parkinson, which broke out and released long-life bulbs to the public.[1]

Since the outlawing of information agreements by the 1968 Restrictive Trade Practices Act, this type of collusive action – long-established in the U.S. as 'open price' agreements or registers, and expanded greatly in the U.K. as a means of by-passing the 1956 ban on price-fixing agreements – has tended to fall into disuse. In its place, however, two other forms of price-fixing collusion expanded. These were 'price-rigging' or collusive tendering (known in the U.S. as 'bid filing') and price-leadership. In 1969 the Registrar of Restrictive Trading Agreements called for an investigation into price-rigging, claiming that they tended to eliminate competition – the main objective of putting work out to tender – by means of a group of companies' effectively sharing the market, by agreeing which would submit the lowest tender. The principal offenders were the electrical and building contractors and the main victims were local authorities and nationalised industries.[2]

---

[1] *Econ.*, 9 Feb. 1963, p. 528 and 7 Dec. 1968, p. 69, 'Lamps: still misbehaving'; *D.T.*, 6 Dec. 1968 and 20 Jan. 1969; *S.T.*, 8 Dec. 1968.
[2] *D.T.*, 12 Jan. 1969.

In 1970 the Electrical Contractors' Association, fearing legislation to outlaw collusive tendering as a restrictive trading agreement, asked its 2,600 members to sign individual declarations that they would not engage in price-rigging and that in future their tenders would be genuine.[1] With regard to price-leadership, two cases are in the cigarette and tyre industries. In October 1970 Imperial Tobacco raised most of its cigarette prices by 1d for 20. This firm had about 67·5% of the market and in the past the other main producers had tended to follow Imperial's lead: they were expected to do so on this occasion and the retailers generally complied.[2] In the case of tyres, Dunlop announced in May 1970 that it would raise most of its tyre prices by $7\frac{1}{2}\%$ and it was expected that all the major U.K. producers would follow its lead. The National Tyre Distributors' Association claimed that some of these increases would be automatically passed on to the consumer. In 1972, however, it was Michelin which led the move towards higher prices, in January. Dunlop, at the time, stated that no increase was necessary, but in March Goodyear and Firestone followed the Michelin lead: Avon was undecided as to which group to follow.[3] Some U.S. examples of price-rigging and price-leadership have been the 1960 General Electric and Westinghouse conspiracy case, when seven senior executives were sent to prison, the 1964 tobacco price-leadership case, and the 1920 U.S. Steel price-leadership case.[4]

Often such trade associations aim at maintaining prices in times of depression, by restricting output, and at retarding the innovation of cheaper substitutes, so as to run down capital sunk in the product. This may slow down the expansion of the market, but permits the price leader to develop comfortably and enables the smaller members to keep afloat. Frequently, the retardation of innovations has the effect of 'buying time' for the price leader, who wishes to amortise his capital investment.

Perhaps an important reason for the relatively high level of productivity in American industry may be the legal obstacles to achieving such collusive restrictions on innovation.

(ii) Resale Price Maintenance agreements

Resale price maintenance (RPM) is a vertical price-fixing device, a specification by the manufacturer of what the retail or wholesale price of the product should be. Before the Restrictive Trade Practices Act of 1956 there used to be collusive enforcement of RPM by trade associations of manufacturers and distributors, with the use of 'black lists' and arbitration courts.[5] RPM was most important and effective with goods which are advertised and/or branded.

Advantages to distributors

(a) Prices tend to be higher than they would otherwise be, with specified profit margins.

---

[1] *Ibid.*, 27 Oct. 1970.
[2] *F.T.*, 26 Oct. 1970.
[3] *F.T.*, 2 May 1970 and 1 March 1972.
[4] G. Owen, *Industry in the U.S.A.*, 1966, pp. 39–40; A. Hunter, ed., *Monopoly and Competition*, 1969, pp. 259–73.
[5] See B. S. Yamey, 'The origins of resale price maintenance: a study of three branches of retail trade', *E.J.*, Sep. 1952, pp. 522–45; B. S. Yamey, ed., *Resale Price Maintenance*, 1966, chs 1 and 8; K. D. George, *Industrial Organization*, pp. 169–73.

(b) Competition and 'loss-leaders'[1] are avoided.

(c) The small distributor is able to hold a share of the market, as the large dealer is unable to sell the produce more cheaply.

(d) As most RPM goods are prepacked and preweighed, less labour, skill and knowledge are required to sell them.

Advantages to the consumer

(a) Constant qualities, consistently packed, can always be expected of particular brands, wherever the customer purchases the product.

(b) The customer knows in advance the price he is expected to pay.

Advantages to the producer

(a) Where there are substitutes, RPM helps to persuade dealers to stock the product, because they are guaranteed a profit margin.

(b) Where there are substitutes, RPM prevents the dealer from raising the price and thus causing the consumer to turn to substitutes.

(c) The manufacturer can use RPM to create confidence in the quality and the stability of the price of the product. For example, if costs rise, he can maintain the price and reduce the profit margins of his dealers, or, as in the case of chocolate bars, reduce the content.

(d) Though the manufacturer would sell more to a dealer who reduced his price, he might sell less to other, less efficient, dealers whose sales fell. On balance, total demand might fall and continuity and dispersion of demand might suffer.

Disadvantages to the distributor

(a) He cannot raise his sales by selling more efficiently at a lower price.

(b) Because of consumers' 'brand loyalty', the dealer must stock a wide range of similar goods, and is prevented from making the maximum possible economies of bulk purchase.

Disadvantages to the consumer

(a) Competitive branding, advertising and RPM may eventually result in higher prices.

(b) Economies made by efficient dealers cannot be passed on to the consumer.

The Lloyd Jacob Committee on Resale Price Maintenance reported in 1949.[2] It noted that in 1938 RPM specifications covered about 30% of goods purchased by consumers. It recommended that individual producers should be able to enforce RPM specifications on their own goods; it found the domestic tribunals, set up by trade associations to enforce RPM by collusive action, to be undemocratic, and recommended steps to render them illegal.

In 1956 the Restrictive Trade Practices Act prohibited collusive RPM enforcement, but gave the individual manufacturer the right to take legal action against price-cutting by dealers.

In July 1964 the Resale Prices Act was passed. This held that RPM clauses were against the public interest and illegal, subject to certain exemptions, which

---

[1] 'Loss-leaders' are articles sold at prices cut drastically below the established retail price, frequently as a form of advertisement for the dealer.

[2] Report of the Committee on Resale Price Maintenance, 1949.

would be considered by the Restrictive Practices Court. In that year it has been estimated that about 25% to 38% of consumer expenditure on goods were affected by RPM. By 1971 nearly 500 classes of goods had been refused exemption by the court and only one (books and maps) had gained exemption under a court order. Although the long run effects are not certain, B. S. Yamey found that short run price reductions of between 10% and 20% had been common by 1966, and Canadian experience of RPM abolition in 1951 supported the view that abolition had promoted the public interest, in terms of the behaviour of retail and wholesale margins.[1] A survey by *The Economist* in 1969 found that the abolition of RPM had removed a major obstacle to structural and behavioural change in retailing, in line with changing circumstances: it was not a simple cure for all ills, however, and could only provide the conditions for price-cutting to aggressive retailers, who actually wanted price competition.[2] In fact, manufacturers evolved numerous practices to circumvent the law, the most common one being 'recommended prices'. In February 1969, after an inquiry lasting twenty months, the Monopolies Commission reported on the practice of recommended prices. It came down against an outright ban, but recommended enabling legislation, giving the Government the power to investigate particular instances and to prohibit them if found to be against the public interest.[3] In 1969 the M.C. was looking into an associated restrictive practice, *viz.* 'withholding (or refusal) of supplies'.[4]

3. MORE FULLY COORDINATED TRADE ASSOCIATIONS – NATIONAL CARTELS

These are associations which involve a higher degree of collusion in the handling of many aspects of their members' activities, including the pooling of advertising efforts; the pooling of technical knowledge; agreements on investment projects; and many of the activities of the less collusive associations. This type of combination is transitional, being more permanent than the above mentioned *ad hoc* forms, but, because they are voluntary, they cannot be considered to be permanent.

Often this type of association takes the form of a federation of several individual product associations, and the degree of collusion ranges up to that of the national cartel. The essence of a cartel is the establishment of a central selling syndicate or of a central body to organise marketing. Market sharing, controlled minimum prices and output quotas are some of the activities sometimes undertaken.

The *general conditions* which foster this type of coordination are as follows:

(*a*) The products concerned are often sold by quotation to industrial users; therefore control over prices, output and capacity is more fruitful than efforts to control the selling channels.

(*b*) The members of the industry think that demand for the product is inelastic, and therefore that price competition would be wasteful.

---

[1] *Econ.*, 29 Feb. 1964; *Brit. O.H.*, 1971, p. 240; R. E. Caves, ed., *Britain's Economic Prospects*, p. 310; Yamey, *Resale Price Maintenance*, pp. 276, 294 and 61; and L. A. Skeoch, 'The abolition of resale price maintenance: some notes on Canadian experience', *Economica*, Aug. 1964.
[2] 'RPM—four years later', *Econ.*, 29 March 1969, pp. 56–7.
[3] *Econ.*, 20 May 1967, p. 827; 'Plugging the loopholes of RPM', *Econ.*, 1 March 1969, pp. 71–2; *F.T.*, 26 Feb. 1969.
[4] *Econ.*, 8 Feb. 1969, p. 112.

(c) Entry into the industry must be difficult, and therefore the possibility of more efficient competitors coming in remote.

(d) Firms involved will usually have a large proportion of their capital locked up in the product or process, with few alternative uses for it.

(e) Most firms in the industry must be prepared to cooperate rather than compete.

The *main motives* for forming such cartel type trade associations are:

(a) To strengthen the position of individual product associations, which may not cover the entire trade.

(b) Fear of excess capacity and ruthless price war, especially when demand is inelastic or low and falling.

(c) To provide a shield of respectability for the small number of dominant firms in the industry and a shield of security for the weaker producers.

(d) The desire to 'speak with one voice' to the Government and to similar industries abroad, on matters affecting the industry.

(e) To perform certain services to the industry on a large scale.

(f) To strengthen the position of producers in conditions where strong bargaining power is present in labour and other factor markets, and/or amongst a few strong purchasers.

Such highly organised associations increased in number and importance during the interwar period, under conditions of falling demand, excess capacity, increased competition in home and export markets, etc. Often such developments received official support and included rationalisation schemes to restrict capacity – as in coal, iron and steel, transport, shipbuilding, shipping, linoleum, agriculture and textiles.

Examples of this type of association are to be found in voluntary agricultural marketing cooperatives, the agricultural marketing boards, the chemicals industry, the cement industry, non-ferrous metals, and, though under public ownership, the nationalised industries. Some interesting recent developments in national cartels have occurred in Japan. The Japanese Fair Trade Commission (F.T.C.) found in 1971 that the Nippon Steel Corporation – the world's second largest steel firm, created in April 1970 by a merger of two large producers – had been governing output reductions and market shares in the industry by way of cartel arrangements, in an effort to limit the fall in prices resulting from demand deficiency and excess capacity. Hitherto, many firms had responded to falling prices by expanding output: the F.T.C. found that the cartel had been successful in halting the deterioration in prices, despite a slowdown in the national economy.[1] In late 1971, following general demand deficiency, stimulated by the U.S. devaluation and foreign trade restrictions, many key Japanese industries sought the permission of the F.T.C. and the Ministry of International Trade and Industry for the creation of 'anti-slump' or 'recession' cartels for a limited period, involving the coordination of production cutbacks where there was excess capacity. They included the steel, paper and pulp, textiles, chemicals and petrochemicals industries.[2]

Generally, a division of functions occurs where the association is federal in form. The individual product associations deal with such matters as the main-

[1] *F.T.*, 11 Feb. 1971.
[2] *Ibid.*, 4 and 11 Nov. 1971.

tenance of prices, 'loyalty rebates' to customers, production quotas, market sharing, standardisation schemes, etc. The federation itself provides common services to the member groups, as in the form of 'official representation at home and abroad'; provision of statistics; joint purchasing and selling agencies abroad; coordination of the price policies of individual product associations; promotion of joint research; provision of information and interpretation of tariff and other legislation; a forum for the coordination of investment policies.

The significance of these collusive organisations may be evaluated in the light of three criteria – efficiency, prices and investment. With regard to general efficiency, the association may help to reduce wasteful competition and may achieve economies in bulk purchase, coordinated production and joint selling. In fixing prices, it is usual for the high-cost producer to be covered. This tends to give the low-cost producer an 'efficiency rent' or bonus, and to foster the continued existence of the least efficient firms. Firms outside the association tend to follow the price leadership of the association, but when demand is low they may break away and engage in price cutting. Indeed, a constant danger is the incentive to the efficient member of the association to break the rules and 'go it alone'. An example of this occurred in late 1967 when the Egg Marketing Board (later disbanded, in March 1971) attempted to bolster its weakening grip on the egg market. Hitherto farmers had been entitled to sell direct to shops, subject to paying the Board a levy of $\frac{1}{2}d$ per dozen: however, in response to retail demand, many farmers had been selling unstamped eggs without a licence and the Board was unable to police the system. The Board sought either to force farmers to restrict private sales to the farm gate – all other eggs going through the Board's packing stations – or to achieve control of imports, a levy on laying fowls, stronger policing action and the abolition of packing station stamping of eggs (with the 'lion' brand), so that the Board could compete in the 'fresh' unstamped egg market.[1] The pooling of contracts and coordinated production might result in cost savings, but these are not always passed on to the consumer. With regard to investment, the over-valuation of existing equipment and the possibilities of retarding innovation would be against the public interest. On the other hand, the pooling of patents could lead to continued improvements in all-round efficiency and reductions of cost.

(b) International cartels

These are voluntary, transitional agreements between independent producers in an industry or closely allied industries, combined in international action for monopolistic control of markets.

There are two distinct types of international agreements and organisations, constituting international cartels. These are agreements on extracted products (agricultural and mineral commodities and raw materials) and agreements on industrial, manufactured goods. The basic conditions underlying both types are inelastic or rigid supply (or demand), uncontrollable shifts in demand (or supply) and a consequent tendency to violent price fluctuations, which result in disjointed growth in national and *per capita* incomes, and disjointed movements in the terms of trade and export earnings, and, also make for difficulties in planning and continuity in investment programmes. Generally, the problems

[1] *D.T.*, 1 Dec. 1967.

with primary products are more severe than in the case of manufactured goods, since extractive plants (fields, plantations, flocks, herds, quarries, mines, etc.) cannot be closed down or switched off as easily as manufacturing plants, nor can the factors of production be, in general, so easily switched to other activities. Furthermore, many primary producing countries have only a narrow range of extractive industries, which must continue to produce, despite adverse market conditions.

In the case of primary products, it is important to distinguish between the basic conditions in tropical and temperate zone food production and those in industrial raw materials or intermediate products. With tropical foodstuffs such as tea, coffee, cocoa and bananas the general problem is one of inelastic or fairly rigid demand (linked to the size of populations, standards of nutrition, etc.), while on the supply side, apart from relative inelasticity in capacity or planned production, the major feature is susceptibility to severe fluctuations in effective or realised supply, which is affected by weather, floods, fire, blight, etc.

In the case of temperate zone foodstuffs and agricultural raw materials such as sugar, wheat, rice, vegetable oils, tobacco and cotton an additional complication is that they are produced not only by developing countries but also by some industrialised countries, which may adopt protectionist policies against imports.[1] With raw materials the general problem is one of inelastic supply, whereas demand, being derived from the ultimate demand for finished goods, is dependent on the general level of activity in the consuming countries: when this falls (or rises) stocks are run down (or built up) and demand may fluctuate severely. In addition, there is the problem that the industrialised consuming countries may increasingly turn to the production of substitute raw materials such as plastics, synthetic rubber and man-made fibres, for reasons of self-sufficiency, and may adopt protectionist policies.

1. PRIMARY PRODUCTS[2]

Some of the problems which fostered cartel type agreements in primary products in both the interwar and postwar periods have been chronic excess capacity in the producing countries; reliance, especially in the underdeveloped countries, on the export to industrialised customers of a narrow range of primary products, whereby factors of production have few alternative applications; the tendency for industrialised customers to aim at self-sufficiency, either by producing the same primary products (as in the case of British and European temperate foodstuffs) or by producing substitutes (as in the case of beet sugar, synthetic rubber, plastics, man-made fibres, etc.).

The trade depression in the interwar period resulted in the developed nations aiming at self-sufficiency and in their contracting imports from the primary producers. The latter, with inelastic supply conditions, were faced with the prospect of falling prices. These factors stimulated numerous cartel agreements, by which efforts were made to stabilise prices by output restrictions, restrictions on capacity, and sales quotas. To stand a chance of success, a commodity

---

[1] For a good survey of these problems see 'UNCTAD 3: Confrontation over commodities', *F.T.*, 11 April 1972.
[2] See J. E. Meade, 'International commodity agreements', *L.B.R.* July 1964; *World conference on development*, *B.B.L.A.*, Apr. 1964; 'Towards a world cereal agreement', *Stat.*, 14 May 1965, p. 1344.

agreement should be for a product in which trade is relatively simple, in which the number of suppliers is small, and for which close substitutes do not exist. These agreements were most effective for commodities produced by a small group of countries, to whom the primary product was an economic mainstay. Examples of these were tin, tea, rubber and diamonds. Where a greater number of countries were involved, or where outsiders were able to break in (perhaps with more efficient methods, as with Rhodesian copper), the efficacy of these agreements was weakened. Under the stress of the depression of the 1930s, many of these agreements broke down because they did not possess enough cohesion to keep members from competing against each other. Agreements were produced for wheat and sugar, but did not pass the discussion stage for cotton, cocoa and coffee.[1] Such agreements may succeed in stabilising prices temporarily, but do not solve the problem of excess capacity. In many countries Government intervention was necessary to preserve the cartels, either in order to stipulate maximum acreages or to conclude official international agreements.

After World War II the United Nations charter made provisions for an International Trade Organisation (I.T.O.). The charter for the I.T.O. has never been ratified, but some of its provisions have been tried out in practice.

The I.T.O. charter aimed at establishing intergovernmental commodity agreements for primary commodities, in an effort to supervise trade in these products and to achieve price stability. Some of the objectives considered were the expansion of consumption by industrial countries; improvements in mobility of factors of production in the primary producing countries; the creation of long-term contracts and buffer stocks, to achieve price stability.

Most of the countries which were to have been members have adopted a less comprehensive scheme, the General Agreement on Tariffs and Trade (G.A.T.T.), which aims at a general lowering of tariffs and the increase of international trade. The United Nations Food and Agriculture Organisation (F.A.O.) helps to sponsor international agreements on maximum and minimum prices for certain agricultural products, such as wheat. It also helps producing countries to build up buffer stocks and provides a statistical service. Its general objectives include the expansion of demand and thus the avoidance of overproduction.

The three main methods adopted by the various international agreements on primary products are:[2]

(i) Multilateral contracts, whereby exporters and importers agree on maximum and minimum prices for the coming season: the exporter guarantees to supply a certain amount when prices are at the maximum and importers guarantee to buy a certain amount when prices are at the minimum. This type of scheme was,

---

[1] Sir Sydney Caine, 'Commodity agreements – a new look', *L.B.R.*, Jan. 1963; *Econ.*, 6 Jan. 1962, p. 61.

[2] M. A. G. van Meerhaeghe, *International Economic Institutions*, 1966, ch. 7; 'International commodity arrangements—a story of slow but helpful progress', *M.B.R.*, Aug. 1966; P. T. Bauer and B. S. Yamey, *Markets, Market Control and Marketing Reform*, 1968, chs 6, 7 and 9; H. G. Johnson, *Economic Policies towards Less Developed Countries*, 1967, ch. 5; 'On the see-saw', *Econ.*, 3 Oct. 1970, pp. 65–6; 'World tea quotas for 1971 agreed', *F.T.*, 9 Dec. 1970; 'Cocoa pact negotiations', *F.T.*, 15 March 1972; 'Russian diamonds may soon be sold on open market', *D.T.*, 18 Oct. 1967; 'Harvest of discontent', *Econ.*, 2 Aug. 1969, p. 55; 'World wheat', *F.T.*, 6 Aug. 1969; 'Coffee under control', *Econ.*, 15 Aug. 1970, pp. 50–1; 'World coffee pact agreed', *S.T.*, 9 April 1972; 'A breakthrough—maybe—in sugar', *Econ.*, 2 Nov. 1968, p. 74; 'Soviet Union to join tin agreement', *F.T.*, 4 Feb. 1971; 'Wool marketing', *F.T.*, 29 Feb. 1972; 'Why no-one wants a showdown', *F.T.*, 19 Jan. 1971.

for a time, adopted for wheat, for which demand is fairly stable. After 1962, however, it only survived by dropping the obligation of consuming countries to purchase guaranteed quantities at a minimum price. From 1962 to 1967 the truncated scheme was operated as the International Wheat Agreement, with a fairly low price range, in view of the high level of world stocks. From 1969 a new scheme for wheat was sponsored by the International Wheat Council, under the International Grain Agreement: the price range for this was pitched higher, as it was thought that world shortages were imminent, and the scheme also incorporated a commitment to provide developing countries with food aid of 4·5 million tons of grain annually. In the event, there was no world shortage, and the main exporters were selling below the minimum price – thus eroding the cartel's cohesion. An interesting version of the multilateral contract, suggested by Professor Meade, is the 'price compensation' scheme, whereby a 'normal trade volume' and 'normal trade price' are agreed, and compensation is paid directly, between Governments, for deviations from the normal levels.

(ii) Restriction schemes, whereby production and/or export quotas are fixed. Such schemes apply in the case of diamonds (organised through the De Beers Central Selling Organisation); coal (through the European Coal and Steel Community); sugar (through the International Sugar Agreement; the first ended in 1961, when the U.S. refused to buy Cuban sugar and Cuba refused to accept a quota cut, and was reconstituted in 1968); cocoa (through the Cocoa Study Group and the proposed – in 1972 – International Cocoa Agreement); coffee (through the 1962 and 1972 International Coffee Agreements); tea (under the 1970 F.A.O. consultative committee agreement); rubber (under the auspices of the U.N. Conference on Trade and Development, U.N.C.T.A.D., and the International Study Group); and oil (through the Organisation of Petroleum Exporting Countries, O.P.E.C.).

(iii) Buffer stock schemes, whereby a central body, such as the International Tin Council (on the basis of the International Tin Agreement – the fourth of which came into effect in July 1971) buys at a standard minimum price when market prices are low and sells at a standard maximum price when market prices are high. An interesting modification of this type of scheme was initiated in February 1972 by the wool boards of the main wool producing countries – Australia, New Zealand and South Africa. The amalgamated boards have powers to buy the total dip: yet the traditional auction sales system would still be retained. The payout to the farmer would be at an average level, determined by the auction, in conjunction with a minimum 'floor' price and deficiency payments if the realised auction price were below this.

Restriction schemes and buffer stock schemes appear to be more effective in the case of industrial raw materials, for which demand is much more likely to fluctuate than in the case of foodstuffs.

The drastic fall in the incomes of primary producers in the interwar period, and the realisation that these countries were still vital as suppliers and as markets for industrial goods, motivated the postwar interest in commodity schemes. Since World War II the share of primary producers in world trade has contracted; since the end of the Korean war primary product prices have been falling, whilst the prices of manufactured goods have steadily risen; political emphasis on the problems of aid to underdeveloped countries has recently intensified. Towards the end of 1962 increased attention was given to the idea of establishing a comprehensive system of worldwide commodity agreements. The main forums for discussion were the European Economic Community, G.A.T.T., the United Nations Commission on International Commodity Trade, the F.A.O., the International Monetary Fund, and the National Farmers' Union of Great Britain.[1]

2. MANUFACTURING

The basic conditions leading to international manufacturing cartels differ from those underlying primary product cartels. Primarily, they lie in the fact that excess capacity tends to be temporary, rather than chronic. This is because supply is much more inelastic in primary production than in manufacturing, as the factors of production involved have fewer alternative uses and are generally committed for longer periods. In manufacturing, resources may more easily be switched from one use to another; industrial plant can, if necessary, be closed down; in conditions of rising overall demand in the long term, industrial factors of production are assured of employment. However, because of the heavy capital investment involved in some industries and the structural decline in some of them, international action is often sought to combat slump conditions in the short term. Restriction schemes for the reduction of capacity may be included, if there is a permanent contraction of demand.

During the interwar period the Government in Britain supported the attempts of many national manufacturing cartels to enter into international agreements with similar bodies abroad. Examples of these international manufacturing cartels were to be found in steel, tubes, phosphates, aluminium, petroleum, textiles, shipbuilding and chemicals. The British Government often cooperated, through the Import Duties Advisory Committee (I.D.A.C.), by using the tariff weapon as a protectionist device for British manufacturers and as a lever for obtaining international cooperation from foreign cartels. Import and export quota systems were often agreed upon, in conjunction with a division of neutral markets. General tariff protection, by reducing foreign competition in home markets, tended to foster internal cohesion in the respective national cartels.

International exchanges of patents, by giving cartel members advantages over non-members, also encouraged cartel cohesion nationally and internationally, as in chemicals. It has been estimated that over a quarter of British exports of manufactured and partly manufactured goods were directly affected, prior to World War II, by international cartel agreements in which British firms were involved.[2]

These cartels tended to be more effective instruments of monopolistic control over price than were those in primary products, largely because of their greater control over, and elasticity of, supply. They were thus able to function with less financial support from their respective governments.

The I.T.O. charter, though never ratified after World War II, has publicised general international opinion on international manufacturing cartels. Its aims have been reflected in G.A.T.T. and other national and international legislation. The I.T.O. charter called for the control, by participating governments, of restrictive trading practices by monopolies and cartels. It called for an inter-

---

[1] *Econ.*, 30 June 1962, p. 1359, 24 Nov. 1962, p. 845, 12 Jan. 1963, p. 131, 9 Feb. 1963, p. 536; *D.T.*, 4 Feb. 1963; *The Times*, 29 Nov. 1962; *L.B.R.*, Jan. 1963.
[2] W. A. Lewis, *Monopoly in British Industry*, Fabian Research Series, No. 91.

national body to deal with cartel policy – a sort of international monopolies commission; it aimed at the maximisation of international trade, the removal of barriers to the flow of capital and materials and the prohibition of subsidies to domestic producers. Though the charter did not outlaw such cartels, it would have provided the weapon of publicity. Failing ratification of the charter, the problem of dealing with international manufacturing cartels was left to individual governments, cooperating through G.A.T.T.

In Britain, the Monopolies and Restrictive Practices Commission was established in 1948 to investigate monopolies in British industry, whether voluntary, cartel type associations or permanent combinations. The Restrictive Practices Court, set up in 1956, tries cases of restrictive trade practice brought before it by the Registrar, to whom all restrictive agreement must be notified.

The European Economic Community favours a similar type of policy towards international manufacturing cartels and price-fixing arrangements.[1] In 1969 the Common Market Commission imposed fines totalling £208,000 on ten chemical companies, which included I.C.I., for secret cartel trading in aniline-based dyes, in contravention of E.E.C. competition rules. They were accused of secret price-fixing and market sharing, under Article 85 of the Treaty of Rome, which applies particularly to 'direct or indirect fixing of purchase or selling prices or of any other trading conditions' and to 'market sharing or the sharing of sources of supply'.[2] In April 1972 the West German Federal Cartel Office took a dramatic step, expected to have worldwide repercussions on the international chemical industry, when it imposed fines totalling about £6 million on nine leading West German man-made fibre manufacturers for operating illegal worldwide cartels. They had been accused of price-fixing and market sharing, which included collusion with Japanese competitors on the demarcation of 'spheres of interest'.[3]

One example of such a cartel was the joint American and British price ring in oil marketing in the Far East, disbanded by the United States courts in November, 1960.[4] In the E.E.C. countries, steel is an industrial product subject to cartel arrangements, by means of the European Coal and Steel Community, to which Britain applied to join in 1962. The E.C.S.C. High Authority pools all the coal, steel, iron ore and scrap of the member countries, and can exercise powers over the constituent national industries. During 1970 and 1971 the large steel groups of the E.E.C. and E.F.T.A. were discussing common cartel-type defence action against the threat of Japanese exports to their home markets. There was excess capacity in Europe and one West German company admitted to requesting the Japanese to enter into an export agreement by joining a cartel which was registered with the West German authorities in 1966.[5] Another industrial cartel agreement was that arranged in February 1962 in cotton textiles. A nineteen-nation meeting at Geneva concluded a five-year agreement on the supply of low cost Asian textiles to the unrestricted U.S. market and the restricted European markets.[6] By 1969 there was a thirty-nation cotton textile committee under the auspices of G.A.T.T. When it met in Geneva in October of that year the U.S. resisted proposals to relax some of the restrictions under what had become the

[1] *D.T.*, 13 Nov. 1961. [2] *D.T.*, 28 July 1969 and 29 July 1969.
[3] *F.T.*, 6 April 1972 and 'A nasty case of fibrositis', *Obs.*, 9 April 1972 and 'The world man-made fibre cartel', *Econ.*, 8 April 1972, pp. 66–7.
[4] *D.T.*, 15 Nov. 1960.
[5] *Econ.*, 7 Nov. 1970, p. 74 and 6 March 1971, p. 91.
[6] *D.T.*, 10 Feb. 1962.

Cotton Textile Agreement (C.T.A.). However, it did not revive its previous proposals to extend the export restriction agreements to wool and man-made fibres. By 1970 and 1971, however, the general downturn in textile demand was resulting in cartel arrangements by some E.E.C. chemical firms engaged in man-made fibre production. Falling demand and over-expanded capacity had resulted in 'information exchanges on capacity, output and prices, and the Common Market Commission was requested to register a cartel in fibre production, so as to foster an 'orderly market'.[1] In July 1964 the Volkswagen company in West Germany announced that it had rejected a plan by the Italian firm of Fiat to form an Italian–West German cartel to keep out U.S. and U.K. vehicles and to share out markets.[2] Another industry in which over-capacity led to attempts at cartel-type agreement was the chemical pulp-making industry. In 1967 European excess capacity equalled about 20% of the world output and price-cutting was creating great price instability.[3]

(c) Combines, trusts or mergers

Throughout the western industrialised economies there has been a growing tendency towards concentration of economic control in big combines, trusts or corporations, by means of formal mergers and acquisitions and by internal growth.

In the U.S., out of about 300,000 manufacturing firms, the 100 largest accounted in 1970 for over one-third of value added by the manufacturing sector (compared with 23% in 1945), employed 25% of manufacturing employees and owned about half of all assets used in manufacturing. The 200 largest manufacturing corporations controlled about 60% of all manufacturing assets (compared with less than 50% in 1950).[4] Studies of the merger movement in the U.S. indicate that this growth in concentration of control after World War II was influenced both by internal growth within large companies and by merger acquisitions: however, the impact of mergers on rising concentration was modest in comparison with that of the merger boom of 1887–1904. Furthermore, mergers tended to occur more frequently during periods of buoyant business activity, rather than as restrictive attempts at rationalisation during slumps.[5] An important factor behind the merger movements, both in the U.S. and the U.K., has been the legal erosion of less formal and permanent methods of coordination.[6] In the U.S. a great stimulus was given by the anti-trust Sherman Act of 1890: in the U.K. this stimulus came later, with the 1948 Monopolies Commission, the 1956 Restrictive Trade Practices Act and subsequent legislation. In the U.K. one study[7] has suggested that recent trends point to a process of continued merger between already important companies (or of their major divisions) which, by the end of the 1970s, could lead to about twenty-one 'national companies' – each in a major sector – together controlling about three-quarters of the private sector of the economy. This trend, it is suggested, is fuelled by certain characteristics of managerial behaviour and motivation – the 'growth ethos' and the desire to avoid the competitive discipline of free market forces.

[1] 'Nylon fixers?', *Econ.*, 12 Dec. 1970, p. 85 and 'Cartel before the horse', *Econ.*, 13 Nov. 1971, p. 88. [2] *D.T.*, 6 July 1964.
[3] *S.T.*, 12 Nov. 1967. [4] Barber, *The American Corporation*, pp. 20–1.
[5] F. M. Scherer, *Industrial Market Structure and Economic Performance*, 1971, pp. 103–12.
[6] Caves, *Britain's Economic Prospects*, pp. 284–5.
[7] G. Newbould and A. S. Jackson, *The Receding Ideal*, 1972.

The implications for market power and for pricing and investment policies would be significant.

In the United Kingdom the number of independent companies quoted on the Stock Exchange fell from 2,900 in 1957 to 2,600 in 1960. Their net assets during this period rose in value by 28% to £13,500 million, the fastest rise being in motor vehicles (39%) and the slowest being in textiles (15%). The 100 largest companies (excluding international firms, such as Royal Dutch-Shell) owned 51% of total net assets in 1957; in 1960 they owned 54%. A Board of Trade investigation, completed in 1962, found that the firms which grew most rapidly were distinguished by three characteristics: they were already large in size; they earned a high rate of return on their assets; and they tended to go to the market for a large proportion of their finance, rather than to 'plough back' from profits.[1]

In 1970 the staff of the Monopolies Commission prepared a report,[2] published by the Department of Trade and Industry, on mergers and acquisitions in manufacturing, distributive and service trades from end-1957 to end-1968, involving 'sizeable' British companies. These were firms which had assets of more than £0·5 million; were 'engaged mainly in the U.K.'; and were quoted on the Stock Exchange. It found that, whereas U.S. companies had tended to concentrate on self-generated or internal growth, U.K. firms had emphasised growth by merger or acquisition. Consequently the number of such companies declined from 2,024 to 1,253 (i.e. by 38%), and the annual average number of mergers involving such firms was 70 – actual numbers varying between 59 and 100. Their net assets more than doubled from £9,711 million to about £20,000 million. The greatest absolute reductions in the number of such firms were in textiles (214 to 126), drink (136 to 51), non-electrical engineering (227 to 145), retail distribution (141 to 94), wholesale distribution (189 to 118) and food (85 to 39): the largest relative reductions in numbers were in drink (63%), food (54%), chemicals (45%), vehicles (44%), bricks, pottery, glass and cement (43%), shipbuilding and marine engineering (42%) and textiles (41%). In manufacturing there was a 40% reduction (from 1,516 to 916) and in distributive and service trades a reduction of 33% (from 508 to 337). Four major findings of the study were as follows:

(a) the very largest firms (the top ten in terms of assets) had the highest overall asset growth rate (trebling their assets from £1,607 m. to £4,728 m.) of which two-fifths was accounted for by acquisitions: the 120 largest firms were involved in half the mergers and thus acquired two-thirds of all the assets involved in these merger activities;

(b) there was a progressively decreasing reliance on internally generated cash to finance acquisitions and an increasing reliance on ordinary shares and long-term loans;

(c) twenty-two main sectors were covered by the report: in fourteen of these the number of 'sizeable' firms, as defined by the report, in which at least 50% of net assets in their sectors were concentrated, declined (e.g. in drink, from twelve to four, and in wholesale distribution, from twenty-one to fourteen): in six sectors the number of such firms accounting for at least a 50% net asset con-

---

[1] *Company Assets, Income and Finance in 1960*, Board of Trade, 1962.
[2] *A Survey of Mergers 1958–1968*. This is well reviewed, with tables, in Chester, 'Large organizations – their role in the U.K. economy', *loc. cit.*, also *F.T.*, 14 Dec. 1970.

centration remained constant, and in only two sectors (timber furniture and miscellaneous services) did the numbers rise (i.e. degree of concentration fell) –
from five to six and four to five, respectively.

(d) although the number of horizontal mergers, within the same classification,
was 55% over the whole period (425 out of 771), vertical and conglomerate
mergers were becoming more important towards the end of the period, indicating
a trend towards consecutive and unrelated diversification.

An analysis made in mid-1970 by Barclays Bank,[1] covering all acquisitions in
industrial and commercial sectors from 1964 to 1969 (including, for 1969,
overseas acquisitions and companies trading mainly overseas), supported the
second finding of the above-mentioned survey (Fig. 4.2).

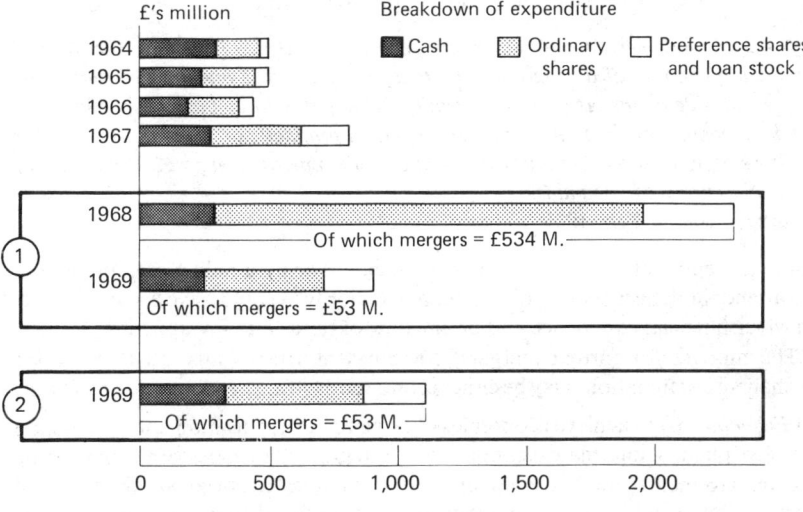

Fig. 4.2. *Value of U.K. acquisitions by industrial and commercial companies,
1964–9*
(Source: *B.B.R.*, May 1970)

One of the most interesting manifestations of the merger movement in recent
years has been the spread of 'conglomerate' mergers – particularly in the U.S.
The strict definition of the conglomerate is integration or diversification into
completely unrelated areas. This trend reached a peak towards the late 1960s
and accounted for almost half of all U.S. mergers in 1968 (Fig. 4.3). Some of
the mergers represented a spread of risks among several industries or the finding
of new growth areas for investment; some represented an infusion of management expertise and ability amongst a diverse collection of subsidiaries; some,

[1] See *B.B.R.*, May 1970.

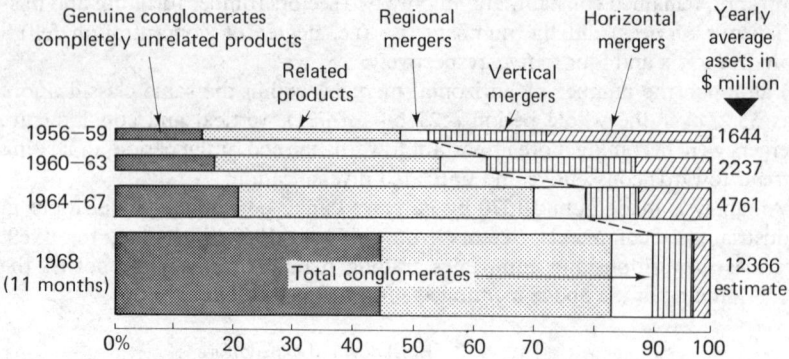

Fig. 4.3. *Conglomerate and other mergers in the U.S., 1956–68. The official American definition of a conglomerate used in this chart is much wider than most people this side of the Atlantic would think. It appears to include every merger in which companies are not either making identical products, or have an interlocking sequence of production. But half the so-called conglomerate mergers in 1968 were of genuinely unrelated companies.*
(Source: *Econ.*, 8 Feb. 1969, p. 68)

however, represented a form of financial juggling or pyramiding of capital, with the attendant danger that a collapse in one major firm could have a serious effect on wider financial confidence and on the flow of funds into investment.[1]

The motives for formal mergers, combines or trusts (alternative terms for permanent combination) may be either economic or strategic, or a mixture of both:

(*a*) *Economic*. (i) to achieve economies of large-scale organisation and production between plants – interplant economies of integration (e.g. research, marketing and management): the efficiency of these economies is not at all clearcut, but they are often publicised by companies advocating takeovers, as in the I.C.I. bid for Courtaulds in 1961;
(ii) to achieve economies of operation within each plant – intraplant economies of scale (e.g. by drawing upon larger financial and technical resources, to operate more efficient equipment and techniques and to concentrate production in the most suitable plants): this reason motivated many mergers in U.S. industry in the early twentieth century, and was often quoted as justification for the rationalisation schemes in Britain during the interwar period; again, the efficiency of these economies is sometimes open to doubt, as changes may not always be made.[2]
(*b*) *Strategic*. (i) to gain a monopolistic power position, by concentrating control over a particular sector of industry (usually by means of lateral integration) and thus increasing bargaining power;
(ii) to act as a substitute for the market controls of a trade association, as in the case of the Calico Printers Association: a merger may miss out the oligopoly (trade association) stage and go straight to the monopoly stage;
(iii) to gain a dominant position in an existing oligopoly, as with the formation of the Imperial Tobacco Company in 1902 and Imperial Chemical Industries in 1926;

[1] See C. F. Pratten, 'A case study of a conglomerate merger', *M. and W.S.R.*, Spring 1970.
[2] For a keen analysis of the scale economies argument, see Scherer, *op. cit.*, pp. 116–17.

(iv) to make an existing oligopoly more secure, as when buying up small members who refuse to conform to the 'rules' (e.g. in the U.S. cement industry large firms bought up small ones, which refused to conform to the 'basing-point' system of freight charges).

In practice it is not easy to separate economic from strategic motives behind particular mergers. In the case of I.C.I., for example, both motives (technical efficiency and bargaining power) were apparent. Vertical integration mergers are often assumed to be for economic reasons, but may often be for strategic reasons also. This was so with the 1947 takeover of Hercules Cycles by Tube Investments: opportunities for economies of scale existed, but an important motive given was the ensuring of a market for T.I. products. The vertical merger between Thorn Electrical and Radio Rentals in 1968 was primarily based on a link-up between Thorn's production expertise in microcircuits and R.R.'s retail and servicing outlets, but fears were expressed at the time that a big sector of the rental market would be 'tied' and thus foreclosed to competing producers.[1]

Horizontal mergers, such as the partial link-up of Dunlop and Pirelli in 1970 may be claimed as leading to benefits of larger scale production and bulk supply economies. Yet both firms operated successful overseas markets and difficult home markets, and it is possible that, apart from coordinating their use of investment resources, they would be exerting market bargaining power through a higher degree of seller concentration.[2] During the takeover bid for Courtaulds, I.C.I. claimed that an important economic reason was to 'avoid duplication of research'. As many of the two firms' products were complementary, it appears that a possible reason was the prospect of controlling most of British man-made fibres production. When renewed merger attempts were hinted at between the two firms in 1970, it was suggested that this would permit economies of scale and vertical integration between the fibre production of both firms and the textile production of Courtaulds. However, the possibility existed of tying outlets, rather than winning them through competition.[3] The £95 million merger of Ranks and Hovis-McDougall in 1961 created one of Britain's largest flour and bakery combines. Both firms were millers and bakers: the merger conferred greater bargaining power on the members, and assured Hovis of a secure retail outlet for its speciality flour. In mid-1969 the President of the Board of Trade suggested that in view of the failure of some mergers to achieve their proclaimed (economic) objectives, such as rationalisation and greater efficiency, there might in future be more stringent vetting of proposed mergers and a periodic review of post-merger performance.[4]

As with voluntary association, there are many forms of formal combination. These range from the outright merger or takeover (as with Ford of America and Ford of England), through holding companies (with dominant voting power in subsidiaries), to the interlocking of minority shareholdings and/or directors.

1. INTERLOCKING MINORITY SHAREHOLDINGS AND/OR INTERLOCKING DIRECTORATES

Combination between companies may take the form of common directors. These representatives may be on the boards of 'dominant' and 'subordinate' companies; they may be on the boards of companies of similar status, on an

[1] *D.T.*, 16 Feb. 1968. [2] *D.T.*, 5 Dec. 1970; *F.T.*, 5 Dec. 1970.
[3] *Econ.*, 10 Jan. 1970, p. 49. [4] *Ibid.*, 28 June 1969, p. 74.

'exchange' basis; or they may be on the board of a 'linking' company, sometimes of minor importance in itself, whilst no obvious connections exist between the separate companies on whose boards the 'link' directors also sit. Often, where the purpose of common directors is to give a measure of control by one or more firms over other firms, there will also be block or minority shareholdings, held by the 'dominant' firms in the subordinate ones. These represent a vested ownership interest and such a combination of common directors and shareholdings constitutes an economical way of exercising control, and may in fact be a prelude to less tenuous forms of combination.

However, not all interlocking directors are decision takers, appointed to exercise control. The common directors may be 'front men' (ex-Cabinet Ministers, aristocrats, etc.), appointed for reasons of prestige to the boards of quite unconnected companies; they may be technical or financial specialists or local worthies, appointed by unrelated companies for their expert knowledge; they may be representatives of interested outside groups, such as banks and insurance companies, who have made investments in, or loans to, several companies. In such cases they will probably have the function of holding a watching brief for the investing firms.

Apart from such coincidental cases, interlocking directorates may be appointed on an exchange basis or to a 'link' firm in order to achieve the coordination of policies by firms in an oligopoly or firms which have technically interconnected activities, as in the Midland metal-using industries.[1] Such appears to be the case with Dupont, General Motors and U.S. Rubber (now Uniroyal), in America. The use of a link firm may very well be to disguise any appearance of direct combination between the firms concerned. Open coordination through common exchange directors may be accompanied by the exchange of interlocking minority shareholdings by the member companies. This would probably serve as an advertisement or token of their mutual interdependence.

Two examples of interlocking minority shareholdings may be noted in microelectronics and in brewing. Before 1969 the Government had been attempting to forge closer links between the three major British companies in micro-electronics, partly to avoid duplication of research and development effort and to combat U.S. domination of this key technological field. One stage in the sequence of cooperation between General Electric – English Electric, Plessey and Ferranti was their coming together as shareholders in International Computers, Ltd (I.C.L.).[2] In 1967, following the new Companies Act provisions for greater disclosure of share ownership, it was revealed that the ramifications of interlocking shareholdings and directors in the brewing industry were quite extensive. In some cases the initiators were dominant firms in the industry, whilst in others there were extensive family connections, expressed through directors' family shareholdings.[3]

During the late 1960s there was a trend towards growing cooperation between firms in the European electronics and heavy electrical engineering industries. This was being manifested in the form of jointly owned, specialised subsidiaries, but, because of the diverging interests of the large companies, it was suggested

[1] M. Beesley, Ph.D. thesis, Birmingham; referred to by P. Sargant Florence, *The Logic of British and American Industry*, 1961, p. 128.
[2] See *D.T.*, 3 Feb. 1969.
[3] See 'The protectors and the protected', *Econ.*, 2 Dec. 1967, p. 991.

that they should mutually interchange shareholdings and directors, rather than try to run subsidiaries in joint harness.[1]

An extensive manifestation of interlocking shareholdings and directors, and of jointly owned subsidiaries occurs in Japan, amongst the three 'zaibatsu' or loosely knit confederations of diversified firms – Mitsubishi, Mitsui and Sumitomo. Within each group, companies are generally part-owned by other companies in the group: the average rates of intra-group interlocking of shares ranges from 13·75% in Mitsui to 29·04% in Mitsubishi. Within each group there are also jointly owned subsidiaries in new areas into which the groups have moved.[2]

An interesting analysis has been made by Dooley of interlocking directorates in the U.S. from 1935 to 1965.[3] Of the 250 largest U.S. corporations in 1965, 233 had interlocks (on average, 9·9 times – although for banks the average was 16·1 times) as compared with 225 in 1935. He found that about one-third of the assets of the 200 largest non-financial firms was financed by credit, and that these firms interlocked 616 times with the fifty largest banks and insurance companies alone. Whilst interlocks tended to be less in firms with a high degree of managerial control – as management finds it easier to isolate itself from other points of view – the board of the typical firm experiences the presence of financial representatives, outside local business representatives and representatives of competitors, all of whom tend to limit the absolute control of the boards and constitute a constraining influence. The phenomenon was both extensive and enduring: most large corporations had been interlocked with others for decades, and the modern corporation was not seen to be an 'independent and self-sufficient organ ruled by its own self-perpetuating management'.[4]

In late-1967 the Federal authorities in the U.S. were attempting to dismantle a complex financial structure which involved the financial 'pyramiding' of control over twenty different companies, including banks, by one man – by way of interlocking directorates and interlocking minority shareholdings.[5] The individual was Victor Muscat, who, in the case of one such pyramid (see Fig. 4.4), only owned 25% of the company at the pinnacle. He was charged with using the system to misappropriate $4·8 million from one of the twice-interlocked firms in the group.

2. HOLDING COMPANIES

This form of combination involves the dominant control by one company over another (which usually retains its individual identity), by means of ownership of over 50% of its voting shares. Whilst not as economical as block-holding and interlocking directorates, it does ensure effective control, and may be preferred when the vital interests of the holding company are involved. However, this form of combination can lead to the 'pyramiding' of control, as illustrated below in Figure 4.5. In such cases, effective control may be achieved by a relatively small company over a tremendous concentration of capital in subsidiary firms, and this combination may not be immediately obvious. The process of 'pyramiding' the concentration of control is heightened by the presence in many firms of non-

---

[1] See 'How will they link?', *Econ.*, 26 Oct. 1968, pp. 82–3.
[2] See 'The zaibatsu regroup', *Econ.*, 20 Feb. 1971, pp. 54–5.
[3] See P. C. Dooley, 'The interlocking directorate', *A.E.R.*, June 1969.
[4] *Ibid.*, p. 322.
[5] See 'Muscat's empire under siege', *S.T.*, 19 Nov. 1967.

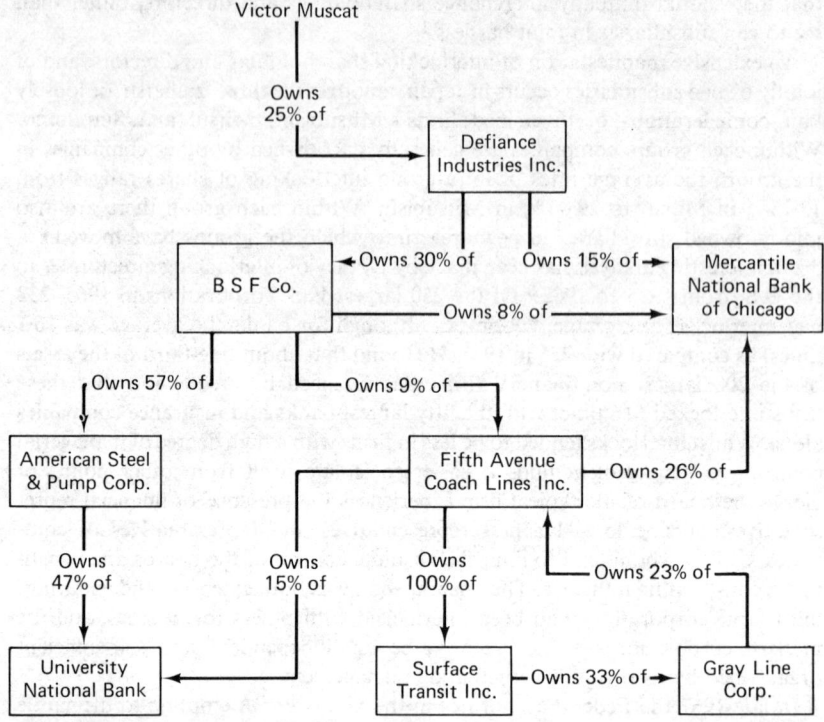

Fig. 4.4. *Financial pyramiding through interlocking minority shareholdings and interlocking directorates*
(Source: *S.T.*, 19 Nov. 1967)

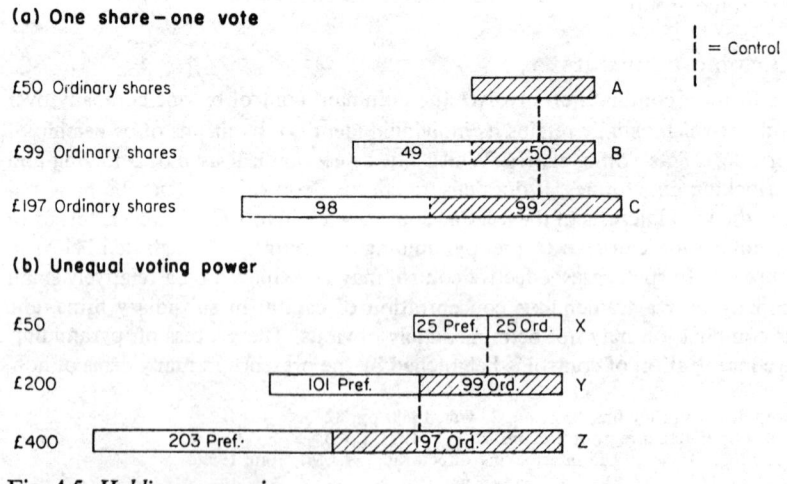

Fig. 4.5. *Holding companies*

voting preference shares and debentures. This form of combination is often to be found in newspapers, cinemas and department stores.

Holding company A may control company C, almost four times as large, where all shares are voting shares. Company X may control company Z, almost eight times as large, merely by means of ownership of vote-carrying ordinary shares.

An extremely interesting example of a holding company in the U.K. is the Rank Organisation. The nominal share capital of this public company in 1969 was £29·6 million and the market value about £300 million. Odeon Cinema Holdings owned 53% of the voting (Ordinary) shares in Rank. All the voting power in O.C.H. rested in one Ordinary (50p) share, held directly by Film Development and Research and in about £50,000 of voting shares, held by Group Holdings (and its subsidiary, F. D. & R. Holdings), which in turn was controlled by £2,500 of voting shares, held by nominees of Film Development and Research (see Fig. 4.6). Thus Film Development and Research, controlled by Lord Rank, had eventual control over the entire Rank Organisation. The system was set up so as to leave the group unaffected by Lord Rank's death and to keep it in British hands.[1]

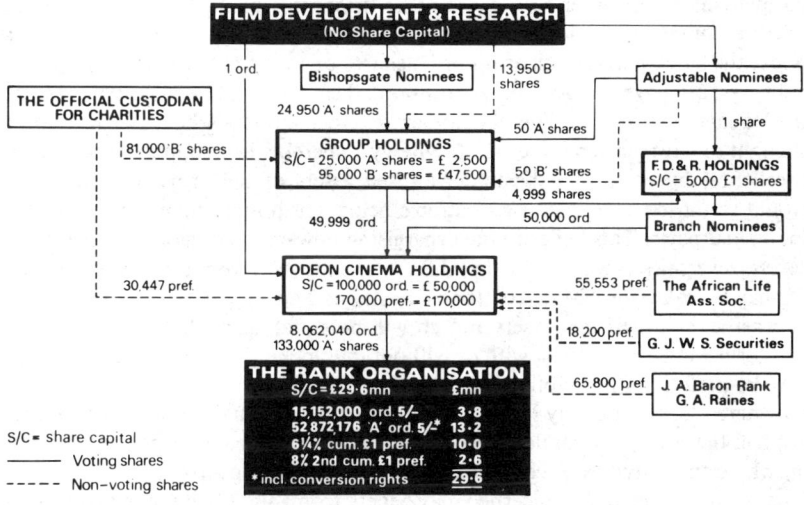

Fig. 4.6. *The Rank Organisation – a holding company, 1969*
(Source: *Econ.*, 11 Jan. 1969, p. 76)

3. OUTRIGHT MERGERS

This is the extreme form of formal, permanent combination, involving the merging of ownership of two separate companies, or the outright acquisition of one company by another. The subsidiary may or may not retain its original name. To all intents and purposes, both companies are one. This relatively expensive method of combination may be preferred for strategic or political reasons, as in the 1961 complete merger of Ford of England into Ford of America. The parent company already had over 50% of voting power, but probably wished to

[1] See 'Rank Organisation: a firm grip', *Econ.*, 11 Jan. 1969, p. 76.

remove any potentially vociferous pressure groups amongst the British share-holders, perhaps with an eye on future investment and production policy.

There are various factors at work influencing the type of combination desired or achieved by participating companies.

Outright mergers or holding companies may be the form used when it is desired to have extensive and effective access to great capital resources, especially when great potential economies of integration seem possible. As between one form and the other, the holding company has the advantage of economy in the use of capital; the outright merger has the advantage of unrestricted control, but there is a danger that the capital structure of the parent company may be weakened (or 'watered down') by the financial strain involved in offering its shares or money for shares in the engulfed company.

In the case of conglomerate acquisitions, these may sometimes take the form of holding companies or of outright mergers. In both cases there has been the danger that they might involve financial juggling and the watering-down of capital, as manifested in the case of Ling-Temco-Vought (L.T.V.) in the U.S. This could happen as a result of the bidding company's issuing loan stock or its own shares, in order to acquire other firms: this might be justifiable if the 'victim' company has under-exploited assets, but if the main effect is simply to boost the stock market valuation of its shares or to increase the takeover firm's debt as part payment for the acquisition, then the whole edifice will rest on inadequate real assets.[1] The conglomerates, in their 1960s heyday, were often thought to have mastered the art of 'synergy', whereby their supposed managerial excellence, by activating the under-utilised assets of the firms they acquired, would result in the whole organisation's being worth more than the sum of the individual parts. This belief in the synergising powers of conglomerates suffered severe reversals, especially in the U.S., when the 1971 recession exposed their financial weaknesses. Many of the acquisitions had apparently been far more expensive than their real assets and growth potential justified.[2]

Interlocking directorates, with or without interlocking minority shareholdings, may be preferred in the following cases:

(a) where a firm is already large enough to achieve internal economies and does not feel the need for complete control of the other company or companies;

(b) where the activities of companies concerned already overlap;

(c) where the companies concerned may benefit from joint planning of production and investment (or the retarding of innovation).[3]

Sometimes a dominant member of an oligopoly may acquire a 'block' of voting shares in a rival firm in order to prevent aggressive outsiders from gaining control and upsetting the status quo. This was the case with the Imperial Tobacco Company, which bought a 51% holding in Gallaher in 1932 to prevent American Tobacco from gaining control. Imperial did not put any of its directors on Gallaher's board. In 1961 the I.T. Company's holding was $42\frac{1}{2}$%. The Monopolies Commission found that this was, in principle, against the public interest, but that Imperial had not actually used its holding to influence Gallaher

---

[1] Scherer, *op. cit.*, p. 113; *Econ.*, 14 June 1969, p. 70; 'Future looks tough for U.S. con-glomerates', *D.T.*, 25 March 1969; 'The logic of always being big', *Obs.*, 25 Jan. 1970.
[2] 'The conglomerates leave synergy behind', *F.T.*, 24 March 1972.
[3] M. Beesley, *op. cit.*

policy.[1] Another example of members of an oligopoly group's forestalling aggressive outsiders was the 1968 merger of the Leyland group with B.M.H., to form B.L.M.C. This was partly to pre-empt further American incursions into the U.K. motor industry.

3. Aims of Social Policy in the Face of Dangers of Monopolistic Concentration

(a) Dangers of monopoly power

The main dangers to society resulting from the power inherent in monopolistic concentration of control may be summarised as follows:

(i) Exploitation: a monopolistic grouping may have the power to exploit its control over supply to the consuming public by restricting output and raising prices; it may also be in a position to exploit the factor markets by its monopsonistic bargaining power (as the dominant purchaser of labour and other factors of production);

(ii) Political consequences: uncontrolled or unsupervised monopoly power may result in political lobbying or indirect interference in the political sphere; social policy must therefore cope with the problem of monopolistic groupings – 'States within the State';[2]

(iii) Unfair competition may result if monopolistic groupings are able to prevent competing producers from entering the field;

(iv) Suppression or retardation of investment and innovation may result from monopolistic control over production; this has short-term effects on the level of economic activity (the trade cycle) and long-term effects on the reduction of industrial efficiency.

The charge of exploiting control over supply (or 'seller concentration') was brought against the U.S. computer firm I.B.M. by the Department of Justice in 1969. I.B.M., with 74% of the U.S. market for the sale and rental of computers, was marketing 'software' or programme packages and services in conjunction with its computers, thus making it virtually impossible for competition to exist from smaller firms in the same areas. It was also accused of giving 'favourable deals' to educational institutions, so as to attain a monopolistic hold over that fast-growing market sector, and of undercutting – with low profit margins – competitors in sectors in which they appeared likely to be successful.[3] In an analysis of Monopolies Commission reports on colour film (Kodak), glass (Pilkington) and cellulosic fibres (Courtaulds), A. Sutherland found that, except for Courtaulds, profits tended to be higher than the average in manufacturing, despite the greater security derived from a high degree of seller concentration.[4]

The 'political consequences' danger was highlighted in the U.S. in 1972 with the case of the International Telephone and Telegraph Corporation (I.T.T.), the world's largest conglomerate. Firstly, I.T.T. was accused of having been involved with the Central Intelligence Agency in plotting to cause economic

[1] Monopolies Commission, *Report on the Supply of Cigarettes and Tobacco and Cigarette and Tobacco Machinery*, 1961.
[2] 'Companies outgrow countries', *Econ.*, 17 Oct. 1964, p. 271.
[3] *D.T.*, 21 Jan. 1969.
[4] See A. Sutherland, *The Monopolies Commission in Action*, 1969, esp. pp. 30–42 and 82–5.

chaos in Chile in 1970, so as to stimulate a military coup d'état, with the object of preventing Allende, a Marxist, from coming to power. The former head of the C.I.A. had become an I.T.T. director: I.T.T. was described as 'a virtual corporate nation in itself with vast international holdings, access to Washington's highest officials, its own intelligence apparatus and even its own classification system'.[1] Secondly, a Senate sub-committee was investigating the allegation that an I.T.T. lobbyist had revealed that I.T.T. had bought off a Department of Justice anti-trust suit in 1971, by guaranteeing several hundred thousand dollars to the Republican party campaign funds.[2]

The dangers of unfair competition by way of barriers to the entry of new competition and of the suppression or retardation of technological innovation were also attributed to I.T.T. by the Justice Department in 1967. The biggest merger in the communications field, between I.T.T. and A.B.C., had been agreed in 1965 and halted by the Justice Department in 1967. One point was that if I.T.T. united with an existing television network, it would cease to be a potential future competing entrant into the broadcasting field. Another was that I.T.T. would have a diminished thirst for technological innovation, as a result of having a 'half-a-billion dollar investment in the status quo'.[3]

With regard to technological change and concentration of control, the evidence is by no means clear. Economists such as S. H. Slichter, J. A. Schumpeter and J. K. Galbraith contend that market dominance is either a prerequisite to, or the best medium for encouraging risky and expensive research and development; others, such as G. J. Stigler and J. Schmookler, consider that the consequent reduction of competitive risk reduces the need and incentive to innovate.[4] J. Enos found that the time intervals between inventions and their adoption (i.e. innovation) were as low as three years for DDT and long-playing records, but as high as six years for the ball point pen, twenty-seven years for the zip fastener and seventy-nine years for the fluorescent lamp.[5] Mansfield found that an industrial firm's speed in using new techniques was directly related to its size and the expectation of profit from the innovation: it did not seem to be related to the firm's rate of growth, profit level, financial liquidity, profit trend or the age of its management personnel.[6] Some highly concentrated firms, as with the Monopolies Commission investigations of Kodak, Pilkingtons and Courtaulds, analysed by Sutherland,[7] appear to have good records in respect of technical efficiency and the elimination of surplus capacity. On the other hand, cartelisation in the U.S. electric lamp industry in the 1920s and 1930s retarded the development of fluorescent lighting, partly in order to amortise and avoid obsolescence in the capital sunk in traditional incandescent lamp production.[8] Another classic case of retardation of innovation was that of power steering in the U.S.: this was

[1] *D.T.*, 22 March 1972.
[2] 'The mysterious case of I.T.T.', *Econ.*, 1 April 1972, pp. 41–2.
[3] *D.T.*, 17 Oct. 1967.
[4] E. Mansfield, ed., *Monopoly Power and Economic Performance* (rev. edn), 1968, for papers by these authors.
[5] Quoted in E. Mansfield, *The Economics of Technological Change*, 1968, pp. 100–1.
[6] *Ibid.*, pp. 123–5, 133.   [7] Sutherland, *op. cit.*, pp. 44–5.
[8] Scherer, *op. cit.*, p. 371; D. Hamberg, 'Invention in the industrial research laboratory', *J.P.E.*, April 1963, esp. p. 106. He shows how it was not until the 1940s, when the last basic patents were expiring, that the General Electric Company was forced to produce fluorescent lamps; this was because a smaller firm, Sylvania Electric, backed by the Justice Department, broke away from the G.E.C. monopoly and forced its introduction. A similar case occurred with the suppression of commercial television by the radio manufacturers in the 1930s.

invented in 1926 and even used in military vehicles during World War II, but the major manufacturers, faced with a seller's market and being under no pressure to install it in private vehicles after the war, held back until 1951, when Chrysler made it available, to be quickly followed by the other firms.[1]

(b) Alternative policies of Reform, Change, or Overall Government Economic Planning and Supervision

The three major lines along which social policy might (and to some extent does) face the problems of monopolistic control over industry – involving as it does questions of size, collusion, efficiency, price policies, the level of economic activity, and 'the public interest' – may be summarised as follows:

1. Reform (or mitigation): 'anti-trust' policy, consumer protection, 'the glare of publicity', etc.;
2. Change: alternative forms of ownership and organisation;
3. Planning: Government supervision and intervention, combined with elements of economic planning.

In practice elements of all three policies co-exist in Britain.

REFORM

The general aim of a reform policy would be to mitigate the undesirable effects of monopoly power, so as to result in what may be described as 'workable competition'.[2] This does not mean unfettered or 'perfect' competition, in which no firm is big enough to exert any influence over supply, but a general state of affairs which would contain the following ingredients:

(i) a substantial number of alternative buyers (of factors of production) and suppliers, with no firm so large that no other could take over part of its trade;
(ii) no actual coercion by large associations or combines;
(iii) firms should be responsive to the market forces of supply and demand;
(iv) firms should make separate decisions on market policy and investment;
(v) new firms should be able to enter without any artificial restrictions.

The U.S. Attorney General's Committee on Anti-Trust Laws, in their 1955 report, defined workable competition by the basic characteristic that 'no group of sellers, acting in concert, has the power to choose its level of profits by giving less and charging more'. This state should be attainable when 'rival sellers, whether existing competitors or new or potential entrants into the field, would keep this power in check by offering or threatening to offer effective inducements'. [3] Since J. M. Clark first coined the phrase, in 1940, there has been a growing literature on the concept of workable competition. Much of this was summarised by S. Sosnick in 1958: using his scheme, F. M. Scherer has set out the major criteria for structure, conduct and performance as follows:[4]

(a) *Structural criteria*
1. Maximum number of sellers permitted by scale economies.
2. No artificial restrictions on mobility and entry.
3. Moderate and price-sensitive quality differentials in products.

[1] See E. Mansfield, *The Economics of Technological Change*, 1968, pp. 103–4.
[2] 'Competition and commonsense', *Stat.*, 3 July 1964, p. 5; M. Spicer, 'The consumer – "a countervailing power" ', *Stat.*, 27 Nov. 1964, p. 532; 'Making Britain competitive', *Stat.*, 5 Mar. 1965, p. 625.
[3] See Hunter, ed., *op. cit.*, p. 71.   [4] Scherer, *op. cit.*, p. 37.

(b) Conduct criteria

1. Uncertainty should exist as to whether rivals will follow price initiatives.
2. Firms should strive to achieve goals independently, without collusion.
3. No unfair, exclusionary, predatory or coercive tactics.
4. No permanent shielding of inefficient suppliers or customers.
5. No misleading sales promotion.
6. No persistent, harmful price discrimination.

(c) Performance criteria

1. Firms' production operations should be efficient.
2. No excessive promotional expenses.
3. Profit levels just sufficient to reward investment, efficiency and innovation.
4. Output levels and quality range should be responsive to consumer demands.
5. Opportunities for introducing new, technically superior products and processes should be exploited.
6. Prices should not intensify periodical market instability.
7. Success should accrue to sellers who best serve consumer wants.

A key problem inherent in such an aim would be to distinguish between size, when technically justified by large-scale output, and size when due to the quest for bargaining power. This hinges on the problem, discussed in Chapter 2, Stage II.9, of integration versus standardisation.

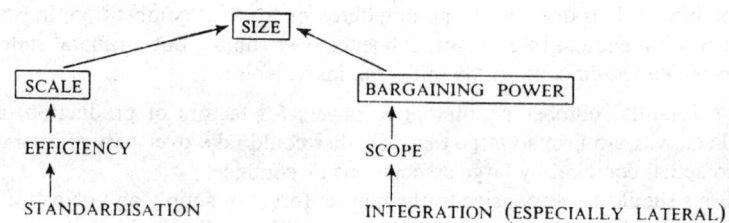

Where large size can be justified on economic and technical grounds, as flowing from the scale of production, this should be permitted, so long as economies are passed on to the consumer. But where size is due to the quest for bargaining power and monopolistic concentration of authority, as frequently occurs in cases of lateral integration, there is a strong case for preserving the public interest by 'trust-busting' or other methods. Professor Hicks once remarked that the greatest monopoly profit was 'a quiet life'.[1] In practice, of course, it may be difficult to disentangle the 'economic' and 'strategic' motives for large size.[2] There appears to be very little evidence that technological (or 'cost of production') economies of scale are only available to the very largest firms. Apart from areas such as electronics and aerospace, where the R & D 'threshold' may be extremely high, it may often be possible for smaller, specialised firms to extract the maximum scale economies. With regard to concentration *via* horizontal integration (whether by merger or agreement), this would be objectionable if the main object or result were to 'rationalise' production by keeping

[1] 'End of the quiet life?', *Stat.*, 24 Jan. 1964, pp. 239–40.
[2] A useful scheme of structural attributes which may affect the conduct of firms, produced by J. W. McKie, may be seen in J. W. Markham and G. F. Papanek, *Industrial Organization and Economic Development*, 1970, pp. 9–10.

inefficient plants in operation for longer than justified by market forces. In the case of concentration by way of vertical integration, by merger or agreement, this would be objectionable if the result were to tie up customers or exert 'leverage' over them, instead of winning them by competition, as a result of more efficient operations.[1] The case for conglomerates is rather more confused. Even where the large conglomerate has little monopoly power in any particular industry, its opportunities for multiple contacts with other large firms are numerous and it may have the ability to mobilise its total resources in a localised attack on smaller firms in a particular market. As C. D. Edwards has put it, 'differentials in size rather than in monopoly power are the source of such advantages. The large concern has a special status, even though it may operate in an industry so large that its percentage of the total market is small'.[2] Some students of the subject have asserted that the conglomerates (and indeed big firms, or 'juggernauts', in general) fail to digest and make use of the complex volume of data generated by their activities, and that they tend to subsidise inefficient activities in some areas of operations: due to this 'X-inefficiency' phenomenon, they thereby fail to achieve a profit-maximising efficiency in resource allocation. Others disagree with this extreme view and find that, potentially, the conglomerates offer scope for top-flight management ability, as long as they avoid an excessively inflexible financial debt structure. *Fortune Magazine*'s review of the top 500 U.S. firms during 1971 found that the median profit margin had fallen to 3·8 % on turnover: the general conclusion was that the process of diversification, mergers and conglomerate development during the previous decade had not paid off, that many of the largest firms had exceeded their optimum size and that size was increasingly involving diseconomies of scale.[3]

An important method by which the consumer may neutralise the monopoly power of producers is the development of what J. K. Galbraith has termed 'countervailing power'. He considers that the function of competition (by rival producers) has been superseded by countervailing power, or the concerted bargaining power of consumers (and labour) on the other side of the market fence. A corollary of his thesis is that countervailing power would more easily break into a multi-firm industry than into an industry dominated by a single-firm monopoly.[4] It must be noted, however, that in its extreme form countervailing power, whether by customer or trade union, may assume monopsonistic proportions, such that the party concerned may be able to exert excessive bargaining power over a weaker producer.[5]

The four main elements of an effective reform policy would be:

(*a*) Publicity: the exposure of monopolistic practices and of cases of monopolistic concentration of control which are against the public interest.

---

[1] For an excellent exposition of the problems of size, see D. Fiennes, 'Is bigger better?', *New Technology*, Sept. 1968.
[2] C. D. Edwards, 'Conglomerate bigness as a source of power' National Bureau of Economic Research report *Business Concentration and Price Policy*, Princeton U.P., 1955, pp. 331–59, quoted in F. M. Scherer, *op cit.*, p. 278.
[3] E. M. Singer, *Antitrust Economics*, 1968, ch. 16 and pp. 259–66; Scherer, *op. cit.*, pp. 27–83; G. Bannock, *The Juggernauts*, 1970; 'Should we believe in giants?', *Econ.*, 10 Jan. 1970, pp. 12–13; 'The ITT expansion: aim is growth – with risks', *F.T.*, 11 April 1972; 'Top companies in U.S. "less profitable" ', *F.T.*, 8 May 1972.
[4] J. K. Galbraith, 'The theory of countervailing power', reprinted in A. Hunter, *op. cit.*, pp. 123–39.
[5] See Scherer, *op. cit.*, pp. 241–2.

(b) An attack upon monopolistic, restrictive practices: a 'norm' of 'workable competition' should be described by law. It would not prohibit specific techniques of restriction, as loopholes might then be found. Official guidance could be given to businessmen, who could adapt their actions to fit in with the general aims of public policy. This would result in a flexible policy, permitting official freedom of action to cope with restrictive practices as they came to light.

(c) An attack upon monopolistic forms of organisation. This would consist, basically, of breaking up combines (where their size was due primarily to the quest for bargaining power), and associations (where they could be shown to operate against the public interest): in both cases the subject for attack would be 'concentration-size', as opposed to 'scale-size'.

(d) The strengthening of consumer bargaining power, by measures to protect the common law rights of the consumer, by providing information on standards of quality and prices, and by energetic and publicised prosecution of infringements of the law relating to weights and measures, etc. Apart from the coordinated growth of consumer protection in the U.K., an interesting phenomenon has been the increasingly effective 'David and Goliath crusade' by Ralph Nader in the U.S.[1]

Extensive strides have been made in Britain since World War II along the lines of a reform policy.

The first White Paper on Employment Policy, published in 1944, outlined the Government's intention of investigating restrictive agreements and the activities of combines, with a view to taking appropriate action if such practices furthered sectional interests, to the detriment of the country as a whole. It also exhorted labour to examine restrictive practices which might constitute an impediment to full employment. The first Economic Survey for 1947 pointed out that there was no place in an expanding economy for industrial arrangements which restrict production, prices or employment.

In 1948, possibly stimulated by the desire to fall into line with the internationally acclaimed principles of the I.T.O. Charter, the Government passed the Monopolies and Restrictive Practices (Inquiry and Control) Act. Under this Act a Monopolies Commission was set up to report to the Board of Trade upon the effect of any monopolistic practices which it specified, insofar as they affected the public interest. It was also instructed to investigate industries referred to it by the Board of Trade, where 'certain conditions' prevailed, and to report upon their effect upon the public interest. Such conditions were held to be present when one-third of a 'class of goods' was supplied by one firm or association of firms under circumstances which restricted competition. The Commission was a fact-finding body, staffed by economists, accountants, a Q.C. and a retired civil servant. It could only investigate and report, when instructed by the Board of Trade: its recommendations could only be enforced by parliamentary sanction. However, its major advantages were its ability to disclose restrictive practices and the great publicity which resulted from such disclosures. The interpretation of 'the public interest' was left to the discretion of the Commission and the Board of Trade.

[1] See 'Naderism spreads its wings', Econ., 29 May 1971, pp. 49–51.

By 1956 the Commission had investigated twenty industries and had reported unfavourably on 'Collective Discrimination'. In seventeen of these industries practices contrary to the public interest were disclosed, and on at least six the Commission made sharp criticisms. The effects of the Commission's much publicised findings were reflected in the voluntary abandonment of many restrictive practices, not only by the industries covered, but also by others in which they were present. An interesting result of the Commission's investigation of costs and profits in relation to size of firm in ten industries was that in only one was the largest producer the most efficient: it appears that in many cases optimum output, with the fullest economies of scale, is reached before the biggest size of firm is achieved.[1] Further growth would seem to be stimulated by strategic reasons.

In 1956 the Government, stimulated by the general disclosures of the Monopolies Commission reports, its specific report on collective discrimination, and the 1949 Lloyd Jacob Committee report (which reported unfavourably on the collective enforcement of resale price maintenance), passed the Restrictive Trade Practices Act. This was the first real step towards control, as opposed to publicity. It did not follow the Commission's advice to prohibit specific restrictive practices, but declared all agreements in restraint of trade to be against the public interest and illegal unless they satisfied certain specified conditions. The onus of establishing the presence of these conditions lay with the firms concerned. All restrictive agreements except those relating exclusively to exports had to be notified to the Registrar of Restrictive Trading Agreements, who could recommend judicial action by the Restrictive Practices Court. The main 'gateway', as the specified conditions were called, was the following: that 'the removal of the restriction would deny to the public as purchasers, consumers or users of any goods specific and substantial benefits or advantages enjoyed or likely to be enjoyed by them as such'. The Act, furthermore, rendered illegal the collective enforcement of RPM agreements by trade association courts, etc., but granted the individual manufacturer the right to uphold his own RPM clauses by court action. The Act also removed from the Monopolies Commission the function of investigating specific restrictive practices. Henceforth it was to report only on the effects of unitary monopolies, *viz.*, single firms which control one-third or more of the supply of a class of goods. Whereas prior to February 1957 most of the M.C.'s reports concerned restrictive agreements and only two of the twenty-one cases reported on were 'dominant firms' (the British Match Corporation and the British Oxygen Company), it completed another six such inquiries between 1958 and 1965. In five of these eight cases they were found not to be against the public interest, and in three of these five some prominence was given to the benefits of economies of scale.[2] By June 1966 2,550 agreements had been registered. Of these, 280 had been referred to the court: 245 of these were settled out of court and of the thirty-five dealt with by judicial process by November 1966 only twelve were found not to be against the public interest. In almost all cases, the 'gateway' pleaded successfully was that the agreement 'benefited consumers'. In a thirteenth case, that of the Yarn Spinners' price agreement, the

[1] *L.B.R.*, Jan. 1961, p. 40.
[2] C. K. Rowley, 'Monopoly in Britain: private vice but public virtue?', *M. and W.S.R.*, Autumn 1968, pp. 53–5. Also see F. V. Meyer, D. C. Corner and J. E. S. Parker, *Problems of a Mature Economy*, 1970, pp. 194–6.

'preventing unemployment' gateway was successfully pleaded, but the agreement failed on the application of the R.T.P. Act 'tailpiece' or overall balancing provision.[1]

As a result of the 1956 Act, collusive agreements were either abandoned or watered down, but the Act was still specific in that it assumed only formal restrictive agreements to be against the public interest. Manufacturers appeared, however, to be exploiting informal methods of collusion, which did not have to be registered. They included price leadership and the notification of prices, turnover and contract bids to trade associations. These methods replaced minimum price agreements, collective price maintenance, quota agreements and the allocation of contracts. The main loophole appeared to be the notification of prices (also known as 'information agreements' or 'open price registers').

The 1968 Restrictive Trade Practices Act subjected information agreements to the Registrar, but included an additional 'gateway' clause, *viz.* that such agreements might be accepted where they did not restrict or deter competition. As has been mentioned earlier, the closing of this loophole led to the greater use of the device of 'price-rigging', 'bid-filing' or collusive tendering and to that of price-leadership. The former device was criticised by the Registrar in his 1969 report. An important source of confusion, cleared up by the 1968 Act, was the apparent inconsistency between the 1956 Act and the work of the E.D.C.s or 'Little Neddies', set up under the National Economic Development Council. The E.D.C. members often felt inhibited in exchanging information, agreeing on objectives, etc., since such activities might have contravened the 1956 Act. Thus the 1968 Restrictive Trade Practices Act exempted 'approved agreements', which were considered reasonably necessary to promote projects or schemes of substantial importance to the national economy.[2] As mentioned earlier, RPM was abolished by the Resale Prices Act of 1964, apart from certain exemptions. As W. B. Reddaway's 1970 report on the distributive trades indicates, the collapse of RPM in sectors where it had been strongly applied (as with confectioners and tobacconists and household goods) was probably largely responsible for the reduction in retail profit margins, despite the selective employment tax, whereas in areas where RPM had been weak (e.g. food, clothing and footwear) margins tended to rise over the period 1965–8. As mentioned previously, the Monopolies Commission was requested, in May 1967, to investigate the practice of 'recommended prices' by manufacturers who had expanded this method of circumventing the law. The M.C. reported in February 1969 to the effect that an outright ban was impracticable but that the Government should reserve the right to investigate and prohibit particular instances.[3] Apart from the possibility of future legislation to amend the law and tighten up loopholes, it is quite likely that the present framework of informal collusion would not be sufficiently rigid or stable to suppress price competition, should severe, competitive strains again appear in the economy.

[1] R. B. Stevens and B. S. Yamey, *The Restrictive Practices Court*, 1965, pp. x–xvii and 68–70; Hunter, *op. cit.*, pp. 285–91; Meyer, *et al.*, *op. cit.*, pp. 181–93, 200–1.
[2] Rowley, *loc. cit.*, pp. 49–50.
[3] W. B. Reddaway, *Effects of the Selective Employment Tax, First Report, the Distributive Trades*, 1970, quoted in George, *op. cit.*, pp. 179–80; Meyer *et al.*, *op. cit.*, p. 193; 'RPM four years later', *Econ.*, 29 March 1969, pp. 56–7; L. A. Skeoch, 'The abolition of resale price maintenance: some notes on Canadian experience', *Economica*, Aug. 1964; 'Without RPM', *Econ.*, 20 May 1967, p. 827; *Econ.*, 1 March 1969, pp. 71–2; *F.T.*, 26 Feb. 1969.

Prior to the 1965 Monopolies and Mergers Act, reform policy had been concerned primarily with conduct detrimental to 'the public interest', but restrictive agreements in the professions and other services and the activities of the nationalised industries were not covered. The 1965 Act brought services within the scope of the Monopolies Commission and in 1967 the Board of Trade referred restrictive agreements in the professions to the M.C., which issued an admonitory report in October 1970.[1] The 1965 Act introduced a more rigorous element into reform policy, particularly in regard to a 'structural' or market dominance criterion of competition. The membership of the M.C. was increased and it was permitted to work in subgroups, in order to handle more cases more quickly. The Board of Trade (later replaced by the Department of Trade and Industry) was given greater powers to act on the M.C.'s reports and was authorised to refer proposed mergers to it (and to prohibit or dissolve them, on the M.C.'s recommendation), in cases where a 'one-third market share' monopoly position would be created or strengthened by the merger or where the value of assets involved exceeded £5 million.[2] From April 1966 to December 1968 the M.C. issued twelve reports; in one of these monopoly conditions were not proved, and in three the public interest was not found to be infringed.[3] From 1966 to 1970 fourteen proposed mergers were referred to the M.C.[4]

In the sphere of consumer protection, various steps have been taken since World War II.

The Merchandise Marks Act, 1953 obliged manufacturers to avoid false or misleading trade marks and descriptions on goods. In 1948 the Board of Trade set up the Hodgson Committee to report on the shortcomings of existing legislation on weights and measures. It reported in 1950, and was followed in 1960 by the Weights and Measures Bill, which did not get through Parliament.

The British Standards Institution tries to set standards on quality, dimensions, testing methods, etc., which are voluntarily accepted by manufacturers, buyers and sellers. A similar service is provided by the Consumers' Association, Ltd, who publish *Which?*[5] The Council of Industrial Design, set up by the Board of Trade in 1944, promotes improvements in the designs of consumer goods.

In 1959 the Board of Trade set up the Molony Committee, to report on the whole field of consumer protection. Its report was published in July 1962, recommending the setting up of a Consumer Council, to serve as a high level, policy forming body on questions of the consumers' interests. It also called for an extension of Citizens' Advice Bureaux, which would be linked with the Council, under a National Citizens' Advice Bureaux Committee. The report also called for an extension of protection to consumers involved in hire purchase agreements, for a consolidation and extension of the Merchandise Marks Acts, and for the restraint of unregistered seals of approval. The Home Office was given power to make regulations to ensure the safety of any class of goods by the 1961 Consumer Protection Act.[6]

[1] J. A. Lincoln, *The Restrictive Society*, 1967, pp. 82–89 and 98–101; Rowley, 'Monopoly in Britain', *loc. cit.*, p. 47; 'Professions: fair practices?', *Econ.*, 31 Oct. 1971, p. 68.
[2] 'Monopoly legislation in Britain', *M.B.R.*, Nov. 1965, pp. 13–22; C. K. Rowley, 'Mergers and public policy in Great Britain', *Journal of Law and Economics*, April 1968.
[3] Rowley, 'Monopoly in Britain', *loc. cit.*, p. 55; Meyer *et al.*, *op. cit.*, pp. 196–7.
[4] *Ibid.*, p. 61 and p. 198, respectively; *F.T.*, 28 Feb. 1970; also 'Monopolies Commission: eight major reports – and how they worked out', *S.T.*, 15 June 1969.
[5] *Brit.*, *O.H.*, 1971, p. 409 and 'Consumers', *Econ.*, 8 Jan. 1972, p. 66.
[6] *Ibid.*, p. 409.

In November 1962 the Government followed up the Molony Report with the Weights and Measures Bill, which attempted to 'create order from a chaotic mass of . . . legislation'. The Government also announced that a Consumer Council would eventually be set up. Both the Bill and the proposed Council were criticised on the grounds that they did not go far enough to protect the consumer as there was inadequate specialised machinery to uphold his common law rights and to fight test cases.[1] The Weights and Measures Act was passed in 1963 and in the same year the Consumer Council was established. The Council's £250,000 annual grant was withdrawn in 1970, on the grounds that other consumer organisations had grown in strength. It had been criticised as ineffectual, but in fact it had limited powers and did useful work in expanding consumer education. The suggestion was raised, in March 1972, that the major consumer protection functions should be administered by district councils under the new local authority reorganisation scheme, on the grounds that officials and premises would be easily accessible.[2] Department of Prices and Consumer Protection was created in March 1974.[3]

In 1965 safeguards to hire-purchase customers were provided by the Hire-Purchase Act and the Hire-Purchase (Scotland) Act.[4]

In 1968 the Trade Descriptions Act gave the weights and measures authorities powers to deal with misdescriptions of goods.[5] The 1973 Supply of Goods (Implied Terms) Act, designed to deal with spurious guarantees and exclusion clauses in consumer sales, was hailed as a first step towards a comprehensive framework of consumer protection legislation.

During 1962 the B.B.C. started a monthly television programme, publicising the findings of *Which?* This went part of the way towards what could be a more general policy, *viz.* the televising of genuine tests on commodities, coordinating such activities with independent research in universities, technical colleges and other such bodies.

Anti-trust legislation in America, based mainly on the Sherman Act of 1890, aims primarily to attack the cause of 'unitary monopoly' power – 'concentration-size'.[6] Anti-monopoly regulations in the Treaty of Rome, adopted by the European Economic Community, go further than British law in prohibiting the 'abuse of a dominant position... affecting trade within the member states' (Art. 86) and 'agreements, decisions and concerted practices that . . . limit competition' (Art. 85).[7] British reform policy does not vigorously tackle the problem of 'concentration – size', the cause of 'unitary monopoly' power. Policy in Britain is directed primarily at providing publicity, prohibiting formal restrictive agreements which result in concentrated control, and strengthening consumer protection. In general, the trend in U.K. reform policy by the end of the 1960s had been fairly consistent with the concept of 'workable competition' outlined above. In March 1969 the President of the Board of Trade summarised the Government's merger policy as one of considering as desirable those mergers which resulted in better management or economies of scale, without eliminating

---

[1] *Econ.*, 17 Feb. 1962, p. 646; 28 July 1962, p. 326; 27 Oct. 1962, p. 333 and 17 Nov. 1962, p. 693.
[2] *Ibid.*, pp. 408–9; *Econ.*, 7 Nov. 1970, p. 26; *F.T.*, 1 March 1972.
[3] See 'The DTI dismembered , *Econ.*, 9th March, 1974, p. 78.
[4] *Brit. O.H.*, 1971, p. 409.
[5] 'No sale under false colours', *D.T.*, 15 Nov. 1968.
[6] *Econ.*, 31 Oct. 1964, p. 526, *re.* Canadian Combines Commission.
[7] *Econ.*, 17 March 1962, p. 1046; D. Swann and D. L. McLachlan, *Concentration or Competition: A European Dilemma?*, P.E.P., 1967; 'E.E.C. laws on competition', *F.T.*, 19 April 1972.

workable competition.[1] In November 1969 the chairman of the City Panel on Take-Overs drew attention to the problems of sanctions and certainty. He considered that the voluntary system of regulating mergers was quite adequate and that publicity and exposure, or 'public reprobation' was in itself a serious sanction. Certainty as to the meaning and interpretation of policy was a more thorny problem in the absence of a statutory system of express rules, but even in the U.S., despite elaborate laws, it was not possible to deal specifically and in advance with all cases.[2] In December 1970 an Industrial Policy Group pamphlet asserted that in most cases the State need do no more than devise and improve general measures for fostering an environment conductive to competition: three exceptions, requiring more direct intervention, were (a) in the event of price- and output-fixing agreements between firms; (b) in the event of statutory monopolies; (c) where technical economies of scale justified high concentration of production.[3]

During 1970 and 1971 a keen debate was raging as to the future form of monopoly policy in Britain. Basically, it centred on the vagueness of the concepts of 'public interest' and 'workable competition'. These have tended to result in a discretionary, 'conduct-orientated' reform policy, which has been criticised for tolerating large firms, which in turn suffer from 'X-inefficiency' or failure to utilise resources effectively in the pursuit of cost-minimisation. The critics have suggested a 'structural' or 'competition-orientated' policy with clear rules concerning maximum market shares, similar to the U.S. 'trust-busting' policy. Certainly, a merger policy requires some sort of 'structural' criterion, as future conduct cannot be proved in advance. Critics of the structural thesis, however, claim that rigid structural rules are clumsy, that structure does not always correlate with behaviour, and that an environment of technological change and product innovation tends to undermine entrenched monopoly power. The general expectation by 1972 was that the new Government policy, deferred through pressure of parliamentary business, would be along 'discretionary' lines, based on 'workable competition' criteria rather than those of 'efficiency' and the nebulous 'public interest': this was expected to involve the abandonment of the rigid structural 'one-third market share' monopoly criterion and the '£5 million assets' merger criterion, and to combine the Registrar of Restrictive Trading Agreements with the Monopolies Commission – with investigatory powers, freer from ministerial control, and with the resources to initiate and pursue research – into a new body, such as a Commission for Competition.[4] In addition, it was expected that restrictive practices in services would be brought within the scope of the Restrictive Practices Court, that anti-competitive practices by individual firms and additional types of restrictive agreement (probably

---

[1] *F.T.*, 1 March 1969. [2] *Ibid.*, 21 Nov. 1969.
[3] *Ibid.*, 2 Dec. 1970.
[4] M. A. Crew and C. K. Rowley, 'Anti-trust policy: economics *versus* management science', *M. and W.S.R.*, Autumn 1970; M. Howe, 'Anti-trust policy: rules or discretionary intervention?', *M. and W.S.R.*, Spring 1971; M. A. Crew and C. K. Rowley, 'Anti-trust policy: The application of rules', *M. and W.S.R.*, Autumn 1971; 'Mergers: bigness ain't bad', *Econ.*, 7 June 1969, pp. 76–7; 'You can be big, provided you behave', *Econ.*, 6 Nov. 1971, p. 72; 'The Tory line on competition', *F.T.*, 3 Nov. 1970; 'Monopolies', *Econ.*, 11 March 1972, p. 86; 'Monopolies and mergers: the Government bares its teeth', *F.T.*, 5 Jan. 1972; 'Bill planned on monopoly law reforms next session', *F.T.*, 13 Oct. 1971; for a useful summary of the conflicting views on policy, see also 'Monopolies: the debate that should be taking place', *F.T.*, 19 April 1972.

including 'price-rigging', 'withholding of supplies' and 'recommended prices') would be made registrable.

It is of interest that in 1964 there were indications that in Canada, where a strict anti-merger policy of the U.S. type had existed since 1889, official policy was beginning to soften towards combines based on technological economies, *viz.*, 'scale/size'.[1]

In December 1972 the Fair-Trading Bill was published. As modified, prior to enactment in late-1973, it tended to emphasise a trend towards a more comprehensive, 'discretionary' party. It proposed the establishment of the post of Director-General of Fair Trading, to look out for practices which may adversely affect the interests of U.K. consumers. The Monopolies Commission was to be extended in size and scope and renamed the Monopolies and Mergers Commission. The Director-General was to take the initiative in referring cases to the M.M.C. Monopoly situations were redefined, in structural terms, to encompass local as well as national *one-quarter* market shares' and the criteria were amended to include the *desirability* of promoting the interests of consumers, purchasers and other users of goods and services. The M.M.C. was enabled to investigate the activities of the nationalised industries. R.T.P. prohibitions were extended to cover 'loophole' practices, such as recommended prices and patent and design posting arrangements. The Director-General was to take over the functions of the Registrar of Restrictive Trading Agreements and was empowered to act with great freedom to investigate, interpret and liaise with the new Consumer Protection Advisory Committee. He was also to chair the M.M.C. Merger Panel.[2]

It appears that in Japan an interesting balance had been achieved, during the 1960s, between collusive factors which might have been thought to stifle competition and efficiency in a different socio-economic environment. Japanese firms, with Government approval, obtained most (generally about 80%) of their capital by bank loans. This avoided the necessity for higher prices to finance, *via* retained earnings, company growth. Thus the more successful firms could obtain bank loans more readily, and this tended to result in a concentration of output into the hands of the lowest-cost producers, with consequent scale economies, rapid growth, narrower profit margins and more competitive prices. The other major factor supporting this was the traditional paternalism in labour relations, such that labour had considerable internal flexibility and mobility – *via* promotions based on length of service – within firms.[3] At the other extreme, it appears that U.S. application of the anti-trust laws was, during the late 1960s, gradually becoming based on the controversial thesis that 'bigness' alone might be a violation of the public interest.[4]

In December 1969 the head of the U.S. Justice Department's anti-trust division suggested that, in order to deal with the complex problems of the multi-national company and cross-frontier mergers, there should be a harmonisation of international anti-trust legislation. Where some countries, such as the U.K.,

[1] 'Controlling mergers', *Econ.*, 31 Oct. 1964, p. 526.
[2] For further details see 'The Fair Trading Bill–a major development in consumer protection', *Trade and Industry*, 7 Dec. 1972, pp. 474–8; 'Consumers', *Econ.*, 7 July 1973, pp. 86–9; G. and P. Polanyi, 'The Fair Trading Bill and Monopoly Policy', *T.B.R.*, June 1973.
[3] 'Why the Japanese economy will continue to expand', *F.T.*, 12 Feb. 1970.
[4] See 'Is G M too big to be trusted?', *S.T.*, 5 Nov. 1967; 'U.S. anti-trust laws keep a tight rein on the conglomerates', *D.T.*, 31 Jan. 1969.

had been encouraging mergers in contracting industries, contrary to U.S. anti-trust policy, there would obviously be great difficulties in reaching common agreement on any supra-national body of law and doctrine relating to size, competition and conflicts of commercial interest.[1]

CHANGE

A policy aimed at combating private enterprise monopoly concentration, by changes in the ownership and administrative organisation of industry, will involve two main lines of approach:

(a) investigation of where control is exercised in the capitalist firm (i.e. locating the 'seat of control') and how it is exercised.

(b) investigation of alternative forms of ownership and organisation, their advantages and disadvantages.

(a) Control

The term 'control' really applies to high policy, and is sometimes referred to as 'top control'. The functions of top control cover planning for investment, type and amount of output, sales promotion and prices; the taking of policy decisions which involve initiative and adjustment; the combining of factors of production; the appointment of top personnel. As industrial organisation has developed, investment, mechanisation and techniques have increased in complexity so that they now involve the specialised management of machines as well as the manage-ment of men. Because of the burden of heavy overheads they also involve greater risk of loss during periods of low activity, and consequently require a large number of supervisory staff. The increasing complexity of activities, as firms have expanded and diversified, has led to much greater reliance on the storage, retrieval and processing of information and to the development of more sophisticated forms of planning and control.[2]

These day-to-day management functions and the high policy functions of top control used to be carried out by the entrepreneur, who also carried the burden of risk and uncertainty. In modern industrial society the entrepreneur – the provider of capital, risk-taker and manager – has given way to a mass of other people, as shown below.

It was estimated by the Chairman of the London Stock Exchange that there were about 1½ million shareholders in 1947, about 3 million in 1961 and that there would be 4 or 5 million by 1971.[3] The spread of share ownership is such that in some firms there are almost as many shareholders as workers. Theoretically,

---

[1] 'The case for a world-wide trust-buster', *S.T.*, 7 Dec. 1969.
[2] F. de P. Hanika, *New Thinking in Management*, 1965; 'New horizons for management', *Stat.*, 19 June 1964, pp. 891–4; M. Ivens and F. Broadway, eds, *Case Studies in Management*, 1965; 'Impoverished British executives', *Stat.*, 28 May 1965, p. 1487. For further discussion of the role of top management, the functions of planning, the qualities and types of director and the importance of information, see also J. R. Morrison, 'The director's real duties', *Management Today*, Dec. 1971; K. Hopper, 'The nature of American management', *M. and W.S.R.*, Autumn 1969; 'What is corporate planning?', *Econ.*, 5 Oct. 1968, pp. 70–1; 'What is management by objectives?', *Econ.*, 25 April 1970, pp. 60–1; Components of company management development', *F.T.*, 28 Feb. 1969; 'No room at the top for specialists', *D.T.*, 8 Jan. 1969; 'Non-executive directors not "window-dressing" ', *F.T.*, 7 Dec. 1970; J. Marsh, 'The managerial convolution', *Management Today*, Sept. 1971; T. E. Chester, 'Mergers and opportunities for managers', *N.W.B.Q.R.*, May 1969.
[3] *Sunday Express*, 12 Nov. 1961.

the 'Golden Rule' of Professor Robertson – that control goes with risk – would ensure that top control would be in the hands of the shareholders. In practice, however, the existence of a great mass of shareholders in some firms reduces the probability of their coalescing into a coordinated instrument of top control.[1] In some huge firms, indeed, an astonishing feature is the apparent absence of any clearly defined 'owner'. As A. Sampson points out,[2] some combines might

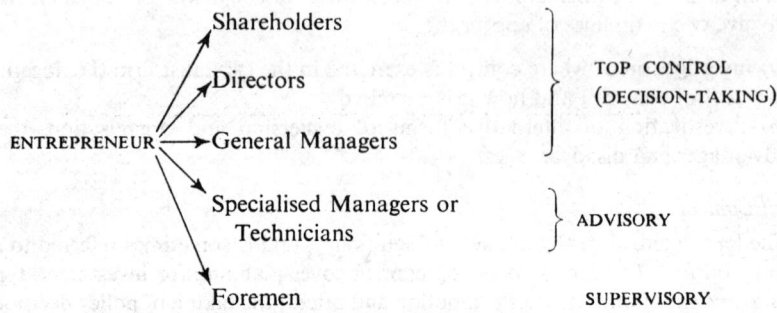

superficially appear to resemble the boy learning to ride a bicycle, who can shout 'Look, Ma, no hands'. Indeed, some combines, large enough to finance themselves and generating their own mystique of autonomous existence, have given rise to a product of the 'managerial revolution', known as the 'corporation man'.

Where, in fact, lies the seat of control, the saddle of high policy? It can be located generally amongst the three strata of shareholders, directors and general managers. It is influenced, however, by the inequality of share distribution, by the presence in some companies of important 'block holders' and by the power of personality amongst members of the Board.

Various investigations into the concentration of shareholding in large British and American companies appear to indicate that the block holder (of voting shares) is the most significant single factor influencing top control.[3] This points to the probability that whereas the small shareholder tends to diversify his holding, thereby spreading his risk (but weakening his control), the large block holder concentrates his resources and his risk, but thereby gains a more effective chance to influence company policy. Professor Sargant Florence, studying a sample of ninety-two out of the 1,700 largest British joint stock companies over the period 1936–51,[4] found that all these companies showed an unequal distribution of vote-holding. This was more unequally distributed than was wealth in the country as a whole. In the twenty-eight largest companies the twenty largest block holders – who included outside companies as well as persons – constituted $\frac{1}{8}$% of the average number of voteholders; in 1936 they held on average 30% of voting shares, and in some cases over 50%. From 1936 to 1951 the average percentage of votes held by the top twenty block holders fell in most of the

[1] See 'Company law reform', *Econ.*, 1 Aug. 1964, p. 496 and *Stat.* 26 June 1964, pp. 987–8.
[2] 'The new leviathans', *Obs.*, 22 Jan. 1961.
[3] Several investigations are reviewed by P. Sargant Florence, *The Logic of British and American Industry*, 1961, pp. 176–95.
[4] P. Sargant Florence, *Ownership, Control and Success of Large Companies*, 1961.

'medium large' and 'very large' companies, but those members of the top twenty who held a smaller proportion of votes in 1951 tended to be the individual persons, not outside firms. Control by personal or family block holdings (amongst the top twenty) was in no case present in the seventeen very largest ('giant') companies, but was present in sixteen out of the twenty-eight 'very large' companies (with capital of £1 to £3 million in 1951). A noticeable factor was the small proportion of voting shares owned by members of boards of directors (in all companies except breweries the average board-holding was 2·3%).[1] In less than one-third of the companies covered was there more than one director who was also on the board of any other large manufacturing or trading company; on average, there were only one and a half directors per very large company covered who were amongst the top twenty vote holders.

Some support for Florence's findings on vote-concentration comes from some recent studies of ownership (or shareholding) concentration, covering the period 1963 to 1970.[2] These indicate a decline in direct share ownership by individuals – although partially substituted with less direct involvement in unit trusts – and a growth in the proportionate share ownership by institutional investors (financial institutions, such as insurance companies and pension funds, and non-financial companies with block holdings in other firms). The personal sector holding of ordinary shares appears to have fallen from about two-thirds in 1957 to less than one-half by 1970 and that of financial institutions to have risen from less than one-fifth to about one-third. According to Revell and Moyle, by 1963 the top twenty block holders in the thirty-nine largest U.K. companies held between 5% and 25% of total shares and in three-quarters of the smaller companies they accounted for more than 50% of market valuation. In the case of the smaller firms, individuals were likely to be an important element: this likelihood was reinforced by the 1970 findings of Moyle, in the sense that the average private investor tended to concentrate his investment into six separate shareholdings, each worth about £1,320. Important implications of the growing share of institutional investors are, firstly, that as their block holding stakes in individual companies grow, they are increasingly obliged to take a more active interest in the management of those firms – to exercise their potential for control, if only to safeguard the capital value of their investment:[3] secondly, this process tends to result in an increasing 'pyramiding' of corporate control – exercised by delegated directors of the institutions over other firms in which they have cross-shareholdings. A similar trend has been noted in the U.S., one manifestation of which has been the development of 'interlocking directorates', referred to earlier.[4]

The dispersion of share ownership throughout industry results in a variety of locations for the seat of control: managerial control appears to be present where block holders are weak; elsewhere, control appears to rest either with influential

[1] For additional reading on this point see Robin Marris, *Managerial Capitalism*, 1964.
[2] See the summary of the 1966 London Stock Exchange Survey and the 1969 Gallup Poll survey, in *F.T.*, 26 Nov. 1969; J. Revell and J. Moyle, *The Owners of Quoted Ordinary Shares: a survey for 1963*, 1966 (summarised in *Stat.*, 9 Dec. 1966, p. 1432); J. Moyle, *The Pattern of Ordinary Share Ownership 1957-70*, 1971; J. H. C. Leach, 'The role of the institutions in the U.K. ordinary share market', *Investment Analyst*, Dec. 1971 (summarised in *Econ.*, 8 Jan. 1972, p. 73).
[3] 'Institutions will need an IRC of their own', *D.T.*, 9 Nov. 1970.
[4] Barber, *op. cit.*, ch. 4; R. J. Larner, 'Ownership and control in the 200 largest nonfinancial corporations, 1929 and 1963', *A.E.R.*, Sept. 1966.

individual block holders or, in a more plutocratic fashion, with a small group of block holders. One of the most significant implications of block holding in the context of the separation of ownership and control lies in the possibility of a change in effective control being achieved, *via* a change in ownership, more economically than by either a 100% acquisition of equity capital or even a 51% acquisition of voting shares. A matter of great interest in this respect, of course, is the question of whether a significant degree of 'owner control' (e.g. by block holders) results in any major difference in performance or profitability, as compared with cases of 'manager control', where share ownership is diffused. The problem centres on theories of managerial motivation: do managers, if free to do so, pursue goals other than profit-maximisation in the interests of share-holders? Do they seek pecuniary and non-pecuniary emoluments; status through market power; long run security instead of short run profits; the promotion of social welfare, rather than the private interests of the shareholders, etc.? Numerous studies have been made into managerial motivation and the effects of the separation of ownership and control on the performance of firms: there is much disagreement as to the results.[1] Monsen, Chiu and Cooley found that large owner-controlled firms had a significantly better record of profitability than large manager-controlled firms, which they attributed to differences in profit motivation. Kamerschen found that, generally, there was no significant difference in profitability, although on balance the advantages of large size might even result in the higher performances of some of the largest manager controlled firms. Mermelstein found that large manager-controlled firms were becoming increasingly successful in stabilising their relative positions, on the basis of asset size. These conflicting views may be reconciled, to some extent, in terms of Hindley's conclusions: he found that there was a 'market for corporate control', whereby if a firm's assets were being under-utilised and the market value of its shares were depressed, investors seeking to change the seat of control could purchase those shares. Thus an efficient market for corporate control should have a chastening effect on wayward managers (and should lead to a reduction in 'X-inefficiency'). However, this market was not fully effective and this could lead to managers' pursuing goals at variance with the maximum interests of the shareholders. Some doubt as to the effectiveness of the market for corporate control has been raised by a recent study by Singh of takeovers in five selected U.K. industries over the period 1955–60. Reddaway's analysis of this study concluded that 'no single explanation can point convincingly to either the likely victim or the likely outcome'.

(b) Alternative forms of ownership and control

(i) *Nationalisation:* There have been various factors at work during the twentieth century, which have made the prospect of public ownership or nationalisation of certain industries more acceptable to public opinion. Some of these factors are as follows:

[1] T. Nichols, *Ownership, Control and Ideology*, 1969; R. J. Monsen, J. S. Chiu and D. E. Cooley, 'The effect of separation of ownership and control on the performance of the large firm', *Q.J.E.*, Aug. 1968; D. R. Kamerschen, 'The influence of ownership and control on profit rates', *A.E.R.*, June 1968; D. Mermelstein, 'Large industrial corporations and asset shares', *A.E.R.*, Sept. 1969; B. Hindley, 'Separation of ownership and control in the modern corporation', *J.L.E.*, April 1970; A. Singh, *Take-overs*, 1971 (analysed by W. B. Reddaway in 'An analysis of take-overs', *L.B.R.*, April 1972).

1. Some industries are 'natural monopolies', which can only be financed in the absence of competition and which can only secure economies of large scale if operated on a coordinated, nationwide basis. Such has been the case with the Post Office, public utilities and public transport. Here, the consumer must be protected against private monopoly abuse.[1]

2. Some industries are 'basic' or vital to other industries and to society or the economy as a whole. This is the case with roads, communications, railways, coal and electricity. Here, the public interest may be protected by State ownership and control.

3. Some industries require great capital investment, either to experiment (as with airlines and atomic energy), or to raise their technical efficiency (as with coal and railways), or to expand to meet growing consumer demand (as with electricity). Where this capital cannot be provided by private enterprise, the State may take over the capital burden.

4. For security reasons or for policy reasons it might be in the public interest to assert State control over certain key sectors of industry. Such is the case with Naval Dockyards, Arsenals and H.M. Stationery Office (security) and the Bank of England (policy).

5. It has often been asserted that where bad labour relations bedevil an important industry, public ownership might provide a new atmosphere of worker participation. Such was the case with coal.

6. Some goods and services are generally recognised as being social 'necessities', which should or must be supplied to all members of society (because they help to maintain or improve the safety, health, welfare or quality of the most valuable assets a nation possesses – people), but for which not all individuals are willing or able to pay. In other words ignorance, apathy or the unequal distribution of wealth and income may cause 'demand' (willingness to pay) to fall short of social needs and wants. Examples of such services are defence, police, health, education, welfare foods, public parks, fire services, museums and, to some extent, housing. Whereas capitalism will only cater for 'demands', under market forces, the State may find it advisable to supply free, or to subsidise, such social necessities, financing their cost out of taxation. The nationalisation or State subsidising of such activities involves a redistribution of income: the wealthy contribute most and the less wealthy benefit most.[2]

Apart from the long-standing public control of such services as defence, police and the Post Office (1660), the nationalisation of entire industries received its greatest impetus and refinement after World War II. During the nineteenth century there was a gradual extension of either private monopolies, operating on a municipal scale, or municipal control and ownership in 'natural monopolies', such as public utilities (gas, water and electricity) and public transport. Early in the twentieth century attempts were made to extend ownership and control beyond the municipal scale, in an effort to improve technical efficiency and reduce costs. The type of commercial and administrative organisation which evolved was the public corporation, essentially a statutory board or commission, responsible to the public interest but with a considerable degree of autonomy in day-to-

---

[1] For a discussion of the theory of 'natural monopolies' and the pros and cons of regulation, see H. Demsetz, 'Why regulate utilities?', *J.L.E.*, April 1968.
[2] For a useful analysis of an efficient market system and of market failure, necessitating collective action, see R. H. Haveman, *The Economics of the Public Sector*, 1970, chs 2 and 3.

day management, and not wholly financed by the Government. Examples of these early twentieth-century public corporations were the Central Electricity Board, established by the Electricity Supply Act of 1926, consisting of a Chairman and seven members, appointed by the responsible minister; the British Broadcasting Corporation, established by Royal Charter in 1927; the London Passenger Transport Board, established in 1933; the Racecourse Betting Control Board, established in 1928 to instal, own, operate and license racecourse totalisators. Their origin lay in the supervisory and administrative statutory boards and commissions, used before the twentieth century, such as Trinity House (lighthouses), the Charity Commission and the Public Trustee, and the local Dock and Harbour Boards of the nineteenth century.

Against the background of industrial strife and trade depression of the 1930s, the Labour Party formulated a policy of nationalisation for public utilities, transport and coalmining, for which the public corporation was to be the model for national ownership and control.[1]

After World War II some entire industries and services came under public ownership and control. These included fuel (coal), power (gas and electricity), iron and steel, transport and communications, the Bank of England, health and education.

The Coal Industry Nationalisation Act 1946 set up the National Coal Board; the Electricity Act 1947 set up the British Electricity Authority; the Gas Act 1948 established the Gas Council, the Iron and Steel Act 1949 set up the Iron and Steel Corporation (replaced, upon denationalisation in 1953, by the supervisory Iron and Steel Board and subsequently replaced, upon renationalisation by the Iron and Steel Act of 1967, by the British Steel Corporation); the Transport Act 1947 established the British Transport Commission; the Civil Aviation Act 1946 reaffirmed the existence of the British Overseas Airways Corporation and established British European Airways, both of which were brought under the unified control of the British Airways Board in 1973.

The general pattern adopted was that of the public corporation, appointed by the responsible Minister (and through him answerable to Parliament), owning the assets of the industry, independent in matters of day-to-day management, able to borrow from the State, and charged with the duties of operating 'in the public interest' and of aiming to 'break even' on costs over a number of years.

Various changes have been made in the administrative structure of these public corporations. The present system of statutory bodies controlling the nationalised fuel, power, transport, communications and iron and steel industries is:

Coal: the National Coal Board, with seventeen area directors and one general manager (for Kent);

Electricity: the Electricity Council (policy-making and advisory, for England and Wales); the Central Electricity Generating Board (for generation and transmission in England and Wales) with twelve Area Electricity Boards; the South of Scotland Electricity Board and the North of Scotland Hydro-Electric Board;

Gas: the Gas Council (advisory and supervisory), with twelve Area Gas Boards;

Transport (other than airlines): after the 1968 Transport Act the *British Railways Board* was to share freight transport with a *National Freight Corporation*:

---

[1] For a detailed review of the development of policy on nationalisation, see R. Kelf-Cohen, *Twenty Years of Nationalisation: the British experience*, 1969, ch. 1.

traffic originating by rail was to be controlled by the B.R.B. and that originating by road was to come under the N.F.C., which also took over that part of road haulage which, after the general denationalisation of road haulage in 1953 onwards, had remained under British Road Services. Supervising both B.R.B.'s freight functions and the H.F.C. was another body – the Freight Integration Council. With regard to passenger transport, the 1968 Act left long distance rail services to the B.R.B., whilst local and commuter rail services were to be run by B.R.B., by agreement with the Passenger Transport Authorities, set up in the four major conurbations outside London. Furthermore, the P.T.A.'s took over the twenty municipal bus services in their areas and made agreements with the *National Bus Company* (established in 1969 and operating in 1970 about 21,000 buses) on the provision of services. A separate *Scottish Transport Group* was set up for bus (and some shipping) services in Scotland. Whereas B.R.B., N.F.C. and the N.B.C. are controlled by the Minister of Transport, the overall planning authority for central bus and underground railway services in the Greater London Council area has been, since 1969, the G.L.C. The services are managed by the London Transport Executive, which took them over from the former London Transport Board: the L.T.B.'s country bus and coach services went to a subsidiary of the N.B.C. Canals come under the British Waterways Board. The British Transport Docks Board runs most of the State-owned ports, which handle about one-fifth of U.K. seaborne trade: some, used mainly in conjunction with railway services, come under the British Railways Board. The Transport Holding Company was left with some peripheral activities, such as hotels and the travel agency, Thomas Cook & Son.[1]

Airlines: the British Overseas Airways Corporation and British European Airways, combined since 1973 under the British Airways Board.

Post and telecommunications: since the 1969 Post Office Act the former Government Department has become a public corporation – the Post Office Corporation – with separate divisions for mail (and the Giro) and for telecommunications: the former Post Office Savings Bank was transferred to the Treasury, as the Department for National Savings.[2]

Iron and steel: since 1967, the British Steel Corporation, with six product divisions.

The organisational changes referred to above have ensued from the ever-present problem of balancing the need for centralisation of control against the need for decentralisation of day-to-day administration. Top controllers are appointed by the responsible minister. In 1957 a House of Commons Select Committee on the Nationalised Industries was set up to examine the reports and accounts of those industries and to report to Parliament, thus improving parliamentary scrutiny.

The nationalised industries have not been static and their evolution has significant implications for the national economy. One of these is the fact that nationalisation increases the concentration of control in the industrial structure: the merits of public ownership and control in this case must be weighed against their performance and efficiency, as compared with that of private enterprise. Furthermore, as some of these industries diversify into peripheral areas (e.g. the N.C.B. and B.S.C. into chemicals), they may be enjoying privileges, denied

[1] For further details see *Brit. O.H.*, 1971, pp. 336–46 and 'Transport reorganised', *D.E.A. Pr. Rep. Econ.*, 47, Dec. 1968.
[2] 'Enter the Post office', *Econ.* 27 Sept. 1969, pp. 68–9.

to private enterprise competitors, and their efficiency in allocating resources must be examined critically. Finally, the very size of the nationalised sector draws attention to the influence which they can exert as employers, customers, suppliers and investors: their use of resources and their costs, prices and investment policies must justify their monopoly status.

Some idea of the relative size of the nationalised industry sector may be gained from the fact that, if the iron and steel sector is included, they employed nearly 2¼ million people in 1966/7 – equivalent to about one-quarter the total employees in manufacturing, or almost 10% of the total in civilian employment. Their capital investment in 1966/7 was about one-quarter of the national total and greater than the total for manufacturing industry: over half of this investment of about £1½ thousand million was financed by Exchequer loans and not from internal sources. They contributed about 10% of the Gross Domestic Product in that year. Excluding the iron and steel sector, their net income (i.e. after allowing for depreciation) was about 3% of their average net assets, between 1955 and 1963, and was about 4% from 1963 to 1967: however, in 1966/7, for example, this 'return on assets' varied from as low as – 4·9% for the British Waterways Board to as high as 21·7% for B.O.A.C. Some of the relevant data for 1966/7 are given in Table 4.1. Fig. 4.7 indicates the size of gross income and its allocation, with percentage rates of return on assets, for the nationalised industries in 1969/70. Figure 4.8 illustrates their capital investment and sources of finance in 1969–70 and Fig. 4.9 illustrates the extent of profits and losses made by the various sectors between 1968 and 1970. It has been estimated that between 1946 and 1971 the total net losses of the nationalised industries amounted to over £1,000 million and it has been suggested that part of the reason has been the over-emphasis on investment in new technology and insufficient emphasis on commercial criteria.[1]

One study[2] has concluded that technical productivity in the nationalised sector as a whole has risen faster than that in manufacturing as a whole, during the period since World War II and especially from 1958 to 1968. These findings may be criticised on the grounds that the capital cost involved in achieving technical efficiency may be unjustified and that technical efficiency itself may be an inferior criterion to that of satisfying consumer wants more successfully and at lower cost than competitors could do. A more recent study[3] has concluded that much of the productivity rise in this sector was accounted for by the rapid output growth in airways and electricity supply – which were not attributable to nationalisation – that during the 1958–68 period the nationalised industries merely tended to catch up with the productivity growth in manufacturing, and that nationalisation was an obstacle to productivity growth, rather than a cause of its achievement.

Two major problems have dominated the debate about the nationalised industries since World War II. *First*, there is the *economic problem* of how far commercial principles of efficiency and resource allocation should be applied, with regard to prices, investment policies and finance and how far social, political and economic goals should be pursued in the national interest. At first, a vague

[1] *D.T.*, 17 May 1971.
[2] R. W. S. Pryke, 'Are nationalised industries becoming more efficient?', *M. and W.S.R.*, Spring 1970.
[3] G. and P. Polanyi, 'The efficiency of nationalised industries', *M. and W.S.R.*, Spring 1972.

348

Table 4.1. *Assets, income, investment and employment in the nationalised industries, 1966-67*

	Average net assets	Net income	Net Income as a percentage of assets	Fixed Investment in the U.K.	Exchequer loans	Exchequer Loans as a percentage of fixed investment[1]	Total employees at March 1967
	£m	£m	%	£m	£m	%	'000s
Post Office	1,584	126·5	8·0	266·4[2]	130·0	48·8	422
National Coal Board[3]	794[4]	29·0	3·7	89·9	37·7	41·9	492
Electricity Council and Boards in England and Wales	3,876	200·4	5·1	664·8	397·0	59·7	229
North of Scotland Hydro-Electric Board	258	12·8	5·0	9·9	21·3[5]	215·2	4
South of Scotland Electricity Board	316	14·7	4·6	47·1	21·4	45·4	16
Gas Council and Area Gas Boards	966	46·5	4·8	215·0	164·4	76·5	124
British Overseas Airways Corporation	134	29·0	21·7	11·8	−2·8	−23·7	19
British European Airways	102	4·8	4·8	17·1	5·6	32·7	20
British Airports Authority	54	5·6	10·3	7·0	—	—	3
British Railways Board[6]	1,931	−70·2	−3·6	106·8	5·0[1]	4·7	361
London Transport Board[6]	218	1·1	0·5	22·1	19·5[1]	88·2	74
British Transport Docks Board[6]	95	5·1	5·4	9·8	3·3	33·7	11
British Waterways Board[6]	13	0·6	4·9	1·0	0·2[1]	20·0	3
Transport Holding Company[6]	175	14·3	8·2	23·3	10·0	42·9	103
Total, all industries	**10,516**	**419·0**	**3·9**	**1,492·0**	**812·6**	**54·4**	**1,881**

[1] These figures exclude deficit grants of £134·7 million for British Railways, £5·9 million for L.T.B. and £1·5 million for British Waterways, but even so do not give directly a self-financing ratio as borrowings may be affected by changes in working capital requirements.
[2] Includes Giro Development Expenses of £0·4 million financed from Exchequer advances.
[3] The N.C.B.'s financial year ran from 27 March 1966 to 25 March 1967.
[4] Reflects only part of the capital reconstruction under the Coal Industry Act 1965. Approximately £156·5 million remained at 25 March 1967, to be written off from the Reserve Fund.
[5] Includes £14·8 million advanced to finance both market purchases of the Board's own stock for cancellation, and the redemption of £13·2 million of the Board's 4½% 1965–6 stock.
[6] For the calendar year 1966.

(Source: *Nationalised Industries: A Review of Economic and Financial Objectives*, Cmnd 3437, 1967)

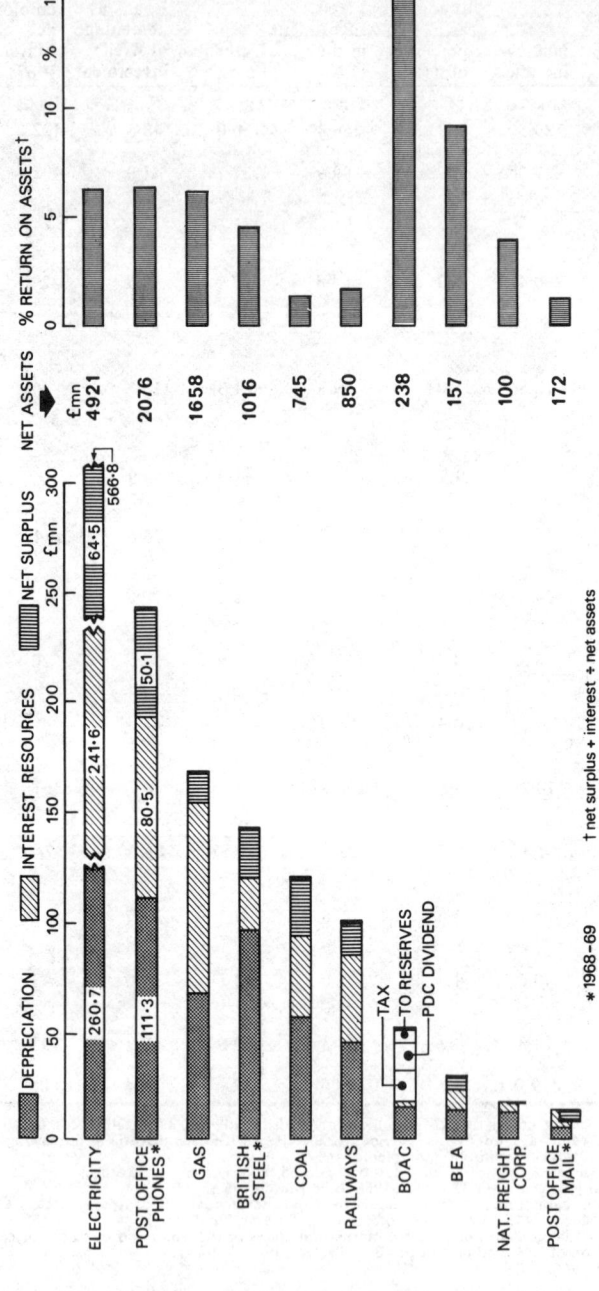

Fig. 4.7. *The nationalised industries 1969–70: allocation of gross income between depreciation, interest repayments and net surplus*
(Source: *Econ.*, 17 Oct. 1970, p. 68)

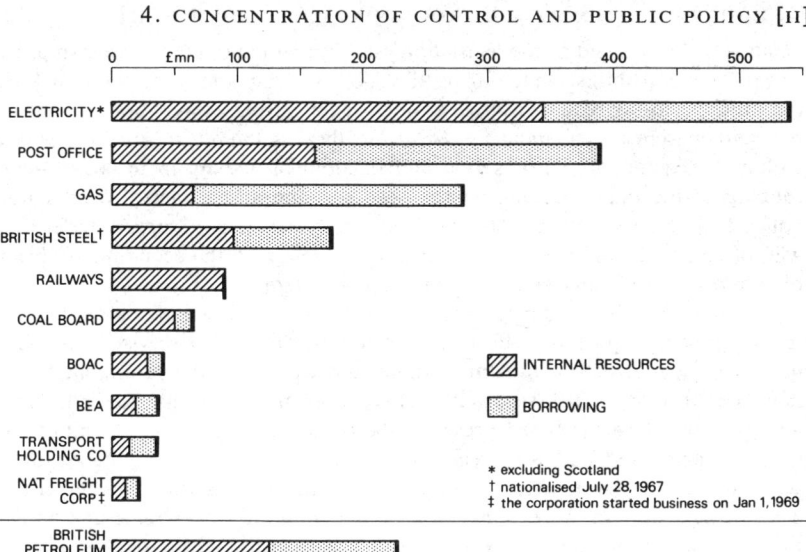

Fig. 4.8. *Extent and sources of capital investment by the nationalised industries, 1969–70*
(Source: *Econ.*, 17 Oct. 1970, p. 69)

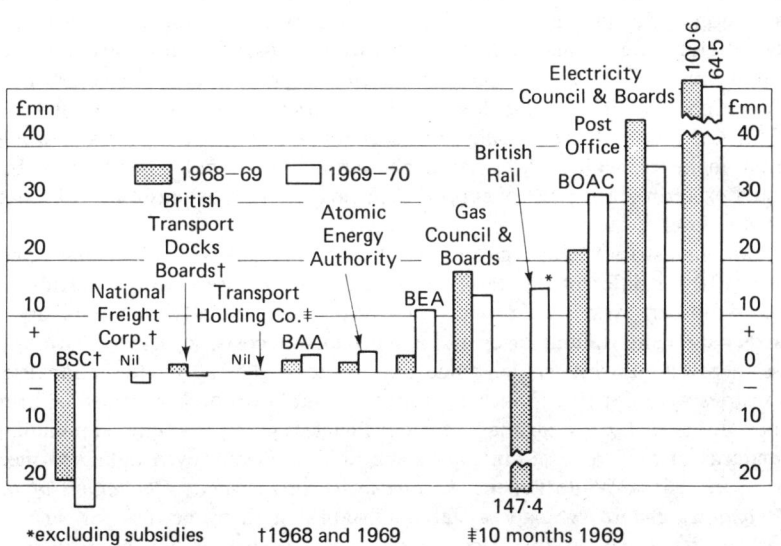

Fig. 4.9. *Profits and losses in the nationalised industries, 1968–70*
(Source: *Econ.*, 26 Dec. 1970, p. 54)

balance was envisaged in the legislation establishing nationalised ownership, by way of a general obligation to pursue 'the public interest' and yet to avoid making a continuous loss extending over a period of years. Surpluses were not prohibited, but neither were they mandatory. *Secondly*, there is the *administrative problem* of how to balance decentralisation and freedom of activity in the day-to-day running of the industries against the need for centralised control over major policy by the Government. This problem of independence *versus* interference will, of course, be influenced by the prevailing policy on the economic problem of commercial self-sufficiency *versus* the public interest.

With regard to the *pricing and investment problem*, it follows, of course, that the pricing policy adopted will affect demand for the product or service, will affect the consequent size and investment plans and will affect the profitability and rate of return on total assets and on new investment projects. At first, most industries in the sector based prices on the overall average cost per unit of the product or process: we have already noted this in the case of coal, and a long-standing example is the pattern of uniform rates for postal services—whether for delivery next door or to distant parts of the country. An extreme alternative would be to charge each successive customer or group of consumers a price which covers the entire addition to total costs resulting from supplying that individual or group. This is referred to as the 'true cost' or the 'marginal cost' (i.e. of producing and supplying at the margin). If successive additions to industry output are at higher and higher cost, the 'marginal cost' will be rising and will be higher than the average cost, which it pulls up behind it. A price based on the marginal cost of the last unit produced would therefore exceed the overall average cost of production and would result in surplus profit: a price based on average cost of all units produced would be lower, would just 'break even', with no profit or loss, but would lead to greater consumption and thus to additional expansion of capacity and investment—which makes a call on scarce resources, needed elsewhere in the economy. If the overall costs for successive units of output are falling, on the other hand, then marginal cost would be less than average cost, which it brings down behind it: prices based on the marginal cost of the last unit produced would not cover the overall average cost and would result in losses, whilst prices based on average cost would 'break even' but would exceed the true cost of supplying the marginal or last customer, at whatever the level of output.

Some industries such as gas and electricity later adopted differential prices (or tariffs) for different classes of consumer: in some cases, two-part tariffs (or even multi-part tariffs) were used, to cover overhead costs (with a standard or fixed charge) and running or operational production costs, separately. Nevertheless, there was no clearcut policy guide for the sector in general, and the nationalised industries were not free to increase prices or to follow purely commercial principles. By 1961 it was clear that the vague financial guidelines only set minimum standards of performance and that some industries were even failing to meet them. In 1961 a White Paper, *The Financial and Economic Obligations of the Nationalised Industries*, made a start on establishing a framework for them to work in. Revenue was to match costs over a five-year period, after allowing for reserves to replace assets at current prices and to finance future capital development. Targets were to be set for five years, subject to annual review, and although cost reductions were seen as the main source of additional revenues, the industries were to have more freedom to increase prices. Targets, usually a percentage return on net assets, were agreed with the boards, varying from $12\frac{1}{2}\%$ for B.O.A.C. to a break-even nil rate for the N.C.B.: the railways were required only to reduce their annual deficit.

By 1967 more advanced investment appraisal methods had been developed and the results of a review of the sector were embodied in the 1967 White Paper, *Nationalised Industries: a review of economic and financial objectives*. This policy document sought an efficient use of resources, directed to activities where the returns were greatest. The *economic* objective was the use of a 'test discount rate of return' on new investment projects (initially 8%, but raised in 1969 to 10%), unless there was some wider economic or special social justification. The *financial* objective was expressed as a target rate of return on net assets: $12\frac{1}{2}\%$ for B.O.A.C., 'break-even' for the N.C.B. and varying rates for the other industries (see Table 4.2). In this respect, prices were of key importance, and one of the most significant points made was that commercial principles were to be adopted, so that weak sectors were not cross-subsidised by profitable sectors: in addition to covering accounting costs (i.e., including interest on capital borrowed and provision for depreciation), prices were to be reasonably related to costs at the margin, designed to promote the efficient use of resources. This was to be accomplished in the following way: for the provision of a continually expanding capacity and production, *long-run marginal costs* (which include fixed overhead charges) should generally form the basis for prices. At any (short run) point in time, however, the capacity in existence may be under-utilised, through deficient demand or over-utilised, through excessive demand. In the former case, *short run marginal cost* – which would be lower than long run marginal cost – would be the basis for prices, so as to stimulate demand; in the latter case, *short run marginal cost* – which would be higher than long run marginal cost – would be the price base, so as to curtail excess demand. Where demand was neither too high nor too low, given the scale of capacity in existence, there would be no difference between long and short run marginal cost. A note of caution was expressed with regard to cases (such as gas or electricity) where new technological developments might lead to falling long run marginal (and average) costs: strict adherence to the principles enunciated above could then lead to temporary but heavy deficits – since prices would not cover average costs – which would need to be subsidised out of general taxation: furthermore, the lower prices might lead to excessive demand, shortages and costly short run measures to increase supply.[1]

In its report for the 1967–8 session, the Select Committee on Nationalised Industries pursued the objective of marginal cost pricing in a seemingly uncritical fashion. There is, in fact, much diversity of opinion as to whether it is theoretically sound, in a world of market imperfections, as a means of ensuring an optimum allocation of resources.[2]

Allied to the long-standing economic problem of pricing and investment policy has been that of the type and source of *finance*. Prior to 1956 most of the nationalised industries were able, within the limits of statutory and Ministerial

[1] Cmnd 3437, paras 17–22. For a useful summary, see 'Guidelines for the nationalised industries', *D.E.A. Pr. Rep. Econ.*, 36, Jan. 1968; also 'Financing the nationalised industries', *M.B.R.*, Aug. 1968.
[2] W. A. Robson, 'Ministerial control of the nationalised industries', *Political Quarterly*, 40, 1969, pp. 105–8.

Table 4.2. *Nationalised industries: financial objectives*

Industry	Objective	Period covered
Post Office	8% net (A)	1963/64–1967/68
National Coal Board	To break even after interest and depreciation including £10 million a year to cover the difference between depreciation at historic cost and replacement cost (B)	
Electricity Boards (England and Wales)	average 12·4% gross (C)	1962/63–1966/67 (F)
North of Scotland Hydro-Electric Board	(see footnote D)	
South of Scotland Electricity Board	12·4% gross (C)	1962/63–1966/67
Gas Boards	Average 10·2% gross (C)	1962/63–1966/67 (F)
British Overseas Airways Corporation	12½% net (A)	1966/67–1969/70
British European Airways Corporation	6% net (A)	1963/64–1967/68
British Railways Board	Have the statutory obligation of reducing their deficit and breaking even as soon as possible	
London Transport Board	(see footnote E)	1963–1967

Targets for the British Airports Authority and the British Transport Docks Board were then under discussion.

Notes

A. Income before interest but after depreciation at historic cost, expressed as a percentage of average net assets.

B. The N.C.B. were relieved of their objective temporarily in April 1965 but this was revived and was to continue in 1967/68.

C. Income before interest and depreciation, expressed as a percentage of average net assets.

D. As an interim measure the N.S.H.E.B. agreed to apply such tariff increases as would give a similar percentage increase in revenue as the tariff increases applied by the S.S.E.B.

E. L.T.B.'s objective was to earn an average balance of revenue of £4 million a year, after interest and depreciation at historic cost. This was equivalent to 5% net. L.T.B.'s target was however in abeyance in view of the Board's financial position.

F. The Minister of Power announced on 19 December 1966, in answer to a Parliamentary Question (O.R. Cols 232–3) that the objectives of these two industries would continue in 1967/68.

(Source: *Nationalised Industries: a review of economic and financial objectives*, 1967)

approval, to borrow for long-term capital investment by issuing fixed-interest stock, guaranteed by the Government: the exception was the N.C.B., which borrowed from the Exchequer. Because of various complications this caused in the gilt-edged market, the practice of stock issues was abandoned in 1956: henceforth, long-term borrowing was to be from the Exchequer, as it had been with the N.C.B. This takes the form of long-term loans – requiring ministerial approval – and appears as payments from the National Loans Fund in the Exchequer accounts.[1] With regard to short-term borrowing for working capital, the Post Office could borrow only from the Bank of England, but the other sectors could borrow from the banks (at Bank rate) and from various other sources, including the foreign exchange market. A further slight easing of controls was announced in May 1972.[2]

With regard to the *administrative problem* of the balance between centralisation and decentralisation – and of the role of public enterprise and the appropriate organisational structure, through which ministerial control should be exercised – the 1960s witnessed an important crystallisation of thought in public debate. The nationalised industries have always had the dual role of functioning as efficient commercial bodies and of functioning in 'the public interest', yet the public interest has been a nebulous concept and the two roles may sometimes conflict. Both roles require ministerial intervention of some sort – on the one hand to scrutinise the efficiency of commercial operation and on the other hand to assess social, political and economic implications and objectives – necessitated by the fact of public ownership.

During the 1950s the public corporations generally enjoyed a large measure of independence: capital requirements were met and there was not much ministerial interference with price policies. With the tightening up of the commercial efficiency criteria, following the 1961 and 1967 White Papers, ministerial intervention tended to increase, as instanced by the September 1967 decision to refer all price increase proposals to the National Board for Prices and Incomes.[3] The Select Committee, in its 1967–8 Report, were highly critical of the confusion about the purposes and methods of Ministerial control, of the increasing tendency for sponsoring departments to encroach on matters of day-to-day operations and to give little or no major policy guidance, and of the incompatibility of the departments' duties to ensure both efficiency and the public interest. The Select Committee proposed the abolition of sponsoring departments and of the Ministry of Power and the creation of a Ministry of Nationalised Industries – primarily responsible for supervising and ensuring their 'efficiency' (a concept defined in very rigid commercial terms). The public interest was to be protected by other interested Ministers, who would have to negotiate with the Boards and pay the cost of non-commercial services, provided at a contracted price. This emphasis on the efficiency role of the Board and the Ministry contrasts with the case of Italy, where a Ministry of State Holdings, created in 1956, promotes commercial

---

[1] Generally, these are fixed-interest loans, but in 1966 an experiment was made with an Exchequer Dividend Capital loan to B.O.A.C. This gave a dividend linked to profits, – as a substitute for equity capital. In 1969 this method became more generally used, and is referred to as 'public dividend capital' (p.d.c.) (see 'They all want P.D.C.', *Econ.*, 12 July 1969, pp. 66–7).

[2] For further details see 'Financing the nationalised industries', *loc. cit.*, pp. 12–18; also *D.T.*, 15 Feb. 1969 and *F.T.*, 4 May 1972.

[3] Kelf-Cohen, *op. cit.*, pp. 315–18.

criteria, but a Committee of Ministers decide issues of major policy. At least one authority considers that the Boards should not be over-preoccupied with commercial criteria and that cross-subsidisation of uncommercial (but otherwise desirable) activities *within* the public corporation would have less drawbacks than subsidies, financed out of general taxation.[1] The essential point seems to be that of allowing the Boards flexibility in balancing their dual role, but with less ministerial interference, as opposed to greater interference in the pursuance of a purely commercial role. A point worthy of mention is that the greater the degree of monopoly power held by a nationalised industry, the easier it is to satisfy investment and pricing efficiency criteria by simply raising prices; other important aspects of efficiency, such as democratic control, consumer satisfaction and cost reduction may be ignored.

A study by Professor Coombes[2] in 1971 found that the basic problem in the administration of the nationalised industries was their uncertain objectives: was State ownership an end in itself, a device for controlling the economy, a device for providing social services or a device for running basic industries more efficiently? He proposed clearer criteria for judging their performance, a reduction in Government involvement and more operational freedom for the Boards – protected from disruptive political changes. Whilst major planning and control functions should be subject to Government influence, day-to-day operation should not. Competition should be encouraged between the nationalised industries themselves and between them and the private sector; the industries should have access to the private capital market, which would act as a monitor on their efficiency and would permit private minority shareholding in the public sector. The Boards would be replaced by holding corporations, which would be interposed between the relevant Government departments and the actual undertakings – which would become joint stock companies.

Some steps in this direction of *mixed ownership* and reduced State interference in operational activities were taken in late 1970, with an evaluation by the Government of the scope and desirability of nationalised gas, steel and electricity activities. The possibility of 'hiving off' profitable sectors and/or allowing private minority participation was being seriously considered. The objective was not outright denationalisation, but rather a 'B.P. solution' (the Government owned 49% of B.P. equity).[3] Mixed ownership developments in the reverse direction have taken place during the 1960s, as with Industrial Reorganisation Corporation and Shipbuilding Industry Board purchases of State shareholdings in some industries. This has been variously described as 'catalysing industrial rationalisation' and as 'creeping nationalisation'.[4] Suggestions have been made for this process to extend to 'joint ventures' other than as rescue operations in problem industries – as in the case of N.C.B. collaboration with appliance manufacturers.[5]

[1] Robson, *loc. cit.*, who refers to W. G. Shepherd, *Economic Performance under Public Ownership: British Fuel and Power*, 1969, pp. 48, 144.
[2] D. Coombes, *State Enterprise: business or politics?*, 1971.
[3] 'Public ownership: what strategy?', *Econ.*, 17 Oct. 1970, pp. 68–9; 'Let them compete', *Econ.*, 5 Dec. 1970, pp. 13–14; 'State industry ancillaries which might be "hived off"', *F.T.*, 5 Jan. 1971.
[4] See W. G. Shepherd, 'Alternatives for public expenditure', ch. 9 in Caves, *op. cit.*, pp. 387–8; F. Broadway, *State Intervention in British Industry, 1964–68*, 1969, pp. 70–2; also W. G. McClelland, 'The Industrial Reorganisation Corporation 1966–71: an experimental prod.', *T.B.R.*, June 1972.
[5] E. Moonman, *Reluctant Partnership*, 1971, pp. 151–2.

4. CONCENTRATION OF CONTROL AND PUBLIC POLICY [II]

With the publication of the Industry Act in August 1972, 'selective financial assistance' was to be made available for firms outside the 'assisted' areas, in the 'national interest'. It was emphasised that although the State would be reluctant to exercise its power to take an equity stake in private sector firms (with their consent), it would not hesitate to do so, even if its were politically distasteful, if job security and the 'national interest' were involved.[1]

During the early 1970s however, a crucial dilemma was becoming apparent. On the one hand, mixed ownership was being viewed as a means of harnessing the financial discipline of the private capital market, in order to promote efficiency in publicly owned (or part-owned) sectors. On the other hand, the nationalised industries were being treated as 'commanding heights' of the economy and were being used to serve the interests of wider national economic and political ends: examples of this were the decision to apply to the nationalised industries the mid-1971 C.B.I. price restraint pledge (which jeopardised their profitability); the pressures put on these industries to expand and bring forward their investment plans as part of the Government's reflationary drive; the pressures exerted on them, at times, to concede high wage increases in order to avoid strike action, and at other times to serve as a bludgeon against inflationary wage claims (with the frequent result that labour disputes became national crises, as with coal, postal services and the railways). The implications seem to be that, whereas proposals such as those of the Select Committee, Professor Coombes and C. Foster[2] call for a reduction in State interference in operational activities – and/or for the introduction of some private capital – combined with greater emphasis on commercial efficiency, the very fact of public ownership brings with it the inevitable involvement of the State with 'public interest' issues, which tends to spill over into direct interference in operational activities. Thus even the suggestions of authorities such as Robson and Shepherd, referred to above, for the Boards to exercise a dual role – but without direct State interference – seem bound to founder on this same inevitability of such interference. Perhaps the solution lies somewhere nearer proposals that all or most of the nationalised industries' assets transfer to private ownership (with Government supervision) and come under market discipline, or that the State retain only those sectors in which political involvement is essential and inevitable.[3]

The democratic problem of worker participation has been tackled by requiring the public corporations to devise a suitable system of collective bargaining for negotiation (on wages, hours and conditions) and for joint consultation (on safety, health, welfare, etc.).

The democratic problem of consumer protection against monopoly abuse has been further tackled by the establishment of representative consumers' councils and consultative committees (for coal, iron and steel, electricity, gas and inland transport), and the Air Transport Advisory Council. There has been much criticism of the lack of effectiveness of the consultative bodies, their lack of staff, finance and expertise and the ignorance and apathy of consumers. In 1968 the Consumer Council published a Report on the Consumer and Consultative

---

[1] See 'Helping the regions,' *E.P.R.*, 32, Oct. 1972.
[2] C. Foster, *Public Enterprise*, 1972. For a useful review of Foster and this debate in general, see also S. Brittan, 'Nationalisation – an old controversy is back', *F.T.*, 27 April 1972.
[3] Brittan, *loc. cit.*; 'Public ownership: what strategy?', *Econ.*, 17 Oct. 1970, p. 69; W. A. Robson, 'Mixed Enterprise', *N.W.B.Q.R.*, Aug. 1972.

Councils, which pointed to these defects but found that, when given the chance, these bodies do try to help the consumer. It is of interest that, during the course through Parliament of the Iron and Steel Bill in 1966, the clause which allowed B.S.C. representation on the Iron and Steel Consumers' Council was deleted, in view of 'the need to increase the independence' of the Council and to indicate its independence.[1]

The dominating economic factors underlying these nationalised industries may be indicated by the symbols B (Basic), M (Monopoly) and C (Capital).[2] Applying these general criteria, the nationalised industries show the following properties:

> Gas, mainly M
> Canals, docks, harbours, mainly M
> Iron and steel, mainly B, C
> Airlines, mainly C
> Coalmining, mainly B, C
> Electricity, mainly B, C, M
> Railways, mainly B, C, M
> Post and telecommunications, mainly B, C, M

The dominant organisational pattern in the public corporations may be represented as shown in Fig. 4.10.

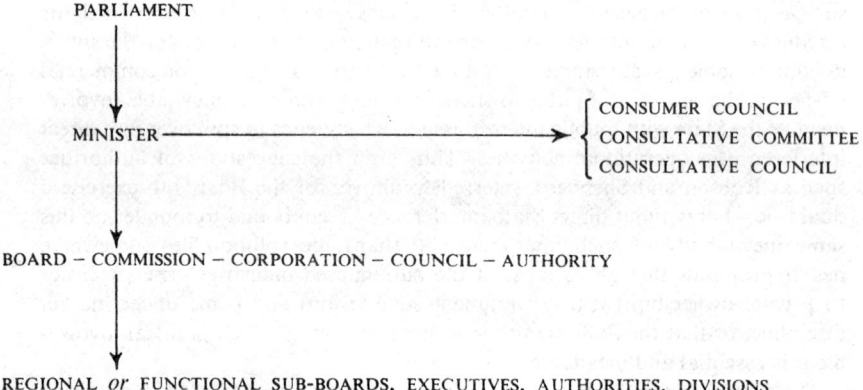

Fig. 4.10. *Organisation of public corporations*

The dominant organisational pattern in the public corporations may be represented as shown opposite.

(ii) *Cooperation.* To achieve stronger bargaining power and/or to secure economies of scale, cooperation may be undertaken by producers, distributors or consumers.

Cooperation by *producers* in the field of production has made little progress in Britain, but in the field of joint marketing there has been much more progress, with a growing trend in agricultural producers' marketing cooperatives. This type of marketing cooperatives by producers does, of course, constitute an element of monopolistic concentration of control by them.

[1] See Kelf-Cohen, *op. cit.*, ch. 12.
[2] A method evolved by Professor Sargant Florence, in *The Logic of British and American Industry*, pp. 222–33.

Cooperation by *distributors* varies from tacit collusion in price-fixing to the banding together of small retailers (usually in an exclusive arrangement with a wholesaler) in order to achieve bulk purchase economies. Cooperatives of this type have been quite active in the grocery business. Whereas the retail turnover share of independent grocers fell from 57% to 43% between 1950 and 1970, the retail members of 'voluntary groups' or 'symbol shop' groups – numerically 32% of independent grocers – accounted by 1970 for a 23% share of retail grocery sales, whilst the non-affiliated independents accounted for only 20%. Retail members of those grocery voluntary groups increased from 50 in 1954 to 31,000 in 1966, since when the number has been fairly stable. Their collective turnover had been rising at about the same rate as that of the multiple grocers, whilst that of non-affiliated independents had declined. Despite these successes, however, some observers have noted that some of the potential advantages of bulk-buying and central services, provided by affiliated wholesalers have been under-utilised, because of 'trading away' by both retailers and wholesalers.[1] While most of these voluntary chains or groups have been sponsored by wholesalers, about one retail member in seven is affiliated to a group sponsored by the retailers themselves. In 1967 the first voluntary group in the drapery trade was launched by three textile wholesalers.[2] Again, as far as the consumer is concerned, this represents a degree of monopolistic concentration of control.

Cooperation by *consumers* has made extensive strides in Britain. Such cooperation has been applied to the retail stage, the wholesale stage and the production stage, as well as action in the political field. The primary aims of consumer cooperation are to increase consumer bargaining power and to achieve a greater degree of democratic control, with the participation of customers, workers and managers alike, all of whom are members.

Consumer retail cooperatives started in Rochdale in 1844. As they had to be self-financing, it was decided to charge 'capitalist' market prices, but to distribute any profit in the form of a dividend to the members, in proportion to the value of their purchases. Each member has one vote, and must have at least one share (usually £1). The maximum investment by members in shares (which receive a low rate of interest) is usually fixed at £1,000. The Co-operative Retail Societies are independent of each other, but they link up in a federal fashion in the central organ of the movement – the Co-operative Union. The whole country is divided up into areas, on the basis of their relative importance in the past, and each area is covered by an independent retail society. The quarterly or half-yearly meetings are open to all members, but are usually dominated by a small proportion of 'activists'. The members elect a spare-time management committee or board (which is split up into specialist sub-committees), and this voluntary committee appoints full-time officials. Following a series of amalgamations and rationalising mergers, the number of independent retail societies fell from 1,015 at the end of 1958 to 257 by 1972. They had about 12.1 million members at end-1970 and 11·35 million at end-1971, but vary in size from a few thousand members to 1·15 million (the London Co-operative Society, with a 1969 turnover of £81 million or about 7½% of the £1,130 million total). The retail societies controlled

---

[1] For further details, see 'Retailers' plan for survival', *Management Today*, Sept. 1971, pp. 105–6; N. A. H. Stacey and A. Wilson, *The Changing Pattern of Distribution*, 1965, pp. 225–9; C. Fulop, *Retailing and the Consumer*, 1968, pp. 15–17.
[2] *Stat.*, 17 March 1967, p. 539 and 31 March 1967, p. 649.

about 25,000 shops in 1969 but only about 13,000 in 1971. In 1971 the twenty-five largest societies accounted for about half the total membership, whilst the hundred smallest had only about 1 % of the total.[1]

The retail societies are free to buy from any supplier, but to secure economies in production and distribution they formed the Co-operative Wholesale Society (C.W.S.) for England and Wales in 1863 and the Scottish Co-operative Wholesale Society (S.C.W.S.) in 1868. These two branches operate about 150 factories and supply about 60% of the goods sold in the co-operative shops.[2] Profits of the wholesale societies are distributed as dividend to the retail societies, according to the value of their purchases. The managements of the wholesale societies are elected by delegates of the retail societies, but the voting power of each delegate is weighted according to the relative importance of his retail society's purchases. The large customers, therefore, carry more weight in elections and discussions. Unlike the management committees of the retail societies, the managements of the wholesale societies are full-time, paid directors. They form specialist sub-committees and are entrusted with both 'top control' and day-to-day management functions. They appoint full-time officials lower down the organisation.

The C.W.S. has run a bank since about 1870, which has become the financial centre of the Co-operative movement. The S.C.W.S. has been engaged in banking since 1948. The C.W.S. also runs an insurance company and, until 1970, was linked with a building society. Financial links are maintained with other institutions, and clients include not only retail society members but also trade unions and local authorities.

The political arm of the consumers' Co-operative movement is the Co-operative Party, which is closely linked to the Labour Party and has representatives in Parliament.

Some of the potential advantages of consumer cooperation in Britain are:

1 The retail 'divi' is an attraction to the consuming public.
2. There is a great deal of consumer loyalty, on ideological grounds.
3. There is a highly democratic element in the system of 'one member, one vote'.
4. Lower financial and operating costs are possible, because:
(*a*) a low rate of interest is paid on members' shares;
(*b*) consumer loyalty reduces the necessity to spend much money on advertising;
(*c*) consumer loyalty permits the societies to open shops in less-frequented streets, where rentals are lower;
(*d*) administrative costs are relatively low, as a result of voluntary work by members;
(*e*) lower merchandise costs are possible, as a result of buying from the wholesale societies and obtaining the wholesale 'dividend'.

Some of the disadvantages of the present system are:

1. Because of the independence of individual retail societies, there is a lack of coordination and planning of activities on a national scale.
2. Little use is made of national advertising.
3. Many consumers use the retail society shops in order to obtain the 'divi' on

---

[1] *Brit. O.H.*, 1971, p. 404; 'Which way for the Co-op?', *Econ.*, 8 May 1971, p. 64 and 31 May 1969, p. 60; *F.T.*, 27 May 1971 and 1 June 1972.
[2] *F.T.*, 27 May 1971; *Econ.*, 8 May 1971, p. 64.

staple commodities, such as milk, or branded articles, subject to RPM, whilst shopping elsewhere for other things.

4. There is little standardisation in the goods produced by the wholesale societies.
5. The 'decentralised democracy' throughout the system tends to result in a deficiency of enterprising people willing to take investment and other risks.
6. The method of electing administrators for top control and day-to-day management often results in the appointment of laymen with unsuitable knowledge or experience.
7. There is a tendency to promote full-time officials according to length of service and not on the basis of business experience and education. This, combined with lower salary scales than those in other branches of retailing and production, tends to result in a deficiency of scientific management.

During the 1960s the movement was subjected to increasing competition from multiples and voluntary groups, particularly in foodstuffs, which account for nearly 75% of retail co-operative turnover (see Fig. 4.11). From 1961 to 1966 co-operative society turnover rose by only 5·9%, whilst that of the multiples rose by 48·8%.[1] The relative shares from 1950 to 1970 in the grocery sector are shown in Fig. 4.12. Much internal self-criticism has been voiced and many profound changes have been made in structure and method of operation.

An independent commission of inquiry in 1958, headed by Mr Gaitskell, suggested that the number of retail societies be reduced by amalgamations to 200 or 300. It also called for the substitution of professional managers for the existing management committees, and for a new, strengthened central organisation – a Co-operative Development Society, with powers to develop chain stores. A minority on the commission recommended a single, national retail society. The President of the Co-operative Union, at the 1961 annual congress, called for much greater competitive retailing by the co-operatives. Some of his suggestions were for a reorganisation of societies into fewer, larger units; the concentration of the production arm on to fewer, standardised products; the employment of specialist, experienced retail officials; fewer and larger retail shops; and an increase in the dividend, as an inducement to shoppers.[2] At the annual Co-operative Union Congress in June 1962, a committee was set up to consider, a new, integrated, central body for the movement, to embrace the Co-operative Union, the C.W.S. and the S.C.W.S. The aim would be to ally the financial strength of the wholesale and production branch with the advisory services of the Co-operative Union. At the same time it was decided to alter the composition of the central executive of the Co-operative Union, to bring in some of the more progressive members from the retail societies and infuse more enterprise and initiative at the centre.[3] Late in 1960 the Co-operative Enterprise Movement was founded, to foster the implementation of the Gaitskell commission's recommendations in the London Co-operative Society.[4]

In May 1967 a plan for amalgamating the independent retail societies into fifty or sixty regional groupings was put to the Co-operative Congress and the Co-operative Union produced a blueprint for this process in 1968. The first such regional grouping was formed out of thirty-one separate societies in the North

[1] For further details of turnover per square foot of sales area, profit margins and financing problems, see 'Which way for the Co-op?', *Econ.*, 8 May 1971, p. 64.
[2] *D.T.*, 23 May 1961.   [3] *Obs.*, 17 June 1962; *D.T.*, 31 July 1962.   [4] *Econ.*, 12 May 1962.

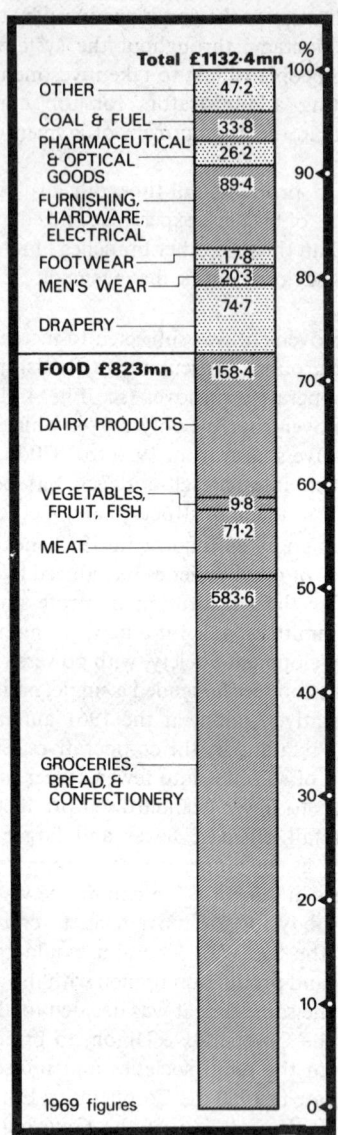

Fig. 4.11. *Co-operative retail sales, by class of goods, 1969*
(Source: *Econ.*, 8 May 1971, p. 65)

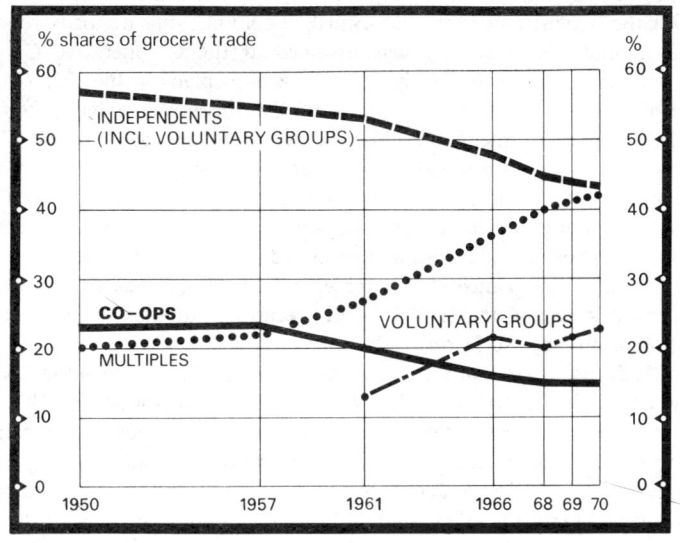

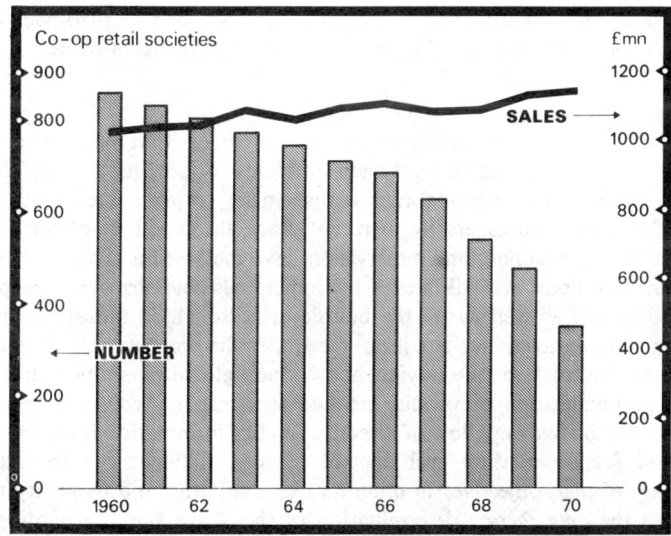

Fig. 4.12. *Shares of grocery turnover and the co-operatives*
(Sources: *Econ.*, 8 May 1971, p. 64; *F.T.*, 10 April 1970; *Management Today*.
Sep. 1971, p. 105)

363

East in 1970: its annual turnover was about £70 million. Discussions were also proceeding in 1969 for the linking of three large societies in the North-West.[1]

In 1971 the suggestion of the 1958 Gaitskell commission's minority report for a single national retail society was dropped at the Co-operative Congress: support was given, however, for the regional groups plan. At the 1972 Congress the idea of a national retail policy, with central control, was revived: the motive was to be that the movement should not be at a disadvantage in the E.E.C.[2]

The 1962 Congress proposal for a merger of the movement's central bodies was reiterated at the 1969 Congress.[3] Later that year it was agreed that the C.W.S. take over the buying for about 1,000 shops run by Co-operative Retail Services. The C.R.S., started in 1934, had amalgamated 150 different societies in thirty-one regions. The significance of this agreement was that it was a step towards a national movement and the C.W.S. would receive a stimulus to its 'own label' production, with large scale orders.[4]

The C.W.S. itself has made progress since 1967, when professional management was brought in, to rationalise production and methods. By 1971 more than eighty factories were closed down; it launched 'operation facelift' – a service to the retail societies for sprucing up their image; it cut down the number of own-brand names under which its products were selling and concentrated on a single national brand, for sale within and outside the movement; it started using spare capacity to produce own-brand products for independent retailers; it moved into the hire-purchase field in 1969; in 1972 it was planning to expand into hypermarkets, in conjunction with the retail societies, and in 1970 had for the first time gone to the open market for finance for its expansion plans.[5]

PLANNING, SUPERVISION AND INTERVENTION

The State has always exercised some elements of supervision over the economy, but has in the past tended to limit such functions to 'holding the ring' for the various sectional interests – labour management, capital, etc. During the twentieth century, and especially in recent years, the functions of the State in overall economic planning and supervision have increased a great deal. Whilst investment decisions are still made by individuals and firms in the private enterprise sector, as well as by the boards of nationalised industries and the consumer co-operatives, the State is not faced with the problem of total economic planning on the scale of the Soviet model. Such global planning results from outright nationalisation of production and services. It involves an elaborate apparatus for the two-way flow of directives and of information for plan formulation and for observation and control of plan fulfilment; it involves the elaboration of plan objectives in quantitative, qualitative and monetary terms; it requires the *ante factum* determination of the Wage Fund, according to a national incomes policy, and this in turn requires the participation of the trade unions in both the formulation and fulfilment of planned objectives; it also involves the ever-present problem of balancing the need for centralisation of

[1] *D.T.*, 29 May 1967, 31 Oct. 1969 and 15 Jan. 1970; *Econ.*, 6 Jan. 1968, p. 45.
[2] *D.T.*, 30 May 1972.
[3] 'Co-operate, or else', *Econ.*, 31 May 1969, p. 60 and *F.T.*, 28 May 1969.
[4] *Econ.*, 22 Nov. 1969, p. 77 and *D.T.*, 21 Jan. 1970.
[5] 'Coping with the Co-op', *Management Today*, Nov. 1969, pp. 100–5; *F.T.*, 27 May 1971, 2 May 1972 and 1 June 1972; *S.T.*, 28 March 1970; *D.T.*, 24 Jan. 1969; *Econ.*, 3 Jan. 1970, p. 49 and 8 May 1971, pp. 64–5.

policy decisions against the need for decentralisation of day-to-day execution, at all levels of the economy.[1]

Since 1965 important experiments in liberalising the economy – using the stimulus of the price mechanism – have been noted in the U.S.S.R. and other Soviet bloc countries.[2]

Since World War II the French system of 'indicative', 'stimulative' or 'permissive' planning has aroused much interest in the Western world.[3]

Swedish experience in the planning of economic growth and of an incomes policy was, in 1965, the subject of study by the British Minister for Economic Affairs.[4]

In the mixed economy of Britain, the State has intensified its supervisory, interventionist and planning activities. Hitherto, its influence was felt largely through monetary and banking policy (Bank rate, etc.) and through indirect taxation. Gradually, the State has become more involved in economic affairs in order to promote the national interest. State planning, intervention and supervision has two aspects – positive (or direct) action and negative (or indirect) action. Both may overlap, in practice, in their application and effect on various sectors of the economy.

Some of the main aims and methods of State interference are as follows:

(*a*) To redistribute income and wealth (as with direct and indirect taxation).

(*b*) To maintain full employment and influence the location of industry (as with the manipulation of budget deficits and surpluses; social security; the Local Employment Acts; the Location of Industry Acts; development certificates; the Town and Country Planning Acts; Employment Exchanges; industrial training and apprenticeship schemes, etc.).

(*c*) To ensure conservation of land and resources (as with the Green Belt policy; the National Trust; Agricultural Grants, etc.).

(*d*) To prevent exploitation of labour and promote industrial peace (as with the Statutory Wages Boards; the Factories and Shops Inspectors; the Joint Industrial 'Whitley' Councils; the D.E.P. conciliation and arbitration machinery, etc.).

(*e*) To manipulate the price mechanism, for reasons of equity or production policy (as with wartime rationing; price controls; raw materials quotas, etc.).

(*f*) To promote planned coordination of the growth of production and productivity throughout the economy.

State interference in economic affairs has evolved in several stages.[5] Each has been characterised, to a greater or less extent, by elements of three basic functions, *viz.* 'holding the ring' (as impartial referee), 'intervention' (as participating coxswain), or more pronounced 'interference' (as tribal chieftain).

---

[1] For the general development and problems of Soviet global planning, see A. Baykov, *The Development of the Soviet Economic System*, 1946. The particular rôle of trade unions in the Soviet planned economy was traced by the author in 'The Rôle of Trade Unions in Soviet Industry', M.Com. thesis, University of Birmingham, 1953.

[2] P. Landy, 'Agonised revisionism in Czechoslovakia', *Stat.*, 15 Jan. 1965, pp. 151–2; 'Czechoslovakia', *Econ.* 3 May 1969, p. 43; 'Russia: planning the unplannable', *Econ.*, 5 Sept. 1970, pp. 84–6; 'Russia: still waiting for the millennium', *F.T.*, 23 Nov. 1970; 'The inefficient Communists', *D.T.*, 19 Feb. 1971.

[3] R. Aron, 'French planning: the facts', *D.T.*, 11 Nov. 1964. For a useful critique, see V. Lutz, *Central Planning for the Market Economy: an analysis of the French theory and experience*, 1969.   [4] 'Brown study in Sweden', *Stat.*, 22 Jan. 1965, p. 233.

[5] For a useful and detailed historical review of State intervention, see A. Skuse, *Government Intervention and Industrial Policy*, 1970.

Before World War I, interventionist emphasis gradually shifted from the protection and fostering of Britain's foreign trade and interference in conditions of employment towards a generally liberal or *laissez faire* approach to trade and industrial relations. Concurrently, however, there was an undertow of protective paternalism towards apprentices and female and child labour and the beginnings of public enterprise. As the period drew to a close, there was a more pronounced move away from *laissez faire*, as the U.K. faced stiffer competition from emerging industrial rivals, as large scale, monopolistic concentration of control in industry was becoming apparent and as municipal and State public enterprise expanded, as was reflected in a continuous rise in public expenditure and revenue.

World War I resulted in the eventual establishment of unprecedented public controls over supplies, production, wages and labour relations – as free market forces failed to meet the requirements of the war effort. Controls involved institutional changes, in the development of central bodies of manufacturers and labour: lasting effects of this were to illustrate the effectiveness of State intervention and to establish precedents for the machinery of intervention. The level of public expenditure remained, after the war, at a very much higher level than at any previous period.

The interwar period was characterised by an increasing degree of protectionism against foreign competition, an increasing State involvement in industrial structure, rationalisation and cartelisation and the beginnings of intervention in industrial location.

World War II saw a speedy imposition of a 'control economy'. This involved controls over industrial finance, production, materials, location, prices and profit margins; the deployment, hours and conditions of labour were subject to price controls; central organisations of labour and employers were fostered, as channels for the mobilisation of resources to the war effort; the bureaucratic State machinery was vastly expanded to administer this control economy, and as the war drew to a close, it turned its attention to the responsibility for planning for peacetime.

Developments since World War II may be broken down into three periods:

(*a*) *1945–50*: continuing controls and nationalisation. This period was overshadowed by the need to rehabilitate the economy and saw the extension of location policy, the beginnings of a monopoly policy and attempts at price controls and a voluntary wages 'freeze'. The level of public expenditure settled down at a higher level than during the period preceding World War II.

(*b*) *1950–61*: dismantling of controls and *laissez faire*. During this period there was a general dismantling of the control apparatus and an increased readiness to give free rein to market forces. However, the slow GNP growth rate and recurrent balance of payments crises gradually led to a climate of opinion which favoured more State intervention and overall economic planning.

(*c*) *1961–70*: planning, supervision and detailed intervention. This period witnessed the most extensive attempts at detailed interference in economic affairs during peacetime, with attempts at national economic 'indicative' planning, numerous locational and regional policy measures, a proliferation of interventionist taxes, agencies and Ministries, attempts at overall supervision of prices and incomes and the evolution of public enterprise and monopoly policy in the mixed economy, outlined above.

After 1970 the Conservative Government, which took over from Labour, embarked on a policy of rationalising the apparatus of intervention and a reduction of intervention and State financial involvement, where possible. The approach was intended to be more pragmatic and less dogmatic than that of the middle and late 1960s.

The debate about the correct balance between State intervention and *laissez faire* market forces has intensified in recent years. At one extreme, critics of State intervention have asserted that positive or direct intervention (such as tax incentives and reorganisation subsidies) in the market mechanism is based on a false supposition that Government knows better than businessmen and trade unionists how to reach the decisions which must be made.[1] Positive, dynamic intervention (such as with I.R.C. subsidising of mergers and State involvement in prestige projects such as Concorde) has been held to dissipate scarce national resources, and the sheltering of nationalised industries and regulated cartels from competition has insulated them from competition, while political super-vision of wage, price and financial policies has not been effective;[2] before the 1970 change of Government, the Conservative spokesman for industry and trade criticised attempts at partnership, collusion or penetration between Government and industry, since their functions were different and the State, whilst sometimes retaining a 'reserve role' for certain industries in need of assistance, should merely create conditions under which industry could function in the national interest.[3] One of the most severe criticisms has been that an advanced industrial economy is far too complex for simplistic solutions and numerous *ad hoc* measures and policies – some of which may conflict with each other in a series of chain reactions. A study of the 1964–68 period[4] found that the biggest failures were the most grandiose attempts at intervention, such as attempts to force industry into higher rates of capital investment by the use of discriminatory taxes against distributed profits, or attempts to hold back wage inflation with an incomes policy. One of the major shortcomings of the period of Labour Government was held to be in the relatively little use of small-scale, practical, well thought-out schemes, and the major use of highly theoretical, grandiose man-datory measures. At the other extreme, the case has been put that the State is inextricably involved in industrial affairs, if only by virtue of the importance of the public sector in the mixed economy and of its major purchasing power as a customer of industries such as construction, pharmaceuticals, electricity and electronics. As a result, State intervention is seen as inevitable in some areas and could be fruitful, in view of the alleged low quality of management in some sectors of industry.[5]

The argument has been put that as economies are not static, the State has continually to steer a course between the pull of various forces, and *laissez faire* is a luxury which only economies on a sound footing can afford.[6] Another recent study has concluded that not only is it necessary for the State to be actively involved in industrial affairs, but also that industry needs the assistance which Government can offer: a partnership, it was considered, should develop between the two parties, but great attention should be paid on the one hand to

[1] M. Zinkin, 'Government and industry', *M. and W.S.R.*, Autumn 1967.
[2] S. Brittan, *Government and the Market Economy*, 1971.
[3] *S.T.*, 25 Jan. 1970.
[4] Broadway, *op. cit.*, esp. pp. 12, 165.
[5] A. Henney, 'Government and industry – a reply', *M. and W.S.R.*, Autumn 1968.
[6] 'No time for a "hands off" policy', *D.T.*, 19 Oct. 1970.

the need for efficient channels of information and communications and on the other hand to the need for farsighted Government planning and consistent policies.[1] Between these two extremes, a consensus appears to be evolving between industry and Government. In late-1967 one respected industrialist called for a change in the institutional background, which caused Ministries to pursue a role of interfering, rather than enterprising, allies; he also noted that business needed the support of Government, provided that each party accepted different responsibilities.[2] In late 1970 the Minister for Trade and Industry, while proposing a process of 'disengagement', nevertheless stressed that excessive reliance on market forces and negative, indirect fiscal and monetary policies might achieve price stability, but only at the cost of excessive unemployment.[3]

The promotion of planned coordination of the growth of production and productivity may be considered to be one of the most far-reaching objectives of State intervention in economic affairs. The keynote of this overall policy was sounded in the 1944 White Paper on Employment Policy (Cmd 6527): it formulated the general objective of maintaining a high level of employment and productivity throughout the economy.

Some of the main strands in State intervention since World War II have been mentioned above and treated at greater length in previous sections: viz. locational and regional policy and intervention in the rationalisation of the industrial structure – as with the Industrial Reorganisation Corporation. The strand with which we are primarily concerned here is the evolution of overall planning and supervision. This has involved three major elements:

(a) The development of statistical data, financial and control techniques and changes in Treasury and Ministerial organisation and roles.

(b) The development of a planning apparatus and attempts at overall economic planning.

(c) Attempts at the supervision and control of prices and incomes.

With regard to **data, techniques** and **financial and administrative machinery,** some of the notable developments have been as follows:

(i) In 1966 the House of Commons estimates committee drew attention to the lack of depth and coordination in the Government statistical services. Increasing State involvement has highlighted the need for more comprehensive, up-to-date and coordinated statistics. In 1968 it was decided to reorganise the Central Statistical Office. Four units were set up, dealing with the planning of the Government's computer developments, the improvement of the classification system, the streamlining of statistical demands made by various Ministries, industries and individuals, and the overall developments and priorities for the State statistical services.[4] Two years later the complaint was still being made, however, that the statistical services were too decentralised and were not paying enough attention to the major magnitudes of income, output and expenditure.[5]

---

[1] Moonman, op. cit., esp. pp. 74–5, 191, 195, 202; J. Jewkes, 'The industrial policy group–an experiment in communication', N.W.B.Q.R., Nov. 1970.

[2] 'What business wants from Government', Obs., 12 Nov. 1967.

[3] D.T., 6 Nov. 1970.

[4] 'The statistical gap', Econ., 11 May 1968, pp. 65–6.

[5] 'Numbers that count', Econ., 29 Aug. 1970, pp. 49–50. For further information about social statistics, the new Business Statistics Office and the general sources and scope of official economic statistics, see also 'Social figures', Econ., 19 Dec. 1970, p. 24; 'Statistics for industry', D.E.A. Pr. Rep., Ind. and Reg., 51, April 1969; 'Economic statistics', E.P.R., 6, Aug. 1970, and 7, Sept. 1970; P. D. Balacs, 'Economic data and economic policy', L.B.R., April 1972.

(ii) In 1961 the Plowden Committee, reporting on Treasury organisation and public spending, called for long-term planning in the public sector of the economy as a means of avoiding disjointed projects, based on year-by-year changes in circumstances and policy. From 1962 to 1969 Plowden-type changes in Treasury organisation resulted in a functional division of responsibilities for overall economic strategy. Two large groups of Divisions conducted most of the work: the Public Sector Group controlled public expenditure in relation to general economic strategy, and the Finance Group had to seek consistency between all aspects of financial policy and overall strategy. A smaller group – the Economic Section – complemented the other two, being responsible for the coordination of economic policy or central economic strategy, in conjunction with the Department of Economic Affairs (created in 1964). A number of smaller Divisions, including a Fiscal and Incomes Policy Division, also contributed. Until the D.E.A. was disbanded in 1969 it concentrated on medium- and long-term strategy, and the Economic Section on short-term and financial aspects. After 1969 overall economic strategy was concentrated in the Treasury. The four main functions involved in this were forecasting, strategy formulation, dissemination of information and cooperation with other Departments in areas of economic activity where the Treasury shared responsibility: they were located in a third large group of Divisions, the National Economy Group, which in turn included an Economic Assessment group of Divisions, a National Economy (General) group, an Industrial and Incomes Policy group and a Fiscal Policy group. The Treasury Information Division was to be closely associated with the functions of these members of the National Economy Group. The general objective was to allocate professional economists between the three main groups: all would be members of the Treasury Economic Service and would interact with each other.[1]

(iii) In April 1969 a Government Green Paper was published, *Public Expenditure: a new presentation*, which introduced two major proposals for improving Parliamentary control over public expenditure. These were, first, that the Government publish a White Paper each autumn, with information on public expenditure plans for five years ahead; second, that the form in which this information was given should be drastically improved, so as to show revenue as well as expenditure and the real costs of public expenditure and their real impact on resources.[2] Such a White Paper was issued in December 1970, the first of the series.[3] In order to plan and monitor public expenditure, the Treasury and other Government Departments have gradually adopted and adapted sophisticated techniques of financial budgeting and control. One of these, arising from D.E.A. work on the 1965 National Plan was the Public Expenditure Survey Committee system (PESC) – whereby Departments make 'rolling' forward estimates of their expenditure plans for four or five years ahead. It is aimed at imposing disciplined priorities, so as to avoid escalation as unanticipated commitments arise. The other major technique, adopted in follow-up studies of the 1970 and 1971 PESC White Papers on long-term expenditure, has been Pro-

---

[1] 'Treasury changes', *E.P.R.*, 2, Feb. 1970; Sir Alec Cairncross, 'Economists in Government', *L.B.R.*, Jan. 1970.
[2] *F.T.*, 30 April 1969.
[3] *Public Expenditure in 1968–69 to 1973–74*, Cmnd 4234; also 'Government policies for public spending', *E.P.R.*, 10, Dec. 1970 for a summary of the second annual White Paper (*New Policies for Public Spending*, Cmnd 4515).

gramme Analysis and Review (PAR), a derivation from the American system called the Planning, Programming, Budgeting system (PPB). This is basically a method of exercising choice and control over the allocation of resources. It consists of three stages: (a) defining *objectives* rigorously; (b) assessing *existing methods* of reaching those objectives (and comparing resources used with achievements); (c) identifying and selecting *alternative ways* of attaining the objectives more effectively.[1]

(iv) During the 1960s a great deal of work was done in the U.K. on the development of econometric (economic measurement) techniques of forecasting and planning. One of these projects has been the Cambridge University Social Accounting Matrix (SAM), which aims, with the use of computers, to establish models of economic growth, showing the effects of changes in the variables.[2] Other models have been developed, dealing with matters such as the determinants of total consumption, dividend behaviour of companies, capital expenditure by manufacturing industry, aggregate commercial bank behaviour and short-term forecasting methods.[3] The Treasury has developed computer facilities in recent years for work on its own econometric models of the economy: these have been the *quarterly model*, for short-term forecasting and the *annual model* for medium-term projections. Each involves numerous variables and analyses the ways in which they interact, by means of a series of mathematical equations.[4] A highly simplified framework for the sort of model used in national income forecasting is shown in Fig. 4.13.

(v) During the 1960s an important series of organisational changes was instituted in Goverment Departments other than the Treasury. The general trend has been for a rationalising of functions and organisation, to cope with the increasing complexity of the economy and the changing relative significance of different areas and types of problem. Major reforms were instituted in the Civil Service, following the 1968 report of the Fulton Committee: a Civil Service Department was set up in 1968, containing a management services section, which provided expert management consultancy facilities to other Departments.[5] Between 1964 and 1969 the major Departments concerned with planning, industry and trade were the Ministry of Technology, the Department of Employment and Productivity, the Department of Economic Affairs and the Board of Trade. In 1969 a policy of rationalisation was adopted to reduce overlapping of functions and to concentrate policy making into better integrated Departments: this included the merging of the Ministry of Power into the Ministry of Technology, the creation of a new Department for Local Government and Regional Planning, the disbanding of the D.E.A. and the reallocation of its functions amongst other Departments. Following the change in Government in 1970 a further process of rationalisation and integration was carried out, involving the recruitment of

---

[1] For more detailed exposition and examples, see 'Mind your Par, Pesc and PPBS', *Econ.*, 4 March 1972, pp. 62–3; 'Planning, programming, budgeting', *E.P.R.*, 6, Aug. 1970; 'PPB applied', *E.P.R.*, 8, Oct. 1970; 'Spending review plans approved by Government', *F.T.*, 15 Jan. 1971.

[2] *D.T.*, 5 Nov. 1962; *Stat.*, 16 July 1965, pp. 167–8; R. J. Ball, 'The Cambridge model of economic growth', *Economica*, May 1963.

[3] K. Hilton and D. F. Heathfield (eds), *The Econometric Study of the United Kingdom*, 1970 (reviewed in *Econ.*, 12 Sept. 1970, p. 55).

[4] 'Treasury computer facilities', *E.P.R.*, 10, Dec. 1970; 'Forecasting a la mode', *Econ.*, 28 Nov. 1970, p. 79.

[5] 'Efficiency in the Civil Service', *D.E.A. Pr. Rep. Ind. and Reg.*, 48, Jan. 1969.

experienced businessmen into Government service. The Department of Trade and Industry was created, replacing the Ministry of Technology and the Board of Trade: it took over responsibility for monopolies and mergers from the Department of Employment and Productivity, but shed aerospace functions to a new Ministry of Aviation Supply. Its vast range of activities presented immense problems of coordination, and in April 1972 its functions were delegated to subordinate Ministries for Industrial Development, Industry and Aerospace (encompassing the former Ministry of Aviation Supply), with Under Secretaries for Trade, Industry, Aerospace and Industrial Development. In 1970 another, new integrated Department was created – the Department of the Environment – which encompassed the functions of the former Ministries of Housing and Local Government, Public Building and Works, and Transport. The D.E.P., shorn of merger and monopoly functions, was renamed the Department of Employment.[1] By March 1974 the DTI had split into Departments of Energy; Industry; Trade; Prices and Consumer Protection.[2]

With regard to the development of a **planning apparatus** and attempts at **overall economic planning** some of the major developments have been as follows: (i) General planning targets for industry were set out in economic 'models'

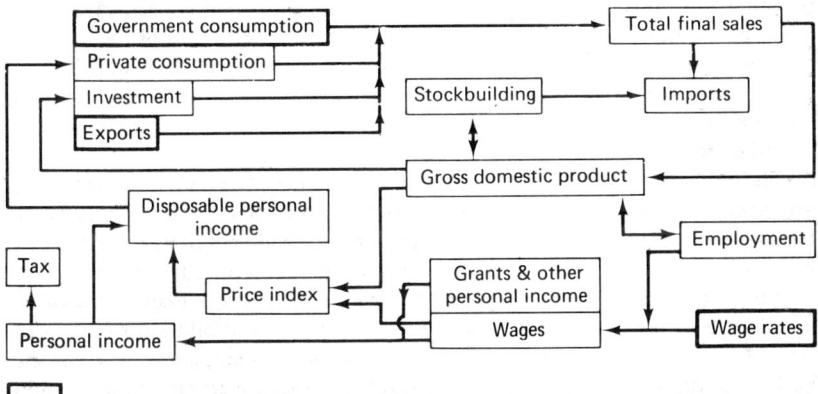

Exogenous (i.e. independently determined)

Fig. 4.13. *General framework for an econometric model used in national income forecasting* (Source: *Econ.*, 22 Nov. 1970, p. 79)

by the 1947 and subsequent Economic Surveys. That for 1947 called for the participation of industry in discussions on the formulation and execution of State policy. Consequently a number of consultative bodies were set up, representing Government, employers' associations and trade unions. They included, at national level, the National Production Advisory Council on Industry (N.P.A.C.I.) and the National Joint Advisory Council (N.J.A.C.). (ii) In November 1960 a conference of the Federation of British Industries called for cooperation between the Government and industry in assessing the needs, and planning the objectives, of economic growth over the next five years.[3]

---

[1] *F.T.*, 6 Oct. 1969; 'The shape of the new Mintech', *F.T.*, 17 Nov. 1969; *D.T.*, 24 June 1970; 'Reorganising central government', *E.P.R.*, 9, Nov. 1970; *D.T.*, 16 Oct. 1970; 'The question of size', *F.T.*, 23 Feb. 1972; *F.T.*, 8 April 1972.
[2] For further details see 'The DTI dismembered', *Econ.*, 9th March, 1974, p. 78.
[3] *Obs.*, 27 Nov. 1960.

(iii) In February 1962 the Government set up the National Economic Development Council (N.E.D.C.) to examine and propose plans for economic stability and future growth in the private and public sectors of the economy, to consider the obstacles to such growth and practical measures required to achieve it. It is a two-tier body, with a top council, under the Chairmanship of the Prime Minister. Other members are Ministers of the main economic Departments, independent members, representatives of management, the trade unions and the nationalised industries and the Director-General of N.E.D.O. (the National Economic Development Office), the N.E.D.C. Secretariat with a permanent staff of economists. The permanent staff do not have the same power as the French *commissariat du plan*, which cannot be vetoed by the *conseil superieur*. They produced a report in 1963, proposing a 4% annual growth rate for National Income.[1]

(iv) Under the auspices of the N.E.D.C., twenty-one Economic Development Councils were set up in various industries – 'Little Neddies' – with representatives of management, the unions and the Government, who were to share responsibility for planning and efficiency in the industry concerned.[2] Gradually, the work of the E.D.C.s assumed more practical relevance than that of the overall planning functions of N.E.D.C. In late 1970, however, it was decided to alter their functions from a preoccupation with industrial sector problems to more general project work. A N.E.D.O. review of the work of the E.D.C.s was thought likely to lead to a reduction in their number: some were likely to be amalgamated and others to be replaced with forecasting groups – so as to maintain contact with the industries concerned.[3]

(v) The entire framework of 'indicative' planning and supervision in the economy was given a stimulus at the end of 1964 when the new Labour Government created the Department of Economic Affairs. The D.E.A. had economic growth as its major objective, and planning as its main tool. It was primarily responsible for long-term aspects of economic policy and with physical resources. Some of its main duties, which had never previously been the responsibilities of any particular Government department, were: macro-economic planning, with the backing of the administrative and fiscal powers of the Government; the creation of operative channels of communication between the central Government and industry, using the industrial apparatus of the N.E.D.C. and the 'Little Neddies'; regional and geographical planning.[4] In 1965 the D.E.A. published a National Plan – much criticised since – aiming at a 2.5% increase in GNP between 1964 and 1970. Another much-criticised attempt at overall planning was *The Task Ahead: economic assessment to 1972*, published in February 1969. After the disbanding of the D.E.A. in 1969 the Treasury, in 1970, published a revised assessment of *The Task Ahead*: this was a more flexible projection than the National Plan, based on alternative 3% and higher growth rates in GNP. This was in line

[1] *Econ.*, 23 Feb. 1963, p. 671; *Obs.*, 3 Feb. 1963.
[2] 'The Little Neddies at work', *D.E.A. Pr. Rep. Ind. and Reg.*, 2, Feb. 1965; 'The Little Neddies and the task ahead', *D.E.A. Pr. Rep. Econ.*, 54, July 1969; Sir Frederick Catherwood, 'Why Neddy survived', *L.B.R.*, April 1971; 'The "Neddy" experiment – a new approach to national planning', *M.B.R.*, Feb. 1968.
[3] See *D.T.*, 11 Feb. 1969 and 11 Sept. 1970; *F.T.*, 14 Nov. 1970 and 30 Nov. 1970.
[4] See S. C. Leslie, 'Whitehall strikes a new balance', *Stat.*, 6 Nov. 1964, pp. 334–5; 'The work of the D.E.A.', *D.E.A. Pr. Rep. Ind. and Reg.* 1, Jan. 1965; 'What does Planning mean?', *D.E.A. Pr. Rep., Econ.*, 4, April 1965; 'The role of the D.E.A.', *D.E.A. Pr. Rep. Econ.*, 50, March 1969.

with current opinion that indicative planning projections should be restricted to medium-term assessments of economic development, continually revised on a 'rolling forward' basis.[1]

With regard to attempts at the **supervision and control** of **prices and incomes,** some of the major developments and problems have been as follows:[2]

(i) Between 1948 and 1950 a policy of vigorous 'wage restraint' was operated in the U.K. by the Labour Government, with the cooperation of the T.U.C. The intention was to keep wage increases in line with the rise in physical output and so keep down the rise in the general price level, to restrain inflationary pressure during a period of high employment levels. This policy achieved a large measure of success but entailed tremendous difficulties, in that the T.U.C. had little control over sectional trade union interests: it was dissolved in 1950.

(ii) From 1956 to 1957 the Conservative Government attempted to establish a 'price plateau' as a corollary to a wage restraint policy. This foundered in 1957, during a period of strikes in the shipbuilding and engineering industries, when the Government conceded inflationary wage increases in order to avoid conflict with the trade unions. In 1957 a three-man Council on Prices, Productivity and Incomes (the Cohen Council, popularly referred to as 'the Three Wise Men'), was established. It reported in 1958, 1959 and 1961, criticising the T.U.C. as being 'obsessed with wages' and of paying insufficient attention to other factors, such as the need for full utilisation of capacity and the raising of productivity.

(iii) In July 1961 came a vigorous attempt to impose a *direct* check on wage and price increases, known as the 'pay pause'. This was associated with the establishment of what became the N.E.D.C., with a February 1962 White Paper on *Incomes Policy: the next step* (Cmnd 1626) and with the establishment in July 1962 of the National Incomes Commission (N.I.C.), which replaced the Cohen Council. It was an advisory body to the Government, examining the implications of wage claims submitted to it, in the light of the national interest. It was not considered a success: a basic problem was the lack of enforcement powers for its recommendations, should they be defied by the trade unions. Between 1962 and 1964 a series of 'guiding lights' or criteria for wage and salary increases was published.

(iv) By 1964 a great deal of public debate was under way about alternatives to 'stop-go' policies of expansion and restraint and opinion generally was in favour of some definite form of incomes policy. Hitherto, the main body of opinion held that inflationary pressure resulted from 'demand-pull' – excessive demand pressure, which resulted in higher prices, followed by trade union wage

---

[1] For a general review of the problems of indicative or voluntary planning in a mixed economy, a critique of the 1965 National Plan and an outline and critique of *The Task Ahead* (1969), see Broadway, *op. cit.*, pp. 18–26; Cairncross, ed., *op. cit.*, pp. 154–9; Caves, ed., *op. cit.*, pp. 118–19; Catherwood, 'Why Neddy survived', *loc. cit.*; G. E. Denton, 'Reflections on economic planning', *The Bankers' Magazine*, Nov. 1968; 'The Task Ahead', *D.E.A. Pr. Rep. Econ.*, 49, Feb. 1969; H. F. R. Catherwood, 'The planning dialogue', *N.W.B.Q.R.*, May 1969; T. S. Barker and J. R. C. Lecomber, *Economic Planning for 1972: an appraisal of 'The Task Ahead'*, 1969, esp. pp. 784–8.

[2] For a fairly comprehensive review and analysis of prices and incomes policy since World War II see: R. Allen, 'Concerning incomes policy', *M. and W.S.R.*, Spring 1970; C. W. Jefferson, K. I. Sams and D. Swann, 'The control of incomes and prices in the United Kingdom, 1964–1967: policy and experience', *The Canadian Journal of Economics*, May 1968; D. C. Smith, 'Incomes policy', ch. 3 in Caves, ed., *op. cit.*; J. Mitchell, 'Why we need a prices policy', *L.B.R.*, April 1969; B. Hollowood, 'Price control – or catastrophe', *N.W.B.Q.R.*, Aug. 1970; 'Do price controls work?', *Econ.*, 29 April 1972, pp. 74–5.

demands and the willingness of employers to concede to them. An alternative theory, however, was gaining acceptance – *viz.*, that of 'cost-push' – which considered rising costs to be the trigger to the wage-cost-prices spiral. This became a more comprehensive theory, taking into account multiple factors, such as trade union militancy and bargaining power, living standard changes, the degree of competition in industry, availability of product substitutes, the height of tariff barriers, etc. All these factors tended to make the cost-push theory somewhat complex and indeterminate. Henceforth, attention was turned to a 'prices and incomes policy', but an alternative term which has been suggested for this is 'direct stabilisation policy' (as opposed to traditional, indirect, monetary and fiscal 'demand management' or 'demand stabilisation policy').

Such direct stabilisation policies may be of four main types:

(*a*) *Indicative planning*, with objectives for wage and price increases, within the context of overall projections for the development of the economy. This depends on the thorough exchange of information and has little or no coercive powers.

(*b*) *'Guidepost' policies*, setting acceptable limits to wage and price increases and using moral pressure against wage increases, and State purchasing power against price increases. This type of policy was attempted in the U.S.A. in 1962 and, with the emphasis on wages, in the U.K. after 1970.

(*c*) *Voluntary (or agreed) direct stabilisation policies*. Such policies were adopted from 1948 to 1950 and from 1964 to 1966 in the U.K. Their basic weakness is that they only last as long as each of the main consenting parties so desires. In December 1964 a Joint Statement of Intent on Prices and Incomes was signed by industry, labour and the Government, declaring willingness to cooperate in the preparation of a general plan for economic development and productivity. In 1965 a National Board for Prices and Incomes (N.B.P.I.) was set up to examine particular cases. Criteria to be used in the application of the policy and the machinery were published in a White Paper on *Prices and Incomes Policy* (Cmnd 2639) in April 1965. This established a 'norm' of 3% to $3\frac{1}{2}$% for annual income rises, consistent with price stability. It was generally considered to have failed in its main objectives.

(*d*) *Statutory (or mandatory) direct stabilisation policies*. Such a policy was enunciated in the Prices and Incomes Acts of August 1966, 1967 and 1968. Part 4 of the composite Act gave the State power to enforce regulations on prices and wages by legal action against contravention by individuals, firms or trade unions. Part 4 was not intended as a permanent piece of legislation, could not be automatically applied, unless by special order of Parliament, and (unless renewed) could only remain in force until August 1967. The Act resulted from the failure of the voluntary policy: it imposed a six-month prices and incomes 'freeze' on the economy, and was followed by a six-month period of 'severe restraint'. The policy was thus based on investigation and delay, rather than on arbitrary control. Suitable cases were referred to the N.B.P.I. and from time to time guidelines on prices and incomes were laid down, which the N.B.P.I. had to bear in mind. Part 4 of the Act expired in August 1967 and in December 1968 the emphasis shifted to Part 2 of the 1966 Act: this imposed a period of thirty days' notice of wage and price increases and a three-month 'standstill' if reference were made to the N.B.P.I. In December 1970 the Act lapsed, when the Conservative Government chose not to renew it.

It is generally considered that the statutory policy achieved some success

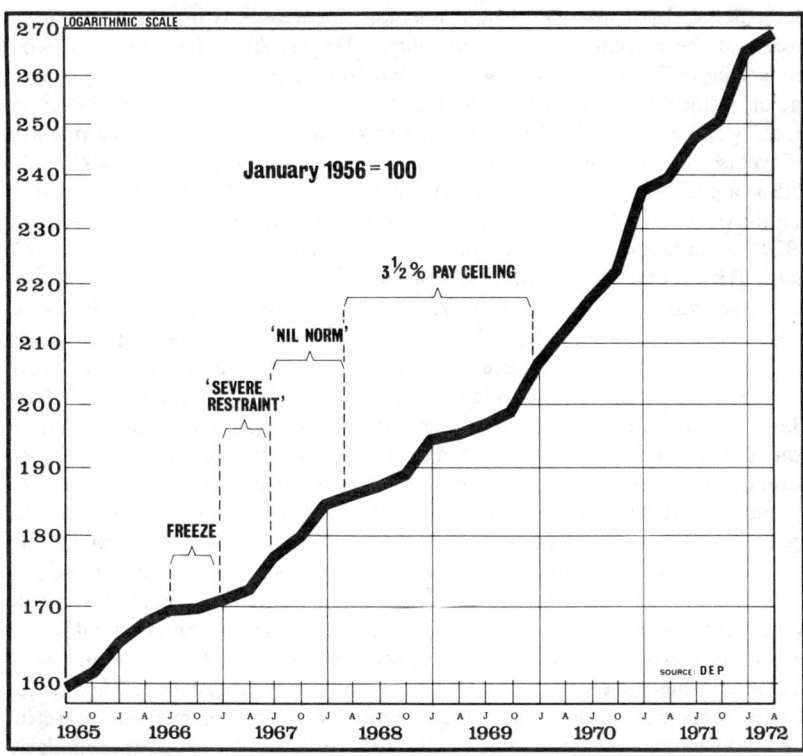

Fig. 4.14. *Hourly wage rates (all workers) with 'policy on' and 'policy off', 1965–72* (Source: *F.T.*, 15 June 1972)

during the first year, but minimal success thereafter. Some of the manifold problems are those of maintaining the credibility of short-term solutions when applied to long-term problems; the possibility of circumvention when either party declines to accept the policy; the complex mixture of political and social factors involved, including effects on unemployment levels, effective demand, traditional wages and incomes differentials, etc.

Some writers, such as Lipsey and Parkin, have concluded that the statutory policy was effective when the unemployment level was low (and thus when wage rate increases might otherwise have been high) but tended to raise wage rates (up to the 'norms') when unemployment was high.[1]

(v) In December 1969 the Labour Government, in its White Paper on *Productivity, Prices and Incomes after 1969* (Cmnd 4237), laid down a $2\frac{1}{2}$ to $4\frac{1}{2}\%$ norm or 'pay ceiling' for wage rises, but by 1970 a series of inflationary increases were being conceded, raising the average hourly rate by 12% per annum.[2] The Conservative Government from 1970 attempted a policy of disengagement and a mixture of market forces and pressure for wage restraint on the public sector:

[1] See M. Parkin, 'Incomes policy: some further results on the determination of the rate of change of money wages', *Economica*, Nov. 1970; 'Why an incomes policy would not work', *F.T.*, 3 Feb. 1971.

[2] See Cairncross, ed., *op. cit.*, p. 138.

nevertheless, both wage levels and unemployment were rising, by 1972, far in excess of the current 7 to $7\frac{1}{2}\%$ guidelines. The especially high award to coal miners in 1972 introduced a new element into wage claims – the 'adjustment factor' – since this concept was applied to the restoration of traditional occupational wage differentials. The N.B.P.I. was disbanded in 1971 and the pressure of events could lead to its restoration in one form or another. In July 1971 the C.B.I. agreed to a voluntary price restraint ceiling of 5%. The background to the introduction of a multi-phase prices and incomes policy during the early 1970s, to some extent modelled on U.S. experience, is outlined in Chapter 12, Stage IIB (Economic Growth), Section 4b.

The general trend in wage rates over the period 1965–72 is shown in Fig. 4.14.

Recent suggestions in the debate about the merits and demerits of direct stabilisation policy include those of the T.U.C., to the effect that central control is not viable, because of the shift to localised, shop floor bargaining; Professor Hayek, to the effect that the only alternative to free market bargaining and a consequent redeployment of labour in the most productive industries is a 'dirigist' planned economy; Professor Weintraub, to the effect that a control agency should supervise prices and wages and that, if the latter rose by more than the specified amount, the employer's profits would be taxed; Professor Meade, to the effect that trade union monopoly bargaining power should be neutralised by paying employers out of an indemnity fund, should they be forced to concede wage increases above a 'norm' as a result of strike action or threats; Hollowood and Jones (ex-N.B.P.I. head), to the effect that the chaos of leapfroging wage claims and high unemployment levels may only be avoided by a joint prices and incomes policy – and that trade unions, with their sometimes powerful monopoly bargaining power, would only agree to restraint if prices were similarly kept down.[1]

(c) Summary

We find that in practice the state has not adopted any one policy of reform, change or planning and supervision, to the exclusion of the others. The British economy is subject to a varied pattern of ownership, ranging from the one-man proprietor to the large joint stock combine, to producers' and consumers' cooperatives, to public ownership by mixed boards (as with docks not owned by the British Transport Docks Board), by municipal authorities (as with public parks, libraries, etc.) and by public corporations (as with fuel, power and transport).[2] Within this mixed economy are exercised elements of the policies of reform, change and planning/supervision.

Professor Sargant Florence has worked out[3] the application of various criteria to control by small capitalist, large capitalist, consumers' cooperation, national-

---

[1] See *F.T.*, 24 Feb. 1972; F. A. Hayek, 'The illusion of a just incomes policy', *F.T.*, 19 April 1972; S. Weintraub, 'An incomes policy to stop inflation', *L.B.R.*, Jan. 1971; 'Judgment of Meade', *Econ.*, 2 Oct. 1971, pp. 24–7; *F.T.*, 30 Sept. 1971; B. Hollowood, 'It could happen here', *N.W.B.Q.R.*, May 1971; A. Jones, 'A policy for prices and incomes now', *L.B.R.*, Jan. 1972.
[2] Professor P. Sargant Florence has worked out an elaborate table of the mixed economy in his book, *The Logic of British and American Industry*, pp. 228–9.
[3] *Ibid.*, p. 251.

isation, and state planning, control and supervision. The criteria which he adopted were:

(i) The 'philosophic' criterion of satisfaction of needs and welfare.
(ii) The 'economic' criteria of consumer sovereignty and satisfaction of demand.
(iii) The 'political' criteria of democracy, national interest and equity.
(iv) The 'business' criteria of efficiency, stability and progress.

Needs were best satisfied by nationalisation and least satisfied by small and large capitalists; consumer sovereignty and the satisfaction of demand were best catered for by the small capitalist and least well catered for by nationalisation; democracy, the national interest and equity were best satisfied by consumers' cooperation and least satisfied by the large capitalist; business efficiency was best ensured by the large capitalist and least ensured by the small capitalist; business stability was best satisfied by nationalisation and least satisfied by large and small capitalists; business progress was best catered for by large and small capitalists and least well catered for by consumers' co-operation. All criteria were satisfied to some extent by state planning, control and supervision, and the highest all-round record was achieved by nationalisation.

These findings, with regard to nationalisation, were supported by a Fabian Society Study, published in 1963.[1] This found that generally the record of Britain's nationalised industries was inconclusive, and that the ideals of the public corporation and its many impressive achievements had been marred by faulty execution, either through a deficiency of resources or imagination or through conflicting objectives. The public corporations were vaguely expected to be accountable to the 'public interest', but this could mean responsibility either to Parliament, the Government or the consumer councils. Furthermore, the balancing of accounts over a number of years posed the problem of price and production policy, the dichotomy between profitability and pruned-down efficiency on the one hand, and the 'needs' of the consumer and the declining industrial areas on the other. The nationalised fuel, power and transport industries in Britain formed a basic part of the nation's economic infrastructure, but they had been existing in a 'commercial no-man's-land', neither fully integrated into a national planned economy, as in the U.S.S.R., nor operating as 'public enterprise free-booters', as in the case of the Italian State Oil Company, under Signor Mattei.[2] In an Aims of Industry study by R. Elvin in 1968,[3] on the other hand, nationalisation was held to be discredited and obsolete. Between 1947 and 1967 they had lost £825 million; they had become monopolies, which became less efficient than comparable enterprises in the private sector, less eager to satisfy consumers and acquire new ones and less able to maintain good labour relations. Gas and electricity had not lost heavily because they had statutory monopoly power over indispensable services and could charge 'what the traffic would bear'. Elvin pointed to the moves, even in the U.S.S.R., towards more pragmatic economic criteria, and in countries such as West Germany away from State control, with the introduction of private capital into Volkswagen, Lufthansa

[1] M. Shanks, ed., *Lessons of Public Enterprise*, 1963.
[2] 'Mixing the enterprise', *Stat.*, 18 June 1965, p. 1684. Also see A. Verrier, 'The Italian industrial State', *Management Today*, Dec. 1969 and 'French State industry assessed', *F.T.*, 6 Nov. 1970.
[3] See Rene Elvin, *Out of Step*, 1968.

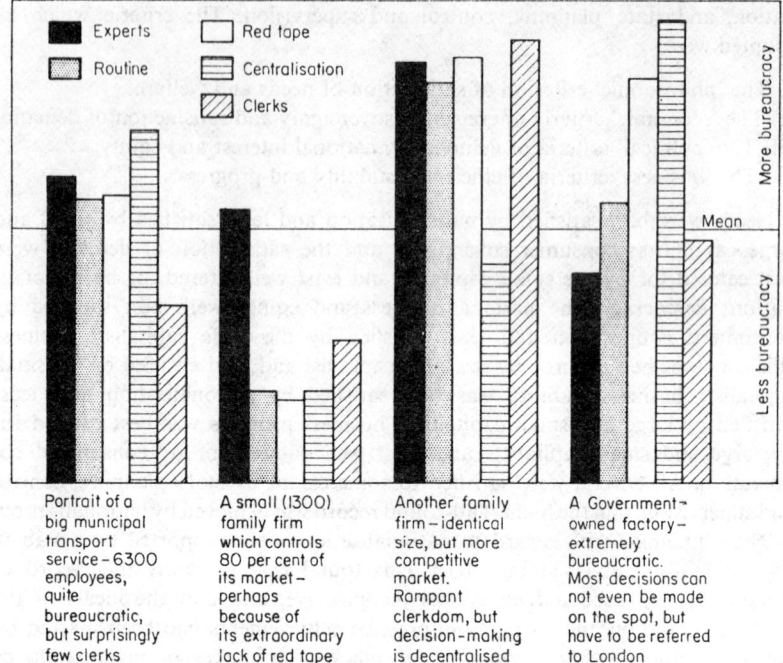

■ Experts	□ Red tape
▦ Routine	▤ Centralisation
	▨ Clerks

Portrait of a big municipal transport service – 6300 employees, quite bureaucratic, but surprisingly few clerks

A small (1300) family firm which controls 80 per cent of its market – perhaps because of its extraordinary lack of red tape

Another family firm – identical size, but more competitive market. Rampant clerkdom, but decision-making is decentralised

A Government-owned factory – extremely bureaucratic. Most decisions can not even be made on the spot, but have to be referred to London

Fig. 4.4. *Degree of bureaucracy: the Pugh-Hickson Bureaucracy Test* (Source: *Obs.*, 11 Apr. 1965)

and the State electricity and mining combine, Preussag AG. In 1964 the suggestion was made, by N. Macrae,[1] that efficiency and service to the consumer might be improved- in the nationalised sector if private enterprise firms were allowed to penetrate (e.g. in broadcasting and aviation) and compete. A step in this direction was taken in October 1970 when the Government encouraged the merger of British United Airways into Caledonian: this was described as creating the nucleus of a 'second force' airline, capable of competing with the two nationalised air corporations, B.E.A. and B.O.A.C. and also as warding off a possible take-over by either of those corporations.[2]

With regard to the 'business' criteria of efficiency, useful research has been conducted by a team of investigators at Aston University. Fifty-two organisations were examined in the Birmingham area, to assess the degree of bureaucracy in them. The first step was to establish factors involved in bureaucratic organisation. The main ones were found to be number of experts, amount of routine administration, 'red tape' paperwork, degree of centralisation of decision-taking, and number of clerical staff.[3] The next stage was to devise measurements of efficiency,

[1] N. Macrae, *A Denationalised Shopping List*, Aims of Industry, 1964, reviewed in *Stat.*, 3 April 1964, p. 17.
[2] See *Econ.*, 24 Oct. 1970, p. 75.
[3] 'The Pugh–Hickson bureaucracy test', *Obs.*, 11 April 1965. Also see D. S. Pugh and D. J. Hickson, 'The facts about "bureaucracy" ', *The Manager*, Dec. 1965, pp. 37–8. N.B. For further analysis of the effect of size of firm and duplication of hierarchical levels on efficiency and bureaucratic 'control loss', which may lead to ultimately diminishing returns, see O. E. Williamson, 'Hierarchical control and optimum firm size', *The Journal of Political Economy*, April 1967.

and to correlate the results to the bureaucracy quotient (or decentralisation quotient). Some of their results are shown in Fig. 4.15.

4. Further Reading and Sources

Footnote references to daily and weekly journals are not repeated.

G. C. ALLEN, *Monopoly and Restrictive Practices*. Allen & Unwin. 1968.

R. ALLEN, 'Concerning incomes policy', *M. and W.S.R.* Spring 1970.

R. BAILEY, 'International corporations and developing countries', *N.W.B.Q.R.* Aug. 1970.

P. D. BALACS, 'Economic data and economic policy', *L.B.R.* April 1972.

R. J. BALL, 'The Cambridge model of economic growth', *Economica*. May 1963.

G. BANNOCK, *The Juggernauts*. Weidenfeld & Nicolson. 1970.

R. J. BARBER, *The American Corporation*. MacGibbon & Kee. 1970.

T. S. BARKER and J. R. C. LECOMBER, *Economic Planning for 1972: an appraisal of 'The Task Ahead'*. P.E.P. Broadsheet 515. Nov. 1969.

P. T. BAUER and B. S. YAMEY, *Markets, Market Control and Marketing Reform*. Weidenfeld & Nicolson. 1968.

A. BAYKOV, *The Development of the Soviet Economic System*. C.U.P. 1946.

BOARD OF TRADE, *Company Assets, Income and Finance in 1960*. H.M.S.O. 1962.

S. BRITTAN, *Government and the Market Economy*. Hobart/I.E.A. 1971.

F. BROADWAY, *State Intervention in British Industry, 1964–68*. Kaye & Ward. 1969.

SIR H. F. R. CATHERWOOD, 'The planning dialogue', *N.W.B.Q.R.* May 1969.

SIR H. F. R. CATHERWOOD, 'Why Neddy survived', *L.B.R.* April 1971.

SIR ALEC CAIRNCROSS, 'Economists in Government', *L.B.R.* Jan. 1970.

R. E. CAVES, ed., *Britain's Economic Prospects*. Allen & Unwin. 1968.

CENTRAL OFFICE OF INFORMATION, *Britain: an official handbook*. H.M.S.O. Annual,

T. E. CHESTER, 'Large organizations – their role in the U.K. economy', *N.W.B.Q.R.* Aug. 1971.

T. E. CHESTER, 'Mergers and opportunities for managers', *N.W.B.Q.R.* May 1969.

COMPANY LAW COMMITTEE. *Report of the Company Law Committee* (Jenkins Report), Cmnd 1749. H.M.S.O. 1962.

'The control of market power', *B.B.R.* May 1970.

D. COOMBES, *State Enterprise: Business or Politics?* P.E.P./Allen & Unwin. 1971.

The Co-operative Movement in Britain, R.5434. C.O.I. 1962.

D. C. CORNER, 'Recent trends in retail distribution', *N.W.B.Q.R.* May 1969.

M. A. CREW and C. K. ROWLEY, 'Anti-trust policy: economics *versus* management science', *M. and W.S.R.* Autumn 1970.

M. A. CREW and C. K. ROWLEY, 'Anti-trust policy: the application of rules', *M. and W.S.R.* Autumn 1971.

G. CYRIAX, *Monopoly and Competition*. Institute of Economic Affairs. 1965. Key Discussion Booklet No. 1.

G. E. DENTON, 'Reflections on economic planning', *The Bankers' Magazine*. Nov. 1968.

DEPARTMENT OF ECONOMIC AFFAIRS:

   D.E.A. Pr. Rep. Nos 1–4, Jan.–Apr. 1965.

   D.E.A. Pr. Rep. Econ., 36, Jan. 1968; 47, Dec. 1968.

4. CONCENTRATION OF CONTROL AND PUBLIC POLICY [11]

'The task ahead', *D.E.A. Pr. Rep. Econ.* 49, Feb. 1969.

'Statistics for industry', *D.E.A. Pr. Rep. Ind. and Reg.* 51, April 1969.

'The Little Neddies and the task ahead', *D.E.A. Pr. Rep. Econ.* 54, July 1969.

DEPARTMENT OF TRADE AND INDUSTRY, 'The Fair Trading Bill—a major development in consumer protection', *Trade and Industry.* 7 Dec. 1972.

P. C. DOOLEY, 'The interlocking directorate', *The American Economic Review.* June 1969.

J. H. DUNNING, 'The multinational enterprise', *L.B.R.* July 1970.

J. H. DUNNING and M. STEUER, 'The effects of United States direct investment in Britain on British technology', *M. and W.S.R.* Autumn 1969.

R. ELVIN, *Out of Step.* Aims of Industry. 1968.

Employers' Associations. H.M.S.O. pamphlet. 1968.

Employment Policy (White Paper), Cmd 6527. H.M.S.O. 1944.

D. FIENNES, 'Is bigger better?', *New Technology.* Sept. 1968.

The Financial and Economic Obligations of the Nationalised Industries, Cmnd 1337. H.M.S.O. 1961.

'Financing the nationalised industries', *M.B.R.* Aug. 1968.

P. SARGANT FLORENCE. *Ownership, Control and Success of Large Companies.* Sweet & Maxwell. 1961.

P. SARGANT FLORENCE, *The Logic of British and American Industry.* Routledge & Kegan Paul. 1961.

C. FOSTER, *Public Enterprise.* Fabian Society. 1972.

C. FULOP, *Retailing and the Consumer.* Longmans/I.E.A. 1968.

J. K. GALBRAITH, *The New Industrial State.* Houghton Mifflin. 1967.

K. D. GEORGE, *Industrial Organization.* Allen & Unwin. 1971.

K. D. GEORGE, 'The changing structure of competitive industry.' *E.J.* (Supplement). March 1972.

M. GORT and T. F. HOGARTY, 'New evidence on mergers', *J.L.E.* April 1970.

D. HAMBERG, 'Invention in the industrial research laboratory', *J.P.E.* April 1963.

F. DE P. HANIKA, *New Thinking in Management.* Hutchinson. 1965.

R. H. HAVEMAN, *The Economics of the Public Sector.* Wiley. 1970.

R. B. HEFLEBOWER and G. W. STOCKING, eds., *Readings in Industrial Organization and Public Policy.* Irwin. 1958.

A. HENNEY, 'Government and industry – a reply', *M. and W.S.R.* Autumn 1968.

K. HILTON and D. F. HEATHFIELD, eds, *The Econometric Study of the United Kingdom.* Macmillan. 1970.

B. HINDLEY, 'Separation of ownership and control in the modern corporation', *J.L.E.* April 1970.

B. HOLLOWOOD, 'Price control – or catastrophe', *N.W.B.Q.R.* Aug. 1970.

B. HOLLOWOOD, 'It could happen here', *N.W.B.Q.R.* May 1971.

K. HOPPER, 'The nature of American management', *M. and W.S.R.* Autumn 1969.

M. HOWE, 'Anti-trust policy: rules or discretionary intervention?', *M. and W.S.R.* Spring 1971.

A. HUNTER, ed., *Monopoly and Competition.* Penguin. 1969.

'International commodity arrangements – a story of slow but helpful progress', *M.B.R.* Aug. 1966.

M. IVENS and F. BROADWAY, eds, *Case Studies in Management.* Business Publications. 1965.

4. CONCENTRATION OF CONTROL AND PUBLIC POLICY [II]

C. W. JEFFERSON, K. I. SAMS and D. SWANN, 'The control of incomes and prices in the United Kingdom, 1964–1967: policy and experience', *The Canadian Journal of Economics*. May 1968.

J. JEWKES, 'British monopoly policy 1944–56', *J.L.E.* Oct. 1958.

J. JEWKES, 'The Industrial Policy Group – an experiment in communication', *N.W.B.Q.R.* Nov. 1970.

H. G. JOHNSON, *Economic Policies Towards Less Developed Countries*. Allen & Unwin. 1967.

A. JONES, 'A policy for prices and incomes now', *L.B.R.* Jan. 1972.

D. R. KAMERSCHEN, 'The influence of ownership and control on profit rates', *A.E.R.* June 1968.

E. KEFAUVER, *In a Few Hands: monopoly power in America*. Penguin. 1965.

R. KELF-COHEN, *Twenty Years of Nationalisation: the British experience*. Macmillan. 1969.

V. KORAH, *Monopolies and Restrictive Practices*. Penguin. 1968.

R. L. LARNER, 'Ownership and control in the 200 largest Nonfinancial Corporations, 1929 and 1963', *A.E.R.* Sept. 1966.

J. H. C. LEACH, 'The role of the institutions in the U.K. ordinary share market', *Investment Analyst*. Dec. 1971.

D. LEE, V. ANTHONY and A. SKUSE, *Monopoly*. Heinemann. 1968.

J. A. LINCOLN, *The Restrictive Society*. Allen & Unwin. 1967.

LLOYDS BANK, *L.B.R.* Jan. 1961, Jan. 1963, July 1964, Oct. 1966.

V. LUTZ, *Central Planning for the Market Economy: an analysis of the French theory and experience*. Longmans/I.E.A. 1969.

P. MCANALLY, *The Economics of the Distributive Trades*. Allen & Unwin. 1971.

W. G. MCCLELLAND, 'The Distributive sector', *T.B.R.* Dec. 1969.

W. G. MCCLELLAND, 'The Industrial Reorganisation Corporation 1966/71: an experimental prod', *T.B.R.* June 1972.

N. MACRAE, *A Denationalised Shopping List*. Aims of Industry. 1964.

E. MANSFIELD, *The Economics of Technological Change*, Longmans. 1968.

E. MANSFIELD, ed., *Monopoly Power and Economic Performance*. Norton. 1968.

J. W. MARKHAM and G. F. PAPANEK, *Industrial Organization and Economic Development*. Houghton Mifflin. 1970.

R. MARRIS, *Managerial Capitalism*. Macmillan. 1964.

M. A. G. VAN MEERHAEGHE, *International Economic Institutions*. Longmans. 1966.

D. MERMELSTEIN, 'Large industrial corporations and asset shares', *A.E.R.* Sept. 1969.

F. V. MEYER, D. C. CORNER and J. E. S. PARKER, *Problems of a Mature Economy*. Macmillan. 1970.

MIDLAND BANK. *M.B.R.* Nov. 1959, Nov. 1965.

J. MITCHELL, 'Why we need a prices policy', *L.B.R.* April 1969.

MONOPOLIES COMMISSION, *A Survey of Mergers 1958–1968*. Department of Trade and Industry. 1970.

Monopolies, Mergers and Restrictive Practices, Cmnd 2299. H.M.S.O. 1964.

R. J. MONSEN, J. S. CHIU and D. E. COOLEY, 'The Effect of Separation of Ownership and Control on the Performance of the Large Firm'. *Q.J.E.* Aug. 1968.

E. MOONMAN, *Reluctant Partnership*. Gollancz. 1971.

J. MOYLE, *The Pattern of Ordinary Share Ownership 1957–70*. C.U.P. 1971.

'Multi-national companies', *B.B.R.* Aug. 1971.

4. CONCENTRATION OF CONTROL AND PUBLIC POLICY [II]

Nationalised Industries: a review of economic and financial objectives. Cmnd 3437. H.M.S.O. 1967.

G. NEWBOULD and A. S. JACKSON, *The Receding Ideal.* Guthstead. 1972.

'The "Neddy" experiment—a new approach to national planning', *M.B.R.* Feb. 1968.

T. NICHOLS, *Ownership, Control and Ideology.* Allen & Unwin. 1969.

M. PARKIN, 'Incomes policy: some further results on the determination of the rate of change of money wages', *Economica.* Nov. 1970.

G. and P. POLANYI, 'The efficiency of nationalised industries', *M. and W.S.R.* Spring 1972.

G. and P. POLANYI, 'The Fair Trading Bill and Monopoly Policy'. *T.B.R.* June 1973.

POLITICAL AND ECONOMIC PLANNING, *Industrial Trade Associations, Activities and Organisation.* Allen & Unwin. 1957.

C. F. PRATTEN, 'A case study of a conglomerate merger', *M. and W.S.R*, Spring 1970.

R. W. S. PRYKE, 'Are nationalised industries becoming more efficient?'. *M. and W.S.R.* Spring 1970.

Public Expenditure: a new presentation, Cmnd 4017. H.M.S.O. 1969. (Government Green Paper)

D. S. PUGH and D. J. HICKSON, 'The facts about "bureaucracy" ', *The Manager.* Dec. 1965.

W. B. REDDAWAY, *Effects of the Selective Employment Tax: First Report, the Distributive Trades.* H.M.S.O. 1970.

W. B. REDDAWAY, 'An analysis of take-overs', *L.B.R.* April 1972.

G. L. REID and K. ALLEN, *Nationalized Industries.* Penguin. 1970.

RESALE PRICE MAINTENANCE COMMITTEE REPORT, Cmd 7696. H.M.S.O. 1949.

J. REVELL and J. MOYLE, *The Owners of Quoted Ordinary Shares: a survey for 1963.* Chapman & Hall. 1966.

W. A. ROBSON, 'Ministerial control of the nationalised industries', *Political Quarterly,* 40. 1969.

W. A. ROBSON, 'Mixed Enterprise', *N.W.B.Q.R.* Aug. 1972.

C. K. ROWLEY, *The British Monopolies Commission.* Allen & Unwin. 1966.

C. K. ROWLEY, 'Mergers and public policy in Great Britain', *J.L.E.* April 1968.

C. K. ROWLEY, 'Monopoly in Britain: private vice but public virtue?', *M. and W.S.R.* Autumn 1968.

R. ROWTHORN and S. HYMER, *International Big Business 1957–1967.* C.U.P. 1971.

F. M. SCHERER, *Industrial Market Structure and Economic Performance.* Rand McNally. 1971.

M. SHANKS, ed., *Lessons of Public Enterprise: a Fabian Society study.* Cape. 1963.

W. G. SHEPHERD, *Economic Performance under Public Ownership: British fuel and power,* Yale University Press, 1969.

E. M. SINGER, *Antitrust Economics.* Prentice-Hall. 1968.

L. A. SKEOCH, 'The abolition of resale price maintenance: some notes on Canadian experience', *Economica.* Aug. 1964.

A. SKUSE, *Government Intervention and Industrial Policy.* Heinemann. 1970.

N. A. H. STACEY and A. WILSON, *The Changing Pattern of Distribution.* Pergamon. 1965.

R. B. STEVENS and B. S. YAMEY, *The Restrictive Practices Court.* Weidenfeld & Nicolson. 1965.

G. J. STIGLER, 'The economic effects of the antitrust laws', *J.L.E.* Oct. 1966.

A. SUTHERLAND, *The Monopolies Commission in Action.* C.U.P. 1969.

D. SWANN and D. L. MCLACHLAN, *Concentration or Competition: A European Dilemma?* P.E.P. Jan. 1967.

TREASURY. *Glossary of Management Techniques.* H.M.S.O. 1967.

TREASURY. 'Treasury changes', *E.P.R.*, 2, Feb. 1970; 'Economic statistics', *E.P.R.*, 6, Aug. 1970; 7, Sept. 1970; 'Reorganising central government', *E.P.R.*, 9, Nov. 1970; 'Government policies for public spending', *E.P.R.*, 10, Dec. 1970; 'Treasury computer facilities', *E.P.R.*, 10, Dec. 1970; 'Helping the regions', *E.P.R.*, 32, Oct. 1972.

M. A. UTTON, *Industrial Concentration.* Penguin. 1970.

S. WEINTRAUB, 'An incomes policy to stop inflation', *L.B.R.* Jan. 1971.

O. E. WILLIAMSON, 'Hierarchical control and optimum firm size', *J.P.E.* April 1967.

B. S. YAMEY, ed., *Resale Price Maintenance.* Weidenfeld & Nicolson. 1966.

G. R. YOUNG, *Mergers and Acquisitions: planning and action.* Routledge & Kegan Paul. 1965.

M. ZINKIN, 'Government and industry', *M. and W.S.R.* Autumn 1967.

M. ZINKIN, 'Multi-national companies', *M. and W.S.R.* Autumn 1968.

5. Past Examination Questions

1. What do you understand by monopoly power? What are the main causes of monopoly? (Summer 1951)
2. What are the causes of monopoly? (Summer 1953)
3. 'Monopoly power is a matter of degree.' Comment. (Autumn 1952)
4. Outline, with examples, the main factors which encourage the growth of monopoly. (Autumn 1956)
5. Why do monopolies arise? Discuss the possible causes of the emergence of monopolistic organisations, with special reference to the United Kingdom. (January 1960)
6. 'Monopolies must be desirable, for they arise from the economies of large-scale production'. Comment. (Summer 1964)
7. What is meant by monopoly power? Classify briefly the causes of monopoly, giving examples. (Summer 1960)
8. Is the number of firms in an industry a good indicator of the strength of the producers' monopoly? (January 1963)
9. Why are some industries more competitive than others? Illustrate your answer with examples drawn from United Kingdom industry. (Summer 1961)
10. 'Monopoly is in the public interest because large-scale production is efficient.' Comment. (Summer 1961)
11. 'The main objective of the government's industrial policy should be the fostering of free competition.' Discuss. (Summer 1961)
12. In what circumstances might it be desirable to control monopolistic practices and how might this be done? (Summer 1956)

13. Discuss the view that it is monopoly practices by groups of producers rather than monopoly as such which are liable to have undesirable effects. (Summer 1954)

14. Why is it necessary to control the activities of monopolies? (Summer 1959)

15. 'A major aim of economic policy should be to restore competition.' Is this, in your view, an adequate policy for dealing with monopolies? (Summer 1953)

16. Outline the methods employed in the United Kingdom to control monopolies and restrictive practices, and consider their adequacy. (Summer 1962)

17. Explain in general terms the working of the 1956 Restrictive Trade Practices Act. (January 1965)

18. What is a public limited liability company? What are the advantages and disadvantages of this form of organisation? (January 1965)

19. What are the advantages and disadvantages of co-operative retailing as compared with other forms? (Summer 1964)

20. What are the advantages of the joint stock form of company? (January 1964)

21. What is the economic basis for the denationalisation of road transport? (Summer 1954)

22. 'The nationalisation of an industry makes little difference to its problems of organisation and management.' Discuss. (Summer 1963)

23. 'Nationalisation of industries is unimportant; the real issues concern public control rather than public ownership.' Discuss. (January 1965)

24. What is meant by economic planning? Discuss its relevance to current problems of the U.K. economy. (Summer 1963)

5. International Trade
Stage I

1. Special Characteristics of International Trade

International trade involves the exchange of goods and services across national frontiers, and it is on this account that special characteristics are involved, which cause it to differ from trade within national boundaries.

(*a*) Whereas within national boundaries there is a fairly standard pattern of laws, customs, habits, living standards, language and currency, there is wide disparity between different countries.

(*b*) Whereas goods, services and factors of production such as labour and capital move fairly freely within national boundaries, the mobility of these factors across national boundaries is lessened because of influences such as increased risks and differences in the laws, customs, etc., mentioned above, and because of government restrictions on the free international flow of goods, services and factors.

(*c*) Because of the forces mentioned above, the rewards to equivalent skills and risks, whilst tending to equality within one country, differ greatly between different countries.

(*d*) Because of the differences in currency between one country and another, international trade transactions involve the added complication of foreign exchange rates, by which one currency is measured in terms of others. The flow of trade between countries and the currency rates of exchange influence each other.

Despite these complications to trade across national frontiers, international trade still takes place because of the differences in skills, specialities, climate, natural resources and acquired advantages of different countries for different products and services. The process by which this happens is the international division of labour, an extension of regional specialisation within a country.

2. The Law of Comparative Costs

Individuals and regions within a country tend to specialise on the production of goods and services for which they are best suited. This process of specialisation or division of labour is based on two important factors. First of all, the person or region which specialises and produces more than sufficient for its own requirements must have a market for the surplus of goods and services produced. Secondly, the person or region which specialises may very well be able to produce other goods and services which it requires, but not so efficiently. In order to specialise, therefore, the possibility must exist of exchanging the resultant goods or services for those produced by other persons or regions. Thus, given a suitable

385

extent of market demand and suitable conditions for exchange, the division of labour has developed to a great extent within most countries, and results in greater efficiency or productivity and therefore a greater total output of goods and services than would be possible if everyone tried to be self-sufficient.

The same process lies behind the international division of labour and international trade. Most countries could produce a wider range of products and services than they do, but if channels of trade are open they find it advantageous to concentrate on the things they do best. This process of specialisation results from the economic Law of Comparative Costs, which states that a country will benefit from concentrating on the production of goods and services for which it has the greatest relative advantage over other countries, provided that it can obtain other goods and services by exchange. It is important to stress the phrase 'greatest relative advantage', because the law holds true even in the case of a country which produces everything more efficiently (at lower cost) than other countries. The super-efficient country will still specialise on its most efficient product or service.

The following examples are used to illustrate the Law of Comparative Costs. In case A two countries are shown, Utopia and Eldorado. Two possible commodities, sugar and steel, are considered. Utopia has a hot climate, plentiful peasant labour and little capital and technical expertise. Eldorado has an industrialised economy, plentiful capital and expertise, but a cold climate and a shortage of agricultural labour. With a given unit of a factor of production (say one man-day) Utopia could produce 10 Utopian 'value-units' of sugar or 2 Utopian value-units of steel. Steel would require a relatively tremendous effort and the devotion of scarce resources, using primitive, inefficient techniques. Eldorado, on the other hand, can produce with 1 unit of the factor of production either 15 Eldorado value-units of steel or 1 Eldorado value-unit of sugar. Sugar, of the beet type, could be produced, but relatively inefficiently. If each country used 2 units of the factor of production, 1 for sugar and 1 for steel, individual and total production would be as follows:

Case A

Country	Units of factor used	Value-units of product	
		Sugar	Steel
Utopia {	1	10	–
	1	–	2
Eldorado {	1	1	–
	1	–	15
Total	4	11	17

However, if each country specialised on the thing it did most efficiently, Utopia would concentrate on sugar and Eldorado on steel. With the same 2 units of factor each, the individual and total outputs would be higher:

Country	Units of factor used	Value-units of product	
		Sugar	Steel
Utopia	2	20	–
Eldorado	2	–	30
Total	4	20	30

The two countries would each use its factors of production most efficiently; total output would be higher; surpluses could be exchanged in international trade.

Whereas in case A each country was shown to have an absolute advantage in the production of its speciality, case B shows that specialisation is still beneficial even to the super-efficient country, Eldorado. Assume that with the same resources as before Utopia could still produce 10 Utopian value-units of sugar and 2 Utopian value-units of steel, but that Eldorado could produce 12 Eldorado value-units of sugar and 15 Eldorado value-units of steel. Although Eldorado is absolutely more efficient in both commodities than Utopia, it is relatively even more efficient in steel production than in sugar production. Without specialisation the results would be:

Case B

Country	Units of factor used	Value-units of product Sugar	Steel
Utopia	{ 1	10	–
	{ 1	–	2
Eldorado	{ 1	12	–
	{ 1	–	15
Total	4	22	17

If Eldorado, however, concentrated between $1\frac{2}{15}$ and $1\frac{5}{8}$ of its two units of factor on steel, at which it was even more efficient than at sugar, and Utopia specialised entirely on sugar, for which it had a greater relative (though not absolute) advantage over Eldorado, the results would be even better. The above-mentioned limits on the amount of factor devoted by Eldorado to steel are such as to result in two alternative total outputs. In either case, the amount of one commodity would be the same as in the absence of specialisation: the additional output of the other commodity thus indicates the surplus value accruing from international specialisation. It is 'the gain from trade', viz. $8\frac{5}{8}$ value-units of sugar or $10\frac{1}{2}$ value-units of steel.

Country	Units of factor used		Value-units of product Sugar	Steel
Utopia	2		20	–
Eldorado	2	{ (a) $1\frac{13}{15}$ on Sugar; $1\frac{2}{15}$ on Steel (a)	$10\frac{3}{5}$	17
		{ (b) $\frac{3}{8}$ on Sugar; $1\frac{5}{8}$ on Steel (b)	2	$27\frac{1}{2}$
Total	4	{ (a) *Either*	$30\frac{3}{5}$	17
		{ (b) *or*	22	$27\frac{1}{2}$

The lowest comparative cost for each country, whether in case A or case B, may be shown by means of a diagram. If sugar and steel, which may be produced by a country with 1 unit of a factor of production, are shown as two sides of a right-angle triangle, then the longer of these two sides (i.e. the side opposite the wider angle) represents the commodity for which that country has the greatest relative advantage in production. If there is another country enjoying a relative advantage in the production of the other commodity, then each may specialise and exchange may take place. (see Fig. 5.1).

Eldorado produces both commodities more efficiently than Utopia, but has lower comparative costs in steel. Utopia would concentrate on sugar, exchanging this against steel from Eldorado.

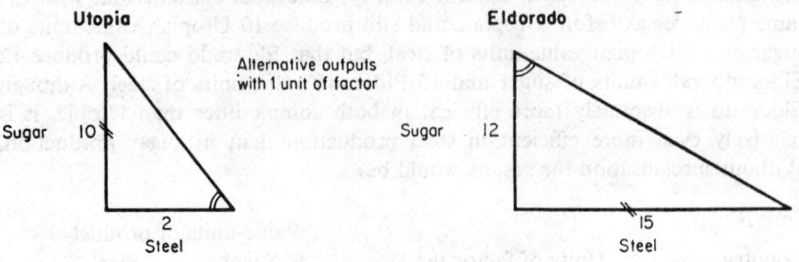

Fig. 5.1. *Diagrammatic representation of the Law of Comparative Costs*

3. Ratio of Exchange

Whereas in case B Utopia could produce sugar at one-fifth the cost of steel, Eldorado was not able to produce steel at one-fifth the cost of sugar, but at four-fifths that cost. How much steel, then, will be exchanged for how much sugar? This question, in fact, asks what the ratio of exchange will be between steel and sugar. Actually, there is no fixed ratio of exchange, but there are fixed limits between which it may vary. These limits are set by the comparative costs of the production of both commodities in each country.

Utopia would be willing *to offer* 10 units of sugar for 2 units of steel, or 5 units of sugar for 1 unit of steel.

Eldorado would be willing *to accept* 12 units of sugar for 15 units of steel, or $\frac{4}{5}$ unit of sugar for 1 unit of steel.

The price of 1 unit of steel in international trade could vary, therefore between 5 units of sugar and $\frac{4}{5}$ unit of sugar. When steel is sold by Eldorado to Utopia in exchange for sugar, Eldorado would *prefer* to obtain 5 units of sugar for each unit of steel, but would be *willing*, if necessary, to obtain $\frac{4}{5}$ unit of sugar for 1 of steel. It would not accept $\frac{2}{5}$ or even $\frac{3}{5}$ unit of sugar, because it could produce those quantities itself with less sacrifice of factors than would be required to make 1 unit of steel.

Whether Eldorado will obtain its best possible terms (5 of sugar for 1 of steel) and thus Utopia its worst terms, or vice versa ($\frac{4}{5}$ of sugar for 1 of steel), or whether some intermediate ratio of exchange is decided upon, depends upon a number of factors:

(*a*) The relative bargaining power of each country – conditions of demand, influenced by factors such as emergency needs, consumer tastes and the pattern of income distribution.

(*b*) The surpluses each has available for export: the ratio of exchange will be such as to equate the *values* of imports and exports, i.e. to balance trade.

4. Complications

This simplified exposition of comparative costs and the ratio of exchange has been based on *certain assumptions*, the absence of which would distort the production and exchange picture:

(*a*) That in fact there would be only two countries involved, in the production and exchange of only two commodities.

(*b*) That perfect competition prevailed, with no monopolistic bargaining power, with no artificial restrictions such as tariffs and quotas, and with perfect knowledge of the other party's costs and prices.

(*c*) That costs of production do not vary with the amount produced.

(*d*) That there are no problems of currency, and therefore that one commodity may be bartered against the other.

(*e*) That there are no transport costs, which might outweigh the benefits of specialisation and exchange.

(*f*) That there are no unused resources in either country.

(*g*) That there are no emergencies (such as war) or political and strategic reasons for producing the commodity with the highest comparative costs.

5. Advantages of International Trade on the Basis of Comparative Costs

Some of the potential advantages of international trade, despite the special characteristics referred to in Section 1, are as follows:[1]

(*a*) Each country is enabled to achieve economies of specialisation in the production of things for which it is best suited, on the basis of the international division of labour.

(*b*) The movement of goods and services across national frontiers opens up wider markets for the products of countries with the lowest comparative costs. This increased extent of markets leads to economies of large-scale production.

(*c*) World output of all goods and services may be greater and more efficient, and world resources more fully utilised.

(*d*) World prices tend to be lower and more stable, the greater is the ease of access to goods and services from countries with the lowest relative costs of production.

(*e*) The volume of goods and services exchanged is increased, and local shortages of supply are more easily satisfied.

(*f*) The variety of commodities available to all participating nations is increased, thus helping to raise the standards of living of all consumers.

(*g*) Factors of production may move from areas where rewards are lowest to areas where they are highest. This increased mobility of factors tends to remove discrepancies between the rewards to factors in different countries.

(*h*) International trade between countries may lead to closer political and cultural ties, may reduce the income gap between the 'haves' and 'have-nots', and may increase international understanding.

A more advanced exposition of comparative cost theory, with 'opportunity cost', exchange ratios and 'relative factor endowment', is given in Stage II, Section 1.

---

[1] *Trade Expansion: Why?*, B.B.L.A., March 1963.

6. Terms of Trade

The terms on which a country exchanges its exports for imports from other countries are, in fact, measured in monetary prices and not as 'so much sugar for so much steel'. These monetary prices in turn depend upon the internal prices of goods in each country and the rates of exchange, or the prices of each currency in terms of others.

In order to show whether a country has been obtaining imports on more favourable or less favourable terms, over a period of years, it is usual to express the relative prices of imports to exports as a percentage, called the 'terms of trade'. A base year is taken, at which the averages of import and export prices are each taken as 1. The terms of trade may thus be expressed as *either* the percentage of average import prices to average export prices *or* the percentage of average export prices to average import prices. The usual convention is to adopt the latter method, whereby the terms of trade =

$$\frac{\text{Average Price of Exports}}{\text{Average Price of Imports}} \times 100$$

If 1900 were taken as the base year, in which the terms of trade were 100, and by 1904 import prices had doubled, whilst export prices fell by one-half, the terms of trade in 1904 would be $\frac{1}{2}/2 \times 100/1 = 25$. Import prices would be 4 times higher than export prices, as compared with 1900, and the terms of trade would have become very unfavourable. If import prices had halved whilst export prices had doubled, the improved terms of trade would be $2/\frac{1}{2} \times 100/1 = 400$.

In the case of the United Kingdom, changes in the terms of trade have been an important factor in her foreign trade transactions, with repercussions on her people's standard of living. If the terms of trade in 1938 are taken as 100, it may be seen that they have varied between 70 and 104 during the period 1913 to 1960, as follows:[1]

1913 – 70. This represents the relatively bad terms on which Britain traded, as compared with 1938.

1921 – 99. During the slump following World War I, Britain's imports of primary products (food and raw materials) fell in price, relative to her exports of manufactured goods.

1928 – 81½. The recovery of world demand and production forced up import prices, relative to the prices of British manufactures.

1933 – 104. The general reduction in world demand during the great depression of the early 1930s affected primary products more adversely than manufactured goods. This was largely due to the relative inability of primary producers to reduce supply.

1951 – 72. Stockpiling of food and raw materials during the Korean War drove up their prices, relative to Britain's manufactured goods.

1960 – 94. Expanded capacity in primary products since 1956, and the greater ability of British manufacturing industry to limit production had resulted in a gradual rise in export prices, relative to import prices.[2]

---

[1] Based on material in *L.B.R.*, July 1961, p. 3.
[2] See Sir Robert Hall, 'Commodity prices and the terms of trade', *L.B.R.*, Jan. 1962, pp. 1–15.

This improvement in Britain's terms of trade during the 1950s may also be seen from the following figures, for which 1954 is taken as the base year.[1]

1951 = 88·5	1954 = 100	1959 = 111
1960 = 112·3	1961 = 116·3	1962 = 117·6

During the 1960s the terms of trade continued to improve for the U.K., on the whole, with minor deteriorations in 1964 and 1969. The general improvement was primarily due to the fairly steady prices of imported fuel and moderate price increases in imported raw materials, as compared with the substantial price increases for manufactured goods exports. This may be seen from Table 5.1, taking 1961 as the base year.[2]

Table 5.1 *U.K. terms of trade, 1960–70*

	Weights (Relative Importance) out of 1,000	1960	1961	1964	1967	1969	1970
Imports							
Total	1,000	102	100	107	109	126	132
Basic materials	222	104	100	103	99	115	121
Fuel	106	101	100	95	92	100	98
Exports							
Total	1,000	100	100	106	114	127	136
Manufactures	824	99	100	106	116	126	140
Terms of Trade	—	**97**	**100**	**99**	**105**	**101**	**104**

(Export prices as a percentage of import prices)
(Source: *Ann. Abs. Stat.*)

7. Freedom of Trade and Restrictions on Trade

'Free trade' is a term used to describe the absence of artificial restrictions to the free international movement of goods, services and factors of production.

Despite the obvious general advantages of free trade – viz. cheapness of goods to all consumers, plentiful supplies, stimulus to economies of scale and the greater gain to the general public than would accrue to any individual, protected industry – most governments have almost always imposed restrictions on international trade. Partly under the influence of Adam Smith's eighteenth-century writings and largely under the stimulus of her expanding industrial potential and relative efficiency in manufacturing, Britain pursued a free trade policy from the 1860s until the Great Depression of the early 1930s. That event gave added force to the arguments for protection of home industries and for restrictions on international trade, both in Britain and elsewhere in the world.

Some of the main arguments for restrictions on trade are as follows:

(*a*) *The Balance of Payments case.* If a country has an adverse balance of payments with the outside world, a quick short-term solution might be to impose restrictions on imports. However, this may result in retaliation against its exports by other

---

[1] *Brit. O.H.*, 1963, p. 419 and *Econ.*, 9 Feb. 1963, p. 555.
[2] *Ann. Abs. Stat.* 104, 1967 and 108, 1971.

countries.[1] A countermove might embody a device for stimulating exports, such as the export rebate scheme, introduced in October 1964.[2]

(b) *The Anti-Dumping case.* Sometimes a foreign monopolist, protected from competition from other producers, is able to supply goods at prices below those in his home market. This would be possible if his home market was protected by a tariff barrier from re-entry of the goods concerned. In effect, the supplier's home market is being exploited and thus subsidises the exporter, so that he has an unfair advantage over producers in the importing countries. Sometimes this dumping is officially subsidised for political, strategic or economic motives. In such cases there is a justifiable argument for restrictions to be imposed by the importing country.

(c) *The Unemployed and/or Immobile Factors of Production case.* Cheaper imports may cause or aggravate unemployment of labour, equipment and other resources in the importing country, and there may be great difficulties in transferring those factors to other uses. The problem may be alleviated in the short-run by imposing restrictions on imports, but in the long-run such protection, by reducing the stimulus to mobility, scrapping and retraining, may hinder the development of more efficient industries and reduce the general productivity of industry.

(d) *The Strategic case.* There may be strong political and strategic reasons for producing goods for which a country does not have the lowest comparative costs. Such reasons may be the desire not to be dependent upon insecure or politically undesirable sources of supply; the desire to be partly or wholly self-sufficient in case of war; the desire to have a bargaining gambit in future discussions with other countries on the international reduction of restrictions on trade.

(e) *The Infant Industry case.* There may be a case for protecting a new industry, in its early stages of development, against competition from established foreign suppliers. However, there is no guarantee that the industry will ever become competitive and it is usually politically difficult to remove protection previously given.

(f) *The Terms of Trade case.* It is sometimes assumed that tariff restrictions on imports compel the supplier to reduce his prices and that this will improve the terms of trade for the importer. However, other countries may retaliate and/or the supplier may only 'swallow' part of the tariff, whilst the remainder is passed on to the consumer. In either case demand for the imported goods and/or demand for the country's exports will be reduced. Thus the volume of international trade will be lower, with all the disadvantages this entails.

(g) *The 'Sweated Labour' and Social Costs case.* It is sometimes claimed that a country's level of employment and high standard of living will be protected if restrictions are imposed on goods from 'sweated labour' low-wage countries. Protagonists claim that this is justified because the high-cost country has the additional burden, reflected in its total costs of production, of providing social services, roads, education, health schemes, town planning, etc., whilst the low-cost country does not. However, tariffs on imports will raise the prices of goods in the importing country, thus raising the cost of living. Furthermore, the level of wages in the exporting country would be depressed even further if its goods were

---

[1] This was the case with the 15% import surcharge, levied by the U.K. Government in November 1964, and the import deposit scheme, introduced in December 1968.
[2] *D.T.*, 31 Jan. 1968.

not bought. This argument was often applied to imports from Italy and other Continental countries, but it ignored the fact that in many of them the workers received substantial 'fringe benefits' in the form of sickness payment, canteen subsidies, subsidised housing, Christmas bonuses, etc., in addition to the monetary wage rate. In 1960 such fringe benefits accounted for 14% of the United Kingdom hourly wage rate of $0·68, but for 74% of the $0·35 Italian hourly wage rate.[1]

8. Forms of Protection or Restrictions on Trade

The most important methods for restricting international trade are tariffs and quotas (or quantitative restrictions).[2]

(i) *Tariffs.* These are charges, levied by governments on imported goods. Their purpose may be either to raise revenue or to restrict the importation of the commodity in question. As a source of revenue, a tariff will only be effective if the additional charge does not deter the home consumer from buying or the foreign exporter from supplying. As a method of restricting imports, the reason may be to give protection to the home producer of similar goods or to prevent the home public from buying, for political or social reasons. Tariffs may be levied either as *ad valorem* charges – a percentage of the import prices – or as 'specific' charges: a fixed sum per unit of the commodity, regardless of its price. Tariffs are, therefore, indirect restrictions on trade. Their effect will depend upon the supply and demand conditions for the product. Sometimes the entire charge will be passed on to the home consumer; sometimes the charge will be 'swallowed' by the foreign producer, stimulated either to greater efficiency or to accept reduced profits; sometimes the charge will be shared between supplier and consumer. The effect on the quantity imported will depend upon the amount of the charge and the way in which it is 'swallowed' and/or passed on. In the United Kingdom the imposition of tariffs is carried on within the framework of the following legislation and agreements:[3]

(*a*) Imperial (or Commonwealth) Preference agreements for reciprocal preferential treatment, concluded with independent Commonwealth countries after the Ottawa Conference of 1932. Most imports into the U.K. from the Commonwealth preference area are free of duty and about 40% in value have a tariff preference of about 11% (expressed as a percentage of the import value). About one-half of British exports to the area are free of duty and about one-half enjoy an average tariff preference of 12%.[4] At the first U.N. Conference on Trade and Development (UNCTAD) in 1964 Britain agreed in principle to the extension of tariff preferences to all the developing countries, subject to certain conditions.[5]

(*b*) Multilateral agreements with other countries, under the auspices of G.A.T.T. (General Agreement on Tariffs and Trade).

(*c*) The 1969 Customs Duties (Dumping and Subsidies) Act.

(*d*) The Import Duties Act, 1958.

---

[1] *The Times,* 6 Dec. 1960.   [2] *Trade expansion: How?, B.B.L.A.,* March 1963.
[3] 'Britain's tariff today and tomorrow', *M.B.R.,* Nov. 1963, pp. 3–10; 'Would tariff preferences help economic development?', G. Patterson, *L.B.R.,* April 1965, pp. 18–30; *Brit. O.H.,* 1972, pp. 364–5.
[4] *Brit. O.H.,* 1971, p. 387.   [5] *Ibid.*

(e) The Stockholm Convention of 1960 governed the reduction of tariffs and quotas between the U.K. and the other 6 members of E.F.T.A. (European Free Trade Association). With British entry into the E.E.C. in 1973 her tariff policy will be determined under the Treaty of Rome, 1957.

Following the 'Kennedy Round' series of tariff negotiations under G.A.T.T., which ended in June 1967, British tariff reductions were implemented between 1968 and 1972. Fig. 5.2 illustrates some of the subsequent tariff levels on imports into the U.K., ranging from 8·4% to 30·0% *ad valorem*.

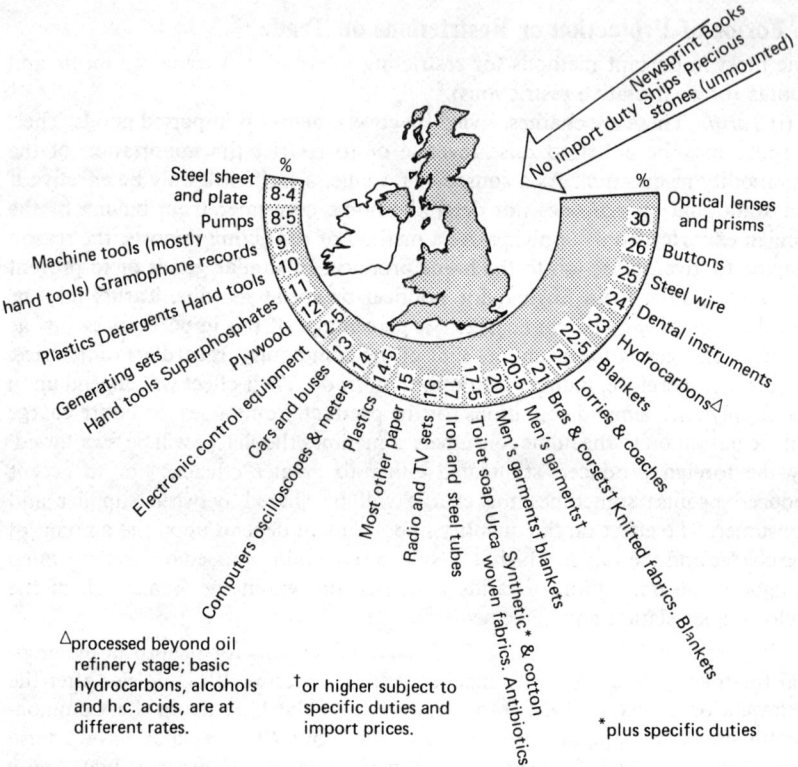

Fig. 5.2 *Britain's post-'Kennedy Round' tariff wall*
(Source: *The Sunday Times*, 23 May 1971)

(ii) *Quotas.* These are direct quantitative restrictions, imposed by Governments either on imports or on exports. A government will fix the amount of the quota for a given period and gives licences to importers or exporters. Some import quotas refer to specific countries; others merely refer to the commodity, regardless of the country of origin. Import licences are granted to importers usually according to their previous share of the trade. Import quotas may be imposed for balance of payments reasons or to restrict the import of a class of goods for social reasons or (when referring to a specific country of origin) for political or foreign currency reasons. The effect of an import quota is to restrict supply in a direct manner, thus causing prices paid by home consumers to be higher than they would otherwise be (especially, in the case of a general quota, if the world price is falling). However, the higher price caused by the shortage of goods will not result in revenue to the government, but in increased profits to importers with the prized licences. The legislative framework within which both import and export quotas may be imposed is the Import, Export and Customs Powers (Defence) Act of 1939. Export quotas may be imposed to supervise the export of goods of military or strategic importance, to conserve scarce resources, to restrict the export of national treasures, or to restrict the transference of capital to foreign countries, in the form of valuable goods.

One interesting example of quotas in recent years was the pressure in the U.S. Congress in late-1967 to impose import quotas on specific products such as steel, oil and textiles. Home production of these goods was under pressure from rising imports, and there was no intention of raising the general tariff wall.[1] Another case was the 1967 attempt by France to protect its domestic appliance manufacturers from further encroachments by Italy, by invoking the 'escape clause' in Article 226 of the Rome Treaty and seeking the right to impose import quota restrictions.[2]

Quotas, in fact, are only the major form of what have come to be termed 'non-tariff trade barriers'. It was noted in 1969[3] that these had become particularly acute since the 'Kennedy Round' tariff reductions and the creation of trading groups such as E.F.T.A. and E.E.C. The eight major barriers of this type are:

(i) Quantitative restrictions on imports and/or exports.
(ii) Customs classifications and customs valuation methods and procedures.
(iii) Public procurement policies and practices.
(iv) Anti-dumping regulations and countervailing duties.[4]
(v) Border tax adjustments.
(vi) Government domestic subsidies to industry, taxation aids and 'adjustment assistance' to import competition.
(vii) Export rebates and export credit subsidies.[5]
(viii) Industrial standards, including technical, health and safety standards.

In 1971 the O.E.C.D. set up a committee to study such protective barriers to international trade.[6]

Professor Baldwin's 1971 study of post-'Kennedy Round' nominal and 'effective' (i.e., after including outlay taxes) levels of protection in the U.K. is summarised in Table 5.2. It probably underestimated the magnitude of the effective rate of protection in the U.K.

In the wake of the U.S. 1971 policy of restrictions on imports, Japan, which had to divert a great deal of its exports to other markets, proposed that other

---

[1] 'What's wrong with quotas?', *Econ.*, 18 Nov. 1967, pp. 727–8.
[2] 'E.E.C. protectionism', *Econ.*, 2 Dec. 1967, p. 979.
[3] *F.T.*, 16 Sept. 1969; 'Why trade barriers still matter', *ibid.*, 18 Feb. 1971; 'Non-tariff distortions of trade', *P.E.P. Broadsheet* 514, Sept. 1969; R. Baldwin, *Non-tariff distortions of international trade*, 1971.
[4] 'Anti-dumping', *Econ.*, 29 April 1972, p. 101; also see, with regard to import surcharges and import deposits, 'Two years on – and off', *Econ.*, 3 Dec. 1966, pp. 1045–6; P. M. Oppenheimer, 'Import deposits', *N.W.B.Q.R.*, Feb. 1969; 'Import deposits', *Econ.*, 18 April 1970, p. 73.
[5] 'Export rebate as reprisal for U.S. action', *D.T.*, 31 Jan. 1968.
[6] *F.T.*, 29 June 1971.

Table 5.2 *Nominal and 'effective' levels of protection*

U.K. RATES OF PROTECTION IN 1972

	Post-Kennedy Round, nominal tariff rates %	Effective rate of protection* %
Radio and Telecommunications	18	44
Cereal foodstuffs	5	42
Cotton and man-made fibres	10	29
Agriculture, forestry and fishing	3	27
Clothing	10	25
China and glassware	12	24
Mechanical engineering	11	23
Precision instruments and jewellery	7	18
Motors and cycles	6	14
Electrical engineering	8	14
Mineral oil refining	0	12
Paper and board	3	9
Chemicals and dyes	2	0
Average, all goods (weighted by domestic supply)	3	13

U.S. and U.K. PROTECTION COMPARED, 1972 RATES

	Tariffs only			
	Nominal rates %		Effective rates* %	
	U.S.	U.K.	U.S.	U.K.
Primary products	7	2	17	18
Intermediate and consumer goods	7	3	18	11
Capital goods	6	8	7	17
Average (weighted by domestic supply)	6	3	15	13

*Excluding non-trading inputs
(Source: *F.T.*, 18 Feb. 1971)

industrialised nations join it in adopting an 'orderly marketing concept', to avoid aggressive competition in overseas markets.[1]

9. Multilateral and Bilateral Trade

A country, for political or currency reasons, may conduct its trade with another country on the basis of direct quantitative agreements and/or indirect tariff methods, so that its imports and exports are of equal value, i.e. so that both countries are in balance of payments equilibrium with each other. This type of trade pattern is termed bilateral, and may, in fact, restrict the volume of international trade. This type of reciprocal, balanced trade has become more important in recent years, especially between the Communist and Western countries.

[1] 'Orderly marketing to avoid trade war', *F.T.*, 4 Nov. 1971.

It is usually termed 'compensation trading' and is, in effect, barter. Many developing countries adopt this system, also, because of their dependence on a narrow range of commodities for the bulk of their foreign exchange earnings. Specialists have evolved, who deal in barter trade deals and in a sophisticated device, referred to as 'switch trading'. This represents a procedure to overcome the lack of mutually compatible needs on the part of both members of a barter deal: despite the frequent presence of clauses prohibiting resale to third parties, specialists undertake this work. One useful function of barter and switch trading is that they permit trade to occur without requiring settlement in foreign exchange: the actual terms on which barter deals take place will differ in different agreements.[1]

On the other hand, if a country (Utopia) has no desire to impose restrictions on its trade with other countries for political, strategic or economic reasons, it may achieve an overall balance of payments with the outside world by permitting a deficit with Eldorado, provided that it achieves a surplus with Subtopia. This pattern of trade is termed multilateral, and permits the maximum volume of international exchange of goods and services. Fig. 5.3 illustrates a possible increase in the volume of international trade on a multilateral basis, as compared with a bilateral system of trade. Free trade and multilateralism increase the opportunities for production and consumption, provided that suitable policies are followed. Such policies may include the deliberate redistribution of incomes, both within and between countries. They may be necessary, as all-round improvements in production, consumption and living standards may not automatically follow, or may be insufficient. The main case for multilateralism lies in the fact that it allows alternative trade patterns to be exploited.

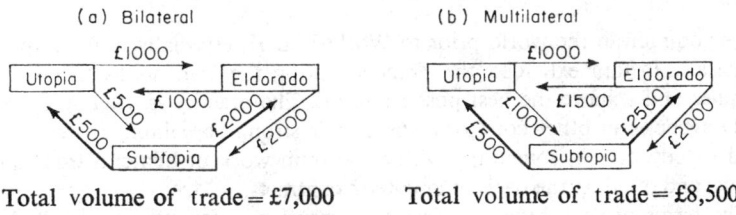

Fig. 5.3. *Bilateral and multilateral trade patterns*

After the depression of the interwar period there was a pronounced trend towards bilateral trading agreements, supported by tariffs and quotas, but since World War II various attempts have been made, through G.A.T.T., to restore more multilateralism into world trade. A summary of the major multilateral trade flows between the main trading nations and blocs, within the blocs and between them and the rest of the world in 1969 is given in Fig. 5.4.

10. Bulk Purchase

Apart from the normal commercial agreements negotiated by trade organisations or large firms for the sale or purchase of goods in bulk, so as to obtain better terms or greater security of supply or outlets, governments sometimes negotiate or sponsor such bulk purchase agreements. This type of transaction became

[1] 'How switch trading works', *Econ.*, 14 Jan. 1967, pp. 143–4; 'Getting back to barter trade', *D.T.*, 22 May 1968; 'Barter trading', *F.T.*, 17 April 1969; *ibid.*, 14 Sept. 1970 and 12 Feb. 1970.

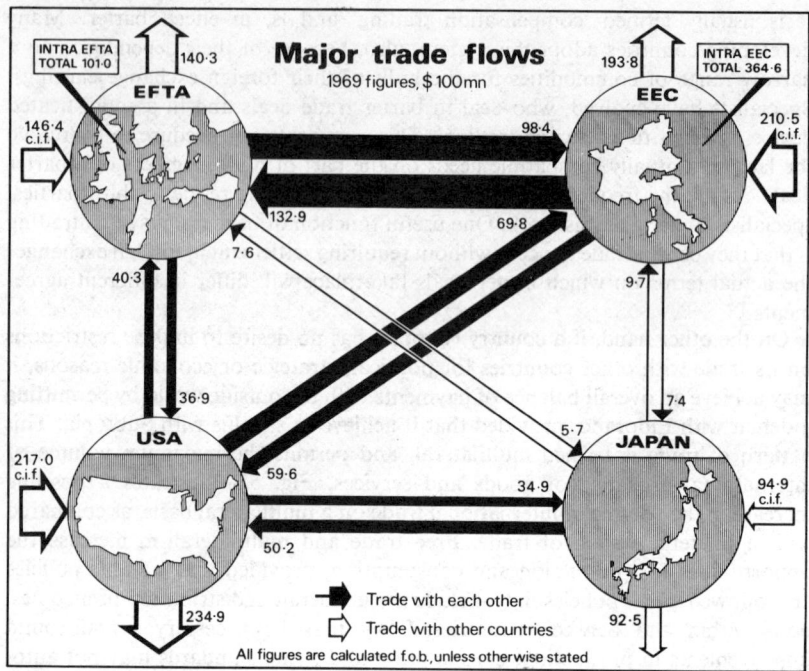

Fig. 5.4 *Multilateral trade flows of the major trading areas, 1969*
(Source: *Econ.*, 1 Aug. 1970, p. 54)

quite common in the world prior to World War II, especially in food and raw materials. Britain extended the practice during the war, so as to guarantee supplies and achieve the best possible terms. The practice is often adopted by State agencies in other countries where their strong bargaining power may be used to buy or sell, sometimes within the framework of bilateral trade agreements, and often on the basis of long-term contracts.

The terms of such bulk purchase agreements will depend upon the relative bargaining powers of seller and purchaser.

The goods may be sold at a low, subsidised price, in an attempt to earn scarce foreign currency; the goods purchased may be resold at a higher or lower price to individual firms. Although the security of outlets may induce the seller to offer at a lower price, he may also be encouraged by the presence of a guaranteed market to neglect innovations and technical efficiency. Furthermore, the buyer may be forced to take other commodities, as part of the agreement. While he may gain if world prices subsequently rise, the buyer may suffer, as a result of being tied to a long-term contractual price, if world prices subsequently fall.

11. Government Promotion of International Trade

Apart from its participation, through G.A.T.T. and other international bodies, in the fostering of trade and the removal of restrictions, the British Government also stimulates trade with more direct methods. Until 1972 export promotion was primarily in the hands of two bodies: the Department of Trade and Industry was the executive body, which actually organised and financed promotional activities, and the British National Export Council was the 'think tank', which handled public relations and conducted research into markets and products. In 1972 the British Export Board was set up (since renamed the British Overseas Trade Board).[1] This body inherited the D.T.I. civil servants formerly involved in export promotion and its board included businessmen and representatives of the D.T.I., the Foreign Office and the Commonwealth Office. The B.O.T.B. henceforth was to replace the previous machinery: its activities included the direction of the whole range of export intelligence and promotion activities; the provision of market intelligence (including the computerised Export Intelligence Service); participation in overseas trade fairs; support in connection with trade missions; individual services to exporters, through the Export Services Branch and Regional Offices; assistance with major overseas projects; assistance in joint representation arrangements overseas by companies making complementary products; aid to non-official export organisations; information and publicity, awards to exporters and forward planning and evaluation.

The Board had access to the services of the Commercial Relations and Exports Divisions of the D.T.I. and could draw upon the trade promotion and information network of the Diplomatic Service abroad. 'British Weeks' held abroad were to continue, subject to careful scrutiny in the light of competing claims for expenditure. The Board was to work through bodies such as trade associations and chambers of commerce and area committees were to be set up. It was expected to continue giving financial support, for the time being, to specialist groups such as the Sino-British Trade Council and the East European Trade Council. The annual budget of the Board was to be about £13·5 million: this was to be approximately one-half of total Government expenditure on export promotion (£28 million). The organisational structure of the Board is shown in Fig. 5.5.

The Export Credits Guarantee Department, established in 1919 under the President of the Board of Trade, provides United Kingdom exporters with an insurance service against the risks of losses in export trading. The E.C.G.D. does not itself provide finance (apart from certain 'last resort' powers which it acquired in 1970): it relies on the cooperation of the banks to do this, whereby they grant favourable terms to exporters who receive E.C.G.D. cover on 95% of the value of their contracts. The banks have been providing loans at only ½% above Bank Rate for finance up to two years, but only about one-third of exporters have been taking advantage of the facility. Although by 1972 less than 10% of British and world exports fell into the category involving credit for more than two years, the proportion has been growing – due to greater competition amongst exporting countries. E.C.G.D. helps to overcome normal banking reluctance to grant long-term credit by giving guarantees to the banks: during the 1950s it also started to give guarantees to the customers, so that exporters might obtain cash from those buyers, who themselves borrow from a British bank against E.C.G.D. cover. This latter device was intended to relieve the exporter from financial problems and allow him to concentrate on production and sales.[2] In May 1972 it was announced that the E.C.G.D. was to double its

---

[1] 'Looking for a new approach', *F.T.*, 11 April 1972; 'The British Overseas Trade Board', *ibid.*, 2 March 1972.
[2] 'Export credits in profusion', *Econ.*, 9 Oct. 1971, pp. 70-1; D. E. Fair, 'Export credit problems', *The Three Banks Review*, Dec. 1970.

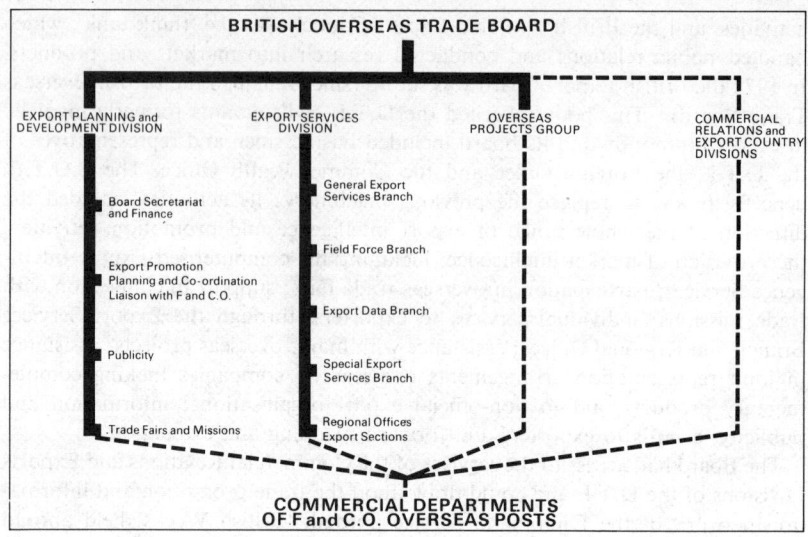

BRITISH OVERSEAS TRADE BOARD

EXPORT PLANNING and
DEVELOPMENT DIVISION

Board Secretariat
and Finance

Export Promotion
Planning and Co-ordination
Liaison with F and C.O.

Publicity

Trade Fairs and Missions

EXPORT SERVICES
DIVISION

General Export
Services Branch

Field Force Branch

Export Data Branch

Special Export
Services Branch

Regional Offices
Export Sections

OVERSEAS
PROJECTS GROUP

COMMERCIAL
RELATIONS and
EXPORT COUNTRY
DIVISIONS

**COMMERCIAL DEPARTMENTS
OF F and C.O. OVERSEAS POSTS**

Fig. 5.5 *Organisational structure of the British Overseas Trade Board, 1972*
(Source: *F.T.*, 3 Nov. 1971)

provincial manpower to 500 and to decentralise some of its London head office
work. The Scholey report recommended more generous terms to exporters,
more discretion to exporters and a more 'commercial' and less bureaucratic
philosophy on the part of the E.C.G.D.[1]

In April 1972 the Midland Bank initiated a new form of export credit which
dispensed with E.C.G.D. guarantees and could, therefore, offer rates under the
6% fixed export finance rate then current.[2]

During the year to end-March 1972 E.C.G.D. insured turnover rose by
18.2% to £3,813 million, of which 8·7% was on 'national interest' account and
91·3% on 'commercial' account: in both sectors there was an increase in bank
advances guaranteed by the E.C.G.D.[3]

12. United Kingdom Visible Imports and Exports

International trade has been of great importance to Britain's economy for over a
century. With less than 2% of the world's population, Britain conducts about
10% of international trade and was the world's third largest trading nation in
1970. By the end of the nineteenth century Britain's share of the world's manufactured exports was about 33%. Because of increasing competition from other
nations, this share fell to 30% in 1914, 24% in 1929, 22% in 1937, 16% in 1961
and 11% in 1968.

Britain still relies upon imports for nearly all its industrial raw materials and
about half its foodstuffs. Exports of goods and services account for about one-
fifth of the Gross National Product. Britain is a major exporter of machinery, road
and railway vehicles, aircraft, metal manufactures, electrical apparatus, chemicals

[1] 'The Scholey Report', *F.T.*, 8 June 1972.
[2] 'Export finance', *F.T.*, 28 April 1972.
[3] *D.T.*, 4 July 1972.

400

and textiles. It is the largest market in the world for foodstuffs, and one of the largest for metals, cotton, wool, petroleum and many other raw materials.

Since 1938, the last full year of trade before World War II, the size and composition of British imports and exports of goods have undergone great changes, as have their geographical distribution.

Official statistics for United Kingdom visible trade are given in the Trade and Navigation Accounts (*Annual Statement of the Trade of the United Kingdom* and *Monthly Overseas Trade Statistics of the United Kingdom*). The system of classification is based on the United Nations Standard International Trade Classification. The basis for the valuation of imports is 'c.i.f.' ('cost-insurance-freight'), which includes shipping, insurance and other expenses involved in delivering goods to the port of entry in Britain. Most of these expenses represent earnings by British firms. Goods exported are valued 'f.o.b.' ('free-on-board'), which represents the sale price of the goods and only those expenses involved in delivering them on board the exporting ship. Due to the time factor and the complex procedures adopted for the recording of exports, something of a scandal came to light in the late 1960s, when it was revealed that for several years exports for the current year had been under-recorded by about 2% to 3%.[1]

There are four categories of visible imports and exports, viz.

A. Food, beverages and tobacco (e.g. meat, sugar, feedingstuffs);

B. Basic materials (e.g. hides, rubber, wool and ores);

C. Mineral fuels and lubricants (e.g. coal, petroleum);

D. Manufactured goods (e.g. finished goods, – textiles, machinery, etc.; semi-finished goods, – yarns, steel, etc.)

At current prices, imports (c.i.f.) were valued at £919 million in 1938, £3,328·1 million in 1953, £4,627·7 million in 1962 and £9,051·5 million in 1970. Exports and re-exports (f.o.b.) were valued at £532 million in 1938, £2,661·1 million in 1953, £4,062·3 million in 1962 and £8,062·8 million in 1970. Because of price changes during this period, the volume of goods involved has not altered as much as these figures might suggest. It has been estimated that, compared with 1962, the volume of imports in 1970 was 55% greater and the volume of exports 52% greater.

The increasing importance of exports may be seen from the fact that whilst imports were equivalent to 16% of Gross National Expenditure at factor costs in 1938, 18% in 1962 and 21·1% in 1970, exports were equivalent to only 10% of Gross National Expenditure in 1938, but rose to 15·8% in 1962 and 18·8% in 1970. The decline in the U.K. share of industrial countries' exports between 1960 and 1970 is shown graphically in Fig. 5.6, as is the relative significance of her major customers. A very thorough study of the structure of U.K. external trade, based on 1968 data, was made by D. F. Lomax in 1970. His comparative table of the U.K. and sixteen other developed countries, giving some of the most important elements, is reproduced in Table 5.3. He found that, generally speaking, the U.K. was a typical country of its size, but had an unusually high level of food imports in relation to G.N.P. and *per capita* income. This he put down to the U.K.'s trading policy, rather than to any inherent abnormality in her situation, involving basic vulnerability or special dependence on food imports and on international trade generally.[2] Another controversial opinion on Britain's

[1] 'The "lost" exports', *F.T.*, 24 June 1969; *ibid.*, 10 Sept. 1969.
[2] D. A. Lomax, 'The United Kingdom's trading position', *N.W.B.Q.R.*, May 1970.

Table 5.3 *The trading position of the U.K. and 16 other developed countries, 1968*

	Population (millions)	Gross National Product (GNP) (millions) ($)	GNP Per head ($)	Exports and imports			Food imports		Raw material imports		Manufacturing exports		Total exports	Population per square mile	
				Value (millions) ($)	As per cent of GNP	Per head of pop. ($)	As per cent of GNP	Per head of pop ($)	As per cent of GNP	Per head of pop ($)	As per cent of GNP	Per head of pop. ($)	Per head ($)		
	(1)	(2)	(3)	(4)	(5)	(6)	(7)	(8)	(9)	(10)	(11)	(12)	(13)	(14)	
U.K.	55·3	102,670	1,850	34,305	33·4	620·3	4·0	74·3	4·9	91·8	12·3	229·1	227·5	585·0	U.K.
Australia	12·0	26,092	2,174	7,908	30·3	659·0	0·5	11·6	2·1	46·4	2·7	58·9	293·8	4·1	Australia
Austria	7·4	11,400	1,550	4,485	39·3	606·1	2·0	30·7	3·8	58·1	14·2	218·9	268·8	226·9	Austria
Belgium/Lux'g	10·0	21,485	2,160	16,497	76·8	1,649·7	4·2	89·2	9·2	197·2	31·2	669·9	816·4	777·7	Belgium/Lux'g
Canada	20·8	62,440	3,010	25,640	41·1	1,232·7	1·2	37·4	2·2	65·7	11·7	352·6	632·6	5·8	Canada
Denmark	4·9	12,390	2,540	5,861	47·3	1,196·1	2·2	54·5	5·1	128·8	10·4	263·3	538·4	293·4	Denmark
France	43·9	126,230	2,530	26,621	21·1	533·4	1·4	35·3	2·9	72·8	7·4	188·1	254·1	234·5	France
W. Germany	60·2	132,480	2,200	45,088	34·0	749·0	2·5	56·1	6·4	86·2	16·8	370·0	412·8	631·3	W. Germany
Ireland	2·9	2,983	1,029	1,973	66·1	680·3	2·5	54·8	4·9	66·2	8·6	88·9	275·2	109·4	Ireland
Italy	52·8	74,980	1,390	20,436	27·3	387·0	2·5	35·2	4·9	69·9	11·2	158·8	192·9	453·6	Italy
Japan	101·1	141,810	1,400	25,961	18·3	256·8	1·3	17·9	5·3	74·6	8·6	120·5	128·3	708·4	Japan
Netherlands	12·7	25,230	1,980	17,632	69·9	1,388·3	4·5	88·9	7·7	153·1	19·4	384·8	656·8	987·8	Netherlands
New Zealand	2·8	4,775	1,740	1,905	39·9	680·4	1·0	17·1	3·0	50·3	1·8	30·4	360·7	26·5	New Zealand
Norway	3·8	9,020	2,360	4,644	51·5	1,222·1	2·2	52·9	5·6	132·4	15·6	371·0	510·0	30·5	Norway
Sweden	7·9	25,570	3,230	10,119	39·6	1,280·9	1·9	62·4	3·7	120·6	14·3	461·3	624·9	49·8	Sweden
Switzerland	6·1	17,160	2,790	8,481	49·4	1,390·3	2·9	82·1	3·4	95·4	21·0	590·2	650·5	386·6	Switzerland
U.S.	201·2	880,770	4,380	70,206	8·0	348·9	0·5	22·7	0·7	29·7	2·7	117·6	172·3	56·6	U.S.

(Source: D. F. Lomax, 'The United Kingdom's trading position', *N.W.B.Q.R.*, May 1970)

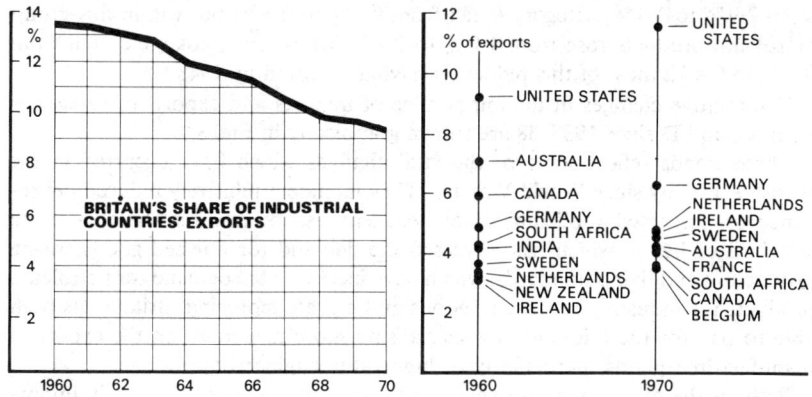

Fig. 5.6 *U.K. share of exports and best customers, 1960 and 1970*
(Source: *Econ.*, 16 Jan. 1971, p. 63)

trading position has been expressed by A. R. Conan. He has concluded that the assumption that the U.K. was failing to pay its way in the 1960s is false, since the officially computed balance included debits incurred on behalf of other countries – including economic aid, some defence costs and particularly 'hidden subsidies' to other countries, resulting from British commercial policy. These latter included the purchase of imports which could be produced in Britain and the purchase, at artificially high prices, of goods subject to international commodity agreements and of goods subject to quota arrangements.[1]

COMPOSITION

There have been marked changes in the composition of visible imports and exports since 1938. With regard to imports, the most significant trend has been the relative fall in the proportion of category A (Food, Beverages and Tobacco) from 44·9% of the total during the period 1935–38 to 23% in 1970, made possible by the big expansion in British agricultural production. Basic Materials (category B) fell from 27·9% of the total during 1935–8 to 15·2% in 1970. Category C (Mineral Fuels and Lubricants) rose from 4·8% to 10·5%, reflecting the increased demand for petroleum and other oil products. Imports of category D (Manufactured Goods) rose from 22·4% in 1935–8 to 51·3% in 1970. Within this general increase, which reflects the trend towards increasingly important world trade in manufactured goods between industrialised countries, since World War II, there has always been a larger proportion of semi-finished goods than of finished products, but the rate of increase has been much faster in the latter group.

With regard to exports, there has always been a heavy preponderance of category D (Manufactured Goods). This proportion increased from 75·7% in 1935–8 to 87·5% in 1970. Within this group the most significant change has been the increase in engineering products from 20·1% of total exports in 1935–38 to 45·0% in 1970. Metals fell from 13·4% of total exports in 1935–38 to 12·3% in 1970. Textiles showed a significant fall, from 24·0% to 5·2%. From the period 1935–38 to 1970 exports of category A fell from 7·4% to 6·5%; category B fell

[1] A. R. Conan, 'Does Britain pay its way?', *N.W.B.Q.R.*, Feb. 1969; A. Franks, 'Does Britain pay its way? – a rejoinder', *ibid.*, May 1969; 'Trade policy', *Econ.*, 15 Feb. 1969, pp. 76–9.

from 7·9% to 3·4%; category C fell from 9·0% to 2·6%, but within this group petroleum products rose from 1·0% to 2·2%, whilst coal, coke, etc., fell from 8·0% to 0·4%, most of this reduction having occurred by 1948.[1]

The relative changes in the importance of imports and exports of categories A, B, C, and D since 1935–38 are shown graphically in Fig. 5.7.

These trends reflect some of the vital changes which have occurred in the British economy since World War II. They include a relatively reduced dependence on imported foodstuffs; more efficient use of raw materials; a rising standard of living, which has increased the demand for finished goods; rising production and living standards, which have increased the demand for petroleum products for industry, carriage of goods and private motoring. Britain has been able to pay for these imports by specialising more and more on the export of manufactured goods, particularly of high-value engineering products.

Perhaps the most significant general development has been the rise in importance of manufactured imports and exports, reflecting the rapid growth in world trade in this category. It has been suggested that the evidence points to a general tendency towards a reduction in the world supply of primary products for export – as instanced by Argentinian beef – and that the reduction in the ratio of world trade in primary products to that in manufactured goods is due more to supply deficiency than to demand deficiency.[2] The apparent paradox of rising U.K. imports of manufactured goods in parallel with rising exports in them has been explained as a manifestation of international specialisation: due to the growing sophistication of mechanical engineering, for example, a home-made product may not always be available for a specific purpose, and may have to be imported.[3] A N.E.D.O. study in 1971 of British export performance during the 1960s sounded a cautionary note worthy of mention. It found that the British economy was weakest in precisely these products in which world trade was growing fastest: these were groups involving the most advanced engineering and chemical products, as with organic chemicals, office machinery, cars and commercial vehicles, electrical machinery, iron and steel and inorganic chemicals. Only in scientific instruments did the U.K. almost hold its own against growing competition. Rising costs were deemed to be less important than lack of change in the industrial structure and in technical competence.[4]

The re-export trade has been declining in relative importance during the twentieth century. Britain has long been conducting an entrepôt trade in raw materials and foodstuffs, particularly involving goods from the Commonwealth and destined for Europe. In 1938 this trade was valued at £61 million f.o.b.; in 1954, £98 million f.o.b.; in 1962, £157·2 million. The most important items were rubber, furs, raw wool, tea, non-ferrous metals, beverages and machinery, including aeroplane engines.

AREA DISTRIBUTION
Since World War II important changes have occurred in the relative importance of different areas as import suppliers and as export customers.[5]

[1] For further data and charts, see 'Britain's overseas trade in 1970', *E.P.R.*, 14, April 1971; 'Into surplus', *E.P.R.*, 5, May 1970; 'The import bill', *D.E.A. Pr. Rep. Econ.*, 44, Sept. 1968; *B.B.R.*, Aug. 1971 and May 1972; *Brit. O. H.*, 1972, pp. 359–61.
[2] E. Devons, 'Understanding international trade', *Economica*, Nov. 1961.
[3] 'Engineering imports', *Econ.*, 22 Feb. 1969, p. 66.
[4] *S.T.*, 2 May 1971.
[5] For an interesting diagrammatic analysis of international export patterns see *Econ.*, 12 Nov. 1966, p. 711.

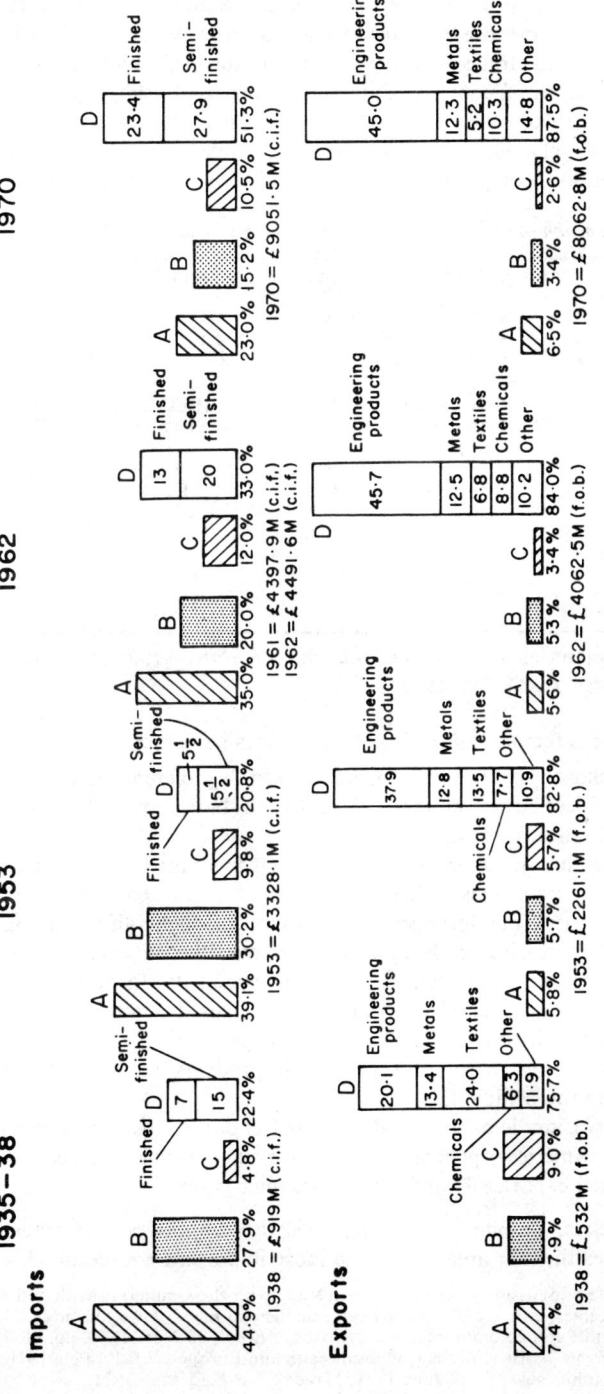

Fig. 5.7. *Changes in the composition of U.K. imports and exports since the period 1935–38* (Based on material in *Britain: an Official Handbook*; *The Economist*, 2 Feb. 1963, p. 467; *Lloyds Bank Review*, July 1961, p. 2; Ann. Abs. Stat.)

5. INTERNATIONAL TRADE [1]

Whereas trade with the Commonwealth[1] accounted for about half U.K. international trade in 1938, it had fallen to less than one-quarter in 1970. Trade with western Europe rose from just over a quarter in 1938, to more than one-third in 1970. Within the trade pattern with western Europe, both imports and exports with the European Economic Community increased relatively by about 70% from 1954 to 1970, whilst with the European Free Trade Association there was about a 30% relative increase in trade (see Table 5.4). The major changes in area distribution, comparing 1971 with 1966, are shown graphically in Fig. 5.8.

Table 5.4 *The changing pattern of U.K. foreign trade: relative shares, by area*

Area	1938 (%)	1954 (%)	1961 (%)	1970 (%)
Commonwealth				
Imports	40·5	47·5	38·0	23·8
Exports	50·0	48·5	39·5	21·0
Western Europe				
Imports	28·5	25·0	30·6	38·0
	(France and northern Europe)	(EEC. 11·6 EFTA. 11·6)	(EEC. 13·1 EFTA. 12·4)	(EEC. 20·0 EFTA. 15·5)
Exports	29·7	27·8	32·4	41·0
	(France and northern Europe)	(EEC. 13·1 EFTA. 12·4)	(EEC. 16·7 EFTA. 13·1)	(EEC. 21·8 EFTA. 15·8)
Rest of world				
Imports	31·0	27·5	31·4	38·2
Exports	20·3	23·7	28·1	38·0

(Based on material in the *Annual Abstract of Statistics*; *Econ.*, 1 Jan. 1972, p. 17 (Survey); *F.T.*, 23 Feb. 1972)

Some of the factors underlying these changes have been:

(*a*) The declining significance of Commonwealth preference margins, which are specific, as prices have risen. Also, G.A.T.T. has been responsible for negotiating reductions in these preference margins.

(*b*) The reduction in the proportion of imports from the Commonwealth of food and basic materials. This is due to increasing self-sufficiency; more efficient use of materials and the increasing importance of high-value manufactures in Britain; the increasing tendency of Commonwealth countries to produce their own manufactured goods, which previously came from Britain.

(*c*) The increasing demand in Britain for specialised manufactures and luxury goods from North America and western Europe.

(*d*) The increasing imports of petroleum products from North and South America and the Middle East.

(*e*) The increasing demand in industrialised countries (such as western Europe and North America), generated by their rising average incomes, for British manufactured exports of capital and consumer goods.

Nevertheless, despite the declining relative importance of trade with the Commonwealth, that area is still the most important source of U.K. imports

1 For a detailed discussion of the changes in trade with the Commonwealth and other areas, with charts, tables, etc., see 'Commonwealth myths and facts', *Econ.*, 9 Jan. 1971, pp. 56–7; 'Commonwealth and common market: the issues', *Econ.*, 28 Nov. 1970, pp. 66–7; *Econ.*, 29 May 1971, pp. 46–7; 'Britain, the Commonwealth and Europe', *B.B.R.*, Feb. 1971; 'Weighing up the opportunities', *F.T.*, 29 June 1971; 'Trade', *F.B.E.*, 5 May 1971.

of categories A, B and C, and the most important customer for U.K. exports of manufactured goods.

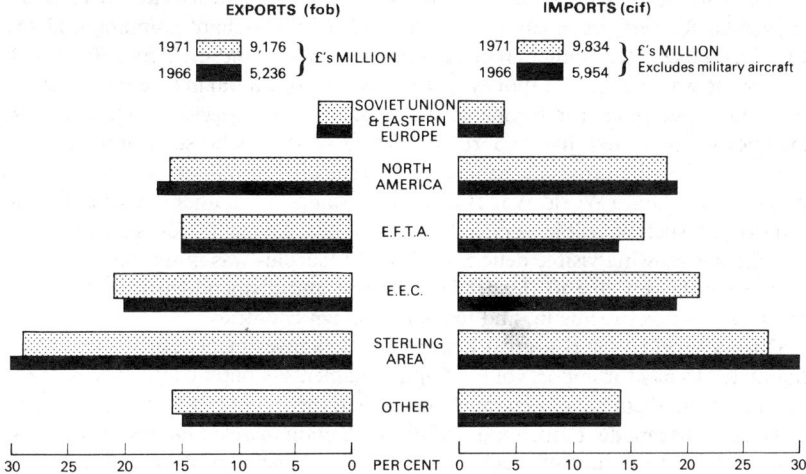

Fig. 5.8. *Changes in the geographical distribution of U.K. external trade, 1966 to 1971.*
(Source: *B.B.R.*, May 1972)

13. Balance of Trade and Balance of Payments

The preceding section dealt with the visible items in Britain's foreign trade, the import and export of goods. Trade, however, also involves the exchange of services of various types. These are referred to as 'invisible' items, and they must be included in any account setting out a country's 'balance of payments' with the outside world.

For about one century Britain's growing population has been enjoying a rising standard of living. This has been accompanied by an increase in imports of food and raw materials, with a less than proportionate increase in exports of goods. The relationship between economic activity and growth, on the one hand, and visible trade, on the other, has been expressed as follows.[1] Imports fall into three broad categories: firstly, basic materials and some manufacturing components, which rise in line with industrial production; secondly, food and fuel, which do not rise in close correlation with industrial production; thirdly, other imports (especially manufactured goods), which rise or fall in close correlation with the competitiveness of the U.K. economy. Exports tend to move in the same way as the third group of imports. Thus, if group 3 imports are subtracted from exports, we may isolate 'net exports'. Instead of seeking to match exports with all three groups and thus to achieve an actual visible balance, it would probably be more economically meaningful if we sought to achieve a 'full growth balance' between 'net exports' (suitably trimmed down by the group 3 imports, which themselves result from the state of economic activity), on the one hand, and group 1 and group 2 imports, on the other. The increasing deficit in visible trade was made

[1] A relationship outlined by Sir Roy Harrod in *E.J.*, Sept. 1967, discussed in Balance of payments', *Econ.*, 7 Oct. 1967, p. 73.

407

possible, up to World War II, by the surplus in earnings from the export of services over payments for the import of services – the 'invisible surplus'. Some of these invisible items in international trade are straightforward earnings (or payments) for services, such as those provided by merchant shipping and the City (insurance, etc.). Others represent interest, profits and dividends, for which the service was the loan of money or the investing of capital in foreign industry.[1] In addition, earnings (or payments) must be made for services such as tourist facilities to foreigners, the 'export' of migrant workers who send home part of their wages, or the provision to foreign governments of military bases, embassy property, etc. Up to World War II Britain's earnings from other countries for the 'export' of such invisible services exceeded her payments for similar items. Despite her growing visible deficit, the invisible surplus was more than sufficient to cover it, largely due to the growing interest and dividend earnings from the great capital investments in, and loans to, foreign countries.

During World War II a great deal of Britain's investments abroad had to be liquidated to pay for imports of food and armaments. Consequently, her postwar earnings from them have been much lower than they would otherwise have been. This factor has made it much more vital that Britain increase her visible exports, and has lain at the root of much of her postwar 'balance of payments crises'. It would be incorrect to blame the reduction in the invisible surplus on wartime losses alone. In 1967 earnings were seven times larger (in money terms) than in 1938: payments, on the other hand, were $15\frac{1}{2}$ times larger – having risen at double the rate of increase in the value of visible imports. The main causes of this increase in payments have been the relative increase in the use of foreign shipping services, especially during the 1960s; the growth of travel and tourism abroad (with 'package holidays', etc.); the growth of Government expenditure abroad – particularly military spending; the growth in payments for interest, profits and dividends – particularly payments for direct investment in the U.K. by foreign companies.[2]

Much attention has centred on the significance of *foreign direct investment*, both by the U.K. abroad and by foreign countries in the U.K. This item is the largest single category of invisible receipts and payments. The most noteworthy recent study was the Reddaway Report in November 1968.[3] The report found that, in manufacturing, direct investment abroad resulted in an 11% immediate or lump sum recoupment, in the form of direct exports of capital equipment, etc. Then there would be 'continuing benefits', such as profits, capital appreciation, a goodwill relationship conducive to exports of services, machinery, components, etc., and an improvement in productivity resulting from the 'feedback' of technical and marketing know-how. Set against these benefits would be the possible loss of direct exports of the goods or services which the overseas subsidiary would replace. The overall continuing benefit in manufacturing – expressed as profits after overseas tax – was estimated at about $5\frac{1}{2}$%, which was much higher than the interest cost of the overseas borrowing, which finances much of this

[1] M. Panić, 'The United Kingdom's exports of long-term capital', *M. and W.S.R.*, Autumn 1968.
[2] M. Panić, 'Britain's invisible balance', *L.B.R.*, July 1968. 'Britain's "invisible" earnings', *E.P.R.*, 9, Nov. 1970.
[3] W. B. Reddaway *et al.*, *Effects of U.K. Direct Overseas Investment: final report*. 'Overseas investment: Reddaway's verdict', *Econ.*, 23 Nov. 1968, pp. 74–5; W. A. P. Manser, 'Professor Reddaway's last word?', *N.W.B.Q.R.*, Feb. 1969.

investment. Some of the main conclusions of the report were that this type of investment tended to earn a higher rate of return, in general, than if put to any alternative use (the average profit rate after overseas tax, excluding the oil industry, was estimated at 8·2%); that it did not tend to take place at the expense of domestic industrial investment; that a net surplus on an investment involving 60% of U.K. finance and 40% external finance (i.e. when the investment has paid for itself and yields a continuous profit) tends to come after about ten years and varies considerably according to the firm or industry sector (see Table 5.5). It follows that policies to restrict capital outflows could have a short-term beneficial effect on the balance of payments and should, if enforced, be applied by a selective, vetting procedure. It also follows, however, that any prolonged stemming of such capital outgoings would severely reduce the long-term receipts or invisible earnings of the U.K.

Table 5.5. *Impact of each £100 of overseas investment, by industry* (£)

Industry	Initial effect	Continuing effects		
	Higher capital exports	Profits after overseas tax	Profits plus *capital appreciation	Additional exports from Britain
Building materials, etc.	16	13·8	18·7	— ½
Chemicals	15	7·7	14·9	— 2
Textiles	20	8·0	11·7	— ½
Food, drink, tobacco, etc.	7	8·5	10·1	1
Vehicles and components	21	5·3	8·0	10½
Metal and metal products	10	6·8	7·5	— ½
Electrical engineering	3	5·6	7·2	3½
Paper	1	6·2	6·1	0
Non-electrical engineering	11	5·3	4·9	18
Total manufacturing	10	7·7	10·1	1½
Manufacturing adjusted*	11	5·5	7·5	1½
Mining	6	12·3	21·6	2
Plantations	18	9·3	7·7	½
Total	9	8·2	10·8	1½

*Adjusted on replacement cost basis and to eliminate the effects of general price rises on inventories and on companies' market valuations.
(Source: *Econ.*, 23 Nov. 1968, p. 75)

Foreign direct investment in the U.K. has been the main reason for the growth in U.K. invisible payments. Estimates of direct investment in and by the U.K. are very tentative, but the following figures may give some idea of the magnitude involved.[1] At end-1967 foreign long-term assets in the U.K. were about £7·8

[1] Extrapolated from *Econ.*, 23 Nov. 1968, p. 74; Panić, 'Britain's invisible balance', *loc. cit.*, p. 21; Panić, 'The United Kingdom's Exports of Long-Term Capital', *loc. cit.*, p. 90; 'America's growing stake in Britain', *F.T.*, 24 Feb. 1969; *Econ.*, 9 May 1970, p. 61; *Economic Trends*, 221, March 1972.

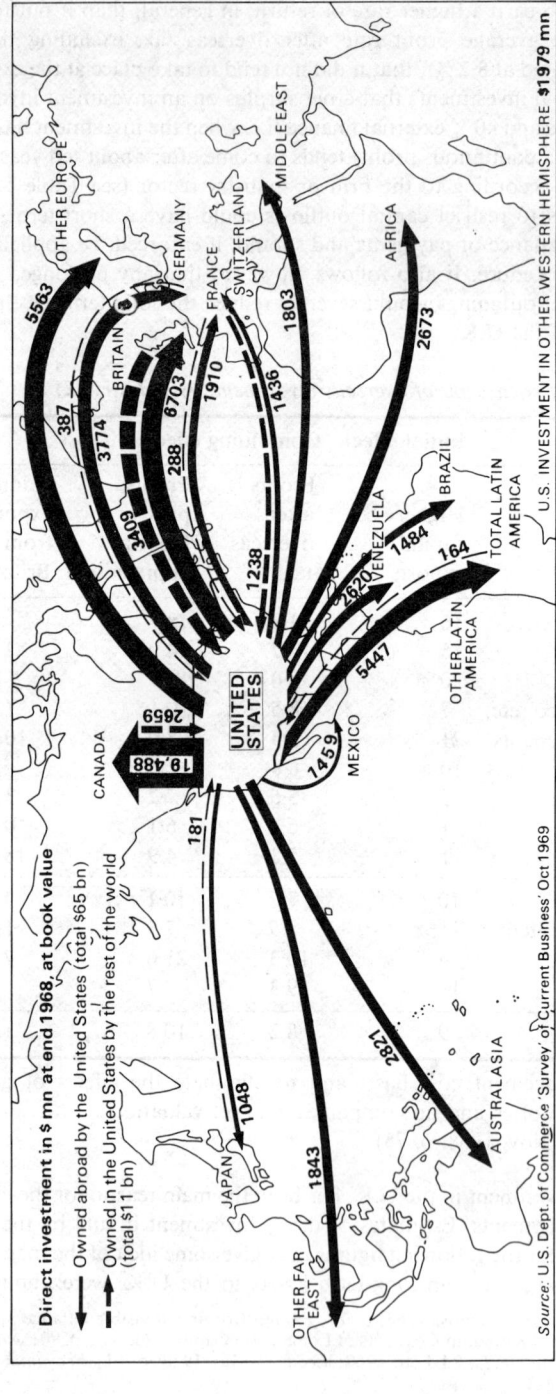

Fig. 5.9. *The pattern of overseas direct investment in and by the U.S., end-1962*
(Source: *Econ.*, 9 May 1970, p. 61)

billion, of which £4·9 billion were privately owned. Foreign direct investment in the U.K. by overseas companies, excluding oil, insurance and banking investments, was valued at £1·4 billion in 1960 and £2·17 billion in 1966 – representing approximately one-half of private long-term assets. This had been built up by about 8% (£180 million) per annum, on average during the period 1960–7. Payments by the U.K. for foreign direct investment in the U.K. were £204 million in 1966 – representing approximately 10% of the value of this direct investment. U.K. long-term assets abroad at end-1967 were about £12·6 billion, of which £11·5 billion were privately owned. A 'guesstimate' of the direct investment element in this would be about £4½ billion to £5 billion. The average annual build-up of U.K. direct investment abroad during the period 1960–7 was about £270 million (approximately 5% per annum – lower than the build-up of foreign direct investment in the U.K.). The U.K. earnings on direct investment abroad were £430 million in 1967 – representing approximately 10% of the value of this direct investment abroad.

By far the major and fastest growing element in foreign direct investment in the U.K. between 1960 and 1966 was by U.S. companies. This, excluding oil, insurance and banking investments, was £613·1 million in 1960 (58·9% of total) and £1,461·7 million in 1966 (67·2% of total) – an increase of 138·3%. Despite the dangers of U.S. control over key industries, this investment has been welcomed on the grounds that it bestows managerial and technical know-how on the U.K. economy, that it results in new industry in the development areas and that U.S. subsidiaries have a high export record.[1] The pattern of U.S. direct investment abroad at end-1968 ($65 billion) and of direct investment in the U.S. by the rest of the world ($11 billion) is shown in Fig. 5.9.

Since 1970 the U.K. accounts with the outside world – her balance of payments accounts – have been split into two major sections. The first section, the 'Total Currency Flow', indicates the net inflow or outflow of international funds. This shows *either* the annual total of money available (if a surplus or net inflow) for adding to the currency reserves and/or for paying off the U.K.'s 'overdraft' of long-term and short-term borrowing, *or* the annual total which must be 'financed' (if a deficit or net outflow) by international borrowing and/or the running down of the official reserves. The Total Currency Flow account is itself subdivided into two main sections: the 'Current Balance' – showing the annual success or failure in paying our way in terms of recurrent sales and earnings – and the 'Total Investment and Other Capital Flows' account – showing the flow of capital receipts and payments, whether long-, medium-, or short-term. This flow of capital, of course, affects the U.K.'s ability to build up reserves or pay off previously-incurred debts. The Current Balance, in turn, consists of two subdivisions: the 'Visible Balance' (or Balance of Trade) on the import and export of goods, and the 'Invisible Balance' on services and other invisible transactions. Thus the Total Currency Flow may be represented in simplified form as follows:

(1)   Visible Balance (Exports+; Imports −)
(2)   + Invisible Balance (Net surplus +; net deficit −)
(1 + 2) = Current Balance
(3)   Current Balance

----

[1] *F.T.*, 24 Feb. 1969.

(4)   + Investment and Other Capital Flows $\begin{cases} + = \text{inflow } or \text{ increase in} \\ \quad \text{liabilities } or \text{ liquidation} \\ \quad \text{of assets abroad} \\ - = \text{outflow } or \text{ decrease in} \\ \quad \text{liabilities } or \text{ acquisition} \\ \quad \text{of assets abroad} \end{cases}$

(3 + 4) = Total Currency Flow

The Total Currency Flow is, in fact, modified by 2 items: the 'E.E.A. loss on forwards' and the 'Balancing Item'. The E.E.A. loss on forwards refers to the loss, if any, incurred by the Exchange Equalisation Account on forward commitments, prior to the devaluation of the pound in 1967. The Balancing Item covers the discrepancies between the recorded capital and current transactions and the precise details of foreign currency movements, known to the Bank of England: such discrepancies are due to time lags and difficulties in making precise, consistent recordings.

Apart from these two modifications, the Total Currency Flow is then subject to two further amendments: the first, when applicable, refers to an inflow due to the operation of Special Drawing Rights from the International Monetary Fund; the other, when applicable, is an outflow, due to the payment of the U.K. gold subscription to the I.M.F. The final result of these modifications is what may be termed the Adjusted Currency Flow: if a surplus, it must somehow be disposed of; if a deficit, it must somehow be financed or paid for. This process of disposal or financing is shown in the second major section of the balance of payments accounts – the 'Official Financing' account. This must always result in a *reversal* of the '+' or '−' on the Adjusted Currency Flow total, with a total of the same magnitude. In this sense, the balance of payments accounts may be said always to balance.

Prior to 1970 the Investment and Other Capital Flows account used to be two separate accounts – the 'Long-term Capital' account and the 'Monetary Movements' (or short-term capital account). The Long-term Capital account balance was added to the Current Balance and the result was referred to as the 'basic balance'. However, it was found that this 'basic balance' was of little economic significance, since the distinction between long-term and short-term capital movements is difficult to ascertain. The concept of an overall Total Currency Flow provides a much clearer indication of the U.K.'s international state of financial affairs, given the increasing variety and intricacy of different forms of capital investment.[1]

Fig. 5.10 illustrates graphically the major components of the balance of payments accounts for 1970.

Table 5.6 shows some of the major changes in recent years in the U.K. balance of payments accounts. Here it must be noted that the figures for import and export totals are not quite the same as those given in the visible trade tables. This is because the Trade and Navigation (visible trade) accounts record values

[1] For further explanatory data and information on definitions, see 'The balance of payments accounts – an ABC', *E.P.R.*, 7, Sept. 1970; 'Balance of Payments', *T.B.B.E.*, 2, May 1971; 'Trade and payments', *E.P.R.*, 14, April 1971; 'Payments progress', *E.P.R.*, 1, Jan. 1970; 'Britain's "invisible" earnings', *E.P.R.*, 9, Nov. 1970; A. R. Conan, 'Britain as creditor', *loc. cit.*; *Ann. Abs. Stat.*, notes on 'Overseas finance'; Notes in *Economic Trends*, 221, March 1972.

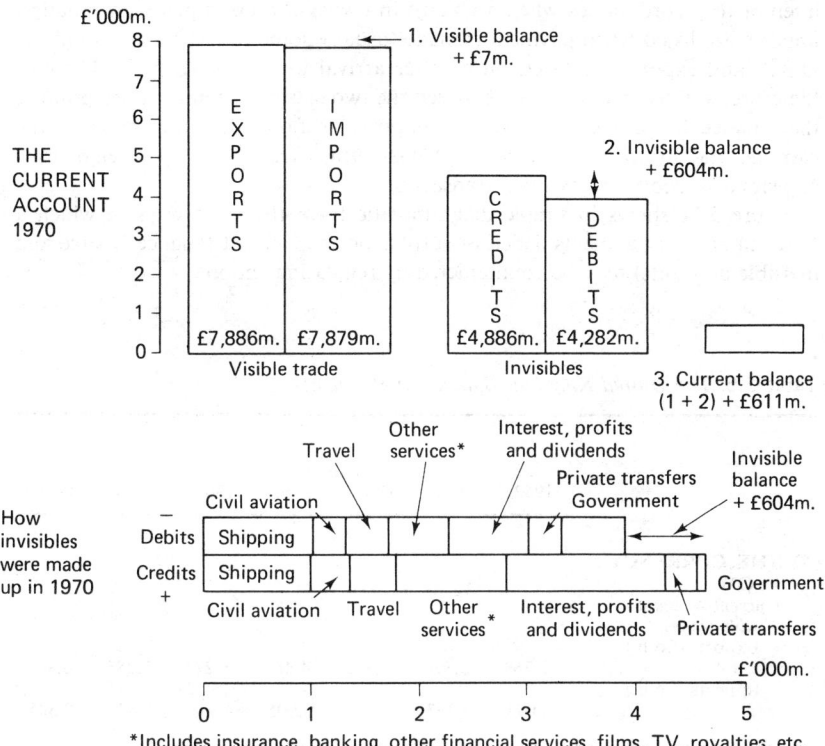

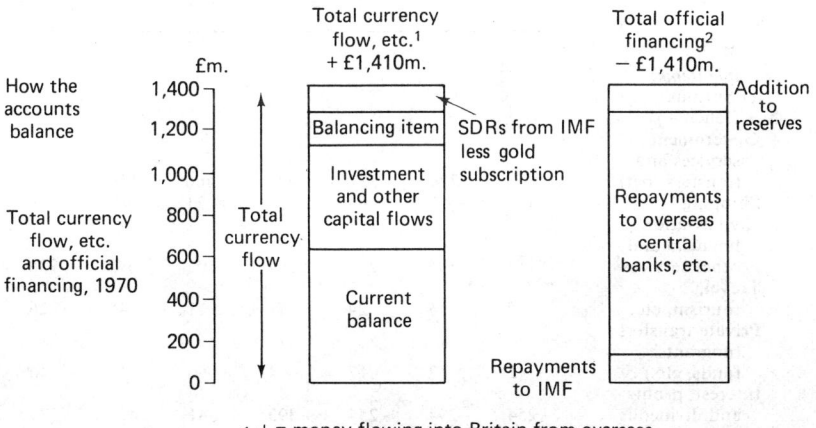

Fig. 5.10. *Charting the balance of payments, 1970*
(Based on material in *T.B.B.E.*, 2, May 1971 and *Economic Trends*, 221, March 1972)

413

of goods at the time they enter or leave Britain. The balance of payments accounts attempt to record values when a change in ownership takes place. In practice, imports are listed when payment is made (usually some time after arrival in the U.K.), and exports are listed on or after arrival in the foreign port. There is, therefore, a difference in timing between the two sets of accounts. Furthermore, the balance of payments figures list imports as f.o.b., because much of the carriage and insurance is done by British firms. That done by foreign firms appears as a debit on 'invisible' transactions.

Figure 5.11 shows in simple diagrammatic form the main ways in which a U.K. balance of payments deficit or surplus on the Current Balance (visible and invisible accounts) may be counteracted by regulating action.

Table 5.6. *The United Kingdom Balance of Payments*

				(£ million)			
	1952	1958	1961	1964	1968	1970	1971
(A) THE CURRENCY FLOW							
Current Account							
Visible trade:							
Exports (f.o.b.) (+)	2,769	3,392	3,891	4,486	6,273	7,886	8,882
Imports (f.o.b.) (−)	3,048	3,357	4,043	5,005	6,916	7,879	8,585
Balance of Trade (Visible)	−279	+35	−152	−519	−643	+7	+297
Invisible items: (Net Surplus +; Net Deficit −)							
Government services and transfers (net)	−54	−224	−332	−432	−466	−486	−521
Shipping ..	+134	+43	−34	−37	+23	−95	−69
Civil aviation, financial and other services	+114	+195	+277	+294	+503	+692	+738
Travel, tourism, etc.	−3	−17	−24	−71	+11	+48	+26
Private transfers (migrants' funds, etc.) ..	−2	+2	+17	−4	−60	−45	−40
Interest, profits and dividends	+254	+294	+254	+393	+341	+490	+521
Invisible Balance	+443	+293	+158	+143	+352	+604	+655
Current Balance ..	+164	+328	+6	−376	−291	+611	+952

Table 5.6 *Continued*   (£ million)

	1952	1958	1961	1964	1968	1970	1971
Investment and Other Capital Flows*							
Official long-term capital			−45	−116	+17	−204	−274
Overseas investment in U.K. public sector			+51	+15	+16	−10	+187
Overseas investment in U.K. private sector			+369	+143	+567	+749	+974
U.K. private investment overseas ..			−313	−399	−727	−761	−762
Foreign currency borrowing (net) by U.K. branches to finance U.K. investment overseas ..	−134	−186		+15	+155	+189	+240
Other foreign currency borrowing or lending (net) by U.K. banks ..				+138	−124	+290	+255
Exchange reserves in sterling: ..		−378					
British Government stocks				+52	−22	+63	+47
Banking and money market liabilities ..				−73	−158	+126	+639
Other external liabilities in sterling ..				+38	−128	+242	+735
Import credit ..				+3	+83	+25	+85
Export credit ..				−48	−331	−237	−360
Other short-term flows ..				−67	−102	+90	+81
Total Investment and Other Capital Flows	−134	−186	−316	−299	−754	+562	+1,847
Balancing Item ..	+65	+60	−29	−20	−114	+114	+429
EEA loss on forwards	—	—	—	—	−251	—	—
TOTAL CURRENCY FLOW†	+95	+202	−339	−695	−1,410	+1,287	+3,228
Allocation of S.D.R.'s ..	—	—	—	—	—	+171	+125
Gold subscription to I.M.F... ..	—	—	—	—	—	−38	—
ADJUSTED CURRENCY FLOW†	+95	+202	−339	−695	−1,410	+1,420	+3,353

Table 5.6 *Continued*   (£ million)

	1952	1958	1961	1964	1968	1970	1971
(B) OFFICIAL FINANCING							
Drawings on I.M.F. —		—	+370	+357	+506	−134	−554
Drawings on other —		—					
monetary authorities —		—	—	+216	+790	−1,161	−1,263
Transfer from —		—					
dollar portfolio to —	−95	−202					
reserves .. .. —			—	—	—	—	—
Drawings on (+) —		—					
or additions to (−) —		—					
official reserves .. —		—	−31	+122	+114	−125	−1,536
TOTAL OFFICIAL FINANCING ..	−95	−202	+339	+695	1,410	−1,420	−3,353

* − = Decrease in Liabilities or Increase in Assets;
  + = Increase in Liabilities or Decrease in Assets;
† − = Outwards;   + = Inwards.

(Based on material in *Ann. Abs. Stat.* and *Economic Trends*, March 1965 and March 1972)

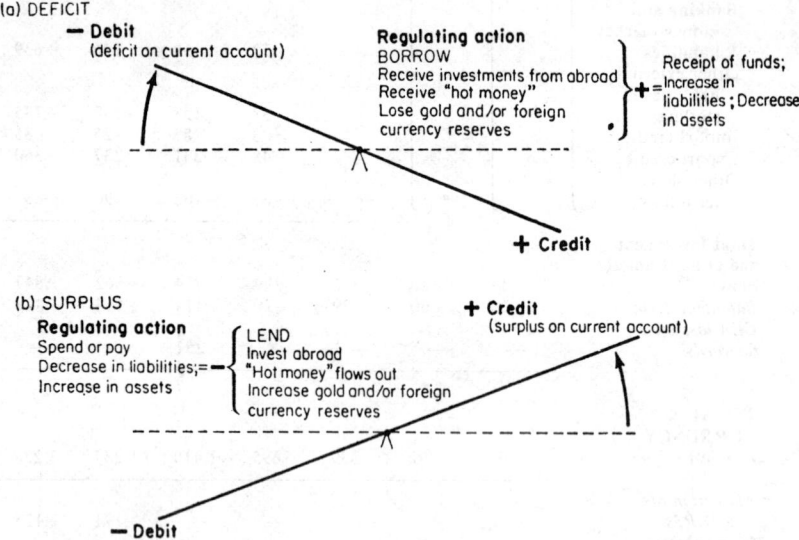

Fig. 5.11. *The balance of payments: financing of a deficit and investing of a surplus on current account*

14. International Trade, Aid and Monetary Cooperation

(a) Sterling area

The members of the sterling area, apart from the United Kingdom, are all the Commonwealth countries (except Canada and Rhodesia), plus Eire, British Trust Territories, Protectorates and Protected States, Iceland, Jordan, Kuwait, South Africa, South West Africa, Samoa and the Yemen P.D.R. In 1972 they constituted sixty countries, with about one-quarter of the world's population.

These are the present members of the group of countries which 'pegged' their currencies to sterling after the abandonment of the gold standard in 1931. They are in voluntary association with Britain with regard to their currency arrangements and rules of conduct.[1] Policies for Commonwealth members are worked out at periodic conferences. They participate in the exchange control policy for sterling. There is freedom of trade amongst members, whilst they finance most of their trade in sterling. This is done by their exchanging foreign currency earnings for sterling, in London. They may also purchase foreign currency as required, in return for sterling. Their reserves are therefore held mainly in sterling, to which their own currencies bear a fixed parity. It follows that when a sterling area member earns (and sells in London) gold or foreign currency, the sterling area 'pool' in London rises by the same amount as do the sterling balances held by overseas (in this case, member) countries. Furthermore, the 'pool' may be tapped at any time by members wishing to convert sterling into gold or foreign currencies, since sterling became freely convertible in 1958. 'External' sterling balances, held by non-sterling area countries were fully convertible, but 'resident', sterling balances, held by sterling area members, were subject to exchange control permission in respect of transfers to 'external' accounts and in respect of capital investment in both the overseas sterling area and in any non-member country. When sterling was allowed to float in June 1972 the restrictions on capital investment in and outside the overseas sterling area member countries were reinforced. To some observers these reductions in preferential monetary arrangements represented the virtual death-knell of the sterling area.[2]

During the 1950s and 1960s sterling lost much of its status as a 'master' or imperial currency – *viz.*, that of a currency buttressed by political factors and a common monetary and currency philosophy. From 1948 to 1971 sterling declined, as a percentage of total world reserves of gold and convertible currencies from 23·6% to 7·4%, whilst the U.S. dollar rose from 6·0% to 37·3%. Even within the overseas sterling area, sterling fell as a proportion of member countries' reserves. This was largely due to the reduction in trade between sterling area countries, from about 50% in 1950 to about 30% in 1970 [3] (see Fig. 5.12). Another factor was the declining importance of Commonwealth preference arrangements. The diversification of world reserves was accentuated during the 1960s by lack of confidence in the correct valuation of sterling at the 1949 parity (and again, during 1972, with regard to the 1967 parity).[4]

[1] 'Sterling as a "key" currency', *M.B.R.*, Aug. 1963, pp. 3–12; for a fairly comprehensive exposition see 'The Evolution of the sterling area – What it signifies today', *M.B.R.*, Feb. 1972.
[2] 'The week the sun set on sterling', *S.T.*, 2 July 1972; 'Floating the Humpty-Dumpty Commonwealth', *Econ.*, 1 July 1972, p. 91.   [3] *M.B.R.*, Feb. 1972, *op. cit.*, p. 13.
[4] *Ibid.*, p. 13; Sir Roy Harrod, 'The Role of Sterling', *D.B.R.*, Dec. 1966; 'The Role of Sterling', *D.E.A. Pr. Rep. Econ.*, 27, April 1967; 'Reinforcing Sterling', *D.E.A. Pr. Rep. Econ.*, 45, Oct. 1968.

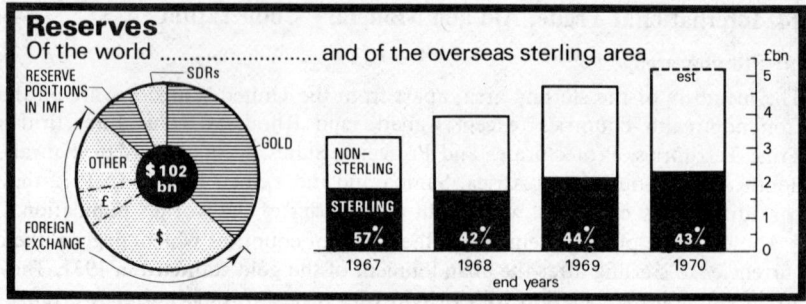

Fig. 5.12 *Sterling and world reserves, 1970*
(Source: *Econ.*, 8 May 1971, p. 49)

The future of sterling as a reserve currency is likely to be greatly influenced by E.E.C. membership.[1] Increasingly, it is expected that trade preferences and capital movement preferences in favour of overseas sterling area countries will decline. The E.E.C. objectives of monetary union would gradually eliminate margins of fluctuation between member countries' exchange rates, and thus sterling would be linked much more closely to European currencies. The major residual problem is the acceptance of responsibility for the debts to other countries, represented by the sterling balances which they hold in their reserves. The Governor of the Bank of England has hinted strongly that the conclusion has been reached that sterling need not be perpetuated as a reserve currency. As for the other major 'external characteristic' of sterling, that of a trading and investment currency, it is expected to converge with that of other European currencies. The role of the City of London as a financial centre of the Euro-currency market is, however, likely to continue.

(b) Bretton Woods Agreement and international liquidity

Towards the end of World War II, in 1944, a United Nations Monetary and Financial Conference was held in Bretton Woods, U.S.A., to discuss ways and means to promote an expansion of world trade with foreign exchange stability and to promote the economic reconstruction of war-shattered economies and the economic development of the underdeveloped nations. The Bretton Woods Agreement, which resulted from this conference of fifty-six member countries, established two specialised agencies – the International Monetary Fund and the World Bank (International Bank for Reconstruction and Development: I.B.R.D.).

INTERNATIONAL MONETARY FUND

The I.M.F., which came into operation in 1946, represented a hybrid, containing elements of exchange control with a sort of international exchange equalisation account, elements of freely fluctuating exchange rates, and elements of a gold standard. It rested on the international cooperation of member countries.

The main aim was to promote multilateral trade, by increasing 'international liquidity' or the availability of foreign currency reserves, which could be tapped

[1] *M.B.R.*, Feb. 1972, *op. cit.*, pp. 17–18; 'The issue of sterling: a political cracker', *Econ.*, 8 May 1971, pp. 48–9.

by deficit countries.[1] This would help to reduce the need either to allow exchange rates to fluctuate wildly or to adopt stringent internal deflationary (if in deficit) or inflationary (if in surplus) economic policies.

The system, basically, functioned as follows: all member currencies were valued in terms of gold and U.S.A. dollars; each member was allotted a quota of drawing rights ($2,800 million in 1971 for the United Kingdom); each member paid into the Fund up to the value of its drawing quota – one-quarter in gold and dollars, the remainder in its own currency; members in chronic payments disequilibrium had to seek the Fund's permission to devalue or revalue, beyond a permissible limit of 10%; a member in need of another member's currency could purchase that currency (with its own) from the Fund, up to a limit of 25% of its quota in any one year, for up to five consecutive years, repaying (in gold, dollars or other convertible currencies) within three to five years; if a member was in chronic surplus (because of an undervalued currency exchange rate) and the Fund runs short of its currency (due to other members' drawings), the Fund could declare it a 'scarce currency' and members could take strict exchange control measures against exports from that country; members were to aim at free convertibility of their currencies (after a transition period) for current transactions, but were to be permitted exchange control on the movement of capital funds.

Members of the I.M.F., who increased from 39 at the outset to 110 by 1970, were committed to maintain their currency exchange rate with 1% either side of the 'par' rate notified to the Fund, except when in 'fundamental disequilibrium', as mentioned above. This rate was to be expressed in terms of gold or of the U.S. dollar (as at 1 July 1944): gold, therefore, remained linked with all the participating currencies, occupying a central position as the common standard of value and ultimate means of debt settlement. The U.S. dollar has been the key 'anchor' or 'intervention' currency, which has been linked with gold at a fixed parity of $35 per fine ounce since 1934.

Particularly since the adoption of free currency convertibility by most major European countries by the end of 1958, the flow of short-term capital between European financial centres, in response to variations in the interest rates which could be earned, tended to speed up. This posed additional burdens on the I.M.F., which could be called upon when a country experienced a large outflow of such 'hot money'. Consequently, the quotas have from time to time been increased. Another factor behind the increase in quotas has been the growth in world trade, which has outstripped the increase in international liquidity or world reserves. It has often been argued that the amount of international liquidity should be related to the volume of world trade. The ratio of total liquidity to world imports has fallen from 68% in 1954 to 33% in 1970: within this falling proportion, the amount of I.M.F. reserves represented by the members' 25% 'gold tranche' deposits rose from $3,570 million in 1960 to $6,488 million in 1968 (see Fig. 5.13), whilst total international reserves rose from $60¼ billion in 1960 to more than $100 billion in 1971.[2]

The general consensus appears to be that from 1959 the 'gold-exchange standard' operated by I.M.F. members resulted in world economic relations

[1] 'The Ghosts of Bretton Woods', *Stat.*, 5 March 1965, pp. 657–8.
[2] 'Progress in International monetary co-operation', *M.B.R.*, Nov. 1969, pp. 14, 16; 'International Liquidity', *B.B.R.*, Feb. 1972, p. 6.

being operated at less than optimum levels: manifestations of this were the growth of national restrictions on trade and the frequent use – especially by some major industrial nations – of domestic price and income adjustment policies. Reasons suggested for this have hinged mainly on the shortage of international liquidity, but also include suggestions that some countries are unwilling to cooperate internationally or to make exchange rate adjustments.

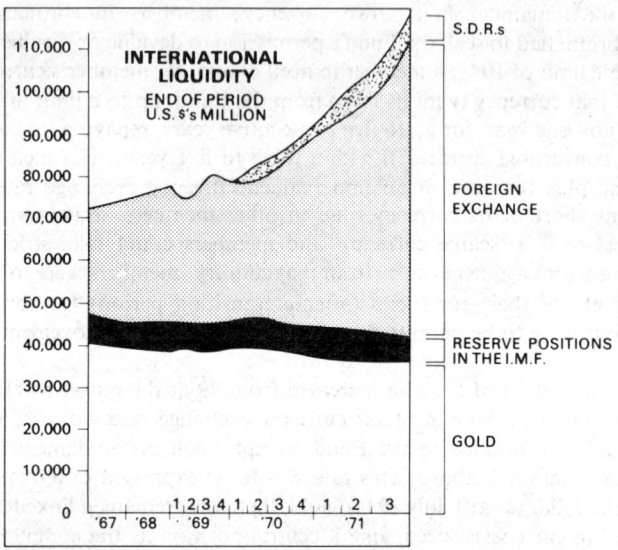

Fig. 5.13 *I.M.F. reserves and international liquidity, 1967–71*
(Source: *B.B.R.*, Feb. 1972, p. 6)

Some of the main developments in the quest for adequate international liquidity, flexibility and exchange rate stability, in order to promote the growth of trade, have been as follows:

(*a*) In 1961 the E.E.C. and the U.K. accepted the status of *Article VIII* of the I.M.F., to the effect that they undertook not to impose restrictions on current transfers and payments without Fund permission. The U.S. and Canada had already done this and others have, since.

(*b*) In 1961 agreement was reached (and first implemented in 1963) on the '*General Arrangements to Borrow*' (*G.A.B.*). This was a device to provide supplementary resources for the Fund, when required, and was an agreement by the '*Group of Ten*' (or 'Paris Club') central banks[1] to lend specified amounts of their currencies to the Fund, for drawings by members of the Group. The original total was equivalent to $6 billion and the arrangements have been used to support sterling and the French franc.

(*c*) In 1961 were inaugurated the *Basle Agreements* or facilities, following a run on sterling, due to speculation on a revaluation (i.e. upward) of the Deutsch-

[1] Belgium, Canada, France, West Germany, Italy, Japan, Holland, Sweden, the U.K. and the U.S., constituting the major financial nations, apart from Switzerland, which is not an I.M.F. member.

mark. Some members of the Bank for International Settlements (B.I.S. or 'Basle club')[1] agreed that each could call upon the others for short-term credits: there would also be close cooperation in the foreign exchange markets, to assist currencies in difficulties because of speculation. The main beneficiary has been sterling, and by this rapid and flexible method the more formal I.M.F. and G.A.B. machinery may be avoided.

(d) In 1962 further measures against speculative runs were taken in the form of 'swap' facilities or 'standby arrangements', made between the U.S. and the central banks of the Group of Ten, plus Austria and Switzerland. These provided for an exchange between dollars and the currency of any participant, up to specified amounts, when called upon by either party. In late 1969 the U.S. Federal Reserve Bank swap network totalled $10⅜ billion and involved fourteen other central banks and the B.I.S. The largest individual facility was for $2 billion with the Bank of England.

(e) In February 1969 the Group of Ten, plus Switzerland and the B.I.S., went farther along the path of alleviating the impact of speculative movements of funds on official reserves. They agreed in principle upon a scheme to 're-cycle' speculative capital movements. The procedures, first used in May 1969 to offset speculative flows into West Germany, in anticipation of a Deutschmark revaluation, involve a 'swap' network between the central banks, with the B.I.S. acting in support. The country losing funds may borrow from the country gaining them, repaying when the speculative flows are reversed. A major problem in differentiating between speculative and normal flows is that the Eurodollar market is used as a main vehicle for the transfer of funds (e.g. by multinational companies) and this makes for difficulties in identifying the original sources of the speculative funds.

(f) With regard to reducing the vulnerability of sterling, due to its role of a reserve currency, as opposed to balance of payments pressures, in 1966 at Basle a number of central banks and the B.I.S. agreed that the U.K. could draw on 'swap facilities' to offset fluctuations in overseas countries' sterling balances. In 1968 this was extended to counteract the diversification of sterling area countries' reserves, involving a movement out of sterling, which was accentuated by the 1967 sterling devaluation. A facility of $2 billion was provided for the U.K.

(g) In 1967 the I.M.F. and the Group of Ten concluded an agreement, which represented the first attempt at the centrally controlled creation of international liquidity reserves. As a means of overcoming the scarcity problem involved in reliance upon gold and the reserve currencies, it was agreed to create 'Special Drawing Rights' (S.D.R.s), which were first allocated in 1970. S.D.R.s were to be allocated to participating countries in proportion to their quotas. A unit of S.D.R. had the same value as the U.S. dollar and had a gold value guarantee. The rights would be exercised when a country loses reserves because of balance of payments difficulties, as opposed to losses due to a change in the composition of its reserves. A country in need informs the Fund that it wishes to exchange some of its S.D.R. units for usable foreign currency, and the Fund specifies

[1] The B.I.S. was originally established after the 1930 Young plan by the central banks of Belgium, Germany, France, Italy, Japan and the U.K. and by a group of U.S. banks. Those members participating in the Basle Agreements were Belgium, West Germany, France, Italy, Holland, Sweden, Switzerland and the U.K.

which countries are to exchange their currency against those S.D.R.s (up to agreed limits). The limit on the country called upon is an S.D.R. total reaching three times its initial allocation: the limit on the deficit country is that it must restore at least 30% of its S.D.R. allocation within a specified period. The initial (1970) issue of S.D.R.s was to be $9½ billion in stages over three years (12·2% of international official reserves). For the U.K. this was $402 million in 1970, $345 million in 1971 and again in 1972.[1]

As may be deduced from the developments noted above, the I.M.F., during the 1960s, was being overshadowed by the parallel growth in influence and activity of the 'Paris Club' (Group of Ten) and the 'Basle Club' (B.I.S.). The Group of Ten was created when the G.A.B. was agreed upon in 1961: the G.A.B. set limits on the power of the I.M.F. to borrow, existing under article VII of the I.M.F., and was a device for avoiding the use of the 'scarce currency' clause. The Basle Club introduced *ad hoc* arrangements among the major European central bankers for the provision of short-term loans for any group member facing speculative currency pressure: this avoided the use of exchange controls on capital account transactions and some potential parity changes.

Thus these parallel bodies were, in effect, propping up the I.M.F. apparatus, avoiding the rigid application of its rules and bringing 'fine tuning' flexibility into the liquidity system. The gold-exchange system, based on key currencies, was enabled to stagger from crisis to crisis without the Fund's devaluation rules being applied, except as a last resort (by the U.K. in 1967 and the U.S. in 1971). The frequent unwillingness of some major trading nations to curb abnormal capital movements led to numerous foreign exchange market crises, which were dealt with not by the use of devaluations and exchange controls, but by the *ad hoc* loans of the Basle Arrangements. In other words, the rules of the Fund were departed from, in order to keep the system in flexible operation. One major result of these departures from Fund rules was the fast growth of the Euro-currency market, especially during the late 1960s: its expansion, although promoting economic expansion in the borrowing countries, exerted speculative pressure on reserve holdings of dollars, especially after 1959, when foreign dollar holdings first exceeded U.S. gold reserves (see Fig. 5.14 and Fig. 5.15).

It may be said that the gold-exchange system lasted for so long, during the 1960s, largely due to the size of U.S. gold stocks at the commencement and to the willingness of other countries to hold dollars. During the early 1970s the international monetary problems have intensified: this has been reflected in the 1971 U.S. decision to suspend dollar convertibility 'temporarily', the use of 'managed' fluctuating exchange rates by Japan and Western Europe, and the political bargaining over realignment of par values for currencies. These developments highlight the extent to which I.M.F. rules have been ignored and also the transitory, makeshift nature of the arrangements of the early 1970s, pending more fundamental reform of the world monetary system. It would seem that the root of the problem is not the Bretton Woods system, but rather the

---

[1] For extensive further data on developments (a to g), see 'Progress in international monetary co-operation', *loc. cit.*, pp. 15–18; 'International liquidity', *loc. cit.*, pp. 5–8; 'International money', *B.B.R.*, May 1969, pp. 30–1; J. H. Richards, *International Economic Institutions*, 1970, pp. 68, 71, 73, 80, 81; M. A. G. van Meerhaeghe, *International Economic Institutions*, 1966, pp. 111–12; 'Special drawing rights', *E.P.R.*, 2, Feb. 1970; 'Special drawing rights', *B.B.R.*, Nov. 1971; 'The A.B.C. of S.D.R.s', *F.T.*, 7 Aug. 1969.

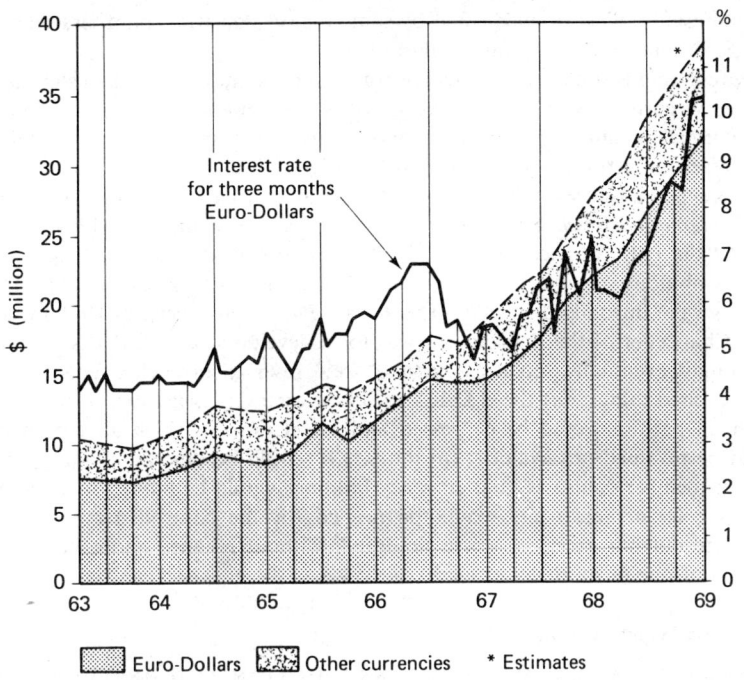

Fig. 5.14 *Euro-currency deposits*
(Source: *Conjoncture*, 118, Aug. 1969)

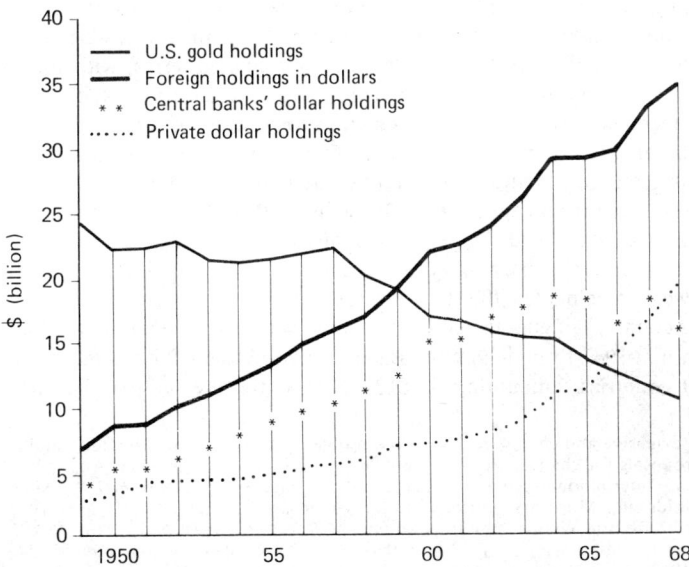

Fig. 5.15 *Growth of the U.S.A.'s gold stocks and foreign engagements* (*liquid*)
(Source: *Conjoncture*, 118, Aug. 1969, p. 6)

423

self-interested policies implemented by some major industrial countries, leading to U.S. deficits and European surpluses.[1]

Because gold is subject to physical restraints and because dollars and sterling – the reserve currencies – are not necessarily managed in a way appropriate to the international community, various proposals for the controlled issue of man-made reserve assets have been made. At the original Bretton Woods negotiations Lord Keynes unsuccessfully proposed a radical scheme for the establishment of an *international clearing union* with a new unit of account, called a bancor. In 1962 the U.K. Chancellor of the Exchequer, Reginald Maudling, suggested a less ambitious scheme, the establishment of a *mutual currency account*. The S.D.R.s were introduced in 1970. The *Barber Plan* – introduced in 1971 by the U.K. Chancellor of the Exchequer – was for a development of S.D.R.s, so that they might eventually replace gold and 'key' reserve currencies. This would involve three things: (*a*) the S.D.R.s could become the *numeraire*, in terms of which all parities would be expressed and in relation to which all currencies would be revalued or devalued; (*b*) the S.D.R. could become the main reserve asset of member countries, and currency holdings would be limited to working balances; (*c*) arrangements would be needed for the controlled creation of 'adequate but not excessive world liquidity', without reliance upon the deficit position of one or more countries.[2]

(*c*) Bretton Woods and international development

INTERNATIONAL BANK FOR RECONSTRUCTION AND DEVELOPMENT (I.B.R.D. – OR WORLD BANK)

The World Bank was established at the same time as the I.M.F., in 1946. Its main aims were to provide longer-term facilities to war-shattered economies; to facilitate capital investment projects between member countries; to channel investment resources into underdeveloped countries. These functions were to operate where private capital was not available on reasonable terms, with the overall intention of promoting the long-range growth of international trade.

Each member of the Bank was made liable for a quota of capital, part of which had to be subscribed and the remainder of which was to be made available when the Bank required it. Out of these quotas the Bank was to make loans. It could also make loans from capital raised by selling I.B.R.D. bonds. The Bank could also guarantee loans made by private persons and bodies. Applications for loans, which carry interest charges, were to be made on a sound commercial basis. Loans were to be made either to a member country or to private enterprise in a member country – if guaranteed by that country's government or central bank.

From mid-1947 to mid-1969 the Bank made 636 loans for specific projects in over 80 countries, amounting to $12⅔ billion: the greater part has been for

---

[1] For an extensive and concise review of the problems of international liquidity and of some major proposals for change, see 'The major currencies', *Conjoncture*, 118, Aug. 1969; A. L. Lougheed, 'International economic relations – past and future', *N.W.B.Q.R.*, May 1972; H. N. Goldstein, 'Monetary reform – the Barber proposals', *N.W.B.Q.R.*, May 1972; 'The retreat from Bretton Woods – the story so far', *M.B.R.*, Nov. 1971; S. Brittan, 'Next steps in world monetary diplomacy', *F.T.*, 20 April 1972; H. G. Grubel, *The International Monetary System*, 1969, ch. 4; 'What to want at the I.M.F.', *Econ.*, 25 Sept., 1971, pp. 12–13; G. Haberler, *Money in the International Economy*, 1965, ch. 5; A. Day, *ABC of International Finance*, 1968, pp. 37–46; G. Haberler, 'Prospects for the dollar standard', *L.B.R.*, July 1972.
[2] 'The retreat from Bretton Woods – the story so far', *loc. cit.*, pp. 18–19.

'infrastructure' projects, which support the various national economies of the borrowing countries. By that time subscriptions totalled $23 billion, as compared with the authorised capital of $24 billion. The major source of lending funds has been the amounts borrowed by the Bank in world capital markets. By mid-1969 it had sold more than 100 issues of securities, valued at more than $7 billion.[1] The president of the Bank, McNamara, announced in 1969 that he would like to see the 1969–73 level of lending double, as compared with the previous 5 years: for the year ending June 1969 the net borrowing of the Bank was estimated to have risen from $215 million to $660 million, whilst loans amounted to about $780 million.[2] A major problem, however, has been the Bank's insistence on making loans only technically and economically sound, well managed projects, valuable to the borrower's economy, and at fairly high rates of interest, repayable over fifteen to twenty-five years.[3]

In 1956 the International Finance Corporation, a subsidiary of the Bank, was established. Its purpose was to make loans to private firms. By mid-1970 the I.F.C. had channelled $476·5 million to 153 firms in forty-three countries: it had outstanding loans of $180·7 million, plus investments in private firms of $98·4 million. In 1966 it had been allowed to borrow $400 million from the Bank for lending. The I.F.C. is a development institution and therefore does much more than just lend out or invest its funds: it helps to reshape investment proposals, helps to recruit private capital and assists in the promotion and development of new enterprises. Its emphasis has gradually shifted to production projects.[4] Its paid-up capital by mid-1969 was a modest $106·5 million.[5] In 1960 the International Development Association was set up as another affiliate of the Bank, with the purpose of providing development finance to the underdeveloped countries on easier and more flexible terms than the Bank loans, repayable over longer periods. This source of untied aid has led to the I.D.A.s being termed the soft-loan agency of the World Bank. The I.D.A. had initial subscriptions of $1 billion, replenished in 1964 and 1967 up to a total of $1·5 billion. Thereafter, it was faced with continual problems of shortages and uncertainty as to sources of finance. By 1968 uncommitted funds had dwindled to $50 million. During 1969 there was great difficulty in securing stage payments of the $1,170 million replenishments, pledged to 1972. The president of the World Bank, in late 1971, called for a more stable basis for stocking-up operations, so that developing countries could plan ahead more effectively. Two basic requirements were: (a) a machinery for equitably sharing out the burden of finance between the developed countries; (b) the principle that aid commitments of this type were a priority charge on the donor countries' foreign exchange resources.[6]

Despite the achievements of the World Bank and its affiliates, the earlier hopes, expressed at Bretton Woods, that it might one day develop into an international control bank, capable of eliminating worldwide financial crises, has not materialised. Even in the context of long-term capital loans, the Bank and its affiliates have faced a continual shortage of funds. Another perennial and growing problem

---

[1] Richards, *op. cit.*, pp. 92, 96–7.
[2] *Econ.*, 14 June 1969, p. 76 and 12 Sept. 1969, p. 75.
[3] *The Guardian*, 2 Apr. 1963; also see 'World Bank "New Style" Loan', *Stat.*, 14 Feb. 1964.
[4] A. E. Davidson, 'International Finance Corporation', *N.W.B.Q.R.*, Nov. 1970.
[5] Richards, *op. cit.*, p. 120.
[6] *Ibid.*, pp. 117–20; 'Halfway house for IDA', *Econ.*, 4 Jan. 1969, p. 50; 'New base for aid is also needed', *F.T.*, 27 Oct. 1971.

has been the escalating indebtedness of some of the developing countries and their repayment difficulties.[1]

(d) International Trade Organisation (I.T.O.) and the General Agreement on Tariffs and Trade (G.A.T.T.)

In 1948 over fifty countries were signatories to the Havana Charter which proposed the establishment of an International Trade Organisation. By that time twenty-three countries had already concluded negotiations for the reduction of tariffs and preferences, and had entered, as a temporary measure, into a General Agreement on Tariffs and Trade. The I.T.O. was not, as had been hoped, ratified by 1951, and thus G.A.T.T. became its 'residuary legatee', or successor.

I.T.O. had aimed at abolishing or reducing tariffs and preferential treatment, at the general banning of quantitative restrictions and at the prohibition of subsidies to domestic producers.[2] Competition was to be free and unfettered by monopolies and restrictive practices. Intergovernmental commodity agreements were to be concluded for primary products, to stabilise their prices and to ensure a rising income for the primary producers. Economic development was to be fostered by the free flow of capital and material resources, and a high level of employment was to be aimed at by the maximisation of international trade. Underdeveloped countries were to be allowed temporary tariff protection, with the permission of the I.T.O.

G.A.T.T. aimed at similar objectives, through reciprocal arrangements between participating countries. The twenty-three participants to the Agreement in 1948 had increased to thirty-eight in 1961, with nine other associates and/or would-be members. They accounted for about 80% of international trade.

During its first three years, G.A.T.T. tended to concentrate on the reduction and stabilisation of tariffs. After 1951 emphasis changed from tariff negotiations to the prevention of direct controls over imports – trade quotas and licences. In 1958 attention shifted to the basic difficulties besetting the primary producers. The Haberler Report of a panel of experts drew attention in 1958 to the unfavourable fact that previous emphasis on the general removal of protective action had affected the primary producers, whose bargaining power was weaker than that of industrialised countries, relatively adversely.[3]

With regard to the development of regional trade groupings (E.E.C., E.F.T.A., etc.), G.A.T.T. has tried to encourage them to develop 'outward-looking' policies, aimed at increasing multilateral trade, and has paid attention to the problems such groupings might raise for the non-industrialised primary producing countries.[4]

As a result of the successful conclusion of the minor 'Dillon Round' (1961) and 'Kennedy Round' (1968) negotiations on tariff reductions, under G.A.T.T. auspices,[5] trade between industrialised nations grew by 55% between 1968 and

---

[1] G. C. Abbott, 'Aid and indebtedness – a proposal', *N.W.B.Q.R.*, May 1972.
[2] For reaction to Britain's decision in Nov. 1964 to give tax rebate to exporters, see 'Volvo hits back at 15 p.c. surcharge: 2 p.c. off British bills', *D.T.*, 11 Nov. 1964.
[3] 'G.A.T.T. offers "new deal" to poorer lands', *ibid.*, 2 Dec. 1964.
[4] 'G.A.T.T. in the world today', *M.B.R.*, Feb. 1961, pp. 10–17; J. Royer, 'World trade: the dangers of regionalism', *L.B.R.*, Oct. 1962, pp. 1–22.
[5] 'The Kennedy Round', *Conjoncture*, 94, Aug. 1967; *Econ.*, 20 May 1967, pp. 813–14; *Econ.*, 6 July 1968, p. 61; 'Tariffs and trade patterns – a resumé of recent developments and trends', *M.B.R.*, May 1968.

1972.[1] Nevertheless, the director-general of G.A.T.T. referred, in late 1970, to 'a resurgence of protectionist measures in a number of countries, which is proving difficult to contain.'[2] Two of the major threats to continuing and expanding liberalism in world trade in recent years have been the growth of protectionism – as reflected in the development of regional trade groupings of industrialised countries and the 1971 import surcharge and quest for voluntary restrictions by the U.S. – and the increase in agricultural protectionism in industrial countries – as in the E.E.C. Common Agricultural Policy (C.A.P.).[3]

In January 1972 it was suggested that Article XII of the G.A.T.T., permitting countries with balance of payments problems to impose import quotas, be abolished or drastically amended.[4] The G.A.T.T. council, in March 1972, endorsed the February joint statements by the U.S. and E.E.C. and by the U.S. and Japan, regarding the initiation of moves towards a new round of multilateral trade negotiations in 1973. Countries dependent upon agriculture were expressing concern at what form the negotiations might take.[5]

(e) United Nations Conference on Trade and Development (U.N.C.T.A.D.)

Growing dissatisfaction with G.A.T.T. and distrust of the developed and industrialised countries' trade and aid policies by the developing countries led, during the early 1960s, to the formation of the 'poor nations club' or the 'group of 77'. This took the form of the United Nations Conference on Trade and Development, first convened in 1964 by the 77 nations who considered themselves underdeveloped and having common interests in their dealings with the developed world.

The emphasis of the 1964 U.N.C.T.A.D. I was on extracting a commitment from the developed nations to devote 1% of their G.N.P. to aid; on commodity agreements to raise and stabilise prices; on easier access to the markets of the developed countries, some of which imposed heavy restrictions, quotas and tariffs on agricultural imports; and on preferential treatment for their manufactured exports.[6] A permanent U.N. secretariat was set up and it was agreed to hold periodic conferences.

U.N.C.T.A.D. II, held in 1968, pursued a similar theme, and helped to encourage a unity of action on the part of the developing nations and a realisation of their needs by the developed ones.

U.N.C.T.A.D. III, held in 1972, was attended by 146 countries. It had less ambitious objectives than the Generalised System of Preferences agreement, adopted by U.N.C.T.A.D. II, but whittled down in practice. The Group A countries (the 77 less developed) and the Group B countries (the developed), represented at the conference, tended to reach compromise agreements on aid and international monetary reform – including the linking of S.D.R.s and develop-

---

[1] 'Tariffs: rounding off', *Econ.*, 8 Jan. 1972, pp. 62–4 and chart on postwar trade in *Econ.*, 28 Feb. 1970, p. 65.
[2] *F.T.*, 13 Nov. 1970.
[3] Lougheed, 'International economic relations – past and future', *loc. cit.*, pp. 37–42; 'U.S. protectionism', *B.B.R.*, May 1972.
[4] *F.T.*, 17 Jan. 1972.
[5] *F.T.*, 8 March 1972 and 'Searching for a formula for freer world trade', *F.T.*, 19 June 1972.
[6] 'UNCTAD and the less developed', *Econ.*, 3 June 1967, pp. 1028–9 and Richards, *op. cit.*, pp. 179–97.

ment finance – and on technological cooperation, tourism and the reduction of restrictive practices by multinational corporations.[1]

(f) Food and Agriculture Organisation (F.A.O.)

As a result of the United Nations Conference on Food and Agriculture at Hot Springs, U.S.A., in 1943, the F.A.O. was established in 1945 as a specialised agency of the United Nations.

The F.A.O. supplies member governments with information relating to world food production forecasts, trends in demand, nutritional standards, etc. It promotes and recommends international action to eliminate fluctuations in agricultural prices. This function is performed by means of advice on commodity agreements and buffer stock schemes, suggestions for improved marketing and distribution facilities, the provision of agricultural credit for improved production methods, and advice on the conservation of agricultural resources. The F.A.O. also gives technical assistance to its members to improve yields, reduce costs, improve rural living conditions and improve nutritional standards by raising levels of consumption.[2]

(g) O.E.E.C. and O.E.C.D.

In 1947 the Organisation for European Economic Cooperation was established to coordinate the economic reconstruction of countries receiving aid from the U.S.A.'s European Recovery Programme – the Marshall Plan.[3] This programme was for financial aid to Western European nations, to help them to restore their economies. The original sixteen members were: the United Kingdom, Norway, Sweden, Denmark, Austria, Switzerland, Portugal, Iceland, Ireland, Turkey, Greece, France, Italy, Holland, Belgium and Luxembourg.

A permanent international secretariat was set up, and so were expert technical committees for such matters as manpower, coal, chemicals, currency and trade liberalisation. In 1955 West Germany became a full member, followed by Spain in 1959. Canada and the U.S.A. were associate members.

In 1960 the eighteen members and two associate members decided to devote more emphasis on aid to the less developed countries of the world, as the original objects of O.E.E.C. had been largely achieved. Consequently, these twenty countries in 1961 formed the Organisation for Economic Cooperation and Development (O.E.C.D.), which replaced O.E.E.C. Its main tasks were to encourage the continued coordination of members' economic policies, to facilitate the expansion of world trade, and to coordinate financial assistance to underdeveloped countries.[4]

In 1950 O.E.E.C. set up the European Payments Union, the main objective of which was to achieve free convertibility between member currencies, so as to

---

[1] 'The undoing of Unctad', *Econ.*, 27 May 1972, pp. 18–23; *Econ.*, 17 June 1972, pp. 4–6; 'Unctad's low profile', *F.T.*, 13 April 1972; 'UNCTAD 3', *F.T.*, 7 April 1972; also see S. Golt, 'UNCTAD: a new approach for developing nations', *M. and W.S.R.*, Spring 1972.
[2] See 'Five-point plan to beat world hunger', *F.T.*, 21 Oct. 1969.
[3] The Marshall Plan was instituted in 1948 in the form of long-term loans and grants. Repayments were made mostly after 1958. Net repayments ceased after 1965 (see A. J. Youngson, *The British Economy, 1920–1957*, 1960, pp. 164–6, 169; A. Maddison, *Economic Growth in the West*, 1964, p. 162; Caves, ed., *op. cit.*, p. 173; 'Outstanding loans to the British Government', *E.P.R.*, 25, March 1972.
[4] See 'Some European organisations', *D.E.A. Pr. Rep. Econ.*, 25, Feb. 1967.

remove impediments to inter-European trade. In 1955 O.E.E.C. concluded the European Monetary Agreement, to provide for a return to full external convertibility of member currencies. The machinery envisaged was to include the Bank for International Settlements (B.I.S.), to operate banking activities in the foreign exchange and gold markets and to provide a forum for European central bankers to discuss matters of common interest. The Agreement also envisaged the setting up of a European Monetary Fund, with reserves of $600 million, to provide short-term dollar credit to members and to facilitate dollar settlements between member central banks. Meanwhile member countries were moving towards free convertibility, and O.E.E.C. set up the European Monetary Fund, envisaged by the European Monetary Agreement, and included with it a Multilateral Clearing System to provide short-term credit in member currencies. When all the main European currencies became freely convertible in 1958, O.E.E.C. decided to terminate the E.P.U. and to bring into force the machinery of the European Monetary Agreement (including the Bank for International Settlements). The cooperation begun between E.P.U. and the I.M.F. was continued with the E.M.A., which operated on a year-to-year renewal basis, within the context, after 1961, of O.E.C.D.[1]

(h) Common Market (E.E.C.)

In 1952 the European Coal and Steel Community was established by France, Italy, Holland, Belgium and Luxembourg (five of the original sixteen O.E.E.C. members) and West Germany (which joined O.E.E.C. in 1955). The object was to abolish trade restrictions on coal and steel between these countries and to coordinate production and price policies. Due to the success of E.C.S.C. the six members set up a committee in 1955 to consider its expansion into a full customs union, with a common external tariff system. Following its optimistic report in 1956, the six members decided to form the European Economic Community, embracing a market of about 170 million people. In 1957 they signed the Treaty of Rome – the constitution of E.E.C. and on 1 January 1958 the Common Market came into being, as did the European Atomic Community (Euratom), the third sister organisation.

The Treaty of Rome provides for the gradual reduction of tariffs between member countries, and the gradual establishment of a common external tariff wall against the rest of the world. By July 1968 the customs union, with internal free trade and a uniform external tariff, had been achieved.[2] Other objectives aimed at include a common policy for agriculture; freedom of labour mobility; common policies for taxation, state subsidies, anti-cartel legislation, anti-dumping legislation, and associated overseas territories; common economic and social security policies. Also, the Treaty of Rome envisages the possibility of an ultimate political federation. The chief institutions within E.E.C. are the Common Market Commission in Brussels (which is generally subordinate to the

---

[1] Van Meerhaeghe, *op. cit.*, ch. 9. For discussion of the future role of O.E.C.D. in monetary and trade negotiations, see 'OECD seeks new monetary bloc', *F.T.*, 23 May 1972.
[2] 'Progress Report on the European Economic Community', *M.B.R.*, Aug. 1970; J. Rey, 'Organizing the European Community', *L.B.R.*, July 1971. For a very useful summary of the Rome Treaty and policy implications of U.K. membership, see also *'What about Europe?': a study of the European Economic Community'*, published by Lloyds Bank, and D. Swann, *The Economics of the Common Market*, 2nd edit.), 1972.

5. INTERNATIONAL TRADE [1]

Council of Ministers); the High Authority of the Coal and Steel Community in Luxembourg; and the Euratom Commission in Brussels (for the joint development of nuclear power). In 1962 Britain applied to join the E.E.C., but negotiations ended unsuccessfully, early in 1963. In 1967 the Labour Government renewed U.K. application for membership and the Conservative Government began negotiations in June 1970, which were successfully concluded in 1971. The date for U.K. entry was fixed at 1 January 1973. Along with Norway, Denmark and Eire – former members of the European Free Trade Association (E.F.T.A.) – the new E.E.C. was to have constituted 'The Ten'.[1]

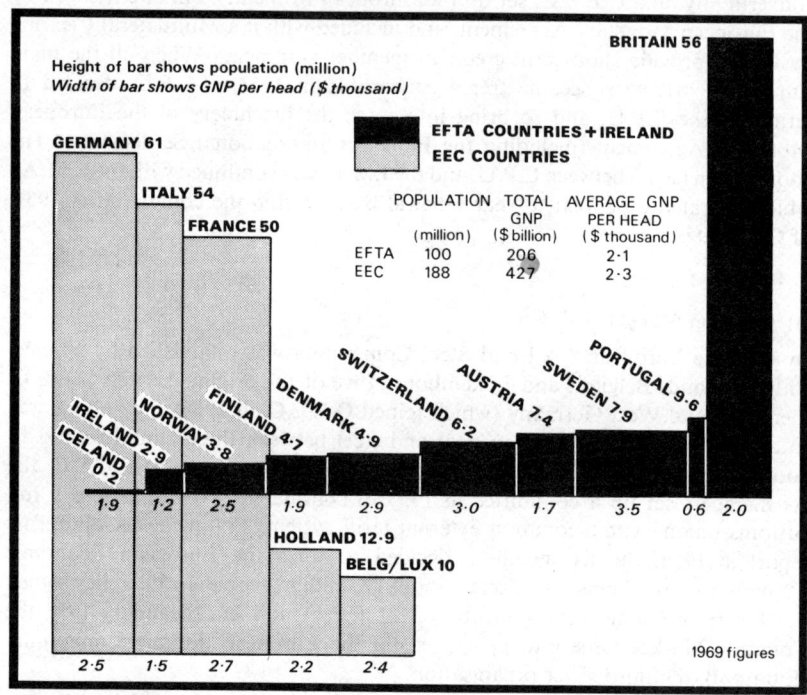

Fig. 5.16. *Population and G.N.P. in the E.E.C. and E.F.T.A., 1969*
(Source: *Econ.*, 26 June 1971, p. 51)

By 1969 the original E.E.C. members ('the Six') had a combined population of about 188 million. E.F.T.A., the (European Free Trade Association) – formed by the U.K. and six other O.E.C.D. members in 1959, after the Stockholm Treaty, and later joined by Finland, Iceland and Eire, as associates – had a combined population of about 104 million. Their populations, G.N.P.s and *per capita* incomes are shown in Fig. 5.16. In 1971 the combined G.N.P. of the

[1] For further details of the negotiations, arguments and implications of U.K. membership, see *Britain and Europe*, H.M.S.O., July 1971; *Factsheets on Britain and Europe*, H.M.S.O., July 1971; 'Negotiations with the EEC', *E.P.R.*, 13, March 1971; 'Economic implications of EEC membership', *E.P.R.*, 18, Aug. 1971; 'Accession to the European Communities', *E.P.R.*, 25, March 1972. A referendum held in Norway in late 1972 resulted in the non-ratification of that country's accession to membership. However, the possibility remained that Norway would join the "Nine" at a later date.

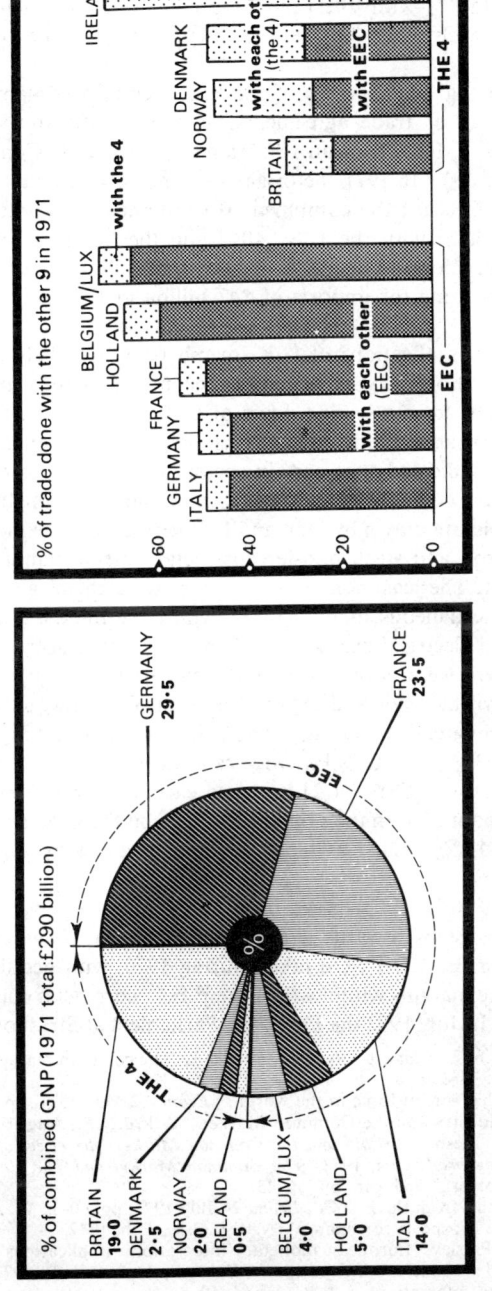

Fig. 5.17. G.N.P. and trade relationships among the E.E.C. and the four candidate members, 1971.

(Source: *Econ.*, 1 July 1972, p. 84)

prospective 'Ten' was £290 billion: of this, the four candidate members contributed 24% (U.K. 19%) and 'the Six' original members accounted for 76% (within which West Germany 29·5%, France 23·5% and Italy 14%). Whilst 'the Six' were conducting between 45% and 65% of their trade with each other in 1971 and only 5% to 8% with 'the Four', the latter were conducting between 10% and 55% with each other, but between 14% and 27% with 'the Six' (see Fig. 5.17).

Apart from the actual membership of the E.E.C. countries, many others are linked with it by way of trade agreements, as E.E.C. African associates, as E.F.T.A. associates, Mediterranean associates or as full Commonwealth associates (see Fig. 5.18).[1] In 1971 the original six members accounted for more than 15% of world G.N.P.: the combined 10 would have accounted for more than 20% (as compared with the U.S., 40% and the U.S.S.R., about 10%). This would have provided the new E.E.C. with tremendous purchasing power in world trade, accounting for imports of $47 billion in 1970 (21·1% of world exports).[2]

Some of the major implications of U.K. membership are likely to be in the field of greater competition and greater scope for economies of scale in production and marketing.[3] Apart from a scaling down of U.K. tariffs to the E.E.C. level, there are problems of agricultural policy, regional policy and taxation policy. Some studies[4] have indicated that certain sectors of U.K. industry are likely to prove more or less competitive, or that specific industries might benefit or suffer. The overall picture drawn by Han and Liesner was that the most competitive sectors were iron and steel, non-ferrous metals, metal manufactures and transport equipment. The least competitive sectors were chemicals, mechanical engineering and miscellaneous manufactures, whilst the middling groups were textiles, clothing and electrical engineering. However, it was noted that in *each* industrial sector there were both strong and weak parts.

With regard to invisible trade and the services of the City, it would appear that the U.K. might benefit greatly from entry. The U.K.'s invisible earnings accounted in 1970 for about 8·3% of its G.N.P., twice as large a share as France or West Germany. More than one-third of U.K. trade earnings came from invisibles, as compared with about 25% in the original E.E.C., and the U.K. share of world invisible trade was 12%, almost as large as those of any two original E.E.C. members.[5]

In December 1969 the E.E.C. agreed on a policy to work towards monetary integration. The first steps towards a *European Monetary Union* or *Economic and Monetary Union* (E.M.U.) were taken during 1970, with decisions to progressively narrow the margins within which the E.E.C. currencies could fluctuate against each other.[6] In July 1972 the European Parliament at Strasbourg adopted

---

[1] 'How are the other nine?', *Econ.*, 1 July 1972, pp. 84–5; 'The common market's backyard', *Econ.*, 6 May 1972, pp. 74–5.

[2] 'A Europe of Ten: what sort of force in the world?', *Econ.*, 22 May 1971, pp. 50–1.

[3] D. J. Ezra, 'British industry and the Common Market', *N.W.B.Q.R.*, Aug. 1971.

[4] S. S. Han and H. H. Liesner, *Britain and the Common Market: the effect of entry on the pattern of manufacturing production*, 1971; *The Common Market and The United Kingdom* (Westminster Bank booklet), 1966, esp. pp. 36–43.

[5] 'London's invisible gains from the E.E.C.', *Econ.*, 24 July 1971, pp. 60–1; W. A. P. Manser, 'UK and the EEC: the prospects for finance', *N.W.B.Q.R.*, Feb. 1972.

[6] P. Coffey and J. R. Presley, 'European monetary integration – implications for the UK', *N.W.B.Q.R.*, Feb. 1971; 'Monetary integration in Europe', *M.B.R.*, Feb. 1971; L. Erhard, 'Prospects for European integration', *L.B.R.*, Jan. 1969.

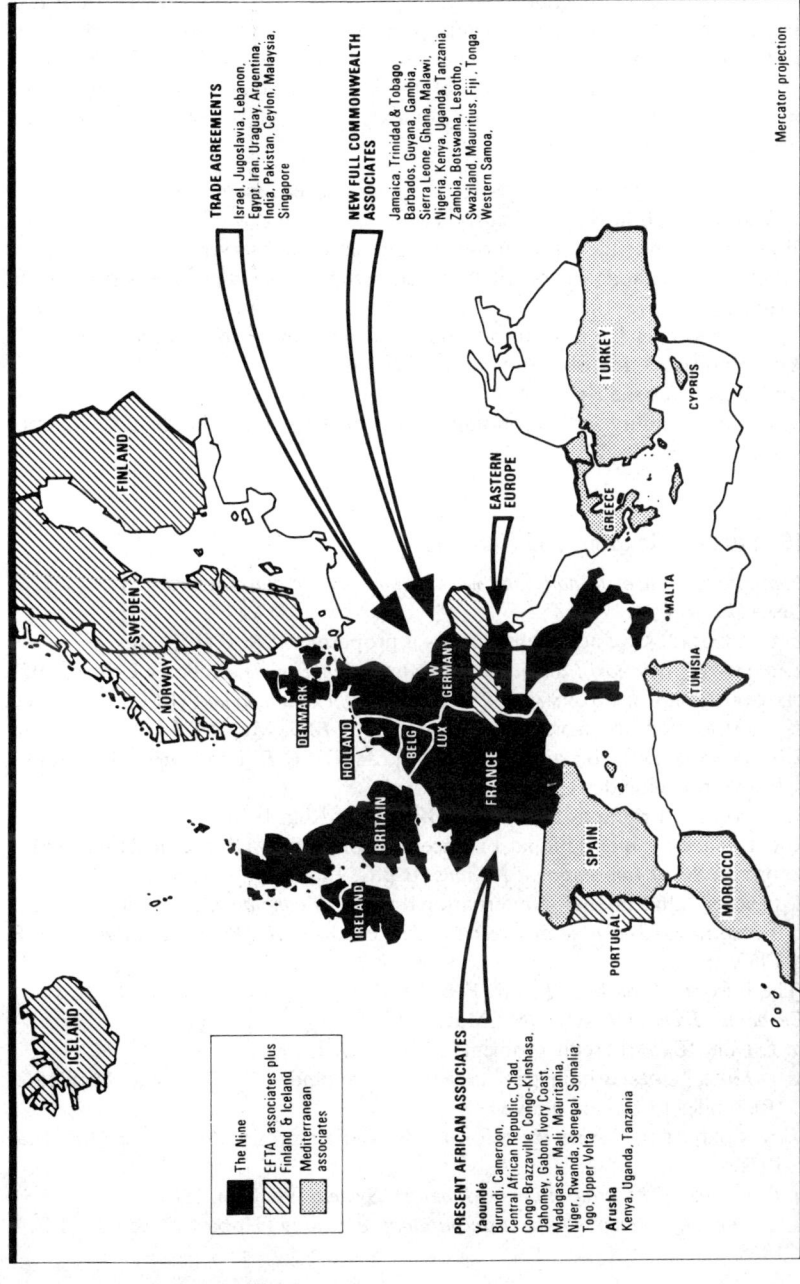

TRADE AGREEMENTS
Israel, Jugoslavia, Lebanon,
Egypt, Iran, Uruguay, Argentina,
India, Pakistan, Ceylon, Malaysia,
Singapore

NEW FULL COMMONWEALTH
ASSOCIATES
Jamaica, Trinidad & Tobago,
Barbados, Guyana, Gambia,
Sierra Leone, Ghana, Malawi,
Nigeria, Kenya, Uganda, Tanzania,
Zambia, Botswana, Lesotho,
Swaziland, Mauritius, Fiji, Tonga,
Western Samoa.

EASTERN EUROPE

Mercator projection

The Nine
EFTA associates plus
Finland & Iceland
Mediterranean
associates

PRESENT AFRICAN ASSOCIATES
Yaoundé
Burundi, Cameroon,
Central African Republic, Chad,
Congo-Brazzaville, Congo-Kinshasa,
Dahomey, Gabon, Ivory Coast,
Madagascar, Mali, Mauritania,
Niger, Rwanda, Senegal, Somalia,
Togo, Upper Volta
Arusha
Kenya, Uganda, Tanzania

Fig. 5.18. *'The Nine' and their associates*
(Source: *Based on material in Econ.*, 1 Jan. 1972, (Survey p. 27))

433

a plan for step-by-step full political and monetary union by the U.K. and 'the Six'. The implications for the U.K. could be quite profound, in regard to her right to devalue or revalue the pound; in regard to the adequacy of E.E.C. reserve facilities to support sterling; and in regard to the form and degree of harmonisation of the U.K. national budget with that of the other members.[1] In July 1972 the Finance Ministers of 'the Ten' reached agreement on eight basic principles for the E.M.U., in the context of the reform of the international monetary system. These were:[2]

(i) Fixed, but adjustable, values for the main currencies;
(ii) Full convertibility for all currencies;
(iii) Controls over the creation of new international reserves;
(iv) Agreed methods for countries to correct balance of payments deficits and surpluses;
(v) Controls over the flow of 'hot money' from country to country;
(vi) Equal rights and obligations for all countries;
(vii) Regard for the rights of the developing countries;
(viii) Compatibility with economic and monetary union inside the Common Market.

15. Further Reading and Sources

Footnote references to daily and weekly journals are not repeated.
General
G. C. ABBOTT, 'Aid and indebtedness – a proposal', *N.W.B.Q.R.* May 1972.
R. BALDWIN, *Non-tariff distortions of international trade.* Allen & Unwin. 1971.
CENTRAL OFFICE OF INFORMATION. *Britain: an official handbook.* H.M.S.O. Annual.
CENTRAL OFFICE OF INFORMATION 'Trade', *F.B.E.* 5, May 1971.
A. R. CONAN, 'Does Britain pay its way?' *N.W.B.Q.R.* Feb. 1969. (See Franks, below, for rejoinder.)
A. R. CONAN, 'Britain as creditor', *N.W.B.Q.R.* Aug. 1970.
A. E. DAVIDSON, 'International Finance Corporation', *N.W.B.Q.R.* Nov. 1970.
A. DAY, *ABC of International Finance.* B.B.C. 1968.
E. DEVONS, 'Understanding international trade', *Economica*, Nov. 1961.
J. H. DUNNING, *The Role of American Investment in the British Economy.* P.E.P. 1969.
'The Eurobond market', *B.B.R.* Feb. 1969.
Economic Trends, March 1965; March 1972.
D. E. FAIR, 'Export credit problems', *T.B.R.* Dec. 1970.
A. FRANKS, 'Does Britain pay its way? – a rejoinder'. *N.W.B.Q.R.* May 1969. (Rejoinder to Conan, above.)
H. N. GOLDSTEIN, 'Monetary reform – the Barber proposals', *N.W.B.Q.R.* May 1972.
H. G. GRUBEL, *The International Monetary System.* Penguin. 1969.
G. HABERLER, *Money in the International Economy.* Hobart Paper 31. I.E.A. 1965.

[1] W. A. P. Manser, *op. cit.*, p. 23; *D.T.*, 6 July 1972; 'Saving the Emu from extinction', *Econ.*, 8 July 1972, pp. 13–14.
[2] 'Money reform agreed', *D.T.*, 18 July 1972.

SIR ROY HARROD, 'The role of sterling', *D.B.R.* Dec. 1966.

'The inescapable problems of international adjustment', *T.B.R.* Sept. 1969.

'International Liquidity', *B.B.R.* Feb. 1972.

'International Money', *B.B.R.* May 1969.

H. G. JOHNSON, 'The Bretton Woods system, key currencies, and the "Dollar crisis" of 1971'. *T.B.R.* June 1972.

D. KERN, 'International finance and the Euro-Dollar market', *N.W.B.Q.R.* Nov. 1971.

D. F. LOMAX, 'The United Kingdom's trading position', *N.W.B.Q.R.* May 1970.

A. L. LOUGHEED, 'Scarce currencies and the contemporary international monetary system', *D.B.R.* Dec. 1968.

A. L. LOUGHEED, 'International economic relations – past and future', *N.W.B.Q.R.* May 1972.

'The major currencies', *Conjoncture*, 118, Aug. 1969.

W. A. P. MANSER, 'Professor Reddaway's last word?' *N.W.B.Q.R.* Feb. 1969.

M. A. G. VAN MEERHAEGHE, *International Economic Institutions.* Longmans. 1966.

F. V. MEYER, D. C. CORNER and J. E. S. PARKER, *Problems of a Mature Economy.* Macmillan. 1970.

P. M. OPPENHEIMER, 'Import deposits', *N.W.B.Q.R.* Feb. 1969.

M. PANIĆ, 'Britain's invisible balance', *L.B.R.* July 1968.

M. PANIĆ, 'The United Kingdom's exports of long-term capital', *M. and W.S.R.* Autumn 1968.

POLITICAL AND ECONOMIC PLANNING, *Non-Tariff Distortions of Trade*, Broadsheet No. 514. P.E.P. 1969.

'Progress in international monetary co-operation', *M.B.R.* Nov. 1969.

W. B. REDDAWAY et al., *Effects of U.K. Direct Overseas Investment: final report.* C.U.P. 1968.

'The retreat from Bretton Woods – the story so far'. *M.B.R.* Nov. 1971.

J. H. RICHARDS, *International Economic Institutions.* Holt, Rinehart & Winston. 1970.

I. O. SCOTT, Jnr., 'That controversial Euro-Dollar market'. *N.W.B.Q.R.* Aug. 1969.

'Special drawing rights', *B.B.R.* Nov. 1971.

M. STAMP, 'The Stamp plan and the present monetary crisis', *M. and W.S.R.* Autumn 1971.

'Tariffs and trade patterns – a resumé of recent developments and trends' *M.B.R.* May 1968.

TREASURY. *E.P.R.*, 1, Jan. 1970; 2, Feb. 1970; 5, May 1970; 6, Aug. 1970; 7, Sept. 1970; 9, Nov. 1970; 11, Jan. 1971; 13, Mar. 1971; 14, Apr. 1971; 18, Aug. 1971; 25, Mar. 1972.

'U.S. protectionism', *B.B.R.* May 1972.

S. J. WELLS, *International Economics.* Allen & Unwin. 1969.

European Economic Community

Britain and Europe, H.M.S.O. July 1971.

'Britain, the Commonwealth and Europe', *B.B.R.* Feb. 1971.

CENTRAL OFFICE OF INFORMATION, *Factsheets on Britain and Europe* (complete series Nos. 1–11), H.M.S.O. July 1971.

P. COFFEY and J. R. PRESLEY, 'European monetary integration – implications for the U.K.', *N.W.B.Q.R.* Feb. 1971.

L. ERHARD, 'Prospects for European Integration'. *L.B.R.* Jan. 1969.

D. J. EZRA, 'British Industry and the Common Market', *N.W.B.Q.R.* Aug. 1971.

S. S. HAN and H. H. LIESNER, *Britain and the Common Market: The Effect of Entry on the Pattern of Manufacturing Production*. C.U.P. (Occasional Paper 27). 1971.

W. A. P. MANSER, 'UK and EEC: the prospects for finance', *N.W.B.Q.R.* Feb. 1972.

Monetary Integration in Europe'. *M.B.R.* Feb. 1971.

'Progress report on the European Economic Community', *M.B.R.* Aug. 1970.

J. REY, 'Organizing the European Community', *L.B.R.* July 1971.

D. SWANN, *The Economics of the Common Market* (2nd edit.). Penguin. 1972.

WESTMINSTER BANK, *The Common Market and the United Kingdom*, Westminster Bank Booklet. 1966.

What About Europe?: a study of the European Economic Community, Lloyds Bank.

16. Past Examination Questions

1. How far, if at all, does international trade differ from domestic trade? (Summer 1955)
2. 'It is only by trade that the physical deficiencies of an area can be made good.' Comment on this statement. (Summer 1961)
3. What are the main advantages of international trade for the United Kingdom? (Autumn 1957)
4. Why must we export to maintain our standard of living? (Summer 1955)
5. Why does it pay Britain to import goods which she can produce herself? (January 1963)
6. British agricultural output per acre is almost the highest in the world. Why then do we not devote more resources to agriculture and produce all our food at home? (Summer 1964)
7. What would be the principal economic effects in the United Kingdom of a complete stoppage of international trade? (Autumn 1953)
8. What would be the likely economic effects in the United Kingdom of a sharp reduction in our export trade? (Summer 1956)
9. The United States is the most important motor-car manufacturing country in the world. Why, then, does the United States import British cars? (Autumn 1952)
10. What is meant by 'the terms of trade'? Why are the terms of trade of considerable importance to Britain? (Summer 1963)
11. Write short notes on . . . the following: (*a*) Sterling area; (*b*) Import quotas. (Summer 1952)
12. Write short notes on . . . the following: (*a*) Export bounties. (Autumn 1952)
13. Outline the composition of the chief British imports and exports of goods. Give some indication of the relative importance of the main items. (Summer 1958)
14. Before 1939 Britain imported the bulk of her food and raw materials for industry. (*a*) How did she pay for them? (*b*) To what extent has the position changed in the post-war years? (January 1963)

15. In order to overcome our balance of payments deficit we are being urged to increase our exports. Write a short report on how you would set about this task, indicating also which of our exports you think could be increased in volume, and where they could go. (Summer 1952)

16. List the principal items which this country exports and indicate briefly their relative importance. How have the size and constitution of our exports changed as compared with pre-war? (Summer 1953)

17. Describe, and account for the location of, the main sources of *either* British imports of tea *or* coffee. (Autumn 1957)

18. 'Whereas the balance of payments must balance, the balance of trade need not.' Comment on this statement. (January 1965)

19. Write short notes on . . . the following: (*a*) Invisible exports. (Summer 1955; Summer 1963)

20. Write short notes on . . . the following: (*a*) Balance of Payments. (Summer 1956; Summer 1964)

21. Distinguish carefully between the following: visible imports and invisible imports. (Summer 1956)

22. Choose *two* of the following three sections, (*a*), (*b*) and (*c*), and distinguish between the terms in each of the two sections you have chosen. (*a*) Balance of trade and Balance of payments. . . . (Summer 1959)

23. Distinguish between the terms in each of the following three sections: (*a*) Visible imports and invisible imports; (*b*) Visible exports and invisible exports; (*c*) Balance of Trade and Balance of Payments. (Summer 1961)

24. Write short notes on . . . the following: (*a*) Invisible imports. (January 1964)

25. There have been (*a*) a decline in overseas earnings by British Insurance companies, and (*b*) an increase in the investment of foreign capital in Britain. Explain the effects of each of these on Britain's balance of payments. (Summer 1960)

26. What do you understand by the Common Market? What are the main points of agreement between its members? (January 1964)

5. International Trade
Stage II

1. Further Development of Comparative Costs, Opportunity Costs, Relative Factor Endowment and Exchange Ratios

(a) Comparative costs

The theory of comparative costs or advantages between countries may be shown diagrammatically. If, as we have assumed in Section 2 of Stage I, each country is using two units of input (or factors of production), then the total value-units of each product which could be produced represent alternatives. In Case A the alternatives for Utopia, by specialisation, are 20 sugar value-units *or* 4 steel value-units: for Eldorado they are 2 sugar *or* 30 steel. In case B, Utopia could produce 20 sugar *or* 4 steel units, while Eldorado could produce 24 sugar *or* 30 steel units. If these alternatives are linked together, as in Fig. 5.19, we have what are termed *production possibility frontiers*. Each country could produce any combination of steel or sugar within its frontier or limit, by making use of its two units of factor of production.

In both cases, the commodity with the longest axis is the one for which the particular country has the comparative advantage, *viz.*, in case A sugar (Utopia) and steel (Eldorado) and in case B sugar (Utopia) and steel (Eldorado).

Production possibility frontiers permit us to illustrate the 'gain from trade' diagrammatically. In case B, for example, if we turn one of the production possibility frontiers upside down, we may construct a box diagram, as in Fig. 5.20. This illustrates sugar on both vertical axes and steel on both horizontal axes. As we have shown, without specialisation (i.e. with each country utilising 50% of its resources on each commodity), each country would be on the half-way point along its 'frontier'. Thus, Utopia would have 10 sugar units *and* 2 steel units, whilst Eldorado would have 12 sugar units *and* 15 steel units. Total combined production would be 22 sugar units *and* 17 steel units. The shaded areas in Fig. 5.20 indicate production without specialisation: Eldorado is at point B on its frontier and Utopia is at point A. since Utopia has no absolute advantage but has a *relative* advantage in sugar, it moves along its frontier to point C, thereby specialising exclusively in sugar and producing 20 value units. As Eldorado has an absolute advantage in both products but a relatively higher advantage in steel, it specialises *to some extent* on steel, within the limits D and E. At D it brings the combined total output of steel up to the non-specialising combined total of 17, but by adding $10\frac{2}{3}$ units of sugar to Utopia's 20 it raises the non-specialising level to $30\frac{2}{3}$: the net gain in terms of sugar is $8\frac{2}{3}$ units. At E, Eldorado brings the combined total output of sugar up to the non-specialising combined total of 22, but its production of steel raises the non-specialising level from 17

438

to $27\frac{1}{2}$: the net gain in terms of steel is $10\frac{1}{2}$. The two *alternative* net gains are shown by the distances DX (for sugar) and EX (for steel).

Case A: Each country has an absolute advantage in a different commodity

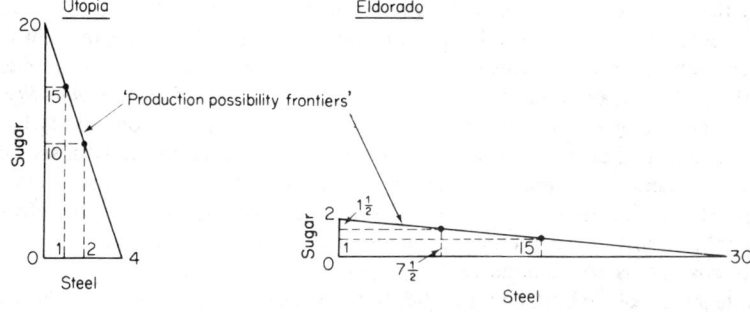

Case B: 1 country has an absolute advantage in both commodities
but each country has a comparative advantage in a different commodity

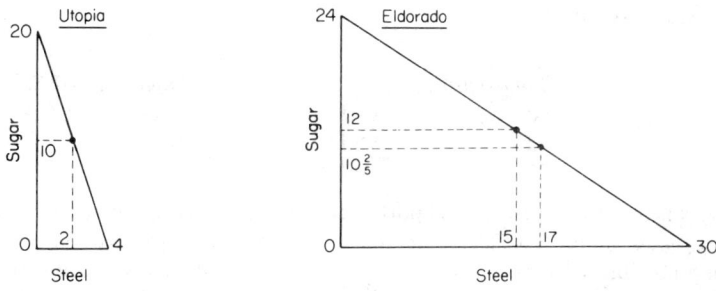

Fig. 5.19. *Production possibility frontiers*

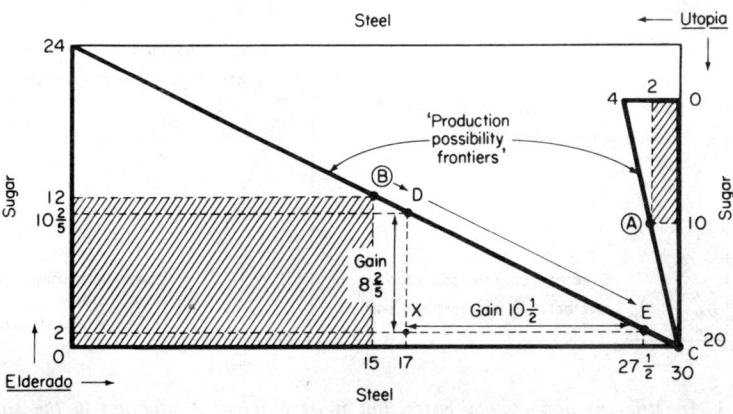

Fig. 5.20. *Comparative advantages and the 'gain from trade'*

439

(b) Opportunity costs

The use of production possibility frontiers enables us to express the advantages of specialisation and trade by means of the concept of 'opportunity cost': we may thus dispense with the assumptions of specific quantities of particular *factors* of production, which, because of their different technological productivities, result in cost differentials in the production of different commodities and thereby in different relative prices. Instead, we may simply refer to the total resources available, which may be used for *alternative* total amounts of each *commodity*: a movement along a 'frontier' indicates the extent to which one commodity has to be sacrificed in order to have more of the other. The 'opportunity costs' or relative sacrifices (or production foregone) are given by the slopes of the production possibility frontiers. The opportunity cost of any commodity is therefore its 'price' in terms of the alternative commodity which has to be foregone.

This enables us to examine case C, a situation in which Eldorado has an absolute advantage in both commodities but in which *both* Eldorado and Utopia are more efficient in the production of the *same* commodity (sugar). Let us suppose that Utopia could have either 20 sugar units or 4 steel units (or any combination of the two) and that Eldorado could produce either 24 sugar units or 8 steel units. On the face of it, both countries would wish to specialise on sugar, and exchange would not be possible. If both countries avoided specialisation, the results would be:

Case C

Country	Value-units of Sugar		Value-units of Steel
Utopia	10	AND	2
Eldorado	12	AND	4
Total	22	AND	6

However, when we compare the opportunity costs for each country, we see that there is room for specialisation and a resultant gain from trade. The production possibility frontiers are as shown in Fig. 5.21. Points A and B show the production and consumption combinations in the absence of specialisation. The opportunity cost to Utopia of producing any unit of sugar will be the

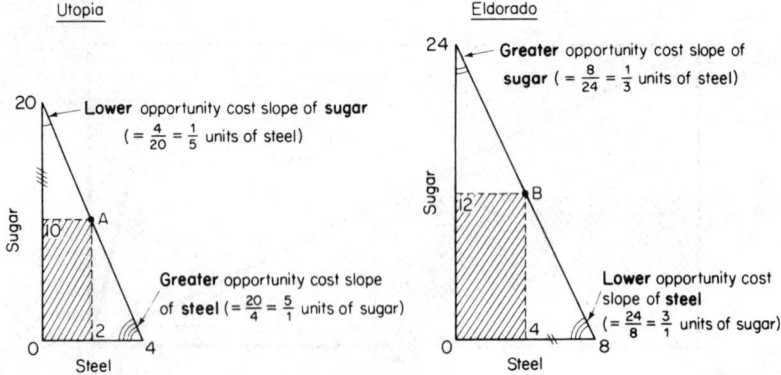

Fig. 5.21 *Different opportunity costs, but most efficient production in the same commodity*

foregone (or sacrificed) steel which could have been produced, *viz*, $\frac{4}{20}$ or $\frac{1}{5}$ unit of steel. Similarly, the opportunity cost of any unit of steel will be $\frac{20}{4} = \frac{5}{1}$ units of sugar. For Eldorado the opportunity cost of sugar will be $\frac{1}{3}$ unit of steel, while that of steel will be $\frac{3}{1}$ units of sugar. Thus we see that Utopia has a *lower* opportunity cost (i.e. $\frac{1}{5}$ unit of steel) in the production of sugar than does Eldorado ($\frac{1}{3}$ unit of steel). This is reflected in Utopia's wider (4-bar) angle *opposite* the sugar axis, as compared with Eldorado and by the shallower slope of its production possibility frontier, originating from the sugar axis. On the other hand, in regard to steel, the commodity in which neither country is most efficient, the opportunity cost to Eldorado ($\frac{3}{1}$ units of sugar) is lower than that to Utopia ($\frac{5}{1}$ units of sugar). This is reflected in Eldorado's wider (2-bar) angle *opposite* its steel axis, as compared with Utopia and in the shallower slope of its production possibility frontier, originating from the steel axis. Thus, what matters is not that both countries produce sugar most efficiently, nor that Eldorado is absolutely more efficient at both commodities than is Utopia, but rather that each has a lower opportunity cost for one commodity than the other country has. There is room for Utopia to specialise completely on sugar and for Eldorado to specialise to some extent on steel. By means of the box diagram in Fig. 5.22 we may see that Utopia will move to point C, producing 20 units of sugar.

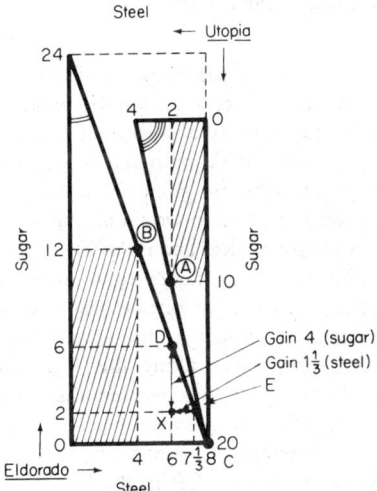

Fig. 5.22 *Opportunity costs and the 'gain from trade' despite relative advantages in the same commodity*

Eldorado would move within the limits of D and E: at D it produces 6 steel units and 6 sugar units (thus creating a 4 sugar unit gain from specialisation and trade), whilst at E it produces 2 sugar units and $7\frac{1}{3}$ steel units (thus creating a $1\frac{1}{3}$ steel unit gain).

(c) Exchange ratios

The range or *limits* to the ratio of exchange when commodities are traded may be illustrated by means of the box diagram in Fig. 5.23. Eldorado's production possibility frontier shows its opportunity cost in steel production as $\frac{4}{5}$ sugar

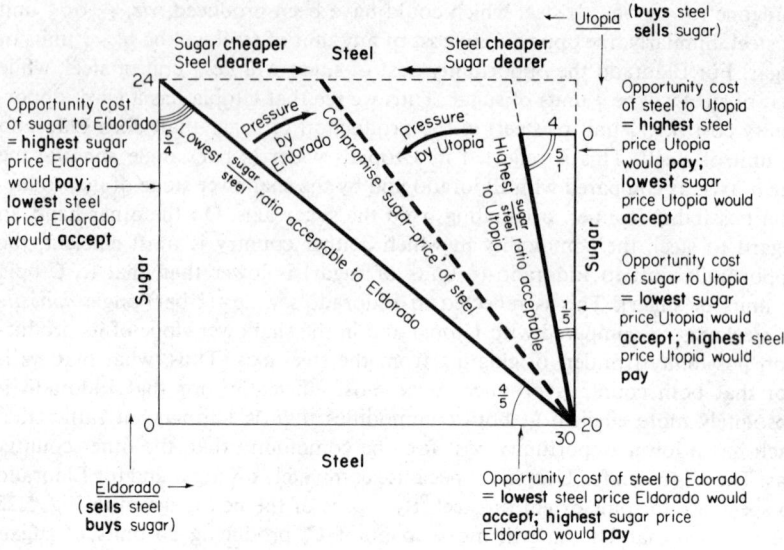

Fig. 5.23 *The ratio of exchange and relative prices*

units per unit of steel (i.e. the slope, originating at the steel axis). This would be Eldorado's 'base line' – the *lowest* sugar payment it would accept for its steel. Utopia's frontier shows its opportunity cost in steel production as $\frac{5}{1}$ sugar units per unit of steel. Utopia would not be prepared to pay more in sugar for the steel it buys than the ratio given by this slope. Thus the two frontiers show the limits to the ratio of exchange. Eldorado would aim at an exchange ratio along Utopia's frontier, thereby selling its steel and obtaining sugar on the best possible terms: Utopia would aim at an exchange ratio along Eldorado's frontier, thereby buying steel and selling its sugar on the best possible terms. One of the various possible compromises is shown by the intermediate ratio of exchange (dotted line). Any trade taking place along this line gives *both* countries a combination of commodities which lies *outside* their production possibility frontiers: both countries benefit, to a greater or less extent.

The significance of these different ratios of exchange, within the limits set by the opportunity costs of each country, lies in the fact that the ratio (or rate of exchange) determines the quantities of each commodity bartered. Thus, in Fig. 5.24, let us suppose that Utopia, concentrating on sugar, was able to devote up to 8 sugar units (distance OA) on a barter deal. It would wish to obtain as much steel as possible for its 8 sugar units, or, conversely, to obtain a given amount of steel units for as few sugar units as possible. Eldorado, specialising on steel, is prepared to devote up to 10 units (distance OB) in a barter for sugar. If Utopia could negotiate an exchange rate on Eldorado's 'frontier' (i.e. $\frac{4}{5}$ sugar units for 1 of steel), it would be able to purchase 10 steel units (AC) with its 8 sugar units (BC). If it had no alternative but to accept its worst possible terms of trade, Utopia would exchange at its own 'frontier' rate (i.e. $\frac{5}{1}$ sugar units for 1 of steel) and would only obtain $\frac{8}{5}$ units of steel (distance AD) with its 8 sugar units (ED). Thus, Eldorado would prefer to exchange at point D, giving AD

442

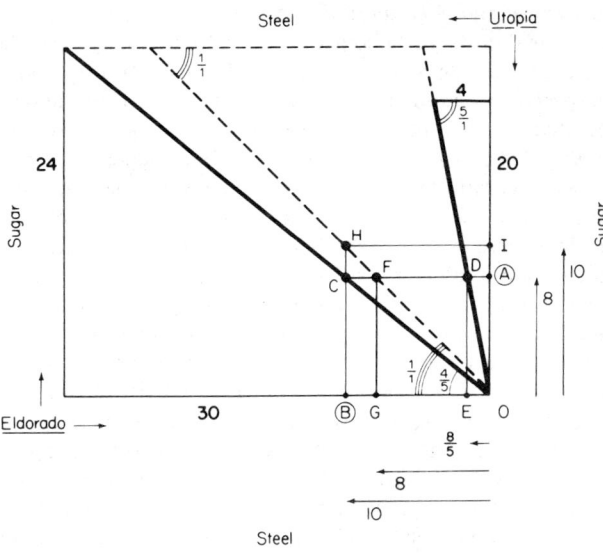

Fig. 5.24 *Effects of differing ratios of exchange*

steel for ED sugar, but would be able, if necessary, to exchange at point C, giving AC steel for BC sugar. The only exchange rate at which the quantities exchanged would be equal would be that shown by the dotted line, at which the ratio is 1 :1. Both countries would be able to achieve combinations lying *outside* their 'frontiers' and both would thus benefit. This, of course, would lie closer to Utopia's most desirable (and Eldorado's least desirable) terms, such that Utopia's 8 units of disposable sugar (OA) secures most of Eldorado's disposable steel (8 units, or OG). Conversely, Eldorado could have obtained 10 sugar units (BH) with its 10 units of disposable steel (OB or IH), if Utopia had been willing to part with them. As Utopia only has 8 sugar units to barter (OA or GF), Eldorado is able to acquire this without using its full surplus of steel, and therefore only needs to barter 8 units (AF or OG) and consequently has 2 units to spare (BG). A further implication might follow: if Eldorado desired such a sugar consumption that it wanted to *buy* 10 sugar units (OI or BH), then, given the $\frac{1}{1}$ exchange rate and Utopia's inability to supply more than 8 units, Eldorado only succeeds in buying 8 sugar units (OA or GF) and has 2 steel units to spare (BG or CF). Eldorado would have to produce the 2 sugar units itself: its own opportunity cost per unit of sugar, however, is $\frac{5}{4}$ steel units, so it has to forego the production of $2\frac{1}{2}$ steel units. This will be greater than the distance BG, which results in its being able to offer only $7\frac{1}{2}$ steel units and to purchase only $7\frac{1}{2}$ sugar units – given the $\frac{1}{1}$ exchange rate. Therefore Eldorado has to *fail* to meet its consumption target for sugar, *or* it has to 'tighten its belt' and divert more of its steel to pay for its sugar target, *or* it has to exert its influence and bargaining power in an attempt to push the exchange rate nearer to Utopia's 'base line'. This would enable Eldorado to acquire Utopia's 8 sugar units with *less* than 8 steel units (OG), so that it could devote $2\frac{1}{2}$ steel unit *resources* to the production of the 2 sugar units which it desires.

(d) Factor endowment and intensity of factor use

Apart from the 'real cost' (or 'labour cost') and 'opportunity cost' theories of comparative advantages – based on the work of David Ricardo and Gottfried Haberler,[1] respectively – another important theory of specialisation and trade is that of 'relative factor endowment', based on the work of Heckscher and Ohlin.[2] Basically, this assumes that countries take advantage of the factors with which they are comparatively well-endowed: some will be labour-intensive and some capital-intensive. Even if two countries have similar factor *endowments*, there may be differences in tastes, institutional arrangements or income distribution: these may result in different patterns of demand for commodities and thus for factors and, thereby, may result in different factor *prices*. Thus, an attempt is made to *explain* the cause of differing comparative advantages.

A more sophisticated exchange model may be constructed, which allows for original relative factor endowments, for differing relative factor prices (and opportunity costs) – according to how intensively each factor is used – and for specialisation, and which shows the compromise exchange rate and the gains from specialisation. In Fig. 5.25(i) Utopia is shown as relatively (and absolutely) better endowed with labour (for sugar production), whilst Eldorado is relatively and absolutely better-endowed with capital (for steel production). Each may select a technique involving more or less of either factor, in the production of either or both commodities. According to the demands it makes on the factors with which it is endowed, a country's technique will cause the relative factor prices to alter. At position A, for example, Utopia uses much of its plentiful labour and less of its scarce capital: the opportunity cost of sugar – given by the slope of the production possibility frontier at A – is therefore lower than that of steel. If Utopia moved to Y, making more capital-intensive steel, for which it is badly suited, then the opportunity cost of steel would be very much higher and that of sugar very much lower – given by the slope of the 'frontier' at Y. Similarly, Eldorado's steel opportunity cost is less at B than at X, indicating that if it moved towards labour-intensive sugar production, its labour (in which it is relatively poorly-endowed) will become expensive, relative to the price of capital. Thus Utopia would tend to move up its 'relative price/production possibility' curve, towards C, and Eldorado would tend to move to more capital-intensive steel production, towards D. At C and D both sets of relative commodity prices are the same: the opportunity cost slopes of their production possibility frontiers are identical. The two countries could therefore specialise to some extent and trade with their surpluses. Utopia sells ZC of sugar in exchange for Eldorado's ZD of steel at the CD exchange rate. To illustrate the potential gain from specialisation and trade in terms of one commodity to one country and the other commodity to the second country, let us assume that Utopia had originally adopted a technique represented by point Y and Eldorado a technique represented by point X. These, of course, represent for each country only one out of numerous alternative factor and commodity combinations open to it. As a result of Utopia's moving to C and Eldorado's moving to D, Utopia thus gains YD *more* of steel than it could have done at Y without specialisation and trade: point D lies beyond its 'frontier'. Eldorado benefits by XC *more*

1 See S. J. Wells, *International Economics*, 1969, pp. 26–33 and 38–43; H. R. Heller, *International Trade*, 1968, pp. 14–15.
2 See Wells, *op. cit.*, pp. 43–7; Heller, *op. cit.*, pp. 37–9.

of sugar than it would otherwise have done at X: point C lies beyond its 'frontier'.

In Fig. 5.25(ii) Eldorado has an absolute advantage in both factors and thus in the available totals of both commodities. The crucial point, however, is that the same *relative* intensities of factor use result in the same relative factor prices and thus the same relative commodity prices (or opportunity costs). Therefore, as the 'relative price/production possibility' curves are parallel and opportunity costs are identical, there is no basis for specialisation and trade. Fig. 5.25(iii) shows Eldorado with an absolute advantage in both factor endowments, but with dissimilar opportunity costs. At any *same* relative commodity 'mix' the opportunity costs for each country are different. At X, for example, Utopia's badly endowed capital is intensively used and relatively expensive: at Y, Eldorado's well-endowed capital is intensively used and relatively cheap.

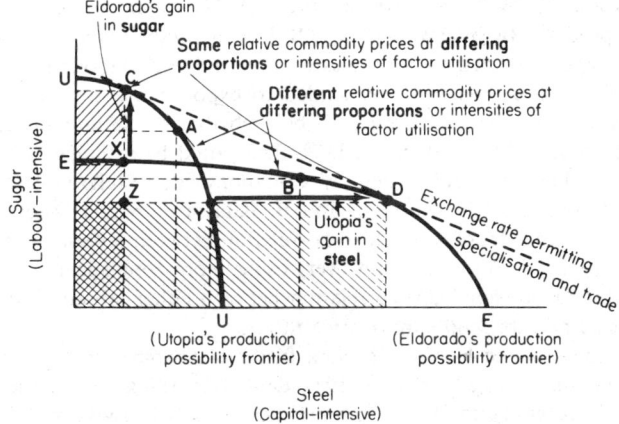

(i) Each country with absolute advantages in a **different** commodity:
differing relative commodity prices and opportunity costs in **both** countries

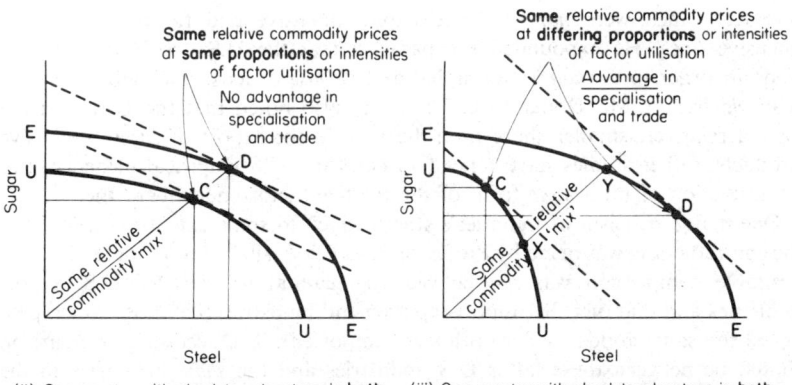

(ii) One country with absolute advantage in **both** commodities: **identical** relative commodity prices and opportunity costs in **both** countries.

(iii) One country with absolute advantage in **both** commodities: **differing** relative commodity prices and opportunity costs in **both** countries.

Fig. 5.25 *Factor endowments, relative commodity prices, opportunity costs and the possibility of specialisation and trade.*

445

Utopia would like to move to C and Eldorado to D. If each specialised in this way, they would find that they would reach points at which their relative commodity price patterns are the same: exchange could take place at the ratio given by C and D, which are parallel.

(e) Some empirical findings

Numerous empirical tests of the comparative costs and factor endowment theories have been attempted: no conclusive evidence seems to be forthcoming – although the comparative costs argument tends to come out with the more satisfactory record.

A major study on the validity of comparative costs was conducted by Sir Donald MacDougall on pre-World War II U.S. and U.K. exports. According to the theory, the country with the highest labour productivity should have the lowest costs and prices for a particular product and should therefore tend to export that product. In general, where U.S. labour productivity was relatively highest, her exports tended to be highest: where the U.K. labour productivity disadvantage was least marked, she tended to export more successfully. The advantage needed by the U.S. tended to be such that her labour productivity had to be at least double that of the U.K. This could be explained by factors such as her higher wage costs, and by Commonwealth Preference for U.K. exports. Postwar studies by R. Stern and B. Balassa amplified MacDougall's conclusions, viz., that there was a high correlation between labour productivity and export shares. J. Bhagwati, however, using more sophisticated statistical techniques, found no significant correlation between either labour productivity or labour costs per unit and export price ratios.[1]

A major study on the Heckscher-Ohlin factor endowment theory was made by W. W. Leontief, based on U.S. 1947 data. According to the theory, we should expect a country to export commodities for which it was relatively well endowed with the major factor: the U.S. was considered to be relatively well-endowed with capital and should have been successfully exporting capital-intensive products. Leontief found that the U.S., in fact, tended to export products which were *not* relatively capital-intensive and to import capital-intensive ones. He expounded the paradox that the U.S. 'resorts to foreign trade in order to *economise* its capital and *dispose* of its surplus labour, rather than *vice-versa*'. MacDougall's earlier study also noted that the U.K. did *not* have a relatively smaller share than the U.S. in the export of capital-intensive products. Other studies have tended to confirm, with empirical evidence, this contradiction of the *simple* form of the relative factor endowment theory.[2]

One major criticism of Leontief's study, which to some extent explains away the contradiction, was made by Professor P. T. Ellsworth.[3] He considered that the desirable comparison was *not* between the capital intensity of U.S. export industries and that of U.S. 'import-replacement' industries (i.e. those which produced the same goods as were primarily imported). The necessary comparison should be between these latter U.S. industries and the *same* industries in the

[1] See Heller, *op. cit.*, pp. 22–5 and Wells, *op. cit.*, pp. 47–9.
[2] See W. W. Leontief, 'Domestic production and foreign trade: the American capital position re-examined', 1953 paper reproduced in J. Bhagwati, ed., *International Trade*, 1969; Wells, *op. cit.*, pp. 49–53; Heller, *op. cit.*, pp. 41–3.
[3] See Wells, *op. cit.*, pp. 51–2.

countries from which those imports originated: according to the Heckscher-Ohlin theory, the industries in the countries of origin should be more labour-intensive than the corresponding U.S. industries. Ellsworth considered that Leontief was implicitly assuming that all countries had the same 'production functions' or production techniques for similar goods. In fact, there are usually numerous methods of production, ranging from the highly capital-intensive to the highly labour-intensive: the U.S. should be expected to adopt the former methods, even in its import-replacement industries. A more recent criticism and explanation of the Leontief paradox was made by J. Vanek,[1] who pointed to the importance of *natural resources*, as well as labour and capital, in influencing trade patterns. The U.S. was relatively under-endowed with natural resources and tended to import goods in which their content was high: since these goods usually required a high capital intensity as well, the U.S. was deemed to be unable to utilise its high capital endowment to the full, and had to import goods of this type. Further evidence in this direction was provided in 1972 by A. E. Fareed,[2] who found that the 'human-capital' component (i.e. representing an investment of capital in the formal schooling of the labour force) of U.S. exports was higher than that of its import-replacement industries. The implication was that Vanek's hypothesis was complemented by the evidence that the U.S. tended to *divert* its strong capital endowment away from export industries with a heavy natural resource component, towards export industries with a heavy human-capital (educated labour force) component.

Some interesting observations on the difficulty involved in finding a completely satisfactory explanation of international trade are as follows:

(i) An important and increasing share of international trade is in manufactured products, between developed manufacturing countries with similar factor endowments and similar economic structures and demand patterns.

(ii) S. Linder[3] has suggested that trade in manufactures is explicable rather by demand pattern *similarities* than by factor endowment *differences*. This would seem to be borne out by the experience of sophisticated products such as motor cars, which require a buoyant home market (permitting scale economies and low, competitive prices) and similar income levels and general economic conditions in the home and export markets. By the early 1970s about 20% of U.K. domestic purchases of motor cars were imports, whilst over 40% of U.K. motor car production was nevertheless exported – primarily to competing countries.

(iii) M. Posner[4] explains the growing proportion of world trade between industrialised countries in terms of the *temporary* advantages which any one country may develop, at any time, through technological inventiveness and change.

(iv) I. B. Kravis[5] suggests that the commodity composition of international trade is mainly determined by 'available' supply at home: a country will tend to import goods which are either unavailable or have a relatively high opportunity cost. He also suggests that the volume and pattern of international trade depends much more on controls and State interventions – such as with agricultural support programmes – than on relative factor endowments.

[1] *Ibid.*, p. 50.
[2] See A. E. Fareed, 'Human-capital intensity of U.S. trade', *E.J.*, June 1972.
[3] Referred to in Wells, *op. cit.*, p. 54.
[4] *Ibid.*, p. 54.
[5] *Ibid.*, p. 55.

2. Foreign Exchange Rates

Every society which has evolved beyond the barter system of trade has found it helpful to use money as a medium of exchange. For a long time gold and silver were used as money, and goods and services were priced in terms of the precious metals. Different countries had different names and magnitudes for the basic units of their currencies, but the intrinsic value of these units of money made it possible to relate the price of a Utopian product to the price of an Eldorado product. Countries paid each other in gold, as their currencies were valued in terms of gold. With the general abandonment, during the twentieth century, of the gold standard and of free convertibility of paper currency, on demand, into gold, problems of equating the value of one currency in terms of others have arisen. Different countries at different times have adopted various currency exchange rate systems for valuing their currencies internationally, to solve balance of payments difficulties.

Basically, the foreign exchange rate for a currency represents its price in terms of other currencies.[1] As with any other commodity, the price of a currency balances the supply of it with the demand for it on the foreign exchange markets of the world.[2] The three main systems of foreign exchange rate are concerned with these factors of price, supply and demand. One method is the freely fluctuating exchange rate, in which the price of a currency is allowed to vary according to its supply and demand conditions. Another is the fixed exchange rate, based on the gold standard, as already mentioned. Here the price is fixed in terms of gold, and changes in supply and demand conditions will affect the gold reserves backing the currency. Thirdly, an exchange rate may be fixed without gold backing, on the basis of 'exchange control'. In this case measures have to be taken to stabilise the conditions of the supply of, and demand for, the currency.

A variety of exchange rate systems was being considered from the end of the 1960s, in the context of international monetary reform. These included the fixed and almost fixed 'peg', the adjustable and 'crawling' peg (or 'gliding parity'), the wider and moveable 'band', the freely floating rate and the 'managed' floating rate (see Fig. 5.26).[3] The relative movements in parities of several major currencies from 1947 to 1970 are illustrated in Fig. 5.27.

When a Utopian citizen needs some Eldorado currency, with which to pay Eldorado citizens for visible goods, invisible services, etc., imported from that country, the demand for Eldorado currency rises. At the same time, the Utopian citizen offers his own currency in exchange for Eldorado money, and so the supply of Utopian currency rises. If there is no reciprocal transaction in the other direction, Utopia will be faced with a balance of payments problem, which will have repercussions on the Utopian rate of exchange.

While noting that an increase in the demand for Eldorado currency (E) entails a corresponding increase in the supply of Utopian currency (U), we may note some of the cases which cause this increase in demand for E.[4]

---

[1] 'The role of exchange rates', *Econ.*, 13 June 1964, p. 1259; also see S. A. Ożga, *The Rate of Exchange and the Terms of Trade*, 1969; A. Day, *ABC of International Finance*, 1968, pp. 9–19; G. Haberler, *Money in the International Economy*, 1965.

[2] 'The foreign exchange market', *E.P.R.*, 20, Oct. 1971 and 'Exchange rates: floating, flexible, fixed', *Econ.*, 19 Sept. 1970, pp. 68–9.

[3] See 'State of play', *Econ.*, 26 July 1969, p. 54, for further explanatory notes.

[4] See 'What happens to the pound', *Obs.* (Colour Supplement), 13 Dec. 1964.

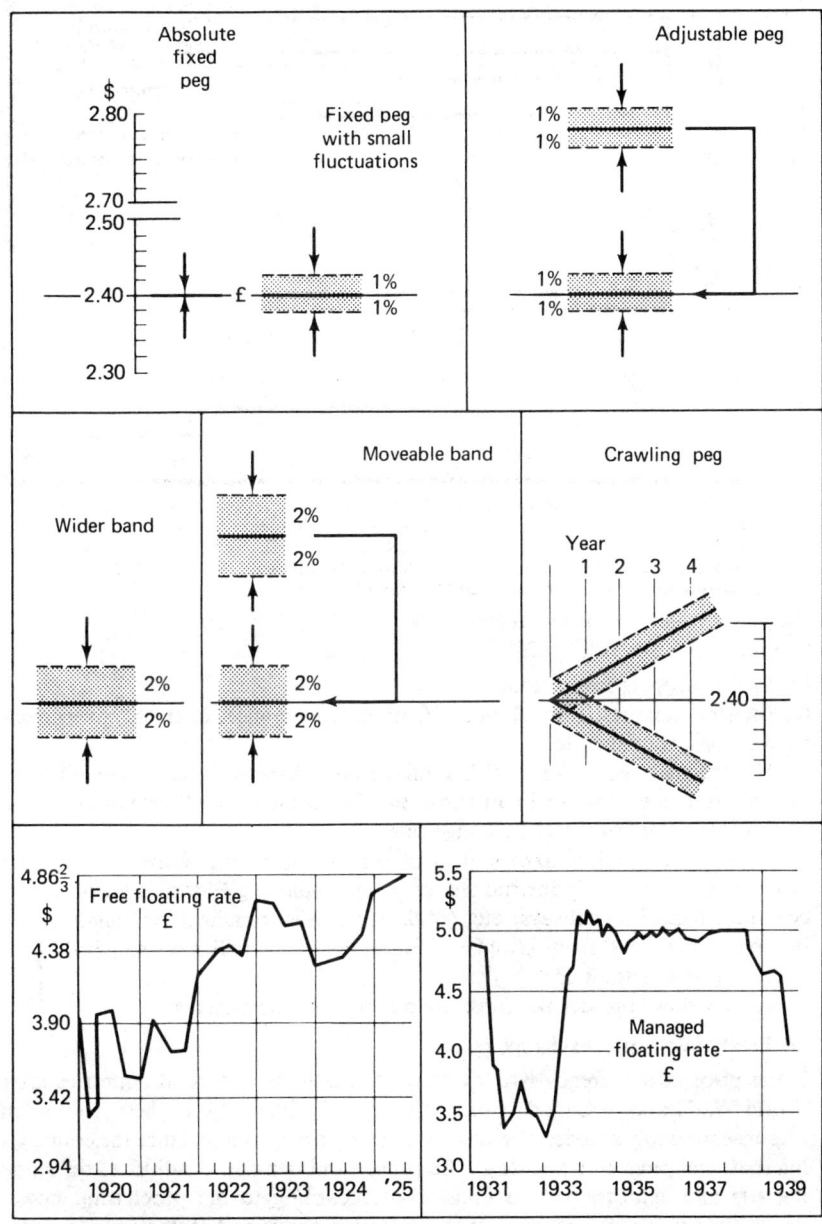

Fig. 5.26. *Exchange rate systems and world monetary reform*
(Source: *S.T.*, 5 Oct. 1969)

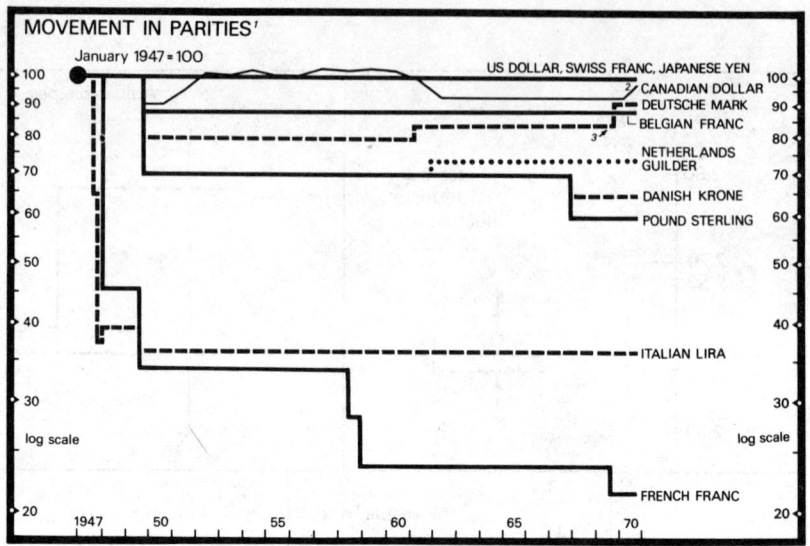

MOVEMENT IN PARITIES'

January 1947 = 100

US DOLLAR, SWISS FRANC, JAPANESE YEN
CANADIAN DOLLAR
DEUTSCHE MARK
BELGIAN FRANC
NETHERLANDS GUILDER
DANISH KRONE
POUND STERLING
ITALIAN LIRA
FRENCH FRANC

log scale

(1) Rates are per values agreed with the IMF except for: Swiss franc (non-member currency); Japanese yen, to May 1953; Italian lira, to March 1960; French franc, January 1948 to December 1960 (Canadian dollar and Deutsche mark see 2, 3 below).
(2) Fluctuating rate, 30 September 1950 to 1 May 1962; and from 1 June 1970.
(3) Fluctuating rate, 29 September to 24 October 1969.

Fig. 5.27. *Major parity movements, 1947 to 1970*
(Source: *Econ.*, 19 Sept. 1970, p. 68)

(*a*) Visible imports from Eldorado.

(*b*) Invisible imports from Eldorado (shipping, insurance, interest, government transactions, tourism, etc.)

(*c*) The speculative flow of 'hot' U money into Eldorado, either to benefit from high interest rates there or in anticipation of a raising of the E rate of exchange and/or a lowering of the U exchange rate.

(*d*) Investment of Utopian capital in Eldorado, either by purchasing Eldorado government bonds or industrial shares or by employing Eldorado resources to construct factories, railways, etc. (*N.B.* This investment will ultimately result in 'invisible exports' from Utopia to Eldorado, which will have to pay Utopia interest, profits and dividends.)[1]

We may now consider the three main exchange rate systems.

(*a*) Freely fluctuating exchange rate

If the price of a currency is allowed to fluctuate (as in several countries after World War I and in Canada from 1950 to 1962), it should, in theory, do so in response to supply and demand changes, in such a way as to balance the country's international payments position. The supply and demand conditions, reflecting imports and exports, will be influenced (according to the purchasing power parity theory) by factors such as the prices of goods and factors in a country and its trading partners, by their costs of production and relative efficiencies, and by the intensity of demand for each other's goods and services.

[1] If Eldorado were already an advanced economy, the future strain on its balance of payments might outweigh the original advantages derived from the inflow of development finance from Utopia. See 'Foreign investment controversy', *Stat.*, 4 June 1965, p. 1558.

If, at the existing exchange rate between U and E, Utopia was in balance of payments equilibrium with Eldorado, some new factor may intrude to upset this balance. Let us suppose that Eldorado was producing woollen pullovers, priced at E6 and that Utopia was producing turkeys, priced at U5, the rate of exchange being E1 = U5. The Utopian importer would have to pay U30 for a pullover, and the Eldorado importer would pay E1 for a turkey. If, because of improved techniques and modern machinery, Eldorado were able to cut costs by half and sell the pullover for E3, then Utopia would be able to buy the article for only U15. This would stimulate increased imports from Eldorado to Utopia. If Utopian demand were very responsive to the price reduction and the number of pullovers purchased more than doubled, Utopia's import bill would increase, causing a balance of payments deficit. This would increase Utopia's demand for E, whilst also increasing her supply of U on the foreign exchange markets. Therefore E would appreciate and U would depreciate in value, relative to each other. Consequently the E3 pullover would cost more than U15, and the U5 turkey would cost less than E1. Utopian demand for pullovers would fall, whilst Eldorado demand for turkeys would rise. This process of moving exchange rates would continue until balance of payments equilibrium was restored, at which point the supply and demand of U and E would be equal, as in Fig. 5.28.

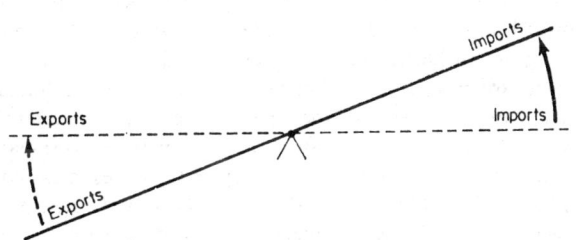

(1) *Result*

Increase in Demand for E

Increase in Supply of U.

(2) *Remedy*

E appreciates: imports from Eldorado FALL

U depreciates: exports to Eldorado RISE.

Fig. 5.28. *Rectification of balance of payments disequilibrium with freely fluctuating exchange rates*

The advantages of this system lie mainly in the fact that in theory balance of payments equilibrium comes about through an external change in the exchange rate, and does not necessitate immediate internal price changes by way of changes in employment and costs in the deficit country. This avoidance of immediate internal economic disruption makes the system politically and socially expedient. It does not follow, however, that a country such as Utopia, if in deficit, can pursue an internal policy completely unrelated to considerations of the balance of payments deficit. Ultimately the internal economic policy, affecting internal prices, will influence exports.

The disadvantages of the system lie primarily in *four* factors.

Firstly, the inability of the system to reflect and compare purchasing power and costs in different countries reliably.

Secondly, if Utopian demand for one Eldorado product increased, this would affect (appreciate) E, due to the increase in imports, whilst U would depreciate.

451

Thus all import prices to Utopia would rise and all export prices to Eldorado would fall, causing market instability.

Thirdly, absence of immediate urgency to lower prices, when in deficit, may result in the pursuance or continuance of an inflationary policy (high employment, costs, prices, etc.), which will aggravate the position.

Fourthly, the psychological factor of international speculation and/or confidence. International trade may be held up, in anticipation of a future exchange rate movement; 'hot' money may flow out of Utopia, in anticipation of U depreciation, thus aggravating the weak status of Utopian currency; international confidence in Utopian currency may be shaken on non-economic grounds, due to political, social or military events in Utopia. Such factors weaken the demand for U, and undermine the purchasing power parity theory. Experience of chaos in international exchange rates following World War I underlined the potential weakness of fluctuating exchange rates.[1]

The 1969 I.M.F. report indicated an opposition to floating exchange rates, but in 1970 amendments to the Fund articles were being considered, with a view to making it easier for countries to change their parities.[2] Following the 'Nixon package' of August 1971 – when the U.S., facing great pressure on the dollar, suspended dollar-gold convertibility, imposed a 10% import surcharge and a 10% reduction in foreign aid, and requested other central banks to allow their currencies to float upwards against the dollar – the G.A.B. Group of Ten central bankers met in Washington. In December 1971 they arrived at the *Smithsonian Agreement*, whereby rates for most member currencies were allowed to fluctuate between margins of $2\frac{1}{4}\%$ on either side of their parities against the dollar: the rate between any two could thus vary by up to $4\frac{1}{2}\%$ from their cross-parity. This range represented the 'tunnel', and the new agreed parities meant that sterling, for example, was 8·57% higher than the pre-August 1971 fixed parity. One major problem was that the E.E.C. bankers had agreed, in 1971, on steps towards a *European Economic and Monetary Union* (E.M.U.). According to this, their member currencies were allowed to fluctuate but not to diverge by more than $2\frac{1}{4}\%$ from their cross-parities. Thus, the agreed E.E.C. $2\frac{1}{4}\%$ band represented a 'snake' in the $4\frac{1}{2}\%$ Smithsonian 'tunnel' (see Fig. 5.29).[3]

This problem became more acute when the U.K. adopted a floating exchange rate in June 1972, following great speculative movements against sterling. As a prospective member of the E.E.C., the U.K. was be expected to keep within the 'snake': yet her 'Smithsonian' parity had probably been fixed too high in December 1971. Thus, pressures by the E.E.C. upon the U.K. to stop floating and fix a new devalued parity, rather than float down to a more realistic level, were generally thought to be undesirable.[4]

---

[1] See P. Bareau, 'The case for exchange flexibility', *Stat.*, 26 Feb. 1965, pp. 595–6, and 'The convertible £', chart of foreign exchange market quotations of sterling from end-1959 to mid-1964, *The Times*, 20 July 1964. also see H. N. Goldstein, 'Further thoughts on floating exchange rates', *N.W.B.Q.R.*, Nov. 1970, and 'The politics of flexible exchange rates', *F.T.*, 28 April 1970.

[2] *F.T.*, 22 Sept. 1969 and 21 Jan. 1970; 'The slow crawl to flexibility', *F.T.*, 14 Sept. 1970.

[3] 'The retreat from Bretton Woods – the story so far', *loc. cit.*, pp. 14–18; 'New exchange rates', *E.P.R.*, 24, Feb. 1972; 'Europe's monetary union', *Econ.*, 21 Nov. 1970, pp. 71–2;·'Europe takes the tube', *Econ.*, 1 Jan. 1972, p. 21 (Survey); 'Can the snake escape?', *Econ.*, 24 June 1972, pp. 71–2; 'Saving the Emu from extinction', *Econ.*, 8 July 1972, pp. 13–14.

[4] 'Float free and low', and 'Floating into Europe', *Econ.*, 1 July 1972, pp. 13–15, 87–8.

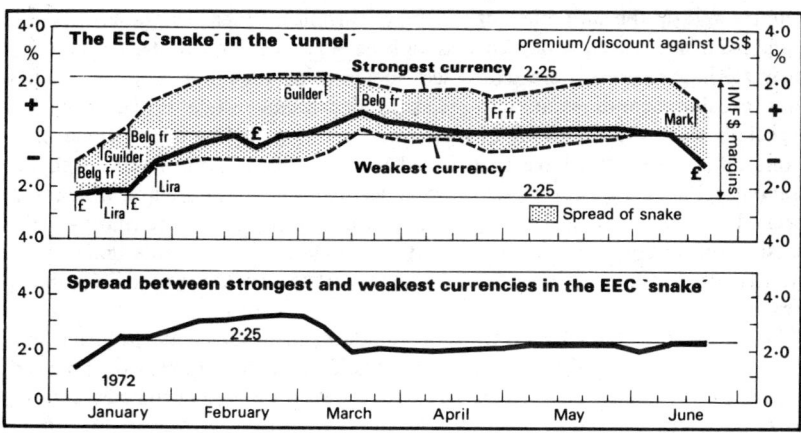

Fig. 5.29. *The E.M.U. 2¼% 'snake' in the Smithsonian 4½% 'tunnel', 1972*
(Source: *Econ.*, 24 June 1972, p. 71)

(b) Fixed exchange rate on the gold standard

In essence, the gold standard represents the fixing of a currency's price in terms of gold, which is internationally accepted as having an intrinsic value of its own. When the supply or demand conditions of that currency alter, its rate of exchange does not appreciate or depreciate because settlement of its balance of payments surplus or deficit is made in gold.

There are three main types of gold standard:

(i) *The Full Gold Standard.* This system, operating in Britain up to 1914, requires that the country's currency should be fully backed by gold, that it should have gold coins, and that its paper money should be fully convertible into gold, upon demand, at a bank. By law, the central bank must buy and sell gold at a fixed price and there must be no restriction on the import and export of gold. Changes in the demand for and supply of gold would not, therefore, affect its price, but would affect the amount of currency in the country.

(ii) *The Gold Bullion Standard.* This system, operating in Britain from 1925 to 1931, differs from the full gold standard in that no gold coins are minted and paper money is convertible only in large sums, for gold bars or bullion (of 400 oz units in Britain). This system is cheaper to operate, as it avoids the cost of minting and replacing gold coins. Also there is a reduced likelihood of the country's paper money being presented for conversion into gold. This imparts a little more stability to the central bank's gold reserves.

(iii) *The Gold-Exchange Standard.* This system, operating in the Scandinavian countries from 1925 to 1931 (whilst Britain was on the gold bullion standard), involves the backing of a country's currency not by gold reserves but by the currency of another country which is itself on the gold standard. The Scandinavian countries held reserves of sterling. The main advantages lie in the fact that reserve stocks of a foreign currency are cheaper to keep than are gold stocks (which must be guarded), and, if invested in securities of the gold standard 'base' country, they also earn interest. The main disadvantage lies in the fact that a country operating this system is dependent on the monetary policy of the 'base' country and on the soundness of the 'base' currency. When Britain left the gold standard in 1931 sterling depreciated and the Scandinavian countries found that their sterling reserves were worth less in terms of gold and other currencies, thus causing Scandinavian currencies to depreciate. Since World War II – especially since the beginning of free convertibility in 1958 – international non-Communist currencies have been based on a modified form of gold exchange standard. They have been based on reserves of sterling[1] and dollars, which were backed to the extent of 25% by gold. In the context of the international discussion on liquidity and the U.K. and U.S. balance of payments deficits, this system was severely criticised in February, 1965, by General de Gaulle of France.[2]

When two countries are on the gold standard, their currencies will each have a fixed value in terms of a given quantity of gold of a certain quality (or fineness). There will thus be a fixed rate of exchange between the two currencies, referred to as the mint (gold coin) or bullion (gold bar) parity of exchange. From 1925 to 1931 1 fine ounce of gold was priced at $20·67 in the U.S.A. and £4·2477 in Britain. Thus the mint (or bullion) parity of exchange between sterling and dollars was $20·67 to £4·2477 or $4·87 to £1.

The statement that a currency on the gold standard cannot appreciate or depreciate because gold flows in or out must be qualified. According to such factors as distance, there will be certain charges for transporting, guarding and insuring gold. Thus if the cost of moving gold between Eldorado and Utopia represented 2% of the price of gold, it would pay those two countries to allow their currencies to fluctuate in terms of each other by an equivalent amount, and to offer and accept currency instead of gold. For example, if Utopia were a deficit country it would not allow U to depreciate more than that amount because it would be cheaper to pay in gold, with a 2% charge. The limits to depreciation and appreciation are termed, respectively, the gold (or specie, or bullion) export and import points.

In theory, the gold standard results in an automatic balancing of a country's payments position. The workings of this process are as follows:

If Utopia (perhaps because of rising internal prices) imports from the rest of the world more than it exports, there would at first be pressures on U (increase in supply) making for its depreciation. The Utopian importer, however, instead of buying foreign currency with what would have been depreciated U, prefers to buy gold from Utopian banks at the fixed price and to send gold to his suppliers. This causes gold to flow out of Utopia, and this has repercussions on Utopian internal economic policy, because the currency is backed by gold reserves. Therefore the quantity of currency is reduced in Utopia. This reduces the banking system's ability to make loans or advances (bank credit), raises interest rates and causes a restriction in borrowing and investment. The level of activity will be reduced by this deflationary process, thus depressing employment, costs and prices in Utopia. As a result of lower prices, foreign demand for Utopian goods will rise, causing an increase in her exports. At the same time, lower incomes and activity will reduce Utopian demand for imports. Thus Utopia will reverse the balance of payments deficit, until she is in equilibrium.

---

[1] 'Sterling as a "key" currency', *M.B.R.*, Aug. 1963, pp. 3–12.
[2] *D.T.*, 5 Feb. 1965; G. S. Relph, 'Gold – a short cut to liquidity', *Stat.*, 25 Dec., 1964, pp. 843–4; P. Bareau, 'Gold and its alternatives', *Stat.*, 16 Oct. 1964, pp. 169–70.

Similarly, a surplus would lead to a net inflow of gold, more currency, more credit easier borrowing, higher investment and activity, competition for labour and other resources, higher wages and other costs, higher prices, reduced exports and increased demand for imports, until the surplus disappeared (see Fig. 5.30).

The main advantages of the gold standard are threefold. First, the 'automatic' process causes changes in the external payments position to react upon the internal economy, which in turn restores external payments equilibrium. Secondly, international trade is facilitated because rates of exchange are stable, thus reducing the likelihood of exchange speculation, market instability and the withholding of transactions, orders, etc. Furthermore, as gold is the medium of payment, debits may be cancelled against equal credits, without gold having to move. Thirdly, the fact that internal currency is backed by gold reduces the

(a) DEFICIT

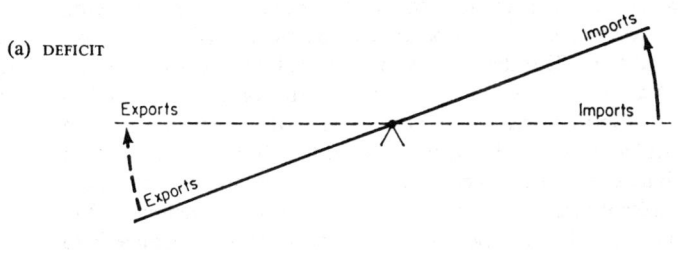

(1) *Result*
1. Pressure on currency to depreciate.
2. Importer purchases gold at fixed price and sends it abroad.
3. Gold flows *out*.
4. Currency and credit restricted. Higher rate of interest.
5. *Lower* investment, employment wages, costs, *prices* (deflation).

(2) *Remedy*
1. *Lower prices* → rise in exports.
2. *Lower incomes* → fall in imports.
3. Exports > Imports.
4. Gold flows *in*, and pressure on currency to depreciate ceases.

(b) SURPLUS

(1) *Result*

1. Gold flows *in*.
2. Currency and credit, expand. Lower rate of interest.
3. *Higher* investment, employment, wages, costs, *prices* (inflation).

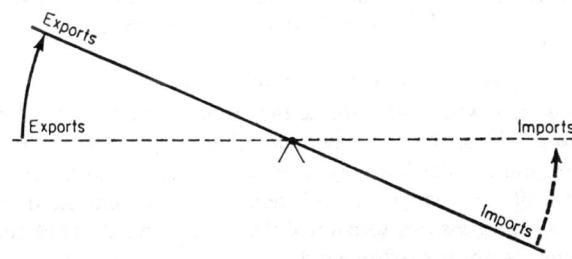

(2) *Remedy*
1. *Higher incomes* → rise in imports.
2. *Higher prices* → fall in exports.
3. Imports > Exports.
4. Gold flows *out*, and pressure on currency to appreciate ceases.

Fig. 5.30. '*Automatic*' *restoration of balance of payments equilibrium with the gold standard*

possibility of 'paper inflation', caused by a government's reckless increase in the note issue.

The main disadvantages of the gold standard are fivefold. First, if a deficit requires a deflationary internal policy, this may not be achieved because of the difficulty encountered in trying to reduce wages, because of trade union opposition, etc. Secondly, a country must surrender control over its internal economic policy to the exigencies of the external payments position. This may prove to be politically and socially unpopular. A country in deficit would be expected to follow a deflationary policy even if there were already unemployment; if in surplus it would be expected to follow an inflationary policy even though full employment might already prevail. Thirdly, 'hot' gold may flow from Utopia to Eldorado for speculative reasons, to earn high interest in 'deficit' Eldorado. Such 'hot' flights may upset Utopia's economy. Fourthly, internal economic expansion and growth in a gold standard country depend upon a gold backing for its currency and credit. Because of a balance of payments deficit gold may be in short supply, and this will restrict the country's ability to expand. Fifthly, a country may fix its exchange rate unrealistically in terms of gold. If it under-values its currency, its export prices will appear to be low, and exports may be high: import prices will appear to be high, and imports may be low. The resultant 'chronic' surplus will be an embarrassment to other countries, and may stimulate inflation and high internal prices. If it overvalues its currency, as Britain did in 1925, its exports will suffer, being expensive to outsiders. This will oblige it to follow a deflationary, unpopular policy, in an attempt to lower wages, costs and prices. The measures required might prove to be inexpedient. Britain, in fact, found it necessary to abandon the gold standard in 1931. Other countries gradually followed suit. A chronic surplus or deficit may be tackled by revaluation or devaluation, respectively, but these measures are unpopular because they involve national currency prestige; they undermine the international stability of the exchange rate pattern; they may be countered by retaliatory action by other countries; or they may induce speculation in further movements, undermining international confidence in the currency concerned.[1]

(c) Fixed exchange rate with exchange control

If a country wishes to stabilise the exchange rate for its currency, to avoid the unpredictability of the freely fluctuating rate, but wishes to avoid the 'tyranny' of the gold standard, it may adopt a form of exchange control.

Basically, exchange control represents the maintenance of exchange rate stability by measures to control the supply and demand conditions, where the currency is not backed by gold.

Many countries introduced some form of exchange control during the 1930s, when the rigid gold standard was abandoned and while the earlier chaos of free rates was still remembered. An important aspect of exchange control is whether or not the rate of exchange fixed upon is *realistic*. If it is not, there will be additional difficulties in controlling supply and demand conditions. In the case of New Zealand, the currency was undervalued, to make its export prices appeal to outsiders. This sort of action makes imports relatively dear, thus penalising consumers of imported goods and services, but tending to encourage a balance of payments surplus. If successful, the currency will be 'hard' or

1 'Gold over a decade – supplies and marketing since 1954', *M.B.R.*, Nov. 1964, pp. 3–9.

strong. In the case of Germany the currency was overvalued, partly to make its imports cheaper, partly to bolster internal confidence and international prestige, and partly to reduce the real cost of Germany's invisible imports (in the shape of debt payments to foreign individuals and governments). Such action makes exports relatively dear and harder to sell, thus tending to encourage a balance of payments deficit. The currency will be under constant pressure, and will be termed 'soft' or weak. Stringent methods are required to limit imports (visible and invisible) by such means as import restrictions on all but essential goods, by restrictions on foreign currency allowances for tourists, and by controls on 'hot' money flights and on investments abroad.

In general, one might say that the degree of exchange control rigidity – the number and stringency of regulations and other measures required to maintain the exchange rate – will depend on two main factors:

(i) Whether or not the exchange rate fixed upon is realistic, in relation to the supply and demand conditions in the international foreign exchange markets.
(ii) The ease with which imports and exports can be kept in balance. With over-valuation, for example, it may be very difficult to boost exports, whilst at the same time it may be just as difficult to restrict imports, especially of essential food and raw materials. Even with undervaluation there may not necessarily be a balance of payments surplus, because foreign demand for exports may be fairly stable or inelastic (unresponsive to the relative cheapness of the exported goods), and home demand for imports (if essential food and raw materials) may likewise be unresponsive to their relatively high price.

When Britain abandoned the gold standard in 1931 she let the exchange rate fluctuate freely, until it stabilised in mid-1932 at about 70% of its gold standard value. Several Commonwealth and other countries 'pegged' their currencies to sterling, forming the 'sterling bloc'. In June 1932 a Government fund was established by the Treasury, operated by the Bank of England. This was the Exchange Equalisation Account and its purpose was to check undue fluctuations in the exchange rate for sterling by intervening in the foreign exchange market, thus influencing supply and demand conditions. The original value of the fund was over £500 million. It was assumed that the sterling exchange rate was 'realistic', and that its supply and demand conditions were fairly stable, reflecting a general balance of payments equilibrium. The purpose of the Account was to counteract 'undue' fluctuations, caused not by import and export changes but by speculative and other capital fluctuations. The method was as follows: if the demand for sterling abroad rose (investments in, and 'hot' flights to the sterling bloc, etc.), the Account would sell sterling in return for foreign currencies. Similarly, if capital flowed out of the sterling bloc into non-sterling countries (causing the supply of sterling to exceed the supply of foreign currencies), the Account would sell some of its holdings of foreign currencies. This system represented a very mild form of exchange control, and when the U.S.A. and France followed suit in 1936, concluding an agreement with Britain on common action, consultation, and support for each other's currency by the sale and purchase of balances for gold, it developed into a simplified modification of the gold standard.

At the outbreak of World War II the Government found it necessary to impose a rigid system of exchange control, for two main reasons. First, foreign trade could not be allowed to operate freely during wartime, nor could capital be allowed to 'flee' the country, thus weakening the sterling exchange rate. Secondly, while imports of food, raw materials, armaments, etc. had to be kept up, resources could not easily be devoted to exports. Consequently, the pound was overvalued, to reduce the import and loan debt burden. As a result, stringent measures had to be taken to control the supply and demand conditions of sterling and foreign currency. These included registration, with the Bank of England, of all holdings of gold and foreign currency and foreign investments, and strict import and export quotas. Sterling was no longer freely convertible into other currencies, and the sterling area (formerly the sterling bloc) became a formally defined currency area for foreign exchange purposes (i.e. sterling earnings by foreigners were 'blocked', and had to be spent in the sterling area).[1]

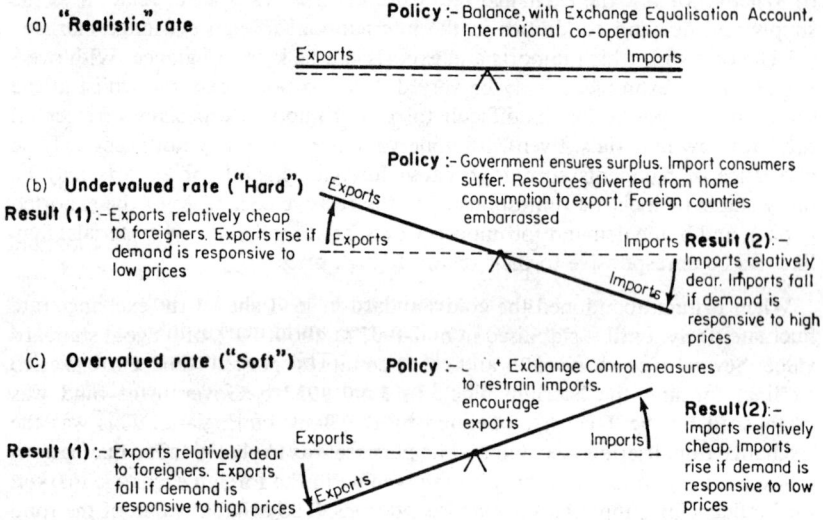

Fig. 5.31. *Balance of payments equilibrium with a fixed rate of exchange supported by exchange control*

After World War II the system was retained, with an overvalued pound, and was consolidated in the 1947 Exchange Control Act. In 1949 sterling was devalued from a parity of $4·03 to $2·80, in an attempt to stimulate exports, reduce imports and bring about a payments equilibrium.[2] Gradually restrictions on visible and invisible transactions have been lifted. The Foreign Exchange Market (195 authorised banks and nine firms of brokers) is still subject to exchange control regulations governing the purchase and sale of foreign currencies, but its activities increased greatly after the introduction of external convertibility for sterling (and other European currencies) in December 1958. An outline of exchange controls on capital movements by sterling area members

1 *Brit. O.H.*, 1963, pp. 409, 427–8, 432–3, 436.
2 A. Shonfield, *British Economic Policy Since the War*, Penguin Books, 1959, p. 200.

has been given in Stage I, Section 14(*a*).[1] Restrictions on foreign currency allowances for tourists have been lifted progressively; restrictions on visible exports to non-sterling countries have been reduced (they are permitted if paid for within six months); import control is now used primarily to ensure that foreign currency granted for imports is, in fact, used for that purpose.[2] The Exchange Equalisation Account is still in operation. It holds the United Kingdom gold and foreign currency reserves, buys and sells foreign exchange when appropriate and buys gold from the sterling area and elsewhere. It intervenes in the foreign exchange market both to prevent undue fluctuations in sterling's exchange value and to safeguard the ability to make payments abroad in foreign currencies. Fig. 5.31 illustrates the basic functioning of an exchange control system.

The system adopted by most countries since World War II has, in fact, been a *dollar standard*, a modified form of *gold-exchange standard*, in which the U.S. dollar – its price fixed in terms of gold and (originally) largely backed by gold reserves – was the 'anchor' or key 'reserve' currency. I.M.F. member currencies, backed by exchange control measures, were given fixed parities in terms of dollars, and the U.S. was committed to uphold the gold value of the dollar by freely converting dollars into gold. After the sterling devaluation of November 1967 a wave of speculation against the dollar – reflected in private hoardings of gold, exchanged for convertible dollars – led to a change in U.S. policy. Since 1961 the U.S., U.K. and some other countries had operated a 'gold pool' on the London market, whereby the price of gold on world markets was kept steady at $35 per fine ounce. With the *Washington Agreement* of March 1968 the gold pool arrangements were ended: henceforth, the U.S. would sell gold at the official price only to central banks, and convertibility of the dollar into gold ceased to be guaranteed to other parties. As a result, a free world market in gold developed alongside the fixed-price central bank market. This was known as the *two-tier gold system*, whereby the central banks agreed not to convert their dollars into gold, except for respectable, official monetary reasons. In August 1971, following renewed speculative pressure on the dollar, continuing balance of payments deficits and a deficiency in gold stocks, as compared with overseas dollar holdings, of $37½ billion, the U.S. ceased converting dollars into gold, except in the interests of monetary stability. This suspension of dollar convertibility led to the virtual suspension of the gold-exchange standard system and to a period of floating currencies: one of the main foundation stones of the postwar fixed parity system had disappeared. Despite concerted efforts to restore fixed parities, a definite 'adjustment process' could be discerned, which may involve many and frequent changes in the pattern of parities and may even lead to a more than temporary experimentation with floating rates.[3]

---

[1] Also see 'Exchange control', *F.T.*, 17 Dec. 1969; 'Is exchange control worth the effort?', *S.T.*, 4 Feb. 1968; 'Exchange control', *Brit. O.H.*, 1972, p. 368.

[2] *Brit. O.H.*, 1972, p. 368.

[3] 'The major currencies', *Conjoncture*, 188, Aug. 1969; 'The retreat from Bretton Woods – the story so far', *loc. cit.*, pp. 13–18; 'Progress in international monetary co-operation'. *loc. cit.*, pp. 15–16; A. L. Lougheed, 'International economic relations – past and future', *loc. cit.*, pp. 36–7; G. Haberler, 'Prospects for the dollar standard', *L.B.R.*, July 1972; H. G. Johnson, 'The Bretton Woods system, key currencies, and the "dollar crisis" of 1971', *T.B.R.*, June 1972.

3. Economic Policy for Balance of Payments and Employment Problems with a Fixed Exchange Rate

In the preceding section the problems of a fixed exchange rate were somewhat simplified by referring to the criterion of the 'realistic' rate. It was pointed out that this rate was such as would equate the international demand for a currency with its supply. In other words, the values of imports and exports would be equal. If, at such a rate, imports and exports could be kept in balance, then the rate would continue to be 'realistic'. If imports subsequently exceeded exports, as in Fig. 5.31(c), the currency would be 'under pressure', 'soft', or overvalued. Alternatively, if exports exceeded imports, as in Fig. 5.31(b), the currency would be 'hard' or undervalued.

Sometimes the balance of payments deficit or surplus might be caused by internal conditions – an inflationary level of economic activity or a deflationary level, which, respectively, cause prices to rise or fall. Such internal conditions would affect the prices of exports and thus their volume and value. The rate of exchange could probably be maintained by the adoption of an internal economic policy to deflate or inflate (e.g. by raising or lowering interest rates), which would tend to lower or raise internal prices. The dangers here, however, would lie in taking excessive measures which might result in extreme fluctuations in the level of activity – i.e. a ponderous 'stop-go' economic policy.

Sometimes, however, a balance of payments deficit (as in Fig. 5.31(c)) or surplus (as in Fig. 5.31(b)) may be 'chronic', seemingly insoluble by means of internal economic policy decisions. For example, there may be a balance of payments deficit whilst a low level of economic activity prevails at home. If an internal deflationary policy were carried out, in order to lower prices and stimulate exports, the internal economic 'slump' situation would be aggravated. The internal position would call for an inflationary policy for full employment, but this would raise prices and aggravate the balance of payments deficit. Alternatively, a balance of payments surplus might be achieved even with a high, inflationary level of internal economic activity. If an internal deflationary policy were embarked upon, this would tend to lower internal prices, increase exports, and further increase the balance of payments surplus, to the added embarrassment of other countries. In both these cases, therefore, the basic cause of the deficit or surplus would be of a monetary nature, due to a faulty exchange rate, and would not be due primarily to the internal level of economic activity. In such cases the country concerned might have to devalue (if in chronic deficit, with low internal activity) or revalue (if in chronic surplus, with high internal activity). The extent and success of devaluation or revaluation would depend largely on world *elasticity of demand* for the country's exports and on its *elasticity of demand* for imports.[1] An interesting finding in a recent study[2] on the results of U.K. devaluation in 1967 was the relatively high exchange rate (or price) *responsiveness* of invisible services and the relatively low price responsiveness of goods. As regards imports of goods, despite the expected low responsiveness of fuel and basic materials imports, manufactures constitute about one-

[1] With regard to devaluation, a deficit would, according to the Marshall-Lerner theory, be rectified if the *sum* of the elasticities of demand for imports and exports is *greater* than one (see van Meerhaeghe, *op. cit.*, pp. 67–8.) This problem is analysed in Chapter 11, II, (A) 4.
[2] National Institute of Economic and Social Research (N.I.E.S.R.), 'The effects of the devaluation of 1967 on the current balance of payments', *E.J.* (Supplement), March 1972, esp. pp. 462–4.

third of goods imports and would be expected to be sensitive to price (exchange rate) changes: nevertheless, the implied elasticity of demand (or price sensitivity) for imports was found to be only $\frac{1}{4}$ rather than within the range of $\frac{1}{2}$ to 1, generally assumed at the time of devaluation. With regard to goods exports, these were found to have an elasticity of demand of only 1·4, rather than of 2 or 3, as had been assumed at and prior to devaluation.[1]

Figure 5.32 illustrates in a simplified manner the four main balance of payments problems, in conjunction with a particular internal economic situation. Each problem is analysed as being 'orthodox' (with internal causes) or as being due to an external monetary (exchange rate) 'crisis'. The relevant internal or external measures required to remedy the problem are then given.

When the U.K. devalued sterling by 14·3% in November 1967, this had followed a period of severe deflationary measures–designed to reduce domestic demand, free resources for export and stem the outflow of 'hot' money. Yet the unemployment level was high (about 2·4%), there was a big margin of unused capacity in the economy, 'hot' money continued to flow out, and the current balance was worsening. The devaluation was accompanied by an increase in Bank Rate, restrictions on home demand and reductions in public expenditure, to divert resources to exports, and by a continuation of the prices and incomes policy. The cut in the parity was kept down to 14·3% (as compared with the 30% devaluation in 1949) by reason of substantial international borrowings and in order not to oblige other major competitors to devalue in competition. Furthermore, most of the countries which also devalued (and there were fewer than in 1949) were primarily *suppliers* to the U.K., rather than *customers:* this tended to keep down the rise in import prices.[2]

The U.S. 'package' of August 1971 effectively led to a devaluation of the dollar, as against other currencies, which floated upwards (until the Smithsonian Agreement of December 1971 again fixed the parities). It had been preceded by a continuing balance of payments deficit, due not so much to a visible deficit as to a capital outflow (in Government spending on the Vietnam war, on massive direct investment overseas and on continued speculative pressures against the dollar). Apart from suspending dollar convertibility, a three-month 'freeze' was imposed on prices, rents, wages and salaries, an import surcharge was imposed, and overseas aid was cut down.[3]

When the U.K. abandoned the 'Smithsonian' fixed parity for sterling in June 1972, there had previously been a sudden rush out of sterling; an uncontrolled wage inflation; steadily worsening U.K. export prices, relative to the rest of the world; a worsening trade deficit; unused resources, represented by the continuing high level of unemployment and the reluctance of industry to invest. Some of the main trends are shown in Fig. 5.33. Speculation against sterling was possibly

[1] See 'Britain's payments choices', *Econ.*, 19 March 1966, pp. 1143–4, for a resumé of the symposium in the *Scottish Journal of Political Economy*, February 1966; Sir Alec Cairncross, ed., *Britain's Economic Prospects Reconsidered*, 1971, pp. 80–92.
[2] A. Day, 'The sterling crisis', *Obs.*, 19 Nov. 1967; 'Business brief' and 'Where 10% counts', *Econ.*, 25 Nov. 1967, pp. 864–5 and 878–81; 'What devaluation means', *D.E.A. Pr. Rep. Econ.*, 35, Dec. 1967; B. J. Cohen, *Balance-of-payments Policy*, 1969, esp. pp. 143–9; 'Devaluation – for the record', *M.B.R.*, Feb. 1968.
[3] 'Background to the dollar crisis', *Obs.*, 9 May 1971; 'New strategy, new pieties' and 'When the dollar was devalued', *Econ.*, 21 Aug. 1971, pp. 39, 53–61; H. N. Goldstein, 'The US deficit – who cares?', *N.W.B.Q.R.*, May 1970; D. C. Redding, 'Closing the U.S. payments gap', *L.B.R.*, April 1967.

External Position (Balance of Payments)	Internal Position (Level of activity)	Type of Problem	Remedy
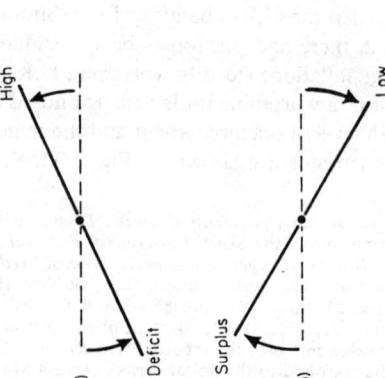		**Orthodox:** *Internal* (i) Inflationary pressure on factors of production. Prices too high. Exports low. (e.g. U.K. in 1960 and 1969.) (ii) Interest rates too low. 'Hot' money flows OUT to earn high interest elsewhere.	**Internal measures** (i) Increase productivity, to lower prices and boost exports. (ii) Deflationary policy; high rates of interest; 'credit squeeze'; high taxation, etc., to *reduce consumption, lower prices and raise exports.* Also, 'hot' money will flow IN.
		Orthodox: internal. (i) Slack in the economy. Prices fairly low. Exports high. (e.g. U.K. in 1958 and 1971.) (ii) Interest rates too high. 'Hot' money flows IN to earn high interest.	*Internal measures* Reflationary policy; low rates of interest; 'easy money' policy; low taxation, etc., to *increase consumption.* This will tend to *raise prices and reduce exports.* Also, 'hot' money will flow OUT.

External Position
(Balance of Payments)

Internal Position
(Level of activity)

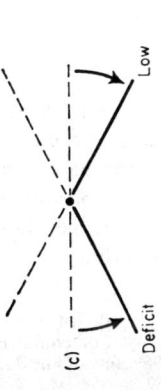

(c)

Low

Deficit

(d)

High

Surplus

Type of Problem

Monetary crisis: external
(i) Drain on reserves, due to too much capital investment abroad, or too much Government aid and/or military spending abroad. (e.g. U.S.A. in 1960 and 1971; U.K. in 1964.)

(ii) Currency *overvalued*, causing export prices to be too high, despite slack in the internal economy. (e.g. U.K. in 1949, 1967 and 1972.)

Monetary crisis: external
Embarrassment to rest of world because currency *undervalued*, causing exports to appear cheap to foreign countries and imports to be expensive. (e.g. West Germany in 1961 and 1969; Japan in 1971.)

Remedy

External measures
(i) Stop or reduce drain, e.g. by cutting foreign aid and/or military expenditure abroad.

(ii) *Devalue*, to make exports cheaper for foreign countries, and to make imports more expensive.

External measures
(i) *Revalue*, to increase imports (which will be cheaper) and to reduce exports (which will be more expensive).
(ii) Increase financial aid to foreign countries.

Fig. 5.32. *Economic policy for balance of payments and employment problems with a fixed exchange rate system*

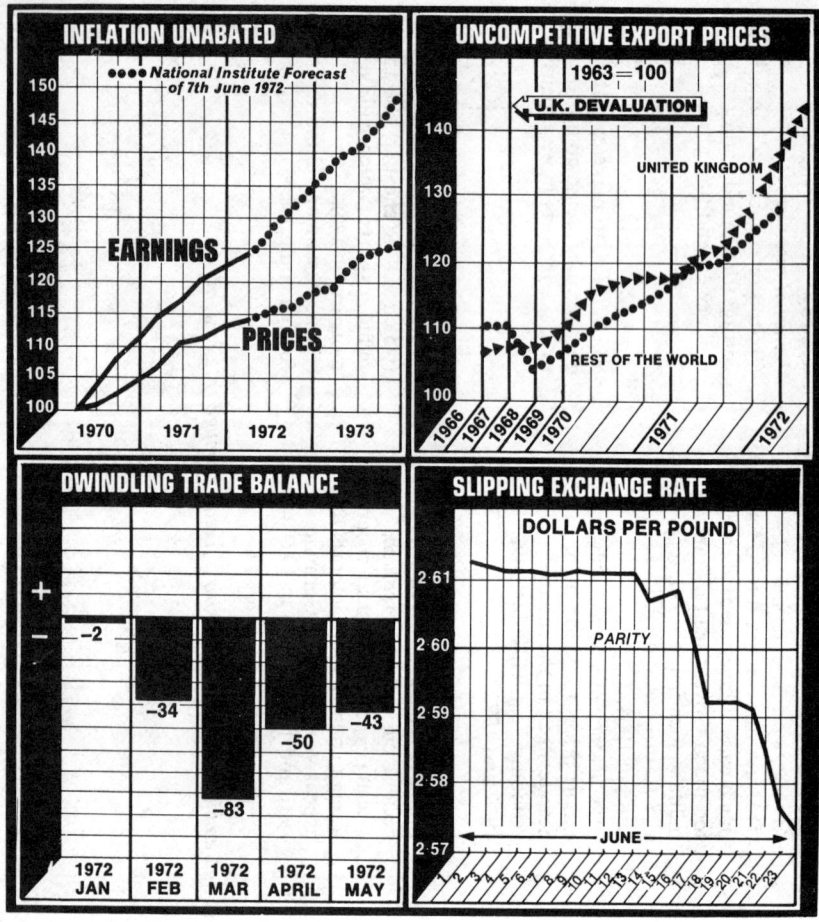

Fig. 5.33. *Factors behind the 1972 abandonment of a fixed sterling parity* (Source: *Obs.*, 25 June 1972)

perennial difficulty in controlling the flow of private international balances of 'hot' money, rendered much more volatile by the ability of multinational companies to switch funds to the most profitable centres. As has been mentioned previously, the decision to float was accompanied by the imposition of exchange control restrictions on the sterling area, ostensibly to prevent speculative outflows through sterling area currencies not directly linked to sterling.[1]

---

[1] See 'Floating: the real causes of the crisis', *F.T.*, 29 June 1972; 'Float free and low', *Econ.*, 1 July 1972, pp. 13–16; 'Floating into Europe', *ibid.*, pp. 87–8. For comments on the revaluations of the West German deutschmark in 1961 and 1969 and of the Japanese yen in 1971, see 'German revaluation: mark two', *Econ.*, 1 Nov. 1969, pp. 58–9; *F.T.*, 5 Nov. 1969· 'The rising yen', *Econ.*, 4 Sept. 1971, pp. 57–9.

4. Further Reading and Sources

Footnote references to daily and weekly journals are not repeated.

J. BHAGWATI, ed., *International Trade*. Penguin. 1969.

SIR ALEC CAIRNCROSS, *Britain's Economic Prospects Reconsidered*. Allen & Unwin. 1971.

B. J. COHEN, *Balance-of-payments Policy*. Penguin. 1969.

R. N. COOPER, ed., *International Finance*. Penguin. 1969.

'Currency crisis – but not for sterling', *M.B.R.* May 1972.

A. DAY, *ABC of International Finance*. B.B.C. 1968.

'Devaluation – for the record', *M.B.R.* Feb. 1968.

E. DEVONS, 'Understanding international trade', *Economica*. Nov. 1961.

F. ELLIOTT and M. SUMMERSKILL, *A Dictionary of Politics*. Penguin, 1961.

A. E. FAREED, 'Human-capital intensity of U.S. trade', *E.J.* June 1972.

H. N. GOLDSTEIN, 'The U S deficit – who cares?', *N.W.B.Q.R.* May 1970.

H. N. GOLDSTEIN, 'Further thoughts on floating exchange rates', *N.W.B.Q.R.* Nov. 1970.

H. G. GRUBEL, *The International Monetary System*. Penguin. 1969.

G. HABERLER, 'Prospects for the dollar standard', *L.B.R.* July 1972.

G. HABERLER, *Money in the International Economy*. Hobart Paper 31. I.E.A. 1965.

H. R. HELLER, *International Trade*. Prentice-Hall. 1968.

P. B. KENEN, *International Economics*, Prentice-Hall. 1967.

LLOYDS BANK. *L.B.R.* July 1963.

M. A. G. van MEERHAEGHE, *International Economic Institutions*. Longmans. 1966.

F. V. MEYER, D. C. CORNER and J. E. S. PARKER, *Problems of a Mature Economy*. Macmillan. 1970.

MIDLAND BANK. *M.B.R.* Aug. 1962; Aug. 1963; Nov. 1964.

NATIONAL INSTITUTE OF ECONOMIC AND SOCIAL RESEARCH (N.I.E.S.R.), 'The effects of the devaluation of 1967 on the current balance of payments', *E.J.* (Supplement). March 1972.

S. A. OŻGA, *The Rate of Exchange and the Terms of Trade*. Weidenfeld & Nicolson. 1969.

S. POLLARD, *The Gold Standard and Employment Policies Between the Wars*. Methuen. 1970.

W. B. REDDAWAY, 'Was $4·86 inevitable in 1925?', *L.B.R.* April 1970.

D. C. REDDING, 'Closing the U.S. payments gap', *L.B.R.* April 1967.

TREASURY, 'The foreign exchange market', *E.P.R.*, 20, Oct. 1971.; 'New exchange rates', *E.P.R.*, 24, Feb. 1972.

S. J. WELLS, *International Economics*. Allen & Unwin. 1969.

5. Past Examination Questions

1. Discuss the importance of the concept of comparative costs in economic analysis. (Summer 1954)
2. 'If one country is more efficient than another in all fields of production, no trade between them is possible.' Discuss. (Summer 1960)
3. 'The international exchange of commodities is a substitute for the international movement of factors of production.' Discuss. (January 1963)

4. Why does one find comparative cost differences between countries? (Summer 1963)

5. Why are there differences in comparative costs of production in different countries? (Summer 1958)

6. What factors should decide the proportion of a country's food supply which is home-produced? (Summer 1960)

7. 'The reasons for specialisation between individuals are essentially the same as the reasons for international trade.' Discuss. (January 1964)

8. 'International trade takes place because each country is differently endowed with resources.' 'International trade takes place because comparative costs of production differ amongst countries.' Are these explanations contradictory? Explain your answer. (Summer 1964)

9. In Malanesia a unit of resources will produce either 100 yards of cloth or 20 units of steel. In Indolaysia a unit of resources will produce 90 yards of cloth or 15 units of steel. Explain the effects of international trade on production of each of the commodities in each country. (January 1965)

10. How does international trade make possible a higher material standard of life? (Summer 1953)

11. What are the factors determining the United Kingdom's terms of trade? (Summer 1952)

12. Does an improvement in the United Kingdom's terms of trade necessarily improve her balance of trade? Explain your answer. (Summer 1960)

13. What are the terms of trade? What is the relationship between the terms of trade and the balance of trade? (January 1963)

14. What is meant by a 'favourable' movement of the Terms of Trade? Is such a movement necessarily desirable? (Summer 1963)

15. What are the possible effects of a change in the terms of trade on the Balance of Payments? (January 1964)

16. What are the advantages and disadvantages of free trade? (Summer 1959)

17. 'The full advantages of international trade can only be reaped if there is free multilateral trade.' Discuss. (Summer 1956)

18. 'When the competitive advantage of foreign goods is due to lower wage rates, tariffs should be imposed to equalise the price of home and imported goods to remove this unfair advantage.' Examine this statement critically. (Summer 1959)

19. Consider the argument that tariffs are justified if their purpose is to 'equalise the cost of production at home and abroad'. (Summer 1961)

20. 'If wages were equal in all countries, then international trade could take place on a fair basis.' Comment. (Summer 1962)

21. 'Raising Japanese wages to U.K. levels would improve U.K. export prospects and improve Japanese living standards at the same time.' Comment. (Summer 1962)

22. 'The duty on fuel oil imported into the United Kingdom should be raised in view of the difficulties which these imports are creating for the United Kingdom's coal industry.' Comment. (Summer 1960)

23. Discuss the relative merits of import duties and subsidies on production as methods of assisting British agriculture. (Summer 1958)

24. 'The more protective are import duties, the less revenue they yield.' Discuss (Summer 1958)

25. By what policy measures can the Government influence the volume of car exports from the United Kingdom? (Summer 1959)

26. To what extent and by what policy measures can a government influence the flow of imports from individual countries? (Summer 1959)

27. 'Tariffs should only be placed on commodities the demand for which is inelastic.' Discuss. (January 1965)

28. What are invisible exports *and* invisible imports? Give examples of both and discuss their relative importance for the United Kingdom. (Summer 1959)

29. What factors determine the level of U.K. exports in any year? (January 1964)

30. Outline the broad changes in the composition of United Kingdom exports over the last fifty years. What is the relationship between these changes and those in the industrial structure of the United Kingdom over the same period? (January 1965)

31. Imports and exports play a much less important part in the American than in the British economy, but the average income per head is higher in the United States than in Great Britain. Does this mean that to raise our standard of living we should reduce our overseas trade? Discuss. (Summer 1959)

32. 'A large home market for a commodity stimulates exports of it.' 'The more of a commodity sold at home, the less there is for export abroad.' Discuss these two statements, and say whether you think they are compatible with one another. (Summer 1961)

33. Under what circumstances may a country continue to import goods of a greater value than the value of goods it exports? (Summer 1957)

34. How might a country continually export goods of greater value than the goods it imports, and yet be losing foreign exchange reserves? (Summer 1958)

35. If the balance of payments must always balance, how is it possible to have a balance of payments problem? (Summer 1959)

36. Is a persistently 'adverse' balance of payments on current account necessarily undesirable? Give reasons for your answer. (Summer 1962)

37. What is meant by the phrase 'Balance of Payments deficit'? What actions could be taken by a government to eliminate a deficit? (Summer 1961)

38. Describe and evaluate the main weapons available to a country seeking to remove an adverse balance of payments. (Summer 1964)

39. If the balance of payments must always balance, why is there any need for a government to take steps to balance it? (Summer 1952)

40. Describe how a balance of payments problem may occur even when there is a favourable balance of trade. (Summer 1960)

41. 'A country's balance of payments must always balance as a matter of book-keeping, so a balance of payments deficit is impossible.' Comment. (Summer 1962)

42. What effect would inflation in the U.S. be likely to have on the U.K. balance of payments? (Summer 1963)

43. How may a country have an adverse balance of payments and yet be exporting goods of a greater value than it is importing? (Summer 1963)

44. Why do countries sometimes borrow from abroad? In your answer distinguish short-term borrowing from long-term borrowing. (January 1964)

45. What is the sterling area and what advantages do countries derive from being members of it? (Summer 1954)

6. Money, Banking and the Capital Market Stage I

Everyone knows what is not money: it is more difficult to describe what money is. This chapter attempts to define and describe money and to show how the monetary system is managed. It introduces the student to some of the far-reaching economic implications of the demand, supply and management of money in a highly developed economic system, based as it is on the specialisation of labour and other factors in the production of goods and services, and on the complex pattern of exchange which ensues.

1. Barter and Money

At the dawn of history Man may have been self-sufficient, making his own primitive tools and weapons, and catering for his own elementary needs for food and clothing by hunting. Gradually, an individual would have noticed that he was better at making tools and weapons than others in his group or in other communities, whereas they might be more adept at hunting or making clothes. A system of 'swapping' or barter developed, which enabled Man to specialise to some extent, thus giving an impetus to the division of labour. The trade caravans of old; Phoenician purple cloth for Cornish tin; the exchange of salt and beads by explorers, against food, porters and guides from local tribesmen; the schoolboy's conker against his classmate's tin badge; these are some examples of the barter system of exchange.

However, there were severe drawbacks to efficiency in the barter system. If A has a cow to sell, and wants to buy small quantities of vegetables, clothing, tools, etc., he is faced first with the problem of finding several suitable suppliers who also want small amounts of meat and who wish to sell the things he wants. Then he is faced with the problem of dividing up his cow (so much for a club; so much for a cabbage, etc.) and he may be left with half a carcase, which will quickly depreciate in value. These drawbacks to barter may be summarised as:

(a) the improbability of exact coincidence of wants by direct exchange;
(b) the imperfect divisibility of different goods;
(c) the absence of any stable measurement of value;
(d) the gradual depreciation of some goods over the course of time.

Most communities eventually turned towards a common tool of exchange, which we call money. Henceforth, A will use units of money to buy his vegetables, etc. He will sell his entire cow to B for several units of money: B will in turn sell quantities of cow for various amounts of money. In this manner the 'exchange

468

barrier' was broken, opening up the way for indirect exchange and the further division of labour or specialisation, first by trades (hunters, shipbuilders, etc.), then by processes (tanners and cobblers; foresters and carpenters; shepherds, spinners, weavers and tailors), then by whole regions (Lancashire cotton; Yorkshire wool, etc.) and finally on an international scale (Britain for manu-factured goods; Canada for wheat; Ghana for cocoa; Malaya for rubber).

2. Functions of Money

In order to serve its prime function as an efficient tool or medium of exchange, money must perform certain other clear functions. First, it must serve as a 'unit of account'. This means that it must be able to represent a clearly recognisable unit of value which can be compared with all other goods, and in terms of which the relative prices or values of all other commodities may be judged. Secondly, it must serve as a 'store of value', by which is meant that money must have lasting properties. It must serve as a medium of exchange and unit of account not only now, but also in the future. Thirdly – as an extension of the other two functions – money must serve as a 'standard of deferred payments'. In other words, it must permit the future settlement of loans and other debts.

3. Properties of Money

Resulting from the need to fulfil its main functions efficiently, a satisfactory form of money should possess the following properties:

(a) The first and all-important property of money, which most clearly dis-tinguishes it from all other commodities, is that it should be generally acceptable as a medium of exchange. If we tried to purchase a packet of cigarettes in Utopia, using some windfall holiday 'money' in the form of Eldorado currency, we might very well be met by blank stares, to say the least.

(b) Stability of value is another important property, but the failure of some forms of money to achieve this property has been the cause of many a monetary headache.

(c) Recognisability: a definite form, appearance, pattern, name, etc.

(d) Homogeneity: the exact equivalence in value of one unit with another.

(e) Divisibility is another important property. Money is less efficient if it can only be used in large units. The debate on decimalisation of the British coinage in 1963 centred largely on this problem.

(f) Durability: the ability to retain its recognisable properties.

(g) Portability: the physical property of being easily transferable.

(h) Scarcity: If money were to be had for the picking by everyone, it would soon break down as a medium of exchange.

4. Forms of Money

Throughout the ages a wide variety of commodities has served, in various places in different circumstances, as money. Nevertheless all were (and sometimes still are) without doubt 'money', because in their particular time and place they were 'generally acceptable'. In some cases they had desirable properties or intrinsic value, and were sought after for their own sake. In all cases, however, their prime function as media of exchange made them desirable because they represented the power to purchase all manner of goods and services, at any time, which were themselves desirable. This, indeed, is the chief characteristic of money. It represents 'liquid' potential purchasing power. The Masai of Kenya use cattle as money (portable and recognisable, but not durable, divisible or really homogeneous); some South Sea Islanders used special round stone discs, punctured with holes, varying in size from a few inches to several feet in diameter (durable and recognisable and divisible, but not always portable or homogeneous); civilian and wartime prisoners have used cigarettes as money and schoolboys have used cigarette cards or foreign stamps.

All these forms of money, being deficient in one or more of the desirable properties, have consequently been less satisfactory media of exchange and have retarded the process of trade.

Since early times Man has been enchanted by the 'precious metals', gold and silver. Before the use of money they were sought after for decorative jewellery. Where it was relatively plentiful, as with the Aztecs, gold was largely used for decoration. Elsewhere their scarcity and attractiveness, plus the fact that they were easily divisible, portable, homogeneous, durable and recognisable, resulted in their being used as money. Gold and silver were sought after for their own sake; they therefore had intrinsic value[1] and were an ideal form of money. In Britain the State took over the function of 'coining' or stamping units of currency, first in silver and later in gold. Until the late eighteenth century Britain was on this bimetallic currency standard. All values were rendered in terms of silver or gold. Then silver, in short supply, became legal tender only up to a certain amount, leaving Britain on the 'gold standard' until 1931.

Gradually, however, other forms of money evolved, some of which had little or no intrinsic value and sometimes no actual physical existence. All, however, were generally acceptable and some, at first, could be exchanged for gold, on which they were based. Due to the process of wear and tear, gold and silver coins often came to have a metallic content lower than their face value; at other times dishonest people used to clip away shavings of precious metal coins; in others, dishonest kings 'debased' the coinage by introducing lead and other impurities, so that the resultant alloy coin was worth less than its nominal value. Later on 'token money' in the form of cupronickel coins came into use, whose intrinsic value was much lower than the nominal value which they represented. The general effect of these developments was that people withdrew and hoarded 'good' precious metal coins, and circulated debased or token coinage, thus giving rise to Gresham's Law (or dictum), the gist of which is that 'bad money drives out good'. A parallel development was the gradual use of paper money, which has no intrinsic value. At first this took the form of the 'deposit receipts', issued by goldsmiths when gold was lodged in their vaults. Eventually the goldsmiths were superseded by commercial banks, which issued their own equivalent, the bank note. This took the form of a note on which the banker 'promises to pay' the bearer. At first they were 'convertible', as the banker promised to pay the bearer an equivalent amount of gold. This promise was temporarily rescinded during the Napoleonic Wars. In fact, banks tended to issue notes in excess of the gold deposited with them – their gold backing – on the assumption that only a small proportion would ever be presented at once for exchange into gold. Many 'rushes' on the banks, due to rumours and panics, underlined the weakness of

[1] See 'Gold at work', *Econ.*, 23 Dec. 1967, pp. 1237–8; 'Meeting the silver shortage', *M.B.R.*, Aug. 1965.

this assumption. After the Bank Charter Act of 1844 the Bank of England gradually became the sole issuer of bank notes for England and Wales. The 'fiduciary' proportion, unbacked by gold, was strictly controlled by Parliament. The Scottish and Northern Ireland banks now have limited rights of note issue, but these issues – apart from amounts specified by legislation for each bank – must themselves be fully covered by holdings of Bank of England notes and coin.[1] Since Britain left the gold standard in 1931 almost the entire issue of bank notes has been fiduciary. Bank notes are now 'inconvertible', so that 'I promise to pay' is now a hollow phrase. What matters, however, is that the bank note is generally acceptable. Even the millionaire will think twice about lighting his cigar with a burning £5 note, however cheap paper may be.

By far the most important form of money in Britain, since the limitations on the paper issue imposed by the 1844 Act, is the bank deposit, which has no physical existence at all, other than as an ink mark on a bank ledger. Deposits, in fact, are the 'credit' granted to a bank's client. He transfers it to other people, if they are willing to accept it in this way, by writing out or 'drawing' a cheque in their favour. Most payments are nowadays made by drawing cheques upon these bank deposits. An interesting phenomenon occurred during the six-month Irish bank strike of 1970. Unofficial, 'homemade' cheques were widely drawn, accepted and negotiated. At the end of the strike it was estimated that about 15 million 'cheques' with a face value of £3,000 million were in the pipeline: many had been drawn and accepted without stating the bank branches at which the drawers' accounts were held, and it was thought that about £3 million worth of these cheques would turn out to be dud.[2]

Trade credit is to some extent another form of money, insofar as the book debts of one firm may be cancelled out against the book debts of another. This avoids the need to use coin, notes or bank deposits (cheques). Reciprocating book debts are thus a form of money acceptable to participating firms. It was noticeable, by the late 1960s, that each successive 'credit squeeze' or restriction on bank credit had the effect of stimulating an expansion of trade credit. This often took the form of 'extending' the period of time taken by trade customers to pay their bills and was found to bear very hardly on small and medium-sized suppliers, dependent on large customers.[3] Bills of Exchange were an early form of cheque, used by traders to transfer debts. Whereas a cheque is an instruction to a bank to pay at once, a bill of exchange is an instruction (to another trader who is in debt, or to a bank) to pay at a future date – usually up to three months. When 'negotiated' and made payable to others, bills of exchange were, in trade circles, as temporary money, acceptable in payment of trade debts. Nowadays they have been largely superseded in the home trade by cheques, but are still used in foreign trade. An interesting parallel to bills of exchange in U.S. banking takes the form of 'Certificates of Deposit'. These were introduced in 1961 as a means of enabling client firms and individuals to tap liquid funds without affecting the banks holding their accounts. They have a 'tenor' or life of from one to twelve months, are restricted to account holders with minimum deposits of $10,000 and are negotiable on the money market like any other bill, with the backing of the certificate holders' banks. Since October 1971 some U.K. banks have issued their own

[1] *Brit. O.H.*, 1972, p. 350.
[2] 'Irish banking: the longest day', *Econ.*, 21 Nov. 1970, pp. 87–8.
[3] 'Squeeze grips the big boys', *S.T.*, 26 May 1968.

negotiable sterling certificates of deposit, thereby operating in their own names in the 'complementary money markets'.[1] Another form of bill (representing the paying party's declared indebtedness and promise to pay) is the Treasury Bill, first initiated in 1877. They are issued by the Government in return for short-term loans from the banks and money market. As in the case of commercial bills of exchange, there is a ready market in which these bills are 'discounted' or bought for ready cash at a price below their value at maturity. Treasury and commercial bills are, therefore, a form of money which is less 'liquid' than ready cash in the form of precious metals, coins,[2] notes or bank deposits. Ultimately, of course, both types of bill mature, and have to be settled in notes, coin or deposits (cheques). It must be remembered that some of these forms of money are only 'generally acceptable' within certain circles. The only forms, known as 'legal tender', whose general acceptability is enforced by law, are Bank of England notes (up to any value) and coins up to limited values. Bank deposits, via cheques, have become almost universally accepted, but are not backed by the force of law. The 1960s saw significant developments, in the U.K. and especially in the United States, away from the physical handling of coinage and cheques. These took the form of various types of 'credit cards', permitting 'cashless' payment by a customer, on presentation of a bank credit card. These constitute a form of single-stage substitute money, which must eventually be backed by the transfer of bank deposits.[3] It is worthy of note that vagueness in the definition of 'money' has been blamed for giving rise to fears about the increase in the U.K. money supply in recent years. Much of the money supply, constituting part of the public's liquidity position, was in fact 'near money' (e.g. deposits with non-bank institutions), which were not considered as part of the 'active money' supply.[4]

We may summarise the various forms of money, as they have developed, as follows:

    (a) *'Generally acceptable' commodities*
    (b) *Precious metals*
      i. by weight;
      ii. in stamped and graded coins:
        'full standard'
        'token' – legal tender, with enforced acceptability
    (c) *Paper money*
      i. goldsmith's deposit receipts;
      ii. bank notes:
        'convertible'
        'inconvertible' or 'fiduciary' or 'token' – legal tender with enforced
                      acceptability

---

[1] 'The American banks', *Conjoncture*, 125, March 1970; A. R. Bennett, 'American commercial banking: the changing scene', *L.B.R.*, July 1971, esp. pp. 43–4; 'Banking enters a new era', *M.B.R.*, May 1972, p. 13.
[2] For further data on the post-1968 U.K. decimal currency and the amounts, uses and locations of the coinage, see 'Decimal currency', *D.E.A. Pr. Rep. Econ.*, 40, May 1968 and 'Coinage', *E.P.R.*, 21, Nov. 1971.
[3] '"Cashless society" in Five Years', *D.T.*, 12 Aug. 1966; 'The cashless society comes closer', *F.T.*, 6 Oct. 1972; 'Credit cards', *F.T.*, 6 May 1972.
[4] See 'Money supply and the banks', *M.B.R.*, Feb. 1969.

(d) *'Substitute' and 'non-physical' money*
   i. bank deposits (or bank credit), transferable by means of cheques ('final' money) and by credit cards;
   ii. commercial bills of exchange – transferring traders' debts ('temporary' money);
   iii. reciprocating trade credit – transferring traders' debts;
   iv. extended trade credit – 'temporary', single-stage money;
   v. Treasury Bills – transferring Government debts ('temporary' money).

5. Quantity of Money and Value of Money

One of the chief properties that a satisfactory form of money should have is 'stability' of value. It was also noted that money should be relatively scarce. Stability of value implies that there should be no change in the 'general level of prices' of the things which money can buy. Over the centuries, however, it has been noticed that the general level of prices (and therefore the value of money) has not been stable. In fact, the average trend in British prices from 1275 to 1959 has shown an increase of $1\frac{1}{2}\%$ per annum.[1] During this period there were 328 years in which the price level fell, and only 343 years in which it rose. There were three major periods of inflation or rising prices, which caused a permanent upward shift; there were two other periods of inflation, which were followed by periods of deflation, or falling prices, of almost equal severity (1790–1813: Napoleonic Wars; 1914–20: World War I).

The three major periods of inflationary price rises were all associated with an increase in the quantity of money (and therefore a reduction in its scarcity). These periods were:

1525–1650, corresponding to a debasement of the coinage and the influx of Spanish gold and silver from the New World.
1750–1790, corresponding to the expansion of the money supply (bank credit, or deposits, and paper money), due to the rapid growth in the number of country banks.
1939–1946, corresponding to the expansion of the money supply (mainly due to 'deficit financing' or Government borrowing) to meet the demands of World War II.

These phenomena draw attention to the link between the quantity of money and its value (the reciprocal of the price level). We shall now examine the factors which influence the value of money.

(a) The Quantity Theory

Professor Irving Fisher gave the most sophisticated form to the Quantity Theory of Money of classical economists, who laid stress on the supply of money as the main influence on the general price level. Fisher noted that it was not only the amount of money in existence which mattered, but also the degree to which it

---

[1] R. G. Lipsey, 'Does money always depreciate?', *L.B.R.*, Oct. 1960, based on material in E. H. Phelps Brown and S. V. Hopkins, 'Seven centuries of the prices of consumables, compared with builders' wage-rates', *Economics*, 23, No. 92; also see E. H. Phelps Brown and S. V. Hopkins, 'Builders' wage-rates, prices and population: some further evidence', *Economica*, Feb. 1959; and J. Burnett, *A History of the Cost of Living*, 1969, esp. p. 328.

was utilised in exchange – its velocity of circulation. For example, a five-pence piece which has dropped behind the back of a gas meter can have no possible effect on the price of gas. It exists; it is a quantity of money; but nobody is exercising his demand for gas with it. However, if the 5p piece is found and popped into the meter, a transaction will have taken place: demand will have been exercised on the amount of gas available. Let us suppose that gas is the only commodity produced for exchange, and that our 5p is the total amount of money. If our gas meter were unlocked, and if we could move fast enough, we could pop that coin into the meter time and time again, until the entire gas supply had been purchased. In other words, the quantity of money (5p), multiplied by the velocity of circulation, represents the amount of money 'used', and would be equivalent to the amount of gas sold, multiplied by its price.

Fisher expressed the equation as follows: $MV = PT$. M represents the total amount of money (of all kinds) in being; V represents the velocity of circulation, or the number of times each unit of money changes hands during a given period; P represents the general price level, or the average price of all goods and services exchanged; T represents the number of transactions which take place, or the volume of goods and services exchanged, during the period. The equation shows that if M rises, whilst V and T remain constant, then P must rise; if M and T remain constant, whilst V rises, then P must also rise; yet even if M and/or V rise, whilst T also rises, then P may remain constant. An interesting episode, in keeping with the gas meter analogy, occurred in Belfast in 1966. Because of a shortage of shillings (pre-decimal era) and the inability of the Gas Department to empty meters fast enough, consumers were unable to purchase as much gas as they desired. Consequently, shillings were being purchased on the black market at prices up to 50% in excess of their face value. In terms of the Fisher equation this might be expressed in the following way: T fell involuntarily and P (price per unit of gas) unofficially rose. Similarly, V was involuntarily reduced and M was unofficially increased, by way of the sale of coins above their face value.[1]

(b) Drawbacks to the Fisher Equation

Whilst the quantity equation as developed by Fisher draws attention to the major variables involved and illustrates how movements in them interact, these movements are in no way precisely calculable. For example, M consists of various types of money, with differing velocities of circulation; P refers to a general level of prices, some of which may move at different rates or even in different directions. Furthermore, we must know three of the four variables, in order to forecast the likely change in the fourth. If, for example, M is increased as a result of deliberate Government policy and we only know T, it may not be possible to forecast the change in P, because velocity of circulation may be unstable. V, in fact, is difficult to calculate in advance and to control, largely because of the element of public confidence in prices and monetary policy – a psychological factor. Finally, the equation $MV = PT$ really *describes* a self-evident truth, whilst failing to *explain* the interaction of the four variables. It shows how *changes* in the price level take place, but fails to explain how the *initial* price level itself was determined. The equation is self-evident, since MV equals the total amount of money exchanged by the community as purchasers, whilst PT equals the total

[1] 'Black market in shillings for the gas', *D.T.*, 3 May 1966.

value of all goods and services sold by the community. The two sides of the equation represent two ways of looking at the same phenomenon, and the equation merely points to the different factors involved.

(c) Alternative or 'liquidity' approach to value of money

An alternative equation of exchange, known as the Cambridge Formula, throws more light on the main weakness of the Fisher Equation (viz. the velocity of circulation) by taking into account a factor which influences V, i.e. the desire to hold money in a 'liquid' form rather than 'freeze' it, or tie it up, or invest it in securities, or spend it on other assets.

During any given period (say the year) a community creates a certain real amount of goods and services, which we call the National Output or National Income, analogous to a 'national cake'. We shall term this volume of 'real income' r, and assume that it represents 1,000 units of gas. The average price per unit of this real income (gas) we shall term p, and assume that it is $5p$. The value of our community's real income (pr) will therefore be $1,000 \times 5p = 5,000p$. Let us assume that the community fears big price rises in the future, in which case every $1p$ held will be worth less later on. The community may therefore decide to retain in the form of liquid or ready money only a fraction of its income (measured in monetary terms), let us say $1/100$ of its income of $5,000p$. This fraction of income held or 'kept' we shall term k. Then M, the total amount of money (of all types) in existence, will be a fraction ($=k=1/100$) of its real income (expressed in monetary terms, viz. $5,000p$). Therefore $M = kpr$, or $M = 1/100 \times 5p \times 1,000 = 50p$. The total quantity of money which people desire to hold in liquid form will be $50p$. If, on the other hand, people expect prices to fall, and thus hold on to a larger proportion of their income (say half), hoping to buy when prices are lower, then M will be $\frac{1}{2} \times 5p \times 1,000 = 5,000p/2 = 2,500p$. The greater the 'liquidity preference' or desire to hold income in the form of money, the greater the quantity of money.

The interaction of the variables M, k, p and r may be seen by representing this Cambridge Formula differently. If $M = kpr$, then $M/kr = p$. In other words, the price level will be increased by either an increase in M (the quantity of money) or a decrease in k (the 'liquidity proportion') or a decrease in r (the amount of goods and services produced). Thus, to use the figures in the last example:

$$\frac{M}{kr} = p; \frac{2,500p}{\frac{1}{2} \times 1,000} = 5p; \frac{10,000p}{\frac{1}{2} \times 1,000} = 20p;$$

$$\frac{2,500p}{\frac{1}{8} \times 1,000} = 20p; \frac{2,500p}{\frac{1}{2} \times 250} = 20p.$$

The similarity between the Fisher (or 'transactions') and Cambridge (or 'income') equations may now be seen. In the equation $MV = PT$ (or $MV/T = P$) if the velocity of circulation (V) rose, the price level (P) would rise. On the other hand, in the equation $M = kpr$ (or $M/kr = p$), if the 'liquidity proportion' (k) fell, the price level would rise. Thus k moves inversely to V. In other words, when the desire to hold on to a proportion of real income in the form of liquid money falls, the velocity of circulation of money in all transactions from one party to another rises. The situation is analogous to that of holding a 'hot penny': the hotter it is the less the desire to hold it, and the faster does it circulate from hand to hand. The Cambridge Formula, or liquidity equation, is of more general use than the Fisher Equation because firstly, changes in V will normally come about as a *result* of changes in k; secondly, the factors which influence k (or liquidity preference) may be investigated more realistically than those which affect V; thirdly, changes in k relate to changes in income.[1]

For many years, largely under the influence of Keynes's theories – developed in the context of the interwar slump and falling incomes – these quantity theories of money became somewhat discredited, especially in the U.K. Keynes noted that increasing M might be neutralised by a fall in V: this would not result in reflationary activity, aimed at expanding the income flow. He laid greater emphasis on the link between rising M and falling rates of interest, which might encourage businessmen to invest and utilise underemployed resources. Thus, in the U.K., post-World War II policies tended to ignore the volume of money and to concentrate on fiscal and monetary controls over the *demand* for money (e.g. by taxation, direct controls on lending, hire purchase regulations, etc.).

During the late 1960s it became apparent that countries such as Japan and West Germany, which continued to emphasise the money *supply* as a key economic factor, were having more success than the U.K. in combating inflation and avoiding balance of payments crises. This has led to a worldwide debate about the role of the money supply, which will be discussed further in Stage II, Section 2.[2] Recent studies indicate that the quantity of money does have a direct effect on price levels and output, *via* its relationship with the public's liquidity preference, rather than merely an indirect effect *via* the interest rate. It used to be thought that the value of money, as reflected in the price level, was influenced more by the level of the income flow (or output, or economic activity) than by the quantity of money. A survey of the period 1880 to 1965, however, indicates that the correlation between the money supply and the price level was far higher than that between the money supply and the real income (or output) level (see Fig. 6.1). The change in emphasis as to the relationship between M and p and r and p may, perhaps, be illustrated as follows:

'Keynesian' view: M *via* interest rates $\rightarrow r$ which, *via* $k \rightarrow p$ (major emphasis on r

'Monetarist' view: M *via* $K \rightarrow p$, which influences r (major emphasis on M).

(d) Value of money – demand and supply

1. DEMAND FOR MONEY: LIQUIDITY PREFERENCE

We noted earlier that the Fisher transaction equation was deficient in that it illustrated the factors which cause changes in the quantity of money and price level to take place, but failed to explain how the original quantity of money and price level came to be determined. We then noted that the Cambridge Formula showed the link between the quantity of money and the National Income, viz. liquidity preference, or the demand for money to hold as a liquid asset.

---

[1] It must be noted that although k moves inversely to V, $-V$ is not quite the same thing as $1/k$. This is because V relates to the velocity of circulation of money in *all* transactions (from producer, through middleman, to consumer, and including the transfer of stocks created in previous periods). It has been likened to a 'transaction-velocity' of money. On the other hand, k is a proportion of the real income *created* during the period and is therefore a proportion of the 'value added' (or 'net income') during that period. However, we could expect V to move in the same direction as $1/k$, which has been likened to the 'income-velocity' of money.

[2] Three useful introductory discussions on this problem may be found in 'The debate over money supply', *Econ.*, 26 Oct. 1968, pp. 16–17; 'The debate over money supply', *Econ.*, 21 June 1969, supplement on banking, pp. iii, ix, x; A. J. Schwartz, 'Why money matters', *L.B.R.*, Oct. 1969.

Fig. 6.1 *Rates of change in incomes, prices and stock of money in U.K.* 1880–1962
(Source: *L.B.R.*, Oct. 1969, p. 16)

In fact, the value of money, as reflected in the price level is, as with any other
commodity, determined by the demand for it and its supply. With regard to the
demand for money *to hold as a liquid asset*, the Cambridge Formula is deficient in
linking this liquidity preference solely to the level of income.

The holding of liquid money entails the sacrifice of satisfaction from services,
consumer goods and other assets which might have been purchased with it: it
also involves the sacrifice of interest and dividends which might have been earned
by spending (i.e. investing) it on less liquid income-earning assets such as bonds
and shares. Lord Keynes distinguished three distinct motives for this liquidity
preference.

(*i*) *The 'transactions' motive.* Individuals and firms require at any given time a
certain amount of liquid money (usually in the form of coin, notes and bank
deposits) to tide them over in their day-to-day transactions in the intervals
between one receipt of income and another. The professional salary earner, paid
monthly, will thus require more than a bricklayer (with perhaps the same annual
income), who is paid weekly. The motor firm of a certain size which buys from
outside accessory firms will need more than it would if its processes were vertically integrated, because money payments between stages would in the latter
case be unnecessary. As well as being influenced by the frequency of income

477

receipts, 'transactions cash' will also be affected by the size of income and the scale of activities. The person with a high income (and probably a high level of consumption) and the firm dealing on a large scale will need more liquid money under the transactions motive than the low-income individual and the small firm.

(*ii*) *The 'precautionary' motive.* This is sometimes referred to as the 'nest egg' motive, and constitutes the desire to hold liquid cash not for planned day-to-day transactions, but for emergencies and contingencies due to faulty planning. The firm may keep liquid cash in case of production delays, increases in the prices of its supplies, or other contingencies. The individual may hold a reserve to cover himself in case of illness, in case the hotel bill is higher than budgeted for, in case his motor car breaks down, or in case his in-laws descend upon him unexpectedly. Of course, to the extent that such contingencies (fire, theft, sickness, etc.) can be insured against with increasing ease, so will the relative importance of the precautionary motive diminish. Again, however, as with 'transactions cash', the amount of 'precautionary cash' held under this motive will probably be stronger as income or the scale of activities rise. The high-income earner will probably wish (and be able) to put by a larger nest egg of liquid cash than the low-income earner.

(*iii*) *The 'speculative' motive.* Keynes described liquid money held over and above the requirements of the transactions and precautionary motives as 'speculative balances'. By this he meant that this money represents a surplus, which is held temporarily, awaiting the right time to purchase speculative assets, which yield interest or dividends. The amount of such speculative money held by someone *at a given time* will be influenced partly by the size of his income and partly by the size of his inherited or accumulated capital, but mainly by factors which make speculative assets more or less desirable *at that moment*. The key factor inducing him to buy speculative assets, or to sell them and hold liquid cash instead, will be the current general level of interest rates and the direction in which he thinks they will move. When interest rates (which could be earned by lending) are high in relation to guaranteed or anticipated yields on securities, security prices fall: their yield becomes less lucrative. Therefore the speculator, who *anticipates* a future rise in interest rates and a consequent fall in security prices, will sell, hoping to repurchase later at the lower price. His liquidity preference, therefore, is higher when he *thinks* interest rates *are* low and that they *will* rise.

2. SUPPLY OF MONEY

The supply of liquid money at any given time consists partly of coin and Bank of England notes, the amount of which is controlled by the Bank, with the sanction of Parliament, in response to the money-handling habits of the public.

The predominant element in the supply of fully liquid money consists of bank deposits, which can be drawn on by cheques. This supply is controlled by the monetary policy of the Treasury and the Bank of England and by the credit policy of the banking system.

The remainder of 'substitute' money consists partly of reciprocating trade credit (or mutually cancelling traders' debts) – dependent upon the business climate and the level of economic activity; partly of fairly liquid Treasury Bills – a temporary form of money, controlled by the Government; partly of fairly liquid commercial bills of exchange – a temporary form of money dependent upon trading habits and the level of economic activity. Both these temporary

478

forms of money, it will be remembered, involve final settlement at maturity in fully liquid money of a more acceptable kind, viz. coin, notes or bank deposits (cheques). Ultimately, therefore, these temporary forms of money must be backed by fully liquid cash. Until maturity, however, they circulate instead of fully liquid cash, and may be considered to add temporarily to the total supply of money.

Whilst the major part of the fully liquid money supply – which is generally acceptable in final settlement of exchange debts – is thus controlled by the monetary authorities and banking system, as will be shown later, these institutions cannot also control the demand for liquid money to hold, nor the velocity of circulation. It is thus the interaction of supply and demand which establishes the value of money and fluctuations in it.[1]

Since 1971 a narrower definition has been adopted for statistics of the money supply. The aim has been to pinpoint money which functions as a medium of exchange, as separate from balances which are not 'active' or closely related to the level of domestic spending. The former element in the money supply or stock is termed M_1 It encompasses notes and coin in circulation and all resident, private, sterling *current* accounts – transferable by cheques – with the major banks and the National Giro. The latter element includes all resident, private, sterling and non-sterling *deposit* accounts and all deposits of the public sector. These, plus M_1 give the total M_3.[2]

From 1969 to 1972 the growth in M_1 and M_3 was as follows:

(£ million)

	M_1	M_3
1969	8,620	16,320
1970	9,430	17,900
1971 (March)	9,820	18,400
1972 (March)	10,624	20,650

Over the period 1963 to 1969 the 'income-velocity' of circulation fluctuated between 2·84 and 2·91 (see Fig. 6.2). This refers to the ratio of the money supply to the G.N.P. and approximates to the factor $\frac{1}{k}$ in the Cambridge Formula. In 1970 G.N.P. was £42,819 million, whilst M_3 was £17,900 million. According to the Cambridge Formula, $M=kpr$, their relationship could be expressed as follows:

$$£17,900 \text{ million} = 42\% \times £42,819 \text{ million}$$
$$M = k \quad \times pr$$

This would give an 'income-velocity' of circulation ($\frac{1}{k}$) for 1970 of about 2·38. For 1971, k was 38·5% and $\frac{1}{k}$ was 2·59.

For 1970 and 1971 the values of Bankers' Clearing House business between banks (i.e. not including about 25% these amounts which were internal clearings between branches of the same bank) were £772,464 million and £843,626 million respectively. On the basis of the Fisher Equation, the 1970 relationship of money

[1] E. V. Morgan, 'Money, liquidity and interest rates', *L.B.R.*, July 1961.
[2] 'Banking enters a new era', *M.B.R.*, May 1972; 'Another look at money supply', *M.B.R.*, Nov. 1970; 'Money supply and the banks', *M.B.R.*, Feb. 1969; 'Monetary glossary', *Econ.*, 6 Sept. 1969, p. 41 (for U.S. definitions).

supply to total transactions (approximating to bank clearings) could be expressed as follows:

$$£17,900 \text{ million} \times 37 \cdot 5 = £772,464 \text{ million}$$
$$M \quad \times \quad V \quad = PT$$

For 1971, V was 45·5. Thus we may see that the 'transactions-velocity' of circulation (V) rose from 37·5 to 45·5, whilst the 'income-velocity' of circulation ($\frac{1}{k}$) also rose, from 2·38 to 2·59. Although not identical, V and $\frac{1}{k}$ move in the same direction.[1]

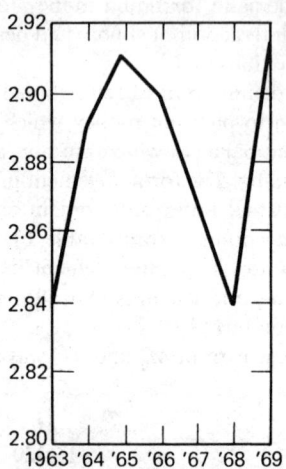

Fig. 6.2 *'Income-velocity' of circulation (average ratio of national income to money supply*
(Source: *F.T.*, 16 April 1970)

6. Effects of Changes in the Value of Money

Changes in the value of money, inversely reflecting movements in the general price level, have effects which may be classified into two main categories:

(*a*) *Effects on the level of economic activity*, and therefore on the use of resources and the resulting size of the National Income or 'national cake'.

(*b*) *Effects on the distribution of the National Income*, the shares of the 'national cake' received by various sections of the community.

(*a*) Level of economic activity

Because of the intense degree of specialisation amongst members of a highly developed economy, goods and services are provided and planned for in expectation of the market demand for them. If, for some reason (e.g. a rise in the amount of money or velocity of circulation, sparked off, perhaps, by big Government

[1] It must be stressed again that the concept of *PT* adopted here refers to ALL transactions, intermediate and final, whereas *pr* refers to 'final' transactions only (i.e. the average price of final goods and services, constituting net output). Some authorities adopt a much more restricted definition of *PT*, to imply G.N.P. (or final output). In such cases, *PT* is the same as *pr* and, tautologically, V would equal $\frac{1}{k}$.

480

orders for roadworks or military materials, financed by borrowing from the banking system) demand for goods and services rises, the pressure of demand might cause prices to rise. Businessmen, who make investment decisions and plan for future demand, will make higher profits than before, and will step up production and use up more factors of production. The climate of business expectations will have improved because of the increased likelihood of making higher profits. In addition, there is added inducement to borrow money for investment projects (new machinery, etc.) because as prices rise and the value of money falls, and as profits and money incomes generally rise, the fixed interest repayments become relatively less onerous. In consequence, the level of activity rises, resources are more fully utilised, and unemployment tends to fall. On the other hand, there is the possibility that the falling value of money might deter people from saving, since the purchasing power of savings would be lower in the future. Such a reduction in the formation of savings would hinder the process of borrowing for investment projects.[1] Furthermore, business firms may find that their financial budgeting becomes unrealistic, because of the distorting effects of falling money values, which may result in the 'capital illusion' and the 'profit illusion'. The former refers to the calculation of depreciation on assets on the basis of outdated prices, such that their replacement is not adequately catered for. The latter refers to the overstatement of profits (resulting from inadequate depreciation), which are consequently over-taxed.[2]

Whilst these results are likely within the home economy, there may, however, be deleterious results in export sales, if prices rise at home. Furthermore, a reduction in monetary stability might lose the confidence of foreign capital, which helps to supplement domestic savings as a source of finance for investment.

In contrast, if prices tend to fall, profits, business expectations, investment decisions and the level of economic activity are likely to fall. The burden of interest repayments is likely to rise and so is the level of unemployment. Outside the home market, however, falling prices will tend to stimulate foreign demand for the community's exports.

(b) Distribution of the national income

Apart from the general effect on the size of the 'national cake', price level fluctuations will have different effects on various sections of the community: where some will benefit, others will suffer.

In the case of generally rising prices, for example, profits will rise fast; wages and the rewards to other factors will tend to rise more slowly, lagging behind price increases; interest repayments will become relatively less onerous; but people on fixed incomes (e.g. pensioners, rent-controlled landlords, and people who have already lent money at fixed rates of interest) will be relatively the worst off. Thus the rising National Income will be redistributed. A larger share will go to entrepreneurs (businessmen and shareholders) as profits and dividends; the share of wages and other factor earnings will tend to fall; the share going to pensioners, fixed salary earners, banks and building societies (with respect to past loans), and to holders of Government gilt-edged securities (lenders, holders of the National Debt) will tend to fall even further. Furthermore, as some prices rise

1 See M. Frère, 'The importance of stable money', *Stat.*, 27 Nov. 1964, pp. 559-60.
2 'How inflation warps accounts', *Econ.*, 16 Jan. 1971, pp. 58-9.

faster than others, there will be a redistribution of incomes between entrepreneurs in favour of those whose prices rise fastest.

In conclusion it might be said, in regard to their relative shares in the national income, that:

(i) *Borrowers*, or debtors – whose repayments on past loans are fixed – tend to gain from rising prices and lose from falling prices.

(ii) *Lenders*, or creditors – whose interest receipts on past loans are fixed – tend to lose from rising prices and gain from falling prices.

(iii) *Groups, such as entrepreneurs* – whose *incomes move faster* than prices and in the same direction – tend to gain most from rising prices and lose most from falling prices.

(iv) *Groups, such as wage earners* – whose *incomes move more slowly* than prices, but in the same direction – tend to suffer somewhat from rising prices and gain somewhat from falling prices.

(v) *Groups, such as pensioners*, fixed salary earners, landlords of rent-controlled property, etc. – whose *incomes are fixed* – tend to lose most from rising prices and gain most from falling prices.

7. Inflation

With regard to changes in the general price level, both the Fisher and Cambridge approaches indicate that such changes take place when there is a disturbance in the balance between the active money *expended* on goods and services (MV or M/k) and the amount of goods and services *available* (PT or pr). It is thus not the actual amount of money which matters, but the amount which is spent – in relation to available goods and services – which causes price changes. An increase in the money supply, for example, if accompanied by a decrease in the velocity of circulation, and/or an increase in liquidity preference, and/or an increase in the number of transactions taking place, and/or an increase in the national income, might leave the price level unaffected.

For this reason, the term 'inflation', as applied to a rising trend in the general price level, has been aptly expressed as 'too much money *chasing* too few goods'. Somewhat ambiguously, however, the term 'inflationary' (and its counterpart 'deflationary') is often used to describe the policy of the monetary authorities when they increase (or decrease) the supply of money, regardless of whether the actual consequences include a rise in the price level. 'Suppressed' inflation is the term used to describe pressure on the price level caused by the community's *desire to spend* too much money, in relation to available goods and services, when this pressure is 'bottled up' by Government controls, such as rationing, quotas, H.P. regulations, etc. 'Persistent' inflation is the term used to describe a continually rising price level, due to continuing business buoyancy, full employment, shortages of key factors of production, rising costs, rising prices and rising money incomes, without a corresponding increase in the actual amount of goods and services produced. In other words, it represents a chronic market instability, where demand exceeds supply, as in the postwar 'cost-price spiral'. According to whether this spiral is caused primarily by the pressure of demand or the pressure of rising costs, this type of inflation is sometimes termed 'demand–pull' inflation or 'cost–push' inflation.[1] Table 6.1 provides a comparison of the annual percent-

[1] W. B. Reddaway, 'Rising prices for ever?', *L.B.R.*, July 1966; A. Seldon, 'What causes inflation?', *D.T.*, 7 Nov. 1972.

Table 6.1 *Annual percentage changes in prices and earnings, analysed by period*

	Selwyn Lloyd vii. 61–vii. 62	Maudling vii. 62–ix. 64	Brown x. 64–vii. 66	Callaghan vii. 66–vii. 67	Wilson-Jenkins vii. 67–xii. 69
Wages	Zero to 2·62%, then 2–2½%	3½% from April, 1963	3–3½%	Zero to end 1966; exceptions in 1967	Zero with 3½% for special cases Then 2½–4½%
Exemptions	Existing deals, productivity	Nothing formal	Low-paid, productivity	None in 1966; productivity, etc., in mid-1967	Productivity
Other provisions	—	—	First attempted price freeze	Public sector, dividend freeze	3½% dividend freeze
Results (annual % increase)					
Prices	5	2½	4½	1	5½
Earnings	3½	6	7½	7½	8½

(Source: *Econ.*, 28 Oct. 1972, p. 78)

age increases in both prices and earnings, during the various periods of 'freeze', 'squeeze', 'stop-go' and prices and incomes policy, between mid-1961 and end-1969.

Following a prolonged period of rising prices in most Western economies and an accelerating trend in the U.K., the term 'expected inflation' has been coined to describe the phenomenon whereby employers, employees, sellers and buyers come to accept future price and cost rises as inevitable.[1] One of the major problems in such a psychological phenomenon is that there is much uncertainty as to the extent of future price rises. This may lead to panic jostling and aggressive behaviour in pricing and in wage bargaining. Perhaps the major ill-effects which ensue are the loss of 'security of contract' and the loss of money's function as a 'store of value'. The former refers to the undermining of contractual agreements: the latter leads to a flight from money into less convenient, less liquid, but more secure forms of asset holdings. The way in which the £ has fallen in value since 1914 is shown in Fig. 6.3. It will be noted that, apart from the period of the inter-war depression, there has been a continuing fall as the price level has risen. This has proceeded even during periods of economic stagnation and has led to the term 'stagflation'. Fig. 6.4 shows some of the main constituents of inflationary price rises in the U.K. from 1970 to 1971 and compares the general change with that in other countries.

The O.E.C.D. secretary-general, in 1970, referred to price inflation as a world-wide problem. He saw this as leading to the danger of reduced international competition amongst companies and saw in it the inadequacy of traditional fiscal and monetary policies.[2] In this respect the experience of Brazil has been most interesting. With a rate of price inflation very much higher than that in the U.K. for many years, Brazil has evolved a series of institutional checks to avoid the economic distortions referred to in Section 6.[3] These include conventional instruments, such as control of budgetary deficits (public expenditure), price controls

[1] Sir John Hicks, 'Expected inflation', *The Three Banks Rev.*, Sept. 1970.
[2] *F.T.*, 6 March 1970.
[3] 'Living with inflation', *Econ.*, 2 Sept. 1972, pp. 37–8.

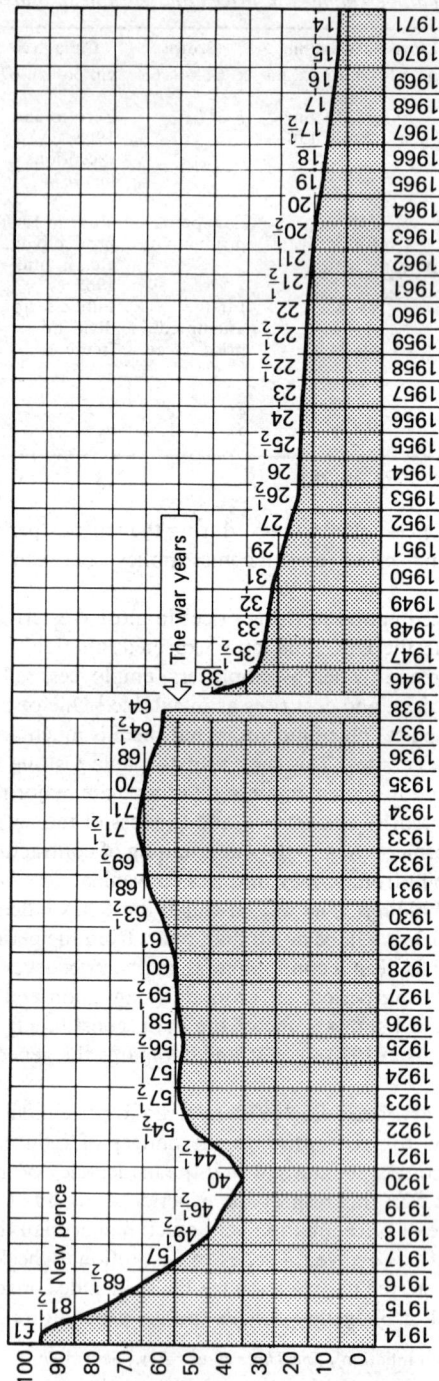

Fig. 6.3 *Changing value of the £, 1914 to 1971*
(Source: *Obs.*, 2 July 1972)

on exports and wage restraint. They also include measures to reduce the uncertainty in 'expected inflation'. Such measures are the 'crawling peg' exchange rate and a scheme of 'monetary correction'. This is aimed at reducing the social and economic distortions of rising prices, by revaluing annually the capital, earnings, savings, loans, fixed assets and securities in the economy, with the intention that no section of the population either benefits or loses as a result of price inflation.

Sometimes inflation is caused primarily by Government action, rather than by actions of the banking system, in response to the community's business activities. For example, the Government may wish to embark on big peacetime investment projects or wartime spending, financed not by 'mopping up' the community's spending power (by taxation and or borrowing from individuals), but by borrowing from the banks, who 'create credit'. Alternatively the Government may wish to 'turn to the printing press', in order to repay and wipe out the internal National Debt or loans from abroad. Such massive creations of paper or bank deposit money result in drastic Fisher-type increases in the price level, to which the terms 'hyperinflation' or 'galloping' or 'runaway' inflation are applied.[1]

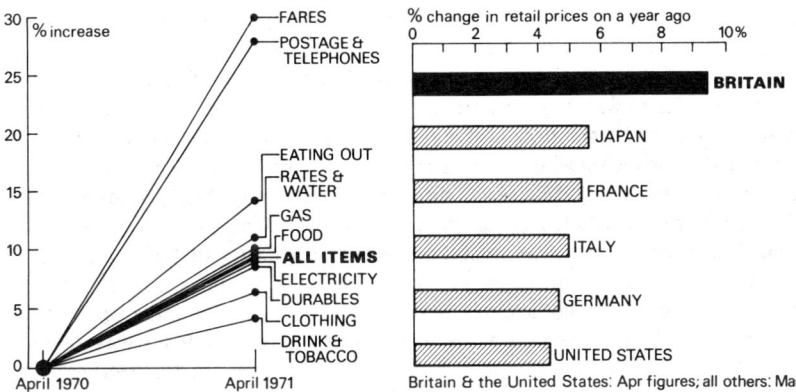

Fig. 6.4 *Inflation and the rise in prices*, 1970–1971
(Source: *Econ.*, 29 May 1971, p. 67)

8. Measurement of Changes in the Value of Money – Price Index Numbers

In the preceding sections changes in the value of money have been referred to as being inverse to fluctuations in the 'general price level'. The Phelps-Brown and Hopkins survey of British prices from 1264 to 1959 – mentioned in Section 5 – traced variations in the composite cost of a constant 'basket' of goods, which were taken as typical elements of general consumer expenditure. The main items were farinaceous products, meat and fish products, butter and cheese, drink, fuel and light, and textiles.

[1] 'The greatest crash of all. *Obs.* (colour supplement), 7 April 1968, pp. 11–14, on the German hyperinflation after World War I. For details of the 'package' of measures adopted by the Government in November 1972, to combat unprecedented price and wage inflation, see 'Controlling inflation', *E.P.R.*, 34, Dec. 1972.

By attaching a certain significance or relative 'weight' to each item in the group, this survey was able to express the composite price, in various years during the period, as percentages of the base year, 1264. Thus, with the basket price taken as 100% or 100 in 1264, the index number, or percentage, in 1959 was more than 4,000, an increase of more than fortyfold.

This method of expressing various price movements as percentages or index numbers in terms of a base year, taken as 100, is used on quite an extensive scale.

Index numbers for a wide selection of wholesale prices (which are eventually reflected in retail prices) are compiled by the Department of Trade and Industry (published in the *Annual Abstract of Statistics*). The Ministry of Agriculture compiles an index for wholesale prices of cereals, farm crops and livestock.

Changes in retail (or consumer) prices are noted in two official indexes, one annual and the other monthly. The annual index is the *Consumer Price Index* (CPI), compiled by the Central Statistical Office. It arises from calculations used to put the G.N.P. figures (for national income and expenditure) on a 'constant price' basis. It has been calculated only for 1938 and for the years 1946 onwards. The monthly index is the *General Index of Retail Prices* (RPI), published by the Department of Employment. It used to be called the *Ministry of Labour Cost of Living (or Retail Price) Index*.[1] This index, until 1947, was based on the 'basket' or pattern of expenditure in a sample of working-class families in 1904, using 1914 prices as the base. After World War II the pattern of expenditure upon which it was based was very outdated, and so an interim index was begun in 1947, based on the mid-1947 prices of a 1938 'basket' or consumption pattern of working-class households. In January 1952 it was again revised, with new 'weights' and items. In January 1956 a new index was started, using '1953 spending habits' of a sample of households as its 'basket', and their January 1956 prices as the base. As a result of the recommendations of the Minister of Labour's Cost of Living Advisory Committee, in February 1962 a new index was started. Its 'basket' was based on the 'average family' expenditure in the three years ended June 1961, and the base year for the prices of items considered was January 1962. For the first time the basket included former luxuries – such as refrigerators, electric cookers, jeans, sherry and thick-knit sweaters – which have become articles of everyday use. In addition, while keeping to January 1962 prices, the weighting pattern or 'basket' is moved forward one year every January, so as to cover a comparatively up-to-date pattern of three years' expenditure.

The selection and weighting of the items are done on the basis of the Family Expenditure Survey. From 1968 the number of main groups in the RPI was raised from ten to eleven, with the inclusion of a separate heading for 'meals bought and consumed outside the home'. In August 1971 the Report of the (renamed) Retail Prices Advisory Committee proposed that regional price indexes – based on regional average expenditure patterns – should be constructed, permitting comparisons with the General R.P.I. and thus furthering the accuracy of that index.[2]

[1] For further details, see 'Measuring the £'s value', *E.P.R.*, 29, July 1972; 'Measuring the cost of living', *D.E.A. Pr. Rep. Econ.*, 17, June 1966; 'Changes in retail prices', *E.P.R.*, 19, Sept. 1971; 'Price indexes: a question of refinement', *F.T.*, 22 Nov. 1971; 'Keeping in step with inflation', *D.T.*, 23 April 1969.
[2] *E.P.R.*, 19, Sept. 1971, *art. cit.*; *F.T.*, 22 Nov. 1971, *art. cit.*; With regard to regional patterns of expenditure on food, see 'Food consumption in the regions', *E.P.R.*, 42, Aug. 1973.

The compiling of index numbers, as the history of the cost of living index illustrates, presents some very serious problems and, as they cannot be ideally solved, the index numbers themselves are limited in their value and reliability as a measurement of changes in the value of money.

The first problem lies in the fact that it is impossible to record the price of every single type of commodity or service. Secondly, the price at which a particular commodity or service is sold may vary from one seller to another, and from one part of the market to another. Thirdly, if certain commodities and services must be selected, we must choose between one quality and another, out of perhaps an immense range. Fourthly, we must decide how much significance or relative weight to give to the items selected. The pattern of expenditure will differ from one locality to another, from one person to another, from one income group to another and from one period to another. Fifthly, the index becomes less meaningful over a long period of time, because the whole pattern of expenditure changes as incomes alter, as the national income changes in size and in the manner of its distribution, as qualities alter, and as new commodities and services come into existence and use. Sixthly, movements in prices will appear to be more or less significant, according to the base year which we select for the prices of items selected. We must therefore aim to select a base year in the past, which experience has shown to be a period of relatively stable prices.

The actual method of constructing a price index, such as the RPI, is to calculate the pattern of expenditure in a sample of consumers (e.g. the 'average family'), and to allocate a relative weight to each item, according to its share of total expenditure in the 'basket'. Then we take a base year for the prices of those items, find the price of each item, and refer to each base year price as 100. We obtain the index for *all* items by multiplying *each* individual price index (100) by its weight, adding up the results obtained, and dividing that figure by the total weight of the 'basket'. In the base year this will give us an index of 100 for all prices. In any subsequent year, we record the new price of each item, and express it as a percentage of the base year price (which was 100). In order to find the new index number for all items, we again multiply each individual price index *in the current year* by its weight, add the results thus obtained, and divide by the total weight of the 'basket'. In this way, the different weightings will influence the overall result, as in Table 6.2 below. We assume here that total expenditure on the 'basket' is £1, broken down into 1,000 parts (or weights), and that all items consist of Food, Clothing and Services.

Had we failed to 'weight' each item, according to its relative importance, we should merely have taken an *average* of the three price movements, *viz.* $150 + 250 + 110 \div 3 = 170$. In fact, the greatest price change was in Clothing, but this item was the least important of the three, with regard to its effect on total expenditure.

The importance of allowing for the changing pattern of expenditure is apparent from the changing weights in the RPI. Thus, for every £1 spent by the 'average household' in 1956, food (including meals outside the home) accounted for 35p, housing for 8·7p, clothing and footwear for 10·6p, and transport and vehicles for 6·8p. In 1971 the comparable expenditure shares had fallen to 29·4p for food and meals outside the home and to 8·7p for clothing and footwear: they had risen to 11·9p for housing and to 13·6p for transport and vehicles.

The main groups of items in the Retail Price or Cost of Living Index, and their

Table 6.2 *Weighted index number of prices*

Item	Base year (e.g. 1945)					Current year (e.g. 1963)		
	Expenditure	Weight	Price per unit (base year)	Index per item (base year)	Index for all items (index × weight per item ÷ total weight)	Price per unit (current year)	Index per item (% of base year)	Index for all items (index × weight per item ÷ total weight)
Food	35p	350	5p	100	35,000	7½p	150	52,500
Clothing	25p	250	12p	100	25,000	30p	250	62,500
Services	40p	400	10p	100	40,000	11p	110	44,000
	£1	1,000			100,000 ÷ 1,000 = 100			159,000 ÷ 1,000 = 159

changing relative weights (as a proportion of a 'basket' of 1,000), are illustrated in Table 6.3 below.

Table 6.3 *Main items of expenditure and their changing relative weights in the Cost of Living Index (RPI)*

Main groups of items	Base years and weights					
	1914 (1904 pattern)	1947 (interim) (1938 pattern)	1952 (interim) (1947/52 pattern)	1956 (1953 pattern)	1962 (1959-61 pattern-'moving')	1962 (1971, with 1968-70 pattern-'moving')
Food						250
Meals outside the home	600	348	399	350	319	44
Alcoholic drink	—	217	78	71	64	65
Tobacco	—		90	80	79	59
Housing	160	88	72	87	102	119
Fuel and light	80	65	66	55	62	60
Durable household goods	—	71	62	66	64	61
Clothing and footwear	120	97	98	106	98	87
Transport and vehicles	—	—	—	68	92	136
Miscellaneous goods	40	35	44	59	64	65
Services	—	79	91	58	56	54
ALL ITEMS	1,000	1,000	1,000	1,000	1,000	1,000

(Source: *Annual Abstract of Statistics*)

It is apparent from Table 6.3 that less emphasis has been placed on the significance of food, over the years. Drink and tobacco were given great significance in the index immediately following World War II – reflecting shortages in other consumer goods – but this emphasis has gradually declined. Transport and vehicles has assumed great importance, reflecting the revolution in private transport, and so has housing, reflecting the relatively high increase in building costs and house prices and the increasing importance placed on housing expenditure by a more affluent and more leisured society.

Consumers' spending constitutes over two-thirds of total expenditure and so the CPI, which records the price level of this expenditure, is generally used to calculate the purchasing power of the pound. The index of the internal purchasing power of the pound is, in fact, the inverse of the CPI. Since the CPI has been compiled only for 1938 and from 1946 onwards, the old Ministry of Labour Cost of Living (Retail Price) Index is used for earlier years and is linked with the CPI to give a continuous series of index numbers for consumer prices and for purchasing power of the pound since 1914 (apart from the World War II period, 1939–45). They give only a rough guide to changes over a long period, because of the different bases used and because of the changes in expenditure patterns. From the data in Fig. 6.5 it may be seen that, taking 1963 as the base year (=100), the price index in 1970 had risen by one-third to 133·5 and the purchasing power of the pound had fallen by one-quarter to 75. Thus, £1 in 1970 would have purchased goods costing only 75p in 1963: alternatively, £1·33½ would have been required in 1970 to purchase goods costing £1 in 1963. In other words, a one-third rise in prices results in a one-quarter fall in purchasing power, or a doubling of prices results in a halving of purchasing power.

Whereas the national income, in monetary terms increased by 56% between 1963 and 1970, from £24,873 million to £38,687 million, the *cost of living* as reflected in the price index, had risen by 33·5%. As a result, the *standard of living*, or national income in real terms, had risen by only $56\% \times \dfrac{100}{132\frac{1}{2}} = 42\cdot26\%$.[1]

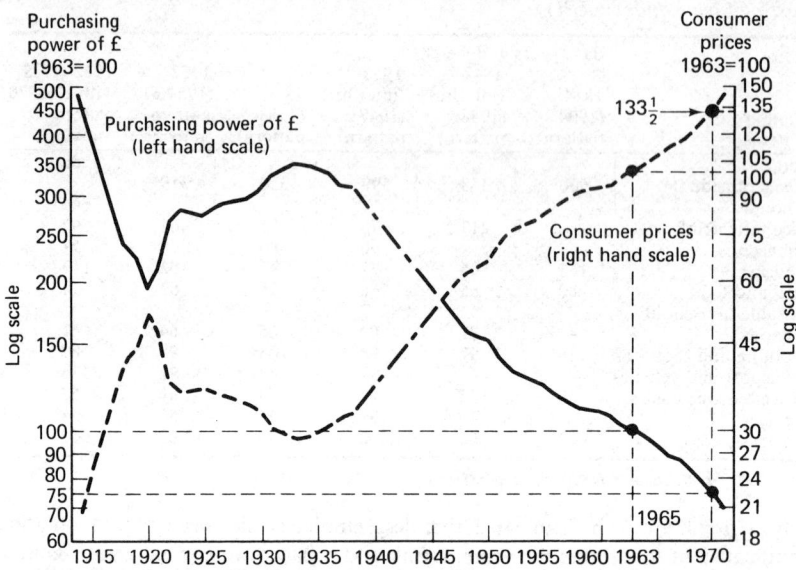

Fig. 6.5. *Indexes of prices and purchasing power of the pound*, 1914–1971 (Source: *E.P.R.*, 29, July 1972)

9. Origins and Development of the Banking System

The dominant element in the supply of money is, as we have seen, non-physical bank deposits (or bank credit, or bank money), transferable by the use of cheques. The banking system is, therefore, of key importance to the supply and management of money.

The three main strands in the origins and development of the present-day banking system are, briefly, as follows:

(a) Early money-lenders, merchants and goldsmiths

During the later Middle Ages merchants from northern Italy – mostly gold-smiths and silversmiths – came to London and, despite the prohibitions against money-lending incorporated in the usury laws, gradually established a service of lending money against some form of security. As the growth of trade led to an increase in the number of people who needed credit for business purposes, the usury laws were eventually repealed in 1545. Apart from serving to establish the legality of lending to businessmen for interest, these early money-lenders have bequeathed the term 'bank' (from their 'bancos' or benches) and the name of Lombard Street – centre of the financial district, where they conducted their business.

[1] For a useful comment on the sub-period changes in living standards from 1961-72, as re-flected in post-tax personal disposable income (at constant prices), see 'Living with inflation', *Econ.*, 28 Oct. 1972, pp. 75–8 and accompanying tables and charts.

(b) Later goldsmiths and the private banks

The expansion of British foreign trade, with the chartered and joint stock companies of the seventeenth century, led to the accumulation of wealth by the merchant venturers. These people and the landed gentry found it convenient to lodge their surplus liquid funds temporarily for safe keeping in the strongboxes and vaults of the goldsmiths, in exchange for 'deposit receipts'.

With experience, the goldsmiths found that they could safely lend out some of the precious metals deposited with them, provided that they retained sufficient to meet any withdrawals by their clients.

Gradually the public gained confidence in the goldsmiths and their deposit receipts, which were titles to the money lodged in their vaults. People began to find it convenient, when paying someone else, to hand over a deposit receipt instead of actually removing a quantity of precious metal from the safe keeping of the goldsmith. Thus, these transferable deposit receipts were an early form of bank note. As certain goldsmiths came to specialise on these financial activities and became banks proper, the deposit receipts gradually became known as bank notes.

The growing custom of leaving deposits untouched, and transferring deposit receipts instead, enabled the goldsmiths to expand the amount of their lending. Eventually they found that they did not have to lend out precious metals, but could lend deposit receipts, which were acceptable. With experience, this led to the goldsmiths being able to lend in excess of the money deposited with them. In effect, these goldsmiths and early banks were 'creating' deposits or granting credit to their borrowers, giving them fiduciary deposit receipts or bank notes to circulate as money. Again they learnt by experience that this credit expansion should be limited in such a way that the actual deposits retained would be sufficient to meet any calls for precious metals as such.

(c) The Bank of England, the evolution of the joint stock deposit banks and the 'secondary banks'

In 1694 the Government required a loan to conduct the war with France. Individual goldsmiths and bankers feared non-repayment, but a group of them lent £1·2 million at 8% interest, in return for a Charter permitting them the privilege of operating as a joint stock bank in London, with the title of 'The Governor and Company of the Bank of England'.

In return for subsequent loans the Government passed an Act in 1708 whereby the Bank of England was the only joint stock bank permitted to operate in London, and the only joint stock bank in England and Wales, with more than six partners, permitted to issue bank notes. Thus only small private banks could operate in London or issue notes in the provinces.

As a result of the 1708 Act and the gradual increase in internal trade and industry towards the end of the eighteenth century, many small, private, 'country banks' became established in the provinces. They had the right to issue notes, which they often abused. These small banks, many of them being offshoots of merchant firms, had a high record of failure. This was in contrast to the larger, more stable joint stock note-issuing banks of Scotland.

Gradually pressure for the right of joint stock note issue built up, and in 1826 this was permitted to larger banks, provided that they operated more than 65 miles away from Charing Cross.

In 1833 joint stock banks were eventually permitted to operate in the London area, but they were still not permitted to issue notes. (In 1858 the joint stock banks were granted the privileges of limited liability companies.)

In 1844 the Government decided on a gradual concentration of the country's note issue in the Bank of England. No additional banks were to be permitted this right: existing rights were to die out gradually, being taken over by the Bank of England.

Towards the end of the eighteenth century a development started which counteracted the restriction on the money supply caused by the 1708 prohibition of joint stock note issue. Following the gradual acceptability of deposit receipts or bank notes, traders began to find it convenient, when paying someone else, not to hand over deposit receipts or bank notes, but to issue written instructions to their bankers to do so. Thus the banker would transfer funds (in ink) from one account to another, or, if the receiver (payee) were the client of another banker, from the payer's account to the other bank. This written instruction was the early form of the cheque – technically a bill of exchange. Eventually the banks issued printed cheque books to their clients. Henceforth the banks could 'create deposits' or lend money simply by making the necessary entries in their ledgers: instead of issuing deposit receipts or bank notes, they would give the borrower a cheque book and allow him to 'draw' cheques up to the amount lent.

The development of the cheque, the gradual restriction of note-issuing rights and the eventual legality of joint stock banking in London gave rise to the main features of the present banking system:[1]

(i) In order to settle the balances owing from one bank to another, due to the presenting or depositing into each bank of cheques drawn upon different banks, a 'clearing house' system developed. By 1773 it was fully fledged, and in that year the London Clearing House was set up in Lombard Street to settle the outstanding balances. This consists of six banks, called the London Clearing Banks (although some of them have headquarters outside London). Some of them perform clearance operations as agents for the smaller banks. There were, until January 1968, twelve major clearing houses in the main provincial cities of England.

(ii) As the Bank of England gradually withdrew from day-to-day commercial banking it added to its functions as the Government's bank that of acting as the banker's bank. The commercial banks came to deposit with it a proportion of their cash reserves (nowadays Bank of England notes and coin). This had the effect of further simplifying the clearing house system, as the banks no longer had to transfer outstanding balances to each other, but simply instructed the Bank of England to transfer (in ink) from the account of one bank to the account of another.

(iii) Joint stock legality, the clearing house system, the expansion of trade and banking transactions and economies of large scale have all led to the establishment of networks of branches and to a process of amalgamations in the banking system, mainly during the latter half of the nineteenth century, the period immediately after World War I and during the 1960s. The 1918 Colwyn Report on bank

[1] For an interesting comparison with developments in U.S. banking, see A. R. Bennett, 'American commercial banking: the changing scene', *L.B.R.*, July 1971 and 'Fed's two birds', *Econ.*, 18 Nov. 1972, p. 58.

amalgamations stressed the dangers of reduced competition and monopolistic collusion. The Prices and Incomes Board 1967 report on Bank Charges,[1] on the other hand, suggested that some advantages might accrue from further mergers amongst the main banks, provided that they abolished their 'cartel-type' fixing of interest rates, competed more vigorously for deposits and revealed their true profits. Several important mergers were completed during the late 1960s. Some of the major reasons were the economies of scale to be derived from computerised data processing; the need to match the borrowing requirements of large industrial mergers with suitably sized banking units; the need to rationalise the pattern of branch banking. Nevertheless, the 1968 Monopolies Commission report found that a projected merger between Barclays, Lloyds and Martins – which would have accounted for about half the banking business in England and Wales – would have been against the public interest. By 1970 the major amalgamations which did take place resulted in the pre-eminence of the 'Big Four'. These were Barclays (including Martins, since 1968); National Westminster (including, since 1968, National Provincial, Westminster and District); Lloyds; Midland. In company with Coutts and Co. and Williams and Glyn's (including, since 1970, National, William Deacon's and Glyn Mills), they constitute the Committee of London Clearing Bankers and operate about 12,000 branches.

(iv) In Scotland and Northern Ireland certain banks have retained limited rights to issue notes, but, apart from an amount specifically authorised by law for each bank, these issues must be fully covered by Bank of England notes and coin.

(v) An important development, resulting from U.K. membership of the E.E.C. was agreed upon in November 1972. The agreement was on the extension of E.E.C. banks' freedom to establish branches to operate in any part of the E.E.C. They would cease to be bound by conflicting national rules: they would be authorised to offer stockbroking services, but were to be limited to capital transactions which had already been liberalised throughout the E.E.C.[2]

(vi) During the 1960s a significant development in U.K. banking was the evolution of the 'non-deposit banks' into a 'secondary banking system'.[3] The joint stock deposit banks (mainly the clearing banks) differ from the non-deposit banks in that the former are concerned with the transfer of payments from one party to another, whilst the latter are much less so. The deposit banks' business is primarily domestic in character and conducted in sterling: more than half the deposits consist of current accounts and the major part of advances takes the form of overdrafts. The non-deposit secondary banks have mostly been established for many years, consisting of accepting houses, other merchant banks, overseas banks and foreign banks. They used to have highly specialised functions, but have recently begun to knit together into a distinguishable group. These banks have been growing at a much faster rate than the deposit banks, and they have been joined by a large influx of foreign (particularly U.S.) banks and by subsidiaries of the deposit banks themselves. Two of the fastest-growing groups of secondary banks have been the U.S. banks in London (providing services for U.S. companies with U.K. subsidiaries and actively tapping the Euro-dollar market for funds for their U.S. clients – in consequence of the protracted U.S.

[1] Cmnd 3292, Report No. 34, 1967; see also 'Revolution for the City', *Econ.*, 27 May 1967, p. 925, and 'Jones points the way', *Econ.*, 10 June 1967, pp. ix–x.
[2] 'More freedom for banks in market', *D.T.*, 8 Nov. 1972.
[3] J. Revell, 'A secondary banking system', paper reprinted in H. G. Johnson, ed., *Readings in British Monetary Economics*, 1972, pp. 422–8.

balance of payments deficit) and the new subsidiaries of the deposit banks themselves. The business of the secondary banks, although encompassing a great
diversity of functions, may generally be said to differ from that of the deposit
banks on the following grounds:

(*a*) They have a *small* number of *large* accounts (in terms of both deposits and
advances).

(*b*) The bulk of deposits are placed for a definite term (or time period).

(*c*) A large proportion of deposits and advances is in non-sterling currencies.

(*d*) Only a small part of advances is of the overdraft type, the rest being 'tailor-
made' to each client's financial problems.

10. The Creation of Credit

The previous section illustrated the steps by which paper money first came to
serve as an alternative form of currency. Later, the supply of money could be
expanded by issuing more of this paper money on a fiduciary basis, by creating
bank deposits or credit. As restrictions were applied to the issue of this paper
alternative money, the deposit banks developed another, non-physical form,
transferable by cheques. Again this involves the creation of a deposit in the client's
account: in other words, the bank creates credit.

The reason why each of these forms of credit is regarded as money lies in the
fact that the deposits are acceptable and transferable from one person to another
by means of paper money or by cheques. Of course, the bank does not create
credit (i.e. create purchasing power) for charity. It does so either by allowing
overdrafts or making loans (backed by the promise and good character of the
borrower, or his lodgement of collateral or security), which earn interest, or by
purchasing securities, which earn dividends. In return, the client is given a
'deposit' in the bank's books, which he can use by drawing out paper money
(and coin) or by drawing cheques.

When the bank creates credit, it has, in fact, created liquidity or purchasing
power. To be more precise, the bank has turned capital, or accumulated illiquid
assets, into ready liquid money. It unlocks or 'melts' less liquid or frozen assets,
giving liquid money or purchasing power in return. The illiquid assets do not,
in fact, have to be physical. They can be physical things of value, represented
by property deeds, life assurance policies or securities (lodged as collateral for
a loan), or securities purchased as an investment by the bank: they can also take
the form, however, of the goodwill or good character, built up by a borrower
who desires a loan, and whose main asset is himself.

The bank, therefore, is a 'creator and purveyor of liquidity', whose main
business is to accept illiquid assets, which are highly profitable, and to create
and give in return liquid bank money in the form of paper money or deposits
or credit. These all represent the bank's debt to its client – its promise to pay –
and, being transferable, they serve as money.

The nearest thing in the way of trade credit to this bank credit form of money
is the bill of exchange. This has a temporary life, but whilst it lasts it represents
a trader's promise to pay (or debt). In the circles in which it is acceptable, it
circulates from hand to hand and finances transactions, thus serving as a temporary form of money. Ordinary trade credit and hire purchase or ordinary debts

are not represented in such a document as the bill of exchange and do not circulate (i.e. are not 'negotiable'). They only serve to finance one transaction, temporarily, between creditor and debtor, and, like the bill of exchange, must eventually be settled in a more acceptable, final form of money. They may be referred to as 'single-stage temporary money'.

It must be noted that there are very real limits to the ability of the banks to create 'deposit money' or credit in this way:

(a) Total stock of illiquid assets (or capital) in the community

There are practical limits to the market value of illiquid physical assets and goodwill which could be 'unfrozen', either by the banks granting loans or by their purchasing investments.

(b) The banks' liquidity ratios

Sometimes a bank's clients may wish to draw out of their deposits sums of legal tender, in coin or notes. The bank must therefore retain a reserve of 'super-liquid' notes and coin and/or other liquid assets, which may be converted into cash (notes and coin) very quickly. Also, the Government monetary authorities may wish to restrict the ability of the banking system to create credit or expand the money supply, and will thus need to relate this ability to a proportion of the banks' total deposits or liabilities.

Over a lengthy period of evolution up to 1946 the banks found that 10% of their total assets in the form of cash constituted an adequate ratio to support public confidence. This voluntary 'first liquidity ratio' had to be backed by a *further* 20% of fairly liquid assets, giving a 'second liquidity ratio' of 30%.[1] From 1946 to 1971 the 'first liquidity (or cash) ratio' was officially reduced to 8% – largely due to the replacement of many physical cash transactions with cheque transactions: the overall 30% second ratio remained voluntary until 1951 and was thereafter officially imposed. From 1963 to 1971 the 'second (or overall) liquidity ratio' was reduced to 28%, which, in effect, permitted the banks to expand their loans (or credit creation).

Against the background of the overall second ratio (i.e. of fairly liquid, but not very profitable, assets) the banks, with an 8% cash ratio, could therefore build up their total assets (and, at the same time, liabilities) to the extent of a *further* 11·5 times this cash base. That portion over and above the (post-1963) 28% liquid ratio was thus in the form of illiquid, longer-term but more profitable assets – investments and advances or loans. An important element in the banks' cash assets has been that part – usually about 35% – lodged in their accounts at the Bank of England. Known as Bankers' Deposits, a rise (or fall) in this item would increase (or decrease) the cash base. Bankers' Deposits are affected by settlement of Clearing House balances between banks and by securities transactions between the banks and the Bank of England (or any agency, such as the Treasury, which has an account at the Bank of England). With the adoption of the 'Competition and Credit Control' (C.C.C.) policy in September 1971, 'Till Money' – that part of banks' cash *not* deposited at the Bank of England – ceased to be eligible as part of the banks' credit base. Instead, 1·5% of total deposits had

---

[1] For an excellent survey of the way in which these ratios evolved, see A. J. Turner, 'The evolution of reserve ratios in English banking', *N.W.B.Q.R.*, Feb. 1972.

to be in the form of Bankers' Deposits at the Bank of England: this compares with the pre-1971 customary proportion of about 2·8% (35%×8%).

Thus there were four main ways in which the 'first liquidity ratio' of 8% could affect an individual bank's creation of bank money, or credit:

(i) Through the increase or decrease of clients' deposits of actual currency for safe keeping.

(ii) Through the increase or decrease of its account (Banker's Deposit) at the Bank of England, resulting from Clearing House activities – the settlement of day-to-day debts between it and other banks. If one bank tried to expand credit whilst other banks refrained, it found that most of its clients' withdrawals or transfers of deposits went to other banks, causing its Banker's Deposit at the Bank of England to fall, following Clearing House settlement. Thus its liquidity ratio fell. If all banks embarked on a credit expansion policy (e.g. by selling investments and using the resulting cash as a basis for credit) they might have succeeded, but one bank attempting such a policy unilaterally would have failed.

(iii) Through the increase or decrease of its account (Banker's Deposit) at the Bank of England, resulting from the sale or purchase of securities to/from the Bank of England or any of its clients.

(iv) Through action of the Bank of England in relation to liquidity ratio policy: this aspect will be examined later, in connection with 'Special Deposits'.

For various reasons which will be discussed later, a change in policy was announced by the Bank of England in May 1971, in its document, 'Competition and Credit Control'. Taking effect from September 1971, the direct imposition of 'ceilings' on bank lending were removed: these had been imposed intermittently since 1965. Of more lasting significance was the radical change in the treatment of liquidity ratios. Henceforth the basis for determining both the reserve requirements and Special Deposits was to be the total of 'eligible liabilities'. These were defined as sterling deposits (with certain technical provisos) and excluded foreign currency deposits, unless these were switched into sterling. A new, single liquidity or reserve ratio was termed the 'eligible reserve assets' ratio, which was to be a minimum of 12·5% of total 'eligible liabilities'. These were defined as a list similar to that of the former 28% liquidity ratio, but *included* Government securities with one year or less to maturity and *excluded* liquid assets not adequately under the control of the authorities to be appropriate as reserve assets: such were 'till money', money 'at call' to some institutions and parts of the commercial bill portfolios. Special Deposits were also excluded. Thus, after 1971, the banking system was permitted to create total deposits to a limit (or by a 'gearing') of eight times the 'eligible reserve assets' base. In other words, they could acquire a *further* seven times as many other, more profitable assets, in return for a parallel creation of credit.

The connection between the new reserve ratio and the old liquidity ratio may, perhaps, be seen from an analysis of the 16 February 1972 statement of the London Clearing Banks.[1] Total Gross Deposits were £12,717·7 million. Liquid assets (on the pre-1971 basis) were £3,113·5 million, or 24·5% of Gross Deposits. If the 28% liquidity ratio had still applied, total gross deposits would have had to be

[1] *F.T.*, 29 Feb. 1972.

contracted to £11,119·6 million: the abolition of the old ruling had permitted an expansion of about £1,600 million in deposits to occur. Total 'eligible reserve assets' amounted to £1,556·9 million (i.e. only about 50% of old-style liquid assets), and were 14·3% of total 'eligible liabilities' (£10,864·5 million). If the strict 12·5% reserve ratio had been taken advantage of, these 'eligible reserve assets' could have formed the base for £12,455·2 million of 'eligible liabilities'. Furthermore, as 'eligible liabilities' only constituted about 86% of total liabilities or gross deposits, the latter could have been as high as about £14,500 million. Thus, whereas on the old basis total gross deposits *should* have been about £11 billion, on the new basis they *could* have been about £14½ billion, or almost one-third higher.

11. Other Banking Functions

Apart from the now practically defunct practice of issuing notes, and the functions of borrowing (or safe keeping) and lending outlined above, the banks provide many other services to their clients.[1]

(a) Savings Accounts, Deposit and Current Accounts

The small private lender to the bank may put his money in a Savings Account. Any amount, however small, may be held in it, and the bank pays interest to the lender. Individuals and companies with larger funds to lend, or who in some other way have a deposit at a bank (either through borrowing from it, through selling securities to it, through paying in a cheque received from someone else, etc.) may hold this money in a Deposit Account. This earns interest, requires notice of withdrawal and may be transferred to a Current Account. Normally it is used when the client does not need the money urgently and probably has a Current Account as well. The Current Account does not earn interest, but can be drawn upon by cheques. The bank makes a periodic charge for handling transfers of money through Current Account. Usually more than 50% of customers' deposits in a bank are held in Current Accounts, but as funds may be switched from these to Deposit Accounts, and vice versa, the distinction is not of great economic significance.

Since October 1971 the clearing banks have been free to compete with each other in the fixing of interest rates paid to depositors and to offer terms other than the previously traditional 'seven days' notice at 2% below Bank Rate'. On the lending side, furthermore, since the 1971 abandonment of collective agreement on interest rates (the 'interest rate cartel'), the banks have quoted rates based on their own individually-fixed 'base rates'. By the end of 1971 these had generally moved to about 0·5 below Bank Rate.[2]

(b) Periodic receipts and payments on behalf of clients

(i) The banks will act as Executors or Trustees of Wills.

(ii) They handle directly with companies the receipt of interest and dividends, on behalf of their clients.

(iii) They handle the income tax payments of their clients to the Inland Revenue.

(iv) They make periodic payments on Banker's Order, on behalf of their clients.

---

[1] For a useful analysis of the various activities of the main clearing banks, see table in *Econ.*, 23 Sept. 1972, p. 17 (survey article on the City).
[2] 'Banking enters a new era', *M.B.R.*, May 1972, p. 13.

(c) Stock Exchange work

The banks provide expert advice on investments for their clients, and buy and sell securities through the stock exchanges on their behalf.

(d) Export and import trade

The banks provide assistance to importers and exporters, including advice, documentation, and the payment or collection of money.

(e) Foreign travel

The banks provide facilities for supplying foreign exchange and Travellers Cheques to their clients, for travel abroad.

(f) Safeguarding of valuables

The banks provide for their clients facilities for the safe keeping of documents, parcels and other valuables in strongrooms.

(g) Information

The banks issue a number of publications on a variety of subjects; their Intelligence and other departments provide reports on worldwide economic, financial and trade conditions; they make enquiries on the financial reputation of firms at home and abroad, with whom their clients wish to do business; they also provide references on behalf of their own clients.

12. Structure of the Banks' Assets and Liabilities

As was noted previously, the major element in the supply of money consists of bank money or bank deposits: at least 87½% of this is really credit created by the banks offering liquid deposits in exchange for less liquid assets. These liquid bank deposits – bank money – in fact represent the banks' promises to pay their depositors: they represent the banks' debts or liabilities to the public. The assets which the banks acquire in exchange consist of cash deposited with them and less liquid but more profitable assets such as securities and the written undertakings of their borrowers to pay back loans.

The structure or composition of the deposit banks' assets and liabilities is important, as this figure represents most of the money supply. It is a factor in the Fisher and Cambridge equations; its rise or fall influences the level of prices and of economic activity; as the use of cheques instead of currency becomes more widespread, so the importance of total bank deposits increases in the financing of trade transactions. The structure of the London Clearing Banks' assets and liabilities as at 16 February 1972 is analysed in Table 6.4.

In addition to deposits, there is a liability of much smaller dimensions, consisting of paid-up capital, provisions and reserves. This is a liability owed to the shareholders, and in 1972 it amounted to £1,564·3 million.

It will be noted that the groups of assets, calculated as percentages of the total, add up to something less than 100%. This is due to the factor of items in transit.

Call money, or 'money at call and short notice', represents very short-term loans (one to seven days) to the money or discount market.

Treasury Bills discounted and other bills represent the short-term debts (up to three months) of the Government and merchants. The banks 'discount' these bills, or pay liquid cash for them – minus interest for the period outstanding – and receive the full amount when the bills 'mature' or become due. As the bills are negotiable instruments, the banks may easily rediscount them (i.e. turn them into liquid cash or use them to pay off debts), should their liquidity ratios fall below the conventional levels.[1]

Special deposits at the Bank of England represents Bankers' Deposits which are *not* counted as constituting part of the banks' $12\frac{1}{2}\%$ reserve assets holdings. Under an agreement between the Bank of England and the Scottish and London Clearing Banks, in 1958, the Bank of England has the right to 'call in' special deposits from the banks. The purpose is to reduce their operative liquidity ratios, forcing the banks to replenish them by selling investments or calling in or curtailing advances. This device was first used in 1960, and by February 1971 it accounted for £378·5 million of the London Clearing Banks' assets. They were repaid in September 1971.

Investments consist of holdings of long-term securities. Although a profitable item, the banks prefer not to invest for long periods, and when they do, they prefer to invest in comparatively safe, fixed-interest Government 'gilt-edged' securities – a form of lending to the State.

Advances represent the most profitable asset of the banks – loans and overdrafts to industry (mainly private enterprise) and to individuals. In 1938 advances constituted 43% of total assets: at the end of the war they were down to 17%. After 1951 they settled down to a level of 26–30%,[2] but since the removal of official requests to restrict bank advances, in 1958, they have tended to rise above the prewar level, stimulated by innovations such as personal loan schemes (advances repayable by fixed monthly instalments); the gradual acquisition by some banks of interests in hire purchase finance companies, the extension of activities in the credit card field, into unit trusts and into investment advisory services; the expansion of international financial operations.[3] In November 1972 an Opinion Research Centre survey noted that both the big banks and the finance houses were beginning to meet strong competition from the 'money-shops'. About sixty of these had been established in the U.K., offering flexible opening hours and a wide range of services under one roof.[4] The overall picture of the banking system's eligible liabilities and reserve assets from October 1971 to March 1972, and the dominating position of the six London Clearing Banks may be seen from Table 6.5. Fig. 6.6 illustrates the distribution of total bank advances in Great Britain as at August 1971.

[1] An increase in activity of this type, in connection with commercial bills, was one of the trends criticised by the Governor of the Bank of England in May 1965. This was one reason for the call for Special Deposits on 30 April 1965 (see *D.T.*, 6 May 1965).
[2] *Brit. O.H.*, 1963, p. 410.
[3] For further details, see 'Hunting for borrowers', *Econ.*, 18 Dec. 1971, pp. 74–5, and 'Clearing the way', *Econ.*, 27 Feb. 1971, p. 85.
[4] *F.T.*, 20 Nov. 1972.

Table 6.4 *Assets and liabilities of the London Clearing Banks, 16 February 1972*

	Barclays £m	%	Coutts £m	%	Lloyds £m	%	Midland £m	%	Nat. West. £m	%	Williams Glyn's £m	%	Totals £m	%
Liabilities														
Capital	156·4		1·0		64·8		64·7		152·4		13·5		452·8	
Reserve funds	326·5		6·4		219·1		160·8		251·2		35·6		999·6	
Provisions §	30·1		0·9		14·2		31·2		31·1		4·4		111·9	
Gross deposits	3,323·2		119·3		2,176·1		3,159·9		3,620·4		318·8		12,717·7	
Total eligible liabilities	3,100·7		72·8		1,855·8		2,296·0		3,268·4		270·8		10,864·5	
Assets														
Cash and balances with Bank of E.	236·0	7·1	1·3	1·1	120·6	5·5	149·2	4·7	215·4	5·9	14·2	4·5	736·7	5·8
Call and short money	315·3	9·5	16·4	13·7	214·4	9·9	245·6	7·8	276·7	7·6	55·6	17·5	1,124·0	8·8
Bills discounted: Treasury	8·8	0·3	1·9	1·6	64·7	3·0	23·7	0·8	101·7	2·8	0·3	0·1	201·1	1·6
Other and refin'ncble credits	237·9	7·2	3·1	2·6	223·4	10·3	298·9	9·5	265·9	7·3	22·5	7·1	1,051·7	8·3
Liquidity ratio		*24·0*		*18·9*		*28·6*		*22·7*		*23·7*		*29·1*		*24·5*
Special deposits*		—		—		—		—		—		—		—
Cheques for collection, etc.	136·2	4·1	4·7	3·9	68·5	3·1	88·3	2·8	125·6	3·4	19·9	6·2	443·2	3·5
Investments	535·2	16·1	21·6	18·1	391·1	18·0	353·0	11·2	635·7	17·6	36·2	11·4	1,972·8	15·5
Advances	2,055·3	61·9	76·2	63·9	1,231·5	56·6	2,101·8	66·5	2,202·2	60·8	201·4	63·2	7,868·4	61·9
Total reserve assets	425·3		10·6		283·2		319·0		480·2		38·6		1,556·9	
Reserve asset ratio ¶		13·7		14·5		15·3		13·9		14·7		14·3		14·3

	Composition of totals £m	Changes on Jan. 1972	Changes on Feb. 1971
Net deposits†	12,086·9	− 30·7	+1,740·4
Gross deposits:			
Current accounts	6,375·8	− 192·5	+ 603·5
Deposit accounts	5,985·2	+ 68·2	+1,272·3
Other accounts ‡	356·6	+ 53·5	+ 44·9
Cash:			
Cash in hand	563·9	− 49·3	− 159·5
Balances with Bank of England	172·8	+ 8·6	− 136·1
Call and short money:			
Discount market	700·4	− 295·9	− 433·6
Other	423·6	− 43·3	− 7·2
Other bills and refinanceable credits:			
U.K.	577·0	+ 25·2	+ 266·4
Other	474·7	+ 0·7	− 14·3
Investments:			
Brit. Gvt. and Gvt. guaranteed	1,793·1	− 47·9	+ 885·2
Other	179·8	+ 0·5	− 11·8
Advances to customers incl. other accounts:			
Gross	7,868·4	+456·8	+1,913·6
Items in transit	187·6	− 21·3	+ 28·4
Net	7,680·8	+478·1	+1,885·2
Nationalised industries	156·7	− 8·4	− 20·5
Other	7,524·1	+486·5	+1,905·7

* Special deposits with the Bank of England were repaid on 15 September. † Gross deposits less 'Cheques for Collection' and items in transit between offices of the same bank included in advances. ‡ Credits in course of transmission and suspense accounts. § These include pensions, taxation and dividends payable. ¶ Reserve assets as a percentage of eligible liabilities. The Reserve Assets system was introduced on 16 September, and figures of Eligible Liabilities and Reserve Assets are not available prior to mid-September.

(Source: *F.T.*, 29 Feb. 1972)

Table 6.5 *Eligible liabilities and reserve assets in the U.K. banking system (£m)*

| | 1971 | | | 1972 | | |
Eligible liabilities	October	November	December	January	February	March
London clearing banks	10,752	10,693	10,946	11,051	10,865	11,135
Scottish clearing banks	1,021	1,027	1,040	1,049	1,038	1,041
Other deposit banks	257	255	256	272	271	283
Accepting houses	1,085	1,068	1,133	1,130	1,054	1,071
Overseas banks	2,613	2,720	2,977	3,017	2,946	2,967
Other banks	1,418	1,460	1,548	1,527	1,460	2,454
Total	17,147	17,224	17,900	18,046	17,633	18,951
Reserve assets						
London clearing banks	1,777	1,640	1,760	1,938	1,557	1,652
Scottish clearing banks	149	162	158	178	150	145
Other deposit banks	34	35	36	45	42	45
Accepting houses	171	176	211	245	223	186
Overseas banks	451	504	699	773	633	567
Other banks	140	178	242	271	247	321
Total	2,721	2,696	3,107	3,450	2,852	2,916
Reserve ratio (%)						
London clearing banks	*16·5*	*15·3*	*16·1*	*17·5*	*14·3*	*14·8*
Scottish clearing banks	*14·6*	*15·7*	*15·2*	*16·9*	*14·4*	*13·9*
Other deposit banks	*13·1*	*13·8*	*14·1*	*16·4*	*15·6*	*16·0*
Accepting houses	*15·7*	*16·5*	*18·6*	*21·7*	*21·1*	*17·4*
Overseas banks	*17·3*	*18·5*	*23·5*	*25·6*	*21·5*	*19·1*
Other banks	*9·9*	*12·2*	*15·6*	*17·8*	*16·9*	*13·1*
Total	*15·9*	*15·7*	*17·4*	*19·1*	*16·1*	*15·4*

(Source: *M.B.R.*, May 1972, p. 14)

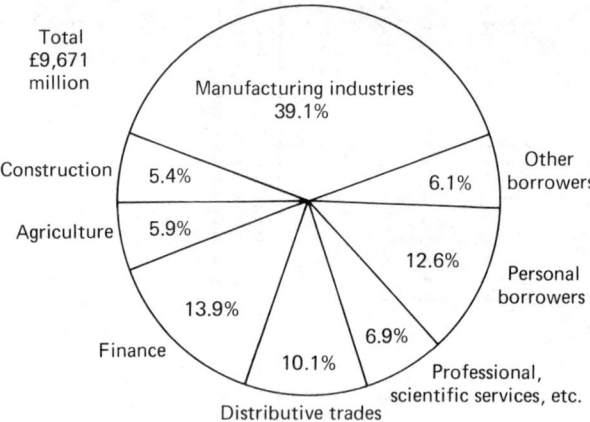

Fig. 6.6. *Analysis of bank advances in Great Britain, August* 1971
(Source: *E.P.R.*, 22, Dec. 1971)

13. The Bank of England

(a) Functions

The Bank of England has gradually assumed the functions of a central bank, and by the Bank of England Act, 1946, was nationalised, its entire capital stock thereby being acquired by the Government. The Act gave the Treasury the legal power to issue directives to the Bank, and gave the Bank the power to 'make recommendations' to the commercial banks.

Its major functions are:

(i) To regulate and coordinate the application of monetary and economic policy as the agent of, and adviser to, the Government.

(ii) To act as the central note-issuing authority.

(iii) To act as banker for the Government's accounts (including the issue and registration of Government loans and management of the National Debt and of the gold reserves in the Exchange Equalisation Account).

(iv) To act as banker to the commercial banks, which deposit part of their bank cash in their accounts at the Bank of England. Any debts owed to them by the Bank of England are added to these Bankers' Deposits, which are regarded as liquid cash by the banks, who can make withdrawals in the form of notes and coin.

(v) To act as the 'lender of last resort' to the short-term money market, by lending to them (by rediscounting approved bills) when the commercial banks 'call in' their short-term loans, if pressed for cash under the liquidity or reserve assets rule.

In addition, the Bank of England still transacts a little conventional banking business for some old customers, usually City of London firms. Also, it undertakes not only the running of the Exchange Equalisation Account, but also relations with foreign central banks, the I.M.F. and the World Bank (I.B.R.D.). The Bank of England is also a shareholder and adviser on the Finance Corporation for Industry Ltd, and the Industrial and Commercial Finance Corporation.

The activities of the Bank of England are conducted in two departments, the Issue Department, which is concerned with the currency issue, and the Banking Department, which administers the accounts of the Government and commercial banks and undertakes the operations which make possible fluctuations in the permitted currency issue. The Bank publishes a Weekly Return, or Account, setting out the assets and liabilities of each department.

(b) Issue and Banking Departments

The assets and liabilities of the Bank's two departments on 18 November 1970 were as follows, in Table 6.6.

With reference to Table 6.6:

(i) It will be noticed that the note issue is fiduciary, i.e. based on 'faith', or backed by holdings of (mainly) Government securities. These have been purchased by the Banking Department and passed on to the Issue Department, which used them to cover new notes, which were passed back in exchange to the Banking Department. The latter then passed them on into circulation when asked for notes by bodies whose deposits it held.

(ii) The assets of the Banking Department consist of notes and coin held in reserve, i.e. not yet passed on into circulation, securities (mainly Government), and short-term loans to, or rediscounted bills from, the money market, which are treated as profitable investments. The 'proportion' or ratio of notes and cash in reserve serves as a regulating factor on the Banking Department's

Table 6.6 *Bank of England return for* 18 *November* 1970

Issue Department:

Liabilities (£m)		Assets (£m)	
Notes issued:		Fiduciary issue:	
In circulation	3488·3	Government Debt and secur-	
Reserve notes held in		ities	3395·3
Banking Dept	61·7	Other securities and coin	
		other than gold coin	154·7
Total	£3,550·0	Total	£3,550·0

Banking Department:

Liabilities (£m)			Assets (£m)		
Capital and undistributed			Securities:		
	profits	18·0	Government	667·4	
Deposits:			Discounts and advances	62·8	
Public accounts	13·7		Other	36·9	
Bankers' deposits	224·4				767·2
Special deposits	386·0		Reserve of coin and notes held		
Others	188·6		for Issuing Dept ('Proportion')		63·5
					(7·64%)
		812·7			
	Total	£830·7		Total	£830·7

(Based on material in *Bank of England Quarterly Bulletin*, Vol. 10, No. 4, Dec. 1970)

acquisition of other assets. When it falls very low – reflecting a desire by the public for added currency to finance 'over-the-counter' transactions, as in the Christmas shopping period – the Bank may be permitted to increase the fiduciary issue, to replenish the reserve.

(iii) The liabilities of the Banking Department represent the deposits of its customers, which include some foreign and colonial banks, members of the money market and a few private customers of long standing (a relic of the days when the Bank still engaged in some commercial activities). The Bankers' Deposits represent the factor most susceptible to monetary control, as they are considered by the banks as part of their liquidity or reserve ratio.

(c) **Weapons of the central bank for the control of monetary and credit policy**

In addition to its power, under the 1946 Act, to issue 'directives' to the banks, on the authority of the Treasury, the Bank of England has the following armoury of monetary and credit controls:[1]

[1] It is of interest to note that following the 7% Bank Rate of November 1964 and the 'directive' of 30 Apr. 1965 for a 'credit squeeze', particularly against the private sector, the commercial banks took the unprecedented step, on 14 May 1965, of writing in protest to the Governor of the Bank (see *D.T.*, 30 April; 6 and 15 May 1965).

The Bank of England has gradually assumed increasing control over the issue of paper money. The 1844 Bank Charter Act, aimed at preventing the over-issue of notes in the economy, which had caused the failure of many note-issuing banks in the past, decreed that no new banks should be allowed note-issuing power. Furthermore, a limit was fixed on the note issue of other banks; only the Bank of England could issue notes in London; provincial banks were to lose note-issuing power if they opened a London branch or amalgamated with a bank which had one. If a bank lost its note issue for these reasons, or voluntarily ceased to issue notes, the Bank of England could increase its fiduciary issue by two-thirds of the abandoned issue. The Bank of England had to back all its notes with gold or silver, other than a fiduciary amount of £14 million (backed by Government securities), which could be increased by the method just described. Since 1921 the Bank of England has been practically the sole note-issuing bank in Britain. The Bank of Scotland and the Bank of Northern Ireland have to back all their notes with Bank of England notes, apart from a minute amount of £4·3 million.

In 1928 the Currency and Bank-notes Act permitted increases in the fiduciary issue, with Treasury consent. On 30 August 1939, just before the outbreak of World War II, the total note issue was about £545 million, of which £282 million was fiduciary and £263 million backed by gold coin and bullion.[1] Following the outbreak of war, almost the entire gold reserve in the Issue Department was transferred to the Treasury, and the note issue became entirely fiduciary.

The significance of the fiduciary issue lies in the fact that it constitutes the legal tender used in cash transactions by the public, and that it is required by the banks as a major element, as part of Bankers' Deposits, in their liquid reserve ratio. Whilst gold coinage was still being used (until 1914) the fiduciary issue was less significant than gold as a limit to the amount of money used in cash transactions, and as a constituent of the liquid cash ratio. Gradually, however, the entire note issue, concentrated in the hands of the Bank of England, has become fiduciary and this fiduciary issue now determines the amount of legal tender (apart from the small amount of coin) available to the public. On the other hand, the development of the cheque and credit card system with bank deposits has to some extent counteracted the shortage of legal tender as a means of settlement. Nevertheless. the extent of bank deposits or bank credit is itself still limited by the 12·5% reserve ratio, which is made up partly of Bankers' Deposits, some of which is legal tender (fiduciary issue and coin), which 'leaks' out of circulation into the banks. Should the fiduciary issue prove to be insufficient to meet the public's requirements for legal tender, the 'leakage' to the banks would dry up, and they would have to restrict bank credit accordingly. Alternatively, should the fiduciary issue be too large, the unnecessary surplus would leak out to the banks, raising their cash ratio and permitting them to expand deposits or bank credit beyond judicious limits.

The Bank of England, in fact, does allow temporary fluctuations in the fiduciary issue for the Christmas shopping period and the summer holiday period, a practice started in 1937. During these two periods the public require more legal tender than usual, to finance unusually large cash transactions. Thus there are

[1] *Ann. Abs. Stat.*, 84, p. 234.

heavy withdrawals of notes and coin from the banks. Eventually, these notes are returned to the banks by businessmen, etc., but in the interim the banks' liquid ratios are depleted. Immediately they call for legal tender to the Bank of England, to replenish their Till Money. The Bank of England pays out notes from the Banking Department reserve, whilst simultaneously Bankers' Deposits fall. The Bank of England's 'proportion' of reserve notes is therefore depleted – a warning signal. The banks, whose cash proportions have fallen, would normally be expected to reduce deposits and bank credit. This would upset the monetary mechanism just at the time when business was at its peak, simply through the technicality that cash had been *temporarily* withdrawn by the public. To avoid this shock to the monetary system, the Bank of England temporarily increases the fiduciary issue towards the end of November (by £50 million in 1963) and in July. The surplus notes are lodged by their holders in the banks, whose cash ratios are restored. The procedure is put into reverse when the original notes start to drift back to the banks – surplus to requirements – at the end of the peak spending periods.

BANK RATE (UNTIL OCTOBER 1972) AND MINIMUM LENDING RATE

Bank Rate was the rate of interest, announced in the Weekly Return, at which the Bank of England was prepared to act as 'lender of last resort' by rediscounting first-class commercial bills or Treasury Bills to approved customers (the Discount Market), when the commercial banks, being short of cash, had to call in loans to the market. At such times the Discount Market was said to be 'in the Bank'. Without the convention of Bank Rate, and the willingness of the Bank of England to supply cash to the Discount Market whenever it was required, the market would have been unable to repay the banks when they called in their short-term loans, because that money would have been spent on the bills which they held. The 'lender of last resort' function therefore made additional cash indirectly available to the banking system, in emergency, and prevented the chaos and instability which would have ensued if the market had been unable to repay the banks.

Its deeper significance lay in the fact that it used to act like a spirit level, since by tradition and interaction the whole complex range of other interest rates moved into line with it. For example, the rate granted by the commercial banks to depositors (on deposit account) used to be 2% below Bank Rate; their rate to borrowers (ordinary customers 'on overdraft') 1% to 1½% above Bank Rate; and to the Discount Market about 1·625% below Bank Rate; the Post Office Savings Bank and the Trustee Savings Bank gave 2½% regardless of Bank Rate; Building Societies gave about 1% below Bank Rate and charged about ⅛% to 2% above: Finance Houses offered about ⅛% above, and charged ½% to ¾% above Bank Rate. A more direct link between Bank Rate and the banks' rates to depositors and lenders was provided by their practice of purchasing very liquid bills (close to maturity) from the Discount Market. As Bank Rate affected the latter, they charged the Banks accordingly, thus causing them to bring their rates into line.

It followed that when Bank Rate rose (making money 'dear'), the banks would raise their interest rates to borrowers, thus tending to reduce the demand for finance for spending on consumer or capital goods and to reduce 'credit' deposits, which are created when loans are made. At the same time the banks offered a higher rate to customers with funds in deposit accounts. This induced some customers to transfer funds from current account to deposit account, and tended to restrict the desire of customers to spend. A further effect of a rise in Bank Rate was to attract foreign capital and 'hot money' to London. It has also been aimed at protecting the balance of payments position, by acting as a brake on internal demand and rising export prices.

The main trends in Bank Rate and in the yield on Consols (Government gilt-edged securities, the yield on which approximates to the long-term interest rate level) are shown in Fig. 6.7 for the period 1800 to 1972, when Bank Rate was abandoned.

In October 1972, for reasons to be discussed in sub-section (d), Bank Rate was replaced with a 'last resort' device called the 'minimum rate for lending to the money market'. This was to be flexibly linked to market rates by the formula 'average rate of discount for Treasury Bills at the weekly tender plus 0·5% and rounded off to the nearest 0·25 above'. Thus, in the first week, the minimum rate was set at 7·25%: this was geared to the 91-day Treasury Bill average rate, which was set at 6·689%. It replaced a Bank Rate of 6% at a time when the base rate of the major clearing banks for lending to prime customers was 7%.

OPEN MARKET OPERATIONS

These functions constitute the buying and selling of short-term liquid securities, usually Treasury Bills, in the discount or money market (through the Special Buyer) or long-term Government securities quoted on the Stock Exchange (through the Government broker). The aim is to supplement or even supersede the effectiveness of the 'last resort' rate, by working on the item Bankers' Deposits, which the banks treat as part of their liquid reserve assets ratio. These day-to-day operations are also carried out to counteract temporary fluctuations in the com-mercial banks' cash ratios, due mainly to irregular Government receipts and payments of large sums of money, which for a while cause a swing from Bankers' Deposits to Public Accounts or *vice versa* in the Banking Department. If, for example, the Bank of England buys bills or securities, the vendors will either be banks, firms or individuals. Simultaneously, the Bank of England will create a deposit in favour of the vendor, or will give the vendor a cheque drawn upon the Bank of England. Where the banks are the vendors, their Bankers' Deposits immediately increase; where the general public are the vendors, they transfer the deposits created in their favour (or their cheques) to their own banks, whose Bankers' Deposits at the Bank of England again rise.

Consequently, when the Bank of England buys through open market opera-tions, the banks' deposits at the Bank of England increase, thus causing the liquid reserve assets ratios of the commercial banks to rise. This permits them to increase other assets (advances, investments, etc.) by 7 times the amount pur-chased by the Bank of England. This simultaneously increases bank deposits or bank credit by an identical amount. As bank deposits are money, then the pur-chase of bills and securities by the Bank of England is termed a 'money-creating' open market operation. A further effect of open market buying is the tendency for the prices of securities to be bid up. As was seen in Section 5 (d) 1 iii (specula-tive liquidity preference), when security prices rise, the level of long-term and medium-term interest rates tends to fall. Furthermore, as the banks' ability to lend increases with the increase in Bankers' Deposits, they are more inclined to reduce their interest rate for loans, in order to encourage borrowers. Consequently, open market *buying* was used to support a *fall* in Bank Rate, and open market

507

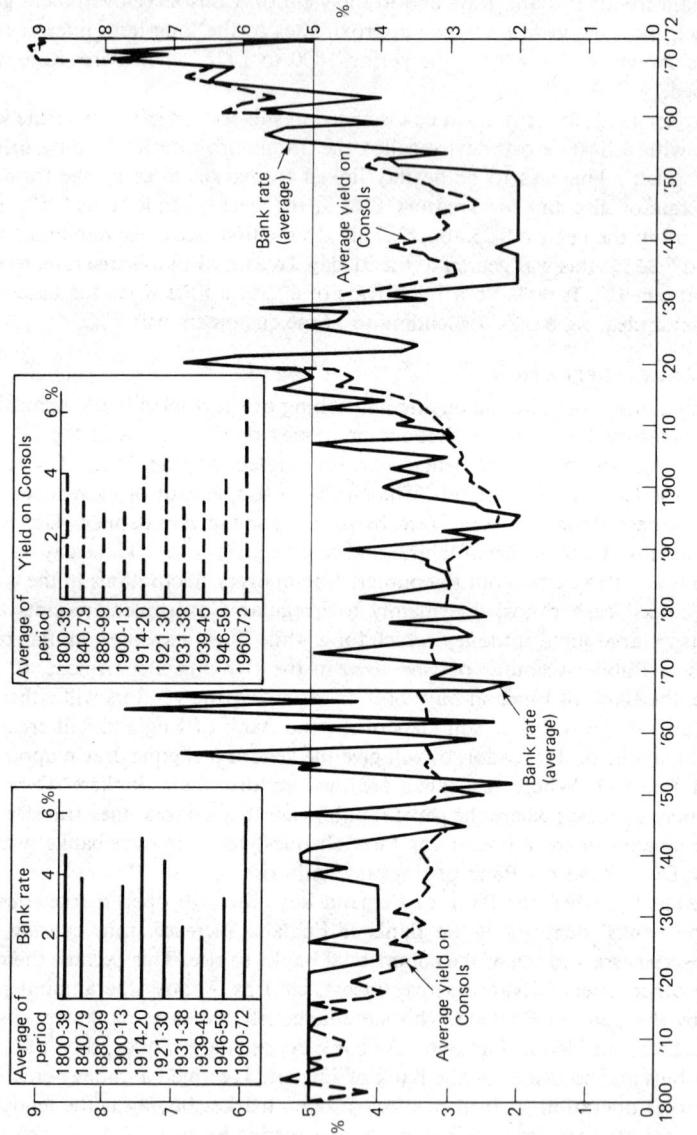

Fig. 6.7. *Bank Rate and Consol yield trends, 1800–1972*
(Sources: *L.B.R.*, April 1970, p. 45, and *B.B.R.*, Aug. 1972, pp. 69, 70)

selling was used to support a *rise* in Bank Rate, both by causing security transactions to influence the rates of interest and by acting directly upon the commercial banks' deposits at the Bank of England, thus directly influencing the
amount of money in the economy.

It must be noted, however, that the effectiveness of open market operations
may be reduced if the 'market' does not wish to sell to the Bank of England, and
especially if it does not wish to buy from it.

SPECIAL DEPOSITS

Under an agreement concluded between the Bank of England, the London
Clearing Banks and the Scottish banks in 1958, the Bank of England reserves the
right (first exercised in April 1960) to 'call on' the banks to lodge 'Special
Deposits' with it. These are notes or part of Bankers' Deposits, which are
'frozen' and are not to be treated as constituting part of the 12·5 reserve assets
ratio.

One or two months' warning is given to the banks, who have to make readjustments in their assets structure, to find the necessary Special Deposits. By September 1971 3·5% of total assets (1·75% for the Scottish Banks) had been called
in. These were all repaid on 15 September 1971.

The aim of Special Deposits is to tie up some of the banks' liquid cash in such
a way that they cannot use it to build up 7 times that extent of other assets, by
'gearing'. Therefore, in theory, the banks would have to cut down customers'
deposits or bank credit by 7 times the amount of Special Deposits. The intention,
therefore, of instituting or raising Special Deposits is to reduce in a direct manner
the amount of money in the economy. In particular, the intention is to oblige the
banks to call in old advances or to restrict new ones, as this item is considered to
be the main element making for inflationary demand pressure on the economy.

The effectiveness of this weapon may be diminished if the banks, not wishing
to lose a great deal of highly profitable assets (securities and advances) in this
way, find the liquid cash for the Special Deposits simply by selling investments
(securities) to an amount equivalent to the Special Deposits. Hitherto the Bank
of England could only appeal to the banks not to do this. On the other hand, the
Bank of England could retaliate by fixing extremely high levels for the Special
Deposits. In June 1969, for example, the Bank of England cut by half the interest
rate paid on Special Deposits, as a penalty for failing to bring their lending down
to the 'ceiling' imposed earlier. In April 1970 the full rate of interest was restored,
but the level of Special Deposits itself was raised – as a more direct control
measure – for the first time since July 1966. In July 1970 the Bank deemed it
necessary to remind the banks firmly to observe the lending guidelines: in
October 1970 it resorted to a further increase in the rate of Special Deposits, to
back up its exhortations.[1] Following the new policy, inaugurated in 1971, Special
Deposits were henceforth to be used flexibly; the rate of calls was to be the same
for all banks; deposits called would be based on all or only some of the eligible
liabilities; the rate of interest paid was to be equivalent to the Treasury Bill rate.[2]
A significant change in Special Deposits policy was announced in the crisis
Budget of December 1973. With the primary objective of securing a firmer
control of the growth in the money supply by the financial authorities – without
causing further increases in interest rates – this measure retained the $12\frac{1}{2}\%$

[1] See *M.B.R.*, May 1971, pp. 27–8.   [2] See 'Controlling bank credit', *E.P.R.*, 17, July 1971.

required liquid assets ratio for the banks and also the Special Deposits already paid in by that date. However, Special Deposits were henceforth to be *automatically payable* whenever a bank's interest-bearing deposits had risen faster than a *specified target rate* (to be fixed periodically). To the extent that such deposits exceeded the current target rate, a proportion of the excess had to be paid to the Bank as Special Deposits *without interest*: the proportion could rise to as much as 50%. The initial target rate up to June 1974 was fixed at 8% above the level for the period at inception of the scheme. It was anticipated that three consequences would occur: firstly, banks would compete to attract current account money; secondly, competition for deposit account money (at higher and higher interest rates) would subside; thirdly, there would be pressures on the banks to sell gilt-edged securities. The last result would tend to raise gilt yields and long term-interest rates, as their prices fell, at a time when short-term money market rates were falling. A limit to the possible fall in money market rates, however, would continue to be set by interest rates abroad.[1]

DETERMINATION OF LIQUIDITY RATIOS

A recent addition to the Bank of England's effective armoury of monetary controls is the power to impose direct control over the banks' liquidity ratios (and thus the total amount of money in the economy), or at least the total amount of money created by an asset of a particular type, such as advances to the public.

In October 1963 the Bank of England announced that the old 'liquidity assets' ratio of the commercial banks was to be reduced to 28% for a trial period, with a view to an eventual reduction to 25%. This permitted the banks to hold a greater proportion of their total assets in the form of securities (investments) and advances. The total amount of money (bank deposits) remained the same, but the manner in which it was created was altered. At a stroke, more money was available as bank loans, highly profitable to the banks, and essential in periods of economic expansion. By the same token, the Bank of England had established its power to interfere directly in liquidity ratios, by raising or lowering them.

This step was followed, during the 1960s, by a series of 'guidelines' or 'lending ceilings', aimed at specifically restricting advances. This proved to be a difficult objective to achieve and had to be bolstered up by an unprecedented, flexible use of Special Deposits.

In 1971 a fairly radical 'package' of measures was inaugurated, with the document 'Competition and Credit Control'. This brought most of the 'non-bank financial intermediaries' – hitherto exempt from many of the Bank of England's controls – into line with the banks. It also inaugurated a more rational system of interest rate competition in the banking system, removed quantitative controls on lending, limited official 'open market' support for gilt-edged securities, and instituted the new concept of 'eligible liabilities' and 'eligible reserve assets'. The ratio of the latter, of course, was fixed at 12·5% but this was to be backed up by flexible use of the Special Deposits weapon. Furthermore, the way has been opened up for flexible use of the reserve assets ratio, which could be raised or reduced, according to the circumstances.[2]

[1] For further details see 'Banking: high cunning', *Econ.*, 22 Dec. 1973, p. 69 and 'Comes the CCC2 banking revolution.' *The Sunday Times*, 23 Dec. 1973.
[2] H. Rose, 'Competition and credit control: the new framework', *T.B.R.*, March 1972, and *M.B.R.*, May 1972, pp. 12–13. Also see 'Controlling bank credit', *E.P.R.*, 17, July 1971 and 'The banks, credit and the value of money', *D.T.*, 6 Dec. 1972.

(d) Effectiveness of the Bank of England on the supply of currency and credit

We may now summarise the general effectiveness of all the Bank's controls over the supply of money – legal tender and credit.

The size of the *fiduciary issue* is at present one of the key factors supporting the pyramid of money in the economy. Out of total notes and coin in circulation, the proportion lodged at the banks (less than one-quarter) constitutes the major part of Bank Cash. Bankers' Deposits at the Bank of England are only about one-quarter of Bank Cash, and most of this element consists of currency lodged at the Bank. The Bank of England's debts (other than for lodgements of currency) to the commercial banks, incurred through the transfer of debts from its other accounts to Bankers' Deposits, or through the purchase of securities from the banks, constitute only a part of the Banker's Deposits item.

On the other hand, the fiduciary issue is strictly controlled by the Treasury, whereas the Bank of England may, through *open market operations*, more easily influence the non-currency element in Bankers' Deposits, which are treated by the banks as part of their reserve assets ratio for the backing of bank deposits. Thus, whilst the main dimensions of the cash basis of the total money supply are determined by the size of the fiduciary issue, fairly important alterations may be engineered by the Bank of England through open market operations. The latter may also be assisted by the manipulation of *Special Deposits* and the varying of the banks' *liquidity (or reserve) ratios.*

Whilst the size of the fiduciary issue and coinage is an important determinant of the total money supply, it is subject to various external counterchecks. The main one is the extent of the 'leakage' into the banking system, where each £1 deposited by clients *permits* the banks to create £7 of credit. This leakage depends very much on seasonal factors such as the Christmas shopping period, when the public needs more currency to make day-to-day transactions. In the main, however, it depends upon the habits and customs of the public. As more and more people and firms use cheques (bank deposits) as a means of payment; as more workpeople are paid by cheque (to avoid payroll snatches); as the practice (widespread in the U.S.A.) of using personal credit cards to purchase all manner of goods and services takes root (whereby the customer gives his credit-card number and then signs the bill), there could be a smaller proportion of notes held by the public, and a larger proportion lodged at the banks, where it may be magnified into bank credit. A further check exists at the point where the 'leakage' has seeped into the banks. Their ability to magnify these deposits (Bank Cash) into bank credit is limited not only by the reserve assets ratio, but also by the willingness of their clients to take up this credit. Even with the weapon of a low Bank Rate (now minimum lending rate), the public, as was found during the interwar depression, may not wish to borrow because of extremely pessimistic business expectations.

The weapon of open market operations, within the limits of existing liquidity ratios, aims at the Bankers' Deposits element in Bank Cash. Its limitations, however, lie in the fact that the market may not wish to buy or sell securities – in which case Bankers' Deposits remain unaltered – and that, again, an increase in this item, whilst increasing the banks' ability to create a magnified amount of credit, may not be matched by a willingness of the public to take up this credit.

Prior to the 1971 changes in monetary policy – limiting the Government's *open market operations*, freeing banks to compete on interest rates and thus leading the way to the eventual abandonment of *Bank Rate* in 1972 – a good deal of controversy had revolved around the usefulness of these weapons.[1] On the one hand, arguments had been presented, during the late 1960s, to the effect that interest rates generally were too high, as compared with earlier years. This, it was contended, discouraged investment which was needed to modernise industry and to promote exports; it was also held to make housing more expensive, because of higher mortgage charges; it penalised holders of fixed-dividend Government securities; it added to the public expenses of 'servicing' the National Debt, as a result of higher interest payments to internal and external lenders to the Government. On the other hand, it has been maintained that as a result of inflationary pressures, rates of interest have failed to keep up with the falling value of money (and thus with capital losses): consequently, these had tended to be 'negative interest rates' in real terms. The fault, it was held, lay in the failure of the Government to pursue orthodox monetary policies, which traditionally relied on Bank Rate and supporting open market operations to alter the price and volume of money. The reason for this lapse lay in the prime concern of the Government to keep down the cost of Government short-term (Treasury Bill) and long-term (gilt-edged) borrowing and to preserve the capital values of gilt-edged securities (*via* high prices), so as to uphold demand for Treasury Bills and gilt-edged and to prevent large scale sales by the public. Attempts to control the volume of money tended to take the indirect form of requests to restrict lending and the use of Special Deposits. During 1971, within an overall policy of stimulating the economy by fiscal reflationary measures, this practice of 'sitting on interest rates' may not have seemed unreasonable. Nevertheless, the pace of inflation, the negative real level of interest rates and the over-valued exchange rate for sterling, fixed by the December 1971 'Smithsonian Agreement', were all exerting pressure to push interest rates up.

During 1972 the role of Bank Rate in determining the structure of interest rates declined, following the 1971 removal of quantitative restrictions on advances, the new liquidity ratio and the increase in banking competition. It became more and more a simple rate of 'last resort' lending to the money market. As such, it was becoming inappropriate to continue to hedge it about with rigid restrictions, as in the past. Furthermore, as market interest rates, from mid-1970, started to move up to levels *above* Bank Rate, the latter was sometimes referred to as a rate of 'first resort' rather than as a penalty 'last resort': the discount market could borrow at Bank Rate and buy Treasury Bills at a profit.[2] Consequently, in October 1972 the device of Bank Rate was officially abandoned. Henceforth there was to be a flexible rate, reflecting the changing conditions of the market, rather than signalling momentous changes in monetary policy.

Bank of England action with regard to *Special Deposits* (as a means of restricting money) appears at first sight to be a more effective control over total Bank Deposits than minimum lending rate, because it acts as an indirect way of varying

---

[1] W. A. Eltis, 'Are interest rates too high?', *L.B.R.*, July 1969; B. Reading, 'Too high interest rates', *N.W.B.Q.R.*, Feb. 1970; W. E. Norton, 'Debt management and monetary policy in the United Kingdom', *E.J.*, Sept. 1969; N. Peera, 'Interest rates: illusion or reality', *N.W.B.Q.R.*, May 1970; P. Wann, 'Lower interest rates?', *N.W.B.Q.R.*, May 1970; 'Managing the gilt-edged market – a temporary change of emphasis?', *M.B.R.*, May 1969; Maxwell Stamp Associates, 'What determines the interest rate?', *M. & W.S.R.*, Spring 1971.

[2] 'A vulgar error', *Econ.*, 14 Oct. 1972, p. 91; 'The half-successful revolution', *Econ.*, 23 Sept. 1972, survey on the City, pp. 9–14.

the liquid reserves asset ratio – 'freezing' sums which would otherwise be part of Bankers' Deposits – part of the 'yeast' of bank credit. Ostensibly, it obliges the banks to wipe out 7 times as much of their other assets (and thereby of their bank credit or deposits), as shown below in Fig. 6.8.

Fig. 6.8.

(i) Assets structure based on £12½ Bankers' Deposits, *before* Special Deposits

(ii) Theoretical assets structure immediately *after* call for 3% Special Deposits

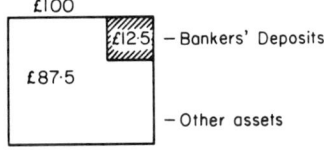

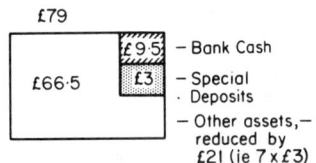

However, the banks may, under the present system, attempt to find the sum to lodge as Special Deposits, not by automatically reducing their Bank Cash (and thereby being forced to reduce Advances), but by liquidating some other assets, such as Investments. This would leave their total assets (and therefore bank credit) virtually unaltered,[1] as shown in Fig. 6.9.

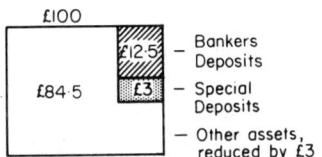

Fig. 6.9. *Possible assets structure if the 3% Special Deposits are* financed *by the liquidation of some other asset and not by the reduction of Bankers'* Deposits

Nevertheless, the Bank of England does have the ultimate power – failing that of instructing the banks as to *how* they should provide the Special Deposits – to step up the percentage of Special Deposits to a penal but effective level, and thereby to force the banks to reduce Advances, etc., or to reduce the interest paid to the banks. By late-1973 the 1971 Competition and Credit Control policy measures – including the traditional Special Deposits weapon – were being criticised as failing to stem the expansion of the money supply without raising interest rates.[2] It was widely anticipated that the authorities would revert to the former device of setting ceilings on advances – abandoned in 1971. Instead, as pointed out above, the crisis Budget of December 1973 introduced a new form

[1] It has been suggested by Norton (*loc. cit.*, p. 492), that the preference of the authorities for short-run stability in interest rates (and thus their willingness to buy securities and uphold their price, rather than passively allow large price falls) has meant that the public and the banks could make sales at small cost. This cast doubts on the efficacy of the Special Deposits device in 1969, but the more forceful use of the device in 1970 and the greater flexibility since 1971 may have done much to increase their effectiveness.

[2] See 'Banking: high cunning', *Economist*, 22 Dec. 1973, p. 69 and 'Comes the CCC2 banking revolution', *The Sunday Times*, 23 Dec. 1973.

of *automatic, non-interest-bearing* Special Deposits, to be levied on interest-bearing liabilities whenever they grew in excess of a specific target rate (initially 8% over the first half-year to June 1974). It was thereby hoped to reduce the pressures on high money market short-term interest rates by inducing banks, at such times, to compete harder for current account money, to compete less for deposit account money and to sell gilts.

Perhaps a more effective, more efficient and less cumbersome tool for influencing the money supply is the Bank of England's power to vary the banking system's liquidity ratios. The exercise of such power may, at a stroke, increase or decrease the banking system's ability to create credit on the basis of the existing 'leakage' from the fiduciary issue and may be used flexibly to alter the whole pattern of short-, medium- and long-term assets.

It must be noted that attempts to alter the pressure of consumer demand *via* changes in the money supply may be neutralised by changes in the velocity of circulation, as mentioned in Section 5(*b*) and (*c*). An interesting example of this occurred in France in May 1968. During a period of widespread strikes there was a shortage of ready cash, as most banks were closed. Yet, despite the fact that a high proportion of the population had no bank accounts, this artificial restriction in the *volume* of money was largely counteracted by the widespread acceptance of cheques as negotiable instruments, the effect of which was to increase the *velocity of circulation*.[1] A similar phenomenon occurred during the Irish bank strike of 1970.

14. The Money Market

The Money Market represents the institutions dealing in the provision and channelling of short-term liquidity. It has been characterised, in recent years, by the development of new techniques, new institutions and the blurring of traditional demarcation lines, according to specialised activities. There is more competition and more variety than used to be the case. The market as a whole is in a state of continuing evolution, but the major elements which may be distinguished are as follows:[2]

(*a*) The Discount Market

The London discount market is an important financial institution, dealing with the short-term lending and borrowing of money, and thus helping to stabilise its supply and demand. It deals mainly in commercial bills of exchange (normally those used in international trade) and Treasury Bills.

A bill of exchange is a device whereby A's promise to pay B (usually in three months) is guaranteed by C. Being guaranteed, the bill is secure, and may be 'negotiated' – handed over in payment by B to D – or 'discounted' for ready cash. The person who discounts the bill offers ready cash, and deducts a small commission to compensate him for the delay until the bill 'matures', when he will receive cash from A. By means of bills of exchange home and international trade were financed for many years. Traders were more willing to give credit, especially

---

[1] See *D.T.*, 29 May 1968.

[2] For further data, see 'Recent developments in London's money markets', *M.B.R.*, Aug. 1969 and Nov. 1969.

to foreign customers, when the debt was guaranteed and when the document could be turned into ready cash at less cost than finance by bank advances.

Treasury Bills, initiated in 1877, are similar devices, by which the Treasury borrows money for short periods (ninety to ninety-two days), to counteract the uneven flow of tax revenue.[1] They, too, may be discounted before maturity. The term 'Money Market', then, is used to refer to the firms concerned in short-term bill transactions, viz. the commercial banks (insofar as they accept and discount bills, and lend to the discounting firms), the Accepting Houses and the Discount Houses.

The guaranteeing (or 'accepting') of commercial bills is done to some extent by ordinary commercial banks – if they have sufficient knowledge of the circum- stances and of A's ability to pay – and by specialist Accepting Houses, who form the Accepting Houses Committee.

These Houses and banks charge a commission for accepting bills. The Houses are sometimes referred to as merchant bankers, and they tend to specialise on certain sections of trade in various parts of the world, so that they may be fully informed as to the acceptance risks. They also perform banking functions on behalf of their (mainly overseas) clients; they deal in bullion and foreign exchange; they issue long-term loans for foreign governments and domestic industrialists. It has been suggested that a more precise description of these firms would be 'accepting and issuing houses'.[2]

The discounting of bills of exchange is undertaken to some extent by the commercial banks, but mainly by the 11 Discount Houses, who are represented by the London Discount Market Association. By convention, the commercial banks do not compete with the discount houses for Treasury Bills, but buy these from them later on. These firms pay for bills partly with their capital, partly with the deposits held on account of clients for whom they perform some banking services, and mainly with short-term loans received from the commercial banks. They are aided by a few 'running brokers', who act as agents between them and sellers. The banks' 'money at call and short notice' is borrowed by the discount houses from day to day, at 'short loan' and 'call money' rates of interest. They then discount bills, charging higher 'market rates', fixed by the Association.

It is at this point that Bank Rate used to exert its influence. When the Bank of England wished to impose a 'dear money' policy of restraint, it raised Bank Rate, which was the penalty rate for 'last resort' lending or rediscounting by it to the Discount Market, when the commercial banks called in loans. The discount houses would already have purchased bills with 'short loans' and 'call money' at the previously lower rates of interest, and would already have entered into com- mitments to discount bills at a slightly higher market discount rate. If Bank Rate were raised, therefore, the market could still obtain funds from the Bank of England, by selling or rediscounting bills to it, in order to repay the banks which 'call in' money, but at such a high rate as to make the transaction unprofitable. The discount houses would thus try to curtail their transactions; money would be 'tight' or dear; the market would henceforth charge a higher market rate to people wishing to discount bills, and short-term finance in bills would be restrained.

1 'The Treasury Bill: the story of an economist's invention', *M.B.R.*, Feb. 1961, pp. 3–9.
2 Sir Edward J. Reid, 'Role of the merchant banks', *Stat.*, 17 May 1963, p. 497; 'Merchant banks and demarcation issue', *Stat.*, 24 Sept. 1965, p. 849 (dealing with novel competition from the Westminster Bank in the field of debenture loan issues).

Over the years, the discount houses have adapted themselves to changing circumstances. With the increasing use of cheques and the decline in home trade commercial bills, they concentrated on foreign bills. As these tended to decline in importance – again due to the use of bank deposits and the cheque system, and also to the rise of foreign commercial centres and to the falling share of Britain in world trade – the discount houses turned to Treasury Bills.

Gradually increasing competition in the discounting of Treasury Bills by foreign institutions has caused the Discount Market to look further afield. It has gradually undertaken the specialist function of buying, selling and holding medium-term (less than five years) Government securities, which give a higher yield than Treasury Bills.[1] The market thus supplies ready cash (borrowed from the banks) to holders of imminently maturing bonds, and by concentrating them into relatively few hands it helps the Government to refinance their conversion into new loans.

During 1971 the banks were showing a greater interest themselves in Treasury Bills, and the holdings of the Discount Houses were lower than in 1970. They were stimulated to expand their business activities into other assets, in particular their holdings of negotiable sterling Certificates of Deposit and of longer-term certificates (of three years and over to maturity).[2] The function of discounting bills is still, nevertheless, of great importance. In carrying it out the Discount Houses make bills available to the commercial banks, who buy them nearer to maturity and hold them as interest-bearing liquid assets. At the same time the supply of short-term money to the market constitutes another interest-bearing, but very liquid bank asset, which can be reclaimed at short notice. As the banks must keep much of their assets in almost cash form ('reserve assets' liquidity rule), bills and money at call and short notice constitute a reasonably profitable way of doing so. During the 1960s there was a great increase in the use of commercial bills and of other generally acceptable liquid assets, which were not readily susceptible to official control. As a result, the efficacy of the old liquidity ratio ruling on the banks was much impaired.[3] Thus the change in monetary control policy, inaugurated in 1971, brought the discount market into line with the banks. While 'last resort' lending continued to be a privilege extended only to the money market and while the banks continued to abstain from tendering for bills on their own account, controls were imposed on the money market. In order to maintain control over the use to which borrowed funds were put, the authorities required the market to keep a minimum of 50% of their assets in the form of public sector debts. Furthermore, the market was obliged to 'cover' the weekly Treasury Bill tender, but had to discontinue the cartel-type practice of tendering as a 'syndicate'. One result of the new 'eligible reserve assets' ratio policy–which was extended to all banks – was that, since 'call money' to the market was to be an eligible reserve asset, many non-clearing banks switched funds to the discount market. From December 1970 to December 1971 total discount market borrowed funds rose by £700 million to almost £3,000 million: the proportion coming from the London Clearing Banks, however, fell from 62% to 42%, while the proportion borrowed

---

[1] 'Discount market in pickle', *Stat.*, 15 Jan. 1965, pp. 167–8; 'Discount houses defences', *ibid.* 29 Jan. 1965, p. 323; 'Discount market's need to diversify', *ibid.*, supplement, 26 June 1964, pp. 34–7; 'Unfurling the umbrella', *Econ.*, 8 Aug. 1970, 'City of London Survey', pp. xii–xv.
[2] See *M.B.R.*, May 1972, p. 19.
[3] For a useful exposition of this problem, see A. B. Cramp, 'The control of bank deposits', *L.B.R.*, Oct. 1967.

from the Accepting Houses, overseas and other banks rose from 23% to nearly 38%. In August 1971 the Discount Houses ended their practice of jointly agreeing the interest rate on fine bank bills, and margins narrowed. This reduction in profitability was offset to some extent by an increased turnover of commercial bills, quantitative restrictions on which had been lifted.[1] As the suppliers of bills and the borrowers of short-term money, the Discount Houses have thus been referred to as the 'repository of liquidity' of the banking system.

(b) Parallel money market

During the 1960s the growth of the 'secondary banking system' was closely linked to the development of the Eurodollar and Euro-currency markets and the newer 'parallel money markets' in sterling.[2] At first, the participants were involved as 'money brokers', but they progressed from broking to 'secondary banking', with the making of medium-term loans and the issue of bonds. The parallel sterling money markets began with the need for local authorities to raise short-term finance, as their long-term bond issue powers were curtailed by Government policy and by the high interest rate cost. They were thus operating in a competitive market for funds, in competition with hire purchase finance houses and other borrowers. The finance houses soon joined the local authorities in their need to tap short-term funds. The brokers – eventually becoming the secondary bankers – tended not to go to the discount market for their liquid funds. The secondary bankers (see Section 9(c)) are competing with the discount houses in these operations, whereby they *provide funds for* the local authority short-term debt market, finance houses and industrial clients. They specialise on 'made to measure' arrangements and *obtain funds from* the Eurodollar and Euro-currency markets, from the 'interbank' market and from the Certificates of Deposit market. Their *clients cover* their borrowings with short-term bonds, bills and temporary deposit receipts, which are negotiable liquid instruments and are discounted. These assets are found by the parallel money market operators to have a wider range of maturities and higher level of yields than those of the conventional discount market (money at call, Treasury Bills and commercial bills).

The major institutional role, as a *source* of funds has been exercised by the interbank market. This constitutes a market in which the secondary banks – the non-deposit banks – borrow from and lend to each other liquid funds (sterling or foreign currency). It thus makes use of the Eurodollar and Euro-currency markets. The institution functions as a result of the tradition that the clearing (deposit) banks do not borrow from each other, and have to secure their loans with a 'cushion' of reserve assets. The secondary banks may thus accept large deposits in the knowledge that some other bank will borrow them: alternatively, it may make a large loan in the knowledge that it may tap the interbank market for idle funds. In this sense, the interbank market has to compete with the local authority market and finance house market in the obtaining of funds or deposits. The major participants in the money market and their interrelationships are shown, in simplified form, in Fig. 6.10.[3]

[1] See *M.B.R.*, May 1972, pp. 12–13, 18–19.
[2] See R. Croome and H. G. Johnson, eds., *Money in Britain*, 1959–1969, 1970, Part IV, ch. 1, pp. 140–6, and H. G. Johnson, ed., *Readings in British Monetary Economics*, pp. 428–30. Also see 'The Inter-bank markets in sterling', *M.B.R.*, Aug. 1973.
[3] An excellent series of notes and summary charts on the institutions and instruments of the money market is available in 'London money markets', *B.B.R.* (centre spread), Nov. 1972. Also see 'The City of London,' *Conjoncture*, 163, May 1973.

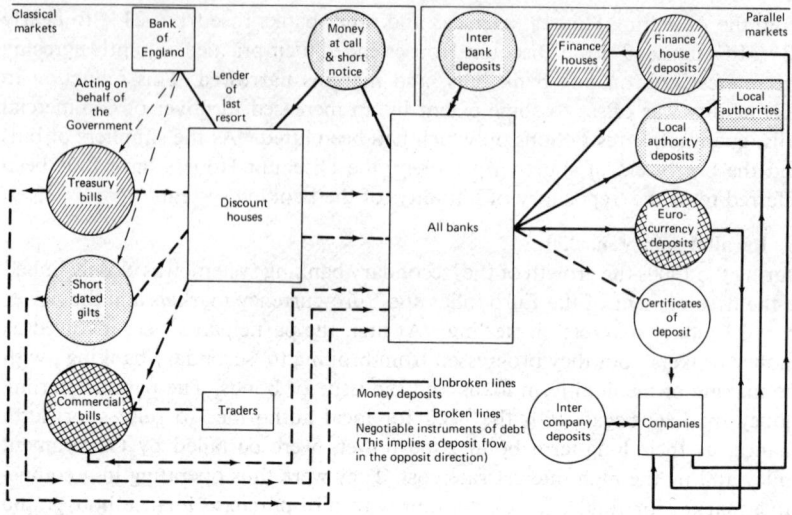

Fig. 6.10. *Primary participants in the money markets*
(Source: *B.B.R.*, Nov. 1972)

15. The Stock Exchange

When public joint stock companies and the Government wish to borrow from the public for long periods, the former give in exchange shares, and the latter give bonds. The shares are sometimes referred to as 'equities', and the bonds as 'gilt-edged'. All may be termed 'securities'.

The Stock Exchange is the institution by means of which holders of long-term securities may turn them into liquid cash by selling them to persons wishing to buy. It is the market in which people buy securities either as a source of income (investment) or in order to resell at a profit (speculation).

The terms 'stocks' and 'shares' are sometimes used indiscriminately with regard to equities and gilt-edged. More precisely, however, 'stock' refers to units of securities issued and quoted at a nominal value of £100. These securities are 'gilt-edged', yielding a fixed rate of interest and issued by British and Commonwealth Governments, local authorites, nationalised industries and public boards, by foreign governments, and as the fixed interest, temporary loan-debt securities of joint stock companies. 'Shares' are the securities of joint stock companies which do not guarantee a fixed return. These are the equities proper, quoted at a nominal (or original) value, such as 25p or 100p. However, in recent years the practice has grown of dealing in units of equity shares, referred to as 'units of stock' or just 'stock'.

The issuing of stocks and shares by the Government and trading firms who needed more money made extensive strides during the seventeenth century. It was an essential prerequisite to the system of borrowing from the public that holders of stocks and shares – the lenders of long-term capital – should be able to liquidate their holdings at will, by selling to available buyers. Agents came into being, who facilitated these transactions, and eventually, in 1773, they opened their first permanent premises, the Stock Exchange.

From 1964 to 1967 the number of provincial stock exchanges in Great Britain was reduced from nineteen to four by a process of amalgamations. By 1971 there were still three separate exchanges in Belfast, Dublin and Cork, but there was a possibility that these might merge. These seven, plus the London Stock Exchange, established a Federation of Stock Exchanges in Great Britain and Ireland in 1965, aimed at rationalisation and standardised procedures and entry requirements.[1] It was also empowered to set up a joint compensation fund to cover the default of any member of any participating exchange. The 1960s witnessed a process of branch office openings and overseas expansion, particularly by the London Stock Exchange.[2]

The London Stock Exchange is the most important member of the Federation, with 364 broking firms and 31 jobbing firms and about 3,800 brokers and 500 jobbers who were either partners or associated members, in 1970. By late-1970 9,180 securities were being quoted (89% of which were British), of which 3,574 were equities (about 80–90% of which were British) and the rest gilt-edged (British and overseas). The market value of all securities dealt with by the London exchange was £120 billion at end-March 1970. More than half of this market value, however, was accounted for by overseas stock and in the case of equity values (£95 million) the proportion accounted for by non-domestic stock was even higher.[3]

At present there are about 2·5 million direct shareholders in Britain, whilst about two-thirds of the population are indirectly shareholders, by way of pension funds, insurance premiums, trade union subscriptions, etc., which are invested by the bodies concerned, the 'institutional investors'.[4]

The 'floor' of the Stock Exchange, where dealings take place, is divided up into sections or 'markets', in each of which a certain type of security is dealt in. Examples of these are 'Oils', 'Aircraft', 'Motors', 'Shipping', etc. On the floor the 'jobbers' or stockjobbers operate in their specialist markets. These people are like wholesalers, buying and selling on their own account. Their link with the outside world – the buyers and sellers of securities – lies in the stockbrokers. These are the agents who act on behalf of their clients. They sell to and buy from the jobbers, who do not deal direct with the outside buyers and sellers.

Market prices for securities quoted on the Stock Exchange fluctuate by reason of changes in supply and demand. In the case of fixed interest securities, the market price will alter as the general level of rates alters. This is because the purchase of the security represents an investment. If it gives a 5% guaranteed rate of interest, whilst the general rate falls to $2\frac{1}{2}$%, then £100 nominal value of stock would yield as much (£5) as would £200 elsewhere. Thus the market price would rise to £200. Demand for a gilt-edged security, therefore, will depend partly on the general level of interest rates and anticipated movements in that level; partly on the length of time still to elapse before the security might become redeemable (or repayable) 'at par' or original, nominal value. In the case of

---

[1] By November 1972 all the U.K. exchanges had agreed in principle to establish a United Stock Exchange by 25 March 1973: the Eire exchanges had, by then, gained Government approval to join the scheme. (See 'Way clear for the United Stock Exchange', *F.T.*, 9 Nov. 1972.)

[2] 'Britain's stock exchanges since the war – a story of adaptation and innovation', *M.B.R.*, Nov. 1968, pp. 18–19.

[3] 'The uncommon market', *Econ.*, 8 Aug. 1970, City of London Survey, p. xx.

[4] *Ibid.*, p. 356, and 'Shareholders', *Econ.*, 2 July 1966, p. 52.

equities, demand and market price would be influenced mainly by the anticipated dividend and thus by the state of business expectations, the type of company, its profitability, the element of risk involved, etc. If anticipated dividend were to rise, the value of the equity as an investment would rise. The net yield on any security is worked out as a percentage of actual income to actual market price (or investment). If the dividend, therefore, is 20% on a nominal value of 100p, whilst market value is 200p, then the actual yield will be $20/100 \times 100p/200p = 10\%$. Consequently, as the investor will compare actual yield with what might be obtained by alternative investment at the general rate of interest, he will offer more for a security when the general interest rate falls. His security will appear to be a more lucrative investment, therefore, both when anticipated dividends rise and when the general level of interest rates falls.

Apart from the purchase of securities as long-term investments, to earn an income or yield on original outlay, some people buy securities primarily as a gamble. They speculate on a future rise in market price, in order to sell later on with a capital gain. Naturally, without an element of speculation as to future prices there would be no buyer wishing to take a security when a seller wishes to dispose of it. A certain modicum of speculation is essential to a free market in securities. The term 'bull' is used to refer to the person who buys, usually when quotations are rising, hoping to sell at a higher price. A 'bear' is a person who sells, usually when quotations are falling, hoping to buy again when prices are lower.

Much public debate has taken place about the evils of speculation, takeover bids and their control. In fact, it will normally be extremely difficult to prove whether a particular security transaction takes place as an investment or as speculation. If the free market were abolished, companies would find great difficulty in tapping funds from a public which knew that the resulting shares could never be turned into liquid cash. On the other hand, ruthless manipulation of the market for speculative purposes must be prevented. False rumours, for example, or sham takeover bids, or deliberate unloading or buying up of securities, to influence security prices, misleads the general public and upsets market stability. Nowadays, however, there exist various general controls over speculation: new issues of securities have to be submitted to the strict scrutiny of the Council of the Stock Exchange; the commercial banks deliberately restrict the proportion of their advances going towards Stock Exchange dealings; a Capital Gains Tax is levied on capital profits made on securities sold within six months of purchase.

The main economic function of the Stock Exchange is that it provides an almost perfect market for the sale and purchase of existing Government and private securities, thus allowing investors to regain liquidity, and so facilitating the flow of capital funds for investment. This function is enhanced by the fact that the Stock Exchange safeguards the interests of the public; helps to eliminate violent fluctuations in security prices, by reason of the specialised jobbers; provides an indication, by way of daily price quotations, of public confidence in Government or private fields of investment, thus facilitating the flow of new capital into suitable sectors of the economy.[1]

---

[1] For an interesting analysis of the problems of attracting finance for firms, see G. P. E. Clarkson and B. J. Elliott, 'Managing capital funds', *N.W.B.Q.R.*, Aug. 1970.

16. The Capital Market

In previous sections we have examined the commercial banking system and the Bank of England, in their rôle as the main source of money. In conjunction with the Accepting Houses and the Discount Houses (or Discount Market) – these institutions constitute the Money Market – in which very short-term loans of liquid cash are made to finance the discounting of short-term, self-liquidating Treasury Bills and commercial bills.

In addition to their participation in the very short-term discounting of bills in the Money Market, the commercial banks also purchase Government securities, but usually those which are quite near to redemption. They do not, therefore, undertake much direct buying of securities from (i.e. long-term lending to) the Government. However, they provide short-term working capital to private industry, by way of advances. To this extent they are participating in the Capital Market, which consists of a wide variety of specialist institutions, existing to channel into Government and industry short-term, medium-term and long-term capital. The Stock Exchange is the institution in the Capital Market where existing securities, given by Government and industry in exchange for long-term finance, may be bought and sold.

Other major institutions in the Capital Market are as follows:

(a) Trustee Savings Banks, the National Savings Bank and the National Savings Movement

These institutions have developed to encourage voluntary savings by the public – to be lent to the Government on short-term and medium-term.

The National Savings Bank, established in 1861 (as the Post Office Savings Bank), attracts deposits from the public. These deposits go into a fund, which is handed to the National Debt Commissioners, who invest it in Government securities. The Government guarantees the repayment of deposits, with interest. Up to £20 may be withdrawn on demand, the balance with a few days' notice. Deposits (to a maximum of £10,000) and withdrawals may be made at any of about 20,000 post offices in the United Kingdom. At the end of June 1971 there were about 22 million active accounts, amounting to £1,794 million in Ordinary and Investment Accounts. Advantages over a deposit account at a commercial bank include the following: a depositor may have more than one account; his 3·5% interest on Ordinary Account (and higher rate on Investment Account) may be higher in a N.S.B. account than in an ordinary bank account; he has to pay no income tax on the first £21 of interest; he has full drawing rights at any participating post office in the country.

The Trustee Savings Banks, established early in the nineteenth century, are local banks, managed by voluntary bodies of local trustees and managers. The Trustee Savings Banks have three departments, for 'ordinary' and 'special' investment and for current accounts. A client may only deposit in one branch of the T.S.B. Deposits (to a maximum of £10,000) in the Ordinary Department are treated in a similar way to N.S.B. deposits. Deposits in the Special Investments Department, to a total of £10,000, are not exempt from income tax on interest; require a month's notice of withdrawal; are not guaranteed by the Government; are invested under the supervision of the National Debt Commissioners; earn a higher interest rate than deposits in the Ordinary Department. In June 1971 there were over 1,500 T.S.B. branches, under the control of 75 independent banks, with

12·5 million accounts, amounting to £1,123 million in the Ordinary Department and £1,542 million in the Special Investments Department. In January 1968 the T.S.B. set up their own unit trust.

The National Savings Movement, originating in the War Savings Committee of World War I, encourages the investment of savings in the N.S.B., the T.S.B. and in National Savings securities. These securities are of four types: National Savings Certificate – introduced during World War I, accumulating 25% tax-free interest over four years, and encashable at short notice; Premium Savings Bonds, to a limit of £2,000, first issued in 1956, are repayable at par with short notice, but, after three months, provide the depositor the chance to win prizes – from £25 to £50,000 – in the monthly draws; British Savings Bonds, bearing 7% interest and repayable at par on one month's notice or with a £3 tax-free bonus, if held to maturity (five years after purchase), to a limit of £10,000; National Savings Stamps of small denominations and withdrawable on demand, which bear no interest. At end-March 1971 National Savings securities were held to the value of £805 million.

In 1969 a contractual form of National Savings was started, known as 'Save As You Earn' (S.A.Y.E.). This involves regular monthly payments into N.S.B. or T.S.B. accounts, provides bonus incentives for long-term deposits and bears tax-free interest.

The total of all these forms of National Savings, with N.S.B., T.S.B., securities and S.A.Y.E. rose from £7,000 million in 1960 to more than £10,000 million at end-1972, having increased sharply by £1,230 million since March 1971. Recent successes have been attributed to higher *per capita* incomes and to the increasingly competitive terms provided by the various forms of investment.[1]

The National Savings Movement's policy is determined by a National Savings Committee for England and Wales, and similar bodies for Scotland and Northern Ireland. These committees are bodies of independent persons, appointed by the Treasury, assisted by small salaried staffs of civil servants. There are about 300,000 voluntary workers in the movement, which works on the basis of small, voluntary savings groups in schools, workplaces, streets and villages – their work being coordinated by voluntary local Savings Committees.

(b) Co-operative Banks

The Co-operative Wholesale Society Bank, legally empowered to function in 1876, was set up to supply capital to the co-operative movement. It is now the financial centre for the movement, but also has clients amongst the trade unions, local authorities and private depositors. In 1948 the Scottish Co-operative Wholesale Society opened its own bank.

(c) Finance companies

The provision of short- and medium-term loans to consumers, to finance hire purchase transactions on consumer goods, became significant after World War I. By the outbreak of World War II about £100 million had been lent out in this way. Credit is given for a fixed term of years, repayable in instalments, interest being charged for the full period on the original amount borrowed. There are about

---

[1] *Brit. O.H.*, 1972, pp. 352–4; 'National Savings on the crest of a wave', *F.T.*, 24 April 1972; 'National Savings hit £10,000 million target', *F.T.*, 20 Nov. 1972.

1,000 hire purchase finance companies in Britain, of whom forty-one – members of the Finance Houses Association – are responsible for the bulk of finance house business.

By the end of 1969 total consumer credit outstanding had reached £2,425 million, excluding long-term credit for house purchases. Of this total about £500 million was owed to finance houses. Restrictions on bank and non-bank consumer credit in recent years has led to a lessening of the relative importance of finance house credit and to an increasing relative share of consumer credit by retailers. This has affected the finance houses in two main ways. Firstly, several large clearing banks have compensated for their loss of business by investing extensively in finance houses, many of which have been absorbed by the banks.[1] Secondly, although loans for car purchase are still the major component, there has been a shift of emphasis away from consumer credit towards the financing of industrial and commercial equipment and of home improvements.[2]

With the 1971 rationalisation of credit policy, the Bank of England brought the finance houses more closely into line with the commercial banks. Henceforth, the F.H.A. members and some finance houses outside the Association (those with more than £5 million of eligible liabilities) were to observe a minimum reserve assets ratio of 10% and could be called upon for Special Deposits. They were to be allowed to seek recognition as banks, and by May 1972 five had succeeded. This has tended to boost the official figures for eligible liabilities of banks.[3]

(d) Finance corporations

The report of the Macmillan Committee on Finance and Industry, published in 1931 (Cmd 3897), noted several 'gaps' in the provision of capital by the various existing institutions. In the main, the gaps were for intermediate credit (one to five years) for all sorts of enterprise – being too long for the banks and too short for new issues *via* the Stock Exchange – and for long-term credit for small and medium-sized firms which could not tap the new-issue institutions. The report stressed the need for the cooperation of the big banks in providing capital and credit facilities to institutions which might be created to bridge the gap. The Bankers' Industrial Development Company, formed in 1930 under the auspices of the Bank of England, played an important part in the reconstruction of the cotton, shipbuilding and steel industries in the 1930s, but it was liquidated voluntarily in 1945.

In 1945 the Finance Corporation for Industry, Limited and the Industrial and Commercial Finance Corporation, Limited were set up, with Government encouragement, to assist in postwar reconstruction and development. They are ordinary limited liability companies, without official representation or recourse to public funds, but the Bank of England subscribed part of their capital.

The F.C.I. was aimed at the re-equipment and development of major industries with loans of £200,000 or more. Its authorised and issued capital is £25 million, but it may increase its resources to £125 million by borrowing. Shares are held as follows: 40% by insurance companies; 30% by trust companies; 30% by the Bank. This share capital provides security for loans from the banks, and the

---

[1] See 'Consumer credit in the United Kingdom', *B.B.R.*, May 1971.
[2] See 'H.P. houses in industrial finance', *Stat.*, 15 Oct. 1965, p. 1049, for details of Finance Houses' entry into the field of loans to industry.
[3] See *M.B.R.*, Nov. 1971, p. 7 and May 1972, p. 13.

F.C.I. has made loans to firms producing steel, oil, chemicals, shipping and electrical components. Loans and investments at end-March 1971 amounted to £70 million.

The I.C.F.C. aims to provide credit and finance, where these are not forthcoming from other institutions, to smaller industrial and commercial firms, by providing long-term loan capital and share capital in amounts from £5,000 to £500,000. Its authorised and issued share capital is £15 million, but it may borrow a further £30 million. It was subscribed mainly by the London Clearing Banks and the Scottish Banks, with token participation of the Bank of England. The I.C.F.C. also provides a range of financial and other specialist services. At end-March 1971 it had about £150 million invested in 2,200 U.K. companies. In January 1970 it took over the Ship Mortgage Finance Company, Limited, which it had managed since 1964. The S.M.F.C. was formed in 1951, mainly to assist in the financing of shipbuilding. In 1962 the I.C.F.C. established a subsidiary, Technical Development Capital, Limited, to provide venture capital for the commercial development of technological innovations. In 1969–70 this function expanded by 44%, to reach an investment of £1·8 million. In 1967 another subsidiary, Industrial Mergers, Limited, was formed to concentrate I.C.F.C. expertise and assistance in the merger field. During its first year, in which it worked in close contact with the Industrial Reorganisation Corporation, it was concerned with thirty-three successfully completed mergers.[1]

Some other specialist finance corporations are as follows:

(i) *The Agricultural Mortgage Corporation, Ltd*[2] – established in 1928 to grant loans for up to sixty years, against mortgages on agricultural lands and buildings in England and Wales. Its share capital is subscribed by the Bank of England and other banks, but most of its funds come from public issues of debentures. In 1969 outstanding loans amounted to about £150 million. In 1933 a similar institution, the Scottish Agricultural Securities Corporation, was established in Scotland, its share capital being subscribed by three Scottish banks;

(ii) *The National Film Finance Corporation* – statutory body, set up in 1949 to make loans to film producers and distributors. Its funds, limited to £13 million, come mainly from Department of Trade and Industry advances and partly from non-Governmental sources;

(iii) *The Commonwealth Development Finance Company Ltd* – established in 1953 as a channel for the investment of private capital in Commonwealth development schemes. Of its total authorised capital of £30 million, £14½ million is in 'A' shares, held by United Kingdom shipping, banking, mining and industrial interests, and £11·75 million is in 'B' shares, held by the Bank of England and various Commonwealth central banks. By end-March 1971 its commitments amounted to about £27 million spread over several industries in more than thirty countries: it is no longer restricted to the Commonwealth.[3]

(e) Building societies

The main function of building societies is to tap personal savings, and to provide long-term mortgage loans to individuals, on the security of owner-occupied dwellings. They occasionally lend on the security of farms and commercial or

[1] See 'I.C.F.C. News-Report 2', *Econ.*, 13 June 1970 and 'I.C.F.C.', *Econ.*, 15 June 1968, p. 67.
[2] 'Finance for farming', *M.B.R.*, Feb. 1965, pp. 3–10 and 'Financing agricultural expansion', *M.B.R.*, May 1972, p. 7.
[3] See *Brit. O.H.*, 1972, p. 355.

industrial premises. General conduct of business is prescribed in the Building Societies Acts of 1874 to 1960, and discretionary powers are exercised by the Chief Registrar of Friendly Societies, who may prevent advertising and the acceptance of deposits in the case of suspected misconduct. Funds are derived mainly from the public, by way of deposits or investment in shares. Shares have a fixed value, are not quoted on the Stock Exchange, and, like deposits, may be withdrawn in cash, usually with one month's notice. Deposits earn a slightly lower rate of interest than shares, but they are given priority over shares in the case of a society winding up. Income tax is not payable on the deposit and share interest received by clients, being deducted at source.

At end 1970 there were 481 societies, with assets of £10,819 million, of which more than half were in the ten largest societies.[1] The amount advanced on mortgages in 1971, £2,741 million, was 36% higher than in 1970. By mid-1971 building societies accounted for about 82% (£9,491 million) of house purchase advances in the U.K., as compared with £1,001 million by local authorities and £1,165 million by insurance companies.[2] These advances constituted, at end-1971, 81% of total assets (£11,750 million) in the building societies: their liquidity reserves (cash and investments) were 19%, as compared with the legally required 7·5% minimum. Two important developments in recent years have been firstly, on the demand side, the rising proportion of owner-occupied houses (42% in 1960, 49·5% in 1970) and secondly, on the supply side, the increasing competition for savings by the various institutions, including the building societies. By 1971 depositors numbered about 11·5 million and borrowers about 3·8 million. It is possible that E.E.C. membership might lead the way to a liberalisation in the lending rules, and to the advancing of international home loans within the E.E.C.[3]

Figure 6.11 illustrates some of the salient points regarding house tenure, the relative importance of the building societies in the attraction of savings from the public, and the trends in building society assets, depositors and borrowers.

(f) Issuing houses and the New Issue Market

When additional long-term finance is required by industrial and commercial firms, whether new, existing, or being converted from private into public companies, the company will issue shares or debentures. Such new issues may be made independently (with Stock Exchange approval) by publishing a prospectus, or by seeking the specialist services of an Issuing House.

The issuing house advises on the type of security to be offered, and maintains close liaison with the Stock Exchange. Most of these firms are members of the Issuing Houses Association, founded in 1945. This body represents the interests of about 60 merchant banking houses, firms of stockbrokers and other institutions acting as issuing houses, maintaining contact with the Bank, the Council of the Stock Exchange, the Council of Foreign Bondholders, the Capital Issues Committee until 1967 and other bodies. About 16 members are also members of the Accepting Houses Committee. The issuing house buys up the whole issue of shares at a discount, and resells the shares to the public at an opportune time. This relieves the company of much financial worry, but the issuing houses, which usually specialise on a particular field, carefully vet all new issues which they

[1] *Brit. O.H.*, 1972, p. 358.
[2] See 'Credit for house purchase', *E.P.R.*, 23, Jan. 1972.
[3] See 'Building societies: mortgages galore', *Econ.*, 19 Feb. 1972, pp. 58–9.

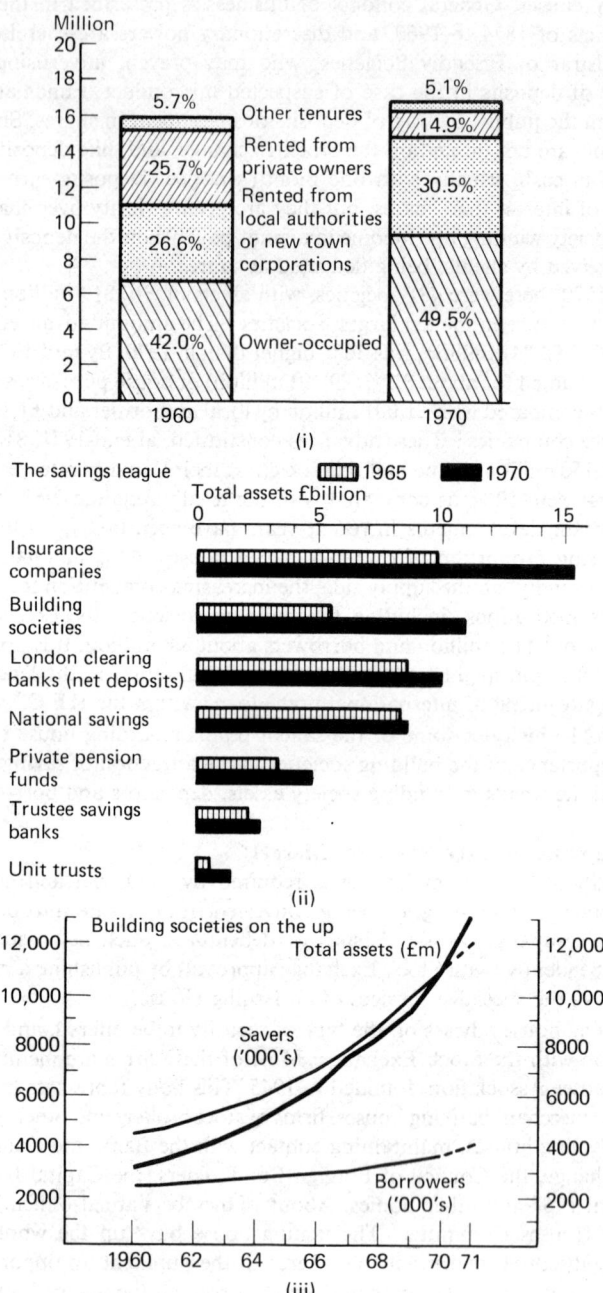

Fig. 6.11. *House tenure, competition for savings and building society assets, depositors and borrowers*
(Sources: *E.P.R.*, 23 Jan. 1972 and *Econ.*, 19 Feb. 1972, pp. 58–9)

handle. The issuing houses are often engaged in the activities of the gold and foreign exchange markets and have many other functions in connection with trade financing, investment management and insurance.[1]

The post-1971 competition in the banking world has heightened the pressure on the merchant banks, exerted by the clearing banks. As they adopt a flexible approach to new fields, the latter have been blurring the traditional demarcation lines around merchant banking activities.[2]

From 1932 to the outbreak of World War II various controls, resulting from public requests by the Chancellor, were exercised over new capital issues in Britain. In 1936 a Foreign Transactions (Advisory) Committee was established to advise the Treasury on issues involving investment abroad, outside the Commonwealth. In 1939 this was renamed the Capital Issues Committee and was given the wider task of advising the Treasury on the subject of statutory control over new capital issues.

After the war the C.I.C. was retained, and permanent control over capital issues was provided in 1946 with the Borrowing (Control and Guarantees) Act. The exemption limit, below which the committee's approval was not required, varied from £10,000 to £50,000. Since 1959 the C.I.C. was concerned with only a few types of application, mainly by overseas residents and local authorities. It was dissolved in November 1967, any residual functions with regard to overseas residents and public sector issues being taken over by the Bank of England.[3]

(g) Investment trusts and Unit trusts

These are institutions through which long-term capital is channelled from small private investors, who, aided by skilled management, may spread their risks over a wide selection of securities.

Investment Trusts were first founded after the granting of limited liability to joint stock companies by the 1862 Companies Act. They are public companies and invest in a wide range of stocks and shares. They acquire their funds by themselves issuing to their clients shares and debentures, which are quoted for resale on the Stock Exchange. Their income results from the dividends received from securities in which they have invested their funds. They distribute an annual dividend to their own shareholders from this income, after deducting administrative expenses (usually $\frac{1}{4}\%$ to $\frac{1}{2}\%$ of total capital), and after making allocations to reserves. The investment trust aims at achieving high and secure income. It does not distribute to its members any capital gains made from the sale of investments.

This form of institution has been prominent in channelling private capital for investment overseas. In 1932 was formed the Association of Investment Trusts, and the Radcliffe Committee found that of its 282 members – 256 had combined assets with a market value of £1,142 million: in 198 trusts there were 200,000 shareholders.[4] About 90% of securities held by the investment trust are equities, whose rising prices have accounted for the major part in the increased market value of investment trust assets. At end-1969 there were about 264 major investment trusts with total assets of about £4,900 million.[5]

[1] *Brit. O.H.*, 1972, pp. 351–2.
[2] 'Merchant banks: life will be a lot less easy in future', *F.T.*, 17 Feb. 1971.
[3] 'The tide turns for new issues', *M.B.R.*, Feb. 1968, p. 4.
[4] *United Kingdom Financial Institutions*, C.O.I. Ref. 24, 1960, p. 28.
[5] E. L. Furness, *An Introduction to Financial Economics*, 1972, p. 30.

The first Unit Trust appeared in London in 1868, but not until the early 1930s did they become fairly important. They are constituted not as public limited companies and by issuing shares, but as trusts, set up by trust deeds, signed by a management company (a limited company) and a trustee company (usually a bank or insurance company). The management company buys a block of securities, spread over a wide range of companies, from a list of stocks quoted in the Trust Deed. It then sells this block of stocks to the public in small units or sub-units, the price including a service charge for the remuneration of the trust managers.[1] The stocks are held by the trustees, who distribute the dividend income received from them to the unit-holders. Units may themselves be bought and sold through banks, stockbrokers, the management company or accountants. Where the list of stocks which may be purchased (known as 'underlying securities') is fixed in the Trust Deed, the unit trust is said to be 'fixed'. Where some variation may be permitted to the managers, the trust is said to be 'flexible'.

Regulation of unit trust activities is provided for in the Prevention of Fraud (Investments) Acts of 1939 and 1958. They are under D.T.I. supervision.

By 1939 there were ninety-eight unit trusts, with total assets of about £80 million. Until 1957 the Capital Issues Committee retarded the offering of units by unit trusts, but since 1957 there has been quite rapid growth. By end-April 1971 there were 2·38 million unit holdings. The value of funds invested in authorised trusts was £60 million in 1958 and doubled from end-1966 to end-April 1971 (to (£1,593 million), greatly influenced by the rising market values of equities and their growth prospects. The Association of Unit Trust Managers publishes monthly sales figures for the industry.

Fig. 6.12 shows the 1970–72 trends in unit trust sales and repurchases and in the index of Stock Exchange and unit trust market prices. The latter would seem

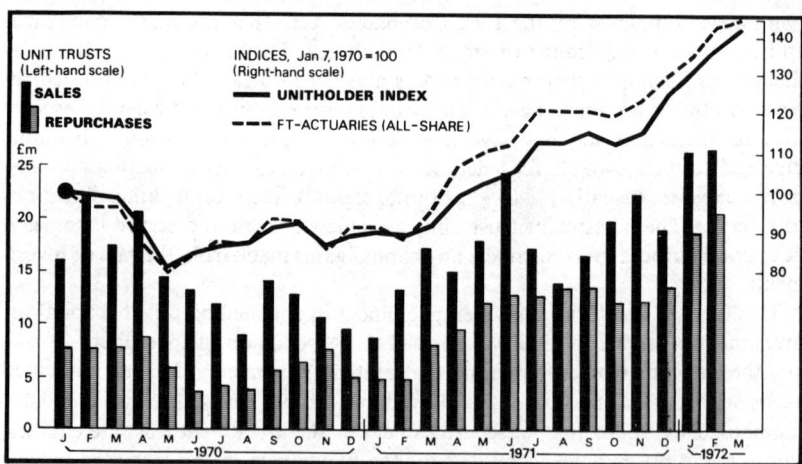

Fig. 6.12 *Trends in Unit Trust rates and repurchases and in Stock Exchange and Unit Trust prices, 1970-72*
(Source: *Econ.*, 15 April 1972 p. 92)

---

[1] For a discussion of the charges, the need for more flexibility in charges and services, and the likely impact of a change in the regulations, see *Econ.*, 19 Feb. 1972, p. 87.

Table 6.7 *Best and worst growth records of unit trusts, 30 March 1972*

Top 20 over three years, three months

Trust	Group	Current size* £m	Growth over three years, three months %	Growth Jan-Mar, 1972 %	Growth 1971 %	Growth 1970 %
Jessel Property & General	Jessel Britannia	9·0	121·8	18·6	59·5	17·0
Scotexempt Growth	Scotbits	1·0	104·3	34·4	47·6	−0·9
Ebor Property & Building	Ebor	0·7	99·0	23·6	77·1	5·3
Target Financial	Target	11·4	87·9	16·7	58·3	10·3
Oceanic Performance	Oceanic	0·6	78·2	14·2	102·9	−6·0
Ebor General	Ebor	2·8	76·7	20·2	65·8	−1·8
Financial Priority	London Wall	1·3	75·1	16·7	57·8	8·3
Scotincome	Scotbits	5·5	72·1	15·5	71·7	−3·8
M & G Midland & General	M & G	5·0	70·2	22·8	67·4	0·8
Scotexempt Yield	Scotbits	2·0	69·5	15·3	58·3	4·5
Raw Materials & General	Janus	2·7	65·9	16·2	42·7	10·9
Scotlaps	Scotbits	1·9	65·7	16·5	59·2	−0·1
Hambro Smaller Companies	Allied-Hambro	6·0	64·9	25·0	52·6	−1·3
Abacus Income	Abacus	1·6	64·4	24·2	51·3	4·5
High Income Priority	London Wall	9·5	63·3	18·6	73·5	−2·5
Jessel Income	Jessel Britannia	3·9	62·6	13·7	56·3	10·9
Stratton	Stratton	2·8	61·2	14·5	34·6	10·9
Schroder Income	Schroder Wagg	6·6	60·9	14·1	41·8	3·0
Ebor Pension	Ebor	1·6	60·7	11·4	38·5	8·6
Discretionary	Discretionary	2·0	60·3	18·8	54·2	3·7
FT-Actuaries all share (income reinvested)		—	**56·2**	**13·0**	**43·4**	**−4·9**

Bottom 10 over three years, three months

Trust	Group	Current size* £m	Growth over three years, three months %	Growth Jan-Mar, 1972 %	Growth 1971 %	Growth 1970 %
Target Growth	Target	9·5	− 7·6	6·3	34·3	−22·7
Vavasseur Oil & Energy	Vavasseur	4·4	− 8·0	14·2	16·6	−15·3
Oceanic Overseas	Oceanic	1·7	− 8·9	16·4	4·6	−23·6
London & Wall Street	London Wall	2·3	−12·6	7·9	25·4	−12·7
Hill Samuel International	Hill Samuel	14·1	−14·3	6·2	9·9	−17·2
Metals Minerals & Commodities	Allied-Hambro	11·3	−17·7	10·8	5·7	−18·8
North American	Ansbacher	0·5	−19·6	2·6	14·1	−5·8
Hill Samuel Dollar	Hill Samuel	3·6	−20·9	7·3	13·6	−16·4
Overseas	Mallet	2·4	−25·4	11·1	1·7	−29·2
Securities of America	Allied-Hambro	1·2	−35·7	1·8	6·1	−21·0

*Size statistics as at 31.12.71, supplied by G. S. Herber

Rankings supplied by Fundex

(Source: *Econ.*, 15 April 1972, p. 93)

to support the criticism that the average unit trust merely performs more or less in line with the market average (reflecting the performance of the 'man-in-the-street' and the institutional investors). Table 6.7 gives details of the top 20 and bottom 10 unit trusts, in terms of current size and growth over a number of years up to 1972.

In recent years the unit trust movement has been broadening out into many areas of the investment market, offering a fairly comprehensive financial service – not limited to the equity market – catering for the differing needs of investors.[1]

(h) Insurance companies

About 570 insurance companies (both British and foreign) are incorporated in the United Kingdom, but most of the insurance business is transacted by about 100 companies. Premiums are received for each of the main types of calculated risk insured against, and these premiums are kept in separate funds, which are then invested according to the needs of the funds. Most of these funds must be invested in fairly liquid, short or medium-term securities, as the funds (e.g. Fire, Marine, Accident, Motor Vehicle, etc.) are drawn upon by claims at regular intervals. Life Assurance, however, in which about 100 companies specialise, gives rise to funds which may be invested in long-term securities – as life premiums represent a long-term form of saving, and actuarial statistics permit the amount of payments out of the Life Funds to be precisely calculated.

Table 6.8 *Structure of the UK insurance market* – 1968

	UK registered	Foreign companies	Total
Insurers			
Companies writing only life and personal accident business	93	25	118
Companies writing only general business	146	106	252
Companies writing life and general	30	6	36
	269	137	406
Lloyd's			
(Marine, plate glass and other specialist non-life mutual associations and companies)	161	—	161
Collecting societies	74	—	74
Other friendly societies	796	—	796
Intermediaries			
Brokers			
(a) firms belonging to the associations (approximately)	2,000		
(b) other firms (estimate)	4,000		
Part-time agents (estimate)	120,000		

(Source: R. L. Carter, 'Britain's Insurance Industry', *L.B.R.*, Jan. 1972, p. 39)

The complex structure of the insurance industry in the U.K. results from an evolution extending over more than three centuries. The number of firms encompassed by the industry was extended by the Insurance Companies Acts of 1958–67, which brought all classes of insurance business under legal supervision. Often, the industry is regarded as comprising 'the companies' and Lloyd's, but many other bodies transact insurance business (see Table 6.8). The collecting societies

---

[1] 'Spreading their wings', *F.T.*, 23 Oct. 1972.

perform about one-sixth of total industrial life assurance business. The friendly societies and trade unions provide personal accident, sickness, unemployment and similar business for their members.[1] Lloyd's is an incorporated society – a *market* for insurance – not a company, and is regulated by special Acts of Parliament. There were, in 1972, about 6,000 underwriting members, grouped into about 280 syndicates and represented by Lloyd's underwriting agents.

In 1968 the total assets of U.K. insurance companies amounted to about £14,832 million, the bulk being in life assurance business.[2]

Table 6.9 illustrates the distribution of premium income of U.K. insurers, from 1945 to 1968, as between Lloyd's and 'the companies' in the various fields of insurance activity.

Table 6.9 *Worldwide premium income of British insurers*, 1948–68

	1945 £m	1955 £m	1965 £m	1968 £m	Growth rate pa 1955–68 %
(a) UK registered companies					
Ordinary life and annuities	117·5	331·0	849·3	1,244·8	10·6
Industrial life	79·4	127·4	204·0	234·8	4·8
Total life	196·9	458·4	1,053·3	1,459·6	9·3
Fire	71·8	218·9	368·2	500·3	6·6
Accident (non-motor)	57·0	258·8	366·1	481·4	4·9
Motor	33·8	180·5	478·2	598·3	9·6
Marine and aviation	22·6	65·4	104·4	210·3	9·4
Total non-life	185·2	723·6	1,286·9	1,790·3	7·2
Total	*382·1*	*1,182·0*	*2,340·2*	*3,249·9*	*8·1*
(b) Lloyd's					
Life	na	—	0·4	0·7	23·6
Fire and accident	na	118·7	257·7	342·3	8·5
Motor	na	8·2	27·2	36·5	12·2
Marine and aviation	na	105·5	176·1	288·7	8·1
Total non-life		232·4	461·0	667·5	8·5
Total		*232·4*	*461·4*	*668·2*	8.5

(Source: R. L. Carter, 'Britain's Insurance Industry', *L.B.R.*, Jan. 1972, p. 45)

Table 6.10 indicates the importance of the investment funds of the insurance companies, as compared with those of public and private sector superannuation funds, investment trusts and unit trusts.

Insurance funds thus constitute one of the major sources of investment funds for the Government, industry and commerce. Investment policy with regard to these funds is not subject to Government regulation. Nearly two-thirds of insurance fund assets are invested in gilt-edged securities. More than one-third are invested in equities and debentures, and this proportion has been increasing in recent years.[3]

[1] For further details, see R. L. Carter, 'Britain's insurance industry', *L.B.R.*, Jan. 1972.
[2] *Brit. O.H.*, 1972, p. 357.   [3] *Brit. O.H.*, 1972, p. 357.

Table 6.10 *Investment funds of institutional investors* – 1970

		£m
Insurance companies:		
life funds	13,781	
general funds	1,671	
		15,452
Superannuation funds:		
public sector, including local authorities	3,009	
private sector	4,607	
		7,616
Investment trusts		4,469
Unit trusts		1,315
		28,852

Notes:
(1) Insurance companies' assets are at book values, except for British government securities and local authorities' securities which are included at nominal values. The assets of the other institutions are at market values. (2) The figures relate mainly to values at the end of 1970, except for insurance companies which take the end of accounting periods and the superannuation funds of local authorities which are at 31 March 1971.

(Source: R. L. Carter, 'Britain's Insurance Industry', *L.B.R.*, Jan. 1972, p. 38)

(*i*) The Euro-capital market

The European market for long-term capital – the Eurobond or Euro-capital market – is an extension of the Euro-currency market, referred to in Section 14(b). Where the latter relates to currencies deposited with banks outside the home country and re-lent to non-bank users, the former relates to Eurobonds – long-term securities used for borrowing in the Euro-currency market. Data on dealings in this market are rare, but data exist on the new issue flow. Total long-term international bond issues rose from negligible proportions in 1963 to more than $3 billion in 1967.[1]

Probably the most serious threat to the market's role are the restrictions and controls on capital movements and transactions by national and international organisations. An example of this is the E.E.C. regulation that the funds of insurance and pension funds must be held in the country of operation. Deficiencies in practices and rules also exist, as in the lack of obligation in some countries to publish consolidated accounts and the wide variation in accountancy practice.[2] A prerequisite for efficient functioning is the elimination of foreign exchange risks.

Nevertheless, the market has shown great resilience in evolving new techniques and instruments, as compared with the traditional domestic capital markets. Such developments are the inception of floating-rate issues – whereby interest rates payable may be adjusted periodically – and issues in European Currency Units (E.C.U.s), which have a fixed parity against the various issue currencies. A proposed development is the Bearer Depository Receipt, which would permit 'secondary' market transactions (i.e. in outstanding, as opposed to new issue bonds) to take place without going through the stock markets.[3]

[1] 'European capital markets', *B.B.R.*, Aug. 1971, p. 54.
[2] 'Euromarkets', *F.T.*, 13 Mar. 1972 and 'Finance for industry', *F.T.*, 10 Jan. 1972.
[3] *B.B.R.*, Aug. 1971, *art. cit.*, p. 54.

17. Further Reading and Sources

Footnote references to daily and weekly journals are not repeated.

V. ANTHONY, *Banks and Markets*. Heinemann. 1972.

BARCLAYS BANK, 'Consumer credit in the United Kingdom'. *B.B.R.* May 1971.

BARCLAYS BANK, 'European capital markets'. *B.B.R.* Aug. 1971.

BARCLAYS BANK, 'London money markets'. *B.B.R.* Nov. 1972.

A. R. BENNETT, 'American commercial banking: the changing scene'. *L.B.R.* July 1971.

E. H. PHELPS BROWN and S. V. HOPKINS, 'Builders' wage-rates, prices and population: some further evidence'. *Economica*. Feb. 1959.

J. BURNETT, *A History of the Cost of Living*. Penguin. 1969.

R. L. CARTER, 'Britain's insurance industry'. *L.B.R.* Jan. 1972.

G. P. E. CLARKSON and B. J. ELLIOTT, 'Managing capital funds'. *N.W.B.Q.R.* Aug. 1970.

A. B. CRAMP, 'The control of bank deposits'. *L.B.R.* Oct. 1967.

R. CROOME and H. G. JOHNSON, eds. *Money in Britain, 1959–1969*. O.U.P. 1970.

DEPARTMENT OF ECONOMIC AFFAIRS, *D.E.A. Pr. Rep. Econ.* 17, June 1966.

W. A. ELTIS, 'Are interest rates too high?', *L.B.R.* July 1961.

E. L. FURNESS, *An Introduction to Financial Economics*. Heinemann. 1972.

R. F. HARROD, *Money*. Macmillan. 1969.

SIR JOHN HICKS, 'Expected inflation'. *T.B.R.* Sept. 1970.

H. G. JOHNSON, ed. *Readings in British Monetary Economics*. O.U.P. 1972.

R. G. LIPSEY, 'Does money always depreciate?' *L.B.R.* Oct. 1960.

LLOYDS BANK, *L.B.R.* Oct. 1960; July 1961.

MAXWELL STAMP ASSOCIATES, 'What determines the interest rate?' *M. & W.S.R.* Spring 1971.

MIDLAND BANK, *M.B.R.* Feb. 1961; May 1963.

MIDLAND BANK, 'Meeting the silver shortage'. *M.B.R.* Aug. 1965.

MIDLAND BANK, 'The tide turns for new issues'. *M.B.R.* Feb. 1968.

MIDLAND BANK, 'Britain's stock exchanges since the war: a story of adaptation and innovation'. *M.B.R.* Nov. 1968.

MIDLAND BANK, 'Money supply and the banks'. *M.B.R.* Feb. 1969.

MIDLAND BANK, 'Managing the gilt-edged market: a temporary change of emphasis?' *M.B.R.* May 1969.

MIDLAND BANK, 'Another look at money supply'. *M.B.R.* Nov. 1970.

MIDLAND BANK, 'Banking enters a new era'. *M.B.R.* May 1972.

'The Inter-bank markets in sterling.' *M.B.R.* Aug. 1973.

NATIONAL BOARD FOR PRICES AND INCOMES, Report No. 34, *Bank Charges*, Cmnd 3292. H.M.S.O. 1967.

W. E. NORTON, 'Debt management and monetary policy in the United Kingdom'. *E.J.* Sept. 1969.

B. READING, 'Too high interest rates'. *N.W.B.Q.R.* Feb. 1970.

W. B. REDDAWAY, 'Rising prices for ever'. *M.B.R.* July 1966.

N. PEERA, 'Interest rates: illusion or reality'. *N.W.B.Q.R.* May 1970.

H. ROSE, 'Competition and credit control: the new framework'. *T.B.R.* March 1972.

R. S. SAYERS, *Modern Banking*, 7th edn. O.U.P. 1967.

A. J. SCHWARTZ, 'Why money matters'. *L.B.R.* Oct. 1969.

SOCIETE GENERALE, 'The City of London', *Conjoncture*, 163 May 1973.

TREASURY, *E.P.R.*, 19, Sept. 1971; 23, Jan. 1972; 29, July 1972; 42, Aug. 1973.

TREASURY, 'Controlling bank credit'. *E.P.R.*, 17, July 1971.

A. J. TURNER, 'The evolution of reserve ratios in English banking'. *N.W.B.Q.R.* Feb. 1972.

P. WANN, 'Lower interest rates?'. *N.W.B.Q.R.* May 1970.

18. Past Examination Questions

1. What is meant by *barter*? What are the defects of barter which make it unsuitable for a modern economy? (Summer 1955)
2. 'Money is *anything* that is *generally acceptable* as a means of exchange and at the same time acts as a measure of value and as a store of wealth.' Describe each of these functions and list the things which perform them in this country. (Autumn 1953)
3. State what you understand to be the functions of money, referring to as many different forms of English money as you can. (Summer 1958)
4. What is meant by a 'period of inflation'? Discuss some of its effects. (Summer 1963)
5. What sections of the community are likely to suffer, or gain, from a progressive decline in the purchasing power of money? Give reasons. (January 1964)
6. Write short notes on . . . the following: . . . (*b*) index number. (January 1965)
7. An old lady called at her bank. The following conversation ensued: *Old Lady:* 'What is the pound worth today?' *Bank Clerk:* 'The pound is worth about ten shillings.'
   Old Lady: 'Here are five ten-shilling notes. Give me five pounds in exchange.' What did the bank clerk mean by his reply to the old lady? (Summer 1953)
8. 'Since the last war there has been a rise in the cost of living.' 'Since the last war there has been a rise in the standard of living.' Explain clearly the meaning of each of these statements, and show how both statements can be true at the same time. (Summer 1962)
9. Payments are often made by cheque. Is a cheque money? Discuss. (Summer 1957)
10. 'Banks create money.' How? (Summer 1952)
11. Explain, and illustrate, the statement: 'A bank both lends and borrows money and makes a profit in either case. It can even lend money it hasn't got.' (Summer 1949)
12. What is a cheque? What are the advantages of using a cheque? Discuss the importance of cheques in the economic system of the United Kingdom today. (Summer 1961)
13. Explain how banks facilitate the exchange of goods. (Autumn 1957)
14. What are the functions of the joint stock banks? (Summer 1962)
15. Describe the credit facilities provided by the commercial banks in the United Kingdom. What considerations does a bank manager take into account when granting a loan? (Summer 1963)

16. The joint stock banks exist to serve both their borrowers and depositors. How do they achieve this, and how do they reconcile their efforts with their liabilities to their shareholders? (January 1964)

17. Write an explanatory account of the following items which are to be found on the assets side of the balance sheet of a commercial bank: (*a*) Cash; (*b*) Money at call and short notice; (*c*) Bills discounted; (*d*) Investments; (*e*) Advances. (Summer 1959)

18. Explain the meaning of the following terms: (*a*) Bankers' Clearing House; (*b*) Deposit account; (*c*) Overdraft; (*d*) Fiduciary Issue. (January 1965)

19. Comment on the following titles: (*a*) the government's bank; (*b*) the bankers' bank; (*c*) the controller of cash and credit; (*d*) the lender of last resort. (Summer 1960)

20. Write short notes on . . . the following: (*a*) Bankers' Bank; . . . (*c*) Stock Jobber; (*d*) Legal tender. (January 1964)

21. How do the functions of the Bank of England differ from those of the commercial (joint stock) banks? (Summer 1955)

22. 'Bank of England Promise to pay the Bearer on Demand the sum of One Pound.'
    The above statement appears on every pound note. What did this mean in the past? What does it mean today? (Autumn 1952)

23. What is meant by 'fiduciary issue'? State precisely how the amount of the issue been altered (*a*) over the past twenty-five years, and (*b*) during the last twelve months? (Summer 1963)

24. What sorts of transactions take place (*a*) between two commercial banks, e.g. Lloyds and Midland, and (*b*) between a commercial bank and the Bank of England? (January 1963)

25. What is the relationship of the Bank of England to the joint stock banks? How, and for what purposes, does the Bank of England control the activities of the joint stock banks? (Summer 1953)

26. Explain the meaning of three of the following:
    (*a*) Legal tender; (*b*) Deposit account; (*c*) Overdraft; (*d*) Cheque; (*e*) Treasury Bill. (January 1963)

27. Write short notes on *three* of the following: (*a*) Cheques; (*b*) Index Number; (*c*) Stock Jobber; . . . (*e*) Unit of Account. (Summer 1960)

28. Write notes on *three* of the following: (*a*) Bankers' Clearing House; (*b*) Current Account; (*c*) Bank loans; (*d*) Cheque; (*e*) . . . (Summer 1964)

29. Write short notes on *three* of the following: (*a*) Fiduciary issue; . . . (*c*) Bank Rate; . . . (*e*) Overdraft. (Summer 1956)

30. Name the chief types of businesses which make up the money market, indicating the work done by each. (January 1965)

31. What do you understand by the term 'London Money Market'? Describe the work of the various institutions (other than banks) which comprise the London Money Market. (Summer 1949)

32. What is the economic importance of the activities of the Stock Exchange? (Summer 1961)

33. What are the functions of the Stock Exchange in the working of the economic system? (Summer 1952)

34. Write short notes on . . . the following: (*c*) Gilt-edged securities; (*d*) Legal tender. (Summer 1955).

535

35. Distinguish carefully between the following: (iii) dividends and interest. (Summer 1956)
36. Write short notes on . . . the following: (*a*) Fiduciary Issue; . . . (*d*) Stock Broker; (*e*) Ordinary Shares. (Summer 1959)
37. Distinguish the functions of a savings bank from those of a commercial joint stock bank. (Autumn 1952)
38. Write short notes on . . . the following: . . . (*b*) Hire purchase; (*c*) Cheques; (*d*) Consols; (*e*) Bulls and Bears. (Summer 1953)
39. Describe the main ways in which firms raise capital. (Summer 1964)
40. Write short notes on . . . the following: (*a*) Lloyd's . . . (Autumn 1952)

6. Money, Banking and the Capital Market Stage II

1. The Radcliffe Report on the Working of the Monetary System

In August 1959 the report of the Committee on the Working of the Monetary System was published.[1] This inquiry, under the chairmanship of Lord Radcliffe, was the first of its kind since the Macmillan Committee report of 1931. It encompassed the activities of the Treasury, the Bank, the commercial banks, the Discount Houses, the merchant banks, the various savings institutions and many others.

With regard to monetary controls in general, the report considered them as furthering five aims of Government policy: a high and stable level of employment; stability of the internal purchasing power of money; steady economic growth and improvement of the standard of living; some contribution, implying a margin in the balance of payments, to the economic development of the outside world; and a strengthening of London's international reserves, implying further margin in the balance of payments.

Perhaps the main contribution of the report was the stress which it laid on the need for monetary policy to consider not only the total supply of money (i.e. 'final settlement' money; coin, notes and bank credit or deposits) but also the ever-expanding volume and types of 'near-money' or money substitutes. Whereas the orthodox conception of money visualised a clearly identifiable group of liquid assets (notes, coin and bank deposits), the report also conceived of a wide range of liquid assets – such as trade credit, hire purchase debt, and deposits with 'non-bank intermediaries', such as building societies and hire purchase finance companies, who subsequently re-lend – which are not closely under the control of the authorities, which are highly substitutable, one for the other, and which, with final money proper, constitute the general liquidity of the economy.[2] This apparent conflict of interpretation and emphasis between the Radcliffe school and the orthodox school bears a striking similarity to the mid-nineteenth-century Currency School *versus* Banking School debate.[3] It would appear, however, that restriction or expansion of final money proper would have sympathetic repercussions on other liquid assets, which, in fact, bear an element of proportionality to conventional money.[4] Following from this analysis, the report considered that the note issue was not of great significance, notes being

---

[1] Cmnd 827, 1959.   [2] Paragraphs 389–95.
[3] Since Radcliffe the evolving debate has resumed prime importance and has centred on money supply *versus* level of activity (with monetary and fiscal stabilisation policies).
[4] For more detailed analysis of this point, see A. B. Cramp, 'Two views on money', *L.B.R.*, July 1962.

'the small change of the monetary system'.[1] Consequently, it did not attach much importance to the banks' cash reserves, which 'leak' out of circulation. It laid much greater emphasis on the second liquidity ratio, the 30% of liquid assets, and in fact noted that the banks had an extra cushion of liquidity in their investment portfolios of short- and medium-term Government bonds close to maturity, which could easily be sold in order to replenish their fully liquid cash reserves.[2] However, the report concluded that the present system of maintaining the two conventional liquidity ratios was justified, and noted with approval that the Bank had, in 1955, exercised a binding power over the banks by insisting on the 30% ratio.[3]

The position with regard to the status and power of the Bank, and its relationship to the Treasury, were considered by the report to be not fully and satisfactorily clear. It considered that as the Bank has a unique relation with the London financial market, it should not be run as a Government department. On the other hand, major policy decisions (such as on Bank Rate) should be made by the Treasury, and the Bank should not be completely independent of political influence, but should pursue policies coordinated in harmony with those of the Government.[4]

Concerning Bank Rate, interest rates generally, and open market operations, the report advocated greater flexibility in the use of Bank Rate, and the setting up of a Standing Committee, advisory in character, to review the coordination of monetary policy as a whole. Bank Rate decisions would then lie between the Governors of the Bank, the Chancellor of the Exchequer and the committee. The report considered that changes in short-term interest rates did not appear to have very much direct influence on borrowers, particularly on big firms, nationalised undertakings and local authorities. The main effect of bank restrictions on lending was to drive borrowers to other, sometimes more onerous, sources of credit.[5] Therefore the monetary authorities should seek to influence the whole structure of interest rates, rather than the basic money supply. It appears that what the committee had in mind was the direction of monetary policy towards influencing the 'intermediaries' or suppliers of 'near-money', by imposing liquidity controls over the whole range of financial institutions, and thereby keeping under control non-banking factors which influence the velocity of circulation of both money and near-money substitutes.[6] Changes in Bank Rate and other rates were seen to be effective mainly in the sense that they influenced the public's conception of the interest rate 'norm', by giving an indication as to the trend in long-term rates.[7]

In order to counteract the gradual depreciation in capital values of gilt-edged, the report favoured the use of public debt (bonds) manipulation, by way of central bank open market operations, to influence long-term rates of interest, bond yields and general liquidity.[8] In the field of commercial bank practice, the report recognised the efficiency and convenience of the cheque service, using

---

[1] Paragraphs 523 and 348.   [2] Paragraph 506.   [3] Paragraphs 505, 351, 429.
[4] Paragraphs 761, 766, 768, 769, 771   [5] Paragraphs 451, 452, 460.
[6] The result of 'idle' bank deposit money being lent to 'intermediaries' such as building societies and finance companies is that these deposits with them are 'near-money' liquid assets. They 'activate' these formerly 'idle' bank deposits – re-lending them to finance other transactions – thus increasing the velocity of circulation and the effective money supply. See 'New light on liquidity', *Econ.*, 19 Mar. 1960, p. 1124. Also see T. M. Podolski, 'The control of non-bank financial intermediaries – I. The need for control', *The Bankers' Magazine*, Jan. 1969.
[7] Paragraphs 442–7.   [8] Paragraphs 982, 148.

current account (or 'demand') deposits. It attached little significance, for the purposes of monetary policy, in distinguishing between deposits on current account and deposit account ('time' deposits), as the latter can so easily be switched to current account, and ultimately add to the total pressure of demand.[1] The report noted that the proportion of advances to total deposits was below the prewar figure, but that the banks would gradually amend their theoretical confinement to short-term lending and, indeed, that they expected to see a decided increase in the proportion of advances. This was viewed as an 'expansionary push'. Measures aimed at restricting advances had to take account of the fact that the banks could quite easily sell investments in order to raise liquid cash, and thereby increase advances. Despite the fact that a restrictive measure against advances (such as increased Bank Rate, backed by open market operations), would induce a fall in security prices and therefore capital losses on such security sales by the banks, the report noted that the banks were tending to insulate themselves from such a risk by adding to their investment portfolios an increasing proportion of bonds with only a few years left to maturity or redemption, these being less vulnerable to a fall in price.[2]

Due to the weakening effect of orthodox measures in influencing bank lending, the report discussed the problem of how best to regulate banking activity. It noted that the power of the Bank, established by the 1946 Act, to issue directions to the banks, upon the authority of the Treasury, had never been used.[3] After supporting the maintenance of the two liquidity rules, it stressed the influence of Treasury Bills on the general liquidity position of the banks. It pointed to the importance of regulating the banks' power to give advances, as 'key lenders in the system', but noted that too severe a restriction on them might lead to the development of 'rival institutions'. It recommended the use of powers to increase the 'reserve requirements' of the banks – favouring the weapon of Special Deposits as a general control of credit – and also recommended the use of powers to vary the liquidity ratios. It also favoured the use of powers to establish a third liquidity rule, that of fixing, in an emergency, limits on the proportion of advances to total deposits. However, the committee suggested that discriminatory action against the banks should be accompanied by general restrictions on all classes of lender and by a combination of controls over capital issues, bank advances and consumer credit.[4]

At the time of the Radcliffe inquiry various questions with regard to the functions of the Discount Market were throwing doubt upon its justification. Having grown up at a time when London was the world's premier financial centre and played a key part in the financing of international trade by commercial bills, did it still have a part to play when these special circumstances had radically altered? Now that Treasury Bills were the main element in the banks' liquidity holdings, was there still justification in the Discount Market acting as an intermediary, especially when they act in unison as a cartel? Was it still reasonable for the Discount Market to have sole right of access to loans from the Bank as 'last resort' lender?[5] The report found that the Bank exercised a 'paternalistic supervision' over the market, and that the Bank considered the market to be efficient and indispensable to Government finance and to London's financial

---

[1] Paragraph 131.   [2] Paragraphs 140–4.   [3] Paragraph 350.
[4] Paragraphs 376, 395, 504, 508, 524, 525, 527.
[5] See 'Lombard Street after Radcliffe', *Econ.*, 19 Sept. 1959, p. 945.

position. The committee itself, however, did not find the market to be indispensable, but thought that it did essential work, which would otherwise have to be done by other agencies, in smoothing out temporary disturbances in the banks' liquidity, thus permitting them to concentrate on their major task. As regards the usefulness of the market as lenders to the Government, the report found that they were not indispensable, but that they did constitute a highly efficient market in instruments which were convenient to the Exchequer. As to the recently developed Discount Market function of dealing as a shock-absorber in short-term bonds, the report considered that the market was an important element in maintaining flexibility in the bond market. Only in respect of the market's restrictive practice in tendering as a syndicate for Treasury Bills was the report slightly critical. Despite the fact that syndicate tendering tended to slow down the movement of Treasury Bill rate towards Bank Rate, thus rendering Bank Rate policy and Treasury Bill policy less effective, the report tolerated the practice, so long as the market did not tend to use it to cause an 'unwarranted fluctuation' in rates, with the aim of discouraging 'outside competition' for bills.

On the subject of availability of credit, particularly long-term credit, in the economy, the report found that, in general, financial institutions were quick to develop in response to changing needs.[1] As mentioned above, it noted the likelihood of the banks' gradually lengthening the term of their lending. It suggested further expansion of longer-term bank lending to farmers and small businesses.[2] In addition, it was suggested that the £200,000 upper limit for loans from the Industrial and Commercial Finance Corporation should be increased, and that the exploitation of technical innovation should be facilitated by the establishment of an Industrial Guarantee Corporation.[3] The committee were impressed by the fact that the market for credit presented a picture of flexibility and overall unity, and that no hard and fast lines seemed to be drawn between the supply of short and long finance.[4]

The committee had many suggestions to make on the subject of the provision of information by the monetary authorities, as an aid to greater understanding, by informed opinion, of monetary affairs. The Bank was urged to provide more and better statistics in the Annual Report and in regular bulletins; its research and intelligence branches should be expanded; it should work in cooperation with the Treasury in this task. Statistics on banking as a whole should be improved and made on a comparable basis with those of the clearing banks, and it would, in fact, be desirable to draw up a single account for financial institutions as a group.[5]

2. The Money Debate: Controversy over the Role of Money

(a) The debate in outline

Since the Radcliffe Report intense debate has been raging over the role of the money supply on the general level of prices and of economic activity and national income. One of the two main schools of thought respresents the 'Keynesians', who consider the money supply to be a passive magnitude which need only be altered by means of a neutral monetary policy, in response to other pressures

---

[1] Paragraph 866. [2] Paragraphs 922, 942. [3] Paragraphs 946, 949.
[4] Paragraph 125. [5] Paragraphs 794, 808, 811, 814, 861, 983, 979.

operating in the economy. The most important influences on the level of prices and economic activity (or national income) are held to be fiscal policy, national debt financing activities and credit controls, which affect expenditures on consumption and investment by way of their effect on interest rates. The other main school of thought represents the 'monetarists' or the 'Chicago school' (or 'new quantity theorists'). They lay much greater emphasis on the more active, direct influence of the money supply (or quantity of money) on prices and the level of activity or income. Both schools use a common terminology and selection of theoretical tools. They are not diametrically opposed to each other, but rather emphasise different aspects of what they both observe. Ignoring the extremist views on either side – that 'money doesn't matter and fiscal policy is all', or that 'money is all that matters' – we might expect to see a gradual diffusion between the two theories, leading to a policy balance between direct money supply controls and 'fine tuning' fiscal and credit controls.

Perhaps a useful starting point in reviewing the debate would be the contention of the Radcliffe Committee that bank deposits and currency were of little importance, as compared with the total liquidity of the economy as a whole, which itself is a nebulous and imprecise concept; that monetary policy (i.e. controls over the money supply) would not have much effect on the levels of expenditure and income unless applied so drastically that it would result in a crisis for the financial institutions; that the aim of monetary policy should be to influence not the basic money supply but the whole structure of interest rates.

This philosophy was greatly influenced by Keynesian ideas. Keynes, during the depression years of the interwar period, had become disillusioned with monetary policies, which *appeared* to have been ineffective in stemming the decline in business activity. Keynes considered that Fisher's equation implied that if M fell, then, since prices tended to be 'sticky' and were determined by costs and by past history, V might be expected to rise and T (an approximation for the level of national income) might be expected to remain constant. He therefore advocated that attention be shifted from the money supply to Government and industrial spending, which was 'autonomous' (i.e. independent of income) and which was 'induced' (by lucrative interest rates and/or by expectations of future profits and/or by political and economic considerations).

Professor Milton Friedman, the leading figure in the 'Chicago school', is of the opinion that the Keynesians have misinterpreted these monetary policies and their effects.[1] In the United States it was found that V did *not* tend to *offset* changes in M, but rather to *reinforce* them: M declined by one-third from 1929 to 1933 and V *also* declined. It would seem that changes in V tend to be fairly slow and delayed (or 'lagged') and are influenced by custom and expectations about the future. Therefore, since prices tend to be rather rigid, the major effect of a reduction in money supply would be felt in the reduction of T. The reduction in M was largely due to a 'rush on the banks', clients withdrawing their deposits and reducing the base for bank money. The monetary authorities failed to increase bank liquidity by counter-measures, and so there was a shortage of credit to finance transactions and investment and thus to maintain income growth. The level of activity, according to this interpretation, therefore declined, not because

[1] Milton Friedman, 'The counter-revolution of monetary theory', First Wincott Memorial Lecture, reproduced in *F.T.*, 17 Sept. 1970.

of the *impotence* of monetary policy, but rather because of its *effectiveness* – its failure to expand *M*.

The apparent failure of Keynesian-type policies – with a fiscal and interest rate emphasis – to procure steady economic growth without price inflation and even to prevent stagnation combined with inflation has heightened the controversy between the monetarists and the Keynesians.[1]

(b) The Keynesian 'transmission mechanism'

It may be of assistance in pinpointing the differences in emphasis and interpretation between the two views, if we start off with a simplified model of the Keynesian 'transmission mechanism' or cause-and-effect relationships. According to this school, investment expenditure (*I*) is one of the major triggers or injections into the income flow, and is itself influenced largely by the level of interest rates: if interest ('*i*') is low, loans for investment are inexpensive and are more likely to be taken up. Thus a reduction in '*i*' leads to an increase in *I*, which generates a rise in income (*Y*) – which is *pr* in the Cambridge Formula and roughly comparable to *PT* in the Fisher Equation. The rise in *Y* results in a rise in liquidity preference (*L*) – the desire for liquid money, under the 'precautionary' and 'transactions' motives. Thus the demand for money (M^d) rises and causes the rate of interest ('*i*') or 'price of liquid money' to rise, *if the supply of money* (M^s) *is fixed*. Furthermore, as the (fixed) *M* is now a smaller fraction of the higher national income (*Y*), the liquidity proportion *k* falls: this is reflected in an increase in the velocity of circulation (*V*), since the same *M* has to service an increased *Y* (or *PT*). In terms of the quantity equation, $MV = PT$, *T* rises, *V* rises and *M* and *P* should stay constant. In terms of the Cambridge Formula, $M = kpr$, *r* rises, *k* falls and *M* and *p* stay constant. The rise in '*i*' will then curtail the rise in *I*.

However, three secondary, short-term booster effects may occur to upset this balance, which may result in an eventual rise in the price level, *P* (see Fig. 6.13).

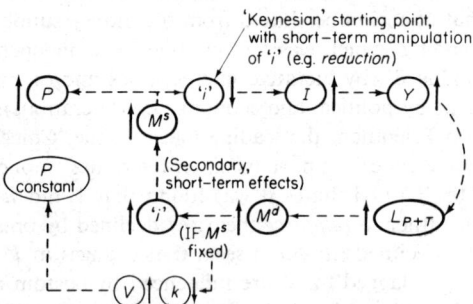

Fig. 6.13 *Simplified Keynesian 'transmission mechanism': interest, investment, income and price level, with* initially *fixed money supply*

[1] For various expositions of aspects of the debate, see Friedman, *op. cit.*; The Bank of England, 'The importance of money' and M. J. Artis and A. R. Nobay, 'The attempt to reinstate money', both reprinted in H. G. Johnson, ed., *Readings in British Monetary Economics*, 1972; J. A. Waters, 'Money supply and credit – theory and practice', *N.W.B.Q.R.*, Nov. 1969; A. J. Schwartz, 'Why money matters', *L.B.R.*, Oct. 1969; P. G. Gschwindt de Gyor, 'The money supply question', *N.W.B.Q.R.*, Aug. 1969; N. Kaldor, 'The new monetarism', *L.B.R.*, July 1970; Milton Friedman, 'The new monetarism: comment', *L.B.R.*, Oct. 1970; K. Brunner, 'The monetarist view of Keynesian ideas', *L.B.R.*, Oct. 1971.

Firstly, the monetary authorities may pursue open market operations, buying gilt-edged securities so as to support their prices and to keep 'i' from rising too much. The former reason is in line with their traditional concern for preserving an 'orderly market', in which they will not prejudice the long-term prospects for selling gilts by allowing the capital values or prices of gilts to fall excessively: the latter reason is in line with 'debt management' considerations, whereby the authorities have tended to step in to bring down interest rates (by buying gilts), so as to keep down the National Debt servicing costs which would be incurred by future issues of gilts at higher rates of interest. *Secondly*, the rise in V, resulting from a rise in L and M^d, might be excessive. This could occur in a situation of 'expected inflation', in which the public rushes into goods and/or financial assets and accelerates its purchases of them, in anticipation of future inflationary price rises and/or capital gains associated with future reductions in 'i'. *Thirdly*, the supply of money may not simply be 'exogenously' (i.e. externally) determined by actions of the monetary authorities on the banking system. As the 'Yale school' pro-Keynesians, under Professor Tobin suggest, the non-bank financial intermediaries may add to the supply of money available as a medium of exchange (for the financing of transactions in real goods): by activating the 'idle balances' or 'store of value' money which resides in the financial circulation, financing securities transactions, they may constitute a link between 'bear' (seller) financial asset markets and real goods purchasers, whose *demand* for transactions each exceeds their current income. Thus, the money supply may be 'endogenously' (i.e. internally) determined, to some extent: the non-bank financial intermediaries extract a 'medium of exchange' function out of activated financial 'idle balances', offering high-yield debt contracts to the holders of financial assets or 'portfolio balances', who thereby rearrange their portfolios. This process constitutes a 'portfolio balances transmission mechanism' between the *financial* and *real goods* markets.[1]

For these reasons, the possibly excessive rise in V and/or eventual indirect increase in M, the 'MV' side of the equation may *more than counteract* the rise in T, thus leading to an inflationary increase in the price level, P. This would be more likely to occur, the more closely the level of activity approached that of full employment or capacity utilisation of resources: the impact of rising MV on income would be reflected in price increases and rising *money* income, rather than in a physical increase in *real* income (T). The monetarist approach to this problem would probably be to short-circuit the rise in 'i' which follows the rise in M^d, and to expand M^s directly and to a more closely controlled extent, thus taking some of the pressure on interest rates ('i') out of the system, retarding the reduction in k and the increase in V, retarding the upward trend in 'i' and thus reducing the likelihood of an increase in the price level (P).

(c) The monetarist 'transmission mechanism'

The monetarists, in fact, tend to state their case for monetary policy – a planned, direct, long-term control over the money supply – by emphasising a *different initial starting point* or locus of sensitivity. This view of the transmission mechan-

[1] For further discussion of this aspect, see H. G. Johnson, 'Recent developments in monetary theory – a commentary', in D. R. Croome and H. G. Johnson, eds., *Money in Britain*, 1959–1969, 1970, pp. 101–5; P. Davidson, 'Money and the real world', *E.J.*, March 1972, esp. pp. 112–14; Schwartz, *op. cit.*, esp. pp. 10–11.

ism hinges on the relationship between M^d – the real value of money balances which the public *desires* to hold – and M^s – the nominal (or current price level) value of money balances which are *available* to hold. Demand for money is envisaged as generally changing slowly, reflecting custom and living standards, or as changing in a delayed response to previous changes in the money supply. The money supply itself is seen as being more frequently altered, often independently of M^d, and as influencing the level of activity and income *via* changes in the prices of a *wide range of assets*, when the actual and desired money balances (M^s and M^d) are *not* in equilibrium. As may be seen in Fig. 6.14, if the process commences with actual M^s higher than M^d (the real balances currently desired by the community), there will be an *initial fall* in 'i' and rise in P (prices of financial *and*

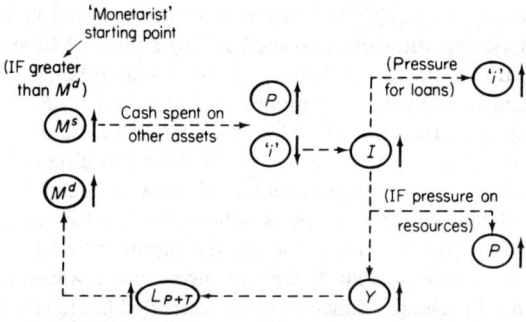

Fig. 6.14 *Simplified monetarist 'transmission mechanism': price levels and income, if 'actual' exceed 'desired' money balances*, initially

other assets). This will be followed by a secondary *reversal* in 'i', which will rise, *perhaps* accompanied by a secondary boost to the rise in P. This occurs as follows: the surplus cash is spent on a variety of *existing* assets, the price of which is bid up (the Keynesian 'liquidity effect', as the public rearranges its asset portfolios to balance out the excess cash element). Consequently, the rise in asset prices brings down the rate of interest, or yield, on assets. This, in turn, encourages investment (I), and the demand for loans and investment resources. It is at this juncture that the current degree of capacity utilisation (or resource utilisation) in the economy is important. As I and the demand for loans rise, 'i' will tend to increase and Y will rise, in money terms: if there are many *under-utilised* resources in men and machines, the rise in Y will be reflected in greater real output, and prices will tend to be steady. If, however, the economy is functioning at a *high degree* of resource utilisation, then the rise in money income will be reflected in further price rises. In either case, money income (Y) will have risen and the demand for money balances (M^d) will be driven up, *via* an increase in 'precautionary' and 'transactions' liquidity preference. Thus, M^d will catch up with M^s, but the price level will have risen, as will have money incomes. According to this reasoning, a steady, controlled rate of growth in M^s would ensure, over the long-term, a steady growth in the level of activity and money income, without straining resources and with less likelihood of boosting the level of prices.

(d) Major differences

Some of the key differences between the two schools of thought may now be noted. Firstly, the Keynesian school emphasises the causal influence of the *interest rate* level on activity and income, whereby '*i*' must be controlled largely by short-term, *indirect* fiscal and budgetary (public spending) measures, supported by monetary (e.g. hire purchase and credit) controls of a neutral nature. The monetarists emphasise the causal nature of the *money supply* and *monetary policy* on activity and incomes, by way of the direct effect on prices, whereby the money supply must be controlled by long-term, *direct* monetary policies. Because of the secondary 'reversal' effect on interest rates, they are held to provide a poor guide to monetary policy. Thus, monetary policy should not be 'discretionary', following or attempting to anticipate short-term fluctuations in the economy by fiscal and monetary measures which stumble from crisis to crisis, but should be decided in advance, on the assumption that changes in the money supply precede and predict, fairly accurately, *future* changes in the level of activity. It must not be assumed from the foregoing, however, that Friedman's prescription for a stable growth in the money supply derives from a belief in a *rigid*, mechanical connection between money supply and national income: on *average* there is a close connection, but in *individual* periods the connection may be loose. He therefore prescribes a 'quasi-automatic' monetary policy, precisely to avoid the instability caused by short-term, badly timed fiscal/monetary mixtures.

The second major difference between the schools lies in their approach to the *range* of alternative assets, which constitute substitutes for liquid money. The monetarists stress a far wider range of substitute assets than do the Keynesians, and include *real* goods, such as houses and durable consumer goods, as well as *financial* assets, as substitutes for money. Consequently, the asset or portfolio balances, which may be rearranged in response to changes in the available money supply, are thought to be much wider than the Keynesians believe: since the rearrangement of portfolio balances becomes translated into effects on income and spending, the spectrum of relevant interest rates, which they reflect, is much wider than the narrow financial market interest rates, stressed by the Keynesians.

(e) Empirical evidence

Empirical evidence has been produced by both sides, to uphold their points of view, but in general it appears that U.S. data, particularly, supports the Chicago school. As was seen in Fig. 6.1 (Stage I, Section 5 (*c*)), U.K. experience during the period 1880–1962 indicates a very close correlation between the money stock, money income and the index of prices.[1]

The importance of the money supply was given added emphasis by the findings of Pepper and Thomas, in 1972.[2] They found a strong relationship between the money supply and equity prices, in which changes in the former always *preceded* changes in the latter. This cast doubt on traditional theories of market forces and *expectations* about future changes in economic activity and interest rates. They also found that the long-term interest rate (the yield on gilt-edged securities) lagged *behind* the level of activity, due to money supply factors. Thus, when gilts

[1] See Schwartz, *op. cit.* This study has been criticised by A. B. Cramp, '*Does* money matter?', *L.B.R.*, Oct. 1970.
[2] G. Pepper and R. Thomas, *The Historical Importance of Money in the U.K.*, reviewed in *F.T.*, 10 May 1972.

reached a 'trough' of low prices (with high interest rates), the market could not anticipate a fall in 'i' and a rise in gilt prices, because of the scarcity of money at the time (M^d greater than M^s). In sum, they found that transactions based on Keynesian-type expectations of cyclical changes in interest rates tended to be insufficient to offset the powerful, conflicting monetary pressures. They did stress, however, that the strong evidence of a 'lead' of money supply over economic activity should not be taken uncritically as proof of causation.

(f) Problems in defining the money supply

Some part in causing confusion over interpretation of the empirical evidence lies in the differing definitions of what money is and what constitutes the money supply.

Five major definitions may be noted, in order of increasing comprehensiveness. Firstly, the concept of 'Reserves available to support Private Deposits' (RPD), adopted by the U.S. Federal Reserve Board in 1972 as an operating target for control over bank deposits: this was to be a monetarist yardstick of money in the private banking system.[1] Secondly, the very similar Chicago school definition, covering currency in circulation and all deposits (private and public) in the commercial banking system. Thirdly, the official U.K. definition of narrow M_1 (currency and private sector *current* accounts with the deposit or commercial banks) and broader M_3 (M_1 *plus* private sector *deposit* or 'time' accounts and public sector current and deposit accounts with the commercial or deposit banks and with accepting houses, overseas banks and the discount market). Fourthly, the official U.K. and I.M.F. definition of Domestic Credit Expansion (DCE), announced by the U.K. in its Letter of Intent to the I.M.F. in May 1969: this was done under pressure from the I.M.F., at a time when the U.K., borrowing from abroad, was under pressure to restrict the growth in the money supply. The DCE concept incorporates the official M_3 *plus* public sector borrowing from abroad— which increases the credit available for use in the U.K.[2] Fifthly, as an alternative to DCE, it has been suggested that the official definition of M_3 should be broadened into M_5.[3] This would incorporate M_3 *plus* deposits with building societies, National Savings and, possibly, private deposits with local authorities and finance houses. The expanded version of M_5 would cover a base almost twice as large as M_3 and might provide a more reliable picture of the overall liquidity and spending power of the private sector of the economy. Table 6.11, opposite, illustrates the differing elements in these various concepts of the money supply.

3. Post-Radcliffe Flexibility in Monetary Controls

Since the appearance of the Radcliffe Committee report there have been noticeable developments towards greater monetary flexibility, which may be said to bring British practice more into line with monetary techniques in the European Economic Community.[4] The importance of flexibility in monetary, as well as

---

[1] See 'Monetarists' gain', *Econ.*, 24 June 1972, p. 53.
[2] See M. J. Artis and A. R. Nobay, 'Two aspects of the monetary debate', *National Institute Economic Review*, Aug. 1969; D. Kern, 'The implications of DCE', *N.W.B.Q.R.*, Nov. 1970.
[3] See Kern, *op. cit.*, p. 39 and '"Incompatible aims" in money supply policy', *F.T.*, 13 Nov. 1972
[4] 'Monetary regulations in Europe', *Econ.*, 24 Nov. 1962, p. 846.

Table 6.11 *Constituent elements in various definitions of the money supply*

Component	RPD	Chicago School	M_1/M_3	DCE	M_5
Currency in circulation	*	*	*	*	*
Private sector *current* account deposits	*	*	*	*	*
Private sector *deposit* account deposits	*	*	*	*	*
Public sector deposits in commercial banks	—	*	*	*	*
Private and public sector deposits with accepting houses, overseas banks and discount market	—	—	*	*	*
Public sector borrowing from abroad	—	—	—	*	—
Private deposits with building societies, National Savings (and, possibly, with local authorities and finance houses)	—	—	—	—	*

(In the M_1/M_3 column, currency in circulation and private sector current account deposits are bracketed as M_1; currency, current and deposit account deposits, public sector deposits, and deposits with accepting houses etc. are bracketed as M_3.)

fiscal, controls was impressed upon observers in late-1966. The U.K. credit 'squeeze' and incomes 'freeze' policy of unmatched severity had begun to depress business investment forecasts alarmingly. Perhaps the need for refinement and opportune timing of monetary controls, to deal with 'overheating' in the economy, could best be summed up by the words of universal wisdom on the salad cream label: 'Keep cool, but don't freeze.'

(a) Information

The committee's report published for the first time a table indicating the sources of net Government borrowing. Henceforth, such figures are being issued, with further detail, on a quarterly basis. During the first year after the report there were notable improvements in information and statistics on monetary conditions. The Bank has continued to issue, in its Report, a comprehensive annual survey of past monetary policy, along the lines of the one submitted to the Radcliffe Committee. Improved banking statistics, introduced before the publication of the report, are now regularly issued. Quarterly balance of payments statistics are now issued, in summary form, in addition to the half-yearly White Papers. Furthermore, the authorities have been much more ready than hitherto to offer official comment and explanation on measures such as Bank Rate changes. All these and other improvements tend to establish a more informed awareness of the trend of monetary policy among the public.

The Bank of England has been seeking to fulfil the objective outlined in the Radcliffe Report (para. 865), *viz.*, that appropriate financial statistics should 'be capable of being fitted together to show the total movements of funds and not merely the flow through individual institutions'. It distinguishes six sectors and links their financial flows to the 'real' magnitudes, represented by the corresponding capital accounts in the national income statistics. Progress towards such a complete 'flow-of-funds matrix' is not, however, a convenient tool for short-term policy manipulation, and other indicators such as M_1, M_3 and DCE have been evolved.[1] As H. G. Johnson pointed out in the mid-1960s,[2] a great deal still remains to be accomplished in regard to the econometric techniques used to study the relationships relevant to the control of monetary policy. Much of the financial data are by-products of reports required by regulatory agencies, rather than tailor-made statistical series: in this context the vagueness and ambiguity surrounding the definition of the money supply represents a problem for policy-making.[3]

(b) Appropriate monetary indicators

The report was concerned not only with the conventional money supply, in terms of 'final settlement' money or 'money in exchange', but with the total liquidity in the economy. The varying definitions which have evolved or been suggested were referred to in Section 2 above. Some authorities are of the opinion that the official concepts of M_1, M_3 and DCE which were in use in 1972 failed to provide an unambiguous indicator of past events and future policies. This defect has been attributed to the fact that Radcliffe had considered the money supply to be only one component in total liquidity and therefore a relatively inadequate economic indicator: it had diverted attention more towards the pattern of interest rates as an indicator for control over the availability of credit.[4]

It appears that from 1969, with the inception of the DCE concept, the money supply became an officially acceptable and publicised economic indicator. However, whilst M_1, M_3 and DCE – the monetary and credit aggregates – have since been used and publicised as an important statistical *measure* of the financial situation, two criticisms may be made, apart from their limitations in comprehensiveness. Firstly, there has been much ambiguity as to whether the authorities, especially since late-1971, have genuinely shifted the focus of their attention from the primary role of interest rates to that of monetary aggregates or whether they really consider that the maintenance of statistical 'tabs' on these aggregates is merely a means of reinforcing the influence of the interest rates structure over liquidity. Secondly, there appears to be little attempt to fix specific target limits to the growth of the money supply, due to unwillingness to permit the sharp short-term fluctuations in interest rates which this might bring about.[5]

(c) Interest rates and open market operations

During the period between Radcliffe and the abandonment of Bank Rate in late-1972 much was done to use Bank Rate more flexibly, with regard to frequency

---

[1] See 'The operation of monetary policy since Radcliffe', paper by B. of E. and Treasury in Croome and Johnson, eds., *op. cit.*, esp. pp. 216–19.

[2] See H. G. Johnson, 'Monetary theory and policy', in A.E.A./R.E.S., *Surveys of Economic Theory*, 1968, p. 40.

[3] See T. C. Gaines, 'Some inadequacies of financial data and theory', *N.W.B.Q.R.*, Nov. 1969.

[4] See D. Kern, 'Monetary policy and CCC', *N.W.B.Q.R.*, Nov. 1972.

[5] *Ibid.*, pp. 41–3.

and timing. Much was done to remove the psychological symbolism and aura of portentous implications for national policy, formerly attaching to it.

Nevertheless, an extensive literature has grown up, which points to the fundamental contradictions in a monetary policy based on the manipulation of interest rates by open market operations. The primary objective of gilt-edged policy was expressed in the June 1966 *Bank of England Bulletin* as being 'to maintain market conditions that will maximise, both now and in the future, the desire of investors to hold British government debt'.[1] This has often led to a clash between a policy of credit restraint and one of supporting an orderly market in gilts. With gilts maturing (becoming repayable and requiring to be 'funded' or replaced with new issues) at the rate of about £1,500 million annually, it became essential for the Government Broker to step in frequently, in order to moderate the fluctuations in prices and yields (which approximate to long-term rates of interest). If interest rates appeared to rise too much, then, on the one hand, 'debt management' considerations might induce the authorities to take action to lower it, and with it the interest cost of new funding. On the other hand, with high interest rates, gilt prices would be low and yields high, but it has often been noted that the public reacts 'perversely' as 'i' rises (and gilt prices fall), because it may expect even further movements, and therefore sells: to counteract such panic selling and unpredictable market reactions, the authorities have, in the past, had to be prepared to deal in gilts and Treasury Bills at all times, at a price, in order to preserve an orderly market and the solvency of the financial institutions.[2] Thus, the unwillingness of the authorities to permit a wide range of interest rate fluctuations, out of concern for 'orderly conditions', has limited the freedom and effectiveness of monetary policy – with regard to interest rates, credit availability and open market operations – as a stabilisation technique. It has become fairly clear that, generally, controls may be effective on *either* interest rates *or* the money supply, but rarely on both simultaneously.

Another factor limiting the effectiveness of interest rate policy has been the possibility of Balance of Payments repercussions. Relatively high interest rates tend to attract 'hot money' into the country, which might add to inflationary pressures, when channelled to borrowers and/or importers – thus neutralising a credit restraint policy and adding to external deficit problems.[3]

A great deal of argument has taken place, in fact, about whether interest rates since Radcliffe really have been as high as they may have appeared to be. Whilst accepting that high interest rates add to the cost of 'debt management' (or of servicing the National Debt) and thereby tend to raise taxation, some authorities maintain that such high *nominal* rates of interest are largely illusory, when seen in *real* terms, related to the changing value of money in inflation and discounted by the tax relief sometimes accruing to interest payers. This concept of observing

---

[1] Croome and Johnson, eds., *op. cit.*, p. 223.
[2] Treasury and B. of E. 'The operation of monetary policy since Radcliffe', in Croome and Johnson, eds., *op. cit.*, pp. 221–5; B. J. Moore, 'Optimal monetary policy', *E.J.*, March 1972, p. 136; 'Managing the gilt-edged market – a temporary change of emphasis?', *M.B.R.*, May 1969; W. E. Norton, 'Debt management and monetary policy in the United Kingdom', *E.J.*, Sept. 1969.
[3] 'Monetary management in the United Kingdom', speech by the Governor of B. of E., Dec. 1970, reprinted in Johnson, ed., *op. cit.*, esp. p. 585; Kern, 'Monetary policy and CCC', *loc. cit.*, p. 37.

nominal monetary magnitudes and failing to consider price-level changes is sometimes referred to as the 'money illusion'.[1]

In 1969 two changes in technique were introduced in gilt-edged open market operations, with the aim of permitting the authorities to adapt more flexibly to market conditions. Firstly, it was announced that whilst the Government Broker continued to be ready to *purchase* stocks within three months of maturity, the official buying price for them was to cease to be tied to the Treasury Bill rate. Secondly, it was announced that the authorities would no longer announce the price at which they would *sell* 'tap' stocks, but would be prepared to sell after considering bids from the market.[2]

Also in 1969 the Governor of the Bank announced[3] that, as inflation had accelerated, unprecedentedly high nominal interest rates appeared to be more appropriate and that open market tactics were becoming more flexible, with the objective of making sharper adjustments than in the past. One writer has suggested[4] that – given the past conflicting pressures in monetary affairs – if a major obstacle to the flexible use of interest rate policy was the potential disruption of the financial mechanism, then perhaps this obstacle could be reduced if the financial mechanism itself were redesigned. Another writer has advocated[5] greater emphasis on a flexible interest rate policy, by means of *abandoning* official 'requests' by the Bank, restrictions on advances and special deposits and by imposing instead a stricter control over the money supply. A third writer has noted[6] that during 1972 the sharp rise in interest rates could have been interpreted as a *tightening* of financial conditions: conversely, however, the acceleration in the growth of money supply – if this were taken as an alternative economic indicator – could have been interpreted as an *easing* of financial stringency. His conclusion was that although more emphasis had been placed on interest rate flexibility, the authorities, up to the abandonment of Bank Rate, had *not* permitted interest rates (i.e. nominal and real) to rise to the very high levels necessary to achieve a significant reduction in the rate of growth of the money supply. The inception of the CCC policy in September 1971 conferred added flexibility to the Bank's operation of open market and interest rate policy: *automatic support* for the gilt-edged market was withdrawn and, whilst reserving the right to purchase gilts with more than one year to maturity, *at its discretion*, the Bank was no longer bound to do so.

After the CCC policy was adopted in late-1971 the Bank was free to determine the day-to-day prices at which it was prepared to deal in Treasury Bills: the authorities announced in September 1972 that an *increase* in their mid-week dealing rates should be taken as a *definite signal* that they anticipated a higher pattern of interest rates. Such a signal had been given for the first time in June 1972. As has been mentioned earlier, Bank Rate was abolished as a monetary tool in October 1972. It was replaced with what was termed a 'minimum lending

[1] W. A. Eltis, 'Are interest rates too high?', *L.B.R.*, July 1969; B. Reading, 'Too high interest rates', *N.W.B.Q.R.*, Feb. 1970; N. Peera, 'Interest rates: illusion or reality?', and P. Wann, 'Lower interest rates?', *N.W.B.Q.R.*, May 1970; Governor of B. of E., *loc. cit.*, Johnson, ed., *op. cit.*, p. 585.
[2] See Croome and Johnson, eds., *op. cit.*, p. 224.
[3] See Johnson, ed., *op. cit.*, p. 585.
[4] See Moore, *op. cit.*, p. 138.
[5] See Norton, *op. cit.*, p. 493.
[6] See Kern, 'Monetary policy and CCC', *loc. cit.*, p. 45.

rate' to the discount market, published each Friday and based on the average discount rate on Treasury Bills at the most recent tender, plus half a per cent, rounded to the nearest (higher) quarter per cent. Whilst aiming to remove any remaining rigidities, psychological effects and symbolism of the Bank Rate, the new instrument could not be considered as a *minimum* rate, since the Bank would continue to assist the market by sometimes dealing in T.B.s and other bills at rates *below* the new rate.[1]

Whilst the pre-October 1972 'signals' represented a form of 'qualitative guidance', which the CCC policy continued to invest in the Bank, the post-October 1972 'minimum lending rate' (or 'market rate') formula was intended to achieve a similar result, through the speedy operation of market trends. Thus, on 22 November 1972, the Bank lent about £20 million to the discount market, some of it at an *increased* minimum lending rate, in line with a general rise in the pattern of interest rates. This should have functioned as a signal to the banks to raise their base rates, which had been low enough to induce favoured borrowers to borrow on overdraft and then relend at a profit. If this signal were not acted upon, the Bank was expected to follow it up with a more forceful pointer, *viz.*, the next Treasury Bill tender rate, which the Bank could influence by means of its control over the supply.[2]

(d) Special deposits

In April 1960 the Bank used for the first time the weapon of calling upon the banks for Special Deposits. By September 1961 the last stage of the third cumulative call had been completed, accounting for 3% (1·5% in Scotland) of gross deposits, or £230 million. They had been accompanied by requests to the banks to restrict their advances and to be much more selective in their lending.

Due to the gradual economic improvement and the desire of the authorities to encourage economic expansion, the Bank announced the first stage in the release of Special Deposits in May 1962. By December 1962 all Special Deposits had been eliminated. Within a period of six months, all the restraints on bank lending had been removed – ensuring 'that adequate finance will be available for expansion'. This was followed by the long-anticipated reduction in Bank Rate, from 4·5% to 4%, in January 1963.

On 29 April 1965 the Bank once again made a call for Special Deposits, as another move in the tightening of the 1965 'credit squeeze'. The call was for 1% (£90 million) from the London Clearing Banks and 0·5% (£5 million) from the Scottish banks. In July 1966 S.D.s were increased by another 1%, in line with renewed calls for lending restraints. At end-May 1969, as a penalty for noncompliance with further calls to limit advances, the interest rate paid on S.D.s was halved. A further S.D. call for 0·5% was made in April 1970 – at which time the interest rate was restored – and a fourth call, for 1%, was made in October 1970, bringing the rate to 3·5% for London Clearing Banks (1·75% for the Scottish banks). All these S.D.s, accounting for £378·5 million from the London Clearing Banks, were released in mid-September 1971, with the introduction of the CCC policy. Henceforth, official CCC policy was to the effect that S.D.s should constitute a major and flexible technique for implementing policy. The interest rate paid on S.D.s was to be equivalent to the Treasury Bill rate. They

[1] *Ibid.*, pp. 46–7.
[2] 'The Bank hints at higher interest rates', *D.T.*, 23 Nov. 1972.

were to be imposed at a uniform rate on *all types of bank* (not merely on the deposit or commercial banks) and would be related to the eligible liabilities (and not to gross deposits, as hitherto). It has been asserted that in the past the S.D. policy instrument has been largely ineffectual.[1] Nevertheless, the spectrum of institutions over which it may operate has been extended and its effectiveness may have been enhanced. When applied for the first time, in its new form, in November 1972 – at a rate of 1%, to be paid over in two stages and netting about £220 million – it affected about 250 banks, including merchant banks and overseas banks, and ten deposit-taking finance houses.[2]

(e) Liquidity ratios and reserve requirements

During the first half-year after the Radcliffe Report, the Chancellor announced that the Government would re-examine the question of using a variable liquidity ratio in conjunction with, or instead of, Special Deposits. The proposal that direct control over the ratio of bank advances should be used only in an emergency was rejected by the Chancellor, who claimed that the Government should be free to use any available and suitable measures to make any change in the economic situation, without the implication that the situation was necessarily an emergency.[3] In October 1963 the Bank asserted its right to announce a change in the banks' second liquidity ratio. It announced a temporary reduction from 30% to 28%, with a view to a further reduction to 25%. Apart from establishing a precedent for making alterations of this sort, and apart from permitting the banks to increase their proportions of advances and investments, it will be remembered that the Radcliffe Committee had considered the proportion of highly liquid assets (easily turned into cash) as being of much greater significance than the single item of 8% actual cash (first liquidity ratio).

The power to change reserve requirements, in principle, gives a central bank an alternative method to open market operations for changing the quantity of bank deposits. The chief differences between the two methods are that variable reserve requirements of liquidity ratios are discontinuous and may have disturbing effects on securities markets, which necessitate rectifying open market operations: also credit expansion by open market purchases may be less costly for the authorities and less profitable for the banks than when achieved by a reduction in reserve requirements. Some authorities consider that variable ratios should be used sparingly, if at all, and that a more equitable procedure would be to establish standardised uniform reserve requirements.[4] The Governor of the Bank, in December 1970, emphasised the point that the great diversity in asset structures of the various types of bank made it extremely difficult to devise an effective and equitable system of credit control, based on liquidity or other asset ratios.[5]

The 1971 CCC policy, as noted earlier, introduced the concept of 'eligible liabilities' (instead of gross deposits) and a *minimum* ratio of 'reserve assets'. These were extended to cover not only the commercial banks, but *all* banks, with the ratio set at 12·5% of eligible liabilities. Furthermore, finance houses with

---

[1] Norton, *op. cit.*, pp. 492–3.
[2] *F.T.* and *D.T.*, 10 Nov. 1972.
[3] *M.B.R.*, May 1960, p. 20.
[4] H. G. Johnson, 'Monetary theory and policy', *loc. cit.*, pp. 38–9.
[5] Johnson, ed., *op. cit.*, pp. 579–80.

more than £5 million of eligible liabilities were subject to a minimum reserve assets ratio of 10%: the Discount Houses were to have a form of reserve assets, in the sense that at least 50% of their assets should be in defined categories of public sector debt. These arrangements have been criticised on grounds of detail.[1] For example, some types of the Discount Houses' public sector debt (eligible reserve assets) are *not* eligible as bank reserve assets, and, if transferred from a bank to a Discount House, would, by 'gearing up' (or 'multiple credit creation'), increase the overall liquidity of the financial system. The combination of a minimum reserve assets concept with S.D.s has been compared with a *variable* reserve assets system, but the fixing of the S.D. interest rate by the authorities deprives the institutions of some freedom to deploy their assets in the most profitable ways and thereby may seem to conflict with the spirit of 'Competition and Credit Control'. It has been suggested that a variable reserve assets ratio principle would have enabled the Bank from taking 'rescue' action during the mid-1972 sterling crisis, which appeared to conflict with the spirit of the CCC system.[2] On this occasion the banks' reserve assets fell sharply and the Bank provided temporary assistance by purchasing from, and then reselling to them, short-dated (near to maturity) gilts. This helped restore the banks' liquidity, but the lowering of a *variable* reserve assets ratio could have achieved the same result within the system, without resort to special, emergency schemes. Nevertheless, the CCC system does cover a wider spectrum of the financial institutions than did the former 'liquid assets ratio' system. Also, the constitution of the lists of eligible reserve assets may be altered, if the authorities see fit, and anomalies may be eliminated.

4. Technique of Altering the Fiduciary Issue

In previous sections mention has been made of the fiduciary issue: its size; how it has developed; the regulations surrounding it; and its significance in the money supply and as a weapon of monetary control. In this section we shall attempt to illustrate, with a simplified model, the technique by which the fiduciary issue is altered.

The sequence of events for an increase is as follows:

(*i*) *Prognosis.* The Bank of England foresees an increased demand for notes in circulation (e.g. before the Christmas period) and/or notices that the 'proportion' or reserve in the Banking Department is being depleted as a result of withdrawals by the commercial banks.

(*ii*) *Permission.* The Bank must obtain Treasury permission to issue more notes and replenish the reserve. In order to do this, it must obtain more securities as backing to the issue.

(*iii*) *Method* (see Fig. 6.15).

(*iv*) *Final result.* The issue Department holds Securities (S) as Assets. The additional notes issued are its Liabilities. The Banking Department holds the new notes – its Assets – as a reserve. The Deposits (D), owing to its clients, are its Liabilities.

---

[1] Kern, 'Monetary policy and CCC', *loc. cit.*, pp. 40–1. Also see D. F. Lomax, 'Reserve assets and Competition and Credit Control', *N.W.B.Q.R.*, Aug. 1973.

[2] Kern, 'Monetary policy and CCC', *loc. cit.*, p. 41.

1. Banking Department *buys* Securities (S), which are its *Assets*.
2. Banking Department *pays* for securities by opening accounts for its clients. These are Deposits (D), which are *liabilities*.
3. Banking Department *gives* its Securities (S) to the Issue Department. They cease to be Banking Department Assets and become *Issue Department Assets*.
4. Issue Department uses these Assets as *backing to an increase* in the Fiduciary Issue. More notes are issued. These are Issue Department *Liabilities*.
5. Issue Department *lodges* these notes, which are still its Liabilities, in the Banking Department, as a reserve. They become *Banking Department Assets*, which take the place of Securities previously surrendered.

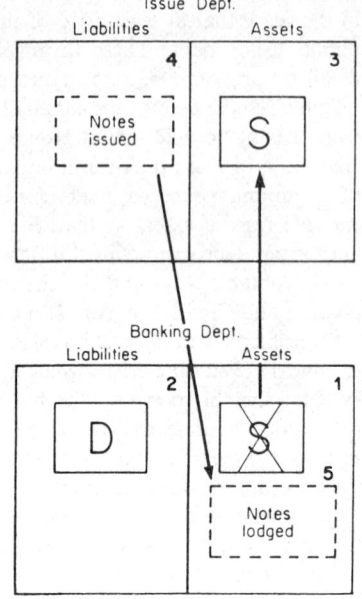

Fig. 6.15. *Stages in increasing the fiduciary issue*

5. Technical Aspects of Open Market Operations

With regard to open market operations, some confusion may arise from a failure to distinguish between the short-term and long-term effects on the money supply. These implications have altered somewhat, over the years, in line with institutional changes in liquidity and reserve ratios and with changes in types of financial assets.

Before the CCC policy of 1971 *three* major phases may be distinguished,[1] each paralleled by an appropriate theory.

Firstly, during the period when an 8% cash ratio and 28% liquid assets ratio were in force, the sequence of events was explained by the '*old-orthodox*' theory. In simplified terms, this implied that there would be a 12½-fold 'credit multiplier' effect from open market *sales* (money-reducing) or *purchases* (money-increasing). According to this theory, if the Bank did *not* impose penal, last-resort interest rates on the discount market, then, when the banks called in cash – following open market *sales* – they would restore their ratios and eventually experience only a *single* reduction in bank deposits. If, however, penal rates were imposed on the discount market, the market would seek to evade these penal rates and borrow from other sources than the Bank and/or by reducing their bills holdings in exchange for cash. Both these actions would lead to further reductions in the banks' cash ratios: the eventual effect would be to reduce bank deposits by a 'credit multiplier' of 12½ (i.e. the reciprocal of the 8% cash ratio). An important element in this process would have been the shrinkage of the total bills supply,

[1] For further details, see A. B. Cramp, 'The control of bank deposits', *L.B.R.*, Oct. 1967.

9. The Yield Gap

During the period since World War II the general inflationary trend in the economy, boosted by official commitment to a policy of full employment, and accompanied by generally high interest rates, has had repercussions on the market prices of gilt-edged and equities and on their actual yields. This has aroused much attention to trends in what is called the 'yield gap' between gilt-edged and equities.[1]

In times of relative general price stability, with periodic trade depressions, which keep business profits and anticipations of future equity dividends low, the fixed dividend on gilt-edged offers security and more or less retains its real value. Despite the fact that rather low interest rates result in high gilt-edged prices, and thus low percentage real or actual yields, gilt-edged in such periods tend to offer stability in the real value of their dividend and also in their real capital value or price. At the same time the risks and uncertainties attaching to equities tend to reduce anticipated dividends and thus their market prices. Although yields are consequently fairly high, there is a heavy risk of capital loss from falling equity prices. Such, in general, was the period before World War II, when gilt-edged (high price, low yield) were preferred to equities (low price, high yield). Investors tended to prefer the fairly stable real capital value in gilt-edged market prices and dividends, despite the 'yield gap' between them and equities, whose dividends were uncertain and whose market prices were thus in much greater danger of falling.

After the war, until 1951, the Government was following a 'cheap money' policy of low interest rates. This tended to boost gilt-edged prices, which reached their peak in 1949. Since 1951 interest rates have been at higher levels, rationing and other consumer restrictions have been lifted, and the economy has been operating at a fairly high level of activity, generating optimism as to anticipated dividends on equities. Consequently equity prices have moved up, especially since 1957, and there has been some movement out of gilt-edged into equities. A 'cult of the equity' grew up, based on the assumption that inflation was part of postwar life, that general prices would always rise and money values fall and that only equities, which could offer ever-higher dividends, could match the fall in money values. As this resulted in rising equity prices, actual percentage dividend yields on equities have fallen, but the equity cult was bolstered by the belief that higher equity prices kept the real capital value of equities ahead of inflation. This attitude was fortified by high levels of taxation, for on gilt-edged the dividend was fixed (and falling in real terms), whilst in the case of equities high taxation could be passed on to the consumer, making possible high profits and high dividends.

Following the post-1951 changes in interest rates, gilt-edged prices and yields moved closely in step, prices in the opposite, and yields in the same direction, until 1962. Meanwhile, equity prices, although moving in the same general direction as gilt-edged prices, tended to fluctuate more violently. Differential profits taxes – higher on distributed profits than on undistributed profits – were in operation from 1947 to 1958. These had the effect of strictly

---

[1] T. Wilson, 'Equities and growth', *L.B.R.*, Oct. 1959, p. 14; 'A turn in gilt-edged?', *Econ.*, 14 July 1962, p. 169; 'Which way for gilt-edged?', *Econ.*, 27 Apr. 1963, p. 342; G. Cummings, *The Complete Guide to Investment*, Penguin Handbook, 1963, pp. 132–5; 'Analysis of "The reverse gap"', *M.B.R.*, May 1960, p. 3.

limiting dividend distribution, and thereby tended to depress equity prices and raise equity yields. The yields on equities remained higher than on gilt-edged, with several fluctuations in the 'gap,' which was small in 1951 (Korean war boom, with high prices and low yields); large in 1956 (monetary restrictions, with low prices and high yields); low in mid-1957 (lower interest rate and higher expectations, with high prices and low yields); large at end-1957 (high interest rate and restrictions, with loss of confidence, low prices and high yields). From 1958 the 'yield gap' narrowed, marking the development of the equity cult. This was stimulated by the 1958 abolition of differential profits taxes[1] and an increase in business confidence, raising equity prices and lowering yields. In the latter half of 1959 came the famous 'intersection', when equity yields fell below gilt-edged yields. This movement into equities, gradually raising their prices, tended to depress gilt-edged prices and raise their yields still further. The willingness to accept lower equity yields was based on the belief that 'growth companies' would eventually be able to pay very much higher dividends.

The big deflationary 'credit squeeze' of mid-1961, with higher interest rates, partly shattered the belief in inevitable inflation, and resulted in a temporary boom in gilt-edged prices (and a fall in yields) during 1962. This was caused partly by the eventual reduction in interest rates – which boosted gilt-edged prices – and partly by a lessened belief in perpetual inflation, and by general fears of a trade depression and falling profits, equity dividends and equity prices (representing capital losses). Consequently, there was a fall in equity prices, reinforced by the Cuban blockade crisis, and a rise in equity yields. The 'yield gap' narrowed considerably. After the end of 1962, however, a more cautious confidence in the future of economic growth and equity dividends returned, stimulating a gradual rise in equity prices and a fall in equity yields. Gilt-edged prices rose early in 1963, following the reduction in Bank Rate to 4%. From then until mid-1963 they fluctuated quite a lot, despite a stable Bank Rate, due partly to a movement out of gilt-edged into equities, partly to an increase in the supply of gilt-edged. In fact, during the latter half of 1963 gilt-edged prices steadily fell under competition from equities.[2] This resulted in a gradual increase in yields,

[1] Some economists believe that differential profits taxes, discriminating against distributed profits, enable inefficient managements to hold up dividend distribution whilst sheltering behind the tax 'wall'. It has been suggested that profits almost in their entirety should be distributed to shareholders, so that future capital for expansion would be channelled in a free market to the successful 'growth' sectors and firms. This point was well made by A. Rubner in *The ensnared shareholder*, 1965. See also *Stat.*, 26 Feb. 1965, p. 570.

[2] Early in 1964 Mr Alan Day outlined a proposal for 'national equities' whose dividend would be linked to the growth of the Gross National Product. The aim would be to counter the drift out of gilt-edged and attract capital for the growth in public investment, whilst the securities would hold a good market price. Thus the yield would be quite low, long-term interest rates would be reduced, and the cost of public borrowing would be kept down. (See 'national equities', *Stat.*, 14 Feb. 1964, p. 470.) In February 1965 it was reported that Sweden was considering the issue of index-linked bonds to check the drift of savings into equities, whereby bond capital values would be linked to a cost-of-living index (*D.T.* 9 Feb. 1965). In May 1970 the Bank was in the invidious position of having to *buy* gilts, which were being dumped by the public – partly due to fears that inflation was making the real yield on gilts unattractive. Yet, at the same time, monetary policy was aimed at decreasing the money supply growth rate: this required substantial net *sales* of gilts, a difficult task in a 'bear' market. *The Economist* suggested that the task be made easier by breaking free of fixed-interest gilts and floating a government equity-type bond. This could have offered a dividend based on a percentage of the GNP: consequently, the dividend would cater for real income growth and for inflationary rises in money income. (See 'A government ordinary share?', *Econ.*, 2 May 1970, pp. 12–13.)

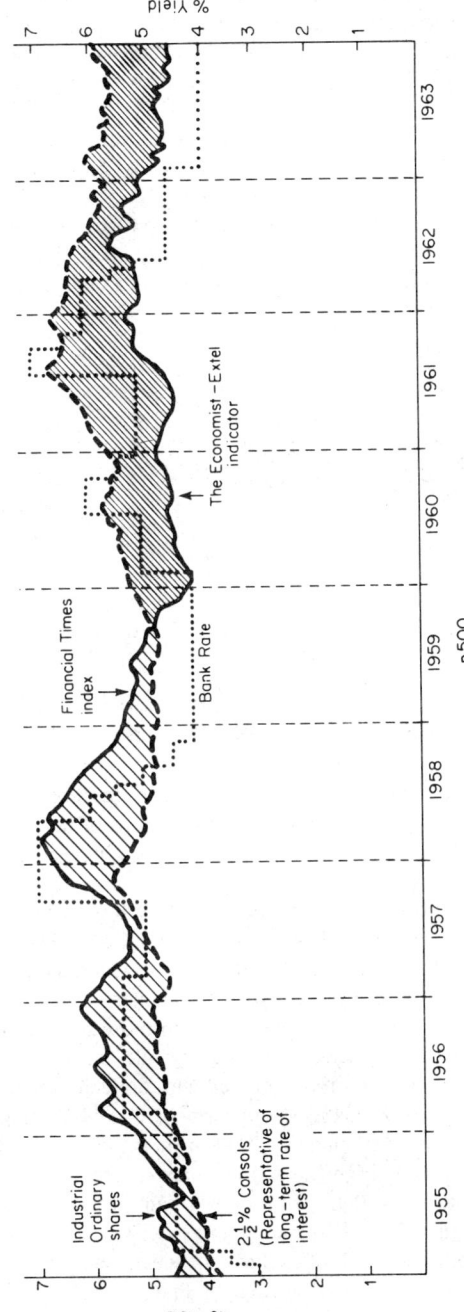

Fig. 6.26. *The 'yield gap' between gilt-edged and equities, 1955–1963*
(Based on material in *L.B.R.*, Oct. 1959; *Econ.*, 27 Aug. and 14 Dec. 1963)

which was in turn reflected in long-term interest rates. Thus, with no change in Bank Rate, the fall in gilt-edged prices, by raising dividend yields, resulted in a rise in long-term interest rates, a process referred to as 'hardening of interest rates in the gilt-edged market'. The rise in gilt-edged dividend yields and the fall in equity dividend yields resulted in a renewed widening of the 'yield gap' (see Fig. 6.26).

During the period from 1963 to early-1972 the main trends in gilt and equity dividend yields and in Bank Rate were as shown in Fig. 6.27. Throughout the period the 'reverse yield gap' was maintained, but several important trends were noticeable. Firstly, until mid-1966 both yields tended to rise, influenced by generally rising interest rates (and lower gilt prices) and by subdued economic expectations and a move from equities to gilts – which tended to depress equity prices.

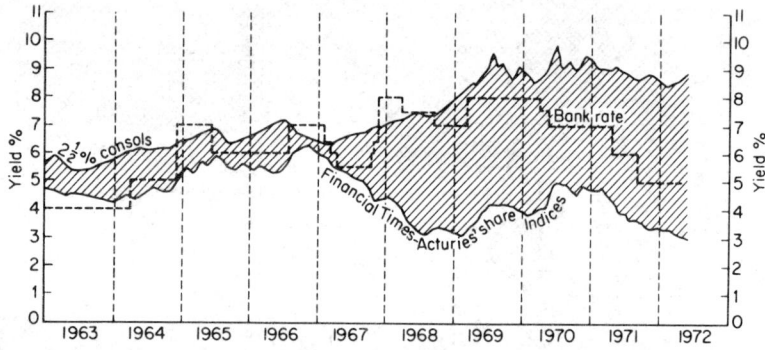

Fig. 6.27. *The 'reverse yield gap' between gilt-edged and equities*, 1963 *to* 1972 (Based on material in *M.B.R.*, Feb. 1966, May 1969 and May 1972)

Secondly, in late-1966 both yields fell: the more pronounced fall in gilt yields almost closed the gap. This was influenced by expectations of imminent interest rate reductions (leading to rising gilt prices and *falling* gilt yields) and to the prices and incomes policy dividend freeze, which depressed equity prices and *raised* dividend yields. Thirdly, from mid-1967 until 1970 the reverse dividend yield gap expanded to about 5%. This was largely caused by the rising trend of interest rates, coupled with an increased supply of gilts, which tended to reduce gilt prices and raise gilt yields, and by the mid-1969 change in debt management policy, whereby gilt prices were allowed to fall much more than hitherto, with less support.[1] It was also influenced by the 'equity cult' and booming equity prices, seen as a 'hedge against inflation', coupled with dividend restraint, which tended to reduce equity yields. Fourthly, from early-1970 to 1972, despite reductions in Bank Rate, gilt yields remained high, at around the 9% to 10% mark: these were affected by relatively high Eurodollar interest rates and by 'inflation-psychosis' and related fears of a 'flight from money' (and falling capital values), which tended to depress gilt prices. At the same time, equity dividend yields, apart from an initial increase early in 1970, tended to fall: these were influenced by the continuing equity price boom. Fifthly, during the first half of 1972 Bank Rate

[1] For further comment see H. McRae, 'Gilt-edged in perspective', *The Banker*, Nov. 1969, esp. p. 1175 and H. Rose, 'Reflections on the Equity Boom, 1966–69', *T.B.R.*, June 1969.

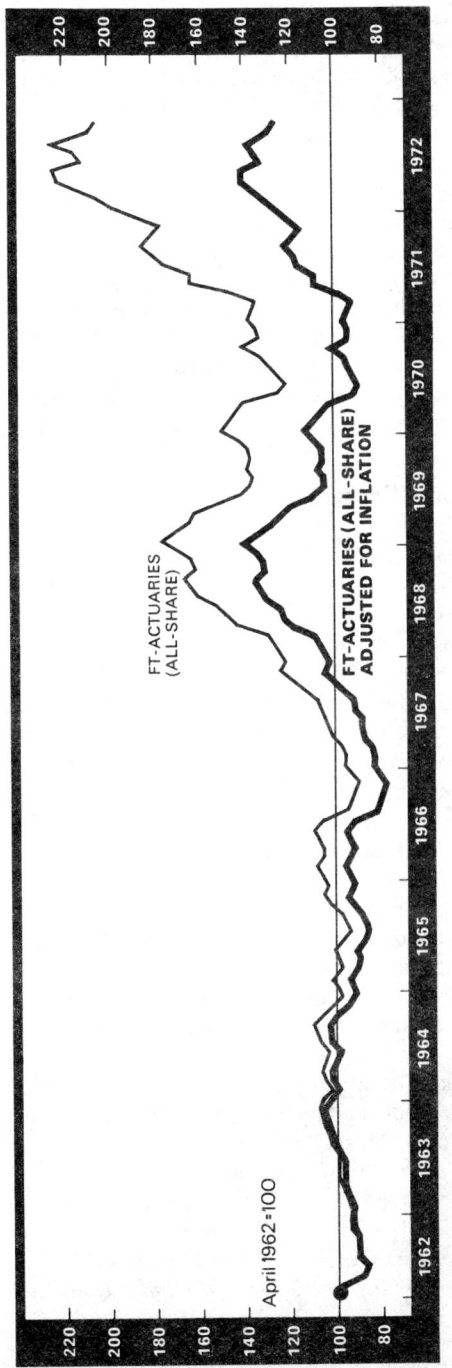

Fig. 6.28. *Monetary and real changes in the stock market price index, 1962 to 1972*
(Source: *Econ.*, 28 Oct. 1972, p. 97)

rose and was accompanied by reduced gilt prices and increased yields and by uncertainty in the equities market, with price reductions and increased yields.

In recent years the 'hedge against inflation' concept of the equity cult has been subjected to some strong criticism. It appears that from 1962 to 1972, despite a doubling of the equity price index, the actual real increase in value was only about one-quarter, after adjusting for inflationary reductions in money values (see Fig. 6.28). Sometimes, as in the United States during 1969, the 'inflation-psychosis' element in the equity cult may be shown to be unfounded.[1] During a period of stringent monetary and fiscal policy, it was generally believed that inflation-psychosis would lead to a rush from cash into equities, thus *raising* their prices. Instead, there was general confidence in the Government's ability to prevent a recession: accordingly, businessmen continued to plan new investment projects; borrowing remained at a high level; and interest rates rose. Consequently, gilt prices fell. Furthermore, institutional lenders diverted funds to fixed-interest gilts – because of their higher yields – rather than to equities: consequently, the demand for equities slackened and their prices *fell*.

10. Further Reading and Sources

Footnote references to daily and weekly journals are not repeated.

M. J. ARTIS and A. R. NOBAY, 'Two aspects of the monetary debate.' *National Institute Economic Review*, Aug. 1969.

M. J. ARTIS and A. R. NOBAY, 'The attempt to reinstate money', reprinted in H. G. Johnson, ed., *Readings in British Monetary Economics*, O.U.P. 1972.

BANK OF ENGLAND, 'The importance of money', reprinted in Johnson, ed., *op. cit.*

K. BRUNNER, 'The monetarist view of Keynesian ideas', *L.B.R.* Oct. 1971.

A. B. CRAMP, 'The control of bank deposits'. *L.B.R.* Oct. 1967.

A. B. CRAMP, '*Does* money matter?' *L.B.R.* Oct. 1970.

D. R. CROOME and H. G. JOHNSON, eds. *Money in Britain*, 1959–1969. O.U.P. 1972.

G. CUMMINGS, *The Complete Guide to Investment*. Penguin Handbook. 1963.

P. DAVIDSON, 'Money and the real world'. *E.J.* March 1972.

W. A. ELTIS, 'Are interest rates too high?' *L.B.R.* July 1969.

MILTON FRIEDMAN, 'The counter-revolution of monetary theory'. First Wincott Memorial Lecture. Reproduced in *F.T.* 17 Sept. 1970.

MILTON FRIEDMAN, 'The new monetarism – comment'. *L.B.R.* Oct. 1970.

T. C. GAINES, 'Some inadequacies of financial data and theory'. *N.W.B.Q.R.* Nov. 1969.

P. G. GSCHWINDT DE GYOR, 'The money supply question'. *N.W.B.Q.R.* Aug. 1969.

H. G. JOHNSON, 'Monetary theory and policy'. Reprinted in A.E.A./R.E.S. *Surveys of Economic Theory*, vol. 1. Macmillan. 1968.

H. G. JOHNSON, ed. *Readings in British Monetary Economics*. O.U.P. 1972.

N. KALDOR, 'The new monetarism'. *L.B.R.* Oct. 1970. (And see Friedman, above.)

D. KERN, 'The implications of DCE'. *N.W.B.Q.R.* Nov. 1970.

D. KERN, 'Monetary policy and CCC'. *N.W.B.Q.R.* Nov. 1972.

I. LITTLE, 'Higgledy-piggeldy growth'. *Bulletin of Oxford University Institute of Statistics*. Nov. 1962.

[1] See 'Inflation defoliates the investor's hedge', *D.T.*, 4 Dec. 1972 and 'Wall Street through the Maginot Line', *Econ.*, 6 Dec. 1969, pp. 81–2.

LLOYDS BANK, *L.B.R.* Oct. 1959; July 1962.

D. F. LOMAX, 'Reserve assets and Competition and Credit Control'. *N.W.B.Q.R.*, Aug. 1973.

MIDLAND BANK, *M.B.R.* Feb. 1966; May 1969; May 1972.

MIDLAND BANK, 'Managing the gilt-edged market – a temporary change of emphasis?' *M.B.R.* May 1969.

B. J. MOORE, 'Optimal monetary policy'. *E.J.* March 1972.

H. MCRAE, 'Gilt-edged in perspective'. *The Banker.* Nov. 1969.

W. E. NORTON, 'Debt management and monetary policy in the United Kingdom'. *E.J.* Sept. 1969.

N. PEERA, 'Interest rates: illusion or reality'. *N.W.B.Q.R.* May 1970.

G. PEPPER and R. THOMAS, *The Historical Importance of Money in the United Kingdom.* 1972. Research Monograph. W. Greenwell & Co. May 1972.

T. M. PODOLSKI, 'The control of non-bank financial intermediaries: I. The need for control; II. Methods of control'. *The Bankers' Magazine,* Jan. and Feb. 1969.

RADCLIFFE REPORT. *Report of the Committee on the Working of the Monetary System.* Cmnd 827. H.M.S.O. 1959.

B. READING, 'Too high interest rates'. *N.W.B.Q.R.* Feb. 1970.

H. ROSE, 'Reflections on the equity boom, 1966–69'. *T.B.R.* June 1969.

A. RUBNER, *The Ensnared Shareholder.* Macmillan. 1965.

A. J. SCHWARTZ, 'Why money matters'. *L.B.R.* Oct. 1969.

B. TAYLOR, 'Investment: art, science or what?' *L.B.R.* Jan. 1969.

J. A. WATERS, 'Money supply and credit – theory and practice'. *N.W.B.Q.R.* Nov. 1969.

J. WHITTAKER, 'What level for share prices?' *L.B.R.* Jan. 1968.

11. Past Examination Questions

1. 'While the accuracy of the quantity equation in the theory of money is beyond dispute its usefulness is not so certain.' Discuss. (Summer 1952)

2. What different items make up the quantity of money in the United Kingdom? How can the government influence the quantity of money? (Summer 1961)

3. What are the chief factors determining the general level of prices in a country? (January 1963)

4. Examine the relationship between the quantity of money and the general level of prices. (Summer 1960)

5. 'Inflation is impossible without an increase in the quantity of money.' Discuss. (January 1965)

6. 'The value of money must be stable if it is to fulfil its functions adequately.' Comment. (Summer 1956)

7. What difficulties lie in the way of making comparisons between the value of money today and its value one hundred years ago? (Summer 1952)

8. 'The value of money is a term which is indispensable to economic discussion but it is one to which it is impossible to attach any exact and precise meaning.' Comment. (Summer 1952)

9. What is meant by inflation? What measures might a government use to combat it? (January 1964)

10. 'Only fixed income recipients gain from deflation.' Explain this statement, and say whether or not you agree with it. (Summer 1961)
11. Discuss the proposition that the only way to end inflation is by bringing about deflation. (Summer 1956)
12. Write an essay on the causes and effects of inflation. (Summer 1953)
13. What are the likely effects of inflation on productivity in a country? (Summer 1957)
14. How would you measure the average level of retail prices? What difficulties are likely to arise in doing so? (January 1965)
15. What is meant by the cost of living? Say how you might measure it, indicating the problems that will be encountered. (January 1964)
16. The Index of Retail Prices published by the Ministry of Labour was 100·0 in June 1947 and 157·0 in June 1956. Account for the difference in the index between the two dates. (Summer 1957)
17. Why was the Index of Retail Prices, published by the Ministry of Labour in the United Kingdom, relatively stable between June, 1958 and September, 1959? (Summer 1960)
18. 'Commercial banks are distinguished from all other institutions by their power of creating credit.' Comment. (Summer 1962)
19. What limits the power of a commercial bank to create credit? (January 1964)
20. Describe the items in a typical commercial bank's balance sheet and account for their relative size. (Summer 1963)
21. What factors influence the distribution of assets of a British joint-stock bank? (Summer 1960)
22. How does a British commercial bank choose between the need for liquidity and the quest for profit? (Summer 1957)
23. What are the functions of a central bank? (Summer 1962)
24. Describe the main functions of the Bank of England. To what extent have these changed since the 'thirties? (Summer 1964)
25. Describe the present relationship between the Bank of England and the Joint Stock banks. (Summer 1956)
26. 'The Bank of England attempts to increase interest rates by open-market operations. These consist of buying bills from the Commercial Banks. This means the Banks have an increased demand for borrowing and can put up their rates.' Comment. (Summer 1961)
27. How are the activities of joint stock banks influenced by the Bank of England? (Summer 1959)
28. 'The Bank of England controls the quantity of cash in circulation and thereby controls the quantity of credit.' How does this come about? (Summer 1952)
29. What is meant by a 'credit squeeze'? In what economic circumstances is it likely to occur? (Summer 1963)
30. What is meant by the 'backing of the Note issue'? Is it a necessary condition of a sound monetary system? (Summer 1959)
31. What is the Bank Rate? Explain the effects of a decrease in Bank Rate. (Summer 1960)
32. How, and in what circumstances, does the Bank of England make Bank Rate effective? (Summer 1957)
33. Outline the main effects of a rise in interest rates. (Summer 1956) ·

34. Why do people hold money balances, if money is only useful when it can be exchanged for goods and services? (Summer 1959)
35. What are the factors which determine the value of a firm's ordinary shares? (Summer 1962)
36. What economic functions are fulfilled by a Stock Exchange? (Summer 1961)
37. 'The Stock Exchange is the hub around which the whole long-term capital market revolves.' Comment. (Summer 1956)
38. Examine the rôle in the national economy of *either* (*a*) the stock exchange *or* (*b*) institutional investors. (Summer 1954)
39. What are the discount houses? Explain their rôle in the London Money Market. (January 1965)

7. Public Finance
Stage I

1. Introduction

During the twentieth century the State has become progressively more involved in economic and social affairs, as well as in matters of defence and diplomacy. Its increasing rôle in the regulation of the economy, the running of nationalised industries, the fostering of industrial and scientific research, the provision of defence facilities, the creation of a large body of 'Welfare State' social services, the development of the road network, and the general administration of these and a host of other activities at local and national level, have led to a vast increase in the importance of the 'public sector' of the economy.[1]

'Public finance' is the term used to cover the whole field of public spending and the raising of revenue by the central Government Exchequer, the local authorities, and special non-Exchequer funds, such as the National Insurance Fund of the Department of Health and Social Security.

By 1971 the public authorities were spending almost £24·5 billion per year, more than 50% of the Gross National Product. Not all of this spending consisted of the purchase of goods and services and investment resources, in competition with the private sector of the economy. Only about 60% consisted of demand-creating expenditure on goods and services – generating Gross National Product – whereas the rest consisted of transfer payments such as debt interest, benefits, pensions, grants and subsidies. Nevertheless, involvement on such a scale has far-reaching implications for the total level of demand, the utilisation of the country's resources, and the level of economic activity. Capital investment and current spending on goods, services and transfer payments for the 'Welfare State' social services accounted for about three-sevenths of the total, more than £10,000 million in 1971, or 22% of the Gross National Product.

2. Main Constituents of Public Expenditure and Revenue

(a) Expenditure

There are various ways in which the main items of public spending might be usefully classified. These include the following:

(i) a distinction between Current expenditure on goods, services, debt interest, benefits, grants and subsidies on the one hand, and Capital expenditure on

---

[1] For a discussion of the rationale of defects in the market system and of public sector activities, see R. H. Haveman, *The Economics of the Public Sector*, 1970, ch. 2; O. Eckstein, *Public Finance*, 2nd edn, 1967, ch. 1; J. F. Due, *Government Finance: economics of the public sector*, 1968, ch. 1; R. A. Musgrave, *The Theory of Public Finance*, 1959, ch. 1.

Table 7.1 *Public expenditure in the United Kingdom, 1971*

Type of expenditure	Amount (£ million)	Analysis	Demand-creating direct purchases of goods and services	Transfers
(A) Capital:				
Public investment:				
(a) Public Corporations	1,859	*Demand-creating Capital Investment* = £4,475 m		
(b) Public Service investment:			£4,475 m	
Miscellaneous	1,251			
Social services (*plus* housing)	1,365			
		Social Services* (*plus* housing)† = £11,335 m		
(B) Current:				
Public current expenditure:		*Current Expenditure* = £19,765m of which:		
(a) Social Services (*plus* housing)	9,970	Demand-creating current expenditure on goods and services = £10,278m	£10,278 m	
(b) Miscellaneous	9,795	Transfer payments = £9,487m		£9,487
TOTAL	24,240		£14,753 m	£9,487

(N.B. 1971 *Gross National Product* = £48,216 m *at factor cost*
  Capital depreciation = £ 5,012 m
  Net National Income = £43,204 m *at factor cost*)

* *Social Services* = Education; health; welfare; social security pensions, benefits and assistance:

  Capital expenditure = £570 m
  Current expenditure = £9,497 m
  Total   = £10,067 m

† *Housing:* Capital expenditure = £795 m; Current expenditure = £473 m; Total = 1,268 m

(Based on material in *National Income and Expenditure*, 1972, H.M.S.O.)

longer-term investment projects on the other (e.g. between pensions, teachers' salaries and medicines, and old people's homes, new schools and new hospitals); (ii) a distinction between expenditure on 'Welfare State' social services and other fields of public spending;
(iii) a distinction between competitive or demand-creating expenditure on current and capital (or investment) consumption of goods and services on the one hand, and non-competitive expenditure on transfer payments on the other.

Table 7.1 illustrates the main outlines of public spending for the calendar year 1971.

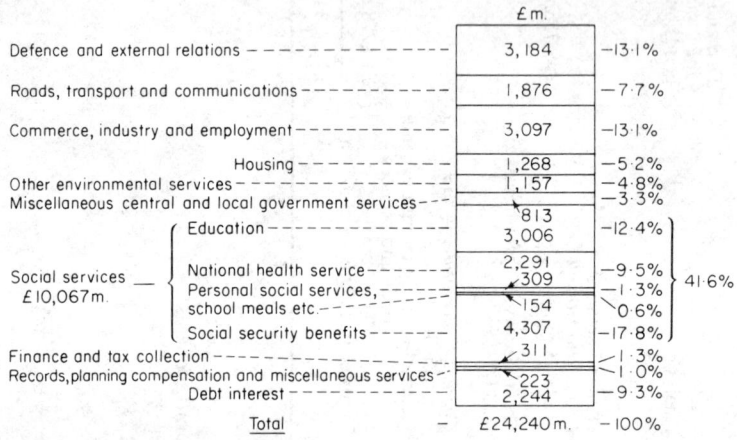

	£m.	
Defence and external relations	3,184	−13·1%
Roads, transport and communications	1,876	−7·7%
Commerce, industry and employment	3,097	−13·1%
Housing	1,268	−5·2%
Other environmental services	1,157	−4·8%
Miscellaneous central and local government services	813	−3·3%
Social services £10,067m. — Education	3,006	−12·4%
National health service	2,291	−9·5%
Personal social services, school meals etc.	309	−1·3%
	154	0·6%
Social security benefits	4,307	−17·8%
Finance and tax collection	311	−1·3%
Records, planning compensation and miscellaneous services	223	−1·0%
Debt interest	2,244	−9·3%
Total	£24,240 m.	−100%

(41·6%)

Fig. 7.1. *Major items of public expenditure*, 1971
(Based on material in *National Income and Expenditure* [*Blue Book*], 1972, H.M.S.O.)

Capital investment in the nationalised industries and public corporations was accounted for mainly by the expansion of the electricity generating industry, the Post Office, the railways and the coal industry. It is worthy of note that this group of industries (fuel, iron and steel, power, transport, airlines and communications) employs more than 2 million people (8 % of the labour force), has net assets worth about £12,000 million, has an output with a gross value of about £9,000 million, and spends almost £2,000 million annually on capital investment projects. Public Service investment was accounted for by such projects as roads, housing, water and sewerage, school and university building, hospitals and welfare services, buildings and equipment for the armed forces, etc.

About 50% of current expenditure was devoted to the social services and housing. About 48% of current expenditure took the form of transfer payments. It is of interest to note that apart from the great expansion in recent years in social service expenditure on pensions, benefits, assistance, education, health and welfare – there have also been significant advances in the provision of council housing. By 1971 it was estimated that almost one-third of dwellings were council houses.[1]

[1] See 'Housing in Britain', *E.P.R.*, 27, May 1972.

A diagrammatic breakdown of public spending for 1971 may be seen from Fig. 7.1 opposite.

(b) Revenue

More than two-thirds of total public spending is financed by the levying of taxes of one sort or another. These range from taxes on income, profits, wealth and expenditure – imposed by the central Government Exchequer – to the rates levied by local authorities. The remainder of public revenue comes from sources such as the National Insurance Funds – maintained by National Insurance contributions, and not under the control of the Exchequer; from public activities of a commercial nature (such as postal services and other nationalised industries, municipal laundries, and council house rents); and from local and central Government borrowing. These main groups of public revenue items are shown diagrammatically in Fig. 7.2.

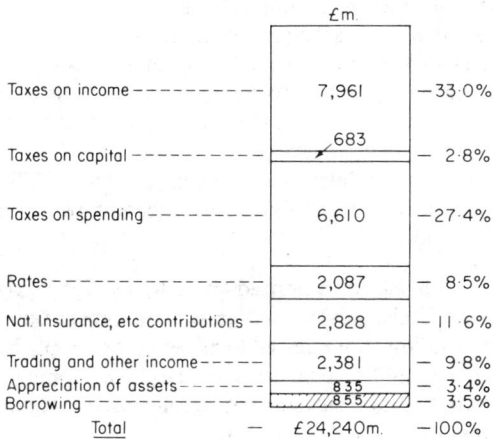

	£m.	
Taxes on income – – – – – – – – –	7,961	— 33·0%
Taxes on capital – – – – – – – – –	683	— 2·8%
Taxes on spending – – – – – – – –	6,610	—27·4%
Rates – – – – – – – – – – – – – –	2,087	— 8·5%
Nat. Insurance, etc contributions —	2,828	— 11·6%
Trading and other income – – – – –	2,381	— 9·8%
Appreciation of assets – – – – – –	835	— 3·4%
Borrowing – – – – – – – – – – – –	855	— 3·5%
Total —	£24,240m.	—100%

Fig. 7.2. *Major items of public revenue*, 1971
(Based on material in *National Income and Expenditure* [*Blue Book*], 1972, H.M.S.O.)

It is important to note that local authority expenditure is not financed entirely by local authority rates and other income. Similarly, expenditure by the National Insurance Funds and other 'social services' expenditure are not financed entirely by National Insurance contributions. In both cases, an important source of finance is in the form of transfers or grants from the central Government, themselves financed by general taxation.[1] It has often been suggested that the whole pattern of financing the social services be rationalised, so that all elements of revenue earmarked for social services should be clearly termed 'social service contributions'. This could result in social service finance being collected and administered more efficiently by one central authority, thus avoiding the clumsy system of internal transfers and the resultant administrative costs.

[1] *Econ.*, 23 June 1962, p. 1198, and W. Hagenbuch, 'The Welfare State and its finances', *L.B.R.*, July 1958.

In the case of taxation and voluntary loans from the public, the authorities are, in effect, transferring purchasing power from the public to themselves. However, if the authorities desired to borrow even more, by selling Treasury Bills to the banks in return for bank deposits, this would increase the total money supply in the economy and would have an inflationary effect. Thus the part of the National Debt held by the public does not create inflationary pressure, but that portion held by the banking system in exchange for Treasury Bills does.

3. Central Government (Exchequer) Finance: the Budget

(a) Introduction

Over the years Parliament has established the right to exercise overriding control over the power of the central Government to spend money and to raise revenue by taxation and borrowing. Apart from the receipt of money into and payments out of special funds such as the National Insurance Funds, all central Government revenue and expenditure accounts are controlled by the Exchequer.[1] Every March or April the Chancellor of the Exchequer makes his major Budget speech to Parliament, in which he presents his Budget, or proposals for raising revenue by changes in taxation and borrowing in order to pay for the expenditure which he anticipates for the coming financial year.

The Budget proposals are later embodied in a Finance Bill, which usually receives the Royal Assent in July.[2] Exchequer expenditure may be divided into three categories, as follows:

(i) Expenditure which must be authorised annually by Appropriation Acts, and which covers defence, social services and general administration of the country. These groups of expenditure are referred to as being for Supply Services – a term which derives from the traditional power of the House of Commons, when voting money to the Crown, to grant 'such aids or supplies as are required to satisfy . . . the pecuniary necessities of the Government'.

(ii) Expenditure which is automatically authorised, by existing Acts of Parliament, as a standing charge to come out of the Consolidated Fund and the National Loans Fund. This covers items such as the interest, reserves and management costs of the National Debt; the financial provisions made for members of the royal family; the salaries and pensions of judges and other high officers, whose independence of political influence is considered to be better guaranteed by a permanent grant than by an annual vote.

(iii) Other expenditure, mainly of a capital (investment, or non-recurrent) nature, which is also automatically authorised by standing Acts of Parliament, for such

[1] See J. M. Buchanan, 'Earmarked taxes', 1963, reprinted in R. W. Houghton, ed., *Public Finance*, 1970.
[2] The interval between the Budget Statement and the Royal Assent, though covered by special legislation (see *Brit. O.H.*, 1972, p. 341), has been criticised by the Law Society as being inadequate to permit serious consideration (see 'Law Society attacks Budget procedure', *D.T.*, 8 March 1967). For further comment on the machinery of authorisation and scrutiny of central government expenditure – including the House of Commons Select Committees on Expenditure (replacing in January 1971 that on Estimates) and on Public Accounts (in conjunction with the Comptroller and Auditor General's Department) – see *Brit. O.H.*, 1972, pp. 339–41; P. D. Clayton, 'Accountability in Government expenditure', *N.W.B.Q.R.*, Nov. 1971; 'MPs call for special committee on tax', *F.T.*, 26 Feb. 1971; 'MPs' committee wants fuller facts on spending', *F.T.*, 14 Sept. 1971; 'Let's have a taxes board', *Econ.*, 29 April 1972, p. 80.

purposes as loans to nationalised industries, local authorities and other public and private concerns. The Exchequer is authorised to finance such expenditure by borrowing, and therefore it does not have to be covered by taxation revenue.

Because of the differences between these three types of expenditure, the Budget accounts used to be divided into two parts – 'Above the line' and 'Below the line'. 'Above the line' consisted of supply services expenditure and Consolidated Fund expenditure, which had to be financed more or less entirely by taxation. 'Below the line' consisted of other receipts and other expenditure, for which, if there was a deficit, the Exchequer was authorised to borrow. By law, the Budget Account had to include virtually all central Government receipts and payments, and the division between Above and Below 'the line' really derived from the conventions and legislation relating to borrowing powers. It had no great economic significance, and did not strictly divide items of a current (or 'ordinary' or day-to-day) nature from those of a capital nature. A White Paper, *Reform of the Exchequer Accounts*,[1] presented in May 1963, suggested future improvements for the modernisation of the Budget Accounts.

The original intention of the Budget was to provide just sufficient 'Above the line' revenue to cover ordinary Government expenditure, including Consolidated Fund standing services. As the Government became progressively more involved in trading activities (nationalised industries) and in local Government finance, tax revenue was enlarged to cover both 'Above' and 'Below the line' expenditure.

Prior to April 1968 the Consolidated Fund was the major Exchequer cash account at the Bank of England: *inflows* consisted of most central government receipts from taxation, loan interest and dividends and borrowing, whilst *outflows* consisted of all Exchequer payments, including service charges on the National Debt and loans. From April 1968 a separate cash account was set up at the Bank – the National Loans Fund – to be responsible for all but residual National Debt service payments, all domestic Exchequer lending (to nationalised and private industries, local authorities, etc.) and all Government borrowing transactions. Thus, the Consolidated Fund (C.F.) henceforth dealt mainly with recurrent receipts and payments (excluding most National Debt servicing charges), whilst the N.L.F. dealt mainly with domestic lending and borrowing – activities of a capital nature – plus National Debt servicing. Any surplus on the C.F. is transferred to the N.L.F. – along with various interest payments and profits of the Bank's Issue Department – where the overall deficit (central government borrowing requirement) or surplus (net repayment of National Debt) is revealed.[2]

The tax changes, announced in the Budget, take account not only of the expenditure requirements and the tax changes needed to yield adequate revenue, but also of tax evasion loopholes, administrative requirements, the 'equity' need for giving the tax system a broader base, etc. Consequently, S. Brittan has suggested an alternative split in the Budget accounts,[3] *viz.*, a Finance Bill section, to give legal effect to the major Budget decisions, and a Tax Management Bill section, dealing with changes in the tax system – which could then be fully debated – and which may not need to be annual.

[1] Cmnd 2014.
[2] For further details see *Brit. O.H.*, 1972, pp. 337–42, 345–6; 'Budget background', *E.P.R.*, 4, April 1970; 'Anatomy of the Budget', *Econ.*, 12 April 1969, pp. 58–9; 'Government finance in the sixties', *B.B.R.*, May 1972.
[3] See *Steering the Economy: the Role of the Treasury*, 1969.

The Budget of the central government Exchequer is nowadays not solely concerned with central government revenue and expenditure: its strategy is in terms of the entire public sector, in the context of the national income accounts, which represent all components of the public sector – including such items as the National Insurance Funds – and not just taxation revenue and tax-financed expenditure. Thus, although Budget decisions may only be implemented within the central government sphere of activity authorised by Parliament and existing statute, the Exchequer accounts are nevertheless of great importance.

Although 'Below the line' expenditure could be financed by borrowing, it used to be considered administratively more sound to secure an 'Above the line' surplus to cover it. Gradually it became apparent, however, that the Budget was a powerful tool for influencing economic activity. The level of taxation and the type of tax influence consumer demand and the pattern of production: the level of total Government expenditure likewise influences the economy, as it competes with the public for goods and services. If the Government desires to stimulate the level of economic activity, it can do so by increasing overall expenditure and/or decreasing taxation. It will deliberately aim at an overall Budget deficit, which will be financed by borrowing. If the Government wishes to restrain the level of activity and the pressure of demand on factors of production, it will aim at an overall Budget surplus, by decreasing expenditure and/or increasing taxation (see Fig. 7.3).

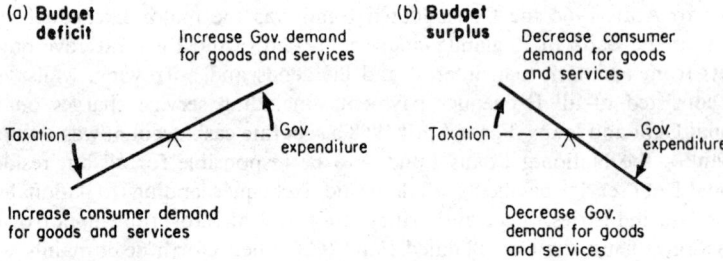

Fig. 7.3. *Budget deficits and surpluses as tools of economic control*

Since the 1944 White Paper on Employment Policy, it has become an established practice to use the Budget consciously as a tool for influencing the level of activity and employment by bringing the total level of demand for goods and services into balance with available resources, by means of overall Budget deficits and surpluses.

Thus, from the economic point of view, the division of the Budget Account into two parts is not of much significance. What really matters is the overall surplus or deficit.

During the 1960s the 'Above-line' (or taxation and other net revenue) surpluses fluctuated considerably, but towards the end of the decade showed a significant increase. This reflected the official preoccupation with balance of payments problems and the desire to curtail domestic spending, so as to switch resources to export-orientated and import-substituting industries. Net lending, on the other hand, was expanding considerably until the late 1960s, since when it has fluctuated between £1,400 million and about £2 billion: this reflected increased lending to local authorities and to nationalised industries – particularly to the

Post Office, electricity and gas industries. The overall borrowing requirement, prior to 1967/68, reflected this rising net lending. Since 1967/68 the rise in the surplus from the C.F. and other sources (e.g. National Insurance Funds, Bank Issue Department profits, etc.) has resulted in a large contraction in the overall borrowing requirement – and at times in a surplus, or net repayment of National Debt – despite the continuing high level of net lending by the N.L.F. Thus, variations in the basic tax revenue surplus have been, in recent years, the major determinant in fluctuations in the central government borrowing requirement.

The key magnitudes in the central government Budget balances, from 1959/60 to 1971/72 are shown in Fig. 7.4.

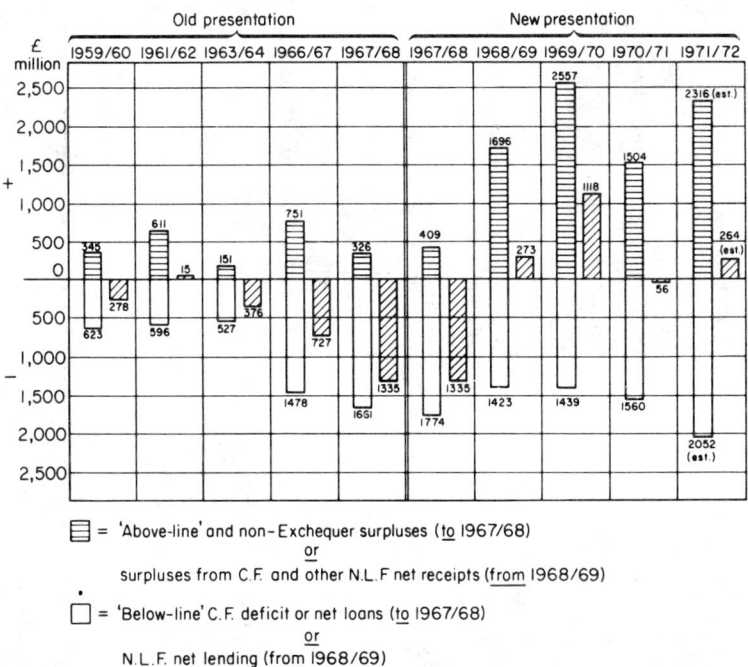

Fig. 7.4. *Central government budgetary deficits and surpluses since* 1959/60 (Based on material in *Ann. Abs. Stat.*, 108, 1971 and *Brit. O.H.*, 1972, p. 346)

(b) Revenue and expenditure

In the C.F. (recurrent or day-to-day revenue and expenditure) section of the 1971/72 Budget estimates £575 million of the £14,446 million total expenditure was for C.F. Standing Services: the remaining 96% (£13,871 million) was for Supply Services. Of the £16,762 million total revenue £16,337 million (about 97½%) was revenue from taxation – including Broadcast Receiving Licence fees, which, although not officially classified as taxes, are, in the economic sense, a tax on spending or on the use of a service. The balance consisted of miscellaneous receipts, such as the interest and dividends from certain loans. Taxes on personal income accounted for 41% of total revenue (£6,851 million); taxes on company incomes accounted for 9·7% (£1,620 million); taxes on wealth (death duties and

583

Table 7.2 Consolidated Fund revenue and expenditure estimates for 1971/72

Revenue	(£ million)	%
Taxes on Income:		
Personal:		
Income Tax[1]	6,491	
Surtax[1]	360	
	6,851	41
Company:		
Corporation Tax	1,620	9.7
Taxes on Wealth:		
Death Duties	375	
Capital Gains Tax	165	
	540	3.2
Outlay Taxes:		
Purchase Tax[2]	1,495	
Oil	1,460	
Tobacco	1,100	
Spirits, Beer, Wine	1,000	
Betting and Gaming	145	
Other Revenue Duties	10	
Protective Duties	265	
Import Deposits	−116	
Stamp Duties	108	
Motor Vehicle Duties	440	
Broadcast Receiving Licences	120	
	6,028	36
Taxes on Employment:		
Selective Employment Tax[2,3] (gross)	1,298	7.8
Total Tax Revenue	16,337	97.5
Interest and Dividends	105	
Other	320	
	425	2.5
TOTAL	16,762	100

Expenditure	(£ million)	%
Defence budget	2,545	15.1
Other military	98	0.59
Overseas aid	246	1.49
Other overseas services	131	0.78
Trade, industry and employment	1,174	7.0
Civil Service pay		
Research Councils, etc.	125	0.75
Agriculture, fisheries, forestry	392	2.35
Roads	403	2.4
Transport	163	0.96
Housing	294	1.76
Miscellaneous local services	57	0.34
Law and order	336	2.0
Arts	28	0.17
Education	444	2.67
Health and personal social services	1,790	10.7
Social security	1,580	9.5
Financial administration	316	1.88
Common Services	295	1.76
Miscellaneous services	69	0.41
S.E.T. refunds	1,183	7.0
Non-specific grants to local authorities	2,480	14.9
Miscellaneous	297	1.76
Surplus transferred to National Loans Fund	2,316	13.9
TOTAL	16,762	100

[1] Income Tax and Surtax replaced after 1972/73 be a unified Personal Tax.
[2] Purchase Tax and S.E.T. replaced after 1972/73 by a Value Added Tax (V.A.T.).
[3] S.E.T. has often been classified as a tax on expenditure (or on the *use* of assets) as it fell mainly on the Services sectors. The *net* yield after refunds was estimated at £219 m.

(Based on material in *Brit. O.H.*, 1972, pp. 346-7.)

capital gains tax) accounted for about 3·2% (£540 million). Outlay taxes (taxes on expenditure or consumption) constituted 36% of total revenue (£6,028 million) and taxes on employment (the Selective Employment Tax – discontinues after 1972/73) constituted 7·8% (£1,298 million). For administrative purposes the Budget revenue items are classified according to *collecting* agency. The Board of Inland Revenue is responsible for taxes on income (personal and company) and wealth and for Stamp Duties. The Board of Customs and Excise is responsible for most of the outlay tax revenue, whilst a variety of authorities are responsible for collecting remaining revenue items – such as the local authorities for Motor Vehicle Duties, the Post Office for Broadcast Receiving Licence fees and the Department of Health and Social Security for the (now abandoned) Selective Employment Tax.

The C.F. revenue estimates for 1971/72, classified according to *economic* significance and expenditure estimates, classified according to *function* are detailed in Table 7.2.

On the N.L.F. account, the total estimate of net lending for 1971/72 was £2,052 million. For 1970/71 it was £1,560·1 million. Of this, £707·4 million (45·5%) constituted loans to the nationalised industries, 9·6% was in loans to other public corporations, such as the New Town Corporations and 44·4% was in loans to local and harbour authorities: £10·5 million was repaid by the private sector.[1]

4. Local Authority Finance

(a) General: revenue and expenditure

Apart from small items of local taxation in the form of licence fees (e.g. for street traders, market stallholders, etc.) the main form of taxation assessed locally, to help finance local authority expenditure, is the local 'rate'. The November 1971 Local Government Bill proposed to reduce the number of local authorities in Great Britain by 1975 from 1,800 by creating 51 county and 375 district authorities in England and Wales, 8 regional and 49 district authorities in Scotland and 6 'metropolitan counties' for the major conurbations. The 424 district authorities – except those in the metropolitan counties – were to lose control of activities considered to be better undertaken on a large scale by the new counties and regions, as in the case of major planning, roads, education and the social services.[2] Local rates contribute about 33% of local authority current revenue. About 45% derives from grants from the central Government, and about 22% from 'trading and rental activities' (council house rents, etc.), dividends and interest.

Central Government capital grants, plus current revenue surpluses, finance about 37% of local authority capital expenditure. Such capital grants are made on approval of specific projects, usually for roads, public lighting and land drainage. Most central Government grants, however, are made on an annual or current basis, either for a particular service, such as police or road maintenance ('specific grants') or as non-specific 'rate support' grants or 'block grants'. The latter constitute about 90% of all annual grants. This is the largest single grant,

---

[1] See *Ann. Abs. Stat.*, 108, 1971, p. 303.
[2] See *Brit. O.H.*, 1972, p. 67. For comment on local government reform, see also J. Wiseman, 'Local government in the twentieth century', *L.B.R.*, Jan. 1966, and Sir Harry Page, 'Local government in decline', *T.B.R.*, June 1971.

Table 7.3 Local government finance, 1960 and 1970

Where the money came from

Current account	1960 £m	per cent of total	1970 £m	per cent of total
Current grants from central government	780	40	2,450	45
Rates	771	39	1,822	33
Gross trading surplus[1]	50	3	77	1
Rent[1]	322	16	1,015	19
Interest, etc.	37	2	110	2
Total current receipts	1,960	100	5,474	100

Capital account	1960 £m	per cent of total	1970 £m	per cent of total
Current surplus[1]	245	37	533	28
Capital grants from central government	44	7	162	9
Net borrowing from central government	−36	−6	722	38
Other identified borrowing (net) Miscellaneous financial receipts (net) and changes in cash balances	406	62	527	28
Total capital receipts	659	100	1,886	100

How it was spent

Current account	1960 £m	per cent of total	1970 £m	per cent of total
Current expenditure on goods and services	1,357	79	3,627	74
of which:				
Education	655	38	1,742	35
Environment	145	8	415	8
Police	116	7	337	7
Roads and lighting	127	7	261	5
Housing subsidies	31	2	118	2
Current grants to personal sector	40	2	159	3
Debt interest	287	17	1,037	21
Total current expenditure	1,715	100	4,941	100
Balance: Current surplus[1]	245		533	
	1,960		5,474	

Capital account	1960 £m	per cent of total	1970 £m	per cent of total
Fixed investment	604	92	1,819	96
of which:				
Housing	255	39	735	39
Education	114	17	288	15
Roads and lighting	54	8	235	12
Environment	101	15	277	15
Capital grants to personal sector	13	2	30	2
Net lending to private sector for hire purchase	42	6	37	2
Total capital expenditure	659	100	1,886	100

[1] On a national accounts basis.

(Source: E.P.R., 22, Dec. 1971)

paid to county and county borough councils in England and Wales by the Minister of Housing and Local Government, and to county and town councils in Scotland by the Secretary of State for Scotland. It is apportioned between the local authorities on the basis of the 'needs' element, based on population size, age distribution, children of school age, etc.; the 'resources' element, based on the available rateable resources, in relation to population size; the 'domestic' element, based on the loss of rate income due to the reduction in rate poundage which must be made to householders. For Northern Ireland there is a system of specific grants for various services, supplemented by a general Exchequer contribution, which takes account of the resources and requirements of individual authorities.

By 1970 local authority spending – both current and capital – had risen to £6,827 million, or about 15% of the G.D.P.[1] The local authorities were employing about 2·5 million people and as a relatively high proportion of local authority

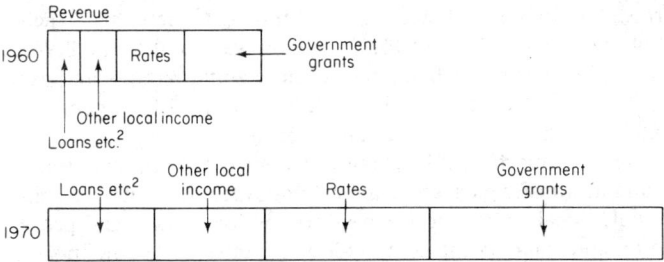

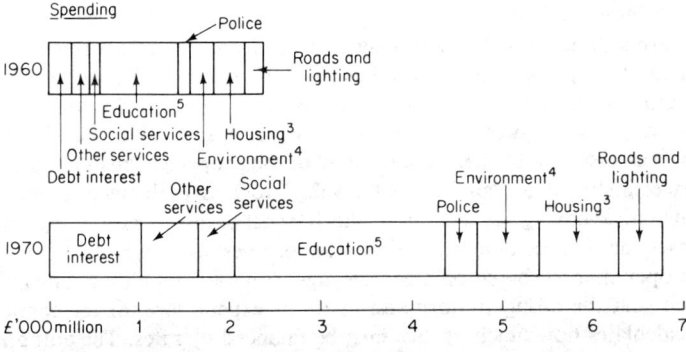

1. Including current and capital spending and revenue
2. Loans and other capital receipts (net)
3. Including net lending to private sector
4. Environmental services (water, drainage, parks, etc.)
5. Including school meals and milk, scholarships and grants

Fig. 7.5. *Local authorities: Total Revenue and Spending,*[1] 1960 *and* 1970 (Source: *E.P.R.*, 22, Dec. 1971)

[1] For further comment, see W. A. Thomas and E. R. Shaw, 'The role of loans bureaux in local authority finance', *M. & W.S.R.*, Autumn 1971, p. 21; 'Financing local government', *E.P.R.*, 22, Dec. 1971.

costs are wages and salaries, the cost of local services has been rising faster than costs in general. Within L.A. spending, that on housing, roads and social services (education, health and welfare), which are partly administered by the L.A.s, has been assuming an increasing share of total public expenditure. Total L.A. spending increased, as a proportion of all public expenditure, from 21% in 1950 to 30% in 1970. About 75% of L.A. current expenditure in 1970 was devoted to direct expenditure on goods and services and about 5% to interest payments on L.A. debt.

Apart from the capital grants from the central Government – 9% of total capital receipts in 1970 – and surpluses from the current account, capital expenditure may also be financed by borrowing. This includes raising loans by issuing mortgages, by issuing securities – which may or may not be quoted on the Stock Exchange – by temporary bank borrowing, within certain limits, and by borrowing from the Public Works Loan Board. The latter acts as lender of last resort to the L.A.s, when they are unable to borrow from the market on reasonable terms. By March 1970 total outstanding L.A. debt had reached about £15,000 million, of which about £5,600 million was owed to the P.W.L.B.[1]

Details of the changes in L.A. current and capital receipts and expenditure, between 1960 and 1970, are given in Table 7.3. In Fig. 7.5 the combined current and capital items are shown in diagrammatic form.

Only a small proportion of local authority current expenditure (on goods and services and in transfer payments) and capital expenditure may be considered to be for purely 'local' aims. Most expenditure is for services and projects which conform to, and complement, central Government activities and policies.

(b) The rating system

Rates are a direct local tax, and may be considered *either* as a recurrent tax on *spending* (if the property concerned has been purchased by the ratepayer), *or* as a recurrent tax on *capital* (if the property has been bequeathed to the ratepayer).[2] Rates are assessed on the 'rateable value' of land and buildings. This 'rateable value' is assessed as the 'net annual value' of the property, which in turn is based on an estimate of its 'annual rental value' to a hypothetical tenant (who is assumed to be paying the actual rate plus the cost of insurance and repairs). Thus the assessment of rateable value is an attempt to establish a realistic rental value in the open market, based on area, size, age, situation, condition, amenities, etc.

Each year the rating authority estimates its expenditure for the coming year, then calculates how much of this must be financed by rates. The authority then decides on a 'rate poundage', or rate to be raised per pound of rateable value. This is calculated by first calculating the revenue from a penny rate, and then dividing this yield into the total rate revenue required. Thus, if total rateable value on the authority's valuation list were £1 million, and the rate revenue required were £500,000 – the formula would be:

---

[1] See 'The role of loans bureaux in local authority finance'; 'Financing local government'; *Brit. O.H.*, 1972, p. 73.

[2] In the National Income and Expenditure (Blue Book) accounts local rates are treated as a tax on *expenditure*, which in turn is treated as an *indirect* tax – being associated with the possession or use of land and buildings (see 'Taxation', *E.P.R.*, 17, July 1971).

(1) Total rateable value: (2) Yield of $1p$ rate: (3) Rate revenue required:

    £1,000,000   1,000,000p £500,000

(4) Rate poundage

$$(3) \div (2) = \tfrac{1}{2} \times 100p = 50p$$

Valuation lists are revised periodically for each rating area, and on these occasions new properties may be inserted, or the values of existing properties altered. At the 1963 revaluation all rateable values (both for private dwellings and other properties) were put on a current rental value basis.[1] The 50% relief on industrial property and freight transport property was abolished, except in Scotland and in Northern Ireland (where there was a 75% relief); the 20% relief on shops, offices and public buildings was abolished. Property occupied by charities for charitable purposes received a 50% relief; agricultural property (except dwellings) was exempt; nationalised industries either made a direct payment in lieu of rates or – as in the case of the railways – made a payment in lieu of rates, which the Ministry of Housing and Local Government distributed to local authorities; the rating authorities also retained the power to reduce or remit rates paid by a wide range of non-profit-making bodies. The share of rates in total revenue has been falling in recent years, while that of central Government grants has been rising, reaching 36% in 1970.

New valuation lists were due to come into force in 1973. These were expected to help bridge the 'revenue gap' noted in the 1971 Green Paper, *The Future Shape of Local Government Finance* (Cmnd 4741). This forecast a gap of about 0·75% between the rise in L.A. spending and that in rate yields and central Government grants. The major alternatives were to charge property occupiers more, increase the grant subsidy from general taxation, or to find new sources of local revenue (such as local income tax, local V.A.T. or sales tax, local payroll tax, etc.)[2] The new valuations were expected to shift the burden more equitably against householders as against flat-dwellers.

The assessment of rateable values in England and Wales is undertaken by officers of the Board of Inland Revenue. In Scotland it is carried out by officers appointed by the county and town councils, and in Northern Ireland by the office of the Commissioner of Valuation, a department of the Ministry of Finance.

5. Taxation: Theory and Practice

(a) Objectives of taxation

When it is realised that more than 83% of total public expenditure in 1971 was financed by taxes of various sorts (central Government taxes, National Insurance contributions and local rates), it is obvious that the main objective of taxation is to raise revenue. This it has always been. Gradually, however, many other (sometimes conflicting)[3] objectives have been superimposed on the tax system,

---

[1] For England and Wales, this increased total rateable value from £713 million (on the 1939 basis) to £2,063 million, an increase of 2·8 times.

[2] For further data, see G. H. Forster, *Local Government Finance, 1971*, 1972; 'Rates shocks ahead', *Econ.*, 23 Jan. 1971, pp. 54–5; 'New taxes to help the rates', *F.T.*, 20 Nov. 1970; 'Spreading the local rates burden more fairly', *F.T.*, 18 Sept. 1972; 'Next year's rates: inflation inevitably the key factor', *F.T.*, 6 Dec. 1972.

[3] See G. S. A. Wheatcroft, 'Inequity in Britain's tax structure', *L.B.R.*, July 1969, esp. pp. 11–15 and 'Tax blueprint', *Econ.*, 4 March 1967, p. 856.

affecting the method of collection, the type of assessment, the diversity of taxes, and the degree of surplus or deficit aimed at.

The traditional view of taxation was that it should be as low as possible, to finance the minimum necessary amount of public authority expenditure, in the belief that income and wealth left 'to fructify' in the pockets of the general public would be more efficiently utilised for the common good. With the increasing scale and scope of public authority involvement in the economy, however, many other social and economic objectives now exert their influence, besides the need to raise revenue for the traditional provision of justice and defence. Taxation has become an important instrument of economic policy. Current objectives of the tax system include the following:[1]

(i) The maintenance of economic stability, a high level of employment, and economic growth.
(ii) The redistribution of income and wealth, with a reduction of inequality in their distribution.
(iii) The reorganisation, re-equipping and expansion of suitable sectors of industry.
(iv) The stimulation of exports and productivity.
(v) The location of industry and population according to public policy.
(vi) The protection of particular industries or sectors of the economy from foreign competition.
(vii) The curtailment of particular industries and/or forms of consumption.
(viii) The preservation of a balance between total demand for goods and services and the resources available, so as to prevent inflation.

By 1970 it was estimated that the Government was spending about £1,000 million per annum on fairly direct financial assistance to private industry, in pursuit of three major policy objectives, viz., stimulation of industrial investment (via investment cash grants), stimulation of technological research and development, and the stimulation of economic activity in the problem regions of the U.K.[2] In his Budget speech of March 1972 the Chancellor emphasised three major aims, which necessitated substantial taxation reforms. These were to stimulate U.K. industrial efficiency prior to E.E.C. entry; to achieve sustained economic growth and rising living standards; to reform the tax system, so as to increase equity and stimulate greater national wealth.[3]

(b) Principles of taxation

The four main canons of taxation enunciated by Adam Smith in the eighteenth century still hold good today. They specified that taxation should be equitable (based on ability to pay), convenient to the taxpayer, economical and certain. These canons have since been added to and enlarged upon, and may be presented as follows:[4]

[1] For further discussion of taxation objectives, see M. H. Cadman, ed., *Taxation Economics*, 1969, ch. 5; *The British System of Taxation*, 1971, pp. 2–3; Due, *op. cit.*, ch. 10; Musgrave, *op. cit.*, pp. 4–6.
[2] See *F.T.*, 19 Jan. 1970.
[3] See *D.T.*, 22 March 1972.
[4] For further elaboration, see L. Hey, *Economics of Public Finance*, 1972, ch. 9; *The British System of Taxation*, 1971, pp. 1–2; Eckstein, *op. cit.*, pp. 58–63; A. R. Prest, *Public Finance in Theory and Practice* 4th edn, 1970, pp. 26–9; Due, *op. cit.*, ch. 14.

Ability to pay. This principle implies an equality of relative sacrifice by taxpayers earning different incomes and possessing different amounts of wealth. It is sometimes referred to as the 'faculty' principle. It has been expanded to imply not only that the more prosperous citizen should pay more than the less prosperous, but that he should also sacrifice a larger proportion of his income and wealth. This is the 'progressive' principle, viz. that as income or wealth rise, the *rate* of tax should become steeper.

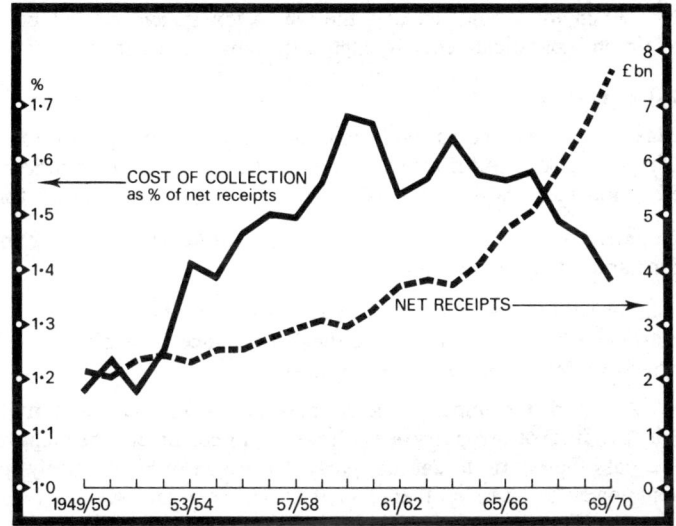

Fig. 7.6. *Higher receipts, lower costs: all Inland Revenue duties*
(Source: *Econ.*, 11 Dec. 1971, p. 69)

Economy. This principle implies that any particular tax should not be wasteful, i.e. that it should not be expensive to administer and that the greatest possible proportion of its yield should accrue to the tax authorities.[1] It has been expanded to imply that the probable yield of the tax should be considered, and that the authorities should consider the possibility that imposition of the tax might result in such a curtailment of taxable income, wealth, spending or other activity that little or insufficient tax may actually be forthcoming. The principle has been further expanded to imply that the community should only be asked to pay taxes for necessary services supplied by the authorities (principle of 'benefits received'); that the tax revenue be used to maximise the welfare of the community ('welfare' principle); that public expenditure should be financed by taxes which involve the minimum of inconvenience and sacrifice of satisfaction on the part of the taxpayers (principle of 'least aggregate sacrifice'). The last two extensions of the

[1] For 1960/61 the cost of Inland Revenue collection was £53·0 million, or 3·54*d* in the pound (1·47%), and the cost of Customs and Excise collection was £22·4 million or 2*d* in the pound (0·94%). See *The British System of Taxation*, C.O.I. Ref. 10, 1962. For further debate on the problem of administrative costs of tax collection, both to the authorities and to taxpayers, see Cadman, ed., *op. cit.*, pp. 81–6. During recent years, while Inland Revenue receipts have been rising, the relative costs of collection have been falling, reaching 1·4% in 1969/70 (see 'How not to collect taxes', *Econ.*, 11 Dec. 1971, pp. 68–9 and Fig. 7.6).

'economy' principle are sometimes referred to together as the principle of 'maximum social advantage'.

Certainty. The type, timing and extent of the tax, the method of assessment, and the liability of the taxpayer should be clearly understood, so as to enable the taxpayer to plan accordingly, without falling foul of the law.

Convenience. The method of payment and its timing should suit the convenience of the taxpayer.

Flexibility. Each individual tax and the whole tax system should be flexible enough to permit of adjustments, to cope with changing circumstances.

(c) Fiscal definitions

Tax. A tax may be defined as the levying by public authorities, with tax jurisdiction, of compulsory contributions to defray the cost of their activities. It may be levied on income, wealth, or goods or services – periodically or once for all.

Legal tax base. This is the net amount upon which the tax is levied, after any legal deductions and allowances have been made.

Impact (or formal incidence) of tax. This indicates the official levying of the tax on the particular taxpayer, who will, in the first instance, be liable to pay. It is of administrative interest to the tax authorities.

'Shifting'. Although the impact of a tax may be on one class of activity (e.g. income or spending) or one party (e.g. wholesaler or customer), the taxpayer may be able to pass the tax on to another party, by reason of his relatively stronger bargaining power, or on to another class of activity (e.g. capital). The theoretical analysis of this phenomenon will be dealt with in Part Two, in the chapter on applications of Supply and Demand theory.

Burden (or effective incidence) of tax. This indicates the eventual sacrifice, borne by the party who in fact suffers the tax payment. If the tax has not been 'shifted', it will coincide with impact or formal incidence. This concept is of *economic* importance, as it involves possible changes in the pattern of production and consumption, and considerations of the ultimate yield and effects of the tax.

Direct and indirect taxes. This is an *administrative* classification. Direct taxes are imposed upon the taxpayer in person by the tax authorities and paid *directly* to them. They include taxes on income, profits and wealth, local rates, stamp duties and all periodic licence duties. Indirect taxes are imposed upon a particular party in the chain of distribution from producer to retailer, who, whether he 'shifts' the tax or not, pays the tax authority in bulk.

Taxes on income and capital and taxes on spending. This is a useful *economic* classification, indicating the *type of activity* upon which the tax is levied, and thus permitting the final effects of the tax to be considered in advance. Furthermore, whereas taxes on spending may be avoided by the consumer's abstinence, taxes on income and capital are much more difficult to avoid.

General and selective taxes. General taxes are levied upon an entire group or range of commodities, services or activities (e.g. all wealth, all incomes, all alcohol, or all tobacco products). Selective taxes are levied on particular items or activities in a group, permitting of flexible manipulation.

Marginal rate of tax. This is the proportion of tax charged on each successive unit of the legal tax base. It may vary at different stages.

Effective rate of tax. This is the average proportion of tax actually charged on the entire income, property or price.

Proportionality and progressiveness. These concepts apply to *changes* in the tax-payer's rate of fiscal sacrifice in relation to his ability to pay (i.e. to his income or wealth). If the particular tax paid by taxpayers with different incomes and wealth represents a fixed *proportion* of that income or wealth, then the burden of the tax is said to be 'constant', e.g. if income tax or the tax paid on drink remove the same, constant proportion of income or wealth from the poor man (who drinks an occasional pint) as from the prosperous man (who drinks whisky liberally). On the other hand, if the actual amount of a particular tax paid represents a smaller proportion of higher incomes and wealth than of lower incomes and wealth, the tax is said to be 'regressive'. If, however, the proportion of income or wealth taken by a particular tax becomes higher as incomes and wealth rise, the

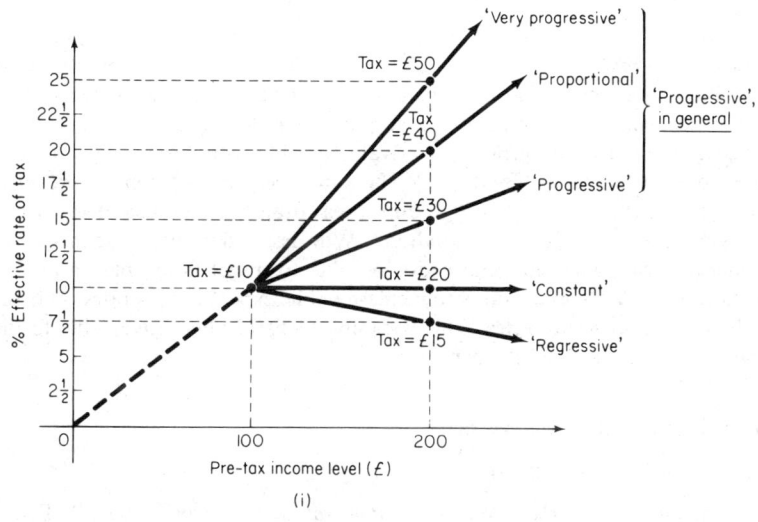

(i)

Pre-tax income level (£)	Tax deduction (£)	Post-tax balance (£)	Effective tax rate (%)	Type of change in tax rate
100	10	90	10	—
200	15	185	$7\frac{1}{2}$	'Regressive'
200	20	180	10	'Constant'
200	30	170	15	'Progressive'
200	40	160	20	'Proportional'
200	50	150	25	'Very progressive'

(ii)

Fig. 7.7. *Rates of change in effective tax burden, at different income levels: proportionality and progressiveness*

tax is said to be, *in general*, 'progressive'. Strictly speaking, if the proportion rises, but not as fast as income or wealth, the tax is 'progressive': if it rises as fast, the tax is 'proportional': if it rises faster, it is 'very progressive' (see Fig. 7.7).[1]

'Full employment' budget surpluses and deficits. With no change in the pattern or incidence of taxes, the actual tax revenue will be affected by changes in the level of economic activity, which affect the G.N.P. and the tax base. Thus, an increase in G.N.P. will result in a broadened tax base, increased revenue and rising budget surpluses (or reduced deficits). Apart from 'automatic stabilisers' of this type, however, revenue may be altered by 'discretionary' fiscal policies, whereby the pattern and/or rates of taxes may be altered. Thus, it is not obvious whether a change in budgetary deficits or surpluses is due to economic factors or policy (discretionary) factors. Hence, the concept of 'full employment' deficits or surpluses has been introduced, to represent the *hypothetical* deficit or surplus which *would* have been produced if the economy were operating at a full employment level, *given* the current fiscal policy. Any deviation between actual surplus or deficit and the full employment, hypothetical level may then be attributed to the automatic budget response to the economic deviations from the full employment level.[2]

'Fiscal drag' and 'fiscal dividend'. If an economy is expanding, over time, then even if public expenditure were constant, tax revenue would rise, thereby resulting in an increasing 'full employment' surplus (or reducing deficit). This, in turn, reduces or retards the growth in private spending (or purchasing power) – a phenomenon known as 'fiscal drag'. There may be periods when the pressure on resources in the economy is high and 'fiscal drag' may be useful in curtailing excessively buoyant private expenditure. With less inflationary circumstances, a moderate increase in budgetary revenue, due to 'fiscal drag', may provide the authorities with an opportunity to increase public expenditure for desirable social ends, or to reduce tax rates. This widening of fiscal alternatives, due to 'fiscal drag', is termed a 'fiscal dividend'.[3]

(d) The principal budgetary taxes

TAXES ON INCOME AND CAPITAL

1. *Personal tax and the tax credit system (or 'negative income tax')*. Personal income taxes, first introduced in the U.K. in 1799, during the war with France, are levied on all personal incomes, whether 'earned' from work or 'unearned' investment income from dividends and interest. They are direct taxes, assessed and collected by the Board of Inland Revenue. Under the P.A.Y.E. (pay-as-you earn) system, most wage and salary earners pay the tax on earned income by way of deductions at source, made by the employer.

Before 1973/74 there was a complex system of marginal rates of tax on earned income, in conjunction with earned income relief and personal allowances. A standard marginal rate of tax then applied to earned and investment incomes.

---

[1] The debate about the 'progressive' principle in taxation may be pursued in H. C. Simmons, 'The case for progressive taxation', in R. W. Houghton, ed., *Public Finance*, 1970; W. J. Blum and H. Kalven, Jr, *The Uneasy Case for Progressive Taxation*, 1966.
[2] Eckstein, *op. cit.*, pp. 105–7.
[3] *Ibid.*, pp. 107–8.

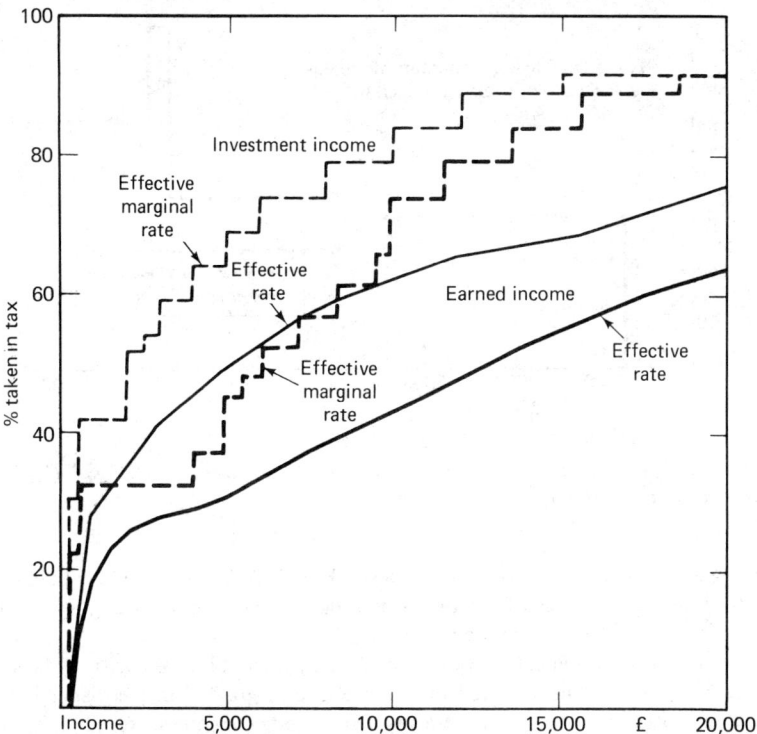

Fig. 7.8. *Effective marginal and overall effective rates of tax on income (single person without dependants)*, 1969/1970
(Source: *L.B.R.*, July 1969)

In addition, when an individual's residual combined income from *all sources*, after all allowances and reliefs, exceeded a certain figure, *additional surtax* rates were charged on successive slices of income, with a rising scale of rates. The standard rate has varied from 4s 6d (22½p) in the pound in 1930/31 to 9s 6d (47½p) in 1951/53 and was reduced from 41·25% (41¼p) in 1965/71 to 38·75% (38¾p) for 1971/73. The latter marginal rate on earned income was reduced to an *effective* marginal rate of 30·14% by the earned income relief of two-ninths. Apart from the changes in standard rate, made for discretionary (economic control) purposes, there have been periodic changes in the incidence of various marginal rates. This has been due to the fact that both economic growth, with rising *real* incomes and inflation, with rising *money* incomes tend to push a larger proportion of tax-payers into nominal income brackets which pay higher tax rates. Fig. 7.8 illustrates the effective (or net-of-allowances) marginal rates and overall effective (or average) rates of tax for one category of taxpayer on earned and investment income after the 1969 Budget. Fig. 7.9 illustrates the changes in the incidence of the effective marginal rates on earned income, made by the 1970/71 Budget, for another category of taxpayer. It will be noted that the tax threshold (at which standard rate applied) was pushed forward and that the next effective marginal

595

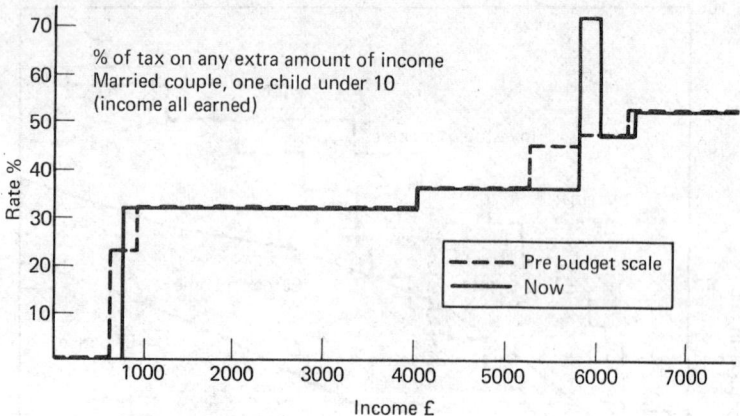

Fig. 7.9. *Changes in effective marginal rates of earned income tax*, 1970/71
(Source: *S.T.*, 19 April 1970)

rate was extended to a higher income level. Fig. 7.10 shows the 1971/72 changes
in overall effective rates of tax on earned income on a sample category of taxpayer, resulting from the reduction in Standard Rate.

The redistributive effect of progressive U.K. personal income tax may be seen
from Fig. 7.11. It will be noted that the 'centre of gravity' in the dispersion of
1968/69 post-tax incomes shifted away from pre-tax incomes exceeding £1,000
per annum. They constituted approximately one-half of all income-earners,

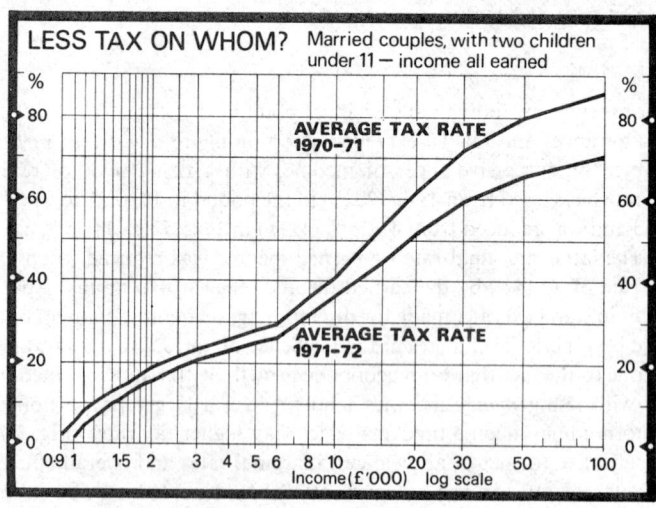

Fig. 7.10. 1971/72 *Budget reduction in the standard rate: changes in overall
effective rates*
(Source: *Econ.*, 3 April 1971, p. 68)

596

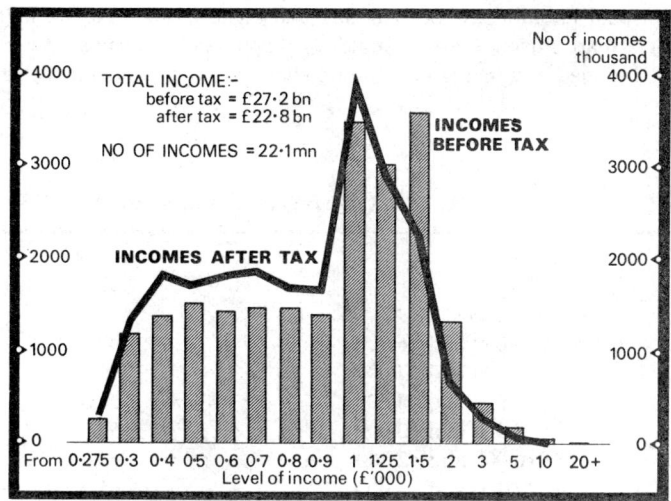

No of incomes
thousand

TOTAL INCOME:–
before tax = £27·2 bn
after tax = £22·8 bn

NO OF INCOMES = 22·1mn

INCOMES BEFORE TAX

INCOMES AFTER TAX

From 0·275 0·3 0·4 0·5 0·6 0·7 0·8 0·9 1 1·25 1·5 2 3 5 10 20+
Level of income (£'000)

Fig. 7.11. *Redistributive effect of U.K. personal income tax*, 1968/69
(Source: *Econ.*, 3 April 1971, p. 69)

accounted for about three-quarters of pre-tax income and contributed about five-sixths of income tax revenue.[1]

The new, *unified* system of a single, graduated *personal tax* was announced in 1971, to take effect in 1973/74. Under the new system there was to be no surtax and only one marginal rate on incomes (net of allowances) up to £5,000. This was provisionally fixed at 30%, which compares with the previous effective Standard Rate of 38·75% less 2/9 earned income relief (up to £4,005). Higher marginal rates were provisionally fixed for net-of-allowance incomes exceeding £5,000 (see Table 7.4). There was to be no earned income relief – only allowances (see Table 7.5) – and a surcharge of 15% was to be levied on investment income exceeding £2,000. An *age allowance* and/or a *small income relief* was designed to restore equity to certain categories of taxpayer, dependent on investment incomes.[2]

In October 1972 proposals were made in a Green Paper (Cmnd 5116) for a *Tax-Credit System*, which was considered to require up to five years to implement. Essentially, this was to be a type of *negative (or reverse) income tax*, about which there had been much debate during the 1960s.[3] According to this scheme, the system of personal allowances in the single personal tax system were to be abolished – thereby simplifying the P.A.Y.E. coding system; National Insurance Family Allowances would be abolished, as would Family Income Supplements, and both would be replaced by a tax credit. Thus, all individuals with the same

[1] See also *Ann. Abs. Stat.*, 108, 1971, Table 339 and R. J. Nicholson, 'The distribution of personal income', *L.B.R.*, Jan. 1967.
[2] For further details, see 'Unified personal tax', *E.P.R.*, 29, July 1972.
[3] D. Lees, 'Poor families and fiscal reform', *L.B.R.*, Oct. 1967; A. Seldon, 'Thaw in the Welfare State', *L.B.R.*, July 1972; 'Negative income tax', *Econ.*, 30 Sept. 1972, pp. 84–9; 'Tax-credit scheme', *E.P.R.*, 33, Nov. 1972; Eckstein, *op. cit.*, pp. 73–5; 'The biggest change since Beveridge', *F.T.*, 11 Oct. 1972.

incomes would initially pay the same tax, but some would receive a higher tax 'claw-back' than others. Some examples of the system, as compared with post-April 1973 unified personal tax (including allowances), are given in Table 7.6.

Table 7.4 *Unified personal tax rates (provisional rates from 6 April* 1973)

Income (£)	Rate (%)
Up to 5,000	30
Excess over 5,000	
between 5,000 and 6,000	40
„ 6,000 and 7,000	45
„ 7,000 and 8,000	50
„ 8,000 and 10,000	55
„ 10,000 and 12,000	60
„ 12,000 and 15,000	65
„ 15,000 and 20,000	70
over 20,000	75
Surcharge on investment income	
Up to 2,000	—
Over 2,000	15

(Source: *E.P.R.*, 29, July 1972)

Table 7.5 *Personal allowances*

	£	
	1972–73	1973–74 provisional
Single person	460	595
Wife's earned income		
Married man	600	775
Child – under 11	155	200
11–16	180	235
over 16	205	265
Additional relief for children	100	130
Dependent relative		
Single woman claimant	110	145
Others	75	100
Housekeeper	75	100
Relative taking charge of		
younger brother or sister	75	100
Daughter's services	40	55
Blind person	100	130

(Source: *E.P.R.*, 29, July 1972)

Table 7.6 *Examples of operation of proposed tax credit system assuming earnings of £25 per week and £50 per week*

	Weekly pay	Present net income of family*†	Position under the proposed tax-credit system			
			Weekly pay	Less tax at 30%	Plus credit	Net income of family*
Single	25	20·93	25	7·50	4	21·50
	50	38·33	50	15	4	39
Married without children	25	21·97	25	7·50	6	23·50
	50	39·47	50	15	6	41
Married with 2 children under 11 ...	25	24·56	25	7·50	10	27·50
	50	42·06	50	15	10	35
Married with 4 children, 2 under 11, 2 11–16 ...	25	27·90	25	7·50	14	31·50
	50	35·48	50	15	14	49

* Represents weekly net income of family after income tax, family allowance and (where appropriate) FIS. The figures assume current rates of family allowance and FIS. Income tax has been calculated on the basis of the provisional unified allowances and basic rate operative from 6 April 1973.

† National insurance contributions have been ignored.

(Source: *E.P.R.*, 33, Nov. 1972)

2. *Corporation Tax*. In the Budget speech of April 1971 the Chancellor announced changes in Corporation Tax – a direct income tax on company profits (introduced in 1966)[1] – to come into force in 1973/74. This was to remove the discrimination against distributed profits. Two alternative methods were suggested for achieving this end, a 'two-rate' system and an 'imputation' system.[2] Prior to 1965 there had been a series of *company profits taxes*, sometimes at a higher rate on distributed, as opposed to retained, profits and sometimes not discriminating against distributed profits. Corporation Tax was introduced at 40% in April 1966, was raised to 42·5% in 1968, 45% in 1969 and was lowered to 42·5% in 1970 and 40% in 1971.

From 1966 to 1973 a company would have paid Corporation Tax on all its profits and would have deducted at source the standard rate of personal income tax on dividends, distributed from profits to shareholders: thus dividends were taxed twice. If approximately one-half of post-tax profits were distributed, the total tax on profits would have been about 52%.

$$\text{i.e.} \quad 40\% \quad + \quad \left(38{\cdot}75\% \quad \times \quad \frac{60\%}{2}\right) \quad = \quad 51{\cdot}6\%$$

(C.T. on all profits)   (Income tax rate)   (Distributed post-tax profits)

The Government accepted the Select Committee Report on the above-mentioned Green Paper, which recommended the 'imputation system' for the new structure. According to this, instead of undistributed profits contributing a relatively smaller share of the overall tax burden than the twice-taxed dividends – as under the previous system – all pre-tax profits would pay a common, higher rate, provisionally fixed at 50%. In simplified form, this highly technical system[3] may be summarised as follows:

(a) Actual dividends distributed are *net* of tax, but the company makes an *advance payment* to the tax authorities, equivalent to $\frac{3}{7}$ of these actual dividends: thus, this payment is equivalent to $\frac{3}{10}$ (or 30%, i.e. the post-1973 personal tax rate) of the *combined* actual dividend *plus* advance payment. In other words, the old pattern of declaring a *gross* dividend, then splitting off personal income tax at the standard rate, then paying out a *net* dividend would be replaced by two separate payments, a net dividend to shareholders and an advance payment to the authorities.

(b) The '*mainstream*' corporation tax, paid at the *end* of a period (at 50% on all profits made during that period) is *reduced* by the amount of *advance payment*, made on dividends distributed *during* that period. This tends to even out the effects of varying profitabilities and of dividend distributions in different periods: the overall 'mainstream' corporation tax remains at 50%, but it is levied with more sophisticated timing.

(c) Along with his actual net dividend, the shareholder receives a *tax credit* for the $\frac{3}{7}$ net dividend (or 30% of gross dividend), paid out as advance payments by the company. These tax credits are then assessed along with his total income so that, according to his overall tax liability, he may receive payment of the credit or be liable to make a further tax payment.

---

[1] See M. Crawford, 'The 1965 reforms in the British tax system', *M. & W.S.R.*, Winter 1965.
[2] Green Paper, *Reform of Corporation Tax*, Cmnd 4630, April 1971.
[3] For further details and comment, see 'Reform of Corporation Tax', *E.P.R.*, 27, May 1972 and 'What do you mean by earnings?', *Econ.*, 4 Dec. 1971, p. 110.

The overall effects are to separate the taxpayer's individual tax liability from the company's corporation tax liability – linking them *via* the advance payment/ tax credit; to permit the company to 'claw back' tax 'advance payments', initially made on account of distributed profits; to spread the overall tax burden on profits equally over retained and distributed profits. In his 1972 Budget speech the Chancellor announced an 'abatement' for about 350,000 small companies: those with profits below £15,000 in any year would pay tax at a special rate, and marginal relief would be available for those with profits between £15,000 and £25,000.

3. Death duties. Sometimes referred to as estate duty, this is a direct tax on the value of property which passes on at death. The deceased does not necessarily have to own such property, as in the case of trust funds, or of gifts made by him less than seven years prior to death (less than one year if for a public or charitable purpose). Estate Duty is an Inland Revenue tax, and as the monetary values of property have gradually risen, the point at which the tax is levied has been successively raised. In 1972 the lower limit was raised to £15,000. There was a range of tax rates on *successive slices* of estates exceeding this amount, ranging up to 75%. In addition, £15,000 in value of an estate left to a surviving spouse was exempted from assessment: thus, the 'threshold' for surviving spouses was raised to £30,000. The Chancellor, in his 1972 Budget speech, indicated that the Government were considering the implications of replacing Estate Duty with an Inheritance Tax.[1]

4. Capital Gains Tax. This is a tax on the capital gain made on *disposal* of an asset and was first introduced in 1965. The 1971 Budget removed the short and long run distinction, referring to period of ownership (with the exception of gilt-edged securities – exempt if held for more than twelve months) and exempted capital gains totalling less than £500 in any one year. There are various other exemptions, including motor cars, principal private residences, chattels worth less than £1,000 and chattels (other than those used in trade) with a predictable life of less than fifty years.[2]

TAXES ON EXPENDITURE

Taxes on spending may be classified as either primarily *revenue-raising* or as primarily *protective* duties. They may also be classified as follows:

(*a*) Customs duties on goods imported from abroad.

(*b*) Excise duties on home-produced goods and services.

(*c*) Purchase tax (replaced in 1973 by the Value Added Tax, or V.A.T.) on both home-produced and imported goods.

(*d*) Selective Employment Tax (S.E.T.) – also replaced in 1973 by V.A.T. – which is a tax on employment but which, as a tax on the *use of labour* in the production of (primarily) services, may be considered as a tax on *expenditure on services*.

(*e*) Stamp duties, motor vehicle duties and broadcast receiving licences, etc.

Local authority rates, referred to earlier, are in some respects a tax on capital and in some respects a tax on expenditure (*via* the *use* of land and buildings).

[1] See *D.T.*, 22 March 1972.
[2] See 'Taxation of capital gains in the United Kingdom – a general survey', *M.B.R.*, Feb. 1971; 'How the 1971 Act affects tax on capital gains', *D.T.*, 2 Oct. 1971; A. J. Merrett, 'The capital gains tax', *L.B.R.*, Oct. 1965.

Except for Stamp Duties (an Inland Revenue *indirect* tax), Motor Duties (a *direct* tax, collected by the county and county borough councils and then transmitted direct to the Exchequer) and Broadcast Licence fees (a *direct* tax collected by the Post Office on behalf of the B.B.C.) all taxes on spending are *indirect* taxes, administered by the Board of Customs and Excise.[1] Taxes on spending may be levied on commodities or services, either once-for-all, or periodically – for *continuing use* of a commodity or service.

1. *Customs and Excise duties.*

Most customs duties and all excise duties are imposed for the prime purpose of raising revenue, though some of these revenue duties have as a secondary aim the protection of British or Commonwealth or E.E.C. member producers (e.g. tobacco, alcoholic drinks and sugar duties), or the protection of a substitute home product (e.g. coal, protected by the hydrocarbon oils duties), or the curtailment of consumption (e.g. the duty on spirits). Some customs duties, however, are primarily protective tariffs. The purchase tax, first introduced in 1940, was to all intents and purposes an extension of the other excise duties.

The most important group of revenue-raising customs and excise duties consists of the *specific* duties (based on quantity, etc.) on *tobacco, alcoholic drinks and hydrocarbon oils.* As with all revenue duties, they apply more or less equally to home-produced and imported goods. The remaining revenue-raising, customs and excise duties are the *specific* duties on matches and mechanical lighters and the *ad valorem* betting and gaming duties on most forms of commercial gambling. It will be noted that nearly all these revenue-raising duties are specific and are levied on things for which demand is fairly inelastic or unresponsive to price increases caused by the duty.

The remaining *customs* duties are almost entirely protective *ad valorem* tariffs under the Import Duties Act, 1958, which consolidated post-1915 protective legislation on such items as motor vehicles, musical instruments, watches, scientific, optical and other 'strategic' goods, silk and man-made fibres, etc.

Purchase tax, until 1973, applied, unlike the selective customs and excise duties, to a wide range of (mainly consumer) goods, whether home-produced or imported. It did not usually apply to items on which there were already revenue-raising customs or excise duties. It was an *ad valorem* tax, applied to different groups of goods at (1972/73) $11\frac{1}{4}\%$, 18% or 25% on wholesale values. It was a very adaptable fiscal instrument, as the tax rates and the ranges of goods could be easily extended – so that the tax could be used as a deterrent to consumption or production, or to mop up surplus purchasing power – or contracted, to stimulate production and consumption. In general, however, it was mainly aimed at providing revenue. Thus it applied mainly to luxuries or goods in fairly inelastic demand. However, so as not to penalise too heavily the lower-income consumers of essentials, it did not apply to food (other than confectionery and ice-cream), fuel, books, newspapers, young children's clothing and footwear, certain non-proprietary drugs and medicines, textiles and some household appliances. During the period of its imposition, purchase tax minimum rates had varied between 5% (1955–62) and $33\frac{1}{3}\%$ (mid-November 1947–April 1953) and maximum rates

---

[1] As mentioned earlier, local rates are a *direct* tax, collected by the local authority from the ratepayer, but in the National Income and Expenditure (Blue Book) accounts are treated as *indirect* taxes on *expenditure* – the two terms being considered there as synonymous.

had ranged from 25% (1972–73) to 125% (mid-November 1947–April 1948).[1] The purchase tax was treated as distinct from the main customs and excise duties because, whilst most of them were specific and related to particular classes of commodity or services, the purchase tax was not only an *ad valorem* tax, but was also applicable to extensive ranges of goods and was used more often as a policy instrument.

In 1961 the Chancellor of the Exchequer was granted the power (which must be renewed each year) to vary the purchase tax and most other customs and excise duties, selectively or generally, by up to a maximum of 10% of the original duty, in either direction. This Customs and Excise Regulator of surcharges and rebates, intended to make the indirect Customs and Excise Department taxes on spending more flexible in response to changing economic circumstances, was first used in July 1961, when the full 10% surcharge was imposed on all purchase tax. In 1964 this provision was extended to apply to a wider range of duties and was made more flexible, becoming applicable at different rates for each group. It was used again in July 1966 (10% on three groups of revenue duties) and in November 1968 (on four groups). In the 1961 and 1966 cases the Regulator surcharges were terminated in the following year's Budget proposals, although the Budget itself simultaneously increased some of the duties. In July 1971, when the existing four rates of purchase tax were cut by 18·2% ($\frac{2}{11}$), i.e. by more than the extent permitted by the Regulator, the reduction was made by special Order, under the Purchase Tax Act of 1963.[2]

Selective employment tax, from 1966 to 1973 was a charge imposed on employers of labour, with rebates and premiums (or bonuses) accruing to employers in particular sectors. One of the major intentions was that it should represent a tax on services, hitherto largely exempt from tax. Another reason was to 'shake out' surplus labour, thought to be 'hoarded' by some industries – particularly service industries – thus releasing labour for supposedly more deserving and productive manufacturing industry.[3]

Value Added Tax was introduced in 1973/74 to replace both purchase tax and S.E.T. The purpose was to come into line with E.E.C. countries and to reduce the distortion of consumer choice, by discriminating less than did the two superseded taxes, as between different types of goods and services.[4] The decision to introduce V.A.T. was announced in the 1972/73 Budget. The standard rate was to be 10% on the value added *at each stage* of production on goods *and* services (as compared to purchase tax, which was levied in a single stage, on the wholesaler), both home-produced and imported. The initial rate was to be 10% on all categories, apart from small companies, certain 'exempted' services and certain 'zero-rated' goods and services. In the case of motor cars, it was considered that as this category was responsible for about £300 million in purchase tax revenue,

[1] See *D.T.*, 22 March 1972; 'Purchase tax' (chart), *L.B.R.*, April 1969; 'The development of purchase tax', *M.B.R.*, Aug. 1969.
[2] For further details, see *The British System of Taxation*, 1971, pp. 4–5.
[3] See E. B. Butler and R. Gidlow, 'The selective employment tax', *M. & W.S.R.*, Autumn 1966.
[4] See Green Paper, *Value-Added Tax*, Cmnd 4621, 1971; 'Value added tax', *E.P.R.*, 28, June 1972; *Value Added Tax: general guide*, Notice No. 700, 1972; *Value Added Tax: scope and coverage*, Notice No. 701, 1972; M. J. MacCormac, 'Turnover taxes – the Irish experience', *L.B.R.*, April 1967; 'V.A.T. – a Common Market tax', *B.B.R.*, Nov. 1971; E. G. Horsman, 'Britain and value-added taxation', *L.B.R.*, Jan. 1972; 'Vat is coming', *Econ.*, 4 Sept. 1971, pp. 54–5; 'Vat in Europe', *Econ.*, 25 March 1972, pp. 64–5; 'The nuts and bolts of Vat', *Econ.*, 8 April 1972, pp. 62–3.

Table 7.7 *Calculation of one firm's V.A.T.*

	Value (excl Vat) £	Vat at 10% £	Value (incl Vat) £
Start with			
Sales:			
to consumers	80,000	8,000	88,000
exports	10,000	—	10,000
to businesses	10,000	1,000	11,000
	£100,000	£9,000	£109,000
Deduct			
Materials etc. bought in	£50,000	£5,000	£55,000
What's left is			
Valued added	£50,000	£4,000	£54,000
Vat payable is therefore £4,000			

(Source: *Econ.*, 4 Sep. 1971, p. 54)

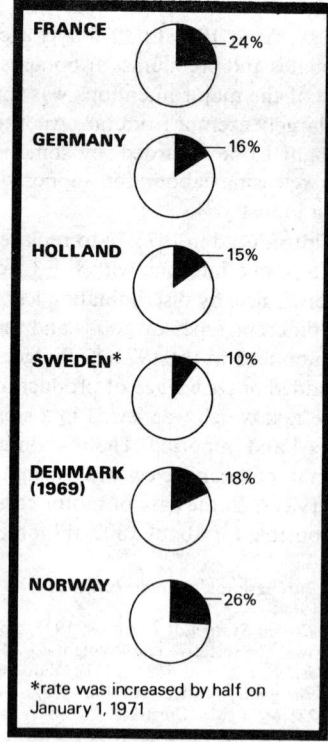

FRANCE — 24%

GERMANY — 16%

HOLLAND — 15%

SWEDEN* — 10%

DENMARK (1969) — 18%

NORWAY — 26%

*rate was increased by half on January 1, 1971

Fig. 7.12. *VAT as % of total tax revenue (including social security contributions),* 1970

(Source: *Econ.*, 25 March 1972, p. 65)

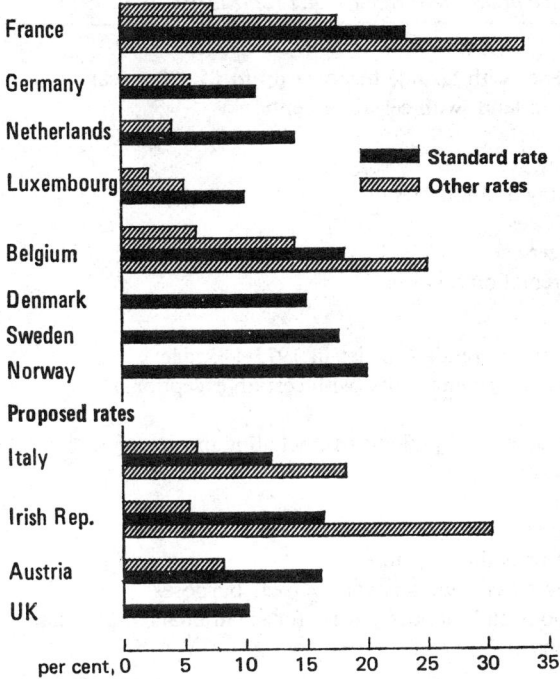

Fig. 7.13. *Some European V.A.T. rates, 1972*
(Source: *E.P.R.*, 28, June 1972)

a special *additional* tax was necessary (10%), to avoid the need to increase the *general* V.A.T. rate. It was announced that the *Regulator* would be retained and applied to V.A.T., but only to the general rate and not to the additional special rate on motor cars. V.A.T. is a tax on expenditure, in that it is added when a good or service is *sold* (except when exported) and thus increases the price. Each firm is charged an 'output tax' on the value added (wage costs plus profit or mark-up) on its sales: it is credited with the 'input tax', which it has paid to its suppliers (who have charged an output tax) for its purchases. As the product or service proceeds through the chain of production, from firm to firm, the *net* V.A.T. accumulates and is eventually paid by the final consumer (see Table 7.7).

For 1971/72 revenue from purchase tax and the *net* revenue from S.E.T. was estimated at about £1,700 million or about 10·5% of total Budget tax revenue. Total tax revenue for the year 1971 was £20,169 million – including central Government taxes, local rates and National Insurance Fund contributions: of this total, £1,948 million (about 9·5%) was accounted for by purchase tax and *net* S.E.T. revenue.[1] Fig. 7.12 illustrates the roughly comparable proportions of total tax revenue from V.A.T. in some European countries during 1970. Fig. 7.13 illustrates the V.A.T. rates in several European countries in 1972 and Table 7.8 lists the main categories of 'exempt' and 'zero-rated' goods and services initially announced.

[1] See *National Income and Expenditure* (Blue Book), 1972, p. 42.

Table 7.8 *Exempt and zero-rated V.A.T. categories, U.K. 1973**

Exempt
Small businesses with taxable turnover up to £5,000 a year
Transactions in land (with certain exceptions)
Insurance
Postal services
Betting, gaming and lotteries
Financial services
Educational services
Burial and cremation services

Zero-rated
Children's clothing (added to list in 1973/4 Budget).
Food and animal feeding stuffs (with certain exceptions)
Water
Books, newspapers and periodicals (including music, maps, charts, etc.)
Newspaper advertisements
News services
Fuel and power
Construction of buildings, etc.
Services to overseas traders or for overseas purposes
Transport goods and services (except for small boats, motor cars, cycles, etc.)
Large caravans
Gold
Bank notes
Drugs and medicines supplied on prescription

* This table is only an approximate guide. For full details see Cmnd 4929, schedules 4 and 5.
(Source: *E.P.R.*, 28, June 1972)

2. *Stamp duties.* These are *ad valorem* or specific indirect taxes, payable on many kinds of legal and commercial document. The tax applies at the time of conclusion of the contract, etc., and the duty is remitted to the Inland Revenue Department.

3. *Motor licence duties.* Motor vehicle duties, payable for licences, are direct specific taxes, paid by the vehicle owner to the licensing local authority, which transmits them to the Exchequer.

4. *Broadcast licence duties.* These are direct specific taxes, paid to the Post Office, which transmits them to the B.B.C.

(e) **The overall burden of taxation**
Towards the end of the nineteenth century most central Government budgetary tax revenue was provided by outlay taxes, which were regressive, and a much smaller proportion of revenue was financed by direct taxes on incomes. Since then, in the interests of equity, the emphasis in the Budget on progressive direct taxes on incomes, profits and capital has been increased and that on regressive (mainly indirect) expenditure taxes has been diminished (see Table 7.9). Nevertheless, because of the disincentive effect of direct income taxes and because of the economy, ease and lack of 'announcement effect' of expenditure taxes, the

Table 7.9 *Relative importance of direct and indirect taxes since 1885 in the U.K. Budget*

Financial year	% Direct	% Indirect
1885–86	39	61
1910–11	58	42
1938–39	62	38
1950–51	56	44
1959–60	58	42
1960–61	58	42
1971–72	58·5	41·5

(Source: *The British System of Taxation*, C.O.I. Ref. 10, 1962; *Ann. Abs. Stat.*, 108, 1971)

latter still constitute a significant proportion of the total. Despite the regressive nature of expenditure taxes, the disincentive effects of direct income taxes have often been considered to be too high in some Western economies: social equity must be balanced against the fact that direct taxes are immediately noticed by the taxpayer as money taken out of his pocket, and by the likelihood that the level of personal savings – essential to finance growth and efficiency – may suffer. In 1969 the Shadow Chancellor called for a switch to indirect (expenditure) taxation on these grounds, claiming that the U.K. system was the most progressive in the developed world.[1] Whilst this might have been true in regard to the effective rates of personal tax on fairly high incomes, the ratio of direct personal and company taxes to national income in the U.K. was by no means the highest (see Fig. 7.14). Norway, with the same such ratio as the U.K. in 1969, decided in that year to make a significant switch from personal income tax to a high rate of V.A.T. (20%).[2]

There is much confusion over the classification of taxes,[3] as between 'direct'

Table 7.10 *Economic and administrative classification of taxes*

ECONOMIC CLASSIFICATION	ADMINISTRATIVE CLASSIFICATION	
	DIRECT	INDIRECT
Taxes on income	Personal income tax Corporation tax	
Taxes on capital	Estate duty Capital gains tax	
Taxes on expenditure	— LOCAL RATES* —	
	Licence fees Stamp duties, etc.	Customs and Excise duties Purchase tax V.A.T. S.E.T.
Indeterminate	Social security contributions by employees (Tax on income?)	Social security contributions by employers (Tax on Expenditure?)

*Paid *directly*, but referred to in international returns as *indirect*.

[1] See *F.T.*, 5 April 1969.   [2] See *D.T.*, 8 April 1969.
[3] For further discussion, see R. A. Musgrave, *Fiscal Systems*, 1969, pp. 173–5.

Table 7.11 *Composition of the total tax burden*, 1962

1962	Britain £m	% Total tax	% G.N.P.	West Germany £m	% Total tax	% G.N.P.	France £m	% Total tax	% G.N.P.
Income and profits taxes:									
on Persons	2,500	29·2	10·0	2,842	26·8	11·0	972	10·8	4·4
on Companies	955	11·2	3·8	1,194	11·2	4·6	550	6·1	2·5
Social security taxes	1,197	14·0	4·8	2,997	28·2	11·6	3,206	35·5	14·6
Outlay taxes (incl. rates and payroll taxes)	3,902	45·6	15·7	3,587	33·8	13·8	4,292	48·6	19·6
Total tax burden*	8,554	100	34·3	10,621	100	41·0	9,020	100	41·1

* Excludes Capital Taxes.

(Based on material in *National Income and Expenditure, 1963*, and *Econ.*, 14 Mar. 1964, p. 1019)

and 'indirect', 'expenditure' or 'income and capital'. This point has already been made with regard to local rates. Another problem case is Social Security Contributions: the part paid by the employee may be considered as a direct tax, whilst that paid in bulk by the employer may be considered as an indirect tax. Perhaps the employee's share should be considered as a sort of income tax and that paid by the employer as a sort of expenditure tax – in the same way as the S.E.T. (i.e. a tax on expenditure on wages and salaries). For most purposes, it is more convenient to dispense with the *administrative* classification and to use the *economic* classification: local rates are generally classed as part of expenditure taxes and Social Security Contributions, because of their complex nature, are classed as a separate group (see Table 7.10).

Table 7.12 *International comparison of taxes and social security contributions, 1968–70*

(a)

Taxes including social security contributions as a percentage of gross national product at factor cost

	Percentages 1968	1969	1970
Austria	41·6	41·9	41·5
Belgium	37·2	37·7	38·2
Canada*	35·8	37·5	37·7
Denmark	41·0	41·8	..
France	42·5	42·9	41·4
W. Germany	39·2	41·9	40·5
Italy	34·1	33·1	32·8
Japan	20·0	20·5	21·3
Netherlands	42·1	42·9	45·0
Norway	43·0	45·6	47·4
Sweden*	45·6	46·0	46·3
Switzerland	24·4	25·5	..
United Kingdom	39·4	41·5	42·7
United States	32·4	33·9	33·0

Table 7.12 *Continued*

(b)

Composition of taxes including social security contributions in 1970

	Taxes on income		Taxes on expendi-ture	Social security contributions	
	House-holds†	Corpora-tions		Total	*of which* paid by employers
As a percentage of total taxes					
Austria	28·8	5·0	43·9	22·3	. .
Belgium	25·6	7·0	37·5	30·0	20·0
Canada*	35·9	11·4	43·8	8·9	. .
Denmark‡	43·9	2·7	48·3	5·1	1·9
France	12·8	6·6	40·5	40·2	28·7
W. Germany	25·5	5·0	37·4	32·2	17·4
Italy	16·3	5·0	41·2	37·5	. .
Japan	21·3	22·8	37·4	18·5	11·3
Netherlands	27·6	6·7	28·9	36·8	26·8
Norway	27·4	3·6	46·5	22·5	11·8
Sweden*	48·0	3·8	29·6	18·7	. .
Switzerland ‡	35·9	9·7	30·7	23·6	21·5
United Kingdom	32·1	8·0	45·6	14·4	7·3
United States	36·6	11·5	32·4	19·5	9·5
As a percentage of gross national product at factor cost					
Austria	11·9	2·1	18·2	9·3	. .
Belgium	9·8	2·7	14·4	11·5	7·7
Canada*	13·5	4·3	16·5	3·3	. .
Denmark‡	18·4	1·1	20·2	2·1	0·8
France	5·3	2·7	16·7	16·6	11·9
W. Germany	10·3	2·0	15·1	13·0	7·0
Italy	5·3	1·7	13·5	12·3	. .
Japan	4·5	4·9	8·0	3·9	2·4
Netherlands	12·4	3·0	13·0	16·6	12·0
Norway	13·0	1·7	22·0	10·7	5·6
Sweden*	22·2	1·7	13·7	8·7	. .
Switzerland‡	9·2	2·5	7·8	6·0	5·5
United Kingdom	13·7	3·4	19·5	6·1	3·1
United States	12·1	3·8	10·7	6·4	3·1

* The figures for Canada and Sweden are based on the revised International System of National Accounts (see May 1969 issue of *Statistical News*) and are therefore not strictly comparable with those for other countries which are still on the former system.
† Households include unincorporated businesses.
‡ The percentages relate to 1969 as 1970 data for Denmark is incomplete and for Switzerland is not available.
. . Not available.

(Source: *Economic Trends*, 228, Oct. 1972, p. lviii)

It is of interest to compare the total tax burden, as a percentage of National Income, as between different countries. For this purpose we usually omit taxes on capital, as they are capital transfers, not related to or levied on the income, output or expenditure *flows* which make up the National Income. Excluding capital taxes and including local rates and employment or payroll taxes (as expenditure taxes) and social security payments, the tax burden (as a percentage of G.N.P.) in 1962 was 34·3 in the U.K., 41·0 in West Germany and 41·1 in France (see Table 7.11). In 1970 the overall tax burden in the U.K. (as a percentage of G.N.P.) was 42·7, as compared with 41·4% in France. Norway had the highest overall burden (47·4%). Both the U.K. and Norway had higher income tax shares than France, which had the highest social security contributions share (see Table 7.12).[4] Fig. 7.14 illustrates graphically some of these international tax burdens and their composition for 1969.

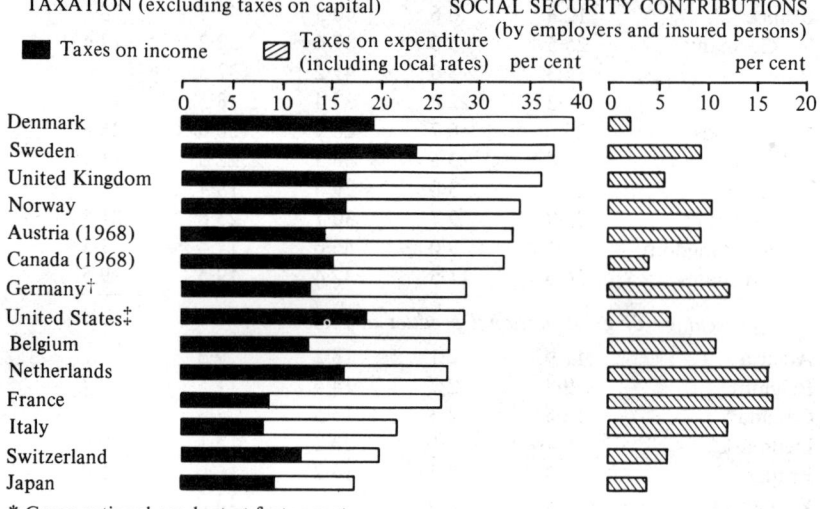

* Gross national product at factor cost.
† Federal Republic of Germany and West Berlin.
‡ Including estate and gift taxes.

Fig. 7.14. *Taxes (excluding Capital taxes) as proportions of national income*, 1969* (Source: *E.P.R.*, 19, Sept. 1971)

As for the way in which the total tax burden falls on individuals with differing levels of income, there will be discrepancies, due to the fact that persons in each income group who neither smoke, drink nor drive escape the outlay taxes on these activities. However, as a general rule we may assume that the burden of indirect outlay taxes, rates and social security contributions is felt at the lowest income level, and falls regressively as income levels rise, because expenditure does not usually rise as fast as income. On the other hand, the burden of direct income tax, though it rises progressively, does not fall on the lowest income groups. Thus the total burden of taxation may tend to fall amongst the lowest income groups (no income tax), but may then tend to rise – particularly on the

[1] For comment on the new O.E.C.D. classification and resulting comparisons, see 'The tax bite is hardest in Scandinavian countries', *F.T.*, 17 Jan. 1973.

higher income groups – as the increasing force of progressive income taxation outweighs the decreasing force of regressive outlay taxation, social security contributions and rates (see Fig. 7.15).

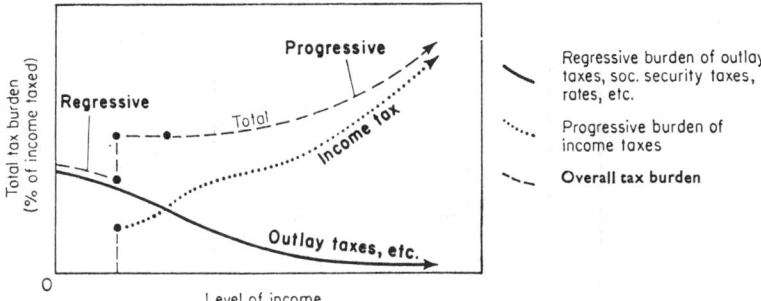

Fig. 7.15. *The total tax burden at different income levels*

It is important to note that individuals do not only pay taxes, but that they also receive benefits in cash and kind (e.g. welfare foods, medical attention, educational grants, family allowances, Social Security allowances, etc.). Furthermore, we should expect that individuals in the lower income groups receive higher benefits than those more prosperous, possibly outweighing their actual tax payments. If so, it would be important to know at what income level each class of taxpayer starts to pay more than he receives, i.e. where the 'real tax burden' begins.

In *Economic Trends*, February 1964, the Central Statistical Office published the second of a series of such estimates for different types of household. The first in the series covered 1959: the second covered 1962. According to these estimates and a later one for 1971, the 'break even' points for one adult, two adults and two adults with two children were as follows:[1]

Year	1 Adult	2 Adults	2 Adults with 2 children
1959	£280	£450	£950
1962	£315–382	£460–559	£676–816
1971	approx. £550	£816–987	approx. £1,000

As money incomes were worth less in later years, taxpayers in the categories '1 adult' and '2 adults' benefited relatively more from the shifting of the 'break even' point to a higher level: those in the other category suffered relatively from its shifting only slightly.

The *Economic Trends* (Nov. 1972) study of taxes and benefits in 1971 concluded that all taxes combined were only mildly progressive: that over a wide range of *incomes* the percentages of total taxes to original income *plus* cash benefits were remarkably constant for any given type of household and did not show very wide variations, even between *households* of different types at any given income level. For example, the average for all households in the sample taken was 35% and the range for all non-retired households was between 32% and 37% (see Table 7.13). The reason given was that, whilst income tax and surtax were certainly

[1] *Economic Trends*, 124, Feb. 1964 and 229, Nov. 1972; *New Contributions to Economic Statistics*, 1964; *Econ.*, 12 Jan. 1963, pp. 143–5; *New Society*, 12 Mar. 1964, p. 20.

Table 7.13 *Total taxes as a percentage of original income plus cash benefits, 1971*

	Range of original income: £ per year								Percentages Average over all income ranges
	Under 381	381–	557–	816–	1,194–	1,749–	2,561–	3,750 and above	
All households in the sample	24	29	29	33	35	35	36	37	35
Retired households									
1 adult	22	26	32	33	35				26
2 adults	25	28	31	32	34	38			30
Non-retired households									
1 adult	26	27	32	36	39	40	43		37
2 adults	28	31	29	35	38	38	36	38	37
2 adults, 1 child	29		24	35	35	35	34	34	34
2 adults, 2 children	24		33	30	33	32	33	32	32
2 adults, 3 children				31	34	34	31	32	33
2 adults, 4 children				25	32	31	34		33

(Source: *Economic Trends*, 229, Nov. 1972, p. ix)

progressive, National Insurance contributions (particularly the flat rate contributions) were mildly regressive and indirect taxes as a whole also tended to be mildly regressive. The social service benefits as a whole were very progressive (in the sense that they formed a larger proportion of low than of high incomes and more so for larger than for smaller households). Flat rate benefits formed a larger proportion of low than of high incomes, thus tending to make *benefits* as a whole *more progressive* than *taxes* as a whole. The general finding was that *all taxes and benefits combined* were progressive in terms of income levels and also in terms of favouring large, as against small, households.[1]

6. The National Debt

The national debt may be considered as the total extent of a central Government's borrowing internally (at home) and externally (abroad). It does not include borrowing by other parts of the public sector, such as local authorities and public corporations, and does not include Bank of England liability on the note issue or accrued interest on National Savings Certificates. The British national debt has the longest continuous history of any. By the end of the Civil War and aftermath, 1689, total indebtedness was over £1 million; by 1691 it was more than £3 million, on which the annual interest charge was under £¼ million. By the beginning of the Industrial Revolution (end of the Seven Years War, 1763) the debt stood at £122 million. By the close of the Napoleonic War, 1815, it stood at £876 million, and would have been higher, had not income tax been introduced to provide finance for the war. By 1914 it had fallen to £650 million, but by the end of World War I it had grown to £7,435 million, of which an appreciable part was in the form of National Savings Certificates. By 1939 it stood at £7,131 million, but by the end of World War II it had reached £23,637 million. By end-March 1971 the total national debt was variously estimated at £33·4 billion by the Treasury and at £32·8 billion by the Bank of England: by end-March 1972 the figure stood at £35·8 billion.

Of the £32·8 billion 1971 total, £9·2 billion represented U.K. official holdings – the investment, by official bodies, of some of their funds in N.D. securities. The major significance of this is not that liability to the public is ultimately decreased, but that control of investment policy concerning such official funds is in the hands of official bodies.

The figures quoted so far refer to 'gross' national debt. In fact, since World War II the process of nationalisation and of Exchequer lending to the nationalised industries, local authorities and the private sector, has resulted in a relatively faster growth in assets, held against the resultant public debt. Thus, the 'net' debt – gross debt *less* assets (held by the National Loans Fund, since 1958) – has tended to fall: the N.L.F. assets stood at about £17½ billion in 1971, thus reducing the £33·4 billion (Treasury estimate) N.D. to £16·0 billion.[2]

Overseas residents – foreign governments, central and other banks, international organisations (mainly the I.M.F.) and private overseas residents – held about £4·6 billion of the £32·8 billion (B. of E. estimate) 1971 national debt. This represented the 'external' debt, on *some* of which interest must be paid and which

[1] See *Economic Trends*, 229, Nov. 1972, pp. x–xi.
[2] See 'Anatomy of the National Debt: the decline in its relative significance', *M.B.R.*, Nov. 1972.

affects the balance of payments. Of this £4·6 billion, about £1·7 billion represented *interest-free* notes, held by the I.M.F. The remaining £2·9 billion represented directly-incurred external debt: of this, about £2 billion was repayable in foreign currencies – £1·7 billion of which was the residue of U.S. and Canadian World War II and post-war 'lend-lease', Marshall Aid and other credits (much of which was also interest-free or repayable at only 2%).[1]

The prime reason for the growth of the national debt has been the finance of budget deficits during or immediately after wars. Other events requiring Government borrowing have been catastrophes (e.g. the Irish famine of 1848), social reforms (e.g. the abolition of slavery in 1836–39) or the building of vast capital projects. In effect, one generation lends to the State and all future generations are involved in paying back the debt.

Traditionally, the debt was looked upon as a necessary nuisance, to be liquidated or paid off as cheaply and quickly as possible. It has become so large, however – exceeding the annual Gross National Product – that the authorities cannot pursue a low interest rate policy (in order to keep debt interest down) without considering its repercussions on the liquidity structure of the whole economy.

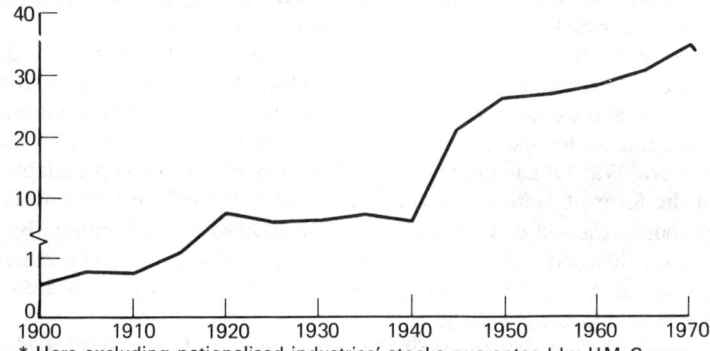

* Here excluding nationalised industries' stocks guaranteed by HM Government and including debts payable in external currencies.

Fig. 7.16. *The National Debt* 1900–70 (£'000 million)*
(Source: *E.P.R.*, 5, May 1970)

Fig. 7.16 traces the growth in 'gross' national debt from 1900 to 1970. Fig. 7.17 traces the *per capita* national debt from 1905 to 1970. Fig. 7.18 compares the national debt (with and without official holdings and I.M.F. notes) as a proportion of G.N.P. in the U.K. and several other countries, as at 1968. That of the U.K. is higher because of the extra debt burden taken on in the two world wars and because of the relatively small proportion wiped out by postwar inflation, as compared with some other countries. The estimated structure of the national debt, by composition and by holder, as at end-March 1971, is illustrated in Fig. 7.19.

Much debate has raged over the question of whether the national debt represents the profligacy of one generation and a burden on future generations.[2] What

[1] See 'Outstanding loans to the British Government', *E.P.R.*, 25, March 1972; 'Anatomy of the National Debt', pp. 4, 6, 9; W. F. Kimball, *The Most Unsordid Act: Lend-Lease, 1939–1941*, 1969.
[2] For further discussion see C. S. Shoup, 'Comment on the Burden of the debt and future generations', reprinted in Houghton, ed., *Public Finance*, 1970.

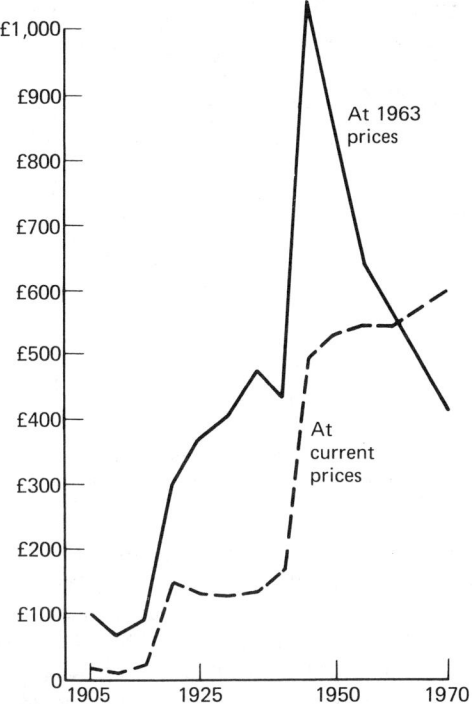

Fig. 7.17. *The National Debt per capita*
(Source: *B.B.R.*, Aug. 1972)

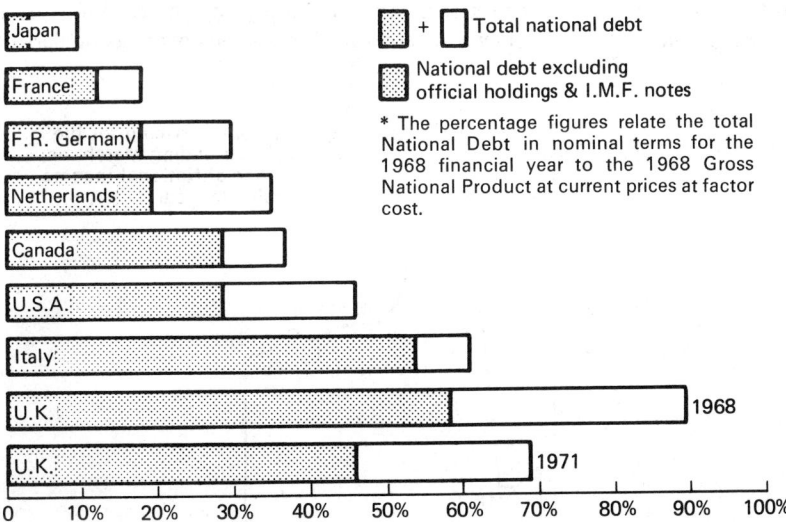

Fig. 7.18. *International comparison of the relation of the National Debt to G.N.P.*,
1968*
(Based on material in *B.B.R.*, Aug. 1972 and *M.B.R.*, Nov. 1972)

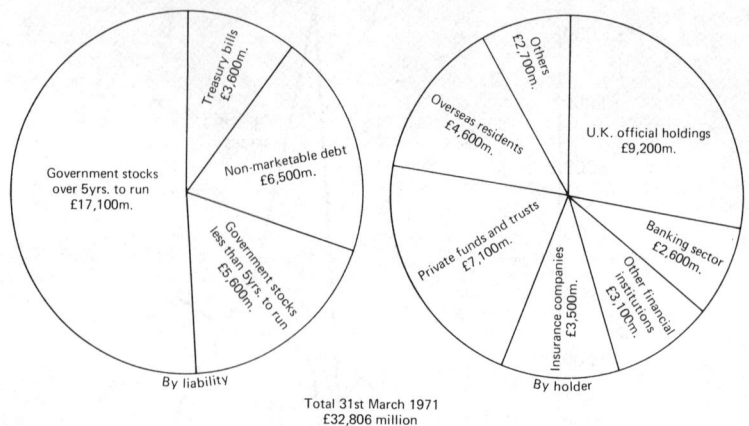

By liability

By holder

Total 31st March 1971
£32,806 million

Fig. 7.19. *Estimated distribution of the National Debt*
(Based on material in *B.B.R.*, Aug. 1972 and *M.B.R.*, Nov. 1972)

really matters is the 'true burden' on the economy. Most of the debt is held *internally*, by U.K. residents or official bodies: repayments to them represent internal transfers within the economy. The overall interest *plus* management charges (i.e. servicing charges) are more relevant than the actual extent of new borrowing or of the cumulative debt. About 95% of servicing charges are interest payments, financed from general taxation. Combined servicing charges as a proportion of National Income have been falling since World War I (see Fig. 7.20) and the interest component fell to 3·0% of G.N.P. on the 'gross' debt and to 0·5% of G.N.P. on the 'net' debt in 1971 (see Table 7.14). Even this low proportion, however, does not represent the 'true burden' on the economy. This concept applies only to the interest charges paid to *external* overseas holders of

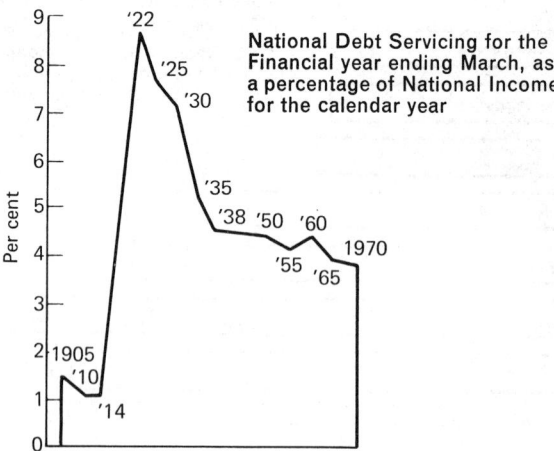

Fig. 7.20. *National Debt servicing as a percentage of national income**
(Source: *B.B.R.*, Aug. 1972)

616

Table 7.14 *National Debt and interest related to G.N.P., 1946–71 (at 31 March)*

	(in £000m) National Debt		Annual Interest		as percentage of G.N.P. National Debt		Annual Interest	
	Gross	Net	Gross	Net	Gross	Net	Gross	Net
1946	23·6	23·6	0·5	0·5	267	267	5·1	5·4
1950	25·8	24·3	0·5	0·5	220	207	4·3	4·0
1955	26·9	23·2	0·7	0·6	158	136	4·0	3·3
1960	27·7	21·1	0·9	0·6	121	94	3·8	2·7
1965	30·4	19·9	1·1	0·6	97	64	3·4	1·9
1970	33·1	17·2	1·5	0·4	77	40	3·4	1·0
1971	33·4	16·0	1·5	0·2	69	33	3·0	0·5

(Source: *M.B.R.*, Nov. 1972, p. 9)

the national debt. As mentioned earlier, they held £4·6 billion of the £32·8 billion debt at end-March 1971, of which only about £1·5 billion to £2 billion was subject to interest charges. The data on such interest charges is fairly vague, but was probably less than the £298 million public sector gross debits shown in the 1971 balance of payments figures (against which could be cancelled out much of the £99 million public sector gross credits for interest *received* from U.K. official holdings of *foreign* national debts).[1]

The problems of debt management were mentioned above, and were dealt with in the chapter on Money and Banking.[2] One interesting effect of postwar inflationary trends, with high interest rates, has been that War Loan securities – issued in 1917 at 5% and converted in 1932 to 3·5% – have plummetted in price in recent years. As high interest rates caused most gilt prices to fall, the low dividend War Loan stock (when gilt yields reached 9–10% in the late 1960s) had to compete: this resulted in drastic price falls and capital losses to investors who held on for too long.[3]

7. Further Reading and Sources

Footnote references to daily and weekly journals are not repreated.
BARCLAYS BANK, 'V.A.T. – a Common Market tax', *B.B.R.*, Nov. 1971.
BARCLAYS BANK, 'Government finance in the sixties', *B.B.R.*, May 1972.
BARCLAYS BANK, 'The National Debt', *B.B.R.* (centre spread), Aug. 1972.
W. J. BLUM and H. KALVEN, jr., *The Uneasy Case for Progressive Taxation*. University of Chicago Press. 1966.
S. BRITTAN, *Steering the Economy: the role of the Treasury*. Secker & Warburg. 1969.
S. BUTLER and R. GIDLOW, 'The Selective Employment Tax', *M. & W.S.R.* Autumn 1966.

[1] 'Anatomy of the National Debt', *loc. cit.*, p. 9.
[2] For further comment, see *ibid.*, pp. 10–11.
[3] For fuller discussion, see 'Inflation defoliates the investor's hedge', *D.T.*, 4 Dec. 1972; 'War Loan since the 1949 devaluation', *Econ.*, 28 Jan. 1967, p. 355; 'The longest running fraud', *Obs.*, 23 Nov. 1969; 'Front line in the war to end War Loan', *S.T.*, 26 Oct. 1969.

7. PUBLIC FINANCE [I]

M. H. CADMAN, ed., *Taxation Economics*. Macmillan. 1969.

CENTRAL OFFICE OF INFORMATION, *The British System of Taxation*. H.M.S.O. 1971.

M. CRAWFORD, 'The 1965 reforms in the British tax system'. *M. & W.S.R.* Winter 1965.

CUSTOMS AND EXCISE, *Value Added Tax: general guide*. Notice No. 700. 1972.

CUSTOMS AND EXCISE, *Value Added Tax: scope and coverage*. Notice No. 701. 1972.

J. F. DUE, *Government Finance: economics of the public sector*. Irwin. 1968.

O. ECKSTEIN, *Public Finance*. 2nd edn. Prentice-Hall. 1967.

G. H. FORSTER, ed. *Local Government Finance*, 1971. Charles Knight. 1972.

W. HAGENBUCH, 'The Welfare State and its finances'. *L.B.R.* July 1958.

R. H. HAVEMAN, *The Economics of the Public Sector*. Wiley. 1970.

N. P. HEPWORTH, *The Finance of Local Government*. Allen & Unwin. 1970.

L. HEY, *Economics of Public Finance*. Pitman. 1972.

E. G. HORSMAN, 'Britain and value-added taxation'. *L.B.R.* Jan. 1972.

R. W. HOUGHTON, ed. *Public Finance*. Penguin. 1970.

W. F. KIMBALL, *The Most Unsordid Act: Lend-Lease, 1939–1941*. Johns Hopkins Press. London I.B.E.G. 1969.

D. LEES, 'Poor families and fiscal reform'. *L.B.R.* Oct. 1967.

M. J. MacCORMAC, 'Turnover taxes: the Irish experience'. *L.B.R.* April 1967.

A. J. MERRETT, 'The Capital Gains tax'. *L.B.R.* Oct. 1955.

MIDLAND BANK, 'The development of purchase tax'. *M.B.R.* Aug. 1969.

MIDLAND BANK, 'Taxation of capital gains in the United Kingdom'. *M.B.R.* Feb. 1971.

MIDLAND BANK, 'Anatomy of the National Debt: the decline in its relative significance'. *M.B.R.* Nov. 1972.

R. A. MUSGRAVE, *The Theory of Public Finance*. McGraw-Hill. 1959.

R. A. MUSGRAVE, *Fiscal Systems*. Yale University Press. 1969.

R. J. NICHOLSON, 'The distribution of personal income'. *L.B.R.* Jan. 1967.

SIR HARRY PAGE, 'Local government in decline'. *T.B.R.* June 1971.

A. R. PREST, *Public Finance in Theory and Practice*. 4th edn. Weidenfeld & Nicolson. 1970.

A. SELDON, 'Thaw in the Welfare State'. *L.B.R.* July 1972.

W. A. THOMAS and E. R. SHAW, 'The role of loans bureaux in local authority finance'. *M. & W.S.R.* Autumn 1971.

TREASURY, *Value Added Tax* [Green Paper]. Cmnd 4621. H.M.S.O. 1971.

TREASURY, *National Income and Expenditure* [Blue Book]. H.M.S.O. 1972.

TREASURY, 'The incidence of taxes and social service benefits in 1971'. *Economic Trends*. 229. Nov. 1972. H.M.S.O.

TREASURY, 'Budget background'. *E.P.R.*, 4, April 1970.

TREASURY, 'The National Debt', *E.P.R.*, 5, May 1970.

TREASURY, 'Taxation'. *E.P.R.*, 17, July 1971.

TREASURY, 'Financing local government'. *E.P.R.*, 22, Dec. 1971.

TREASURY, 'Outstanding loans to the British Government. *E.P.R.*, 25, March 1972.

TREASURY, 'Reform of Corporation Tax'. *E.P.R.*, 27, May 1972.

TREASURY, 'Value added tax'. *E.P.R.*, 28, June 1972.

TREASURY, 'Unified personal tax'. *E.P.R.*, 29, July 1972.

TREASURY, 'Tax credit scheme'. *E.P.R.*, 33, Nov, 1972.

G. S. A. WHEATCROFT, 'Inequity in Britain's tax structure'. *L.B.R.*, July 1969.

J. WISEMAN, 'Local government in the twentieth century'. *L.B.R.*, Jan. 1966.

8. Past Examination Questions

1. Mention some of the more important objects of government expenditure. Who pays for these objects of expenditure and how? (Autumn 1953)
2. Outline the main sources of revenue to the Exchequer and the objects on which the revenue is spent. (Autumn 1957)
3. Outline the benefits which a citizen may enjoy in return for taxation he is called upon to pay. (Summer 1958)
4. What do you consider to be the qualities of a good tax? How far do these qualities conflict with one another in practice? (January 1963)
5. In what ways has the Government tried to reduce the cost that parents incur in rearing children? (Summer 1955)
6. What is meant by a progressive tax? To what extent are the following of Britain's taxes progressive: (a) Income Tax, (b) Customs and Excise Duties, (c) Purchase Tax? (Summer 1959)
7. What are the main causes of the inequality of incomes in our society? (Summer 1955)
8. Distinguish, with examples, between direct and indirect taxes. What are the advantages of each of these types (a) for the taxpayer, (b) for the government? (Autumn 1953)
9. Give an example of (a) a direct tax, and (b) an indirect tax. Describe each in detail. (Summer 1964)
10. Name one indirect tax and examine the probable economic effects of an increase in it. (Summer 1955)
11. Distinguish carefully between the following:
    (i) direct taxes and indirect taxes. . . . (Summer 1956)
12. What are the advantages and disadvantages of very heavy taxation on personal incomes? (January 1964)
13. 'The income tax is a progressive tax'. Explain the meaning of this. (Autumn 1957)
14. Write short notes on . . . the following: (a) Death Duties. . . . (Summer 1952)
15. What is the Purchase Tax? State the advantages and disadvantages of this tax in this country at the present time. (Autumn 1952)
16. Assume that the duty on tobacco were to be further increased. In which circumstances would you expect the total yield of the duty (a) to increase, (b) to decrease? (Summer 1952)
17. 'In imposing taxes account must be taken not only of the revenue to be raised by them, but of their general economic effects.' Relate this statement to the following taxes at present levied in the United Kingdom: (a) income tax, (b) purchase tax, (c) customs duties. (Summer 1961)
18. Compare the probable economic effects of raising the income tax and of raising the tax on tobacco. (January 1965)
19. Examine the probable economic effects of (a) an increase in the standard rate of income tax, and (b) an increase in the tax on beer. (Summer 1953)
20. Discuss the likely economic effects of an increase in the tax on petrol. (Autumn 1953)
21. What economic effects would follow if there were a substantial decline in smoking in Great Britain? (Summer 1964)
22. Discuss the likely economic effects of the imposition of a high tax on butter. (Summer 1956)

23. 'Bank rate up; purchase tax up.' What effect would the Chancellor of the Exchequer expect these changes to have on (*a*) manufacturers, and (*b*) individual expenditure? (January 1964)

24. The Hon. Ivor Castle, a gentleman of leisure, has two residences, a large holding of government stock, and one child, a son at public school. Mr Will Needham, a postman, rents a council house, and has six children under the age of sixteen. Compare the effects upon their standards of living of government taxation and expenditure. (Summer 1960)

25. Giving clear explanations in each case, state which taxes you expect to pay during your first year of full-time employment, and also state which taxes at present levied by the government you do not expect to pay. (Summer 1962)

26. John Citizen has a wife and four children, enjoys his pipe and an occasional visit to the local public house, and earns £1,200 a year. In all these respects, his eldest child, Jim, who has just started earning at £250 a year, has nothing in common with his father. Describe a friendly argument in which John puts forward the view that Jim's contribution to the government revenue is only a fraction of his own. What arguments might Jim advance to show that his father is not so badly treated after all by the budgetary policy of the government? (Summer 1963)

27. Write short notes on . . . the following: (*a*) National Debt. . . . (Autumn 1953)

7. Public Finance
Stage II

1. The Growth in Public Spending

Since World War II a great deal of attention has been paid to the rise in the level of public spending, both in absolute terms and as a percentage of the Gross National Product. In monetary terms the amount of public spending increased more than eightyfold from £130·6 million in 1890 (excluding debt interest) to more than £12,000 million in 1963/64. In real terms, making allowance for wage and price increases over the period, the rise was about fourteenfold.[1] In 1971 public expenditure had risen by a factor of about 185 in monetary terms (to £24,240 million), or of about 21 in real terms, as compared with 1890. As a percentage of the Gross National Product at factor prices, public spending has risen from 9% in 1890 (excluding debt interest) to about 50% in 1971. It will be remembered that not all this expenditure represents a direct call upon goods and services by current and capital expenditure: with the spread of social services there has been a faster relative rise in transfer payments (grants, benefits, loans and subsidies) than in the direct purchase of goods and services. However, the latter used to account for 7% of the Gross National Product in 1890, and had grown to about $30\frac{1}{2}\%$ in 1971, direct *current* expenditure by public authorities accounting for about $21\frac{1}{4}\%$ of the G.N.P. and direct *capital* expenditure for about $9\frac{1}{4}\%$.

When comparisons are made between the U.K. and other countries, in respect of the relationship between *per capita* incomes and the ratio of current expenditure to G.N.P., it appears that the U.K. is fairly typical of similar countries. Fig. 7.21, which probably understates the level of current expenditure in the U.K., illustrates the relativities for several countries in 1967. It will be noted that the group with higher incomes had a lower average ratio of current public expenditure to G.N.P. When the current direct (goods and services) elements are isolated from current transfer payments, it appears again that the U.K. is fairly typical of similar countries. Higher-income countries (with generally lower current expenditure ratios) have tended to devote a greater proportion of such spending to goods and services and a lesser proportion to transfer payments (see Fig. 7.22).

Dire warnings have been voiced by authorities such as Professor Parkinson ('Expenditure rises to meet income'), who in 1961 foresaw the pound as being relatively worthless by 1975, unless public departments worked to strict budgets

[1] Estimate based on material in A. T. Peacock and J. Wiseman, *The Growth of Public Expenditure in the United Kingdom*, 1961; Peacock and Wiseman 'The past and future of public spending', *L.B.R.*, Apr. 1961; *Public Expenditure in 1963–64 and 1967–68*, Cmd 2235, 1963.

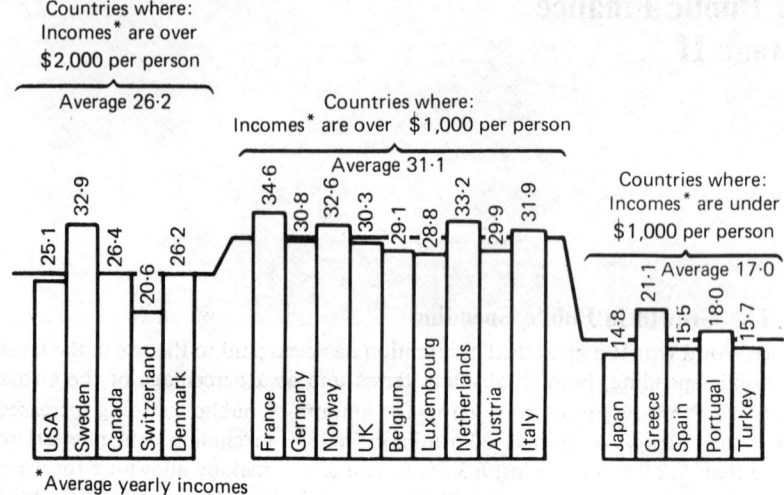

Fig. 7.21. *Current public expenditure as a percentage of G.N.P., 1967: an international comparison*
(Source: *B.B.R.*, Feb. 1968)

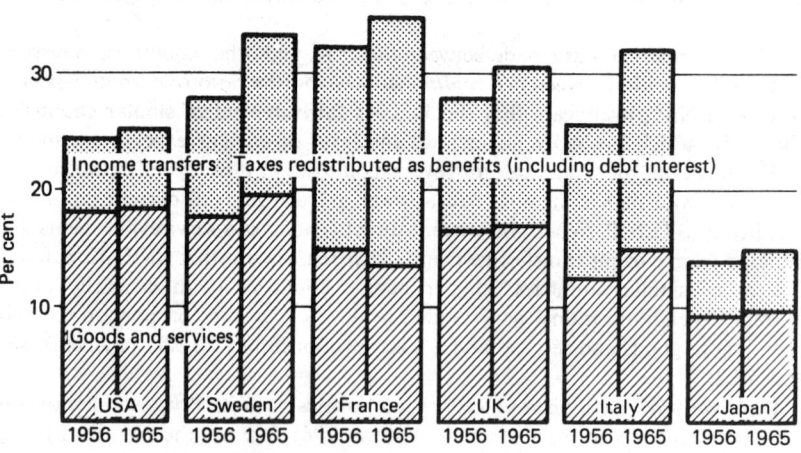

Fig. 7.22. *Current expenditure and the direct claim on resources as a percentage of G.N.P., 1967: an international comparison*
(Source: *B.B.R.*, Feb. 1968)

and total public expenditure was held down to 20% or less of the Gross National Product.[1]

The process of parliamentary scrutiny of public expenditure was intensified by the creation, in January 1971, of the Public Expenditure Survey Committee (P.E.S.C.). This body replaced the former Estimates Committee and had sub-committees representing all the major spending departments and covering all the major areas of expenditure policy.[2]

An important area in which the authorities have the opportunity to economise is that of public purchasing. In 1968 the Institute of Purchasing and Supply criticised a 1967 Government White Paper[3] on *Public Purchasing and Industrial Efficiency* as paying lip service to the possibility of the public sector's being able to use its bargaining power to promote industrial efficiency and competitiveness: little indication was given as to how this power might be exercised. The Institute criticised the Government's naïve purchasing policy and its failure to adopt even the simpler techniques of stock control, cost effectiveness, etc.[4] The scope for rationalisation and economies may be seen from Fig. 7.23, which illustrates the main classes of goods and services accounted for by central government net current expenditure alone. These amounted to £2,276 million in 1969, excluding the wages, salaries, S.E.T., National Insurance contributions, etc., of direct employees: they accounted for four-fifths of total public expenditure in this category, $17\frac{1}{2}$% of all central government current expenditure and 4·1% of all U.K. final expenditure on goods and services. For 1970 the total was £2,379 million, 16·7% and 3·9%, respectively). By 1970 it was claimed that the purchasing divisions of central government departments, which had been advised by experts from private sector distributive firms, had undertaken drastic programmes of product rationalisation, centralised purchasing, bulk purchase economies, and computerised stock control.[5] In April 1972 the Joint Advisory Committee on Local Authority Purchasing, set up at the request of the Government eighteen months previously, reported to the effect that the failure of local authorities to rationalise their purchasing methods represented substantial penalties, paid by ratepayers.[6]

In July 1961 was published the report of the Plowden Committee on the Control of Public Expenditure.[7] It called for regular surveys of public expenditure as a whole for a period of years ahead, balanced against available resources, so that the Government could cease to confine financial policy to the annual budget and take a longer view.

In December 1963 the Government issued the first such forward estimate in the White Paper *Public Expenditure in 1963–64 and 1967–68* (Cmd 2235). According to this survey, public expenditure was analysed into functional blocks (omitting debt interest, because of uncertainty in its calculation resulting from future borrowing, taxation and interest rates), and it was estimated that

[1] See *D.T.*, 21 Aug. 1961 and 25 May 1962, and views of Colin Clark, reported in *Stat.*, 10 July 1964, p. 86.
[2] See 'Control of public expenditure', *E.P.R.*, 31, Sept. 1972; 'First fruits of a democratic innovation', *F.T.*, 26 Nov. 1971.
[3] Cmnd 3291.
[4] '"Naïve" purchasing', *D.T.*, 13 Feb. 1968.
[5] 'Whitehall's buying policy brought up-to-date', *F.T.*, 29 Jan. 1970.
[6] 'Bulk buying could save £10 m.', *D.T.*, 3 April 1972.
[7] Cmnd 1432.

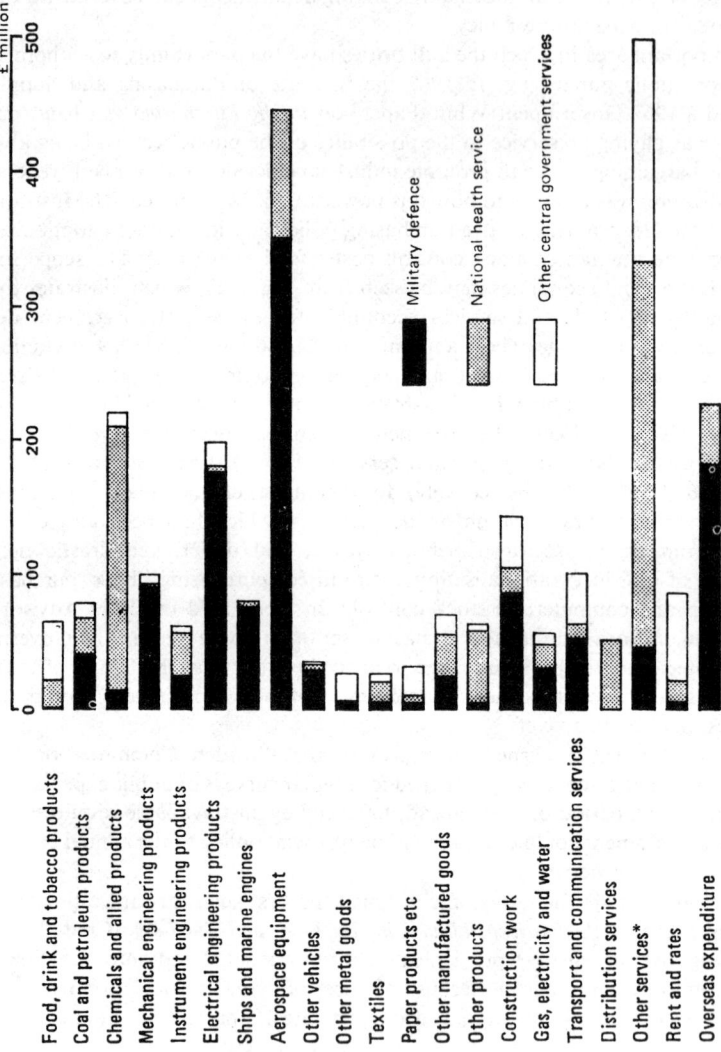

Fig. 7.23. *Commodity analysis of central government net current expenditure on goods and services in 1969* (Source: *E.P.R.*, 21, Nov. 1971)

*includes insurance, banking, finance, business services, professional and scientific services and miscellaneous services during the four-year period expenditure would rise by £1,915 million (17½%) or 4·1% per annum, as compared with a planned growth in the G.N.P. of 4% per annum. 'It is unlikely', the White Paper records, 'that a development of public expenditure on the scale implied will leave much scope for a reduction in the burden of taxation.'[1]

Stimulated by the Plowden report and the subsequent need to plan effectively for several years ahead, Government departments – starting with the Ministry of Defence in 1964 – have developed planning and review procedures for public expenditure projects, such as the 'planning, programming, budgeting' (PBB) system.[2] In January 1971 the Prime Minister announced the introduction of a modified procedure for planning and monitoring public expenditure, following the recommendations of a team of advisers from private enterprise firms. This was PAR ('programme analysis and review')[3] which involves analytical studies of individual programmes, selected annually, with emphasis on objectives, on costs and returns, and on alternative ways of achieving objectives.

Research by A. T. Peacock and J. Wiseman,[4] published in 1961, has thrown much light on the reasons for the rise in public spending during the twentieth century and on the stages in which it has grown. They found that during this period public expenditure reached successively higher peaks (absolutely and as percentages of G.N.P.) during World Wars I and II, which in both cases were followed by peacetime levels of expenditure which were permanently higher than before the wars (see Fig. 7.24).

Peacock and Wiseman noted certain permanent factors and other once for all influences which seem to have caused this growth in public spending. The permanent factors include the growth in population and the increasing complexity or urban society, requiring increasing public involvement; rising money incomes, of which progressive taxation takes an increasing share; rising real incomes, which make this increasing share appear less onerous to the community; the rising level of employment, which has involved State expenditure on public works and other measures to increase the level of activity. However, it appears that the main, decisive influences have been the two war periods, during which public spending rose sharply, and which had a lasting effect in conditioning the community to higher levels of taxation and greater State involvement in social service expenditure. Here, the main impetus has not been defence expenditure, which declined after each war: nor was it ancillary postwar costs, such as war damage compensation, pensions, etc.: nor was it the burden of national debt interest, which has in fact become relatively less important. The main factor has been the permanent increase in social service expenditure, pushed to successively higher levels during and after each war, and made acceptable to the community by reason of massive social disturbance and the rousing of social unity and the social conscience.

The rise in social service costs has been reflected in the doubling of social services expenditure in eight years, from about £3·5 billion in 1960/61 to about £7·6 billion in 1968/69.[5] The December 1972 White Paper forecasts for 1966/77

---

1 Par. 40.
2 For further details see 'Planning, programming, budgeting', *E.P.R.*, 6, Aug. 1970; 'PBB applied', *E.P.R.*, 8, Oct. 1970.
3 See 'Control of public expenditure', *loc. cit.*, p. 2.   4 *Op. cit.*
5 See *D.T.*, 11 June 1969. For comment on a similar trend in E.E.C. countries, over the period 1962–71, see *F.T.*, 23 Jan. 1973.

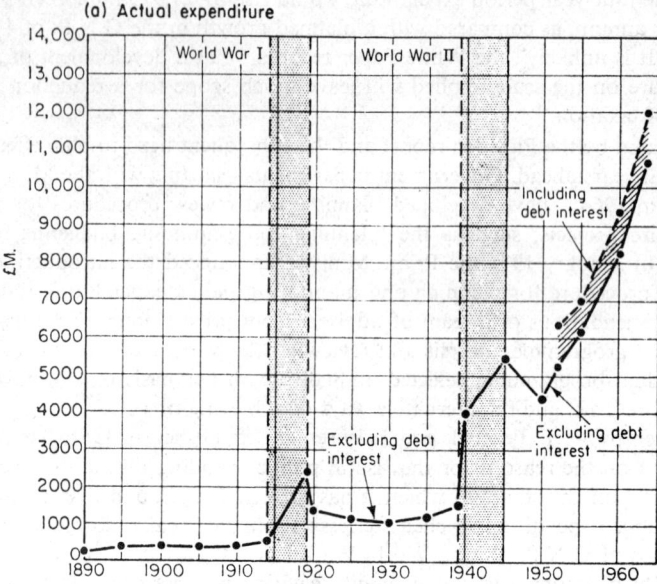

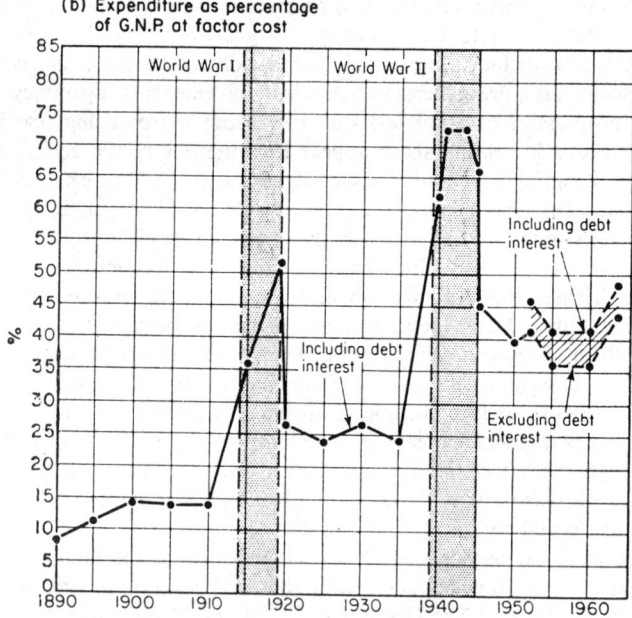

Fig. 7.24. *Public expenditure, 1890–1963/64*
(Source: material in A. T. Peacock and J. Wiseman, *The
Growth of Public Expenditure in the United Kingdom*, 1961,
Chart I, pp. 43 and 166; and *Public Expenditure in 1963–
64 and 1967–68*, H.M.S.O.)

projected the figure for the next eight years to about £13 billion, at 1972/73 prices and allowing for relative price adjustments between various types of expenditure.[1] The *health* and *social security* element in social services public expenditure is influenced by the fact that in the U.K. a far higher proportion of the cost is borne by the Government, *via* general taxation, than is the case in most other E.E.C. countries[2] (see Fig. 7.25). It is of interest that the graduated State pension scheme, announced in November 1971 to come into force in April 1975, was likely to result in an elimination of the National Insurance Fund deficit by 1980/81. On the basis of constant earnings at October 1972 levels the Fund was likely to achieve a surplus of about £500 million by 2005–06.[3]

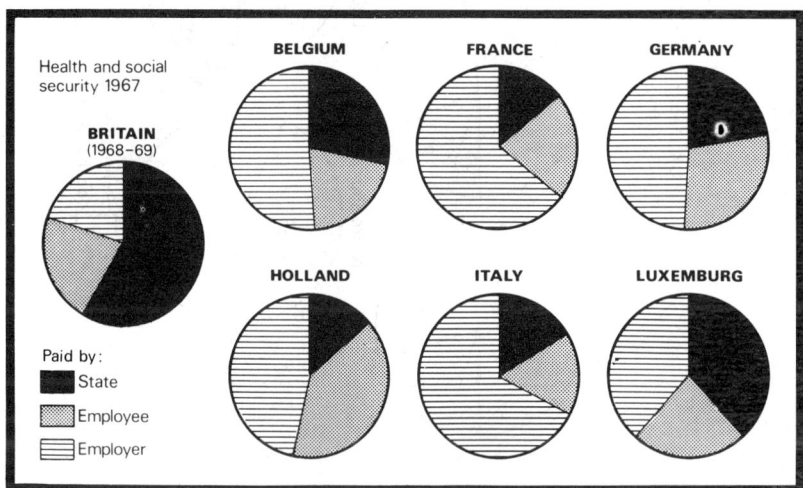

Fig. 7.25. *The financing of health and social security: an international comparison* (Source: *Econ.*, 3 July 1971, p. 44)

Housing has constituted another important growth area in welfare-type public expenditure in recent years. 'Environmental services' expenditure on housing expanded from £494·6 million in 1960/61 to £1,105·3 million in 1968/69: the December 1972 forecasts to 1976/77, at 1972/73 prices, envisaged a figure of £1,241 million. While the proportion of all dwellings in Great Britain which were rented from local authorities rose from 18·0% in 1950 to 30·7% in 1971, the proportion of owner-occupied dwellings rose from 29·5% to 50·1% (see Fig. 7.26). The White Paper envisaged further encouragement of private sector building, encouragement of the sale of council houses and the improvement of older houses to modern standards, rather than a further growth in expenditure on expanding the council house sector.[4]

From 1950 to 1972 expenditure on *education* more than doubled, in real terms, as the population increased and as facilities improved. Total spending on the social services increased from 35% of all public expenditure in 1950 to about 42% in

---

[1] See *Public Expenditure to 1976–77*, Cmnd 5178, Dec. 1972.
[2] See 'Social security', *F.B.E.*, 6, May 1971.
[3] For details and chart, see *Econ.*, 11 Nov. 1972, pp. 72–3.
[4] See Cmnd 5178, p. 54.

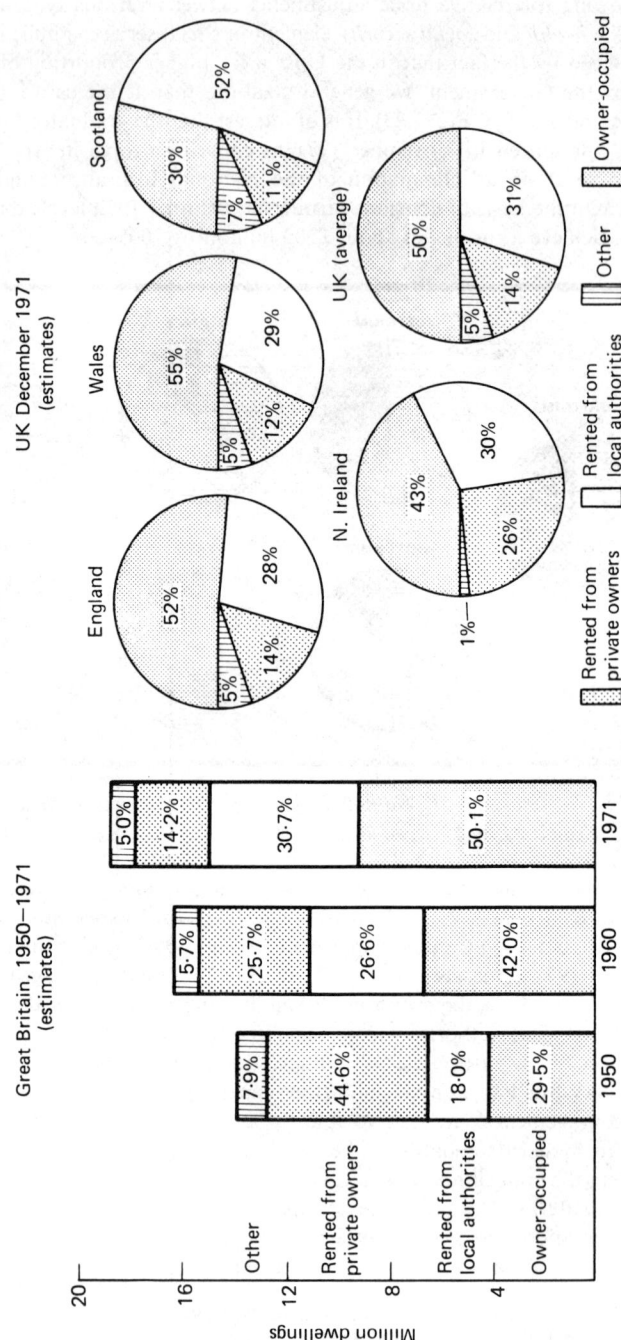

Fig. 7.26. *Ownership of dwellings, 1950 to 1971*
(Source: *E.P.R.*, 27, May 1972)

1970: as many of these services are partly administered by local authorities, the share of the local authorities in total expenditure rose from 21 % in 1950 to 30 % in 1970.

Expenditure on *commerce and industry* increased from 9 % of the total in 1950 to 12 % in 1970, influenced by regional policy incentives, grants and subsidies and by research aid and other industrial services.

Nationalised industry capital investment expanded until the late 1960s, whilst spending on *defence and external relations* was gradually cut back to 13 % of the total in 1970, as compared with 20 % in 1950.[1]

In December 1969 the first of a new series of annual White Papers appeared, representing public expenditure programme estimates for the ensuing five-year period.[2] Two innovations were the estimation of the effect of public sector direct demand for goods and services and an estimation of what is called the 'relative price effect'. This entails an adjustment of constant price estimates (i.e. in 'volume' terms) to take account of changing relative costs, due to the presence in some expenditure programmes of cost elements which rise faster or slower than the general price index. The aim is to present 'volume' estimates in relative 'cost' terms.[3] Criticisms have been levelled at this method of expenditure projections,[4] *viz.*, that projections of changes in prices and tax rates, to which the projected financing of expenditure must be linked, are not shown; that comparability with other available statistics is made more confusing by the introduction of new sources of non-comparability – such as the 'relative price effect' calculations in constant price tables; that public expenditure and taxation plans should really be integrated with plans for the economy as a whole; that the Plowden Committee's call for the presentation of alternative uses of national resources, to permit the public to take a balanced view, was not fulfilled by such expenditure projections.

The projections to 1973–74 envisaged an average annual percentage increase (at 1969 prices) of 3 %, with reductions in Defence and External Relations and in Nationalised Industries' capital expenditure. The two White Papers of October 1970 and January 1971[5] envisaged an average annual increase (at 1970/71 prices) of 2·6 % by 1974/75, with an average annual *reduction* of $6\frac{1}{2}$ % in Commerce and Industry expenditure and of about $3\frac{1}{2}$ % in Debt interest: Nationalised Industries' capital expenditure was planned to increase – in contrast to the projections made in the previous year – particularly in telecommunications and electricity. The third annual forward projection to 1975/76,[6] published in November 1971, forecast a 2·7 % average annual increase, at 1971/72 prices. Some of the major changes were further reductions in Commerce and Industry (annual average reduction about $9\frac{1}{2}$ %), due to the anticipated rundowns in investment grants, regional employment premiums and finance for the Concorde aircraft project; an increase in the growth of Defence and External Relations expenditure, reflecting estimated

[1] For further comments, see W. G. Shepherd, 'Alternatives for public expenditure', in R. E. Caves, ed., *Britain's Economic Prospects*, 1968; 'Public spending', *T.B.B.E.*, 4, Nov. 1971; 'Public expenditure', *B.B.R.*, Feb. 1970; 'Public expenditure', *E.P.R.*, 1, Jan. 1970.
[2] *Public Expenditure 1968–69 to 1973–74*, Cmnd 4234.
[3] For further details, see *Public Expenditure White Papers: Handbook on Methodology*, 1972, pp. 23–5.
[4] T. S. Barker and J. R. C. Lecomber, 'Public expenditure and the public', *M. & W.S.R.*, Autumn 1970; 'Public spending and your tax bill', *F.T.*, 25 Jan. 1973.
[5] Cmnd 4515 and Cmnd 4578, respectively.
[6] *Public Expenditure to 1975–76*, Cmnd 4829.

Table 7.15 *Public expenditure: 1972–73 and 1976–77*

	£ million at 1972–73 outturn prices (including the relative price effect)		
	1972–73	1976–77	Average annual growth rate per cent
Defence and external relations:			
1. Defence Budget	3,003	3,304	2·4
2. Other military defence	61	98	12·6
3. Overseas aid	275	324	4·2
4. EEC and other overseas services	205	362	1·2
Commerce and industry:			
5. Agriculture, fisheries and forestry	582	479	−4·7
6. Research Councils, etc.	141	137	−0·7
7. Trade, industry and employment	1,670	1,070	−5·5
Nationalised industries:			
8. Nationalised industries capital expenditure	1,811	2,184	4·8
Environmental services:			
9. Roads	1,013	1,256	5·5
10. Surface transport	287	238	−4·6
11. Housing	1,415	1,241	−3·2
12. Miscellaneous local services	1,257	1,456	3·7
13. Law and order	847	1,079	6·2
14. Arts	41	50	5·1
Social services:			
15. Education and libraries	3,569	4,331	5·0
16. Health and personal social services	2,917	3,525	4·8
17. Social security	5,050	5,325	1·3
Other services:			
18. Financial administration	446	354	−5·6
19. Common services	326	403	5·4
20. Miscellaneous services	101	114	3·1
21. Northern Ireland	711	715	0·1
Total programmes	25,728	28,045	2·5
22. Debt interest	2,350	2,225	−1·4
23. Contingency reserve	—	700	
24. Shortfall	−200	−200	
25. Price adjustments	6	−331	
Total	27,884	30,439	2·5

(Source: *Public Expenditure to 1976–77*, White Paper, Cmnd. 5178, Dec. 1972)

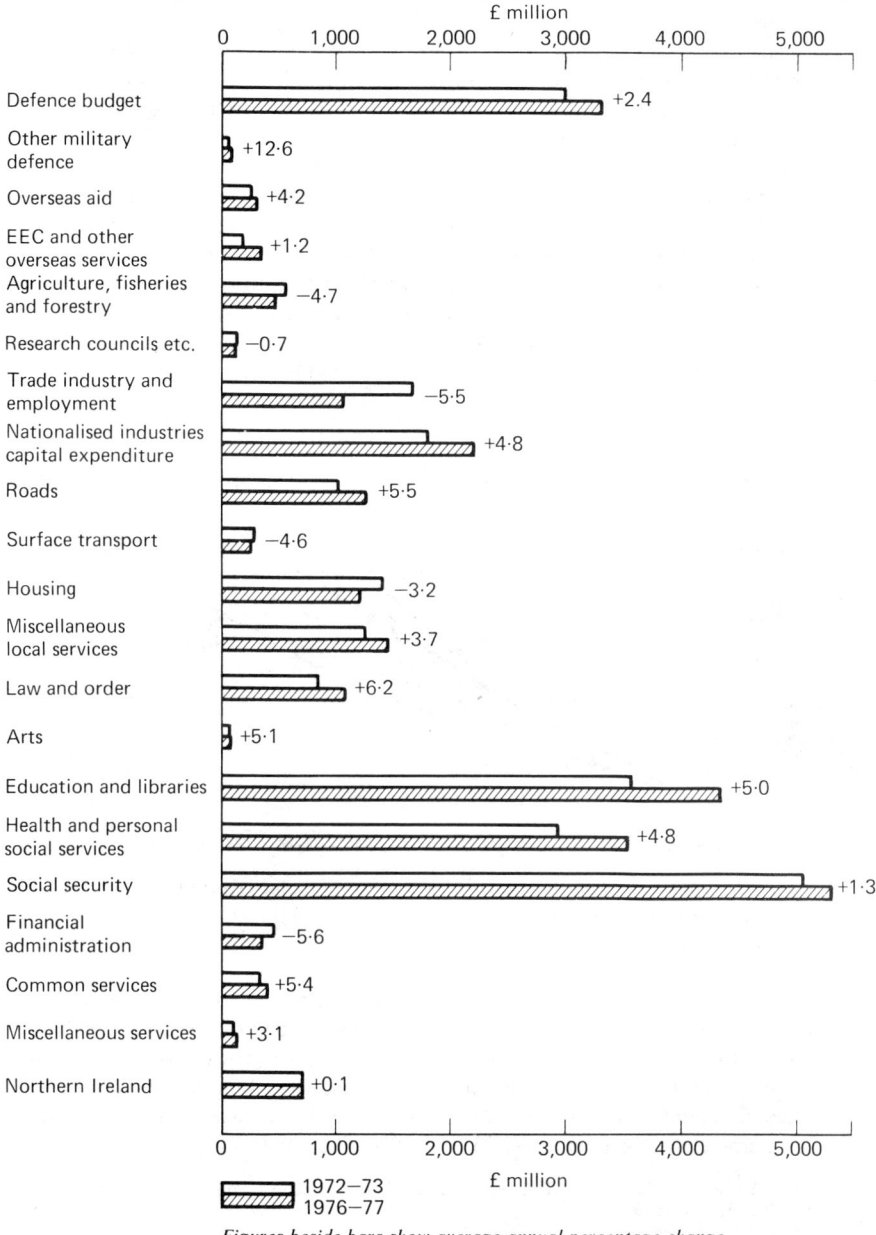

£ million

Defence budget +2.4
Other military defence +12·6
Overseas aid +4·2
EEC and other overseas services +1·2
Agriculture, fisheries and forestry −4·7
Research councils etc. −0·7
Trade industry and employment −5·5
Nationalised industries capital expenditure +4·8
Roads +5·5
Surface transport −4·6
Housing −3·2
Miscellaneous local services +3·7
Law and order +6·2
Arts +5·1
Education and libraries +5·0
Health and personal social services +4·8
Social security +1·3
Financial administration −5·6
Common services +5·4
Miscellaneous services +3·1
Northern Ireland +0·1

☐ 1972–73
▨ 1976–77

£ million

Figures beside bars show average annual percentage change

Fig. 7.27. *The public expenditure programmes: 1972–73 and 1976–77*
(Source: *Public Expenditure to 1976–77*, White Paper, Cmnd 5178, Dec. 1972)

contributions to the E.E.C. budget and related institutions;[6] a reduction in the rate of decline in Debt interest, reflecting the trend towards higher rates of interest.

The five-year projections to 1976/77, published in December 1972,[2] envisaged an annual rate of increase averaging 2·5% at 1972/73 prices, to reach a total of £30,439 million. The direct demand on resources was estimated to rise at an annual rate of between 3·0% and 3·4%. Current priorities reflected much greater assistance to 'Trade, industry and employment' in the Commerce and Industry programme than had been envisaged in earlier years. This was expected to *rise* to a peak in 1973/74 and subsequently decline, reflecting regional and industrial assistance measures in the 1972 Industry Act, related countercyclical developments and additional Government commitments (e.g. to the nationalised industries) resulting from the 1972/73 prices and incomes 'standstill' policy.[3] The general policy expressed in the White Paper was to provide short-term countercyclical measures to stimulate growth, to provide for the modernisation of

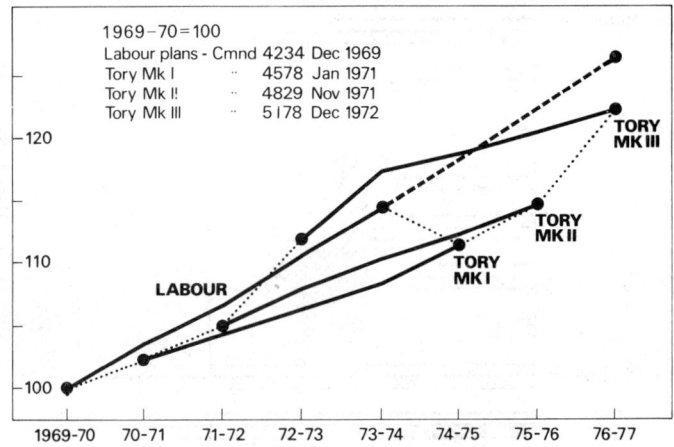

Fig. 7.28. *Public expenditure projections, 1969–77 and realised levels, 1969–73, corrected for price changes*
(Source: *Econ.*, 23 Dec. 1972, p. 54)

industry in the regions, expand employment, improve the environment and improve the social services facilities: these aims entailed the control of inflation, the restriction of public expenditure within a rate of growth which would not prejudice other objectives, and the furtherance of a compassionate and fair society.[4] Table 7.15 and Fig. 7.27 indicate the main changes in the expenditure programmes, as between 1972/73 and 1976/77 at 1972/73 prices, adjusted for

[1] For further details of the E.E.C. Budget, see 'The European Communities' Budget, 1973', *E.P.R.*, 35, Jan. 1973.
[2] *Public Expenditure to 1976–77*, Cmnd 5178.
[3] For further comment, see 'Now for that budget', *Econ.*, 23 Dec. 1972, pp. 53–4 and 'Treasury taking a harder look at public spending', *F.T.*, 13 Nov. 1972. For a graphical breakdown of the allocation of expenditure for the year 1973/74, according to Cmnd 5178 and adjusted for subsequent revisions in the 1973/74 Budget, see 'Public expenditure,' *E.P.R.*, 42, Aug. 1973.
[4] Cmnd 5178, paras 2, 3.

'relative price effects'. It was estimated that U.K. net contributions to the E.E.C., at 1972 prices, would rise to £195 million by 1976/77.[1]

Fig. 7.28 shows the relative projections and realised starting points on the four White Papers since 1969/70, corrected for price changes. The interesting points which emerge are that despite the early attempts to cut back the growth in public expenditure, the realised starting point for 1972/73 was higher than the level projected in 1969/70; the final-year projections, after an initial deceleration, have accelerated; by 1974/75 expenditure was expected to be as high as if the first White Paper's trend had continued; on the basis of past experience, the final-year figure for 1976/77 might prove to be higher than that indicated by the first White Paper's trend projection.

The main purpose of this forward planning has been to enable the Government to balance the physical requirements of the public sector for goods and services against the G.N.P. (or resources available). As regards the fiscal approach to the problem, the raising of finance, it should be noted that if the G.N.P. does not rise fast enough to keep pace with the requirements of the public sector, private consumption would have to be held down either by increased taxation (local and central), increased national insurance contributions, or increased borrowing. If the level of personal savings can be stimulated by the Government to uphold an adequate pace of growth, it would be easier for the Government to borrow (in order to raise revenue and hold down private consumption) and there would be less need to raise the level of taxation. Of course, difficulties would arise from an under-estimation of the future cost of Government policies and/or an over-estimation of the future growth of the G.N.P.[2]

2. The Economic Effects of Taxation

As will be apparent from the foregoing sections, taxes are only one element – albeit an important one – in the package of fiscal measures and policies open to the public sector authorities. It would be admirable if the precise economic effects of any particular tax could be analysed and foreseen, and compared with the various objectives and principles of taxation. Unfortunately, some of these objectives may be found to conflict with others. Also, there may be important practical, political and social, as well as economic effects, which must be balanced out. Furthermore, there is a lack of descriptive, statistical and empirical knowledge about the various effects of taxes in a complex and changing social, political and economic environment.

In December 1970 an independent research body – the Institute for Fiscal Studies – was founded to investigate and consider the various implications of fiscal problems and of suggestions for tax reforms.[3] This had been preceded by numerous private and public studies of taxation and tax reform, notably by the Allen Committee on rates (1965), the Royal Commission on the Taxation of Profits and Incomes (1955) and the Canadian Royal Commission on Taxation (1966).[4]

[1] *Ibid.*, Table 2.4 and *D.T.*, 20 Dec. 1972.
[2] This point was forcefully made by the Second Secretary at the Treasury at a Stamp Memorial Lecture on 1 Dec. 1964 (*D.T.*, 2 Dec. 1964).
[3] See *F.T.*, 17 Dec. 1970.
[4] See R. W. Houghton, ed., *Public finance*, 1970, pp. 46–84 and 142–67.

7. PUBLIC FINANCE [II]

(a) Local rates

In the sense that the ratepayer may have purchased his property, the rate may be considered as a tax on spending. Whether or not it satisfies the equity criterion (i.e. based on ability to pay) depends on whether or not the person with lower income or wealth purchases property with a *correspondingly* lower rateable value than the person with a higher level of income or wealth. Generally, this is not likely to be so, and as the tax is at a standard rate, and no allowances or reliefs are permitted, it may fairly be considered to bear regressively on the less prosperous ratepayers.[1] As a capital tax (on inherited property), it draws no distinction between the income and other wealth of the prosperous and less prosperous ratepayer, and so again may be considered to be regressive. This point was underlined by the report of the Allen Committee (on the impact of rates on different income groups). It found rates to be a regressive form of tax, taking an average of 8% of the lowest incomes, but less than 2% of high incomes.[2]

An important economic effect of this regressive recurrent tax on spending or capital will be to encourage the less prosperous purchasers to opt for lower value property and to oblige many otherwise unprosperous legatees of property to sell, so as to avoid the tax. An increase in the rate poundage will thus tend to reduce the demand for property and to increase its supply on the market – trends which may lower or retard the rise in property prices.

(b) Taxes on personal and company incomes:

1. Redistribution of income. An important economic effect of the progressive system of personal income tax and surtax is that it cannot be avoided (except by the decision not to gain income) and it removes a large proportion of high incomes, so that much of the proceeds may be distributed to the recipients of low incomes as transfer payments in cash or services (e.g. pensions, assistance, welfare foods, defence, etc.). It thus results in important changes in the distribution of personal incomes before and after tax, as was noted in Stage One, Section 5 (c). The effect in 1969 was estimated[3] to have raised the average income of the lowest family income 'quintile' (i.e. the lowest one-fifth) from 35% to 53% of the average income level for all families.

It is of interest to note, however, that the U.K. system of personal income tax tends to be 'proportional' (strictly speaking, 'constant'), except on the lowest and highest income groups, especially when account is taken of the neutralising effects of benefits and expenditure taxes.[4] Furthermore, some incisive studies of the case for 'progressiveness' in the tax system[5] conclude that *technical* arguments, on the grounds of benefit, sacrifice, ability to pay, etc., prove to be weaker than the *general equity* case, based on the reduction of economic inequalities. As Blum and Kalven put it: 'Ultimately a serious interest in progression stems from the fact that a progressive tax is perhaps the cardinal instance of a democratic community struggling with its hardest problem.'[6]

[1] See G. S. A. Wheatcroft, 'Inequity in Britain's tax structure', *L.B.R.*, July 1969, p. 25.
[2] See Prof. A. Peacock, 'Rates: Relief for the retired', *Stat.*, 5 Mar. 1965, pp. 628–9.
[3] See *Brit. O.H.*, 1972, p. 199.
[4] See P.E.P. Broadsheet, *Personal Taxation, Incentive and Taxation Reform*, Jan. 1969 and *F.T.*, 29 Jan. 1969.
[5] See H. C. Simmons, 'The case for progressive taxation', reprinted in Houghton, ed., *op. cit.*; W. J. Blum and H. Kalven, Jr., *The Uneasy Case for Progressive Taxation*, 1953.
[6] *Op. cit.*, p. 104.

2. Disincentive to work. The progressive system of personal taxation, with its successively higher marginal rates of tax, is often considered to act as a deterrent to work or effort. This disincentive effect has been noticed in the case of coal-mining, for example, where absenteeism was quite high because leisure and sunlight were preferable to unpleasant extra work, the income from which might be taxed at a high and/or rising rate. The disincentive effect might also be felt on overtime in general and on the acceptance of more highly paid work, involving greater strain and responsibility. However, it is by no means a general rule that existing or increased rates of income tax must necessarily act as a disincentive to earn income, so as to avoid the tax. An increase in the general level of tax rates, or the prospect of becoming liable to the next (higher) marginal rate will have two conflicting effects, one of which may outweigh the other, or both of which may cancel out.

Firstly, an increase in the marginal rate of tax on earned income, either through an increase in the general level or through the existing progressive system, will oblige the taxpayer to work harder or longer, in order to achieve a certain level of 'retained' or post-tax income, as he retains less and less of each successive increment of income. This is termed the 'income effect'.

Secondly, as the marginal rate of tax rises, the taxpayer finds that by not working (i.e. by enjoying leisure) he sacrifices less and less retained income. Leisure, in other words, becomes 'cheaper' in relation to retained income, and the taxpayer may tend to work less and have more leisure instead (i.e. substitute leisure for work). This is termed the 'substitution effect'. Both effects work in opposite directions, but the key to the problem of which will be strongest is the 'target' level of retained income which the taxpayer finds 'necessary', either to keep body and soul together, or to meet his financial (e.g. H.P.) commitments, or to maintain a conventional standard of living. If his retained income is below this level, an increase in the tax rate applicable to extra income will lead to more work ('income effect' stronger than 'substitution effect'): if he has already passed the 'necessary' level of retained income, he will work less ('substitution effect' stronger than 'income effect'), as shown in Fig. 7.29.[1]

Empirical findings on the disincentive effects of progressive income taxation on work differ widely.[2] Most point to little significant disincentive effect on the (limited) groups of persons investigated, as in the 1966 U.S. study by R. Barlow *et al.* on higher income groups; the 1962 U.S. survey of wage earners, by J. N. Morgan *et al.*; the 1951 U.S. study of executives by T. H. Sanders; the 1956 study of solicitors and accountants in Great Britain by G. Break; the 1955 study of workers in Great Britain by the Royal Commission on the Taxation of Profits and Incomes, which found that income taxation affected only about 20%, equally divided between those who tended to work less and those who tended to work harder. On the other hand, the Royal Commission found that there was a stronger tax disincentive on those paying a marginal rate of 70% than on those at lower rates; Sanders found that some executives postponed retirement (whereas the Barlow *et al.* study did not).

[1] Compare with comments made by D. Walker, 'Direct *v* indirect taxes', reprinted in Houghton, ed., *Public Finance*, p. 356; G. S. A. Wheatcroft, 'A taxation policy for growth', in M. H. Cadman, ed., *Taxation Economics*, 1969, p. 91; R. A. Musgrave, *The Theory of Public Finance* (International Student Edition), 1959, p. 244; P. R. Kaim-Caudle, 'Selectivity and the social services', *L.B.R.*, April 1969, p. 33.
[2] See J. F. Due, *Government Finance: economics of the public sector*, 4th edn., 1968, pp. 176–8; A. R. Prest, *Public Finance in Theory and Practice*, 4th edn., 1970, pp. 277–82.

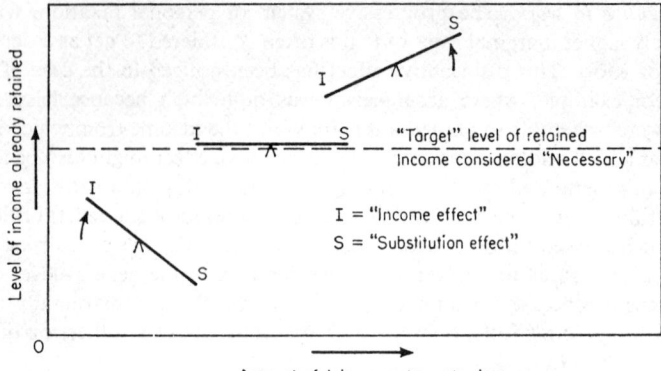

Fig. 7.29. *Income tax and the incentive to work: 'Income effect' and 'Substitution effect'*

A. J. Merrett's 1967 study[1] of British executive remuneration and saving approached the problem from a different angle: not questioning whether executives would *volunteer* to work harder with less taxation, but rather whether more effective results (by comparison with other countries) are *obtainable* from executive talent. He found that directors with inherited wealth had a privileged position in respect of wealth, hours worked and pre-tax remuneration; that the tax system was a contributory factor to the lack of management incentive; that work incentives were most deficient in the middle management income range; that the latter factor, especially when U.S. executive remuneration comparisons were made, suggested a conservative approach by U.K. companies to executive pay, from which numerous problems flowed. He suggested a trimodal approach, linked to much higher pre-tax pay, such that:

(a) firms must *require* greater efficiency, to recoup the added cost;

(b) the better-paid managers would be more prepared to accept higher standards of discipline and penalties for failure;

(c) that a higher calibre of executive would be attracted.

Numerous findings have lent subsequent support to Professor Merrett's thesis:

(i) In September 1969 a survey by Associated Industrial Consultants (A.I.C.) on executive remuneration in 1,200 international firms found[2] that British executives were tending to be more highly taxed than their counterparts elsewhere: the U.K. executive with £3,000 gross income (and a wife and two children), for example, retained 77% after personal tax, as compared with 93·8% (France), 91% (Switzerland) and 86% (West Germany).

(ii) The management consultants, Hay-MSL, conducted a survey of executive pay policies in seventy-five of the largest U.K. firms in 1969, covering 150,000 posts. Its general finding was that, because of the high personal tax burden on executives, firms tended to reward key executives with more leisure, rather than with further, taxable remuneration.[3]

---

[1] A. J. Merrett, *Executive Remuneration in the United Kingdom*, 1967; also see 'Brains and the cost of efficiency', *D.T.*, 2 Jan. 1968; 'The real case for incentives', *Econ.*, 2 March 1968. pp. 36–7.

[2] *F.T.*, 15 Sep. 1969.

[3] 'Top executives are losing out', *F.T.*, 3 Oct. 1969.

(iii) A 1970 survey, by A.I.C., of executive salary trends between 1963 and 1969 in Western European countries[1] found that whereas the pre-tax earnings of executives in most comparable countries had risen by 20% to 30% in *real* terms, those of British executives rose by only 4% (see Fig. 7.30).

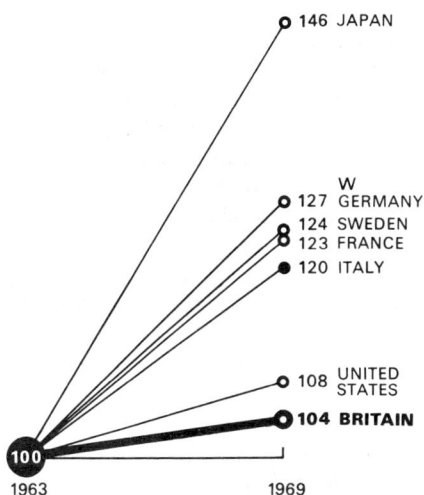

Fig. 7.30. *Pre-tax executive salaries: Real gains (net of cost-of-living rises), 1963–69*
(Source: *Econ.*, 15 Aug. 1970, p. 60)

3. Disincentive to investment, enterprise and risk-taking. Progressive systems of tax on unearned personal income, of tax on company profits (especially where these bear more heavily on distributed profits, as in the case of Corporation Tax, until 1973), and of tax on earned income, in the case of the small firm which does not pay profits tax, may tend to discourage initiative and enterprise – the taking of risks.[2] The rewards for such risk-taking are profits, dividends and interest, and these rewards are taxed progressively. Again, however, the disincentive effect must be considered in relation to the level of retained income *desired* and already *achieved.* There is a conflict between the 'income effect' (encouragement towards greater enterprise) and the 'substitution effect' (discouragement to enterprise and encouragement of security).

A study of profitability in U.S. and U.K. industry by Merrett and Whittaker[3] concluded that, although difficult to quantify, the role of post-tax profitability was of great importance to investment decisions; that official policy should be to support corporate profitability; that a norm equivalent to the pre-Corporation Tax figure would have required a 12·5% level in net-of-Corporation Tax profitability, as compared with the 1965 preliminary level of 10·0%. In contrast, U.S.

[1] 'The boss is falling well behind', *Econ.*, 15 Aug. 1970, p. 60.
[2] Compare with comments by Due, *op. cit.*, pp. 182–5; E. D. Domar and R. A. Musgrave, 'The effects of income taxes on risk taking', in Houghton, ed., *op. cit.*, esp. pp. 376–80; 'Corporation tax: how not to encourage investment', *Econ.*, 19 April 1969, p. 89.
[3] A. J. Merrett and J. Whittaker, 'The profitability of British and American industry', *L.B.R.*, Jan. 1967.

studies in 1949 and 1966 indicated that the financial investment decisions of *individuals* in higher income groups were little affected by U.S. taxes, whereas two 1967 U.S. studies indicated that in 1959 and 1962 business investment by *companies* was substantially increased when the rates of depreciation allowances were accelerated – this having the effect of relieving the company income tax burden.[1]

Two related topics of interest are firstly, the possibility that part of the burden of company profits taxes might be 'shifted' on to the employee or the consumer. A 1964 study of this problem concluded[2] that the general impression was of the probability, in the U.S., of a substantial amount of shifting, even in the short run, but that no definite conclusion was possible. A significant implication would be that the disincentive effect on investment and risk-taking might be reduced if shifting occurs. Secondly, opinion for several years has been divided over the question of equal or unequal tax rates on distributed profits: those in favour of a discriminatory burden on dividends – as with the Corporation Tax system from 1965 to 1973 – consider that this discourages high dividend distribution and encourages a higher proportion of retentions, which may be available for plough-back investment, whilst others consider that this provides an excuse for inefficient management, when making low dividend distributions, that a larger proportion of profits should be distributed and that the capital market should monitor company efficiency and channel investment funds to the most efficient, highest-profit/dividend firms. Crawford[3] maintains that, even in the pre-1965 years of non-discrimination and high dividend distribution, firms tended to be almost 75% self-financing; that the initial Corporation Tax system plus personal tax on dividends might induce a higher percentage of retained profits, but that, except for firms in declining industries or for badly managed firms – for which the best remedy would be takeover – tax policy should encourage profit retentions.

4. Disincentive to saving and incentive to spending. Unearned income is considered by some authorities to be not simply another form of income, but rather a reflection of the unequal distribution of capital or wealth – resulting in income accruing from the possession of wealth: on these terms it has been suggested that unearned income should be taxed more heavily than earned income.[4] Others, however,[5] stress the differences between the inequalities in income and wealth and the difficulties in establishing criteria for assessing these differences.

Most authorities tend to the view[6] that the higher level of personal and company taxation, the lower will be retained income and the possibility of saving (or accumulating reserves). This effect is increased by the fact that tax is levied on personal unearned incomes resulting from past saving, thus encouraging individuals to spend and enjoy their incomes immediately. Furthermore, the

---

[1] See Due, *op. cit.*, pp. 190–1.
[2] M. Krzyzaniak and R. A. Musgrave, 'The shifting of the Corporation Income Tax', in Houghton, ed., *op. cit.*, esp. pp. 429–30, 450–51; also see Prest, *op. cit.*, pp. 354–5.
[3] M. Crawford, 'The 1965 reforms in the British tax system', *M. & W.S.R.*, Winter 1965; also see comments by Prest, *op. cit.*, pp. 356–61.
[4] See G. S. A. Wheatcroft, 'Inequity in Britain's tax structure', *loc. cit.*, pp. 19–20.
[5] For example, see J. B. Bracewell-Milnes, 'Saving and inequality', *M. & W.S.R.*, Autumn 1969, esp. pp. 77–8.
[6] *Ibid.*, esp. p. 75; G. S. A. Wheatcroft, 'A taxation policy for growth', in Cadman, ed., *op. cit.*, pp. 89, 92–4; V. Tanzi, J. B. Bracewell-Milnes and D. R. Myddleton, *Taxation: a radical approach*, 1970.

redistribution of the National Income resulting from progressive personal and company taxes affects the proportion of the National Income which may be saved. This is because the proportion of a person's income which is saved tends to be higher on large than on small incomes. If a large part of the National Income were concentrated (and retained) in the hands of a prosperous minority, the proportion saved would probably be greater than if these large incomes were decimated and distributed thinly to the vast majority. On the other hand, this effect would be more pronounced in a poor, underdeveloped country (where the general level of existing incomes is low) than in a wealthy developed country, where standards of living and incomes are higher.

5. *Disincentive to efficiency.* The progressive tax on the small businessman's income (or profits) and the high proportional tax on company profits may very well discourage efficiency in the reduction of expenses. This is because any given expense which reduces profits only involves the ultimate sacrifice of the amount of such profit that would be *retained* after tax. The true cost of an expense such as a £10 business lunch to the businessman paying surtax at an overall rate of 90p in the pound would only be £1 ($10 \times 10p$ retained): to the company paying Corporation Tax at the rate of 50p in the pound, the true cost in 'sacrificed post-tax profit' would be £5 ($10 \times 50p$ retained). This has led in the past to much criticism of lavish 'expense-account' business spending and of the 'golden hand-shakes' (lavish severance payments) to retiring or deposed executives.

6. *Inflationary consequences.* During periods of high economic activity and high pressure of demand, an increase in personal and/or company taxation might aggravate the inflationary pressure. Individuals, especially those in short supply, might press for higher wages and salaries: companies might try to pass the tax on in higher prices. In both cases the incidence of the tax might be 'shifted', on to employers and consumers, respectively.[1]

Another consequence of inflation on personal income tax and surtax is that, due to 'fiscal drag', as money incomes rise, people automatically become liable to higher marginal rates of tax, thus paying a higher proportion of their incomes. If incomes have only risen in money and not in real terms, this will involve unnecessary hardship. For this reason existing marginal rates are, from time to time, 'pushed on' or applied to higher levels of income.

(c) Negative (reverse) income taxes and selective benefits:

1. 'Selectivity' and 'universality' in benefits: the 'poverty trap'
There has been a great deal of debate in recent years as to the pros and cons of 'selective' and 'universalist' benefits. Some protagonists conclude that *selectivity* of individuals (e.g. by 'means testing') or of groups (e.g. widows, the disabled, parents of large families, etc.) humiliates the individual, offends social conscience and results in incomplete 'take-up' (i.e. unwillingness by some eligible beneficiaries to assert their rights). Others believe that *universality* of benefits – where the benefit or service is available to all, regardless of whether or not the cost is 'clawed back' from the recipient in the form of a price or in taxation – is more

---

[1] Krzyzaniak and Musgrave, *op. cit.*; Prest, *op. cit.*, pp. 354–5.

compassionate, more equitable and less costly, and constitutes less disincentive to work and earn than does selectivity.[1]

Where a benefit is to any extent selective, in the sense of being related to the income level of the recipient, there is likely to be a disincentive effect on the willingness to work. Kaim-Caudle estimated that in 1969 a married man with three children, living in a house with a £2·75p weekly rent and a £61·50 annual rate, would lose £2·68p of a £3 increase in income (i.e. about 90p in the pound) from £15 to £18 weekly, due to reduced rent rebate, loss of free school meals and liability to social insurance contributions.[2] A 1972 analysis of the impact of the six most important selective benefit schemes operating in the U.K. disclosed a great deal of overlap in these schemes and also disclosed a number of 'poverty traps'.[3] A 'poverty trap' or 'poverty surtax' refers to the situation in which a low wage-earner, receiving an *increase in earnings*, actually suffers a *loss in benefits*, as in the example cited above. If this loss exceeds the rise in earnings and leads to a fall in disposable income, the marginal effective rate of tax he experiences would exceed 100% and would act as a deterrent to the wage-earner's willingness to work harder and to earn more – which may or may not be neutralised by feelings of pride and self-respect and by the presence of social conventions to earn more. The 1972 survey found anomalies even with a £1 *increase* in family allowances: it might only shift, and in some cases deepen, the poverty traps and one case even resulted in such a potential loss in other benefits that disposable income could have *fallen* by £1·02p.

2. 'Negative income tax', the 'poverty gap' and disincentives to work and saving. One important suggestion – usually attributed first to Professor Milton Friedman in 1962, since discussed and refined by others and accepted in principle by the U.K. Government in 1972 – for removing some of the indignities, complexities and administrative costs of many selective benefits and for introducing an element of universality and equity, is the 'negative' or 'reverse' income tax (R.I.T.), involving tax credits.

Most R.I.T. schemes relate to the concept of a 'poverty line' or level of disposable post-tax income, considered to be the minimal requirement for various categories of citizen (e.g. married man with wife and two children under eleven years of age). A progressive income tax system would incorporate a 'threshold' level of income, below which no tax would be paid. The threshold may or may not be at the poverty line. Assuming that it is at the poverty line, persons below the threshold level of income would, in the *absence* of benefits, experience the full extent of the 'poverty gap' – a deficiency in their disposable incomes. In Fig. 7.31(*a*) the heavy line indicates a zero tax rate on incomes below the 'poverty' level and a tax rate of $33\frac{1}{3}\%$ on additional income above that level: it represents the levels of post-tax *disposable* income, corresponding to various levels of pre-

---

[1] For fuller discussion of these concepts and their implications, see D. Lees, 'Poor families and fiscal reform', *L.B.R.*, Oct. 1967, esp. pp. 9–11; O. Eckstein, *Public Finance*, 2nd edn., 1967, p. 74; R. H. Haveman, *The Economics of the Public Sector*, 1970, pp. 199–200; P. R. Kaim-Caudle, 'Selectivity and the social services', *L.B.R.*, April 1969, pp. 30–41; A. B. Atkinson, *Poverty in Britain and the Reform of Social Security*, 1969, pp. 22, 193; A. Seldon, 'Thaw in the Welfare State', *L.B.R.*, July 1972, pp. 20–5; 'Poverty: what has been done?', *Econ.*, 19 Dec. 1970, pp. 62–3; A. B. Atkinson, 'Policies for poverty', *L.B.R.*, April 1971.
[2] Kaim-Caudle, *op. cit.*, p. 41.
[3] 'Uncovering the traps', *Econ.*, 30 Sept. 1972, p. 26; 'Selectivity: problems for Parliament', *Econ.*, 14 Oct. 1972, p. 28; 'Ending poverty surtax', *Econ.*, 30 Sept. 1972, p. 89.

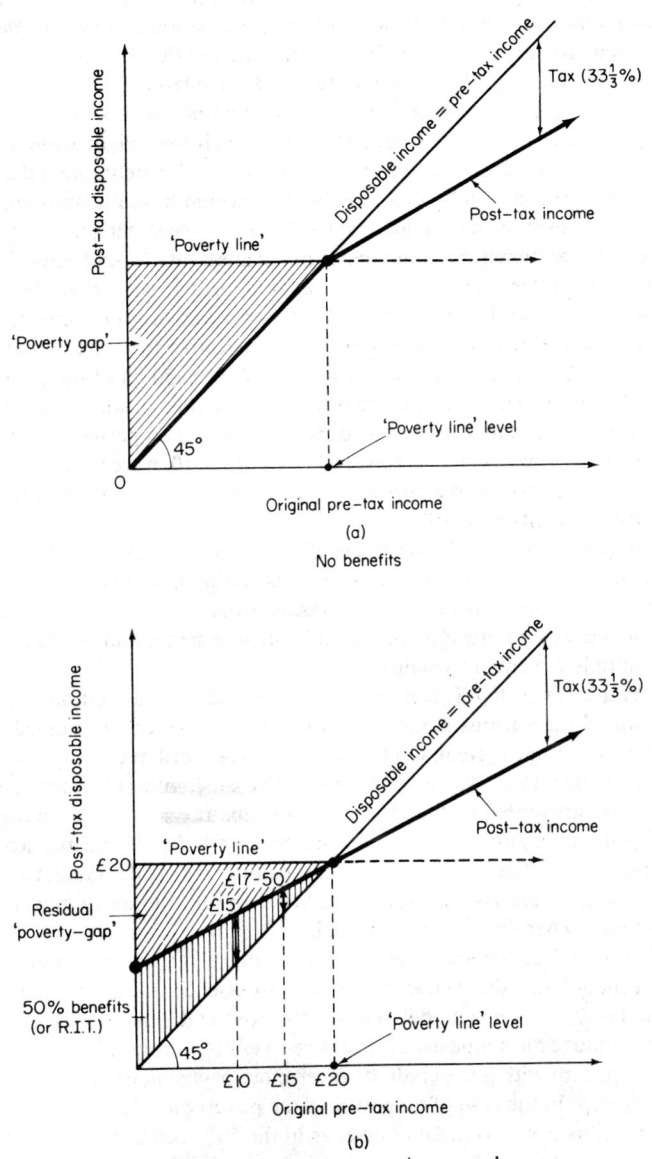

Fig. 7.31. *'Poverty line', 'poverty gap' and benefits (or Friedman-type proportional R.I.T.)*

tax income. The 45° line indicates equality of pre-tax and disposable income levels. In practice, it is most unlikely that an individual or family would be permitted to remain at a near-zero level of income: various forms of selective or universal benefits might be available which, allied with the zero tax rate, raise disposable income *above* the original pre-tax income level.

One of the major problems involved in 'topping up' low incomes to bridge the poverty gap is the possible disincentive effect which this might have, regarding willingness to work harder or longer and earn more. If benefits were designed to eliminate the gap completely, then the recipient would have a disposable income at poverty line level, whatever income he earned between zero and poverty line level. It is often assumed that human nature, laziness, etc. would outweigh pride, self-respect and other incentives to be self-supporting, such that the recipient would prefer leisure and maximum benefits to work and 'top-up' benefits. A fairly typical suggestion for reducing this alleged disincentive to effort is that benefits should be scaled so as to bridge a *proportion only* (e.g. 50%) of the poverty gap. Thus, as shown in Fig. 7.31(*b*), if the poverty line were considered to be £20 per week for a married man with wife and two children, then persons in that group earning £10 (pre-tax) would receive 50% of the £10 poverty gap as top-up benefits, giving a disposable income of £15 weekly. Pre-tax earnings of £15 would attract benefits of £2·50.

Other major problems relating to benefits are such as were referred to in subsection 1, including the humiliation of means testing and incomplete 'take-up', in the case of selective benefits; unnecessary expense in the case of universal benefits; and chaos, confusion and administrative expense and inefficiency in the case of multiple benefits of whatever type.

The negative tax or R.I.T. is generally understood to be a method of replacing some or all of the various benefits with tax credits, which are unified into the personal 'positive' tax system. On the basis of various criteria credits (or 'pluses') – some of which may be flat-rate and universalist, others means-tested and selective – are attributed to the individual. Income tax is assessed on *all* income and not just on income above a zero-rated threshold. If the tax assessment *exceeds* the credits, the individual *pays* a 'positive' tax: if the credits exceed the tax assessment, he *receives* a 'negative' or reverse income tax. A poverty line is borne in mind, when credits are designed.

Two major R.I.T. schemes, against which others may be compared, are the Friedman model and the Theobald model.[1] In essence, the Friedman model is similar to the 50% benefits model, referred to above and illustrated in Fig. 7.31(*b*). In order to reduce the supposed disincentive to effort, earnings *below* the poverty line are topped up with a tax credit or reverse tax payment, equivalent to 50% of the poverty gap. In the case of taxpayers *at* the poverty line level, their tax assessment and credits cancel out. Of course, as in the 50% benefits case, the taxpayer experiences a 50% *cut* in benefit or credit for every dollar or pound he earns: this is sometimes held to constitute a 50% rate of tax and to be itself a disincentive, but it must be noted that most individuals involved will be below their 'target' level of income and may thus be expected to prefer income to leisure. It should be noted that the 50% tax on effort is less disincentive than the sometimes 100% 'poverty surtax' inherent in some benefits which are reduced in line with income.

[1] For further elaboration, see Haveman, *op. cit.*, pp. 199–206.

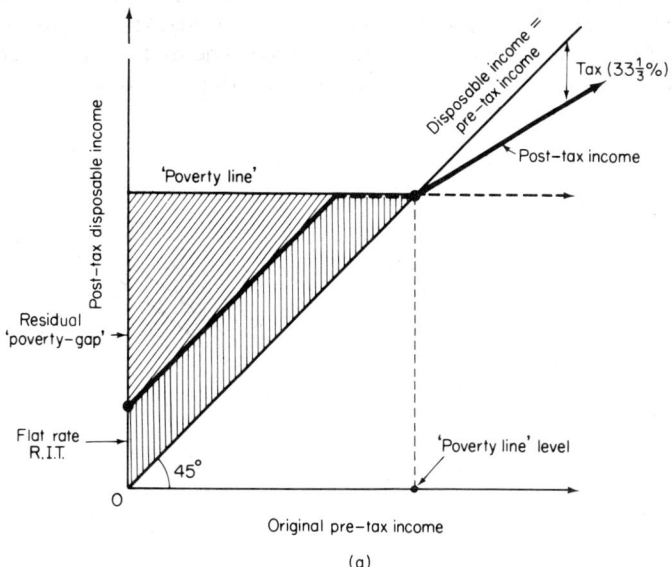

(a)

Flat rate R.I.T. up to poverty line

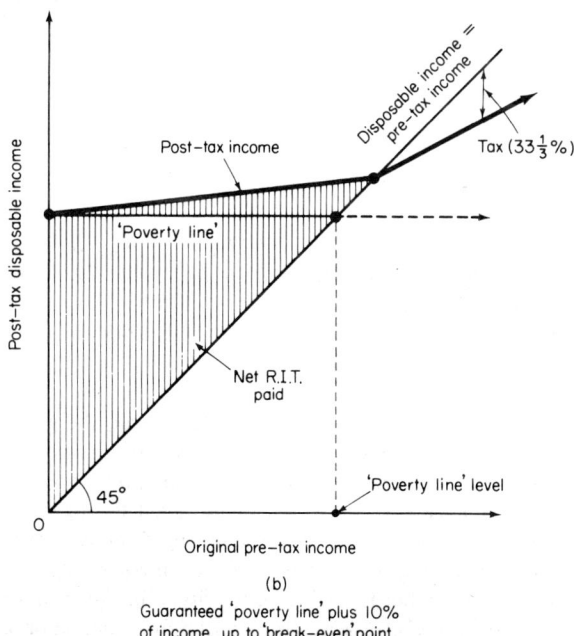

(b)

Guaranteed 'poverty line' plus 10%
of income, up to 'break-even' point

Fig. 7.32. *'Flat rate' (sub-poverty line) R.I.T. and Theobald-type (supra-poverty line) R.I.T.*

Even if 'flat-rate' tax credits of constant amount were given on all incomes below poverty line level, until disposable income reached that level, it would leave a range of pre-tax incomes approaching the poverty line level with a 100% tax rate: see Fig. 7.32(a). Furthermore, a 'progressive' element is retained in the 50%

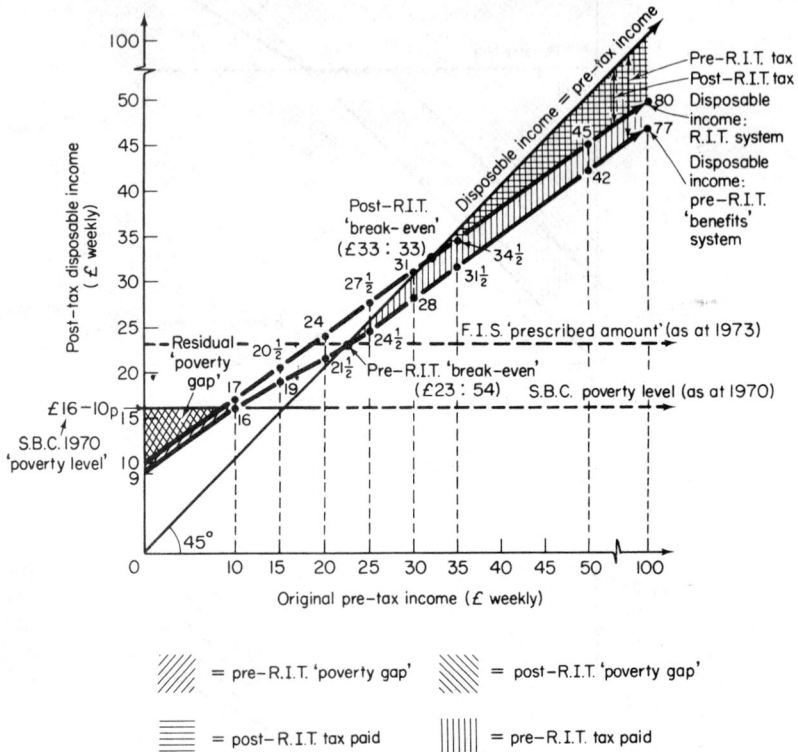

Fig. 7.33. *Pre-R.I.T. benefits (F.A. and F.I.S.) and tax and proposed R.I.T. credits and tax, against S.B.C. 1970 'poverty level' and F.I.S. 1973 'prescribed amount': family with two children under eleven*
(Based on material in *Econ.*, 19 Dec. 1970, pp. 62–3 and *Proposals for a Tax-Credit System*, Cmnd 5116, Oct. 1972.)

system, in the sense that the lower the income level, the greater the R.I.T. received. This seems to be borne out by the New Jersey Experiment, commencing in 1968 in the U.S. The reactions of most of the families involved indicated that there was no evidence that the R.I.T. discouraged the recipients from earning: furthermore, there was no lack of 'take-up' by families entitled to the R.I.T., since the tax credits were primarily based on income rather than on complex means tests, and were thus free of all selectivity, other than that which is inherent in different income levels.[1] A key feature of the Friedman approach is that it does not aim to *eliminate* 'poverty' but rather to *reduce* it by topping up the incomes of the poor and hard-pressed, whilst preserving some incentive to effort. The

[1] A. Seldon, 'Reverse taxes to abolish poverty', *D.T.*, 14 July 1971.

Theobald model, by contrast, aims to *eliminate* poverty by *guaranteeing* a basic poverty line level of income, even to zero income earners. It then aims to provide some incentive to effort by means of levying a 90% tax on *all* incomes below the poverty line level and permitting 10% retentions – thus permitting income earners within that range to have post-R.I.T. disposable incomes equivalent to the poverty line level *plus* 10% of pre-R.I.T. income. Thus, the 'break-even' point, at which tax assessment and R.I.T. cancel out – i.e. at which the individual is zero rated – is *higher* than the poverty line: see Fig. 7.32(*b*). Of course, whilst zero income earners would receive an R.I.T. equivalent to 100% of the poverty gap, incomes between zero and poverty line level would contribute 90% in 'assessed tax', by which amount the actual R.I.T. payment (or cost to the Exchequer) would be reduced. Thus, someone at poverty line pre-tax income would have 110% poverty level disposable income: the R.I.T. would be 10% of poverty line level (the other 90% having been cancelled out by 'notional' tax assessed).

Both the proposed negative income tax scheme for the U.K., outlined in the 1972 Green Paper[1] and attributed to A. Cockfield and the benefits system which it was intended partially to replace appear to share features common to both the Friedman and Theobald models (see Fig. 7.33). Taking as a typical example the family with two children under eleven years of age, and applying the appropriate 'poverty level' standard for that category, as set by the Supplementary Benefits Commission (S.B.C.) for 1970, it may be seen that assisted disposable income in both cases starts below the poverty line – Friedman-style. In both cases, however, the poverty line level of disposable income is reached before the equivalent level of original pre-tax income: thereafter, disposable income continues to rise until the break-even (or tax-exemption) limits are reached. In the pre-R.I.T. benefits case, which incorporated Family Allowance (F.A.) and Family Income Supplement (F.I.S.), the zero income earner received benefits of £9 (or 56% of the poverty level). At higher incomes, up to £25 per week, the marginal rate of 'notional' tax first rose, then fell as retentions first fell, then rose. Beyond £25 per week (and beyond the tax-exemption limit) the marginal tax rate fell to 30%. Thus, the Theobald-type incentive to effort was inconsistent, in its fluctuations, and regressive, in the sense that the marginal tax rate increased, up to the break-even point. The proposed R.I.T. system was not intended to replace all benefits, but merely the F.A. and F.I.S. However, as net tax credits were to be paid weekly, they were to constitute an additional form of income supplement, automatically paid to the recipient. Furthermore, whereas the 'poverty surtax' element in the preceding scheme ranged up to 50%, the R.I.T. scheme was to constitute a straight 30% marginal rate on all income and a flat-rate £10 tax credit. This was designed to raise the zero income threshhold to £10 (62½% of the poverty level), to raise disposable incomes to a level £3 higher (on pre-tax incomes of £25 and over) than on the preceding scheme, and to raise the tax-exemption limit or break-even point from £23·54 to £33·33. A comparison of the marginal tax rates (or poverty surtax rates, in the case of sub-poverty level disposable incomes) is made in Table 7.16. It was estimated that the additional revenue cost would be £1,300 million annually, which it was hoped would be forthcoming as a result of 'fiscal drag'. Future changes in the levels of credits for various categories of

[1] *Proposals for a Tax-Credit System*, Cmnd 5116, Oct. 1972.

Table 7.16 *Marginal tax rates and 'poverty surtax' at different income levels in the pre-R.I.T. benefits system and R.I.T. system: family with two children under eleven*

£ per week — Benefits system (F.A. and F.I.S.)				£ per week — R.I.T. system			
Pre-tax income range	Increase in pre-tax income	Amount of increase retained	Marginal rate of tax (%)	Pre-tax income range	Increase in pre-tax income	Amount of increase retained	Marginal rate of tax (%)
0	—	9	—	0	—	10	—
0–10	10	7	30	0–10	10	7	30
10–15	5	3	40	10–15	5	3½	30
15–20	5	2½	50	15–20	5	3½	30
20–25	5	3	40	20–25	5	3½	30
25–30	5	3½	30	25–30	5	3½	30
30–35	5	3½	30	30–35	5	3½	30
35–50	15	10½	30	35–50	15	10½	30
50–100	50	35	30	50–100	50	35	30

(The rows 10–15, 15–20, 20–25 in the benefits system are marked 'high "poverty surtax"'.)

(Based on material in *Proposals for a Tax-Credit System*, Cmnd 5116, Oct. 1972.)

citizen would be the subject of Budgetary decisions, estimates of changing poverty levels, etc.[1] It was envisaged that cash benefits such as National Insurance benefits, rent rebates and rate rebates would continue alongside R.I.T. These, plus direct 'benefits in kind' or 'public goods', such as educational and health facilities, would raise *real* income levels above the pre-R.I.T. and post-R.I.T. *cash disposable income* threshold levels.

(d) Taxes on capital:[2]

1. Incentive to spend. The payment of death duties and any such tax on capital will probably have the effect of encouraging 'consumption of capital', or spending, so as to avoid the tax and enjoy wealth accumulated in the past. During inflationary periods this may tend to *add* to the pressure of demand on prices: during periods of low economic activity it might stimulate spending beneficially.

2. Equalisation of opportunity. In so far as capital enables its holders to acquire educational and other advantages which facilitate the earning of income, and also gains for its holders unearned income (dividends, interest, etc.), the progressive system of capital taxation breaks down these inherent privileges and reduces inequalities of opportunity to gain earned and unearned income.

3. Disintegration of economic units. As much of the burden of capital taxation may be avoided by the judicious practice of bequests and grants, this may result in the decimation of economically efficient units of financial control or of property. This process is accentuated by the above-mentioned incentive to spend out of existing capital.

(e) Taxes on expenditure (and employment):

The economist has much to contribute in terms of public debate and political interest, on various aspects of different forms of taxation. These include the effects on saving; incentives to effort and to risk-taking; the extent of post-tax income differentials; the differentiation between earned and unearned (investment) income; problems of administrative cost and the possibilities of evasion or avoidance; the policy discrimination between different categories of goods and services. However, it has been maintained that the analysis of problems and effects of direct (income and wealth) as opposed to indirect (expenditure) taxation, whilst intensely interesting to the economist, may have little hope of a serious audience in the realities of practical politics. Firstly, the descriptive and statistical data for precise analysis is lacking. Secondly, tax policy is a part of economic *policy* and economic policy is an integral part of *politics*. Thirdly, the finer points of economic welfare considerations about various tax structures tend to be

---

[1] Cmnd. 5116, p. 29. For comment, see 'The biggest change since Beveridge', *F.T.*, 11 Oct. 1972. For further comment, see 'Tax Credits—some questions answered', *E.P.R.*, 43, Sept. 1973; G. and P. Polanyi, 'Tax credits a Reverse Income Tax' *N.W.B.Q.R.*, Feb. 1973. It is of interest that the F.I.S. poverty level (termed the 'prescribed amount') for a family with 2 children under 11 in 1973 was £23-50. Thus the pre-R.I.T. break even point merely reached the *current* poverty level (see Department of Health and Social Security, 'Family Income Supplement; Leaflet F.I.S.1', Feb. 1973).

[2] For further comment see Wheatcroft, 'Inequity in Britain's tax structure', *loc. cit.*; Bracewell-Milnes, *op. cit.*; Tanzi *et al.*, *op. cit.*; A. J. Merrett, 'The Capital Gains Tax', *L.B.R.*, Oct. 1965, esp. pp. 48–57; 'Taxation of capital gains in the United Kingdom – a general survey', *M.B.R.*, Feb. 1971; 'Wealth tax would not halt spending', *D.T.*, 5 Nov. 1968.

subordinated to political realities and expedience, in the formulation of tax policy.[1]

1. Regressive burden on the less prosperous and the indulgent. Some taxes on spending are *specific*, and unrelated to the amount of expenditure involved. Such is the case with motor duties, broadcasting licences, and the customs and excise duties on tobacco, hydrocarbon oils, alcoholic drinks, matches and cigarette lighters. These items are in fairly inelastic demand (unresponsive to price changes), and therefore consumption does not increase in proportion to income, or ability to pay. A partial exception occurs in the case of specific taxes on tobacco and alcoholic drinks, where the higher income earner may purchase cigars and whisky (bearing high specific taxes) instead of cigarette tobacco and beer (bearing lower specific taxes). The burden of these taxes is, therefore, very regressive on the lower income groups. In the case of specific (or flat-rate) road fund licences, for example, the point has been made that it is regressive on two grounds. Firstly, as a tax on *ownership*, it bears more heavily on the (probably lower income) owner of a small car than on the (probably higher income) owner of a larger car. Secondly, as a tax on *use of a product*, it does not distinguish between the low-mileage user and the high-mileage user.[2] In the case of *ad valorem* taxes, such as purchase tax, protective tariffs, stamp duties, betting and television advertising taxes, there is more likelihood of expenditure (and therefore tax) being higher with the more prosperous income groups. Even so, as most of these items are in inelastic demand, it is unlikely that the tax paid rises in proportion to the taxpayer's level of prosperity (income and capital).[3]

Furthermore, all these taxes may be avoided by the individual in each income group who abstains from the taxed form of expenditure (e.g. the non-smoking, teetotal pedestrian). Thus these taxes are also regressive in respect of the indulgent, as opposed to the abstinent.

The V.A.T.-type tax is sometimes held to be regressive if there is no gradation in rates, according to ability to pay.[4] On the other hand, if it is designed with lower rates on essentials, such as food, or if such items are exempt (or zero rated), much of this regressive element may be removed. The V.A.T. introduced in the U.K. in 1973 did exempt food, but it seemed probable that by 1975 V.A.T. would be imposed, in view of the E.E.C. policy on member contributions from V.A.T. revenue, and the consequent standardisation of the range of affected items and of the basis on which they are assessed, which this implied.[5] One authority, nevertheless, has asserted[6] that, while compensation for the lowest-paid should be taken into account, a V.A.T. system with differential rates should be economic-

---

[1] For further discussion of this problem, see D. Walker, 'Direct *v*. Indirect taxes', paper reprinted in Houghton, ed., *Public Finance*, esp. pp. 373–4.

[2] 'Car licence duty: the one that got away', *Econ.*, 13 Jan. 1973, pp. 48–9.

[3] It is of interest that the commission which reported on the Swedish tax system in July 1964 recommended a switch in emphasis from direct (income) to indirect (outlay) taxation, so that the proportion of revenue accruing to the latter would rise from 33% in 1964 to 43% by 1970. The main reason given was that the rapid rise in family incomes (doubling in real value between 1948 and 1960) and the more equitable distribution of incomes had tended to weaken the regressive element in indirect taxation. Also, there would be a reduction in the disincentive effect of direct taxation. (See *Econ.*, 8 Aug. 1964, p. 573.)

[4] M. J. MacCormac, 'Turnover taxes – the Irish Experience', *L.B.R.*, April 1967, p. 9.

[5] *Ibid.*, p. 9; 'VAT again', *Econ.*, 30 Dec. 1972, p. 44. For further discussion of the problem of conformity of member countries tax systems, see D. Dosser, 'Tax harmonisation in the European Community', *T.B.R.*, June 1973.

[6] Professor A. R. Ilersic, reported in 'VAT's potential as a revenue raiser', *F.T.*, 6 March 1972.

ally and socially suitable for a consumption-orientated society such as in the U.K. He based this argument on the current *pattern* of consumer expenditure, in which food accounted for only 20% and housing, fuel and light for about 17½%, whilst 'affluent'-type expenditure on travel, entertainment and other services accounted for more than 19% and alcohol and tobacco for about 12½% – as much as on housing.

2. Ease and economy of collection. Most taxes on spending, or outlay taxes, are indirect. Being collected from a few intermediaries instead of from each consumer 'at the point of sale', they are much more easily controlled and much less expensive to collect. In the case of multi-stage taxes such as V.A.T. and turnover (or general sales) taxes, however, the administrative complexity and cost of collection may be much higher than in the case of the single-stage purchase tax, levied on the wholesaler. Much of the costs of V.A.T. administration is, of course, borne by the various firms in the sequence of production and distribution, but it is probable that they might attempt to pass much of their additional costs on to the consumer.

3. 'Invisible burden': lack of 'announcement effect'. As the indirect taxes on spending are included in the final price to the consumer, he is less likely to be aware of paying a tax, and less likely to react accordingly in adjusting his pattern of expenditure. In other words, the 'announcement effect' of these taxes is less pronounced than in the case of direct outlay taxes (e.g. licences of various types) and direct taxes on income, capital and company profits.

4. 'Excess burden' through distortion of expenditure pattern. As will be shown in Part Two (Chapter 11, Theory of Value or Price), the immediate loss of consumer satisfaction to the individual appears to be higher in the case of an outlay tax than in the case of a lump sum tax on income or capital. The basic reason is that an outlay tax, being reflected in increased prices, obliges the consumer to make readjustments in his pattern of expenditure. The whole pattern of relative prices of substitutes is altered by the outlay tax, whereas with a lump sum income or capital tax there is less dislocation in relativities. However, one authority has concluded that theoretical studies could throw little light on the magnitudes of the 'excess burden' of sacrificed consumer satisfaction and, therefore, could not contribute much to the debate on the relative welfare merits of income taxes, as opposed to expenditure taxes.[1]

5. Inflationary effect. Whereas progressive income tax is equitable, does not disturb the pattern of relative prices, and may not lead to intensified, inflationary wage demands, such pressure is a much more likely result of taxes on spending. Such taxes, unless entirely 'absorbed' by producers, are immediately reflected in higher market prices, and, being usually on items in inelastic demand, they cannot easily be avoided. Thus they affect the Cost of Living Index and/or will be accompanied by pressure for higher wages and salaries. Such pressure will be stronger during periods of high economic activity, when labour's bargaining power is strong, but it can be reduced by increased productivity (lower per unit costs) on the part of producers, who may thus be able to absorb or cushion the tax.

[1] H. P. Wald, referred to by Walker, 'Direct v. indirect taxes', *loc. cit.*, p. 358.

The introduction of the turnover tax (or general sales tax) in Eire in 1963 was held, by one author, to have resulted in raising retail prices and to have precipitated the inflationary round of wage increases in 1964.[1] An analysis of consumer price levels, following the introduction of V.A.T. in eight European countries, revealed increases of between $1 \cdot 5\%$ and $7 \cdot 8\%$ within six months, but in only a minority of cases could this be attributed to V.A.T. itself, rather than to pressures and trends already noticeable before its introduction.[2]

6. *Distortion of market mechanism and allocation of resources.* Whether an outlay tax is levied in the first instance (i.e. formal incidence, or impact) on the producer (or the middleman) or on the consumer, each of these parties will attempt to 'shift' the final burden on to the other party. Each will react to the prospect of a reduction in profit or increase in price, and each will exercise his relative bargaining power.

On the supply side, the producer or middleman may be 'elastic' (having several alternative uses for his equipment and abilities) or 'inelastic' (having few alternative prospects). On the demand side, the consumer may be elastic (having several competitive substitutes to choose from) or inelastic (if the item is a necessity, with no substitutes). As regards the final market price, the tax will be shared according to the relative inelasticities (bargaining weaknesses) of the two parties. If both are equally strong or both equally weak, market price to the consumer will be higher by half the tax, and the reward to the producer (or middleman) will be lower by half the tax. If one is weaker than the other, he will suffer the greater share of the final burden. However, there will also be a reduction in the final quantity produced and sold, which involves both a redistribution of expenditure by the consumer and a different pattern of production by producers. This decrease in output (with its repercussions on other industries and on the use of resources in the economy) will be related to the sum of the bargaining strengths (or elasticities) of both parties. The reduction will be large if either is elastic: it will be greater still if both are elastic. (Diagrammatic treatment of this problem may be seen in Chapter 11.) High elasticity involves a reduction in consumption and/or production. The free working of the market price mechanism upon the allocation of resources is distorted, but this may be politically more expedient than the possible 'disincentive effect' which might be caused by a direct income or capital tax.

There may be quite subtle differences in the effects of different types of expenditure taxes[3] – turnover taxes, V.A.T., retail sales tax, purchase tax – but certain features of the V.A.T. are likely to be noticeable. Being fairly general, it is likely to be less disruptive in its effects upon any one product or service market, but may result in some realignment between different markets, which are affected in varying degrees. If the rate of V.A.T. is raised generally, on all sectors, there seems to be a greater likelihood of the increased tax being passed on to consumers, than if certain products or sectors only were affected by the tax increase. This passing on of an increased tax on all final output is likely because prices tend to be *flexible* upwards, whilst labour costs, in particular, tend to be *inflexible* down-

[1] MacCormac, *op. cit.*, p. 9.
[2] E. G. Horsman, 'Britain and value-added taxation', *L.B.R.*, Jan. 1972, pp. 33–4.
[3] For further discussion, see R. Turvey, 'A tax system without company taxation', *L.B.R.*, Jan. 1963, esp. pp. 33–6; D. K. Stout, 'The tax on value added', reprinted in Houghton, ed., *op. cit.*, esp. pp. 417–23.

wards – the 'ratchet' effect of trade union pressure in wage bargaining.[1] Of course, in view of the differing relative bargaining strengths of producers and customers in different sectors, some firms may be stimulated to further endeavours to increase productivity and reduce costs as, for example, by a search for substitute materials and changes in the factor 'mix'.

Some elements of this 'productivity' response are claimed to have been noted in some services sectors, following the period in which S.E.T. was levied (on services, distribution and construction).[2] In the distributive trades the 1970 Reddaway Report indicated that some of the 'unexpected', additional 5·1 % rise in productivity between 1965 and 1968 was probably due to more efficient labour utilisation and the trend to self-service retailing. Gross profit margins were lower than had been expected. There have been criticisms of the Report's interpretation of the data,[3] one of which relates to the possible reduction in the *quality* of retail service, as opposed to its quantity, in terms of turnover per employee, etc.

3. Further Reading and Sources

Footnote references to daily and weekly journals are not repeated.

BARCLAYS BANK, 'Public expenditure'. *B.B.R.* Feb. 1970.

A. B. ATKINSON, *Poverty in Britain and the Reform of Social Security*. Cambridge University Press. 1969.

A. B. ATKINSON, 'Policies for poverty'. *L.B.R.* April 1971.

T. S. BARKER and J. R. C. LECOMBER, 'Public expenditure and the public'. *M. & W.S.R.* Autumn 1970.

W. J. BLUM and H. KALVEN jr., *The Uneasy Case for Progressive Taxation*. University of Chicago Press. 1966.

J. B. BRACEWELL-MILNES, 'Saving and inequality'. *M. & W.S.R.* Autumn 1969.

E. B. BUTLER and R. GIDLOW, 'The Selective Employment Tax'. *M. & W.S.R.* Autumn 1966.

M. H. CADMAN, ed., *Taxation Economics*. Macmillan. 1969.

M. CRAWFORD, 'The 1965 reforms in the British tax system'. *M. & W.S.R.* Winter 1965.

B. CRICK and W. A. ROBSON, *Taxation Policy*. Penguin. 1972.

DEPARTMENT OF HEALTH AND SOCIAL SECURITY, *Family Income Supplement:* Leaflet FIS 1. H.M.S.O. Feb, 1973.

D. DOSSER, 'Tax harmonisation in the European Community'. *T.B.R.* June 1973.

J. F. DUE, *Government Finance: Economics of the Public Sector*, 4th edn. Irwin. 1968.

O. ECKSTEIN, *Public Finance*, 2nd edn. Prentice-Hall. 1967.

R. H. HAVEMAN, *The Economics of the Public Sector*. Wiley. 1970.

E. G. HORSMAN, 'Britain and value-added taxation'. *L.B.R.* Jan. 1972.

---

[1] Compare with comments in Turvey, *op. cit.*, p. 34, and Horsman, *op. cit.*, p. 34.

[2] E. B. Butler and R. Gidlow, 'The selective employment tax', *M. & W.S.R.*, Autumn 1966; 'The effects of SET', *E.P.R.*, 3, March 1970. Also see R. D. Sleeper, 'SET and the shake out: a note on the productivity effects of the selective employment tax', *Oxford Economic Papers*, vol. 24, No. 2, July 1972.

[3] See 'SET: Counter Reddaway', *Econ.*, 11 April 1970, p. 67; 'SET and the shop assistant', *Econ.*, 7 March 1970, pp. 57–8; 'Report "strengthens case for abolishing SET"', *F.T.*, 12 March 1970.

7. PUBLIC FINANCE [II]

R. W. HOUGHTON, ed., *Public Finance*. Penguin. 1970.

P. R. KAIM-CAUDEL, 'Selectivity and the social services'. *L.B.R.* April 1969.

D. LEES, 'Poor families and fiscal reform'. *L.B.R.* Oct. 1967.

M. J. MacCORMAC, 'Turnover taxes – the Irish experience'. *L.B.R.* April 1967.

A. J. MERRETT, 'The Capital Gains Tax'. *L.B.R.* Oct. 1965.

A. J. MERRETT, *Executive Remuneration in the United Kingdom.* Longmans. 1967.

A. J. MERRETT and J. WHITTACKER, 'The profitability of British and American industry'. *L.B.R.* Jan. 1967.

R. A. MUSGRAVE, *The Theory of Public Finance* (International Student edition). McGraw-Hill. 1959.

A. T. PEACOCK and J. WISEMAN, *The Growth of Public Expenditure in the United Kingdom.* Princeton University Press. 1961.

A. T. PEACOCK and J. WISEMAN, *The Past and Future of Public Spending. L.B.R.* April 1961.

PLOWDEN REPORT, *Report of the Plowden Committee on the Control of Public Expenditure.* Cmnd 1432. H.M.S.O. 1961.

G. AND P. POLANYI, 'Tax credits: a Reverse Income Tax' *N.W.B.Q.R.*, Feb 1973.

POLITICAL AND ECONOMIC PLANNING, *Personal Taxation, Incentive and Taxation Reform.* P.E.P. Broadsheet. Jan. 1969.

A. R. PREST, *Public Finance in Theory and Practice*, 4th edn. Weidenfeld & Nicolson. 1970.

A. SELDON, 'Thaw in the Welfare State', *L.B.R.* July 1972.

W. G. SHEPHERD, 'Alternatives for public expenditure', in R. E. Caves, ed., *Britain's Economic Prospects.* Allen & Unwin. 1968.

R. D. SLEEPER, 'SET and the shake-out: a note on the productivity effects of the selective employment tax'. *Oxford Economic Papers*, Vol. 24, No. 2. July 1972.

V. TANZI, J. B. BRACEWELL-MILNES and D. R. MYDDLETON, *Taxation: a radical approach.* Institute of Economic Affairs. 1970.

TREASURY, *Public Expenditure 1968–69 to 1973–74*, White Paper. Cmnd 4234. H.M.S.O. 1969.

TREASURY, *New Policies for Public Spending*, White Paper. Cmnd 4515. H.M.S.O. 1970.

TREASURY, *Public Expenditure 1969–70 to 1974–75*, White Paper. Cmnd 4578. H.M.S.O. Jan. 1971.

TREASURY, *Public Expenditure to 1976–77*, White Paper. Cmnd 5178. H.M.S.O. Dec. 1972.

TREASURY, *Public Expenditure White Papers: Handbook on Methodology.* H.M.S.O. 1972.

TREASURY, *Proposals for a Tax-Credit System*, Green Paper. Cmnd 5116. Oct. 1972.

TREASURY, *E.P.R.* 10, Dec. 1970; 13, March 1971; 23. Jan. 1972.

TREASURY, 'Public expenditure'. *E.P.R.* 1. Jan. 1970.

TREASURY, 'The effects of SET', *E.P.R.* 3. March 1970.

TREASURY, 'Planning, programming, budgeting', *E.P.R.* 6. Aug. 1970.

TREASURY, 'PBB applied'. *E.P.R.* 8. Oct. 1970.

TREASURY, 'What the Government buys'. *E.P.R.* 21. Nov. 1971.

TREASURY, 'Control of public expenditure'. *E.P.R.* 31. Sept. 1972.

TREASURY, 'The European Communities budget'. *E.P.R.* 35. Jan. 1973.

TREASURY, 'Public expenditure'. *E.P.R.* 42. Aug. 1973.

TREASURY, 'Tax credits—some questions answered'. *E.P.R.* 43. Sept. 1973.
R. TURVEY, 'A tax system without company taxation'. *L.B.R.* Jan. 1963.
G. S. A. WHEATCROFT, 'Inequity in Britain's tax structure'. *L.B.R.* July 1969.

4. Past Examination Questions

1. Discuss the relative importance of the main items of United Kingdom government expenditure. (Summer 1959)
2. Examine the rôle of the Budget in the national economy. (Summer 1953)
3. What would be the likely effects on the U.K. economy of the building of considerably greater mileage of new roads every year for the next ten years? (Summer 1963)
4. 'We must regard roads as a public service in the same class as law and order and defence.' Discuss. (January 1964)
5. What are the main categories of Government expenditure in Britain? To what extent has their relative importance changed in the past twenty-five years? (Summer 1964)
6. Compare the aims of fiscal policy today with those of the 19th century. (Summer 1952)
7. 'The criterion for expenditure on the National Health Service should be the best medical treatment technically possible for everyone.' Comment. (January 1963)
8. Write a note on the economic problem of rearmament. (Summer 1952)
9. How can the government influence the distribution of income? Refer in your answer to the actual conditions in the United Kingdom. (Summer 1959)
10. By what methods can the government influence the prices and outputs of an industry? (January 1965)
11. Distinguish between direct and indirect taxation and discuss the relative merits of each type. (Summer 1952)
12. Compare and contrast direct and indirect taxes as sources of government revenue. (January 1965)
13. What is the difference between an income tax and a purchase tax? Discuss the advantages and disadvantages of each. (Summer 1961)
14. Explain the meaning of 'the incidence of taxation' and explain under what circumstances the incidence of a purchase tax on cotton cloth might fall on (*a*) the manufacturer, (*b*) the buyer. (Summer 1953)
15. 'Indirect taxes are useless as a measure against inflation because they bring about the very rise in prices which it is intended to prevent.' Discuss. (Summer 1962)
16. What would be the probable economic effects of a 100 per cent excess profits tax levied on all profits in excess of 5 per cent of capital employed in a firm? (Summer 1964)
17. Trace as far as you can the economic effects of an increase in the tax on cigarettes so that they sell for 4*s* 0*d* for 20, instead of for 3*s* 6*d* for 20. (Summer 1951)
18. 'The duty on fuel oil imported into the United Kingdom should be raised in view of the difficulties which these imports are creating for the United Kingdom's coal industry.' Comment. (Summer 1960)

19. 'A profits tax lowers the level of capital investment in a country.' Discuss. (Summer 1963)

20. How would a tax on profits affect the level of private investment in a country? In what ways can a government influence the level of private investment? (Summer 1961)

21. Examine the short run and long run effects of (*a*) a high income tax, and (*b*) a high profits tax. (Summer 1953)

22. 'A high rate of income tax is inflationary because it lowers the incentive to work.' Discuss. (January 1963)

8. Stages in the Flow of Goods and Services to the Final Consumer
Stage I

1. Channels of Distribution

As was seen in Chapter 1, the sector of the economy engaged in the production of goods is supported by a large and increasing sector producing services, of which commercial services are an important element. This chapter will be dealing with the distributive trades – the main links in the flow of goods and services from producer to consumer – though these links in turn are supported by and dependent upon ancillary commercial services, such as transport, communications and financial services (banking, insurance, etc.).

Without the division of labour between the production of goods and that of commercial services, total output, efficiency and consumer satisfaction would have remained at a much lower level. Specialisation has made it possible for producers of goods to concentrate on what they do best – acting on advice, information and orders received from the wholesale, import, export and retail trades. These trades in turn, helped by the ancillary services, ascertain the requirements of the consumer and see that they are met. The pattern of activities, from producer to consumer, is outlined in Fig. 8.1.

In mid-1970 the main body of the distributive trades group in Great Britain had 2,702,000 employees, or 12·2% of total employees, of whom the greater part were employed in the retail trade (1·9 million in 1970).[1]

In recent years a number of official statistical inquiries have been made into the distributive trades. In 1950 the Board of Trade undertook its first full Census of Distribution of Great Britain, covering the wholesale trade, retail trade and related services. This was followed by the second full Census of Distribution in 1961, inquiries into the wholesale trades (1965) and the retail and some service trades (1966). The latest full Census of Distribution was taken in 1972 (covering the year 1971). In 1964 was set up the Economic Development Committee for the Distributive Trades – the 'Little Neddy' – to advise on productivity, assess trends, etc.

Retail-type related distributive services constitute a complementary group, which belongs partly to Private Direct Services and partly to Distributive Trades (Commercial Services). Employment in this group in 1970 totalled about 1,450,000 people, of whom about 532,000 were in hotels and catering, 405,000 in garages and motor repairs and the remainder in such services as laundries and

---

[1] *Ann. Abs. Stat.*, 108, 1971. *N.B.* Including employers and self-employed, the number of persons *engaged* in retail shops alone was 2,562,045 in 1971 (see 'Provisional results of the Census of Distribution for 1971', *Trade and Industry*, 21 Dec. 1972, p. 621).

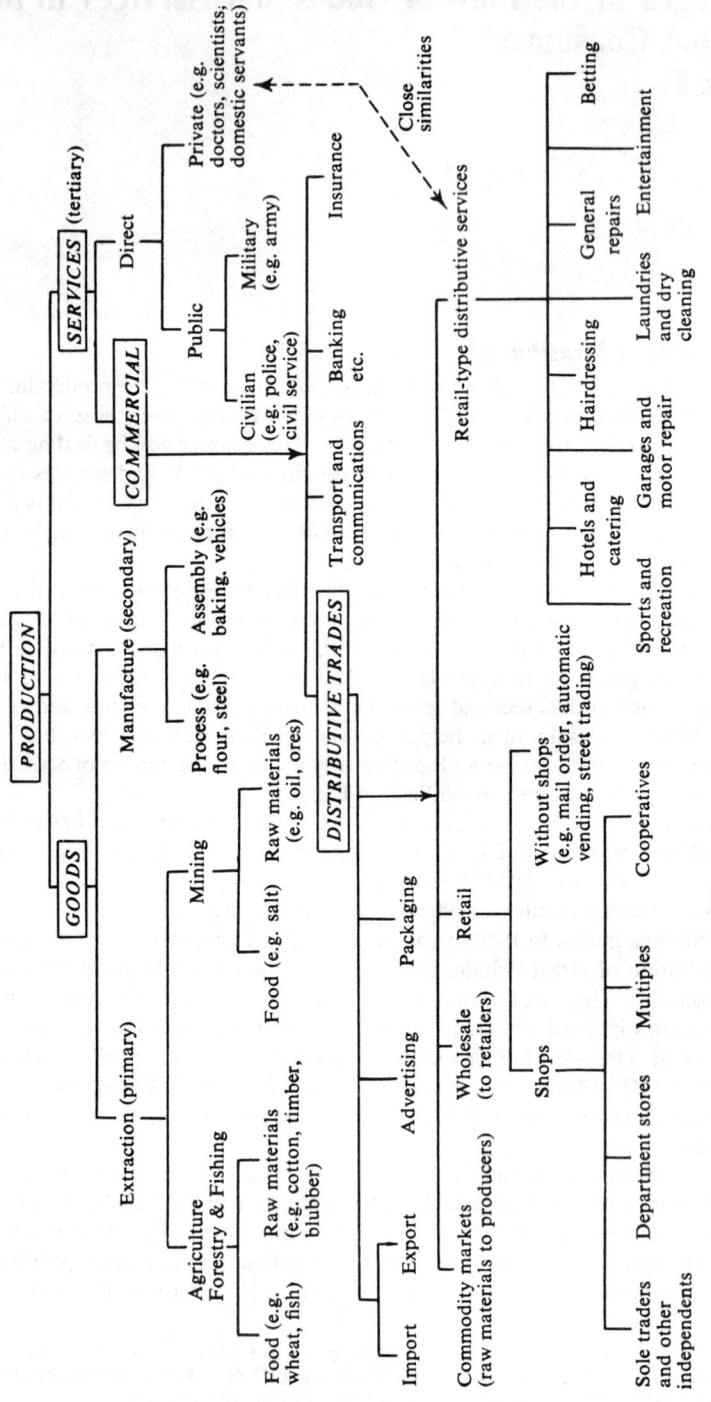

Fig. 8.1. *The pattern of productive activity*

dry cleaning (113,000), entertainment, sports, recreation and betting (305,000), hairdressing (87,000) and boot and shoe repair (7,000).

2. Retail Trade and Recent Developments

(a) Economic functions of the retailer

Retailing is the final link in the chain of distribution of goods to the final consumer. Most retail trade is conducted through shops, but there is a growing proportion of retailing without shops.

Some of the main economic functions of the retailer may be summarised as follows:

(i) *'Test-bed'*. To test consumer reaction to new products and to act upon information thus obtained.

(ii) *'Sounding-board'*. To 'keep an ear to the ground' regarding present and future consumer requirements, and to pass on information thus acquired.

(iii) *Variety*. To satisfy consumer tastes by stocking the widest possible variety required by customers.

(iv) *Form*. To stock commodities in the form (e.g. packed, loose, fresh, frozen, etc.) and in the quantities or sizes required by consumers.

(v) *Prices*. To supply goods to consumers at the lowest possible competitive prices.

(vi) *Location*. To offer the above services in such places (or 'points of sale') as will best suit consumers (e.g. local shops, city-centre shops, out-of-town shopping centres, etc.).

(vii) *Time*. To offer the above services during such hours as will best suit the convenience of consumers (e.g. late-night closing, Saturday and Sunday opening, etc.).

(viii) *Method of purchase*. To offer the consumer the most convenient method of making his purchases (e.g. self-service, 'drive-in', delivery service, etc.).

(ix) *Method of payment*. To offer the consumer the most convenient method of paying for his purchases (e.g. cash, cheques, credit, instalments, etc.).

(x) *General service*. To give the consumer expert advice, 'after-sales service', 'satisfaction or money back', courtesy, the impression that 'the customer is always right', and generally efficient service.

A reflection upon the manner in which these functions are being fulfilled has been the notable increase in competition in recent years – with new types of product, new types of shop, method of payment and location pattern – and the improvement in consumer protection. There is now, on average, about one retail shop for every 112 persons in Great Britain.

(b) The pattern of retail trade

Some interesting comparisons may be drawn between the general pattern of retailing in Britain, western Europe generally and the U.S.A.[1] Throughout western Europe the rate of growth of employment in the distributive trades has been about twice as fast as in manufacturing and agriculture. However, by 1960 the west European labour force engaged in these trades was about 20% the size of the labour force engaged in the production of goods, construction and public utilities (in Britain the proportion in mid-1961 was 26%). In the U.S.A.,

1 See 'Retailing in Europe' and 'Retailing in Britain', *Econ.*, 23 Feb. 1963, pp. 716–18.

on the other hand, this stage was reached in 1930, and by 1950 the percentage had reached 40–41. There appears to be a general correlation between, on the one hand, rising standards of living (high *per capita* consumption), the decline in agriculture, the concentration of production and lengthening of distributive channels, the reduction in the hours worked per distributive employee, and the slower rise in productivity in distribution than in production of goods, and, on the other hand, an increase in the proportion of working populations engaged in distribution.

With regard to the volume and value of retail spending in Britain, turnover increased by 22·4% from 1966 to 1970, but the real volume only rose by 4·2%, after allowing for the increase in the general price level. By 1971 turnover had risen by 36·8%, but continuing inflation had caused prices to rise by 28%, since 1966. The real volume increase was about 7%. A significant increase in volume occurred during 1972, influenced by fiscal and monetary relaxation and 'expected inflation'. Between 1966 and end-1972 the volume increase in total consumer expenditure was 1.8%, but, as shown in Fig. 8.2, this was much less than in some

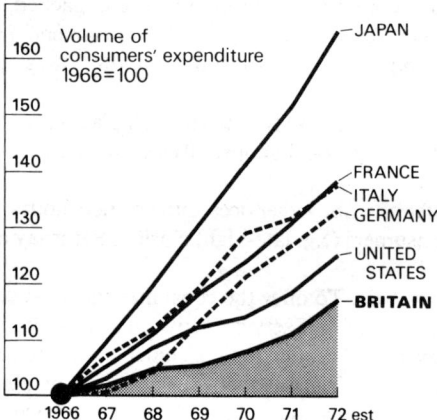

Fig. 8.2. *Increase in volume of total consumer expenditure, 1966 – end-1972: Britain and other countries*
(Source: *Econ.*, 10 Feb. 1972, p. 74)

other advanced countries. The number of retail shop outlets fell by 11·0% between 1961 and 1971 – the greatest absolute and relative reductions occurring in the Grocers and Provision Dealers section, which fell by 39,214 or 26·7% and the greatest absolute and relative increases occurring in Household Goods shops which rose by 13,321 or 22·0% (see Table 8.1).[1] Both types of General Stores – Department and Variety – reversed the 1961–66 reductions and had increased by 1971 to the extent of 16·5% and 14·1%, respectively.

[1] For further details and comment see 'Provisional results of the Census of Distribution for 1971', *Trade and Industry*, 21 Dec. 1972 and 25 Jan. 1973; 'The 1971 Census of Distribution', *Trade and Industry*, 21 Sept. 1972, pp. 516-18; 'You can't keep a good shopkeeper down', *Econ.*, 23 Sept. 1972, pp. 85-6; 'Retail trade: present and future', *B.B.R.*, Nov. 1971; D. C. Corner, 'Recent trends in retail distribution', *N.W.B.Q.R.*, May 1969; W. G. McClelland, 'The distributive sector', *T.B.R.*, Dec. 1969. Also see 'The changing pattern of retail trade,' *E.P.R.*, 40, June 1973 for a useful graphical analysis commentary.

Table 8.1 Retail and distributive service trades by number and turnover, Great Britain, 1961–1971 (a)

SECTOR	No. of Establishments				Turnover				Volume
	1961	1966	1971	% change 1961–71	% change 1957–61	% change 1961–66	% change 1966–71	£ million 1971	% change 1966–70
Shops: Total	*542,301*	*504,412*	*485,346*	*–11*	*+18*	*+26.5*	*+36.8*	*15,218*	*+4.2*
Grocers and provision dealers	146,777	123,385	107,563	–26.7	+16	+23.6	37.2	+3,993	+3.3
Other food shops	114,655	104,359	94,281	–17.8	+16	+20.4	25.2	+2,606	} +3
Confectioners, tobacconists, newsagents	70,108	63,333	54,024	–22.7	+14	+31.1	24.0	+1,297	
Clothing, footwear, soft furnishings and household textiles shops	86,555	83,095	81,139	–6.3	+18	+25.6	+31.6	2,248	+3
Household goods shops	60,343	65,850	73,664	+22.0	+25	+25.6	+50.0	1,939	+7
Other non-food shops	60,113	61,381	70,371	+17.0	+21	+44.2	+54.1	1,573	+7
General stores: total	3,750	3,009	4,304	+14.8	+21	+14.7	+46.5	1,562	+3 } +5.0
of which:									
Department stores (b)	784	760	914	+16.5	—	+19.7	+43.7	938	—
Variety and general (c)	2,966	2,249	3,390	+14.1	—	+7.8	+50.7	624	—
Non-shop									
Market stalls and mobile shops	35,006	—	24,343	–32.8	—	—	+7.3 (1961–71)	97.8	—
Electricity and Gas Board showrooms	2,791	3,012	2,359	–15.4	—	+78	+52.5	283	—
Mail order businesses (d)	556	495	676	+21.6	—	+89	+44.4	619	—
Automatic vending machine operators	26	56	60	+132.6	—	+167	0	10.9	—
Total retail trade	—	—	—	—	—	+27	+38	16,229	—
Distributive service trades									
Footwear repairing establishments	11,154	8,769	6,304	–43.6	+12	+2.4	–2.7	25.3	—
Hairdressing establishments	40,152	47,632	47,093	+17.3	+57	+39.6	+21.7	165	—
Sundries, launderette operators and dry cleaners (d)	4,573	5,621	8,040	+76.3	—	+53.2	+16.1	200	—
Total retail and service trades	—	—	—	—	—	+27.7	+37.2	16,620	—

(a) Including estimates for non-response.
(b) At least 25 employees.
(c) Turnover of at least £15,000, but smaller than Department stores.
(d) Organisations, not simply establishments.

(Based on material in *Brit. O.H.*, 1964 and 1972; *Ann. Abs. Stat.*, 108, 1971; *Trade and Industry*, 21 Sept. 1972 and 21 Dec. 1972)

Table 8.2 *The changing pattern of household expenditure*

Expenditure on commodity or service as a percentage of total weekly household expenditure			
	1959-61	1964-66	1969-71
Housing	9·3	11·4	12·6
Fuel, light and power	6·0	6·3	6·3
Food	31·0	28·3	25·9
Alcoholic drink	3·4	4·1	4·5
Tobacco	6·0	5·7	4·7
Clothing and footwear	10·1	9·4	9·0
Durable household goods	6·9	6·4	6·4
Other goods	7·2	7·0	7·4
Transport and vehicles	10·4	11·7	13·8
Services	9·3	9·4	9·1
Miscellaneous	0·4	0·4	0·3
TOTAL	100·0	100·0	100·0

(Source: *E.P.R.*, 36, Feb. 1973)

These changes reflect the gradual shift in emphasis away from the small shop to the large supermarkets and general stores – seen most clearly in the Grocers and Provisions sector and the Confectioners, Tobacconists and Newsagents sector and to a lesser extent in the Other Food and the Clothing, Footwear, etc., sectors. The positive trends in Household Goods etc., and Other Non-Food groups reflect the growth in 'do-it-yourself' shops, antique shops, fashion boutiques, electrical goods shops, television rental shops, card shops, fancy goods and sports goods shops, pet food shops and garden centres. This, in turn, reflects the changing pattern of spending, as rising affluence and leisure lead to the desire for novelty

Table 8.3 *Changing relative significance of turnover by main forms of retail organisation, Great Britain*

Sector	Type					
		Independents	Multiples	Retail Co-operaative societies	Department stores	Mail order firms	ALL
	1950	62·2(a)	21·2(a)	11·4(a)	5·2(c)	—	100
Percentage shares in	1957	59·2(a)	23·9(a)	11·9(a)	5·0(c)	—	100
Total Retail Trade	1961	59·9(b)	29·2(b)	10·9(b)	5·0(d)	—	100
	1966	56·4(b)	34·5(b)	9·1(b)	5·6(d)	3·7(d)	100
	1971	52·9(b)	39·8(b)	7·2(b)	5·8(d)	3·8(d)	100
Percentage changes in Turnover, 1966–1970:						
(a) Total Trade		+16	+35	+7	+25	+32	+22·4
(b) Food		+16	+40	+9	—	—	+22·2
(c) Non-Food:						
i Clothing and footwear		+13	+33	−6	—	—	+21
ii Durable goods		+17	+36	+5	—	—	+23

(a) *Excluding* department stores and mail order subsidiaries.
(b) *Including* department stores and mail order subsidiaries.
(c) *Not included* in totals for Independents, Multiples and Retail Co-operative societies.
(d) *Included* in totals for Independents, Multiples and Retail Co-operative societies.

(Based on material in *E.P.R.*, 40 June 1973. *Ann. Abs. Stat.*, 108, 1971; *Brit. O.H.* 1964 and 1972; *Trade and Industry*, 21 Dec. 1972; *F.T.*, 1 June 1972 and 12 Sept. 1972)

and consumer participation, as opposed to basic consumer goods. Table 8.2 indicates the main features in the changing pattern of household expenditure between 1959 and 1971. The reversal in the upward trend for Hairdressers may be a misleading result of the changes in methods of classification after 1966: the 1961 and 1966 figures include 4,172 and 2,380 shops, respectively, classified as hairdresser-tobacconists.

The changes in retail turnover were by no means evenly spread over all forms of retail organisation. We may distinguish five main types of retail organisation: (i) Independent traders (including sole proprietors, small chains of stores with nine or less branches, and market and street traders).
(ii) Department store organisations.
(iii) Multiple traders (chains of stores with ten or more branches).
(iv) Retail co-operative societies.
(v) Mail order businesses.

Some of the main trends in relative shares and rates of growth in major sectors may be seen in Table 8.3. The most significant trend has been the expansion in the relative share accounted for by the multiple groups. The smaller independents have continued to receive a falling share, but have retained nearly one-half of total trade, by means of adapting themselves to self-service methods and by forming voluntary buying chains. The department stores seem to have reversed the decline in their share of trade: they, too, have adapted to new methods, with the introduction of some self-service elements and the creation of specialist boutiques within their organisations. Mail order firms have continued to make some progress, but still account for only a small percentage of the total retail turnover. The retail co-operatives have been the least adaptable type of organisation and have continued to drop behind in all sectors, especially in Clothing and Footwear.

As will be noted from Table 8.1 and Fig. 8.3, the share of retail trade attributable to food fell from 45% in 1966 to 43·4% in 1971. The number of grocery outlets has been reduced during the 1960s to about one for every 500 people – one of the lowest ratios in Europe, apart from the Netherlands (see Fig. 8.4). The retail co-operatives reduced their share of total food sales from 15·1% in 1966 to 12·2% in 1971, but retained a fairly stable proportion of grocery sales. The

£ (millions)

	Total retail sales £7,550m.	£11,391m.	£12,613m.
All food shops	47·4%	45·1%	45·5%
Confectioners, tobacconists & newsagents	9·3	9·5	9·3
Clothing & footwear	15·6	15·6	15·4
Durable goods	10·5	12·1	11·9
Chemists	2·9	3·5	3·5
General stores, Photographic dealers, Other non-food stores	14·3	14·2	14·4
	1957	1967	1969

Fig. 8.3. *Retail sales by type*, *Great Britain*
(Source: *F.T.*, 17 Dec. 1970)

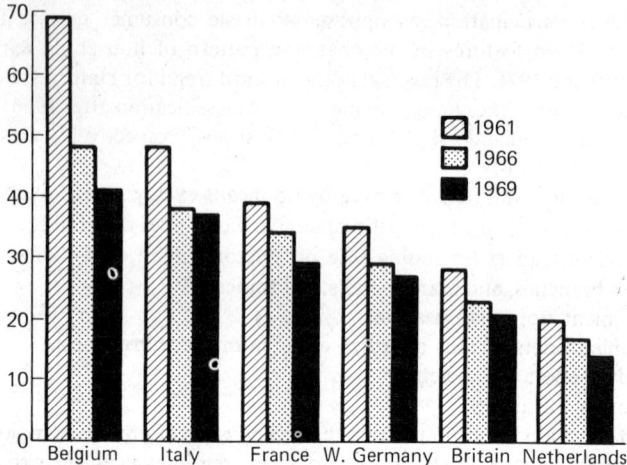

Fig. 8.4. *Grocery outlets per 10,000 people, 1961–69*
(Source: *F.T.*, 3 Nov. 1970)

multiples and the voluntary buying groups of independents (the 'symbol' shops) increased their shares. The share of the non-aligned small independents contracted to about 21% (see Fig. 8.5). These changes reflect the trend towards quick turnover, self-service and price competition, with fewer and larger grocery outlets, as compared with most E.E.C. countries, other than the Netherlands.[1]

Since 1967 the Business Statistics Office has asked 'large retail organisations', in its Annual Inquiries into the Distributive and Service Trades, to provide an analysis of their turnover, in respect of fifteen groups of commodities. Large

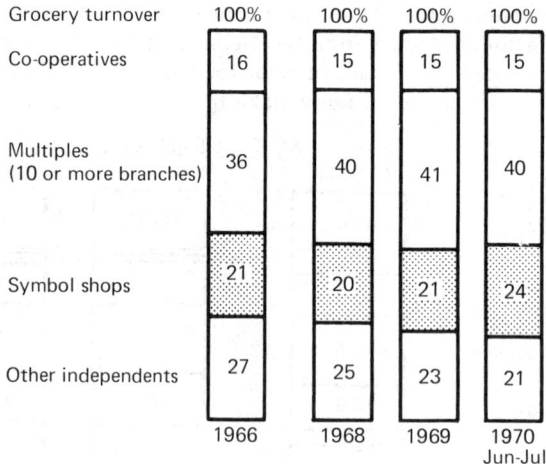

Fig. 8.5. *Relative shares of the grocery trade*
(Source: *F.T.*, 23 Oct. 1970)

[1] 'Prices will not go up that much', *Econ.*, 30 Jan. 1971, p. 57.

Table 8.4 *Relative significance of large organisations in total retail turnover and in turnover by classes of retail firm, Great Britain, 1966*

Type of large retail organisation	Turnover 1966 (£ m.)	% of 1966 total retail turnover (£11,757 m.)	% of 1966 retail turnover by particular type of retailer
Retail co-operative societies	916·9	7·9	84
Grocers	954·4	8·2	40
Other food shops	321·5	2·8	17
Clothing and footwear shops	813·6	7·0	48
Durable goods shops	294·9	2·5	22
Other non-food shops	724·5	6·2	30
Department stores	464·9	4·0	85
General mail order firms	362·6	3·1	95
ALL TYPES	4,851·4	42 (a)	42 (a)

(a) Allowing for incomplete returns from some large retail organisations.

(Based on material in *Trade and Industry*, 21 Sept. 1972, p. 621 and 14 Dec. 1972, p. 555)

retail organisations are defined as those with a turnover exceeding £1 million in 1966.[1] Turnover of such organisations, including some multiples, department stores, mail order firms and retail co-operatives was estimated at 42% of total retail trade turnover in 1966 and rose, in monetary terms, by 33·3% by 1970 – as compared with the 22·4% increase in total retail turnover during that period. The proportions of total retail turnover, in the fifteen commodity groups, which was accounted for by the large organisations ranged in 1966 ₁ ·m 69% in footwear and 58% in women's, girls' and children's wear to 25% in newspapers, books and stationery and 20% in cigarettes and tobacco. Table 8.4 summarises the shares of each type of large organisation in total retail turnover and also the relative importance of large organisations in relation to the turnover of all sizes of firm of each type. It will be noted that, while representing only small proportions of total retail turnover, the *large* retail co-operatives, department stores and mail order firms accounted for 84%, 85% and 95% of turnover by their respective *type* of retail outlet: the degree of market concentration was high amongst those types of retailers. Forty per cent of grocery turnover was accounted for by large grocers, but amongst non-grocery food shops, durable goods and 'other non-food' shops the degree of large firm market concentration was much lower.

With regard to the management of the retail sector and planning for future change, two points may be made. Firstly, the Distributive Trades E.D.C. ('Little Neddy') in 1969 drew attention to continuing defects in management quality and training in modern techniques and human relations.[2] Secondly, as a 1970 study of retailing methods indicated,[3] the various specialised retailing techniques of the present and of the future should be visualised in terms of a product life cycle. The implication is that companies which are too fully committed to any particular method – self-service, mail order, general department store, etc. – may become beneficiaries or involuntary victims of that particular technique's life cycle. They may become too inflexible to adapt to changes in consumer spending patterns and shopping habits.

[1] 'Commodity analysis of the turnover of large retailers', *Trade and Industry*, 14 Dec. 1972, pp. 550–5.
[2] *D.T.*, 22 Oct. 1969.
[3] Reported in 'Life cycles among the retail groupings', *F.T.*, 7 Dec. 1970.

(c) Types of shop organisation

INDEPENDENT TRADERS

This form of shop organisation ranges from the one-man firm (or sole trader, or 'unit trader') to small multiples (less than ten branches) and general department and variety stores. They numbered about 403,876 in 1966 (80% of all shops) and about 402,814 in 1971 (83% of all shops). There had been a reduction of about 11,000 in the number of food shops, but an increase of about 10,000 in the non-food sector. In 1966 227,000 shops had an annual turnover of less than £10,000. The Distributive Trades E.D.C. suggested in 1970 that the ability of these smallest traders to develop and increase their efficiency was limited by their very smallness: their continued survival would depend upon their offering services which could not be matched by other organisations – in terms of location and opening hours. The larger independents were seen to be capable of making a positive contribution to the economy by providing competition, new entry to the retail trade and willingness to adopt new ideas and methods.[1]

During the period 1966 to 1970 the independents as a whole increased their turnover by about 16%, as compared with an average for all major retail types of 22·4%. By 1971 the independents (*including* their 369 department stores) still accounted for about 52·9% of total retail trade (about £8,000 million), but this had fallen from 56·4% in 1966 and 59·9% in 1961.[2]

Such small retailers have sprung up, and continue to come into being largely because of the ease of entry. Very limited capital may suffice to open up a 'front parlour' shop, especially for the sale of perishable foods, where stocks are small. Sometimes the shop is not relied upon as the sole source of income; family help in staffing keeps down overhead costs; the traditional pattern of 'spheres of influence' or differentiation in types of product sold in different shops has also made it easier for the small newcomer to open up. Some of the advantages of small-scale retailing are that the working proprietor may offer the consumer a high standard of personal service; he may open up in localities convenient to a small local market – which would not attract the larger firm; he has comparatively low overheads; he is helped financially by obtaining goods on credit from wholesalers; he may be prepared to supply 'cheap labour' by working long hours for small reward. Some of the disadvantages of small-scale retailing are the difficulty in accumulating enough capital to expand; the lack of resources to advertise; the small size of turnover and orders, which prevent the securing of bulk-purchase economies which could lead to lower prices and greater turnover. Yet, despite the disadvantages of small size, the relatively high bankruptcy 'death rate', and the stepping up of competition in the retail trade, the small retailers appear to be surviving remarkably well. One of the reasons is the development, particularly in the grocery section, of voluntary buying chains of retailers, linked to wholesalers in exclusive trading contracts. This process has made great strides on the Continent, and is following suit in Britain.

In both the Grocers and Provisions sector and the Confectioners, Tobacconists and Newsagents (CTN) sector – in which the small independents predominate – the reduction in the number of outlets was more than double the average for all shops, between 1961 and 1971. However, in the CTN sector, the abolition of

[1] '"Save efficient small retail businesses" call to inquiry', *F.T.*, 19 May 1970.
[2] *Trade and Industry*, 25 Jan. 1973, p. 185.

RPM and the trends towards larger scale and out-of-town locations does not appear to have affected numbers and turnover as much as was feared. By 1971 about 2,000 CTN shops – roughly 4% of the total – had been drawn into *small* multiple chains, using modern methods of stock control. Although a fully fledged multiple is officially classified as having at least ten units, a more realistic figure in CTN might be fifty, as average shop turnover in CTN was only about £25,000 in 1971. A further 4,000 CTN shops (8% of the total) were estimated to have been reorganised into this *latter* category of multiples: the process of further rationalisation of CTN independents into fully fledged multiples was expected to continue.[1] In the grocery section, the independents which joined voluntary buying chains appear to have held their own against the competition from multiples. From fifty in 1954, the number of independent members reached 31,000 in 1966 and then levelled off. Whilst constituting only 32% of independent grocers, these 'symbol' shops accounted for more than 50% of independent grocery trade in 1970 – 24% of all grocery trade, as compared with 21% by the non-affiliated independents (see Fig. 8.5).[2] They face the problem of balancing democratic procedures against the need for efficient management control.[3]

As the turnover figures for the CTN and grocery sectors might imply, the switch towards self-service, the economies of voluntary chain buying and the flexibility and personal service, which the independents seek to foster, have resulted in an increase in turnover per shop. Also, the average floor space of the independents has tended to rise.[4]

DEPARTMENT STORE ORGANISATION

Department stores, which started in France and America and which are often grouped under holding companies to obtain further economies of scale, are essentially complex clusters of shops (departments) under one roof and one management. They may contain up to 300 different departments and have a turnover of several million pounds each, employing as many as 5,000 persons. They have two main sections, the selling departments and the non-selling. The latter range from the administrative, welfare and accounts offices to the warehousing, delivery, cleaning, security, publicity, display and complaints departments. These centralised sections provide services for all the selling departments, and may therefore be provided economically – if fully utilised. Such stores aim to provide a comprehensive selection of goods to consumers, and also offer attractions such as banking facilities snack-bars and restaurants, exhibitions, etc. Generally they are limited companies (public joint stock companies). The management of each store is divided into two main sections, both under the General Manager. These sections are:

(i) Administrative – covering all the service sections.

(ii) Merchandise. This section is the 'front-line' or productive section of store management. There is an Assistant General Manager, mainly responsible for the control of buying and selling. Under him are several Merchandise Managers or Group Controllers, each in charge of a whole floor or connected group of sales departments. Under each of these persons are the individual Department Sales

[1] 'An unsung success story in the High Street', *F.T.*, 27 Nov. 1972.
[2] 'Retailers plan for survival', *Management Today*, Sept. 1971, p. 105.
[3] 'Keeping the small retailer in line', *F.T.*, 29 Jan. 1969; and 'You can't keep a good shopkeeper down', *Econ.*, 23 Sept. 1972, p. 85.
[4] *Brit. O.H.*, 1972, p. 382; and 'Retail trade: present and future', *B.B.R.*, Nov. 1971, p. 72.

Managers (or Buyers). According to the type of central control, these latter will have different responsibilities. In some organisations with several stores there is a Central Buying Office. Here, Central Buyers are each responsible for the bulk-purchase of goods for a particular department (e.g. floor coverings) in every store. Each has a similar status to the Merchandise Managers in each store. Under such a system great economies of large-scale buying are possible; ranges and prices are fairly uniform throughout like departments in every store; each Sales Manager will be responsible for stock control, reordering and sales promotion in his department. In other firms, the head of each department is a Buyer, who is responsible for making his own selection of goods, as well as for sales promotion. Sometimes, under this system of individual department buying bulk-purchase economies may still be obtained from manufacturers by arrangements for assessing cumulatively the orders from a given department in each store.

Of course, such stores require a large clientele to support the tremendous capital outlay and heavy overheads involved. This has tended to result in their being located mainly in the centres of large cities (e.g. the West End of London). Some, however, have moved outwards to busy suburbs (and less competition), whilst yet others have moved outside the dense urban areas, in order to attract customers from the adjacent slice of urban area and from far afield outside it. Such a trend has been noticeable in the U.S.A. and has been advocated in Britain as an answer to the congestion and parking problems of the city centres.

Each department works according to a financial budget, based on past performance. Great flexibility between departments is possible by the reallocation of floor space when one department's sales are rising and those of another falling, either through seasonal factors or differences in relative efficiency. Sales promotion programmes are organised on the basis of Major Events (January and July Sales, etc.), Minor Events (e.g. Fashion Festival, Household Event, etc.), Target Weeks (for individual departments) and Departmental Promotions (e.g. 'Spotlight' on Umbrellas, etc.).

Advantages include the attractions of a comprehensive selection; the concentration of consumer purchasing power; bulk buying economies; great capital resources; efficient utilisation of special services; the possibility of catering for a wide range of incomes either in one store or with different stores under one holding company. Disadvantages include the heavy capital outlay; high overheads; the tendency for the proportion of non-selling personnel to rise as the number of departments increases; the long-term danger of falling future importance, as concentrated city centre location conflicts with increasing traffic congestion.

Of the 760 department stores in 1966, 308 were owned by independents, 214 by multiples and 238 by retail co-operatives. Of the 914 in 1971 369 were owned by independents, 296 by multiples and 249 by retail co-operatives. They are therefore not a distinctive form of *ownership* – as are the independents, the multiples and the retail co-operatives – but rather of a type of *organisation*. Their number had fallen from 784 in 1961, but rose to 914 in 1971. Many have adopted new methods, such as layouts similar to self-service stores and the incorporation of distinctive boutiques, within the general store.[1] The official classification of department stores was changed in 1971. Whilst still retaining the minimum of twenty-five

[1] 'Retail trade: present and future', *loc. cit.*, p. 72; 'Sweden's "do-it-yourself" department stores', *F.T.*, 26 Sept. 1969; 'Changing image of department stores', *D.T.*, 1 Dec. 1967.

persons engaged in selling a wide range of commodities, the classification specified sales of at least £15,000 in *each* of five or more commodity groups, of which
at least one must be in *each* of three commodity group categories.[1]

Whereas in 1966 department stores accounted for about 5·6% of total retail
trade (and 5·8% in 1971), 'large' department stores were responsible for 4·0%
of the total and for 85% of all department store turnover (see Tables 8.3 and 8.4).
The forces in play seem to be such that, on the one hand, the large department
store acts as a shopping focus or magnet, so that city centre or out-of-town
shopping centres will increasingly tend to have one: on the other hand, to operate
efficiently, the large department store needs to be in a large shopping centre. The
likelihood is that there will eventually be fewer but larger department stores.

MULTIPLE STORE ORGANISATION

The chief characteristic of multiple organisations is uniformity throughout the
branches, which are usually of normal, unit-shop size. The number of branches
ranges from 10 to 1,300 and more (e.g. Boots Pure Drug Co.) all under the same
financial management.[2]

Generally they are limited companies, which may have grown up out of smaller
independent traders. Some are regional and others are nationwide. There are
three main types of multiple:

(i) Those owned by manufacturers and intended mainly as outlets for their own
particular narrow range of products (e.g. Freeman, Hardy and Willis in footwear; Montague Burton in men's tailoring; Boots in pharmaceuticals, etc.).
(ii) Those· which confine themselves to a particular range of products in one
sector of trade and buy on a large scale from several manufacturers – sometimes
under contract and with their own labels on the goods (e.g. Sainsbury's in the
grocery trade; Halfords in cycle equipment; Marks and Spencer in clothing).
(iii) The 'variety chain stores', which offer a wide, 'bazaarlike' selection of goods,
obtained in bulk from many manufacturers (e.g. Woolworth, British Home
Stores, International Stores, etc.).

In all cases, economies of scale and integration are possible, making it possible
to offer goods at low, competitive prices. In all cases there is uniformity in the
external appearance of the branches, fixtures and fittings, range of stock, and
prices, so as to present an 'image' of continuity and stability in the minds of
consumers.

With this uniformity comes a high degree of centralised control. The ordering
of goods from suppliers, the keeping of accounts and statistical records, price
policy, stock-keeping (or warehousing) and transportation are all controlled by
headquarters, though sometimes there may be a little decentralisation of some
functions to regional headquarters. The branch manager is primarily responsible
for turnover and for sending regular reports of sales results and stock requirements to head office.

Some of the economies of large scale multiple retailing, apart from bulk
purchase at advantageous terms, are as follows:

(i) Continuity of range and supply.

---

[1] *Trade and Industry*, 21 Dec. 1972, pp. 622–3.
[2] See G. Burlton, 'Managing a multiple', *Stat.*, 19 Mar. 1965, pp. 797–9.

(ii) Economy through the pooling of stocks centrally, so that duplication is avoided. Only enough need be held to cope with emergencies throughout the group, and greater flexibility in satisfying the requirements of a particular branch may be secured.

(iii) The central pooling of profits and resources from all branches, which may be tapped to open up a new branch and/or to subsidise it during the initial period.

(iv) The pooling of management and skilled personnel – who may be available for service in any branch of the firm, if required.

With regard to the economy to be made by efficient central stock control, Boots have in recent years introduced computers to replace clerks and to speed up stock control at their Nottingham headquarters. There, orders come in daily from the 1,300 branches for the 60,000 different items held in stock. The new system requires a fraction of the clerical staff previously used, and enables stock records to be brought up to date within one hour, thus preventing the wastage of capital which might otherwise lie idle in the form of unnecessary stocks. Such methods are increasingly being adopted by other multiple organisations.

Many multiple firms have, in recent years, been in the forefront of the self-service and supermarket developments in the grocery trade, which have been revolutionising the British retail food sector.[1]

As mentioned above, many department stores are owned by multiples. There has been a trend for multiples to open large scale units and out-of-town and shopping centre 'superstores'. There was a reversal in the trend of multiple shop numbers by 1971. The number, including department stores, rose from 66,701 in 1961 to 73,852 in 1966, but fell to 67,479 in 1971 – a fall of about 9%. During the period 1966–71 they increased their turnover by 58%, reflecting the trend towards fewer and larger units. In the food sector their numbers fell by 16%, whilst turnover rose by 55%. During this period the multiples, particularly in drapery and clothing, were examining the possibilities of expansion into the E.E.C. countries.[2]

The April 1971 Prices and Incomes Board report on food distribution found that the multiples, in particular, had been exercising their power and competitive strategies to the advantage of the consumer, in regard to prices and profit margins.[3]

The share of multiples in total retail turnover rose from 29·2% in 1961 to 39·8% in 1971 (see Table 8.3). They had the fastest rates of growth in all retail trade, between 1966 and 1970 (35%) – especially in food (40%) and durable goods (36%). As was mentioned above, by 1971 they had begun to make a noticeable impact on the CTN sector, with about 4,000 stores (almost 8% of CTN shops) in groups of at least fifty. This traditional 'independent' sector was expected to experience further encroachments and rationalisation by the multiples.[4]

---

[1] See 'A treat in store for Portsmouth', *F.T.*, 29 Nov. 1972; 'Marks & Spencer lead plastics pack revolution', *D.T.*, 13 Feb. 1969; 'First train your farmer, then sell his chickens', *S.T.* (colour supplement), 12 May 1968; G. Rees, *St Michael: a history of Marks and Spencer*, 1968.
[2] See 'Sainsbury seeks large shops but few', *F.T.*, 22 Oct. 1969; 'Fifth Woolco superstore to open on Oct. 5', *F.T.*, 18 Sept. 1971; *Trade and Industry*, 25 Jan. 1973, pp. 184–5; see 'Cautiously to the Continent go the British retailers', *F.T.*, 10 Feb. 1973.
[3] 'Pat on the back for the multiples', *F.T.*, 21 April 1971.
[4] 'An unsung success story in the High Street', *F.T.*, 27 Nov. 1972.

RETAIL CO-OPERATIVE SOCIETIES

These societies are consumer co-operatives, owned and managed by members of the purchasing public so as to obtain economies of bulk purchase from manufacturers and financial economies in the pooling of capital resources. They are voluntary, non-profit-making organisations, which started in Rochdale in 1844; any net profits made are distributed to the members as a dividend, according to the value of their purchases. The general public may also use the stores of the societies, but they have no vote and receive no dividend. Membership of a society entails the payment of a deposit on a £1 minimum share. A maximum of £1,000 may be invested in a society's shares, on which a low rate of interest is paid.

Details of the organisation, trends and problems of the retail co-operative societies are given earlier in the book, in Chapter 4, Section 3 (b), under CHANGE, (ii) *Cooperation*.

The movement played an important part in the initial development of supermarkets and smaller self-service and mobile food shops in Britain, but it has since been losing ground to the multiples.

Between 1961 and 1971 the share of the retail co-operatives in total retail trade fell from 10·9% to 7·2% (see Table 8.3), There was a drop in co-op shops of 44% between 1966 and 1971, reflecting amalgamations and rationalisation. Whereas they constituted 5·3% of all shops in 1966, the share had fallen to 3·1% in 1971. Between 1966 and 1971 turnover (*including* department stores) rose by only 8% and their share fell from 9·1% to 7·2%.[1] Between 1966 and 1970 turnover – before allowing for price rises – rose by only 7% (9% in food, and an actual reduction of 6% in clothing and footwear). In 1966 the 'large' co-operative societies accounted for 7·9% of total retail trade, but for 84% of the 9·1% of retail trade achieved by all retail co-operatives.

By late-1972 the co-operatives had two 'superstores' – out-of-town units with at least 25,000 square feet of shopping space on one floor – and planned to have about twenty by 1975.[2] Also in late-1972 the decision was taken to increase the advertising budget by one-third, to £3·5 million, in order to undertake more aggressive marketing and make better use of potential market power.[3]

Some of the advantages of consumer retail co-operatives are as follows:

(i) Consumer loyalty, on political or moral grounds.
(ii) Economies of scale and integration (e.g. bulk purchase, pooled capital, 'divi' from C.W.S., etc.).
(iii) The incentive of the dividend to members.
(iv) Possibility for a high degree of democracy in internal management.

Some of the disadvantages are:

(i) Inexperienced, voluntary and sometimes inefficient retail society management committees.
(ii) Promotion based on length of service rather than ability: this, combined with the relatively low salaries paid to personnel and executive management in all sections, tends to result in a lack of efficient management and personnel and useful new ideas.

[1] *Trade and Industry*, 25 Jan. 1973, pp. 184–5.
[2] *F.T.*, 30 Nov. 1972.
[3] 'Co-op starts to show its muscle', *F.T.*, 30 Nov. 1972 and 'Co-op retail societies: the slow decline', *Obs.*, 17 Dec. 1972.

(iii) The hard core of consumer loyalty tends to lead to complacency and lack of competitiveness and initiative: this in turn sometimes leads to inefficient levels of production, slow stock turnover in the shops, and a low level of profitability.

(d) Retailing without shops

The many forms of non-shop retailing, some of long standing and others of more recent origin, have been making significant strides in recent years. The main types are as follows:

ITINERANT SALESMEN, MANUFACTURERS' CANVASSERS, STREET TRADERS (HAWKERS, ETC.), MARKET STALLHOLDERS AND MOBILE SHOPS

Itinerant salesmen vary from gypsies to bicycle-mounted onion sellers, and appear to be largely vestigial survivors on the retail scene.

Manufacturers' canvassers are one medium of direct selling from manufacturers to the public. They operate in such commodities as domestic electrical goods, encyclopaedias, carpets, soft drinks, brushes and polishes, etc. It was estimated that in 1961 such salesmen accounted for about 56% of the £144 million sales direct from manufacturers to consumers.[1]

Street traders or hawkers range from the 'barrow-boys' (fruit and vegetables) to flower sellers, and newspaper vendors, with a more or less fixed 'pitch', to unlicensed salesmen operating out of an open suitcase, ready to 'close up' and move off at a moment's notice.

Market stallholders operate on market squares and other pitches, controlled by local authorities, who usually provide for the setting up of stalls and charge a stallage fee. Some of these markets (markets 'overt') are of long standing and are covered by Royal Charters or statute. Markets are usually held on set days, which vary from town to town, so that the traders can move round to a different point on a circuit on each day of the week.[2]

Of the 35,000 market stallholders and mobile shops in 1961, 11,700 were estimated to have been mobile shops. Combined turnover for both was £90·7 million. By 1971 the combined numbers had fallen by 32·8% to 24,343 and turnover had risen by only 7·3% to £97·8 million (see Table 8.1). Nearly 25% of the mobile shop sales are estimated to take place in Scotland, as compared with only about 10% of total retail turnover. The retail co-operatives were responsible for about 39% of mobile shop sales – mainly food retailing (42% grocers, 28% greengrocers and 21% butchers) – as compared with its share of about 16% in all food retailing.[3]

AUTOMATIC VENDING MACHINES

Although coin-operated vending machines were used before World War II for the sale of cigarettes, chocolate, etc., the number and range of such machines has been increased greatly in recent years. They offer the consumer a twenty-four-hour per day service, and may be conveniently located in places which do not require a shop or kiosk. Operating overheads are very low. Such machines have been adapted for the sale of hot and cold beverages, ready prepared foodstuffs, ladies' stockings, etc., and have been set up on streets and in stations, cinemas,

[1] *Brit. O.H.*, 1964, p. 442.
[2] 'Street traders', *Econ.*, 12 April 1969, p. 26.
[3] *Brit. O.H.*, 1972, p. 384.

factories and offices. It was estimated that in 1970 there were more than 400,000 such machines in use in Britain, with a total turnover of about £170 million annually – including £35 million on hot drinks and £100 million on cigarettes. Another form of automatic vending is the self-service petrol pump, sometimes completely automated, with regard to payment.[1] The Census of Distribution data is for the sale of automatic vending *machines* by organisations *not* otherwise engaged in retail trade. These increased from 26 to 56 between 1961 and 1966, with a turnover increase of 167 %, but between 1966 and 1971 they only rose to 60, with a turnover of £10·9 million (a zero percentage increase over 1966, see Table 8.1).

MAIL-ORDER RETAILING AND 'DIRECT MAIL' SELLING

In recent years retail trading through the post, on the basis of full- and part-time agents, catalogues, and newspaper, TV and other advertising, has been growing very rapidly. There are four main forms of mail-order retailing:[2]

(i) Large, general, specialist MO retailers – mainly in clothing, footwear and household textiles, offering a wide range of goods through catalogues, agents and advertisements.
(ii) Small, specialist MO retailers – generally concerned with a single commodity and dealing mainly in seeds, plants and horticultural goods.
(iii) Large retail shops – usually department stores, which advertise their goods through catalogues and press and TV advertisements.
(iv) Manufacturers, selling direct to the public through TV and press advertisements.

One of the main advantages of this type of retailing is the possibility of achieving large scale economies in bulk buying. Another is the absence of the need to maintain expensive retail outlets at every selling point. Others are the possibility of delaying orders to suppliers until goods have been ordered by customers, and the possibility of keeping warehouses, offices and staff on relatively cheap provincial sites, where labour is not scarce. The large, specialist MO retailers usually offer customers the incentive of being able to make instalment payments without the usual hire purchase charges. This is made possible by the reduced overheads and by favourable bulk purchase discounts from suppliers.

One of the growing disadvantages of mail order retailing is the increasing cost element of postal charges. Whilst the MO firms have not been heavily involved in food retailing and used to complement other forms of trading, they have been meeting increasing competition from the latter. This, with rising postal costs and increasing difficulty in recruiting agents, has led to a slowing down in the growth rate of the MO retailers. The number of MO organisations grew by 21·6 %, to 676, between 1961 and 1971: turnover, however, which grew by 89 % between 1961 and 1966, rose by only 44·4 % between 1966 and 1971, reaching £619 million (3·8 % of total retail turnover, as compared with 3·7 % in 1966).[3] According to the annual inquiry figures for 'large' firms, large MO firms were responsible for

1 'Vending', supplement in *F.T.*, 8 Jan. 1971.
2 See 'The group that made good', *Stat.*, 1 Jan. 1965, pp. 46–7 and 'Growth in the medium-sized companies', *ibid.*, pp. 47–8.
3 'Middle-class mail order', *Management Today*, April 1971, pp. 43–6; 'Spending: mail order's battle to keep up with the boom', *F.T.*, 6 Sept. 1972.

95% of all MO trade in 1966. It seems that a figure of 84% might be more likely.

'Direct mail' sales by manufacturers to the public reached about £100 million in 1971, with an annual growth rate of about 10%.[1] The business is divided between manufacturers (or publishers), who handle their own direct mail campaigns – such as *Reader's Digest*, the leading exponent – who account for about 95% of turnover, and forty or so firms, which undertake to organise campaigns on behalf of clients. The British Direct Mail Advertising Association held its first national conference in January 1961.

(e) Recent developments

Some of the most significant trends noticeable in retailing in recent years have been in the following spheres:

Hire purchase.
Consumer protection.
Stamp trading and promotional offers.
Locational movements – suburban fringe 'hypermarkets', city centre and regional 'shopping centres', etc.
Diversification – the breakdown of traditional ranges, spheres of influence and methods.
Flexibility in shopping hours.
Modernisation of techniques – packaging, advertising, stock control, etc.
Cut-price retailing – with self-service stores, supermarkets and 'cash and carry' discount houses and 'own brand' retailing.

HIRE-PURCHASE

As the Radcliffe Report on the monetary system noted in 1959, hire purchase (or instalment payment, or retail credit) was becoming as important a source of credit for equipping homes as was the system of building society mortgages for purchasing them. This form of retail sale has made great strides in recent years, particularly in household and other durable consumer goods, such as private and commercial vehicles, furniture, refrigerators, TV sets, washing machines and cookers. This form of transaction has become an important factor in the sales of these products, and the Government has exerted a great influence over them by means of its power to regulate the terms of hire purchase and credit sales agreements. Interest is charged on the total original amount on credit until the last payment has been made.

Hire-purchase finance may be provided directly by household goods shops (sometimes rediscounted, or guaranteed, by finance houses) and directly by finance houses, which cover some household goods sales but concentrate mainly on motor vehicles and industrial, farm and commercial vehicles. Most finance house business is concentrated in a small number of firms.

At end-December 1971 the total of HP and other instalment credit outstanding was £1,628 million, of which 62% was owing to finance houses directly and the remainder to retailers. Table 8.5 shows the distribution of such debt from 1965 to 1971. It will be noticed that whilst the share of durable goods shops has been

[2] 'Direct mail', supplement in *F.T.*, 24 Oct. 1972 and 'Direct mail', *F.T.*, 26 Jan. 1971.

Table 8.5 *Hire-purchase and other instalment debt outstanding at end of period*
(£m)

	1965	1966	1967	1968	1969	1971	1972
Total*	1,431	1,302	1,266	1,311	1,295	1,628	2,064
Owing to:							
durable goods shops ⎱	⎱ 360	⎱ 278	248	250	245	—	—
department stores ⎰		⎰ 29	28	31	31	—	—
other instalment credit retailers†	190	198	208	222	232	—	—
Total amount owing to retailers	550	505	484	503	508	618	—
as percentage of total	*38·4*	*38·8*	*38·2*	*38·4*	*39·2*	*38·0*	—
Amount owing to finance houses*	881	797	782	808	787	1,010	—
as percentage of total	*61·6*	*61·2*	*61·8*	*61·6*	*60·8*	*62·0*	—

*Including debt arising from transactions in cars and industrial equipment.
† Comprising general stores (other than department stores), general mail-order houses and co-operative society non-durable goods departments.

(Based on material in *M.B.R.*, Aug. 1970; *Trade and Industry*, 9 Nov., 1972; *D.T.*, 6 Feb. 1972)

falling, that of general stores, mail order houses and co-operative retail stores has increased. By end-December 1972 the total of HP and other instalment credit by finance houses and retailers rose by 27% to £2,064 million – influenced by the 1972 'soft' budget and tax and credit relaxations and by fears of future price rises resulting from inflation and the introduction of VAT in 1973. These figures probably under-estimated the extent of retail credit, since they did not include bank loans for the financing of retail purchases, nor did they include 'credit card' buying – a form of temporary bank loan.[1]

Other forms of consumer credit have been waxing and waning, causing the overall pattern to alter. Some of the finance raised by second mortgages on homes is increasingly being used to finance consumer purchases. Some of the traditional purveyors of consumer credit, such as check and voucher trading firms, are moving into new kinds of business. The use of credit cards, noted in earlier chapters, has been growing.[2]

In July 1971 the temporary removal of all restrictions on the terms of hire purchase, credit sales and rental agreements came into effect.

Substantial losses were suffered through bad debts in the early 1960s by the finance houses, and measures have since been taken to check the standards of credit-worthiness of clients. These include the establishment of 'credit bureaux', which keep registers of borrowers' credit histories.[3]

The 1965 Hire-Purchase Act and Hire-Purchase (Scotland) Act provided some safeguards to buyers on hire-purchase or credit terms, on agreements up to £2,000. The Crowther Committee on Consumer Credit, reporting in March 1971, advocated the establishment of a Credit Commissioner to monitor all consumer credit activities and also proposed a Consumer Sale and Loan Act, regulating all consumer credit transactions and extending the safeguards which operated on H.P. agreements to all loans.[4]

[1] 'Biggest increase for ten years in consumer spending', *D.T.*, 6 Feb. 1973.
[2] 'Credit', *E.P.R.*, 22 Dec. 1971.   [3] *Econ.*, 13 July 1963, p. 155.
[4] Credit,' *loc. cit.*, 'Credit after Crowther', *Econ.*, 27 March 1971, pp. 69–70 and 'Britain in hock', *Econ.*, 27 March 1971, pp. 66–7.

Resale Price Maintenance – the system whereby manufacturers have been able to insist on the final retail price of their branded products – made extensive strides during the interwar and post-World War II period. It was claimed on behalf of the manufacturers that it made for stability of consumer demand, the protection of the consumer from overcharging, and the protection of small retailers from unscrupulous price-cutting by competitors. In effect, it tended to shelter the inefficient retailer from competition, as the fixed price was usually high enough to provide him with a safe profit margin.[1] It also gave the efficient retailer no possibility to increase sales by offering lower prices. This simply meant that the manufacturer was assured of the maximum number of outlets – as all had to sell at the same price. In 1956 the Restrictive Trade Practices Act gave individual manufacturers the right to uphold their fixed prices by legal action, but made it generally illegal for groups of manufacturers to combine collusively to fix prices. In February 1964 the Government introduced a Resale Prices Bill, to make any resale price maintenance agreement illegal – subject to certain considerations of 'public interest'. The resultant Resale Prices Act came into effect at the end of April 1965.

It is worthy of note that the spread of 'cut-price' selling in recent years, especially in the grocery trade, had already reduced the power of RPM agreements. By 1964 it was estimated that 60% of retail trade was no longer covered by RPM.[2] Other retailers (e.g. Marks and Spencer in clothing and Sainsbury's in foodstuffs) had partly bypassed RPM by arranging to have their own brand name put on goods supplied to them. The significance of RPM may be seen from Table 8.6.

Table 8.6 *The influence of price-fixing (RPM) on retail trade*

Wholly free	Prices mainly fixed	Prices partly fixed	Prices 'recommended'
Meat	Cars	Stationery	Bread and cakes
Greengroceries	Electrical goods	Ironmongery	Carpets and
Pet foods	TV, etc.	Furniture	floorcoverings
Farm chemicals	Drugs and cosmetics	Branded clothes	Branded groceries
Unbranded goods	Books, etc.	Leather	Branded textiles
Most imports	Cigarettes and	Clocks	Petrol
Except:	tobacco	Toys	
		Tools	
Cars	Sweets and ice-cream		
Tape recorders	Drink		
Cameras	Cameras		
Books	Seeds, sprays, etc.		
Typewriters	Perambulators		

(Source: *Econ.*, 29 Feb. 1964, p. 812)

The main outlines of Resale Price Maintenance (RPM), its abolition in 1964 and subsequent effects and developments were given earlier, in Chapter 4, Section 2(a), 2(ii). The outlines of consumer protection – covering the 1953 Merchandise Marks Act, the 1963 Weights and Measures Act, the coming and

---

[1] For gross profit margins in various sectors of the retail trade from 1950 to 1960, see 'Will prices and margins be lower?', *Stat.*, 26 Mar. 1965, pp. 861–2.

[2] *D.T.*, 26 Feb. 1964.

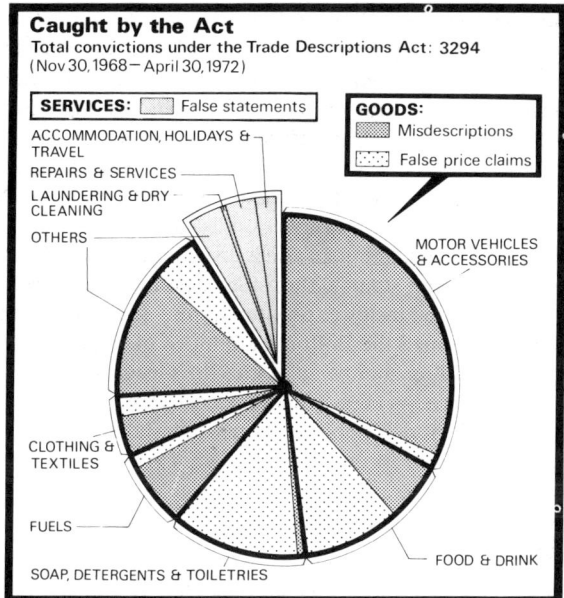

Caught by the Act
Total convictions under the Trade Descriptions Act: 3294
(Nov 30, 1968 – April 30, 1972)

SERVICES: False statements

GOODS:
Misdescriptions
False price claims

ACCOMMODATION, HOLIDAYS &
TRAVEL
REPAIRS & SERVICES
LAUNDERING & DRY
CLEANING
OTHERS

MOTOR VEHICLES
& ACCESSORIES

CLOTHING &
TEXTILES

FUELS

SOAP, DETERGENTS & TOILETRIES

FOOD & DRINK

Fig. 8.6. *Total convictions under the Trade Descriptions Act:* 3294
(30 *Nov.* 1968 – 30 *April* 1972)
(Source: *Econ.*, 28 Oct. 1972, p. 69)

going of the Consumer Council and the 1968 Trade Descriptions Act – were also
given earlier, in Chapter 4, Section 3(*b*), under REFORM. An analysis of the 3,294
convictions under the Trade Descriptions Act, from end-November 1968 to end-
April 1972, is given in Fig. 8.6. It will be noted that about one-third were for false
price claims. In this respect it is of interest that in January 1973 the Consumer
Safeguards Group, set up by the Metrication Board, suggested that foodstuffs
and other suitable goods should be subject to 'unit pricing' – whereby they are
marked with the cost per unit of measurement or weight – so as to permit
value-for-money comparisons.[1]

In December 1972 the Government introduced the Fair Trading Bill,[2] which
became law in August 1973. This proposed the establishment of a Director-
General of Fair Trading, to protect consumers from unfair and shoddy goods
and services, and the setting up of a Consumer Protection Advisory Committee,
to act as a channel for consumers' complaints. In February 1973, when the
Supply of Goods (Implied Terms) Bill was given its Second Reading – it dealt
with 'phony guarantees' and exclusion clauses in consumer sales – it was
described as the first step towards the proposed creation of a comprehensive
programme of consumer protection legislation.[3] In March 1974 the Department
of Prices and Consumer Protection was created.[4]

[1] *F.T.*, 24 Jan. 1973.
[2] 'The Fair Trading Bill – a major development in consumer protection', *Trade and Industry*,
7 Dec. 1972, pp. 474–8; *Econ.*, 9 Dec. 1972, pp. 85–6; 'Watchdog for the wicked businessman',
S.T., 3 Dec. 1972.
[3] *F.T.*, 14 Feb. 1973.
[4] See 'The DTI dismembered', *Econ.*, 9 March 1974, p. 78.

TRADING STAMPS AND PROMOTIONAL OFFERS

Since World War II the practice by which retailers gave their clients, with every purchase, free trading stamps – which could later be exchanged for free goods – has made fairly steady progress. During the 1960s several multiple food and other organisations decided to offer trading stamps in lieu of, or as well as, price reductions. In 1968 Cadbury became the first U.K. manufacturer to give trading stamps with its goods at point-of-sale outlets.[1] By 1969 Green Shield, the major stamp sponsoring firm, claimed a turnover on its stamps of £21 million – 75% of the market – access to 20,000 retailers and a growth rate of 24% per annum.[2] If, eventually, all retailers offer stamps, the added cost may be passed on in higher prices, but may be absorbed by lower profit margins.[3] In this respect the National Chamber of Trade informed the Bolton Committee of Inquiry on Small Firms, in March 1970, that trading stamps, gifts and 'loss-leaders' were a form of 'destructive competition'. They claimed that the cost was in fact passed on to the consumer, that in their absence competition would be adequate to keep down prices and that they worked to the disadvantage of small businesses.[4]

LOCATIONAL MOVEMENTS: SUBURBAN 'HYPERMARKETS' *versus* CITY CENTRE AND REGIONAL 'SHOPPING CENTRES'

The 1961 Census of Distribution revealed that one-third of total retail trade in Britain was done in the 272 main 'shopping centres' in towns with populations exceeding 50,000. Shopping centres were areas 'characterised by the presence of department stores or other large shops which attract shoppers from a wide area'. It was found, furthermore, that large towns had a greater proportion of their retail sales in a concentrated shopping area than did the larger conurbations. In smaller market towns the proportion went up to 60·1%; in towns from 50,000 to 100,000 it averaged 52·4%; in conurbations it ranged from 28·1% (south-east Lancashire) to 48·8% (Greater London). This seemed to indicate the lower concentration of shopping in densely populated areas, where traffic congestion and allied problems in town centres are deterrents to shoppers.

In November 1961 an attempt was made to gain permission for the building of the first part of a ring of shopping centres at Watford, on the fringe of the Greater London Area.[5] It was turned down, but the economic pressures which led to the proposal still remain, and may be expected to lead to this sort of development, as has happened in motorised America. The reasoning behind such projects – which, in America, are often financed by city centre department stores – is that the traditional concentrated shopping centre of a conurbation attracts shoppers from all over the area. This leads to increasing congestion, delays and costs. If the conurbation were divided up into radial segments, a fraction of the traditional city centre shops, located on the fringe of each segment, would serve the whole segment. Furthermore, the flow of consumers would be outwards, to less restricted parts of the segment, where parking space and site costs would be lower. The principles of such 'self-contained urban segment' shopping centre location may be seen from Fig. 8.7.

[1] See 'Cadbury joins the stamp set', *D.T.*, 2 May 1968.
[2] See 'Green Shield grows fast', *D.T.*, 15 Feb. 1969.
[3] See H. Unger, 'U.S. tires of trading stamps', *Stat.*, 24 Sept. 1965, pp. 833–4.
[4] See *F.T.*, 14 March 1970.
[5] 'The shops move out', *Obs.*, 19 Nov. 1961.

(a) Traditional city centre concentration

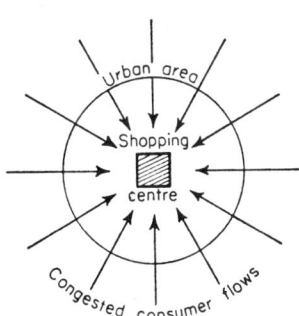

(b) Dispersed shopping centres in self-contained urban segments

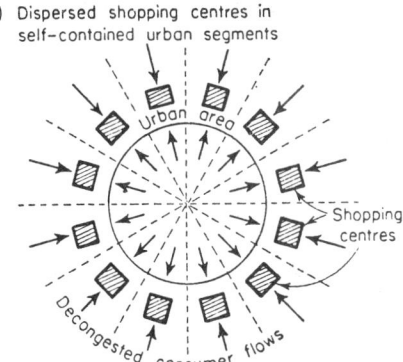

Fig. 8.7. *The dispersed location of shopping centres in 'self-contained urban segments'*

By mid-1964 the Minister of Housing and Local Government had approved 113 schemes for central area redevelopment in several towns, whilst another 72 schemes were under consideration. In addition, more than 200 schemes were in the early stages of local authority planning. Most of these schemes included proposals for new shopping facilities, ranging from a few shops in small towns to the multi-million pound Bull Ring development in Birmingham.[1]

During the 1960s there has been a crystallisation of trends and arguments in the debate about retail location and retail planning. On the one hand, as noted above, a great deal of redevelopment has taken place in some *city centres*, such as Birmingham, Coventry, Wolverhampton and Plymouth. These, allied with the provision of parking facilities and pedestrian precincts, are an attempt to build upon the acknowledged attractions of city centres – with their variety of stores and cultural and recreational facilities – whilst also attempting to minimise the congestion problems. On the other hand, there has been a great deal of interest in out-of-town *hypermarkets* (clusters of stores with a total of more than 25,000 square feet of selling area) – an extension of the self-service and cut-price supermarket. By mid-1971 there were 368 in West Germany, 128 in France and 34 in Belgium,[2] but the first one had only just received planning permission in the U.K. – outside Telford in Shropshire.[3] Some of the major advantages claimed were the cheaper site costs, as compared with town centres – particularly relevant for goods requiring a lot of space, as with furniture; convenience for shoppers, with parking facilities, reduced congestion and potentially lower prices. Some of the disadvantages, however, were that they might drain custom away from nearby town centre retailers, create new congestion problems on approach roads, and aesthetically spoil the rural landscape. In 1970 one of the biggest multiple cut-price grocers, Tesco, was planning to concentrate future superstore developments on out-of-town sites, selling a wide range of goods.[4] The Co-op opened its second superstore (50,000 square feet) outside Birkenhead at end-1972 and planned to

[1] 'Changes in retail distribution', *Bull. Ind.*, 174, May 1964.
[2] See 'Shopping goes out-of-town', *Econ.*, 15 April 1972, pp. 60–1.
[3] See 'Act now to avoid a shops surplus', *F.T.*, 22 April 1971.
[4] *F.T.*, 25 Nov. 1970.

have several more by 1975.[1] Several large retailers appeared to be assuming that the future lay in U.S.-style motorised shopping and felt frustrated by the reluctance of planning authorities to grant permission for superstores or hypermarkets. In April 1971 the Distributive Trades E.D.C. published a report on the future pattern of shopping, which drew attention to the possible wastage of national resources on unlimited hypermarket proliferation, leading to future excess capacity. It strengthened the case for city centre developments and pointed to the need for a coordinated national policy on retail planning.[2] The Department of the Environment, in May 1971, finally laid down guidelines for policy.[3] Whilst accepting the need to avoid increasing city centre congestion, accepting the rising trend towards motorised shopping, and accepting the need for out-of-town sites for suburban areas with poor shopping facilities, it made some provisos. Firstly, the 25% or so of families who might *lack* cars by 1980 would have to be catered for. Secondly, large scale 'green field' shopping sites, *without* the associated commercial and social facilities of the town or city centre, might be of less use to the community than a *district* centre in or near a built-up area. In future, all applications for stores exceeding 50,000 square feet were to be submitted to the Ministry for approval. This policy statement was followed by a wave of plans for stores below the 50,000 square feet limit, which might appear to lead to future excess capacity, whilst not achieving the 'comprehensive magnet' or focal point attributes of the traditional city centre.

The possible outcome of these conflicting objectives and trends might be along the following lines. Many of the 'superstores' might prove to be uneconomic at or below the 50,000 square feet limit. (Many of the French hypermarkets have more than 100,000 square feet. Furthermore, many of the applications for stores in excess of 50,000 square feet are *not* for 'green field' sites but for edge-of-town, semi-industrial sites.[4] This indicates that they recognise the weakness of their limited size as a countermagnet to the attractions of the city centre).[5] The logical development might be for local authorities and groups of firms to collaborate in the planning of true 'green field' sites, not as isolated 50,000 square feet stores, but as much larger regional shopping centres, incorporating department stores, numerous superstores and smaller stores on sites of about 1 million square feet, with adjacent cultural and sporting amenities.

The *regional shopping centre* (or *shopping market*), based on American models, has been widely adopted in France. Designed to serve catchment areas with 0·3 to 0·5 million people and more, they incorporate new and traditional forms of retailing, with restaurants, cinemas, etc., and have less need for price-cutting as an attraction. In the U.S., by 1972, 13,000 shopping centres of all sizes accounted for about 44% of all retail distribution. France was planning to have twenty or thirty regional centres by 1987 (see Fig. 8.8). Sweden already had 1 per 2 million inhabitants; Switzerland had 1 per 3·1 million and West Germany 1 per 3·4 million.[6]

In Britain the first three RSC projects were the Runcorn 'shopping city' (a

[1] See 'Hypermarkets: Still waiting', *Econ.*, 2 Dec. 1972, p. 97.
[2] See 'Act now to avoid a shops surplus', *loc. cit.*
[3] See 'Out-of-town shopping centres: Ministry's planning note', *F.T.*, 19 May 1971.
[4] See 'Hypermarkets: Still waiting', *loc. cit.*
[5] See 'Retail trade: present and future', *loc. cit.*, p. 74.
[6] See 'Shopping centres in France', *Conjoncture*, 148, Feb. 1972; *F.T.*, 17 Jan. 1972; 'Retail trade: present and future', *loc. cit.*, pp. 73–4.

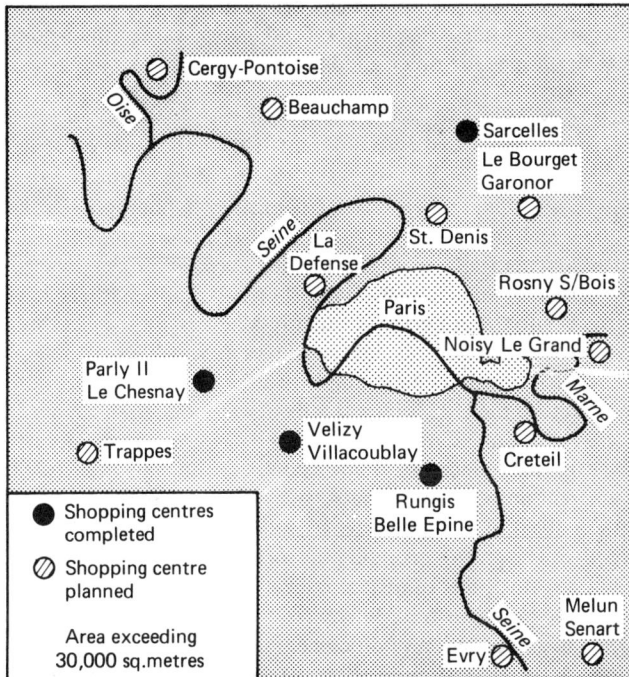

Fig. 8.8. *Completed and planned Regional Shopping Centres, Paris region, 1972* (Source: *Conjoncture*, 148, Feb. 1972)

£10 million development, opened in November 1971, to serve 1·5 million persons within a 12·5 mile radius of Runcorn), the Northampton shopping centre (220,000 square feet, planned to open in late-1974) and the Brent Cross development (800,000 square feet, a £12 million project, planned for 1975). All these were planned for the outskirts of urban areas, however, and not as truly peripheral countermagnets.[1]

A great deal of research needs to be conducted on consumer shopping habits and the criteria for retail planning. The Distributive Trades E.D.C. announced, in October 1972, the creation of a data-collecting and research unit to examine all aspects of retail planning.[2] It was noted in 1969 that shopping trends in the U.K. were *not*, in fact, following the U.S. pattern, in which about half of all shopping takes place in the suburbs. A 1970 survey suggested that more than 44% of housewives preferred the inconvenience of city centre shopping, with its choice, intimacy and excitement, as against 7½% who preferred 'one-stop', out-of-town shopping. This was supported by a 1971 Building Research Centre study of shopping patterns in Watford. This found that only 5% of shoppers practised once-a-week shopping; at least 42% shopped nearly every day; about 40% pur-

[1] See *F.T.*, 4 Nov. 1971; *S.T.*, 6 Feb. 1972; *F.T.*, 23 Jan. 1973.
[2] See *F.T.*, 25 Oct. 1972. In February 1973 the Chairman of this new Retail Planning Unit was appointed. The unit, expected to start work in late-1973 with an initial Government grant of £60,000 over three years, was to function within the framework of the Centre for Environmental Studies. It was to conduct some of its research for local authorities and retailers and it was hoped to be eventually self-supporting (*F.T.*, 5 Feb. 1973).

chased a quarter of their food in the city centre and 80% of these were prepared to make separate journeys for minor food items, rather than combine such purchases with outings for other goods.[1]

DIVERSIFICATION

Increasing competition and the abolition of RPM and some restrictive practices have been accompanied by an erosion of the traditional limits to the ranges of goods stocked by different retailers. Chemists sell photographic equipment; cinemas sell sweets and tobacco; grocers sell drugs and medicines; fish shops sell poultry; butchers sell frozen fish, etc. Perhaps grocers, faced with the stiffest competition of all from self-service shops and supermarkets, have made the greatest inroads into the preserves of other retailers. In most cases this involved a rational desire to utilise point-of-sale resources as widely as possible, to achieve maximum possible turnover. An example of this, by mobile distributors, was the decision by Unigate, the U.K.'s largest milk distributors, to sell canned beer from its milk floats:[2] this type of multiple-product distribution from mobile points-of-sale may be expected to increase. Some examples of the breakdown in traditional product demarcation may appear less rational, as in the case when the author asked at a Sandbach (Cheshire) greengrocery store if they stocked chicory, for adding to coffee. The greengrocer did not stock this vegetable, which may be used in coffee, but did stock tins of instant coffee.

Apart from the breakdown of differences in *product* ranges, another aspect of diversification is the reduction of differences in *techniques* and practices between retail outlets. As more and more shops – food and non-food – change over to some form of self-service, so do the differences between the multiples, supermarket chains, 'corner store' independents and department stores dissolve.[3]

FLEXIBILITY IN SHOPPING HOURS

Since World War II many retailers have experimented with variations on conventional shopping hours, so as to cater for working housewives and city workers. Some shops operate late night closing on one day of the week. Many shops now stay open during office lunch hours. In February 1964 the Government started consultations with shopkeepers, trade unions and consumers' councils about possible legislation for greater flexibility on Sunday opening, late night opening, suspension of weekly half-day closing, etc.[4] It appeared that the small shopkeeper might find the possibility, in such flexibility, to offer a better service to his clients and thus be able to face the increasing price competition which might follow the abolition of RPM.

As was mentioned above, U.S.-style one-stop motorised shopping was *not* assuming significant proportions in Britain during the 1960s. Factors such as the one-car family head driving to work; the more accessible U.K. town centres; the post-slum clearance and post-bomb damage city centre redevelopments; the 68% of shoppers (1968) who shop on foot, while only 17% shop by car; these and similar factors have tended to result in fairly frequent shopping, which concen-

[1] 'Britain's high streets survive', *Econ.*, 4 Jan. 1969, pp. 38–9; 'Planners thwart move out-of-town', *F.T.*, 26 Nov. 1970; 'A fresh and surprising look at how we shop', *S.T.*, 25 July 1971.
[2] See *F.T.*, 10 Jan. 1973.
[3] See 'Retail Trade: Present and Future', *loc. cit.*, p. 75.
[4] *D.T.*, 6 Feb. 1964; 'Open – or closed – for shopping?', *Stat.*, 10 Sept. 1965, pp. 709–10.
[5] See 'Britain's high streets survive', *Econ.*, 4 Jan. 1969, pp. 38–9.

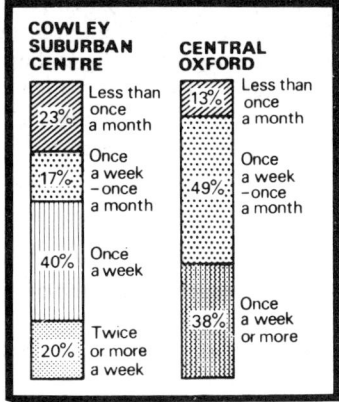
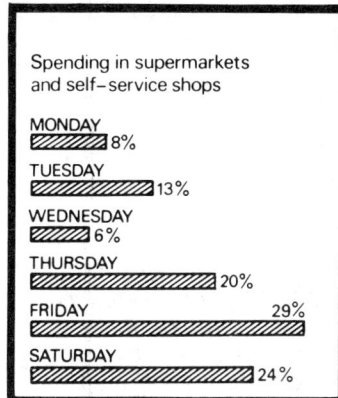

Fig. 8.9. *Shopping patterns in Cowley and central Oxford, 1968*
(Source: *Econ.*, 4 Jan. 1969, p. 38)

trates into evenings (especially late-opening nights) and weekends (see Fig. 8.9 on the pattern in Cowley and central Oxford).[5] Thus, a great deal of retail resources are not fully utilised for much of the time: greater flexibility in hours of opening might, therefore, be expected to provide an important area of competition, in which the smaller retailers might find a further means of survival – particularly as larger stores face increasing problems of labour recruitment.

MODERNISATION OF TECHNIQUES

The ferment accompanying the increase in retail competition in recent years has resulted in new ideas on modernisation and productivity. Equipment has been improved, as an aid to self-selection, and clerical work has been pruned down to reduce costs, as in the case of Marks and Spencer and Boots. One of the most ingenious ideas, being pursued in the U.S.A. and studied in Britain,[1] is for the use of push-button telephones for remote control ordering, by customers, from a fully automatic warehouse-supermarket. Automated, computer-controlled warehouse stock-keeping had already made much headway in France by the end of the 1960s:[2] such techniques must inevitably find many applications in British retailing as competitive cost reductions are sought.

The Institute of Packaging estimates that expenditure on *packaging* increased by 50% during the 1950s, to £500 or £600 million annually. By 1970 it was estimated to have reached £900 million (a 12% increase over the 1969 level). This development has been caused by the increase in self-service retailing and in the sale of prepackaged, standardised and branded goods and the use of aerosols.[3]

The increase in the choice of goods made available during recent years has also been accompanied by a rise in expenditure on *advertising* – to £525 million in 1970. Of this total, about £365 million was in press advertising, £125 million (including taxation) in television advertising, and the rest on posters, films, catalogues, exhibitions, window displays and free sample or gift schemes. Most

[1] 'Shopping by push-button telephone', *Obs.*, 5 Nov. 1961.
[2] See 'Storage and Warehousing III', *F.T.*, 5 Jan. 1972; 'Why more stores are switching to automated stock-keeping', *F.T.*, 28 May 1969; 'Computerised Stock Control', *F.T.*, 20 Oct. 1969.
[3] See *Brit. O.H.*, 1972, p. 386, for further details.

advertising is carried out through specialist agencies, many of whom carry out consumer research. The Advertising Association – the trade association in this field – was responsible for setting up in 1962 the Advertising Standards Authority to promote and enforce high standards and integrity. The central body in advertising is the Institute of Practitioners in Advertising.[1] In 1969 about 23% of advertising was conducted by retail shops and mail-order firms as such: 90% of this was press advertising.[2]

CUT-PRICE RETAILING

Expansion in retail sales, especially in the multiples, has been stimulated primarily by the spread of *self-service* methods. Aimed at reducing costs, these have been accompanied, especially in the grocery trade, by cut-price selling. In 1969 it was estimated that there were about 23,000 self-service shops in Britain, as compared with about 9,500 at end-1961 and less than 500 in 1950.

An important development in self-service retailing has been the establishment of *supermarkets* (self-service shops with at least 2,000 square feet of selling space – dealing in foodstuffs and some household goods). These started in Britain in 1956 – the initiative coming largely from the retail co-operatives. By mid-1971 there were about 4,400 supermarkets in Britain – an increase of 500 over the beginning of 1970. Average selling area was 4,400 square feet – 1,700 having more than 4,000 square feet and some as much as 40,000 square feet – but the average size of supermarkets opened in 1970 was over 7,000 square feet.[3] Several multiple organisations were planning extensive supermarket developments for the 1970s, including a programme for 1,000 new supermarkets, between 1970 and 1980, by the Allied Suppliers group. It already had 470 supermarkets and intended to replace its 1,500 other shops, without any increase in staff.[4] In late-1969 the chairman of the Fine Fare group forecast that by 1980 there might be 7,500 supermarkets in Britain, responsible for about 60% of food retailing and controlled by about four major supermarket groups (compare the 25% of grocery turnover accounted for by supermarkets in 1970). His own firm planned to open 250 by 1975, averaging 5,000 square feet each.[5] Tesco, in late-1970 announced that all its future supermarket projects would have at least 20,000 square feet of selling area.[6] Fig. 8.10 illustrates the past changes and likely trends in the total number of grocery outlets, the reduction in counter-service outlets, the increase in self-service outlets and the increase in supermarket numbers. As the supermarkets face increasing problems of site costs and competition, some have made innovations in breaching the demarcation between food and other goods, in an attempt to increase turnover. One of the leaders in this respect has been the Tesco group, which in 1968 persuaded Hoover to supply electrical goods for cut-price retailing and had already diversified into furniture and clothing.[7] Some of the main *problems* for the supermarket firms, posed by this rapid expansion, have been the strain on their accounting, transport and warehousing resources,

[1] *Ibid.* Also see 'Advertising sheds its glamour', *Econ.*, 16 May 1970, pp. 54–5, for details and charts on the problems and structure of the industry and the breakdown of advertising expenditure in 1969.
[2] See 'Advertising sheds its glamour', *loc. cit.*, p. 55.
[3] See 'Supermarkets', supplement in *F.T.*, 25 May 1971.
[4] See *F.T.*, 29 Nov. 1969.
[5] See 'Future belongs to supermarkets', *D.T.*, 15 Oct. 1969.
[6] See 'Supermarkets', *loc. cit.*
[7] See 'Tesco-Hoover deal breaks new ground for supermarkets', *D.T.*, 28 Aug. 1968.

Fig. 8.10. *Trends in the number of grocery outlets of different types, 1959–79* (Source: *F.T.*, 6 Oct. 1971)

and the shortage of skilled management and staff.[1] Some of the main *problems* for their suppliers and for the public generally stem from the increasing concentration of selling points into the hands of the supermarket firms and the possibility of their curtailing price competition and of their exercising great bargaining power in buying from their suppliers at unduly advantageous discount rates, without necessarily passing on these cost reductions to the consumer.[2] The Minister of Food, in February 1970, pointed out that bargaining power in the market place had passed to the distributors, particularly the large food retailers. Manufacturers' margins were being eroded and they often had to pay supermarkets high flat-rate fees for promoting their products. At the same time, the degree of price competition was less pronounced than in the U.S., such that U.K. multiples were earning, by 1970, pre-tax profits of about $3\cdot25\%$ on turnover, as compared with the 1967/68 level of $1\cdot87\%$ in the U.S.[3]

The advantages of large scale retailing, bulk buying and the ability to offer cut-price goods has not been confined to supermarkets situated in busy shopping centres. There has been in recent years a development of '*cash and carry*' *discount houses* (or 'economy stores'), which are a combination of retail supermarket and wholesale warehouse, dealing in all sorts of goods, often situated on lower-rent sites outside the busy shopping areas, and specialising in the sale of branded goods at low prices. By bulk buying, spartan surroundings, cash sales and no delivery facilities, they offer significant discounts to retailers and retail customers. The number rose from 400 in 1967, with a turnover of £164 million, to about 550

---

[1] 'Growth has its problems', *Econ.*, 8 June 1963, p. 1056.
[2] See 'Who loses out in the supermarket battle?', *D.T.*, 27 April 1970.
[3] See 'Guarding against an abuse of power now supermarkets hold the reins', *F.T.*, 24 Feb. 1970.

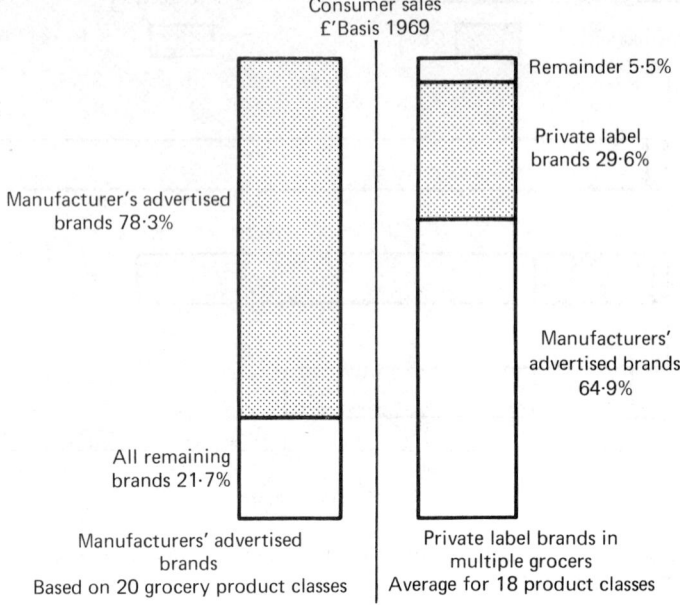

Fig. 8.11. *Manufacturers' advertised brands and 'own label' brands in groceries: relative shares in product classes, 1969* (Source: *F.T.*, 13 Jan. 1971)

in May 1971, with a turnover of £477 million.[1] A note of caution, with regard to continued growth, was sounded by the Retail Outlet Research Unit of the Manchester Business School, in its 1972 report.[2] Apart from the perennial problem of finding cheap, convenient sites, the report noted that some areas were becoming saturated, that secondary sites might have to be turned to, and that the 1972 projection (of the 9·5 million square feet of selling space then in use) to 34 million square feet of selling space by 1975 was a considerable overestimate.

Apart from the different types of outlet, interest was aroused during the 1960s by the growth of a hitherto little-publicised marketing technique used by multiple retailers, *viz.*, *'own label'* retailing. This represented the exploitation, by large retailers, of their prestige with consumers and of their bargaining power with suppliers, so as to market products with their own company image, rather than solely the manufacturers' advertised branded goods. Whilst some of these products may be produced by manufacturing subsidiaries of the retailers themselves, most are supplied by producers of branded products. By 1971 all the Marks and Spencer food lines and about 50% of Sainsbury's lines were 'own label' products. Fig. 8.11 shows the relative shares of 'own label' sales in several grocery product classes in 1969. Advantages to the retailer include the cutting of costs, by preferential bulk purchase terms, and the propagating and intensifying of consumer loyalty. For the consumer, the advantages include significant price

---

[1] See *Brit. O.H.*, 1972, p. 384; 'Cash and carry boom', and 'Discount shopping', *F.T.*, 25 May 1971.
[2] See 'Slowdown for cash and carry', *F.T.*, 20 April 1972.

reductions (usually 10% to 20%), as compared with branded products, and the ability to complain directly to the retailer, if dissatisfied. For the manufacturer, the advantages include the possibility of utilising excess capacity or the tail-ends of production runs, and of securing bulk orders. His disadvantages include the possibility of becoming dependent on a small number of customers, vulnerability to 'thumbscrew' pressures, and the increasing difficulty in securing volume turn-over and 'shelf space' for his branded products. By mid-1971 it appeared that the rate of growth in 'own label' retailing was slowing down. Of course, the possibility arises in some products that 'own label' price reductions may not be accompanied by proportionate increases in the volume of goods sold, such that turnover may actually fall.[1]

3. Wholesale Trade

The wholesaler is a link between producers and retailers. By no means all goods pass through the wholesale network. There has been a growing tendency for large manufacturers (especially of branded goods) to set up their own retail outlets, to provide security through vertical integration. This may take the form of shops or a mail-order system. Other manufacturers have their own sales network direct to retailers, again to guarantee outlets. Many large retailers have found it profitable to buy in bulk from manufacturers, thus missing out the wholesaler.

The 1965 inquiry into the wholesale trades found that there were 23,643 firms engaged in wholesale distribution in Great Britain. These included 3,435 in clothing, footwear and textiles; 2,007 in grocery and provisions; 2,630 in vegetables and fruit; 3,469 in other food and in drink. In addition to these 23,643 *wholesalers* there were 8,282 *dealers* – involved in a mixture of wholesale and retail activities – in coal, builders' materials, grain or agricultural supplies and 9,117 *dealers* in other industrial materials and machinery. At end-1970 the value of stocks held by wholesalers and dealers was estimated at £1,670 million and 1970 expenditure on capital assets was about £124 million.[2]

The June 1970 report of the Distributive Trades E.D.C. considered that there were too many, too small and too inefficient wholesale firms. It pinpointed the problems of 'squeezed' profit margins, large numbers of small, unprofitable orders and difficulties in operating modern handling equipment (because of the frequent use of old, unsuitable buildings). Unawareness and non-use of management science techniques, depressed salaries and inadequate staff training schemes tended to result in an unenterprising managerial approach to capital investment. It suggested wide changes, possibly by means of mergers – although many small firms were not inefficient, whilst some recent mergers had failed to achieve suitable reorganisation, making full use of potential scale economies. Its Wholesale Sub-Committee was commissioning a guide to the collection and use of management information and a study of the best methods of labour utilisation in wholesaling.[3]

[1] See 'Profits in "own label"', *F.T.*, 25 May 1971; 'Marketing', *Management Today*, Dec. 1971, pp. 91–2.
[2] See *Brit. O.H.*, 1972, p. 381.
[3] See 'Too many in wholesale trade says Little Neddy', *F.T.*, 9 June 1970.

Some of the main economic functions performed by the wholesaler are as follows:

(i) By virtue of buying to resell to several retailers, he may buy economically in bulk and 'break bulk', or sell in small quantities to each retailer, working on a small profit margin, thus enabling the retailer to stock a wide range of goods.

(ii) By allowing credit terms or a period for repayment, he provides capital, in effect, to the small retailer.

(iii) By taking over the distribution function, he allows the small manufacturer to concentrate on production.

(iv) By providing specialist warehousing facilities, he may buy in times of plentiful supply, in anticipation of sales in times of shortage, thus helping to maintain price stability and relieving producers of the burden (space and costs) of holding stocks.

(v) By keeping abreast of the retailers' requirements, he transmits orders to manufacturers, which enable them to plan ahead for production, thus helping to maintain continuity and stability of supply.

(vi) By acting as an intermediary between producers and retailers, he minimises the costs of transport and communications.

(vii) By providing specialist services, such as blending, bottling, packing, processing, etc., he is able to meet the detailed needs of his market.

(viii) By virtue of making purchases from a wide range of manufacturers, he acts as a buffer against monopolistic pressure, by individual producers, upon small retailers.

Despite the bypassing of wholesalers by large retailers who buy direct from manufacturers, and despite the fact that branding and 'own label' production have led many manufacturers to bypass the wholesaler, in the quest to guarantee security of outlets, the financing, 'bulk-breaking', warehousing and other functions must still be carried out by the firms concerned – albeit without a middleman. Furthermore, the establishment of a sales network (representatives, shops, warehouses, etc.) may only be worth while if fully utilised on a large scale. In most other cases the specialist wholesaler might very well perform the service more efficiently and cheaply. Even in the function of relieving the manufacturer of sales network expenses, however, there are indications that outsiders may usurp the wholesaler. Such is the case with *food brokers*. These are specialist sales agents who provide a sales and merchandising force, on a commission basis, for several non-competing manufacturers. The staff may sell numerous products at the same call. Manufacturers are relieved of administrative overheads, recruiting and training expenses, etc., and may calculate selling costs on any given volume of sales. By 1967 more than 50% of grocery products in the U.S. were handled by the more than 4,000 food brokers – of whom almost 3,000 were affiliated to brokers in Canada, Sweden and other countries. However, there were only four members of the association in the U.K., where the field was opened up by two firms in 1962.[1]

Another intrusion into the field of activity of the private enterprise specialist wholesaler has, of course, been the development, by the retail co-operative movement, of the C.W.S. and Scottish C.W.S.

[1] See 'Year of the broker?', *The Statist*, 28 April 1967, p. 903.

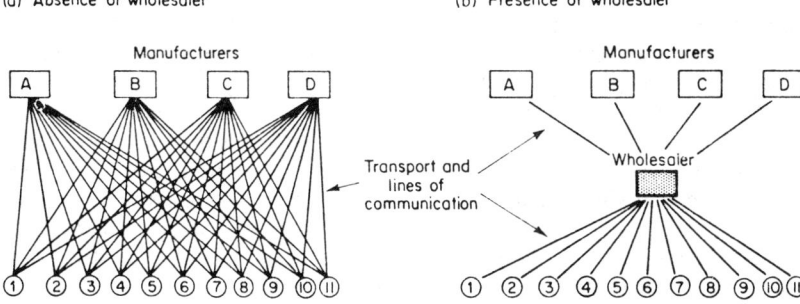

Fig. 8.12. *The wholesaler in the distributive system*

The logic of the wholesaler's position in the distributive services may be seen from Fig. 8.12.

In the grocery trade, the development of voluntary buying chains has helped to enable both independents and wholesalers to survive and benefit from economies of large scale buying and selling, as mentioned previously. One example of such developments is Wheatsheaf Distribution and Trading, a food-grocery wholesale group, which, in 1955, decided to abandon traditional wholesaling and to enter 'voluntary group' trading. The VG group was started in 1955, was joined by four outside firms and by March 1972 was linked with 2,800 shops with retail sales exceeding £100 million per annum. Low prices in return for guaranteed custom provided security and made possible bulk purchase negotiations with manufacturers.[1]

Both in grocery products and consumer durables wholesalers have found new ways of providing a service, by means of the 'cash and carry' discount warehouses, referred to earlier.[2]

The methods of wholesale produce marketing vary according to the type of merchandise. Some wholesalers sell by mail-order. In the case of fish, it is first auctioned to port wholesalers, who then sell it at the main inland distribution centres to other wholesalers or direct to retailers or, increasingly, by contract to fryers and processors. Fruit and vegetables may first be sold by growers to commission agents, who then sell to wholesalers or direct to retailers – or may be sold by growers direct to wholesalers. Most of the principal wholesale produce markets in foodstuffs are in London. Covent Garden used to deal in about 1·2 million tons of fruit, vegetables and flowers annually, before the market was moved in the early 1970s to a new site at Nine Elms in south London; Smithfield market handles about 340,000 tons of meat and poultry; the principal British fish distribution centre is Billingsgate; Leadenhall deals in poultry and Spitalfields in fruit and vegetables.[3]

---

[1] 'Wheatsheaf takes on the supermarkets', *F.T.*, 7 March 1972.
[2] 'Grocery wholesalers stage a fighting comeback', *F.T.*, 8 Dec. 1969.
[3] *Brit. O.H.*, 1972, p. 381.

4. Specialised Commodity Markets

Apart from the retail markets in county towns, the wholesale produce markets which sell to retailers, and the specialist financial markets such as Lloyd's (insurance and shipping), the stock exchanges (equities and bonds), the money and capital markets and the foreign exchange markets, there are many specialised markets in Britain in which imported commodities (as opposed to ready-to-consume produce) are sold at wholesale prices to manufacturers. Two very important commodity markets – raw cotton and wheat – are centred in Liverpool; the Manchester Royal Exchange deals in cotton and rayon yarn and cloth and other goods; the Bradford Wool Exchange deals in tops and noils; most others are situated within a small area in the City of London.

The business transacted in these markets is international, both because many of the commodities dealt in are re-exported and because consumers in other parts of the world buy at prices based on London quotations.[1]

Some of the main London markets are as follows:

The London Commodity Exchange, a group of 'futures' or 'terminal' markets at Plantation House, consisting of: (*a*) the London Rubber Market; (*b*) the Cocoa Terminal Market; (*c*) the Coffee Terminal Market; (*d*) Oils and fats; (*e*) General produce (pepper and spices); (*f*) Jute, (*g*) the Terminal Sugar Market.

The London Metal Exchange, for copper, tin, lead and zinc.

The Baltic Exchange, for coarse grains, grains for shipment, oils and oil seeds.

The Corn Exchange, for mainly English wheat, barley, oats and rye.

The London Wool Exchange, for wool auctions arranged by the Committee of London Wool Brokers.

The Diamond Trading Company and London Diamond Club (for sales of uncut diamonds) and Hatton Garden (for cut and uncut diamonds).

The Fur Market, at Beaver House.

The possibility was noted, in 1972, that some of the existing commodity markets might eventually move to the London world trade centre – a complex of facilities for exhibitions, offices, trading floors, etc., due to be completed near Tower Bridge by 1976.[2]

The methods of commodity market trading depend largely on the type of product and also on the conditions of supply and demand. One way of classifying these markets is according to the *manner* of trading. Thus there are *auctions* for goods which vary in quality from one batch to another, and must first be inspected, as with wool, furs, tea and coffee. Then there is the *private deal* method (also used in the Stock Exchange), used for commodities which may easily be graded and classified and bought on description. This method is used in the Baltic Exchange for oils, oil seeds, and grains. Thirdly, there is the *ring trading* method, as used in the Metal Exchange, whereby the forty ring members sit in a circle, bidding for one metal at a time, until the five minute limit is announced by the ringing of a bell. Fourthly, there is the *sights* method, which may be described as a 'take it or leave it' method adopted by the producer, who shows his commodity and asks a certain price. If the buyers do not agree to his

---

[1] For further details and comment, see G. Rees and J. Wiseman, 'London's commodity markets', *L.B.R.*, Jan. 1969; 'Uncertain futures', *Econ.*, 8 Aug. 1970, pp. lviii–lxiii; 'London metal exchange', *F.T.* (supplement), 27 Oct. 1970; 'Commodity markets', *F.T.* (supplement), 6 April 1972.
[2] 'The trade centre boom', *Econ.*, 12 Feb. 1972, pp. 56–7.

price, he withdraws the product from the market. This method is adopted with diamonds by the Diamond Trading Company for gem stones and by the Industrial Distributors for industrial diamonds, in which commodities production is controlled by the De Beers diamond cartel, which keeps up prices by offering diamonds in small batches.

Another way of classifying commodity markets is by the *timing* of the sale. Some commodities are offered for immediate sale and delivery. Markets for such products are said to be *spot* markets. In other commodities the sale relates to future deliveries of goods. In such cases the buyer wants to guarantee a fixed price for his future supply of materials and the seller a fixed price for his goods. Both are in fact 'hedging' against future price movements. Such markets are called *futures* or *terminal* markets. A prerequisite is that the commodity must be standardised and capable of grading and sale by description, as in metals, grains, cotton, sugar, etc. Goods ordered 'forward' (i.e. as futures) may eventually be resold 'spot' if the general price tends to rise.

The main economic functions performed by commodity markets may be classified as follows:

(i) To make possible worldwide commodity dealings in specialist markets, where buyers and sellers may meet, where goods may be warehoused, and where specialist services may be performed.

(ii) To achieve greater stability in worldwide commodity prices, both by the operation of 'futures' and 'spot' trading and by the fact that market quotations serve as the basis for contracts all over the world.

It will have been noted by the student that a market may be in a building, in a district, or be worldwide. The relevant characteristic is that it is a *situation* in which buyers and sellers are in communication with one another.

5. Further Reading and Sources

Footnote references to daily and weekly journals are not repeated.
Annual Abstract of Statistics, H.M.S.O.
BARCLAYS BANK, 'Consumer credit in the United Kingdom'. *B.B.R.* May 1971.
BARCLAYS BANK, 'Retail trade: present and future'. *B.B.R.* Nov. 1971.
CONJONCTURE, 'Shopping centres in France'. *Conjoncture.* 148. Feb. 1972.
D. C. CORNER, 'Recent trends in retail distribution'. *N.W.B.Q.R.* May 1969.
Department of Employment Gazette, H.M.S.O.
C. FULOP, *Retailing and the Consumer*. Longmans I.E.A. 1968.
P. MCANALLY, *The Economics of the Distributive Trades*. Allen & Unwin. 1971
W. G. MCCLELLAND, 'The distributive sector', *T.B.R.* Dec. 1969.
MIDLAND BANK, 'Credit in retail trade: sources and use of funds'. *M.B.R.* Aug. 1970.
DISTRIBUTIVE TRADES E.D.C., *A Look at Wholesaling*. National Economic Development Office. 1970.
G. REES, *St Michael: a history of Marks and Spencer*. Weidenfeld & Nicolson. 1968.
G. REES and J. WISEMAN, 'London's commodity markets'. *L.B.R.* Jan. 1969.
N. A. N. STACEY and A. WILSON, *The Changing Pattern of Distribution*. Pergamon. 1965.

TREASURY, 'Credit'. *E.P.R.* 22. Dec. 1971.
TREASURY, 'Household spending'. *E.P.R.* 36. Feb. 1973.
TREASURY, 'The changing pattern of retail trade.' *E.P.R.* 40. June 1973.

6. Past Examination Questions

1. Trace the production of a manufactured commodity from the earliest stages in its production to its sale to the final consumer, and show how division of labour in industry and trade facilitates the process. (Summer 1963)
2. Wheat harvested by the farmers reaches the consumers in the form of bread. Describe the main stages in this process. (Autumn 1957)
3. What are the economic functions of the retailer? To what extent may these functions be exercised by the manufacturer? (Summer 1952)
4. Describe the economic functions of the retailer. In what ways have these functions changed during this century? (Summer 1958)
5. Classify retail businesses into a few main types, and assess the advantages enjoyed by each type of store. (Summer 1962)
6. Why do we find both very large and very small organisations in the retail trade? (January 1963)
7. Discuss the advantages and disadvantages of large-scale operations in the retail trade. (Summer 1963)
8. Write short notes on . . . the following: (*e*) Department Stores. (Summer 1961)
9. What are the advantages enjoyed by a department store which are not equally available to a store selling one line of goods only? (Summer 1955)
10. How does a retail co-operative society differ from a public joint-stock company owning a chain of stores? (Summer 1960)
11. Write an account of the Co-operative Movement as it exists in Britain today. (Summer 1961)
12. Write short notes on . . . the following: (*a*) Co-operative societies; (*b*) Hire-purchase . . . (Summer 1953)
13. What are the economic functions of the wholesaler? In what circumstances might a manufacturer or retailer find it profitable to perform these functions? (Summer 1956)
14. What are the functions of the wholesale merchant? What are the forces making for his (*a*) elimination, (*b*) survival? (Summer 1959)
15. There is a tendency for the wholesaler to be eliminated. How do you account for this? Under what circumstances is the wholesaler likely to survive? (Autumn 1952)
16. What is meant in economics by a 'market'? Give examples of different types of market in economic life and indicate how they aid production. (Autumn 1953)
17. What are the conditions of a perfect market? Discuss the extent to which typical retail, wholesale and commodity markets are perfect markets. (Summer 1956)
18. What are the differences between (*a*) retail markets, (*b*) wholesale markets, and (*c*) commodity markets? Explain how these markets facilitate the flow of goods from the producers to the final consumer. (January 1964)

19. What are the advantages and disadvantages to (*a*) manufacturers, (*b*) retailers and (*c*) consumers of (i) the 'branding' of goods and (ii) the sale at fixed prices? (January 1965)

Chapter 8 has no Stage II

691

Index